UNIVERSITY CASEBOOK SERIES®

DISABILITY RIGHTS LAW

CASES AND MATERIALS

SECOND EDITION

by

SAMUEL R. BAGENSTOS
Professor of Law
University of Michigan Law School

FOUNDATION PRESS

University Casebook Series is a trademark registered in the U.S. Patent and Trademark Office.

© 2010 by THOMSON REUTERS / FOUNDATION PRESS
© 2014 by LEG, Inc. d/b/a West Academic
  444 Cedar Street, Suite 700
  St. Paul, MN 55101
  1-877-888-1330

Printed in the United States of America

ISBN: 978–1–60930–353–2

Mat #41433441

To my mother, Naida Tushnet, a great teacher

PREFACE TO THE SECOND EDITION

This second edition includes many revisions designed to bring the book up to date, as well as to respond to the many helpful comments of students and colleagues who used the first edition. I would like to thank those colleagues and students very much for their comments. My perspective on some of the key questions addressed in this book was no doubt affected by my service, from 2009 to 2011, as a senior political appointee in the Civil Rights Division of the United States Department of Justice. Many thanks are due to Tom Perez, John Wodatch, and the many terrific colleagues I had in the Division—and to the University of Michigan Law School for offering me the opportunity to take a leave to serve in the Department.

SAMUEL R. BAGENSTOS

Ann Arbor, MI
October 2013

PREFACE TO THE FIRST EDITION

In this casebook, I aim to provide an introduction to the key debates in disability rights law. I have taught disability rights law for a decade, and I have practiced disability rights law for even longer. Increasingly through the years, I have felt that the field needs a text that focuses on the large questions of doctrine, theory, and policy that disability rights law raises. I have designed this casebook with that need in mind.

My focus on the big questions, I think, makes this casebook different in several respects from the other fine texts in the field. First, in choosing cases I have tried less to find those that apply the basic rules in a myriad of contexts than to find those that illustrate the key issues in disability rights law in some distinctive way. For example, this text, unlike some of the others, contains no separate chapter on the Fair Housing Act. Fair Housing Act cases are included in Chapters Four (addressing disability discrimination by government) and Five (addressing disability discrimination in businesses' sale of goods and services), where they provide a distinctive perspective on the questions at hand. But a separate chapter on housing tempts an author to include, for the sake of "completeness," various Fair Housing Act cases that raise issues that were fully addressed in other parts of the book. Similarly, where it is important for students to understand the rule structure in a particular area, but the rules raise no especially difficult doctrinal questions, I have eschewed the use of cases and instead am presenting the material in relatively short, straightforward textual notes. (The rules governing medical examinations by employers are an example of this.) And I rarely use long notes with many squibs; I use notes like that only in the rare areas, like the application of the standard for reasonable accommodation in employment, where a student's understanding will benefit from seeing the same standard applied to a multiplicity of different factual contexts.

Second, many of the notes introducing various sections of the book (and following the cases) focus on major theoretical and policy controversies in disability rights law, with extensive citation to and excerpts from the secondary literature. A few examples: Chapter Three includes discussions of the justifications in antidiscrimination theory for, and the critiques of, the reasonable accommodation requirement, as well as of the theoretical and empirical arguments regarding the employment effects of disability discrimination law and alternative disability employment policies. Chapter Four includes materials on the "unfunded mandates" critique of the ADA as applied to state and local governments, as well as on the policy questions and political dynamics of deinstitutionalization litigation and the Baby Doe cases. Chapter Five includes discussions of the justification for the physical accessibility requirements of the ADA and Fair Housing Act, as well as of the controversy surrounding serial ADA litigation. And Chapter Six includes discussions of the policy controversies surrounding the IDEA's integration mandate and its private-school reimbursement rule, as well as the normative and policy questions involved in requests for accommodated testing. In these and other notes throughout the book, I try to present each of the contending arguments fairly. Although my disability rights practice experience comes exclusively from representing plaintiffs (the federal government, various disability rights organizations, and a number of individuals with disabilities), I have always found disability rights law fascinating precisely because it raises such difficult and complex theoretical, empirical, and policy questions. I have tried in this book to provide sufficient materials on both sides of the relevant controversies to provide the fodder for many classroom debates.

Third, and related, I have structured the normative and policy material so that it nearly always appears either immediately before or immediately after a series of cases. In my experience, discussions in law school classrooms are easiest, and most fruitful, if the class can go back and forth between more abstract normative and policy arguments and the concrete application of the law to particular cases. The discussion of the abstract questions can then shed light on what is really at stake (if perhaps unspoken) in the decision of concrete cases, while the cases themselves can offer a reality-check on, and a more nuanced texture to, the abstract arguments. I hope that this casebook will promote that back-and-forth process.

Finally, by avoiding repetition in the choice of cases, I have been able to use fewer cases than some other casebooks—while at the same time providing longer excerpts from the ones I have included. In addition to the normative and policy questions, disability rights law raises difficult and complex questions of doctrine and interpretation. I have found that longer case excerpts enable students to obtain a deeper understanding of those questions by puzzling through them right along with the judges. And when cases are severely edited, it is often necessary to cut out the portions of judges' opinions that are not part of the syllogistic logic of legal doctrine but that often shed light on the normative commitments and social vision of the judges.

In short, this is not a book for those who want to learn "the rules" of disability rights law—at least if "the rules" means the bottom-line holdings of each of the many different federal courts that have resolved questions in each of the many contexts in which that body of law applies. This book is not an encyclopedia or a treatise. But it does, I think, serve the pedagogical purpose of exposing students to the major doctrinal, theoretical, and empirical debates in the disability discrimination field and enabling them to understand the principles of the law in this area, apply those principles to new fact settings, and develop a position on the important normative and policy questions this body of law raises.

I should note a couple of housekeeping matters about the book. First, I indicate deletions from cases by placing brackets around the first letter (or entire word, if that word is an acronym) of the word that follows the deletion. I find it far easier to read edited cases when they don't contain lots of strings of asterisks. I indicate deletions from other materials the same way, except on a couple of occasions in which I thought three asterisks looked better. Second, as I note in Chapter One, I use people-first language (*e.g.*, not "the disabled" but "people with disabilities") throughout the book, except when it makes the writing clunky. I have made no effort to alter the language of those I quote, however, and many of them refer to people with disabilities in other terms.

I'd like to thank a number of people who have helped me with and supported me in this project. I took a draft version of this casebook "out on the road" as a visiting professor at the UCLA School of Law in the Spring Semester, 2009; I'd like to thank the students in my Disability Rights class there for helping me work through a number of issues with the book. And I'd like to thank the students in my disability rights law classes through the years at UCLA, Washington University, and Harvard for helping me to better understand the doctrinal, theoretical, and empirical questions this body of law raises. I'd also like to thank my many colleagues in disability rights teaching, scholarship, and litigation, from whom I've learned more than I can possibly recall. I owe a special thanks to the deans who supported this project, intellectually as well as financially: Kent Syverud, Mike Schill, and Evan Caminker. But my biggest thanks, as always, go to my family, for their love, support, and intellectual engagement.

I should note that, to the extent that anything expressed in this book reflects *anyone*'s views (as opposed to merely being provocations), those views are mine alone, and not those of any employer including the University of Michigan Law School and the United States Department of Justice.

SAMUEL R. BAGENSTOS

Ann Arbor, MI
July 2009

SUMMARY OF CONTENTS

TABLE OF CONTENTS

TABLE OF CASES

The principal cases are in bold type.

TABLE OF AUTHORITIES

DISABILITY RIGHTS LAW

CASES AND MATERIALS

SECOND EDITION

CHAPTER 1

INTRODUCTION

The disability rights laws that you will study in this book emerged from a particular history, and they raise significant theoretical and policy questions. This chapter provides a general introduction to the historical background to the disability rights laws, as well as two key theoretical and policy questions that those laws pose. For a more extensive discussion, see Samuel R. Bagenstos, Law and the Contradictions of the Disability Rights Movement 12–33 (2009).

A. The Disability Rights Movement and the Development of Disability Rights Law

One might begin the history of the American disability rights movement at almost any point in the history of the United States. But probably the most sensible place to begin is with the eugenics movement. The eugenics movement, which drew substantial support from elite opinion and popular politics from the 1890s into the 1920s, aimed to use law, medicine, and public policy to promote procreation among those with "good genes" (positive eugenics) and to impede procreation among those with "bad genes," who were often referred to by the elastic term "feebleminded" (negative eugenics). See generally Daniel Kevles, In the Name of Eugenics: Genetics and the Uses of Human Heredity (1998). Perhaps not surprisingly, the determination of who had "bad" genes often exhibited a strong racial, ethnic, and class bias. See, *e.g.*, Edwin Black, War Against the Weak: Eugenics and America's Campaign to Create a Master Race 63–86 (2004). As a result of the eugenic movement, states throughout the country adopted laws providing for the institutionalization and sterilization of people with various disabilities, and prohibiting them from marrying. See Kevles, *supra*, at 98–112. The Supreme Court upheld compulsory sterilization laws in *Buck v. Bell*, 274 U.S. 200 (1927) (a principal case in Chapter Four), and institutionalization of people with various disabilities continues to this day, despite the successes of the deinstitutionalization movement of the 1970s and 1980s. Although the Nazis' reliance on eugenic ideas brought those ideas into disrepute, disability rights activists often argue that the vestiges of eugenics remain in various policies and practices that deny equality and full citizenship to people with disabilities.*

Probably the next significant event in the history of disability rights in America took place before the eugenics movement had fully waned. After World War I, the federal government created a vocational rehabilitation program for disabled veterans. This program, which was soon extended to working-aged men with disabilities generally, marked the beginnings of a shift in disability policy—one not fully completed

---

* Throughout this book, except where it makes the writing clunky, I use people-first terminology (e.g., "people with disabilities," not "the disabled"), because most politically active Americans with disabilities believe that it is more respectful and less objectifying.

even today—from pure custodialism to a focus on moving people with disabilities into productive work and life in the community.

Two important precursors of the disability rights movement—one that was short-lived, one that has become an enduring part of the movement—were formed in the 1930s and 1940s. In 1935, an organization in New York that called itself the League of the Physically Handicapped held what could probably be regarded as the first protests for disability rights in the United States. The League challenged the exclusion of people with disabilities from New Deal work programs, though it died out after a few years. See Paul K. Longmore, Why I Burned My Book and Other Essays on Disability 53–101 (2003). In 1940, a number of blind people (led by the constitutional scholar Jacobus tenBroek) formed the National Federation of the Blind, which successfully advocated for the adoption of state laws requiring drivers to stop for people using white canes and requiring businesses to allow blind customers to bring guide dogs with them. Both of these organizations were formed by and for people with disabilities—which marked a self-conscious contrast with the paternalism of most charitable disability organizations.

In the 1960s, four important events took place that would lead, in the 1970s, to the beginning of a full-fledged American disability rights movement. First, in 1962 the University of California at Berkeley admitted Ed Roberts, who had quadriplegia as a result of polio, into its undergraduate program. Roberts slept in an iron lung at night, and the University allowed him to live in Cowell Hospital on campus. Other college-aged people with quadriplegia heard about Roberts's arrangement, and over the next few years a number of students with quadriplegia matriculated at Berkeley and lived in Cowell Hospital. These students formed a campus political group for disability rights. And that group, in turn, became the core of the Independent Living Movement, an important part of the disability rights movement that emerged in the early 1970s with Roberts as a key leader. See Edward D. Berkowitz, Disabled Policy: America's Programs for the Handicapped 197–207 (1987); Joseph P. Shapiro, No Pity: People with Disabilities Forging a New Civil Rights Movement 49–54 (1993).

Second, in 1966, Professor Jacobus tenBroek wrote two key articles (one coauthored) that put forward a set of basic principles that, he argued, should guide disability rights law. Those principles began with an important insight:

> The actual physical limitations resulting from the disability more often than not play little role in determining whether the physically disabled are allowed to move about and be in public places. Rather, that judgment for the most part results from a variety of considerations related to public attitudes, attitudes which not infrequently are quite erroneous and misconceived. These include public imaginings about what the inherent physical limitations must be; public solicitude about the safety to be achieved by keeping the disabled out of harm's way; public feelings of protective care and custodial security; public doubts about why the disabled should want to be abroad anyway; and public aversion to the sight of them and the conspicuous reminder of their plight.

Jacobus tenBroek, *The Right to Live in the World: The Disabled in the Law of Torts*, 54 Cal. L. Rev. 841, 842 (1966). See also Jacobus tenBroek & Floyd W. Matson, *The Disabled and the Law of Welfare*, 54 Cal. L. Rev. 809, 814 (1966) ("In practice, however, the psychological and socio-economic handicap suffered by disabled persons far outweighs the actual physical restrictions resulting from their impairment. Their dependent and segregated status is not an index merely of their physical condition; to an extent only beginning to be recognized it is the product of cultural definition—an assumptive framework of myths, stereotypes, aversive responses, and outright prejudices, together with more rational and scientific evidence."). Arguing against the "custodial attitude [that] is typically expressed in policies of segregation and shelter, of special treatment and separate institutions," *id.* at 816, he contended that disability law "should be controlled by a policy of integrationism—that is, a policy entitling the disabled to full participation in the life of the community and encouraging and enabling them to do so," tenBroek, *supra*, at 843. These articles enormously influenced the legal thinking of the disability rights movement.

Third, the successes of the black civil rights movement in the 1960s generated a civil rights consciousness among other marginalized and disadvantaged groups and spurred them to frame calls for change in civil rights terms. See generally John D. Skrentny, The Minority Rights Revolution (2002). Sometimes, in fact, the influence was quite direct: The students with quadriplegia at Berkeley during the 1960s were clearly influenced by participation in the political life of the campus, and Jacobus tenBroek was an important theorist for the civil rights and welfare rights movements.

Fourth, many Vietnam War veterans returned to the United States with disabilities. Those veterans provided a politically active constituency for disability rights. See Ann Hubbard, A Military-Civilian Coalition for Disability Rights, 75 Miss. L.J. 975, 984 (2006) ("The widespread anti-war protests 'helped to legitimate social activism,' and the 'large number of disabled veterans who were activists' provided models for disability rights activism.") (quoting Richard K. Scotch, From Good Will to Civil Rights: Transforming Federal Disability Policy 7 (1984)).

By the early 1970s, the American disability rights movement had begun in earnest. Although all social movements are complex and contradictory, it is fair to say that, in the main, the American disability rights movement was driven by two big ideas. The first big idea was antipaternalism—a challenge to the widespread societal view that people with disabilities should be "objects of pity or charity," or were "people who 'inspire' those without disabilities by 'overcoming' the hardships imposed by fate." Samuel R. Bagenstos, *Justice Ginsburg and the Judicial Role in Expanding "We the People"*: The Disability Rights Cases, 104 Colum. L. Rev. 49, 50 (2004). These benevolent feelings, disability rights activists argued, were not in fact beneficial for people with disabilities: "At best (as when individuals with disabilities were seen as inspirations), these attitudes placed people with disabilities on a pedestal that is in fact a cage. Far more often, these attitudes labeled people with disabilities as straightforwardly lesser persons—people who must be cared for because they cannot, or cannot be expected to, care for themselves." *Id.* at 50–51. This set of arguments drew directly from Jacobus tenBroek's critique of custodialism. (And the pedestal-as-cage argument was clearly influenced by the antipaternalist arguments of the women's rights movement as well.)

The second big idea has come to be known as the "social model" of disability. The social model posits that disability is not something that is inherent in the body of the person with a disability; instead, disability results from the interaction between an individual's physical or mental characteristics and the social choices and attitudes that attach disadvantage to those characteristics. In this view, the inability to walk is not what makes paraplegia disabling; paraplegia is disabling only because so much of the built environment—buildings with stairs, and with doorways that are too narrow, for example—is inaccessible to people with that condition. To be sure, the recognition that disability results from an interaction between individual and society carries no *logical* implications about the proper policy response. See Adam M. Samaha, What Good is the Social Model of Disability?, 74 U. Chi. L. Rev. 1251 (2007). But the social model denaturalizes disability, and many disability rights activists saw it as pointing the way to a new policy approach. If disability is understood as something inherent in the person with a disability, they argued, then the proper policy response will appear to be one that is focused on the person: efforts to cure the disability, or provide care for the person whose disability cannot be cured. But if disability is understood as something to which the individual and society both contribute, then we are more likely to see the proper response as one that requires *society* to change its aspects that make some mental or physical conditions disabling.

Disability rights activists in the 1970s derived from the social model a particular prescription: They argued that the proper approach to disability was not cure, charity, and welfare, but was instead civil rights legislation that would prohibit discrimination against people with disabilities. Crucially, they understood discrimination capaciously—to design buildings or routines in ways that excluded people with disabilities, they argued, was itself a form of discrimination.

Disability rights advocates had no direct role in the enactment of the first major American disability rights statute, Section 504 of the Rehabilitation Act of 1973, 29 U.S.C. § 794. Section 504, which remains on the books, prohibits disability-based discrimination by recipients of federal financial assistance. The provision was placed in a complex rehabilitation services bill by congressional staffers and did not draw much attention at the time. But when the Nixon and Ford Administrations delayed issuing regulations to implement the statute, and the Carter Administration's new Health, Education, and Welfare Secretary, Joe Califano, suggested publicly that he would delay the regulations even further, the disability rights movement mobilized. In protests at Califano's office, his house, and locations in nine other cities (including HEW's San Francisco Regional Office, where protesters sat in for 25 days), activists urged Califano to sign the Section 504 regulations that the department's staff had drafted. Califano relented. The newly adopted regulations were far reaching. They prohibited intentional discrimination on the basis of disability, and they also required federal funding recipients to make reasonable accommodations to—and to conduct their programs in a way that was accessible to—people with disabilities. For a discussion of the protests and the regulations, see Scotch, *supra, passim.*

Until Congress enacted the Americans with Disabilities Act in 1990, Section 504 was the most significant and broad-ranging disability discrimination law on the books. But Congress passed two important disability rights statutes in the interim. In 1975, Congress enacted the Education for All Handicapped Children Act, 20 U.S.C. § 1400 *et seq.* (now entitled the Individuals with Disabilities Education Act). That statute, supported by a coalition of civil rights advocates, special-education teachers, and parents' groups, guarantees all children with disabilities a free appropriate public education in the least restrictive environment. And in 1988, Congress added disability to the prohibited grounds of discrimination under the Fair Housing Act, 42 U.S.C. § 3604. The Fair Housing Act Amendments of 1988 specifically required new multifamily dwellings to be physically accessible to people with disabilities, and it required the owners of older dwellings to permit disabled tenants to make reasonable physical modifications. See *id.*

Throughout the 1980s, disability rights advocates prepared the groundwork for the enactment of their (mist) significant legislative priority—a comprehensive disability discrimination law. Robert Burgdorf, a disability rights lawyer who served in a succession of government positions (and now teaches at the University of the District of Columbia's law school), played a key role. In 1983, Burgdorf coauthored a report of the federal Civil Rights Commission which defended disability discrimination law as an application of the same principles as race discrimination law. See U.S. Comm'n on Civil Rights, Accommodating the Spectrum of Individual Abilities (1983). In 1986, he wrote a report of the National Commission on the Handicapped (now the National Commission on Disability), which argued for the adoption of a comprehensive disability discrimination law. See Nat'l Council on the Handicapped, Toward Independence (1986). Two years later, he wrote another report that provided the text of a proposed statute—the text that would form the basis for the initial ADA bill that was introduced in Congress that year. See Nat'l Council on Disability, On the Threshold of Independence (1988).

After an intensive two-year process of negotiation, Congress adopted the ADA, and President George H.W. Bush signed it, in 1990. The statute as adopted prohibits disability discrimination in employment, in the activities of state and local government, and in retail good-and-service providers' treatment of their customers. Much of the material in this book examines the interpretation and impact of the ADA.

B. MAJOR POLICY DEBATES

1. IS DISABILITY RIGHTS LAW CIVIL RIGHTS LAW?

As the previous section indicated, disability rights advocates have understood disability discrimination law—with its requirement of accommodation—as fundamentally continuous with previous antidiscrimination laws. But there seems to be a real difference of cost. To cease discriminating on the basis of race (and usually sex), one need not bear any cost; all that is necessary is to change one's attitude. But to make the accommodations necessary to stop discriminating on the basis of disability might be quite costly indeed. See Berkowitz, *supra*, at 221 ("To admit James Meredith's handicapped counterpart to a university would cost money rather than save it. It would mean that the physical plant would need to be expanded or modified, and it would require the university to pay the administrative costs of complying with the federal regulations.").

Pointing to this difference of cost, a number of commentators argue that disability rights laws really are not antidiscrimination laws:

> Fundamentally the ADA is not an antidiscrimination law. By forcing employers to pay for work site and other job accommodations that might allow workers with impairing conditions defined by the law to compete on equal terms, it would require firms to treat unequal people equally, thus discriminating in favor of the disabled.

Sherwin Rosen, *Disability Accommodation and the Labor Market, in* Disability and Work: Incentives, Rights, and Opportunities 18, 21 (Carolyn L. Weaver ed., 1991). These commentators argue that antidiscrimination law merely prohibits irrational conduct, but that disability rights law goes beyond the requirement of rationality to demand redistribution in favor of people with disabilities. See, *e.g.,* Samuel Issacharoff & Justin Nelson, *Discrimination with a Difference: Can Employment Discrimination Law Accommodate the Americans with Disabilities Act?*, 79 N.C. L. Rev. 307, 314–15 (2001); Mark Kelman, *Market Discrimination and Groups*, 53 Stan. L. Rev. 833 (2001). And the redistribution is problematic, they argue, because it is cloaked in the language of rights, which may politically exempt it from being traded off against other (potentially more socially valuable) uses of resources. See Kelman, *supra*.

Some commentators have responded by highlighting similarities between the disability accommodation requirement and the prohibition of race and sex discrimination in Title VII of the Civil Rights Act of 1964, 42 U.S.C. § 2000e *et seq.*. Professors Christine Jolls and Michael Stein, for example, point out that the disparate-impact branch of Title VII law imposes something that is analytically quite similar to an accommodation requirement. See Christine Jolls, Antidiscrimination and Accommodation, 115 Harv. L. Rev. 642 (2001); Michael Ashley Stein, *Same Struggle, Different Difference: ADA Accommodations as Antidiscrimination*, 153 U. Pa. L. Rev. 579 (2004). And Samuel R. Bagenstos, *"Rational Discrimination," Accommodation, and the Politics of (Disability) Civil Rights*, 89 Va. L. Rev. 825 (2003), argues that the accommodation requirement is continuous with Title VII's prohibition of rational *intentional* discrimination. Cf. *City of L.A., Dep't of Water & Power v. Manhart*, 435 U.S. 702, 708 (1978) (Title VII case stating that "[e]ven a true generalization about the class" cannot justify discrimination). The *"Rational Discrimination"* article contends that the failure to provide reasonable accommodations, like rational intentional discrimination, will sometimes reflect animus, often reflect "selective sympathy and indifference," and always "represents an employer's participation in constructing and maintaining the structure of occupational segregation that undergirds a system of subordination—participation the employer could avoid at relatively modest cost." Bagenstos, *"Rational Discrimination," supra*, at 866–870.

As you read the cases and materials in the following chapters, consider whether the accommodation requirement, as interpreted and applied in various contexts, operates in a way that is similar to or different from "classic" antidiscrimination laws. Does the requirement, in these contexts, impose appropriate costs on the appropriate entities? Or does it impose excessive costs, on entities that ought to bear no responsibility? These issues recur throughout the materials in this book, and the answers may well depend on the context.

2. IS CIVIL RIGHTS LAW SUFFICIENT?

As the discussion above pointed out, disability rights advocates have argued that the proper response to disability is not cure or care—not social welfare—but instead civil rights. But is civil rights law a sufficient tool to address the disadvantage attached to disability? Even if we accept the social model's insight that societal choices, not inherent individual characteristics, are what creates disability, it will be hard in many cases to attribute those societal choices to any particular defendant. If an individual with a disability needs personal assistance services to get out of bed, get dressed, and go to work, whom can she sue if she cannot find personal assistance services and is thus unable to work? As some of the material in Chapter Three shows, the law on the books reflects an intuition that it is not the employer's responsibility to provide services like personal assistance that help an individual with a disability both in and out of the workplace. But it is difficult to say that antidiscrimination law requires the state to pay for such services. Antidiscrimination law thus will be insufficient to promote independence and empowerment for people who need personal assistance services. Widespread access to personal assistance services will be difficult to achieve without an expansion of disability welfare programs.

This is not a minor concern. As the materials in Chapter Three show, the employment rate for people with disabilities has barely increased—if it has increased at all—during the time that the Americans with Disabilities Act has been in effect. As those materials show, some commentators argue that the ADA has actually harmed the employment prospects for people with disabilities. But even if it has not harmed those prospects, has it helped them? Has it helped them enough?

As you read the case in the chapters that follow, consider whether antidiscrimination law (with the reasonable-accommodation embellishment) is the best way of addressing the problems that the plaintiffs are raising? Does antidiscrimination law impose too much and achieve too little, as many critics contend? Or are there important advantages to employing an antidiscrimination strategy?

CHAPTER 2

WHAT IS DISABILITY?

INTRODUCTORY NOTE

The major disability rights statutes—the Americans with Disabilities Act, the Rehabilitation Act, the Fair Housing Act, and the Individuals with Disabilities Education Act—generally limit their protections to individuals who have a "disability." In that respect, the disability rights laws are very different from the laws that prohibit race and sex discrimination. Title VII of the Civil Rights Act, for example, protects everyone—black, white, Latino, Asian, or any other race; woman or man—from race and sex discrimination. See *McDonald v. Santa Fe Trail Transp. Co.*, 427 U.S. 273 (1976).

Why the difference? The Supreme Court's decision in *City of Cleburne v. Cleburne Living Center, Inc.*, 473 U.S. 432 (1985), which appears as a principal case in Chapter Four, suggests some possible answers. The *Cleburne* Court held that discrimination against people with mental retardation is not subject to heightened scrutiny under the Fourteenth Amendment. The Court reasoned that there are "real and undeniable differences between the retarded and others," and that "governmental consideration of those differences in the vast majority of situations is not only legitimate but also desirable." *Id.* at 444. Government agencies, the Court thought, often have good reason to exclude people with mental retardation from some opportunities. And, the Court said, "a civilized and decent society" would appropriately pass legislation that "singl[es] out the retarded for special treatment." *Id.*

Applying the *Cleburne* Court's reasoning more broadly, perhaps the disability rights laws protect only those with "disabilities" because discrimination based on ability is typically considered unproblematic—and is in fact encouraged in many sectors of our market economy. Disability rights laws thus carve out a class of people who may not be discriminated against on the basis of their abilities—people who meet the "disability" definition—in order to ensure that those laws do not pose a fundamental challenge to the general prerogative of employers and other economic actors to make ability-based distinctions. In the *Sutton* case, discussed below, the Supreme Court read the ADA's "disability" definition narrowly; the Court did so, at least in part, to preserve employers' general prerogative "to decide that physical characteristics or medical conditions that do not rise to the level of an impairment—such as one's height, build, or singing voice—are preferable to others, just as it is free to decide that some limiting, but not *substantially* limiting, impairments make individuals less than ideally suited for a job." (Congress pretty much completely overturned *Sutton* in the ADA Amendments Act of 2008, which is also discussed below.)

Picking up on another theme in *Cleburne*, perhaps disability rights laws are framed in terms of a protected class simply in order to avoid "reverse discrimination" claims. Although race and sex discrimination laws permit affirmative action for minorities and women under certain circumstances, those circumstances are limited. See, *e.g.*, *Taxman v. Board of Educ.*, 91 F.3d 1547 (3d Cir.1996). The limitation of disability rights protections to individuals with "disabilities" may simply reflect a view that affirmative action does not raise the same concerns in the disability context as it does in the race and sex context.

Finally, perhaps disability rights laws are framed in terms of a protected class because members of the class are the only ones who are understood to "need" the protections of those laws. The IDEA, which is the subject of Section B below, highlights the point: It explicitly limits its protections to those who "need[ ] special education and related services" because of their conditions. The ADA might be understood in a similar way: as giving civil rights protections to individuals who are subject to systematic discrimination, see Samuel R. Bagenstos, *Subordination, Stigma, and "Disability,"* 86 Va. L. Rev. 397 (2000) (arguing, prior to the ADA Amendments Act, that the ADA should be understood this way); as granting special benefits, as a form of welfare or forced charity, to the "unfortunates" who need it, see Matthew Diller, *Judicial Backlash, the ADA, and the Civil Rights Model*, 21 Berkeley J. Emp. & Lab. L. 19 (2000) (arguing that the ADA should *not* be understood in this way); or, in the employment setting particularly, as giving workplace accommodations to those who need them to stay in the labor force and off of welfare, see Samuel R. Bagenstos, *The Americans with Disabilities Act as Welfare Reform*, 44 Wm. & Mary L. Rev. 921 (2003) (arguing, prior to the ADA Amendments Act, that the ADA's disability definition has been interpreted in this way).

These possible purposes are not mutually exclusive, nor are they exhaustive. As you read the cases in this chapter, try to identify the courts' understandings (even if they are only implicit) of the purpose of limiting disability rights protection to a particular class. Consider what those understandings might tell us about the courts' views of the overall purpose of disability rights laws.

A. UNDER THE ADA, REHABILITATION ACT, AND FAIR HOUSING ACT

The ADA contains a three-pronged definition of disability:

The term "disability" means, with respect to an individual

   (A) a physical or mental impairment that substantially limits one or more major life activities of such individual;

   (B) a record of such an impairment; or

   (C) being regarded as having such an impairment[.]

42 U.S.C. § 12102(1). The Rehabilitation Act uses the same definition, 29 U.S.C. § 705(20)(B), and the Fair Housing Act uses essentially the same definition, 42 U.S.C. § 3602(h). Prior to the enactment of the ADA Amendments Act, the statute did not elaborate on that three-pronged definition. The ADAAA added a number of provisions that gave additional content to the statute's disability category, though it retained the same basic three-pronged definition. Congress enacted the ADAAA in direct response to a series of Supreme Court and lower court decisions that had read the ADA's definition narrowly. So that you can understand what Congress was responding to, this section begins by

discussing the key pre-ADAAA decisions. It then turns to the changes worked by the ADAAA.

1. THE PRE-ADA AMENDMENTS ACT CASES

Before Congress enacted the ADA Amendments Act, the Supreme Court decided five key cases addressing the definition of disability: *Bragdon v. Abbott*; *Sutton v. United Air Lines*; *Murphy v. United Parcel Service*; *Albertson's v. Kirkingburg*; and *Toyota v. Williams*. These decisions addressed a number of key questions in the interpretation of the ADA's disability category.

1. Bragdon v. Abbott. In BRAGDON v. ABBOTT, 524 U.S. 624 (1998), the Court addressed "whether HIV infection is a disability under the ADA when the infection has not yet progressed to the so-called symptomatic phase." Sidney Abbott, who had asymptomatic HIV, went to the office of Dr. Randon Bragdon, a dentist, to have a cavity filled. Because she had HIV, Bragdon refused to fill the cavity in his office. Abbott sued under Title III of the ADA, which prohibits disability discrimination in public accommodations (including the offices of health-care providers). The district court granted summary judgment to Abbott, and the First Circuit affirmed. In an opinion by Justice Kennedy, the Supreme Court affirmed the holding that Abbott had a disability. (The Court's ruling on a second question—whether Bragdon could properly exclude Abbott because of a risk that filling her cavity might pose to health and safety—appears in Chapter Three.)

The Court began by noting that the "ADA's definition of disability is drawn almost verbatim from the definition of 'handicapped individual' included in the Rehabilitation Act of 1973, and the definition of 'handicap' contained in the Fair Housing Amendments Act of 1988," and that Congress specifically directed, in 42 U.S.C. § 12201(a), that the ADA not be construed "to apply a lesser standard" than that applied under Rehabilitation Act or the federal regulations implementing that statute. Accordingly, the Court focused its legal analysis on the Rehabilitation Act regulations as they existed prior to the enactment of the ADA.

The Court next concluded that, "[i]n light of the immediacy with which the virus begins to damage the infected person's white blood cells and the severity of the disease," HIV "is an impairment from the moment of infection":

> [I]nfection with HIV causes immediate abnormalities in a person's blood, and the infected person's white cell count continues to drop throughout the course of the disease, even when the attack is concentrated in the lymph nodes. In light of these facts, HIV infection must be regarded as a physiological disorder with a constant and detrimental effect on the infected person's hemic and lymphatic systems from the moment of infection. HIV infection satisfies the statutory and regulatory definition of a physical impairment during every stage of the disease.

The Court also concluded that, at least in Abbott's case, HIV infection substantially limited major life activities. Abbott contended that HIV infection substantially limited "her ability to reproduce and to bear children." The Court adopted the First Circuit's interpretation that "[t]he plain meaning of the word 'major' denotes comparative importance," and rejected the argument that "Congress intended the ADA only to cover those aspects of a person's life which have a public, economic, or daily character." Because "[r]eproduction and the sexual dynamics surrounding it are central to the life process itself," it fell "well within the phrase 'major life activity.'"

On the substantial limitation question, the Court concluded that Abbott's HIV "substantially limited her ability to reproduce in two independent ways":

> First, a woman infected with HIV who tries to conceive a child imposes on the man a significant risk of becoming infected. The cumulative results of 13 studies collected in a 1994 textbook on AIDS indicates that 20% of male partners of women with HIV became HIV-positive themselves, with a majority of the studies finding a statistically significant risk of infection. (Studies report a similar, if not more severe, risk of male-to-female transmission.)

> Second, an infected woman risks infecting her child during gestation and childbirth, *i.e.,* perinatal transmission. Petitioner concedes that women infected with HIV face about a 25% risk of transmitting the virus to their children. Published reports available in 1994 confirm the accuracy of this statistic. Petitioner points to evidence in the record suggesting that antiretroviral therapy can lower the risk of perinatal transmission to about 8%. The United States questions the relevance of the 8% figure, pointing to regulatory language requiring the substantiality of a limitation to be assessed without regard to available mitigating measures. We need not resolve this dispute in order to decide this case, however. It cannot be said as a matter of law that an 8% risk of transmitting a dread and fatal disease to one's child does not represent a substantial limitation on reproduction.

> The Act addresses substantial limitations on major life activities, not utter inabilities. Conception and childbirth are not impossible for an HIV victim but, without doubt, are dangerous to the public health. This meets the definition of a substantial limitation. The decision to reproduce carries economic and legal consequences as well. There are added costs for antiretroviral therapy, supplemental insurance, and long-term health care for the child who must be examined and, tragic to think, treated for the infection. The laws of some States, moreover, forbid persons infected with HIV to have sex with others, regardless of consent.

> In the end, the disability definition does not turn on personal choice. When significant limitations result from the impairment, the definition is met even if the difficulties are not insurmountable.

The Court found its holding "confirmed by a consistent course of agency interpretation before and after enactment of the ADA." The Court noted that "[e]very agency to consider the issue under the

Rehabilitation Act found statutory coverage for persons with asymptomatic HIV." It placed particular weight on a 1988 opinion issued by the Department of Justice's Office of Legal Counsel—an opinion explicitly discussed in the ADA's legislative history—which concluded that asymptomatic HIV was an impairment that substantially limited the major life activity of reproduction. Moreover, it noted, "[e]very court which addressed the issue before the ADA was enacted in July 1990 [had] concluded that asymptomatic HIV infection satisfied the Rehabilitation Act's definition of a handicap." And after the enactment of the ADA, both the Department of Justice and the Equal Employment Opportunity Commission had issued technical assistance documents that stated that asymptomatic HIV was a disability.

In a concurring opinion, Justice Ginsburg made a broader argument for reading asymptomatic HIV as included within the statute's definition:

> The disease inevitably pervades life's choices: education, employment, family and financial undertakings. It affects the need for and, as this case shows, the ability to obtain health care because of the reaction of others to the impairment. No rational legislator, it seems to me apparent, would require nondiscrimination once symptoms become visible but permit discrimination when the disease, though present, is not yet visible. I am therefore satisfied that the statutory and regulatory definitions are well met. HIV infection is "a physical . . . impairment that substantially limits . . . major life activities," or is so perceived, 42 U.S.C. §§ 12102(2)(A)–(C), including the afflicted individual's family relations, employment potential, and ability to care for herself.

Chief Justice Rehnquist dissented, joined on this issue by Justices Scalia and Thomas. He emphasized that the statute requires "an individualized inquiry" into whether a plaintiff has a disability. In his view, there was "not a shred of record evidence indicating that, prior to becoming infected with HIV, respondent's major life activities included reproduction." At most, he concluded, "the record indicates that after learning of her HIV status, respondent, whatever her previous inclination, conclusively decided that she would not have children. There is absolutely no evidence that, absent the HIV, respondent would have had or was even considering having children."

In any event, he argued, reproduction is not like the illustrative list of major life activities that appeared in the Rehabilitation Act regulations ("functions such as caring for one's self, performing manual tasks, walking, seeing, hearing, speaking, breathing, learning, and working"):

> No one can deny that reproductive decisions are important in a person's life. But so are decisions as to who to marry, where to live, and how to earn one's living. Fundamental importance of this sort is not the common thread linking the statute's listed activities. The common thread is rather that the activities are repetitively performed and essential in the day-to-day existence of a normally functioning individual. They are thus

quite different from the series of activities leading to the birth of a child.

And, Chief Justice Rehnquist argued, asymptomatic HIV infection did not substantially limit reproduction, because "those so infected are still entirely able to engage in sexual intercourse, give birth to a child if they become pregnant, and perform the manual tasks necessary to rear a child to maturity."

In a brief dissent, Justice O'Connor agreed with the Chief Justice that "the act of giving birth to a child, while a very important part of the lives of many women, is not generally the same as the representative major life activities of all persons—'caring for one's self, performing manual tasks, walking, seeing, hearing, speaking, breathing, learning, and working'—listed in regulations relevant to the Americans with Disabilities Act of 1990.

2.   The Sutton Trilogy. The Court took up the ADA's definition of disability again the next year, in three cases decided on the same day. The major case, SUTTON v. UNITED AIR LINES, INC., 527 U.S. 471 (1999), was brought by twin sisters with severe but correctable myopia: 20/200 vision in one eye, and 20/400 in the other, but 20/20 or better when they wore glasses or contact lenses. The sisters, both certified pilots, applied for jobs with United as global airline pilots.   The company rejected them because they did not meet its vision standards for the position: "uncorrected visual acuity of 20/100 or better."   The lower courts dismissed the case on the ground that the sisters had no disability. The Supreme Court affirmed.

In an opinion by Justice O'Connor, the Court began by addressing whether the Suttons were covered under the first prong of the disability definition. Because any limitation on their ability to see was eliminated while the sisters were wearing corrective lenses, the Court considered whether the analysis of substantial limitation should take account of such mitigating measures. "Interpretive guidance" issued by the EEOC stated that "[t]he determination of whether an individual is substantially limited in a major life activity must be made on a case by case basis, without regard to mitigating measures such as medicines, or assistive or prosthetic devices." 29 CFR pt. 1630, App. § 1630.2(j) (1998).   The Department of Justice had issued virtually identical guidance.

But although the statute gave the EEOC authority to issue regulations implementing Title I of the ADA, and it gave the DOJ authority to issue regulations implementing Title III and parts of Title II of the statute, the Court concluded that "[n]o agency has been given authority to issue regulations implementing the generally applicable provisions of the ADA, see §§ 12101–12102, which fall outside Titles I–V."   Because the disability definition appeared in those general provisions, the Court held that "no agency has been delegated authority to interpret the term 'disability.'"

Turning to the statutory text, the Court held that "[t]he approach adopted by the agency guidelines—that persons are to be evaluated in their hypothetical uncorrected state—is an impermissible interpretation of the ADA."   The Court offered three reasons for this conclusion. First, "[b]ecause the phrase 'substantially limits' appears in the Act in the present indicative verb form," the Court thought "the language is properly read as requiring that a person be presently—not potentially or hypothetically—substantially limited in order to demonstrate a disability. Second, the Court believed that "[t]he agency guidelines' directive that persons be judged in their uncorrected or unmitigated state runs directly counter to the individualized inquiry mandated by the ADA":

> The agency approach would often require courts and employers to speculate about a person's condition and would, in many cases, force them to make a disability determination based on general information about how an uncorrected impairment usually affects individuals, rather than on the individual's actual condition. For instance, under this view, courts would almost certainly find all diabetics to be disabled, because if they failed to monitor their blood sugar levels and administer insulin, they would almost certainly be substantially limited in one or more major life activities. A diabetic whose illness does not impair his or her daily activities would therefore be considered disabled simply because he or she has diabetes. Thus, the guidelines approach would create a system in which persons often must be treated as members of a group of people with similar impairments, rather than as individuals. This is contrary to both the letter and the spirit of the ADA.

Third, the Court looked to Congressional findings, included in the text of the ADA as adopted in 1990, that "some 43,000,000 Americans have one or more physical or mental disabilities, and this number is increasing as the population as a whole is growing older." Examining various sources of disability statistics as of the 1980s, the Court found that an approach to the definition of disability that took account of mitigating measures would embrace something close to 40 million people, but that an approach that ignored those measures would "produce significantly larger numbers."

The Court emphasized that the "use of a corrective device does not, by itself, relieve one's disability." For example, the Court said, "individuals who use prosthetic limbs or wheelchairs may be mobile and capable of functioning in society but still be disabled because of a substantial limitation on their ability to walk or run," and "individuals who take medicine to lessen the symptoms of an impairment so that they can function" may "nevertheless remain substantially limited." But the Sutton sisters could fully eliminate any limitation wearing their glasses or contact lenses. Accordingly, their impairments did not substantially limit any major life activity.

The Court next considered whether the sisters were covered under the definition's third prong, as individuals "regarded as having" a disability. The sisters argued that United's rejection of their applications demonstrated that the company regarded them as substantially limited in the major life activity of working. But the Court rejected that argument:

> When the major life activity under consideration is that of working, the statutory phrase "substantially limits" requires, at a minimum, that plaintiffs allege they are unable to work in a broad class of jobs. Reflecting this requirement, the EEOC

uses a specialized definition of the term "substantially limits" when referring to the major life activity of working:

> "significantly restricted in the ability to perform either a class of jobs or a broad range of jobs in various classes as compared to the average person having comparable training, skills and abilities. The inability to perform a single, particular job does not constitute a substantial limitation in the major life activity of working." § 1630.2(j)(3)(i).

[T]o be substantially limited in the major life activity of working, then, one must be precluded from more than one type of job, a specialized job, or a particular job of choice. If jobs utilizing an individual's skills (but perhaps not his or her unique talents) are available, one is not precluded from a substantial class of jobs. Similarly, if a host of different types of jobs are available, one is not precluded from a broad range of jobs.

Because the parties accept that the term "major life activities" includes working, we do not determine the validity of the cited regulations. We note, however, that there may be some conceptual difficulty in defining "major life activities" to include work, for it seems "to argue in a circle to say that if one is excluded, for instance, by reason of [an impairment, from working with others] . . . then that exclusion constitutes an impairment, when the question you're asking is, whether the exclusion itself is by reason of handicap." Tr. of Oral Arg. in *School Bd. of Nassau Co. v. Arline,* O.T.1986, No. 85–1277, p. 15 (argument of Solicitor General).

[A]ssuming without deciding that working is a major life activity and that the EEOC regulations interpreting the term "substantially limits" are reasonable, petitioners have failed to allege adequately that their poor eyesight is regarded as an impairment that substantially limits them in the major life activity of working. They allege only that respondent regards their poor vision as precluding them from holding positions as a "global airline pilot." Because the position of global airline pilot is a single job, this allegation does not support the claim that respondent regards petitioners as having a *substantially limiting* impairment. Indeed, there are a number of other positions utilizing petitioners' skills, such as regional pilot and pilot instructor to name a few, that are available to them. Even under the EEOC's Interpretative Guidance, to which petitioners ask us to defer, "an individual who cannot be a commercial airline pilot because of a minor vision impairment, but who can be a commercial airline co-pilot or a pilot for a courier service, would not be substantially limited in the major life activity of working." 29 CFR pt. 1630, App. § 1630.2 (1998).

Petitioners also argue that if one were to assume that a substantial number of airline carriers have similar vision requirements, they would be substantially limited in the major life activity of working. Even assuming for the sake of argument that the adoption of similar vision requirements by other carriers would represent a substantial limitation on the major life activity of working, the argument is nevertheless flawed. It is not enough to say that if the physical criteria of a single employer were *imputed* to all similar employers one would be regarded as substantially limited in the major life activity of working *only as a result of this imputation.* An otherwise valid job requirement, such as a height requirement, does not become invalid simply because it *would* limit a person's employment opportunities in a substantial way *if* it were adopted by a substantial number of employers. Because petitioners have not alleged, and cannot demonstrate, that respondent's vision requirement reflects a belief that petitioners' vision substantially limits them, we agree with the decision of the Court of Appeals affirming the dismissal of petitioners' claim that they are regarded as disabled.

In a brief concurrence, Justice Ginsburg emphasized the 43 million figure, as well as Congress's finding that that "individuals with disabilities are a discrete and insular minority," persons "subjected to a history of purposeful unequal treatment, and relegated to a position of political powerlessness in our society." She said that "the inclusion of correctable disabilities within the ADA's domain would extend the Act's coverage to far more than 43 million people. And persons whose uncorrected eyesight is poor, or who rely on daily medication for their well-being, can be found in every social and economic class; they do not cluster among the politically powerless, nor do they coalesce as historical victims of discrimination."

Justice Stevens, joined by Justice Breyer, dissented:

> [T]his case [i]s not about whether petitioners are genuinely qualified or whether they can perform the job of an airline pilot without posing an undue safety risk. The case just raises the threshold question whether petitioners are members of the ADA's protected class. [H]ence, this particular case, at its core, is about whether, assuming that petitioners can prove that they are "qualified," the airline has any duty to come forward with some legitimate explanation for refusing to hire them because of their uncorrected eyesight, or whether the ADA leaves the airline free to decline to hire petitioners on this basis even if it is acting purely on the basis of irrational fear and stereotype.
>
> I think it quite wrong for the Court to confine the coverage of the Act simply because an interpretation of "disability" that adheres to Congress' method of defining the class it intended to benefit may also provide protection for "significantly larger numbers" of individuals, than estimated in the Act's findings. It has long been a "familiar canon of statutory construction that remedial legislation should be construed broadly to effectuate its purposes." *Tcherepnin v. Knight,* 389 U.S. 332, 336 (1967). Congress sought, in enacting the ADA, to "provide a . . . comprehensive national mandate for the discrimination against individuals with disabilities." 42 U.S.C. § 12101(b)(1). The ADA, following the lead of the Rehabilitation Act before it, seeks to implement this mandate

by encouraging employers "to replace . . . reflexive reactions to actual or perceived handicaps with actions based on medically sound judgments." [*School Bd. v.*] *Arline,* 480 U.S. [273], 284–285 [(1987)].

[I]t seems to me eminently within the purpose and policy of the ADA to require employers who make hiring and firing decisions based on individuals' uncorrected vision to clarify why having, for example, 20/100 uncorrected vision or better is a valid job requirement. So long as an employer explicitly makes its decision based on an impairment that in some condition is substantially limiting, it matters not under the structure of the Act whether that impairment is widely shared or so rare that it is seriously misunderstood. Either way, the individual has an impairment that is covered by the purpose of the ADA, and she should be protected against irrational stereotypes and unjustified disparate treatment on that basis.

I do not mean to suggest, of course, that the ADA should be read to prohibit discrimination on the basis of, say, blue eyes, deformed fingernails, or heights of less than six feet. Those conditions, to the extent that they are even "impairments," do not substantially limit individuals in any condition and thus are different in kind from the impairment in the case before us. While not all eyesight that can be enhanced by glasses is substantially limiting, having 20/200 vision in one's better eye is, without treatment, a significant hindrance. Only two percent of the population suffers from such myopia. Such acuity precludes a person from driving, shopping in a public store, or viewing a computer screen from a reasonable distance. Uncorrected vision, therefore, can be "substantially limiting" in the same way that unmedicated epilepsy or diabetes can be. Because Congress obviously intended to include individuals with the latter impairments in the Act's protected class, we should give petitioners the same protection.

Justice Breyer also filed a brief dissent, in which he argued that the EEOC had regulatory authority to interpret the disability definition in cases brought under Title I of the ADA.

In MURPHY v. UNITED PARCEL SERVICE, INC., 527 U.S. 516 (1999), the Court held (by the same 7–2 vote as in *Sutton*) that Vaughn Murphy, a UPS mechanic who was fired because of his hypertension, did not have an ADA disability. Quoting Murphy's physician, the Court described Murphy's medical condition this way: "Unmedicated, his blood pressure is approximately 250/160. With medication, however, petitioner's 'hypertension does not significantly restrict his activities and . . . in general he can function normally and can engage in activities that other persons normally do.'" One thing he could not do, however, is drive commercial motor vehicles for UPS. United States Department of Transportation regulations demand that "the driver of a commercial motor vehicle in interstate commerce have 'no current clinical diagnosis of high blood pressure likely to interfere with his/her ability to operate a commercial vehicle safely.'" UPS believed that Murphy's "blood pressure exceeded the DOT's requirements for drivers of commercial motor vehicles." Because his mechanic's job required him to drive commercial motor vehicles, UPS fired him.

The Court affirmed the lower courts' grant of summary judgment to UPS. Murphy had argued that his hypertension, when considered in its unmedicated state, substantially limited major life activities, but the Court relied on *Sutton*'s "mitigating measures" holding to reject that analysis. The Court gave more extensive consideration to the argument that UPS erroneously "regarded" Murphy's disability as substantially limiting, but it ultimately found *Sutton* to be dispositive of that issue as well:

> The evidence that petitioner is regarded as unable to meet the DOT regulations is not sufficient to create a genuine issue of material fact as to whether petitioner is regarded as unable to perform a class of jobs utilizing his skills. At most, petitioner has shown that he is regarded as unable to perform the job of mechanic only when that job requires driving a commercial motor vehicle—a specific type of vehicle used on a highway in interstate commerce. 49 CFR § 390.5 (1998) (defining "commercial motor vehicle" as a vehicle weighing over 10,000 pounds, designed to carry 16 or more passengers, or used in the transportation of hazardous materials). Petitioner has put forward no evidence that he is regarded as unable to perform any mechanic job that does not call for driving a commercial motor vehicle and thus does not require DOT certification. Indeed, it is undisputed that petitioner is generally employable as a mechanic. Petitioner has "performed mechanic jobs that did not require DOT certification" for "over 22 years," and he secured another job as a mechanic shortly after leaving UPS. Moreover, respondent presented uncontroverted evidence that petitioner could perform jobs such as diesel mechanic, automotive mechanic, gas-engine repairer, and gas-welding equipment mechanic, all of which utilize petitioner's mechanical skills.

> Consequently, in light of petitioner's skills and the array of jobs available to petitioner utilizing those skills, petitioner has failed to show that he is regarded as unable to perform a class of jobs. Rather, the undisputed record evidence demonstrates that petitioner is, at most, regarded as unable to perform only a particular job. This is insufficient, as a matter of law, to prove that petitioner is regarded as substantially limited in the major life activity of working. [Citing *Sutton*.]

In ALBERTSON'S, INC. v. KIRKINGBURG, 527 U.S. 555 (1999), the plaintiff, Hallie Kirkingburg, was a truck driver who was fired after his employer discovered that he had monocular vision. Although the Court ultimately ruled against Kirkingburg on other grounds (which are discussed in Chapter Three), it went out of its way to state that the court of appeals had been "too quick to find a disability." In particular, the court of appeals had erred by "suggest[ing] that in gauging whether a monocular individual has a disability a court need not take account of the individual's ability to compensate for the impairment." Although Kirkingburg did not use any medications or devices to mitigate his visual impairment, the court of appeals noted that his "brain has developed subconscious mechanisms for coping with [that] impairment and thus his body compensates for his disability." The Court saw "no principled basis for distinguishing between measures undertaken with artificial aids, like medications and devices, and measures undertaken, whether consciously or not, with the body's own systems." The Court also emphasized the individualized nature of the disability determination:

> Finally, and perhaps most significantly, the Court of Appeals did not pay much heed to the statutory obligation to determine the existence of disabilities on a case-by-case basis. The Act expresses that mandate clearly by defining "disability" "with respect to an individual," and in terms of the impact of an impairment on "such individual." [Citing *Sutton*.] While some impairments may invariably cause a substantial limitation of a major life activity, cf. *Bragdon* (declining to address whether HIV infection is a *per se* disability), we cannot say that monocularity does. That category, as we understand it, may embrace a group whose members vary by the degree of visual acuity in the weaker eye, the age at which they suffered their vision loss, the extent of their compensating adjustments in visual techniques, and the ultimate scope of the restrictions on their visual abilities. These variables are not the stuff of a *per se* rule. While monocularity inevitably leads to some loss of horizontal field of vision and depth perception, consequences the Ninth Circuit mentioned, the court did not identify the degree of loss suffered by Kirkingburg, nor are we aware of any evidence in the record specifying the extent of his visual restrictions.

> This is not to suggest that monocular individuals have an onerous burden in trying to show that they are disabled. On the contrary, our brief examination of some of the medical literature leaves us sharing the Government's judgment that people with monocular vision "ordinarily" will meet the Act's definition of disability, and we suppose that defendant companies will often not contest the issue. We simply hold that the Act requires monocular individuals, like others claiming the Act's protection, to prove a disability by offering evidence that the extent of the limitation in terms of their own experience, as in loss of depth perception and visual field, is substantial.

Toyota Motor Mfg., Ky., Inc. v. Williams

Supreme Court of the United States, 2002.
534 U.S. 184.

■ JUSTICE O'CONNOR delivered the opinion of the Court.

[R]espondent, claiming to be disabled because of her carpal tunnel syndrome and other related impairments, sued petitioner, her former employer, for failing to provide her with a reasonable accommodation as required by the ADA. See § 12112(b)(5)(A). The District Court granted summary judgment to petitioner, finding that respondent's impairments did not substantially limit any of her major life activities. The Court of Appeals for the Sixth Circuit reversed, finding that the impairments substantially limited respondent in the major life activity of performing manual tasks, and therefore granting partial summary judgment to respondent on the issue of whether she was disabled under the ADA. We conclude that the Court of Appeals did not apply the proper standard in making this determination because it analyzed only a limited class of manual tasks and failed to ask whether respondent's impairments prevented or restricted her from performing tasks that are of central importance to most people's daily lives.

I

Respondent began working at petitioner's automobile manufacturing plant in Georgetown, Kentucky, in August 1990. She was soon placed on an engine fabrication assembly line, where her duties included work with pneumatic tools. Use of these tools eventually caused pain in respondent's hands, wrists, and arms. She sought treatment at petitioner's in-house medical service, where she was diagnosed with bilateral carpal tunnel syndrome and bilateral tendinitis. Respondent consulted a personal physician who placed her on permanent work restrictions that precluded her from lifting more than 20 pounds or from "frequently lifting or carrying . . . objects weighing up to 10 pounds," engaging in "constant repetitive . . . flexion or extension of [her] wrists or elbows," performing "overhead work," or using "vibratory or pneumatic tools."

In light of these restrictions, for the next two years petitioner assigned respondent to various modified duty jobs. [U]pon her return, petitioner placed respondent on a team in Quality Control Inspection Operations (QCIO). QCIO is responsible for four tasks: (1) "assembly paint"; (2) "paint second inspection"; (3) "shell body audit"; and (4) "ED surface repair." Respondent was initially placed on a team that performed only the first two of these tasks, and for a couple of years, she rotated on a weekly basis between them. In assembly paint, respondent visually inspected painted cars moving slowly down a conveyor. She scanned for scratches, dents, chips, or any other flaws that may have occurred during the assembly or painting process, at a rate of one car every 54 seconds. When respondent began working in assembly paint, inspection team members were required to open and shut the doors, trunk, and/or hood of each passing car. Sometime during respondent's tenure, however, the position was modified to include only visual inspection with few or no manual tasks. Paint second inspection required team members to use their hands to wipe each painted car with a glove as it moved along a conveyor. The parties agree that respondent was physically capable of performing both of these jobs and that her performance was satisfactory.

During the fall of 1996, petitioner announced that it wanted QCIO employees to be able to rotate through all four of the QCIO processes. Respondent therefore received training for the shell body audit job, in which team members apply a highlight oil to the hood, fender, doors, rear quarter panel, and trunk of passing cars at a rate of approximately one car per minute. The highlight oil has the viscosity of salad oil, and employees spread it on cars with a sponge attached to a block of wood. After they wipe each car with the oil, the employees visually inspect it for flaws. Wiping the cars required respondent to hold her hands and arms up around shoulder height for several hours at a time.

A short while after the shell body audit job was added to respondent's rotations, she began to experience pain in her neck and shoulders. Respondent again sought care at petitioner's in-house medical service, where she was diagnosed with myotendinitis bilateral periscapular, an inflammation of the muscles and tendons around both of her shoulder blades; myotendinitis and myositis bilateral forearms with nerve compression causing median nerve irritation; and thoracic outlet compression, a condition that causes pain in the nerves that lead to the upper extremities. Respondent requested that petitioner accommodate her medical conditions by allowing her to return to doing only her original two jobs in QCIO, which respondent claimed she could still perform without difficulty.

[O]n December 6, 1996, the last day respondent worked at petitioner's plant, she was placed under a no-work-of-any-kind restriction by her treating physicians. On January 27, 1997, respondent received a letter from petitioner that terminated her employment, citing her poor attendance record.

Respondent based her claim that she was "disabled" under the ADA on the ground that her physical impairments substantially limited her in (1) manual tasks; (2) housework; (3) gardening; (4) playing with her children; (5) lifting; and (6) working, all of which, she argued, constituted major life activities under the Act. Respondent also argued, in the alternative, that she was disabled under the ADA because she had a record of a substantially limiting impairment and because she was regarded as having such an impairment.

After petitioner filed a motion for summary judgment and respondent filed a motion for partial summary judgment on her disability claims, the District Court granted summary judgment to petitioner. The court found that respondent had not been disabled, as defined by the ADA, at the time of petitioner's alleged refusal to accommodate her, and that she had therefore not been covered by the Act's protections.

[T]he Court of Appeals for the Sixth Circuit reversed the District Court's ruling on whether respondent was disabled at the time she sought an accommodation. [T]he Court of Appeals held that in order for respondent to demonstrate that she was disabled due to a substantial limitation in the ability to perform manual tasks at the time of her accommodation request, she had to "show that her manual disability involve[d] a 'class' of manual activities affecting the ability to perform tasks at work." Respondent satisfied this test, according to the Court of Appeals, because her ailments "prevent[ed] her from doing the tasks associated with certain types of manual assembly line jobs, manual product handling jobs and manual building trade jobs (painting, plumbing, roofing, etc.) that require the gripping of tools and repetitive work with hands and arms extended at or above shoulder levels for extended periods of time." In reaching this conclusion, the court disregarded evidence that respondent could "ten[d] to her personal hygiene [and] carr[y] out personal or household chores," finding that such evidence "does not affect a determination that her impairment substantially limit[ed] her ability to perform the range of manual tasks associated with an assembly line job." Because the Court of Appeals concluded that respondent had been substantially limited in performing manual tasks and, for that reason, was entitled to partial summary judgment on the issue of whether she was disabled under the Act, it found that it did not need to determine whether respondent had been substantially limited in the major life activities of lifting or working, or whether she had had a "record of" a disability or had been "regarded as" disabled.

We granted *certiorari* to consider the proper standard for assessing whether an individual is substantially limited in performing manual tasks. We now reverse the Court of Appeals' decision to grant partial summary judgment to respondent on the issue of whether she was substantially limited in performing manual tasks at the time she sought an accommodation. We express no opinion on the working, lifting, or other arguments for disability status that were preserved below but which were not ruled upon by the Court of Appeals.

[III]

[T]he question presented by this case is whether the Sixth Circuit properly determined that respondent was disabled under subsection (A) of the ADA's disability definition at the time that she sought an accommodation from petitioner. The parties do not dispute that respondent's medical conditions, which include carpal tunnel syndrome, myotendinitis, and thoracic outlet compression, amount to physical impairments. The relevant question, therefore, is whether the Sixth Circuit correctly analyzed whether these impairments substantially limited respondent in the major life activity of performing manual tasks.

[O]ur consideration of this issue is guided first and foremost by the words of the disability definition itself. "[S]ubstantially" in the phrase "substantially limits" suggests "considerable" or "to a large degree." See Webster's Third New International Dictionary 2280 (1976) (defining "substantially" as "in a substantial manner" and "substantial" as "considerable in amount, value, or worth" and "being that specified to a large degree or in the main"); see also 17 Oxford English Dictionary 66–67 (2d ed.1989) ("substantial": "[r]elating to or proceeding from the essence of a thing; essential"; "[o]f ample or considerable amount, quantity, or dimensions"). The word "substantial" thus clearly precludes impairments that interfere in only a minor way with the performance of manual tasks from qualifying as disabilities.

"[M]ajor" in the phrase "major life activities" means important. See Webster's, *supra,* at 1363 (defining "major" as "greater in dignity, rank, importance, or interest"). "Major life activities" thus refers to those activities that are of central importance to daily life. In order for performing manual tasks to fit into this category—a category that includes such basic abilities as walking, seeing, and hearing—the manual tasks in question must be central to daily life. If each of the tasks included in the major life activity of performing manual tasks does not independently qualify as a major life activity, then together they must do so.

That these terms need to be interpreted strictly to create a demanding standard for qualifying as disabled is confirmed by the first section of the ADA, which lays out the legislative findings and purposes that motivate the Act. See 42 U.S.C. § 12101. When it enacted the ADA in 1990, Congress found that "some 43,000,000 Americans have one or more physical or mental disabilities." § 12101(a)(1). If Congress intended everyone with a physical impairment that precluded the performance of some isolated, unimportant, or particularly difficult manual task to qualify as disabled, the number of disabled Americans would surely have been much higher. Cf. [*Sutton*].

[A]n individualized assessment of the effect of an impairment is particularly necessary when the impairment is one whose symptoms vary widely from person to person. Carpal tunnel syndrome, one of respondent's impairments, is just such a condition. While cases of severe carpal tunnel syndrome are characterized by muscle atrophy and extreme sensory deficits, mild cases generally do not have either of these effects and create only intermittent symptoms of numbness and tingling. Studies have further shown that, even without surgical treatment, one quarter of carpal tunnel cases resolve in one month, but that in 22 percent of cases, symptoms last for eight years or longer. When pregnancy is the cause of carpal tunnel syndrome, in contrast, the symptoms normally resolve within two weeks of delivery. Given these large potential differences in the severity and duration of the effects of carpal tunnel syndrome, an individual's carpal tunnel syndrome diagnosis, on its own, does not indicate whether the individual has a disability within the meaning of the ADA.

IV

The Court of Appeals' analysis of respondent's claimed disability suggested that in order to prove a substantial limitation in the major life activity of performing manual tasks, a "plaintiff must show that her manual disability involves a 'class' of manual activities," and that those activities "affec[t] the ability to perform tasks at work." Both of these ideas lack support.

The Court of Appeals relied on our opinion in *Sutton v. United Air Lines, Inc.,* for the idea that a "class" of manual activities must be implicated for an impairment to substantially limit the major life activity of performing manual tasks. But *Sutton* said only that "*[w]hen the major life activity under consideration is that of working,* the statutory phrase 'substantially limits' requires . . . that plaintiffs allege they are unable to work in a broad class of jobs." Because of the conceptual difficulties inherent in the argument that working could be a major life activity, we have been hesitant to hold as much, and we need not decide this difficult question today. In *Sutton,* we noted that even assuming that working is a major life activity, a claimant would be required to show an inability to work in a "broad range of jobs," rather than a specific job. But *Sutton* did not suggest that a class-based analysis should be applied to any major life activity other than working. Nor do the EEOC regulations. In defining "substantially limits," the EEOC regulations only mention the "class" concept in the context of the major life activity of working. 29 CFR § 1630.2(j)(3) (2001).

While the Court of Appeals in this case addressed the different major life activity of performing manual tasks, its analysis circumvented *Sutton* by focusing on respondent's inability to perform manual tasks associated only with her job. This was error. When

Broad Range of Jobs not Specific Job

addressing the major life activity of performing manual tasks, the central inquiry must be whether the claimant is unable to perform the variety of tasks central to most people's daily lives, not whether the claimant is unable to perform the tasks associated with her specific job. Otherwise, *Sutton*'s restriction on claims of disability based on a substantial limitation in working will be rendered meaningless because an inability to perform a specific job always can be recast as an inability to perform a "class" of tasks associated with that specific job.

There is also no support in the Act, our previous opinions, or the regulations for the Court of Appeals' idea that the question of whether an impairment constitutes a disability is to be answered only by analyzing the effect of the impairment in the workplace. Indeed, the fact that the Act's definition of "disability" applies not only to Title I of the Act, which deals with employment, but also to the other portions of the Act, which deal with subjects such as public transportation and privately provided public accommodations, demonstrates that the definition is intended to cover individuals with disabling impairments regardless of whether the individuals have any connection to a workplace.

Even more critically, the manual tasks unique to any particular job are not necessarily important parts of most people's lives. As a result, occupation-specific tasks may have only limited relevance to the manual task inquiry. In this case, "repetitive work with hands and arms extended at or above shoulder levels for extended periods of time," the manual task on which the Court of Appeals relied, is not an important part of most people's daily lives. The court, therefore, should not have considered respondent's inability to do such manual work in her specialized assembly line job as sufficient proof that she was substantially limited in performing manual tasks.

At the same time, the Court of Appeals appears to have disregarded the very type of evidence that it should have focused upon. It treated as irrelevant "[t]he fact that [respondent] can . . . ten[d] to her personal hygiene [and] carr[y] out personal or household chores." Yet household chores, bathing, and brushing one's teeth are among the types of manual tasks of central importance to people's daily lives, and should have been part of the assessment of whether respondent was substantially limited in performing manual tasks.

[A]ccordingly, we reverse the Court of Appeals' judgment granting partial summary judgment to respondent and remand the case for further proceedings consistent with this opinion.

So ordered.

NOTES ON THE *PRE-ADA AMENDMENTS ACT* CASES

1. **Medical and Social Models of Disability.** Recall the discussion in Chapter One of the medical and social models of disability. Which, if either, of these two models is most salient in the cases in this section? *Bragdon* contains extensive discussion of the physiological effects of HIV (most of it edited out of the squib above), but it also focuses, crucially, on the disease's effect on Sydney Abbott's reproductive choices. Justice Ginsburg's concurrence emphasizes the way that "the reaction of others" limits the opportunities available to people with HIV.

Why should people be protected against discrimination because they have severe medical conditions? Because their medical conditions turn ordinary life choices into potentially tragic ones? Or because others react to their conditions by excluding them from opportunities? Perhaps disability discrimination laws should be understood as an act of beneficence for people who, due to their medical impairments, have suffered enough. Or perhaps those laws should be seen as identifying a stigmatized, systematically disadvantaged class and protecting them against the discrimination that instantiates and constructs that stigma and disadvantage. How do these different perspectives bear on the interpretive question in *Bragdon*?

How does *Sutton* address these questions? Justice O'Connor's opinion for the Court seems to reflect a medical model of disability. In concluding that the "disability" determination must take account of mitigating measures, Justice O'Connor focuses on the medical effects of those measures—by wearing glasses, the Sutton sisters eliminated the physical effects of their impairment and thus no longer had a disability. A medical model is also apparent in Justice O'Connor's skepticism of "working" as a major life activity. At every point, the analysis in the majority opinion focuses on the medical rather than the social effects of impairment.

As in *Bragdon*, Justice Ginsburg's separate concurrence seems to reflect far more of a social model of disability. Justice Ginsburg argues that the "disability" determination must take account of mitigating measures because "persons whose uncorrected eyesight is poor, or who rely on daily medication for their well-being, can be found in every social and economic class; they do not cluster among the politically powerless, nor do they coalesce as historical victims of discrimination." That analysis, although deployed in support of a result that many disability rights advocates oppose, is very much in tune with the notion that it is social choices, and not medical facts, that determine what impairments are disabling. Many disability rights advocates argue that disability defines a disadvantaged, minority group, and Justice Ginsburg's analysis is explicitly geared toward identifying the contours of that group.

And what of *Toyota*? The Court's unanimous opinion there seems most concerned with the medical-physiological effects of Williams's carpal tunnel syndrome and tendinitis. But would a focus on stigma and systematic disadvantage lead to a different result? Or, as with eyeglass wearers in *Sutton*, would it point in the same direction as the Court's more medicalized approach?

Justice Ginsburg's approach, of course, does not exhaust the ways one might give content to the social model:

> The social model recognizes that all people's abilities lie on a spectrum, and there is no *a priori* line that divides the level of ability we call "normal" from the level we call "disability." Instead, it is society that explicitly and implicitly draws that line. But that diagnosis hardly dictates the proper prescription for disability policy. To the contrary, it could call for one of two diametrically opposed policy responses. One possible response would be to take society's construction of disability and go with it:

through prejudice, stereotypes, and neglect, one might say, society has created a distinct (though not *naturally* distinct) minority group of people with disabilities. By analogy to the affirmative action remedies that were adopted in the race context, one might then argue that the proper policy response is to direct resources and accommodations at that group. The work of the scholar-activist Harlan Hahn articulates that "minority group" model of disability, and many disability rights activists have operated on the basis of that model.

The opposite policy prescription, equally consistent with the social model of disability, would be to declare that the disability label is arbitrary and useless, and to pursue (in the words of Irving Zola, another prominent scholar-activist) "universal policies that recognize that the entire population is 'at risk' for the concomitants of chronic illness and disability." To continue with the affirmative action analogy, this universalist position might be akin to William van Alstyne's call to "get[ ] beyond racism by getting beyond it *now*." It might see people with socially identified disabilities as canaries in the coal mine, whose incompatibility with existing physical or social structures calls our attention to problems that all individuals can face in dealing with a world that often fails to take individualized needs into account. But the proper response would not be disability specific—it would be the universal design of the built environment to embrace the largest variety of potential users, as well as a general rule of flexibility to recognize that all people are different.

Samuel R. Bagenstos, Law and the Contradictions of the Disability Rights Movement 20-21 (2009). Justice Ginsburg's understanding is consistent with the minority-group interpretation of the social model of disability. The approach taken by Justice Stevens's *Sutton* dissent, by contrast, resonates with the universalist interpretation of that model. Whether or not the Sutton sisters' visual impairments were generally disabling, he argued, they were incompatible with the rules that United Air Lines set for its global pilots. That incompatibility, he said, demands interrogation and justification. How would that approach apply in *Toyota*?

Which of these approaches do you find most compelling?

2. **Major Life Activities.** The *Bragdon* Court holds that "major life activities" are activities that are comparatively important to people's lives, but that they need not be engaged in daily, and they need not be of a public or economic character. In reaching that conclusion, Justice Kennedy's majority opinion relies on the plain meaning of the term "major" and the illustrative list of major life activities in the Rehabilitation Act regulations. Chief Justice Rehnquist's dissent relies on the same materials, but concludes that "major" life activities are those important activities that are performed by normal people on a day-to-day basis. Who has the better of the argument?

Why is the Court skeptical in *Sutton* that working can be a major life activity? Following the definition applied in *Bragdon* ("comparative importance," "significance"), is there any doubt that working is a "major" activity in most people's lives? As the "argue in a circle" quote from the oral argument in *Arline* suggests, the Court appears concerned about bootstrapping: An individual could claim that because an employer discriminated against her, she had a statutory disability and could therefore challenge the discrimination. If that were true, the "substantially limits one or more of the major life activities" language would be superfluous in employment cases—any time an employer discriminates against an individual with an impairment, that impairment would become, *ipso facto*, a disability.

But the *Arline* Court itself rejected the bootstrapping point: "The argument is not circular, however, but direct. Congress plainly intended the [Rehabilitation] Act to cover persons with a physical or mental impairment (whether actual, past, or perceived) that substantially limited one's ability to work. '[T]he primary goal of the Act is to increase employment of the handicapped.' " *School Board v. Arline*, 480 U.S. 273, 283 n.10 (1987) (quoting *Consolidated Rail Corp. v. Darrone*, 465 U.S. 624, 633 n.13 (1984)). Why was the *Sutton* Court unmoved by that argument? Is it because of medical-model thinking—that inability to work is the result of an interaction between a person's physical or mental endowments and what workplaces need, while the other major life activities listed in the regulations seem to look purely at the endowments themselves? Or is it just because the Court feared, as Justice Stevens suggested in dissent, that accepting working as a major life activity would open the door to too many plaintiffs?

Is *Toyota*'s interpretation of "major life activities"—"those activities that are of central importance to daily life"—consistent with the interpretation in *Bragdon* and *Sutton*? After its sharp divisions in the earlier cases, why do you think the Court was unanimous in *Toyota*?

3.   The Major Life Activity of Reproduction. The major life activity of reproduction was the clearest path to holding that asymptomatic HIV is a disability in *Bragdon*: The 1988 OLC memorandum interpreting the Rehabilitation Act had relied on limitations in reproduction in concluding that asymptomatic HIV was a disability; OLC's interpretation was specifically presented to Congress during its consideration of the proposed ADA; and the committee reports accompanying the statute endorsed that interpretation. But the Court's reliance on the major life activity of reproduction raises a number of questions.

For one thing, HIV will not lead to substantial limitations in reproduction for every individual who acquires the disease. Consider a post-menopausal woman, a woman who was infertile to begin with, or a nun who acquires HIV in a blood transfusion. Sydney Abbott testified that her HIV disease was the reason she chose not to have a child; would the Court's reproduction-focused analysis apply even in the case of an individual who would not have had a child even before she acquired HIV? Does it make sense for civil rights protection of individuals with HIV to turn on whether the disease affected the individual's childbearing choices? What is the normative justification for protecting individuals with HIV from discrimination *only* when those individuals would have had children had they not contracted the disease?

For another thing, the Court's analysis seems to extend well beyond HIV. If HIV is a disability because it substantially limits the major life activity of reproduction, then infertility should, *a fortiori*, be a disability as well. Some lower courts have followed that logic and stated flatly that infertility is a disability. See, e.g., *Yindee v. CCH Inc.*, 458 F.3d 599, 601 (7th Cir.2006). But, to pick up Justice Ginsburg's analysis, would a rational legislator want to provide antidiscrimination protection to *all* individuals with infertility but only *some* individuals with HIV?

4.   Substantially Limits. What is the scope of *Bragdon*'s substantial limitation holding? Sydney Abbott could not bear and beget a child without facing an (at least) 8% risk of passing HIV along to the child (and some risk of passing the disease along to a partner if artificial insemination were not used). These are burdens that most people probably would not want to assume (and that, as Justice Kennedy points out, there is a public interest in avoiding). Is the point that the inability to engage in a major life activity without assuming such a burden is a substantial limitation in that activity? If so, how does one avoid Chief Justice Rehnquist's *reductio*—that under the Court's view "every individual with a genetic marker for some debilitating disease" would have a disability, even if the individual *never* acquired that disease? Is the point that the genetic marker would not be an "impairment"? Cf. EEOC Compliance Manual, Section 902: Definition of the Term Disability (individuals discriminated against because of their own genetic susceptibility to illness are covered under the "regarded as" prong of the disability definition).

The Genetic Information Nondiscrimination Act of 2008, Pub. L. No. 110–233, 122 Stat. 881 (2008), prohibits employers and health insurers from discriminating on the basis of genetic information. But unlike the ADA and Rehabilitation Act, GINA does not require reasonable accommodation. See, *e.g.*, *id.* § 202(a) (to be codified at 42 U.S.C. § 2000ff–1(a)). Note that the congressional statement of purposes for GINA invokes some purposes that seem quite consonant with purposes typically attributed to disability rights law, *e.g.*, *id.* § 2(2) (expressing concern that new advances in genetic information might be used in a way reminiscent of the eugenics movement of the early 20th Century), as well as some that seem quite distinct, *e.g. id.* § 2(3) (noting that "many genetic conditions and disorders are associated with particular racial and ethnic groups and gender" and expressing concern that "members of a particular group may [therefore] be stigmatized or discriminated against as a result of that genetic information"); *id.* § 2(5) (seeking to "allay [public] concerns about the potential for discrimination, thereby allowing individuals to take advantage of genetic testing, technologies, research, and new therapies"). Mark Rothstein notes one major limitation of the statute: "GINA prohibits discrimination based on genotype, but not phenotype. Thus, GINA only applies to individuals who are asymptomatic. In the health insurance context, individuals are protected from discrimination based on their genetic risk of disease, but they are not protected if they develop the disease." Mark A. Rothstein, *GINA, the ADA, and Genetic Discrimination in Employment*, 36 J.L. Med. & Ethics 837, 838 (2008). The ADA extends to some symptomatic individuals, but only (as subsequent chapters will discuss) if they can show that they are "qualified" for the job or benefit they seek.

Is *Bragdon*'s interpretation of substantial limitation consistent with *Sutton*'s? To show that she is substantially limited in working, the *Sutton* Court held, a plaintiff must prove that she is "unable to work in a broad class of jobs." And "[i]f jobs utilizing an individual's skills (but perhaps not his or her unique talents) are available, one is not precluded from a substantial class of jobs." Is that consistent with *Bragdon*, where the Court emphasized that "[t]he Act addresses substantial limitations on major life activities, not utter inabilities"?

Why should an individual be denied ADA protection if "jobs utilizing [his or her] skills" but "not his or her unique talents" are available? Consider the Court's application of that principle in *Sutton* and *Murphy*. In *Sutton*, the Court held that the plaintiffs' inability to work as a "global airline pilot" was not a substantial limitation on working, because the plaintiffs could still work as regional airline pilots or flight instructors. But regional pilots "can earn a great deal less than—perhaps as little as a third of the salaries of—their counterparts at the major carriers." *Samuel R. Bagenstos, Subordination, Stigma, and "Disability,"* 86 Va. L. Rev. 397, 510 (2000). And "flight instructor jobs typically represent the lowest-paid first rung on a pilot's career ladder." *Id.* In *Murphy*, the Court held that the plaintiff's inability to work in jobs requiring a commercial driver's license was not a substantial limitation on working, because the plaintiff could still work in other jobs. But Murphy's inability to obtain a commercial driver's license "would disqualify him from literally millions of jobs." *Id.* Professor Samuel Issacharoff and Justin Nelson have criticized this aspect of *Sutton* for "essentially presum[ing] the fungibility of jobs, a strikingly odd presumption in the context of a statutory scheme designed to end occupational segregation." Samuel Issacharoff & Justin Nelson, *Discrimination with a Difference: Can Employment Discrimination Law Accommodate the Americans with Disabilities Act?*, 79 N.C. L. Rev. 307, 329–330 (2001).

The Court might simply be attempting to avoid the bootstrapping problem—if an individual cannot perform a large number of jobs, then there is no reason to fear that she is using a single employer's adverse job decision as the basis for arguing that she has a disability. But that concern could be satisfied by holding that substantial limitation in working requires more than the inability to perform a single job. Neither *Sutton* nor *Murphy* was a case in which a plaintiff was disqualified from only a single job for idiosyncratic reasons, and the Court's "jobs utilizing an individual's skills" standard excludes far more people from ADA coverage than is necessary to avoid bootstrapping. Is the notion that any "real" disability would likely manifest itself as a substantial limitation of some other major life activity, so the concept of substantial limitation in working should be as narrow as possible? Relatedly, is the concern one of fakery—that individuals with only minor limitations will otherwise be able to slip into the disability category by pointing to work restrictions?

Matthew Diller has argued that *Sutton*'s substantial-limitation-in-working analysis improperly "transmutes the ADA from an equal access measure into a means of providing some threshold level of access to the job market." Matthew Diller, *Judicial Backlash, the ADA, and the Civil Rights Model*, 21 Berkeley J. Emp. & Lab. L. 19, 29 (2000). Linda Krieger has similarly argued that *Sutton* demonstrates that the Court does "not understand that the ADA, even with its redistributive reasonable accommodation provisions, is an anti-discrimination statute, not a social welfare benefits program like social security." Linda Hamilton Krieger, Socio-Legal Backlash, 21 Berkeley J. Emp. & Lab. L. 476, 516 (2000). But the Court's concern about access to the job market clearly resonates with the arguments of many ADA supporters that the statute was necessary to move people with disabilities off of welfare and into the workforce; by limiting protection to those who need the ADA to stay in the workforce, *Sutton* seems to serve that welfare-reform purpose (a purpose that may or may not be normatively attractive). See Samuel R. Bagenstos, *The Americans with Disabilities Act as Welfare Reform*, 44 Wm. & Mary L. Rev. 921, 976–980 (2003).

5.   The Mitigating Measures Issue. *Sutton* was heavily criticized by the disability rights community. Much of that criticism focused on the Court's holding that the disability determination must take account of the measures an individual uses to mitigate the effects of her impairment. As Justice Stevens's dissent shows, that holding is inconsistent with some quite specific statements in the committee reports accompanying the ADA. But didn't Justice O'Connor have a point that mitigating measures can have a significant effect on whether an impairment currently "substantially limits" a major life activity? The facts of *Sutton* highlight the concern.

Once we move beyond eyeglasses, however, the Court's decision may appear more problematic. Epilepsy, diabetes, and schizophrenia, among other conditions, may be controlled by medication, but, even when controlled, they are frequent targets of discrimination. A person may be able to walk with a prosthetic leg but frequently experience discrimination anyway. The *Sutton* Court suggests that people with these conditions will still be covered if the mitigating measures themselves impose substantial limitations (*e.g.*, the side effects of medication) or if the mitigating measures do not eliminate the substantial limitations imposed by the underlying impairment (the Court suggests individuals who have prosthetic legs might meet this test). But does that lead to sensible results?

In *Branham v. Snow*, 392 F.3d 896, 903 (7th Cir.2004), for example, the court applied *Sutton* to hold that the plaintiff's diabetes constituted a "disability" even though it was "undisputed" that the plaintiff's "treatment regimen allows him to avoid severe hypoglycemic and hyperglycemic episodes, and protects him from the long-term consequences of Type I diabetes." The court determined that the "negative side effects" of the plaintiff's treatment regime were "many" (*id.* at 903–904):

> His dietary intake is dictated by his diabetes, and must respond, with significant precision, to the blood sugar readings he takes four times a day. Depending upon the level of his blood sugar, Mr. Branham may have to eat immediately, may have to wait to eat, or may have to eat certain types of food. Even after the mitigating measures of his treatment regimen, he is never free to eat whatever he pleases because

he risks both mild and severe bodily reactions if he disregards his blood sugar readings. He must adjust his diet to compensate for any greater exertion, stress, or illness that he experiences.

In *Scheerer v. Potter*, 443 F.3d 916 (7th Cir.2006), by contrast, the court concluded that the plaintiff's diabetes was not a "disability." The court explained that "[d]uring the pertinent time period, Scheerer did not experience many of the more severe symptoms of diabetes, including severe hypoglycemia, seizures, or loss of consciousness." *Id.* at 920. Although the plaintiff "relied on a cumbersome protective boot for a period of time because of his diabetic ulcers and experienced intermittent episodes of significant neuropathy," the court concluded that "he nonetheless was generally able to walk and stand during the pertinent time period." And although the plaintiff faced "dietary restrictions," the court concluded that his "predominant purpose" in following those restrictions "was to lose weight—as millions of other non-disabled individuals seek to do—rather than to control rapid fluctuations of his blood sugar levels that could lead to immediate and dire consequences." *Id.* Does it make sense to treat these two individuals with diabetes so differently—protecting one but not the other from discrimination—simply because one individual's "diabetes had not yet worsened to such a stage where it severely restricted his major life activities" (*id.*)?

6.   "Regarded As." Consider the following critique of *Sutton*'s interpretation of the "regarded as" prong:

> The best evidence of what an employer regards to be necessary to perform a job is the set of minimum requirements it actually imposes on those who seek that job. If an employer disqualifies all people with asthma from bicycle courier positions, for example, one can rationally infer that the employer regards asthma as sufficiently interfering with an individual's ability to perform that job to disqualify her from all bicycle courier positions. If disqualification from all bicycle courier jobs amounts to a substantial limitation on working, it should not matter whether asthma is in fact substantially limiting. The "regarded as" analysis should be satisfied by the fact (inferred from the employer's imposition of the job requirement) that the employer regards asthma as imposing a limitation that would be substantial.

> For the same reason, the employer's job criteria ought to be imputed to all other employers for purposes of the "regarded as" analysis. In a "regarded as" case where the plaintiff alleges that the defendant regarded her as disabled, it should be irrelevant whether other employers have adopted similarly disqualifying criteria. The issue should instead turn on whether the defendant believed that the plaintiff's impairment was incompatible with the safe and economical performance of a sufficient number of jobs to constitute a substantial limitation. Unless the employer acknowledges that its selection criteria are irrational—that they do not serve the purpose of screening out those who are incapable of performing the job safely and economically—there is every reason to believe that the employer regards applicants who fail its criteria as unable to perform similar jobs for all other employers.

Samuel R. Bagenstos, *Subordination, Stigma, and "Disability,"* 86 Va. L. Rev. 397, 515–516 (2000). How do you think Justice O'Connor would respond to that critique?

2.   The ADA Amendments Act

Rico v. Xcel Energy, Inc.
United States District Court for the District of New Mexico, 2012.
893 F.Supp.2d 1165.

■ Martha Vazquez, District Judge.

THIS MATTER comes before the Court on Defendants' Motion to Dismiss First Amended Complaint. The Court, having considered the motion, briefs, relevant law and being otherwise fully informed, finds that the Motion [w]ill be [D]ENIED[.]

BACKGROUND

For purposes of this motion, the Court accepts as true the facts as alleged in the First Amended Complaint (the "Complaint"). Plaintiff has been an employee of Southwestern Public Service Company ("Southwestern") since 1999. In or about January of 2009, he suffered a work injury, which required him to undergo back surgery. After his surgery, in or about February or March of 2010, his physician released him to resume employment with "modest lifting restrictions" and "no utility pole climbing." At that time, he was working as a "third year apprentice lineman."

In or about March or April of 2010, Plaintiff requested a transfer to a job for which he was qualified, and for which he would not be required to climb utility poles or lift more than sixty pounds. Defendants refused this request, and instead recommended that Plaintiff apply for long-term disability benefits, terminated his employment, and required him to apply for an open position, in competition with other job applicants. Plaintiff notified his union of Southwestern's actions; the union declined to initiate a grievance procedure.

Thereafter, Southwestern offered Plaintiff a job as a "substation electrician," at a lower rate of pay than he had been earning in his previous position. Southwestern also eliminated Plaintiff's three years of seniority as a third year apprentice lineman. Plaintiff accepted the employment offer, and has held the substation electrician position since June 1, 2011.

On January 19, 2012, Plaintiff filed his First Amended Complaint for Damages Arising from Violation of Americans with Disabilities Act against Southwestern and Xcel Energy, Inc. ("Xcel"). The Complaint alleges a claim under the Americans with Disabilities Act ("ADA") (Count I). [O]n February 15, 2012, Defendants filed the instant motion to dismiss. Plaintiff filed a response on February 29, 2012.

[D]ISCUSSION

[T]he ADA prohibits employment discrimination against "a qualified individual on the basis of disability" with regard to "the hiring, advancement, or discharge of employees . . . and other terms, conditions, and privileges of employment" on the basis of such disability. 42 U.S.C. § 12112(a). The term "discriminate" includes the failure to make "reasonable accommodations to the known physical or mental limitations of an otherwise qualified individual with a disability," unless the employer demonstrates that such accommodations would impose an "undue hardship" on the operation of their business. 42 U.S.C. § 12112(b)(5)(A).

[P]laintiff alleges that Defendants' refusal to reasonably accommodate his disability by allowing him to transfer to a position that does not require heavy lifting constitutes a violation of the ADA. Defendants argue that Count I fails to state a claim under the ADA because it is devoid of facts that, if proven, would establish that Plaintiff is disabled.

For purposes of the ADA, an individual is disabled if he: (1) has "a physical or mental impairment that substantially limits one or more major life activities of such individual;" (2) has "a record of such an impairment;" or (3) is "regarded as having such an impairment." 42 U.S.C. § 12102(1). Plaintiff argues that his back injury is an impairment that substantially limits his ability to lift, and that he thus has adequately alleged a disability under the ADA. Defendants counter that the allegations of Plaintiff's impairment are insufficient to allege a disability under the ADA, because limitations on heavy lifting and climbing are not, as a matter of law, "substantial limitations" of major life activities.

"Ultimately, whether an individual is substantially limited as to a major life activity is a question of fact." *Mills v. Temple Univ.*, 869 F.Supp.2d 609, 621 (E.D.Pa.2012). Before Congress amended the ADA in 2008, courts construed the Act strictly, finding that an individual was "substantially limited" only if he had "an impairment that prevents or severely restricts the individual from doing activities that are of central importance to most people's daily lives." Toyota v. Williams. In another leading ADA case, the Supreme Court held that the degree of limitation caused by an individual's impairment should be determined with reference to the ameliorative effects of mitigating measures. *Sutton.*

On January 1, 2009, however, Congress passed the ADA Amendments Act of 2008 ("ADAAA"), rejecting *Toyota* and *Sutton*. Pub. L. No. 110–325, § 2(b)(1)–(6), 122 Stat. 3553 (2008). With the ADAAA, Congress explicitly lowered the standard for "substantially limits," noting that "lower courts have incorrectly found in individual cases that people with a range of substantially limiting impairments are not people with disabilities." Pub. L. No. 110–325, § 2(a)(6), 122 Stat. at 3553. Congress declared that "the primary object of attention in cases brought under the ADA should be whether entities covered under the ADA have complied with their obligations," and that "the question of whether an individual's impairment is a disability under the ADA should not demand extensive analysis." Pub. L. No. 110–325, § 2(b)(5), 122 Stat. at 3554. Notably, the ADA, as amended, explicitly defines "major life activities" to include lifting. 42 U.S.C. § 12102(2)(A).

The post-ADAAA regulations promulgated by the EEOC similarly caution that the term "substantially limits": is "not meant to be a demanding standard"; shall be construed broadly in favor of expansive coverage, to the "maximum extent permitted by the ADA"; and shall "be applied to require a degree of functional limitation that is lower than the standard for 'substantially limits' applied prior to the ADAAA." 29 C.F.R. § 1630.2(j)(i), (iv). While noting that "not every impairment will constitute a disability within the meaning of [the ADA]," the regulations make clear that "[a]n impairment need not prevent, or significantly or severely restrict, the individual from performing a major life activity in order to be considered substantially limiting." 29 C.F.R. § 1630.2(j)(ii). Rather, the relevant inquiry is whether a disability "substantially limits the ability of an individual to perform a major life activity as compared to most people in the general population." *Id.* While this inquiry "usually will not require scientific, medical, or statistical analysis," such evidence may be presented in order "to make such a comparison where appropriate." 29 C.F.R. § 1630.2(j)(v).

"Few courts have had occasion to consider the effects of the ADAAA. Those that have, apply it broadly to encompass disabilities that previously might have been excluded." Harty v. City of Sanford, No. 11–cv–1041, 2012 WL 3243282, *5 (M.D.Fla. Aug. 8, 2012). Of particular relevance here, in light of the new standards outlined in the ADAAA and its implementing regulations, courts have declined to dismiss, under Rule 12(b)(6), ADA claims for failure to allege facts that, if proven, would establish an impairment that "substantially limits" a major life activity. *See* Lapier v. Prince George's County, Md., No. 10–CV–2851, 2012 WL 1552780, *7–8 (D.Md. Apr. 27, 2012) (holding that plaintiff's allegations of a blood disorder that caused decreased oxygen in his blood were sufficient to state a claim of a disability that substantially limited his major life activities); Johnson v. Farmers Ins. Exch., No. CIV–11–963, 2012 WL 95387, *1 (W.D.Okla. Jan. 12, 2012) (holding that, under the broader definition of disability set forth in the ADAAA, Plaintiff's allegations that she suffered from sleep apnea were sufficient to state a claim that she had a disability that substantially limited a major life activity); *Coffman v. Robert J. Young Co., Inc.*, No. 3:10–1052, 2011 WL 2174465 (M.D.Tenn. June 1, 2011) (recommending that district court deny motion to dismiss, as plaintiff sufficiently pleaded that she was an individual with a disability within the meaning of the ADA where she alleged that she suffered serious injuries that required, after a six-month medical leave, lifting restrictions and limited motions affecting her ability to work), *report and recommendation adopted,* No. 3:10–1052, 2011 WL 2416745 (M.D.Tenn. June 14, 2011); *see also Farina v. Branford Board of Educ.*, No. 09–CV–49, 2010 WL 3829160, *11 (D.Conn. Sept. 23, 2010) (stating that, in light of the fact that the ADAAA lowered the threshold requirement to establish a disability, and specifically included lifting as a major life activity, "it is possible that even a relatively minor lifting restriction could qualify as a disability within the statute"), *aff'd,* 458 Fed.Appx. 13 (2d Cir.2011).

While acknowledging the broadened standards of the ADAAA, Defendants nonetheless argue that neither heavy lifting nor climbing utility poles is an activity that can be accomplished by "most people in the general population," and thus that Plaintiff's inability to perform these tasks, as a matter of law, does not constitute a "substantial limitation" on a major life activity. In support of this argument, Defendants point to Tenth

Circuit cases finding that lifting restrictions even more stringent than the 60–pound lifting restriction at issue here did not substantially limit major life activities. *See Rakity v. Dillon Cos.,* 302 F.3d 1152 (10th Cir.2002) (40-pound lifting restriction); *Lusk v. Ryder Integrated Logistics,* 238 F.3d 1237 (10th Cir.2001) (same); *Huckans v. U.S.P.S.,* 201 F.3d 448, 1999 WL 1079619 (10th Cir. Nov. 30, 1999) (35-pound lifting restriction); *McCoy v. USF Dugan, Inc.,* 42 Fed.Appx. 295, 2002 WL 1435908 (10th Cir. July 3, 2002) (25-pound lifting restriction). While admitting that these cases were all decided under pre-ADAAA standards, Defendants contend that they remain "valid guidance for this Court," as they were not decided based on the principles set forth in the *Toyota* and *Sutton* decisions specifically discussed and rejected by Congress in the ADAAA.

The Court does not read the ADAAA's repudiation of prior case law so narrowly. Indeed, in the ADAAA, Congress specifically noted that *"lower courts* have incorrectly found in individual cases that people with a range of substantially limiting impairments are not people with disabilities." Pub. L. No. 110–325, § 2(a)(6), 122 Stat. at 3553 (emphasis added). In response to these lower court decisions, Congress passed the ADAA for the express purpose of lowering the threshold for the term, "substantially limits," and the EEOC has instructed that courts now apply that term to require a degree of functional limitation that is lower than the standard applied prior to the ADAAA. The express language of the ADAA and its interpretative regulations thus call into question the continued precedential value of pre-amendment cases, such as those cited by Defendants, which well might have applied a higher degree of functional limitation than is now permissible under the statute to determine whether lifting restrictions are stringent enough to qualify an individual as disabled.

Moreover, none of the cases cited by Defendants involved a motion to dismiss an ADA claim based on the insufficiency of the factual allegations in a complaint; rather, each of those cases had reached the summary judgment stage, and the Court's decision therein, based on a fully developed factual record, addressed the sufficiency of the plaintiff's evidence of a disability. *See Lusk,* 238 F.3d at 1241 ("agree[ing] with the district court that Plaintiff failed to produce sufficient evidence to establish (for the purpose of defeating summary judgment) that his lifting restriction is substantially limiting."); ***1170** Rakity,* 302 F.3d at 1159 ("The most favorable interpretation of Mr. Rakity's medical and employment records does not suggest he is substantially impaired in performing manual tasks."); *Huckans,* 1999 WL 1079619, at *3 n. 4 ("Huckan's failure to present [evidence comparing his lifting restriction with the capabilities of an average person] reinforces the conclusion that his impairment is not substantially limiting."); *McCoy,* 42 Fed.Appx. at 298 (affirming summary judgment for employer where employee "ha[d] not shown that she was substantially limited in the major life activity of lifting"). In contrast, Plaintiff herein has not yet had an opportunity to present evidence of the limitations on his major life activities as compared to "most people in the general population." Accordingly, even if the cases cited by Defendants continue to have precedential value after the ADAAA as to what evidence is required in order to survive summary judgment, they provide little guidance to the Court in determining whether Plaintiff's allegations are sufficiently pled to survive the instant motion to dismiss.

Under the broadened standards of the ADAAA, the Court finds Plaintiff's allegations as to his disability sufficient to withstand the pleading requirements of Rule 12(b)(6). According to the Complaint, Plaintiff's condition renders him unable to climb utility poles or engage in heavy lifting. Post-surgery, his doctor limited him to work that did not involve lifting over sixty pounds or climbing utility poles. Moreover, Southwestern recommended that Plaintiff apply for long-term disability benefits. These allegations, read in the light most favorable to Plaintiff, are sufficient to raise an inference that Plaintiff was disabled at the time of his termination. Accordingly, the Court would be premature in dismissing Plaintiff's ADA claim at this stage of the litigation.

[C]ONCLUSION

[T]he Complaint contains sufficient factual matter, accepted as true, to state a claim to relief under [t]he ADA [t]hat is plausible on its face[.]

Norton v. Assisted Living Concepts, Inc.

United States District Court for the Eastern District of Texas, 2011.
786 F.Supp.2d 1173.

■ RICHARD A. SCHELL, CHIEF JUDGE.

[T]his is an employment discrimination suit brought under [t]he Americans with Disabilities Act (ADA). Plaintiff Michael J. Norton began working for Defendant ALC in May of 2008. Operating over 200 facilities in twenty states, ALC provides assisted living services to the elderly. Norton worked at ALC's "Hopkins House" facility in Sulphur Springs, Texas as a "Residence Sales Manager" and was responsible for attracting people to reside at the facility.

In April of 2009, Norton was diagnosed with a cancerous tumor on his left kidney. After obtaining permission from ALC, Norton went on medical leave and underwent surgery on May 22, 2009. Norton returned to work on July 1, 2009. On August 5, 2009, ALC fired Norton. ALC alleges that Norton was fired because of his poor job performance. Norton alleges that he was fired for taking medical leave and because he suffered from cancer.

[I]n its motion, ALC argues that Norton did not have an actual disability as that term is defined in the Act and that Norton has failed to show that ALC regarded Norton as having such a disability. Therefore, ALC argues, Norton has failed to make a prima facie case of discrimination under the ADA. Accordingly, ALC seeks summary judgment on Norton's ADA claim.

[T]he sole issue before the court is whether ALC's motion for summary judgment should be granted on the basis of Norton not having an actual disability, as that term is defined in the Act. Norton argues that Congress' recent amendments to the ADA operate to qualify his renal cancer as a disability under the Act, and, therefore, summary judgment is not warranted. For the following reasons, the court agrees with Norton and finds that ALC's motion for summary judgment should be denied.

The ADA Amendments Act of 2008 (ADAAA) was signed into law by President George W. Bush on September 25, 2008, with a statutory effective date of January 1, 2009. Pub.L. No. 110–325, 122 Stat 3553. Passed in response to decisions by the U.S. Supreme Court that, according to Congress, had "created an inappropriately high level of limitation necessary to obtain coverage under the ADA," the ADAAA sought to reinstate "a broad scope of protection . . . available under the ADA." *Id.* at 3554 (citing *Sutton* and *Toyota*).

The primary way in which Congress chose to broaden the scope of ADA coverage was to expand the law's definition of the term disability. Congress' stated purpose in expanding the definition of disability was to "convey that the question of whether an individual's impairment is a disability under the ADA should not demand extensive analysis." *Id.* This is because "the primary object of attention in cases brought under the ADA should be whether entities covered under the ADA have complied with their obligations." *Id.*

While the ADAAA retained the three prong definition of disability, it significantly expanded the meaning of terms included in that definition. Thus, the Act expanded the meaning of terms under the actual disability prong, which, as stated previously, defines a person with a disability as one who has an actual "physical or mental impairment that substantially limits one or more major life activities of such individual." 42 U.S.C. § 12102(1). For purposes of this case, the most significant changes to the ADA are as follows:

(1) The ADA now states that "[t]he definition of 'disability' [under the Act] shall be construed in favor of broad coverage of individuals . . . to the maximum extent permitted by the terms [of the Act]." 42 U.S.C. § 12102(4)(A).

(2) The definition of "major life activities" under the Act's actual disability prong was expanded to include the operation of "major bodily functions." 42 U.S.C. § 12102(2)(B). The Act now includes a sample list of major bodily functions that constitute a major life activity; this list includes "normal cell growth." *Id.*

(3) The Act emphasizes that the term "substantially limit" under the actual disability prong shall be interpreted as broadly as possible. 42 U.S.C. § 12102(4)(A) & (B).

(4) The Act now clarifies that as long as an impairment substantially limits one major life activity, such as normal cell growth, it need not limit other major life activities, such as working, in order to be considered a disability. 42 U.S.C. § 12102(4)(C).

(5) Finally, the Act explains that "[a]n impairment that is episodic or in remission is a disability if it would substantially limit a major life activity [such as normal cell growth] when active." 42 U.S.C. § 12102(4)(D).

Applying the amended definition of disability under the actual disability prong to the facts in this case, the court concludes that Norton's renal cancer is capable of qualifying as a disability under the ADA. Neither side disputes that renal cancer, when active, constitutes a "physical impairment" under the statute. Further, the court finds that renal cancer, when active, "substantially limits" the "major life activity" of "normal cell growth." *See* 42 U.S.C. § 12102(4)(A) & (B); 42 U.S.C. § 12102(2)(B).

Therefore, that Norton may have been in remission when he returned to work at ALC is of no consequence. *See* 42 U.S.C. § 12102(4)(D). Finally, Norton's renal cancer qualifies as a disability even if the only "major life activity" it "substantially limited" was "normal cell growth." *See* 42 U.S.C. § 12102(4)(C).

The court's conclusion that Norton's renal cancer is capable of qualifying as a disability under the ADA is bolstered by the EEOC's interpretation and implementation of the ADAAA. The EEOC's final regulations implementing the amendments provide a list of impairments that, because they substantially limit a major life activity, will "in virtually all cases, result in a determination of coverage under [the actual disability prong]." 29 C.F.R. § 1630.2(j)(3)(ii) (effective May 24, 2011). One of the impairments listed is "cancer" because it "substantially limits [the major life activity] of normal cell growth." *Id.* at *§ 1630.2(j)(3)(iii)*. *See also* the EEOC's interpretive guidance accompanying its final regulations, 76 FR 16978–01 (citing examples in the legislative history of the ADAAA where Congress named cancer as the kind of impairment that would qualify as a disability under the amended Act).

Because the ADAAA has only been effective since January 1, 2009, and did not apply retroactively, there is a scarcity of decisions analyzing the ADA as amended by the ADAAA. However, the court decisions that have been made support the court's conclusion in this case. For purposes of this case, the most persuasive of these decisions is *Hoffman v. Carefirst of Fort Wayne, Inc.,* 737 F.Supp.2d 976 (N.D.Ind.2010). In *Hoffman,* an employee who suffered from renal cancer brought suit against his employer alleging that the employer violated the ADA when it fired him. The employer moved for summary judgment, arguing that the employee had failed to establish a prima facie case of discrimination because the employee's cancer was in remission and, therefore, did not substantially limit a major life activity. Relying on the language quoted above from 42 U.S.C. § 12102(4)(D) and the EEOC's proposed regulations implementing the ADAAA, the court denied the motion. The court held that because the employee's renal cancer, when active, substantially limited the major life activity of normal cell growth, the employee was disabled under the ADA as amended.[6]

See also Feldman v. Law Enforcement Assocs. Corp., No. 5: 10–cv–08–BR, 779 F.Supp.2d 472, 2011 WL 891447 (E.D.N.C. March 10, 2011) (holding that employee who suffered from episodic flare ups of multiple sclerosis (MS) had plausible claim of disability under the ADA as amended because when active, the MS substantially limited the employee's normal neurological functions, which is a major life activity under the amended Act); *Chalfont v. U.S. Electrodes,* No. 10–2929, 2010 WL 5341846 (E.D.Pa. Dec. 28, 2010) (holding that employee with leukemia, heart disease and remissive cancer had plausible claim of disability under the ADA as amended because his maladies substantially limited his normal cell growth

---

[6] ALC argues that the *Hoffman* case is inapposite because the plaintiff in that case had Stage III renal cancer and because neither party disputed that Stage III renal cancer, when active, constitutes a disability. The record in this case is unclear as to the stage of Norton's cancer. Nevertheless, the court finds the distinction immaterial because cancer at any stage "substantially limits" the "major life activity" of "normal cell growth." And while it is true that neither party in the Hoffman case disputed that when active Sta[g]e III renal cancer constitutes a disability, this court fails to see, nor does ALC explain, how that fact should dissuade the court from its holding.

and circulatory functions, both of which are major life activities under the amended Act); *Horgan v. Simmons,* 704 F.Supp.2d 814 (N.D.Ill.2010) (holding that employee with HIV positive status had plausible claim of disability under the ADA as amended because the normal functioning of his immune system, a major life activity under the amended Act, was substantially limited).

Therefore, because Norton's cancer is capable of being classified as a disability under the ADA as amended, ALC's motion for partial summary judgment is **DENIED.**

Darcy v. City of New York

United States District Court for the Eastern District of New York, 2011.
2011 WL 841375.

■ DEARIE, CHIEF JUDGE.

Plaintiff James Darcy, a lieutenant with the New York City Police Department, brings this action pursuant to the Americans with Disabilities Act (the "ADA"), 42 U.S.C. §§ 12101 *et seq.* [B]efore the Court is defendants' motion for summary judgment. For the reasons set forth below, the motion is denied[.]

FACTUAL BACKGROUND

Plaintiff was appointed to the NYPD on January 20, 1987. On or about October 10, 1997, he was elevated to the level of lieutenant, the rank at which he continues to serve. On February 20, 1999, he was first assigned to the Narcotics Division. Following assignments in the Bronx and Brooklyn Narcotics, plaintiff was assigned on August 23, 2001 to Queens Narcotics, which plaintiff describes as a "very prestigious assignment." Defendants do not dispute this characterization. Plaintiff continued to serve in Queens Narcotics from August 2001 until he was transferred, in late 2004, to the NYPD Transit Division, District # 11, in the Bronx, where he now serves as platoon commander. According to plaintiff, the assignment in Transit is less prestigious than Queens Narcotics, and offers him considerably fewer overtime hours than his former position and thus adversely impacts his eventual retirement benefits.

It was when plaintiff first arrived at the 112th precinct in Queens in October of 1997 that he first met Police Officer John Doe, who was also assigned there. It is undisputed that Doe and plaintiff socialize as friends. The parties' papers occasionally withhold Officer Doe's true name to protect his privacy, but they also discuss openly the fact that Doe is the brother of Three-Star Deputy Chief Hall and the son of retired Two–Star Chief Francis Hall.

On or about June 3, 2004, according to plaintiff, he was called into Deputy Chief Hall's office. The two had a conversation during which Hall said to plaintiff, "You are a lowly lieutenant and you suffer from the same disease as my brother." Plaintiff's papers refer to this disease as "alcoholism" and "alcohol dependence" while defendants employ the term "alcoholic." Plaintiff's complaint alleges that, upon information and belief, Officer Doe has undergone rehabilitative treatment for his disease in conjunction with programs under the auspices of the NYPD but that Doe still struggles with his disease. Defendants are unable to confirm or deny

Doe's participation in any programs concerning alleged alcohol use or rehabilitation due to applicable regulations concerning privacy.

According to plaintiff, during the June 3 conversation Hall also expressed disapproval of plaintiff's friendship with Doe, threatened to ruin plaintiff if he ever went near Doe again, and reminded plaintiff that Hall's father also disapproved of plaintiff's friendship with Doe. The record contains no affidavit from Deputy Chief Hall or any other evidence purporting to contradict plaintiff's account of the conversation.

Plaintiff promptly reported Hall's remarks to both Deputy Director John Essig, the Commanding Officer of Queens Narcotics (and also Doe's commanding officer), and Captain Matthew Hyland.

Approximately five months later, by Memorandum dated November 7, 2004, Captain Hyland formally requested that Darcy be transferred from the Queens Narcotics Bureau "to a less sensitive position within the Patrol Services Bureau." Hyland's memorandum states that for "the past several months," Darcy "has engaged in a pattern of contemptuous and questionable behavior that has impaired his ability, integrity and judgment to supervise a narcotics module in a safe and effective manner." The memorandum outlines the incidents of alleged misconduct and, for most of the incidents, the explanations offered by Darcy that Hyland or others found to be unsatisfactory. In addition to the explanations summarized in Hyland's memo, plaintiff also addressed the particulars of Hyland's memorandum in his deposition. With one exception, the alleged performance deficiencies involve incidents or reviews occurring after the June 3, 2004 incident with Deputy Chief Hall; the one exception is the noting of deficiencies, during a review conducted on May 28, 2004, with respect to plaintiff's attitude toward case management.

The result of Hyland's memorandum was plaintiff's transfer from Queens Narcotics to Bronx Transit in December of 2004. Prior to and other than the accusations in Hyland's memorandum, no formal discipline was imposed on plaintiff during his time in Queens Narcotics. For the years 2001 and 2002 plaintiff received a "highly competent" 4.0 rating. Defendants were unable to produce plaintiff's 2003 performance evaluation, and no evaluation appears to have been completed for 2004.

Plaintiff claims that he was discriminated against by being transferred out of Queens Narcotics because he was regarded as suffering from alcoholism (*i.e.,* the "same disease as" Doe). [T]he record of misconduct chronicled in Hyland's memorandum, he further claims, is pretext, assembled in order to justify the transfer but not the real reason for it. In their motion, defendants quarrel principally not with the facts but instead with plaintiff's legal theory: they claim that plaintiff cannot, as a matter of law, invoke the ADA solely on a "perceived as" [t]heory without an accompanying actual or perceived impairment in a major life activity[.]

DISCUSSION

"[I]n order to establish a prima facie case of discrimination under the ADA, a plaintiff must show (a) that his employer is subject to the ADA; (b) that he is disabled within the meaning of the ADA *or perceived to be so by his employer;* (c) that he was otherwise qualified to perform the essential functions of the job with or without reasonable accommodation; and (d) that he suffered an adverse employment action because of the disability." *Brady v. Wal-Mart Stores, Inc.,* 531 F.3d 127, 134 (2d Cir.2008) (emphasis added).

[D]efendants do not dispute that alcoholism has been recognized as a "disability" within the meaning of the ADA. Defendants insist, however, that plaintiff's claim must fail as a matter of law because, even assuming he was "regarded as having" alcoholism, he was not regarded as being "substantially limit[ed][in] one or more major life activities" within the meaning of section 12122(a)(A). Defendants argue that plaintiff has not even sought to show that he was regarded as being "substantially limit[ed][in] one or more major life activities," and that, in any event, the fact that the NYPD assigned plaintiff to the position of platoon commander in the Bronx precludes a jury from concluding that the NYPD regarded plaintiff as being so limited.

But defendants' arguments do not take account of the statute's current language. Added to the definition of disability in the 2008 amendments is a paragraph that expressly exempts "regarded as" claimants from having to show that the disability they are perceived as having substantially limits a major life activity. To wit, "[d]isability" includes "being regarded as having such an impairment (as described in paragraph 3)," and the referenced paragraph 3 provides:

(3) Regarded as having such an impairment

> For purposes of paragraph (1)(C):

> (A) An individual meets the requirement of "being regarded as having such an impairment" if the individual establishes that he or she has been subjected to an action prohibited under this chapter because of an actual or perceived physical or mental impairment *whether or not the impairment limits or is perceived to limit a major life activity*

42 U.S.C. § 12102(3) (emphasis added).[2]

Thus, under the plain language of the statute, an employee making a "regarded as" claim is not required to show that the disability he is perceived as suffering from is one that actually limits, or is perceived to limit, a major life activity. To the contrary, cognizable ADA injury occurs when an employer takes an adverse employment action against an employee because of its perception that the employee suffers from a recognized disability. Defendants cling to the notion that ADA protections are not triggered unless there in fact exists an underlying impairment, but this theory is irreconcilable with the plain statutory language. "[B]eing regarded as having" an impairment is singled out as a distinct, alternative definition of disability, and individuals making such a claim are expressly relieved of having to show an actual or the perception of an actual impairment. Obviously, the statute recognizes that perceptions about disabilities carry stigma enough and that, when these perceptions are the motivating force in an employment decision, they often become agents of the improper biases and prejudices associated with the disability (real or imagined) in question. The statute does not require that an individual seeking its protections show that the employer had a reasonable basis for perceiving him as suffering from a disability; it merely requires him to show that the employer did so perceive him. Indeed, the fact that plaintiff

---

[2] The referenced "paragraph 3" was added by the ADA Amendments Act of 2008, PL 110–325 which became effective January 1, 2009. The section expressly overruled *Sutton*, under which "perceived as" claimants were required to show that their employers believed them to be impaired in a major life activity or unable to work in a broad class of jobs[.]

does not (or at least has not claimed to) suffer from the disability he is regarded as having, rather than militating against him, serves instead to expose the action taken against him to have been all the more the result of the biases associated with the disability rather than legitimate concerns. In short, defendants' focus on the import of an actual disability to the present analysis misses the point of "perceived as" disability claims, namely, that they often reflect a *mistaken* perception.

Returning to the facts here, defendants all but conceded at oral argument, and I now conclude for purposes of the summary judgment motion, that a rational jury could find that plaintiff was regarded as suffering from alcoholism. I further conclude that the record permits a jury to infer that that mistaken perception motivated the ensuing employment actions taken against plaintiff. Deputy Chief Hall's remarks speak for themselves, plaintiff relayed the substance of those remarks to his two supervisors, and it was one of them (Hyland) who was instrumental in having plaintiff transferred out of narcotics. To be sure, it may also have been the case that Hall, because of the nature of his relationship to Doe, was motivated by other considerations and did not, despite his remarks, harbor a genuine belief that plaintiff was an alcoholic. But that is a matter for the jury to decide.

Furthermore, on this record, the question of pretext is for the jury rather than this Court to decide. Despite the number of incidents of unsatisfactory performance chronicled in Hyland's memorandum requesting plaintiff's transfer, all but one of the incidents post-date the June 3, 2004 exchange between plaintiff and Hall, and other than that document, plaintiff's record was more than satisfactory (as noted, for the years 2001 and 2002 plaintiff was rated 4.0 or highly competent; defendant was unable to produce plaintiff's 2003 performance evaluation; and no evaluation appears to have been completed in 2004). The inference in plaintiff's favor speaks for itself; *i.e.,* the record permits a jury to infer that, following the June 3 incident, Hall and Hyland harbored a desire to have plaintiff transferred out of Queens Narcotics, and to advance that goal, caused plaintiff to be assessed, and his deficiencies to be documented, more thoroughly than they would have were they not seeking to build a case against him. At the very least, I cannot conclude that "the evidence to support [plaintiff's claim of pretext] is so slight" that "no rational jury could find in [his] favor."

[C]ONCLUSION

Defendants' motion for summary judgment is [d]enied.

[S]O ORDERED.

NOTES ON THE ADA AMENDMENTS ACT

1.   **The ADAAA's Provisions.** For an insider's account of the drafting and negotiation of the ADAAA, see Chai R. Feldblum, Kevin Barry & Emily A. Benfer, *The ADA Amendments Act of 2008*, 13 Tex. J. on C.L. & C.R. 187 (2008). The statute makes a number of changes to the ADA's definition of disability:

a.   **Broad Construction.** The ADAAA specifically lists a purpose "to reject" *Toyota*'s "need to be interpreted strictly" statement. § 2(b)(4) (codified at 42 U.S.C. § 12101 note). And the operative provisions add a new "rule of construction" to the ADA's definitional section, a rule that provides that "[t]he definition of 'disability' . . . shall be construed in favor of broad coverage of individuals under this Act, to the maximum extent permitted by the terms of this Act." § 4(4)(A) (codified at 42 U.S.C. § 12102(4)(A)). The EEOC's regulations implementing the ADAAA echo the point. See 29 C.F.R. § 1630.2(i)(2) ("In determining other examples of major life activities, the term 'major' shall not be interpreted strictly to create a demanding standard for disability."); *id.* § 1630.2(j)(1)(i) ("The term 'substantially limits' shall be construed broadly in favor of expansive coverage, to the maximum extent permitted by the terms of the ADA. 'Substantially limits' is not meant to be a demanding standard."). These sections directly reverse *Toyota*'s rule of narrow construction. To the extent that judges' narrow reading of the ADA's disability definition rested on their belief that Congress intended it that way—or their belief that Congress was silent on the question—Congress's clear statement in favor of broad construction will make a difference. But can such a provision constrain judges who remain skeptical of broad ADA coverage?

     b.   Mitigating Measures. The ADAAA unambiguously eliminates *Sutton*'s rule that courts must take account of mitigating measures when determining whether an impairment substantially limits a major life activity. The findings that appear in the statutory text specifically state that "the holdings of the Supreme Court in Sutton v. United Air Lines, Inc., and its companion cases have narrowed the broad scope of protection intended to be afforded by the ADA, thus eliminating protection for many individuals whom Congress intended to protect." § 2(a)(4) (codified at 42 U.S.C. § 12101 note) (citation omitted). The statute lists a "purpose[ ]" to "reject the requirement enunciated by the Supreme Court in Sutton v. United Air Lines, Inc., and its companion cases that whether an impairment substantially limits a major life activity is to be determined with reference to the ameliorative effects of mitigating measures." § 2(b)(2) (codified at 42 U.S.C. § 12101 note) (citation omitted). And the operative provisions of the statute state that "[t]he determination of whether an impairment substantially limits a major life activity shall be made without regard to the ameliorative effects of mitigating measures." § 3(4)(E)(i) (codified at 42 U.S.C. § 12102(4)(E)(i)). See also 29 C.F.R. § 1630.2(j)(1)(vi) (EEOC regulation implementing this provision). The ADAAA makes an exception to this new rule for "ordinary eyeglasses and contact lenses," § 3(4)(E)(ii) (codified at 42 U.S.C. § 12102(4)(E)(ii)), so it seems to leave *Sutton*'s holding intact on the facts of that case. But the statute adds another new section, which provides that "[n]otwithstanding" the mitigating measures provision referring to ordinary eyeglasses and contact lenses, "a covered entity shall not use qualification standards, employment tests, or other selection criteria based on an individual's uncorrected vision unless the standard, test, or other selection criteria, as used by the covered entity, is shown to be job-related for the position in question and consistent with business necessity." § 5(b) (codified at 42 U.S.C. § 12113(c)). See also 29 C.F.R. § 1630.10(b) (EEOC regulation implementing this provision). Thus, even though the new statute would leave intact the Sutton holding that the plaintiff sisters had no present disability, it would give them what they sought—a determination whether United Air Lines' requirement of

20/100 uncorrected vision was job-related and consistent with business necessity.

c. Substantially Limits Major Life Activities. As *Rico* and *Norton* illustrate, the ADAAA also makes changes to the definitions of "substantially limits" and "major life activities." The statute provides, as a "rule of construction," that "[t]he term 'substantially limits' shall be interpreted consistently with the findings and purposes of the ADA Amendments Act of 2008." § 4(a)(4)(B) (codified at 42 U.S.C. § 12102(4)(B)). The statute's findings and purposes, in turn, contain a number of provisions that speak to the definition of "substantially limits." One finding and one purpose each refer specifically to *Toyota*'s interpretation of that term: the finding that "the Supreme Court, in the case of Toyota Motor Manufacturing, Kentucky, Inc. v. Williams, interpreted the term 'substantially limits' to require a greater degree of limitation than was intended by Congress," § 2(a)(7) (citation omitted); and the purpose "to convey congressional intent that the standard created by the Supreme Court in the case of Toyota Motor Manufacturing, Kentucky, Inc. v. Williams for 'substantially limits,' and applied by lower courts in numerous decisions, has created an inappropriately high level of limitation necessary to obtain coverage under the ADA," § 2(b)(5) (citation omitted). And one finding and one purpose each refer specifically to the EEOC's "substantially limits" regulations, which defined the term as "significantly restrict[s]": the finding that "the current Equal Employment Opportunity Commission ADA regulations defining the term 'substantially limits' as 'significantly restricted' are inconsistent with congressional intent, by expressing too high a standard," § 2(a)(8); and the purpose "to express Congress's expectation that the Equal Employment Opportunity Commission will revise that portion of its current regulations that defines the term 'substantially limits' as 'significantly restricted' to be consistent with this Act, including the amendments made by this Act," § 2(b)(6). A separate provision of the new statute makes clear that the EEOC has authority to promulgate, and presumably obtain *Chevron* deference for, regulations interpreting the definition of disability for purposes of the ADA's employment provisions. § 6(a)(2) (codified at 42 U.S.C. § 12205a). And the new statute also provides that "[a]n impairment that substantially limits one major life activity need not limit other major life activities," and that "[a]n impairment that is episodic or in remission is a disability if it would substantially limit a major life activity when active." § 3(a)(4)(C), (D) (codified at 42 U.S.C. § 12102(4)(C), (D)). See also 29 C.F.R. § 1630.2(j)(1)(vi), (vii) (EEOC regulation implementing these statutory provisions).

As noted above, the EEOC's ADAAA regulations provide for generous construction of the "substantially limits" definition. See 29 C.F.R. § 1630.2(j)(1)(i). See also *id.* § 1630.2(j)(1)(iii) ("The primary object of attention in cases brought under the ADA should be whether covered entities have complied with their obligations and whether discrimination has occurred, not whether an individual's impairment substantially limits a major life activity. Accordingly, the threshold issue of whether an impairment 'substantially limits' a major life activity should not demand extensive analysis."). The regulations also give some further content to that definition. They provide that the inquiry into substantial limitation must be made by reference to the abilities of "most people in the general population," 29 C.F.R. § 1630.2(j)(1)(ii), and that "it may be useful in appropriate cases to consider * * * the condition under which the individual performs the major life activity; the manner in which the individual performs the major life activity; and/or the duration of time it takes the individual to perform the major life activity, or for which the individual can perform the major life activity." *Id.* § 1630.2(j)(4)(i). In this regard, a factfinder may consider "difficulty, effort, or time required to perform a major life activity; pain experienced when performing a major life activity; the length of time a major life activity can be performed; and/or the way an impairment affects the operation of a major bodily function." *Id.* § 1630.2(j)(4)(ii). The factfinder may also consider "the non-ameliorative effects of mitigating measures, such as negative side effects of medication or burdens associated with following a particular treatment regimen." *Id.* The regulations emphasize that "[a]n impairment need not prevent, or significantly or severely restrict, the individual from performing a major life activity in order to be considered substantially limiting." *Id.* § 1630.2(j)(1)(ii). Thus, "the focus is on how a major life activity is substantially limited, and not on what outcomes an individual can achieve. For example, someone with a learning disability may achieve a high level of academic success, but may nevertheless be substantially limited in the major life activity of learning because of the additional time or effort he or she must spend to read, write, or learn compared to most people in the general population." *Id.* § 1630.2(j)(4)(iii).

In addition to its changes to the "substantially limits" prong, the ADAAA provides a nonexclusive list of "major life activities," and it also states that major life activities include "the operation of a major bodily function." § 4(a)(2) (codified at 42 U.S.C. § 12102(2)). The list of major life activities resolves the question, reserved in *Sutton* and *Toyota*, whether "working" is a major life activity by stating specifically that it is. § 4(a)(2)(A) (codified at 42 U.S.C. § 12102(2)(A)). The statute also resolves disputes in the lower courts and provides that "sleeping," "lifting," "bending," "concentrating," and "thinking" are major life activities. *Id.* See also 29 C.F.R. § 1630.2(i)(1)(i) (EEOC regulation adding "sitting," "reaching," and "interacting with others" to the statutory list). The addition of "major bodily functions" to the major life activity definition expands the ADA's coverage still further, as *Norton* illustrates. The ADAAA provides that major bodily functions include, but are "not limited to," the following: "functions of the immune system, normal cell growth, digestive, bowel, bladder, neurological, brain, respiratory, circulatory, endocrine, and reproductive functions." § 4(a)(2)(B) (codified at 42 U.S.C. § 12102(2)(B)). See also 29 C.F.R. § 1630.2(i)(1)(ii) (EEOC regulation adding functions of the "special sense organs and skin," and "genitourinary," "hemic," "lymphatic," and "musculoskeletal" functions to the statutory list). Like the new major life activities provision, the new major bodily functions provision directly responds to the suggestion of the Supreme Court in *Toyota* that a condition cannot be a disability unless it affects activities of daily life. Under the new statute, a condition that substantially limits some internal bodily function will be a disability even if it has no particular effect (or an insubstantial effect) on an individual's ability to go about her daily life. And the EEOC regulations expressly state that "[w]hether an activity is a 'major life activity' is not determined by reference to whether it is of 'central importance to daily life.' " 29 C.F.R. § 1630.2(i)(2).

The EEOC's regulations recognize that the determination whether an impairment substantially limits major life activities will require an "individualized assessment," even after the ADAAA. 29 C.F.R. § 1630.2(j)(1)(iv). But they also recognize that, under the broadened definition of disability, the individualized assessment will be both easy and predictable in many cases. In particular, the regulations list certain impairments that "will, as a factual matter, virtually always be found to impose a substantial limitation on a major life activity." *Id.* § 1630.2(j)(3)(ii). For those impairments, the regulations state, "the necessary individualized assessment should be particularly simple and straightforward." *Id.* The regulations provide the following list:

> For example, * * * it should easily be concluded that the following types of impairments will, at a minimum, substantially limit the major life activities indicated: Deafness substantially limits hearing; blindness substantially limits seeing; an intellectual disability (formerly termed mental retardation) substantially limits brain function; partially or completely missing limbs or mobility impairments requiring the use of a wheelchair substantially limit musculoskeletal function; autism substantially limits brain function; cancer substantially limits normal cell growth; cerebral palsy substantially limits brain function; diabetes substantially limits endocrine function; epilepsy substantially limits neurological function; Human Immunodeficiency Virus (HIV) infection substantially limits immune function; multiple sclerosis substantially limits neurological function; muscular dystrophy substantially limits neurological function; and major depressive disorder, bipolar disorder, post-traumatic stress disorder, obsessive compulsive disorder, and schizophrenia substantially limit brain function.

Id. § 1630.2(j)(3)(iii). And, the regulations emphasize, "[t]he types of impairments described in this section may substantially limit additional major life activities not explicitly listed above." *Id.*

d. Regarded As. Under *Sutton*, an individual would not be "regarded as" disabled if her employer merely thought her medical condition disqualified her from the particular job she held or sought; instead, the employer needed to perceive the impairment as disqualifying for a substantial number of jobs (or as substantially limiting some other major life activity). Responding to that holding, the new statute provides that "[a]n individual meets the requirement of 'being regarded as having such an impairment' if the individual establishes that he or she has been subjected to an action prohibited under this Act because of an actual or perceived physical or mental impairment whether or not the impairment limits or is perceived to limit a major life activity." § 4(a)(3)(A) (codified at 42 U.S.C. § 12102(3)(A)). (The statute makes an exception to this provision for "transitory and minor impairments." *Id.* § 4(a)(3)(B) (codified at 42 U.S.C. § 12102(3)(B)).) This provision is phrased somewhat infelicitously.

Strictly speaking, there cannot be "an action prohibited under this Act" in the employment context unless the employer discriminates against an individual "on the basis of disability." § 5(a) (codified at 42 U.S.C. § 12112(a)). To discriminate "on the basis of disability" would seem to require that the person discriminated against have a disability. But if a court already has concluded that the plaintiff has a disability, there is no need to invoke the new "regarded as" provision; and if the court has not yet decided whether the plaintiff has a disability, then it cannot invoke the new "regarded as" provision by concluding that the employer has discriminated "on the basis of disability."

If "an action prohibited under this Act" in the new "regarded as" provision were read as requiring the plaintiff to show that the defendant violated the ADA in order to establish ADA coverage, it would be meaningless. The language is best read as referring to what might be called the statute's "act element." When an employer discriminates against an individual because of an actual or perceived physical or mental impairment, that individual will be covered under the new "regarded as" provision (and therefore entitled to challenge the discrimination). The EEOC's regulations adopt this interpretation. The regulations provide that an individual will be covered under the "regarded as" prong "if the individual is subjected to a prohibited action because of an actual or perceived physical or mental impairment," they define "prohibited actions" as including, but not limited to, "refusal to hire, demotion, placement on involuntary leave, termination, exclusion for failure to meet a qualification standard, harassment, or denial of any other term, condition, or privilege of employment," and they make clear that "a prohibited action" will suffice to cover an individual "even if the [defendant] asserts, or may or does ultimately establish, a defense to such action." 29 C.F.R. § 1630.2(*l*)(1), (2). The new "regarded as" regime openly embraces the phenomenon that the *Sutton* Court worried was circularity—the phenomenon of an act of discrimination triggering coverage, which in turn triggers a prohibition on that discrimination. *Darcy* illustrates how the new "regarded as" provision operates.

But the new "regarded as" provision is limited in a significant respect. Although the original ADA drew no distinction between individuals with present disabilities and those with perceived disabilities in the protections it afforded, and a number of lower courts had specifically held that individuals covered under the perceived-disability prong were entitled to reasonable accommodation, the ADAAA specifically provides that individuals "who meet[ ] the definition of disability . . . solely under [the 'regarded as' provision]" are not entitled to accommodation. § 6(a)(1) (codified at 42 U.S.C. § 12201(h)).

2. The ADAAA's Implications. The ADAAA reveals a clear congressional desire for courts to interpret the ADA's disability definition more broadly than they had before. For an argument that courts have largely gotten that message, see Kevin M. Barry, *Exactly What Congress Intended?*, 17 Employee Rts. & Emp. Pol'y J. ___ (forthcoming 2013) (noting that since Congress adopted the ADAAA, "lower courts have found the following impairments to be covered disabilities under the ADA: alcoholism, ankle injury, anxiety disorder, autoimmune disorder, back injury, bipolar disorder, brain tumor, broken legs, cancer, carp[a]l tunnel syndrome, depression, diabetes, eating disorder, fibromyalgia, Friedreich's Ataxia (a degenerative neurological condition), gastrointestinal problems, heart disease, HIV infection, insomnia, monocular vision and other vision problems, multiple sclerosis, obesity, obsessive compulsive disorder, pain in hands, joints, and hip, psoriatic arthritis, sleep apnea, stuttering, and TSI (mini-strokes)").

Thanks to the ADAAA's "regarded as" provision, the ADA now protects anyone with an actual or perceived "impairment" against disparate-treatment discrimination, regardless of whether the impairment does or is perceived to limit major life activities. For arguments that the ADAAA thus incorporates, to a significant extent, a universalist approach to disability, see Kevin Barry, *Toward Universalism: What the ADA Amendments Act Can and Can't Do For Disability Rights*, 31 Berkeley J. Emp. & Lab. L. 203 (2010); Michelle A. Travis, *Impairment as Protected Status: A New Universality for Disability Rights*, 46 Ga. L. Rev. 937 (2012).

This development—along with the ADAAA's expansion of the concepts of substantial limitation and major life activity—will put substantial pressure on the statute's definition of impairment. See Travis, *supra*, at 959 (noting the "retrenchment risk" that judges hostile to the ADAAA's broader disability definition can respond by adopting restrictive understandings of impairment). None of the Supreme Court's cases has presented a difficult question regarding whether a condition was an impairment. The EEOC's regulations define the term as encompassing "[a]ny physiological disorder or condition, cosmetic disfigurement, or anatomical loss affecting one or more body systems, such as neurological, musculoskeletal, special sense organs, respiratory (including speech organs), cardiovascular, reproductive, digestive, genitourinary, immune, circulatory, hemic, lymphatic, skin, and endocrine," as well as "[a]ny mental or psychological disorder, such as an intellectual disability (formerly termed 'mental retardation'), organic brain syndrome, emotional or mental illness, and specific learning disabilities." 29 C.F.R. § 1630.2(h).

What is the principle that defines an impairment? Consider *Bragdon*'s facts in this regard. Is it the mental or physical effect of the condition (the flu-like symptoms and the attack on white blood cells, in the case of asymptomatic HIV disease)? Is it the presence of a discrete, identifiable, physiological cause (infection with the human immunodeficiency virus)? Or is it the blessing of organized medicine (the fact that the medical profession has recognized a particular diagnosis of "HIV disease")?

This question is important in cases involving conditions that do not have a discrete, identifiable physiological cause, like some cases of morbid obesity, chronic fatigue syndrome, or psychiatric disability. In most of these cases, the medical or psychological professions have recognized diagnoses that are defined by a set of symptoms. But those diagnostic categories inevitably reflect not just the underlying scientific facts but the professional community's normative views about what ought to be considered abnormal. For a discussion of the point in the context of psychiatric diagnoses, see Herb Kutchins & Stuart A. Kirk, Making Us Crazy: DSM: The Psychiatric Bible and the Creation of Mental Disorders

(1997). For an instructive discussion in the context of autism, see Kevin Barry, *Gray Matters: Autism, Impairment, and the End of Binaries*, 49 San Diego L. Rev. 161 (2012). Psychiatric professionals may define all sorts of socially unacceptable behaviors as disorders; does that mean that the law protects people against discrimination on the basis of those behaviors—and even requires reasonable accommodation of them? What some laypeople see as laziness or listlessness, medical professionals may see as chronic fatigue syndrome. Does the law incorporate those professionals' determinations?

These are normative questions. They require some sort of theory about whom the ADA should protect and why. (For a good general discussion of these issues, see Bradley A. Areheart, *Disability Trouble*, 29 Yale L. & Pol'y Rev. 347 (2011).) But the statutory and regulatory definitions do not give courts any clear guidance about the normative theory that should underlie interpretation of the term "impairment"; those definitions make the impairment inquiry appear to be a purely medical one, and they do not acknowledge the normative nature of many diagnostic choices. Faced with conditions that meet professional definitions of "disorder" but do not seem to them to warrant protection, some courts (particularly prior to the ADAAA's enactment) have looked to other medical concepts to narrow the ADA's coverage.

The Sixth Circuit's decision in *EEOC v. Watkins Motor Lines, Inc.*, 463 F.3d 436 (6th Cir.2006), suggests some of the problems with that strategy. The employee in *Watkins* met the established medical standards for a diagnosis of "morbid obesity"—his body weight was over 100% above the norm. See *id.* at 441. But the court held that his obesity was not an "impairment" under the ADA, because he could not establish that it was "related to any physiological cause" or "the result of a physiological condition." *Id.* at 438, 443. But what does it mean to say that morbid obesity has a "physiological cause"? All of our behavior has some physiological cause, if only from hormones and brain chemistry. Brain proteins that alter appetite and activity levels, not to mention genetics, are substantial contributors to morbid obesity. More broadly, every fact about our body is by definition physiological. And morbid obesity, being a condition of one's physiology, is by definition a "physiological condition." The *Watkins Motor* decision seems to call for an inquiry into whether a condition has an *identifiable* organic etiology, but it is not clear why that should matter. Given the evolving state of medical knowledge, doctors still do not know the precise etiology of any number of conditions that they diagnose and treat. What normative theory would exclude people with those conditions from the protection of the ADA?

By broadening the concepts of substantial limitation and major life activity, the ADAAA should expand the availability of reasonable accommodations under the ADA. But the amended statute expressly denies any right to accommodation to individuals who are covered only under the "regarded as" prong of the disability definition. Does it make sense to divide the statute's protections in this way? Perhaps those who are covered only under the "regarded as" prong do not really "need" accommodations. But if an employer could reasonably accommodate an individual with an impairment, and the failure to provide the accommodation denies that individual a job, why shouldn't the employer be required to make that accommodation? And why should it matter whether the impairment substantially limits major life activities? For arguments that the law should apply a broader definition of disability in disparate treatment cases than in accommodation cases (as the ADAAA does), see Michelle T. Friedland, Note, *Not Disabled Enough: The ADA's "Major Life Activity" Definition of Disability*, 52 Stan. L. Rev. 171 (1999); Travis, *supra*. For defenses of using the broad impairment-only standard in all ADA cases, see Claudia Center & Andrew J. Imparato, *Redefining "Disability" Discrimination: A Proposal to Restore Civil Rights Protections for All Workers*, 14 Stan. L. & Pol'y Rev. 321 (2003); Robert L. Burgdorf Jr., *"Substantially Limited" Protection from Disability Discrimination: The Special Treatment Model and Misconstructions of the Definition of Disability*, 42 Vill. L. Rev. 409 (1997). For an argument that the ADAAA, at least in this respect, "repudiates a strong form of the social model of disability and accedes to a hierarchy of discrimination that treats the failure to accommodate as a different and lesser form of bias than direct discrimination," see Elizabeth F. Emens, *Disabling Attitudes: U.S. Disability Law and the ADA Amendments Act*, 60 Am. J. Comp. L. 205 (2012).

3. A Comparative Perspective. Other nations take a variety of approaches to defining the protected class in their disability discrimination laws. In Great Britain, the Disability Discrimination Act of 1995 (DDA) defines "disability" as "a physical or mental impairment which has a substantial and long-term adverse effect on his ability to carry out normal day-to-day activities." Disability Discrimination Act (1995) § 1(1). (Severe disfigurement is conclusively treated as having such an effect. *Id.*, Sch. 1 § 3(1).) The statute does not cover perceived disabilities—there is no "regarded as" provision—but it does cover past disabilities. See *id.* § 2. The DDA specifically provides, in contrast to the *Sutton* case, that the effects of mitigating measures are to be disregarded in the disability determination. *Id.*, Sch. 1 § 6.

The definition of disability in Australia's Disability Discrimination Act of 1992 (DDA) is broader than that in both the ADA and the British DDA. Under the Australian DDA, "disability" means:

(a) total or partial loss of the person's bodily or mental functions; or

(b) total or partial loss of a part of the body; or

(c) the presence in the body of organisms causing disease or illness; or

(d) the presence in the body of organisms capable of causing disease or illness; or

(e) the malfunction, malformation or disfigurement of a part of the person's body; or

(f) a disorder or malfunction that results in the person learning differently from a person without the disorder or malfunction; or

(g) a disorder, illness or disease that affects a person's thought processes, perception of reality, emotions or judgment or that results in disturbed behaviour; and includes a disability that:

(h) presently exists; or

(i) previously existed but no longer exists; or

(j) may exist in the future; or

(k) is imputed to a person.

Disability Discrimination Act (1992) § 4. There is good reason to believe that the broad definition of disability in the Australian DDA has not led to a flood of litigation. See Samuel R. Bagenstos, *Comparative Disability Employment Law From an American Perspective*, 24 Comp. Lab. L. & Pol'y J. 649, 666 (2003) (discussing Australian Productivity Commission report that "conclude[d] that the DDA's benefits outweigh its costs, and that the statute's broad disability definition may actually reduce litigation burdens by eliminating the need for a costly and time-consuming inquiry into whether the claimant is disabled").

B. UNDER THE INDIVIDUALS WITH DISABILITIES EDUCATION ACT

Mr. I. v. Maine School Administrative District No. 55

United States Court of Appeals for the First Circuit, 2007.
480 F.3d 1.

■ Before TORRUELLA, CIRCUIT JUDGE, CYR, SENIOR CIRCUIT JUDGE, and HOWARD, CIRCUIT JUDGE.

■ HOWARD, CIRCUIT JUDGE.

This case presents an issue of eligibility for benefits under the Individuals with Disabilities Education Act, 20 U.S.C. § 1400 *et seq.* (the "IDEA"). We have previously noted that such issues can require a "difficult and sensitive" analysis. This case is no exception. The appellant, Maine School Administrative District No. 55 ("the district"), appeals the district court's determination that the appellees' daughter ("LI") qualifies as a "child with a disability" eligible for special education and related services under the IDEA as a result of her Asperger's Syndrome. [W]e affirm the judgment of the district court.

I.

We begin with an overview of the statutory framework. The IDEA provides funding to each state "to assist [it] to provide special education and related services to children with disabilities," 20 U.S.C. § 1411(a)(1), provided that "[a] free appropriate public education is available to all children with disabilities residing in the state. . . . " *Id.* § 1412(a)(1)(A). In this sense, a "free appropriate public education" encompasses "special education and related services," *id.* § 1401(9), including "specially designed instruction, at no cost to parents, to meet the unique needs of a child with a disability. . . . " *Id.* § 1401(29).

To receive special education and related services under the IDEA, a child must qualify as a "child with a disability." In relevant part, a "child with a disability" is a child

(i) with mental retardation, hearing impairments (including deafness), speech or language impairments, visual impairments (including blindness), serious emotional disturbance (referred to in this chapter as "emotional disturbance"), orthopedic impairments, autism, traumatic brain injury, other health impairments, or specific learning disabilities; and

(ii) who, by reason thereof, needs special education and related services.

Id. § 1401(3)(A). The Secretary of Education has promulgated a regulation defining each of the categories of disability set forth in § 1401(3)(A)(i). Those definitions, so far as they are relevant here, require that each of the enumerated conditions "adversely affect[ ] a child's educational performance" to constitute a disability. 34 C.F.R. §§ 300.8(c)(1)(i) (2006) (autism), (c)(4)(i) (emotional disturbance), (c)(9)(ii) (other health impairment).

II.

A.

LI attended Cornish Elementary School in Cornish, Maine, until 2003. Though she excelled academically, by the fourth grade she began to experience sadness, anxiety, and difficulty with peer relationships. These problems persisted into the fifth grade, when LI sought to distance herself physically from most of her classmates. Her parents sought psychological counseling for LI and she started taking a prescription anti-depressant. Her grades also dropped from "high honors" to "honors." As the school year progressed, however, LI became more successful at interacting with her peers and participating in class.

[B]y mid-September [of 2003, her sixth-grade year], LI was "slacking off" in her academic work and regularly missing school, prompting a meeting between her teacher and Mrs. I. At this meeting, also attended by LI, Mrs. I noticed cuts or scratches on her daughter's arms; the teacher offered that LI might have inflicted those wounds on herself during her "lengthy bathroom breaks" from class. According to the teacher, LI was also having continued trouble relating with her peers due to a "serious lack of awareness" of their social and emotional states, which bordered on "hostility." The teacher added that she could not "reach" LI, who had refused to complete assignments and shown a "passive resistance to meeting learning goals." Yet the teacher considered LI "a very bright young girl with strong language and math skills . . . capable of powerful insights in her reading and writing. . . ."

[O]n October 1, following an argument with Mrs. I over one of LI's academic assignments, LI deliberately ingested excessive quantities of one her prescription drugs and two over-the-counter medications in a suicide attempt. [I]n the wake of her attempted suicide, LI met with a new counselor, who, suspecting that LI might suffer from Asperger's Syndrome, referred her to Dr. Ellen Popenoe for neuropsychological testing. Mr. and Mrs. I conveyed this information, as well as the news of LI's suicide attempt, to the district's director of special services, Jim McDevitt. They added that LI would not return to Cornish Elementary "for the time being" and that they were looking at other options, including TCS [The Community School, a local private school]. At [a] meeting [held later that month], the PET [pupil evaluation team] decided that LI should receive up to ten hours of tutoring outside of school each week pending completion of her neuropsychological testing.

The testing, finished by early November, further suggested that LI had Asperger's Syndrome, as well as adjustment disorder with depressed mood. Popeneo, the neuropsychologist, observed that LI "experiences significant limitations in many areas of adaptive skills" and executive skills, "which likely contribute[s] to her behavioral and emotional difficulties." These behavioral difficulties, particularly LI's poor pragmatic language abilities and restricted range of social interests, supported a diagnosis of Asperger's. Popeneo recommended that LI begin seeing both a social skills coach, who would help her develop social abilities and judgment, and a therapist familiar with Asperger's, who would use a cognitive-behavioral approach.

[I]n the meantime, McDevitt told Mrs. I that he would attempt to find LI a tutor in accordance with the PET's decision. Mrs. I had not heard back from him by November 10, however, so she started home-schooling LI. Despite additional prodding by Mrs. I in November and December, the district never provided a tutor as ordered by the PET, nor explained its failure to do so. [O]n January 5, 2004, LI began attending TCS. Although she was withdrawn and isolated at the outset, over time LI developed positive relationships with some of her peers. She also thrived academically, completing assignments at the seventh- and eighth-grade level with ease. TCS, however, provided LI with neither the direct teaching of social skills nor the cognitive behavioral therapy that had been recommended as treatment for her Asperger's.

When the PET reconvened in early March, it accepted Popenoe's conclusion that LI suffered from both Asperger's and adjustment disorder with depressed mood. The PET also agreed that LI needed social skills and pragmatic language instruction. The PET, however, could not reach consensus on whether LI qualified as a "child with a disability" under the IDEA. The district's representatives argued that LI's condition, whether denominated "autism," "emotional disturbance," or "other health impairment," 20 U.S.C. § 1401(3)(A)(i), had not affected her academic performance "to a marked degree" or "over a long period of time," which they deemed essential to IDEA eligibility. The district then issued a "prior written notice," *id.* § 1415(b)(3), announcing its refusal to offer special education services on the stated basis of "no significant adverse effect on education." The district instead asked the PET to consider LI's eligibility for services under the Rehabilitation Act, 29 U.S.C. § 794.

At its next meeting, the PET identified LI as a "qualified individual with a disability" under the Rehabilitation Act, *id.* § 794(a), and recommended an array of services. These included close supervision throughout the school day; instruction in "social pragmatics"; access to the district's existing gifted and talented programming as well as additional programming provided through a consultant to be hired by the district; and placement in any elementary school within the district. The district also offered to supply a tutor to work with LI for three hours each day to ease her eventual transition back to the classroom.

Mr. and Mrs. I objected to this proposal as inadequate and unduly restrictive, given LI's success in a classroom environment at TCS and her apprehension over returning to public school. They wanted LI to remain at TCS for the balance of the academic year with a view toward beginning her transition back to public school in September 2004, and notified the district that they intended to seek reimbursement under the IDEA for LI's attendance at TCS. LI completed the 2003–2004 academic year at TCS, and stayed on for the 2004–2005 and 2005–2006 school years as well. While she has done well academically, she continues to experience "atypical" peer relationships and spent the summer of 2004 shunning her TCS classmates in favor of solitary pursuits. LI also generally refuses to go outdoors or to eat more than a severely limited variety of foods. Her current social worker believes that, without social skills coaching, LI is unlikely to master the flexible thinking, problem solving, teamwork, and communication abilities she will need for employment in the future.

B.

[T]he district court [c]onclud[ed] that LI's "condition did adversely affect her educational performance as Maine defines that term and that the events of the fall of 2003 cannot be isolated from [her] underlying condition." The district court determined that LI's Asperger's had exerted an adverse effect on her educational performance as measured by state criteria, most significantly in the areas of socialization and communication. [T]urning to the second prong of the IDEA's eligibility standard, 20 U.S.C. § 1401(3)(A)(ii), the district court concluded that LI needed special education and related services by reason of her disability. [B]ased on its determination that LI satisfied both elements of the IDEA eligibility test, the district court ordered the district "to convene a PET meeting . . . to develop an IEP for [LI] that meets her unique needs as a student with Asperger's Syndrome and a depressive disorder."[7]

III.

A.

1.

[T]hough the IDEA "establishes a basic floor of education" for children with disabilities, guaranteeing them "[a] free appropriate public education," 20 U.S.C. § 1412(a)(1)(A), it does not displace the states from their traditional role in setting their own educational policy. Each state thus remains free to calibrate its own educational standards, provided it does not set them below the minimum level prescribed by the statute.

As we have seen, the right to special education and related services under the IDEA extends to children "with" one or more of a variety of disabilities, 20 U.S.C. § 1401(3)(A)(i), "who, by reason thereof, need[ ] special education and related services." *Id.* § 1401(3)(A)(ii). The IDEA does not itself define any of the qualifying disabilities listed in § 1401(3)(A)(i), though the Department of Education has issued a regulation fleshing them out. 34 C.F.R. § 300.8(c). The regulatory definitions, with one exception not relevant here, state, among other requirements, that each condition must "adversely affect[ ] a child's educational performance." *Id.* § 300.8(c)(1)–(c)(13). In keeping with the

---

[7] The state must develop and implement an "individualized education program," or "IEP," to meet the particularized needs of each child with a disability. 20 U.S.C. §§ 1412(a)(4), 1414(d)(1)(A)(i).

IDEA's respect for state policy judgments, however, the regulation does not expand upon this phrase, "leaving it to each State to give substance to these terms."

It is here that the district's argument as to the proper scope of § 1401(3)(A) begins to encounter difficulty. While Maine's Department of Education has promulgated its own regulation defining the disabilities recognized under the IDEA, those definitions simply ape their federal counterparts, including the requirement that a disability "adversely affect[ ] the student's educational performance." 05–071–101 Me.Code.R. §§ 3.2–3.14 (2006). The regulation, like its federal cousin, also does not further elaborate on this phrase, although Maine has adopted its own definition of "educational performance" for IDEA purposes:

> The term "educational performance" includes academic areas (reading, math, communication, etc.), non-academic areas (daily life activities, mobility, etc.), extracurricular activities, progress in meeting goals established for the general curriculum, and performance on State-wide and local assessments.

Id. § 2.7. Despite this expansive notion of educational performance, and in the absence of any regulatory guidance as to the term "adversely affects," the district asks us to hold that a child meets the first criterion of IDEA eligibility in Maine "only if the student's condition imposes a significant negative impact on the child's educational performance . . . limited to those areas of performance actually being measured and assessed by the local unit, in accordance with law." We decline to do so.

At the outset, Maine does not look only at "areas of performance actually being measured and assessed by the local unit" when determining whether a child has a disability under the IDEA. That much is clear from the regulatory definition of "educational performance" itself, which counts "performance on state-wide and local assessments" as just one of a number of different indicators embraced by the concept. [A]s the magistrate judge and the district court observed, Maine's broad definition of "educational performance" squares with the broad purpose behind the IDEA: "to ensure that all children with disabilities have available to them a free and appropriate public education that emphasizes special education and related services designed to meet their unique needs and prepare them for further education, *employment,* and *independent living.*" 20 U.S.C. § 1400(d)(1)(A) (emphases added). We have likewise held that the IDEA entitles qualifying children to services that "target '*all* of [their] special needs,' whether they be academic, physical, emotional, or social."

[I]n light of Maine's broad notion of "educational performance" as the standard of IDEA eligibility, we see no basis for restricting that standard to "areas of performance actually being measured and assessed by the local unit." Indeed, "there is nothing in IDEA or its legislative history that supports the conclusion that . . . 'educational performance' is limited only to performance that is graded." *See* Robert A. Garda, Jr., *Untangling Eligibility Requirements Under the Individuals with Disabilities Education Act,* 69 Mo. L. Rev. 441, 471 (2003). To be sure, some states have adopted more circumscribed criteria for identifying children with disabilities under the IDEA, requiring, for example, that a student perform poorly in a specific area of "basic skills." Maine, however, has chosen not to do so.

[T]he district also argues that the district court misconstrued the "adversely affects" component of the test to include disabilities with "any adverse effect on educational performance, however slight. . . . " *Id.* at 160. The correct formulation, the district urges, requires "some significant impact on educational performance." In rejecting this proposal, the district court reasoned that the phrase "adversely affects," as it appears in the relevant regulations, "has no qualifier such as 'substantial,' 'significant,' or 'marked,'" and declined to infer such a limitation "from Maine's regulatory silence." *Id.* We agree with this interpretation of the "adversely affects" standard.

Though the district marshals a number of arguments in support of its contrary position, they all sound a common theme: that an unlimited definition of "adversely affects" will qualify every child with one of the listed disabilities—no matter how minor—for IDEA benefits. This contention, however, overlooks the structure of the IDEA's eligibility standard, which requires not only that a child have one of the listed conditions, § 1401(3)(A)(i), but also that, "by reason thereof," the child "needs special education and related services," *id.* § 1401(3)(A)(ii). So a finding that a child meets the first criterion because his or her disability adversely affects educational performance—to whatever degree—does not itself entitle the child to special education and related services under the IDEA. *See* Mark C. Weber, *Special Education Law and Litigation Treatise* § 2.2(1), at 2:4 (2d ed.2002); Garda, *supra,* at 490–91. The child must also need special education and related services by reason of the disability.

In fact, an adverse effect on educational performance, standing alone, does not even satisfy the first prong of the eligibility test. The child's condition must also possess the additional characteristics required by the regulatory definitions of each of the disabilities enumerated in § 1401(3)(A)(i). Thus, the "adversely affects educational performance" requirement serves as but one of a list of factors that must be present for a child's condition to qualify as a disability under § 1401(3)(A)(i)—and, to receive IDEA benefits, the child must also need special education and related services by reason of the disability under § 1401(3)(A)(ii). The district court's interpretation of "adversely affects," then, is unlikely to loose the torrent of IDEA claims forecast by the district and its *amici.*

The district's specific arguments fare no better. The district contends that § 1401(3)(a)(i) fails to put the states on notice that, as a condition of accepting federal money under the IDEA, they are required to provide benefits to children whose conditions have merely an "adverse effect" on their educational performance. It is true that "when Congress attaches conditions to a State's acceptance of federal funds" pursuant to its Spending Clause authority, "the conditions must be set out unambiguously" so that each state can intelligently decide whether to take the money and its accompanying obligations. Based on this principle, the Supreme Court has held that whether the IDEA imposes a particular obligation on the states depends, at the outset, on whether the IDEA "furnishes clear notice regarding the liability at issue. . . . "

[citing *Arlington Central Sch. Dist. v. Murphy*, a principal case in Chapter Six.]

The principal place to look for such notice, of course, is the text of the IDEA itself. [T]o properly understand "disability" as it appears in the IDEA, we do not, as the district implores, resort to dictionary definitions of the word "disable," but to § 1401(3)(A)(i), which functions as the first part of the statutory definition of "child with a disability." Section 1401(3)(A)(i), as the district court observed, does not include the qualifying language urged upon us by the district, but simply defines "child with a disability" as a child "with" one of a number of specific conditions.[12]

The district also directs us to the more restrictive meaning of the term "disability" under Title II of the Americans with Disabilities Act and the Rehabilitation Act. Because the IDEA contains its own definition of the term, however, its appearance in other acts of Congress is of little moment. Putting aside the difference between the legislative goals of the IDEA and these other acts, then, the IDEA simply defines "disability" differently than they do. *Compare* 20 U.S.C. § 1401(3)(A) *with* 29 U.S.C. § 705(9)(B) *and* 42 U.S.C. § 12102(2)(A) (defining "disability" as "physical or mental impairment that substantially limits one or more major life activities").

[G]iven the express definition of "disability" set forth in § 1401(3)(A)(i), we need look no further to conclude that the statute sufficiently articulates the first prong of the standard for IDEA eligibility and, in so doing, adequately informs the states of the extent of their obligations. *Murphy*. The district and its *amici* nevertheless argue that this standard, as interpreted by the district court, flies in the face of congressional admonishments against identifying too many students as "children with disabilities" under the IDEA. It is true that, in amending the Act in 1997, Congress voiced concern about "over identifying children as disabled when they may not be truly disabled . . . particularly in urban schools with high proportions of minority students. . . . " H.R.Rep.No.105–95, at 89 (1997), *reprinted in* 1997 U.S.C.C.A.N. 78, 86. To remedy this problem, Congress changed the formula for calculating the funds due each state under the IDEA from one "based on the number of children with disabilities to a formula based on census and poverty. . . . " *Id.* at 88, 1997 U.S.C.C.A.N. at 85.

Notably, though, Congress thought this shift—rather than any alteration to the eligibility criteria—sufficient to address the over-identification problem. *Id.* at 89, 1997 U.S.C.C.A.N. at 87. Congress specifically stated, in fact, that the change to the funding formula "should in no way be construed to modify the obligation of educational agencies to identify and serve students with disabilities." *Id.* at 88, 1997 U.S.C.C.A.N. at 85.[13]

---

[12] Contrary to the district's suggestion, that § 1401(3)(A)(i) uses the words "impairment" or "serious" in naming some of the disabilities set forth provides no basis for inferring that *any* condition must be a "serious impairment" to meet the statutory standard, let alone a "significant impact" requirement.

[13] Moreover, Congress took this course of action despite the presidential committee report touted by the district and its *amici* in support of their proffered standard. President's Comm'n on Excellence in Special Educ., *A New Era: Revitalizing Special Education for Children and Their Families* (2002). This report not only further expressed concern about

The legislative history, then, only strengthens our conviction that § 1401(3)(A)(i), as construed by the district court, does not offend the Spending Clause by springing hidden liabilities upon participating states. Furthermore, as the district acknowledges, states deciding whether to enter into the IDEA bargain also have the benefit of the federal regulation defining the disabilities set forth in § 1401(3)(A)(i). Those definitions, again, specifically require that each disability (save one) "adversely affect[ ] a child's educational performance." 34 C.F.R. §§ 300.8(c)(1)–(c)(13). They do not contain the limiting language urged by the district, *i.e.,* "significantly impacts educational performance."

[M]aine's regulation, cribbed from 34 C.F.R. § 300.8, also requires no particular degree of impact on educational performance. 05–071–101 Me. Code R. §§ 3.2–3.14. This fact alone distinguishes this case from the decisions of other courts, cited by the district, which derived a higher standard from state law. *See* J.D. [v. Pawlet Sch. Dist.], 224 F.3d [60,] 66–67 [(2d Cir.2000)]. In *J.D.,* [t]he Second Circuit considered a Vermont regulation that defined "adverse effect of the disability on educational performance" to require a determination "that the student is functioning significantly below expected age or grade norms, in one or more of the basic skills." This provision further required that the "determination of adverse effect, usually defined as 1.0 standard deviation or its equivalent, shall be documented and supported by two or more measures of school performance," which were themselves specified by the regulation. Based on this standard, the Second Circuit concluded that the child did not qualify for IDEA benefits because he was "unable to identify at least two school performance measures that point to an adverse effect," despite his emotional-behavioral disability.

[S]tates wishing to put meat on the bones of the "adversely affects" standard are free to do so—provided, of course, they do not transgress the "floor" of substantive protection set by the IDEA. On its own, however, the federal regulation does not contain the "significant impact" requirement the district desires, and we cannot put it there. The district court correctly ruled that any negative impact, regardless of degree, qualifies as an "adverse effect" under the relevant federal and state regulations defining the disabilities listed in § 1401(3)(A)(i).

2.

Because the district court applied the right standard, we review its determination that LI has one of the disabilities included in § 1401(3)(A)(i) "for clear error on the record as a whole." We find none. As the hearing officer noted, the parties agree that LI suffers from Asperger's, manifested in her poor pragmatic language skills and social understanding difficulties, as well as from a depressive disorder brought on by the stress of managing these problems; indeed, the district has never questioned the opinions of LI's neuropsychologist and speech therapist in this regard. The parties disagree, however, on whether these conditions have adversely affected LI's educational performance in light of her strong grades, generally nondisruptive classroom behavior, and what the district court called her "undisputed

over-identification, as the district and its *amici* point out, but strongly criticized the regulatory definitions of the disabilities recognized by the IDEA. *Id.* at 22. Because neither Congress nor the Department of Education appears to have acted on the commission's recommendations, however, the report is of little use in construing the eligibility standards that have endured.

intellectual ability." In a lengthy written opinion, the district court tackled this issue head on, ultimately finding that, despite LI's above-average academic performance, "many of [her] social and communication deficits, including her isolation, inflexibility, and self-mutilation during schooltime, are precisely in the content areas and skills that Maine mandates educationally." This finding, the district court reasoned, compelled the conclusion that LI's disability had exerted an adverse effect on her educational performance under the governing standard.

B.

The district also argues that the district court misapplied § 1401(3)(A)(ii), which requires that a child "need[ ] special education and related services" as a result of his or her disability in order to qualify for them under the IDEA. The district asserts two errors: first, the district court used the wrong definition of "special education," and, second, it found that the district had waived any argument that LI does not "need" special education based on the position it took before the PET and the hearing officer. We believe the district court correctly defined "special education" under § 1401(3)(A)(ii). We do not decide, however, whether the district court properly treated the "need" issue as waived, because the district has not adequately explained to us why LI does not need special education, even under its view of the proper standard for making that determination.

1.

The IDEA defines "special education," in relevant part, as "specially designed instruction, at no cost to parents, to meet the unique needs of a child with a disability. . . . " 20 U.S.C. § 1401(29). A federal regulation, promulgated by the Department of Education, elaborates:

> Specially designed instruction means adapting, as appropriate to the needs of an eligible child . . . , the content, methodology, or delivery of instruction—
>
> (i) To address the unique needs of the child that result from the child's disability; and
>
> (ii) To ensure access of the child to the general curriculum, so that the child can meet the educational standards within the jurisdiction of the public agency that apply to all children.

34 C.F.R. § 300.39(b)(3) (2006).

[T]he district court ruled that a number of the interventions [i]ncluded in the services offered by the PET under the Rehabilitation Act, were "special education" within the meaning of federal law. [M]ost significantly, the district court reasoned that "extra instructional offerings such as social-skills and pragmatic-language instruction are 'specially designed instruction' to ensure [LI's] 'access . . . to the general curriculum.' " The district protests that its proffered "social pragmatics instruction," which "was aimed more at counseling LI at how she could better interact with others" than at traditional "speech services," qualifies as a "related service," not "special education," under the IDEA. The district has it backwards, however. While "speech-language pathology services" comprise a category of "related services," 20 U.S.C. § 1401(26)(A), directly teaching social skills and pragmatic language to LI amounts to adapting the content of the usual instruction to address her unique needs and to ensure that she meets state educational standards, *viz.,* those defining educational performance to include "communication" and requiring progress in "career preparation." The district court did not err in ruling that the services recommended for LI by her neuropsychologist and speech-language pathologist, and agreed to by the PET as part of its Rehabilitation Act plan, are "special education."

2.

The district also challenges the district court's resolution of whether LI "needs" the special education in question. [T]he district argues, based on McDevitt's testimony and LI's performance at TCS, that she does not need special education "to benefit from school" or "to do well in school."

But whether a child requires special education "to do well in school," or even "to benefit from school," presents a different question from whether the child requires special education "to benefit in those areas of educational performance that are adversely affected by her disability." The former inquiry considers the effect of special education on the child's overall achievement in school, while the latter focuses on the effect of special education on the components of that achievement hampered by the child's disability. Indeed, a child may "do well in school" without special education, accumulating a high grade point average, but may nevertheless perform below acceptable levels in other areas, such as behavior. The questions of whether such a child "needs special education" under a proper interpretation of § 1401(3)(A)(ii)—and how to articulate that interpretation in the first instance—have generated a cacophony of different answers. *See* Garda, *supra,* at 491–507 (surveying divergent authority).

[T]he district has not directed us to any error undermining the district court's determination that LI meets the second prong of the standard for IDEA eligibility, 20 U.S.C. § 1401(3)(A)(ii). Having found that the district court's ruling as to the first prong also holds up, we affirm the district court's decision that LI is eligible for services under the IDEA.

V.

[F]or the foregoing reasons, we ***affirm*** the judgment of the district court in its entirety.

NOTES ON *MR. I. V. MAINE SCHOOL ADMINISTRATIVE DISTRICT*

1. Civil Rights Versus Public Benefits. The IDEA, like the ADA, Rehabilitation Act, and Fair Housing Act, protects only a defined class of individuals with disabilities. But unlike those other statutes, the IDEA expressly defines its protected class in terms of medical diagnoses. One reason is that the IDEA has both a civil rights and a public benefits purpose. As Chapter Six will show, much of the impetus behind the original passage of the Education for All Handicapped Children Act—the statute that became the IDEA—came from advocates who were challenging the wholesale exclusion of many children with disabilities from public education or the segregation of children with disabilities into separate, inferior placements. These concerns fit easily with traditional understandings of civil rights law, and the statute responds to them by requiring states to provide a "free appropriate public education" in the "least restrictive environment" to all children with disabilities in their jurisdictions. 20 U.S.C. § 1412(a)(1)(A), (a)(5).

But the IDEA is also a public benefits statute. The statute does not just require that children with disabilities receive an education; it requires that they receive "special education and related services." 20 U.S.C. § 1401(9). The statute makes clear that special education must be "specially designed . . . to meet the unique needs of [the] child." 20 U.S.C. § 1401(29). And "related services" can include expensive nursing and personal care services, as the *Garret F.* case, which appears as a principal case in Chapter Six, demonstrates. It may therefore seem inevitable that the IDEA's definition of disability will rest heavily on medical diagnoses. The point, one might say, is not to identify the class of people who are marked by society as disabled, but the point is instead to identify the people who, because of their medical conditions, "need" the special benefits guaranteed by the statute.

How different is the IDEA from the ADA in this regard? The IDEA's requirement that schools provide children with disabilities special education and related services might be seen as just an application of the disability rights laws' general mandate of "reasonable accommodation." As Chapter Six will show, however, the mandates of the IDEA require states to provide accommodations that would never be considered "reasonable" under the ADA. The statute requires states to provide all children with disabilities access to education that will benefit them—even if it is incredibly costly to do so. How ought that difference affect the interpretation of the IDEA's definition of disability? If the courts have read the ADA's definition of disability narrowly because they see the ADA as a kind of welfare, for which eligibility should be carefully policed, does the more expensive nature of the benefits provided by the IDEA suggest that courts will interpret that statute's disability definition even more narrowly?

2. Normative Issues. What is the normative justification for limiting the IDEA's protections to children with a "disability"? Surely every student would benefit from education "specially designed" to meet their "unique needs." The normative questions are particularly pointed in the context of learning disabilities. The IDEA lists "specific learning disabilities" as among the conditions that, if they cause a child to need special education, constitute "disabilities" entitling the child to the statute's protections. 20 U.S.C. § 1401(3)(A)(i). Mark Kelman and Gillian Lester note that learning disabilities are typically diagnosed by identifying a significant discrepancy between an individual's IQ score and her observed achievement—if a child reads much less well than we would expect given her IQ score, for example, she will be diagnosed as having a learning disability. Kelman and Lester argue that devoting additional resources to individuals diagnosed with learning disabilities under that "discrepancy" makes no normative sense: As between two children whose performance is identical, they contend, there is no good reason to give more resources to one of them simply because she has a higher IQ. They also contend that the learning disability diagnosis is very malleable, and that giving additional resources to children with learning disabilities effects a wealth transfer to the relatively rich—who have the resources to get their children such a diagnosis. See Mark Kelman & Gillian Lester, Jumping the Queue: An Inquiry into the Legal Treatment of Students with Learning Disabilities (1997). For a similar argument, focused on the ADA, see Craig S. Lerner, *"Accommodations" for the Learning Disabled: A Level Playing Field or Affirmative Action for Elites?*, 57 Vand. L. Rev. 1043 (2004).

Is there a good answer to Kelman and Lester's normative challenge? One might argue, in a utilitarian vein, that focusing our resources on students with learning disabilities provides more bang for the buck—we can easily teach them strategies to circumvent the limitations their disabilities impose, and they will then achieve at a higher level than their fellow poor achievers who do not have learning disabilities. One might argue, in a more egalitarian vein, that schools uniquely disregard the needs of children with learning disabilities; to provide those children what seems like "special" interventions is really to rectify the inequality in the way they are treated. As Chapter Three shows, that sort of egalitarian argument is one of the key rationales for the general requirement to accommodate individuals with disabilities. But both of these arguments rest on empirical premises that one might doubt (and that Kelman and Lester attempt to disprove). Is there a persuasive reason to give children with learning disabilities extra attention in school, above and beyond nondisabled children who achieve at the same level? For a response to Kelman and Lester, see Andrew Weis, Jumping to Conclusions in "Jumping the Queue," 51 Stan. L. Rev. 183 (1998).

CHAPTER 3

DISABILITY DISCRIMINATION IN EMPLOYMENT

A. "REASONABLE ACCOMMODATIONS"

U.S. Airways, Inc. v. Barnett
Supreme Court of the United States, 2002.
535 U.S. 391.

■ JUSTICE BREYER delivered the opinion of the Court.

The Americans with Disabilities Act of 1990 prohibits an employer from discriminating against an "individual with a disability" who, with "reasonable accommodation," can perform the essential functions of the job. [42 U.S.C.] §§ 12112(a) and (b). This case, arising in the context of summary judgment, asks us how the Act resolves a potential conflict between: (1) the interests of a disabled worker who seeks assignment to a particular position as a "reasonable accommodation," and (2) the interests of other workers with superior rights to bid for the job under an employer's seniority system. In such a case, does the accommodation demand trump the seniority system?

In our view, the seniority system will prevail in the run of cases. As we interpret the statute, to show that a requested accommodation conflicts with the rules of a seniority system is ordinarily to show that the accommodation is not "reasonable." Hence such a showing will entitle an employer/defendant to summary judgment on the question—unless there is more. The plaintiff remains free to present evidence of special circumstances that make "reasonable" a seniority rule exception in the particular case. And such a showing will defeat the employer's demand for summary judgment.

I

In 1990, Robert Barnett, the plaintiff and respondent here, injured his back while working in a cargo-handling position at petitioner U.S. Airways, Inc. He invoked seniority rights and transferred to a less physically demanding mailroom position. Under U.S. Airways' seniority system, that position, like others, periodically became open to seniority-based employee bidding. In 1992, Barnett learned that at least two employees senior to him intended to bid for the mailroom job. He asked U.S. Airways to accommodate his disability-imposed limitations by making an exception that would allow him to remain in the mailroom. After permitting Barnett to continue his mailroom work for five months while it considered the matter, U.S. Airways eventually decided not to make an exception. And Barnett lost his job.

Barnett then brought this ADA suit claiming, among other things, that he was an "individual with a disability" capable of performing the essential functions of the mailroom job, that the mailroom job amounted to a "reasonable accommodation" of his disability, and that U.S.

Airways, in refusing to assign him the job, unlawfully discriminated against him. US Airways moved for summary judgment. It supported its motion with appropriate affidavits, contending that its "well-established" seniority system granted other employees the right to obtain the mailroom position.

The District Court found that the undisputed facts about seniority warranted summary judgment in U.S. Airways' favor. [A]n en banc panel of the United States Court of Appeals for the Ninth Circuit reversed. It said that the presence of a seniority system is merely "a factor in the undue hardship analysis." And it held that "[a] case-by-case fact intensive analysis is required to determine whether any particular reassignment would constitute an undue hardship to the employer."

II

In answering the question presented, we must consider the following statutory provisions. First, the ADA says that an employer may not "discriminate against a qualified individual with a disability." 42 U.S.C. § 12112(a). Second, the ADA says that a "qualified" individual includes "an individual with a disability who, with or without reasonable accommodation, can perform the essential functions of" the relevant "employment position." § 12111(8) (emphasis added). Third, the ADA says that "discrimination" includes an employer's "not making reasonable accommodations to the known physical or mental limitations of an otherwise qualified . . . employee, unless [the employer] can demonstrate that the accommodation would impose an undue hardship on the operation of [its] business." § 12112(b)(5)(A) (emphasis added). Fourth, the ADA says that the term " 'reasonable accommodation' may include . . . reassignment to a vacant position." § 12111(9)(B).

The parties interpret this statutory language as applied to seniority systems in radically different ways. In U.S. Airways' view, the fact that an accommodation would violate the rules of a seniority system always shows that the accommodation is not a "reasonable" one. In Barnett's polar opposite view, a seniority system violation never shows that an accommodation sought is not a "reasonable" one. Barnett concedes that a violation of seniority rules might help to show that the accommodation will work "undue" employer "hardship," but that is a matter for an employer to demonstrate case by case. We shall initially consider the parties' main legal arguments in support of these conflicting positions.

A

US Airways' claim that a seniority system virtually always trumps a conflicting accommodation demand rests primarily upon its view of how the Act treats workplace "preferences." Insofar as a requested accommodation violates a disability-neutral workplace rule, such as a seniority rule, it grants the employee with a disability treatment that other workers could not receive. Yet the Act, U.S. Airways says, seeks only "equal" treatment for those with disabilities. See, e.g., 42 U.S.C. § 12101(a)(9). It does not, it contends, require an employer to grant preferential treatment. Cf. H.R.Rep.No.101–485, pt. 2, p. 66 (1990), U.S.Code Cong. & Admin.News 1990, pp. 303, 348–349; S.Rep.No.101–

116, pp. 26–27 (1989) (employer has no "obligation to prefer applicants with disabilities over other applicants"). Hence it does not require the employer to grant a request that, in violating a disability-neutral rule, would provide a preference.

While linguistically logical, this argument fails to recognize what the Act specifies, namely, that preferences will sometimes prove necessary to achieve the Act's basic equal opportunity goal. The Act requires preferences in the form of "reasonable accommodations" that are needed for those with disabilities to obtain the same workplace opportunities that those without disabilities automatically enjoy. By definition any special "accommodation" requires the employer to treat an employee with a disability differently, *i.e.,* preferentially. And the fact that the difference in treatment violates an employer's disability-neutral rule cannot by itself place the accommodation beyond the Act's potential reach.

Were that not so, the "reasonable accommodation" provision could not accomplish its intended objective. Neutral office assignment rules would automatically prevent the accommodation of an employee whose disability-imposed limitations require him to work on the ground floor. Neutral "break-from-work" rules would automatically prevent the accommodation of an individual who needs additional breaks from work, perhaps to permit medical visits. Neutral furniture budget rules would automatically prevent the accommodation of an individual who needs a different kind of chair or desk. Many employers will have neutral rules governing the kinds of actions most needed to reasonably accommodate a worker with a disability. See 42 U.S.C. § 12111(9)(b) (setting forth examples such as "job restructuring," "part-time or modified work schedules," "acquisition or modification of equipment or devices," "and other similar accommodations"). Yet Congress, while providing such examples, said nothing suggesting that the presence of such neutral rules would create an automatic exemption. Nor have the lower courts made any such suggestion.

In sum, the nature of the "reasonable accommodation" requirement, the statutory examples, and the Act's silence about the exempting effect of neutral rules together convince us that the Act does not create any such automatic exemption. The simple fact that an accommodation would provide a "preference"—in the sense that it would permit the worker with a disability to violate a rule that others must obey—cannot, in and of itself, automatically show that the accommodation is not "reasonable." As a result, we reject the position taken by U.S. Airways and JUSTICE SCALIA to the contrary.

U.S. Airways also points to the ADA provisions stating that a " 'reasonable accommodation' may include . . . reassignment to a vacant position." § 12111(9)(B) (emphasis added). And it claims that the fact that an established seniority system would assign that position to another worker automatically and always means that the position is not a "vacant" one. Nothing in the Act, however, suggests that Congress intended the word "vacant" to have a specialized meaning. And in ordinary English, a seniority system can give employees seniority rights allowing them to bid for a "vacant" position. The position in this case was held, at the time of suit, by Barnett, not by some other worker; and that position, under the U.S. Airways seniority system, became an "open" one. Moreover, U.S. Airways has said that it "reserves the right to change any and all" portions of the seniority system at will. Lodging of Respondent 2 (U.S. Air Personnel Policy Guide for Agents). Consequently, we cannot agree with U.S. Airways about the position's vacancy; nor do we agree that the Act would automatically deny Barnett's accommodation request for that reason.

B

Barnett argues that the statutory words "reasonable accommodation" mean only "effective accommodation," authorizing a court to consider the requested accommodation's ability to meet an individual's disability-related needs, and nothing more. On this view, a seniority rule violation, having nothing to do with the accommodation's effectiveness, has nothing to do with its "reasonableness." It might, at most, help to prove an "undue hardship on the operation of the business." But, he adds, that is a matter that the statute requires the employer to demonstrate, case by case.

In support of this interpretation Barnett points to Equal Employment Opportunity Commission (EEOC) regulations stating that "reasonable accommodation means. . . . [m]odifications or adjustments . . . that enable a qualified individual with a disability to perform the essential functions of [a] position." 29 CFR § 1630(*o*)(ii) (2001). See also H.R.Rep.No.101–485, pt. 2, at 66, U.S.Code Cong. & Admin.News 1990, pp. 303, 348–349; S.Rep.No.101–116, at 35 (discussing reasonable accommodations in terms of "effectiveness," while discussing costs in terms of "undue hardship"). Barnett adds that any other view would make the words "reasonable accommodation" and "undue hardship" virtual mirror images-creating redundancy in the statute. And he says that any such other view would create a practical burden of proof dilemma.

The practical burden of proof dilemma arises, Barnett argues, because the statute imposes the burden of demonstrating an "undue hardship" upon the employer, while the burden of proving "reasonable accommodation" remains with the plaintiff, here the employee. This allocation seems sensible in that an employer can more frequently and easily prove the presence of business hardship than an employee can prove its absence. But suppose that an employee must counter a claim of "seniority rule violation" in order to prove that an "accommodation" request is "reasonable." Would that not force the employee to prove what is in effect an absence, *i.e.*, an absence of hardship, despite the statute's insistence that the employer "demonstrate" hardship's presence?

These arguments do not persuade us that Barnett's legal interpretation of "reasonable" is correct. For one thing, in ordinary English the word "reasonable" does not mean "effective." It is the word "accommodation," not the word "reasonable," that conveys the need for effectiveness. An ineffective "modification" or "adjustment" will not accommodate a disabled individual's limitations. Nor does an ordinary English meaning of the term "reasonable accommodation" make of it a simple, redundant mirror image of the term "undue hardship." The statute refers to an "undue hardship on the operation of the business." 42 U.S.C. § 12112(b)(5)(A). Yet a demand for an effective accommodation could prove unreasonable because of its impact, not on business operations, but on fellow employees—say, because it will lead to dismissals, relocations, or modification of employee benefits to which an employer, looking at the matter from the perspective of the business itself, may be relatively indifferent.

Neither does the statute's primary purpose require Barnett's special reading. The statute seeks to diminish or to eliminate the stereotypical thought processes, the thoughtless actions, and the hostile reactions that far too often bar those with disabilities from participating fully in the Nation's life, including the workplace. See generally §§ 12101(a) and (b). These objectives demand unprejudiced thought and reasonable responsive reaction on the part of employers and fellow workers alike. They will sometimes require affirmative conduct to promote entry of disabled people into the work force. They do not, however, demand action beyond the realm of the reasonable.

Neither has Congress indicated in the statute, or elsewhere, that the word "reasonable" means no more than "effective." The EEOC regulations do say that reasonable accommodations "enable" a person with a disability to perform the essential functions of a task. But that phrasing simply emphasizes the statutory provision's basic objective. The regulations do not say that "enable" and "reasonable" mean the same thing. And as discussed below, no court of appeals has so read them.

Finally, an ordinary language interpretation of the word "reasonable" does not create the "burden of proof" dilemma to which Barnett points. Many of the lower courts, while rejecting both U.S. Airways' and Barnett's more absolute views, have reconciled the phrases "reasonable accommodation" and "undue hardship" in a practical way.

They have held that a plaintiff/employee (to defeat a defendant/employer's motion for summary judgment) need only show that an "accommodation" seems reasonable on its face, *i.e.*, ordinarily or in the run of cases. [O]nce the plaintiff has made this showing, the defendant/employer then must show special (typically case-specific) circumstances that demonstrate undue hardship in the particular circumstances. [I]n our opinion, that practical view of the statute, applied consistently with ordinary summary judgment principles, avoids Barnett's burden of proof dilemma, while reconciling the two statutory phrases ("reasonable accommodation" and "undue hardship").

III

The question in the present case focuses on the relationship between seniority systems and the plaintiff's need to show that an "accommodation" seems reasonable on its face, *i.e.*, ordinarily or in the run of cases. [Barnett] has requested assignment to a mailroom position as a "reasonable accommodation." We [a]ssume that normally such a request would be reasonable within the meaning of the statute, were it not for one circumstance, namely, that the assignment would violate the rules of a seniority system. See § 12111(9) ("reasonable accommodation" may include "reassignment to a vacant position"). Does that circumstance mean that the proposed accommodation is not a "reasonable" one?

In our view, the answer to this question ordinarily is "yes." The statute does not require proof on a case-by-case basis that a seniority system should prevail. That is because it would not be reasonable in the run of cases that the assignment in question trump the rules of a seniority system. To the contrary, it will ordinarily be unreasonable for the assignment to prevail.

A

Several factors support our conclusion that a proposed accommodation will not be reasonable in the run of cases. Analogous case law supports this conclusion, for it has recognized the importance of seniority to employee-management relations. This Court has held that, in the context of a Title VII religious discrimination case, an employer need not adapt to an employee's special worship schedule as a "reasonable accommodation" where doing so would conflict with the seniority rights of other employees. *Trans World Airlines, Inc. v. Hardison*, 432 U.S. 63, 79–80 (1977). The lower courts have unanimously found that collectively bargained seniority trumps the need for reasonable accommodation in the context of the linguistically similar Rehabilitation Act. And several Circuits, though differing in their reasoning, have reached a similar conclusion in the context of seniority and the ADA. All these cases discuss collectively bargained seniority systems, not systems (like the present system) which are unilaterally imposed by management. But the relevant seniority system advantages, and related difficulties that result from violations of seniority rules, are not limited to collectively bargained systems.

For one thing, the typical seniority system provides important employee benefits by creating, and fulfilling, employee expectations of fair, uniform treatment. These benefits include "job security and an opportunity for steady and predictable advancement based on objective standards." They include "an element of due process," limiting "unfairness in personnel decisions." And they consequently encourage employees to invest in the employing company, accepting "less than their value to the firm early in their careers" in return for greater benefits in later years.

Most important for present purposes, to require the typical employer to show more than the existence of a seniority system might well undermine the employees' expectations of consistent, uniform treatment—expectations upon which the seniority system's benefits depend. That is because such a rule would substitute a complex case-specific "accommodation" decision made by management for the more uniform, impersonal operation of seniority rules. Such management decisionmaking, with its inevitable discretionary elements, would involve a matter of the greatest importance to employees, namely, layoffs; it would take place outside, as well as inside, the confines of a court case; and it might well take place fairly often. Cf. ADA, 42 U.S.C. § 12101(a)(1) (estimating that some 43 million Americans suffer from physical or mental disabilities). We can find nothing in the statute that suggests Congress intended to undermine seniority systems in this way. And we consequently conclude that the employer's showing of violation of the rules of a seniority system is by itself ordinarily sufficient.

B

The plaintiff (here the employee) nonetheless remains free to show that special circumstances warrant a finding that, despite the presence of a seniority system (which the ADA may not trump in the run of cases), the requested "accommodation" is "reasonable" on the particular facts. That is because special circumstances might alter the important expectations described above. The plaintiff might show, for example, that the employer, having retained the right to change the seniority system unilaterally, exercises that right fairly frequently, reducing employee expectations that the system will be followed—to the point where one more departure, needed to accommodate an individual with a disability, will not likely make a difference. The plaintiff might show that the system already contains exceptions such that, in the circumstances, one further exception is unlikely to matter. We do not mean these examples to exhaust the kinds of showings that a plaintiff might make. But we do mean to say that the plaintiff must bear the burden of showing special circumstances that make an exception from the seniority system reasonable in the particular case. And to do so, the plaintiff must explain why, in the particular case, an exception to the employer's seniority policy can constitute a "reasonable accommodation" even though in the ordinary case it cannot.

IV

[B]ecause the lower courts took a different view of the matter, and because neither party has had an opportunity to seek summary judgment in accordance with the principles we set forth here, we vacate the Court of Appeals' judgment and remand the case for further proceedings consistent with this opinion.

It is so ordered.

■ JUSTICE STEVENS, concurring.

While I join the Court's opinion, my colleagues' separate writings prompt these additional comments.

A possible conflict with an employer's seniority system is relevant to the question whether a disabled employee's requested accommodation is "reasonable" within the meaning of the Americans with Disabilities Act of 1990. For that reason, to the extent that the Court of Appeals concluded that a seniority system is only relevant to the question whether a given accommodation would impose an "undue hardship" on an employer, or determined that such a system has only a minor bearing on the reasonableness inquiry, it misread the statute.

Although the Court of Appeals did not apply the standard that the Court endorses today, it correctly rejected the *per se* rule that petitioner has pressed upon us and properly reversed the District Court's entry of summary judgment for petitioner. The Court of Appeals also correctly held that there was a triable issue of fact precluding the entry of summary judgment with respect to whether petitioner violated the statute by failing to engage in an interactive process concerning respondent's three proposed accommodations. This latter holding is untouched by the Court's opinion today.

■ JUSTICE O'CONNOR, concurring.

I agree with portions of the opinion of the Court, but I find problematic the Court's test for determining whether the fact that a job reassignment violates a seniority system makes the reassignment an unreasonable accommodation under the Americans with Disabilities Act of 1990. Although a seniority system plays an important role in the workplace, for the reasons I explain below, I would prefer to say that the effect of a seniority system on the reasonableness of a reassignment as an accommodation for purposes of the ADA depends on whether the seniority system is legally enforceable. But [i]n order that the Court may adopt a rule, and because I believe the Court's rule will often lead to the same outcome as the one I would have adopted, I join the Court's opinion despite my concerns. Cf. *Bragdon v. Abbott*, 524 U.S. 624, 655–656, (STEVENS, J., joined by BREYER, J., concurring).

The ADA specifically lists "reassignment to a vacant position" as one example of a "reasonable accommodation." 42 U.S.C. § 12111(9)(B). In deciding whether an otherwise reasonable accommodation involving a reassignment is unreasonable because it would require an exception to a seniority system, I think the relevant issue is whether the seniority system prevents the position in question from being vacant. The word "vacant" means "not filled or occupied by an incumbent [or] possessor." Webster's Third New International Dictionary 2527 (1976). In the context of a workplace, a vacant position is a position in which no employee currently works and to which no individual has a legal entitlement. For example, in a workplace without a seniority system, when an employee ceases working for the employer, the employee's former position is vacant until a replacement is hired. Even if the replacement does not start work immediately, once the replacement enters into a contractual agreement with the employer, the position is no longer vacant because it has a "possessor." In contrast, when an employee ceases working in a workplace with a legally enforceable seniority system, the employee's former position does not become vacant if the seniority system entitles another employee to it. Instead, the employee entitled to the position under the seniority system immediately becomes the new "possessor" of that position. In a workplace with an unenforceable seniority policy, however, an employee expecting assignment to a position under the seniority policy would not have any type of contractual right to the position and so could not be said to be its "possessor." The position therefore would become vacant.

Given this understanding of when a position can properly be considered vacant, if a seniority system, in the absence of the ADA, would give someone other than the individual seeking the accommodation a legal entitlement or contractual right to the position to which reassignment is sought, the seniority system prevents the position from being vacant. If a position is not vacant, then reassignment to it is not a reasonable accommodation.

[P]etitioner's Personnel Policy Guide for Agents, which contains its seniority policy, specifically states that it is "not intended to be a contract (express or implied) or otherwise to create legally enforceable obligations," and that petitioner "reserves the right to change any and all of the stated policies and procedures in [the] Guide at any time, without advanc[e] notice." Lodging of Respondent 2. Petitioner conceded at oral argument that its seniority policy does not give employees any legally enforceable rights. Because the policy did not give any other employee a right to the position respondent sought, the position could be said to have been vacant when it became open for bidding, making the requested accommodation reasonable.

[A]lthough I am troubled by the Court's reasoning, I believe the Court's approach for evaluating seniority systems will often lead to the same outcome as the test I would have adopted. Unenforceable seniority systems are likely to involve policies in which employers "retai[n] the right to change the seniority system," and will often "contai[n] exceptions," ibid. They will also often contain disclaimers that "reduc[e] employee expectations that the system will be followed." Thus, under the Court's test, disabled employees seeking accommodations that would require exceptions to unenforceable seniority systems may be able to show circumstances that make the accommodation "reasonable in the[ir] particular case." Because I think the Court's test will often lead to the correct outcome, and because I think it important that a majority of the Court agree on a rule when interpreting statutes, I join the Court's opinion.

■ JUSTICE SCALIA, with whom JUSTICE THOMAS joins, dissenting.

The principal defect of today's opinion [g]oes well beyond the uncertainty it produces regarding the relationship between the ADA and the infinite variety of seniority systems. The conclusion that any seniority system can ever be overridden is merely one consequence of a mistaken interpretation of the ADA that makes all employment rules and practices—even those which (like a seniority system) pose no distinctive obstacle to the disabled—subject to suspension when that is (in a court's view) a "reasonable" means of enabling a disabled employee to keep his job. That is a far cry from what I believe the accommodation provision of the ADA requires: the suspension (within reason) of those employment rules and practices that the employee's disability prevents him from observing.

I

[The ADA's] provisions order employers to modify or remove (within reason) policies and practices that burden a disabled person "because of [his] disability." In other words, the ADA eliminates workplace barriers only if a disability prevents an employee from overcoming them—those barriers that would not be barriers but for the employee's disability. These include, for example, work stations that cannot accept the employee's wheelchair, or an assembly-line practice that requires long periods of standing. But they do not include rules and practices that bear no more heavily upon the disabled employee than upon others—even though an exemption from such a rule or practice might in a sense "make up for" the employee's disability. It is not a required accommodation, for example, to pay a disabled employee more than others at his grade level—even if that increment is earmarked for massage or physical therapy that would enable the employee to work with as little physical discomfort as his co-workers. That would be "accommodating" the disabled employee, but it would not be "making . . . accommodatio[n] to the known physical or mental limitations" of the employee, § 12112(b)(5)(A), because it would not eliminate any workplace practice that constitutes an obstacle because of his disability.

So also with exemption from a seniority system, which burdens the disabled and nondisabled alike. In particular cases, seniority rules may have a harsher effect upon the disabled employee than upon his co-workers. If the disabled employee is physically capable of performing only one task in the workplace, seniority rules may be, for him, the difference between employment and unemployment. But that does not make the seniority system a disability-related obstacle, any more than harsher impact upon the more needy disabled employee renders the salary system a disability-related obstacle. When one departs from this understanding, the ADA's accommodation provision becomes a standardless grab bag—leaving it to the courts to decide which workplace preferences (higher salary, longer vacations, reassignment to positions to which others are entitled) can be deemed "reasonable" to "make up for" the particular employee's disability.

Some courts, including the Ninth Circuit in the present case, have accepted respondent's contention that the ADA demands accommodation even with respect to those obstacles that have nothing to do with the disability. Their principal basis for this position is that the definition of "reasonable accommodation" includes "reassignment to a vacant position." § 12111(9)(B). This accommodation would be meaningless, they contend, if it required only that the disabled employee be considered for a vacant position. [T]his argument seems to me quite mistaken. The right to be given a vacant position so long as there are no obstacles to that appointment (including another candidate who is better qualified, if "best qualified" is the workplace rule) is of considerable value. If an employee is hired to fill a position but fails miserably, he will typically be fired. Few employers will search their organization charts for vacancies to which the low-performing employee might be suited. The ADA, however, prohibits an employer from firing a person whose disability is the cause of his poor performance without first seeking to place him in a vacant job where the disability will not affect performance. Such reassignment is an accommodation to the disability because it removes an obstacle (the inability to perform the functions of the assigned job) arising solely from the disability.

The phrase "reassignment to a vacant position" appears in a subsection describing a variety of potential "reasonable accommodation[s]":

> "(A) making existing facilities used by employees readily accessible to and usable by individuals with disabilities; and

> "(B) job restructuring, part-time or modified work schedules, reassignment to a vacant position, acquisition or modification of equipment or devices, appropriate adjustment or modifications of examinations, training materials or policies, the provision of qualified readers or interpreters, and other similar accommodations for individuals with disabilities." § 12111(9).

Subsection (A) clearly addresses features of the workplace that burden the disabled because of their disabilities. Subsection (B) is broader in scope but equally targeted at disability-related obstacles. Thus it encompasses "modified work schedules" (which may accommodate inability to work for protracted periods), "modification of equipment and devices," and "provision of qualified readers or interpreters." There is no reason why the phrase "reassignment to a vacant position" should be thought to have a uniquely different focus. It envisions elimination of the obstacle of the current position (which requires activity that the disabled employee cannot tolerate) when there is an alternate position freely available. If he is qualified for that position, and no one else is seeking it, or no one else who seeks it is better qualified, he must be given the position. But "reassignment to a vacant position" does not envision the elimination of obstacles to the employee's service in the new position that have nothing to do with his disability—for example, another employee's claim to that position under a seniority system, or another employee's superior qualifications.

Unsurprisingly, most Courts of Appeals addressing the issue have held or assumed that the ADA does not mandate exceptions to a "legitimate, nondiscriminatory policy" such as a seniority system or a consistent policy of assigning the most qualified person to a vacant position.

[S]adly, this analysis is lost on the Court, which mistakenly and inexplicably concludes that my position here is the same as that attributed to U.S. Airways. In rejecting the argument that the ADA creates no "automatic exemption" for neutral workplace rules such as "break-from-work" and furniture budget rules, the Court rejects an argument I have not made.

II

Although, as I have said, the uncertainty cast upon bona fide seniority systems is the least of the ill consequences produced by today's decision, a few words on that subject are nonetheless in order. Since, under the Court's interpretation of the ADA, all workplace rules are eligible to be used as vehicles of accommodation, the one means of saving seniority systems is a judicial finding that accommodation through the suspension of those workplace rules would be unreasonable. The Court is unwilling, however, to make that finding categorically, with respect to all seniority systems. Instead, it creates (and "creates" is the appropriate word) a rebuttable presumption that exceptions to seniority rules are not "reasonable" under the ADA, but leaves it free for the disabled employee to show that under the "special circumstances" of his case, an exception would be "reasonable." The employee would be entitled to an exception, for example, if he showed that "one more departure" from the seniority rules "will not likely make a difference."

I have no idea what this means. When is it possible for a departure from seniority rules to "not likely make a difference"? Even when a bona fide seniority system has multiple exceptions, employees expect that these are the only exceptions. One more unannounced exception will invariably undermine the values ("fair, uniform treatment," "job security," "predictable advancement," etc.) that the Court cites as its reasons for believing seniority systems so important that they merit a presumption of exemption.

One is tempted to impart some rationality to the scheme by speculating that the Court's burden-shifting rule is merely intended to give the disabled employee an opportunity to show that the employer's seniority system is in fact a sham—a system so full of exceptions that it creates no meaningful employee expectations. The rule applies, however, even if the seniority system is "bona fide and established." And the Court says that "to require the typical employer to show more than the existence of a seniority system might well undermine the employees' expectations of consistent, uniform treatment. . . . " How could deviations from a sham seniority system "undermine the employees' expectations"?

I must conclude, then, that the Court's rebuttable presumption does not merely give disabled employees the opportunity to unmask sham seniority systems; it gives them a vague and unspecified power (whenever they can show "special circumstances") to undercut bona fide systems. The Court claims that its new test will not require exceptions to seniority systems "in the run of cases," but that is belied by the disposition of this case. The Court remands to give respondent an opportunity to show that an exception to petitioner's seniority system "will not likely make a difference" to employee expectations, despite the following finding by the District Court:

> "[T]he uncontroverted evidence shows that [petitioner's] seniority system has been in place for 'decades' and governs over 14,000 . . . Agents. Moreover, seniority policies such as the one at issue in this case are common to the airline industry. Given this context, it seems clear that [petitioner's] employees were justified in relying upon the policy. As such, any significant alteration of that policy would result in undue hardship to both the company and its non-disabled employees."

■ JUSTICE SOUTER, with whom JUSTICE GINSBURG joins, dissenting.

"[R]eassignment to a vacant position," 42 U.S.C. § 12111(9), is one way an employer may "reasonabl[y] accommodat[e]" disabled employees under the Americans with Disabilities Act of 1990. The Court today holds that a request for reassignment will nonetheless most likely be unreasonable when it would violate the terms of a seniority system imposed by an employer. Although I concur in the Court's appreciation of the value and importance of seniority systems, I do not believe my hand is free to accept the majority's result and therefore respectfully dissent.

Nothing in the ADA insulates seniority rules from the "reasonable accommodation" requirement, in marked contrast to Title VII of the Civil Rights Act of 1964 and the Age Discrimination in Employment Act of 1967, each of which has an explicit protection for seniority. See 42 U.S.C. § 2000e–2(h) ("Notwithstanding any other provision of this subchapter, it shall not be an unlawful employment practice for an employer to [provide different benefits to employees] pursuant to a bona fide seniority . . . system . . . "); 29 U.S.C. § 623(f) ("It shall not be unlawful for an employer . . . to take any action otherwise prohibited [under previous sections] . . . to observe the terms of a bona fide seniority system [except for involuntary retirement] . . . "). Because Congress modeled several of the ADA's provisions on Title VII, its failure to replicate Title VII's exemption for seniority systems leaves the statute ambiguous, albeit with more than a hint that seniority rules do not inevitably carry the day.

In any event, the statute's legislative history resolves the ambiguity. The Committee Reports from both the House of Representatives and the Senate explain that seniority protections contained in a collective-bargaining agreement should not amount to more than "a factor" when it comes to deciding whether some accommodation at odds with the seniority rules is "reasonable" nevertheless. H.R.Rep.No.101–485, pt. 2, p. 63 (1990) U.S.Code Cong. & Admin.News 1990, pp. 303, 345, (existence of collectively bargained protections for seniority "would not be determinative" on the issue whether an accommodation was reasonable); S.Rep.No.101–116, p. 32 (1989) (a collective-bargaining agreement assigning jobs based on seniority "may be considered as a factor in determining" whether an accommodation is reasonable). Here, of course, it does not matter whether the congressional committees were right or wrong in thinking that views of sound ADA application could reduce a collectively bargained seniority policy to the level of "a factor," in the absence of a specific statutory provision to that effect. In fact, I doubt that any interpretive clue in legislative history could trump settled law specifically making collective-bargaining agreements enforceable. See, e.g., § 301(a), Labor Management Relations Act, 1947, 29 U.S.C. § 185(a) (permitting suit in federal court to enforce collective-bargaining agreements). The point in this case, however, is simply to recognize that if Congress considered that sort of agreement no more than a factor in the analysis, surely no greater weight was meant for a seniority scheme like the one before us, unilaterally imposed by the employer, and, unlike collective-bargaining agreements, not singled out for protection by any positive federal statute.

This legislative history also specifically rules out the majority's reliance on *Trans World Airlines, Inc. v. Hardison*, 432 U.S. 63 (1977), a case involving a request for a religious accommodation under Title VII that would have broken the seniority rules of a collective-bargaining agreement. We held that such an accommodation would not be "reasonable," and said that our conclusion was "supported" by Title VII's explicit exemption for seniority systems. The committees of both Houses of Congress dealing with the ADA were aware of this case and expressed a choice against treating it as authority under the ADA, with its lack of any provision for maintaining seniority rules. E.g., H.R.Rep.No.101–485, pt. 2, at 68, U.S.Code Cong. & Admin.News 1990, pp. 303, 350 ("The Committee wishes to make it clear that the principles enunciated by the Supreme Court in TWA v. Hardison . . . are not applicable to this legislation"); S.Rep.No.101–116, at 36 (same).

Because a unilaterally imposed seniority system enjoys no special protection under the ADA, a consideration of facts peculiar to this very case is needed to gauge whether Barnett has carried the burden of showing his proposed accommodation to be a "reasonable" one despite the policy in force at U.S. Airways. The majority describes this as a burden to show the accommodation is "plausible" or "feasible," and I believe Barnett has met it.

He held the mailroom job for two years before learning that employees with greater seniority planned to bid for the position, given U.S. Airways's decision to declare the job "vacant." Thus, perhaps unlike ADA claimants who request accommodation through reassignment, Barnett was seeking not a change but a continuation of the status quo. All he asked was that U.S. Airways refrain from declaring the position "vacant"; he did not ask to bump any other employee and no one would have lost a job on his account. There was no evidence in the District Court of any unmanageable ripple effects from Barnett's request, or showing that he would have overstepped an inordinate number of seniority levels by remaining where he was.

In fact, it is hard to see the seniority scheme here as any match for Barnett's ADA requests, since U.S. Airways apparently took pains to ensure that its seniority rules raised no great expectations. In its policy statement, U.S. Airways said that "[t]he Agent Personnel Policy Guide is not intended to be a contract" and that "USAir reserves the right to change any and all of the stated policies and procedures in this Guide at any time, without advanced notice." While I will skip any state-by-state analysis of the legal treatment of employee handbooks (a source of many lawyers' fees) it is safe to say that the contract law of a number of jurisdictions would treat this disclaimer as fatal to any claim an employee might make to enforce the seniority policy over an employer's contrary decision.

NOTES ON *U.S. AIRWAYS V. BARNETT*

1.   What is the Accommodation Mandate For? The requirement of reasonable accommodation occupies a central place in disability discrimination law. What is the justification for treating the failure to make accommodations for people with disabilities as discrimination against them? There are several possible answers to this question, each of which might have implications for the interpretation of the accommodation mandate.

    a.   The Failure to Accommodate as Simple Discrimination. Employers accommodate (nondisabled) employees all the time. A supervisor may, for example, give an employee time off to attend a child's little league championship or to play in the finals of a club golf tournament. And accommodation to nondisabled employees is built into the workplace itself. As the disability studies scholar Harlan Hahn explains, "[p]erhaps the clearest, though not the most costly, example is chairs which, for wheelchair users who are considerate enough to bring our own, represent a significant concession to the nondisabled segment of society." Harlan Hahn, *Accommodations and the ADA: Unreasonable Bias or Biased Reasoning?*, 21 Berkeley J. Emp. & Lab. L. 166, 178 n.61 (2000). Indeed, accommodations of nondisabled employees are far more extensive than that. As Professor Burgdorf argues, the physical layout and facilities of a workplace, as well as its policies and schedules, are all designed "with the standard employee in mind"—an employee who has no disability. Robert L. Burgdorf Jr., *"Substantially Limited" Protection from Disability Discrimination: The Special Treatment Model and Misconstructions of the Definition of Disability*, 42 Vill. L. Rev. 409, 530–531 (1997).

    From this perspective, accommodations for employees with disabilities do not offer them anything "special." Instead, they merely rectify an inequality: Nondisabled employees get their needs accommodated, but employees with disabilities do not (at least not to the same extent). And that is because the people who designed workplaces and job tasks were not thinking of people with disabilities as potential workers (something that may itself be a legacy of a long history of shunting away and institutionalizing individuals with disabilities). Under this view, the ADA's accommodation mandate is justified in the same way as a classic antidiscrimination requirement. By demanding that employers arrange their physical and institutional structures to take account of people with disabilities, that mandate prohibits employers from denying employees with disabilities the same accommodations as they give to nondisabled employees, and it provides a remedy for past discrimination against individuals with disabilities. Perhaps that is what Justice Breyer means when he writes, "The Act requires preferences in the form of 'reasonable accommodations' that are needed for those with disabilities to obtain the same workplace opportunities that those without disabilities automatically enjoy."

But if avoiding this sort of simple discrimination is the justification for the accommodation requirement, what implications might that justification have for the proper scope of that requirement? Perhaps the requirement should be read to require only those sorts of accommodations that the employer would provide to any valued (nondisabled) employee. Or perhaps we should engage in counterfactual reasoning and ask whether, if an employer had been thinking of people with disabilities as potential employees, it would have imposed the barrier that the employee with a disability is challenging. Would these inquiries be analytically tractable? Are they normatively attractive? How would *Barnett* have come out if the accommodation requirement were limited to cases involving some sort of simple discrimination? Robert Barnett wasn't just asking for what any valued employee would get, was he? But cf. Samuel R. Bagenstos, US Airways v. Barnett and the Limits of Disability Accommodation, in Civil Rights Stories 323, 344 (Myriam E. Gilles & Risa L. Goluboff, eds., 2008) ("[E]ven if disability does not limit the amount of seniority a person can accrue, a workplace that took people with disabilities into account as 'normal' workers would recognize their more frequent need for flexibility in the application of a seniority system.").

b. Antisubordinationist Justifications. *Barnett* highlights the limitations of a simple-discrimination model of the ADA's accommodation requirement. As Professor Verkerke has noted, that requirement seems to call on employers to adopt measures whose cost and inconvenience "frequently goes well beyond the sort of assistance they would provide as a matter of course to any valued employee." J.H. Verkerke, *Disaggregating Antidiscrimination and Accommodation*, 44 Wm. & Mary L. Rev. 1385, 1400 (2003). Can the accommodation mandate be justified as something other than a response to simple discrimination?

One justification might rest on the subordinated status of people with disabilities. People with disabilities, in the aggregate, face significant and widespread disadvantage in society and barriers to employment. In part, this is because many aspects of employers' physical and social environment are not accessible to them. The systematic lack of opportunities for people with disabilities imposes stigmatic harm, and it may discourage people with disabilities from developing their human capital. It may also lead to market inefficiencies. See J.H. Verkerke, Is the ADA Efficient?, 50 UCLA L. Rev. 903 (2003) (describing socially inefficient "churning" and "scarring" experienced by workers with disabilities). The employer, by granting an accommodation, is the only one in a position to undermine this system of subordination and occupational segregation; where the accommodation will not be unduly costly, we might characterize the duty to provide it as part of an employer's duty not to participate in entrenching a subordinating system. For an extended version of this argument, see Samuel R. Bagenstos, *"Rational Discrimination," Accommodation, and the Politics of (Disability) Civil Rights*, 89 Va. L. Rev. 825 (2003). What might this antisubordinationist account suggest about the proper scope of the accommodation mandate? Should the mandate be limited to cases in which accommodation is necessary to avoid systematic disadvantage? How could we tell which cases fit that description?

   c.   **Dependency Costs.** The drafters and supporters of the ADA as it passed through Congress offered a variation on the concern with subordination and systematic disadvantage. They argued that accommodations were necessary to keep people with disabilities from relying on welfare and other governmental cash benefits programs. "In official reports, in congressional hearings, on the floor of Congress, and in the popular press, supporters of the proposed ADA argued that the statute was necessary to reduce the high societal cost of dependency—that people with disabilities were drawing public assistance instead of working, and that a regime of 'reasonable accommodations' could move people with disabilities off of the public assistance rolls and into the workforce in a way that would ultimately save the nation money." Samuel R. Bagenstos, *The Americans with Disabilities Act as Welfare Reform*, 44 Wm. & Mary L. Rev. 921, 926–927 (2003). If the goal of the accommodation mandate is to save society the costs of dependency, what implications does that have for the proper scope of the mandate? Ought it to be limited to cases in which the accommodation is necessary to keep an individual with a disability in the workforce? In this light, consider the accommodation Robert Barnett sought—the right to stay in the mailroom, and therefore continue working for the company. Was that accommodation necessary to enable Barnett to keep off of the disability benefits rolls? "[S]tudents of disability benefits programs have arrived at a consistent empirical finding: Disability benefits recipients only rarely return to work. If that is right, then an effort to avoid the social costs of dependency should focus on keeping people off of the disability rolls in the first place." *Id.* at 982. What does that suggest about the proper scope of the accommodation requirement?

   d.   **Pure Redistribution or Charity.** Justice Scalia accuses the Court of requiring employers to do whatever seems "reasonable" to "make up for" an employee's disability. He thus suggests that the Court is treating the accommodation requirement as a sort of *ad hoc* forced charity. The majority seems to deny the charge and defend a principle of "equal opportunity." Both majority and dissent thus seem to treat forced-charity as an improper purpose for the ADA. As Chapter One shows, disability rights activists have tended to take the same position. But why? Cf. Bonnie Poitras Tucker, *The ADA's Revolving Door: Inherent Flaws in the Civil Rights Paradigm*, 62 Ohio St. L.J. 335, 339 (2001) (stating that "[t]he ADA appears to waffle on" the question whether it requires employers "to act as good Samaritans"). Among disability rights advocates, the position reflects the sense that if the accommodation mandate is understood as pure redistribution, it will be morally and politically weaker than if it is understood as part and parcel of a right against discrimination. Professor Mark Kelman, one of the leading academic skeptics of the accommodation requirement, illustrates their fears. He argues that "[v]ictims of simple [*i.e.*, irrational] discrimination possess * * * a fairly strong, uncircumscribed 'right' to be free from such treatment, while those seeking accommodation possess, in essence, a colorable 'claim' on social resources that competes with a variety of other claims on such resources, a policy 'argument' to be balanced against other prudential arguments." Mark Kelman, *Market Discrimination and Groups*, 53 Stan. L. Rev. 833, 834 (2001). How might we assess whether a particular accommodation claim should defeat other claims to social resources? Do the statutory requirements that the accommodation be "reasonable" and carried out without "undue hardship" strike the balance appropriately? For critique of Professor Kelman's argument, see Bagenstos, *"Rational Discrimination," supra*, at 870–900; Ravi Malhotra, *The Law and Economics Tradition and Workers with Disabilities*, 39 Ottawa L. Rev. 239, 265–267 (2008). For a rejoinder and further discussion, see Mark Kelman, *Defining the Antidiscrimination Norm to Defend It*, 43 San Diego L. Rev. 735 (2006).

If the ADA is understood as a form of forced charity, what sorts of accommodations should be required? Is Justice Scalia right that the ADA would become a "standardless grab-bag" if understood in this way? Is Justice Breyer persuasive in denying that he treats the accommodation requirement as a form of forced charity, particularly given the facts of the case?

e. Why Should the Employer Pay? As Professor Samuel Issacharoff and Justin Nelson observe, the ADA's accommodation mandate turns on the seemingly arbitrary "fact that a potential employee selected one employer rather than another to apply to for a job. Thus, any individual employer may be subject to costs of unknown dimensions while her competitors are not. In turn, the extent of the accommodation standard is defined not by a uniform obligation across all employers, but by the ability of any employer to pay, regardless of fault or ensuing competitive disadvantage." Samuel Issacharoff & Justin Nelson, *Discrimination with a Difference: Can Employment Discrimination Law Accommodate the Americans with Disabilities Act?*, 79 N.C. L. Rev. 307, 344–345 (2001). See also Jerry L. Mashaw, *Against First Principles*, 31 San Diego L. Rev. 211, 230–231 (1994) ("The incidence of the ADA antidiscrimination 'tax' will depend upon the choices of impaired applicants and potential litigants. Who pays to accommodate the needs of the disabled depends on where the disabled work or apply for work. One can easily imagine that the firms who have done the most to accommodate the disabled will be the most attractive to potential job seekers and, therefore, will bear the greatest costs of accommodation.").

What is the justification for imposing the costs of accommodations on the particular employer whom a job applicant with a disability chooses, rather than spreading the costs through public subsidies for those accommodations? Professor Julie Roin argues that public financing would be inefficient, because it will be difficult for the government to determine whether the subsidies are being spent by employers "in a cost-effective manner. Employers who were paid by the government to take these steps might often make wasteful expenditures that they would never incur with their own money even when required to meet the same ends. Opportunities for corrupt arrangements would abound." Julie A. Roin, *Reconceptualizing Unfunded Mandates and Other Regulations*, 93 Nw. U. L. Rev. 351, 365 (1999). As a result, imposing a mandate on employers may be the only practical means of preventing systematic exclusion of people with disabilities from important opportunities. See generally Bagenstos, *"Rational Discrimination," supra*; see also Elizabeth F. Emens, *The Sympathetic Discriminator: Mental Illness, Hedonic Costs, and the ADA*, 94 Geo. L.J. 399, 480 (2006) ("The employer faced with an individual applicant or worker with a mental illness is the person currently in a position to contribute or not to contribute to systematic exclusion and so, to the extent that the employer can do so without suffering significant hardship, she should bear the costs of including rather than excluding.").

The law does in fact allow employers to spread some accommodations-related costs through two tax incentives: a credit of up to $5,000 per year for small businesses, 26 U.S.C. § 44, plus a deduction of up to $15,000 per year, *id.* § 190. Moreover, a number of studies suggest that most accommodations are quite inexpensive. See, e.g., Peter David Blanck, *Empirical Study of Disability, Employment Policy, and the ADA*, 23 Mental & Physical Disability L. Rep. 275, 276–78 (1999) (collecting studies finding that in most cases disability accommodations imposed no direct costs and that the costs only very rarely exceeded $1000); Michael Ashley Stein, *Empirical Implications of Title I*, 85 Iowa L. Rev. 1671, 1674–77 (2000) (same). But these studies do not take full account of *indirect* costs, and they look to accommodations that employers provided *voluntarily*—which one would expect to be the accommodations that were relatively cheap for the employers to provide. See generally Thomas N. Chirikos, *Will the Costs of Accommodating Workers with Disabilities Remain Low?*, 17 Behav. Sci. & L. 93 (1999). As you read the accommodation fact patterns in the next series of notes, consider whether you think it is fair to impose the costs of the requested accommodation on the employer at issue.

2. **"Disability-Specific Obstacles."** In an effort to keep the ADA from becoming a requirement of charity, Justice Scalia argues that the accommodation mandate should apply only to remove "disability-specific obstacles" to working. In his view, stairs are a disability-specific obstacle for a person who uses a wheelchair—absent the disability, the person could climb them—but a seniority system is not. Is Justice Scalia correct to limit the accommodation requirement to disability-specific obstacles? Is he right that U.S. Airways' seniority system was *not* such an obstacle? Consider the following response to Justice Scalia:

> Justice Scalia concluded that the seniority system was not "disability-specific," because he believed that Barnett's disability had nothing to do with his lack of seniority. But that is not right: Barnett's disability is what made him unable to work in the cargo position and thus forced him to put himself at the mercy of the

seniority system before he had accumulated enough seniority to hold a position that would enable him to keep working. Both Barnett's need for seniority and his lack of seniority at the time he needed it were the product of his disability.

Barnett's case really looks just like a paradigm case for reasonable accommodation. Imagine a 9-person secretarial pool in which all of the secretaries do typing and filing, but one—always the newest hire—is also required to relieve the receptionist at the lunch hour. The pool hires a new secretary, who is deaf. Under Justice Scalia's analysis, the employer would never be required even to consider whether it is reasonable to reallocate the receptionist duties from the new hire to someone else: Sure, her disability is what keeps her from performing the receptionist duties of the secretarial position (just as Barnett's disability kept him from performing the lifting duties of the cargo position), but it's her lack of seniority—which has nothing to do with her disability—that forces her to perform the receptionist duties.

Bagenstos, *U.S. Airways v. Barnett and the Limits of Disability Accommodation, supra.*

NOTES ON REASONABLE ACCOMMODATION

The ADA's accommodation mandate applies in a diverse array of circumstances to require a variety of possible accommodations. The statutory definition of "reasonable accommodation" makes that clear. The statute provides that reasonable accommodations "may include" the following: "making existing facilities used by employees readily accessible to and usable by individuals with disabilities," and "job restructuring, part-time or modified work schedules, reassignment to a vacant position, acquisition or modification of equipment or devices, appropriate adjustment or modifications of examinations, training materials or policies, the provision of qualified readers or interpreters, and other similar accommodations for individuals with disabilities." 42 U.S.C. § 12111(9).

How can an employer tell when one of these possible accommodations is in fact required? The Court's opinion in *U.S. Airways v. Barnett* holds that the "reasonable accommodation" inquiry has two steps. First, the plaintiff must show that the proposed accommodation is "reasonable on its face, i.e., ordinarily or in the run of cases." If the plaintiff satisfies that burden, the employer "must show special (typically case-specific) circumstances that demonstrate undue hardship in the particular circumstances." As the Court's formulation makes clear, determining whether an accommodation is required demands a fact-sensitive, context-specific inquiry. Accordingly, to understand the scope of the ADA's accommodation mandate requires examination of how it applies to an array of different fact situations. Some important fact situations are set forth in this note.

1. The *Vande Zande* and *Borkowski* Cases. Shortly after the ADA took effect, two leading appellate decisions on the scope of the accommodation requirement were issued. Are these cases consistent with each other? Are they consistent with the Supreme Court's later decision in *U.S. Airways v. Barnett*?

a.   In VANDE ZANDE V. WISCONSIN DEPARTMENT OF ADMINISTRATION, 44 F.3d 538 (7th Cir.1995), the plaintiff, Lori Vande Zande, worked for the State of Wisconsin as a program assistant. She was "paralyzed from the waist down as a result of a tumor of the spinal cord," and her paralysis made her "prone to develop pressure ulcers, treatment of which often require[d] that she stay at home for several weeks." Vande Zande acknowledged that her employer had made a number of accommodations for her condition:

> As examples, in her words, "they paid the landlord to have bathrooms modified and to have a step ramped; they bought special adjustable furniture for the plaintiff; they ordered and paid for one-half of the cost of a cot that the plaintiff needed for daily personal care at work; they sometimes adjusted the plaintiff's schedule to perform backup telephone duties to accommodate the plaintiff's medical appointments; they made changes to the plans for a locker room in the new state office building; and they agreed to provide some of the specific accommodations the plaintiff requested in her October 5, 1992 Reasonable Accommodation Request."

In two significant respects, however, she contended that her employer had failed to accommodate her. First, during an eight-week period when Vande Zande's pressure ulcers forced her to stay home from work, her supervisor denied her the use of a desktop computer that would have enabled her to do all of her work at home. Although Vande Zande "was able to work all but 16.5 hours in the eight-week period" anyway, she was forced to take those 16.5 hours as sick leave. In his opinion for the Seventh Circuit, Judge Posner concluded that "[n]o jury" could "be permitted to stretch the concept of 'reasonable accommodation' so far." He explained:

> Most jobs in organizations public or private involve team work under supervision rather than solitary unsupervised work, and team work under supervision generally cannot be performed at home without a substantial reduction in the quality of the employee's performance. This will no doubt change as communications technology advances, but is the situation today. Generally, therefore, an employer is not required to accommodate a disability by allowing the disabled worker to work, by himself, without supervision, at home. [N]o doubt to this as to any generalization about so complex and varied an activity as employment there are exceptions, but it would take a very extraordinary case for the employee to be able to create a triable issue of the employer's failure to allow the employee to work at home.

More recent decisions have disagreed with *Vande Zande* and held that working at home can be a reasonable accommodation. See, *e.g., Humphrey v. Memorial Hosp. Assn.*, 239 F.3d 1128, 1136–1137 & n.15 (9th Cir.2001) (collecting cases). But *cf. Mason v. Avaya Communications, Inc.*, 357 F.3d 1114, 1124 (10th Cir.2004) ("Although some courts have described the

Ninth Circuit's approach to at-home accommodations as different from the majority of circuits, we perceive the difference, if any, as largely illusory. The Ninth Circuit in *Humphrey* was presented with the 'unusual' or 'extraordinary' case where evidence supported the employee's contention that he could perform the essential functions of his employment position from home because physical attendance in the workplace was not an essential function of his employment position.").

Second, "[b]oth the sink and the counter in each of the kitchenettes [in Vande Zande's office building] were 36 inches high, which is too high for a person in a wheelchair. The building was under construction, and the kitchenettes not yet built, when the plaintiff complained about this feature of the design. But the defendants refused to alter the design to lower the sink and counter to 34 inches, the height convenient for a person in a wheelchair." Vande Zande's employer agreed to install a 34-inch-high shelf in the kitchenette for her to use as a counter. But it refused to install a 34-inch-high sink there, because the sinks in the bathroom were 34 inches high. According to Judge Posner, "it would have cost only about $150 to lower the sink on Vande Zande's floor; to lower it on all the floors might have cost as much as $2,000, though possibly less." But he nonetheless concluded that it would not be "reasonable" to require the employer to bear that cost:

> Given the proximity of the bathroom sink, Vande Zande can hardly complain that the inaccessibility of the kitchenette sink interfered with her ability to work or with her physical comfort. Her argument rather is that forcing her to use the bathroom sink for activities (such as washing out her coffee cup) for which the other employees could use the kitchenette sink stigmatized her as different and inferior; she seeks an award of compensatory damages for the resulting emotional distress. We may assume without having to decide that emotional as well as physical barriers to the integration of disabled persons into the workforce are relevant in determining the reasonableness of an accommodation. But we do not think an employer has a duty to expend even modest amounts of money to bring about an absolute identity in working conditions between disabled and nondisabled workers. The creation of such a duty would be the inevitable consequence of deeming a failure to achieve identical conditions "stigmatizing." That is merely an epithet.*

b. In Borkowski v. Valley Central School District, 63 F.3d 131 (2d Cir.1995), the Second Circuit reversed a grant of summary judgment to the defendant school district. The plaintiff, Kathleen Borkowski, was an elementary school library teacher who had experienced neurological damage as the result of a traumatic injury. Her injury limited her ability to stand and maintain control of the classroom, and the school district fired

---

* Judge Posner's opinion in *Vande Zande* has been the subject of significant criticism. See, *e.g.*, Lennard J. Davis, *Bending Over Backwards: Disability, Narcissism, and the Law*, 21 Berkeley J. Emp. & Lab. L. 193 (2000); Linda Hamilton Krieger, *Socio–Legal Backlash*, 21 Berkeley J. Emp. & Lab. L. 476–518 (2000); Cass R. Sunstein, *Cost–Benefit Analysis Without Analyzing Costs or Benefits: Reasonable Accommodation, Balancing, and Stigmatic Harms*, 74 U. Chi. L. Rev. 1895 (2007).

her as a result. Borkowski asked the school district to accommodate her disability by assigning a teacher's aide to her room; the aide, she submitted, would assist her with classroom control and enable her to perform the essential functions of her job. The school district refused, Borkowski sued, and the district court entered summary judgment for the district.

In an opinion reversing the district court, Judge Guido Calabresi wrote for the Second Circuit that "having someone else do part of a job may sometimes mean eliminating the essential functions of the job. But at other times providing an assistant to help with a job may be an accommodation that does not remove an essential function of the job from the disabled employee."

> Thus, for example, a visually impaired administrator or clerk may be provided with a reader. What matters to that individual's job is not the ability to read *per se*, but rather the ability to take in, process, and act on information. The provision of a reader in these circumstances does not eliminate an essential function, but rather permits the individual with a disability to perform that essential function.

> The accommodation suggested by Ms. Borkowski appears, at first blush, to resemble more closely one that would eliminate an essential function of a library teacher in a classroom setting than one that would permit Ms. Borkowski to perform that function. Yet, viewing the record at this stage of the proceedings in the light most favorable to Ms. Borkowski, we cannot say that no reasonable jury could conclude otherwise. This is especially so since the regulations implementing Section 504 [of the Rehabilitation Act] explicitly contemplate that teachers with disabilities may require the assistance of teachers' aides.

> A number of factors might be relevant in the present case. One might be the age of the students that Ms. Borkowski taught. We know that they were elementary school students, but, within that category, children of different ages may require different degrees of supervision. Another would be the availability of teacher's aides within the School District. We know from the record that Ms. Borkowski was provided with an aide to assist her in the performance of her library duties, although not of her teaching duties. But were other teachers within the school system provided with teacher's aides to assist in maintaining appropriate student behavior? If so, then classroom management might not be considered an essential function.

Judge Calabresi noted that "[b]oth the regulations implementing Section 504 and the cases applying the Rehabilitation Act contemplate the possibility that the use of assistants may be reasonable accommodations," thereby making the proposed accommodation at least facially reasonable. Because the school district had presented no evidence that providing a teacher's aide to Borkowski would cause undue hardship, Judge Calabresi's opinion concluded that the district court had erred in granting summary judgment to the district: "It may be that the School District can show that the benefits that an aide would give are too small in relation to the cost of an aide. It may also be that the District can demonstrate that in this and other districts provision of an aide would impact school budgets sufficiently as to be an unreasonable or undue burden. It may even be that the School District can show these so powerfully that a judgment as a matter of law would be appropriate. But in the absence of evidence regarding school district budgets, the cost of providing an aide of this sort, or any like kind of information, we are unable to conclude that unreasonableness or undue hardship has been established, and we certainly cannot say that either has been established as a matter of law."

2. Accommodations with Significant, Ongoing Costs. One paradigm case for reasonable accommodation is the installation of a ramp—an accommodation with a one-time cost. Vande Zande's request that the sinks be lowered exemplifies that sort of one-time accommodation with no ongoing costs. But that does not exhaust the category of required accommodations. In a number of cases, courts have mandated that employers provide accommodations with significant, ongoing costs.

a. Readers. *Borkowski* held that an employer may be required to provide an assistant to an individual with a disability to enable him or her to perform job functions. The court relied in part on NELSON V. THORNBURGH, 567 F.Supp. 369 (E.D.Pa.1983), a Rehabilitation Act case in which Judge Louis Pollak (like Judge Calabresi a former dean of the Yale Law School) ruled that the state was required to provide readers to assist blind individuals who worked for it as welfare caseworkers. The caseworkers' job required them to interview welfare clients to determine their eligibility for benefits. Caseworkers entered the results of those interviews onto standardized forms, and the plaintiffs had hired readers to assist them in filling out those forms. The court held that a half-time reader for each plaintiff was necessary to enable them to perform the essential functions of their jobs, and that the cost of those readers (about $6,600.00 per year for each of the plaintiffs) was reasonable and did not impose undue hardship. The court explained:

> [I]n view of DPW's $300,000,000 administrative budget, the modest cost of providing half-time readers, and the ease of adopting that accommodation without any disruption of DPW's services, it is apparent that DPW has not met its burden of showing undue hardship. To be sure, DPW's financial resources are limited. But there is no principled way of distinguishing DPW on this basis from the large school district employing an aide for a blind teacher, or from the state welfare agency providing an interpreter for a deaf employee.

b. Parking Spaces and Personal Items. In LYONS V. LEGAL AID SOCIETY, 68 F.3d 1512 (2d Cir.1995), the plaintiff was a legal aid attorney who, after injuries experienced when a car hit her, was significantly limited in her ability to walk long distances. Upon returning to work, she was unable to walk from the subway, and she asked her employer to provide her a parking space close to her office in Manhattan. The space cost between $300 and $520 per month, 15–26 percent of Lyons's monthly net salary. The employer argued that "Lyons's claim for financial assistance in parking her car amounts to a demand for unwarranted preferential treatment because the requested accommodation is merely 'a matter of personal convenience that she uses regularly in daily life,' " and that it did "not provide parking facilities or any other commuting assistance to its nondisabled employees."

The Second Circuit held that Lyons's complaint stated a claim upon which relief could be granted. The court explained that "[a]ccording to the complaint, whose factual allegations must be taken as true, Lyons cannot fulfill her responsibilities as a staff attorney at Legal Aid without being able to park her car adjacent to her office." Notwithstanding the cost of the requested accommodation, the court concluded that "there is nothing inherently unreasonable . . . in requiring an employer to furnish an otherwise qualified disabled employee with assistance related to her ability to get to work."

The Equal Employment Opportunity Commission has stated that that an ADA accommodation must be "job-related" rather than a "personal item." 29 C.F.R. pt. 1630 app. § 1630.9. Under this rule, an employer might be required to provide a disabled individual with an accommodation that "specifically assists the individual in performing the duties of a particular job" (so long as the accommodation is reasonable and can be provided without undue hardship). *Id.* But the employer will never be required to provide "an adjustment or modification [that] assists the individual throughout his or her daily activities, on and off the job." *Id.* The EEOC has said that this rule excuses employers from any obligation to provide assistive technology that people with disabilities need to get to work—at least if that technology also helps them outside of the workplace. See EEOC, A Technical Assistance Manual on the Employment Provisions (Title I) of the Americans with Disabilities Act § 3.4 (1992). Courts have held that employers need not provide medical treatment or rehabilitation that would make an individual with a disability able to work, see Brookins v. Indianapolis Power & Light Co., 90 F.Supp.2d 993, 1003–04 (S.D.Ind.2000); Burnett v. Western Resources, Inc., 929 F.Supp. 1349, 1358 (D.Kan.1996); paid leave to attend training for a new service animal that would enable an individual with a disability to come to work, see Nelson v. Ryan, 860 F.Supp. 76, 82–83 (W.D.N.Y.1994); or training that would enable an individual to perform a new job when she has become unable to perform her old job because of a disability, see Williams v. United Ins. Co., 253 F.3d 280, 282–83 (7th Cir.2001).

Is the *Lyons* case consistent with the rule requiring reasonable accommodations to be "job related" and not "personal items"? Does that rule make sense? Consider the following critique:

> [T]he rule seems to rest on a rough-and-ready notion of corrective justice. Under this view, an employer can be held responsible only for the obstacles it erects to the employment of people with disabilities; if an individual with a disability cannot come to work because of factors that go beyond any particular employer's workplace or work rules, no individual employer can rightly be held responsible for those factors. In essence, the rule imposes a kind of act/omission distinction: Employers are responsible for

their own acts, and they must take "reasonable" care to assure that those acts "accommodate" employees with disabilities. But employers are not responsible for simply failing to help employees with disabilities overcome obstacles that stem from the government's failure to extend social provision. Indeed, the people who interjected the "job-related" concept into the congressional deliberations surrounding the ADA's accommodation requirement—lobbyists for hotel and small-business employer groups—appear to have had precisely this kind of act/omission distinction in mind. Urging that employers not be required to provide accommodations whose usefulness extended outside of the workplace, they contended that such accommodations were the responsibility of the social welfare system rather than individual employers.

Like all act/omission distinctions, the "job-related" rule is subject to serious critique. The mere fact that an accommodation removes an obstacle that the employer did not impose cannot be determinative, for ADA-mandated accommodations always require employers to alleviate disadvantages that are caused by the interaction between conditions the employer created and conditions the employer played no role in creating. That is true even of core accommodations. When an employer provides a ramp in a building that formerly had only stairs, for example, it removes an obstacle that results from the interaction between the design of its facilities (facilities the employer either created or chose to move in to) and the inability of people who use wheelchairs to climb stairs (an inability the employer played no role in creating). If wheelchair users could climb stairs, the lack of a ramp would not be an obstacle. And when an employer modifies work schedules for an individual with diabetes, it removes an obstacle that results from the interaction between its general work schedules (schedules the employer created) and the need of people with diabetes to take unusually frequent breaks for self-monitoring and medication (a need the employer played no role in creating).

Samuel R. Bagenstos, *The Future of Disability Law*, 114 Yale L.J. 1, 42–43 (2004) (footnotes omitted).

3. Reallocation of Job Tasks. Another paradigm case of reasonable accommodation is the reallocation of some job tasks from an employee with a disability to other employees. The statute defines "reasonable accommodation" to include "job restructuring." 42 U.S.C. § 12111(9)(B). Whether a reallocation of tasks constitutes a reasonable accommodation in a particular case turns on whether the tasks are best understood as essential or marginal job functions. See 29 C.F.R. Part 1630 App. § 1630.2(o) ("An employer or other covered entity may restructure a job by reallocating or redistributing nonessential, marginal job functions. For example, an employer may have two jobs, each of which entails the performance of a number of marginal functions. The employer hires an individual with a disability who is able to perform some of the marginal functions of each job but not all of the marginal functions of either job. As an accommodation, the employer may redistribute the marginal functions so that all of the marginal functions that the individual with a disability can perform are made a part of the position to be filled by the individual with a disability. The remaining marginal functions that the individual with a disability cannot perform would then be transferred to the other position.").

Consider MILLER V. ILLINOIS DEPARTMENT OF TRANSPORTATION, 643 F.3d 190 (7th Cir.2011). Miller, who worked on a bridge maintenance crew, had a fear of heights. That fear did not prevent him from working 80 feet above the ground in a "snooper bucket" or from crawling on the arch of a bridge on a catwalk, but it did make him unable to work above 20 to 25 feet "in an extreme, exposed position" such as walking on a bridge beam. The district court granted summary judgment to the employer, but the Seventh Circuit reversed. The court addressed the question whether it was a reasonable accommodation to reallocate the extreme, exposed, high-level work to Miller's coworkers with the following analysis:

> As in other "team" environments, the individual members took on tasks according to their capacities and abilities. Here, a reasonable fact-finder would have to conclude that *some* members of the bridge crew had to be able to work at heights in exposed or extreme positions so that the bridge crew—as a unit—could do its job, just as some members of the crew had to be able to weld, ride in the snooper bucket, spray, mow, and rake. That conclusion does not mean that the fact-finder would be required to conclude that *each* member of the bridge crew had to be able to do *every* task required of the entire team. In terms of the regulation, the evidence of actual experience of past and present incumbents in the job and similar jobs conflicts with the employer's judgment about which functions are essential. See 29 C.F.R. § 1630.2(n)(3). On this record, a reasonable jury could find that working at heights in an exposed or extreme position was not an essential function for Miller as an individual member of the bridge crew.

> From this same evidence, a reasonable jury could find that Miller's request for accommodation—that other members of his team substitute for him when a task required working above 25 feet in an exposed or extreme position—was reasonable.

> [T]he ADA does not give employers unfettered discretion to decide what is reasonable. The law requires an employer to rethink its preferred practices or established methods of operation. Employers must, at a minimum, consider possible modifications of jobs, processes, or tasks so as to allow an employee with a disability to work, even where established practices or methods seem to be the most efficient or serve otherwise legitimate purposes in the workplace. See, *e.g.,* Vande Zande ("It is plain enough what 'accommodation' means. The employer must be willing to consider making changes in its ordinary work rules, facilities, terms, and conditions in order to enable a disabled individual to work.").

When considering other work environments, we have upheld determinations that requests for a "helper" employee and requests to rotate work tasks were unreasonable. For instance, in *Lenker v. Methodist Hospital,* 210 F.3d 792 (7th Cir.2000), a nurse with multiple sclerosis was unable to lift patients. He requested that he be permitted to use assistive devices or call for help when he was unable to lift a patient. On review, we upheld the jury's verdict in favor of the employer. We found sufficient evidence in the record from which the jury could reasonably find (a) that assistive devices might help to lift a patient out of bed but would not help a patient walk down the hall or to the bathroom, and (b) that other staff would not be able to assist at all times, particularly in a staff shortage or a hospital emergency.

In another case, we upheld summary judgment against an equipment operator who suffered a shoulder injury and was no longer able to lift or carry anything over fifty pounds. See *Peters v. City of Mauston,* 311 F.3d 835, 840 (7th Cir.2002). That employee also requested that his employer permit another employee to help him with the lifting requirements of his job. We found that the request was unreasonable because lifting and carrying were essential functions of his job as an equipment operator. Making the accommodation would have required another person to perform an essential function of the employee's job. See *id.* at 845; see also *Miller v. Illinois Department of Corrections,* 107 F.3d 483, 485 (7th Cir.1997) ("if an employer has a legitimate reason for specifying multiple duties for a particular job classification, duties the occupant of the position is expected to rotate through, a disabled employee will not be qualified for the position unless he can perform enough of these duties to enable a judgment that he can perform its *essential* duties") (emphasis in original); *Cochrum v. Old Ben Coal Co.,* 102 F.3d 908, 912 (7th Cir.1996) (holding that employee's request that employer hire a helper to perform essential function was unreasonable; "hiring a helper to perform the overhead work would mean the helper would de facto perform [the employee's] job. We cannot agree that [the employee] would be performing the essential functions of his job with a helper.").

These cases teach that task reassignments within a job can be unreasonable in situations where the reassigned task is an essential function of the job. In those situations, reassignment or delegation of the task would equate, essentially, to reassignment or delegation of the job itself.

What sets this case apart from those earlier cases is Miller's evidence that it was in fact the normal course for individual members of the bridge crew to substitute and reassign tasks among themselves according to individual abilities, preferences, and limitations. Miller's request for reasonable accommodation did not ask IDOT to do anything it was not already doing (or, at least, anything it had not been doing up until March 2006). The record on summary judgment, taken in the light reasonably most favorable to Miller, does not compel a finding that IDOT required every employee working as a highway maintainer on a bridge crew to be able to work in an exposed or extreme position above 25 feet in the air or that being able to do so was an essential function of the job. To the contrary, the record confirms that it was a regular occurrence for individuals on the bridge team to share and swap tasks according to their individual capacities, abilities, and limitations. Miller's request that task assignments be adjusted among the bridge crew members so that he would not be confronted with a task requiring him to work above 25 feet in an exposed or extreme position did not amount to a request that another member of the team perform an essential, non-delegable task. A jury should be permitted to consider Miller's actual work environment and IDOT's past flexibility in delegating tasks amongst the bridge team members in deciding whether Miller's request for accommodation was reasonable.

Does this analysis persuade you? See also *Kiphart v. Saturn Corp.*, 251 F.3d 573 (6th Cir.2001) (plaintiff presented sufficient evidence that employer's nominal requirement that work team members rotate fully across all of the team's job tasks was not an essential function).

4. Leaves of Absence. Might a leave of absence be a reasonable accommodation? The statutory list of reasonable accommodations (which does not purport to be exclusive) says nothing about leaves. And the statutory definition of "qualified individual with a disability"—"an individual with a disability who, with or without reasonable accommodation, can perform the essential functions of the employment position," 42 U.S.C. § 12111(8)—might be read to suggest that a leave of absence is not a proper accommodation. If an individual is seeking a leave of absence, she is necessarily stating that she cannot perform the essential functions of her job until she can return. And the statutory language is phrased in the present tense ("can perform"), which suggests that an accommodation must enable the individual to perform essential job functions immediately. See *Myers v. Hose*, 50 F.3d 278, 283 (4th Cir.1995) ("[R]easonable accommodation is by its terms most logically construed as that which presently, or in the immediate future, enables the employee to perform the essential functions of the job in question.").

Nonetheless, the EEOC and the federal courts have stated that an employer may be required to grant a leave of absence as a reasonable accommodation in some circumstances. For a discussion, see Stephen F. Befort, *The Most Difficult ADA Reassignment Issues: Reassignment and Leaves of Absence*, 37 Wake Forest L. Rev. 439, 459–468 (2002). Generally, courts have held that an *indefinite* leave of absence is not a reasonable accommodation, but that a leave for a specified period might be. See *id*. But two major questions remain: How certain must the employee be that at the end of her leave period she will be able to do the job? And how long may the leave period be before it becomes unreasonable?

In HUMPHREY V. MEMORIAL HOSPITALS ASSOCIATION, 239 F.3d 1128 (9th Cir.2001), the court addressed the first of these questions. The plaintiff, a medical transcriptionist who had obsessive compulsive disorder, "engaged in a series of obsessive rituals that hindered her ability to arrive at work on time":

> She felt compelled to rinse her hair for up to an hour, and if, after brushing her hair, it didn't "feel right," she would return to the shower to wash it again. This process of washing and preparing her hair could take up to three hours. She would also feel compelled to dress very slowly, to repeatedly check and recheck for papers she needed, and to pull out strands of her hair and examine them closely because she felt as though something was crawling on her scalp. She testified that these obsessive thoughts and rituals made it very difficult to get to work on time. Once she realized that she was late, she would panic and become embarrassed, making it even more difficult for her to leave her house and get to work.

Humphrey's doctor wrote the following to Humphrey's employer: "I believe that we can treat this, although, the treatment may take a while. I do believe that she would qualify under the Americans with Disability Act, although, I would like to see her continue to work, but if it is proving to be a major personnel problem, she may have to take some time off until we can get the symptoms better under control." Notwithstanding this letter, the hospital for which she worked did not grant Humphrey a leave of absence, and, after additional incidents of absenteeism and tardyism, it fired her.

Humphrey sued. She argued, among other things, that the hospital was required to grant her a leave of absence instead of terminating her. The district court granted summary judgment to the employer, but the Ninth Circuit reversed. The court of appeals explained:

> A leave of absence for medical treatment may be a reasonable accommodation under the ADA. See 29 C.F.R. 1630 app. § 1630.2(o). We have held that where a leave of absence would reasonably accommodate an employee's disability and permit him, upon his return, to perform the essential functions of the job, that employee is otherwise qualified under the ADA. See *Nunes v. Wal-Mart Stores, Inc.*, 164 F.3d 1243, 1247 (9th Cir.1999).
>
> [The employer] contends that Humphrey is not otherwise qualified because the results of the leave of absence were speculative. However, the ADA does not require an employee to show that a leave of absence is certain or even likely to be successful to prove that it is a reasonable accommodation. [T]he statements in Dr. Jacisin's letter that Humphrey's condition was treatable and that "she may have to take some time off until we can get the symptoms better under control" are sufficient to satisfy the minimal requirement that a leave of absence could plausibly have enabled Humphrey adequately to perform her job.

Is this decision consistent with the Fourth Circuit's ruling in *Myers*, 50 F.3d at 283, that "[n]othing in the text of the reasonable accommodation provision requires an employer to wait an indefinite period for an accommodation to achieve its intended effect"? If they are in tension with one another, which approach is correct?

In GARCIA-AYALA V. LEDERLE PARENTERALS, INC., 212 F.3d 638 (1st Cir.2000), the court addressed the question of the length of an ADA-required leave. Zenaida García-Ayala worked in a clerical position for Lederle when she was diagnosed with breast cancer and took leave to obtain treatment. Lederle's medical leave policy provided that an individual on medical leave would retain the right to her old job for up to one year, after which she would be terminated. According to the company, Garcia began her medical leave in March of 1995; on June 10, 1996, the company informed her "that her one-year period for job reservation had elapsed in March 1996, and that her employment was terminated. García asked that her job be reserved until July 30th, when her doctors expected her to return to work, but to no avail." In the event, Garcia's doctors released her to return to work on August 22, after Lederle had terminated her.

García sued. Lederle argued that any leave that went beyond its one-year job-reservation policy was *per se* unreasonable. But the First Circuit rejected that argument and ruled that García was entitled to the extended leave as a matter of law:

> While on different facts, a request for an extended leave could indeed be too long to be a reasonable accommodation and no reasonable factfinder could conclude otherwise, that is not this case for a number of reasons. It does not appear that García expected to be paid for the additional weeks away from work beyond those allowed under the employer's disability benefits program and while her job functions were being performed by temporary help. There is no evidence that the temporary employees were paid more than García or were less effective at her job than she. Indeed, Lederle's continued use of temporary employees and Lederle's failure to replace García indicates the contrary. There was, therefore, no financial burden on the employer from paying an employee who was not performing. It is true that an employer usually needs to have the functions of a job filled, and the fact that essential functions have gone unfilled for a lengthy period could well warrant judgment for an employer. But here, the essential functions of the job were filled, to all indications satisfactorily, by temporary employees. The use of temporary employees is not, of course, always a satisfactory or even a possible solution. But here, there is no evidence that Lederle was under business pressure to fill the slot with another permanent employee (indeed, it never did). In other situations, temporary replacements may be unavailable or unsuited to the position; here, the available evidence is all to the contrary. In addition, as said, there is no evidence that the cost of the temporary help was greater than the cost of a permanent employee; one might suppose it was less. Thus, the requested accommodation of a few additional months of unsalaried leave, with the job functions being satisfactorily performed in the meantime, is reasonable.

> The employer presented the court with no evidence of any hardship, much less undue hardship. On this record, we see no

basis for the court to do other than enter judgment for García. [W]e stress that the Act does not require employers to retain disabled employees who cannot perform the essential functions of their jobs without reasonable accommodation. Applying this rule to the prolonged disability leave situation is tricky, however. An absent employee obviously cannot himself or herself perform; still, the employer may in some instances, such as here, be able to get temporary help or find some other alternative that will enable it to proceed satisfactorily with its business uninterrupted while a disabled employee is recovering. In situations like that, retaining the ailing employee's slot while granting unsalaried leave may be a reasonable accommodation required by the ADA. If, however, allowing the sick employee to retain his or her job places the employer in a hardship situation where it cannot secure in some reasonable alternative way the services for which it hired the ailing employee, and yet is blocked from effecting a rehire, the ADA does not require the retention of the disabled person. Hence, where it is unrealistic to expect to obtain someone to perform those essential functions temporarily until the sick employee returns, the employer may be entitled to discharge the ill employee and hire someone else. An exception to this might be if the requested disability leave was so brief that no undue business harm could reasonably be expected to occur from not filling the vacancy. We add that our analysis, while applicable to these facts, may not be applicable in other cases. Undue hardships are not limited to financial impacts; the term includes accommodations that are unduly extensive, substantially disruptive, or that would fundamentally alter the nature or operation of the business. See 29 C.F.R. pt. 1630, App.

Other factors to be considered as to whether requests for leaves of absence are unreasonable include, for example: where the employee gave no indication as to when she might be able to return to work, and, instead, she simply demanded that her job be held open indefinitely; where the employee's absences from work were "erratic" and "unexplained"; where, upon the employee's return to work, she would be unqualified; and where the employee was hired to complete a specific task. In addition, this court has inquired into whether the company had made earlier policy decisions that it was more profitable to permit an employee additional leave than to hire and train a new employee.

These are difficult, fact intensive, case-by-case analyses, ill-served by per se rules or stereotypes. We emphasize that the stipulated record here contains no evidence whatever of any form of hardship to Lederle as a result of the requested accommodation. Were this not so, we would feel obligated to return the case to a factfinder for further evaluation. But given the employer's failure to meet, even minimally, its burden of proof on the issue of hardship, we award judgment to García as a matter of law.

Judge O'Toole dissented:

> It seems to me that the following proposition can be extrapolated from the cases: For a proposed period of leave to constitute an effective accommodation, it must meet at least two conditions. First, it must be instrumental to effect or advance a change in the employee's disabled status with respect to the job, so that the employee is enabled to do it. A period of leave would meet this criterion if it permitted the employee to receive therapy or treatment that would succeed in removing the obstacle to employment the particular disability posed. In *Criado [v. IBM Corp.*, 145 F.3d 437 (1st Cir.1998)], for example, the court noted that the employee's physician believed that "the leave would ameliorate her disability." 145 F.3d at 444. Similarly, an EEOC interpretive guideline suggests that leave "for necessary treatment" could be a reasonable accommodation, 29 C.F.R. pt. 1630, app., and the Department of Labor advises that leave might be a reasonable accommodation "when the disability is of a nature that it is likely to respond to treatment." 29 C.F.R. pt. 32, app. A(b). Simply the possibility of improvement is not enough, however; the recovery must be reasonably likely. Further, the prospect of recovery (or enablement) should be judged not by hindsight, but by what reasonably appears at the time the leave is requested. *Id.*

> Second, the employee's return to work must be relatively proximate in a temporal sense. The cases do not speak with one voice on this subject, and some give little attention to it, except to imply that the temporal element will figure in the jury's assessment of reasonableness. Although there seems to be general agreement that a leave period cannot be indefinite, the leave periods that have been explicitly or implicitly approved vary in length. Some variation is not inappropriate; that is consistent with the need to evaluate each case on its particular facts.

> In the end, however, the leave must not only be one that serves a proper medical purpose; it must also be one that serves the statutory purpose, which is to enable the employee to perform the essential functions of her job. It cannot be overlooked that the statute speaks in the present tense, indicative mood. A "qualified individual with a disability" entitled to the statute's protection is a person who "*can perform* the essential functions of the employment position" with reasonable accommodation. 42 U.S.C. § 12111(8) (emphasis added). "Can perform," as in "now." I would not contend that the statute requires literally instantaneous effectiveness of an accommodation. By approving the idea that some leaves might qualify as reasonable accommodations, courts, including this one, have properly rejected such a cramped and unrealistic reading of the statute. However, fidelity to both the language and purpose of the statute requires that the time within which the proposed accommodation accomplishes its intended purpose—enabling the employee to perform the job—must be such that the accommodation is tolerably consistent with the statutory words, "can perform."

I would conclude that the plaintiff did not carry her burden of proffering evidence that the leave she requested was "effective" in these two essential ways. She asked that the employer abide her continued recuperation for an additional period, but she offered little—essentially an unelaborated prognostic estimate—that would enable an objective assessment either of the realistic prospect of recovery as of the time of the request or of the likely duration of her absence. Further, I do not think the requested leave could legitimately be said to be an accommodation enabling her, more or less contemporaneously, to perform the essential functions of the job. It may have given her an opportunity to become able again a couple of months down the road, but that is something that this statute, properly construed, does not address.

Who has the better of this argument? Which position is more consistent with *Barnett*'s discussion of neutral workplace rules?

5.   Reassignment. Reassignment raises some questions that are similar to those raised by leaves of absence—in both cases, the worker with a disability is unable to perform the essential functions of her then-current position at the time she seeks the accommodation—but "reassignment to a vacant position," unlike leave, is specifically listed in the statute as a form of reasonable accommodation. 42 U.S.C. § 12111(9)(B). In *Barnett*, the Court held that the reassignment duty does not, "in the run of cases," require an employer to override a seniority system to reassign an employee with a disability. But what if the employer does not have a seniority system and simply hires the "best" applicant for all openings? If a worker with a disability can no longer perform the essential functions of her present position, but she is qualified for a vacant position, must the employer disregard its best-applicant policy and automatically transfer the disabled worker to that position? Or does the statute merely require that the employer give the incumbent disabled worker the opportunity to apply for the new position?

Prior to *Barnett*, the courts of appeals had divided over that question. In EEOC V. HUMISTON-KEELING, INC., 227 F.3d 1024 (7th Cir.2000), the employer refused to transfer an injured warehouse worker to an open clerical position. Although the company acknowledged she was qualified to perform a number of open clerical jobs, it gave each of them to an applicant it deemed more qualified. In an opinion by Judge Posner, the court ruled that the employer had satisfied its obligations, and it rejected contrary decisions from two other courts of appeals:

> The EEOC does not deny that in every case the applicant chosen for the job was better than Houser in the sense of likely to be more productive. Nor does it deny that the company had a bona fide policy, consistently implemented, of giving a vacant job to the best applicant rather than to the first qualified one. Nor does it suggest that Houser's disability played any role in the decisions favoring her competitors. None of the jobs involved a degree of lifting that her disability would have interfered with her performing, and it is not suggested that the defendant harbors any animus toward disabled workers. Rather the Commission

interprets the "reassignment" form of reasonable accommodation to require that the disabled person be advanced over a more qualified nondisabled person, provided only that the disabled person is at least minimally qualified to do the job, unless the employer can show "undue hardship," a safe harbor under the statute. The fact that the disability isn't what makes the disabled person unable to perform the job as well as the person who got it is, in the Commission's view, irrelevant.

We do not agree with the Commission's interpretation of the statutory provision on reassignment. The interpretation requires employers to give bonus points to people with disabilities, much as veterans' preference statutes do. Houser's disability, we repeat, had nothing to do with the office jobs for which she applied. The Commission asserts that her unrelated disability, a disability that put her at no disadvantage in competing for an opening in an office job, nevertheless entitled her to be given more consideration than nondisabled workers. It is easy to imagine situations in which under the Commission's view one disabled worker would be entitled to get a job ahead of a worker with a more serious disability. Suppose that A and B are both applying for the same job, Job X. A was severely disabled years ago and placed in an office job with the company. B was less severely disabled, and not being able to work in his present job has also applied for X. A is not only more severely disabled than B; he is also, let us assume, certain to perform the job much better than B, although B meets the minimum qualifications for the job. Under the Commission's view, B is entitled to the job.

Or suppose, to take a variant case, that B is a 29-year-old white male with severe tennis elbow, just like Houser, and A is a 62-year-old black woman with no disability, and again they are applying for the same job. Under the Commission's view, even though A is not only the better applicant but also a member of one of the minority groups that the laws administered by the EEOC are supposed to be protecting, B, the white male, is entitled to the job. Thus on the Commission's view there is a hierarchy of protections for groups deemed entitled to protection against discrimination, with the disabled being placed ahead of the members of racial minorities.

The Commission thinks these odd and counterintuitive results compelled by the structure of the statute. If all that Houser's employer had to do by way of a reasonable accommodation was to allow Houser to compete for jobs for which she was qualified and to obtain any job for which she was the best applicant, what is left of the duty to reassign a disabled worker to a vacant position? Plenty is left. Without the reassignment provision in the statute, an employer might plausibly claim that "reasonable accommodation" refers to efforts to enable a disabled worker to do the job for which he was hired or for which he is applying, rather than to offer him another job. The reassignment provision makes clear that the employer must also consider the feasibility of assigning the worker to a different job in which his disability will not be an impediment to full performance, and if the reassignment is feasible and does not require the employer to turn away a superior applicant, the reassignment is mandatory. That is not the same thing as requiring the employer to give him the job even if another worker would be twice as good at it, provided only that this could be done without undue hardship to the employer.

The Commission presses on us two recent en banc decisions in other circuits, *Smith v. Midland Brake, Inc.*, 180 F.3d 1154, 1164–68 (10th Cir.1999); *Aka v. Washington Hospital Center*, 156 F.3d 1284, 1303–05 (D.C.Cir.1998). *Aka* is distinguishable. It does not address the situation in which a nondisabled person is the superior applicant for the job to which the disabled person seeks reassignment and the employer has a consistent policy of preferring the best candidate for a vacancy rather than merely hiring the first qualified person to apply, as is often done for routine low-skilled jobs. The court assumed that the alternative to a duty to reassign a person who is minimally qualified is a duty of the employer just to "consider" the person for the job, with no obligation actually to reassign him even if there is no competing applicant, let alone one no better than the disabled person. On that assumption the statute's provision that reassignment can be a mandatory accommodation would indeed be meaningless. *Aka* merely rejects an "interpretation of the reassignment provision as mandating nothing more than that the employer allow the disabled employee to submit his application along with all of the other candidates," an interpretation that the court thought "would render that provision a nullity." That is not the same thing as holding that the employer must pass over the superior applicant who, as we have emphasized, might himself or herself be disabled or belong to some other protected class.

The Tenth Circuit cases are not distinguishable from the present case, but they are inconsistent with decisions of this court that hold that the Americans with Disabilities Act is not a mandatory preference act. [We have] held that an employer is not required "to reassign a disabled employee to a position when such a transfer would violate a legitimate, nondiscriminatory policy of the employer. . . . The contrary rule would convert a nondiscrimination statute into a mandatory preference statute, a result which would be both inconsistent with the nondiscriminatory aims of the ADA and an unreasonable imposition on the employers and coworkers of disabled employees." A policy of giving the job to the best applicant is legitimate and nondiscriminatory. Decisions on the merits are not discriminatory. See also *Malabarba v. Chicago Tribune Co.*, 149 F.3d 690, 699–700 (7th Cir.1998), where we said that "the ADA does not mandate a policy of 'affirmative action in favor of individuals with disabilities, in the sense of requiring that disabled person be given priority in hiring or reassignment over those who are not disabled,' " and *Matthews v. Commonwealth Edison Co.*, 128 F.3d 1194, 1196 (7th Cir.1997), where we said that "the Americans with Disabilities Act does not command affirmative action in hiring or firing."

It is true that antidiscrimination statutes impose costs on employers. That is obvious in disparate-impact cases, when the employer is told to change a policy that may not have been adopted for discriminatory reasons (though that is its effect) and so presumably is efficient. The duty of accommodation operates in a similar way. It requires the employer to incur (if it need be) an expense rather than just to desist from invidious discrimination. The requirement is implicit in the ADA's creating an "undue hardship" safe harbor for employers; the safe harbor would be otiose if the employer's only duty were to stop doing something.

But there is a difference, one of principle and not merely of cost, between requiring employers to clear away obstacles to hiring the best applicant for a job, who might be a disabled person or a member of some other statutorily protected group, and requiring employers to hire inferior (albeit minimally qualified) applicants merely because they are members of such a group. That is affirmative action with a vengeance. That is giving a job to someone solely on the basis of his status as a member of a statutorily protected group. It goes well beyond enabling the disabled applicant to compete in the workplace, or requiring the employer to rectify a situation (such as lack of wheelchair access) that is of his own doing.

Does Judge Posner's analysis leave any room for a reasonable accommodation claim (as opposed to a straightforward disparate treatment claim) in the reassignment context? It appears that the only circumstances in which an employer would be required to make a reassignment are circumstances where the failure to do so would constitute intentional discrimination—where the employer refuses to assign a disabled employee to a vacant position *even though she is the most qualified candidate*. On the other hand, doesn't Judge Posner have a point? It is clear that, at the initial hire stage, an employer has no obligation to hire an applicant with a disability if that applicant is less qualified than other candidates. Why should the rule be any different where the disabled applicant is an incumbent employee seeking reassignment? Is the answer that once an individual with a disability is out of work, it may be too late to bring her back into the workforce, so the law's intervention must be targeted at incumbent employees who acquire disabilities? Is that a proper consideration for an antidiscrimination law?

Is Judge Posner's analysis consistent with *Barnett*? In HUBER V. WAL-MART STORES, INC., 486 F.3d 480 (8th Cir.2007), the Eighth Circuit expressly agreed with Judge Posner's holding in *Humiston-Keeling*, and held that "the ADA is not an affirmative action statute and does not require an employer to reassign a qualified disabled employee to a vacant position when such a reassignment would violate a legitimate nondiscriminatory policy of the employer to hire the most qualified candidate." The court found its conclusion "bolstered" by *Barnett*'s holding that seniority systems ordinarily trump the claim to reassignment. The Supreme Court granted *certiorari* in *Huber*, but the parties settled the case before argument and the Court dismissed the writ. See *Huber v. Wal-Mart Stores, Inc.*, 552 U.S. 1136 (2008).

After the Supreme Court dismissed the writ in *Huber*, the Seventh Circuit overruled its earlier *Humiston-Keeling* decision in EEOC V. UNITED AIRLINES, INC., 693 F.3d 760 (7th Cir.2012):

> The EEOC points out that U.S. Airways relied heavily on *Humiston-Keeling* and, more importantly, that the *Barnett* Court flatly contradicted much of the language of *Humiston-Keeling*. U.S. Airways argued that it was not required to grant a requested accommodation that would violate a disability-neutral rule, using the argument from *Humiston-Keeling* that the ADA is "not a mandatory preference act" but only a "nondiscrimination statute." The *Barnett* Court rejected this anti-preference interpretation of the ADA, noting that this argument "fails to recognize what the Act specifies, namely, that preferences will sometimes prove necessary to achieve the Act's basic equal opportunity goal." Merely following a "neutral rule" did not allow U.S. Airways to claim an "automatic exemption" from the accommodation requirement of the Act. Instead, U.S. Airways prevailed because its situation satisfied a much narrower, fact-specific exception based on the hardship that could be imposed on an employer utilizing a seniority system.
>
> The analysis of *Barnett's* impact on *Humiston-Keeling* is further complicated by the fact that we are not the first panel to consider this issue. This court considered *Barnett's* relationship to *Humiston-Keeling*, albeit in an abbreviated fashion and without the benefit of briefing, in *Mays v. Principi*, 301 F.3d 866 (7th Cir.2002). In *Mays*, this court relied on *Humiston-Keeling* in finding that an employer did not violate the duty of reasonable accommodation in the Rehabilitation Act of 1973, 29 U.S.C. § 701 *et seq.*, by giving an administrative nursing position to a better qualified applicant, rather than to a disabled employee needing reassignment. The *Mays* Court interpreted the recently handed down *Barnett* decision actually to bolster *Humiston-Keeling* by equating seniority systems with any other normal method of filling vacancies.
>
>> [*Barnett*] holds that an employer is not required to give a disabled employee superseniority to enable him to retain his job when a more senior employee invokes an entitlement to it conferred by the employer's seniority system. If for "more senior" we read "better qualified," for "seniority system" we read "the employer's normal method of filling vacancies," and for "superseniority" we read "a break," *U.S. Airways* becomes our case.
>
> The EEOC argues, and we agree, that the *Mays* Court incorrectly asserted that a best-qualified selection policy is essentially the

same as a seniority system. In equating the two, the *Mays* Court so enlarged the narrow, fact-specific exception set out in *Barnett* as to swallow the rule. While employers may prefer to hire the best qualified applicant, the violation of a best-qualified selection policy does not involve the property-rights and administrative concerns (and resulting burdens) presented by the violation of a seniority policy. To strengthen this critique, the EEOC points out the relative rarity of seniority systems and the distinct challenges of mandating reassignment in a system where employees are already entitled to particular positions based on years of employment.

The Supreme Court has found that accommodation through appointment to a vacant position is reasonable. Absent a showing of undue hardship, an employer must implement such a reassignment policy. The *Mays* Court understandably erred in suggesting that deviation from a best-qualified selection policy always represented such a hardship.

[F]or its part, United argues that this court should not abandon *Humiston-Keeling,* in part because the Eighth Circuit explicitly adopted the reasoning of *Humiston-Keeling* in Huber v. Wal-Mart. The Eighth Circuit's wholesale adoption of *Humiston-Keeling* has little import. The opinion adopts *Humiston-Keeling* without analysis, much less an analysis of *Humiston-Keeling* in the context of *Barnett.* Two of our sister Circuits have already determined that the ADA requires employers to appoint disabled employees to vacant positions, provided that such accommodations would not create an undue hardship (or run afoul of a collective bargaining agreement): the Tenth in *Smith v. Midland Brake, Inc.,* 180 F.3d 1154 (10th Cir.1999) (en banc) and the D.C. in *Aka v. Washington Hospital Center,* 156 F.3d 1284 (D.C.Cir.1998) (en banc). We feel that in light of *Barnett,* [w]e must adopt a similar approach.

Do you find the Seventh Circuit's *United Airlines* analysis persuasive?

6. Nexus. The ADA requires employers to "mak[e] reasonable accommodations to the known physical or mental *limitations* of an otherwise qualified individual with a disability," 42 U.S.C. § 12112(b)(5)(A) (emphasis added). The statute does not speak of accommodating the "substantial limitations on major life activities" or the "disabilities" of a qualified individual with a disability. Does this mean that, if an employee has a disability, her employer must accommodate any known physical or mental limitations she has, whether or not they stem from the disability? Or is the employer required only to accommodate limitations that stem from the disability that triggers statutory coverage?

Determining what physical or mental limitations stem from the disability may not be obvious—and may well depend on the level of generality at which a judge chooses to describe the plaintiff's disability. Consider FELIX V. NEW YORK CITY TRANSIT AUTHORITY, 324 F.3d 102 (2d Cir.2003). Felix, a railroad clerk for the NYCTA, was diagnosed with post-traumatic stress disorder after being stuck in a train while a fellow clerk was killed in a firebombing. The PTSD caused insomnia, which, the NYCTA agreed, sufficiently limited Felix's major life activities to satisfy the ADA's definition of disability. The condition also caused Felix acute anxiety when working in the subway, and her doctor "specified that she was not to do any subway work, but could do clerical work." Felix requested to be reassigned to a position that did not require her to work in the subway, but the NYCTA refused.

Felix sued, the district court granted summary judgment to the NYCTA, and the Second Circuit affirmed:

> The statutory language prohibits discrimination against an employee "because of the disability of such individual." 42 U.S.C. § 12112(a). Although "discriminate" is defined in very broad terms, that expansive definition does not change the requirement that to be actionable the discrimination must be "because of the disability." Reading the requirement of reasonable accommodation in this light, an employer discriminates against an employee with a disability only by failing to provide a reasonable accommodation for the "disability" which is the impairment of the major life activity. Other impairments that do not amount to a "disability" as defined by 42 U.S.C. § 12102(2)(a) do not require accommodation under the ADA.

> The principle is not altered by the fact that the disability (which must be accommodated) is caused by another impairment (which need not be accommodated). In this case, her disability was her insomnia which substantially limited her ability to sleep. Felix's inability to work in the subway did not substantially limit any major life activity. She was fully able to work, just not in the subway. Her inability to work in the subway was related to her insomnia because they both stemmed from the same traumatic incident and resultant psychological disorder, the PTSD. But this common traumatic origin alone does not mean that the non-disability impairment is entitled to an accommodation.

> A simple hypothetical of a car accident illustrates the point well. A passenger in a car is badly injured in an accident. The passenger loses the ability to walk, a major life activity and thus has a "disability" that qualifies him for accommodation. The passenger also suffers some injury to his arms, which lower his typing speed from one-hundred words per minute to forty words per minute, without seriously limiting his ability to perform the major life activity of working in general. Because his arm injuries do not substantially limit any major life activity, these injuries are not a disability. His employer terminates him from a position doing data entry and word processing because his productivity has decreased. The fact that the disability, the inability to walk, and the limitation of his typing stem from the same accident does not change the fact that he was not discriminated against "because of [his] disability." Similarly, Felix's inability to sleep (a significant limitation on a major life activity) is separate from her inability to work in the subway (not a significant limitation on the

major life activity of working in general), even though both were caused by the subway firebombing and the resultant PTSD.

In *Bragdon v. Abbott* [Chapter Two, *supra*] the Supreme Court held that for purposes of receiving a public accommodation of dental treatment, a person with AIDS is a person with a disability because AIDS interferes with the major life activity of reproduction. Although the right to the public accommodation of dental treatment is secured by Title III of the ADA, not by Title I, the definition of "disability" applies to all of the ADA. However, contrary to Felix's argument, the dentist in *Bragdon* denied services to the plaintiff purely because of Bragdon's disability, her infection with HIV. Although the life activity of reproduction was not directly connected to the dentist's unreasonable failure to accommodate *Bragdon*, the same specific medical condition—the risk of HIV transmission—was responsible for both the impairment of her reproductive capacity and the dentist's unreasonable failure to accommodate her. Thus, the discrimination was because of her disability.

[F]elix seeks a workplace accommodation for a mental condition which does not flow directly from her disability—the mental condition of insomnia that prevents her from sleeping. Felix did not argue to the NYCTA that she was unable to work in the subway because such work aggravated her insomnia; she told the NYCTA that she could not work in the subway because she was "terrified of being alone and closed in." Thus, in contrast to the cases upon which she relies, the impairment for which Felix seeks accommodation does not arise "because of the disability." If the requested accommodation addressed a limitation caused by Felix's insomnia, it would be covered by the ADA. Adverse effects of disabilities and adverse or side effects from the medical treatment of disabilities arise "because of the disability." However, other impairments not caused by the disability need not be accommodated.

Felix contends that her case falls within our precedents by arguing that her insomnia and her fear of being in the subway are part of the same singular mental disability, the PTSD, and thus her inability to work in the subway is also "because of the disability." However, we do not view her insomnia and fear of the subway as a singular mental condition: They are two mental conditions that derive from the same traumatic incident. In cases involving conditions like AIDS that are discrete diseases with pervasive effects, it will frequently be obvious that the lesser impairment is caused by the disability. However, in situations like plaintiff's where it is not clear that a single, particular medical condition is responsible for both the disability and the lesser impairment, the plaintiff must show a causal connection between the specific condition which impairs a major life activity and the accommodation. Felix has not done so here.

Finally, we note that our interpretation of the language of the statute is supported by policy considerations. The ADA serves the important function of ensuring that people with disabilities are given the same opportunities and are able to enjoy the same benefits as other Americans. The ADA mandates reasonable accommodation of people with disabilities in order to put them on an even playing field with the non-disabled; it does not authorize a preference for disabled people generally [citing *Barnett*]. The interpretation advanced by Felix and the EEOC would transform the ADA from an act that prohibits discrimination into an act that requires treating people with disabilities better than others who are not disabled but have the same impairment for which accommodation is sought. We think that the ADA deliberately speaks in terms of eliminating discrimination and thus do not interpret it so broadly as to require the accommodation of impairments that do not limit major life activities whenever the person with an impairment happens to also have a disability.

Adopting this principle would effectively eviscerate the statutory definition of a disability as an impairment of a major life activity—a significant threshold for seeking redress under the ADA. An ADA plaintiff who is not otherwise impaired in a major life activity but suffers debilitating anxiety or stress from a particular job could get to a jury merely by alleging that the job causes insomnia, difficulty breathing, or some other set of disabling symptoms that can be characterized as a syndrome. We decline to adopt such an expansive reading of the ADA that frustrates its plain statutory meaning.

Judge Leval dissented. He noted that "Felix's medical evaluations recommended work above ground, stating that below-ground assignments would aggravate her PTSD, the condition that caused the sleep disorder." He concluded that "[a]lthough the doctors did not state this with optimal clarity, a fact finder could easily find on the basis of the medical opinions that work below ground would aggravate the sleep disorder."

The majority described Felix's disability at a low level of generality: Her disability, according to the majority, was her insomnia. In this view, she could demand accommodations for her insomnia, but not for her PTSD more generally. But why is that the proper level of generality? One could just as readily describe Felix's disability as consisting of her PTSD, which (among other things) substantially limited her major life activity of sleeping. When Felix's disability is described at that, higher, level of generality, the majority's effort to distinguish *Bragdon* seems much less successful. Just like Sydney Abbott's HIV infection, Ms. Felix's PTSD had at least two symptoms: one that substantially limited a major life activity (Abbott's inability to safely reproduce, Felix's insomnia), and a distinct one that was the basis for the discrimination against her (Abbott's alleged contagiousness, Felix's anxiety in subway tunnels). The *Felix* decision, then, turns entirely on the majority's decision to describe Felix's disability at a low rather than a high level of generality. What is the justification for that decision? Does the expansion of the definition of disability in the ADA Amendments Act undermine that justification? As a practical matter, the new statute should make the issue in *Felix* less important at any rate. For an instructive discussion of the nexus requirement, see Note, *Three Formulations of the Nexus Requirement in Reasonable Accommodations Law*, 126 Harv. L. Rev. 1392 (2013).

   7.   Interactive Process. The EEOC's regulations implementing the ADA's employment provisions state that "[t]o determine the appropriate reasonable accommodation it may be necessary for the covered entity to initiate an informal, interactive process with the qualified individual with a disability in need of the accommodation. This process should identify the precise limitations resulting from the disability and potential reasonable accommodations that could overcome those limitations." 29 C.F.R. § 1630.2(o)(3). A number of courts have held that this regulation imposes a requirement on both the employer and the worker with a disability to engage in an interactive process to determine the proper accommodation. But the sanction for violating this obligation is less clear, because the statute by its terms prohibits the denial of reasonable accommodation, not the failure to engage in an interactive process. 42 U.S.C. § 12112(b)(5)(A). If no reasonable accommodation was possible, the statute does not appear to authorize liability simply because the employer failed to engage in the preferred process. See, *e.g.*, *Taylor v. Phoenixville School Dist.*, 184 F.3d 296, 317 (3d Cir.1999) ("The interactive process does not dictate that any particular concession must be made by the employer; nor does the process remove the employee's burden of showing that a particular accommodation rejected by the employer would have made the employee qualified to perform the job's essential functions."). Courts may, however, be less likely to grant summary judgment to an employer who refused to engage in the interactive process:

   When an employee has evidence that the employer did not act in good faith in the interactive process, however, we will not readily decide on summary judgment that accommodation was not possible and the employer's bad faith could have no effect. To assume that accommodation would fail regardless of the employer's bad faith would effectively eliminate the requirement that employers must participate in the interactive process. An employer who acted in bad faith would be in essentially the same, if not better, position than one who participated; that is, both employers would be arguing that the employee failed to find an accommodation making him or her able to perform the essential function of the job. The less the employer participated, the easier this would become, and as a result, the requirement that employers participate in the interactive process would be toothless. Thus, where there is a genuine dispute about whether the employer acted in good faith, summary judgment will typically be precluded. When the disability involved is one that is heavily stigmatized in our society—as is true when the employee is voluntarily or involuntarily committed to a mental institution— courts should be especially wary on summary judgment of underestimating how well an employee might perform with accommodations or how much the employer's bad faith may have hindered the process of finding accommodations.

Id. Because the statute requires accommodation only of "known" disabilities, 42 U.S.C. § 12112(b)(5)(A), the *employee*'s failure to engage in the interactive process will often be fatal to her claim. The employee's burden in this regard is not very great, however. See, *e.g.*, *id.* at 319 ("What matters under the ADA are not formalisms about the manner of the request, but whether the employee or a representative for the employee provides the employer with enough information that, under the circumstances, the employer can be fairly said to know of both the disability and desire for an accommodation.").

B. "QUALIFIED INDIVIDUAL WITH A DISABILITY"

1. "QUALIFIED INDIVIDUAL" VERSUS "QUALIFICATION STANDARDS"

Albertson's, Inc. v. Kirkingburg

Supreme Court of the United States, 1999.
527 U.S. 555.

■ JUSTICE SOUTER delivered the opinion of the Court.*

The question posed is whether, under the Americans with Disabilities Act of 1990 (ADA or Act), 104 Stat. 327, as amended, 42 U.S.C. § 12101 *et seq.*, an employer who requires as a job qualification that an employee meet an otherwise applicable federal safety regulation must justify enforcing the regulation solely because its standard may be waived in an individual case. We answer no.

I

In August 1990, petitioner, Albertson's, Inc., a grocery-store chain with supermarkets in several States, hired respondent, Hallie Kirkingburg, as a truckdriver based at its Portland, Oregon, warehouse. Kirkingburg had more than a decade's driving experience and performed well when petitioner's transportation manager took him on a road test.

Before starting work, Kirkingburg was examined to see if he met federal vision standards for commercial truckdrivers. For many decades the Department of Transportation and its predecessors have been responsible for devising these standards for individuals who drive commercial vehicles in interstate commerce. Since 1971, the basic vision regulation has required corrected distant visual acuity of at least 20/40 in each eye and distant binocular acuity of at least 20/40. Kirkingburg, however, suffers from amblyopia, an uncorrectable condition that leaves him with 20/200 vision in his left eye and monocular vision in effect. Despite Kirkingburg's weak left eye, the doctor erroneously certified that he met the DOT's basic vision standards, and Albertson's hired him.

In December 1991, Kirkingburg injured himself on the job and took a leave of absence. Before returning to work in November 1992, Kirkingburg went for a further physical as required by the company.

---

*   JUSTICE STEVENS and JUSTICE BREYER join Parts I and III of this opinion.

This time, the examining physician correctly assessed Kirkingburg's vision and explained that his eyesight did not meet the basic DOT standards. The physician, or his nurse, told Kirkingburg that in order to be legally qualified to drive, he would have to obtain a waiver of its basic vision standards from the DOT. The doctor was alluding to a scheme begun in July 1992 for giving DOT certification to applicants with deficient vision who had three years of recent experience driving a commercial vehicle without a license suspension or revocation, involvement in a reportable accident in which the applicant was cited for a moving violation, conviction for certain driving-related offenses, citation for certain serious traffic violations, or more than two convictions for any other moving violations. A waiver applicant had to agree to have his vision checked annually for deterioration, and to report certain information about his driving experience to the Federal Highway Administration (FHWA or Administration), the agency within the DOT responsible for overseeing the motor carrier safety regulations. See 57 Fed.Reg. 31458, 31460–31461 (1992). Kirkingburg applied for a waiver, but because he could not meet the basic DOT vision standard Albertson's fired him from his job as a truckdriver. In early 1993, after he had left Albertson's, Kirkingburg received a DOT waiver, but Albertson's refused to rehire him.

Kirkingburg sued Albertson's, claiming that firing him violated the ADA. Albertson's moved for summary judgment solely on the ground that Kirkingburg was "not 'otherwise qualified' to perform the job of truck driver with or without reasonable accommodation." The District Court granted the motion, ruling that Albertson's had reasonably concluded that Kirkingburg was not qualified without an accommodation because he could not, as admitted, meet the basic DOT vision standards. The court held that giving Kirkingburg time to get a DOT waiver was not a required reasonable accommodation because the waiver program was "a flawed experiment that has not altered the DOT vision requirements."

A divided panel of the Ninth Circuit reversed.

II

[Part II of the Court's opinion, which is discussed in Chapter Two above, addressed the definition of disability.]

III

[P]etitioner's primary contention is that even if Kirkingburg was disabled, he was not a "qualified" individual with a disability, see 42 U.S.C. § 12112(a), because Albertson's merely insisted on the minimum level of visual acuity set forth in the DOT's Motor Carrier Safety Regulations, 49 CFR § 391.41(b)(10) (1998). If Albertson's was entitled to enforce that standard as defining an "essential job functio[n] of the employment position," see 42 U.S.C. § 12111(8), that is the end of the case, for Kirkingburg concededly could not satisfy it.

Under Title I of the ADA, employers may justify their use of "qualification standards . . . that screen out or tend to screen out or otherwise deny a job or benefit to an individual with a disability," so long as such standards are "job-related and consistent with business necessity, and . . . performance cannot be accomplished by reasonable accommodation. . . . " § 12113(a). See also § 12112(b)(6) (defining discrimination to include "using qualification standards . . . that screen out or tend to screen out an individual with a disability . . . unless the standard . . . is shown to be job-related for the position in question and is consistent with business necessity").

Kirkingburg and the Government argue that these provisions do not authorize an employer to follow even a facially applicable regulatory standard subject to waiver without making some enquiry beyond determining whether the applicant or employee meets that standard, yes or no. Before an employer may insist on compliance, they say, the employer must make a showing with reference to the particular job that the waivable regulatory standard is "job-related . . . and . . . consistent with business necessity," see § 12112(b)(6), and that after consideration of the capabilities of the individual a reasonable accommodation could not fairly resolve the competing interests when an applicant or employee cannot wholly satisfy an otherwise justifiable job qualification.

The Government extends this argument by reference to a further section of the statute, which at first blush appears to be a permissive provision for the employer's and the public's benefit. An employer may impose as a qualification standard "a requirement that an individual shall not pose a direct threat to the health or safety of other individuals in the workplace," § 12113(b), with "direct threat" being defined by the Act as "a significant risk to the health or safety of others that cannot be eliminated by reasonable accommodation," § 12111(3); see also 29 CFR § 1630.2(r) (1998). The Government urges us to read subsections (a) and (b) together to mean that when an employer would impose any safety qualification standard, however specific, tending to screen out individuals with disabilities, the application of the requirement must satisfy the ADA's "direct threat" criterion, see Brief for United States *et al.* as *Amici Curiae* 22. That criterion ordinarily requires "an individualized assessment of the individual's present ability to safely perform the essential functions of the job," 29 CFR § 1630.2(r) (1998), "based on medical or other objective evidence," *Bragdon [v. Abbott]*, 524 U.S.[624,] 649 [(1998)].

[T]he Court of Appeals majority concluded that the waiver program "precludes [employers] from declaring that persons determined by DOT to be capable of performing the job of commercial truck driver are incapable of performing that job by virtue of their disability," and that in the face of a waiver an employer "will not be able to avoid the [ADA's] strictures by showing that its standards are necessary to prevent a direct safety threat." [B]ut the reasoning underlying the Court of Appeals's decision was unsound, for we think it was error to read the regulations establishing the waiver program as modifying the content of the basic visual acuity standard in a way that disentitled an employer like Albertson's to insist on it. To be sure, this is not immediately apparent. If one starts with the statutory provisions authorizing regulations by the DOT as they stood at the time the DOT began the waiver program, one would reasonably presume that the general regulatory standard and the regulatory waiver standard ought to be accorded equal substantive significance, so that the content of any general regulation would as a matter of law be deemed modified by the terms of any waiver standard thus applied to it. Compare 49 U.S.C.App. § 2505(a)(3) (1988 ed.) ("Such regulation shall . . . ensure that . . . the physical condition of operators of commercial motor vehicles is adequate to enable them to operate the vehicles safely"), with 49 U.S.C.App. § 2505(f) (1988 ed.) ("After notice and an opportunity for comment, the Secretary may waive, in whole or in part, application of any regulation issued under this section with respect to any person or class of persons if the Secretary determines that such waiver is not contrary to the public interest and is consistent with the safe operation of commercial motor vehicles"). Safe operation is supposed to be the touchstone of regulation in each instance.

As to the general visual acuity regulations in force under the former provision, affirmative determinations that the selected standards were needed for safe operation were indeed the predicates of the DOT action. Starting in 1937, the federal agencies authorized to regulate commercial motor vehicle safety set increasingly rigorous visual acuity standards, culminating in the current one, which has remained unchanged since it became effective in 1971. When the FHWA proposed it, the agency found that "[a]ccident experience in recent years has demonstrated that reduction of the effects of organic and physical disorders, emotional impairments, and other limitations of the good health of drivers are increasingly important factors in accident prevention"; the current standard was adopted to reflect the agency's conclusion that "drivers of modern, more complex vehicles" must be able to "withstand the increased physical and mental demands that their occupation now imposes." Given these findings and "in the light of discussions with the Administration's medical advisers," the FHWA made a considered determination about the level of visual acuity needed for safe operation of commercial motor vehicles in interstate commerce, an "area [in which] the risks involved are so well known and so serious as to dictate the utmost caution."

For several reasons, one would expect any regulation governing a waiver program to establish a comparable substantive standard (albeit for exceptional cases), grounded on known facts indicating at least that safe operation would not be jeopardized. First, of course, safe operation was the criterion of the statute authorizing an administrative waiver scheme, as noted already. Second, the impetus to develop a waiver program was a concern that the existing substantive standard might be more demanding than safety required. When Congress enacted the ADA, it recognized that federal safety rules would limit application of the ADA as a matter of law. Accordingly, two [congressional] Committees asked "the Secretary of Transportation [to] undertake a thorough review" of current knowledge about the capabilities of individuals with disabilities and available technological aids and devices, and make "any necessary changes" within two years of the enactment of the ADA. Finally, when the FHWA instituted the waiver program it addressed the statutory mandate by stating in its notice of final disposition that the scheme would be "consistent with the safe operation of commercial motor vehicles," just as 49 U.S.C.App. § 2505(f) (1988 ed.) required.

And yet, despite this background, the regulations establishing the waiver program did not modify the general visual acuity standards. It is not that the waiver regulations failed to do so in a merely formal sense, as by turning waiver decisions on driving records, not sight requirements. The FHWA in fact made it clear that it had no evidentiary basis for concluding that the pre-existing standards could be lowered consistently with public safety. When, in 1992, the FHWA published an "[a]dvance notice of proposed rulemaking" requesting comments "on the need, if any, to amend its driver qualification requirements relating to the vision standard," it candidly proposed its waiver scheme as simply a means of obtaining information bearing on the justifiability of revising the binding standards already in place. The agency explained that the "object of the waiver program is to provide objective data to be considered in relation to a rulemaking exploring the feasibility of relaxing the current absolute vision standards in 49 CFR part 391 in favor of a more individualized standard." As proposed, therefore, there was not only no change in the unconditional acuity standards, but no indication even that the FHWA then had a basis in fact to believe anything more lenient would be consistent with public safety as a general matter. After a bumpy stretch of administrative procedure, see *Advocates for Highway and Auto Safety v. FHWA*, 28 F.3d 1288, 1290 (C.A.D.C.1994), the FHWA's final disposition explained again that the waivers were proposed as a way to gather facts going to the wisdom of changing the existing law. The waiver program "will enable the FHWA to conduct a study comparing a group of experienced, visually deficient drivers with a control group of experienced drivers who meet the current Federal vision requirements. This study will provide the empirical data necessary to evaluate the relationships between specific visual deficiencies and the operation of [commercial motor vehicles]. The data will permit the FHWA to properly evaluate its current vision requirement in the context of actual driver performance, and, if necessary, establish a new vision requirement which is safe, fair, and rationally related to the latest medical knowledge and highway technology." And if all this were not enough to show that the FHWA was planning to give waivers solely to collect information, it acknowledged that a study it had commissioned had done no more than " 'illuminat[e] the lack of empirical data to establish a link between vision disorders and commercial motor vehicle safety,' " and " 'failed to provide a sufficient foundation on which to propose a satisfactory vision standard for drivers of [commercial motor vehicles] in interstate commerce,' " *Advocates for Highway and Auto Safety*, *supra*, at 1293 (quoting 57 Fed.Reg. 31458 (1992)).

In sum, the regulatory record made it plain that the waiver regulation did not rest on any final, factual conclusion that the waiver scheme would be conducive to public safety in the manner of the general acuity standards and did not purport to modify the substantive content of the general acuity regulation in any way. The waiver program was simply an experiment with safety, however well intended, resting on a hypothesis whose confirmation or refutation in practice would provide a factual basis for reconsidering the existing standards.

Nothing in the waiver regulation, of course, required an employer of commercial drivers to accept the hypothesis and participate in the Government's experiment. The only question, then, is whether the ADA should be read to require such an employer to defend a decision to decline the experiment. Is it reasonable, that is, to read the ADA as requiring an employer like Albertson's to shoulder the general statutory burden to justify a job qualification that would tend to exclude the disabled, whenever the employer chooses to abide by the otherwise clearly applicable, unamended substantive regulatory standard despite the Government's willingness to waive it experimentally and without any finding of its being inappropriate? If the answer were yes, an employer would in fact have an obligation of which we can think of no comparable example in our law. The employer would be required in effect to justify de novo an existing and otherwise applicable safety regulation issued by the Government itself. The employer would be required on a case-by-case basis to reinvent the Government's own wheel when the Government had merely begun an experiment to provide data to consider changing the underlying specifications. And what is even more, the employer would be required to do so when the Government had made an affirmative record indicating that contemporary empirical evidence was hard to come by. It is simply not credible that Congress enacted the ADA (before there was any waiver program) with the understanding that employers choosing to respect the Government's sole substantive visual acuity regulation in the face of an experimental waiver might be burdened with an obligation to defend the regulation's application according to its own terms.

The judgment of the Ninth Circuit is accordingly reversed.

It is so ordered.

■ JUSTICE THOMAS, concurring.

[DOT]'s visual acuity standards might also be relevant to the question whether respondent was a "qualified individual with a disability" under 42 U.S.C. § 12112(a). That section provides that no covered entity "shall discriminate against a qualified individual with a disability because of the disability of such individual." Presumably, then, a plaintiff claiming a cause of action under the ADA bears the burden of proving, inter alia, that he is a qualified individual. The phrase "qualified individual with a disability" is defined to mean:

> "an individual with a disability who, *with or without reasonable accommodation*, can perform the *essential functions* of the employment position that such individual holds or desires. For the purposes of this subchapter, consideration shall be given to the employer's judgment as to what functions of a job are essential, and if an employer has prepared a written description before advertising or interviewing applicants for the job, this description shall be considered evidence of the essential functions of the job." § 12111(8) (emphasis added).

[A]s the Court explains, DOT's Motor Carrier Safety Regulations have the force of law and bind petitioner—it may not, by law, "permit a person to drive a commercial motor vehicle unless that person is qualified to drive." 49 CFR § 391.11 (1999). But by the same token, DOT's regulations bind respondent, who "shall not drive a commercial motor vehicle unless he/she is qualified to drive a commercial motor vehicle." Given that DOT's regulation equally binds petitioner and respondent, and that it is conceded in this case that respondent could not meet the federal requirements, respondent surely was not "qualified" to perform the essential functions of petitioner's truckdriver job without a reasonable accommodation. The waiver program might be thought of as a way to reasonably accommodate respondent, but for the fact, as the Court explains, that the program did nothing to modify the regulation's unconditional requirements. For that reason, requiring petitioner to make such an accommodation most certainly would have been unreasonable.

The result of this case is the same under either view of the statute. If forced to choose between these alternatives, however, I would prefer to hold that respondent, as a matter of law, was not qualified to perform the job he sought within the meaning of the ADA.

NOTES ON ALBERTSON'S, INC. V. KIRKINGBURG

1. "Qualified Individual" versus "Qualification Standards." The ADA's employment provisions prohibit discrimination against a "qualified individual with a disability." 42 U.S.C. § 12112(a). The statute defines a "qualified individual" as one "who, with or without reasonable accommodation, can perform the essential functions of the employment position that such individual holds or desires." 42 U.S.C. § 12111(8). Thus, the statute requires an employment discrimination plaintiff to show, as part of her case-in-chief, that she can perform "essential" job tasks (if only with reasonable accommodation, see Section A, *supra*). In addition to requiring that the plaintiff prove that she is "qualified," the ADA offers employers a defense for applying certain "qualification standards, tests, or selection criteria that screen out or tend to screen out or otherwise deny a job or benefit to an individual with a disability." 42 U.S.C. § 12113(a). An employer can defend such "qualification standards" if it shows that they are "job-related and consistent with business necessity," and that no "reasonable accommodation" to them is possible. *Id.*

Are these provisions merely two sides of the same coin? In his *Albertson's* concurrence, Justice Thomas certainly suggests that he thinks so. But is Justice Thomas correct that Kirkingburg could not "perform the essential functions" of the truck driver job? The Court's recitation of the facts seems to make clear that Kirkingburg was *physically* able to perform those functions. And once he received his waiver from the Department of Transportation, he was also *legally* able to perform those functions. Kirkingburg's failure to satisfy the federal regulation's general visual acuity standards thus does not seem to have anything to do with whether he was "qualified" under the ADA's definition of that term. By contrast, it seems clear that Albertson's requirement that its drivers meet the general visual acuity standard was a "qualification standard[ ]" or "selection criteri[on]," and Justice Souter's opinion for the Court proceeds on that basis.

2. "Reinventing the Government's Own Wheel"? If Albertson's requirement that its drivers satisfy the FHWA's general visual acuity standards was a "qualification standard," as the Court indicates, the statutory text seems to say that Albertson's must "show[ ]" that the requirement was "job-related and consistent with business necessity." 42 U.S.C. § 12113(a). This language, drawn from disparate impact doctrine under Title VII of the Civil Rights Act of 1964, see 42 U.S.C. § 2000e–2(k), is not defined in Title VII or the ADA, and its interpretation is uncertain at best. See generally Michael Selmi, *Was the Disparate Impact Theory a Mistake?*, 53 UCLA L. Rev. 701 (2006). Even so, the *Albertson's* Court held that the employer had satisfied its burden without requiring it to prove that its refusal to accept DOT waivers was "job-related and consistent with business necessity."

If the law were to require Albertson's to justify its refusal to accept waivers as business necessity, the Court reasoned, employers "would be required on a case-by-case basis to reinvent the Government's own wheel when the Government had merely begun an experiment to provide data to consider changing the underlying specifications." But was Kirkingburg demanding that Albertson's "reinvent the Government's own wheel."? It was the government itself that created the waiver program and gave Kirkingburg a waiver that permitted him to drive. From his perspective, he was asking Albertson's to justify its refusal to let him work in the face of the government's decision to permit him to drive. See Samuel R. Bagenstos, *The Supreme Court, the Americans with Disabilities Act, and Rational Discrimination*, 55 Ala. L. Rev. 923, 929 (2004) ("It is only by disregarding the existence and legality of the waiver regulation that one could think that Kirkingburg was calling on Albertson's to defend the government's—rather than the company's—own decision.").

What is wrong with requiring employers to justify, on a case-by-case basis, their refusal to hire individuals who had received waivers from the government? The Court relies on the government's acknowledgment "that contemporary empirical evidence was hard to come by" to suggest that it would be unfair to require employers to shoulder that burden. But might the government's acknowledgement suggest the opposite? If people with monocular vision are uniformly excluded from jobs driving commercial vehicles, despite the lack of a significant body of "contemporary empirical evidence" to support that exclusion, wouldn't it be consistent with the general principles of disability discrimination law to require employers to consider the claims of particular individuals with monocular vision that, whatever is true of the broad class of people with monocular vision, those individuals are safe drivers? Cf. Samuel Issacharoff & Justin Nelson, *Discrimination with a Difference: Can Employment Discrimination Law Accommodate the Americans with Disabilities Act?*, 79 N.C. L. Rev. 307, 325 (2001) ("Perhaps showing its frustration with the potential sweep of ADA claims, the Court virtually abandoned the narrow statutory structure and interposed a broader policy concern about the statute" in *Albertson's*.).

Recall the Supreme Court's decision in *Sutton v. United Air Lines, Inc.* (excerpted in Chapter Two). There, in holding that the determination of whether a plaintiff has a "disability" must take account of any mitigating measures the individual plaintiff uses, the Court emphasized the ADA's core purpose of requiring employers to treat people with disabilities as individuals, rather than as members of medical-diagnostic categories. The Court decided *Albertson's* on the same day it decided *Sutton*, yet *Albertson's* permits employers to make precisely the sorts of categorical judgments *Sutton* rejects. What can explain the difference?

3. Disability Rights versus Public Safety? One might think of disability discrimination law as prohibiting employers from making categorical determinations of *incapacity*—*i.e.*, that all people with some class of disability are incapable of performing the tasks required by the job—but not as prohibiting employers from making categorical determinations about *safety*—*i.e.*, that all people with some class of disability pose an unjustified risk of physical harm to themselves or others. The ADA contains specific language governing discrimination on the basis of safety risks, to which the *Albertson's* Court refers, and which is discussed in depth in Section C below. Nevertheless, the public-safety overtones of *Albertsons*'s seem at the least to have made the Court more comfortable with endorsing a categorical exclusion. But was the Court right to give decisive weight to the Federal Highway Administration's determination that it is generally unsafe for people with monocular vision to drive commercial vehicles? The FHWA acted pursuant to a statute that required the agency to resolve all uncertainty in favor of accident prevention. See *Advocates for Highway and Auto Safety v. Federal Highway Admin.*, 28 F.3d 1288, 1294 (D.C.Cir.1994). Under such a regime, an agency has an incentive to respond to uncertainty with rules categorically excluding people with disabilities from even potentially risky activities. See, *e.g.*, Paula E. Berg, *When the Hazard is Human: Irrationality, Inequity, and Unintended Consequences in Federal Regulation of Contagion*, 75 Wash. U. L.Q. 1367, 1389–1392 (1997) (describing how the Occupational Safety and Health Administration, which operates under a similar statute, has encouraged employers to simply exclude workers with actual or suspected tuberculosis from entering their facilities). Ought a disability rights law like the ADA to be read to defer to the judgments of these sorts of single-minded regulatory agencies?

Bates v. United Parcel Service, Inc.

United States Court of Appeals for the Ninth Circuit, *en banc*, 2007.
511 F.3d 974.

■ McKEOWN, CIRCUIT JUDGE:

This appeal under the Americans with Disabilities Act (ADA) requires us to consider the intersection of a safety-based qualification standard and the "business necessity" defense. United Parcel Service (UPS) imposes a Department of Transportation (DOT) hearing standard on all package-car drivers, even though the DOT standard is federally mandated only for higher-weight vehicles. A class of hearing-impaired UPS employees and applicants who cannot meet the DOT hearing requirement challenges UPS's policy under Title I of the ADA, 42 U.S.C. §§ 12101–12213[.]

Bates accepts, as he must, that UPS may lawfully exclude individuals who fail the DOT test from positions that would require them to drive DOT-regulated vehicles, *i.e.*, vehicles exceeding a gross vehicle weight rating (GVWR) of 10,000 pounds. *See Albertson's*. Bates contends, however, that UPS may not lawfully exclude hearing-impaired individuals from consideration for positions that involve vehicles whose GVWR is less than 10,001 pounds.

After a bench trial on liability, the district court found UPS liable, [e]njoined UPS from using the blanket qualification standard, and required individualized assessment of candidates for the package-car driver positions. [W]e granted rehearing *en banc* to consider the contours of a claim that an employer's safety qualification standard discriminates against otherwise "qualified" persons with disabilities, *see* 42 U.S.C. § 12112(a), (b)(6), and the showing required of an employer to successfully assert the business necessity defense to use of such qualification under 42 U.S.C. § 12113(a). [W]e vacate and remand for further proceedings.

[B]ACKGROUND

UPS AND PACKAGE-CAR DRIVERS

UPS package-car drivers deliver and pick up packages for UPS in the familiar brown UPS trucks. UPS employs more than 320,000 employees in the United States, over 70,000 of whom are package-car drivers.

When an opening for a driving position becomes available, UPS contacts the individual in that UPS center with the highest seniority who has bid on such a position. If that person is not interested, UPS moves down the list in descending seniority order until it finds an interested employee. The applicant must satisfy several requirements, which vary from district to district, but generally include (1) having completed an application; (2) being at least twenty-one years of age; (3) possessing a valid driver's license; and (4) having a "clean" driving record. Once the seniority threshold and other prerequisites to employment are met, all applicants for a package-car driver position must pass both UPS's road test and the DOT physical examination required of drivers of commercial vehicles over 10,000 pounds. UPS has a policy of hiring only drivers who can satisfy DOT standards.

At issue in this appeal is the hearing standard that is part of the DOT physical. An individual satisfies the DOT hearing standard if he

> [f]irst perceives a forced whispered voice in the better ear at not less than 5 feet with or without the use of a hearing aid or, if tested by use of an audiometric device, does not have an average hearing loss in the better ear greater than 40 decibels at 500 Hz, 1,000 Hz, and 2,000 Hz with or without a hearing aid when the audiometric device is calibrated to American National Standard (formerly ASA Standard) Z24.5–1951.

49 C.F.R. § 391.41(b)(11). According to the district court, the forced-whispered standard requires that potential drivers not only hear the sounds made but understand the words spoken.

Unlike UPS, which requires drivers of all package cars to pass the DOT physical, the DOT imposes this standard only for those driving vehicles with a GVWR of at least 10,001 pounds. *See* 49 U.S.C. § 31132(1)(A); 49 C.F.R. § 391.41. A "gross vehicle weight rating" is the actual weight of the vehicle plus any cargo capacity. As of October 2003, UPS's fleet contained 65,198 vehicles, of which 5,902 vehicles had a GVWR of less than 10,001 pounds. The GVWR of the lighter vehicles ranged from 7,160 to 9,318 pounds, with the majority of these vehicles weighing 8,600 pounds. By way of comparison, automobiles, which include passenger cars, sport utility vehicles, light trucks and minivans, average 3,240 pounds.

PROCEEDINGS IN THE DISTRICT COURT

In November 2001, the district court certified a nationwide federal class on the ADA claim that includes "[t]hose persons throughout the United States who (i) have been employed by and/or applied for employment with [UPS] at any time since June 25, 1997, up through the conclusion of this action, (ii) use sign language as a primary means of communication due to a hearing loss or limitation, and (iii) allege that their rights have been violated under Title I of the ADA on account of [UPS's] policies and procedures." The federal class was certified under Federal Rule of Civil Procedure 23(b)(2) to seek primarily injunctive and declaratory relief. As part of its post-trial findings and conclusions, the district court modified the composition of the class on the "driving issue" to include "only those individuals who failed or would fail the DOT hearing test." *See* Fed.R.Civ.P. 23(c)(1)(C) ("An order [certifying an action as a "class action"] under Rule 23(c)(1) may be altered or amended before final judgment.").

Phase one of the bifurcated bench trial was conducted over several weeks in the spring and fall of 2003. [F]ollowing phase one of the trial, the district court issued detailed findings of fact and conclusions of law. The district court found that Bates satisfied his prima facie case based upon a combination of two factors: first, UPS's policy operated as a blanket exclusion of deaf individuals, and second, at least one named plaintiff, Babaranti Oloyede, and at least one class member, Elias Habib, were "qualified" individuals with a disability with standing to sue under the ADA by virtue of having satisfied all prerequisites for the driving position other than the DOT hearing requirement. The court further concluded that Bates did not have the burden to establish at that stage that any plaintiffs were "qualified" in the sense that they were capable of driving safely. Accordingly, the district court denied UPS's motions for judgment under Rule 52(c) and to decertify the class.

Critical to its ruling, the district court next found that [U]PS failed to satisfy its burden under the business necessity defense. Thus, the court reasoned, UPS's categorical exclusion of individuals who do not meet the DOT hearing requirement violates the ADA. [T]he district court entered an injunction requiring UPS to "cease using the DOT hearing standard to screen applicants for package-car driver positions" with respect to vehicles weighing 10,000 pounds or less and to "perform an individualized assessment" of applicants that meet the threshold qualifications, other than the hearing standard. Upon UPS's motion, the district court stayed all further proceedings pending UPS's interlocutory appeal.

ANALYSIS

[III]. LEGAL FRAMEWORK APPLICABLE TO A "QUALIFICATION STANDARD" CLAIM UNDER THE ADA

[B]. APPLICABLE PROVISIONS OF THE ADA

[T]here is no dispute that the class members, who are hearing impaired, are disabled. Instead, we focus on the two other key terms in the statute: "qualified individual" and "discriminate." To unpack the meaning of these terms, we look to the statute. [W]e turn first to the qualified individual inquiry and then to the question of discrimination.

C. QUALIFIED INDIVIDUAL WITH A DISABILITY

As the plaintiff, Bates bears the burden to prove that he is "qualified." Qualification for a position is a two-step inquiry. The court first examines whether the individual satisfies the "requisite skill, experience, education and other job-related requirements" of the position. The court then considers whether the individual "can perform the essential functions of such position" with or without a reasonable accommodation. 29 C.F.R. § 1630.2(m); 42 U.S.C. § 12111(8).

1. JOB REQUISITES

The package-car driver job requires an applicant to meet UPS's threshold seniority requirements for the package-car driver position, complete an application, be at least twenty-one years of age, possess a valid driver's license, and have a clean driving record by UPS's local standards. The district court's finding that named plaintiff Oloyede and class member Elias Habib meet these prerequisites is not clearly erroneous.

2. ESSENTIAL FUNCTIONS

To prove that he is "qualified," the applicant also must show that he can perform the "essential functions" of the job. 42 U.S.C. § 12111(8). As noted earlier, a job's "essential functions" are "fundamental job duties of the employment position . . . not includ[ing] the marginal functions of the position." 29 C.F.R. § 1630.2(n)(1); *see also id.* § 1630.2(n)(2)-(3) (elaborating on reasons and evidence relevant to an essential function showing). "Essential functions" are not to be confused with "qualification standards," which an employer may establish for a certain position. Whereas "essential functions" are basic "duties," 29 C.F.R. § 1630.2(n)(1), "qualification standards" are "personal and professional attributes" that may include "physical, medical [and] safety" requirements. *Id.* § 1630.2(q). The difference is crucial.

The statute does not require that a person meet each of an employer's established "qualification standards," however, to show that he is "qualified." And, indeed, it would make little sense to require an ADA plaintiff to show that he meets a qualification standard that he undisputedly *cannot* meet because of his disability and that forms the very basis of his discrimination challenge.

Although the plaintiff bears the ultimate burden of persuading the fact finder that he can perform the job's essential functions, we agree with the Eighth Circuit's approach that "an employer who disputes the plaintiff's claim that he can perform the essential functions must put forth evidence establishing those functions." *EEOC v. Wal-Mart*, 477 F.3d 561, 568 (8th Cir.2007). The genesis of this rule is the recognition that "much of the information which determines those essential functions lies uniquely with the employer." *Benson v. Nw. Airlines, Inc.*, 62 F.3d 1108, 1113 (8th Cir.1995). In addition, the ADA and implementing regulations direct fact finders to consider, among other things, "the employer's judgment as to what functions of a job are essential," 42 U.S.C. § 12111(8); job descriptions prepared before advertising or interviewing applicants, *id.*; "[t]he amount of time spent on the job performing the function," 29 C.F.R. § 1630.2(n)(3)(iii); "[t]he consequences of not requiring the [applicant or employee] to perform the function," *id.* § 1630.2(n)(3)(iv); and the work experience of current and former employees. *Id.* § 1630.2(n)(3)(vi), (vii). Thus, to the extent that an employer challenges an ADA plaintiff's claim that he can perform the job's essential functions, we think it appropriate to place a burden of production on the employer to come forward with evidence of those essential functions.

At trial the parties agreed that two of the "essential functions" of the package-car driver position are (1) "the ability to communicate effectively" and (2) "the ability to drive safely." UPS urged that "the ability to drive DOT-regulated vehicles" was another essential function. The district court rejected that contention, finding that UPS permits other drivers who cannot drive all DOT-regulated vehicles to drive package cars. For example, UPS has protocols in place for driver applicants who cannot pass certain DOT certification requirements because of their vision impairments or insulin-dependent diabetes, but who can pass less stringent physical requirements. UPS has not shown that the district court's determination that DOT certification is not an essential job function was clearly erroneous.

Only the second essential function, "safe driving," is at issue in this appeal. UPS argues that "hearing" at a level sufficient to pass the DOT hearing standard is either a stand-alone essential job function or part and parcel of being a safe driver. This point illustrates the critical difference between a job's essential functions—"effective communication" or "safe driving"—versus a qualification standard based on "personal or professional attributes," such as hearing at a certain level. The question, then, is whether plaintiffs established that they meet the essential function of safe driving.

The district court found that Oloyede met UPS's threshold requirements of having no accidents or moving violations within the last year, no DUI within the last three years, and no more than three moving violations in the last three years. Habib also met the prerequisites to apply for the position: a valid driver's license, twenty-seven years of driving experience, and no evidence of even a minor traffic accident.

UPS urges that Oloyede and Habib are required to show not only that they are "safe" drivers in the sense that they have a "clean driving record," but also that they are safe drivers even though they are hearing impaired. The district court rejected that argument, stating that imposing this burden would require plaintiffs to disprove the employer's business necessity affirmative defense, *i.e.*, that the employer is justified in imposing a qualification standard that facially screens out individuals with a specific disability.

Because UPS has linked hearing with safe driving, UPS bears the burden to prove that nexus as part of its defense to use of the hearing qualification standard. The employees, however, bear the ultimate burden to show that they are qualified to perform the essential function of safely driving a package car. In so doing, Oloyede and Habib need not disprove the validity of the hearing standard, but must demonstrate their safe driving ability vis-à-vis package cars. The inquiry is not whether Oloyede and Habib are capable of safely driving their personal cars, but rather whether they can drive the package cars at issue in this litigation. The district court did not make a finding with respect to plaintiffs' ability to drive package cars safely. Merely finding an absence of evidence with respect to driving a package car is insufficient. In short, Oloyede and Habib bear the burden of proving that they are qualified individuals with disabilities. They must show that they can perform the essential job function of safely driving package cars. Only if they meet this burden does the question become whether the qualification standard used by the employer satisfies the business necessity defense.

By requiring UPS to justify the hearing test under the business necessity defense, but also requiring plaintiffs to show that they can perform the essential functions of the job, we are not saying, nor does the ADA require, that employers must hire employees who cannot safely perform the job, particularly where safety itself is an essential function. Nor are we saying that an employer can never impose a safety standard that exceeds minimum requirements imposed by law. However, when an employer asserts a blanket safety-based qualification standard—beyond the essential job function—that is not mandated by law and that qualification standard screens out or tends to screen out an individual with a disability, the employer—not the employee—bears the burden of showing that the higher qualification standard is job-related and consistent with business necessity, and that performance cannot be achieved through reasonable accommodation. 42 U.S.C. § 12113(a).

This approach is parallel to the one adopted in a "direct threat" case under the ADA. 42 U.S.C. § 12113(b) ("The term 'qualification standards' may include a requirement that an individual shall not pose a direct threat to the health or safety of other individuals in the workplace."). Although the specifics of proof in direct threat and business necessity cases may vary, the frameworks are parallel. We emphasize that UPS is not required to meet the requirements of the direct threat defense, but rather that cases under that section of the ADA illuminate our analysis.

[T]he employee does not bear the burden to invalidate the employer's safety-based qualification standard. Nor is the employee required to disprove UPS's contention that, in order to be safe, the driver must pass the DOT hearing standard—the very qualification standard disputed in this case. [W]e conclude that an employee who shows that he meets the basic qualifications for the package-car driver position (seniority, twenty-one years of age, and holding a valid driver's license) and can drive a package car safely, including having a clean driving record and passing the driving test, is an otherwise qualified individual.

The last step of the "qualified individual" inquiry requires a plaintiff to show that he is qualified "with or without reasonable accommodation." 42 U.S.C. § 12111(8). If the plaintiff proves that he can perform the job's essential functions either without a reasonable accommodation or with such an accommodation, then he has met his burden to show he is qualified. Here, the district court did not explicitly discuss reasonable accommodation, although in finding that Oloyede and Habib met the job requisites and could perform the essential function of safe driving, it implicitly found that no accommodation was necessary to meet those baseline requirements for UPS package-car driver applicants.

Because the district court did not analyze whether Oloyede and Habib are "qualified individuals" capable of performing the "essential function" of safely driving a package car in the framework discussed above, nor did it directly undertake the "qualified individual" inquiry, we remand to the district court for the employees to prove that they are so qualified and for an analysis of reasonable accommodation. Thus, we vacate the district court's order denying UPS's motion for judgment on partial findings under Rule 52(c), and in the alternative to decertify the nationwide class under Rule 23(c)(1) and (d).

D. DISCRIMINATION BECAUSE OF DISABILITY

An employee bears the burden of proving that he was discriminated against "because of" a disability. 42 U.S.C. § 12112(a). The qualification standard at issue—the DOT hearing standard—is facially discriminatory and falls squarely within the ADA's definition of discrimination. 42 U.S.C. § 12112(b)(6) ("discrimination" includes using qualification standards, employment tests or other selection criteria that screen out or tend to screen out an individual with a disability or a class of individuals with disabilities).

The district court found, and UPS does not contest, that UPS applies a qualification standard that has the effect of discriminating on the basis of disability and/or screens out the class of employees who cannot pass the DOT hearing standard. *See* 42 U.S.C. § 12112(b)(6). Such discrimination violates the ADA *unless* UPS can prove a valid defense to its use of the DOT hearing standard. We therefore turn to UPS's defense that its reliance on the DOT hearing standard is justified under the business necessity defense.

E. EMPLOYER'S "BUSINESS NECESSITY" DEFENSE

Under the ADA, an employer may assert an affirmative defense to a claim that application of a qualification standard, test or selection criteria discriminates on the basis of disability. *See* 42 U.S.C. § 12113(a); *Albertson's.* Although the shorthand reference is the "business necessity" defense, the defense also incorporates requirements of job-relatedness and reasonable accommodation.

[W]e look first and foremost to the text of the ADA:

> It may be a defense to a charge of discrimination under this chapter that an *alleged application of qualification standards, tests, or selection criteria* that screen out or tend to screen out or otherwise deny a job or benefit to an individual with a disability has been shown to be *job-related and consistent with business necessity,* and such performance *cannot be accomplished by reasonable accommodation,* as required under this subchapter.

42 U.S.C. § 12113(a) (emphasis added). To successfully assert the business necessity defense to an allegedly discriminatory application of a qualification standard, test or selection criteria, an employer bears the

burden of showing that the qualification standard is (1) "job-related," (2) "consistent with business necessity," and (3) that "performance cannot be accomplished by reasonable accommodation." *Id.*

[T]o show "job-relatedness," an employer must demonstrate that the qualification standard fairly and accurately measures the individual's actual ability to perform the essential functions of the job. When every person excluded by the qualification standard is a member of a protected class—that is, disabled persons—an employer must demonstrate a predictive or significant correlation between the qualification and performance of the job's essential functions. *Albemarle Paper Co. v. Moody,* 422 U.S. 405, 431 (1975); *Cf. Clady v. County of Los Angeles,* 770 F.2d 1421, 1432 (9th Cir.1985) ("As a general principle, the greater the test's adverse impact, the higher the correlation which will be required.") (analyzing business necessity defense to Title VII disparate impact claim).

To show that the disputed qualification standard is "consistent with business necessity," the employer must show that it "substantially promote[s]" the business's needs. *Cripe [v. City of San Jose],* 261 F.3d [877,] 890 [(9th Cir. 2001)] (quoting *Bentivegna v. U.S. Dep't of Labor,* 694 F.2d 619, 621–22 (9th Cir.1982) (interpreting the term "business necessity" for purposes of the Rehabilitation Act of 1973)). As we observed in *Cripe:* "The 'business necessity' standard is quite high, and is not to be confused with mere expediency." For a safety-based qualification standard, "[i]n evaluating whether the risks addressed by . . . [the] qualification standard constitute a business necessity, the court should take into account the magnitude of possible harm as well as the probability of occurrence." *EEOC v. Exxon Corp.,* 203 F.3d 871, 875 (5th Cir.2000) (noting that "[t]he acceptable probability of an incident will vary with the potential hazard posed by the particular position: a probability that might be tolerable in an ordinary job might be intolerable for a position involving atomic reactors, for example").

Finally, to show that "performance cannot be accomplished by reasonable accommodation," the employer must demonstrate either that no reasonable accommodation currently available would cure the performance deficiency or that such reasonable accommodation poses an "undue hardship" on the employer. *See* 42 U.S.C. §§ 12113(a), 12111(10) (defining "undue hardship").

[I]n rejecting UPS's business necessity defense to application of the DOT hearing standard to all package-car driving positions, the district court concluded that "UPS has demonstrated neither that all or substantially all deaf drivers pose a higher risk of accidents than non-deaf drivers nor that there are no practical criteria for determining which deaf drivers pose a heightened risk and which do not. Additionally, UPS has not demonstrated that it would be impossible to develop empirical evidence that would be sufficient to make either showing." This finding does not track the statutory elements of the business necessity defense. [W]e vacate the finding that UPS violated Bates's rights under the ADA, vacate the injunction, and remand for proceedings consistent with this opinion.

[T]he district court also rejected UPS's reliance on the DOT's hearing standard. [U]PS offered up the DOT standard as evidence that, for safety purposes, a certain level of hearing is necessary to drive non-DOT-regulated vehicles. According to UPS, there is complete congruity between the positions of driving a DOT-regulated package car (more than 10,000 pounds) and driving a vehicle that weighs a little less. UPS argued that package cars weighing almost five tons do not have operating characteristics similar to passenger cars and pose greater risks than do passenger cars.

To be sure, DOT's regulation does not apply to the category of vehicles at issue in this case. However, that circumstance does not mean that the standard has no relevance to the employer's safety argument. UPS is entitled to use as some evidence of its business necessity defense the fact that it relied on a government safety standard, even where the standard is not applicable to the category of conduct at issue. [C]f. Albertson's (holding that an employer is not required to justify its decision to require that employees meet an *applicable* government safety regulation, even if the government permits waiver of the applicable requirements under an experimental policy). The parallel consideration applies to an employee; that is, an employee may offer as evidence challenging the validity or applicability of a safety standard the government's refusal to adopt such standard to govern the conduct at issue. *See, e.g.,* 53 Fed.Reg. 18042, 18044 (discussing DOT's rejection of UPS's attempt to apply DOT's physical requirements to trucks under 10,000 pounds because (1) smaller trucks and vans have "operating characteristics" more comparable to cars; and (2) smaller trucks and vans pose a lesser "safety risk" than large trucks).

Thus, while certainly not dispositive of UPS's showing of job-relatedness, business necessity or the reasonableness of potential accommodations, UPS's reliance on the government safety standard with respect to other vehicles in its fleet should be entitled to some consideration as a safety benchmark. Whether, as UPS puts it, "non-DOT package cars in the UPS fleet share significant risk characteristics with their slightly larger cousins" is a factual question of the congruity between vehicles and drivers in UPS's non-DOT fleet and those regulated by DOT. We leave it to the fact finder to determine how much weight to give such evidence.

[V]. INJUNCTION

The district court stayed enforcement of its injunction pending UPS's interlocutory appeal. We vacate the injunction and remand to the district court for further proceedings consistent with this opinion.

VACATED IN PART, REVERSED IN PART, AND REMANDED.
Each party shall bear its own costs on appeal.

■ BERZON, CIRCUIT JUDGE, WITH WHOM CIRCUIT JUDGE REINHARDT JOINS, CONCURRING IN PART, DISSENTING IN PART, AND CONCURRING IN THE JUDGMENT:

I would approach the "qualified individual" and Department of Transportation (DOT) hearing standard inquiries differently than does the majority, but do agree that this case must be remanded for re-examination under the majority's statement of the business necessity framework. I therefore concur only in Parts I, II, III(A)-(C)(1), III(D), III(E), IV(B), and V of the majority opinion, and in the judgment.

I.

The majority holds that to be "qualified individuals with disabilities" Oloyede and Habib (or some other member of the class) must show that they can "perform the essential job function of safely driving package cars." The majority opinion is entirely unclear, however, as to how they are to do so. In my view, such a requirement can be squared with the statute and with the complaint in this case, if at all, only if understood as imposing a definable, threshold burden.

1.

Oloyede and Habib ask in their complaint just that the district court order UPS to "individually assess ... hearing disabled workers to determine if they are able to safely drive vehicles where DOT regulations are not applicable." In other words, although the plaintiffs certainly hope eventually to become package car drivers, they are *not* seeking to bypass UPS's package car driver testing, training, and probation programs and be placed directly into the driver's seat. The district court explicitly limited its relief to mandating individual assessment.

UPS's requirements and programs are extensive. First, applicants must have adequate seniority and clean driving records to begin the application process. Then, in addition to the DOT physical, applicants must pass a driving test to enter the program. If they pass, they enter a driving training course with both on-the-road and classroom components. If they pass *that* course, they embark on a thirty-day probationary period, with supervisors sometimes riding along. Only if they pass all these hurdles do those who enter the program become UPS package car drivers.

The majority opinion would require the plaintiffs to bear the ultimate burden of proving that they will be safe package car drivers, so as to show that they are qualified persons with disabilities. But, perhaps because it does not recognize the limited nature of the relief sought, the majority leaves unclear what it is asking of the district court and of the parties on remand with regard to that requirement.

Requiring the plaintiffs to prove that they will be safe package car drivers, as the majority opinion does, will unnecessarily complicate this litigation on remand. "Safe" is not a self-defining term, and particularly is not so in the context of industrial safety decisions; nor is it self-evident whether any particular scheme for predicting whether a person who has never driven a package car safely will be able to do so is likely to yield valid results. Thus, asking Oloyede and Habib to prove that they are "safe" without providing guidance as to how they are to do so, or as to how "safe" is "safe" in this context, presents the litigants and the district court with an ill-defined and complicated puzzle. Yet, such a requirement is extraneous given the limited nature of the relief Oloyede and Habib seek. UPS has designed evaluation methods using its own vehicles to test for the degree of safety it requires, so it makes little sense to suggest that Oloyede and Habib must devise, validate, and pass their *own* safety tests and training programs before they may sue to take *UPS's* tests and training programs—which, again, is all that they seek to do.

Here, what makes sense is to require the plaintiffs to meet UPS's threshold requirements for entry into the package car driver testing and training program. UPS itself will then be able individually to evaluate them for the job they desire, according to UPS's own standards and methods (with appropriate accommodations, if requested and if the need for them is proven, *see* 42 U.S.C. § 12111(8)-(9) (defining "qualified individual" and "reasonable accommodation"); *Dark v. Curry County,* 451 F.3d 1078, 1088 (9th Cir.2006) (explaining the reasonable accommodation process).

Practically speaking, under the approach I suggest, once a deaf applicant shows that he meets the normal threshold qualifications for eligibility—that he is at least twenty-one years of age, possesses a valid driver's license, and has a clean driving record by UPS's local standards—he has met his burden of proof in this regard. It is then UPS's burden to show, if it desires to adopt as a threshold requirement a minimum hearing level such as the DOT standard, that it can establish under the business necessity test that deaf applicants as a group who do not meet that requirement cannot drive package cars safely. Unless UPS can establish a business necessity supporting such a blanket requirement, either by validating the application of the DOT standard to deaf drivers or by adopting some other validated standard for such drivers, it must allow hearing impaired applicants to take the same initial driving test, benefit from the same training program, and be subject to the same final test as all other applicants, all with reasonable accommodations if necessary.

This approach in no way compromises the safety of UPS's driving force, as there are other stages, after applicants are deemed qualified to commence training, at which drivers, including deaf drivers who cannot safely drive package trucks, may be weeded out. If the final test, for example, shows that a deaf applicant is fully capable of driving safely, regardless of the extent of his hearing impairment, he should not be disqualified from employment. If, however, it reveals that an applicant's hearing impairment results in an inability to avoid accidents to the same extent as drivers without hearing impairments, he should be deemed to have failed the test. The key, accordingly, is to design a training and testing program that will eliminate all applicants who pose a safety hazard regardless of whether the cause is hearing impairment, inadequate vision, lack of judgment, slow reflexes, lack of intelligence, or some disability other than a hearing impairment.

In this case, should the plaintiffs prevail and be allowed to undergo the training program, UPS would be free to design a test to be administered following its completion. By doing so, it would test the ability of all potential employees, including those who are hearing-impaired, to drive in a safe manner. Oloyede and Habib would be allowed, if they pass the initial driving test, to enroll in the training program and take the final test upon its completion. Those who fail the testing and training program for reasons related to their hearing impairment, would, of course, be entitled to challenge it on the ground that it did not properly measure whether such employees could perform the essential functions of the position. But, absent such a challenge, and absent UPS proof of the DOT standard or some other hearing impairment standard as a business necessity, plaintiffs and other deaf drivers would demonstrate that they are safe drivers in the same manner as all other employees who desire to be package car drivers.

As I read the district court's opinion, it is consistent with this basic approach. I would not, therefore, vacate the district court's holding on the "qualified individual" point.

2.

The majority opinion holds, instead, that the district court erred by not specifically examining whether Oloyede and Habib are now capable of *driving* a package car safely, rather than just whether they can drive safely enough to be eligible for UPS's package car driver assessment program. Still, the majority opinion may not require significantly more proof of Oloyede and Habib than they have already adduced, except in one respect.

UPS does not decide whether participants in its training program can drive a package car safely enough to meet UPS's risk standards until the *end* of the program. Instead, it uses the entry requirements and the initial phases of the training program—most notably, a driving test—to decide whether applicants are, at a first cut, *likely* to be able to perform that essential job function and so should be allowed to continue training for the job. Surely, Oloyede and Habib, who have never driven package cars, are not required to show that they are *more* able to perform the essential job function of ultimately driving a package car safely than any other similarly inexperienced UPS employee who successfully passes the initial screening for the training program. Instead, they must simply be as qualified as hearing employees must be at that initial stage. The majority's description of its required evidentiary showing suggests as much, as it would include meeting UPS's entrance requirements and tests, including "having a clean driving record," *and* "passing the driving test," not more.

So, on remand, the district court may approach the qualified individual inquiry under the majority opinion by deciding whether the plaintiffs can show that they are likely to be able to drive package cars as safely as other training program *entrants*. The district court, on remand, may rely upon the evidence already provided by Oloyede and Habib, or on any other evidence they may introduce. Also, the district court may order discovery on the UPS driving test given to program entrants to allow Oloyede or Habib (or some other class representative) to reconstruct and then take the same test. Members of the class who meet all valid requirements and can pass that test, with or without reasonable accommodations, would then be as qualified to be package car drivers as other employees entering the training program, and will meet their burden of proof in this litigation.

To require the plaintiffs to show any more to meet their burden of proof would be to suppose that UPS's training program is a useless formality in no way essential to teaching strategies and skills necessary to drive package cars safely. UPS obviously does not believe that, and neither should we. As deaf potential drivers have not had the opportunity to learn those skills and strategies, they cannot fairly be measured for safety against drivers who have. And, there is no way potential deaf drivers can reproduce and prove that they can pass a several-week program supervised by experienced UPS trainers. So, as far as I can tell, deaf drivers should be able to show they can drive a package car safely and so are "qualified persons with a disability," as the majority requires, simply by passing a driving test equivalent to the one UPS requires to enter its package car driver training program.

II.

The majority opinion is also somewhat unclear on how the district court should review the evidence supporting UPS's business necessity defense of the DOT hearing standard. The majority remands on this question, directing the district court to give "some consideration" to the DOT's use of the standard for larger vehicles as evidence for business necessity.

It appears to me that the district court has largely already done so. It devoted several pages of careful analysis to explaining the empirical and statistical deficiencies inherent in extending the DOT hearing standard beyond the area in which it now applies. It examined the studies supporting such an extension, noting that the data supporting their conclusions is "extremely dated," that the studies used different definitions and methodologies and so are not easily comparable, and that the studies do not, themselves, tie the DOT hearing standard to particular risk levels.

[I]n any event, the majority does not disapprove of the district court's factual findings on this point, and instead only remands to the district court for it to consider the question under the business necessity framework that the majority opinion today enunciates. That directive is perfectly proper, because it is possible—although, I suggest, not probable— that the analysis will come out differently under the business necessity standard as we enunciate it today. But nothing in the majority opinion prevents the district court from examining in that context the same methodological and empirical flaws it previously discussed.

Those flaws may well be significant under today's standard. As the majority demonstrates, "business necessity" is not an easy hurdle for an employer to surmount, particularly when using discriminatory employment tests or qualification standards. As we have held in the Title VII context, "[a]s a general principle, the greater the test's adverse impact [on protected individuals], the higher the correlation [between the qualification standard and the essential functions of the job] which will be required." *Clady v. County of Los Angeles,* 770 F.2d 1421, 1432 (9th Cir.1985). Here, UPS's use of the DOT hearing standard excludes, if not 100% of deaf individuals (as a few may pass), then at least the vast majority of such individuals. Under our law, such a facially-discriminatory qualification standard must be well-justified indeed. The district court's initial analysis demonstrates the thinness of the data supporting UPS's use of the DOT hearing standard. On remand, the district court will have to decide whether the business necessity framework, as described in the majority opinion, can tolerate such serious impacts justified with such scanty data.

Only if the district court decides that the DOT hearing standard is supported by business necessity could UPS use the hearing standard to exclude deaf individuals as a group. Any other result would leave in place the barriers, based in group stereotypes rather than in thoughtful individual consideration, that the ADA seeks to root out of American society[.]

NOTES ON BATES V. UPS

How does *Bates* reconcile the ADA's "qualified individual" and "qualification standards" terms? Unlike Justice Thomas in *Albertson's*, the *Bates* court does seem to draw a conceptual distinction between the two terms: To be a "qualified individual" for the driver position at issue, the plaintiffs must carry the burden of demonstrating that they can drive package cars safely If they satisfy that burden, but fail to satisfy the employer's selection criteria (here, the criterion that drivers must satisfy the DOT requirements for vehicles with a GVWR of over 10,000 pounds), the employer must carry the burden of demonstrating that the criteria are job-related and consistent with business necessity and that no reasonable accommodation is available. One way of understanding this holding is as requiring the individual plaintiff to establish that she can in fact do the job (perhaps with reasonable accommodation) but at the same time allowing the employer to nonetheless exclude such capable individuals pursuant to rules that sort a broad mass of applicants—so long as those rules have, in general, a sufficient basis.

Does *Bates*'s analysis of the interaction of the "qualified individual" and "qualification standards" provisions conform to the statutory text? Does the resulting scheme make sense? What precise burden does it place on employers to justify their exclusionary "qualification standards"? By placing on employers in cases challenging "qualification standards" the burden to show the *absence* of any reasonable accommodation, did the *Bates* court contradict the Supreme Court's opinion in *Barnett*?

2.   JUDICIAL ESTOPPEL

Cleveland v. Policy Management Systems Corp.

Supreme Court of the United States, 1999.
526 U.S. 795.

■ JUSTICE BREYER delivered the opinion of the Court.

The Social Security Disability Insurance (SSDI) program provides benefits to a person with a disability so severe that she is "unable to do [her] previous work" and "cannot . . . engage in any other kind of substantial gainful work which exists in the national economy." § 223(a) of the Social Security Act, as set forth in 42 U.S.C. § 423(d)(2)(A). This case asks whether the law erects a special presumption that would significantly inhibit an SSDI recipient from simultaneously pursuing an action for disability discrimination under the Americans with Disabilities Act of 1990(ADA), claiming that "with . . . reasonable accommodation" she could "perform the essential functions" of her job. § 101, 104 Stat. 331, 42 U.S.C. § 12111(8).

We believe that, in context, these two seemingly divergent statutory contentions are often consistent, each with the other. Thus pursuit, and receipt, of SSDI benefits does not automatically estop the recipient from pursuing an ADA claim. Nor does the law erect a strong presumption against the recipient's success under the ADA. Nonetheless, an ADA plaintiff cannot simply ignore her SSDI contention that she was too disabled to work. To survive a defendant's motion for summary judgment, she must explain why that SSDI contention is consistent with her ADA claim that she could "perform the essential functions" of her previous job, at least with "reasonable accommodation."

I

After suffering a disabling stroke and losing her job, Carolyn Cleveland sought and obtained SSDI benefits from the Social Security Administration (SSA). She has also brought this ADA suit in which she claims that her former employer, Policy Management Systems Corporation, discriminated against her on account of her disability. The two claims developed in the following way:

August 1993: Cleveland began work at Policy Management Systems. Her job required her to perform background checks on prospective employees of Policy Management System's clients.

January 7, 1994: Cleveland suffered a stroke, which damaged her concentration, memory, and language skills.

January 28, 1994: Cleveland filed an SSDI application in which she stated that she was "disabled" and "unable to work."

April 11, 1994: Cleveland's condition having improved, she returned to work with Policy Management Systems. She reported that fact to the SSA two weeks later.

July 11, 1994: Noting that Cleveland had returned to work, the SSA denied her SSDI application.

July 15, 1994: Policy Management Systems fired Cleveland.

September 14, 1994: Cleveland asked the SSA to reconsider its July 11th SSDI denial. In doing so, she said: "I was terminated [by Policy Management Systems] due to my condition and I have not been able to work since. I continue to be disabled." She later added that she had "attempted to return to work in mid April," that she had "worked for three months," and that Policy Management Systems terminated her because she "could no longer do the job" in light of her "condition."

November 1994: The SSA denied Cleveland's request for reconsideration. Cleveland sought an SSA hearing, reiterating that "I am unable to work due to my disability," and presenting new evidence about the extent of her injuries.

September 29, 1995: The SSA awarded Cleveland SSDI benefits retroactive to the day of her stroke, January 7, 1994.

On September 22, 1995, the week before her SSDI award, Cleveland brought this ADA lawsuit. She contended that Policy Management Systems had "terminat[ed]" her employment without reasonably "accommodat[ing] her disability." She alleged that she requested, but was denied, accommodations such as training and additional time to complete her work. And she submitted a supporting affidavit from her treating physician. The District Court did not evaluate her reasonable accommodation claim on the merits, but granted summary judgment to the defendant because, in that court's view, Cleveland, by applying for and receiving SSDI benefits, had conceded that she was totally disabled. And that fact, the court concluded, now estopped Cleveland from proving an essential element of her ADA claim, namely, that she could "perform the essential functions" of her job, at least with "reasonable accommodation." 42 U.S.C. § 12111(8).

The Fifth Circuit affirmed the District Court's grant of summary judgment. [W]e granted *certiorari* in light of disagreement among the Circuits about the legal effect upon an ADA suit of the application for, or receipt of, disability benefits.

II

[A]n SSA representation of total disability differs from a purely factual statement in that it often implies a context-related legal conclusion, namely, "I am disabled for purposes of the Social Security Act." And our consideration of this latter kind of statement consequently leaves the law related to [a] purely factual [k]ind of conflict where we found it.

The case before us concerns an ADA plaintiff who both applied for, and received, SSDI benefits. [T]he Court of Appeals thought, in essence, that claims under both Acts would incorporate two directly conflicting propositions, namely, "I am too disabled to work" and "I am not too disabled to work." And in an effort to prevent two claims that would embody that kind of factual conflict, the court used a special judicial presumption, which it believed would ordinarily prevent a plaintiff like Cleveland from successfully asserting an ADA claim.

In our view, however, despite the appearance of conflict that arises from the language of the two statutes, the two claims do not inherently conflict to the point where courts should apply a special negative presumption like the one applied by the Court of Appeals here. That is because there are too many situations in which an SSDI claim and an ADA claim can comfortably exist side by side.

For one thing, as we have noted, the ADA defines a "qualified individual" to include a disabled person "who . . . can perform the essential functions" of her job "with reasonable accommodation." [B]y way of contrast, when the SSA determines whether an individual is disabled for SSDI purposes, it does not take the possibility of "reasonable accommodation" into account, nor need an applicant refer to the possibility of reasonable accommodation when she applies for SSDI. The omission reflects the facts that the SSA receives more than 2.5 million claims for disability benefits each year; its administrative resources are limited; the matter of "reasonable accommodation" may turn on highly disputed workplace-specific matters; and an SSA misjudgment about that detailed, and often fact-specific matter would deprive a seriously disabled person of the critical financial support the statute seeks to provide. The result is that an ADA suit claiming that the plaintiff can perform her job with reasonable accommodation may well prove consistent with an SSDI claim that the plaintiff could not perform her own job (or other jobs) without it.

For another thing, in order to process the large number of SSDI claims, the SSA administers SSDI with the help of a five-step procedure that embodies a set of presumptions about disabilities, job availability, and their interrelation. The SSA asks:

Step One: Are you presently working? (If so, you are ineligible.) See 20 CFR § 404.1520(b) (1998).

Step Two: Do you have a "severe impairment," i.e., one that "significantly limits" your ability to do basic work activities? (If not, you are ineligible.) See § 404.1520(c).

Step Three: Does your impairment "mee[t] or equa[l]" an impairment on a specific (and fairly lengthy) SSA list? (If so, you are eligible without more.) See §§ 404.1520(d), 404.1525, 404.1526.

Step Four: If your impairment does not meet or equal a listed impairment, can you perform your "past relevant work?" (If so, you are ineligible.) See § 404.1520(e).

Step Five: If your impairment does not meet or equal a listed impairment and you cannot perform your "past relevant work," then can you perform other jobs that exist in significant numbers in the national economy? (If not, you are eligible.) See §§ 404.1520(f), 404.1560(c).

The presumptions embodied in these questions—particularly those necessary to produce Step Three's list, which, the Government tells us, accounts for approximately 60 percent of all awards—grow out of the need to administer a large benefits system efficiently. But they inevitably simplify, eliminating consideration of many differences potentially relevant to an individual's ability to perform a particular job. Hence, an individual might qualify for SSDI under the SSA's administrative rules and yet, due to special individual circumstances, remain capable of "perform[ing] the essential functions" of her job.

Further, the SSA sometimes grants SSDI benefits to individuals who not only can work, but are working. For example, to facilitate a disabled person's reentry into the workforce, the SSA authorizes a 9-month trial-work period during which SSDI recipients may receive full benefits. Improvement in a totally disabled person's physical condition, while permitting that person to work, will not necessarily or immediately lead the SSA to terminate SSDI benefits. And the nature of an individual's disability may change over time, so that a statement about that disability at the time of an individual's application for SSDI benefits may not reflect an individual's capacities at the time of the relevant employment decision.

Finally, if an individual has merely applied for, but has not been awarded, SSDI benefits, any inconsistency in the theory of the claims is of the sort normally tolerated by our legal system. Our ordinary Rules recognize that a person may not be sure in advance upon which legal theory she will succeed, and so permit parties to "set forth two or more statements of a claim or defense alternately or hypothetically," and to "state as many separate claims or defenses as the party has regardless of consistency." Fed. Rule Civ. Proc. 8(e)(2). We do not see why the law in respect to the assertion of SSDI and ADA claims should differ.

[I]n light of these examples, we would not apply a special legal presumption permitting someone who has applied for, or received, SSDI benefits to bring an ADA suit only in "some limited and highly unusual set of circumstances."

Nonetheless, in some cases an earlier SSDI claim may turn out genuinely to conflict with an ADA claim. [A]n ADA plaintiff bears the burden of proving that she is a "qualified individual with a disability"— that is, a person "who, with or without reasonable accommodation, can perform the essential functions" of her job. 42 U.S.C. § 12111(8). And a plaintiff's sworn assertion in an application for disability benefits that she is, for example, "unable to work" will appear to negate an essential element of her ADA case—at least if she does not offer a sufficient explanation. For that reason, we hold that an ADA plaintiff cannot simply ignore the apparent contradiction that arises out of the earlier SSDI total disability claim. Rather, she must proffer a sufficient explanation.

[W]hen faced with a plaintiff's previous sworn statement asserting "total disability" or the like, the court should require an explanation of any apparent inconsistency with the necessary elements of an ADA claim. To defeat summary judgment, that explanation must be sufficient to warrant a reasonable juror's concluding that, assuming the truth of, or the plaintiff's good-faith belief in, the earlier statement, the plaintiff could nonetheless "perform the essential functions" of her job, with or without "reasonable accommodation."

III

In her brief in this Court, Cleveland explains the discrepancy between her SSDI statements that she was "totally disabled" and her ADA claim that she could "perform the essential functions" of her job. The first statements, she says, "were made in a forum which does not consider the effect that reasonable workplace accommodations would have on the ability to work." Moreover, she claims the SSDI statements were "accurate statements" if examined "in the time period in which they were made." The parties should have the opportunity in the trial court to present, or to contest, these explanations, in sworn form where appropriate. Accordingly, we vacate the judgment of the Court of Appeals and remand the case for further proceedings consistent with this opinion.

It is so ordered.

NOTES ON CLEVELAND V. POLICY MANAGEMENT SYSTEMS

1.   **Rights versus Welfare.** *Cleveland* highlights the differences and tensions between a rights-oriented approach to disability policy, like that embodied in the ADA, and a welfare-oriented approach, like that embodied in the Social Security Disability Insurance program. The ADA treats disability as a status that is often compatible with work; in keeping with the social model of disability, it targets the prejudice, stereotypes, and denials of accommodation that keep many people with disabilities from working. Disability welfare programs have long rested on a very different

understanding—that disability is a status defined by the inability to work. This understanding stemmed from the fear of undermining the rules of a market economy; unless welfare programs are strictly limited to those who cannot work, the thinking went, they will undermine the work ethic of those who can. For an excellent discussion of the impact of this understanding on the development of disability welfare programs in the United States, Great Britain, and Germany, see Deborah A. Stone, The Disabled State (1984).

In recent years, as the *Cleveland* opinion makes clear, the SSDI program has incorporated a number of rules—such as the allowance for a trial work period—that recognize that disability is not *inherently* inconsistent with work. And the various administrative rules for defining disability under the SSDI statute—including the Step Three list, and the refusal to consider the possibility of reasonable accommodations—mean that the Social Security Agency will determine that many people who can in fact work are, for statutory purposes, "under a disability." But the statute still defines disability as the inability to perform "any . . . substantial gainful work." It thus continues to rest, to a significant extent, on a model of disability as the inherent inability to work. Given the tension between that model and the ADA's model of disability as only contingently inconsistent with work, it is perhaps not surprising that many lower courts before *Cleveland* sought to divide people with disabilities into two mutually exclusive classes: (1) those who could work, who could invoke the benefits of the ADA but not disability welfare programs; and (2) those who could not work, who could invoke the benefits of disability welfare programs but not the ADA. For a good pre-*Cleveland* discussion, see Matthew Diller, *Dissonant Disability Policies: The Tensions Between the Americans with Disabilities Act and Federal Disability Benefit Programs*, 76 Tex. L. Rev. 1003 (1998).

2.   The Scope of the Court's Holding. Professor Diller echoed a common sentiment when he predicted that the *Cleveland* decision "should put an end to the widespread practice of barring disability benefit recipients from bringing cases under Title I of the ADA." Matthew Diller, *Judicial Backlash, the ADA, and the Civil Rights Model*, 21 Berkeley J. Emp. & Lab. L. 19, 30 (2000). Why would one predict that result? The *Cleveland* Court did clearly state that claims under the ADA and the SSDI statute "do not inherently conflict to the point where courts should apply a special negative presumption" against the ADA claims of SSDI recipients. The Court explained that "there are too many situations in which an SSDI claim and an ADA claim can comfortably exist side by side" to justify such a presumption. But the Court then turned around and said that "[w]hen faced with a plaintiff's previous sworn statement asserting 'total disability' or the like, the court should require an explanation of any apparent inconsistency with the necessary elements of an ADA claim." Note that the Court was not speaking about purely factual conflicts—specific, conflicting factual assertions made by the plaintiff—but about the potentially inconsistent implications of SSDI and ADA claims. Does *Cleveland*'s requirement that the plaintiff "expla[in] . . . any apparent inconsistency" give lower courts the room to continue the old practice of barring SSDI recipients from bringing cases under the ADA?

Some post-*Cleveland* lower-court cases seem very consistent with the old practice. Consider MOTLEY V. NEW JERSEY STATE POLICE, 196 F.3d 160 (3d Cir.1999). Motley was a New Jersey state police detective who had been severely injured in a work-related incident in 1990. He continued to work and received excellent performance evaluations, but because of his injuries, the department refused to permit him to take the physical examination that would make him eligible for promotion. After three years of being deemed ineligible for promotion, Motley applied for and received a disability pension from the state. In his application, Motley said that "he was 'permanently and totally disabled' as a result of the events of January 1990." Although Motley's statements, like Cleveland's, " 'were made in a forum which does not consider the effect that reasonable workplace accommodations would have on the ability to work,' " the court held that "simply averring that the statutory schemes differ is not enough to survive summary judgment in light of *Cleveland*."

Compare MURPHEY V. CITY OF MINNEAPOLIS, 358 F.3d 1074 (8th Cir.2004). There, the court found no inconsistency between an ADA claim and an application for permanent disability benefits from the Minnesota Public Employee Retirement Association—even though the relevant state law, like the SSDI statute, defined "permanent disability" as "the inability to engage in any substantial gainful activity." Minn.Stat. § 353.01, subd. 19. The benefits application included a statement from Murphey's doctor that Murphey satisfied the statutory requirement for permanent disability. But the court noted that "the physician's opinion does not amount to a 'sworn statement' or representation *by Murphey* that he is totally and permanently disabled and unable to work." The court also found "a critical distinction between the eligibility requirements for PERA disability benefits and SSDI benefits. The essential difference between the two statutory schemes is that a person receiving PERA disability benefits based on total and permanent disability is allowed to return to work without losing his benefits." Accordingly, the court "conclude[d] that there [wa]s no inconsistency between Murphey's successful application for and receipt of PERA disability benefits and his ADA claim that he could perform the essential functions of his job." Does this analysis adequately distinguish the PERA program from the SSDI program (under which, as *Cleveland* explains, some recipients can work without losing their benefits)?

3. DRUG AND ALCOHOL USE

Raytheon Co. v. Hernandez
Supreme Court of the United States, 2003.
540 U.S. 44.

■ JUSTICE THOMAS delivered the opinion of the Court.

[W]e are asked to decide in this case whether the ADA confers preferential rehire rights on disabled employees lawfully terminated for violating workplace conduct rules. The United States Court of Appeals for the Ninth Circuit held that an employer's unwritten policy not to rehire employees who left the company for violating personal conduct rules contravenes the ADA, at least as applied to employees who were lawfully forced to resign for illegal drug use but have since been rehabilitated. Because the Ninth Circuit improperly applied a disparate-impact analysis in a disparate-treatment case in order to reach this holding, we vacate its judgment and remand the case for further proceedings consistent with this opinion. We do not, however, reach the question on which we granted *certiorari*.

I

Respondent, Joel Hernandez, worked for Hughes Missile Systems [now part of Raytheon] for 25 years. On July 11, 1991, respondent's appearance and behavior at work suggested that he might be under the influence of drugs or alcohol. Pursuant to company policy, respondent took a drug test, which came back positive for cocaine. Respondent subsequently admitted that he had been up late drinking beer and using cocaine the night before the test. Because respondent's behavior violated petitioner's workplace conduct rules, respondent was forced to resign. Respondent's "Employee Separation Summary" indicated as the reason for separation: "discharge for personal conduct (quit in lieu of discharge)."

More than two years later, on January 24, 1994, respondent applied to be rehired by petitioner. Respondent stated on his application that he had previously been employed by petitioner. He also attached two reference letters to the application, one from his pastor, stating that respondent was a "faithful and active member" of the church, and the other from an Alcoholics Anonymous counselor, stating that respondent attends Alcoholics Anonymous meetings regularly and is in recovery.

Joanne Bockmiller, an employee in the company's Labor Relations Department, reviewed respondent's application. Bockmiller testified in her deposition that since respondent's application disclosed his prior employment with the company, she pulled his personnel file and reviewed his employee separation summary. She then rejected respondent's application. Bockmiller insisted that the company had a policy against rehiring employees who were terminated for workplace misconduct. Thus, when she reviewed the employment separation summary and found that respondent had been discharged for violating workplace conduct rules, she rejected respondent's application. She testified, in particular, that she did not know that respondent was a former drug addict when she made the employment decision and did not see anything that would constitute a "record of" addiction.

Respondent subsequently filed a charge with the Equal Employment Opportunity Commission (EEOC). [Petitioner's] response, together with evidence that the letters submitted with respondent's employment application may have alerted Bockmiller to the reason for respondent's prior termination, led the EEOC to conclude that petitioner may have "rejected [respondent's] application based on his record of past alcohol and drug use." The EEOC thus found that there was "reasonable cause to believe that [respondent] was denied hire to the position of Product Test Specialist because of his disability." The EEOC issued a right-to-sue letter, and respondent subsequently filed this action alleging a violation of the ADA.

Respondent proceeded through discovery on the theory that the company rejected his application because of his record of drug addiction and/or because he was regarded as being a drug addict. See 42 U.S.C. §§ 12102(2)(B)–(C). In response to petitioner's motion for summary judgment, respondent for the first time argued in the alternative that if the company really did apply a neutral no-rehire policy in his case, petitioner still violated the ADA because such a policy has a disparate impact. The District Court granted petitioner's motion for summary judgment with respect to respondent's disparate-treatment claim. However, the District Court refused to consider respondent's disparate-impact claim because respondent had failed to plead or raise the theory in a timely manner.

The Court of Appeals agreed with the District Court that respondent had failed timely to raise his disparate-impact claim. In addressing respondent's disparate-treatment claim, the Court of Appeals proceeded under the familiar burden-shifting approach first adopted by this Court in *McDonnell Douglas Corp. v. Green*, 411 U.S. 792 (1973). First, the Ninth Circuit [h]eld that with respect to respondent's prima facie case of discrimination, respondent had proffered sufficient evidence to preclude a grant of summary judgment.

[T]he Court of Appeals then moved to the next step of *McDonnell Douglas*, where the burden shifts to the defendant to provide a legitimate, nondiscriminatory reason for its employment action. Here, petitioner contends that Bockmiller applied the neutral policy against rehiring employees previously terminated for violating workplace conduct rules and that this neutral company policy constituted a legitimate and nondiscriminatory reason for its decision not to rehire respondent. The Court of Appeals, although admitting that petitioner's no-rehire rule was lawful on its face, held the policy to be unlawful "as applied to former drug addicts whose only work-related offense was testing positive because of their addiction." The Court of Appeals concluded that petitioner's application of a neutral no-rehire policy was not a legitimate, nondiscriminatory reason for rejecting respondent's application:

> "Maintaining a blanket policy against rehire of all former employees who violated company policy not only screens out persons with a record of addiction who have been successfully rehabilitated, but may well result, as [petitioner] contends it did here, in the staff member who makes the employment decision remaining unaware of the 'disability' and thus of the fact that she is committing an unlawful act. . . . Additionally, we hold that a policy that serves to bar the reemployment of a drug addict despite his successful rehabilitation violates the ADA."

In other words, while ostensibly evaluating whether petitioner had proffered a legitimate, nondiscriminatory reason for failing to rehire respondent sufficient to rebut respondent's prima facie showing of disparate treatment, the Court of Appeals held that a neutral no-rehire policy could never suffice in a case where the employee was terminated for illegal drug use, because such a policy has a disparate impact on recovering drug addicts. In so holding, the Court of Appeals erred by conflating the analytical framework for disparate-impact and disparate-treatment claims. Had the Court of Appeals correctly applied the disparate-treatment framework, it would have been obliged to conclude that a neutral no-rehire policy is, by definition, a legitimate, nondiscriminatory reason under the ADA. And thus the only remaining question would be whether respondent could produce sufficient evidence from which a jury could conclude that "petitioner's stated reason for respondent's rejection was in fact pretext." *McDonnell Douglas, supra,* at 804.

II

This Court has consistently recognized a distinction between claims of discrimination based on disparate treatment and claims of discrimination based on disparate impact. The Court has said that "'[d]isparate treatment' . . . is the most easily understood type of discrimination. The employer simply treats some people less favorably than others because of their race, color, religion, sex, or [other protected characteristic]." Liability in a disparate-treatment case "depends on whether the protected trait . . . actually motivated the employer's decision." By contrast, disparate-impact claims "involve employment practices that are facially neutral in their treatment of different groups but that in fact fall more harshly on one group than another and cannot be justified by business necessity." Under a disparate-impact theory of discrimination, "a facially neutral employment practice may be deemed [illegally discriminatory] without evidence of the employer's subjective intent to discriminate that is required in a 'disparate-treatment' case."

Both disparate-treatment and disparate-impact claims are cognizable under the ADA. See 42 U.S.C. § 12112(b) (defining "discriminate" to include "utilizing standards, criteria, or methods of administration . . . that have the effect of discrimination on the basis of disability" and "using qualification standards, employment tests or other selection criteria that screen out or tend to screen out an individual with a disability"). Because "the factual issues, and therefore the character of the evidence presented, differ when the plaintiff claims that a facially neutral employment policy has a discriminatory impact on protected classes," courts must be careful to distinguish between these theories. Here, respondent did not timely pursue a disparate-impact claim. Rather, the District Court concluded, and the Court of Appeals agreed, that respondent's case was limited to a disparate-treatment theory, that the company refused to rehire respondent because it regarded respondent as being disabled and/or because of respondent's record of a disability.

Petitioner's proffer of its neutral no-rehire policy plainly satisfied its obligation under *McDonnell Douglas* to provide a legitimate, nondiscriminatory reason for refusing to rehire respondent. Thus, the only relevant question before the Court of Appeals, after petitioner presented a neutral explanation for its decision not to rehire respondent, was whether there was sufficient evidence from which a jury could conclude that petitioner did make its employment decision based on respondent's status as disabled despite petitioner's proffered explanation. Instead, the Court of Appeals concluded that, as a matter of law, a neutral no-rehire policy was not a legitimate, nondiscriminatory reason sufficient to defeat a prima facie case of discrimination. The Court of Appeals did not even attempt, in the remainder of its opinion, to treat this claim as one involving only disparate treatment. Instead, the Court of Appeals observed that petitioner's policy "screens out persons with a record of addiction," and further noted that the company had not raised a business necessity defense, factors that pertain to disparate-impact claims but not disparate-treatment claims. By improperly focusing on these factors, the Court of Appeals ignored the fact that petitioner's no-rehire policy is a quintessential legitimate, nondiscriminatory reason for refusing to rehire an employee who was terminated for violating workplace conduct rules. If petitioner did indeed apply a neutral, generally applicable no-rehire policy in rejecting respondent's application, petitioner's decision not to rehire respondent can, in no way, be said to have been motivated by respondent's disability.

[O]nce respondent had made a prima facie showing of discrimination, the next question for the Court of Appeals was whether petitioner offered a legitimate, nondiscriminatory reason for its actions so as to demonstrate that its actions were not motivated by respondent's disability. To the extent that the Court of Appeals strayed from this task by considering not only discriminatory intent but also discriminatory impact, we vacate its judgment and remand the case for further proceedings consistent with this opinion.

It is so ordered.

■ JUSTICE SOUTER took no part in the decision of this case. JUSTICE BREYER took no part in the consideration or decision of this case.

NOTES ON *RAYTHEON CO. V. HERNANDEZ*

1. **Subsequent History.** On remand from the Supreme Court in *Raytheon*, the Ninth Circuit reinstated its earlier judgment for the plaintiff. The Ninth Circuit found "a genuine issue of material fact as to whether Raytheon failed to re-hire Hernandez because of his 'status as an alcoholic,' rather than in reliance on a uniform no re-hire policy." The court reasoned that "[a] reasonable juror could find that, despite Bockmiller's testimony to the contrary, she was aware of the fact that Hernandez had been a substance-abuser and based her decision on that ground." And "the jury could infer from the fact that nobody at Raytheon could identify the origin, history, or scope of the alleged unwritten policy, that it either did not exist or was not consistently applied. A juror could also infer from the fact that Hughes has specific written policies regarding drug abuse, which, unlike the policy on which it now relies, are very favorable to temporary and part-time employees, that those written policies are the relevant policies regarding the matter before us." *Hernandez v. Hughes Missile Systems Co.,* 362 F.3d 564 (9th Cir.2004).

2. **Drug and Alcohol Use and the ADA.** Title I of the ADA contains detailed provisions addressing the statute's coverage of drug and alcohol users. See 42 U.S.C. § 12114. The statute provides that "the term 'qualified individual with a disability' shall not include any employee or applicant who is currently engaging in the illegal use of drugs, when the covered entity acts on the basis of such use." 42 U.S.C. § 12114(a). In other words, an employer may fire or refuse to hire someone simply because of that person's current use of illegal drugs—even if that drug use has no effect on job performance. (Note that this provision applies only to the illegal use of drugs—alcoholics remain protected by the statute unless their alcohol use

has an effect on job performance.) But that general exclusion does not apply to an individual who "has successfully completed a supervised drug rehabilitation program and is no longer engaging in the illegal use of drugs, or has otherwise been rehabilitated successfully and is no longer engaging in such use"; "is participating in a supervised rehabilitation program and is no longer engaging in such use"; or "is erroneously regarded as engaging in such use." 42 U.S.C. § 12114(b).

Courts have tended to read the "safe harbor" for participation in a supervised rehabilitation program quite narrowly, however. In ZENOR V. EL PASO HEALTHCARE SYSTEM, LTD., 176 F.3d 847 (5th Cir.1999), the court upheld the termination of a pharmacist who had admitted an addiction to cocaine. Although Zenor had entered a supervised rehabilitation program and had not used cocaine for five weeks by the time of his termination, the court held that he was nonetheless "currently engaging in the illegal use of drugs." "Such a short period of abstinence," the court concluded, "particularly following such a severe drug problem, does not remove from the employer's mind a reasonable belief that the drug use remains a problem." As for the safe harbor provision, the court explained, "the mere fact that an employee has entered a rehabilitation program does not automatically bring that employee within the safe harbor's protection." Instead, the court read that provision as applying "only to individuals who have been drug-free for a significant period of time."

Did *Zenor* correctly interpret the statute's exclusion of "current" drug users and its safe harbor provision? As to the "currently using" language, see *Shafer v. Preston Memorial Hosp. Corp.*, 107 F.3d 274 (4th Cir.1997):

> [T]he ordinary or natural meaning of the phrase "currently using drugs" does not require that a drug user have a heroin syringe in his arm or a marijuana bong to his mouth at the exact moment contemplated. Instead, in this context, the plain meaning of "currently" is broader. Here, "currently" means a periodic or ongoing activity in which a person engages (even if doing something else at the precise moment) that has not yet permanently ended.

Would a broader interpretation of the safe harbor provision ensure that "an employee discovered engaging in the illegal use of drugs could escape responsibility for his actions by immediately enrolling in a drug rehabilitation program," *id.*? Is that necessarily contrary to the language or purpose of the statute?

Where the use of alcohol *or* illegal drugs affects job performance, the statute gives an employer even greater latitude. Thus, an employer "may prohibit the illegal use of drugs and the use of alcohol at the workplace by all employees"; "may require that employees shall not be under the influence of alcohol or be engaging in the illegal use of drugs at the workplace"; and "may hold an employee who engages in the illegal use of drugs or who is an alcoholic to the same qualification standards for employment or job performance and behavior that such entity holds other employees, even if any unsatisfactory performance or behavior is related to the drug use or alcoholism of such employee." 42 U.S.C. § 12114(c). This provision creates what might be thought of as an act/status distinction:

Employers may not discriminate against individuals because of their *status* as alcoholics or recovering drug addicts, but it may but they may discriminate against individuals because of job-related *acts* that they undertake because of that status. See, *e.g.*, *Nielsen v. Moroni Feed Co.*, 162 F.3d 604 (10th Cir.1998) ("[U]nsatisfactory conduct caused by alcoholism and illegal drug use does not receive protection under the ADA or the Rehabilitation Act. However, the mere status of being an alcoholic or illegal drug user may merit such protection.").

Do these elaborate rules make sense? Maybe they afford too much protection to illegal drug users. Why should employers be forbidden to discriminate against individuals who have engaged in illegal conduct? A history of illegal drug use carries the risk of other illegal conduct (including theft from the employer or customers) as well as risks to the safety of coworkers and others. Why should employers be forced to face these risks? Perhaps the goal is to encourage rehabilitation and reformation. If addicts will be stigmatized and discriminated against on the job market long after they stop using, they have less reason to stop. Protecting former drug users against discrimination gives current users an incentive to turn their lives around. But the line between "current" and "former" users may be a hazy one in practice, as recovering addicts constantly face the risk of relapse. In the end, the question may be how much of a burden we wish to place on private employers to provide an incentive for drug users to turn their lives around. The cases interpreting the ADA's drug-addiction provisions suggest that an employer should be forced to bear this burden only when the risk of relapse is very low and when no workplace effects are present—in other words, when it would be irrational for the employer to discriminate against a person with a history of drug addiction. As the following section indicates, the ADA imposes on employers a significantly greater burden to accommodate other sorts of disabilities.

C. DIRECT THREAT

Bragdon v. Abbott

Supreme Court of the United States, 1998.
524 U.S. 624.

■ JUSTICE KENNEDY delivered the opinion of the Court.

[Plaintiff Sydney Abbott, who had asymptomatic HIV disease, went to defendant Dr. Randon Bragdon's dental office to have a cavity filled. Bragdon refused to fill the cavity in his office, though he offered to fill the cavity in a hospital (with Abbott paying the extra cost of the facilities). Abbott sued under the public accommodations provisions of the ADA. In Part II of the opinion, the Court held that the plaintiff's asymptomatic HIV disease was a "disability."]

III

[N]otwithstanding the protection given respondent by the ADA's definition of disability, petitioner could have refused to treat her if her infectious condition "pose[d] a direct threat to the health or safety of others." 42 U.S.C. § 12182(b)(3). The ADA defines a direct threat to be "a significant risk to the health or safety of others that cannot be eliminated by a modification of policies, practices, or procedures or by the provision of auxiliary aids or services." Ibid. Parallel provisions appear in the employment provisions of Title I. §§ 12111(3), 12113(b).

The ADA's direct threat provision stems from the recognition in School Bd. of Nassau Cty. v. Arline, 480 U.S. 273, 287 (1987), of the importance of prohibiting discrimination against individuals with disabilities while protecting others from significant health and safety risks, resulting, for instance, from a contagious disease. In *Arline*, the Court reconciled these objectives by construing the Rehabilitation Act not to require the hiring of a person who posed "a significant risk of communicating an infectious disease to others." Congress amended the Rehabilitation Act and the Fair Housing Act to incorporate the language. See 29 U.S.C. § 706(8)(D) (excluding individuals who "would constitute a direct threat to the health or safety of other individuals"); 42 U.S.C. § 3604(f)(9) (same). It later relied on the same language in enacting the ADA. See 28 CFR pt. 36, App.B, p. 626 (1997) (ADA's direct threat provision codifies *Arline*). Because few, if any, activities in life are risk free, *Arline* and the ADA do not ask whether a risk exists, but whether it is significant. *Arline, supra*; 42 U.S.C. § 12182(b)(3).

The existence, or nonexistence, of a significant risk must be determined from the standpoint of the person who refuses the treatment or accommodation, and the risk assessment must be based on medical or other objective evidence. *Arline, supra*; 28 CFR § 36.208(c) (1997); id., pt. 36, App.B, p. 626. As a health care professional, petitioner had the duty to assess the risk of infection based on the objective, scientific information available to him and others in his profession. His belief that a significant risk existed, even if maintained in good faith, would not relieve him from liability. [P]etitioner receives no special deference simply because he is a health care professional. It is true that *Arline* reserved "the question whether courts should also defer to the reasonable medical judgments of private physicians on which an employer has relied." At most, this statement reserved the possibility that employers could consult with individual physicians as objective third-party experts. It did not suggest that an individual physician's state of mind could excuse discrimination without regard to the objective reasonableness of his actions.

[I]n assessing the reasonableness of petitioner's actions, the views of public health authorities, such as the U.S. Public Health Service, CDC, and the National Institutes of Health, are of special weight and authority. *Arline, supra*; 28 CFR pt. 36, App.B, p. 626 (1997). The views of these organizations are not conclusive, however. A health care professional who disagrees with the prevailing medical consensus may refute it by citing a credible scientific basis for deviating from the accepted norm. See W. Keeton, D. Dobbs, R. Keeton, & D. Owen, Prosser and Keeton on Law of Torts § 32, p. 187 (5th ed.1984).

[F]or the most part, the Court of Appeals followed the proper standard in evaluating petitioner's position and conducted a thorough review of the evidence. Its rejection of the District Court's reliance on the Marianos affidavits was a correct application of the principle that petitioner's actions must be evaluated in light of the available, objective evidence. The record did not show that CDC had published the conclusion set out in the affidavits at the time petitioner refused to treat respondent.

A further illustration of a correct application of the objective standard is the Court of Appeals' refusal to give weight to petitioner's offer to treat respondent in a hospital. Petitioner testified that he believed hospitals had safety measures, such as air filtration, ultraviolet lights, and respirators, which would reduce the risk of HIV transmission. Petitioner made no showing, however, that any area hospital had these safeguards or even that he had hospital privileges. His expert also admitted the lack of any scientific basis for the conclusion that these measures would lower the risk of transmission. Petitioner failed to present any objective, medical evidence showing that treating respondent in a hospital would be safer or more efficient in preventing HIV transmission than treatment in a well-equipped dental office.

We are concerned, however, that the Court of Appeals might have placed mistaken reliance upon two other sources. In ruling no triable issue of fact existed on this point, the Court of Appeals relied on the 1993 CDC Dentistry Guidelines and the 1991 American Dental Association Policy on HIV. This evidence is not definitive. As noted earlier, the CDC Guidelines recommended certain universal precautions which, in CDC's view, "should reduce the risk of disease transmission in the dental environment." U.S. Dept. of Health and Human Services, Public Health Service, CDC, Recommended Infection-Control Practices for Dentistry, 41 Morbidity and Mortality Weekly Rep. No. RR–8, p. 1 (May 28, 1993). The Court of Appeals determined that, "[w]hile the guidelines do not state explicitly that no further risk-reduction measures are desirable or that routine dental care for HIV-positive individuals is safe, those two conclusions seem to be implicit in the guidelines' detailed delineation of procedures for office treatment of HIV-positive patients." In our view, the Guidelines do not necessarily contain implicit assumptions conclusive of the point to be decided. The Guidelines set out CDC's recommendation that the universal precautions are the best way to combat the risk of HIV transmission. They do not assess the level of risk.

Nor can we be certain, on this record, whether the 1991 American Dental Association Policy on HIV carries the weight the Court of Appeals attributed to it. The Policy does provide some evidence of the medical community's objective assessment of the risks posed by treating people infected with HIV in dental offices. It indicates:

> "Current scientific and epidemiologic evidence indicates that there is little risk of transmission of infectious diseases through dental treatment if recommended infection control procedures are routinely followed. Patients with HIV infection may be safely treated in private dental offices when appropriate infection control procedures are employed. Such infection control procedures provide protection both for patients and dental personnel."

We note, however, that the Association is a professional organization, which, although a respected source of information on the dental profession, is not a public health authority. It is not clear the extent to which the Policy was based on the Association's assessment of dentists' ethical and professional duties in addition to its scientific assessment of the risk to which the ADA refers. Efforts to clarify dentists' ethical obligations and to encourage dentists to treat patients with HIV infection with compassion may be commendable, but the question under the statute is one of statistical likelihood, not professional responsibility. Without more information on the manner in which the American Dental Association formulated this Policy, we are unable to determine the Policy's value in evaluating whether petitioner's assessment of the risks was reasonable as a matter of law.

We acknowledge the presence of other evidence in the record before the Court of Appeals which, subject to further arguments and examination, might support affirmance of the trial court's ruling. For instance, the record contains substantial testimony from numerous health experts indicating that it is safe to treat patients infected with HIV in dental offices. We are unable to determine the import of this evidence, however. The record does not disclose whether the expert testimony submitted by respondent turned on evidence available in September 1994.

There are reasons to doubt whether petitioner advanced evidence sufficient to raise a triable issue of fact on the significance of the risk. Petitioner relied on two principal points: First, he asserted that the use of high-speed drills and surface cooling with water created a risk of airborne HIV transmission. The study on which petitioner relied was inconclusive, however, determining only that "[f]urther work is required to determine whether such a risk exists." Johnson & Robinson, Human Immunodeficiency Virus-1 (HIV-1) in the Vapors of Surgical Power Instruments, 33 J. of Medical Virology 47 (1991). Petitioner's expert witness conceded, moreover, that no evidence suggested the spray could transmit HIV. His opinion on airborne risk was based on the absence of contrary evidence, not on positive data. Scientific evidence and expert testimony must have a traceable, analytical basis in objective fact before it may be considered on summary judgment.

Second, petitioner argues that, as of September 1994, CDC had identified seven dental workers with possible occupational transmission of HIV. See U.S. Dept. of Health and Human Services, Public Health Service, CDC, HIV/AIDS Surveillance Report, vol. 6, no. 1, p. 15, tbl. 11 (Mid-year ed.June 1994). These dental workers were exposed to HIV in the course of their employment, but CDC could not determine whether HIV infection had resulted from this exposure. Id., at 15, n. 3. It is now known that CDC could not ascertain how the seven dental workers contracted the disease because they did not present themselves for HIV testing at an appropriate time after this occupational exposure. Gooch *et al.*, Percutaneous Exposures to HIV–Infected Blood Among Dental Workers Enrolled in the CDC Needlestick Study, 126 J. American Dental Assn. 1237, 1239 (1995). It is not clear on this record, however, whether this information was available to petitioner in September 1994. If not, the seven cases might have provided some, albeit not necessarily sufficient, support for petitioner's position. Standing alone, we doubt it would meet the objective, scientific basis for finding a significant risk to the petitioner.

[W]e conclude the proper course is to give the Court of Appeals the opportunity to determine whether our analysis of some of the studies cited by the parties would change its conclusion that petitioner presented neither objective evidence nor a triable issue of fact on the question of risk. In remanding the case, we do not foreclose the possibility that the Court of Appeals may reach the same conclusion it did earlier. A remand will permit a full exploration of the issue through the adversary process.

The determination of the Court of Appeals that respondent's HIV infection was a disability under the ADA is affirmed. The judgment is vacated, and the case is remanded for further proceedings consistent with this opinion.

It is so ordered.

■ JUSTICE STEVENS, with whom JUSTICE BREYER joins, concurring.

[T]he Court's discussion in Part III of the relevant evidence has persuaded me that the judgment of the Court of Appeals should be affirmed. I do not believe petitioner has sustained his burden of adducing evidence sufficient to raise a triable issue of fact on the significance of the risk posed by treating respondent in his office. The Court of Appeals reached that conclusion after a careful and extensive study of the record; its analysis on this question was perfectly consistent with the legal reasoning in JUSTICE KENNEDY's opinion for the Court; and the latter opinion itself explains that petitioner relied on data that were inconclusive and speculative at best.

There are not, however, five Justices who agree that the judgment should be affirmed. Nor does it appear that there are five Justices who favor a remand for further proceedings consistent with the views expressed in either JUSTICE KENNEDY's opinion for the Court or the opinion of THE CHIEF JUSTICE. Because I am in agreement with the legal analysis in JUSTICE KENNEDY's opinion, in order to provide a judgment supported by a majority, I join that opinion even though I would prefer an outright affirmance. Cf. Screws v. United States, 325 U.S. 91, 134 (1945) (Rutledge, J., concurring in result).

■ JUSTICE GINSBURG, concurring.

[I] agree, in view of the "importance [of the issue] to health care workers," that it is wise to remand, erring, if at all, on the side of caution. By taking this course, the Court ensures a fully informed determination whether respondent Abbott's disease posed "a significant risk to the health or safety of [petitioner Bragdon] that [could not] be eliminated by a modification of policies, practices, or procedures . . . . " 42 U.S.C. § 12182(b)(3).

■ CHIEF JUSTICE REHNQUIST, with whom JUSTICE SCALIA and JUSTICE THOMAS join, and with whom JUSTICE O'CONNOR joins as to Part II, concurring in the judgment in part and dissenting in part.

I

[Part I of Chief Justice Rehnquist's dissent addressed the question whether Abbott had a "disability." That part is excerpted in Chapter Two above.]

II

I disagree with the Court [t]hat "[i]n assessing the reasonableness of petitioner's actions, the views of public health authorities . . . are of special weight and authority." Those views are, of course, entitled to a presumption of validity when the actions of those authorities themselves are challenged in court, and even in disputes between private parties where Congress has committed that dispute to adjudication by a public health authority. But in litigation between private parties originating in the federal courts, I am aware of no provision of law or judicial practice that would require or permit courts to give some scientific views more credence than others simply because they have been endorsed by a politically appointed public health authority (such as the Surgeon General). In litigation of this latter sort, which is what we face here, the credentials of the scientists employed by the public health authority, and the soundness of their studies, must stand on their own.

[I]t is clear to me that petitioner has presented more than enough evidence to avoid summary judgment on the "direct threat" question. In June 1994, the Centers for Disease Control and Prevention published a study identifying seven instances of possible transmission of HIV from patients to dental workers. While it is not entirely certain whether these dental workers contracted HIV during the course of providing dental treatment, the potential that the disease was transmitted during the course of dental treatment is relevant evidence. One need only demonstrate "risk," not certainty of infection. See *Arline, supra* (" '[T]he probabilities the disease will be transmitted' " is a factor in assessing risk). Given the "severity of the risk" involved here, *i.e.*, near certain death, and the fact that no public health authority had outlined a protocol for eliminating this risk in the context of routine dental treatment, it seems likely that petitioner can establish that it was objectively reasonable for him to conclude that treating respondent in his office posed a "direct threat" to his safety.

In addition, petitioner offered evidence of 42 documented incidents of occupational transmission of HIV to health-care workers other than dental professionals. The Court of Appeals dismissed this evidence as irrelevant because these health professionals were not dentists. But the fact that the health care workers were not dentists is no more valid a basis for distinguishing these transmissions of HIV than the fact that the health care workers did not practice in Maine. At a minimum, petitioner's evidence was sufficient to create a triable issue on this question, and summary judgment was accordingly not appropriate

NOTES ON SIGNIFICANT RISK

1.   *Bragdon* on Remand. On remand, the First Circuit conducted the reexamination of the evidence the Supreme Court called for. It concluded, once again, that treating Abbott would pose no direct threat to health and safety. The First Circuit made these specific comments about the evidence:

> The CDC did not write the 1993 Guidelines in a vacuum, but, rather, updated earlier versions issued in 1986 and 1987, respectively. The 1986 text calls the universal precautions "effective for preventing hepatitis B, acquired immunodeficiency syndrome, and other infectious diseases caused by bloodborne viruses." The 1987 edition explains that use of the universal precautions eliminates the need for additional precautions that

the CDC formerly had advocated for handling blood and other bodily fluids known or suspected to be infected with bloodborne pathogens. Neither the parties nor any of the *amici* have suggested that the 1993 rewrite was intended to retreat from these earlier risk assessments, and we find no support for such a position in the Guidelines' text. Thus, we have again determined that the Guidelines are competent evidence that public health authorities considered treatment of the kind that Ms. Abbott required to be safe, if undertaken using universal precautions.

Second, the Court questioned the appropriate weight to accord the Policy, expressing concern that the Policy might be based in whole or in part on the Association's view of dentists' ethical obligations, rather than on a pure scientific assessment. The supplemental briefing that we requested yielded a cornucopia of information regarding the process by which the Policy was assembled. We briefly recount the undisputed facts.

The Association formulates scientific and ethical policies by separate procedures, drawing on different member groups and different staff complements. The Association's Council on Scientific Affairs, comprised of 17 dentists (most of whom hold advanced dentistry degrees), together with a staff of over 20 professional experts and consultants, drafted the Policy at issue here. By contrast, ethical policies are drafted by the Council on Ethics, a wholly separate body. Although the Association's House of Delegates must approve policies drafted by either council, we think that the origins of the Policy satisfy any doubts regarding its scientific foundation.

For these reasons, we are confident that we appropriately relied on the Guidelines and the Policy. Moreover, as the Supreme Court acknowledged, these two pieces of evidence represent only a fraction of the proof advanced to support Ms. Abbott's motion.

[I]n [our earlier opinion], we canvassed eight items of evidence adduced by Dr. Bragdon in an effort to demonstrate a genuine issue of material fact. The Supreme Court suggested that one such piece of evidence—the seven cases that the CDC considered "possible" HIV patient-to-dental worker transmissions—should be reexamined.

[T]he Court noted that the CDC marks an HIV case as a "possible" occupational transmission if a stricken worker, who had no other demonstrated opportunity for infection, simply failed to present himself for testing after being exposed to the virus at work. See id. The Court speculated that if this definition of "possible" was not available in September 1994, the existence of seven "possible" cases "might have provided some, albeit not necessarily sufficient, support for [Dr. Bragdon's] position." In other words, if a dentist knew of seven "possible" occupational transmissions to dental workers without understanding that "possible" meant no more than that the CDC could not determine whether workers were infected occupationally, he might reasonably regard the risk of treating an HIV-infected patient to be significant.

Upon reexamination of the record, we find that the CDC's definition of the word "possible," as used here, had been made public during the relevant period. The record contains two scientific articles published before Ms. Abbott entered Dr. Bragdon's office which explained this definition. See Louise J. Short & David M. Bell, *Risk of Occupational Infection With BloodBorne Pathogens in Operating and Delivery Room Settings*, 21 Am. J. Infection Control 343, 345 (1993); John A. Molinari, *HIV, Health Care Workers and Patients: How to Ensure Safety in the Dental Office*, 124 J. Am. Dental Ass'n 51, 51–52 (1993).

Abbott v. Bragdon, 163 F.3d 87 (1st Cir.1998).

2. "Risk Free." It is easy to understand how Ms. Abbott might infect Dr. Bragdon. All Dr. Bragdon would have to do is accidentally stick himself with a needle after giving Ms. Abbott a shot of Novocain—a hardly unheard-of occurrence. It is unlikely that the needle would contain enough blood—and enough of the virus—to infect Dr. Bragdon, but the risk is not zero. And the potential harm is of the highest order—infection with a debilitating and fatal disease. If treating Ms. Abbott poses *any* risk of imposing such a severe harm, why shouldn't Dr. Bragdon be permitted to turn her away?

A pre-*Bragdon* series of cases that upheld the dismissal of HIV-infected heath-care workers adopted just that sort of zero-risk approach. See, *e.g.*, *Bradley v. University of Tex. M.D. Anderson Cancer Ctr.*, 3 F.3d 922, 924 (5th Cir.1993) ("A cognizable risk of permanent duration with lethal consequences suffices to make a surgical technician with Bradley's responsibilities not 'otherwise qualified.' "); *Doe v. University of Md. Med. Sys. Corp.*, 50 F.3d 1261, 1266 (4th Cir.1995) ("We hold that Dr. Doe does pose a significant risk to the health and safety of his patients that cannot be eliminated by reasonable accommodation. Although there may presently be no documented case of surgeon-to-patient transmission, such transmission clearly is possible."); *Leckelt v. Board of Comm'rs.*, 909 F.2d 820, 829 (5th Cir.1990) (upholding firing of nurse who refused to take an HIV test "[e]ven though the probability that a health care worker will transmit HIV to a patient may be extremely low" because "the potential harm of HIV infection is extremely high").

Justice Kennedy's opinion for the Court in *Bragdon* explicitly rejects the zero-risk approach. He explains that "[b]ecause few, if any, activities in life are risk free, *Arline* and the ADA do not ask whether a risk exists, but whether it is significant." But even if employers, coworkers, and customers should be required to bear a *financial* cost to ensure the integration of people with disabilities into the workplace, should they also be required to face risks to life and health? Justice Kennedy's answer reflects the common wisdom among students of risk regulation that *all* actions (and refusals to act) pose risks, so it makes no sense to say that one could avoid all risk.

But Justice Kennedy's rejection of the zero-risk approach raises a further question: If it is only significant risks that can justify excluding otherwise qualified individuals with disabilities from job opportunities, what counts as significant? This is not a question that can be answered technocratically. "[T]he question whether a risk is 'significant' is not simply a factual question. To ask whether a risk is 'significant' is at least in part to ask whether the risk is 'acceptable,' and 'the issue of acceptable risk lies,' as Mary Douglas has noted, not simply within the realm of facts, but 'with the principles of valuation itself, that is, with culture.' " Barry Sullivan, *When the Environment is Other People: An Essay on Science, Culture, and the Authoritative Allocation of Values*, 69 Notre Dame L. Rev. 597, 601 (1994) (quoting Mary Douglas, Risk Acceptability According to the Social Sciences 14–15 (1985)).

How ought a judge to decide what risks are significant in the disability discrimination context? A prominent approach to risk regulation looks to cost-benefit analysis. See, *e.g.*, Stephen Breyer, Breaking the Vicious Circle: Toward Effective Risk Regulation (1993); W. Kip Viscusi, Rational Risk Policy (1998). Perhaps the judge should attempt to assess whether the benefits that will be gained from prohibiting discrimination against an individual will be worth the expected cost of permitting the individual to work in the risky job. The expected cost would be the risk that the harm would eventuate, multiplied by the dollar value of the harm should it eventuate. Regulators and economists have (controversial) techniques for attaching costs to the value of a life, and it would be possible to create (equally controversial) monetary measures of the benefits of integration.

But these valuation questions themselves demand normative judgments. And they would impose a significant informational burden on judges. Is a judge, who depends on the arguments and evidentiary presentations of the parties, likely to be able to take the sort of synoptic view of society-wide costs and benefits that cost-benefit analysis demands? Can the party- and transaction-based nature of litigation exacerbate the sorts of prejudice and stigma that lead to unjustifiable exclusion of people with disabilities? Samuel R. Bagenstos, *The Americans with Disabilities Act as Risk Regulation*, 101 Colum. L. Rev. 1479, 1493–1494 (2001), argues that "[t]he same prejudices and fears that lead a restaurant to determine that it is unsafe to hire people with HIV may also influence the judge or (particularly) the jury who decides that the restaurant acted properly in refusing to hire people with that condition," and that "[t]he identification of the party who must bear the consequences only exacerbates the 'zero-risk mentality' that leads people to demand an elimination of all risk." Do the pre-*Bragdon* HIV cases support that argument?

3.   Deference to Public Health Professionals. Justice Kennedy's opinion for the Court in *Bragdon* sidesteps the value questions inherent in determining whether a risk is significant. The opinion does so by demanding deference (though not unqualified deference) to "the views of public health authorities, such as the U.S. Public Health Service, CDC, and the National Institutes of Health." Does such deference make sense? "Even if we assume that public health officials are uniquely capable of determining the 'true' extent of the risk imposed by allowing a person with a disability to participate in a given opportunity, we still need to know something else: Is the risk worth running? [And] that is at bottom a value question." Bagenstos, *ADA as Risk Regulation*, *supra*, at 1496. "[P]eople with disabilities would seem to have a lot to fear from a policy of leaving safety determinations to the public health 'experts' ": " '[S]ome of the worst abuses against vulnerable groups have occurred in the name of public health.' Public health measures have been marked by racism, classism, homophobia, and the hysteria associated with whatever epidemic is most dreaded at the moment." *Id.* at 1496–1497 (footnotes omitted).

Given these facts, what is the justification for deferring to public health officials? Perhaps the professional culture of public health agencies operates as a check against bias: "The epidemiological-probabilistic orientation of modern public health practice exerts a strong pressure on public health officials to gather enormous amounts of information from a variety of sources and then to tally up and weigh the society-wide costs of a proposed course of action against the society-wide benefits. That tallying exercise itself operates as a guard against heuristics and biases that might otherwise result in the unjustified denial of opportunities to people with disabilities." *Id.* At 1499. Judges and juries, who look at a single fact pattern at a time, are plausibly more likely to be driven by bias and stigma. Or perhaps people with disabilities are likely to have unusually strong access to and influence over public health agencies. That is certainly what happened in the case of the HIV epidemic in the 1980s, when public health officials became strong allies of gay rights and HIV support groups in the fight against discrimination. See *id.* at 1499–1503.

Are these sufficient justifications for the rule of deference?

Chevron USA, Inc. v. Echazabal

Supreme Court of the United States, 2002.
536 U.S. 73.

■ JUSTICE SOUTER delivered the opinion of the Court.

A regulation of the Equal Employment Opportunity Commission authorizes refusal to hire an individual because his performance on the job would endanger his own health, owing to a disability. The question in this case is whether the Americans with Disabilities Act of 1990 permits the regulation. We hold that it does.

I

Beginning in 1972, respondent Mario Echazabal worked for independent contractors at an oil refinery owned by petitioner Chevron U.S.A. Inc. Twice he applied for a job directly with Chevron, which offered to hire him if he could pass the company's physical examination. See 42 U.S.C. § 12112(d)(3). Each time, the exam showed liver abnormality or damage, the cause eventually being identified as Hepatitis C, which Chevron's doctors said would be aggravated by continued exposure to toxins at Chevron's refinery. In each instance, the company withdrew the offer, and the second time it asked the contractor employing Echazabal either to reassign him to a job without exposure to harmful chemicals or to remove him from the refinery altogether. The contractor laid him off in early 1996.

Echazabal filed suit, ultimately removed to federal court, claiming, among other things, that Chevron violated the Americans with Disabilities Act (ADA or Act) in refusing to hire him, or even to let him continue working in the plant, because of a disability, his liver condition. Chevron defended under a regulation of the Equal Employment Opportunity Commission (EEOC) permitting the defense that a worker's disability on the job would pose a "direct threat" to his health, see 29 CFR § 1630.15(b)(2) (2001). Although two medical witnesses disputed Chevron's judgment that Echazabal's liver function was impaired and subject to further damage under the job conditions in the refinery, the District Court granted summary judgment for Chevron. It held that Echazabal raised no genuine issue of material fact as to whether the company acted reasonably in relying on its own doctors' medical advice, regardless of its accuracy.

On appeal, the Ninth Circuit asked for briefs on a threshold question not raised before, whether the EEOC's regulation recognizing a threat-to-self defense exceeded the scope of permissible rulemaking under the ADA. The Circuit held that it did and reversed the summary judgment. The court rested its position on the text of the ADA itself in explicitly recognizing an employer's right to adopt an employment qualification barring anyone whose disability would place others in the workplace at risk, while saying nothing about threats to the disabled employee himself. The majority opinion reasoned that "by specifying only threats to 'other individuals in the workplace,' the statute makes it clear that threats to other persons—including the disabled individual himself—are not included within the scope of the [direct threat] defense," and it indicated that any such regulation would unreasonably conflict with congressional policy against paternalism in the workplace.

II

The statutory definition of "discriminat[ion]" covers a number of things an employer might do to block a disabled person from advancing in the workplace, such as "using qualification standards . . . that screen out or tend to screen out an individual with a disability." § 12112(b)(6). By that same definition, as well as by separate provision, § 12113(a), the Act creates an affirmative defense for action under a qualification standard "shown to be job-related for the position in question and . . . consistent with business necessity." Such a standard may include "a requirement that an individual shall not pose a direct threat to the health or safety of other individuals in the workplace," § 12113(b), if the individual cannot perform the job safely with reasonable accommodation, § 12113(a). By regulation, the EEOC carries the defense one step further, in allowing an employer to screen out a potential worker with a disability not only for risks that he would pose to others in the workplace but for risks on the job to his own health or safety as well: "The term 'qualification standard' may include a requirement that an individual shall not pose a direct threat to the health or safety of the individual or others in the workplace." 29 CFR § 1630.15(b)(2) (2001).

[E]chazabal [a]rgues that as a matter of law the statute precludes the regulation, which he claims would be an unreasonable interpretation even if the agency had leeway to go beyond the literal text.

A

As for the textual bar to any agency action as a matter of law, Echazabal says that Chevron loses on the threshold question whether the statute leaves a gap for the EEOC to fill. Echazabal recognizes the generality of the language providing for a defense when a plaintiff is screened out by "qualification standards" that are "job-related and consistent with business necessity" (and reasonable accommodation would not cure the difficulty posed by employment). 42 U.S.C. § 12113(a). Without more, those provisions would allow an employer to turn away someone whose work would pose a serious risk to himself. That possibility is said to be eliminated, however, by the further specification that " 'qualification standards' may include a requirement that an individual shall not pose a direct threat to the health or safety of other individuals in the workplace." § 12113(b); see also § 12111(3) (defining "direct threat" in terms of risk to others). Echazabal contrasts this provision with an EEOC regulation under the Rehabilitation Act of 1973, 87 Stat. 357, as amended, 29 U.S.C. § 701 *et seq.*, antedating the ADA, which recognized an employer's right to consider threats both to other workers and to the threatening employee himself. Because the ADA defense provision recognizes threats only if they extend to another, Echazabal reads the statute to imply as a matter of law that threats to the worker himself cannot count.

The argument follows the reliance of the Ninth Circuit majority on the interpretive canon, *expressio unius est exclusio alterius*, "expressing one item of [an] associated group or series excludes another left unmentioned." The rule is fine when it applies, but this case joins some others in showing when it does not.

The first strike against the expression-exclusion rule here is right in the text that Echazabal quotes. Congress included the harm-to-others provision as an example of legitimate qualifications that are "job-related and consistent with business necessity." These are spacious defensive categories, which seem to give an agency (or in the absence of agency action, a court) a good deal of discretion in setting the limits of permissible qualification standards. That discretion is confirmed, if not magnified, by the provision that "qualification standards" falling within the limits of job relation and business necessity "may include" a veto on those who would directly threaten others in the workplace. Far from supporting Echazabal's position, the expansive phrasing of "may include" points directly away from the sort of exclusive specification he claims.[3]

Just as statutory language suggesting exclusiveness is missing, so is that essential extrastatutory ingredient of an expression-exclusion demonstration, the series of terms from which an omission bespeaks a negative implication. [S]trike two in this case is the failure to identify any such established series, including both threats to others and threats to self, from which Congress appears to have made a deliberate

---

[3] In saying that the expansive textual phrases point in the direction of agency leeway we do not mean that the defense provisions place no limit on agency rulemaking. Without deciding whether all safety-related qualification standards must satisfy the ADA's direct-threat standard, we assume that some such regulations are implicitly precluded by the Act's specification of a direct-threat defense, such as those allowing "indirect" threats of "insignificant" harm. This is so because the definitional and defense provisions describing the defense in terms of "direct" threats of "significant" harm, 42 U.S.C. §§ 12113(b), 12111(3), are obviously intended to forbid qualifications that screen out by reference to general categories pretextually applied. Recognizing the "indirect" and "insignificant" would simply reopen the door to pretext by way of defense.

choice to omit the latter item as a signal of the affirmative defense's scope. The closest Echazabal comes is the EEOC's rule interpreting the Rehabilitation Act of 1973, 87 Stat. 357, as amended, 29 U.S.C. § 701 *et seq.*, a precursor of the ADA. That statute excepts from the definition of a protected "qualified individual with a handicap" anyone who would pose a "direct threat to the health or safety of other individuals," but, like the later ADA, the Rehabilitation Act says nothing about threats to self that particular employment might pose. 42 U.S.C. § 12113(b). The EEOC nonetheless extended the exception to cover threat-to-self employment, 29 CFR § 1613.702(f) (1990), and Echazabal argues that Congress's adoption only of the threat-to-others exception in the ADA must have been a deliberate omission of the Rehabilitation Act regulation's tandem term of threat-to-self, with intent to exclude it.

But two reasons stand in the way of treating the omission as an unequivocal implication of congressional intent. The first is that the EEOC was not the only agency interpreting the Rehabilitation Act, with the consequence that its regulation did not establish a clear, standard pairing of threats to self and others. While the EEOC did amplify upon the text of the Rehabilitation Act exclusion by recognizing threats to self along with threats to others, three other agencies adopting regulations under the Rehabilitation Act did not. See 28 CFR § 42.540(*l*)(1) (1990) (Department of Justice), 29 CFR § 32.3 (1990) (Department of Labor), and 45 CFR § 84.3(k)(1) (1990) (Department of Health and Human Services).[4] It would be a stretch, then, to say that there was a standard usage, with its source in agency practice or elsewhere, that connected threats to others so closely to threats to self that leaving out one was like ignoring a twin.

[I]nstead of making the ADA different from the Rehabilitation Act on the point at issue, Congress used identical language, knowing full well what the EEOC had made of that language under the earlier statute. Did Congress mean to imply that the agency had been wrong in reading the earlier language to allow it to recognize threats to self, or did Congress just assume that the agency was free to do under the ADA what it had already done under the earlier Act's identical language? There is no way to tell. Omitting the EEOC's reference to self-harm while using the very language that the EEOC had read as consistent with recognizing self-harm is equivocal at best. No negative inference is possible.

There is even a third strike against applying the expression-exclusion rule here. It is simply that there is no apparent stopping point to the argument that by specifying a threat-to-others defense Congress intended a negative implication about those whose safety could be considered. When Congress specified threats to others in the workplace, for example, could it possibly have meant that an employer could not defend a refusal to hire when a worker's disability would threaten

---

[4] In fact, we have said that the regulations issued by the Department of Health and Human Services, which had previously been the regulations of the Department of Health, Education, and Welfare, are of "particular significance" in interpreting the Rehabilitation Act because "HEW was the agency responsible for coordinating the implementation and enforcement of § 504 of the Rehabilitation Act, 29 U.S.C. § 794," prohibiting discrimination against individuals with disabilities by recipients of federal funds. Unfortunately for Echazabal's argument, the congruence of the ADA with the HEW regulations does not produce an unequivocal statement of congressional intent.

others outside the workplace? If Typhoid Mary had come under the ADA, would a meat packer have been defenseless if Mary had sued after being turned away? See 42 U.S.C. § 12113(d). *Expressio unius* just fails to work here.

B

Since Congress has not spoken exhaustively on threats to a worker's own health, the agency regulation can claim adherence under the rule in *Chevron*, so long as it makes sense of the statutory defense for qualification standards that are "job-related and consistent with business necessity." 42 U.S.C. § 12113(a). Chevron's reasons for calling the regulation reasonable are unsurprising: moral concerns aside, it wishes to avoid time lost to sickness, excessive turnover from medical retirement or death, litigation under state tort law, and the risk of violating the national Occupational Safety and Health Act of 1970, 84 Stat. 1590, as amended, 29 U.S.C. § 651 *et seq.* Although Echazabal claims that none of these reasons is legitimate, focusing on the concern with OSHA will be enough to show that the regulation is entitled to survive.

Echazabal points out that there is no known instance of OSHA enforcement, or even threatened enforcement, against an employer who relied on the ADA to hire a worker willing to accept a risk to himself from his disability on the job. In Echazabal's mind, this shows that invoking OSHA policy and possible OSHA liability is just a red herring to excuse covert discrimination. But there is another side to this. The text of OSHA itself says its point is "to assure so far as possible every working man and woman in the Nation safe and healthful working conditions," § 651(b), and Congress specifically obligated an employer to "furnish to each of his employees employment and a place of employment which are free from recognized hazards that are causing or are likely to cause death or serious physical harm to his employees," § 654(a)(1). Although there may be an open question whether an employer would actually be liable under OSHA for hiring an individual who knowingly consented to the particular dangers the job would pose to him, see Brief for United States *et al.* as *Amici Curiae* 19, n. 7, there is no denying that the employer would be asking for trouble: his decision to hire would put Congress's policy in the ADA, a disabled individual's right to operate on equal terms within the workplace, at loggerheads with the competing policy of OSHA, to ensure the safety of "each" and "every" worker. Courts would, of course, resolve the tension if there were no agency action, but the EEOC's resolution exemplifies the substantive choices that agencies are expected to make when Congress leaves the intersection of competing objectives both imprecisely marked but subject to the administrative leeway found in 42 U.S.C. § 12113(a).

Nor can the EEOC's resolution be fairly called unreasonable as allowing the kind of workplace paternalism the ADA was meant to outlaw. It is true that Congress had paternalism in its sights when it passed the ADA, see § 12101(a)(5) (recognizing "overprotective rules and policies" as a form of discrimination). But the EEOC has taken this to mean that Congress was not aiming at an employer's refusal to place disabled workers at a specifically demonstrated risk, but was trying to get at refusals to give an even break to classes of disabled people, while claiming to act for their own good in reliance on untested and pretextual stereotypes.[5] Its regulation disallows just this sort of sham protection, through demands for a particularized enquiry into the harms the employee would probably face. The direct threat defense must be "based on a reasonable medical judgment that relies on the most current medical knowledge and/or the best available objective evidence," and upon an expressly "individualized assessment of the individual's present ability to safely perform the essential functions of the job," reached after considering, among other things, the imminence of the risk and the severity of the harm portended. 29 CFR § 1630.2(r) (2001). The EEOC was certainly acting within the reasonable zone when it saw a difference between rejecting workplace paternalism and ignoring specific and documented risks to the employee himself, even if the employee would take his chances for the sake of getting a job.[6]

Finally, our conclusions that some regulation is permissible and this one is reasonable are not open to Echazabal's objection that they reduce the direct threat provision to "surplusage." The mere fact that a threat-to-self defense reasonably falls within the general "job related" and "business necessity" standard does not mean that Congress accomplished nothing with its explicit provision for a defense based on threats to others. The provision made a conclusion clear that might otherwise have been fought over in litigation or administrative rulemaking. It did not lack a job to do merely because the EEOC might have adopted the same rule later in applying the general defense provisions, nor was its job any less responsible simply because the agency was left with the option to go a step further. A provision can be useful even without congressional attention being indispensable.

---

[5]   Echazabal's contention that the Act's legislative history is to the contrary is unpersuasive. Although some of the comments within the legislative history decry paternalism in general terms, see, e.g., H.R.Rep.No.101–485, pt. 2, p. 72 (1990), U.S.Code Cong. & Admin.News 1990, pp. 303, 354 ("It is critical that paternalistic concerns for the disabled person's own safety not be used to disqualify an otherwise qualified applicant"); ADA Conf. Rep., 136 Cong.Rec. 17377 (1990) (statement of Sen. Kennedy) ("[A]n employer could not use as an excuse for not hiring a person with HIV disease the claim that the employer was simply 'protecting the individual' from opportunistic diseases to which the individual might be exposed"), those comments that elaborate actually express the more pointed concern that such justifications are usually pretextual, rooted in generalities and misperceptions about disabilities. See, e.g., H.R.Rep.No.101–485, at 74, U.S.Code Cong. & Admin.News 1990, pp. 303, 356 ("Generalized fear about risks from the employment environment, such as exacerbation of the disability caused by stress, cannot be used by an employer to disqualify a person with a disability"); S.Rep.No.101–116, p. 28 (1989) ("It would also be a violation to deny employment to an applicant based on generalized fears about the safety of the applicant. . . . By definition, such fears are based on averages and group-based predictions. This legislation requires individualized assessments"). Similarly, Echazabal points to several of our decisions expressing concern under Title VII, which like the ADA allows employers to defend otherwise discriminatory practices that are "consistent with business necessity," 42 U.S.C. § 2000e–2(k), with employers adopting rules that exclude women from jobs that are seen as too risky. See, e.g., Dothard v. Rawlinson, 433 U.S. 321, 335 (1977); Automobile Workers v. Johnson Controls, Inc., 499 U.S. 187, 202 (1991). Those cases, however, are beside the point, as they, like Title VII generally, were concerned with paternalistic judgments based on the broad category of gender, while the EEOC has required that judgments based on the direct threat provision be made on the basis of individualized risk assessments.

[6]   Respect for this distinction does not entail the requirement, as Echazabal claims, that qualification standards be "neutral," stating what the job requires, as distinct from a worker's disqualifying characteristics. Brief for Respondent 26. It is just as much business necessity for skyscraper contractors to have steelworkers without vertigo as to have well-balanced ones. Reasonableness does not turn on formalism.

Accordingly, we reverse the judgment of the Court of Appeals and remand the case for proceedings consistent with this opinion.

It is so ordered.

NOTES ON *CHEVRON USA, INC. V. ECHAZABAL*

1.   *Chevron* on Remand. On remand in *Chevron*, the Ninth Circuit once again reversed the district court's grant of summary judgment to the defendant. The court of appeals explained:

> Echazabal has raised a material issue of fact as to whether Chevron's decision was "based on a reasonable medical judgment that relies on the most current medical knowledge and/or the best available objective evidence." 29 C.F.R. § 1630.2(r). As part of the physical examinations ordered by Chevron, Dr. Baily, and later Dr. McGill, administered and relied upon tests that measure the levels of three enzymes in the bloodstream. Based on results demonstrating abnormally high levels of certain enzymes, Drs. Baily and McGill concluded that Echazabal's liver was not functioning properly, and recommended that Echazabal not be exposed to chemicals that could be toxic to his liver. Neither Dr. Baily nor Dr. McGill has any special training in liver disease. Baily's area of medical expertise is in preventive medicine, while McGill is a generalist, with no board certification in any specialty. In contrast, Echazabal's experts, Dr. Fedoruk and Dr. Gitnick, are specialists in toxicology and liver disease. Their opinions demonstrate that enzyme tests do not produce information regarding liver function. Rather, enzyme tests reflect only that an infection is ongoing. According to Fedoruk and Gitnick, the only tests that do measure liver function—blood albumin levels and prothrombin time—revealed that Echazabal's liver was functioning properly. Far from showing "cutting edge research," as Chevron argues, these opinions offered the unequivocal assessment that Echazabal could work at the refinery without facing a substantial risk of harm, beyond that faced by other workers. The required assessment could not be based upon "common sense," as Chevron argues, but rather only after—at a minimum—a consultation with a medical professional who had made an "objective, scientific" judgment. [*Bragdon.*]

> Echazabal presents evidence that there was no scientific basis for the contrary opinions of Chevron's doctors. Both Dr. Gitnick and Dr. Fedoruk stated that "there is no medical or scientific evidence" supporting a finding that Echazabal's chemical exposures from working as a plant helper or in the coker unit would present an appreciable or clinically significant risk. Dr. Fedoruk indicated that for some of the chemicals identified as potentially risky for Echazabal, an individual would receive a higher dosage from a daily multivitamin tablet than Echazabal would receive from working in the refinery. Based on the opinions of Drs. Fedoruk and Gitnick, a reasonable jury could conclude that Chevron failed to rely upon a "reasonable medical judgment that relies on the

most current medical knowledge and/or on the best available objective evidence."

In addition, the record does not support the district court's conclusion that the medical opinion letters from Echazabal's doctors evaluating his specific position all concurred that the job posed a "serious, immediate risk to him." On April 5, 1993, Dr. Ha wrote: "In my opinion the patient is now capable of carrying on with the work that he has applied for and there is no restriction on his activity at work as outlined by the working condition sheet GO 308 that was sent to me." Dr. Ha stated that Echazabal's prognosis "should be very good." Dr. Ha's opinion, based on her knowledge of Echazabal's potential work environment, does not support the view that she concurred in Chevron's assessment. On November 10, 1993, and July 20, 1994, Dr. Suchov wrote two letters indicating that there was "no limitation" on Echazabal's ability to work and that he could return to his "usual duties." Although the district court dismissed these letters because they did not address Echazabal's specific job duties, Echazabal's declaration states that he informed all of his doctors of the type of work that he performed. These letters, together with Echazabal's own declaration, raise a material issue of fact as to the objective reasonableness of Chevron's opinion.

The dissent describes as "clincher" the communications between Dr. McGill and Dr. Weingarten, one of Echazabal's treating physicians, in which Dr. Weingarten recommended against exposure to hepatotoxic hydrocarbons. The sum total of the recommendation was as follows:

> In your letter, it is mentioned that Mr. Echazabal has applied for return of his job and it mentioned that "this may entail exposure to hepatotoxic hydrocarbons." This, of course, is recommended not to be the case.

This general statement, which followed a statement that Echazabal was in good health and showed no sign of liver failure, is insufficient to carry Chevron's burden of establishing that it relied on the "most current medical knowledge and/or the best available objective evidence" and that it considered the likelihood of harm, its possible severity, and imminence. Notably missing from this statement is any indication that Dr. Weingarten was asked to consider the specific chemical exposures, to indicate the levels at which they would become dangerous or the likelihood that they would injure Echazabal, or even whether the risk to Echazabal was any greater than that for a healthy individual. (Indeed, it is difficult to imagine that any responsible doctor would recommend exposure of even his healthiest patient to an unspecified amount of hepatotoxic chemicals.) The district court notably found that "Dr. Weingarten was not informed by Dr. McGill about the specific chemicals to which plaintiff would be exposed, or the levels of concentration of those chemicals."

Chevron was required to do more than consider generalized statements of potential harm. Before refusing to hire Echazabal, Chevron was required, under the terms of 29 C.F.R. § 1630.2(r), to consider the severity, imminence, and potential likelihood of harm. Based on consideration of these factors, Chevron had the burden of demonstrating at least a "significant risk of substantial harm" to Echazabal. *Id.* The EEOC's Interpretive Guidance for this section explains that where the employer invoking the direct threat defense relies on threats to the employee, the employer must determine that there is a "high probability of substantial harm" to the individual. 29 C.F.R. pt. 1630 App. (EEOC Interpretive Guidance on Title I of the ADA) ("Interpretive Guidance"). Echazabal has raised a material question of fact as to whether Chevron made an adequate analysis. Dr. Weingarten's general statement, unrelated to the demands and conditions of the particular position or the likelihood, imminence, or potential severity of harm (or even whether Echazabal was at greater risk than a healthy individual), would not preclude a reasonable juror from concluding that Chevron failed to make the required assessment.

Echazabal died of an unrelated illness before the case could proceed to trial.

2. A "Dissent" from *Chevron*. Consider this response to the Supreme Court's opinion in *Chevron*, from the author of this casebook (who argued the losing side):

What Congress includes also gives a clue as to what Congress excludes. Can there be any doubt, for example, that by saying qualification standards "may include" a requirement that the employee pose no "direct threat" or "significant risk," that Congress prohibited employers from refusing to hire individuals with disabilities based on indirect threats or insignificant risks? [S]imilarly, one can make a strong argument that the textual limitation of the "direct threat" provision to cases involving risks to others, when considered in the light of the prohibition of paternalistic discrimination under Title VII and Congress's clear recognition of paternalism as a major target of the ADA, implies a clear rejection of the EEOC's earlier endorsement of a threat-to-self defense under the Rehabilitation Act.

[Moreover,] there has indeed been a longstanding "pairing of threats to self and others" in disability law—most notably in the law governing civil commitment. "General civil commitment statutes ordinarily require mental illness and dangerousness to self or others as criteria of commitment." When the normative justification for involuntary commitment based on "dangerousness to self" has been challenged, the challenges have been framed and understood as attacks on paternalism.

[T]he Court was simply wrong to assert that the EEOC's threat-to-self regulation under the Rehabilitation Act represented an interpretation of the "direct threat" language in that earlier statute. To the contrary, that regulation expressly purported to interpret the Rehabilitation Act's requirement that the plaintiff be "qualified" for the position he or she seeks—while the statutory "direct threat" provisions appeared in a portion of the statute that defined the term "handicapped person." Indeed, the EEOC's Rehabilitation Act regulation had a far broader scope than the direct threat provisions that existed in that earlier statute. The statutory provisions expressly applied only to two classes of people with disabilities: (1) alcoholics or drug abusers "whose employment, by reason of such current alcohol or drug abuse, would constitute a direct threat to property or the safety of others"; and (2) individuals with a "currently contagious disease or infection," who, "by reason of such disease or infection, would constitute a direct threat to the health or safety of other individuals." The EEOC's Rehabilitation Act regulation applied to all individuals with disabilities who posed risks to themselves or others—not just alcoholics, drug abusers, and people with contagious diseases. Moreover, the Rehabilitation Act's two "direct threat" provisions were not adopted until after the EEOC promulgated its regulations. It is therefore implausible to suggest that the EEOC's threat-to-self regulation in any way interpreted the "direct threat" language in that statute.

Thus, by defining the term "qualified individual with a disability" in the ADA solely by reference to present abilities to perform job tasks, Congress removed the statutory basis on which the EEOC had rested its threat-to-self regulation. Congress moved consideration of safety risks from the threshold "qualified individual" inquiry, where the EEOC's Rehabilitation Act regulation had put it, to the new general "direct threat" defense. And Congress expressly tailored that defense—in contrast to the EEOC's earlier approach—to cases involving threats to others. When viewed in this light, the omission of threat-to-self language from the ADA seems far more telling than the Chevron opinion suggests.

Samuel R. Bagenstos, *The Supreme Court, the Americans with Disabilities Act, and Rational Discrimination*, 44 Ala. L. Rev. 923 (2004). Which side do you find persuasive?

3. Is Direct Threat the Exclusive Safety-Based Defense? In *Albertson's*, the Court reserved the question whether all safety-based qualifications standards must satisfy the requirements of the direct threat defense. There is a reasonable argument that the direct threat defense is exclusive: If employers can justify safety-based qualification standards without showing a significant risk based on objective evidence and the most current medical knowledge, then what is the point of including that defense in the statute? *Chevron* also reserves the question, but two aspects of the Court's analysis suggest that the direct threat defense is *not* exclusive: First, the Court upholds an EEOC regulation that extends the defense to risks that are not specified in the statute's direct threat provision. Second, the Court emphasizes the breadth and inclusiveness of the "job related and consistent with business necessity" defense ("spacious defensive categories"). Can an employer apply a safety-based qualification standard to individuals whose disabilities do not pose a direct threat to the health and safety of others, simply by satisfying the more lenient business necessity standard? See, *e.g.*, *E.E.O.C. v. Exxon Corp.*, 203 F.3d 871, 875 (5th Cir.2000) ("We have found nothing in the statutory language, legislative history or case law that persuades that the direct threat provision addresses safety-based qualification standards in cases where an employer has developed a standard applicable to all employees of a given class. We hold that an employer need not proceed under the direct threat provision of § 12113(b) in such cases but rather may defend the standard as a business necessity. The direct threat test applies in cases in which an employer responds to an individual employee's supposed risk that is not addressed by an existing qualification standard."). Note that *Bates v. UPS*, a principal case above, applies the business-necessity analysis, and not the direct threat test, to a safety-based qualification standard.

D. SPECIAL PROBLEMS

1. MEDICAL EXAMINATIONS

Employer-required medical examinations can be an important location of discrimination against applicants and employees with disabilities. Employers can use them to identify employees with undisclosed disabilities, and they can use them to harass employees with known disabilities. But medical examinations also can serve legitimate employer interests in workplace safety and productivity. The ADA balances these concerns through a detailed series of provisions that regulate, but do not prohibit, employer-sponsored medical examinations.

The statute imposes different rules depending on *when* in the employment relationship an employer administers a medical exam:

a. *Job applicants*: Before an employer makes a conditional offer of employment (discussed immediately below), an employer is prohibited from "conduct[ing] a medical examination or mak[ing] inquiries of a job applicant as to whether such applicant is an individual with a disability or as to the nature or severity of such disability." 42 U.S.C. § 12112(d)(2)(A). The employer may, however, "make preemployment inquiries into the ability of an applicant to perform job-related functions." Id. § 12112(d)(2)(B).

b. *Employment entrance examination*: *After* an employer makes an offer of employment to a job applicant, the employer may require the applicant to submit to a medical examination, so long as "all entering employees are subjected to such an examination regardless of disability." 42 U.S.C. § 12112(d)(3)(A). The statute does not limit the scope of such an examination; it does, however, impose certain confidentiality requirements, and it prohibits using such an exam to discriminate. *Id.* § 12112(d)(3)(B), (C). An employer may condition the offer of employment on the results of the examination—but because the employer may not administer the exam until after it extends a conditional offer of employment, discrimination based on the results of the exam should be easy for a rejected applicant to identify.

c. *Incumbent employees*: Once an individual begins work, the employer may neither "require a medical examination" nor "make inquiries . . . as to whether such employee is an individual with a disability or as to the nature or severity of the disability, unless such examination or inquiry is shown to be job-related and consistent with business necessity." *Id.* § 12112(d)(4)(A).

The statutory provisions concerning medical examinations thus give employers one free shot to conduct a full-scale medical examination—though at a time, after a conditional offer of employment has been extended, that disability discrimination should be easy to spot. Before extending a conditional offer, the employer may not conduct a medical examination or make inquiries about disability; after an employee has begun work, the employer may conduct such an exam or make such inquiries only if it can establish job-relatedness and business necessity. An important, emerging question concerns the application of the ADA's medical examination provisions to workplace wellness programs. That question is addressed in the section on insurance in Chapter Five.

On the application of the ADA's medical examination provisions generally, consider the Eleventh Circuit's decision in OWUSU-ANSAH V. COCA-COLA CO., 715 F.3d 1306, 2013 WL 1896978 (11th Cir., May 8, 2013). At the time at issue in the case, Owusu-Ansah worked for Coca-Cola as a quality assurance person for customer service representatives in the company's call center. In that position, he worked mostly from home. In December 2007, however, he went to the office for a routine management meeting with his supervisor. At the meeting, according to the record as reviewed by the court, Owusu-Ansah complained about a number of instances of national origin discrimination and harassment he said he had experienced at the hands of his supervisors and coworkers. His supervisor "observed that Mr. Owusu-Ansah became agitated during the meeting, banged his hand on the table where they sat, and said that someone was 'going to pay for this.'"

Concerned about Owusu-Ansah's behavior, company management asked him to be interviewed by a consulting psychologist. After the interview, the company placed Owusu-Ansah on paid leave to enable him to be further evaluated as a potential safety threat. The company directed him to undergo a psychiatric evaluation, which included taking the Minnesota Multiphasic Personality Inventory (MMPI). He first refused to take the MMPI, but eventually took the test in March 2008. After reviewing the results of the test, Coca-Cola allowed Owusu-Ansah to return to work in April.

Owusu-Ansah claimed that the requirement that he take the MMPI was an impermissible medical examination or inquiry. The Eleventh Circuit affirmed a grant of summary judgment to the employer. The court held that the psychological evaluation, including the requirement that Owusu-Ansah take the MMPI, was "job-related and consistent with business necessity":

> The evaluation was "job-related" because an "employee's ability to handle reasonably necessary stress and work reasonably well with others are essential functions of any position." Ms. Cabral [the supervisor] reported that Mr. Owusu-Ansah—in the course of complaining about

discrimination and harassment—banged his fist on the table and said in a raised voice that someone was "going to pay for this." When he was deposed, Mr. Owusu-Ansah denied having behaved that way during his meeting with Ms. Cabral, and he now points out that there were no prior incidents showing that he had a propensity for workplace violence. That, however, is not dispositive. Although Coca-Cola apparently never asked Mr. Owusu-Ansah for his version of what happened at the meeting, it did not rely solely on Ms. Cabral's account in ordering the evaluation. Coca-Cola knew that Mr. Owusu-Ansah had refused to speak to Ms. Welsh [a company HR manager] and Dr. Riddell [a psychiatrist] about his workplace problems. In addition, Dr. McElhaney—the consulting psychologist—expressed "significant concerns" to Coca-Cola about Mr. Owusu-Ansah's emotional and psychological stability, and recommended a psychiatric/psychological fitness-for-duty evaluation.

On this record, we conclude that Coca-Cola had a reasonable, objective concern about Mr. Owusu-Ansah's mental state, which affected job performance and potentially threatened the safety of its other employees. Though Mr. Owusu-Ansah worked from home, he had access to and was required to attend meetings at the Dunwoody call center.

For basically the same reasons, the evaluation was also "consistent with business necessity." Though it may not be one of the traditional canons of statutory construction, common sense is not irrelevant in construing statutes, and in our view an employer can lawfully require a psychiatric/psychological fitness-for-duty evaluation under § 12112(d)(4)(A) if it has information suggesting that an employee is unstable and may pose a danger to others.

Does the court's analysis persuade you? Is Owusu-Ansah's conduct, as described by the court, sufficient to make a psychological examination job-related and consistent with business necessity?

Note that the ADA's medical examination provisions are not limited to individuals with disabilities. As every appellate court to have addressed the issue has noted, they protect any employee or applicant, regardless of whether she has an ADA-qualifying "disability." See, *e.g.*, *Conroy v. New York State Dept. of Correctional Services*, 333 F.3d 88, 94–95 (2d Cir.2003) (agreeing "with our sister circuits that a plaintiff need not prove that he or she has a disability unknown to his or her employer in order to challenge a medical inquiry or examination"). What damages would an applicant or employee have if she were subjected to a medical examination that violated these provisions but, because the exam revealed no disability, she suffered no adverse employment action?

Title II of the Genetic Information Nondiscrimination Act (GINA), 42 U.S.C. § 2000ff *et seq.*, also imposes limitations on medical examinations and inquiries, though it makes no distinction between applicants and incumbent employees. See 42 U.S.C. § 2000ff(2)(A)(i) (defining covered employees to include "an employee (including an applicant)" as defined in Title VII of the Civil Rights Act of 1964).

GINA generally prohibits employers from "request[ing], requir[ing], or purchas[ing] genetic information with respect to an employee or a family member of the employee." 42 U.S.C. § 2000ff-1(b). The statute defines "genetic information" to include information about "genetic tests" of the employee or a family member, as well as information about "the manifestation of a disease or disorder in family members of such individual." 42 U.S.C. § 2000ff(4)(A)(iii). The statute also contains a number of exceptions to this general prohibition, including for certain voluntary workplace wellness programs. See 42 U.S.C. § 2000ff-1(b)(2). And GINA imposes confidentiality requirements, which cross-reference the ADA's requirements for employment entrance examinations, on employers who validly receive their employees' genetic information. See 42 U.S.C. § 2000ff-5. For discussion of GINA, see Jessica L. Roberts, *The Genetic Information Nondiscrimination Act as an Antidiscrimination Law*, 86 Notre Dame L. Rev. 597 (2011); Jessica L. Roberts, *Preempting Discrimination: Lessons from the Genetic Information Nondiscrimination Act*, 63 Vand. L. Rev. 439 (2010).

2. DISPARATE IMPACT

The ADA's employment provisions prohibit more than just intentional discrimination or the failure to accommodate individual employees with disabilities. The statute also, by its terms, prohibits selection criteria that have an unjustified disparate impact on any "class of individuals with disabilities." 42 U.S.C. § 12112(b)(6). Since roughly the time the ADA was adopted, few disparate impact cases have been brought in *any* area of employment discrimination law, and such cases are especially scant in the disability area: "Under the Americans with Disabilities Act (ADA), individual claims to accommodate specific impairments in particular jobs have all but eclipsed a coherent theory of disability-related disparate impact law. Moreover, the class action device, which historically played a central role in group-based discrimination theory (while often going hand in hand with robust disparate impact litigation), has been virtually nonexistent under the statute's employment provisions." Michael Ashley Stein & Michael E. Waterstone, *Disability, Disparate Impact, and Class Actions*, 56 Duke L.J. 861, 864 (2006).

Professors Stein and Waterstone argue that an invigorated disparate impact doctrine, enforced through class actions, can be essential to eliminating the workplace practices that impose barriers to people with disabilities. Invoking pandisability theory, they argue that an individual with one disability ought to be able to sue an employer on behalf of potential employees with all sorts of disabilities: If an employer's workforce has a "near-complete absence of people with disabilities" (of any kind), they argue, an applicant with a disability will establish "a prima facie case that some official policy or practice has made [the employer] an unwelcoming employer for disabled persons." The employer, in their view, should then be required to show that its existing practices are job-related and consistent with business necessity. See *id.* at 914. Is the proposal of Professors Stein and Waterstone practical? Is it attractive?

3. HARASSMENT

The Supreme Court has held that "sexual harassment so 'severe or pervasive' as to 'alter the conditions of [the victim's] employment and create an abusive working environment' " violates Title VII of the Civil Rights Act of 1964. *Faragher v. City of Boca Raton*, 524 U.S. 775, 786 (1998) (quoting *Meritor Savings Bank, FSB v. Vinson*, 477 U.S. 57, 67 (1986)). Like Title VII, the ADA prohibits discrimination in the "terms, conditions, and privileges of employment." 42 U.S.C. § 12112(a). The courts have therefore held that the ADA prohibits discriminatory workplace harassment of individuals with disabilities to the same extent as Title VII prohibits race- or sex-based harassment. See Mark C. Weber, *Workplace Harassment Claims Under the Americans with Disabilities Act: A New Interpretation*, 14 Stan. L. & Pol'y Rev. 241, 243 (2003) ("Courts have uniformly concluded that the ADA furnishes a cause of action to remedy a work environment that is hostile to persons with disabilities.").

Professor Weber argues that the Title VII standard affords insufficient protection to people with disabilities in the workplace:

> The result of applying the severe-or-pervasive standard to ADA cases is that co-workers and supervisors can ridicule, threaten, verbally abuse, and otherwise harass persons with disabilities with impunity, so long as the mistreatment does not rise to the level the courts have established. Harassment punishes workers with disabilities for simply showing up, and it works. It keeps people with disabilities out of the workplace.

Id. at 249. He argues that litigants and courts should look to 42 U.S.C. § 12203(b) as offering a more generous standard for harassment plaintiffs. That section provides:

> It shall be unlawful to coerce, intimidate, threaten, or interfere with any individual in the exercise or enjoyment of, or on account of his or her having exercised or enjoyed, or on account of his or her having aided or encouraged any other individual in the exercise or enjoyment of, any right granted or protected by this chapter.

Professor Weber argues that Section 12203(b), by its terms, prohibits (non-severe, non-pervasive) harassment because "[v]erbal abuse and physical harassment are highly effective tools of coercion and intimidation." Weber, *supra*, at 251. He argues that "Co-worker and supervisor conduct that harasses—under a common-sense, not a Supreme Court, definition of that word—interferes with" the statutory rights of "taking a job on an equal basis, working every day the same way that others work, and participating as an equal in the workplace." *Id.* at 252. Is Professor Weber's reading of the statute persuasive? Does it respond to a real problem?

4. ASSOCIATIONAL DISCRIMINATION

In addition to prohibiting discrimination against people with disabilities themselves, the ADA bars employers from "excluding or otherwise denying equal jobs or benefits to a qualified individual because of the known disability of an individual with whom the qualified individual is known to have a relationship or association." 42 U.S.C. § 12112(b)(4). Does this provision require employers to provide *accommodations* to the nondisabled relatives or associates of individuals with disabilities? See *Den Hartog v. Wasatch Academy*, 129 F.3d 1076, 1084–85 (10th Cir.1997) (answering that question in the negative).

E. REMEDIES

Title I of the ADA incorporates by reference the remedies and procedures that apply under Title VII of the Civil Rights Act of 1964. See 42 U.S.C. § 12117(a). Aggrieved individuals must first file a charge with the Equal Employment Opportunity Commission or the equivalent state antidiscrimination agency. The EEOC will investigate the charge and may attempt to resolve it through conciliation or, occasionally, file a lawsuit. If the EEOC does not resolve the charge to the complainant's satisfaction within 180 days, it will issue a "right to sue" letter; the complainant may then file an action in federal district court.

A successful plaintiff in a Title I action may be entitled to up to two years' back pay, reinstatement, and damages (up to a statutory cap). The plaintiff may recover punitive damages (subject to the cap) if she can show that the employer "engaged in a discriminatory practice or discriminatory practices with malice or with reckless indifference to [her] federally protected rights." 42 U.S.C. § 1981a(b)(1). In reasonable accommodation cases (but not cases involving intentional discrimination), the employer will not be required to pay damages if it "demonstrates good faith efforts, in consultation with the person with the disability who has informed the covered entity that accommodation is needed, to identify and make a reasonable accommodation that would provide such individual with an equally effective opportunity and would not cause an undue hardship on the operation of the business." 42 U.S.C. § 1981a(a)(3). This provision gives employers an incentive to pursue the interactive process that, as discussed above, some courts say the statute requires.

There is some dispute regarding whether Title VII's so-called mixed-motives provisions apply to ADA cases. The first of those provisions states that "an unlawful employment practice is established when the complaining party demonstrates that race, color, religion, sex, or national origin was a *motivating factor* for any employment practice, even though other factors also motivated the practice." 42 U.S.C. § 2000e-2(m) (emphasis added). The second provides that, once the plaintiff establishes liability under the first provision, the employer can nonetheless avoid back pay, damages, and reinstatement if it can demonstrate that it "would have taken the same action in the absence of the impermissible motivating factor." 42 U.S.C. § 2000e-5(g)(2)(B).

In LEWIS V. HUMBOLDT ACQUISITION CORP., INC., 681 F.3d 312 (6th Cir.2012) (*en banc*), a divided court held that these mixed-motives provisions do not apply to cases brought under the ADA. Instead, the court held, the plaintiff must prove that disability was the but-for cause of her adverse employment action:

> [I]n 1989, the Court considered how a because-of standard of causation worked in mixed-motives cases—cases where

permissible and impermissible considerations played a role in the employer's adverse employment action. *Price Waterhouse v. Hopkins,* 490 U.S. 228, 232 (1989). The decision splintered four ways. As later characterized by the Court, the lowest common denominator of *Price Waterhouse* was the creation of a burden-shifting framework to determine causation in mixed-motive cases: "[I]f a Title VII plaintiff shows that discrimination was a 'motivating' or a 'substantial' factor in the employer's action, the burden of persuasion should shift to the employer to show that it would have taken the same action regardless of that impermissible consideration."

Two years after *Price Waterhouse,* Congress passed the Civil Rights Act of 1991, which added two relevant provisions to Title VII. The first says: "Except as otherwise provided in this title, an unlawful employment practice is established when the complaining party demonstrates that race, color, religion, sex, or national origin was *a motivating factor* for any employment practice, even though other factors also motivated the practice." Pub.L. No. 102–166, § 107, 105 Stat. 1071, 1075 (1991) (codified at 42 U.S.C. § 2000e–2(m)) (emphasis added). The second provides limited remedies—declaratory relief, injunctive relief and attorney's fees, but not damages or reinstatement—if the claimant meets the motivating factor standard but the employer shows it would have taken the same adverse employment action anyway. *Id.* (codified at 42 U.S.C. § 2000e–5(g)(2)(B)). The two provisions "responded to *Price Waterhouse*" by adding new standards for mixed-motives cases to the text of Title VII. *Desert Palace, Inc. v. Costa,* 539 U.S. 90, 94 (2003).

There are two ways to look at this history. One is that *Price Waterhouse* established the meaning of "because of" for Title VII *and* other statutes with comparable causation standards, with Congress essentially ratifying *Price Waterhouse:* Namely, a "because of" causation standard permits a plaintiff to show that the prohibited characteristic was "a motivating factor" of the adverse employment action, shifting the burden of persuasion to the employer to show that the characteristic was not a "but-for" cause of the action because it would have taken the same action anyway for legitimate reasons. The other is that by amending Title VII to provide recovery under a "motivating factor" theory, Congress made this theory available to Title VII claimants but not to claimants under other civil rights statutes given that Congress did not extend this framework to the other statutes.

Enter *Gross v. FBL Financial Services,* 557 U.S. 167 (2009). It adopted the second theory and refused to expand the reach of Title VII's "motivating factor" amendments to another civil rights statute that contained a "because of" standard of causation. At stake in *Gross* was whether to apply Title VII's "motivating factor" standard for proving employment discrimination, 42 U.S.C. §§ 2000e–2(m) and 2000e5(g)(2)(B), to disputes under the Age Discrimination in Employment Act,

29 U.S.C. § 623(a)(1). Although both statutes concern employment discrimination and both statutes share common goals, the Court reasoned that it would not casually "apply rules applicable under one statute to a different statute." *Gross,* 557 U.S. at 174. Unlike Title VII, *Gross* observed, the ADEA does not allow a plaintiff to prove discrimination merely by showing that her disability was *a motivating factor* behind her adverse employment action; the ADEA requires discrimination to be *because of* a disability, which means "but-for" causation. *Id.* at 177–78. Making this difference in language particularly salient was the reality that Congress amended both statutes in 1991, but added the "motivating factor" language only to Title VII, not to the ADEA. Civil Rights Act of 1991, Pub.L. No. 102–166, § 107, 105 Stat. 1071; *see also id.* § 115; Gross, 557 U.S. at 174–75.

This rationale applies with equal force to the ADA. The ADEA prohibits discrimination "because of [an] individual's age," 29 U.S.C. § 623(a)(1), and does "not provide that a plaintiff may establish discrimination by showing that age was simply a motivating factor" in the adverse employment decision. *Gross,* 557 U.S. at 174. So too with the ADA, which makes unlawful "discriminat[ion] . . . *because of* " a person's disability, 42 U.S.C. § 12112(a), (b)(1), and which says nothing about allowing a plaintiff to prevail because a disability was a "motivating factor" in the adverse employment decision.

[G]ross resolves this case. No matter the shared goals and methods of two laws, it explains that we should not apply the substantive causation standards of one antidiscrimination statute to other anti-discrimination statutes when Congress uses distinct language to describe the two standards.

[L]ewis insists she is not asking us to read anything into the text of the ADA that is not already there. A section of the ADA, she points out, cross-references Title VII:

> The powers, remedies, and procedures set forth in sections 2000e–4, 2000e–5, 2000e–6, 2000e–8, and 2000e–9 of [Title VII] shall be the powers, remedies, and procedures this subchapter provides to the [EEOC], to the Attorney General, or to any person alleging discrimination on the basis of disability in violation of any provision of this chapter, or regulations promulgated under section 12116 of this title, concerning employment.

42 U.S.C. § 12117(a). But this cross-reference, which predates the 1991 amendments, accounts for the reality that the ADA does not have any enforcement provisions of its own. *Id.* That is why the provision has the label "Enforcement," *id.,* and why the Title VII cross-reference invoked by Lewis, 42 U.S.C. § 2000e–5, has the label "Enforcement provisions." That also is why these enforcement mechanisms apply only to remedies for "discrimination on the basis of disability in violation of any provision of *this chapter* " (emphasis added), as opposed to violations of some other standard of care under *another* chapter. A disability claimant may not use the "powers,

remedies, and procedures" of Title VII without establishing a violation of the ADA.

Confirming the point, the companion enforcement provision of this section of the ADA, labeled "Coordination," directs the agencies with enforcement authority under the ADA and the Rehabilitation Act to create "procedures" that "prevent[ ] imposition of inconsistent or conflicting standards for the same requirements." 42 U.S.C. § 12117(b). Congress took the same path with the coordination provision of Title II of the ADA, which incorporates "[t]he remedies, procedures, and rights" of section 505 of the Rehabilitation Act. 42 U.S.C. § 12133. Just as the provisions of the ADA incorporating the Rehabilitation Act's enforcement provisions do not bring that Act's standard of care into the ADA, neither does the provision of the ADA incorporating Title VII's enforcement provisions.

There is another reason the incorporation of Title VII's enforcement "powers, remedies, and procedures" into the ADA does not pull the "motivating factor" standard along with them. The part of Title VII that contains the "motivating factor" test—§ 2000e–2—is *not* included in the list of enforcement provisions identified in the ADA but appears (unsurprisingly) in a section of Title VII captioned "Unlawful employment practices." That Congress did not incorporate § 2000e–2 into the ADA ought to give a court pause before doing so itself.

Keep looking, Lewis tells us. Although the ADA's cross-references do not mention § 2000e–2, they do mention § 2000e–5, which itself contains a cross-reference to the "motivating factor" provision when it provides a limited set of remedies for Title VII claimants who demonstrate motivating-factor discrimination. But this cross-cross-reference argument contains problems of its own. One is that § 2000e–5 does not direct judges to apply the substantive "motivating factor" standard from § 2000e–2(m); it permits them only to provide a remedy for plaintiffs who "prove[ ] a violation under section 2000e–2(m)." 42 U.S.C. § 2000e–5(g)(2)(B). No ADA plaintiffs will prevail under § 2000e–2(m), because that provision is a substantive standard that applies only to Title VII plaintiffs, not to ADA plaintiffs, as it speaks to "[i]mpermissible consideration of race, color, religion, sex, or national origin" but says nothing about disability status. Nor does this reading make the ADA's incorporation of § 2000e–5 meaningless. That subsection contains more than a dozen other provisions detailing procedures that remain applicable under the ADA. In incorporating a wide range of Title VII enforcement procedures and remedies into the ADA, it is hardly surprising that some of those provisions (in truth some *parts* of those provisions) apply by their terms only to Title VII cases.

Still another problem with this argument is that § 2000e–5(g)(2)(B) cross-references *all* of § 2000e–2(m). It applies the "motivating factor" standard of causation to "race, color, religion, sex, or national origin" discrimination in employment.

That means an ADA claimant could win only by showing discrimination based on *another* protected ground. Even with a lower standard of causation, that is no benefit to claimants seeking relief premised on disability-based discrimination. Surely the ADA does not impose liability based on other forms of discrimination or, worse, make other forms of discrimination a precondition for establishing disability-based discrimination.

Judges Clay, Stranch, and Donald dissented in relevant part. Judge Clay explained:

> It is unnecessary to resort to a lengthy explanation of the legislative history of the ADA and other civil rights statutes or an extended statutory construction analysis, because the authority setting forth the application of Title VII to the ADA is clear and forthright. Simply put, the ADA was enacted to expand the protection against discrimination beyond that afforded by Title VII, in order to provide the same remedies offered to individuals discriminated against on the basis of race, color, religion, sex, and national origin to those discriminated against on the basis of their disabilities. *See* 42 U.S.C. § 12101. The ADA explicitly cross-references and adopts Title VII's enforcement section, including "powers, remedies, and procedures." 42 U.S.C. § 12117(a) ("The powers, remedies, and procedures set forth in sections 2000e–4, 2000e–5, 2000e– 6, 2000e–8, and 2000e–9 of this title shall be the powers, remedies, and procedures [of] this subchapter . . . ."). Title VII's remedies thus apply to the ADA with equal force and validity; this includes the changing interpretation of Title VII and any amendments made thereto. As noted by the House of Representatives Report on the ADA, "[b]ecause of the cross-reference to title VII" in the ADA, "any amendment to Title VII that may be made" with respect to Title VII's powers, remedies, and procedures "would be fully applicable to the ADA." H.R. Rep. No. 101–485, pt. 3, at 48 (1990). In other words, "[b]y retaining the cross-reference to Title VII, the Committee's intent is that the remedies of Title VII, currently and as amended in the future, will be applicable to persons with disabilities." *Id.* "Thus, if the powers, remedies, and procedures change in title VII of the 1964 Act, they will change identically under the ADA for persons with disabilities." *Id.* The fact that Title VII employs the motivating-factor standard of causation informs us that the meaning of the ADA's "because of" language should correspondingly be interpreted to invoke the motivating-factor standard. 42 U.S.C. § 2000e–2(m).

> The shortcomings of the "but-for" standard employed by the majority become clear when one considers, in this context, how the "but-for" concept is narrowly circumscribed by its own definition. "But-for cause," also referred to as "actual cause" or "cause in fact," means "[t]he cause without which the event could not have occurred." Black's Law Dictionary 212 (7th ed.1999). It is "[t]he doctrine that causation exists only when the result would not have occurred without the [relevant] conduct." *Id.* at 192–93. In other words, but-for cause means

that the relevant factor was *necessary* for the consummation of an event. As the Supreme Court has described it, "[b]ut-for causation is a hypothetical construct." *Price Waterhouse.* "In determining whether a particular factor was a but-for cause of a given event, we begin by assuming that that factor was present at the time of the event, and then ask whether, even if that factor had been absent, the event nevertheless would have transpired in the same way." *Id.*

A motivating-factor standard, which is in accord with the requirements of the ADA, requires a plaintiff to show that her protected trait, disability in this case, was one of the considerations that the defendant took into account when taking action against the plaintiff. A but-for standard requires proof that even if that consideration was absent, the adverse action "nevertheless would have transpired in the same way."

[I]magine that a disabled plaintiff seeks remedy under the ADA following the termination of her employment, which she believes was on the basis of her disability. The plaintiff admits evidence that the employer wished to terminate her because the employer believed her disability was troublesome to its business; but the employer admits other evidence that the plaintiff's work was less than exemplary. Under a motivating-factor standard, the plaintiff could easily satisfy her causation burden by presenting evidence that her disability provided one of the reasons for her termination. However, under the but-for standard, the plaintiff is obligated to prove that without the disability, her allegedly poor performance would not have been enough to motivate her employer to terminate her. In practice, a plaintiff will rarely discover objective evidence of her employer's state of mind or internal motivations that would satisfy this extremely heavy burden. The plaintiff must instead resort to conjectural inquiry of the employer's thoughts and purposes, which the employer can simply and succinctly reject by offering a myriad of other subjective reasons for her termination. As the Supreme Court stated in *Price Waterhouse,* it is contrary to "our common sense" that "Congress meant to obligate a plaintiff to identify the precise causal role played by legitimate and illegitimate motivations in the employment decision she challenges." When taking into account the purpose of the ADA to ameliorate discrimination against people with disabilities and its relationship to other civil rights statutes, it becomes clear that the less burdensome motivating-factor standard of causation should apply.

The majority relies on the Supreme Court's recent decision in *Gross,* which held that claims under the Age Discrimination in Employment Act of 1967 (ADEA), 29 U.S.C. §§ 621–634, are governed by the but-for standard and not the motivating-factor standard, as conclusive support for the proposition that the but-for standard must apply to ADA claims as well. However, *Gross* is inapplicable to our analysis of the appropriate standard of causation under the ADA because *Gross* examined the issue in the context of the ADEA, which involves discrimination under a different analytical rubric. [B]ecause the ADA is explicitly tied to Title VII's remedies provisions— unlike the ADEA—a careful examination of the two statutes makes clear that a plaintiff alleging discrimination under the ADA must only prove that the discrimination was a motivating factor for the adverse action.

Judge Stranch similarly argued:

In 1989, the Supreme Court decided Price Waterhouse v. Hopkins, determining what the statutory language "because of" meant in Title VII. The Court held that where a plaintiff proved gender played "a motivating part" in an employment decision, along with other legitimate factors, the plaintiff established that the decision was "because of" sex in violation of Title VII. This method of proof became known as the "mixed-motive" analysis, or the "motivating factor" standard. Thus, when Congress enacted the ADA shortly thereafter and chose both to include the "because of" language and to cross-reference Title VII, it knew that using the Title VII language in an analogous and closely related employment anti-discrimination statute created a "motivating factor" standard.

F. DISABILITY RIGHTS LAW AND EMPLOYMENT POLICY

NOTES ON DISABILITY RIGHTS LAW AND EMPLOYMENT POLICY

1. **The Employment Effects of the ADA.** When the ADA was pending in Congress, the bill's supporters argued that it would move people off of the disability benefits rolls and into the workforce in large numbers. See generally Samuel R. Bagenstos, *The Americans with Disabilities Act as Welfare Reform*, 44 Wm. & Mary L. Rev. 921 (2003). But, more than two decades after the bill's enactment into law, the employment rate for people with disabilities remains extremely low. According to the Bureau of Labor Statistics, 20.7% of people with disabilities were in the labor force in April 2013, compared with 68.8% of people without disabilities. Data from the Census Bureau's American Community Survey tell a similar story. That survey found that, in 2011, 33.1% of working-age men and women with disabilities were working, compared with 69.3% of those *without* disabilities.[a] (The numbers differ because the different surveys use different definitions of disability, as well as different sampling and estimating techniques.)

During the 2007-2009 recession, employment rates for people with disabilities dropped significantly more than for people without disabilities. Between October 2008 and October 2010, the employment rate for people with disabilities dropped by 9.9 percent, while the employment rate for people without dropped by only 4.9 percent. See H. Stephen Kaye, *The Impact of the 2007–09 Recession on Workers with Disabilities*, Monthly Lab. Rev., Oct. 2010, at 19, 24. And "[n]umerous studies have found that the employment rate for people with disabilities declined or remained stagnant throughout the 1990s—a period that overlapped with both the

---

[a] Up-to-date disability statistics can be found at http://www.disabilitystatistics.org or http://www.dol.gov/odep/topics/DisabilityEmploymentStatistics.htm.

implementation of the ADA and a booming economy." Samuel R. Bagenstos, *The Future of Disability Law*, 114 Yale L.J. 1, 19 (2004). During that period, "[a]lthough the employment rates for men and women without disabilities increased with the economic boom of the 1990s, the employment rates for those with disabilities did not. As a result, 'in the 1990s the relative employment rates of both men and women with disabilities also declined dramatically.'" *Id.* at 20 (quoting Richard V. Burkhauser *et al.*, *A User's Guide to Current Statistics on the Employment of People with Disabilities*, *in* The Decline in Employment of People with Disabilities: A Policy Puzzle 23, 41 (David C. Stapleton & Richard V. Burkhauser, eds., 2003)). Why has the ADA not led to an improvement in the employment rate of people with disabilities? Why, indeed, did the employment rate of (some classes of) people with disabilities *drop* on some measures during the 1990s economic boom, when employment rates were increasing for most groups in the economy? Cf. Alan S. Blinder & Janet L. Yellen, *The Fabulous Decade: Macroeconomic Lessons From the 1990s*, *in* The Roaring Nineties: Can Full Employment Be Sustained? 91 (Alan B. Krueger & Robert M. Solow eds., 2001).

Some commentators have suggested that the ADA *itself* is the problem. See Daron Acemoglu & Joshua D. Angrist, *Consequences of Employment Protection? The Case of the Americans with Disabilities Act*, 109 J. Pol. Econ. 915 (2001); Thomas DeLeire, *The Wage and Employment Effects of the Americans with Disabilities Act*, 35 J. Hum. Res. 693 (2000); Christine Jolls, *Accommodation Mandates*, 53 Stan. L. Rev. 223, 273–76 (2000). Extending an argument first made in the context of Title VII of the Civil Rights Act of 1964,[b] they contend that the ADA imposes on employers a net economic incentive to refuse to hire individuals with disabilities.

The point may seem counterintuitive at first, but in fact it is straightforward. Although the ADA prohibits discrimination against job *applicants* with disabilities, that prohibition is likely to prove difficult to enforce. It is often difficult to determine with any certainty whether discriminatory intent factored into an employer's decision to choose one applicant (who had no disability) over another (who had a disability). That fact poses a barrier to enforcement of Title VII's prohibition of hiring discrimination as well, but the problem is more acute in the disability context. Because there are so many different disabilities, and so few applicants with any given disability, it is far more difficult to muster statistical proof of disability discrimination than of race or sex discrimination. And the prospective damages recovery for a disappointed applicant (who must mitigate damages, and typically can find some other job) will often be too little to entice an attorney to take her case.

By contrast, the prohibitions on discrimination against *incumbent* employees with disabilities (who are discharged or denied accommodations) are likely to be far more effectively enforced. An individual who has been doing a job satisfactorily for years is an attractive plaintiff before a jury, and she is likely to be earning more—and thus have a higher prospective

---

[b] See, e.g., John J. Donohue III & Peter Siegelman, *The Changing Nature of Employment Discrimination Litigation*, 43 Stan. L. Rev. 983, 1026–27 (1991); Richard A. Posner, *The Efficiency and Efficacy of Title VII*, 136 U.Pa. L. Rev. 513, 519 (1987).

damages recovery—than a disappointed entry-level applicant. (Not to mention that she can afford an attorney's retainer.) Not surprisingly, claims of discriminatory discharge have far outpaced claims of hiring discrimination in ADA litigation. See Steven L. Willborn, *The Nonevolution of Enforcement under the ADA: Discharge Cases and the Hiring Problem*, in Employment, Disability, and the Americans with Disabilities Act: Issues In Law, Public Policy, And Research 103, 103–04 (Peter David Blanck ed., 2000) (observing that "over the short life of the ADA, the ratio of discharge to hiring cases has been about 10 to 1, a ratio that is substantially higher than for Title VII cases").

If employers are, as a practical matter, unlikely to face much consequence if they discriminate against job applicants with disabilities, but they will be required to provide accommodations to—and be less free to fire—employees with disabilities, they will have an incentive, all else equal, *not* to hire disabled job applicants. Three significant empirical studies of the ADA's employment effects have concluded that the statute had precisely this sort of perverse effect when it initially came into force. See Acemoglu & Angrist, *supra*; DeLeire, *supra*; Christine Jolls & J.J. Prescott, Disaggregating Employment Protection: The Case of Disability Discrimination (working paper, 2005). Professors Acemoglu and Angrist found that the number of weeks worked among adults with disabilities reduced significantly after the ADA came into effect in 1992, and that the effect was most pronounced during the statute's first two years of implementation. Professor DeLeire found that the employment rate for men with disabilities began dropping when the ADA was adopted in 1990, and that the rate continued to decline through the end of his study period in 1995.

Probably the richest analysis comes from Professors Jolls and Prescott, who examined whether the changes in disability employment differed across the states that did and did not have their own reasonable accommodation laws prior to the enactment of the ADA. They found states that had *no* such laws prior to the ADA experienced a significant drop in 1993 and 1994 in the number of weeks worked by people with disabilities compared to people without disabilities in 1993 and 1994 (but no significant employment effect thereafter). In states that *had* such laws, they found no significant employment effect of the ADA.

Professors Donahue, Stein, Griffin & Becker, examining data regarding the employment of male heads of household in the Panel Study of Income Dynamics from 1981 through 1996, found that "the ADA had a *negative* impact on the employment levels of the disabled relative to the nondisabled but no impact on relative earnings." John J. Donohue III, Michael Ashley Stein, Christopher L. Griffin, Jr., & Sascha Becker, 8 J. Emp. Leg. Stud. 477, 501 (2011). But when they restricted their sample to the 1,437 individuals who appeared in the PSID throughout the entire 16-year period, Professor Donahue and his colleagues found "little evidence of adverse effects on weeks worked," but "strong evidence of wage decline for the disabled, albeit one that began in 1986, well prior to the adoption of the ADA." *Id.*

These studies are controversial. One significant criticism relates to the measure of disability that they employed. Those studies relied on government data that defines disability as a "work limitation"—a condition that limits the type or amount of work one can do. When compared to the definition of disability employed by the ADA at the time, the "work limitation" definition is both over- and under-inclusive. As studies using different definitions of disability show, the ADA seems to have led to a significant increase in employment among those individuals whose disabilities do not limit the type or amount of work they can do. See Julie L. Hotchkiss, The Labor Market Experience of Workers with Disabilities: The ADA and Beyond 23–27 (2003); Douglas Kruse & Lisa Schur, *Employment of People with Disabilities Following the ADA*, 42 Indus. Rel. 31 (2003).

Another significant criticism looks to other policy changes that occurred at roughly the same time as the ADA was enacted. In particular, the eligibility criteria for Social Security Disability Insurance loosened in significant ways beginning in 1984. In the recession of 1990–1991, many people with disabilities were pushed to take advantage of the loosened criteria and joined the SSDI rolls for the first time. It was the push of a weak economy combined with the pull of easier access to SSDI, a number of commentators argue, that led to the decline in employment among people with disabilities around the time the ADA was enacted. One significant study found "an almost one to one correspondence between the numbers moving onto SSDI and the numbers showing up in the work limited and not employed category." Nanette Goodman & Timothy Waidmann, *Social Security Disability Insurance and the Recent Decline in the Employment Rate of People with Disabilities, in* The Decline in Employment, *supra,* at 339, 352. And a study by Professor Richard Burkhauser and his colleagues concluded that the decline in employment of people with disabilities began before the ADA was enacted, as a direct result of the expansions in SSDI eligibility. See Richard V. Burkhauser *et al.*, Accounting for the Declining Fortunes of Working-Age People with Disabilities (working paper 2006).

What is the upshot of these various studies? In a separate work, the author of this casebook concludes that the ADA "has probably already had a demonstrably positive effect on the employment of individuals whose disabilities do not require accommodation, and it is likely ultimately to have a positive effect on the employment of individuals whose disabilities require accommodation as well." Samuel R. Bagenstos, Law and the Contradictions of the Disability Rights Movement 122 (2009). But when considering the results to date for people with disabilities considered in the aggregate, however, "it is clear that the statute hasn't *increased* employment for people with disabilities to any significant extent." *Id.* at 121. Do you agree with these conclusions? What do the data suggest about whether the ADA reflects a helpful or a harmful approach to disability policy? Compare *id.* at 122–123 (arguing that a "great deal of reform is necessary" but that "the case for abandonment of the statute has not been made"), with Richard A. Epstein, Forbidden Grounds: The Case against Employment Discrimination Laws 493–94 (1992) (arguing for repeal of the ADA), and Jerry L. Mashaw, *Against First Principles*, 31 San Diego L. Rev. 211, 231–237 (1994) (arguing that the ADA is a "deeply-flawed statute" that should be replaced with a system of tradable quotas).

2.   The Quota Alternative. European countries—and other countries throughout the world—have traditionally relied heavily on quota systems to promote the employment of individuals with disabilities. See Lisa Waddington & Matthew Diller, *Tensions and Coherence in Disability Policy: The Uneasy Relationship Between Social Welfare and Civil Rights Models of Disability in American, European, and International Employment Law*, *in* Disability Rights Law and Policy: International and National Perspectives 241, 256 (Mary Lou Breslin & Sylvia Yee eds., 2002). A number of commentators have suggested that the United States should adopt such a system. Professor Mark Weber, for example, argues that a quota system—imposed by the federal government on private industry—is the only way to move people with disabilities into the workforce in significant numbers. See Mark C. Weber, *Beyond the Americans with Disabilities Act: A National Employment Policy for People with Disabilities*, 46 Buff. L. Rev. 123 (1998).

Other commentators argue for the quota system on the grounds of fairness and efficiency. Professor Jerry Mashaw proposes a scheme of tradable quotas analogous to the emissions trading schemes that have been adopted in environmental law in recent decades. Professor Mashaw's proposal would require the government to "estimate the number of disabled workers who might with reasonable accommodation be employed; divide that number by the total number of workers in the economy; and require that each employer hire that percentage of its workforce from the pool of 'disabled' workers. Employers who fail to hire their share of disabled workers would have to buy a waiver from employers who are employing more than their share." Mashaw, *supra*, at 232. Professor Mashaw argues that such a scheme would promote both fairness and efficiency, because employers who faced high accommodations costs would pay, and employers who faced lower accommodations costs would accommodate (and be subsidized by the high-cost employers). Professor Issacharoff and Justin Nelson similarly defend the German "pay or play" quota scheme on the ground that "the ability to opt out of employing disabled workers in exchange for paying a fee to the government means that all employers must contribute toward the admirable societal goal of full employment of disabled workers" while giving "an employer the flexibility to decide, for example, whether it is worth employing a person who has a history of hypertension or paying a fee in lieu of employing that person." Issacharoff & Nelson, *supra*, at 355–356.

But the evidence suggests that European quota systems have not succeeded in improving employment for people with disabilities. "During a period when the law required employers to fill six percent of their positions with people who have 'severe handicaps,' the percentage of people with such conditions who were actually employed in Germany fell from a high of 5.9% in 1982 to 3.7% in 1999." Samuel R. Bagenstos, *Comparative Disability Employment Law from an American Perspective*, 24 Comp. Lab. L. & Pol'y J 649, 654 (2003). Professor Lisa Waddington, a leading European student of disability rights law, is especially pessimistic about quota systems. She argues that "systems which are not effectively enforced have little or no effect in terms of generating employment, while those which are based on the levy-grant system are incapable of meeting the set targets in this period of high unemployment, at least where the levy is set at a low level," and that "[t]he political will does not exist to enforce quota systems, or to set a high levy." Lisa Waddington, Reassessing the Employment of People with Disabilities in Europe: From Quotas to Anti-Discrimination Laws, 18 Comp. Lab. L.J. 62, 100 (1996). See also Vai Io Lo, *Promotion of the Employment of Persons with Disabilities in Japan, the United States, and China: Carrot, Stick, or Both?*, 29 Ariz. J. Int'l & Comp. L. 557, 562-575 (2012) (discussing lack of compliance with quota system in Japan). Moreover, tradable quota systems have enhanced the segregation of people with disabilities. See Katharina C. Heyer, *The ADA on the Road: Disability Rights in Germany*, 27 Law & Soc. Inquiry 723, 729 (2002) (discussing German experience with tradable quotas); Katharina Heyer, *From Special Needs to Equal Rights: Japanese Disability Law*, 1 Asian-Pac. L. & Pol'y J. 7:1, 7:8 (2000) (discussing Japanese experience with tradable quotas).

In December 2011, the Department of Labor issued a Notice of Proposed Rulemaking that proposed to establish disability hiring goals for federal contractors under Section 503 of the Rehabilitation Act, 29 U.S.C. § 793. See Dep't of Labor, Off. of Fed. Contract Compliance Progs., *Affirmative Action and Nondiscrimination Obligations of Contractors and Subcontractors Regarding Individuals with Disabilities*, 76 Fed. Reg. 77,056 (2011). Section 503 requires entities that receive federal contracts worth more than $10,000 to "take affirmative action to employ and advance in employment qualified individuals with disabilities," with "disability" defined as it is in the ADA. Until the 2011 Notice, the Department of Labor and the courts had not significantly enforced the statute's "affirmative action" language but had tended to treat Section 503 as simply applying a nondiscrimination-plus-reasonable-accommodation requirement. In its 2011 Notice, the Department explained the reasons for and proposed scope of its new hiring goals:

Section 60–741.46 Utilization Goals

This section of the proposed rule is new and proposes to establish a single, national utilization goal for individuals with disabilities.[8] A utilization goal is neither a hiring quota, nor a restrictive hiring ceiling. Rather, it is an equal employment opportunity objective, and an important tool for measuring the contractor's progress toward equal employment opportunity and assessing where barriers to equal employment opportunity remain.

The Need for a Goal

Before considering the appropriate methodology for such a goal, OFCCP first considered the option of not having any goal. The current section 503 regulations require affirmative action but lack a goal. This has been the case since their inception in the 1970's. As discussed, below, the intervening years have resulted in little improvement in the unemployment and workforce

---

[8] This provision [a]pplies only to those contractors that have 50 or more employees and a contract of $50,000 or more.

participation rates of individuals with disabilities. In light of the long-term and intractable nature of the substantial employment disparity between those with and without disabilities, we concluded that process requirements, without a quantifiable means of assessing whether progress toward equal employment opportunity is occurring, are insufficient. We concluded, therefore, that the establishment of a utilization goal for individuals with disabilities is warranted. Though aspirational, establishing a goal would create more accountability within the contractor's organization and might be key to ensuring that the goal is achieved.

Little Government data measuring the unemployment and workforce participation rates of individuals with disabilities exists prior to the 2000 Census. However, illustrative data can be found in the 1989 legislative history of the Americans with Disabilities Act. Explaining the need for inclusion of employment provisions in the then- pending legislation, the Senate reported that individuals with disabilities "experience staggering levels of unemployment." Senate Committee on Labor and Human Resources, S. Rep. No. 101–116, 101st Cong, 1st Sess. (1989) at 9. More specifically, the Senate reported that two-thirds of all disabled Americans of working age were not working at all, even though a large majority of those not working (66%) wanted to work. Id. (citing a poll by the Lou Harris company).

Today, more than twenty years later, there continues to be a substantial discrepancy between the workforce participation and unemployment rates of working age individuals with and without disabilities. According to the U.S. Department of Labor's Bureau of Labor Statistics (BLS), just 21.8% of working age individuals with certain functional disabilities were in the labor force in 2010, compared with 70.1% of working age individuals without such disabilities. This same data also indicates that the unemployment rate for those with these disabilities was 14.8%, compared with a 9.4% unemployment rate for those without a disability.

Similarly, according to the U.S. Census Bureau's 2009 American Community Survey (the most recent year for which data are available), just 23% of individuals with certain functional disabilities age 16 and over were employed, compared to 65.8% of those 16 and over without such disabilities. The survey also reported that nearly three-quarters of individuals with these disabilities (72.2%) age 16 and over were not in the labor force, compared with just 27.3% of those age 16 and over without such disabilities.

The establishment of a utilization goal for individuals with disabilities is not, by itself, a "cure" for this longstanding problem. We believe, however, that the goal proposed in this section is a vital element that, in conjunction with other requirements of this part, will enable contractors and OFCCP to assess the effectiveness of specific affirmative action efforts, and to identify and address specific workplace barriers to employment.

Methodology for Setting the Utilization Goal

The utilization goal established in this section is derived, in part from the disability data collected as part of the American Community Survey. The American Community Survey (ACS) was designed to replace the census "long form" of the decennial census, last sent out to U.S. households in 2000, to gather information regarding the demographic, socioeconomic and housing characteristics of the nation. Whereas the Census Bureau now only administers a very short survey for the decennial census, a more detailed view of the social and demographic characteristics of the population is provided by the ACS, which collects data from a sample of 3 million residents on a continuing basis.

The ACS was first launched in 2005, after a decade of testing and development by the Census Bureau. Refinement of the questions designed to characterize disability status has been continuous, with the current set of disability-related questions incorporated into the ACS in 2008. Taken together, the six dichotomous ("yes" or "no") disability-related questions comprise the function-based definition of "disability," used in the ACS and by most of the other major surveys administered by the Federal Statistical System.

The definition of disability used by the ACS, however, is clearly not as broad as that of the Rehabilitation Act and the ADA. For example, since the ACS questions do not say that one should respond without considering mitigating measures (e.g., medication or aids), some individuals with disabilities that are well-controlled by medication (e.g., depression or epilepsy) or in remission might respond to the ACS in a way that leads them not to be coded as "disabled." Likewise, since the ACS questions do not include major bodily functions, an individual who has a disability that substantially limits a major bodily function such as HIV, cancer, or diabetes but does not limit an activity such as hearing, seeing or walking, might respond that he or she does not have a disability on the ACS. Despite its limitations, the ACS is the best source of nationwide disability data available today, and, thus, an appropriate starting place for developing a utilization goal.

In developing the utilization goal proposed in this section, OFCCP considered two general approaches. The first approach OFCCP considered aimed to mirror precisely the goals framework for minorities and women that is used by supply and service (non-construction) contractors subject to Executive Order (EO) 11246. Accordingly, it would require individual contractor establishments to set their own goals for each of their job groups based on the percentage of individuals with disabilities available in the particular recruitment area from which the contractor sought to fill the jobs in the job group. Where there are fewer than expected incumbent disabled employees in a job group given their availability percentage, a contractor would be required to establish a goal for the specific job group that is at least equal to the availability percentage in the job group's recruitment area. See 41 CFR 60–2.12—60–2.16 for a more detailed description of the EO 11246 goals provisions for supply and service contractors.

After careful consideration of the available data and consultation with the U.S. Census Bureau regarding the level of geographic aggregation at which the data could be analyzed, OFCCP became concerned that replicating the supply and service goals framework might not be the most effective approach for the establishment of goals for individuals with disabilities. Supply and service contractors establishing goals for minorities and women typically use the Special EEO Tabulation of census data to assist them. The results of the 2000 decennial census can be tabulated for 472 occupation categories and thousands of geographic areas. However, the ACS disability data, which is based on sampling, cannot be broken down into as many job titles, or as many geographic areas as the data for race and gender based on the decennial census. That is, the confidence intervals on such estimates are large and the estimates are not statistically significant when broken down to the degree of detail required by the supply and service goals framework. Contractors therefore would not be able to use the job groups established under EO 11246 to establish goals for individuals with disabilities, and would often be unable to utilize the geographic recruitment areas established under the Executive Order when determining the availability of individuals with the disabilities (as queried in the ACS). In addition, the Executive Order supply and service goals framework does not include consideration of discouraged workers in computing availability, a factor particularly important in the context of disability, as discussed below.

In light of the difficulties replicating the supply and service goals approach in the context of disability, OFCCP considered other options. For a variety of reasons, OFCCP believes that the establishment of a single, national goal for all jobs in all geographic areas is a more viable approach to the establishment of a goal for individuals with disabilities. This approach would also allow for the continued use of the contractor's EO 11246 job groups, and require that those job groups be used to measure the representation of individuals with disabilities in the contractor's workforce.

OFCCP proposes to set a goal for individuals with disabilities, based on the most recent 2009 ACS disability data for the "civilian labor force" and the "civilian population," first averaged by EEO–1 job category, and then averaged across EEO–1 category totals. Specifically, we use the mean across these EEO–1 groups (5.7%) as a starting point for deriving a range of values upon which we will take comment. 5.7% is OFCCP's estimate of the percentage of the civilian labor force that has a disability as defined by the ACS. However, OFCCP acknowledges that this number does not encompass all individuals with disabilities as defined under the broader definition in section 503 and the ADAAA; therefore, 5.7% should not be construed as an affirmative action goal for individuals with disabilities under these authorities, nor to convey a false sense of precision. Even if the 5.7% represented a complete availability figure for all individuals with disabilities as defined under the ADAAA, we are concerned that such an availability figure does not take into account discouraged workers, or the effects of historical discrimination against individuals with disabilities that has suppressed the representation of such individuals in the workforce. Discouraged workers are those individuals who are not now seeking employment, but who might do so in the absence of discrimination or other employment barriers. There are undoubtedly some individuals with disabilities who, for a variety of reasons, would not seek employment even in the absence of employment barriers. However, given the acute disparity in the workforce participation rates of those with and without disabilities, it is reasonable to assume that at least a portion of that gap is due to a lack of equal employment opportunity.

One way one might go about estimating the size of the discouraged worker effect would be to compare the percent of the civilian population with☐a disability (per the ACS definition) who identified as having an occupation to the percent of the civilian labor force with a disability who identified as having an occupation. Though not currently seeking employment, it might be reasonable to believe that those in the civilian population who identify as having an occupation, but who are currently not in the labor force, remained interested in working should job opportunities become available. Using the 2009 ACS EEO–1 category data, the result of this comparison is 1.7%.

Adding this figure to the 5.7% availability figure above, results in 7.4%. OFCCP uses this level, rounded to 7% to avoid implying a false level of precision, as its initial approximation of the availability for employment of individuals with disabilities. Because of the various data limitations and underlying measurement issues discussed above, OFCCP requests comment on using 7% as its utilization goal as well as on a range of values between 4% and 10%. The lower and upper bounds of this range are designed to take into account the variability across the EEO–1 categories, the potential for geographic variation in availability, and whether or not a discouraged worker effect should be taken into account.

OFCCP also takes comment on whether there might be other approaches for setting a utilization goal, particularly approaches to setting ranges that recognize that in some geographic areas and some occupations, there may be fewer people with disabilities. OFCCP requests comment on whether and, if so, how to take into account discouraged workers in assessing the availability of workers with disabilities. OFCCP is also very interested in public comment on whether there are empirically-based approaches that recognize that there are many more people who have disabilities as characterized by the ADAAA than the ACS and that there is likely a discouraged worker effect.

OFCCP recognizes that including a discouraged worker component in the establishment of a proposed goal is a new approach. We therefore invite public comment on the methodology used to calculate the discouraged worker effect, and on the application of the discouraged worker effect in the goal-setting context.

OFCCP believes that a single-goal approach will serve the equal opportunity and affirmative action objectives of the Rehabilitation Act and this part better than the supply and service approach of EO 11246. It will allow contractors to use their existing job groups and not require the use of multiple geographic availability comparisons as would the supply and service goals approach. OFCCP invites public comment on the impact of this proposal on contractors. In particular, we invite small businesses with current federal prime contracts or subcontracts, or those interested in future prime or subcontract work with the federal government, to identify any impacts unique to small businesses and to propose potential alternatives to alleviate the difficulties identified.

Section-by-Section Analysis

Paragraph (a) of the proposed rule states that the utilization goal for employment of individuals with disabilities is 7% for each job group in the contractor's workforce.

Proposed paragraph (b) states that the purpose of this section is to establish a benchmark against which contractors can measure the representation of individuals with disabilities within each of their job groups. The goal serves as an equal opportunity objective that should be attainable by complying with all of the affirmative action requirements of part 60–741.

Proposed paragraph (c) provides that the Director of OFCCP will periodically review and update, as appropriate, the utilization goal established in proposed paragraph (a) of this section.

Proposed paragraph (d) sets out the steps that the contractor must use to determine whether it has met the utilization goal. Proposed paragraph (d)(1) states that the purpose of a utilization analysis is to evaluate the representation of individuals with disabilities in each job group within a contractor's workforce and compare the rate against the utilization goal set forth in § 60–741.46(a).

Proposed paragraph (d)(2) clarifies that in evaluating the representation of individuals with disabilities in its workforce, the contractor must use the same job groups it established pursuant to EO 11246, either as prescribed in 41 CFR 60–2.12, or in accordance with 41 CFR part 60–4. OFCCP considered permitting contractors to compare the individuals with disabilities in its workforce as a whole with the proposed 7% goal. We decided against this approach because of its potential for masking discrimination and segregation. For example, a contractor that has segregated all of its employees with disabilities into one or two low-paying jobs might be able to conceal this discrimination and satisfy the 7% goal☐if only a single whole-workforce comparison were required by this section. Nevertheless, as we are mindful of the burden required of contractors in making the job group-by-job group comparisons required in this proposed paragraph, we are mandating the use of the EO 11246 job groups for this purpose, by eliminating the need for any geographic assessment, and by providing the single goal to which each job group will be compared.

Proposed paragraph (d)(3) requires that the contractor evaluate its utilization of individuals with disabilities in each job group annually.

When the percentage of employees with disabilities in one or more job groups is less than the utilization goal proposed in paragraph (a) of this section, proposed paragraph (e) requires that the contractor must develop and execute "action-oriented programs" designed to correct any identified problems and attain the established goal. Such programs may include additional efforts from among those listed in §§ 60–741.44(f)(1) and (f)(2) and/or any other appropriate actions.

Paragraph (f) of the proposed rule clarifies that a contractor's determination that it has not attained the utilization goal in one or more job groups does not constitute either a finding or admission of discrimination in violation of this part. It is also important to point out that such a determination, whether by OFCCP or the contractor, will not impede or prevent OFCCP from finding that one or more unlawful discriminatory practices caused the contractor's failure to meet the utilization goal. In such a circumstance, OFCCP will take appropriate enforcement measures.

Lastly, proposed paragraph (g) states that the goal proposed in this section shall not be used as a quota or ceiling that limits or restricts the employment of individuals with disabilities.

Sub-Goal Option

OFCCP is considering the option of including within the 7% goal for individuals with disabilities a sub-goal of 2% for individuals with certain particularly severe disabilities. The federal government currently monitors internal hiring with respect to a list of particularly severe disabilities, referred to as "targeted disabilities" in furtherance of its affirmative action obligation to employ and advance in employment individuals with disabilities in the Government pursuant to section 501 of the Rehabilitation Act. The list of targeted disabilities is defined in the President's July 2010 Executive Order "Increasing Federal Employment of Individuals with Disabilities," as set forth in Standard Form 256 (SF256). Subject to updating, SF 256 currently identifies the following as "targeted/severe disabilities:" Total deafness, blindness, missing extremities (hand, foot, arm or leg), partial paralysis, complete paralysis, epilepsy, severe intellectual disability, psychiatric disability, and dwarfism.18 If such a sub-goal is adopted, the Director would similarly prescribe the language and manner in which contractors should invite applicants and employees to self- identify. This will ensure consistency in all pre-offer invitations that are made, and will reassure applicants that the request is routine and executed pursuant to obligations created by OFCCP.

OFCCP invites comments from the public on this sub-goal option. If OFCCP adopts the use of a sub-goal, it will be included in the Final Rule. We are seeking public input and comment on both the concept of a sub-goal, as well as the disabilities to be included within that sub-goal. Comments on the questions below will be especially helpful.

1. What data or research is available that informs the design of an appropriate sub-goal including, but not limited to which severe disabilities should be covered by the sub-goal, and the appropriate sub-goal target?

2. How does a sub-goal further the overall objective of increasing employment opportunities for individuals with severe disabilities?

3. What data or research is available on the need for a sub-goal for specific disabilities?

On August 27, 2013, the Department of Labor announced final rules that adopt a 7% hiring goal, using the ADAAA's definition of disability. The final rules include no sub-goals for individuals with more significant disabilities. See Final Rule, Section 503 of the Rehabilitation Act, available at http://www.dol.gov/ofccp/regs/compliance/section503.htm. Does the Department of Labor's notice persuade you of the need for hiring goals? Do you think the proposed goals are well designed? Are they likely to be effective? Given the breadth of the disability definition in the ADAAA, as incorporated in Section 503, will the proposed hiring goals lead to the enhanced hiring of people with relatively mild disabilities, perhaps at the expense of those with more significant disabilities? Is the Notice's sub-goal option a sufficient means of dealing with that problem? Will the sub-goal option disrupt solidarity within the community of people with disabilities?

3.   Expanding Access to Health Insurance. Deep-rooted structural barriers, including lack of accessible transportation, personal assistance, and assistive technology, keep many people with disabilities out of the workforce well before any employer has the opportunity to discriminate against them. See Bagenstos, Law and the Contradictions, *supra*, at 128–130. Perhaps the most significant of these barriers is the structure of our health care system: "In its current form, our health insurance system affirmatively disserves the interest of people with disabilities in moving into the workforce. * * *. [P]rivate insurance—on which most nondisabled people rely for their health needs—fails to cover the services people with disabilities most need for independence and health. And public insurance is saddled with requirements that lock people with disabilities out of the workforce." *Id.* at 129.

A number of potential efforts to improve the employment rates of people with disabilities might focus on expanding access to health insurance. The Ticket to Work and Work Incentives Improvement Act of 1999, Pub.L.No.106–170, 113 Stat. 1860 (codified in scattered sections of 26 and 42 U.S.C.), expanded the circumstances in which people with disabilities could return to work and retain Medicare benefits, and it authorized states, at their option, to allow people with disabilities to buy into the Medicaid program. See Bagenstos, Law and the Contradictions, *supra* at 141 (arguing that the statute "marks a major step forward in promoting independence and work for people with disabilities" but that it is limited by not guaranteeing access to Medicaid, the program that is better designed for the needs of nonelderly people with disabilities, and by not targeting people with disabilities who are still in the workforce).

The Patient Protection and Affordable Care Act (ACA), Pub. L. No. 111-148, 124 Stat. 119 (2010), *amended by* Health Care and Education Reconciliation Act of 2010, Pub. L. No. 111-152, 124 Stat. 1029 (2010), might make a significant dent in this problem. The ACA prohibits health insurers from imposing preexisting conditions exclusions or lifetime caps on coverage for particular conditions or treatments. It also imposes guaranteed-issue and guaranteed-renewal requirements for health insurance policies, and it prohibits discrimination based on health status. The ACA creates two key means by which individuals who do not receive health insurance through their employers can obtain coverage: First, the statute sets up health insurance exchanges, in which individuals can purchase private coverage. Individuals whose families earn between 100% and 400% of the Federal Poverty Level will receive subsidies to purchase insurance on those exchanges. Second, the statute encourages states to expand their Medicaid programs to cover all individuals with family incomes up to 133% of the Federal Poverty Level. See *Nat'l Federation of Independent Business v. Sebelius*, 132 S. Ct. 2566 (2012) (holding, across two opinions, that Congress could not withhold *all* Medicaid funds from a state that refused to expand its Medicaid program per the ACA, but that it could withhold Medicaid funds earmarked for that expansion). For further discussion of the ACA, see the material on insurance in Chapter Five.

CHAPTER 4

GOVERNMENT (AND GOVERNMENT-FUNDED) SERVICES, PROGRAMS, AND ACTIVITIES

A. COVERAGE OF THE ADA, REHABILITATION ACT, AND FAIR HOUSING ACT

Pennsylvania Department of Corrections v. Yeskey

Supreme Court of the United States, 1998.
524 U.S. 206.

■ JUSTICE SCALIA delivered the opinion of the Court.

The question before us is whether Title II of the Americans with Disabilities Act of 1990 (ADA), 104 Stat. 337, 42 U.S.C. § 12131 *et seq.*, which prohibits a "public entity" from discriminating against a "qualified individual with a disability" on account of that individual's disability, see § 12132, covers inmates in state prisons. Respondent Ronald Yeskey was such an inmate, sentenced in May 1994 to serve 18 to 36 months in a Pennsylvania correctional facility. The sentencing court recommended that he be placed in Pennsylvania's Motivational Boot Camp for first-time offenders, the successful completion of which would have led to his release on parole in just six months. See Pa.Stat.Ann., Tit. 61, § 1121 *et seq.* (Purdon Supp.1998). Because of his medical history of hypertension, however, he was refused admission. He filed this suit against petitioners, the Commonwealth of Pennsylvania's Department of Corrections and several department officials, alleging that his exclusion from the Boot Camp violated the ADA. The District Court dismissed for failure to state a claim, holding the ADA inapplicable to inmates in state prisons; the Third Circuit reversed; we granted *certiorari*.

Petitioners argue that state prisoners are not covered by the ADA for the same reason we held in *Gregory v. Ashcroft*, 501 U.S. 452 (1991), that state judges were not covered by the Age Discrimination in Employment Act of 1967 (ADEA), 29 U.S.C. § 621 *et seq. Gregory* relied on the canon of construction that absent an "unmistakably clear" expression of intent to "alter the usual constitutional balance between the States and the Federal Government," we will interpret a statute to preserve rather than destroy the States' "substantial sovereign powers." 501 U.S., at 460–461 (citations and internal quotation marks omitted). It may well be that exercising ultimate control over the management of state prisons, like establishing the qualifications of state government officials, is a traditional and essential state function subject to the plain-statement rule of *Gregory*. "One of the primary functions of government," we have said, "is the preservation of societal order through enforcement of the criminal law, and the maintenance of penal institutions is an essential part of that task." "It is difficult to imagine an activity in which a State has a stronger interest."

Assuming, without deciding, that the plain-statement rule does govern application of the ADA to the administration of state prisons, we think the requirement of the rule is amply met: the statute's language unmistakably includes State prisons and prisoners within its coverage. The situation here is not comparable to that in *Gregory*. There, although the ADEA plainly covered state employees, it contained an exception for " 'appointee[s] on the policymaking level' " which made it impossible for us to "conclude that the statute plainly cover[ed] appointed state judges." Here, the ADA plainly covers state institutions without any exception that could cast the coverage of prisons into doubt. Title II of the ADA provides:

> "Subject to the provisions of this subchapter, no qualified individual with a disability shall, by reason of such disability, be excluded from participation in or be denied the benefits of the services, programs, or activities of a public entity, or be subjected to discrimination by any such entity." 42 U.S.C. § 12132.

State prisons fall squarely within the statutory definition of "public entity," which includes "any department, agency, special purpose district, or other instrumentality of a State or States or local government." § 12131(1)(B).

Petitioners contend that the phrase "benefits of the services, programs, or activities of a public entity," § 12132, creates an ambiguity, because state prisons do not provide prisoners with "benefits" of "programs, services, or activities" as those terms are ordinarily understood. We disagree. Modern prisons provide inmates with many recreational "activities," medical "services," and educational and vocational "programs," all of which at least theoretically "benefit" the prisoners (and any of which disabled prisoners could be "excluded from participation in"). See *Block v. Rutherford*, 468 U.S. 576, 580 (1984) (referring to "contact visitation program"); *Hudson v. Palmer*, 468 U.S. 517, 552 (1984) (discussing "rehabilitative programs and services"); *Olim v. Wakinekona*, 461 U.S. 238, 246 (1983) (referring to "appropriate correctional programs for all offenders"). Indeed, the statute establishing the Motivational Boot Camp at issue in this very case refers to it as a "program." Pa.Stat.Ann., Tit. 61, § 1123 (Purdon Supp.1998). The text of the ADA provides no basis for distinguishing these programs, services, and activities from those provided by public entities that are not prisons.

We also disagree with petitioners' contention that the term "qualified individual with a disability" is ambiguous insofar as concerns its application to state prisoners. The statute defines the term to include anyone with a disability

> "who, with or without reasonable modifications to rules, policies, or practices, the removal of architectural, communication, or transportation barriers, or the provision of auxiliary aids and services, meets the essential eligibility

requirements for the receipt of services or the participation in programs or activities provided by a public entity." 42 U.S.C. § 12131(2).

Petitioners argue that the words "eligibility" and "participation" imply voluntariness on the part of an applicant who seeks a benefit from the State, and thus do not connote prisoners who are being held against their will. This is wrong on two counts: First, because the words do not connote voluntariness. See, *e.g.*, Webster's New International Dictionary 831 (2d ed.1949) ("eligible": "Fitted or qualified to be chosen or elected; legally or morally suitable; as, an eligible candidate"); *id.*, at 1782 ("participate": "To have a share in common with others; to partake; share, as in a debate"). While "eligible" individuals "participate" voluntarily in many programs, services, and activities, there are others for which they are "eligible" in which "participation" is mandatory. A drug addict convicted of drug possession, for example, might, as part of his sentence, be required to "participate" in a drug treatment program for which only addicts are "eligible." And secondly, even if the words did connote voluntariness, it would still not be true that all prison "services," "programs," and "activities" are excluded from the ADA because participation in them is not voluntary. The prison law library, for example, is a service (and the use of it an activity), which prisoners are free to take or leave. In the very case at hand, the governing law makes it clear that participation in the Boot Camp program is voluntary. See Pa. Stat. Ann., Tit. 61, § 1126(a) (Purdon Supp.1998) ("An eligible inmate may make an application to the motivational boot camp selection committee for permission to participate in the motivational boot camp program"); § 1126(c) ("[c]onditio[n]" of "participa[tion]" is that applicant "agree to be bound by" certain "terms and conditions").

Finally, petitioners point out that the statute's statement of findings and purpose, 42 U.S.C. § 12101, does not mention prisons and prisoners. That is perhaps questionable, since the provision's reference to discrimination "in such critical areas as . . . institutionalization," § 12101(a)(3), can be thought to include penal institutions. But assuming it to be true, and assuming further that it proves, as petitioners contend, that Congress did not "envisio[n] that the ADA would be applied to state prisoners," Brief for Petitioners 13–14, in the context of an unambiguous statutory text that is irrelevant. As we have said before, the fact that a statute can be " 'applied in situations not expressly anticipated by Congress does not demonstrate ambiguity. It demonstrates breadth.' "

Our conclusion that the text of the ADA is not ambiguous causes us also to reject petitioners' appeal to the doctrine of constitutional doubt, which requires that we interpret statutes to avoid "grave and doubtful constitutional questions." That doctrine enters in only "where a statute is susceptible of two constructions." And for the same reason we disregard petitioners' invocation of the statute's title, "Public Services," 104 Stat. 337. "[T]he title of a statute . . . cannot limit the plain meaning of the text. For interpretive purposes, [it is] of use only when [it] shed[s] light on some ambiguous word or phrase."

We do not address another issue presented by petitioners: whether application of the ADA to state prisons is a constitutional exercise of

Congress's power under either the Commerce Clause or § 5 of the Fourteenth Amendment. Petitioners raise this question in their brief, but it was addressed by neither the District Court nor the Court of Appeals, where petitioners raised only the Gregory plain-statement issue. "Where issues are neither raised before nor considered by the Court of Appeals, this Court will not ordinarily consider them." We decline to do so here.

* * *

Because the plain text of Title II of the ADA unambiguously extends to state prison inmates, the judgment of the Court of Appeals is affirmed.

It is so ordered.

NOTES ON THE COVERAGE OF GOVERNMENT SERVICES

1. **The reach of *Yeskey*.** *Yeskey* appears to give Title II of the ADA a sweep as broad as its language—any activity, of any state or local government entity, seems to be covered by the statute. As one court has explained, "the word 'activities,' on its face, suggests great breadth and offers little basis to exclude any actions of a public entity." *Johnson v. City of Saline*, 151 F.3d 564, 570 (6th Cir.1998); see also *Innovative Health Sys., Inc. v. City of White Plains*, 117 F.3d 37, 44 (2d Cir.1997) ("the plain meaning of 'activity' is a 'natural or normal function or operation,' " and thus the ADA encompasses any "normal function of a governmental entity") (citation omitted), overruled in part on other grounds, *Zervos v. Verizon N.Y., Inc.*, 252 F.3d 163, 171 n.7 (2d Cir.2001). *Yeskey* appears to hold that courts may not exempt some of these activities from Title II's coverage, because no such exemption appears in the statutory text.

a. **Termination of Parental Rights Proceedings.** Nevertheless, even after *Yeskey*, a number of lower courts have held that Title II does not apply to state-court proceedings to terminate parental rights. See, *e.g.*, *In re Kayla N.*, 900 A.2d 1202, 1208 (R.I.2006) (holding "that a termination-of-parental-rights proceeding does not constitute the sort of service, program, or activity that would be governed by the dictates of the ADA") (citing cases), cert. denied, 549 U.S. 1252 (2007). These courts have explained that such "proceedings are held for the benefit of the child, not the parent. Therefore, the ADA is inapplicable when used as a defense by the parent(s) in [those] proceedings." *Id.* (internal quotation marks omitted).

This is not an obscure class of cases. As of 2005, statutes in 30 states made "mental deficiency," "mental illness," or similar disabilities a factor in termination decisions. See National Adoption Information Clearinghouse, Grounds for Involuntary Termination of Parental Rights: Summary of State Laws (2005). According to one commentator, these statutes are often "interpreted such that the mere label of mental disability constitutes grounds for parental rights termination." Susan Kerr, *The Application of the Americans with Disabilities Act to the Termination of the Parental Rights of Individuals with Mental Disabilities*, 16 J. Contemp. Health L. & Pol'y 387, 403 (2000). Other commentators have described common patterns of discrimination against parents with various disabilities. See, *e.g.*, Martha A. Field & Valerie A. Sanchez, Equal Treatment for People

With Mental Retardation: Having and Raising Children 5, 273 (1999) ("Often state authorities move to terminate the parental rights of persons with mental retardation because of generalized fears that retardation makes for parental inadequacy. Often their rights actually are terminated, even though the parents' conduct would have seemed acceptable to state authorities had the parents not been considered 'mentally retarded.' [A]ny broad selection of opinions suggests that judges are peculiarly unacquainted with and unsympathetic to the problems of persons with mental retardation and are particularly fearful of allowing them to parent."); Michael Ashley Stein, *Mommy Has a Blue Wheelchair: Recognizing the Parental Rights of Individuals with Disabilities*, 60 Brook. L. Rev. 1069, 1083 (1994) (stating that judicial bias "often manifests itself in different guises for different disabilities: deaf parents are thought to be incapable of effectively stimulating language skills; blind parents cannot provide adequate attention or discipline; and parents with spinal cord injuries cannot adequately supervise their children") (footnotes omitted). And indeed, the House Judiciary Committee report on the ADA specifically stated that "discriminatory policies and practices affect people with disabilities in every aspect of their lives," including "securing custody of their children." H.R.Rep.No.101–485, Part 3 at 25 (1990).

Is it consistent with *Yeskey* to hold that the ADA does not apply to state termination-of-parental-rights proceedings? Many, though not all, of the state courts that have held that the ADA does not apply to such proceedings have acknowledged that the statute requires the state "to accommodate the parents' special needs in its provision of services *prior to*" a termination proceeding. *In re Adoption of Gregory*, 434 Mass. 117, 122 (2001). And they have suggested that parents with disabilities may enforce these rights by filing "a separate action for discrimination under the ADA." *Id.* at 124. Is it consistent with *Yeskey* to hold that Title II does not apply to the termination proceedings themselves but only to family reunification services that are provided prior to the initiation of those proceedings?

b.   Police Practices. Some courts have also held that "Title II does not apply to [a police] officer's on-the-street responses to reported disturbances or other similar incidents, whether or not those calls involve subjects with mental disabilities, prior to the officer's securing the scene and ensuring that there is no threat to human life":

> Law enforcement personnel conducting in-the-field investigations already face the onerous task of frequently having to instantaneously identify, assess, and react to potentially life-threatening situations. To require the officers to factor in whether their actions are going to comply with the ADA, in the presence of exigent circumstances and prior to securing the safety of themselves, other officers, and any nearby civilians, would pose an unnecessary risk to innocents. While the purpose of the ADA is to prevent the discrimination of disabled individuals, we do not think Congress intended that the fulfillment of that objective be attained at the expense of the safety of the general public.

Hainze v. Richards, 207 F.3d 795, 801 (5th Cir.2000). Is that holding consistent with *Yeskey*? Do the court's concerns require that Title II be held not to apply to on-the-street police decisions? Would those concerns be better addressed by giving great deference to those decisions in the discrimination and reasonable accommodation inquiries? Cf. *Bircoll v. Miami-Dade County*, 480 F.3d 1072, 1085 (11th Cir.2007) ("The exigent circumstances presented by criminal activity and the already onerous tasks of police on the scene go more to the reasonableness of the requested ADA modification than whether the ADA applies in the first instance."); *Gohier v. Enright*, 186 F.3d 1216, 1222 (10th Cir.1999) (holding that police officer did not discriminate against disabled plaintiff, because the plaintiff's "threatening conduct [d]id warrant the police response at issue in this case, *i.e.*, the use of force in self-defense").

2. Section 504 of the Rehabilitation Act. In addition to Title II of the ADA, two other statutes prohibit disability-based discrimination by public entities. Section 504 of the Rehabilitation Act of 1973 provides that "[n]o otherwise qualified individual with a disability in the United States * * * shall, solely by reason of her or his disability, be excluded from the participation in, be denied the benefits of, or be subjected to discrimination under any program or activity receiving Federal financial assistance." 29 U.S.C. § 794(a). As the similarity in language suggests, the operative provision of ADA Title II was drawn from Section 504. But where Title II applies to all state and local government entities (and only state or local government entities), Section 504 applies only to "programs" or "activities" that receive federal financial assistance. An amendment added by the Civil Rights Restoration Act of 1987 defines "program or activity" very broadly to include:

(1)(A) a department, agency, special purpose district, or other instrumentality of a State or of a local government; or

(B) the entity of such State or local government that distributes such assistance and each such department or agency (and each other State or local government entity) to which the assistance is extended, in the case of assistance to a State or local government;

(2)(A) a college, university, or other postsecondary institution, or a public system of higher education; or

(B) a local educational agency, [s]ystem of vocational education, or other school system;

(3)(A) an entire corporation, partnership, or other private organization, or an entire sole proprietorship—

(i) if assistance is extended to such corporation, partnership, private organization, or sole proprietorship as a whole; or

(ii) which is principally engaged in the business of providing education, health care, housing, social services, or parks and recreation; or

(B) the entire plant or other comparable, geographically separate facility to which Federal financial assistance is extended, in the case of any other corporation, partnership, private organization, or sole proprietorship; or

(4) any other entity which is established by two or more of the entities described in paragraph (1), (2), or (3);

any part of which is extended Federal financial assistance.

29 U.S.C. § 794(b). Because some part of nearly every state and local government department or entity receives at least some federal money, Section 504 generally covers at least as much conduct as does Title II of the ADA, though the plaintiff has to prove the receipt of federal funds to establish her claim. Indeed, because virtually all *private* institutions of higher education receive federal financial assistance, Section 504 extends to them as well.

3.   The Fair Housing Act. The Fair Housing Act, too, prohibits some disability-based discrimination by state and local governments. The statute makes it unlawful

(1) To discriminate in the sale or rental, or to otherwise make unavailable or deny, a dwelling to any buyer or renter because of a handicap of—

(A) that buyer or renter,

(B) a person residing in or intending to reside in that dwelling after it is so sold, rented, or made available; or

(C) any person associated with that buyer or renter.

(2) To discriminate against any person in the terms, conditions, or privileges of sale or rental of a dwelling, or in the provision of services or facilities in connection with such dwelling, because of a handicap of—

(A) that person; or

(B) a person residing in or intending to reside in that dwelling after it is so sold, rented, or made available; or

(C) any person associated with that person.

42 U.S.C. § 3604(f). The statute defines "handicap" in the same way the ADA, prior to the enactment of the ADA Amendments Act of 2008, defined "disability." See 42 U.S.C. § 3602(h). As the zoning cases discussed below show, these provisions apply to any entity, including a state or local government, that discriminates against a person with a disability in housing or "otherwise make[s]" a dwelling "unavailable" to a person with a disability.

Frame v. City of Arlington

United States Court of Appeals for the Fifth Circuit, *en banc*, 2011.
657 F.3d 215, cert. denied, 132 S.Ct. 1561.

■ BENAVIDES AND PRADO, CIRCUIT JUDGES:

Title II of the Americans with Disabilities Act (ADA), like § 504 of the Rehabilitation Act, provides that individuals with disabilities shall not "be denied the benefits of the services, programs, or activities of a public entity, or be subjected to discrimination by any such entity." For nearly two decades, Title II's implementing regulations have required cities to make newly built and altered sidewalks readily accessible to individuals with disabilities. The plaintiffs-appellants in this case, five individuals with disabilities, allege that defendant-appellee the City of Arlington (the City) has recently built and altered sidewalks that are not readily accessible to them. The plaintiffs brought this action for injunctive relief under Title II and § 504.

We [m]ust determine whether Title II and § 504 (and their implied private right of action) extend to newly built and altered public sidewalks. We hold that the plaintiffs have a private right of action to enforce Title II and § 504 with respect to newly built and altered public sidewalks[.]

I

The plaintiffs in this case depend on motorized wheelchairs for mobility. They allege that certain inaccessible sidewalks make it dangerous, difficult, or impossible for them to travel to a variety of public and private establishments throughout the City. Most of these sidewalks allegedly were built or altered by the City after Title II became effective on January 26, 1992. The plaintiffs sued the City on July 22, 2005, claiming that the inaccessible sidewalks violate Title II of the ADA and § 504 of the Rehabilitation Act. The complaint was most recently amended on August 9, 2007. The plaintiffs seek injunctive relief but not damages.

The district court dismissed the plaintiffs' complaint on statute-of-limitations grounds. [O]n appeal, a panel of this Court began by considering whether the plaintiffs had a private right of action to enforce Title II with respect to inaccessible sidewalks. The panel unanimously held that the plaintiffs had such a right because public sidewalks are "services, programs, or activities" of a public entity within the plain meaning of Title II. The panel next considered whether the plaintiffs' claims were barred by Texas's two-year personal-injury statute of limitations. The panel determined that the statute of limitations is an affirmative defense on which the defendant has the burden of proof, and that the district court erred in requiring the plaintiffs to plead dates of construction in their complaint. The panel would have remanded for further proceedings. One member of the panel dissented, however, with respect to the panel majority's finding that the plaintiffs' claims "accrued on the date the City completed the construction or alteration of any noncompliant" sidewalk. According to the dissenting judge, the plaintiffs' claims did not accrue until the plaintiffs "physically encounter [ed], or actually learn[ed] of and [were] deterred from attempting to access, a noncompliant sidewalk."

Both parties petitioned for rehearing en banc. The panel majority withdrew its initial opinion and issued a revised opinion. In the revised opinion, the panel majority determined that sidewalks were not "services, programs, or activities of a public entity" within the meaning of Title II. The panel majority thus held that the plaintiffs did not have a private right of action to enforce Title II with respect to sidewalks "in instances where these facilities do not prevent access to some [other] service, program, or activity." The panel majority would have remanded the case "only to the extent [the plaintiffs] have alleged a noncompliant sidewalk, curb, or parking lot denies them access to a program, service, or activity that does fall within the meaning of Title II." With respect to the statute of limitations, however, the panel unanimously found that the plaintiffs' claims did not accrue until the plaintiffs "knew or should have known" they were denied the benefits of the City's services, programs, or activities. A member of the panel again dissented, asserting that the construction, alteration, and maintenance of public sidewalks unambiguously are services, programs, or activities of a public entity within the plain meaning of Title II.

We granted the plaintiffs' second petition for rehearing en banc. At oral argument, the plaintiffs unequivocally abandoned any claims with respect to sidewalks built on or before (and not altered after) January 26, 1992. Accordingly, we deem the plaintiffs' claims with respect to such sidewalks waived and abandoned. All that remain to be considered are the plaintiffs' claims with respect to sidewalks built or altered after January 26, 1992. We refer to such sidewalks as newly built or altered sidewalks.

[III]

It is established that Title II of the ADA and § 504 of the Rehabilitation Act are enforceable through an implied private right of action. The issue is whether these statutes (and their established private right of action) extend to newly built and altered public sidewalks. Based on statutory text and structure, we hold that Title II and § 504 unambiguously extend to newly built and altered public sidewalks. We further hold that the plaintiffs have a private right of action to enforce Title II and § 504 to the extent they would require the City to make reasonable modifications to such sidewalks.

[W]e begin by determining whether the plain meaning of Title II extends to newly built and altered sidewalks. [T]itle II provides that disabled individuals shall not be denied the "benefits of the services, programs, or activities of a public entity, or be subjected to discrimination by any such entity." The Supreme Court addressed this same statutory provision in *Pennsylvania Department of Corrections v. Yeskey,* and held that it "unambiguously" permitted a prisoner to sue a state prison. The Supreme Court considered the text of Title II as it is "ordinarily understood," and reasoned that "prisons provide inmates with recreational 'activities,' medical 'services,' and educational and vocations 'programs,' all of which at least theoretically 'benefit' the prisoners." The Supreme Court noted that "in the context of an unambiguous statutory text," it is "irrelevant" whether Congress specifically envisioned that the ADA would benefit state prisoners. That a statute may be "applied in situations not expressly anticipated by Congress does not demonstrate ambiguity. It demonstrates breadth."

The ADA does not define the "services, programs, or activities of a public entity." The Rehabilitation Act, however, defines a "program or activity" as "all of the operations of . . . a local government." [W]e interpret Title II and the Rehabilitation Act *in pari materia.* Accordingly, like the Supreme Court in *Yeskey,* we must determine whether newly built and altered city sidewalks are benefits of "all of the operations" and "services" of a public entity within the ordinary meaning of those terms.

[B]uilding and altering city sidewalks unambiguously are "services" of a public entity under any reasonable understanding of that term. The Supreme Court has broadly understood a "service" to mean "the performance of work commanded or paid for by another," or "an act done for the benefit or at the command of another."[37] Webster's Dictionary additionally defines a "service" as "the provision, organization, or apparatus for . . . meeting a general demand."[38] For its part, Black's Law Dictionary defines a "public service" as work "provided or facilitated by the government for the general public's convenience and benefit."[39]

Under each of these common understandings, building and altering public sidewalks unambiguously are services of a public entity. The construction or alteration of a city sidewalk is work commanded by another (i.e., voters and public officials), paid for by another (i.e., taxpayers), and done for the benefit of another (e.g., pedestrians and drivers). When a city builds or alters a sidewalk, it promotes the general public's convenience by overcoming a collective action problem and allowing citizens to focus on other ventures. Moreover, when a city builds or alters a sidewalk, it helps meet a general demand for the safe movement of people and goods. In short, in common understanding, a city provides a service to its citizens when it builds or alters a public sidewalk.

A "service" also might be defined as "[t]he duties, work, or business performed or discharged by a public official."[41] Under this definition too, newly built and altered public sidewalks are services of a public entity. Cities, through their officials, study, debate, plan, and ultimately authorize sidewalk construction. If a city official authorizes a public sidewalk to be built in a way that is not readily accessible to disabled individuals without adequate justification, the official denies disabled individuals the benefits of that sidewalk no less than if the official poured the concrete himself.

Furthermore, building and altering public sidewalks easily are among "all of the operations" (and thus also the "programs or activities") of a public entity. Webster's Dictionary broadly defines "operations" as "the whole process of planning for and operating a business or other organized unit," and defines "operation" as "a doing or performing esp[ecially] of action."[43] In common understanding, the operations of a public entity would include the "whole process" of "planning" and "doing" that goes into building and altering public sidewalks.

In sum, in common understanding, building and altering public sidewalks are services, programs, or activities of a public entity. When a city decides to build or alter a sidewalk and makes that sidewalk inaccessible to individuals with disabilities without adequate justification, disabled individuals are denied the benefits of that city's

---

[37] *Holder v. Humanitarian Law Project,* __ U.S. __, 130 S.Ct. 2705, 2721–22, 177 L.Ed.2d 355 (2010) (quoting WEBSTER'S THIRD NEW INTERNATIONAL DICTIONARY 2075 (1993)).

[38] WEBSTER'S THIRD NEW INTERNATIONAL DICTIONARY 2075 (1993).

[39] BLACK'S LAW DICTIONARY 1352 (9th ed. 2009).

[41] *See supra,* n. 38.

[43] WEBSTER'S THIRD NEW INTERNATIONAL DICTIONARY 1581 (1993).

services, programs, or activities. Newly built and altered sidewalks thus fit squarely within the plain, unambiguous text of Title II.

[E]ven if we focus on a public sidewalk *itself,* we still find that a sidewalk unambiguously is a service, program, or activity of a public entity. A city sidewalk itself facilitates the public's "convenience and benefit" by affording a means of safe transportation. A city sidewalk itself is the "apparatus" that meets the public's general demand for safe transportation. As the Supreme Court has observed, sidewalks are "general government services"[47] "provided in common to all citizens"[48] to protect pedestrians from the "very real hazards of traffic."[49] The Supreme Court also has recognized that public sidewalks are "traditional public fora" that "time out of mind" have facilitated the general demand for public assembly and discourse. When a newly built or altered city sidewalk is unnecessarily made inaccessible to individuals with disabilities, those individuals are denied the benefits of safe transportation and a venerable public forum.

[W]ere there any doubt that the plain meaning of § 12132 extends to newly built and altered sidewalks, other provisions in Title II confirm that it does. Congress directed DOJ to "promulgate regulations" that "implement" § 12132.[51] Congress also required those implementing regulations to be consistent with Rehabilitation Act coordination regulations codified at 28 C.F.R. pt. 41.[52] Notably, the Rehabilitation Act regulations that Congress sought to replicate under Title II require new and altered facilities, including sidewalks, to be accessible in most circumstances.[53] That Congress directed DOJ to "implement" § 12132 by promulgating regulations governing newly built and altered sidewalks strongly suggests that Congress thought § 12132 would extend to such sidewalks.

In fact, the ADA actually prohibits courts from construing Title II to apply a lesser standard than the Rehabilitation Act *and its implementing regulations.*[54] As the Supreme Court has recognized, Congress's "directive requires us to construe the ADA to grant at least as much protection as provided by the regulations implementing the Rehabilitation Act."   [*Bragdon.*] Because the Rehabilitation Act regulations require new and altered facilities, including sidewalks, to be

---

[47] *Everson v. Bd. of Educ. of Ewing,* 330 U.S. 1, 17–18 (1947).

[48] *Comm. for Pub. Educ. & Religious Liberty v. Nyquist,* 413 U.S. 756, 781–82 (1973).

[49] Everson, 330 U.S. at 17–18.

[51] 42 U.S.C. § 12134(a); *see also* 28 C.F.R. § 35.101 (2010) ("The purpose of this part is to effectuate subtitle A of title II of the [ADA], which prohibits discrimination on the basis of disability by public entities."). DOJ's regulations were amended effective March 11, 2011. The parties do not assert that the amended regulations apply to this case, and we assume that the earlier regulations continue to apply.

[52] 42 U.S.C. § 12134(b). The coordination regulations "implement Executive Order 12250, which requires the [DOJ] to coordinate the implementation of section 504 of the Rehabilitation Act" among federal agencies. 28 C.F.R. § 41.1.

[53] 28 C.F.R. § 41.58(a) (requiring new facilities to be accessible, and altered facilities to be accessible "to the maximum extent feasible"); *id.* § 41.3(f) (defining "facility" to include "roads, walks, [and] parking lots").

[54] 42 U.S.C. § 12201(a) (requiring that "nothing in this chapter shall be construed to apply a lesser standard than the standards applied under title V of the Rehabilitation Act of 1973 . . . or the regulations issued by Federal agencies pursuant to such title").

accessible in most circumstances, our construction of § 12132 requires no less.

[T]he City draws our attention to a purported distinction between "transportation barriers" and "services" in Title II's definition of a "qualified individual with a disability." A qualified individual with a disability is defined as:

> an individual with a disability who, with or without reasonable modifications to rules, policies, or practices, the removal of architectural, communication, or transportation barriers, or the provision of auxiliary aids and services, meets the essential eligibility requirements for the receipt of services or the participation in programs or activities provided by a public entity.[58]

According to the City, because Congress included transportation barriers and services in the same sentence, Congress must have contemplated that newly built and altered sidewalks (and other facilities) are not services, programs, or activities within the meaning of § 12132.

As an initial matter, if our focus is on building and altering sidewalks, as opposed to sidewalks themselves, the City's distinction breaks down immediately. Even if the definition of a qualified individual with a disability suggests that sidewalks and services are mutually exclusive, the definition certainly does not suggest (contrary to any ordinary understanding) that building and altering sidewalks are not services.

In any event, Title II's definition of a qualified individual with a disability does not suggest that sidewalks and services are mutually exclusive. The phrase "with or without . . . the removal of architectural, communication, or transportation barriers" simply clarifies that the necessity of a reasonable accommodation does not disqualify a disabled individual from invoking Title II in the first place. Drawing from the complaint in this case, a transportation barrier might be a ditch. The definition thus tells us that a newly built or altered sidewalk implicates Title II even if making that sidewalk readily accessible would require reasonably removing the ditch. In other words, a disabled individual's right not to be denied access to a newly built or altered sidewalk does not turn on his ability to access that sidewalk in the first place. This in no way suggests that newly built and altered sidewalks are exempt from § 12132's plain, unambiguous meaning.

[T]hough unnecessary to resolve this case, legislative purpose and history confirm that Congress intended Title II to extend to newly built and altered sidewalks. Congress anticipated that Title II would require local governments "to provide curb cuts on public streets" because the "employment, transportation, and public accommodation sections of [the ADA] would be meaningless if people who use wheelchairs were not afforded the opportunity to travel on and between streets."[61] Implicit in this declaration is a premise that sidewalks are subject to Title II in the first place. Congress's specific application of Title II is consistent with its statutory findings. In enacting Title II, Congress found that

---

[58] 42 U.S.C. § 12131(2).

[61] H.R.REP. NO. 101–485(II), at 84, 1990 U.S.C.C.A.N. at 367.

individuals with disabilities suffer from "various forms of discrimination," including "isolat[ion] and segregat[ion],"[62] and that inaccessible transportation is a "critical area[ ]" of discrimination.[63] Moreover, Congress understood that accessible transportation is the "linchpin" that "promotes the self-reliance and self-sufficiency of people with disabilities."[64] Continuing to build inaccessible sidewalks without adequate justification would unnecessarily entrench the types of discrimination Title II was designed to prohibit.

Title II does not only benefit individuals with disabilities. Congress recognized that isolating disabled individuals from the social and economic mainstream imposes tremendous costs on society. Congress specifically found that disability discrimination "costs the United States billions of dollars in unnecessary expenses resulting from dependency and nonproductivity." Congress also anticipated that "the mainstreaming of persons with disabilities will result in more persons with disabilities working, in increasing earnings, in less dependence on the Social Security system for financial support, in increased spending on consumer goods, and increased tax revenues." The Rehabilitation Act was passed with similar findings and purpose. Continuing to build inaccessible sidewalks without adequate justification would unnecessarily aggravate the social costs Congress sought to abate.

[T]hat Title II extends to newly built and altered sidewalks does not mean that it, or its private right of action, requires cities to employ "any and all means" to make such sidewalks accessible. A city's obligation to make newly built and altered sidewalks readily accessible is not "boundless." As the Supreme Court stated in *Tennessee v. Lane* [a principal case later in this chapter], Title II imposes an "obligation to accommodate," or a "reasonable modification requirement."

On their face, DOJ's regulations governing new and altered facilities are congruous with Title II's reasonable modification requirement. Under DOJ's regulations, each new sidewalk must be made "readily accessible" to individuals with disabilities.[72] This is because, as Congress recognized, the marginal costs of making a new sidewalk readily accessible "are often nonexistent or negligible." With respect to altered sidewalks, the "altered portion" must be made "readily accessible" "to the maximum extent feasible" if it "could affect the usability of the facility."[74] Again, this is because once a public entity decides to alter a sidewalk, it generally is not a significant burden to make the altered portion of that sidewalk accessible. In any event, a public entity is not "required to undertake measures that would impose an undue financial or administrative burden, threaten historic preservation interests, or effect a fundamental alteration in the nature of the service."[76] Thus, DOJ's regulations do not require cities to achieve accessibility at any cost. Instead, the regulations require only that

---

[62] 42 U.S.C. § 12101(a)(2), (5)[.]

[63] 42 U.S.C. § 12101(a)(3)[.]

[64] H.R.REP. NO. 101–485(II), at 37.

[72] 28 C.F.R. § 35.151(a); *id.* § 35.104 (defining a "facility" to include, inter alia, "roads, walks, passageways, [and] parking lots").

[74] 28 C.F.R. § 35.151(b).

[76] Lane, 541 U.S. at 532; *see also* 28 C.F.R. §§ 35.130(b)(7), 35.150(a)(2)–(3), (b)(1), 35.151(b), (d).

when a city chooses to construct a new sidewalk or alter an existing one, the city must take reasonable measures to ensure that those sidewalks are readily accessible to individuals with disabilities. This is the same thing Title II requires.

[A]t least three other circuits have upheld a private right of action to enforce DOJ's regulations governing newly built and altered sidewalks. In *Ability Center of Greater Toledo v. City of Sandusky,* the Sixth Circuit upheld a private right of action to enforce DOJ's regulations with respect to newly built and altered sidewalks.[81] Similarly, in *Barden v. City of Sacramento,* the Ninth Circuit permitted a private plaintiff to enforce DOJ's regulations with respect to newly built and altered (and existing) sidewalks.[82] And in *Kinney v. Yerusalim,* the Third Circuit permitted a private plaintiff to enforce DOJ's regulations with respect to altered sidewalks. Although the Tenth Circuit's decision in *Chaffin v. Kansas State Fair Board* did not concern sidewalks, it too upheld a private right of action to enforce DOJ's regulations with respect to other facilities.[84]

On occasion, a plaintiff may attempt to enforce DOJ's regulations beyond what those regulations and even Title II require. In such cases, DOJ's regulations would not "simply apply" Title II's mandate, and thus would not be privately enforceable. Such cases generally should be dealt with at summary judgment or trial. If the City can show that making its newly built and altered sidewalks accessible would have been unreasonable when those sidewalks were built or altered, the City would be entitled to an affirmative defense. Of course, the district court also will have discretion to craft an appropriate injunction based on the particular facts of the case, and thus will be able to ensure that the City's alleged violations are remedied in a reasonable manner. On the face of the plaintiffs' complaint, however, we cannot say that the plaintiffs' remaining claims are unreasonable as a matter of law.

[T]he panel majority in *Frame II* would have limited Title II's private right of action to sidewalks that serve as "gateways" to other public services, programs, or activities. As already discussed, we find no statutory basis for such a limitation. [W]ere there any ambiguity in DOJ's regulations (and we believe there is not), DOJ has filed an amicus brief confirming that newly built and altered sidewalks "are a subset of services, programs, or activities," and that such sidewalks need not "serve as a gateway to a service, program, or activity in order to be covered by Title II." According to DOJ, §§ 35.149–51 "simply explain how the Act applies when the service, program, or activity is a facility, or takes place in a facility." We observe that DOJ's position is consistent with its amicus briefs in similar cases. Because DOJ's amicus brief corroborates our own analysis, we need not determine precisely how much deference it deserves.

As a final matter, limiting Title II's private right of action to sidewalks that serve as gateways to other public services, programs, or activities would create an unworkable and arbitrary standard. Even on the panel majority's view in *Frame II,* "there should be no set proximity

---

[81] 385 F.3d 901, 906–07 (6th Cir.2004).

[82] 292 F.3d 1073, 1076 (9th Cir.2002).

[84] 348 F.3d 850, 861 (10th Cir.2003).

limitation of the sidewalk to the benefit." But without a proximity limitation, the standard provides no guidance to courts or local governments about when a newly built or altered sidewalk must be accessible[.]

IV

There remains the issue of whether the plaintiffs' claims are barred by the statute of limitations. [The court held that the plaintiffs' claims were not barred. This aspect of the opinion is discussed in the materials on statutes of limitations in Chapter Five.]

V

For the reasons stated, we hold that the plaintiffs have a private right of action to enforce Title II of the ADA and § 504 of the Rehabilitation Act with respect to newly built and altered sidewalks. We further hold that the plaintiffs' private right of action accrued at the time the plaintiffs first knew or should have known they were being denied the benefits of the City's newly built and altered sidewalks. Accordingly, we VACATE the district court's judgment and REMAND for further proceedings.

■ E. GRADY JOLLY, CIRCUIT JUDGE, JOINED BY EDITH H. JONES, CHIEF JUDGE, AND JERRY E. SMITH, EMILIO M. GARZA, EDITH BROWN CLEMENT, PRISCILLA OWEN AND JENNIFER WALKER ELROD, CIRCUIT JUDGES, DISSENTING IN PART AND CONCURRING IN PART:[1]

[I]f one concludes, as the majority does, that somehow a sidewalk is a "service," then one concludes that the subject matter of a private cause of action against a public entity under Title II is unlimited; if one concludes that under the ADA a sidewalk is a public "facility," and that an inanimate and static public facility is distinguishable from a public service, then a private cause of action is thus limited to services and does not extend to facilities.

Finally, and with no apparent discomfort, the majority finds it necessary to recast the issue that Richard Frame has stated for the en banc court. Specifically, Frame states that the sidewalks he seeks to alter constitute a service. The majority says it is not determinative whether a sidewalk is itself a service, because the labor that produced the sidewalk is a service. The majority, however, fails to recognize that the ADA provides a cause of action only if a service is denied "by reason of" disability.

In other words, the majority's alternative argument necessarily assumes that the plaintiffs were denied access to the service of the city's labor force on account of their respective disabilities. This assumption ignores that the city's labor services are not accessible to the general population as a whole; that is to say that no individual—able bodied or disabled—can commandeer the labor force of a city to construct or reconstruct *any* facility, sidewalk or otherwise. In short, neither facts, nor policies, nor law, supports granting the plaintiffs a right of access to the city's labor force.

For these reasons, and for the reasons that follow, I respectfully dissent.

---

[1] This dissent challenges only the majority's conclusion that a sidewalk constitutes a service under 42 U.S.C. § 12132.

I.

The bottom-line question presented for en banc consideration is whether private plaintiffs generally have a cause of action to require the city to reconstruct sidewalks built or repaired after January 26, 1992 (the effective date of the ADA). The question is resolved by the following analysis.

First, Title II's anti-discrimination provisions do not specifically provide that a private cause of action may be brought against a municipality to enforce ADA-compliant sidewalk construction or reconstruction. Second, although the regulations that accompany the ADA address sidewalk construction and reconstruction, *see* 28 C.F.R. § 35.149–151, regulations are not privately enforceable unless they effectuate a statutory mandate, because "private rights of action to enforce federal law must be created by Congress." *Alexander v. Sandoval,* 532 U.S. 275, 286 (2001). That is, as applicable in this case, the statute does not guarantee access to facilities, but only to "services, programs, or activities."

Third, the ADA mandates equal access to governmental *services,* and it therefore provides a disabled individual with a private cause of action if he is being effectively denied meaningful access to a service. *See Alexander v. Choate,* 469 U.S. 287, 301 (1985) (stating in the context of the Rehabilitation Act that a benefit cannot be offered in a way that "effectively denies otherwise qualified handicapped individuals the meaningful access to which they are entitled"). Fourth, the question of whether the plaintiffs have a private cause of action to enjoin the City to construct or reconstruct a sidewalk is resolved by determining whether a sidewalk constitutes a service. Fifth, the ADA does not define "service" in specific terms.

Sixth, turning to examine the statute and regulations for guidance, we see that the statute suggests that sidewalks constitute either a barrier to transportation, or a facility, or both. *See* 42 U.S.C. §§ 12131(2), 12146–12147. Additionally, the regulations specifically define sidewalks as a "facility." 28 C.F.R. § 35.104 ("Facility *means* all or any portion of . . . roads, walks, [and] passageways. . . .") (emphasis added). Furthermore, the regulations draw a distinction between services and facilities at the behest of Congress: DOJ is required to model the relevant regulations after the "regulations and analysis as in part 39 of title 28 of the Code of Federal Regulations[,]" *see* 42 U.S.C. § 12134(b), which differentiate "program[s] or activiti[es]" from "facilities." 28 C.F.R. § 39.150.

Seventh, in the light of the statute and regulations, there is no mandate for accessibility to facilities; on the other hand, there is the express mandate of the statute and the regulations to universal accessibility of services, programs, and activities. Stated differently, facilities are specifically excluded from the access demands of the private cause of action provided in Section 12132. Because a sidewalk is a facility—not a service—the sidewalk regulations are privately enforceable only if an inaccessible sidewalk effectively denies a disabled individual meaningful access to a public service. Although the majority holds that the wheelchair-disabled have no rights of access to a sidewalk constructed or last repaired before 1992, irrespective of whether that sidewalk effectively denies a disabled person access to a city's services, this dissent would hold that if a noncompliant sidewalk effectively denies meaningful access to a service available to the general public, there is a private cause of action.

II.

[A.]

Even though the statute does not explicitly define the term "services," the statute makes a few suggestions to aid our interpretation of the term. First, Title II deals with "transportation barriers," which include unfriendly sidewalks. Specifically, a "qualified individual with a disability" is defined as a disabled individual "who, *with or without* . . . the removal of *architectural,* . . . or *transportation* barriers . . . meets the essential eligibility requirements for the receipt of *services or the participation in programs or activities* . . ." 42 U.S.C. § 12131(2) (emphasis added). Thus, we get some indication as to the meaning of services by reference to what services are *not*. Obviously, the noncompliant sidewalks are alleged by the plaintiffs to be barriers to transportation for the wheelchair disabled. Consequently, it is plain that transportation barriers are treated as barriers to accessing a service, and that sidewalks are not classified as a service.

We are not alone in reaching the conclusion that transportation barriers are distinguishable from services: the Supreme Court has held that the necessary implication of Section 12131(2) is that in some circumstances, local governments must "remove architectural and other barriers to [the] accessibility [of judicial services]." *Tennessee v. Lane,* 541 U.S. 509, 531 (2004). Thus, if transportation barriers, *i.e.*, facilities, and services are coextensive as the majority argues, the ADA requires local governments to "remove" services, *i.e.*, transportation barriers, so that disabled individuals will have access to services. This is the nonsensical reading that follows from the majority's reasoning; we should strive to avoid such absurdity. *See Dunn-McCampbell Royalty Interest, Inc. v. Nat'l Park Serv.,* 630 F.3d 431, 439 (5th Cir.2011).

In sum: although Title II of the ADA does not define services in express terms, it tells us that a service is not an inaccessible sidewalk, which is instead treated as a facility that is a *barrier* to access of a public service.

B.

We continue to look to the statute for guidance on what a service is not, but we now turn to Part B of Title II, which deals not with public services generally, but with the specific subset of public *transportation* services. *See generally* 42 U.S.C. §§ 12141–12165. Within this part, Congress required that local governments make accessible their new and altered facilities, but only those that are "to be used in the provision of designated public transportation services . . ." 42 U.S.C. § 12146. Thus, as the majority concedes, the ADA explicitly requires facilities to be made accessible in (and only in) "the *unique context* of 'designated public transportation services' . . . ." Majority Op. (emphasis added).

Given that the statute requires that facilities be accessible to disabled individuals only in this limited context, it is plain that, despite the majority's argument to the contrary, facilities are not merely a "subset of services." I reiterate: under the ADA, disabled individuals shall not "be excluded from participation in or be denied the benefits of" public *services.* 42 U.S.C. § 12132. Thus, all services must be made accessible in all contexts. Again, the primary implication of Sections 12146 and 12147 is that facilities need only be made equally accessible *in the specific and limited context* of "designated public transit services." Thus, because facilities are not subject to the universal equal accessibility requirement, they are not—as the majority argues— enfolded within the term services.

Moreover, relevant precedent teaches that when Congress included the term "facilities" in Sections 12146 and 12147, it indicated that it had purposefully excluded that term from the private cause of action included in Section 12132. *See Russello v. United States,* 464 U.S. 16, 23 (1983) ("[W]here Congress includes particular language in one section of a statute but omits it in another section of the same Act, it is generally presumed that Congress acts intentionally and purposely in the disparate inclusion or exclusion.") (alteration in original). Thus, we should reject the majority's argument that the use of the term facilities in Sections 12146 and 12147 demonstrates that Congress intended to include the term facilities in Section 12132.

To sum up, Section 12132 provides a private cause of action when disabled individuals are denied access to public "services, programs, or activities." *See* 42 U.S.C. § 12132 (Requiring local governments to provide equal access to its "services, programs, or activities . . . ."). The use of three—and only three—terms indicates the statute was intended to have a structured meaning. Congress could easily have expressed its intent to prohibit local governments from denying disabled individuals equal access to *all* "facilities, services, programs, or activities." It did not. Instead, it required that local governments make their facilities accessible only in the context of transportation services.

Thus, the ADA, without explicitly defining the term services, identifies two things that a service is not: a transportation barrier and a facility. Applying those distinctions here, it seems that under the statute itself, a noncompliant sidewalk is a transportation barrier and that sidewalks in general, are—like other static, inanimate, immobile infrastructure—facilities.

III.

We now turn to the regulations to resolve any remaining doubt that facilities are distinguishable from services.

A.

Although the majority turns to the regulations hoping to smooth off the rough incongruities of its statutory interpretation of "service" as unambiguous, the regulations, for the reasons below, actually—and compellingly—suggest that a sidewalk itself does not constitute a service.

First, the regulations define and designate a sidewalk as a "facility"—not as a "service, program, or activity." 28 C.F.R. § 35.104.

Second, the regulations mirror the statute and require that all *services* shall be accessible to the disabled. 28 C.F.R. § 35.130(a).

Third, the regulations further provide that no disabled individual "shall, *because a public entity's facilities are inaccessible . . .* or unusable

. . . be excluded from participation in, or be denied the benefits of the *services,* programs, or activities . . . ." 28 C.F.R. § 35.149 (emphasis added). Thus, under the regulations, as under the statute, all services are mandated to be accessible, but facilities, e.g., sidewalks, may remain inaccessible—a crucial distinction that tells us, contrary to the majority's assertion, that facilities and services are two distinctly separate categories under Title II. Stated differently, under Section 35.149, a city violates the law by having inaccessible facilities *only if* those facilities deny disabled individuals access to a service.

Fourth, the regulations further provide that a city is not "[n]ecessarily require[d] . . . to make each . . . existing facilit[y] accessible to and usable by individuals with disabilities." 28 C.F.R. § 35.150. Indeed, a municipality is granted the discretion to choose how best to make its services accessible; "alteration of existing facilities and construction of new facilities" is merely one potential method. 28 C.F.R. § 35.150(b)(1). Still further, *if* a city elects to provide access to its services by making "structural change[s] to facilities[,]" that city must "develop . . . a transition plan setting forth the steps necessary to complete such changes [,]" and the plan must "include a schedule for providing curb ramps . . . giving priority to walkways serving entities covered by the Act . . . ." 28 C.F.R. § 35.150(d)(1)-(2). If sidewalks are— as the majority urges—services, one would abandon good sense to say— as the regulations would then say—that local governments should focus their *reconstruction efforts* on services, services that "*serve* entities covered by the Act" because the sidewalks would *themselves* be "entities covered by the Act."

Finally, the regulations require only that a city make *newly constructed* or *reconstructed* sidewalks handicapped-accessible. 28 C.F.R. § 35.151. As we have said more than once, all *services* of the city must be made accessible; if the regulations characterized sidewalks a service, no sidewalk would be allowed to be inaccessible. Section 35.151 is not privately enforceable unless it effectuates a *statutory* mandate. Here, the statutory mandate, requiring accessibility for the disabled, specifically omits facilities. "[P]rivate rights of action to enforce federal law must be created by Congress." Sandoval, 532 U.S. at 286. This principle means that agencies, as well en banc courts, cannot "conjure up a private cause of action that has not been authorized by Congress. Agencies may play the sorcerer's apprentice but not the sorcerer himself." *Id.* at 291. Because—as discussed at length above—the statute mandates access to services, not facilities, Section 35.151's requirements are not enforceable in a private suit, but instead are left to other enforcement mechanisms as might be employed by the Attorney General.

In short, the *regulations expressly define sidewalks as facilities,* not as services. And, furthermore, by requiring that all services be made accessible, while requiring facilities to be made accessible only in specific and limited circumstances, the regulations are compelling that a facility—such as a sidewalk—is not a service.

B.

Nor is the regulatory distinction between "facilities" and "services" the result of oversight, mistake, or confusion, but derives from congressional mandate. Indeed, Congress directed that the regulations differentiate between facilities and services.

The ADA—statutorily and specifically—requires that the DOJ regulations regarding " 'program accessibility, existing facilities,' . . . be consistent with regulations and analysis as in part 39 of title 28 of the Code of Federal Regulations." 42 U.S.C. § 12134(b).

[T]he statute further requires that the regulations regarding new and altered facilities track the language from the "coordination regulations under part 41 of title 28, Code of Federal Regulations . . . ." 42 U.S.C. § 12134(b). The majority correctly argues that the "regulations that Congress sought to replicate under Title II require new and altered facilities, including sidewalks, to be accessible in *most* circumstances." The majority's wobble, *i.e.*, "most," proves the point. If facilities, *i.e.*, sidewalks, are services, they must be equally accessible in *all* circumstances, not in "most circumstances." 42 U.S.C. § 12132 ("[*N*]*o qualified individual with a disability shall* . . . be excluded from participation in or be denied the benefits of the services, programs, or activities, ...") (emphasis added). Thus, the fact that, pursuant to Congress's direct instructions, the regulations require only that *new*— but not all—facilities be accessible in *most*—but not all—circumstances again suggests that "facility" is not a term that replicates the statutory term "service." The clear mandate of the ADA is the unequivocal right of access to services, programs, and activities, and Congress required that the regulations clarify that this private right of action to demand access does not extend to facilities, a term not mentioned in § 12132.

[V.]

Finally, we turn to address the majority's attempt to reframe the issue presented, and to thereby shift our focus from the actual sidewalks that the plaintiffs seek to modify, to the labor services employed to construct those sidewalks. [T]his alternative argument leaves unaddressed that, under Section 12132 the denial of the construction worker's "service" must be by "reason of disability," that is, the *disability* must preclude access to the service of the labor of public employees. Furthermore, the argument falsely assumes that the public generally is provided access to commandeer the service of governmental employees. Here, for example, the non-disabled citizens have no individual right to direct the services of public construction workers to any construction project, including a sidewalk. An illustration, which is perhaps apt to our understanding, is that although the legal department of a city provides legal services in the public interest and on public matters, those public services are not available to the public at large and are not denied to the disabled by reason of their disability.

The majority vigorously contends, and we do not disagree, that Congress passed the ADA with the aim of granting disabled citizens the same access to public services that able-bodied citizens enjoy; but the majority does not contend that the ADA provides disabled individuals with *greater* access to public services. Plainly said, no citizen has access to a city's labor force for the construction of a sidewalk. So, surely, any denial of access to the sidewalk construction crew cannot be "by reason of . . . disability."

Thus, the majority is demonstrably incorrect when it insists that it does not matter how broadly we analyze the statute. The proper question is whether a sidewalk is itself a service. The answer is that it is not.

VI.

From reading the majority opinion and this dissent, it is evident that the statute has not been drawn with preciseness. Nevertheless, this dissent has demonstrated that the statute itself differentiates services from facilities, and has addressed sidewalks only as transportation barriers and facilities, but never as a service. The regulations that implement the statute, however, define sidewalks as a facility. Like the statute, these regulations never refer to sidewalks as a service.

This dissent has thus shown that the majority errs when it conflates services and facilities. This error is further demonstrated because the statute and the regulations allow facilities to be inaccessible to the disabled in many circumstances but require all services to be made equally accessible. Thus, a proper reading of the statute makes clear that facilities and services are treated with distinct and separate meanings. When the statute and regulations are considered as a whole, it should be clear, except perhaps to the most intractable, that Congress never intended for sidewalks to constitute a service, accompanied by a private cause of action.

Finally, this dissent has shown the non-functionality of the majority's abstract argument that the labor construction services morph into the sidewalk itself.

For the reasons stated above, I respectfully dissent. I would remand to allow the district court to determine whether the plaintiffs can show that particular sidewalks deny access to services that are not otherwise accessible.

NOTES ON FRAME V. CITY OF ARLINGTON

Which of the opinions in *Frame*, the majority or the dissent, is most consistent with the statutory text? Which is most consistent with the Supreme Court's decision in *Yeskey*?

B. THE ACCESS/CONTENT DISTINCTION

Alexander v. Choate

Supreme Court of the United States, 1985.
469 U.S. 287.

■ JUSTICE MARSHALL delivered the opinion of the Court.

In 1980, Tennessee proposed reducing the number of annual days of inpatient hospital care covered by its state Medicaid program. The question presented is whether the effect upon the handicapped that this reduction will have is cognizable under § 504 of the Rehabilitation Act of 1973 or its implementing regulations. We hold that it is not.

I

Faced in 1980–1981 with projected state Medicaid[1] costs of $42 million more than the State's Medicaid budget of $388 million, the directors of the Tennessee Medicaid program decided to institute a variety of cost-saving measures. Among these changes was a reduction from 20 to 14 in the number of inpatient hospital days per fiscal year that Tennessee Medicaid would pay hospitals on behalf of a Medicaid recipient. Before the new measures took effect, respondents, Tennessee Medicaid recipients, brought a class action for declaratory and injunctive relief in which they alleged, *inter alia*, that the proposed 14-day limitation on inpatient coverage would have a discriminatory effect on the handicapped. Statistical evidence, which petitioners do not dispute, indicated that in the 1979–1980 fiscal year, 27.4% of all handicapped users of hospital services who received Medicaid required more than 14 days of care, while only 7.8% of nonhandicapped users required more than 14 days of inpatient care.

Based on this evidence, respondents asserted that the reduction would violate § 504 of the Rehabilitation Act of 1973, 87 Stat. 394, as amended, 29 U.S.C. § 794, and its implementing regulations. Section 504 provides:

> "No otherwise qualified handicapped individual . . . shall, solely by reason of his handicap, be excluded from the participation in, be denied the benefits of, or be subjected to discrimination under any program or activity receiving Federal financial
> assistance. . . . " 29 U.S.C. § 794.

Respondents' position was twofold. First, they argued that the change from 20 to 14 days of coverage would have a disproportionate effect on the handicapped and hence was discriminatory.[3] The second, and major, thrust of respondents' attack was directed at the use of any annual limitation on the number of inpatient days covered, for respondents acknowledged that, given the special needs of the handicapped for medical care, any such limitation was likely to disadvantage the handicapped disproportionately. Respondents noted, however, that federal law does not require States to impose any annual durational limitation on inpatient coverage, and that the Medicaid programs of only 10 States impose such restrictions.[4] Respondents therefore suggested that Tennessee follow these other States and do away with any limitation on the number of annual inpatient days covered. Instead, argued respondents, the State could limit the number

---

[1] Medicaid was established by Title XIX of the Social Security Act of 1965, 79 Stat. 343, as amended, 42 U.S.C. § 1396 *et seq.* Medicaid is a joint state-federal funding program for medical assistance in which the Federal Government approves a state plan for the funding of medical services for the needy and then subsidizes a significant portion of the financial obligations the State has agreed to assume. Once a State voluntarily chooses to participate in Medicaid, the State must comply with the requirements of Title XIX and applicable regulations.

[3] The evidence indicated that, if 19 days of coverage were provided, 16.9% of the handicapped, as compared to 4.2% of the nonhandicapped, would not have their needs for inpatient care met.

[4] As of 1980 the average ceiling in those States was 37.6 days. Six States also limit the number of reimbursable days per admission, per spell of illness, or per benefit period. See App. B to Brief for United States as *Amicus Curiae.*

of days of hospital coverage on a per-stay basis, with the number of covered days to vary depending on the recipient's illness (for example, fixing the number of days covered for an appendectomy); the period to be covered for each illness could then be set at a level that would keep Tennessee's Medicaid program as a whole within its budget. The State's refusal to adopt this plan was said to result in the imposition of gratuitous costs on the handicapped and thus to constitute discrimination under § 504.

A divided panel of the Court of Appeals for the Sixth Circuit held that respondents had indeed established a prima facie case of a § 504 violation. The majority apparently concluded that any action by a federal grantee that disparately affects the handicapped states a cause of action under § 504 and its implementing regulations. Because both the 14-day rule and any annual limitation on inpatient coverage disparately affected the handicapped, the panel found that a prima facie case had been made out, and the case was remanded to give Tennessee an opportunity for rebuttal. According to the panel majority, the State on remand could either demonstrate the unavailability of alternative plans that would achieve the State's legitimate cost-saving goals with a less disproportionate impact on the handicapped, or the State could offer "a substantial justification for the adoption of the plan with the greater discriminatory impact." We granted *certiorari* to consider whether the type of impact at issue in this case is cognizable under § 504 or its implementing regulations, and we now reverse.

II

The first question the parties urge on the Court is whether proof of discriminatory animus is always required to establish a violation of § 504 and its implementing regulations, or whether federal law also reaches action by a recipient of federal funding that discriminates against the handicapped by effect rather than by design. The State of Tennessee argues that § 504 reaches only purposeful discrimination against the handicapped.

[D]iscrimination against the handicapped was perceived by Congress to be most often the product, not of invidious animus, but rather of thoughtlessness and indifference—of benign neglect.[12] Thus, Representative Vanik, introducing the predecessor to § 504 in the House, described the treatment of the handicapped as one of the country's "shameful oversights," which caused the handicapped to live among society "shunted aside, hidden, and ignored." Similarly, Senator Humphrey, who introduced a companion measure in the Senate, asserted that "we can no longer tolerate the invisibility of the handicapped in America. . . . " And Senator Cranston, the Acting Chairman of the Subcommittee that drafted § 504, described the Act as a response to "previous societal neglect." Federal agencies and commentators on the plight of the handicapped similarly have found that discrimination against the handicapped is primarily the result of apathetic attitudes rather than affirmative animus.

---

[12] To be sure, well-cataloged instances of invidious discrimination against the handicapped do exist. See, *e.g.*, U.S. Comm'n on Civil Rights, Accommodating the Spectrum of Individual Abilities, Ch. 2 (1983); Wegner, *The Antidiscrimination Model Reconsidered: Ensuring Equal Opportunity Without Respect to Handicap Under Section 504 of the Rehabilitation Act of 1973*, 69 Cornell L.Rev. 401, 403, n. 2 (1984).

In addition, much of the conduct that Congress sought to alter in passing the Rehabilitation Act would be difficult if not impossible to reach were the Act construed to proscribe only conduct fueled by a discriminatory intent. For example, elimination of architectural barriers was one of the central aims of the Act, yet such barriers were clearly not erected with the aim or intent of excluding the handicapped. Similarly, Senator Williams, the chairman of the Labor and Public Welfare Committee that reported out § 504, asserted that the handicapped were the victims of "[d]iscrimination in access to public transportation" and "[d]iscrimination because they do not have the simplest forms of special educational and rehabilitation services they need. . . . " And Senator Humphrey, again in introducing the proposal that later became § 504, listed, among the instances of discrimination that the section would prohibit, the use of "transportation and architectural barriers," the "discriminatory effect of job qualification . . . procedures," and the denial of "special educational assistance" for handicapped children. These statements would ring hollow if the resulting legislation could not rectify the harms resulting from action that discriminated by effect as well as by design.

At the same time, the position urged by respondents—that we interpret § 504 to reach all action disparately affecting the handicapped—is also troubling. Because the handicapped typically are not similarly situated to the nonhandicapped, respondents' position would in essence require each recipient of federal funds first to evaluate the effect on the handicapped of every proposed action that might touch the interests of the handicapped, and then to consider alternatives for achieving the same objectives with less severe disadvantage to the handicapped. The formalization and policing of this process could lead to a wholly unwieldy administrative and adjudicative burden. Had Congress intended § 504 to be a National Environmental Policy Act for the handicapped, requiring the preparation of "Handicapped Impact Statements" before any action was taken by a grantee that affected the handicapped, we would expect some indication of that purpose in the statute or its legislative history. Yet there is nothing to suggest that such was Congress' purpose. Thus, just as there is reason to question whether Congress intended § 504 to reach only intentional discrimination, there is similarly reason to question whether Congress intended § 504 to embrace all claims of disparate-impact discrimination.

Any interpretation of § 504 must therefore be responsive to two powerful but countervailing considerations—the need to give effect to the statutory objectives and the desire to keep § 504 within manageable bounds. Given the legitimacy of both of these goals and the tension between them, we decline the parties' invitation to decide today that one of these goals so overshadows the other as to eclipse it. While we reject the boundless notion that all disparate-impact showings constitute prima facie cases under § 504, we assume without deciding that § 504 reaches at least some conduct that has an unjustifiable disparate impact upon the handicapped. On that assumption, we must then determine whether the disparate effect of which respondents complain is the sort of disparate impact that federal law might recognize.

III

To determine which disparate impacts § 504 might make actionable, the proper starting point is *Southeastern Community College v. Davis*, 442 U.S. 397 (1979), our major previous attempt to define the scope of § 504. *Davis* involved a plaintiff with a major hearing disability who sought admission to a college to be trained as a registered nurse, but who would not be capable of safely performing as a registered nurse even with full-time personal supervision. We stated that, under some circumstances, a "refusal to modify an existing program might become unreasonable and discriminatory. Identification of those instances where a refusal to accommodate the needs of a disabled person amounts to discrimination against the handicapped [is] an important responsibility of HEW." We held that the college was not required to admit Davis because it appeared unlikely that she could benefit from any modifications that the relevant HEW regulations required, and because the further modifications Davis sought—full-time, personal supervision whenever she attended patients and elimination of all clinical courses—would have compromised the essential nature of the college's nursing program. Such a "fundamental alteration in the nature of a program" was far more than the reasonable modifications the statute or regulations required. *Davis* thus struck a balance between the statutory rights of the handicapped to be integrated into society and the legitimate interests of federal grantees in preserving the integrity of their programs: while a grantee need not be required to make "fundamental" or "substantial" modifications to accommodate the handicapped, it may be required to make "reasonable" ones.[20]

The balance struck in *Davis* requires that an otherwise qualified handicapped individual must be provided with meaningful access to the benefit that the grantee offers. The benefit itself, of course, cannot be defined in a way that effectively denies otherwise qualified handicapped individuals the meaningful access to which they are entitled; to assure meaningful access, reasonable accommodations in the grantee's program or benefit may have to be made.[21] In this case, respondents

---

[20] In *Davis*, we stated that § 504 does not impose an "affirmative-action obligation on all recipients of federal funds." Our use of the term "affirmative action" in this context has been severely criticized for failing to appreciate the difference between affirmative action and reasonable accommodation; the former is said to refer to a remedial policy for the victims of past discrimination, while the latter relates to the elimination of existing obstacles against the handicapped. See *[D]opico v. Goldschmidt*, 687 F.2d 644, 652 (CA2 1982) ("Use of the phrase 'affirmative action' in this context is unfortunate, making it difficult to talk about any kind of affirmative efforts without importing the special legal and social connotations of that term."). Regardless of the aptness of our choice of words in *Davis*, it is clear from the context of Davis that the term "affirmative action" referred to those "changes," "adjustments," or "modifications" to existing programs that would be "substantial," or that would constitute "fundamental alteration[s] in the nature of a program . . . ," rather than to those changes that would be reasonable accommodations.

[21] As the Government states: "Antidiscrimination legislation can obviously be emptied of meaning if every discriminatory policy is 'collapsed' into one's definition of what is the relevant benefit." At oral argument, the Government also acknowledged that "special measures for the handicapped, as the *Lau* case shows, may sometimes be necessary. . . ." Tr. of Oral Arg. 14–15 (referring to *Lau v. Nichols*, 414 U.S. 563 (1974)). The regulations implementing § 504 are consistent with the view that reasonable adjustments in the nature of the benefit offered must at times be made to assure meaningful access. See, *e.g.*, 45 CFR § 84.12(a) (1984) (requiring an employer to make "reasonable accommodation to the known physical or mental limitations" of a handicapped individual); 45 CFR § 84.22 and § 84.23

argue that the 14-day rule, or any annual durational limitation, denies meaningful access to Medicaid services in Tennessee. We examine each of these arguments in turn.

A

The 14-day limitation will not deny respondents meaningful access to Tennessee Medicaid services or exclude them from those services. The new limitation does not invoke criteria that have a particular exclusionary effect on the handicapped; the reduction, neutral on its face, does not distinguish between those whose coverage will be reduced and those whose coverage will not on the basis of any test, judgment, or trait that the handicapped as a class are less capable of meeting or less likely of having. Moreover, it cannot be argued that "meaningful access" to state Medicaid services will be denied by the 14-day limitation on inpatient coverage; nothing in the record suggests that the handicapped in Tennessee will be unable to benefit meaningfully from the coverage they will receive under the 14-day rule.[22] The reduction in inpatient coverage will leave both handicapped and nonhandicapped Medicaid users with identical and effective hospital services fully available for their use, with both classes of users subject to the same durational limitation. The 14-day limitation, therefore, does not exclude the handicapped from or deny them the benefits of the 14 days of care the State has chosen to provide.

To the extent respondents further suggest that their greater need for prolonged inpatient care means that, to provide meaningful access to Medicaid services, Tennessee must single out the handicapped for more than 14 days of coverage, the suggestion is simply unsound. At base, such a suggestion must rest on the notion that the benefit provided through state Medicaid programs is the amorphous objective of "adequate health care." But Medicaid programs do not guarantee that each recipient will receive that level of health care precisely tailored to his or her particular needs. Instead, the benefit provided through Medicaid is a particular package of health care services, such as 14 days of inpatient coverage. That package of services has the general aim of assuring that individuals will receive necessary medical care, but the benefit provided remains the individual services offered— not "adequate health care."

The federal Medicaid Act makes this point clear. The Act gives the States substantial discretion to choose the proper mix of amount, scope, and duration limitations on coverage, as long as care and services are provided in "the best interests of the recipients." 42 U.S.C.

(1984) (requiring that new buildings be readily accessible, building alterations be accessible "to the maximum extent feasible," and existing facilities eventually be operated so that a program or activity inside is, "when viewed in its entirety," readily accessible); 45 CFR § 84.44(a) (1984) (requiring certain modifications to the regular academic programs of secondary education institutions, such as changes in the length of time permitted for the completion of degree requirements, substitution of specific courses required for the completion of degree requirements, and adaptation of the manner in which specific courses are conducted).

[22] The record does not contain any suggestion that the illnesses uniquely associated with the handicapped or occurring with greater frequency among them cannot be effectively treated, at least in part, with fewer than 14 days' coverage. In addition, the durational limitation does not apply to only particular handicapped conditions and takes effect regardless of the particular cause of hospitalization.

§ 1396a(a)(19). The District Court found that the 14-day limitation would fully serve 95% of even handicapped individuals eligible for Tennessee Medicaid, and both lower courts concluded that Tennessee's proposed Medicaid plan would meet the "best interests" standard. That unchallenged conclusion indicates that Tennessee is free, as a matter of the Medicaid Act, to choose to define the benefit it will be providing as 14 days of inpatient coverage.

Section 504 does not require the State to alter this definition of the benefit being offered simply to meet the reality that the handicapped have greater medical needs. To conclude otherwise would be to find that the Rehabilitation Act requires States to view certain illnesses, *i.e.,* those particularly affecting the handicapped, as more important than others and more worthy of cure through government subsidization. Nothing in the legislative history of the Act supports such a conclusion. Section 504 seeks to assure evenhanded treatment and the opportunity for handicapped individuals to participate in and benefit from programs receiving federal assistance. *Southeastern Community College v. Davis,* 442 U.S. 397 (1979). The Act does not, however, guarantee the handicapped equal results from the provision of state Medicaid, even assuming some measure of equality of health could be constructed.

Regulations promulgated by the Department of Health and Human Services (HHS) pursuant to the Act further support this conclusion. These regulations state that recipients of federal funds who provide health services cannot "provide a qualified handicapped person with benefits or services that are not as effective (as defined in § 84.4(b)) as the benefits or services provided to others." 45 CFR § 84.52(a)(3) (1984). The regulations also prohibit a recipient of federal funding from adopting "criteria or methods of administration that have the purpose or effect of defeating or substantially impairing accomplishment of the objectives of the recipient's program with respect to the handicapped." 45 CFR § 84.4(b)(4)(ii) (1984).

While these regulations, read in isolation, could be taken to suggest that a state Medicaid program must make the handicapped as healthy as the nonhandicapped, other regulations reveal that HHS does not contemplate imposing such a requirement. Title 45 CFR § 84.4(b)(2) (1984), referred to in the regulations quoted above, makes clear that

> "[f]or purposes of this part, aids, benefits, and services, to be equally effective, are not required to produce the identical result or level of achievement for handicapped and nonhandicapped persons, but must afford handicapped persons equal opportunity to obtain the same result, to gain the same benefit, or to reach the same level of achievement. . . . "

This regulation, while indicating that adjustments to existing programs are contemplated, also makes clear that Tennessee is not required to assure that its handicapped Medicaid users will be as healthy as its nonhandicapped users. Thus, to the extent respondents are seeking a distinct durational limitation for the handicapped, Tennessee is entitled to respond by asserting that the relevant benefit is 14 days of coverage. Because the handicapped have meaningful and equal access to that benefit, Tennessee is not obligated to reinstate its 20-day rule or to provide the handicapped with more than 14 days of inpatient coverage.

B

We turn next to respondents' alternative contention, a contention directed not at the 14-day rule itself but rather at Tennessee's Medicaid plan as a whole. Respondents argue that the inclusion of any annual durational limitation on inpatient coverage in a state Medicaid plan violates § 504. The thrust of this challenge is that all annual durational limitations discriminate against the handicapped because (1) the effect of such limitations falls most heavily on the handicapped and because (2) this harm could be avoided by the choice of other Medicaid plans that would meet the State's budgetary constraints without disproportionately disadvantaging the handicapped. Viewed in this light, Tennessee's current plan is said to inflict a gratuitous harm on the handicapped that denies them meaningful access to Medicaid services.

Whatever the merits of this conception of meaningful access, it is clear that § 504 does not require the changes respondents seek. In enacting the Rehabilitation Act and in subsequent amendments, Congress did focus on several substantive areas—employment, education, and the elimination of physical barriers to access—in which it considered the societal and personal costs of refusals to provide meaningful access to the handicapped to be particularly high. But nothing in the pre– or post–1973 legislative discussion of § 504 suggests that Congress desired to make major inroads on the States' longstanding discretion to choose the proper mix of amount, scope, and duration limitations on services covered by state Medicaid. And, more generally, we have already stated that § 504 does not impose a general NEPA-like requirement on federal grantees.

The costs of such a requirement would be far from minimal, and thus Tennessee's refusal to pursue this course does not, as respondents suggest, inflict a "gratuitous" harm on the handicapped. On the contrary, to require that the sort of broad-based distributive decision at issue in this case always be made in the way most favorable, or least disadvantageous, to the handicapped, even when the same benefit is meaningfully and equally offered to them, would be to impose a virtually unworkable requirement on state Medicaid administrators. Before taking any across-the-board action affecting Medicaid recipients, an analysis of the effect of the proposed change on the handicapped would have to be prepared. Presumably, that analysis would have to be further broken down by class of handicap—the change at issue here, for example, might be significantly less harmful to the blind, who use inpatient services only minimally, than to other subclasses of handicapped Medicaid recipients; the State would then have to balance the harms and benefits to various groups to determine, on balance, the extent to which the action disparately impacts the handicapped. In addition, respondents offer no reason that similar treatment would not have to be accorded other groups protected by statute or regulation from disparate-impact discrimination.

It should be obvious that administrative costs of implementing such a regime would be well beyond the accommodations that are required under *Davis*. As a result, Tennessee need not redefine its Medicaid program to eliminate durational limitations on inpatient coverage, even if in doing so the State could achieve its immediate fiscal objectives in a way less harmful to the handicapped.

IV

The 14-day rule challenged in this case is neutral on its face, is not alleged to rest on a discriminatory motive, and does not deny the handicapped access to or exclude them from the particular package of Medicaid services Tennessee has chosen to provide. The State has made the same benefit—14 days of coverage—equally accessible to both handicapped and nonhandicapped persons, and the State is not required to assure the handicapped "adequate health care" by providing them with more coverage than the nonhandicapped. In addition, the State is not obligated to modify its Medicaid program by abandoning reliance on annual durational limitations on inpatient coverage. Assuming, then, that § 504 or its implementing regulations reach some claims of disparate-impact discrimination, the effect of Tennessee's reduction in annual inpatient coverage is not among them. For that reason, the Court of Appeals erred in holding that respondents had established a prima facie violation of § 504. The judgment below is accordingly reversed.

It is so ordered.

NOTES ON ALEXANDER V. CHOATE

Choate highlights an important difference between the employment and public services settings. In private employment, determining the function of the defendant's enterprise is relatively straightforward—the function is typically the production, distribution, or sale of goods and services, with the purpose of making a profit. To apply the reasonable accommodation requirement to the employment context, we simply need to ask whether a modification to job duties, employer policies, or physical facilities will enable the plaintiff to perform his or her role in the function of the enterprise, at reasonable cost. Although application of the accommodation mandate in employment is sometimes controversial, the accommodation inquiry is relatively uncomplicated. (The inquiry is slightly more complicated in the nonprofit setting, but even in that setting an individual's job serves some function in achieving the overall enterprise's goals.)

But things can be very different in the public services context. Although public benefits programs serve many ultimate purposes, their proximate function is to provide benefits, in the amount specified in statutes and regulations, to those individuals the law deems eligible. But if the role of accommodation is to enable a person with a disability to perform the function of the enterprise at issue, how can *any* accommodation to a benefits program be reasonable (beyond such requirements as making the facilities where benefits are awarded physically accessible)? In his opinion for the Court, Justice Marshall quotes with approval the Solicitor General's statement that "[a]ntidiscrimination legislation can obviously be emptied of meaning if every discriminatory policy is 'collapsed' into one's definition of what is the relevant benefit." That statement suggests that plaintiffs can challenge *disability-specific* benefits rules—for example, a rule that denies blind people Medicaid benefits that are available to everyone else. Must disability-neutral benefits rules ever be modified at the instance of individuals with disabilities?

If so, how is a court supposed to determine what modifications are reasonable? Must it ask what the ultimate purpose of the benefits program is, at a high level of generality, and then determine whether it is reasonable, in light of that purpose, to extend the program on behalf of the plaintiff? On the facts of *Choate*, for example, a court might first decide that the ultimate purpose of the Tennessee Medicaid law is to provide essential care for poor people at a reasonable cost. Then, it might decide that more than fourteen days of hospitalization constitutes essential care for many individuals with disabilities, and that the cost of removing the cap on hospitalization reimbursements is reasonable in light of the ultimate purpose of the Tennessee Medicaid law. But how can a court determine what is *the* purpose of the Medicaid law, when the particular provisions and exclusions of that law must necessarily reflect a compromise that accommodates the different and potentially conflicting purposes of many legislators?

Justice Marshall's opinion for the Court attempts to avoid this problem by invoking an access/content distinction—the distinction that now, as a doctrinal matter, structures the reasonable accommodation inquiry in cases challenging government discrimination. Justice Marshall wrote that the Rehabilitation Act requires only "that an otherwise qualified handicapped individual must be provided with meaningful access to the benefit that the grantee offers." Although he recognized that "reasonable accommodations * * * may have to be made" in order "to assure meaningful access," he nonetheless emphasized that access is all that the statute requires. And he upheld the 14-day limitation because "[t]he reduction in inpatient coverage will leave both handicapped and nonhandicapped Medicaid users with identical and effective hospital services fully available for their use, with both classes of users subject to the same durational limitation."

But doesn't this conclusion turn entirely on the level of generality at which the benefit offered by the state is defined? Justice Marshall stated that "the benefit provided through Medicaid is a particular package of health care services, such as 14 days of inpatient coverage. That package of services has the general aim of assuring that individuals will receive necessary medical care, but the benefit provided remains the individual services offered—not 'adequate health care.' " Consider the following argument:

> Why must the opportunity provided by the Tennessee Medicaid program be described at that level of generality? The state does not provide the package of services that it does because there is anything magical in that particular bundle of services, but because the package meets some basic needs of members of the target population at an affordable cost. Viewed at that level of generality, people whose basic needs are more extensive because of disability (such as those who, because of their disability, need more hospital care than the average person) should have those basic needs satisfied to the same extent as the average person.

The Court appears to have rejected that higher level of generality out of a reluctance to second-guess the state's resource allocation decisions. But that same reluctance could in fact lead us to take the level of generality even lower. For example, why define the opportunity provided by the Tennessee Medicaid program as the opportunity to receive fourteen days of inpatient hospitalization? Why not define it as the opportunity to receive fourteen days of inpatient hospitalization as provided by the particular delivery system the state has set up? Medical care under the Tennessee Medicaid program may be provided in inaccessible buildings, and Medicaid recipients may be required to file forms that blind people cannot use. But making those aspects of the delivery system accessible may draw significant resources away from other state priorities.

Samuel R. Bagenstos, *The Future of Disability Law*, 114 Yale L.J. 1, 47–48 (2004). Is there a response to that critique? Consider whether the following case is consistent with *Choate*.

Olmstead v. L.C. ex rel. Zimring

Supreme Court of the United States, 1999.
527 U.S. 581.

■ JUSTICE GINSBURG announced the judgment of the Court and delivered the opinion of the Court with respect to Parts I, II, and III–A, and an opinion with respect to Part III–B, in which JUSTICE O'CONNOR, JUSTICE SOUTER, and JUSTICE BREYER join.

This case concerns the proper construction of the anti-discrimination provision contained in the public services portion (Title II) of the Americans with Disabilities Act of 1990 (ADA), 104 Stat. 337, 42 U.S.C. § 12132. Specifically, we confront the question whether the proscription of discrimination may require placement of persons with mental disabilities in community settings rather than in institutions. The answer, we hold, is a qualified yes. Such action is in order when the State's treatment professionals have determined that community placement is appropriate, the transfer from institutional care to a less restrictive setting is not opposed by the affected individual, and the placement can be reasonably accommodated, taking into account the resources available to the State and the needs of others with mental disabilities. In so ruling, we affirm the decision of the Eleventh Circuit in substantial part. We remand the case, however, for further consideration of the appropriate relief, given the range of facilities the State maintains for the care and treatment of persons with diverse mental disabilities, and its obligation to administer services with an even hand.

I

This case, as it comes to us, presents no constitutional question. The complaints filed by plaintiffs-respondents L.C. and E.W. did include such an issue; L.C. and E.W. alleged that defendants-petitioners, Georgia health care officials, failed to afford them minimally adequate care and freedom from undue restraint, in violation of their rights under the Due Process Clause of the Fourteenth

Amendment. But neither the District Court nor the Court of Appeals reached those Fourteenth Amendment claims. Instead, the courts below resolved the case solely on statutory grounds. Our review is similarly confined. Mindful that it is a statute we are construing, we set out first the legislative and regulatory prescriptions on which the case turns.

In the opening provisions of the ADA, Congress stated findings applicable to the statute in all its parts. Most relevant to this case, Congress determined that

> "(2) historically, society has tended to isolate and segregate individuals with disabilities, and, despite some improvements, such forms of discrimination against individuals with disabilities continue to be a serious and pervasive social problem;

> "(3) discrimination against individuals with disabilities persists in such critical areas as . . . institutionalization . . . ;

> . . .

> "(5) individuals with disabilities continually encounter various forms of discrimination, including outright intentional exclusion, . . . failure to make modifications to existing facilities and practices, . . . [and] segregation. . . . " 42 U.S.C. §§ 12101(a)(2), (3), (5).

Congress then set forth prohibitions against discrimination in employment (Title I, §§ 12111–12117), public services furnished by governmental entities (Title II, §§ 12131–12165), and public accommodations provided by private entities (Title III, §§ 12181–12189). The statute as a whole is intended "to provide a clear and comprehensive national mandate for the elimination of discrimination against individuals with disabilities." § 12101(b)(1).

There is no dispute that L.C. and E.W. are disabled within the meaning of the ADA.

This case concerns Title II, the public services portion of the ADA. The provision of Title II centrally at issue reads:

> "Subject to the provisions of this subchapter, no qualified individual with a disability shall, by reason of such disability, be excluded from participation in or be denied the benefits of the services, programs, or activities of a public entity, or be subjected to discrimination by any such entity." § 201, as set forth in 42 U.S.C. § 12132.

Title II's definition section states that "public entity" includes "any State or local government," and "any department, agency, [or] special purpose district." §§ 12131(1)(A), (B). The same section defines "qualified individual with a disability" as

> "an individual with a disability who, with or without reasonable modifications to rules, policies, or practices, the removal of architectural, communication, or transportation barriers, or the provision of auxiliary aids and services, meets the essential eligibility requirements for the receipt of services or the participation in programs or activities provided by a public entity." § 12131(2).

[C]ongress instructed the Attorney General to issue regulations implementing provisions of Title II, including § 12132's discrimination proscription. See § 204, as set forth in § 12134(a) ("[T]he Attorney General shall promulgate regulations in an accessible format that implement this part."). The Attorney General's regulations, Congress further directed, "shall be consistent with this chapter and with the coordination regulations . . . applicable to recipients of Federal financial assistance under [§ 504 of the Rehabilitation Act]." § 204, as set forth in 42 U.S.C. § 12134(b). One of the § 504 regulations requires recipients of federal funds to "administer programs and activities in the most integrated setting appropriate to the needs of qualified handicapped persons." 28 CFR § 41.51(d) (1998).

The ADA contains several other provisions allocating regulatory and enforcement responsibility. Congress instructed the Equal Employment Opportunity Commission (EEOC) to issue regulations implementing Title I, see 42 U.S.C. § 12116; the EEOC, the Attorney General, and persons alleging discrimination on the basis of disability in violation of Title I may enforce its provisions, see § 12117(a). Congress similarly instructed the Secretary of Transportation and the Attorney General to issue regulations implementing provisions of Title III, see §§ 12186(a)(1), (b); the Attorney General and persons alleging discrimination on the basis of disability in violation of Title III may enforce its provisions, see §§ 12188(a)(1), (b). Each federal agency responsible for ADA implementation may render technical assistance to affected individuals and institutions with respect to provisions of the ADA for which the agency has responsibility. See § 12206(c)(1).

As Congress instructed, the Attorney General issued Title II regulations, see 28 CFR pt. 35 (1998), including one modeled on the § 504 regulation just quoted; called the "integration regulation," it reads:

> "A public entity shall administer services, programs, and activities in the most integrated setting appropriate to the needs of qualified individuals with disabilities." 28 CFR § 35.130(d) (1998).

The preamble to the Attorney General's Title II regulations defines "the most integrated setting appropriate to the needs of qualified individuals with disabilities" to mean "a setting that enables individuals with disabilities to interact with non-disabled persons to the fullest extent possible." 28 CFR pt. 35, App.A, p. 450 (1998). Another regulation requires public entities to "make reasonable modifications" to avoid "discrimination on the basis of disability," unless those modifications would entail a "fundamenta[l] alter[ation]"; called here the "reasonable-modifications regulation," it provides:

> "A public entity shall make reasonable modifications in policies, practices, or procedures when the modifications are necessary to avoid discrimination on the basis of disability, unless the public entity can demonstrate that making the modifications would fundamentally alter the nature of the service, program, or activity." 28 CFR § 35.130(b)(7) (1998).

We recite these regulations with the caveat that we do not here determine their validity. While the parties differ on the proper construction and enforcement of the regulations, we do not understand petitioners to challenge the regulatory formulations themselves as outside the congressional authorization.

II

With the key legislative provisions in full view, we summarize the facts underlying this dispute. Respondents L.C. and E.W. are mentally retarded women; L.C. has also been diagnosed with schizophrenia, and E.W. with a personality disorder. Both women have a history of treatment in institutional settings. In May 1992, L.C. was voluntarily admitted to Georgia Regional Hospital at Atlanta (GRH), where she was confined for treatment in a psychiatric unit. By May 1993, her psychiatric condition had stabilized, and L.C.'s treatment team at GRH agreed that her needs could be met appropriately in one of the community-based programs the State supported. Despite this evaluation, L.C. remained institutionalized until February 1996, when the State placed her in a community-based treatment program.

E.W. was voluntarily admitted to GRH in February 1995; like L.C., E.W. was confined for treatment in a psychiatric unit. In March 1995, GRH sought to discharge E.W. to a homeless shelter, but abandoned that plan after her attorney filed an administrative complaint. By 1996, E.W.'s treating psychiatrist concluded that she could be treated appropriately in a community-based setting. She nonetheless remained institutionalized until a few months after the District Court issued its judgment in this case in 1997.

In May 1995, when she was still institutionalized at GRH, L.C. filed suit in the United States District Court for the Northern District of Georgia, challenging her continued confinement in a segregated environment. [L.C.] alleged that the State's failure to place her in a community-based program, once her treating professionals determined that such placement was appropriate, violated, inter alia, Title II of the ADA. L.C.'s pleading requested, among other things, that the State place her in a community care residential program, and that she receive treatment with the ultimate goal of integrating her into the mainstream of society. E.W. intervened in the action, stating an identical claim.

The District Court granted partial summary judgment in favor of L.C. and E.W. The court held that the State's failure to place L.C. and E.W. in an appropriate community-based treatment program violated Title II of the ADA. In so ruling, the court rejected the State's argument that inadequate funding, not discrimination against L.C. and E.W. "by reason of" their disabilities, accounted for their retention at GRH. Under Title II, the court concluded, "unnecessary institutional segregation of the disabled constitutes discrimination per se, which cannot be justified by a lack of funding."

In addition to contending that L.C. and E.W. had not shown discrimination "by reason of [their] disabilit[ies]," the State resisted court intervention on the ground that requiring immediate transfers in cases of this order would "fundamentally alter" the State's activity. The State reasserted that it was already using all available funds to provide services to other persons with disabilities. Rejecting the State's "fundamental alteration" defense, the court observed that existing state programs provided community-based treatment of the kind for which

L.C. and E.W. qualified, and that the State could "provide services to plaintiffs in the community at considerably less cost than is required to maintain them in an institution."

The Court of Appeals for the Eleventh Circuit affirmed the judgment of the District Court, but remanded for reassessment of the State's cost-based defense. As the appeals court read the statute and regulations: When "a disabled individual's treating professionals find that a community-based placement is appropriate for that individual, the ADA imposes a duty to provide treatment in a community setting— the most integrated setting appropriate to that patient's needs"; "[w]here there is no such finding [by the treating professionals], nothing in the ADA requires the deinstitutionalization of th[e] patient."

The Court of Appeals recognized that the State's duty to provide integrated services "is not absolute"; under the Attorney General's Title II regulation, "reasonable modifications" were required of the State, but fundamental alterations were not demanded. The appeals court thought it clear, however, that "Congress wanted to permit a cost defense only in the most limited of circumstances." In conclusion, the court stated that a cost justification would fail "[u]nless the State can prove that requiring it to [expend additional funds in order to provide L.C. and E.W. with integrated services] would be so unreasonable given the demands of the State's mental health budget that it would fundamentally alter the service [the State] provides." Because it appeared that the District Court had entirely ruled out a "lack of funding" justification, the appeals court remanded, repeating that the District Court should consider, among other things, "whether the additional expenditures necessary to treat L.C. and E.W. in community-based care would be unreasonable given the demands of the State's mental health budget."

We granted *certiorari* in view of the importance of the question presented to the States and affected individuals.[8]

III

Endeavoring to carry out Congress' instruction to issue regulations implementing Title II, the Attorney General, in the integration and reasonable-modifications regulations, made two key determinations. The first concerned the scope of the ADA's discrimination proscription, 42 U.S.C. § 12132; the second concerned the obligation of the States to counter discrimination. As to the first, the Attorney General concluded that unjustified placement or retention of persons in institutions, severely limiting their exposure to the outside community, constitutes a form of discrimination based on disability prohibited by Title II. See 28 CFR § 35.130(d) (1998) ("A public entity shall administer services . . . in the most integrated setting appropriate to the needs of qualified individuals with disabilities."); Brief for United States as *Amicus Curiae* in *Helen L. v. DiDario*, No. 94–1243 (C.A.3 1994), pp. 8, 15–16 (unnecessary segregation of persons with disabilities constitutes a form of discrimination prohibited by the ADA and the integration regulation). Regarding the States' obligation to avoid unjustified isolation of individuals with disabilities, the Attorney General provided

---

[8]   Twenty-two States and the Territory of Guam joined a brief urging that *certiorari* be granted. Ten of those States joined a brief in support of petitioners on the merits.

that States could resist modifications that "would fundamentally alter the nature of the service, program, or activity." 28 CFR § 35.130(b)(7) (1998).

The Court of Appeals essentially upheld the Attorney General's construction of the ADA. As just recounted, the appeals court ruled that the unjustified institutionalization of persons with mental disabilities violated Title II; the court then remanded with instructions to measure the cost of caring for L.C. and E.W. in a community-based facility against the State's mental health budget.

We affirm the Court of Appeals' decision in substantial part. Unjustified isolation, we hold, is properly regarded as discrimination based on disability. But we recognize, as well, the States' need to maintain a range of facilities for the care and treatment of persons with diverse mental disabilities, and the States' obligation to administer services with an even hand. Accordingly, we further hold that the Court of Appeals' remand instruction was unduly restrictive. In evaluating a State's fundamental-alteration defense, the District Court must consider, in view of the resources available to the State, not only the cost of providing community-based care to the litigants, but also the range of services the State provides others with mental disabilities, and the State's obligation to mete out those services equitably.

A

We examine first whether, as the Eleventh Circuit held, undue institutionalization qualifies as discrimination "by reason of . . . disability." The Department of Justice has consistently advocated that it does.[9] Because the Department is the agency directed by Congress to issue regulations implementing Title II, its views warrant respect. We need not inquire whether the degree of deference described in *Chevron U.S.A. Inc. v. Natural Resources Defense Council, Inc.*, 467 U.S. 837, 844 (1984), is in order; "[i]t is enough to observe that the well-reasoned views of the agencies implementing a statute 'constitute a body of experience and informed judgment to which courts and litigants may properly resort for guidance.' " *Bragdon v. Abbott*, 524 U.S. 624, 642 (1998) (quoting *Skidmore v. Swift & Co.*, 323 U.S. 134, 139–140 (1944)).

The State argues that L.C. and E.W. encountered no discrimination "by reason of" their disabilities because they were not denied community placement on account of those disabilities. See Brief for Petitioners 20. Nor were they subjected to "discrimination," the State contends, because " 'discrimination' necessarily requires uneven treatment of similarly situated individuals," and L.C. and E.W. had

---

[9] See Brief for United States in *Halderman v. Pennhurst State School and Hospital*, Nos. 78–1490, 78–1564, 78–1602 (CA3 1978), p. 45 ("[I]nstitutionalization result[ing] in separation of mentally retarded persons for no permissible reason . . . is 'discrimination,' and a violation of Section 504 [of the Rehabilitation Act] if it is supported by federal funds."); Brief for United States in *Halderman v. Pennhurst State School and Hospital*, Nos. 78–1490, 78–1564, 78–1602 (CA3 1981), p. 27 ("Pennsylvania violates Section 504 by indiscriminately subjecting handicapped persons to [an institution] without first making an individual reasoned professional judgment as to the appropriate placement for each such person among all available alternatives."); Brief for United States as *Amicus Curiae* in *Helen L. v. DiDario*, 46 F.3d 325, 335 (C.A.3 1994), ("Both the Section 504 coordination regulations and the rest of the ADA make clear that the unnecessary segregation of individuals with disabilities in the provision of public services is itself a form of discrimination within the meaning of those statutes."); *id.*, at 337–339.

identified no comparison class, i.e., no similarly situated individuals given preferential treatment. We are satisfied that Congress had a more comprehensive view of the concept of discrimination advanced in the ADA.[10]

The ADA stepped up earlier measures to secure opportunities for people with developmental disabilities to enjoy the benefits of community living. The Developmentally Disabled Assistance and Bill of Rights Act, a 1975 measure, stated in aspirational terms that "[t]he treatment, services, and habilitation for a person with developmental disabilities . . . should be provided in the setting that is least restrictive of the person's personal liberty." 89 Stat. 502, 42 U.S.C. § 6010(2) (1976 ed.) (emphasis added); see also *Pennhurst State School and Hospital v. Halderman*, 451 U.S. 1, 24 (1981) (concluding that the § 6010 provisions "were intended to be hortatory, not mandatory"). In a related legislative endeavor, the Rehabilitation Act of 1973, Congress used mandatory language to proscribe discrimination against persons with disabilities. See 87 Stat. 394, as amended, 29 U.S.C. § 794 (1976 ed.) ("No otherwise qualified individual with a disability in the United States . . . shall, solely by reason of her or his disability, be excluded from the participation in, be denied the benefits of, or be subjected to discrimination under any program or activity receiving Federal financial assistance.") Ultimately, in the ADA, enacted in 1990, Congress not only required all public entities to refrain from discrimination, see 42 U.S.C. § 12132; additionally, in findings applicable to the entire statute, Congress explicitly identified unjustified "segregation" of persons with disabilities as a "for[m] of discrimination." See § 12101(a)(2) ("historically, society has tended to isolate and segregate individuals with disabilities, and, despite some improvements, such forms of discrimination against individuals with disabilities continue to be a serious and pervasive social problem"); § 12101(a)(5) ("individuals with disabilities continually encounter various forms of discrimination, including . . . segregation").[11]

---

[10] The dissent is driven by the notion that "this Court has never endorsed an interpretation of the term 'discrimination' that encompassed disparate treatment among members of the same protected class," that "[o]ur decisions construing various statutory prohibitions against 'discrimination' have not wavered from this path," and that "a plaintiff cannot prove 'discrimination' by demonstrating that one member of a particular protected group has been favored over another member of that same group." The dissent is incorrect as a matter of precedent and logic. See *O'Connor v. Consolidated Coin Caterers Corp.*, 517 U.S. 308, 312 (1996) (The Age Discrimination in Employment Act of 1967 "does not ban discrimination against employees because they are aged 40 or older; it bans discrimination against employees because of their age, but limits the protected class to those who are 40 or older. The fact that one person in the protected class has lost out to another person in the protected class is thus irrelevant, so long as he has lost out because of his age."); cf. *Oncale v. Sundowner Offshore Services, Inc.*, 523 U.S. 75, 76 (1998) ("[W]orkplace harassment can violate Title VII's prohibition against 'discriminat[ion] . . . because of . . . sex,' 42 U.S.C. § 2000e–2(a)(1), when the harasser and the harassed employee are of the same sex."); *Jefferies v. Harris County Community Action Assn.*, 615 F.2d 1025, 1032 (C.A.5 1980) ("[D]iscrimination against black females can exist even in the absence of discrimination against black men or white women.").

[11] Unlike the ADA, § 504 of the Rehabilitation Act contains no express recognition that isolation or segregation of persons with disabilities is a form of discrimination. Section 504's discrimination proscription, a single sentence attached to vocational rehabilitation legislation, has yielded divergent court interpretations. See Brief for United States as *Amicus Curiae* 23–25.

Recognition that unjustified institutional isolation of persons with disabilities is a form of discrimination reflects two evident judgments. First, institutional placement of persons who can handle and benefit from community settings perpetuates unwarranted assumptions that persons so isolated are incapable or unworthy of participating in community life. Cf. *Allen v. Wright*, 468 U.S. 737, 755 (1984) ("There can be no doubt that [stigmatizing injury often caused by racial discrimination] is one of the most serious consequences of discriminatory government action."); *Los Angeles Dept. of Water and Power v. Manhart*, 435 U.S. 702, 707, n. 13 (1978) (" 'In forbidding employers to discriminate against individuals because of their sex, Congress intended to strike at the entire spectrum of disparate treatment of men and women resulting from sex stereotypes.' ") (quoting *Sprogis v. United Air Lines, Inc.*, 444 F.2d 1194, 1198 (C.A.7 1971)). Second, confinement in an institution severely diminishes the everyday life activities of individuals, including family relations, social contacts, work options, economic independence, educational advancement, and cultural enrichment. See Brief for American Psychiatric Association *et al.* as *Amici Curiae* 20–22. Dissimilar treatment correspondingly exists in this key respect: In order to receive needed medical services, persons with mental disabilities must, because of those disabilities, relinquish participation in community life they could enjoy given reasonable accommodations, while persons without mental disabilities can receive the medical services they need without similar sacrifice. See Brief for United States as *Amicus Curiae* 6–7, 17.

The State urges that, whatever Congress may have stated as its findings in the ADA, the Medicaid statute "reflected a congressional policy preference for treatment in the institution over treatment in the community." Brief for Petitioners 31. The State correctly used the past tense. Since 1981, Medicaid has provided funding for state-run home and community-based care through a waiver program. See 95 Stat. 812–813, as amended, 42 U.S.C. § 1396n(c); Brief for United States as *Amicus Curiae* 20–21. Indeed, the United States points out that the Department of Health and Human Services (HHS) "has a policy of encouraging States to take advantage of the waiver program, and often approves more waiver slots than a State ultimately uses." *Id.*, at 25–26 (further observing that, by 1996, "HHS approved up to 2109 waiver slots for Georgia, but Georgia used only 700").

We emphasize that nothing in the ADA or its implementing regulations condones termination of institutional settings for persons unable to handle or benefit from community settings. Title II provides only that "qualified individual[s] with a disability" may not "be subjected to discrimination." 42 U.S.C. § 12132. "Qualified individuals," the ADA further explains, are persons with disabilities who, "with or without reasonable modifications to rules, policies, or practices, . . . mee[t] the essential eligibility requirements for the receipt of services or the participation in programs or activities provided by a public entity." § 12131(2).

Consistent with these provisions, the State generally may rely on the reasonable assessments of its own professionals in determining whether an individual "meets the essential eligibility requirements" for habilitation in a community-based program. Absent such qualification, it would be inappropriate to remove a patient from the more restrictive setting. See 28 CFR § 35.130(d) (1998) (public entity shall administer services and programs in "the most integrated setting appropriate to the needs of qualified individuals with disabilities"); cf. *School Bd. of Nassau Cty. v. Arline*, 480 U.S. 273, 288 (1987) ("[C]ourts normally should defer to the reasonable medical judgments of public health officials."). Nor is there any federal requirement that community-based treatment be imposed on patients who do not desire it. See 28 CFR § 35.130(e)(1) (1998) ("Nothing in this part shall be construed to require an individual with a disability to accept an accommodation . . . which such individual chooses not to accept."); 28 CFR pt. 35, App. A, p. 450 (1998) ("[P]ersons with disabilities must be provided the option of declining to accept a particular accommodation."). In this case, however, there is no genuine dispute concerning the status of L.C. and E.W. as individuals "qualified" for noninstitutional care: The State's own professionals determined that community-based treatment would be appropriate for L.C. and E.W., and neither woman opposed such treatment.[14]

B

The State's responsibility, once it provides community-based treatment to qualified persons with disabilities, is not boundless. The reasonable-modifications regulation speaks of "reasonable modifications" to avoid discrimination, and allows States to resist modifications that entail a "fundamenta[l] alter[ation]" of the States' services and programs. 28 CFR § 35.130(b)(7) (1998). The Court of Appeals construed this regulation to permit a cost-based defense "only in the most limited of circumstances," and remanded to the District Court to consider, among other things, "whether the additional expenditures necessary to treat L.C. and E.W. in community-based care would be unreasonable given the demands of the State's mental health budget."

The Court of Appeals' construction of the reasonable-modifications regulation is unacceptable for it would leave the State virtually defenseless once it is shown that the plaintiff is qualified for the service or program she seeks. If the expense entailed in placing one or two people in a community-based treatment program is properly measured for reasonableness against the State's entire mental health budget, it is unlikely that a State, relying on the fundamental-alteration defense, could ever prevail. Sensibly construed, the fundamental-alteration component of the reasonable-modifications regulation would allow the State to show that, in the allocation of available resources, immediate relief for the plaintiffs would be inequitable, given the responsibility the State has undertaken for the care and treatment of a large and diverse population of persons with mental disabilities.

When it granted summary judgment for plaintiffs in this case, the District Court compared the cost of caring for the plaintiffs in a community-based setting with the cost of caring for them in an

---

[14] We do not in this opinion hold that the ADA imposes on the States a "standard of care" for whatever medical services they render, or that the ADA requires States to "provide a certain level of benefits to individuals with disabilities." Cf. *post* (THOMAS, J., dissenting). We do hold, however, that States must adhere to the ADA's nondiscrimination requirement with regard to the services they in fact provide.

institution. That simple comparison showed that community placements cost less than institutional confinements. As the United States recognizes, however, a comparison so simple overlooks costs the State cannot avoid; most notably, a "State . . . may experience increased overall expenses by funding community placements without being able to take advantage of the savings associated with the closure of institutions."

As already observed, the ADA is not reasonably read to impel States to phase out institutions, placing patients in need of close care at risk. Nor is it the ADA's mission to drive States to move institutionalized patients into an inappropriate setting, such as a homeless shelter, a placement the State proposed, then retracted, for E.W. Some individuals, like L.C. and E.W. in prior years, may need institutional care from time to time "to stabilize acute psychiatric symptoms." For other individuals, no placement outside the institution may ever be appropriate. See Brief for American Psychiatric Association *et al.* as *Amici Curiae* 22–23 ("Some individuals, whether mentally retarded or mentally ill, are not prepared at particular times—perhaps in the short run, perhaps in the long run—for the risks and exposure of the less protective environment of community settings"; for these persons, "institutional settings are needed and must remain available."); Brief for Voice of the Retarded *et al.* as *Amici Curiae* 11 ("Each disabled person is entitled to treatment in the most integrated setting possible for that person—recognizing that, on a case-by-case basis, that setting may be in an institution."); *Youngberg v. Romeo*, 457 U.S. 307, 327 (1982) (Blackmun, J., concurring) ("For many mentally retarded people, the difference between the capacity to do things for themselves within an institution and total dependence on the institution for all of their needs is as much liberty as they ever will know.").

To maintain a range of facilities and to administer services with an even hand, the State must have more leeway than the courts below understood the fundamental-alteration defense to allow. If, for example, the State were to demonstrate that it had a comprehensive, effectively working plan for placing qualified persons with mental disabilities in less restrictive settings, and a waiting list that moved at a reasonable pace not controlled by the State's endeavors to keep its institutions fully populated, the reasonable-modifications standard would be met. See Tr. of Oral Arg. 5 (State's attorney urges that, "by asking [a] person to wait a short time until a community bed is available, Georgia does not exclude [that] person by reason of disability, neither does Georgia discriminate against her by reason of disability"); see also *id.*, at 25 ("[I]t is reasonable for the State to ask someone to wait until a community placement is available."). In such circumstances, a court would have no warrant effectively to order displacement of persons at the top of the community-based treatment waiting list by individuals lower down who commenced civil actions.

For the reasons stated, we conclude that, under Title II of the ADA, States are required to provide community-based treatment for persons with mental disabilities when the State's treatment professionals determine that such placement is appropriate, the affected persons do not oppose such treatment, and the placement can be reasonably accommodated, taking into account the resources available to the State and the needs of others with mental disabilities. The judgment of the Eleventh Circuit is therefore affirmed in part and vacated in part, and the case is remanded for further proceedings.

It is so ordered.

■ JUSTICE STEVENS, concurring in part and concurring in the judgment.

[I]n my opinion, [w]e should simply affirm the judgment of the Court of Appeals. But because there are not five votes for that disposition, I join the Court's judgment and Parts I, II, and III–A of its opinion.

■ JUSTICE KENNEDY, with whom JUSTICE BREYER joins as to Part I, concurring in the judgment.

I

Despite remarkable advances and achievements by medical science, and agreement among many professionals that even severe mental illness is often treatable, the extent of public resources to devote to this cause remains controversial. Knowledgeable professionals tell us that our society, and the governments which reflect its attitudes and preferences, have yet to grasp the potential for treating mental disorders, especially severe mental illness. As a result, necessary resources for the endeavor often are not forthcoming. During the course of a year, about 5.6 million Americans will suffer from severe mental illness. E. Torrey, Out of the Shadows 4 (1997). Some 2.2 million of these persons receive no treatment. *Id.,* at 6. Millions of other Americans suffer from mental disabilities of less serious degree, such as mild depression. These facts are part of the background against which this case arises. In addition, of course, persons with mental disabilities have been subject to historic mistreatment, indifference, and hostility.

Despite these obstacles, the States have acknowledged that the care of the mentally disabled is their special obligation. They operate and support facilities and programs, sometimes elaborate ones, to provide care. It is a continuing challenge, though, to provide the care in an effective and humane way, particularly because societal attitudes and the responses of public authorities have changed from time to time.

Beginning in the 1950's, many victims of severe mental illness were moved out of state-run hospitals, often with benign objectives. According to one estimate, when adjusted for population growth, "the actual decrease in the numbers of people with severe mental illnesses in public psychiatric hospitals between 1955 and 1994 was 92 percent." Brief for American Psychiatric Association *et al.* as *Amici Curiae* 21, n. 5 (citing Torrey, *supra,* at 8–9). This was not without benefit or justification. The so-called "deinstitutionalization" has permitted a substantial number of mentally disabled persons to receive needed treatment with greater freedom and dignity. It may be, moreover, that those who remain institutionalized are indeed the most severe cases. With reference to this case, as the Court points out, it is undisputed that the State's own treating professionals determined that community-based care was medically appropriate for respondents. Nevertheless, the depopulation of state mental hospitals has its dark side. According to one expert:

"For a substantial minority . . . deinstitutionalization has been a psychiatric Titanic. Their lives are virtually devoid of 'dignity' or 'integrity of body, mind, and spirit.' 'Self-determination' often means merely that the person has a choice of soup kitchens. The 'least restrictive setting' frequently turns out to be a cardboard box, a jail cell, or a terror-filled existence plagued by both real and imaginary enemies." Torrey, *supra*, at 11.

It must be remembered that for the person with severe mental illness who has no treatment the most dreaded of confinements can be the imprisonment inflicted by his own mind, which shuts reality out and subjects him to the torment of voices and images beyond our own powers to describe.

It would be unreasonable, it would be a tragic event, then, were the Americans with Disabilities Act of 1990 (ADA) to be interpreted so that States had some incentive, for fear of litigation, to drive those in need of medical care and treatment out of appropriate care and into settings with too little assistance and supervision. The opinion of a responsible treating physician in determining the appropriate conditions for treatment ought to be given the greatest of deference. It is a common phenomenon that a patient functions well with medication, yet, because of the mental illness itself, lacks the discipline or capacity to follow the regime the medication requires. This is illustrative of the factors a responsible physician will consider in recommending the appropriate setting or facility for treatment. JUSTICE GINSBURG's opinion takes account of this background. It is careful, and quite correct, to say that it is not "the ADA's mission to drive States to move institutionalized patients into an inappropriate setting, such as a homeless shelter. . . . "

In light of these concerns, if the principle of liability announced by the Court is not applied with caution and circumspection, States may be pressured into attempting compliance on the cheap, placing marginal patients into integrated settings devoid of the services and attention necessary for their condition. This danger is in addition to the federalism costs inherent in referring state decisions regarding the administration of treatment programs and the allocation of resources to the reviewing authority of the federal courts. It is of central importance, then, that courts apply today's decision with great deference to the medical decisions of the responsible, treating physicians and, as the Court makes clear, with appropriate deference to the program funding decisions of state policymakers.

II

With these reservations made explicit, in my view we must remand the case for a determination of the questions the Court poses and for a determination whether respondents can show a violation of 42 U.S.C. § 12132's ban on discrimination based on the summary judgment materials on file or any further pleadings and materials properly allowed.

At the outset it should be noted there is no allegation that Georgia officials acted on the basis of animus or unfair stereotypes regarding the disabled. Underlying much discrimination law is the notion that animus can lead to false and unjustified stereotypes, and vice versa. Of course, the line between animus and stereotype is often indistinct, and it is not always necessary to distinguish between them. Section 12132 can be understood to deem as irrational, and so to prohibit, distinctions by which a class of disabled persons, or some within that class, are, by reason of their disability and without adequate justification, exposed by a state entity to more onerous treatment than a comparison group in the provision of services or the administration of existing programs, or indeed entirely excluded from state programs or facilities. Discrimination under this statute might in principle be shown in the case before us, though further proceedings should be required.

Putting aside issues of animus or unfair stereotype, I agree with JUSTICE THOMAS that on the ordinary interpretation and meaning of the term, one who alleges discrimination must show that she "received differential treatment vis-à-vis members of a different group on the basis of a statutorily described characteristic." In my view, however, discrimination so defined might be shown here. Although the Court seems to reject JUSTICE THOMAS' definition of discrimination, it asserts that unnecessary institutional care does lead to "[d]issimilar treatment." According to the Court, "[i]n order to receive needed medical services, persons with mental disabilities must, because of those disabilities, relinquish participation in community life they could enjoy given reasonable accommodations, while persons without mental disabilities can receive the medical services they need without similar sacrifice."

Although this point is not discussed at length by the Court, it does serve to suggest the theory under which respondents might be subject to discrimination in violation of § 12132. If they could show that persons needing psychiatric or other medical services to treat a mental disability are subject to a more onerous condition than are persons eligible for other existing state medical services, and if removal of the condition would not be a fundamental alteration of a program or require the creation of a new one, then the beginnings of a discrimination case would be established. In terms more specific to this case, if respondents could show that Georgia (i) provides treatment to individuals suffering from medical problems of comparable seriousness, (ii) as a general matter, does so in the most integrated setting appropriate for the treatment of those problems (taking medical and other practical considerations into account), but (iii) without adequate justification, fails to do so for a group of mentally disabled persons (treating them instead in separate, locked institutional facilities), I believe it would demonstrate discrimination on the basis of mental disability.

Of course, it is a quite different matter to say that a State without a program in place is required to create one. No State has unlimited resources, and each must make hard decisions on how much to allocate to treatment of diseases and disabilities. If, for example, funds for care and treatment of the mentally ill, including the severely mentally ill, are reduced in order to support programs directed to the treatment and care of other disabilities, the decision may be unfortunate. The judgment, however, is a political one and not within the reach of the statute. Grave constitutional concerns are raised when a federal court is given the authority to review the State's choices in basic matters such as establishing or declining to establish new programs. It is not reasonable to read the ADA to permit court intervention in these decisions. In addition, as the Court notes, by regulation a public entity is required only to make "reasonable modifications in policies, practices, or procedures" when necessary to avoid discrimination and is not even required to make those if "the modifications would fundamentally alter the nature of the service, program, or activity." 28 CFR § 35.130(b)(7) (1998). It follows that a State may not be forced to create a community-treatment program where none exists. Whether a different statutory scheme would exceed constitutional limits need not be addressed.

Discrimination, of course, tends to be an expansive concept and, as legal category, it must be applied with care and prudence. On any reasonable reading of the statute, § 12132 cannot cover all types of differential treatment of disabled and nondisabled persons, no matter how minimal or innocuous. To establish discrimination in the context of this case, and absent a showing of policies motivated by improper animus or stereotypes, it would be necessary to show that a comparable or similarly situated group received differential treatment. Regulations are an important tool in identifying the kinds of contexts, policies, and practices that raise concerns under the ADA. The congressional findings in 42 U.S.C. § 12101 also serve as a useful aid for courts to discern the sorts of discrimination with which Congress was concerned. Indeed, those findings have clear bearing on the issues raised in this case, and support the conclusion that unnecessary institutionalization may be the evidence or the result of the discrimination the ADA prohibits.

Unlike JUSTICE THOMAS, I deem it relevant and instructive that Congress in express terms identified the "isolat[ion] and segregat[ion]" of disabled persons by society as a "for[m] of discrimination," §§ 12101(a)(2), (5), and noted that discrimination against the disabled "persists in such critical areas as . . . institutionalization," § 12101(a)(3). These findings do not show that segregation and institutionalization are always discriminatory or that segregation or institutionalization are, by their nature, forms of prohibited discrimination. Nor do they necessitate a regime in which individual treatment plans are required, as distinguished from broad and reasonable classifications for the provision of health care services. Instead, they underscore Congress' concern that discrimination has been a frequent and pervasive problem in institutional settings and policies and its concern that segregating disabled persons from others can be discriminatory. Both of those concerns are consistent with the normal definition of discrimination-differential treatment of similarly situated groups. The findings inform application of that definition in specific cases, but absent guidance to the contrary, there is no reason to think they displace it. The issue whether respondents have been discriminated against under § 12132 by institutionalized treatment cannot be decided in the abstract, divorced from the facts surrounding treatment programs in their State.

The possibility therefore remains that, on the facts of this case, respondents would be able to support a claim under § 12132 by showing that they have been subject to discrimination by Georgia officials on the basis of their disability. This inquiry would not be simple. Comparisons of different medical conditions and the corresponding treatment regimens might be difficult, as would be assessments of the degree of integration of various settings in which medical treatment is offered. For example, the evidence might show that, apart from services for the mentally disabled, medical treatment is rarely offered in a community setting but also is rarely offered in facilities comparable to state mental hospitals. Determining the relevance of that type of evidence would require considerable judgment and analysis. However, as petitioners observe, "[i]n this case, no class of similarly situated individuals was even identified, let alone shown to be given preferential treatment." Without additional information regarding the details of state-provided medical services in Georgia, we cannot address the issue in the way the statute demands. As a consequence, the judgment of the courts below, granting partial summary judgment to respondents, ought not to be sustained. In addition, as JUSTICE GINSBURG's opinion is careful to note, it was error in the earlier proceedings to restrict the relevance and force of the State's evidence regarding the comparative costs of treatment. The State is entitled to wide discretion in adopting its own systems of cost analysis, and, if it chooses, to allocate health care resources based on fixed and overhead costs for whole institutions and programs. We must be cautious when we seek to infer specific rules limiting States' choices when Congress has used only general language in the controlling statute.

I would remand the case to the Court of Appeals or the District Court for it to determine in the first instance whether a statutory violation is sufficiently alleged and supported in respondents' summary judgment materials and, if not, whether they should be given leave to replead and to introduce evidence and argument along the lines suggested above.

For these reasons, I concur in the judgment of the Court.

■ JUSTICE THOMAS, with whom THE CHIEF JUSTICE and JUSTICE SCALIA join, dissenting.

[T]he majority concludes that petitioners "discriminated" against respondents—as a matter of law—by continuing to treat them in an institutional setting after they became eligible for community placement. I disagree. Temporary exclusion from community placement does not amount to "discrimination" in the traditional sense of the word, nor have respondents shown that petitioners "discriminated" against them "by reason of" their disabilities.

Until today, this Court has never endorsed an interpretation of the term "discrimination" that encompassed disparate treatment among members of the same protected class. Discrimination, as typically understood, requires a showing that a claimant received differential treatment vis-à-vis members of a different group on the basis of a statutorily described characteristic. This interpretation comports with dictionary definitions of the term discrimination, which means to "distinguish," to "differentiate," or to make a "distinction in favor of or against, a person or thing based on the group, class, or category to which that person or thing belongs rather than on individual merit." Random House Dictionary 564 (2d ed.1987); see also Webster's Third New International Dictionary 648 (1981) (defining "discrimination" as "the making or perceiving of a distinction or difference" or as "the act, practice, or an instance of discriminating categorically rather than individually").

Our decisions construing various statutory prohibitions against "discrimination" have not wavered from this path. [U]nder Title VII, a finding of discrimination requires a comparison of otherwise similarly situated persons who are in different groups by reason of certain characteristics provided by statute. See, *e.g.*, *Newport News Shipbuilding & Dry Dock Co. v. EEOC*, 462 U.S. 669, 683 (1983) (explaining that Title VII discrimination occurs when an employee is treated " 'in a manner which but for that person's sex would be different' ") (quoting *Los Angeles Dept. of Water and Power v. Manhart*, 435 U.S. 702, 711 (1978)). [C]ourts interpreting Title VII have held that a plaintiff cannot prove "discrimination" by demonstrating that one member of a particular protected group has been favored over another member of that same group. See, *e.g.*, *Bush v. Commonwealth Edison Co.*, 990 F.2d 928, 931 (C.A.7 1993), cert. denied, 511 U.S. 1071 (1994) (explaining that under Title VII, a fired black employee "had to show that although he was not a good employee, equally bad employees were treated more leniently by [his employer] if they happened not to be black").

Our cases interpreting § 504 of the Rehabilitation Act of 1973, 87 Stat. 394, as amended, which prohibits "discrimination" against certain individuals with disabilities, have applied this commonly understood meaning of discrimination. [I]n keeping with the traditional paradigm, we have always limited the application of the term "discrimination" in the Rehabilitation Act to a person who is a member of a protected group and faces discrimination "by reason of his handicap." Indeed, we previously rejected the argument that § 504 requires the type of "affirmative efforts to overcome the disabilities caused by handicaps," *Southeastern Community College v. Davis*, 442 U.S. 397, 410 (1979), that the majority appears to endorse today. Instead, we found that § 504 required merely "the evenhanded treatment of handicapped persons" relative to those persons who do not have disabilities. [S]imilarly, in *Alexander v. Choate*, 469 U.S. 287, 302 (1985), we found no discrimination under § 504 with respect to a limit on inpatient hospital care that was "neutral on its face" and did not "distinguish between those whose coverage will be reduced and those whose coverage will not on the basis of any test, judgment, or trait that the handicapped as a class are less capable of meeting or less likely of having." We said that § 504 does "not . . . guarantee the handicapped equal results from the provision of state Medicaid, even assuming some measure of equality of health could be constructed."

Likewise, in *Traynor v. Turnage*, 485 U.S. 535, 548 (1988), we reiterated that the purpose of § 504 is to guarantee that individuals with disabilities receive "evenhanded treatment" relative to those persons without disabilities. In *Traynor*, the Court upheld a Veterans' Administration regulation that excluded "primary alcoholics" from a benefit that was extended to persons disabled by alcoholism related to a mental disorder. In so doing, the Court noted that "[t]his litigation does not involve a program or activity that is alleged to treat handicapped persons less favorably than nonhandicapped persons." Given the theory of the case, the Court explicitly held: "There is nothing in the

Rehabilitation Act that requires that any benefit extended to one category of handicapped persons also be extended to all other categories of handicapped persons."

This same understanding of discrimination also informs this Court's constitutional interpretation of the term. [D]espite this traditional understanding, the majority derives a more "comprehensive" definition of "discrimination," as that term is used in Title II of the ADA, one that includes "institutional isolation of persons with disabilities." It chiefly relies on certain congressional findings contained within the ADA. To be sure, those findings appear to equate institutional isolation with segregation, and thereby discrimination. The congressional findings, however, are written in general, hortatory terms and provide little guidance to the interpretation of the specific language of § 12132. In my view, the vague congressional findings upon which the majority relies simply do not suffice to show that Congress sought to overturn a well-established understanding of a statutory term (here, "discrimination"). Moreover, the majority fails to explain why terms in the findings should be given a medical content, pertaining to the place where a mentally retarded person is treated. When read in context, the findings instead suggest that terms such as "segregation" were used in a more general sense, pertaining to matters such as access to employment, facilities, and transportation. Absent a clear directive to the contrary, we must read "discrimination" in light of the common understanding of the term. We cannot expand the meaning of the term "discrimination" in order to invalidate policies we may find unfortunate.

Elsewhere in the ADA, Congress chose to alter the traditional definition of discrimination. Title I of the ADA, § 12112(b)(1), defines discrimination to include "limiting, segregating, or classifying a job applicant or employee in a way that adversely affects the opportunities or status of such applicant or employee." Notably, however, Congress did not provide that this definition of discrimination, unlike other aspects of the ADA, applies to Title II. Ordinary canons of construction require that we respect the limited applicability of this definition of "discrimination" and not import it into other parts of the law where Congress did not see fit. The majority's definition of discrimination— although not specifically delineated—substantially imports the definition of Title I into Title II by necessarily assuming that it is sufficient to focus exclusively on members of one particular group. Under this view, discrimination occurs when some members of a protected group are treated differently from other members of that same group. As the preceding discussion emphasizes, absent a special definition supplied by Congress, this conclusion is a remarkable and novel proposition that finds no support in our decisions in analogous areas.

[A]t bottom, the type of claim approved of by the majority does not concern a prohibition against certain conduct (the traditional understanding of discrimination), but rather concerns imposition of a standard of care. As such, the majority can offer no principle limiting this new species of "discrimination" claim apart from an affirmative defense because it looks merely to an individual in isolation, without comparing him to otherwise similarly situated persons, and determines that discrimination occurs merely because that individual does not receive the treatment he wishes to receive. By adopting such a broad view of discrimination, the majority drains the term of any meaning other than as a proxy for decisions disapproved of by this Court.

Further, I fear that the majority's approach imposes significant federalism costs, directing States how to make decisions about their delivery of public services. [T]he majority's affirmative defense will likely come as cold comfort to the States that will now be forced to defend themselves in federal court every time resources prevent the immediate placement of a qualified individual. In keeping with our traditional deference in this area, see *Alexander*, the appropriate course would be to respect the States' historical role as the dominant authority responsible for providing services to individuals with disabilities.

The majority may remark that it actually does properly compare members of different groups. Indeed, the majority mentions in passing the "[d]issimilar treatment" of persons with and without disabilities. [But] the majority neither specifies what services persons with disabilities might need nor contends that persons without disabilities need the same services as those with disabilities, leading to the inference that the dissimilar treatment the majority observes results merely from the fact that different classes of persons receive different services—not from "discrimination" as traditionally defined.

Finally, it is also clear petitioners did not "discriminate" against respondents "by reason of [their] disabili[ties]," as § 12132 requires. Respondents do not contend that their disabilities constituted the proximate cause for their exclusion. Nor could they—community placement simply is not available to those without disabilities. Continued institutional treatment of persons who, though now deemed treatable in a community placement, must wait their turn for placement does not establish that the denial of community placement occurred "by reason of" their disability. Rather, it establishes no more than the fact that petitioners have limited resources.

For the foregoing reasons, I respectfully dissent.

NOTES ON OLMSTEAD V. L.C.

1.   The Access/Content Distinction. Is *Olmstead* consistent with *Choate*? The state argued that requiring it to move people with disabilities into community placements that did not yet exist did more than provide *access* to the "particular package of health care services" the state provided—a package that included mental health treatment in an available bed in a state hospital or an existing community placement. Rather, the state argued, such a requirement forced it to change the *content* of the package of services it provided. Justice Thomas essentially adopts that argument in his dissent. Justice Ginsburg offers the following reply:

> We do not in this opinion hold that the ADA imposes on the States a "standard of care" for whatever medical services they render, or that the ADA requires States to "provide a certain level of benefits to individuals with disabilities." We do hold, however, that States must adhere to the ADA's nondiscrimination requirement with regard to the services they in fact provide.

Is that a sufficient answer? As its program existed at the time of the lawsuit, Georgia did not "in fact provide" community mental health services to *all* individuals with disabilities for whom those services would be appropriate. Justice Ginsburg must be defining the relevant services at a higher level of generality: If the state provides mental health services in an institution, it must provide those services in a community setting as well for those individuals who have been institutionalized but for whom "the State's treatment professionals have determined that community placement is appropriate, the transfer from institutional care to a less restrictive setting is not opposed by the affected individual, and the placement can be reasonably accommodated, taking into account the resources available to the State and the needs of others with mental disabilities." Is that understanding of the relevant services an appropriate one? For an argument that *Olmstead*, despite Justice Ginsburg's protestations, *does* grant "positive rights" to people with disabilities at risk of institutionalization, see Mark C. Weber, *Home and Community-Based Services, Olmstead, and Positive Rights: A Preliminary Discussion*, 39 Wake Forest L. Rev. 269 (2004).

2. Theories of Discrimination. Much of the discussion in the various opinions addresses the basic question of what constitutes "discrimination." Justice Thomas argues, in his dissent, that Georgia clearly did not discriminate against the plaintiffs because of their disabilities by denying them community placements; to the contrary, "community placement simply is not available to those without disabilities." Justice Kennedy, in his concurrence in the judgment, seems to embrace the same understanding of discrimination as does Justice Thomas—different treatment of similarly situated persons—but, unlike Justice Thomas, he concludes that the plaintiffs *might* have been able to establish discrimination *if* they could show "that Georgia (i) provides treatment to individuals suffering from medical problems of comparable seriousness, (ii) as a general matter, does so in the most integrated setting appropriate for the treatment of those problems (taking medical and other practical considerations into account), but (iii) without adequate justification, fails to do so for a group of mentally disabled persons (treating them instead in separate, locked institutional facilities)."

In her opinion for the Court, Justice Ginsburg concludes "that Congress had a more comprehensive view of the concept of discrimination advanced in the ADA." In particular, she offers two reasons for concluding "that unjustified institutional isolation of persons with disabilities is a form of discrimination." First, she says, "institutional placement of persons who can handle and benefit from community settings perpetuates unwarranted assumptions that persons so isolated are incapable or unworthy of participating in community life." And second, "confinement in an institution severely diminishes the everyday life activities of individuals, including family relations, social contacts, work options, economic independence, educational advancement, and cultural enrichment." Moreover, she points out that "[d]issimilar treatment correspondingly exists in this key respect: In order to receive needed medical services, persons with mental disabilities must, because of those disabilities, relinquish participation in community life they could enjoy given reasonable accommodations, while persons without mental disabilities can receive the medical services they need without similar sacrifice."

Is Justice Ginsburg's response to Justices Kennedy and Thomas persuasive? How can Justice Kennedy's and Justice Thomas's position be reconciled with *Choate*'s recognition that disability discrimination laws treat the failure to provide reasonable accommodation as a form of discrimination? As Carlos Ball explains, the debate between Justice Ginsburg and Justices Kennedy and Thomas reflects a "fundamental disagreement . . . as to what equality means and what it requires": The dissent, like the State, "relied on a rather formalistic approach to equality, asking whether there were parties who were similarly situated to the plaintiffs but who were nonetheless treated differently by the State." Carlos A. Ball, *Looking for Theory in All the Right Places: Feminist and Communitarian Elements of Disability Discrimination Law*, 66 Ohio St. L.J. 105, 155 (2005). But the Court, Professor Ball argues, "explicitly incorporate[d] communitarian principles" and "reasoned that if the ADA was about nothing more than making sure that the State provides disabled individuals with the same services and benefits that it makes available to the nondisabled, the statute would fail to address the significant harms associated with the isolation and segregation of individuals with mental disabilities." *Id.*

3.   **Fundamental Alteration.** The Court remands for the lower courts to reconsider whether Georgia can establish that deinstitutionalizing the plaintiffs would effect a "fundamental alteration" of the state's program. Speaking only for a plurality in this part of her opinion, Justice Ginsburg explains that the state can establish a fundamental alteration if it can "show that, in the allocation of available resources, immediate relief for the plaintiffs would be inequitable, given the responsibility the State has undertaken for the care and treatment of a large and diverse population of persons with mental disabilities." For example, a state might "demonstrate that it had a comprehensive, effectively working plan for placing qualified persons with mental disabilities in less restrictive settings, and a waiting list that moved at a reasonable pace not controlled by the State's endeavors to keep its institutions fully populated."

Olmstead has been called the "*Brown v. Board of Education* of the disability rights movement." *E.g.*, Samuel R. Bagenstos, *Justice Ginsburg and the Judicial Role in Expanding "We the People": The Disability Rights Cases*, 104 Colum. L. Rev. 49, 49 (2004); see also Nestor M. Davidson, *Rights as a Functional Guide for Service Provision in Homeless Advocacy*, 26 St. Louis U. Pub. L. Rev. 45, 60–61 (2007) ("*Olmstead*, with its sweeping language about the harms that segregation causes for individuals with disabilities, has become one of those decisions that transcends the context in which it arises to become a cultural symbol. The decision has had significant practical implications as well, as advocates have rallied around *Olmstead*'s endorsement of integration as a practical tool for galvanizing providers of services for those with mental illness, for those experiencing or at risk of homelessness, and for individuals facing institutionalization more generally."). Continuing the analogy, is Justice Ginsburg's formulation of the fundamental alteration defense the disability rights movement's "all deliberate speed"? See, *e.g.*, Susan Stefan, *The Americans with Disabilities*

Act and Mental Health Law: Issues for the Twenty-First Century, 10 J. Contemp. Legal Issues 131 (1999) (characterizing Justice Ginsburg's formulation of the fundamental alteration defense as "clearly not what Congress intended" and observing that "[d]epending on how the lower courts interpret the requirement of a 'comprehensive, effectively working plan' and a 'reasonable pace' of placements, this requirement could be either sensible or fatal to any kind of progress in placement of inappropriately institutionalized people into the community"); Ruth Colker, *Anti-Subordination Above All: A Disability Perspective*, 82 Notre Dame L. Rev. 1415, 1448 (2007) (criticizing post-*Olmstead* law as "muddled": States have been given the opportunity to move through their waiting lists at a "reasonable pace," sacrificing the liberty interests of those who are mildly disabled and could live in the community so that the state can afford to maintain its disability-only institutions for those with more severe disabilities. Further, success is measured by the rate of deinstitutionalization rather than by the quality of life for those who are deinstitutionalized.).

One might offer several possible defenses of Justice Ginsburg's formulation. Carlos Ball suggests that Justice Ginsburg's analysis is admirably communitarian, because "the rights of the plaintiffs in *Olmstead* were determined, at least in part, by the needs of other disabled individuals who were not parties to the case. * * * In this way, the plurality linked together the interests of those who are best treated outside of institutions with those who are best treated inside of them." Ball, *supra*, at 163. For a critique of Professor Ball's argument, see Colker, *supra*, at 1447 ("Ball's justification, however, is problematic because it does not explain why individuals with mild disabilities should have to bear the burden of finding financial resources to assist those with severe disabilities who need to live in residential institutions. Why is their liberty less valuable than the liberty of any other individuals in society?").

Both Professor Ball and Professor Colker seem to take it as a given that some people with "severe" disabilities "need to live in residential institutions" (as opposed to community settings like small group homes). Is that assumption justified?

> Consider Nicholas Romeo, the plaintiff in *Youngberg v. Romeo*, 457 U.S. 307 (1982) [a principal case later in this chapter]. Romeo had what the Court characterized as "profound[ ]" mental retardation, "with an I.Q. between 8 and 10." *Id.* at 309. His own counsel had conceded, "in light of the severe character of his retardation," that Romeo could never live outside of an institution. *Id.* at 317–18. Yet "ten months after the Court's decision, Nicholas Romeo moved to a community residence in Philadelphia." Timothy M. Cook, *The Americans with Disabilities Act: The Move to Integration*, 64 Temp. L. Rev. 393, 443 (1991). Eight years later, Cook observed that "[s]ince April 1983, Romeo has been living, receiving services, and working part-time in his neighborhood." *Id.* Nicholas Romeo's experience was typical of those released from Pennhurst, the institution where he had been confined. See James W. Conroy & Valerie J. Bradley, The Pennhurst Longitudinal Study: Combined Report of Five Years of Research and Analysis 84, 118, 142 (1985) (discussing three separate

case studies of Pennhurst residents and their improvements in quality of life and ability after moving into community living arrangements after Pennhurst's closing).

Samuel R. Bagenstos & Margo Schlanger, *Hedonic Damages, Hedonic Adaptation, and Disability*, 60 Vand. L. Rev. 745, 782 n.177 (2007). For a different defense of Justice Ginsburg's formulation, one that does not assume that any people with disabilities must necessarily be institutionalized, consider the following argument:

> Where efforts at swift, judicially imposed deinstitutionalization in the 1970s created a political, professional, and ultimately judicial backlash, Justice Ginsburg's measured approach offers two reasons for hope that such a negative reaction can be avoided. First, by crediting the decisions of states' treating professionals, the Justice's opinion enlisted a group of people who, by disciplinary training and inclination, are often supportive of less institutionalized settings but who would object to having courts dictate professional decisions to them. Second, by emphasizing the liability-avoiding power of "a comprehensive, effectively working plan" for deinstitutionalization, Justice Ginsburg—just like the Court in the gender discrimination cases—urged state legislatures to "rethink ancient positions on these questions" without removing the ball from their court.

Bagenstos, *Justice Ginsburg*, *supra*, at 58.

C. APPLICATION TO SPECIFIC AREAS OF STATE GOVERNMENT

1. DISABILITY-SERVICES SYSTEMS AND UNNECESSARY INSTITUTIONALIZATION

Fisher v. Oklahoma Health Care Authority

United States Court of Appeals for the Tenth Circuit, 2003.
335 F.3d 1175.

■ LUCERO, CIRCUIT JUDGE.

Plaintiffs, three disabled individuals receiving state-funded medical care as part of Oklahoma's Home and Community-Based Services ("HCBS") Waiver Program, the "Advantage Program," ask us to decide whether the defendants, the Oklahoma Health Care Authority ("OHCA")—the state agency that administers the Medicaid program for Oklahoma—and Mike Fogarty, in his official capacity as CEO of the OHCA, are violating federal law by the manner in which they operate their HCBS program. Specifically, plaintiffs object to the defendants' recent decision to limit prescription medications for participants in the waiver program to five per month, irrespective of medical necessity, and seek declaratory and injunctive relief against the imposition of the five-prescription cap. Plaintiffs assert that due to their precarious medical and financial circumstances, imposition of the five-prescription cap will force them out of their communities and into nursing homes in order to obtain the care that is medically necessary. The district court granted summary judgment to the defendants, holding that the plaintiffs could not maintain a claim under the Americans with Disabilities Act ("ADA"), 42 U.S.C. § 12101 *et seq.,* because they are not presently institutionalized and face no risk of institutionalization. Because we conclude that the plaintiffs may have a meritorious ADA claim, we exercise jurisdiction under 28 U.S.C. § 1291, and reverse and remand for further consideration.

I

Medicaid is a joint federal-state program designed to provide medical assistance to low-income families and individuals "to help such families and individuals attain or retain capability for independence or self-care." 42 U.S.C. § 1396. Once a state enters into a partnership with the federal government, Congress requires the state to provide a minimum level of benefits known as the mandatory program. § 1396a(10)(A)(i); 42 C.F.R. §§ 440.210, .220. Mandatory services include nursing home care. 42 U.S.C. § 1396a(10)(A) (incorporating § 1396d(a)(4)(A)). Pharmacy benefits, the focus of the instant case, are not part of the mandatory program, and are considered an optional program under Title XIX. §§ 1396a(a)(10), 1396d(a)(12). Along with every other state, Oklahoma has elected to provide prescription drugs as part of its Medicaid program. Persons institutionalized in nursing homes receive all the prescriptions that are medically necessary. Okla. Admin. Code. § 317:35–3–2(15)(B).

As an alternative to institutionalization, Congress provides for home and community-based services as part of an optional waiver program.[1] 42 U.S.C. § 1396n(c)(1). Once a state obtains a waiver, this program allows individuals who meet the level of care required for institutionalization in a nursing facility to live at home and receive state-funded medical care. *Id.* "[T]he department of Heath and Human Services (HHS) has a policy of encouraging States to take advantage of the waiver program, and often approves more waiver slots than a State ultimately uses." *Olmstead v. Zimring,* 527 U.S. 581, 601 (1999) (quotation omitted). To obtain a waiver, a state must certify that placement of an individual in a waiver program will be cost-neutral, meaning that costs for persons in the waiver program will be less than if those persons were in an institution.[2] § 1396n(c)(2)(D). Oklahoma obtained such a waiver from the federal government for its Advantage Program. Okla. Admin. Code. § 317:30–5–760.

Oklahoma has elected to provide prescription benefits to Advantage participants as well as residents in nursing homes. Until recently, Advantage participants were entitled to an unlimited number of medically necessary prescriptions paid for by the state. However, in September 2002, the state notified participants that it would impose a cap of five prescriptions per month on Advantage participants, effective October 1, 2002, while continuing to provide unlimited prescriptions to patients in nursing facilities. This decision was based on a budgetary

---

[1] The program is referred to as a "waiver" because, with express authorization by a federal agency, the state is exempted from certain Title XIX statutory requirements.

[2] In Oklahoma, it costs approximately $28,000 per year to provide care to a disabled individual in a nursing home, and $14,000 to provide care through the Home and Community Based Waiver program.

shortfall; defendants anticipated that capping the number of prescriptions available would save the state $3.2 million.

On the same day that the five-prescription cap came into effect, plaintiffs Katherine Fisher, Earlee Heath, and Karol Loy, participants in Oklahoma's Advantage program, filed suit in federal court against the OHCA and its CEO, Mike Fogarty. In their complaint, plaintiffs allege that defendants' five-prescription cap violates the integration requirements of the ADA, 42 U.S.C. § 12101 *et seq.,* and section 504 of the Rehabilitation Act ("RA"), 29 U.S.C. § 794, because it will force them out of their communities and into nursing homes in order to obtain the care that is medically necessary. Plaintiffs further assert that the cap violates Title XIX of the Social Security Act, 42 U.S.C. § 1396 *et seq.* All three plaintiffs meet the medical and financial requirements for nursing facility care and would be eligible for admission to a nursing home.

Earlee Heath is 73 years old, uses a wheelchair, and suffers from insulin-dependant diabetes, hypertension, asthma, congestive heart failure, residual bilateral paresis and deep-vein thrombosis. She uses a portable oxygen machine to assist her in breathing. She takes approximately sixteen prescription medications that cost a total of $839 per month, all of which are prescribed by her doctors, who monthly review and monitor them. Assuming that defendants pay for the five most expensive medications, plaintiffs contend that Heath will have to pay $256 per month for the remainder out of her monthly income of $313.

Katherine Fisher is 48 years old, uses a wheelchair, has suffered from cerebral palsy since birth, and has had two strokes that required hospitalization. Fisher takes approximately twenty-one medications that cost a total of $858 per month. Her treating physicians re-evaluate her medications on a monthly basis. Assuming that defendants pay for the five most expensive medications, plaintiffs assert that Fisher, whose monthly income is $725, will have to pay $274 per month for the remainder.

Karol Loy is 46 years old, has difficulty walking and standing, and has acute mixed connective tissue disease with seizure disorder, residual from a stroke and cardiac malfunction. She has been hospitalized for two strokes and a heart attack. Loy takes twenty-four prescriptions daily that cost a total of $2,808 per month. Assuming that defendants pay for the five most expensive medications, plaintiffs claim that Loy will have to pay $644 per month, out of a monthly income of $547, for the remainder.

Defendants contest these figures. According to defendants, adjusting the schedule under which medication is purchased and eliminating drug interactions could reduce the amount plaintiffs would have to pay under the cap. By rescheduling and eliminating drugs that have adverse interactions with other drugs defendants argue that Fisher's monthly cost could be reduced to $45–60 per month; Heath's monthly cost could be reduced to $25 per month; and Loy's monthly cost could be reduced to "an admittedly still high two hundred dollars." Because the plaintiffs do not contest these projected cost savings, we assume that defendants' projections are correct.

Plaintiffs filed a motion for a preliminary injunction, which the district court converted into a motion for a permanent injunction. After receiving briefing and conducting a hearing on the matter, the district court granted summary judgment to the defendants, concluding that the plaintiffs could not maintain a claim under the ADA because they are not presently institutionalized and face no risk of institutionalization. This appeal followed.

II

A

[U]nder Title II of the ADA, a public entity may not discriminate against qualified individuals based on a disability:

> [N]o qualified individual with a disability shall, by reason of such disability, be excluded from participation in or be denied the benefits of the services, programs, or activities of a public entity, or be subjected to discrimination by any such entity.

42 U.S.C. § 12132. Pursuant to congressional authority, the Attorney General issued regulations implementing provisions of Title II, including the discrimination proscription of § 12132. Central to the instant case are two such regulations. The first, known as the "integration regulation" or "integration mandate," provides that "[a] public entity shall administer services, programs, and activities in the *most integrated setting appropriate* to the needs of qualified individuals with disabilities," 28 C.F.R. § 35.130(d) (emphasis added). In *Olmstead,* the Supreme Court construed the ADA's integration mandate and concluded that the discrimination forbidden under Title II of the ADA includes "[u]njustified isolation" of the disabled. Thus, "the ADA and its attendant regulations clearly define unnecessary segregation as a form of illegal discrimination against the disabled." *Helen L. v. DiDario,* 46 F.3d 325, 333 (3d Cir.1995).

Although public entities are required to "make reasonable modifications in policies, practices, or procedures" in order to avoid the discrimination inherent in the unjustified segregation of the disabled, the second regulation at issue, the so-called "fundamental alteration regulation," relieves a public entity of its duties under the ADA's integration mandate if "the public entity can demonstrate that making the modifications would *fundamentally alter* the nature of the service, program, or activity." 28 C.F.R. § 35.130(b)(7) (emphasis added); *see Townsend v. Quasim,* 328 F.3d 511, 517–18 (9th Cir.2003). Thus, under *Olmstead* and the applicable ADA regulations, when treatment professionals have determined that community placement is appropriate for disabled individuals, those individuals do not oppose the placement, and the provision of services would not constitute a "fundamental alteration," states are required to place those individuals in community settings rather than institutions.[7]

Arguing that the integration regulation, as interpreted in *Olmstead,* renders the imposition of the five-prescription cap a violation of the ADA because it will force them to enter nursing facilities in order to obtain necessary prescriptions, the plaintiffs sought declaratory and

---

[7] There is no dispute in the instant case as to whether community placement is appropriate for the plaintiffs.

injunctive relief before the district court. Rejecting this argument, the district court held that *Olmstead* is "factually and materially distinguishable" from the instant case, in that, unlike the plaintiffs in *Olmstead,* Fisher, Heath, and Loy are not presently living in an institution and are free to remain in the community.

Upon *de novo* review, we conclude that the district court was incorrect in its reading of *Olmstead* and the integration mandate. First, there is nothing in the plain language of the regulations that limits protection to persons who are currently institutionalized. The integration regulation simply states that public entities are to provide "services, programs, and activities in the most integrated setting appropriate" for a qualified person with disabilities. 28 C.F.R. § 35.130(d). Those protections would be meaningless if plaintiffs were required to segregate themselves by entering an institution before they could challenge an allegedly discriminatory law or policy that threatens to force them into segregated isolation. Second, while it is true that the plaintiffs in *Olmstead* were institutionalized at the time they brought their claim, nothing in the *Olmstead* decision supports a conclusion that institutionalization is a prerequisite to enforcement of the ADA's integration requirements. [O]lmstead does not imply that disabled persons who, by reason of a change in state policy, stand imperiled with segregation, may not bring a challenge to that state policy under the ADA's integration regulation without first submitting to institutionalization.

As we have elaborated, under *Olmstead,* the failure to provide Medicaid services in a community-based setting may constitute a form of discrimination. Because the OHCA does not allow the plaintiffs to receive services for which they are qualified unless they agree to enter a nursing home, the plaintiffs have presented a genuine issue of material fact as to whether they can prove that the defendants have violated the integration requirement of Title II of the ADA. However, our conclusion that the five-prescription cap may violate the ADA's integration regulation does not end our inquiry, for "[t]he State's responsibility, once it provides community-based treatment to qualified persons with disabilities, is not boundless," *Olmstead,* and states are permitted "to resist modifications that entail a 'fundamenta[l] alter[ation]' of the State's services and programs," *id.* (quoting 28 C.F.R. § 35.130(b)(7)).

In expounding upon the meaning of "fundamental alteration," the *Olmstead* Court rejected a construction of the fundamental-alteration defense that required *only* a comparison of the cost of the community services for the plaintiffs with the state's budget. Rather, courts are to consider whether "in the allocation of available resources, immediate relief for the plaintiffs would be inequitable, given the responsibility the State has undertaken for the care and treatment of a large and diverse population of persons with . . . disabilities." *Id.* With this standard in mind, we proceed to consider whether the plaintiffs have created a genuine issue of material fact as to whether elimination of the five-prescription cap would constitute a fundamental alteration.

Recognizing that the fundamental-alteration regulation can serve as a defense to the requirements of the integration regulation, the district court noted two things: (1) the waiver program is optional; and (2) "[g]iven . . . the State financial crisis, . . . [d]efendants have made a reasonable move to reduce the optional program rather than eliminate it altogether as the State could." Regarding the fact that the Advantage waiver program is optional, we note that, under Title II of the ADA, a state may not amend optional programs in such a way as to violate the integration mandate. *See, e.g., Helen L.,* 46 F.3d. at 336, 339 (requiring the requested community-based service, attendant care, even though it is an optional Medicaid service). Thus, the mere fact that a program is optional does not support a fundamental-alteration defense; rather, it merely begs the question whether provision of that service would constitute a fundamental alteration.

As to the second fundamental-alteration factor cited by the district court, that the decision "to reduce the optional program rather than eliminate it altogether" was "reasonable" because of the reality of Oklahoma's financial crisis, we note that public entities have a defense when a modification "would fundamentally alter the nature of the service, program, or activity," 28 C.F.R. § 35.130(d); that their actions were merely "reasonable" does not constitute a defense. Moreover, the fact that Oklahoma has a fiscal problem, by itself, does not lead to an automatic conclusion that preservation of unlimited medically-necessary prescription benefits for participants in the Advantage program will result in a fundamental alteration. In passing the ADA, Congress was clearly aware that "[w]hile the integration of people with disabilities will sometimes involve substantial short-term burdens, both financial and administrative, the long-range effects of integration will benefit society as a whole." H.R.Rep. No. 101–485, pt.3, at 50, *reprinted in* 1990 U.S.C.C.A.N. 445, 473. If every alteration in a program or service that required the outlay of funds were tantamount to a fundamental alteration, the ADA's integration mandate would be hollow indeed.

The district court appears to have found Oklahoma's decision "reasonable," and, by implication, that the elimination of the five-prescription cap would constitute a fundamental alteration, because the alternative to the imposition of the five-prescription cap was to eliminate the entire HCBS Waiver program. However, there is no evidence in the record to suggest that the state considered eliminating the entire program. Fogarty testified that "[the] agency is absolutely committed to [the waiver] program . . . It's a program that's needed." Given that the cost of institutional care is nearly double that of community-based care, it seems unlikely that the option cited by the district court, elimination of the waiver program, would have solved Oklahoma's fiscal crisis, because it could have served only to drive participants into nursing homes.

In opposing summary judgment below, the plaintiffs proffered a number of alternatives to the five-prescription-cap, such as requiring prior authorization for prescriptions or reducing nursing home payments by $160 per year per patient, as examples that would allow the state to save money while preserving unlimited prescription benefits for participants in the Advantage program. Thus, it is not clear from the record or the district court's summary analysis that the expenses involved in preserving unlimited prescriptions under the Advantage program will "in fact, compel cutbacks in services to other Medicaid recipients," or be "inequitable, given the responsibility the

State has undertaken for the care and treatment of a large and diverse population of persons with . . . disabilities." Nor is it clear why the preservation of a program as it has existed for years and as approved by the federal government would "fundamentally alter the nature" of the program. 28 C.F.R. § 35.130(b)(7). Plaintiffs are simply requesting that a service for which they would be eligible under an existing state program, unlimited medically necessary prescriptions, be provided in a community-based setting rather than a nursing home. They are not demanding a separate service or one not already provided by the state. Given that Oklahoma has, until recently, provided unlimited prescriptions to participants in the Advantage program, and continues to do so for those living in nursing homes, receiving medically necessary prescriptions is clearly in the nature of Oklahoma's HCBS program.[8] The district court's cursory fundamental-alteration analysis cannot stand up to logical inquiry.

In sum, in granting summary judgment to the defendants on the plaintiffs' ADA claim, the district court made errors of law and ignored disputed issues of material fact. There are genuine issues of material fact concerning whether reasonable modifications to Oklahoma's program must be made under the ADA. If reasonable modifications are required, there are genuine issues of material fact concerning whether they would fundamentally alter the program. Thus, we remand the matter for further consideration.

B

The state argues on appeal that the plaintiffs are not entitled to declaratory or injunctive relief because they cannot show that they will be harmed by the five-prescription cap. Because plaintiffs can reduce the cost of their prescriptions through scheduling and discontinuance of drugs with harmful interactions, the OHCA argues, the plaintiffs will not suffer irreparable harm absent the issuance of an injunction. On this point, the district court observed that "with appropriate scheduling of drug purchases, management of prescriptions to avoid drug interactions, and alternative community resources, Plaintiffs could completely avoid institutional care."

Under defendants' figures, plaintiff Loy will face out-of-pocket expenses of $200 per month, which defendants acknowledge to be "admittedly still high." Given that Loy's income is limited to $547 per month, an extra $200 per month—36.6% of her income—in drug costs will place a severe burden on her finances and could easily force her to enter a nursing home. Thus, there can be no question that plaintiff Loy will be irreparably harmed absent the issuance of an injunction.

Whether plaintiffs Fisher and Heath will be irreparably harmed under defendants' figures is a closer question. Defendants assert that Fisher's expenses will be reduced to $60 per month, and Heath's costs can be reduced to $25 per month. Fisher's income is $725 a month, which means that her prescription expenses will constitute 8.28% of her income under defendants' projections. Although Heath's costs will be

---

[8] An inescapable irony of the decision to cap prescriptions for participants in the Advantage program is that, given that the cost of institutional care is approximately twice as high as community-based care, if the plaintiffs are indeed forced to enter a nursing home to obtain necessary medical services, any cost savings achieved by the prescription cap will be quickly eroded.

small under defendants' projections, so too is her income—$313 per month. Her prescription expenses will constitute about 8% of her income under defendants; projections. This may not be devastating, but it will likely have a real effect on Fisher's and Heath's finances given their poverty.

The state further argues that the plaintiffs cannot show that they will be harmed by the five-prescription cap because all three plaintiffs stated at a hearing conducted by the district court either that they would rather die than be placed in a nursing home, or that they would not enter a nursing home because they feared they "wouldn't last long" due to the fact that "they don't take care of people [there] any more." By their own admission, the state argues, the plaintiffs do not face the segregation and isolation from the community that constitutes discrimination under the ADA. We note, however, that given the plaintiffs' precarious health and finances, the five-prescription cap places them at "high risk for premature entry into a nursing home." That they have emphatically stated their desire to remain in the community does not mean that they do not face a substantial risk of harm. An expert witness testified that under the prescription cap, "some . . . would just choose to stay at home and die a premature death. Others will wait until their health has deteriorated and then there will be a hospital admission. Some will eventually end up in a nursing home."

We conclude that plaintiffs have raised a genuine issue of material fact as to irreparable harm even if their expenses can be lowered as suggested by defendants.

III

[I]n sum, in granting summary judgment to the defendants on the plaintiffs' ADA claim, the district court relied on incorrect legal assumptions and ignored genuine issues of material fact. We therefore **REVERSE** the judgment of the district court granting summary judgment to the defendants and **REMAND** the matter for further proceedings consistent with this opinion.

Lane v. Kitzhaber

United States District Court for the District of Oregon, 2012.
841 F.Supp.2d 1199.

■ STEWART, UNITED STATES MAGISTRATE JUDGE.

INTRODUCTION

Plaintiffs filed this class action alleging violations of Title II of the Americans with Disabilities Act of 1990 ("ADA"), 42 U.S.C. §§ 12131–34 ("First Claim") and Section 504 of the Rehabilitation Act of 1973, 29 U.S.C. § 794(a) ("Second Claim") against the Oregon Department of Human Services ("DHS") and various state officials including Oregon's governor (John Kitzhaber), the Director of DHS (Erinn Kelley-Siel), the Administrator of the Office of Developmental Disability Services ("ODDS") (Mary Lee Fay), and the Administrator of the Office of Vocational Rehabilitation Services ("OVRS") (Stephaine Parrish Taylor).

Plaintiffs are eight individuals with intellectual or developmental disabilities, each of whom qualifies for and receives employment services from DHS. Each plaintiff is able and would prefer to work in an integrated employment setting. Plaintiffs allege that, despite their preference to work in such a setting, they and thousands of similarly situated individuals remain unnecessarily segregated in sheltered workshops and are denied virtually all contact with nondisabled persons in these workshops as a result of DHS's administration, management, and funding of its employment service system.

Defendants have now filed a Motion to Dismiss. [F]or the reasons that follow, defendants' motion is GRANTED and plaintiffs' claims are DISMISSED WITH LEAVE TO AMEND.

DISCUSSION

[T]he eight individual plaintiffs are intellectually or developmentally disabled persons who reside in the community. Complaint, ¶¶ 112 (Paula Lane lives in an apartment with staff support), 120 (Andres Paniagua lives with his mother), 129 (Elizabeth Harrah lives in an adult foster home), 135 (Angela Kehler lives in a group home with other disabled individuals), 144 (Gretchen Cason lives with her parents), 154 (Lori Robertson lives in a group home), 162 (Sparkle Green lives in an adult foster home), 170 (Zavier Kinville lives with his father). Plaintiffs do not allege that defendants' alleged actions or inactions have created a risk that any of them will be forced to live in an institution.

Seven of the eight plaintiffs work in sheltered workshops. *Id.,* ¶¶ 113, 121, 130, 136, 155, 163, 171. Ms. Cason, worked at a sheltered workshop in and prior to December 2010. *Id.,* ¶¶ 146–48. Sheltered workshops are segregated employment settings that employ people with disabilities or where people with disabilities work separately from others. *Id.,* ¶ 3. Plaintiffs prefer to receive supported employment services[1] which would prepare and allow them to work in an "integrated employment setting," which they define as a "real job in a community-based business setting, where employees have an opportunity to work alongside non-disabled coworkers and earn at least minimum wage." *Id.,* ¶¶ 2, 4, 119, 125–28, 132–34, 140–43, 151–53, 159–61, 166–68, 174–76.

DHS has developed, adopted, and promoted an "Employment First Policy" premised on data indicating that integrated employment has better outcomes than segregated employment and that through a person-centered planning process, individuals with disabilities can and do succeed at integrated employment. *Id.,* ¶ 84. It is actively pursuing goals to expand access to supported employment services for intellectually and developmentally disabled Oregonians. *Id.,* ¶¶ 84, 96, 101–02. As part of that effort, DHS commissioned the preparation of the "Call to Action" report in order to help develop strategies for implementing its "Employment First" policy at the community level. *Id.,* ¶ 89; *see* Community Leadership for Employment First in Oregon

---

[1] Plaintiffs define supported employment services as "vocational training services that prepare and allow people with intellectual and developmental disabilities to participate in integrated employment." Complaint, ¶ 4.

(2010),   http://www.dhs.state.or.us/dd/supp_emp/docs/wise.pdf,   p.   12 (last accessed May 17, 2012).

[D]efendants seek dismissal of plaintiffs' claims because: (1) employment claims are not cognizable under Title II of the ADA; (2) even if plaintiffs get past that hurdle, the integration mandate does not apply because the denial of employment services does not place any plaintiff at risk of institutionalization; (3) plaintiffs' claims improperly seek to require defendants to provide a service that the state does not and cannot provide, namely integrated employment in a community business; and (4) plaintiffs' claims improperly seek to impose a certain standard of care on the state's provision of employment services.

A. *Employment Claims Under Title II*

In their Reply, defendants seek dismissal of the ADA claim on the basis that plaintiffs are raising an "employment claim" not cognizable under Title II of the ADA. Plaintiffs rely on *Zimmerman v. Oregon Dept. of Justice,* 170 F.3d 1169, 1176 (9th Cir.), *reh'g en banc denied,* 183 F.3d 1161 (1999), *cert. denied,* 531 U.S. 1189 (2001), which upheld dismissal of a Title II claim premised upon an allegation that the state refused to accommodate his visual impairment and then terminated him. Based on a contextual reading of the structure of the ADA, the Ninth Circuit concluded that Congress had "unambiguously expressed its intent that Title II not apply to employment" and granted "no weight" to the Attorney General's implementing regulation which found that Title II applied to employment. Defendants contend that *Zimmerman* mandates dismissal of plaintiffs' ADA claim because it similarly involves employment, employment training, and employment services.

However, contrary to defendants' argument, this case does not involve "employment," but instead involves the state's provision (or failure to provide) "integrated employment *services,* including supported employment programs." Complaint, ¶¶ 2, 6 (emphasis added). Even a cursory review of the "inputs" versus "outputs" analysis cited in *Zimmerman* reveals that the integrated employment services sought by plaintiffs are "services, programs, and activities" offered by defendants, not merely the "means to deliver the services, programs, and activities." Plaintiffs simply do not seek to become state employees or contend that the state discriminates against them in employing them. Instead, they contend that the state has failed to provide services to them which would make it possible for them to become and remain competitively employed in the community.

Thus, this court concludes that *Zimmerman* is no barrier to plaintiffs' claim under Title II of the ADA.

B. *Applicability of Integration Mandate to Employment-Related Services*

Defendants also contend that the integration mandate does not apply to the provision of employment-related services. They raise several arguments to support this contention.

First, defendants contend that the court should give no deference to the Department of Justice's recent interpretation of the integration mandate which prohibits the unnecessary provision of services to persons with disabilities in non-residential settings, including segregated sheltered workshops. "Statement of the Department of

Justice on Enforcement of the Integration Mandate of Title II of the Americans with Disabilities Act and *Olmstead v. L.C.*," p. 3 (June 22, 2011) ("2011 DOJ Statement"), available at: http://www.ada.gov/olmstead/q&a_olmstead.htm (last accessed May 17, 2012).

[I]n the 2011 DOJ Statement under Question 1, "What is the most integrated setting under the ADA and Olmstead," the Department of Justice states:

> Integrated services are those that provide individuals with disabilities opportunities to live, work, and receive services in the greater community, like individuals without disabilities. Integrated settings are located in mainstream society; offer access to community activities and opportunities at times, frequencies and with persons of an individual's choosing; afford individuals choice in their daily life activities; and provide individuals with disabilities the opportunity to interact with non-disabled persons to the fullest extent possible . . . . Segregated settings include, but are not limited to, . . . settings that provide for daytime activities primarily with other individuals with disabilities.

The Department of Justice further states that a "comprehensive, effectively working plan" written pursuant to *Olmstead* must "include commitments for each group of persons who are unnecessarily segregated," including "individuals spending their days in sheltered workshops or segregated day programs." Finally, the Department of Justice states that appropriate remedies under the integration mandate include "supported employment."

Although the Ninth Circuit recently accorded deference to another portion of the 2011 DOJ Statement in *M.R. v. Dreyfus,* 663 F.3d 1100, 1117 (9th Cir.2011), defendants argue that it should be given no weight here because it is inconsistent with the Department of Justice's earlier proclamation in 1991 when the integration mandate regulation was promulgated. The 1991 commentary to the publication of the proposed regulation stated that: "These provisions should not be construed to jeopardize in any way the continued viability of separate schools providing education for particular categories of children with disabilities, *sheltered workshops,* special recreational programs, and other similar programs." Nondiscrimination on the Basis of Disability in State and Local Government Services, 56 Fed.Reg. 8538–01, 8543 (proposed Feb. 28, 1991), 1991 WL 311707 (emphasis added). Defendants contend that this language means that the Department of Justice did not consider sheltered workshops to violate the proposed integration mandate regulation. However, that contention plainly is at odds with the next two paragraphs of the 1991 commentary which unequivocally demonstrate that the Department of Justice also did not consider it appropriate to strip disabled individuals of the opportunity to choose participation in integrated activities over participation in special programs such as sheltered workshops:

> At the same time, *individuals with disabilities cannot be denied the opportunity to participate in programs that are not separate or different.* This is an important and overarching principle of the Americans with Disabilities Act. *Separate, special, or different programs* that are designed to provide a

benefit to persons with disabilities *cannot be used to restrict the participation of persons with disabilities in general, integrated activities.*

For example, a person who is blind may wish to decline participating in a special museum tour that allows persons to touch sculptures in an exhibit and instead tour the exhibit at his or her own pace with the museum's recorded tour. It is not the intent of this section to require the person who is blind to avail himself or herself of the special tour. Modified participation for persons with disabilities must be a choice, not a requirement.

As in these examples, plaintiffs contend that sheltered workshops—ostensibly "designed to provide a benefit to persons with disabilities"—cannot be used to restrict the participation of persons with disabilities in general, integrated employment. Plaintiffs do not argue that sheltered workshops must be eliminated because they are *per se* illegal, but instead argue that, in most instances, a more integrated setting is appropriate and, therefore, required by the integration mandate. Complaint, ¶ 33 ("most" of the members of the plaintiff class could and would prefer to work in an integrated employment setting). Accordingly, participation for persons with disabilities in sheltered workshops "must be a choice, not a requirement." No meaningful conflict exists between the 1991 commentary by the Department of Justice on the integration mandate and the recent 2011 DOJ Statement on its enforcement following *Olmstead.*

Next, citing *Dreyfus,* defendants contend that the integration mandate does not apply to plaintiffs' claims. In *Dreyfus,* the Ninth Circuit granted a preliminary injunction to Medicaid beneficiaries with severe mental and physical disabilities on their ADA claims against the state for reducing the available amount of in-home personal care services which placed them at serious risk of institutionalization. Applying *Olmstead,* the Ninth Circuit held that in order to state a violation of the integration mandate, "a plaintiff need only show that the challenged state action creates a serious risk of institutionalization." *Dreyfus,* 663 F.3d at 1116 Because plaintiffs in this case do not allege that they are at risk for institutionalization, defendants contend that the integration mandate simply does not cover their claims.

[A]s defendants correctly note, no other case has applied the integration mandate in a context other than one in which the state's action places plaintiffs at risk for institutionalization. However, that dearth of authority does not lead inexorably to the conclusion that the integration mandate is inapplicable to plaintiffs' claims. To the contrary, the broad language and remedial purposes of the ADA, the corresponding lack of any limiting language in either the ADA or the integration mandate itself, and the lack of any case law restricting the reach of the integration mandate suggest just the opposite conclusion. It is particularly noteworthy that the Supreme Court levied the following criticisms against institutionalization in *Olmstead:*

Recognition that unjustified institutional isolation of persons with disabilities is a form of discrimination reflects two evident judgments. First, institutional placement of persons who can handle and benefit from community settings perpetuates unwarranted assumptions that persons so isolated are incapable or unworthy of participating in community life. Second, confinement in an institution severely diminishes the everyday life activities of individual, including family relations, social contacts, work options, economic independence, educational advancement, and cultural enrichment.

Those same criticisms apply equally to offering no choice of employment services other than working in a sheltered workshop. This case is notably different than any prior case, including *Dreyfus,* because it does not involve a claim to restore services in order to prevent confinement in a residential institution. Instead, it seeks to ensure the provision of available employment-related services in order to prevent unnecessary segregation in employment. Although the means and settings differ, the end goal is the same, namely to prevent the "unjustified institutional isolation of persons with disabilities." Thus, this court concludes that the risk of institutionalization addressed in both *Olmstead* and *Dreyfus* includes segregation in the employment setting.

Defendants also argue that the integration mandate is inapplicable in this context because plaintiffs do not allege that they are working against their will, unlike the plaintiffs in other cases who faced involuntary institutionalization by the state's action. They also argue that several of the plaintiffs work as little as a couple of hours per week, which they contend does not qualify as "institutionalization." This argument improperly attempts to shift the focus of the inquiry toward plaintiffs' choices and away from the issue of defendants' actions relative to the services provided. Defendants' obligation is to administer their services and programs "in the most integrated setting appropriate to the needs of qualified individuals with disabilities." 28 C.F.R. §§ 35.130(d), 41.51(d). Plaintiffs allege that they are "unnecessarily segregated"— *i.e.* forced to work in a segregated setting if they are to work at all—due to defendants' overreliance on sheltered workshops and corresponding "failure to timely develop and adequately fund integrated employment services, including supported employment programs." Complaint, ¶¶ 2, 5–6, 34–37, 81, 88–92, 97–98, 107. Those allegations sufficiently assert that defendants have failed to meet their obligation under the integration mandate.

C. *Imposition of a Standard of Care or Demand for Level of Benefits*

[T]he central theme of plaintiffs' claims is that defendants are violating the antidiscrimination laws by dedicating a disproportionate amount of their resources to fund sheltered workshops at the expense of supported employment services. Complaint, ¶¶ 2, 5–6, 34–37, 81, 85 (describing problem as a "capacity" issue), 88–92, 97–99, 107. Nevertheless, defendants contend that plaintiffs' ultimate goal is to obtain two forms of impermissible relief. First, defendants argue that the ultimate goal of "integrated employment," as that term is defined by plaintiffs, is not a "service" that the state does or can provide. They point out that some allegations—read literally and collectively—seek the ultimate goal of a "real job in a community-based business setting" for all plaintiffs and class members. *See* Complaint, ¶ 4 (defining "integrated employment" as a "real job in a community-based business setting"); Prayer, ¶ 2 ("failing to provide [plaintiffs] with supported employment programs in integrated settings"); Prayer, ¶ 3(b) (seeking "supported employment programs in integrated employment settings for all qualified class members"). Second, defendants contend that plaintiffs seek either to impose a standard of care on the services defendants provide or seek to obtain a particular level of benefits, neither of which is a permissible form of relief. Again, some of the allegations in the pleadings support this argument. *Id.,* ¶¶ 184 (failing to "offer an *adequate array* of integrated employment and supported employment services to qualified persons with disabilities") (emphasis added), 192 (same), and Prayer, ¶ 3(a) (same).

As defendants acknowledge, *Olmstead* admonishes that a disability discrimination claim may not be premised upon allegations that defendants failed to meet a particular standard of care with regard to the services provided or upon a request for a particular level of benefits:

> We do not in this opinion hold that the ADA imposes on the States a "standard of care" for whatever medical services they render, or that the ADA requires States to "provide a certain level of benefits to individuals with disabilities." . . . We do hold, however, that States must adhere to the ADA's nondiscrimination requirement with regard to the services they in fact provide.

Thus, a claim survives only if it truly alleges a "discriminatory denial of services" and must be dismissed if it instead concerns the "adequacy" of the services provided. Accordingly, claims by qualified individuals who both meet the eligibility requirements for a particular program and are willing participants may properly allege a claim for a denial of the services provided by a program, but not a claim for providing inadequate services.

At oral argument, plaintiffs clarified that they are not seeking a guarantee that the employment services they desire will result in community-based or competitive employment. Instead, they seek the provision of employment services that would allow them the opportunity to work in an integrated setting. *Id.,* ¶¶ 4 (defining "[s]upported employment services" as those "vocational training services that *prepare and allow* people with intellectual and developmental disabilities to participate in integrated employment") (emphasis added), 85 (alleging that ODDS has failed "to ensure there is a sufficient capacity of supported employment services *to allow* persons with intellectual and developmental disabilities to *work in integrated settings*") (emphasis added), 119 (Lane not offered supported employment services that would allow her to work in an integrated environment), 128 (Peniagua), 132–34 (Harrah), 142 (Kehler), 152 (Cason), 161 (Robertson), 168 (Green), 175–76 (Kinville). In particular, plaintiffs seek to have defendants reallocate their available resources in a way that does not unjustifiably favor segregated employment in sheltered workshops at the expense of providing supported employment services to qualified individuals. Accordingly, they seek a court order mandating: (1) a treatment planning process that properly and fairly assesses the individuals' ability and interest in supported employment; (2) provision of supported employment services to those individuals who qualify for and are interested in them; and (3) a supported employment program that complies with CMS and other national accrediting standards.

However, some of allegations in the Complaint go beyond the clarification offered by plaintiffs at the hearing and seek the forbidden remedy of requiring defendants to provide an adequate level of employment services to enable plaintiffs to obtain a competitive job. In particular, plaintiffs allege that defendants are violating Title II of the ADA and the Rehabilitation Act by failing "to offer an *adequate array* of integrated employment and supported employment services" (Complaint, ¶¶ 184, 192) (emphasis added) and "to provide them with supporting employment services that *would enable them to work in integrated employment settings*" (*id.,* ¶¶ 185, 193) (emphasis added). These allegations are subject to dismissal because they demand that defendants provide a competitive job in the community and a certain standard of care or level of benefits. Instead, to comply with the scope of plaintiffs' claims as described at the hearing, these allegations (and other related allegations) must be amended to clarify that defendants are violating Title II of the ADA and the Rehabilitation Act by denying employment services to plaintiffs for which they are eligible with the result of unnecessarily segregating them in sheltered workshops.

ORDER

For the reasons stated above, defendants' Motion to Dismiss is GRANTED. Plaintiffs' claims are dismissed WITHOUT PREJUDICE and WITH LEAVE TO AMEND. Plaintiffs shall file their First Amended Complaint to cure the problems identified in this Opinion and Order on or before May 29, 2012.*

NOTES ON OLMSTEAD LITIGATION

1. Deinstitutionalization—The Policy History. In the late 1960s through the 1970s, an effort to move people with mental disabilities out of congregate institutions and into community settings had significantly effects on public policy. These efforts were driven by two quite distinct motivations. From one side came civil libertarians, who were influenced by Erving Goffman's argument that congregate, institutional living was inherently dehumanizing, Erving Goffman, Asylums: Essays on the Social Situation of Mental Patients and Other Inmates (1961), and by the journalistic exposés of horrendous conditions in state mental hospitals and facilities for people with mental retardation. See, *e.g.*, Burton Blatt & Fred Kaplan, Christmas in Purgatory: A Photographic Essay on Mental Retardation (1966). From the other side came fiscal conservatives, who sought to balance state budgets by moving people out of costly institutions. See Paul S. Appelbaum, Almost a Revolution: Mental Health Law and the Limits of Change 50 (1992); James W. Trent, Inventing the Feeble Mind: A History of Mental Retardation in the United States 256–257 (1994).

---

* [The plaintiffs subsequently filed an amended complaint, and the district court then granted certification of the plaintiff class. See *Lane v. Kitzhaber*, 283 F.R.D. 587 (D. Or. 2012). —ed.]

With support from the civil libertarian left and the conservative right, the deinstitutionalization policy succeeded in dramatically reducing the number of people with psychiatric and intellectual and developmental disabilities who were confined to congregate institutions:

> The number of people with developmental disabilities confined to state-operated institutions in the United States peaked at just under 200,000 in 1967. Since that time, states have closed hundreds of their institutions, and they have downsized many others. Institutions like the Pennhurst State School and Hospital in Pennsylvania (peak census: 3500 in 1955), the Lincoln State School and Colony in Illinois (peak census: over 5000 in the 1950s), and Letchworth Village in New York (peak census: over 4000 in the mid-1960s) are now closed. The state-operated institutions that remain are much smaller, housing at most hundreds, not thousands, of residents. As of June 30, 2009, according to statistics compiled by the Research and Training Center on Community Living at the University of Minnesota (RTC), "nine states had closed all state operated residential facilities with 16 or more residents with [intellectual or developmental disabilities]." And "[o]f the 354 large state operated facilities operating at any time between 1960 and 2008, only 162 facilities (45.7%) in 42 states remained open on June 30, 2009."
>
> Although every state has significantly reduced its reliance on large state-operated facilities for people with intellectual disabilities, some states still have very large numbers of residents in those facilities. The RTC reports that the average daily population in these facilities across the country has dropped 74.4% between 1980 and 2009, from 131,345 to 33,682. Twenty-four states and the District of Columbia have reduced the population in these facilities by more than 80% over this period of time. These states, which are geographically and demographically diverse, are: Alabama, Alaska, Arizona, Colorado, Delaware, Hawaii, Indiana, Kentucky, Maine, Maryland, Massachusetts, Michigan, Minnesota, New Hampshire, New Mexico, New York, North Dakota, Oklahoma, Oregon, Pennsylvania, Utah, Vermont, West Virginia, and Wyoming. Of the states not on this list, thirteen continued as of 2009 to confine more than 900 people in congregate, state-operated institutions: Arkansas (1083); California (2391); Florida (1040); Georgia (915); Illinois (2161); Louisiana (1174); Mississippi (1323); New Jersey (2841); North Carolina (1629); Ohio (1455); Texas (4629); Virginia (1276); and Washington (936). In Mississippi, the population of these facilities decreased by only 20.3% between 1980 and 2009; in Arkansas, it decreased by only 30.1%. Perhaps not surprisingly, a number of states on this list have been the targets of enforcement actions by the Department of Justice as it has stepped up its Olmstead program in recent years.
>
> In the psychiatric disability area, the numbers are even more stark. The end-of-year inpatient census in public psychiatric hospitals in the United States peaked in 1955 at just under

560,000 individuals. By 2003, the number had decreased by more than 90% to just under 50,000. As Professors Grob and Goldman point out, "[t]he decline was even more dramatic if general population growth is taken into account. Had the proportion remained stable and the mix constant, mental hospitals would have had about 950,000 patients in 2000." The total number of admissions to these hospitals was significantly higher than this number might suggest, as 60% of adults admitted to state psychiatric hospitals in 2007 were discharged within thirty days; average length of stay has gone down dramatically since the 1950s as well. And the total number of public psychiatric hospitals in the United States also decreased substantially, from 310 as late as 1970 to 220 in 2000. As with developmental disabilities, there is substantial variation across the states in the numbers, but the overall trend is clear.

Samuel R. Bagenstos, *The Past and Future of Deinstitutionalization Litigation*, 34 Cardozo L. Rev. 1 (2012).

But left and right divided over what to do next. The civil libertarians urged the full financing of group homes, mental health clinics, and other services in the community. But full funding would not serve the purposes of the fiscal conservatives who supported deinstitutionalization as a way of cutting costs. Particularly in the context of psychiatric disabilities, the fiscal conservatism of the 1970s and 1980s led to a serious underinvestment in community-based services: "Ultimately, once discharged from the state hospitals, former in-patients in many jurisdictions were essentially abandoned." Appelbaum, *supra*, at 50. Deinstitutionalization of people with intellectual and developmental disabilities has been far more successful—as the Pennhurst experience demonstrates. See Cook, *supra*, at 444 (collecting studies showing the success of people with mental retardation who had been deinstitutionalized). But it has not been without problems. See Trent, *supra*, at 271 ("[S]ome people once labeled mentally retarded have had trouble integrating into 'normal' patterns of community life. Some have thrived in new and exciting living arrangements; others [h]ave been reinstitutionalized in 'community institutions' operated not by the state but by various nonprofit and for-profit organizations; still others have also been reinstitutionalized, this time in jails and prisons.").

In his concurrence in the judgment in *Olmstead*, in a portion of his opinion joined by Justice Breyer, Justice Kennedy endorses a common critique of the deinstitutionalization efforts of the 1970s—that many people with severe psychiatric disabilities need institutionalization, and that deinstitutionalization is simply a way of abandoning them. Justice Kennedy cites extensively to the work of E. Fuller Torrey to support that critique. See E. Fuller Torrey, Out of the Shadows: Confronting America's Mental Illness Crisis (1997). Advocates of deinstitutionalization argue that Torrey's work is "terribly flawed," and that "social structures exist to transition patients from an institutional setting into the community and to create treatment programs that may ultimately be more effective than institutionalized treatment settings." Michael L. Perlin, *"Their Promises of Paradise": Will Olmstead v. L.C. Resuscitate the Constitutional "Least*

Restrictive Alternative" Principle in Mental Disability Law?, 37 Hou. L. Rev. 999, 1041 n.296 (2000). The problem, they contend, is not in deinstitutionalization itself but in the failure to fund services and supports in the community:

> To be sure, we could solve the problem of homelessness among people with psychiatric disabilities by simply institutionalizing them for the long term. But other policies could solve that problem just as well—notably supportive housing, in which individuals obtain tenancy in apartments linked with supportive services. And yet, as homelessness was increasing in the 1980s, the federal and state governments were cutting Supplemental Security Income (SSI) and housing assistance—the very programs that could pay for community-based housing for people with psychiatric disabilities. The indictment of deinstitutionalization, as opposed to the failure to invest in community-based services and supports, does not rest on an empirical determination of what happened in the world so much as on a normative premise that institutionalization is preferable to community-based housing and supports.

Bagenstos, *Past and Future of Deinstitutionalization*, *supra*. As that discussion suggests, the dispute between the two positions rests partly on different interpretations of the empirical evidence of the effects of deinstitutionalization and partly on different normative views about questions of liberty versus paternalism. Is it appropriate for courts to treat the ADA as resolving these disputes? Ought the states have the power to weigh the empirical and normative questions for themselves?

2.   The Scope of the *Olmstead* Holding. Recall that *Olmstead* itself was a case brought by two individuals, L.C. and E.W., who argued that Georgia inappropriately required them to be institutionalized in a state psychiatric hospital if they wished to receive services. *Fisher* and *Lane* applied *Olmstead*'s holding to quite different contexts.

In *Fisher*, the court applied *Olmstead* to protect individuals who are not institutionalized but were merely at risk of unnecessary institutionalization. If Oklahoma's cuts to prescription drug reimbursements put individuals at sufficient risk of needless institutionalization, the court held, those cuts would violate *Olmstead*. In *Fisher* itself, the risk of institutionalization stemmed from a difference in the way the state treated people who did and did not live in nursing homes. Those who did not live in nursing homes would be subject to the limitations on prescription drug reimbursement, while those who lived in nursing homes (including privately operated nursing homes reimbursed by Medicaid) would not. That disparity, the plaintiffs argued, made it likely that individuals who had more extensive prescription drug needs would be required to move into nursing homes in order to satisfy those needs—even though there was nothing intrinsic about their disabilities that made them unable to be served while living in their own homes in the community.

The *Fisher* risk-of-institutionalization theory opens up the possibility for plaintiffs to challenge a far broader array of institutionalization problems than the paradigm case of an individual unjustifiably confined to a state mental hospital:

The new doctrine enables challenges to institutionalization in private facilities (such as nursing homes, adult care homes, and ICF/MRs ["intermediate care facilities for the mentally retarded"]), for example, because state funding decisions often are the force driving people with disabilities into those facilities. A state might, for example, pay for adult diapers for people with disabilities living in nursing homes but not for those living in the community, [o]r it might pay for adult care homes for people with psychiatric disabilities but not integrated supported housing, even though the two cost roughly the same.

Olmstead also enables advocates to obtain high-quality community services for people with disabilities, precisely because the state's failure to provide such services will predictably lead many individuals to become institutionalized, whether in state facilities or private nursing homes. Recent judgments and consent decrees demonstrate the array of services courts are willing to require under the *Olmstead* doctrine. In the *Disability Advocates* case, recently vacated by the Second Circuit on standing grounds (but sure to be refiled), the District Court for the Eastern District of New York ordered the State of New York to provide at least 1500 integrated, scattered-site supported housing units per year to individuals currently residing in private adult homes. [See *Disability Advocates, Inc. v. Paterson*, No. 03-CV-3209, 2010 WL 786657, at *6 (E.D.N.Y. Mar. 1, 2010), vacated, 675 F.3d 149 (2d Cir. 2012).] And the United States Department of Justice has recently reached *Olmstead* settlements with a number of states. Those settlements contain extensive and detailed provisions governing the types of services the states must provide in the community to those who have been institutionalized or are at risk of institutionalization, the number of individuals who must receive those services, and timetables specifying when those services must be provided.

For example, the recent settlement with the Commonwealth of Virginia provides a detailed schedule according to which the state will add over 4000 home and community-based waivers for people with intellectual and developmental disabilities to its Medicaid program over nine years. Just over 800 of these waiver slots will be dedicated to individuals currently living in state institutions; nearly 3000 will be dedicated to individuals with intellectual disabilities who currently live outside of state institutions but who are either on the state's "urgent waitlist" for a waiver (indicating that they are at substantial risk of institutionalization) or are children who live in private nursing homes or intermediate-care facilities; and the remainder will be dedicated to individuals with other developmental disabilities who are on the state's waiting list for a waiver or who are children who live in private nursing homes or intermediate-care facilities. The agreement also provides support for 1000 families who are currently providing for family members with intellectual and developmental disabilities at home. These are individuals who might not need all of the services available under a Medicaid waiver but who do need some supports to prevent institutionalization. The agreement also contains detailed provisions for a statewide crisis system for people with intellectual and developmental disabilities, so that the response to a behavioral or other crisis is not institutionalization or criminalization but instead is an intervention that ensures that the individual can remain successfully in the community. The agreement also includes a number of provisions to ensure that "the community" is truly integrated for people receiving services under it. Those provisions require a commitment to integrated day activities and supported employment, they put a priority on ensuring that individuals receive services in their own homes or apartments or their family's home, and they erect a strong presumption against placing individuals in group homes containing more than four residents. The agreement also contains significant provisions to ensure that community-based services meet key quality measures.

The recent Department of Justice *Olmstead* settlements that involve services for people with psychiatric disabilities take a similar structure. They contain detailed timetables governing the specific community-based services specified numbers of people will receive to ensure that they can leave or avoid admission to institutions. In psychiatric disability cases, these services generally fall into four key categories: integrated supported housing; intensive community-based treatment (like ACT [Assertive Community Treatment] or forms of case management); community-based crisis services; and integrated supported employment. Like the Virginia settlements, the psychiatric disability settlements also contain extensive provisions ensuring the quality of community-based services.

Crucially, in times of budget retrenchment, the *Olmstead* doctrine also enables advocates to challenge cuts to community services, because those cuts, too, will put people with disabilities at risk of institutionalization. *Olmstead*, [so construed,] does not incentivize states simply to turn people out of institutions and onto the streets. It incentivizes states to provide the array of services people need to thrive in the community—at least so long as a state remains enrolled in Medicaid, which requires states to pay for nursing home and other institutionalized placements for those individuals.

Bagenstos, *Past and Future of Deinstitutionalization, supra.* Especially when considered in light of these broad-ranging consequences, is *Fisher* a proper application of the Supreme Court's decision in *Olmstead*?

Olmstead, Fisher, and the subsequent cases just discussed focused on the effects of state decisions on *where* people with disabilities live. The plaintiffs in each case argued that the state's decision (to place an individual in an institution or to allocate resources in a particular way) effectively forced individuals with disabilities to live in a setting that was not the most integrated setting appropriate to the needs of those individuals. *Lane* applied *Olmstead* to state decisions that are not about where people with disabilities live but about *how* they live. In particular, the court accepted that the plaintiffs could make out an *Olmstead* violation if they could show that the state provided employment services in unnecessarily segregated settings such as sheltered workshops. Is this a proper application of *Olmstead?*

On the controversy over the use of sheltered workshops to provide employment services to people with disabilities, see Laura C. Hoffman, *An Employment Opportunity or a Discrimination Dilemma? Sheltered Workshops and the Employment of the Disabled,* 16 U. Pa. J. L. & Soc. Change 151 (2013); Susan Stefan, *Beyond Residential Segregation: The Application of Olmstead to Segregated Employment Settings,* 26 Ga. St. U. L. Rev. 875 (2010).

3. Conflicts in Deinstitutionalization Litigation. Deinstitutionalization litigation often provokes conflicts—between different groups of people with disabilities (and, often, their parents or guardians), and between people who want to live outside of institutions and the people who work in those institutions. Consider the following discussion of those conflicts:

> As the process of deinstitutionalization has ground on, conflict between deinstitutionalization advocates and family and union groups has intensified. The reason is simple economics. State-run institutions have very high fixed costs of operation. As people leave those institutions and are not replaced with new people coming in, per-resident costs rise significantly and compare less and less favorably to the costs of serving current residents in the community. Once an institution's population drops below a tipping point, closure of the entire institution becomes almost a fiscal necessity. To parents and family members who want their loved ones to remain in an institution, and to unions who want to preserve their jobs in an institution, it becomes equally imperative to keep the institution from reaching that tipping point—or, if it has already reached that point, to apply extraordinary political and legal pressure to delay or forestall what seems fiscally inevitable. In the new politics of deinstitutionalization, then, parents and unions can be expected to wage epic battles to keep states and courts from downsizing institutions—even if the downsizing efforts focus entirely on people who affirmatively want (and whose families affirmatively want them) to live in the community. In a time of fiscal retrenchment, as those who support and oppose deinstitutionalization are fighting over shares of a shrinking pie, the battles become ever so much more intense.

> This intensified conflict has played out in deinstitutionalization litigation across the country. Parents' organizations have often intervened (sometimes successfully) to oppose agreements that would merely allow people who choose to receive services in the community to leave institutions. In a number of these cases, such as the original settlement of the *Ligas* litigation in Illinois,[229] these settlements would not require an individual to leave an institution if she (or her guardian) did not want to leave. But the parents' organizations quite understandably feared that, if too many people were allowed to

---

[229] See Ligas v. Maram, No. 05 C 4331, 2010 WL 1418583, at *1 (N.D. Ill. Apr. 7, 2010) (describing the court's decertification of the plaintiff class in response to guardians' objections to the initial consent decree).

leave the institutions in question, the choice of keeping one's child in that institution would soon be unavailable as a practical matter. As I discussed above, the rhetoric of choice is incomplete in the context of competing claims on scarce resources.

Similar dynamics have arisen when states have proposed to close institutions outside of the context of litigation. When Massachusetts responded to fiscal concerns by seeking to close Fernald Developmental Center, its oldest institution for people with developmental disabilities—even though it offered residents and guardians a choice of transferring to another state institution—Fernald parents sought to reopen a long-closed pre-*Olmstead* case that had been settled in 1993. The parents argued that the closure actually violated *Olmstead*, because it deprived them of the opportunity to oppose placement in the community. The district court seemed to express support for this argument: it restored the case to its active docket; required the Commonwealth to "carefully assess the needs and wishes of each resident, and provide a genuine and meaningful opportunity for their guardians to participate in their placement decisions" before closing the institution; and stated that its ruling "simply ensur[ed]" that the Commonwealth determine whether each individual's new placement "is appropriate and whether it 'is not opposed by the affected individual' ' under *Olmstead*. The First Circuit reversed on the ground that there was no basis for reopening the old decree; the appellate court cited *Olmstead* for the proposition that the law had in fact "moved in a direction disfavoring institutionalization of residents" since the decree was first entered.[233]

But the battle did not end there. Evidently blaming the Massachusetts government's decision on the pressures caused by the threat of litigation, Representative Barney Frank, who represented the district in which Fernald was located, responded by introducing legislation that would limit the ability of federally funded Protection and Advocacy agencies—the source of much *Olmstead* litigation—to bring cases that could lead to the closing and downsizing of institutions. Both VOR [a parents' organization, formerly known as the Voice of the Retarded] and AFSCME [a union that represents the employees at many state-operated institutions] have vocally supported this legislation. Though the legislation has not moved in Congress, the support by one of its most stereotypically liberal members for a bill that would limit public interest lawsuits highlights the unusual political alliances that continue to surround deinstitutionalization litigation.

Despite the intensified conflict, the new politics of deinstitutionalization open up the possibility for alliances between parent and union groups and deinstitutionalization advocates. In a meta-analysis of studies of parental attitudes published in 1991, the researchers Sheryl Larson and K. Charlie Lakin found that "prior satisfaction with institutional care and reservations about community care in time turns into satisfaction

---

[233] Ricci v. Patrick, 544 F.3d 8, 21 (1st Cir. 2008), cert. denied, 129 S. Ct. 1907 (2009).

with community settings for the majority of families." These systematic findings have been replicated in the studies of implementation of particular deinstitutionalization decrees. These studies concluded that many parents initially opposed deinstitutionalization because they believed that their children could not benefit from community services but ultimately found that their children flourished in the community. These parents have often become vigorous advocates of deinstitutionalization.

Nor have all unions followed AFSCME's lead in opposing **deinstitutionalization**. The Service Employees International Union (SEIU), for example, filed an amicus brief supporting Massachusetts's decision to close Fernald, and it and its locals have served as plaintiffs in a number of *Olmstead* cases. Not coincidentally, it is the SEIU that has had the greatest success in organizing the dispersed workers who provide community-based services. Advocates of deinstitutionalization can build on this alliance with an important and dynamic part of the labor movement.

Bagenstos, *Past and Future of Deinstitutionalization, supra.* How ought a court presiding over *Olmstead* litigation to address these sorts of conflicts? As the quoted excerpt suggests, these conflicts can arise at a number of different points in an *Olmstead* litigation: at the time of class certification (as in *Ligas*); in determining whether to allow parents or guardians who oppose deinstitutionalization to intervene (see, for example, *Benjamin v. Dep't of Public Welfare*, 432 Fed.Appx. 94 (3d Cir.2011) (affirming denial of intervention at liability stage to parents who objected to deinstitutionalization of their children, because the plaintiff class was limited to those who did not oppose deinstitutionalization: "The current parties have deliberately defined the class and the relief sought so that Intervenors' right to choose institutional treatment would not be affected."); and *Benjamin v. Dep't of Public Welfare*, 701 F.3d 938 (3d Cir.2012) (reversing denial of intervention to objecting parents at the remedy stage of the same case, because the settlement agreement between class plaintiffs and the state would as affect the intervenors' interests)); and in determining whether a deinstitutionalization remedy itself violates *Olmstead* (as in *Ricci*). Based on what you know, did the courts in *Ligas*, *Benjamin*, and *Ricci* properly resolve these questions?

Recall that *Olmstead* presumptively requires the state to serve an individual in a community-based setting only if "the transfer from institutional care to a less restrictive setting is not opposed by the affected individual." How ought this standard to take account of guardianship? When an individual with a disability is placed under guardianship, and the individual does not object to community treatment but the guardian does object, whose preference should control?

Olmstead itself spoke of the choice of the "patient[ ],"[197] and it relied on regulations that refer to the choice of the "individual with a disability"[198]—as well as the language in the preamble to those regulations which states that "persons with disabilities

---

[197] Olmstead, 527 U.S. at 602.

[198] 28 C.F.R. §35.130(e)(1) (2012).

must be provided the option of declining to accept a particular accommodation."[199] These sources would support the argument that it is the choice of the individual with a disability herself that should control, but one could argue to the contrary that they should be interpreted in light of the background state-law principle that guardians can make decisions for their wards. The courts have not definitively resolved this question, though a number have suggested that it is the guardian's choice that matters.[200]

Bagenstos, *Past and Future of Deinstitutionalization, supra.* For a provocative argument that guardianship itself at least presumptively violates *Olmstead*, see Leslie Salzman, *Rethinking Guardianship (Again): Substituted Decision Making as a Violation of the Integration Mandate of Title II of the Americans with Disabilities Act*, 81 U. Colo. L. Rev. 157 (2010).

2. CIVIC PARTICIPATION

Nelson v. Miller

United States Court of Appeals for the Sixth Circuit, 1999.
170 F.3d 641.

■ BATCHELDER, CIRCUIT JUDGE.

This class action was brought on behalf of all blind registered voters in the State of Michigan who cannot independently read or mark election ballots provided for them. The Plaintiffs claim that the Michigan Constitution provides all Michigan voters with a right to "secrecy of the ballot." Because the Secretary of State, according to Plaintiffs, is "the Chief Election Officer for the State of Michigan ha[ving] the ultimate responsibility to administer the Michigan Election Law," and has refused to implement methods by which the Plaintiffs could cast their votes unassisted by another person,[1] they argue that she is violating their rights under the Americans with Disabilities Act of 1990 and the Rehabilitation Act of 1973. Plaintiffs request that she be permanently enjoined from failing to implement such methods in the future.

[W]e hold that Plaintiffs' complaint must be dismissed because Plaintiffs can state no facts tending to establish that they are being denied any right in violation of the ADA and the RA.

[T]he Michigan Constitution provides:

The legislature shall enact laws to regulate the time, place and manner of all nominations and elections, except as otherwise

---

[199] *Id.* §35 app. B (Guidance on ADA Regulation on Nondiscrimination on the Basis of Disability in State and Local Government Services, Originally Published July 26, 1991).

[200] *See, e.g.,* People First of Tenn. v. Clover Bottom Developmental Ctr., 753 F. Supp.2d 701, 713-15 (M.D. Tenn.2010); Ligas v. Maram, No. 05 C 4331, 2010 WL 1418583 (N.D. Ill. Apr. 7, 2010).

[1] Plaintiffs' complaint alleges the existence of "inexpensive technologies that are currently in commercial use which permit persons who are blind to read and mark ballots without involving a third party, including brailed ballot overlays or templates, taped text or phone-in voting systems."

> provided in this constitution or in the constitution and laws of
> the United States. The legislature shall enact laws to preserve
> the purity of elections, to preserve the *secrecy of the ballot*, to
> guard against abuses of the elective franchise, and to provide
> for a system of voter registration and absentee voting.

Mich.Const. art. 2, § 4 (emphasis added). Appellants claim that this
creates a constitutional right to secrecy of the ballot, or a "secret voting
program," for all of Michigan's voters. This is a legal conclusion, rather
than a factual allegation, which this Court need not accept as true for
purposes of reviewing the district court's 12(b)(6) dismissal.

> Michigan statutory law provides:

> When at an election an elector shall state that the elector
> cannot mark his or her ballot, the elector shall be assisted in
> the marking of his or her ballot by 2 inspectors of election. If
> an elector is . . . disabled on account of blindness, the elector
> may be assisted in the marking of his or her ballot by a
> member of his or her immediate family or by a person over 18
> years of age designated by the blind person.

Mich.Comp.Laws Ann. § 168.751. Because the Secretary of State
refused their request to implement a system by which blind voters could
vote without third-party assistance of their choosing, Appellants allege
that she has denied Michigan's blind voters the benefit of complete
secrecy of the ballot enjoyed by Michigan's sighted voters. Accordingly,
Appellants claim that the State has violated the ADA and RA by
"exclud[ing them] from participation in or . . . den[ying them] the
benefits of" the State's constitutionally mandated "secret voting
program."

> [A]ppellants' claim [c]an be stated another way: the special benefits
extended to Appellants under Mich.Comp.Laws Ann. § 168.751 do not
comply with the constitutionally required benefits to which they are
entitled, and which sighted voters receive, under Mich. Const. art. 2,
§ 4. For such a claim to be true, Appellants essentially must show that
the Michigan legislature, by providing blind voters with third-party
voting aid, rather than unassisted voting aid, has violated the Michigan
Constitution's mandate that it "enact laws to . . . preserve the secrecy
of the ballot," Mich.Const. art. 2, § 4. The question, then, is whether the
Michigan Constitution requires more secrecy than the Michigan
legislature has provided for in Mich.Comp.Laws Ann. § 168.751.

> The Michigan Supreme Court, if faced with this question, certainly
could interpret the language of Article 2, § 4, as requiring the state
legislature to modify its election laws when the technology becomes
available that would allow blind voters to exercise their voting rights
without third-party assistance. Not only might the text of Article 2, § 4,
support such a reading, but so also could the following Constitutional
Convention Comment made concerning Article 2, § 4:

> This is a version of Sec. 8, Article III, of the present [1908]
> constitution and vests in the legislature the full authority over
> election administration, subject to other provisions of this
> constitution and to the U.S. constitution and laws. The
> legislature is specifically directed to enact corrupt practices
> legislation.

The provision regarding the secrecy of the ballot is designed to insure that in the future the legislature will be empowered to adopt any new techniques of casting and recording voter choices, so long as the secrecy of the ballot is preserved.

Mich.Comp.Laws Ann., Constitution of 1963, art. 2, § 4 (Convention Comment). The court could just as easily, however, interpret the "secrecy of the ballot" requirement of Article 2, § 4, as being satisfied by the present system of allowing blind voters the assistance of a person of their choosing. Article 2, § 4 of the Michigan Constitution clearly vests in the legislature the power to enact the laws to preserve the undefined "secrecy of the ballot;" as the Comment notes, Article 2, § 4 thus empowers the legislature to interpret how best to do the job. Between the two plausible outcomes we are inclined to conclude, for the following reasons, that the Michigan Supreme Court would find that the statute fulfills the requirements of Article 2, § 4.

First, no Michigan court has ever found that Mich.Comp.Laws. Ann. § 168.751 violates the state constitution's mandate that the legislature "preserve the secrecy of the ballot." Older cases, however, have mentioned that permitting blind voters to have someone aid them in voting is perfectly in keeping with the purpose of Article 2, § 4's predecessor (Mich.Const. art. 7, § 6 (1850)), which was preserving "the purity of elections." See, e.g., Common Council v. Rush, 82 Mich. 532, 46 N.W. 951, 953 (1890) ("The secrecy of the ballot is the great safeguard to the purity of elections.") In fact in *Rush*, a voting law which was silent on the issue of third-party assistance for disabled voters was specifically interpreted to permit such assistance so as to avoid having to strike the voting law down as unconstitutional, which the court indicated it would have had to do had it been unable to read such assistance into the act. This holding certainly indicates to us that third-party voting assistance to the blind has, at least in the past, been seen by the Michigan Supreme Court as complying with the requirements of the Michigan Constitution, rather than violating them.

In *Ellis ex rel. Reynolds v. May*, 99 Mich. 538, 58 N.W. 483 (1894), the Supreme Court of Michigan addressed the constitutionality of a statute that allowed voters, who could not read English or because of physical disability could not mark their ballots, to have assistance in marking their ballots. Specifically, the statute required those who could not read English to take an oath swearing their illiteracy before they would be permitted to receive assistance in marking their ballots; the respondent contended that this requirement was unconstitutional because it placed an unreasonable restriction upon the right to vote. Affirming the constitutionality of the statute, the court said, "The regulations are to preserve the purity of the election, and we see no constitutional objections to them as prescribed by the act." It further stated:

> The law aims to secure secrecy in the ballot, and does not attempt to disenfranchise any voter. At the expense of this secrecy, and in order to enable voters who are physically incapacitated from marking their ballots, the law provides a method for such aid, as well as to those who cannot read the English language. The law does not deprive these voters of any right, but rather secures to them aid in voting intelligently; it

is plain and simple in its provisions. Every voter, however illiterate or however much incapacitated physically, has a method pointed out by which he may exercise his right of franchise. The law does not shut off any class of voters from the ballot, and, we think, was designed by the legislature to accomplish the purpose specified in the constitution.

Thus, whatever the phrase "secrecy of the ballot" in the Michigan Constitution means, the only Michigan precedent we could find even tangentially addressing the issue indicates at least a previous understanding that third-party assistance to blind voters was within its ambit.

Second, we note that the Michigan Supreme Court has "long . . . held that a statute comes clothed in a presumption of constitutionality." [A]ccordingly, when the issue could reasonably go either way, the directive we read in the Michigan Supreme Court's precedent is to presume constitutionality.

Third, and closely associated with the second point, is that it appears to us that the state legislature has clearly interpreted Article 2, § 4 as not meaning "absolute secrecy" in all instances. We note that Article 2, § 4 is a direct mandate to the state legislature, and that the legislators have all sworn to uphold Michigan's Constitution, see Mich. Const. art. 11, § 1. The respect that the Michigan Supreme Court has declared is due "to the wisdom, the integrity, and the patriotism of the legislative body," leads us to presume that the legislature, when enacting the predecessor to Mich.Comp.Laws Ann. § 168.751 over 100 years ago and continuing to recodify and amend it throughout this century, see Mich.Comp.Laws Ann. § 168.751 (Historical Note) (West 1989) (mentioning the numerous previous codifications of the statute's precursors), has believed that the statutory provision satisfies the mandate contained within Article 2, § 4 and its predecessors, and thus that it interprets the phrase "secrecy of the ballot" in Article 2, § 4 as not meaning "absolute secrecy from everyone in all instances." Our understanding of the state legislature's interpretation of Article 2, § 4 is further supported by the legislature's amendment in 1996 of Mich.Comp.Laws Ann. § 168.786. That section, at least since 1955, has stated in pertinent part, "The operating of the voting machine by the elector while voting shall be secret and obscure, from all other persons, except as provided by this act in cases of assisted electors"; the 1996 amendment added to the exception for assisted electors a minor child accompanying an elector into the voting booth. Clearly, the legislature does not contemplate the constitutional requirement of secrecy as being absolute.

[III]. CONCLUSION

For these reasons we conclude that the Appellants are not being denied their state constitutional right to "secrecy of the ballot" as that right has, up to this point, been understood by those charged with interpreting Michigan's constitution. We find no clear indication that the Michigan Supreme Court, if faced with the question, would hold otherwise. We therefore conclude that and Secretary of State of Michigan, by refusing to provide Appellants with voting assistance other than that already extended to them under Mich.Comp.Laws Ann. § 168.751, does not discriminate against them in violation of the ADA and/or the RA. Accordingly, we AFFIRM the judgment of the district court dismissing the complaint.

NOTES ON NELSON V. MILLER

1.   The Access/Content Distinction. The *Nelson* court treats the relevant question as whether the plaintiffs are "being denied their state constitutional right to 'secrecy of the ballot' as that right has, up to this point, been understood by those charged with interpreting Michigan's constitution." But why is that the relevant question? The plaintiffs alleged violations of the ADA and the Rehabilitation Act, not of state law. These federal statutes specifically regulate state conduct. They do not, by their terms, permit a state to invoke state law as a defense. Any such defense would be inconsistent with the statutory requirement that states must make reasonable modifications to rules, policies, and practices in order to avoid discriminating. Why, then, does the court treat the state's compliance with *state* law as dispositive of the plaintiffs' *federal*-law claims? (After the Sixth Circuit's decision in *Nelson*, Congress adopted the Help America Vote Act, which authorized grants to states to make polling places accessible to, among others, "the blind and visually impaired, in a manner that provides the same opportunity for access and participation (including privacy and independence) as for other voters." 42 U.S.C. § 15421(b)(1).)

The court's opinion applies a form of the access/content distinction. The court first identifies the right to which everyone is entitled under state law, and then it asks whether the challenged practices deny people with disabilities access to that right. As in all cases in which the access/content distinction is applied, how the relevant right is described makes all the difference. Looking to the broad statements in the Michigan Constitution regarding the "secrecy of the ballot," the plaintiffs described the relevant right as the right to cast a secret ballot. But the court rejects that characterization. Just as the *Choate* Court stated that the Medicaid Act provides not "adequate health care" generally but instead the specific services set forth in the Tennessee's Medicaid plan, the *Nelson* court states that Michigan law provides not "secrecy of the ballot" generally but rather the specific voting conditions prescribed under the state statutes. Is the court's analysis consistent with the requirement that states must sometimes modify their existing rules and practices?

2.   Physical Accessibility Requirements for Public Buildings. Must a state provide polling places that are physically accessible to people with disabilities? The ADA Title II regulations require that all newly constructed and renovated state and local government facilities (those in which construction or renovation commenced after January 26, 1992) must be "readily accessible to and usable by individuals with disabilities." 28 C.F.R. § 35.151(a), (b). Except in unusual circumstances, those facilities must be completely accessible. To the extent that polling places are in new (or recently renovated) government buildings, then, the statute requires them to be accessible.

Where polling places are in private buildings, or in older public buildings that have not been recently renovated, the Title II regulations impose the more lenient standard of *program accessibility*: "A public entity shall operate each service, program, or activity so that the service, program, or activity, *when viewed in its entirety*, is readily accessible to and usable by individuals with disabilities." 28 C.F.R. § 35.150(a) (emphasis added). This requirement does not necessarily demand that "a public entity . . . make each of its existing facilities accessible to and usable by individuals with disabilities," nor does it "[r]equire a public entity to take any action that would threaten or destroy the historic significance of an historic property" or "to take any action that [the entity] can demonstrate would result in a fundamental alteration in the nature of a service, program, or activity or in undue financial and administrative burdens." *Id.* Is it necessary for *all* polling places to be accessible in order to satisfy this program accessibility requirement? Is it enough that a jurisdiction has at least *one* polling place that is accessible? Must a jurisdiction provide *any* accessible polling places if it offers the opportunity to vote on an absentee ballot?

The Voting Accessibility for the Elderly and Handicapped Act, 42 U.S.C. § 1973ee *et seq.*, imposes detailed accessibility requirements that govern elections for federal office. That statute imposes a general requirement that political subdivisions "assure that all polling places for Federal elections are accessible to handicapped and elderly voters." *Id.* § 1973ee–1(a). If the chief state election officer determines that it is impossible to provide an accessible polling place in a particular precinct, the state must "assure[ ] that any handicapped or elderly voter assigned to an inaccessible polling place, upon advance request of such voter" will either "be assigned to an accessible polling place" or "be provided with an alternative means for casting a ballot on the day of the election." *Id.* § 1973ee–1(b)(2). As noted above, the Help America Vote Act provides for federal grants to enable states to make their polling places accessible. See 42 U.S.C. § 15421.

3. **Voting Qualifications.** To what extent do the ADA and the Rehabilitation Act restrict states' power to establish disability-linked voting qualifications? A number of courts have suggested that those statutes (and perhaps also the Fourteenth Amendment) bar a state from categorically disenfranchising voters with particular mental or physical disabilities without a particularized inquiry into their ability to understand the nature and effect of voting. See *Missouri Protection and Advocacy Services, Inc. v. Carnahan*, 499 F.3d 803 (8th Cir.2007); *Doe v. Rowe*, 156 F.Supp.2d 35 (D.Me.2001). See also *Tennessee v. Lane*, 541 U.S. 509, 524 (2004) ("Congress enacted Title II against a backdrop of pervasive unequal treatment in the administration of state services and programs, including systematic deprivations of fundamental rights. For example, '[a]s of 1979, most States . . . categorically disqualified "idiots" from voting, without regard to individual capacity.' The majority of these laws remain on the books, and have been the subject of legal challenge as recently as 2001.").

Galloway v. Superior Court

United States District Court for the District of Columbia, 1993.
816 F.Supp. 12.

■ JOYCE HENS GREEN, DISTRICT JUDGE.

Individuals with disabilities . . . have been faced with restrictions and limitations, subjected to a history of purposeful unequal treatment, . . . based on characteristics that are beyond the control of such individuals and resulting from stereotypic assumptions not truly indicative of the individual ability of such individuals to participate in, and contribute to, society.

42 U.S.C. § 12101(a)(7) (1992). Declaring that he has been the subject of precisely this type of discrimination, plaintiff Donald Galloway ("plaintiff" or "Galloway") initiated this action, alleging that defendants' policy and practice of refusing to permit persons who are blind to serve on juries of the Superior Court of the District of Columbia ("Superior Court") violates the Rehabilitation Act of 1973 ("Rehabilitation Act"), as amended, 29 U.S.C. § 794, regulations implementing that law. [P]laintiff subsequently filed a second amended complaint, which added a cause of action alleging a violation of Title II of the Americans with Disabilities Act ("ADA"), 42 U.S.C. § 12132.

Presently pending are cross-motions for summary judgment, in which plaintiff seeks, inter alia, declaratory and injunctive relief. Specifically, Galloway asks that the Court declare the policy of excluding blind jurors from Superior Court juries discriminatory, and accordingly enjoin defendants from barring blind persons from participating in the jury pool. Defendant, on the other hand, continues to maintain that blind persons cannot be deemed "qualified" to perform the essential functions of a juror. After consideration of all of the pleadings and for the reasons stated below, plaintiff's motion is granted, and defendants' motion is denied.

BACKGROUND

Plaintiff Galloway is a United States citizen, who lives in and is registered to vote in the District of Columbia. He is also blind and has been blind since the age of sixteen. Presently, he is employed as a Special Assistant and Manager by the District of Columbia Department of Housing and Community Development. Prior to attaining his current position, Galloway received both a Bachelors of Arts degree in sociology and a Masters of Arts in social work. After completing his education, he held a variety of research and supervisory positions in both the private and public sectors. For instance, early in his career, Galloway worked for the University of California, assisting the establishment of a prepaid health care program and health care centers. Later, Galloway served for three years as the Director of the Peace Corps for Jamaica, and then became assistant to the Deputy Director of the Peace Corps. In his current position with the District of Columbia government, as well as in his past positions, Galloway has had "to evaluate facts and people and to weigh evidence and make judgments based on this information."

Like many registered voters in the District of Columbia, Galloway received a notice from the Superior Court indicating that he had been selected for jury duty. Accordingly, accompanied by his guide dog, he duly reported to Superior Court at 8:00 a.m. on the specified date, March 1, 1991. Although he attempted to register for the jury pool, Galloway was informed by Superior Court personnel that he was barred from serving as a juror because he is blind—the official policy of the Superior Court excludes all blind persons from jury service.

DISCUSSION

[A]fter careful consideration of the statutes invoked and the pleadings submitted, it is clear that defendants have violated the Rehabilitation Act [and] the ADA [b]y implementing a policy that categorically excludes blind individuals from jury service.

A. The Rehabilitation Act

"[T]he basic purpose of § 504 . . . is to ensure that handicapped individuals are not denied jobs or other benefits because of the prejudiced attitudes or ignorance of others." *School Bd. of Nassau County, Florida v. Arline*, 480 U.S. 273, 284 (1987). Accordingly, "mere possession of a handicap is not a permissible ground for assuming an inability to function in a particular context." *Southeastern Community College v. Davis*, 442 U.S. 397, 405 (1979). In promulgating the Rehabilitation Act, Congress was concerned not only with "archaic attitudes" held by the general populace, but also with archaic laws. Arline, 480 U.S. at 279.

[D]efendant bases its policy of excluding blind persons from jury service on the assertion that no blind person is ever "qualified" to serve as a juror because he or she is not able to assess adequately the veracity or credibility of witnesses or to view physical evidence and thus cannot participate in the fair administration of justice. Defendants' position is not only profoundly troubling, but clearly violates the Rehabilitation Act.

Without doubt, there exists "the tendency on the part of officialdom to overgeneralize about the handicapped." The policy at issue here is an excellent example of this penchant for overgeneralization. It is furthermore the reason why a court "must look behind the qualifications [invoked by defendants]. To do otherwise reduces the term 'otherwise qualified' and any arbitrary set of requirements to a tautology." Thus, two questions exist: What are the essential attributes of performing jury duty, and can Galloway or other blind persons meet these requirements?

Defendants' policy is based on the assumption that visual observation is an essential function or attribute of a juror's duties. In reaching this conclusion[4], however, defendants failed to examine any studies or review any literature on the ability of blind individuals to serve on juries or the ability of these individuals to assess credibility. Even now, defendants only conclusorily contend that plaintiff "is not capable of performing all of the essential aspects of jury service."

---

[4] The manner in which defendants decided not to permit blind jurors to serve is also disturbing. When questioned how the policy arose, the Clerk of the Superior Court, Frederick B. Beane, Jr. stated:

> Well, the policy came in to [sic] being because I had the question raised by the director of the Special Operations Division regarding service by blind jurors, and I at that time informed him that my policy was that we would not utilize blind jurors—blind persons to serve on the jury.

He added that the decision

> was based on my previous experience in the court, and it may well have been influenced by some information that I had read over the years or have come to know about, but not with any specific document in mind.

Indeed, this conclusion that blind jurors are not qualified appears based on exactly the archaic attitudes and unsubstantiated prejudices Congress wished to eradicate.

However, plaintiff has offered uncontradicted testimony that blind individuals, like sighted jurors, weigh the content of the testimony given and examine speech patterns, intonation, and syntax in assessing credibility. Thus, "[t]he nervous tic or darting glance, the uneasy shifting or revealing gesture is almost always accompanied by auditory correlates[, including inter alia,] clearing the throat, pausing to swallow, voice quavering or inaudibility due to stress or looking downward," Kaiser, Juries, *Blindness and the Juror Function*, 60 Chicago Kent Law Review 191, 200 (1984), and permits a blind juror to make credibility assessments just as the juror's sighted counterparts do.

Interestingly, at least ten states—Oklahoma, California, Virginia, Oregon, Texas, South Carolina, Washington, Massachusetts, Wisconsin, and New York—have enacted statutes that forbid the exclusion of blind persons from jury pools solely because of their disability. Similarly, the United States District Court for the District of Columbia allows blind persons to serve as jurors, if they so elect. In many of these jurisdictions, visual impairment is not a *per se* disqualification, but may result in the exclusion of a blind individual from the jury pool if the case involves a significant amount of physical evidence or if the right to a fair trial is otherwise threatened by that juror's service.

Similarly, in the United States, there are several active judges who are blind. Indeed, it is highly persuasive that Judge David Norman, a blind person, served as a judge on the Superior Court of the District of Columbia and presided over numerous trials where he was the sole trier of fact and had to assess the credibility of the witnesses before him and evaluate the documentation and physical evidence. Defendants have never claimed that "those trials were invalid because [Judge Norman] was blind." It is thus illogical to suggest that all blind persons are unqualified to sit on a jury when a blind judge in the same Superior Court successfully fulfilled those very duties a blind juror would have to discharge. No distinction can be drawn between a blind judge's ability to make factual findings and the abilities of a blind juror.

In addition, the Superior Court admits persons who are deaf to jury panels and has never suggested that simply because they cannot hear, they cannot serve. In fact, the Superior Court accommodates those individuals by providing sign language interpreters. Yet, a deaf juror cannot hear a witness' words and cannot make credibility determinations based on inflection and intonation of voice, but still is able to make the requisite credibility determinations. Defendants obviously recognize deaf individuals' qualifications to serve on a Superior Court jury since no policy excluding deaf jurors exists. Applying the same logic to a blind individual demonstrates that although a blind juror cannot rely on sight, the individual can certainly hear the witness testify, hear the quaver in a voice, listen to the witness clear his or her throat, or analyze the pause between question and answer, then add these sensory impressions to the words spoken and assess the witness' credibility. Defendants' policy toward deaf jurors evidences a lack of prejudice towards those with hearing impairments and demonstrates their ability to look behind archaic stereotypes thrust upon disabled persons; it is thus difficult to fathom why the policy differs toward blind jurors.

Moreover, even if the individual does not initially appear to be "otherwise qualified," it must still be determined whether reasonable accommodation would make the individual otherwise qualified. In the instant case, no accommodation was offered to Galloway or to any other blind person. According to Galloway he was turned away after being expressly informed that blind jurors could not be accommodated. Plaintiff has established that, in many instances, accommodation could indeed result in an "otherwise qualified" individual. As noted above, sign language interpreters are provided to deaf individuals serving on Superior Court juries. A similar service could be employed for blind jurors.[11] With this type of "reasonable accommodation," a blind juror such as plaintiff should be able to serve satisfactorily in most cases.

In addition to the evidence presented showing that visual observation is not necessarily an essential function of a juror, Galloway introduced substantial evidence to support his individual qualifications to serve competently on a jury. Plaintiff's educational and employment history underscores the fact that he can, and does, make credibility determinations daily. Galloway has served in a number of executive positions in the private sector, the federal government, and the state government and is presently responsibly employed by the District of Columbia, one of the defendants herein. In these capacities, Galloway has been called upon to evaluate facts, weigh evidence, and make judgments. He assesses credibility by listening carefully to the content and consistency of a person's speech and pays particular attention to auditory clues: the rhythm of a person's breathing and the sounds of a person moving, for example.

Yet, just as no *per se* rule of exclusion should be employed against blind persons who wish to serve as jurors, no *per se* rule of inclusion should apply either. Plaintiff has never argued that he should be permitted to participate in every trial. Rather, he has consistently conceded that there may be cases in which it would be inappropriate for a blind person to serve as a juror—cases in which there is a substantial amount of documentary evidence, for example—and that the decision as to whether he should be empaneled in any particular case should be left to the Judge, the attorneys, and the *voir dire* process. In many cases, a blind juror can certainly provide competent jury service.

B.   The Americans with Disabilities Act

[H]ere, too, the question under the ADA turns on an individual's qualification to sit on a jury. And once again, defendants' policy that all blind persons cannot not serve on any Superior Court jury is unavailing. For substantially the same reasons as earlier set forth, the Court finds that blindness alone, does not disqualify an individual from

---

[11] An organization called "Metropolitan Washington Ear, Inc." employs "audio describers"—individuals, trained to describe physical movements, dress, and physical settings for the blind. This or a similar service could be utilized in the Superior Court or the attorneys could be reminded to take special care in questioning witnesses to ensure accurate and complete descriptions of exhibits or diagrams. Moreover, if necessary, documentary evidence could be read to a blind juror by a sighted person and physical evidence could be described. In fact, the Library of Congress utilizes a device called a Kurzweil Reading Machine, which translates printed material into audio. Nevertheless, these suggestions are just that, suggestions—because no accommodation was offered to Galloway, the Court takes no position on the reasonableness of any particular accommodation other than to note that solutions are as limitless as a willing imagination can conceive.

serving on many juries. Moreover, with reasonable accommodation, the number of cases for which a blind person could be chosen increases even further. Consequently, the policy of categorical exclusion of all blind persons from Superior Court juries violates the ADA.

[C]ONCLUSION

As the Supreme Court noted in *Powers v. Ohio*:

> Jury service preserves the democratic element of the law, as it guards the rights of the parties and insures continued acceptance of the laws by all the people. . . . It "affords ordinary citizens a valuable opportunity to participate in a process of government, an experience fostering, one hopes, a respect for the law." . . . Indeed, with the exception of voting, for most citizens the honor and privilege of jury duty is their most significant opportunity to participate in the democratic process.

Thus, "the honor and privilege of jury duty" may not be abridged simply because an individual is blind. The Rehabilitation Act and the ADA were enacted to prevent old-fashioned and unfounded prejudices against disabled persons from interfering with those individuals' rights to enjoy the same privileges and duties afforded to all United States citizens.

NOTES ON GALLOWAY V. SUPERIOR COURT

1. **The Law and Public Attitudes.** The year before Judge Green issued her decision in *Galloway*, Senator Alphonse D'Amato recommended that President George H.W. Bush nominate Richard Casey to the United States District Court for the Southern District of New York. Casey, a former Assistant United States Attorney who lost his sight as a result of retinitis pigmentosa, had been a successful lawyer before and after he became blind. But the New York Times editorialized that "[e]ven in this age of increased opportunities for the disabled," Casey's possible nomination "pushes the outer boundaries of what the judicial system can accommodate." Editorial, *A Blind Judge?*, N.Y. Times, Feb. 6, 1992, at A22. The Times explained that "[t]he ability to make eye contact has almost universally been assumed indispensable for the task of trial judging," because a trial judge must assess credibility, detect "illicit attempt[s] at improperly influencing a jury," and "see for himself what impact a trial exhibit, say an inflammatory poster, might have on a viewer." *Id.* How different are these arguments from the ones Judge Green rejects in *Galloway*?

The Times editorial provoked a number of critical letters in response. James Cohen, a clinical professor at the Fordham Law School, wrote that eye contact was "overrated. As a lawyer I have examined hundreds of witnesses and found that most witnesses who lie do so easily with a straight face. Voice, manner of speech and consistency or lack of it are probably more reliable indicators of credibility." Letter, N.Y. Times, Feb. 18, 1992, at A18. Allen Fischer, an attorney in New York, wrote to inform the Times that a judge on the New York Supreme Court (the major trial-level court) was "totally blind," and that "[h]aving tried several complicated cases before Justice [Gilbert] Ramirez in the Supreme Court, as well as numerous cases before him while he was sitting in Family Court, I can assure you that there is nothing that takes place in the courtroom of Justice Ramirez that escapes his attention." Letter, N.Y. Times, Mar. 1, 1992, § 4 at 14. And Judge Ramirez wrote to remind the Times that it had in fact endorsed his "candidacy for a new 14-year term"! Letter, N.Y. Times, Mar. 13, 1992, at A30.

President Bill Clinton ultimately nominated Mr. Casey for the position in 1997, and Casey served as a judge on the Southern District for nearly a decade before he died in 2007. The obituary for Judge Casey that ran in the Times noted that he "had to overcome skeptics when he took on a load of 300 to 400 cases beginning in late 1997," and that "[s]ome questioned whether a blind judge could accurately assess the credibility of a witness he could not see." *Richard Conway Casey, 74, Blind Federal Judge, Dies*, N.Y. Times, Mar. 24, 2007. The obituary did not explain that the Times' editorial board had been among the "some." But it did offer Judge Casey's response: that "truth could be found by following the facts to see if they held together in a coherent, logical way." *Id.* It also noted that Judge Casey "did occasionally swap a trademark case with a colleague because it depended on visual observation." *Id.*

2. Courthouse Accessibility. *Galloway* involved an intentional exclusion of individuals with some disabilities from serving as jurors. But the problem of physically inaccessible courthouses is at least as significant for people with disabilities. Consider this excerpt from the plaintiffs' brief in *Tennessee v. Lane*, 541 U.S. 509 (2004) (which is a principal case in the last section of this chapter):

> The record Congress compiled in developing the ADA makes clear that courthouses throughout the country were inaccessible at the time of the statute's enactment. A Civil Rights Commission report that provided much of the basis for Congress's consideration of the statute declared that seventy-six percent of all state buildings open to the general public were inaccessible to people with disabilities. U.S. Comm'n on Civil Rights, Accommodating the Spectrum of Individual Abilities 39 (1983). Congress had every reason to conclude that courthouses were no exception. Hearings held by congressional committees and by the congressionally designated Task Force on the Rights and Empowerment of Americans with Disabilities discussed inaccessible courthouses and court proceedings in at least eighteen states—including Tennessee.

> Even today, thirteen years after enactment of the ADA, there is ample evidence that the problem of inaccessible courthouses persists in every corner of the Nation. Published studies have identified serious and pervasive denials of accessibility in a number of state court systems. In Tennessee, the state's own commission on the future of its judicial system warned in 1996 that "[f]or persons with physical or mental impairment, the system can be quite literally inaccessible." Comm'n on the Future of the Tenn. Judicial Sys., *supra*, at 31. Similar reports addressing courthouse accessibility in California, Florida, Missouri, New York, Texas, and Washington State have echoed that warning;

those reports have often provided detailed accounts of the barriers faced by people with disabilities who seek to participate in court proceedings.

[T]he United States Department of Justice's published enforcement records [d]emonstrate that the inaccessibility of courthouses is a nationwide problem. On its website, http://www. usdoj.gov/crt/ada/enforce.htm, the Department posts periodic status reports that provide a snapshot of its enforcement activities; it also posts the full text of selected settlement agreements. A review of the posted reports and agreements reveals over 120 instances in forty-one states (including at least six in Tennessee) in which state courts and court proceedings were inaccessible, and the court system agreed to make its facilities and proceedings more accessible only after the federal government intervened (typically in response to a citizen complaint). Given the limitations on the federal government's enforcement resources (and the fact that the Department of Justice's published status reports do not purport to be comprehensive), these enforcement actions likely represent only the tip of the iceberg. But they demonstrate in any event that courthouse inaccessibility is a problem of nationwide scope.

3. TRAVEL FROM PLACE TO PLACE

Kinney v. Yerusalim

United States Court of Appeals for the Third Circuit, 1993.
9 F.3d 1067.

■ ROTH, CIRCUIT JUDGE:

This appeal requires us to determine whether 28 C.F.R. 35.151(e)(1) (1992), issued by the Attorney General pursuant to Section 204 of the Americans with Disabilities Act (the "ADA"), 42 U.S.C. § 12134, requires the City of Philadelphia (the "City") to install curb ramps at intersections when it resurfaces city streets. At issue is whether resurfacing constitutes an "alteration" within the scope of the regulation. The district court held that it does and ordered the City to install curb ramps on those portions of city streets for which resurfacing bids had been taken since January 26, 1992, the effective date of the ADA. On appeal, the City challenges the district court's reading of the term "alteration." Alternatively, it suggests that if resurfacing is, indeed, an alteration, it is entitled to raise an "undue burden" defense under 28 C.F.R. 35.150(a)(3) (1992).

We agree with the district court's interpretation of the regulation and, consequently, we will affirm. Moreover, we agree that the applicability of the "undue burden" defense has been carefully limited to existing facilities and programs. Thus, that defense is not available in the context of alterations.

I.

Plaintiffs are Disabled in Action, a non-profit organization, and twelve individuals with ambulatory disabilities who live and work in

Philadelphia. In their complaint, plaintiffs sought injunctive relief [f]or alleged violations of the ADA. These allegations were based on the City's practice of installing curb cuts only when work on the city streets otherwise affected the curb or sidewalk or when a complete reconstruction of the street was required.

The lack of curb cuts is a primary obstacle to the smooth integration of those with disabilities into the commerce of daily life. Without curb cuts, people with ambulatory disabilities simply cannot navigate the city; activities that are commonplace to those who are fully ambulatory become frustrating and dangerous endeavors. At present, people using wheelchairs must often make the Hobson's choice between travelling in the streets—with cars and buses and trucks and bicycles—and travelling over uncut curbs which, even when possible, may result in the wheelchair becoming stuck or overturning, with injury to both passenger and chair.

The City of Philadelphia has some 2,400 miles of streets, roads and highways. These streets typically consist of three components: a sub-base of stone, covered by a concrete base, finished with a layer of asphalt. For routine maintenance—patching, pothole repairs, and limited resurfacing—the City maintains a crew of roughly 300 people. For more extensive work, including most resurfacing, bids are solicited from outside contractors.

Resurfacing of the streets is done in a variety of ways, affecting different parts of the street structure. Resurfacing at its simplest is "paving," which consists of placing a new layer of asphalt over the old. In other instances, a more complicated process of "milling" is used to ensure proper drainage or contouring of the road. Milling requires the use of heavy machinery to remove the upper 2 to 3 1/2 inches of asphalt. During an ordinary milling and resurfacing job, cracks in the concrete base may be discovered, and, if so, repaired. The most extensive form of resurfacing is "reconstruction," which involves removal and replacement of both the asphalt and the concrete or stone layers.

Whatever the extent of work performed under a contract, the City has certain minimum requirements for resurfacing. Thus, by the City's own specifications, resurfacing requires laying at least 1 1/2 inches of new asphalt, sealing open joints and cracks, and patching depressions of more than one inch. At issue in this appeal are those resurfacings which cover, at a minimum, an entire street from intersection to intersection. Thus, we are not called upon to decide whether minor repairs or maintenance trigger the obligations of accessibility for alterations under the ADA.

At present the City does not include the installation of curb cuts in its milling and resurfacing contracts unless the curb is independently intended to be altered by the scope of the contract. Thus, only those contracts calling for alterations to curbs include curb cuts; contracts for alterations limited to the street surface itself do not.

Plaintiffs brought this class action against Alexander Hoskins, the Commissioner of the Philadelphia Streets Department, and Howard Yerusalim, the Secretary of the Pennsylvania Department of Transportation ("PennDOT"), to compel the installation of curb cuts on all streets resurfaced since the effective date of the ADA.[2] After the parties filed cross-motions for summary judgment, the district court granted plaintiffs' motion, ordering the City to "install curb ramps or slopes on every City street, at any intersection having curbs or other barriers to access, where bids for resurfacing were let after January 26, 1992." The City brought a timely appeal.

[III.]

Title II of the ADA prohibits discrimination in the provision of public services. [C]ongress' concern with physical barriers is apparent in both the history and the text of the legislation. For example, the findings section of the Act recounts:

(2) historically, society has tended to isolate and segregate individuals with disabilities . . . ;

(3) discrimination against individuals with disabilities persists in such critical areas as . . . transportation . . . and access to public services;

(5) individuals with disabilities continually encounter various forms of discrimination, including . . . the discriminatory effects of architectural, transportation and communication barriers. . . .

42 U.S.C. § 12101. These general concerns led to a particular emphasis on the installation of curb cuts. The House Report for the legislation noted that "[t]he employment, transportation, and public accommodation sections of this Act would be meaningless if people who use wheelchairs were not afforded the opportunity to travel on and between the streets." H.Rep.No.485, 101st Cong., 2d Sess., pt. 2, at 84 (1990), reprinted in 1990 U.S.C.C.A.N. 267, 367. As such, "under this title, local and state governments are required to provide curb cuts on public streets." *Id.*

The Act itself does not set forth implementing standards, but rather directs the Attorney General to do so. 42 U.S.C. § 12134(a). As guidance, Congress directed that the regulations be consistent both with the ADA and with the coordination regulations issued by the Department of Health, Education, and Welfare under Section 504 of the Rehabilitation Act of 1973, 29 U.S.C. § 794, concerning nondiscrimination by recipients of federal financial assistance. 42 U.S.C. § 12134(b). These regulations are now codified at 28 C.F.R. pt. 41 (1992). With regard to program accessibility in existing facilities and communications, Congress directed that the regulations be consistent with the Department of Justice's Section 504 regulations for federally conducted activities. See 28 C.F.R. pt. 39 (1992).

Following this mandate, the Department of Justice issued regulations maintaining the previously established distinction between existing facilities, which are covered by 28 C.F.R. 35.150, and new construction and alterations, which are covered by 28 C.F.R. 35.151. With limited exceptions, the regulations do not require public entities to retrofit existing facilities immediately and completely. Rather, a flexible concept of accessibility is employed, and entities are generally excused

---

[2]   Plaintiffs and defendant Yerusalim entered into a stipulation of settlement, requiring the installation of curb ramps at locations resurfaced by PennDOT since January 26, 1992. The district court approved the agreement. Defendant Yerusalim is not a party to this appeal.

from making fundamental alterations to existing programs and bearing undue financial burdens. 28 C.F.R. 35.150(a) & (b). In contrast, the regulations concerning new construction and alterations are substantially more stringent. When a public entity independently decides to alter a facility, it "shall, to the maximum extent feasible, be altered in such a manner that the altered portion of the facility is readily accessible to and usable by individuals with disabilities." 28 C.F.R. 35.151(b). This obligation of accessibility for alterations does not allow for non-compliance based upon undue burden.

Consistent with the emphasis on architectural barriers, the installation of curb cuts is specifically given priority in both the "existing facilities" and the "new constructions and alterations" sections of the regulations. Streets are considered existing facilities under the regulations,[3] and, as such, they are subject to the more lenient provisions of § 35.150. However, because of the importance attributed to curb cuts, the regulations direct public entities to fashion a transition plan for existing facilities, containing a "schedule for providing curb ramps or other sloped areas where pedestrian walks cross curbs, giving priority to walkways serving entities covered by the Act." 28 C.F.R. 35.150(d)(2). These changes must be completed by January 26, 1995. 28 C.F.R. 35.150(c).

The existence of a transition plan for the installation of curb cuts on existing streets does not, however, negate the City's obligations under § 35.151, governing alterations. In addition to the general provision in subpart (b), § 35.151 has a second subpart addressed solely to the installation of curb ramps. This subpart provides that when a public entity undertakes to construct new streets or to alter existing ones, it shall take that opportunity to install curb ramps.

> Newly constructed or altered streets, roads, and highways must contain curb ramps or other sloped areas at any intersection having curbs or other barriers to entry from a street level pedestrian walkway.

28 C.F.R. 35.151(e). The City does not dispute the literal requirement that the regulation mandates the installation of curb cuts when the City "alters" a street. The City does, however, protest the notion that the resurfacing of a street constitutes an "alteration."

Subpart (e) does not explicitly define "alteration," either in general or as applied in particular instances. Our focus here is the specific application of the general provision in subpart (b) (alterations to existing facilities) to one subject in subpart (e) (streets). We will look first to subpart (b) for guidance:

> Alteration. Each facility or part of a facility altered by, on behalf of, or for the use of a public entity in a manner that affects or could affect the usability of the facility or part of the facility shall, to the maximum extent feasible, be altered in such a manner that the altered portion of the facility is readily accessible to and usable by individuals with disabilities, if the alteration was commenced after January 26, 1992.

---

[3] The regulations define "facility" to include "all or any portion of . . . roads, walks, [or] passageways." 28 C.F.R. 35.104. See also 28 C.F.R. pt. 35, app. A.

28 C.F.R. 35.151(b). In addition, subpart (c) provides that alterations made in conformity with the Americans with Disabilities Act Accessibility Guidelines for Buildings and Facilities (the "ADAAG") or with the Uniform Federal Accessibility Standards (the "UFAS") shall be deemed to comply with the requirements of this section. Both guidelines provide technical and engineering specifications. The ADAAG definition of "alteration" is substantially the same as that in the regulation: "a change to a building or facility . . . that affects or could affect the usability of the building or facility or part thereof." 28 C.F.R. pt. 36, app.A. It continues: "[n]ormal maintenance . . . [is] not [an] alteration[ ] unless [it] affect[s] the usability of the building or facility." *Id.*

These provisions lead one to the conclusion that an "alteration" within the meaning of the regulations is a change that affects the usability of the facility involved. If we then read the "affects usability" definition into subpart (e), the regulation serves the substantive purpose of requiring equal treatment: if an alteration renders a street more "usable" to those presently using it, such increased utility must also be made fully accessible to the disabled through the installation of curb ramps.

Subpart (e) effectively unifies a street and its curbs for treatment as interdependent facilities. If a street is to be altered to make it more usable for the general public, it must also be made more usable for those with ambulatory disabilities. At the time that the City determines that funds will be expended to alter the street, the City is also required to modify the curbs so that they are no longer a barrier to the usability of the streets by the disabled. This interpretation helps to implement the legislative vision, for Congress felt that it was discriminatory to the disabled to enhance or improve an existing facility without making it fully accessible to those previously excluded.

Although there is limited analysis of the "alterations" sections of Title II, the discussion of the parallel provision in Title III (addressing public accommodations) is helpful in our analysis here.[6] In the context of Title III, Congress' discussion of "affecting usability" focused on the "primary function" of a facility. "Areas containing primary functions refer to those portions of a place of public accommodations where significant goods, services, facilities, privileges, advantages or accommodations are provided." H.Rep.No.485, 101st Cong., 2d Sess., pt. 2, at 112 (1990), reprinted in 1990 U.S.C.C.A.N. 445, 486. For example, "the path of travel[,] . . . bathrooms, telephones, and drinking fountains [must be] . . . readily accessible to and usable by individuals with disabilities." Id. at 394.

Thus, while Congress chose not to mandate full accessibility to existing facilities, it required that subsequent changes to a facility be undertaken in a non-discriminatory manner. The use of such changes must be made available to all. The emphasis on equal treatment is

---

[6] Like Title II, Title III bears the distinction between existing and new or altered facilities. Congress intended that the provisions of both titles be read consistently. The House Report states "The Committee intends . . . that the forms of discrimination prohibited by [Title II] be identical to those set out in applicable provisions of Titles I and III of this legislation." H.Rep.No.485, 101st Cong., 2d Sess., pt. 2, at 84 (1990), reprinted in 1990 U.S.C.C.A.N. 267, 367.

furthered, as well, by an expansive, remedial construction of the term "usability." "Usability should be broadly defined to include renovations which affect the use of a facility, and not simply changes which relate directly to access." H.Rep.No.485, 101st Cong., 2d Sess., pt. 3, at 64 (1990), reprinted in 1990 U.S.C.C.A.N. 445, 487.

With this directive, we must now determine whether resurfacing a street affects its usability. Both physically and functionally, a street consists of its surface; from a utilitarian perspective, a street is a two-dimensional, one-plane facility. As intended, a street facilitates smooth, safe, and efficient travel of vehicles and pedestrians—in the language above, this is its "primary function."

As such, we can only agree with the district court that resurfacing a street affects it in ways integral to its purpose. As discussed above, "resurfacing" involves more than minor repairs or maintenance. At a minimum, it requires the laying of a new asphalt bed spanning the length and width of a city block. The work is substantial, with substantial effect. As the district court described in its opinion granting plaintiffs' motion for summary judgment:

> Resurfacing makes driving on and crossing streets easier and safer. It also helps to prevent damage to vehicles and injury to people, and generally promotes commerce and travel. The surface of a street is the part of the street that is "used" by both pedestrians and vehicular traffic. When that surface is improved, the street becomes more usable in a fundamental way.

[IV.]

As a final argument, the City contends that, even if resurfacing is an "alteration" requiring the installation of curb cuts, it is entitled to assert an "undue burden" defense excusing compliance. There is no general undue burden defense in the ADA. Rather, following the Section 504 regulations for program access in existing facilities, as Congress intended, the ADA regulations provide for the defense only in limited circumstances. For example, § 35.150(a)(3), governing "existing facilities," excuses a public entity from taking "any action that it can demonstrate would result in a fundamental alteration in the nature of a service, program, or activity or in undue financial and administrative burdens."

As discussed above, there are logical reasons for the distinction between existing and new or altered facilities. Allowance of an undue burden defense for existing facilities serves as recognition that modification of such facilities may impose extraordinary costs. New construction and alterations, however, present an immediate opportunity to provide full accessibility. Congress recognized the competing social interests at stake: "While the integration of people with disabilities will sometimes involve substantial short-term burdens, both financial and administrative, the long-range effects of integration will benefit society as a whole." H.Rep.No.485, 101st Cong., 2d Sess., pt. 3, at 50 (1990), reprinted in 1990 U.S.C.C.A.N. 445, 473. Balancing these interests, Congress acknowledged the existence of an undue burden defense for existing facilities but clearly warned, "[n]o other limitation should be implied in other areas."

The City acknowledges that the defense is not available for alterations. Nonetheless, it makes a last-ditch attempt at characterizing a street and its curbs as separate facilities. As such, a curb would remain an existing facility susceptible to the "undue burden" defense even while the street that it abuts is being altered. [T]he express language of § 35.151(e) refutes this reasoning. That section requires the installation of curb ramps if a street is altered. When the City decides that funds are available for the alteration of the street, the City must now understand that such a determination is to be made with the awareness that subpart (e) also requires alteration of the curbs. Thus, once the City undertakes to resurface a street, the accompanying curbs are no longer to be considered as existing facilities, subject to the "undue burden" defense of § 35.150(a)(3). They are now, pursuant to the language of subpart (e), incorporated with a facility under alteration, pursuant to § 35.151, so that the "undue burden" defense is no longer available.

V.

For the foregoing reasons, we find that resurfacing of the city streets is an alteration within the meaning of 28 C.F.R. 35.151(b) which must be accompanied by the installation of curb cuts under 28 C.F.R. 35.151(e). We will affirm the decision of the district court.

NOTES ON *KINNEY V. YERUSALIM*

1. **The Competing Interests.** *Kinney* presents a conflict between two interests of great importance. One is the interest of wheelchair and scooter users in living in the world. Without curb cuts, many people with disabilities will be unable (absent great effort) to take advantage of the life of the community. But the other interest is also weighty—the interest of a self-governing municipality in choosing how best to allocate scarce resources for the good of all of the municipality's residents. And the cost of accessibility can be significant. Boston Globe columnist Thomas Oliphant, relating criticisms raised by Philadelphia's then-Mayor Edward Rendell, argued in response to *Kinney* that "[i]t's one thing to vigorously implement the Americans with Disabilities Act, but it's ridiculous to require curb cuts and ramps at all 80,000 intersections in Philadelphia next year. The cost, about $140 million, is three times this year's city budget for all street improvements." Thomas Oliphant, *A Mayor's Message*, Boston Globe, Apr. 20, 1994, at 15.

How ought these interests to be weighed against one another? To be sure, Philadelphia brought some of the $140 million cost on itself: If the city had complied with the ADA and constructed curb cuts at the same time it was resurfacing the streets, it would not have had to go back and tear up the streets a second time, incurring additional cost, to place the curb cuts. But the fact is that "[m]ore money for curb ramps has to come from somewhere." Ross Sandler & David Schoenbrod, Democracy By Decree: What Happens When Courts Run Government 43 (2003). As Professors Sandler and Schoenbrod note, New York City was already spending $32 million each year on curb cuts at the time the ADA was adopted. "With the same money," they observe, "the New York City Department of Transportation could annually fill every pothole in the streets, thereby preventing the accidents and injuries they cause." *Id.* at 43–44. How ought courts to assess such "question[s] of priorities," *id.*? Professors Sandler and Schoenbrod argue that Congress is to blame for adopting a general rule requiring accessibility that requires the states to fund it and (in part as a result) is inattentive to the necessary tradeoffs.

But is that right? Absent the ADA, do we believe that the states would take appropriate account of the interests of people with disabilities? Professors Sandler and Schoenbrod seem to assume that people with disabilities can fend for themselves in local pluralist bargaining. How does the widespread paternalism toward people with disabilities affect that assumption? Perhaps the charitable feelings toward people with disabilities will lead local governments to overvalue their interests in allocating public funds; perhaps, however, those feelings will lead local governments to believe that charitable maintenance is more important for people with disabilities than what Professor tenBroek called "the right to live in the world." Jacobus tenBroek, The Right to Live in the World: The Disabled in the Law of Torts, 54 Cal. L. Rev. 841 (1966).

2.   The ADA and Public Transportation. In the years leading up to the enactment of the ADA, many disability rights activists made access to public transportation a top priority issue. See generally To Ride the Public's Buses: The Fight that Built a Movement (Mary Johnson & Barrett Shaw, eds., 2001). In the 1980s, the federal Department of Transportation issued regulations to implement Section 504 of the Rehabilitation Act. Those regulations required recipients of federal funds to make their mass transit systems accessible, but they limited the requirement in two ways: (1) they permitted transit systems to satisfy the requirement by making their mainstream services accessible or by providing a separate accessible paratransit service, at their option; and (2) they gave transit systems whose accessibility expenditures exceeded 3% of their operating costs a safe harbor from further obligations to make their services accessible. The disability rights organization ADAPT (which then stood for Americans Disabled for Accessible Public Transportation, and now stands for Americans Disabled for Attendant Programs Today) sued. In *Americans Disabled for Accessible Public Transp. v. Skinner*, 881 F.2d 1184 (3d Cir.1989) (*en banc*), the Third circuit upheld the paratransit option regulation but invalidated the 3% safe harbor.

The ADA responded to the disputes over the application of disability discrimination principles to public transportation by including a number of transportation-specific provisions. These provisions require *both* that transit systems take steps toward making their mainstream services accessible *and* that they provide paratransit. As for mainstream services, the statute provides that all new buses, subway cars, and light rail cars must be "readily accessible to and usable by individuals with disabilities, including individuals who use wheelchairs." 42 U.S.C. § 12142(a). When a public transportation system buys or leases a used vehicle, it must "make[ ] demonstrated good faith efforts" to purchase or lease one "that is readily accessible to and usable by individuals with disabilities, including individuals who use wheelchairs." *Id.* § 12142(b). And except for historic vehicles, any vehicle that is remanufactured to extend its life for five or more years must "to the maximum extent feasible," be "readily accessible to and usable by individuals with disabilities, including individuals who use wheelchairs." *Id.* § 12142(c). The statute also requires newly constructed transit facilities to be "readily accessible to and usable by individuals with disabilities, including individuals who use wheelchairs." *Id.* § 12146. When transit systems make physical alterations to their facilities, those alterations must be designed so that, "to the maximum extent feasible, the altered portions of the facility are readily accessible to and usable by individuals with disabilities, including individuals who use wheelchairs." *Id.* § 12147(a). And systems were required to make their "key stations" readily accessible "as soon as practicable but in no event later than the last day of the 3-year period beginning on July 26, 1990," unless the time was extended by the Secretary of Transportation. *Id.* § 12147(b). The statute also imposes a general requirement of program accessibility on transit programs, and it provides that, within five years of the effective date of the statute, at least one car per train (that contains two or more cars) must be accessible. *Id.* § 12148. The statute imposes similar, if more detailed, rules to govern intercity and commuter rail accessibility. *Id.* § 12162.

As for paratransit, the statute requires public transit systems to provide "paratransit and other special transportation services to individuals with disabilities, including individuals who use wheelchairs, that are sufficient to provide to such individuals a level of service (1) which is comparable to the level of designated public transportation services provided to individuals without disabilities using such system; or (2) in the case of response time, which is comparable, to the extent practicable, to the level of designated public transportation services provided to individuals without disabilities using such system." *Id.* § 12143(a).

Some critics charge that the ADA's transportation provisions harm public transit systems by imposing unfunded mandates that require those systems to cut back services. One commentator, for example, reports an estimate that "in the mid-1990s thirty-one percent of American transit agencies reduced service, raised fares or laid off employees in order to pay costs imposed by the Americans with Disabilities Act." Michael Lewyn, *Campaign of Sabotage: Big Government's War Against Public Transportation*, 26 Colum. J. Envtl. L. 259, 278 (2001). Assuming this estimate is correct, is it a problem? Again, even if one grants that paying for accessibility requires tradeoffs, do we believe that state and local governments were giving adequate and appropriate consideration to the interests of people with disabilities before the enactment of the ADA?

4. ZONING

Wisconsin Community Services, Inc. v. City of Milwaukee

United States Court of Appeals for the Seventh Circuit, *en banc*, 2006.
465 F.3d 737.

■ RIPPLE, CIRCUIT JUDGE.

Wisconsin Community Services ("WCS"), a provider of treatment to mentally ill patients, brought this action under Title II of the

Americans with Disabilities Act ("ADA") and section 504 of the Rehabilitation Act of 1973. The WCS sought an injunction ordering the City of Milwaukee ("the City") to issue a zoning permit that would allow it to move its mental health clinic to an area of Milwaukee, Wisconsin, where health clinics are permitted only on a case-by-case basis. The district court granted partial summary judgment to WCS, concluding that the ADA and the Rehabilitation Act obligated the City to accommodate the disabilities of WCS' patients by allowing WCS to move to its desired location. For the reasons set forth in this opinion, we reverse the judgment of the district court and remand for proceedings consistent with this opinion.

I

BACKGROUND

[WCS] is a private, non-profit organization that provides a variety of inpatient and outpatient services to individuals afflicted with severe mental illnesses. WCS provides patients, who cannot live alone without substantial assistance, with psychiatric treatment, counseling, medication monitoring, transportation and help in finding housing and employment. A number of WCS' patients have a history of substance abuse, and a majority have had previous run-ins with the criminal justice system; WCS often accepts patient referrals from court-related agencies such as the United States Probation Service. Although WCS staff sometimes will treat patients in their homes, most of WCS' services are administered in a 7,500 square-foot mental health clinic located at 2023 West Wisconsin Avenue in the City of Milwaukee. Originally, WCS shared this facility with other non-profit organizations, but, as its clientele grew, WCS expanded to occupy the entire building. In 1994, at the time of this initial expansion, WCS employed twenty full-time employees and served 250 patients.

By 1998, the staff at WCS' 2023 West Wisconsin Avenue facility had grown to approximately forty full-time employees serving approximately 400 patients. This increase in clients, services and personnel had caused a shortage in space available for employee parking, client treatment, group therapy sessions and other services. Faced with the shortage, WCS at first considered remodeling, but finally concluded that such a project would be too costly and would interfere with client care. WCS then began searching for a new building. Despite having a limited budget, WCS needed a facility that was located in a safe neighborhood and had adequate floor space, parking and access to public transit. After searching for three years, WCS was able to find two buildings that met its criteria. Neither property, unfortunately, was located in a neighborhood zoned for health clinics. Both were in areas where health clinics are permitted only as "special uses" that require issuance of a permit by the Milwaukee zoning authorities.

WCS previously had received this type of special use permit for some of its other facilities. It therefore made an offer of purchase for one of the properties, contingent on obtaining the necessary special use permit from the Milwaukee zoning board. The seller of this property, concerned about this contingency, declined to accept the offer. WCS then abandoned its efforts to purchase that property and instead made a similar contingent offer on the other identified property. This facility was an 81,000 square-foot building located about one mile from its current facility at 3716 West Wisconsin Avenue. The larger facility is located in an area zoned as a "local business district." Milwaukee, Wis.Code § 295–703–1. According to the City Code's "use table," health care clinics, except for nursing homes, are deemed "special uses" for this zone. *Id.* § 295–603–1. Incidentally, the same zone allows foster homes, shelter care facilities, community living arrangements and animal hospitals either as "permitted" or "limited" (no special approval required) uses. *Id.* The seller accepted WCS' offer.

[M]ilwaukee's City Code defines "special use" as "[a] use which is generally acceptable in a particular zoning district but which, because of its characteristics and the characteristics of the zoning district in which it would be located, requires review on a case by case basis to determine whether it should be permitted, conditionally permitted, or denied." Special use designations are instruments of municipal planning that allow city officials to retain review power over land uses that, although presumptively allowed, may pose special problems or hazards to a neighborhood.

In Milwaukee, an applicant for a special use permit must present its plans to the Department of City Development ("the DCD"), where they are reviewed by a plan examiner. If the DCD denies the special use application, the applicant may appeal the decision to the Milwaukee Board of Zoning Appeals ("BOZA"), where the application is reviewed, a public hearing is held and evidence is heard. Consistent with this procedure, WCS submitted a plan to DCD, outlining its intent to relocate the mental health clinic and several of its administrative offices to the new building. The plan stated that WCS would occupy 32,000 out of the 81,000 square feet of space in the building. An additional 12,000 square feet, according to the plan, would be occupied by two existing tenants, a Walgreens pharmacy and an office of the Social Security Administration. The remaining 37,000 square feet, the plan stated, would be rented out for use as office space or for other commercial purposes.

[DCD rejected the plan.] Specifically, DCD expressed concern over the second factor, protection of neighboring property value. It stated that use of the property as a mental health clinic would jeopardize the commercial revitalization that the neighborhood currently was undergoing. WCS, availing itself of its right to administrative review, then appealed the DCD's decision to Milwaukee's BOZA.

On March 22, 2001, BOZA held a hearing on WCS' appeal. [WCS] presented evidence in an effort to refute the perception that the mental health clinic posed a safety threat and would discourage businesses from locating in the neighborhood. This evidence included testimony from a security official who told BOZA that, based on his own investigation, WCS' patients had not been the source of any safety problems in WCS' current neighborhood. WCS also presented letters from its current neighbors to the same effect. Finally, WCS submitted evidence of an award it had received from the National Institute of Justice for exemplary care of previously institutionalized individuals with mental health needs.

BOZA then heard testimony in opposition to the permit. An attorney representing several area businesses testified that opening a mental health clinic that serves a large number of young, unemployed males with histories of mental illness and illegal behavior substantially increases the chance of crime and anti-social behavior in the neighborhood. In a similar vein, a nearby high school voiced its fear that WCS' clients would be riding public transit alongside its "young and vulnerable" students. Additionally, a neighborhood organization encouraged residents to object to WCS' request; it circulated leaflets that argued that the clustering of WCS' clientele "in one location on a daily basis raises a serious risk for the health and well being of people living and working in surrounding neighborhoods."

On May 9, 2001, BOZA voted unanimously to deny WCS' application for a special use permit. The accompanying written decision said only that the proposed use was inconsistent with the considerations set forth in the zoning code. However, several board members orally announced the reasoning behind their decision. One member noted that the "overwhelming" opposition from neighborhood residents convinced him that the WCS clinic would have "a damaging effect upon neighboring business." Another member stated that WCS' clientele, with its large number of convicted criminals, raised "red flags" for local residents. These board members did not think that BOZA had the duty to question the "perceptions" of local residents regarding the possible dangers presented by WCS' patients.

[The district court ordered BOZA to hold another hearing to address whether the ADA and the Rehabilitation Act required an accommodation to the normal zoning criteria. BOZA held that hearing on September 12, 2002.] Jill Fuller, WCS' clinic administrator, was the first to testify. She described the state of overcrowding at WCS' current facility and the effect that these conditions were having on WCS' patients. Individuals with severe mental disabilities, Fuller explained, are particularly sensitive to external stimuli and often have poor social skills. Overcrowding in the common area of WCS' facility—a room described by another WCS administrator as noisy, smoky and packed—created an extremely stressful environment for these patients and caused their symptoms to become more acute. Additionally, Fuller testified that overcrowding compromised the privacy of one-on-one therapy sessions, which represent a primary component of WCS' treatment.

WCS then presented testimony from its executive director, Stephen Swigart. He described the search process under-taken by WCS to find a new facility that, in addition to being of adequate size, would satisfy the clinic's need for a central location, access to public transit, a serviceable floor plan, low renovation costs and a safe neighborhood. Swigart testified that, after being denied the special use permit, WCS had worked with city planners to locate a suitably zoned property, but that its efforts had been unsuccessful. Any potential alternatives, Swigart explained, were either unavailable or too costly.

Finally, WCS presented expert testimony from Dr. Nancy Frank, the Chair and Associate Dean of the Department of Architecture and Urban Planning at the University of Wisconsin-Milwaukee. She opined that locating the mental health clinic at WCS' desired location, 3716 West Wisconsin Avenue, would have a positive rather than an adverse effect on the surrounding neighborhood. Pointing out that a properly zoned health clinic already was located directly across the street from the proposed site, Frank noted that WCS' clinic would be a consistent addition to the neighborhood and encourage commercial uses of a similar nature. In addition, Frank testified that the building at 3716 West Wisconsin Avenue had been mostly vacant for some time. According to Frank, the goal of city planners seeking to revitalize a commercial area should be to fill vacant space as quickly as possible. Frank predicted that relocating WCS and all of its employees to the area would attract businesses such as "restaurants, dry cleaners [and] coffee shops" eager to serve the new influx of professionals. Frank further stated that "[i]t's actually a strategy in urban redevelopment to try to get a good non-profit anchor in an area first because they're often less dependant on having an area that already has a lot of consumer demand, and you can then build on that employee base." When asked about safety concerns, Frank stated that four of the six parole offices in the City of Milwaukee were located in areas zoned for business use. Frank saw no reason why WCS' clinic would present any more of a safety risk than these offices.

BOZA then heard testimony from Michael Murphy, an alderman representing the area in which WCS was seeking to relocate its clinic. Steadfastly opposed to WCS' plans, Alderman Murphy stated that "WCS' thrust to rip an 81,000 square foot building out of the heart of this emerging business district could be fatal to this area." When pressed on whether the new clinic conceivably could bring economic benefits to the neighborhood, Alderman Murphy conceded that the influx of professionals potentially could draw new businesses. He stated, nevertheless, that he objected to the plan because it meant that WCS, as a non-profit, would not pay tax on the space used for its clinic and operations; Alderman Murphy preferred a tax-paying commercial tenant in the space. Notably, the only submission on whether WCS' patients were a safety risk to the community were affidavits from business owners near the proposed site. None of these opinions, however, was supported by actual evidence.

On December 22, 2002, BOZA issued a written decision denying the special use permit to WCS. [WCS challenged that action in the district court, and the court concluded that BOZA had violated the ADA and the Rehabilitation Act.]

II

DISCUSSION

[W]e must decide whether, and to what extent, the Rehabilitation Act and Title II require the City to modify its zoning practices in order to accommodate the needs of the disabled individuals served by WCS.

WCS submits that the City must waive application of its normal special-use criteria for WCS because it has shown that granting the permit will ameliorate overcrowding, a condition that particularly affects its disabled clients. Before accepting this position, however, we must ask whether WCS has satisfied the "necessity" element contained in the Rehabilitation Act as interpreted by [*Alexander v.*] *Choate* and in the Title II regulation, see 28 C.F.R. § 35.130(b)(7). WCS contends that the necessity element is satisfied simply when a modification helps the disabled, regardless of whether it is necessary to alleviate discrimination. Implicit in this position is that the federal accommodation obligation reaches not only rules that create barriers "on the basis of" a person's disability, but also rules that are not disability-based and create obstacles to persons because of some factor unrelated to disability.

[W]ith respect to the Rehabilitation Act, *Choate* held that a modification is "necessary" only when it allows the disabled to obtain benefits that they ordinarily could not have by reason of their disabilities, and not because of some quality that they share with the public generally. The inquiry is the same under the ADA regulation, which asks whether a modification is "necessary to avoid discrimination on the basis of disability." 28 C.F.R. § 35.130(b)(7). Framed by our cases as a causation inquiry, the element is satisfied only when the plaintiff shows that, "but for" his disability, he would have been able to access the services or benefits desired.

On the present record, WCS' inability to meet the City's special use criteria appears due not to its client's disabilities but to its plan to open a non-profit health clinic in a location where the City desired a commercial, taxpaying tenant instead. As far as this record indicates, the City would have rejected similar proposals from non-profit health clinics serving the non-disabled. WCS contends that Title II's accommodation requirement calls, in such a situation, for " 'preferential' treatment and 'is not limited only to lowering barriers created by the disability itself.' " WCS' view, however, is inconsistent with the "necessity" element as it has been defined under the Rehabilitation Act, the FHAA and Title II of the ADA. On this record, because the mental illness of WCS' patients is not the cause-in-fact of WCS' inability to obtain a suitable facility, the program that it seeks modified does not hurt persons with disabilities "by reason of their handicap."

WCS responds that the Supreme Court's decision in *U.S. Airways, Inc. v. Barnett*, 535 U.S. 391 (2002), has overruled the principle, central to previous Title II accommodation decisions, that the proposed modification must be necessary to avoid discrimination on the basis of a disability. In Barnett, a case decided under Title I of the ADA, a U.S. Airways baggage handler injured his back and requested transfer to a mailroom position that recently had become available. U.S. Airways refused because, under its seniority policy, the company was required to award the position to a more senior employee. Recognizing that U.S. Airways' seniority policy must yield, under certain circumstances, to the needs created by the plaintiff's disability, the Supreme Court held that the plaintiff should be permitted to rebut the presumption that his requested modification to the neutral seniority policy was unreasonable.

According to WCS' characterization, in *Barnett*, the seniority policy treated the disabled and non-disabled alike, and it was a non-disability characteristic (seniority) that denied Barnett the job. WCS sees no distinction between *Barnett* and the present case: Just as the plaintiff in *Barnett* was ineligible for the mail room position because of his seniority rather than his disability, WCS was ineligible for a special use permit because it was a non-profit health clinic, not because its clients were disabled. Because the Supreme Court allowed Barnett's claim to go forward, albeit with a heightened burden of persuasion, WCS submits that it has satisfied the necessity element of its accommodation claim.

We cannot accept this argument. *Barnett* and the present case simply deal with different analytical problems. Fairly read, *Barnett* did not deal with the issue of necessity-causality. [R]ather, it dealt with the second question that courts must confront in Title II accommodation cases: whether the accommodation was reasonable. Yet, this element cannot be reached until it has been determined that an accommodation is necessary because a person's disability is the cause for his being denied the service or benefit. As we explained earlier, to satisfy Title II's necessity element, a plaintiff must show that, "but for" its disability, it would have received the ultimate benefit being sought—which, in WCS' case, is a larger facility. The same is true under the Rehabilitation Act. See *Choate*, 469 U.S. at 302. If the City's zoning rules are to be compared to the seniority policy in *Barnett*, WCS must demonstrate that, because of its clients' disabilities, it cannot relocate to a suitable site. Only then will the unmodified policy hurt the disabled on account of their disability. Only then will the modification be "necessary to avoid discrimination on the basis of disability." 28 C.F.R. § 35.130(b)(7).

The district court assumed that the proposed modification could be deemed "necessary" even if the disabilities suffered by WCS' patients were not the cause-in-fact of its inability to find a larger building. The district court failed to apply a "but for" causation standard in determining the necessity element of WCS' accommodation claim. Choosing this course was error in light of the prevailing standards under our case law. We therefore must remand to the district court so that it may afford the parties the opportunity to develop the question of whether WCS has been prevented, because of its clients' disabilities, from locating a satisfactory new facility.

Reversed and Remanded.

■ EASTERBROOK, CIRCUIT JUDGE, concurring.

One question on which the parties have disagreed is whether 28 C.F.R. § 35.130(b)(7), which was promulgated under Title II of the Americans with Disabilities Act, establishes an accommodation requirement in addition to the statutory rules that prohibit disparate treatment and limit disparate impact. The district judge said "yes," the panel said "no," and now the *en banc* court says "yes." Having written the panel's opinion saying "no," I now join the en banc opinion saying "yes," because further consideration has led me to conclude that the right question is what this regulation means rather than what label to attach to its provisions.

The regulation provides:

A public entity shall make reasonable modifications in policies, practices, or procedures when the modifications are necessary to avoid discrimination on the basis of disability, unless the public entity can demonstrate that making the modifications would fundamentally alter the nature of the service, program, or activity.

A proposed accommodation is required only if it is "necessary" to "avoid discrimination". That an alteration in zoning rules would be convenient or helpful to a plaintiff does not make the change "necessary." Moreover, "discrimination" exists only if the zoning regulation (or other rule at issue) hurts "handicapped people by reason of their handicap, rather than . . . by virtue of what they have in common with other people, such as a limited amount of money to spend" (maj.). That was the panel's view as well.

In a brief *amicus curiae* filed at the court's request, the Civil Rights Division of the Department of Justice told us that this regulation creates an accommodation requirement distinct in the sense that disparate impact may be established by case-specific as well as statistical evidence. In employment-discrimination litigation under Title VII of the Civil Rights Act of 1964 or the Age Discrimination in Employment Act, a "disparate impact" means a statistically significant adverse effect of a rule that is neutral in its terms. There is no good reason, however, why a regulation may not take a different approach to disparate-impact theories in disability-discrimination cases, where the circumstances of the affected persons may be so different—and the number of zoning or housing-code rules so numerous—that statistical analysis would be impractical. Title II does not specify a regimen for disparate-impact analysis, which means that a regulation requiring local zoning rules to yield when "necessary" to avoid applicant-specific disparate impacts that occur by reason of disability is a reasonable way to implement the statute. So I accept the Civil Rights Division's reading of this regulation, and I understand the court's opinion to do so too.

Hovsons, Inc. v. Township of Brick

United States Court of Appeals for the Third Circuit, 1996.
89 F.3d 1096.

■ COWEN, CIRCUIT JUDGE.

In this case we must decide whether the Township of Brick's refusal to grant a variance to Hovsons, Inc. ("Hovsons") to build a nursing home in the Township's R–R–2 zone, an area the district court found to be predominantly residential, violates the mandate of the Fair Housing Amendments Act of 1988 ("FHAA"), 42 U.S.C. § 3601 *et seq.*, that all municipalities provide "reasonable accommodations" to handicapped persons. *Id.* § 3604(f)(3)(B). The district court rejected Hovsons' FHAA claims and denied its request for declaratory and injunctive relief.

We conclude that the accommodation Hovsons has put forward would not impose an undue financial or administrative burden upon Brick Township. Nor would building a nursing home in the R–R–2 zone fundamentally undermine the Township's zoning scheme. We therefore hold that the finding of the district court that the Township complied with the FHAA's "reasonable accommodations" provision cannot stand.

I.

A.

Hovsons is a developer of nursing homes and other forms of senior citizen housing, such as adult retirement communities. Hovcare of Brick, Inc., a corporation affiliated with Hovsons, owns a 32.73-acre parcel of land on the Brick Township-Lakewood Township border in

New Jersey. Hovsons has proposed to build a nursing home facility on that parcel. Approximately twenty-two (21.96) of the acres are located in Brick Township; the remaining (10.77) acres are in Lakewood Township. Hovsons' developmental plan calls for site construction only on the Brick Township portion of the property. Brick Township has steadfastly opposed the construction of such a development within the R–R–2 zone.

The nursing home facility Hovsons has envisioned is intended for persons who will require some form of nursing care for the rest of their lives. Referred to as "Holiday Village," it would have the capacity to house 210 residents. The density, architecture and design features of the proposed development are comparable to that of the surrounding planned retirement communities in Brick Township. The structure and its associated parking and access facilities would cover six to seven acres. The remaining land area would consist of open spaces, landscaped areas and preserved tree buffers.

Under New Jersey law, nursing homes may not be built unless the need for a home within the applicable health service area is established through a certificate of need process. See N.J. Stat. Ann. §§ 26:2H–7–:2H–8. On December 2, 1989, the New Jersey Department of Health approved Hovsons' application for a certificate of need which authorized construction of a 150-bed nursing home in Brick Township. Hovsons' certificate was amended on August 12, 1991 to increase the authorized number of beds from 150 to 210.

In its August 12, 1991, approval letter to Hovsons authorizing this sixty-bed increase, the New Jersey Department of Health cited the acute need for nursing home facilities in Brick Township. New Jersey Commissioner of Health Frances J. Dunston declared that building another nursing home in Brick Township would "help to maintain balance in the distribution of long-term care beds throughout Ocean County, thereby promoting geographical access to care for area residents. Brick Township has approximately 6.7 long-term care beds per 1,000 population, compared to the County average of 12 beds per 1,000 population." In addition, the State prioritized Hovsons' application on account of its agreement to have Medicaid-eligible patients comprise no less than fifty-five percent of its patient population.

[H]ovsons has proposed to construct Holiday Village in Brick Township's R–R–2 or "Rural Residential-Adult Community Zone." The district court found that the R–R–2 zone is "primarily, although not exclusively, for residential use," and that this region was zoned by community planners with the intention of "minimiz[ing] traffic" and bringing about an environment that was both "quiet" and "seclu[ded]." In the R–R–2 zone, Brick Township permits the following land uses as of right and without conditions: (1) customary and conventional farming activities; (2) one-family dwellings; (3) public schools and accredited private schools; (4) municipal parks, playgrounds and other municipally owned facilities; and (5) planned residential retirement communities.

The Brick Township R–R–2 zone also allows for a number of conditional uses, including: (1) public utilities installations; (2) hospitals; (3) public and quasi-public philanthropic and charitable uses; (4) quasi-public buildings and recreation areas; (5) golf courses; (6)

single-family residential dwellings with a maximum density of 1.5 dwelling units per acre; (7) single-family residential dwellings with open space; and (8) churches, parish houses, convents and cemeteries. The only area in Brick Township where nursing homes can be constructed is the hospital support zone. Other permitted uses in the hospital support zone are doctors' offices, clinics, emergency treatment facilities, pharmacies, retail establishments for the sale of medical and surgical supplies, motels and hospitals. The hospital support zone is commercial in nature. No single or multiple-family residences may be built in this area without first obtaining a variance.

Brick Township's hospital support zone has already been developed extensively. Less than thirty undeveloped acres remain. The remaining vacant land consists of small, noncontiguous, separately owned parcels, the largest site being 8.6 acres. The record is unclear as to whether any of the undeveloped land in the hospital support zone is currently on the market or otherwise available for purchase.

B.

In 1990, Hovsons applied for a variance to the Brick Township Zoning Board of Adjustment ("Zoning Board"), to build a nursing home in the R–R–2 zone. Hovsons' application was debated extensively (a total of seventeen public hearings were conducted over a two-year period) and was ultimately denied in April of 1992.

[O]n September 6, 1994, Hovsons filed suit in the United States District Court for the District of New Jersey against the Township of Brick and the Zoning Board. Hovsons alleged, inter alia, that the defendants had violated the FHAA. Hovsons maintained that the Township and its Zoning Board had discriminated against handicapped persons by denying its application for a variance to construct a nursing home in the R–R–2 zone. Specifically, Hovsons contended [t]hat the defendants had refused to comply with the FHAA's requirement that they provide "reasonable accommodations" to handicapped persons.[2]

Hovsons sought both declaratory and injunctive relief to prevent the Township of Brick and its Zoning Board from interfering with its plans to build a nursing home in the R–R–2 zone. [A] one-day bench trial was held on July 12, 1995. On August 16, 1995, the district court issued its findings of fact and conclusions of law. The court [h]eld that Brick Township was not in violation of the "reasonable accommodations" provision of the FHAA. The district court opined that § 3604(f)(3)(B) does not require municipalities "to disregard their own zoning requirements in order to provide sufficient opportunities and accommodations for the disabled." In so holding, the court relied upon the fact that Brick Township permitted the construction of nursing homes in another area of the Township. Moreover, the nursing home would, in the district court's view, be inconsistent with the residential

---

     [2] In so doing, Hovsons was raising the claims of the "John Doe" plaintiffs who would reside in the nursing home facility that Hovsons plans to construct. The Fair Housing Act has been interpreted to permit such broad assertions of third-party standing. See *Havens Realty Corp. v. Coleman*, 455 U.S. 363, 372 (1982) ("[T]he sole requirement for standing to sue under [the Fair Housing Act] is the Art. III minima of injury in fact[.]"); *Growth Horizons, Inc. v. Delaware County, Pennsylvania*, 983 F.2d 1277, 1282 n.6 (3d Cir.1993) (Under the FHAA, " 'an aggrieved person' does not necessarily have to be the person discriminated against.").

character of the R–R–2 zone and would not adequately "service the immediate surrounding community."

[III.]

[T]he Township of Brick contends that this case should not be considered under the FHAA because nursing homes are not "dwellings" as defined in the Act. Hovsons maintains that the district court erred in finding that Brick Township complied with the "reasonable accommodations" provision of the FHAA. We will address these issues in turn.

A.

Section 3604 of the FHAA proscribes discrimination "in the sale or rental" of "a dwelling." 42 U.S.C. § 3604(f)(1). The FHAA defines the term "dwelling" as

> any building, structure, or portion thereof which is occupied as, or designated or intended for occupancy as, a residence by one or more families, and any vacant land which is offered for sale or lease for the construction or location thereon of any such building, structure, or portion thereof.

42 U.S.C. § 3602(b). [T]he Township of Brick's argument that the proposed nursing home is not a "dwelling" under the FHAA is without merit. To the handicapped elderly persons who would reside there, Holiday Village would be their home, very often for the rest of their lives. We therefore hold that the proposed nursing home is a "dwelling" within the meaning of § 3602(b).

B.

1.

[S]ection 3604(f)(1) of the FHAA provides that it is unlawful

[t]o discriminate in the sale or rental, or to otherwise make unavailable or deny, a dwelling to any buyer or renter because of a handicap of—

> (A) that buyer or renter,

> (B) a person residing in or intending to reside in that dwelling after it has been sold, rented, or made available; or

> (C) any person associated with that buyer or renter.

42 U.S.C. § 3604(f)(1). Section 3604(f)(3)(B) further provides that "[f]or the purposes of this subsection, discrimination includes . . . a refusal to make reasonable accommodations in rules, policies, practices, or services, when such accommodations may be necessary to afford such person equal opportunity to use and enjoy a dwelling[.]" *Id.* § 3604(f)(3)(B).[3] [W]e now turn to the question of whether there is a sufficient foundation in the record to support the factual finding of the district court that Brick Township complied with the FHAA's "reasonable accommodations" provision.

---

[3] The parties do not dispute that the nursing home patients at Holiday Village would be "handicapped" within the meaning of the FHAA.

2.

The conclusion of the district court that the Township of Brick satisfied the FHAA's mandate that "reasonable accommodations" be provided to handicapped persons was clear error. Brick Township does not permit the construction of nursing homes in any of its residential areas. The Township nonetheless contends that the authorization for nursing home construction within its hospital support zone, an area zoned for hospitals and other medical support facilities, suffices to satisfy its legal obligation to handicapped persons. We disagree.

The reasoning and analysis of the district court evinces a fundamental misunderstanding of the intent of Congress in enacting the FHAA. The district court's statement that the FHAA "does not ask [municipalities] to disregard their own zoning requirements in order to provide sufficient accommodations for the disabled" runs counter to the entire thrust of the FHAA. The Township of Brick's blanket exclusion of nursing homes from its residential areas in general, and its refusal to permit the construction of the specific facility in question, is precisely the sort of isolation of handicapped persons from the mainstream of society that the FHAA was enacted to forbid. Furthermore, there is a dearth of evidence in the record to support Brick Township's sweeping claim as to the fundamental incompatibility of nursing homes and residential areas in general and the R–R–2 zone in particular.

A review of the record, case law interpreting the meaning of "reasonable accommodations" and the legislative history of the FHAA leads us to conclude that the Township of Brick failed to satisfy the requirements of § 3604(f)(3)(B) as a matter of law. [T]he FHAA's "reasonable accommodations" provision prohibits the enforcement of "zoning ordinances and local housing policies in a manner that denies people with disabilities access to housing on par with that of those who are not disabled." Laurie C. Malkin, *Troubles at the Doorstep: The Fair Housing Amendments Act of 1988 and Group Homes for Recovering Substance Abusers*, 144 U. Pa. L. Rev. 757, 804 (1995) (hereinafter *Fair Housing Amendments Act*). Pursuant to § 3604(f)(3)(B), the Township of Brick has "an affirmative duty" to make reasonable accommodations on behalf of handicapped persons.

"The reasonable accommodation inquiry is highly fact-specific, requiring a case-by-case determination." As in Rehabilitation Act cases, we must view the reasonable accommodations requirement "in light of two countervailing legislative concerns: (1) effectuation of the statute's objectives of assisting the handicapped; and (2) the need to impose reasonable boundaries in accomplishing this purpose." We keep in mind the principle that satisfaction of the FHAA's reasonable accommodation requirement "can and often will involve some costs."

[I]t was clear error for the district court to conclude that Hovsons' request for a variance could not be accommodated. Granting a variance to Hovsons would not have saddled the Township of Brick with "undue financial and administrative burdens," or otherwise resulted in the imposition of an "undue hardship." On the contrary, the proprietors of Holiday Village will become taxpaying members of the local community. Furthermore, the district court acknowledged the "considerable efforts [Hovsons has made] to work with the township in order to make the site feasible. . . . " Holiday Village intends to manage its own affairs with a minimum of local governmental involvement. Hovsons has agreed to have Holiday Village arrange for its own garbage collection, street maintenance and snow removal. The nursing home would rely upon the municipal fire, police and emergency services, but its use of these services would be no different from that of the surrounding retirement developments. The mere fact that the employees and residents of Holiday Village will at times require the assistance of the local police and other emergency services does not rise to the level of imposing a cognizable administrative and financial burden upon the community.

Nor would granting a variance to Hovsons fundamentally undermine the Brick Township zoning scheme. The Supreme Court has observed that, in broad general terms, the purpose of zoning law is "to prevent problems caused by the 'pig in the parlor instead of the barnyard.'" *City of Edmonds v. Oxford House, Inc.*, 514 U.S. 725 (1995) (quoting *Village of Euclid, Ohio v. Ambler Realty Co.*, 272 U.S. 365, 388 (1926)). As the record makes clear, however, permitting the construction of a nursing home in the R–R–2 zone would cause no such problems.

We reject the Township of Brick's contention that nursing homes are fundamentally incompatible with the other permitted uses in the R–R–2 zone. Brick Township appears to rely upon the blanket proposition that nursing homes are clearly out of place in residential zones. This is precisely the type of land use planning that the FHAA was enacted to prevent and, if necessary, overrule. Furthermore, the design construction of Holiday Village is similar to that of the local planned residential retirement communities, a permitted use in the R–R–2 zone. As both of these types of facilities cater to the elderly, Holiday Village could provide a useful resource to members of the local retirement communities who do not want to locate in a new area, but who are no longer able to care for themselves.

As the Court of Appeals for the Sixth Circuit has observed, "the handicapped may have little choice but to live in a commercial home if they desire to live in a residential neighborhood. To provide the handicapped with equal housing opportunities, the City must make the necessary 'reasonable accommodations.'" We hold that under the facts in this case, § 3604(f)(3)(B) requires that the Township of Brick permit Hovsons to proceed with its plans to build a nursing home in its R–R–2 zone.

[I]t is uncontroverted that the Township of Brick has a substantial interest in enforcing its zoning code and that, under appropriate circumstances, local zoning codes are entitled to a considerable amount of deference. We are also mindful of the fact that "[i]n requiring reasonable accommodation, . . . Congress surely did not mandate a blanket waiver of all facially neutral zoning policies and rules, regardless of the facts." Nor did Congress intend to "give handicapped persons *carte blanche* to determine where and how they would live regardless of zoning ordinances to contrary." Nonetheless, the FHAA's promise that "reasonable accommodations" be provided to handicapped persons would be an empty one indeed if Brick Township were permitted to do nothing to accommodate the elderly disabled who are in need of nursing home care and desire to live in one of the Township's residential zones.

The House Report to the FHAA expressly states that the Act "is intended to prohibit . . . [the imposition of] terms or conditions . . . which have the effect of excluding . . . congregate living arrangements for persons with handicaps." H.R.Rep.No.711, 100th Cong., 2d Sess. 23, reprinted in 1988 U.S.C.C.A.N. 2173, 2184. As one court has explained, "strict adherence to a rule which has the effect of precluding handicapped individuals from residing in the residence [of their choice] was precisely the type of conduct which the Fair Housing Amendments Act sought to overcome with the enactment of § 3604(f)(3)(B)."

IV.

We will reverse the August 16, 1995 order of the district court and remand this matter with instructions to enjoin the Township of Brick from interfering with the construction of the nursing home facility under the terms, conditions and specifications agreed to by the State of New Jersey.

New Directions Treatment Services v. City of Reading

United States Court of Appeals for the Third Circuit, 2007.
490 F.3d 293.

■ SMITH, CIRCUIT JUDGE.

This case presents the familiar conflict between the legal principle of non-discrimination and the political principle of not-in-my-backyard. New Directions Treatment Services, a reputable and longstanding provider of methadone treatment, sought to locate a new facility in the City of Reading. A Pennsylvania statute that facially singles out methadone clinics gave the City of Reading the opportunity to vote to deny the permit. The City of Reading availed itself of that opportunity.

New Directions and individual methadone patients brought suit on constitutional and federal statutory grounds, raising both facial and as applied challenges to the statute. The City of Reading successfully moved for summary judgment against all of plaintiffs' claims. New Directions and the individual plaintiffs' appeal is before us.

I.   Summary of facts and procedural history

New Directions Treatment Services ("NDTS") operates several methadone clinics throughout Pennsylvania, including one in West Reading.[1] NDTS provides methadone maintenance for adults who have

---

[1]   The National Institute on Drug Abuse (part of the National Institutes of Health) describes methadone treatment: Methadone treatment has been used for more than 30 years to effectively and safely treat opioid addiction. Properly prescribed methadone is not intoxicating or sedating, and its effects do not interfere with ordinary activities such as driving a car. The medication is taken orally and it suppresses narcotic withdrawal for 24 to 36 hours. Patients are able to perceive pain and have emotional reactions. Most important, methadone relieves the craving associated with heroin addiction; craving is a major reason for relapse. Among methadone patients, it has been found that normal street doses of heroin are ineffective at producing euphoria, thus making the use of heroin more easily extinguishable. Methadone's effects last four to six times as long as those of heroin, so people in treatment need to take it only once a day. Also, methadone is medically safe even when used continuously for 10 years or more. Combined with behavioral therapies or counseling and other supportive services, methadone enables patients to stop using heroin (and other opiates)

been addicted to heroin for at least a year. NDTS's Executive Director, Glen Cooper, contacted the City of Reading ("the City") to discuss opening an additional treatment center, as their West Reading facility had developed a waiting list for treatment. NDTS met with City officials on January 24, 2001, to discuss potential sites within the City. NDTS met with the City Council two months later to continue the discussion. Although NDTS had not yet obtained an operating permit from the City, NDTS signed a ten-year lease on a property located at 700 Lancaster Avenue. NDTS then submitted a zoning permit application.

The Lancaster Avenue property is located on a commercial highway that is interspersed with 40–75 private residences. The Berks Counseling Center previously occupied the site, providing treatment to patients with mental health problems and drug addictions. It did not provide methadone treatment. NDTS intended to serve "a couple hundred or so" methadone patients at the new facility. NDTS proposed a 4,000 square foot addition to the property to accommodate this increased usage. NDTS planned to operate the new facility from 5:30 a.m. to 6:00 p.m. on weekdays, as well as more limited hours on weekends.

In 1999, Pennsylvania adopted 53 Pa. Cons. Stat. Ann. § 10621, a zoning statute regulating locations of methadone treatment facilities. The statute provides that "a methadone treatment facility shall not be established or operated within 500 feet of an existing school, public playground, public park, residential housing area, child-care facility, church, meetinghouse or other actual place of regularly stated religious worship established prior to the proposed methadone treatment facility," unless, "by majority vote, the governing body for the municipality in which the proposed methadone treatment facility is to be located votes in favor of the issuance of an occupancy permit." *Id.* at § 10621(a)(1) and (b). The Lancaster Avenue property falls within the ambit of the statute. When NDTS inquired about sites not covered by the statute, a City zoning official referred them to three sites, including a cemetery and a heavy industrial area, all of which NDTS considered unsuitable.

The City notified NDTS that it would hold a hearing on January 14, 2002. Glen Cooper, the Executive Director of NDTS, appeared at the hearing and described NDTS's history and its proposed treatment center. He also answered questions from the City Council. NDTS acknowledged that it had experienced some loitering and littering at its West Reading facility. At a second hearing on February 28, 2002, the Council heard additional public comments. At a March 25, 2002 Council meeting, the City heard more comments and then unanimously voted against NDTS's application.

[NDTS] and several individual plaintiffs proceeding in pseudonym filed suit in the United States District Court for the Eastern District of Pennsylvania on March 25, 2004. [NDTS] alleged that the [Pennsylvania] statute, both facially and as applied, violates § 504 of the Rehabilitation Act. 29 U.S.C. § 794. [NDTS also] alleged that the

---

and return to more stable and productive lives. http://www.nida.nih.gov/researchreports/ heroin/heroin5.html#treatment.

statute, both facially and as applied, violates Title II of the Americans with Disabilities Act ("ADA"). 42 U.S.C. § 12132.

[T]he City moved for summary judgment. NDTS filed a cross-motion for partial summary judgment on their claims against the validity of the statute. The District Court granted the City's motion in its entirety and denied NDTS's cross-motion on August 22, 2005. NDTS timely appealed.

II.   Discussion

Section 12132 of Title II of the ADA provides that "[s]ubject to the provisions of this subchapter, no qualified individual with a disability shall, by reason of such disability, be excluded from participation in or be denied the benefits of the services, programs, or activities of a public entity, or be subjected to discrimination by any such entity." 42 U.S.C. § 12132. This statement constitutes a general prohibition against discrimination by public entities, regardless of activity. *Bay Area Addiction Research and Treatment, Inc. v. City of Antioch*, 179 F.3d 725, 730–31 (9th Cir.1999) (striking down a ban on methadone clinics within 500 feet of a residential area). Section 504 of the Rehabilitation Act similarly provides that "[n]o otherwise qualified individual with a disability . . . shall, solely by reason of her or his disability, be excluded from the participation in, be denied the benefits of, or be subjected to discrimination under any program or activity receiving Federal financial assistance." 29 U.S.C. § 794(a). We have noted that "[a]s the ADA simply expands the Rehabilitation Act's prohibitions against discrimination into the private sector, Congress has directed that the two acts' judicial and agency standards be harmonized" and we will accordingly analyze the two provisions together.

The Sixth and Ninth Circuits have considered the issue of whether a municipal ordinance prohibiting methadone clinics within 500 feet of a residential area violated the general proscription contained in the ADA and Rehabilitation Act. See *MX Group, Inc. v. City of Covington*, 293 F.3d 326, 342 (6th Cir.2002); *Bay Area, 179 F.3d at 737*. Both Courts concluded that the ordinances were "facially discriminatory laws" and therefore "present[ed] per se violations of § 12132."

The Ninth Circuit confronted many of the issues presented in this case when the Bay Area Addiction Research and Treatment, Inc. ("BAART") and California Detoxification Programs, Inc. ("CDP") tried to relocate their methadone clinic to the City of Antioch, California. BAART had been operating a methadone clinic near the courthouse in Pittsburg, California for 13 years. BAART and CDP received notice from Antioch that the proposed location could be used for a methadone clinic under Antioch's zoning plan. However, the Antioch City Council enacted an urgency ordinance banning methadone clinics within 500 feet of residential areas, thereby barring use of the proposed site. BAART and other plaintiffs alleged that Antioch had violated both Title II of the ADA and § 504 of the Rehabilitation Act. The District Court denied Bay Area's motion for a preliminary injunction enjoining the ordinance. BAART appealed.

[T]he Ninth Circuit analyzed whether the District Court had abused its discretion by denying the preliminary injunction in part because BAART did not have a likelihood of success on the merits. [T]he

Ninth Circuit first held that the District Court erred by applying the "reasonable modification" test to a facially discriminatory law. U.S. Department of Justice regulations require that would-be plaintiffs request reasonable modifications to avoid discrimination unless the modification would fundamentally alter the program, activity, ordinance, or statute. 28 C.F.R. § 35.130(b)(7). However, where the "statute discriminates against qualified individuals on its face rather than in its application," the applicable regulation interpreting Title II, which only requires "reasonable" accommodation, makes little sense. *Bay Area*, 179 F.3d at 734. The only way to alter a facially discriminatory ordinance is to remove the discriminating language. The Antioch ordinance could only have been "rendered facially neutral by expanding the class of entities that may not operate within 500 feet of a residential neighborhood to include all clinics at which medical services are provided, or by striking the reference to methadone clinics entirely," and, "[e]ither modification would fundamentally alter the zoning ordinance, the former by expanding the covered establishments dramatically, and the latter by rendering the ordinance a nullity." *Id.* Therefore, the reasonable modifications test could not apply to a facially discriminatory ordinance. See *id.* at 735 (holding that "facially discriminatory laws present *per se* violations of § 12132").

The Ninth Circuit noted that this determination does not end the inquiry, however, as both statutes withhold protection from any "individual who poses a significant risk to the health or safety of others that cannot be ameliorated by means of a reasonable modification." *Id.* Although the Ninth Circuit disclaimed any conclusion about the outcome of this inquiry or the ultimate merits of the claim, it repeatedly emphasized that [the significant risk test] was designed to "ensure[ ] that decisions are not made on the basis of 'the prejudiced attitudes or the ignorance of others,' " and that "[t]his is particularly important because, as with individuals with contagious diseases, '[f]ew aspects of a handicap give rise to the same level of public fear and misapprehension,' as the challenges facing recovering drug addicts." *Bay Area*, 179 F.3d at 736. The Ninth Circuit held that, in order for a methadone clinic to fail the significant risk test, it must present "severe and likely harms to the community that are directly associated with the operation of the methadone clinic." *Id.* at 736–37. Such alleged harms must be supported by evidence and "may include a reasonable likelihood of a significant increase in crime." *Id.* The Ninth Circuit noted that courts should be mindful of the ADA and Rehabilitation Act's goals of eliminating discrimination against individuals with disabilities and protecting those individuals "from deprivations based on prejudice, stereotypes, or unfounded fear." *Id.* at 737. Therefore, "it is not enough that individuals pose a hypothetical or presumed risk"—the evidence must reflect a risk that is significant and harm that is serious. *Id.*

[A]lthough *Bay Area* [d]ealt with [an] outright ban[ ], we believe that the reasoning of those cases is equally applicable here. The Pennsylvania statute imposes a ban on the establishment of methadone clinics within 500 feet of many structures, including schools, churches, and residential housing developments. See 53 Pa. Cons. Stat. Ann. § 10621(a)(1). The Pennsylvania law differs from those in *Bay Area* and *MX Group* in that the "the governing body for the municipality in which the proposed methadone treatment facility is to be located" can waive the ban if, and only if, it approves the issuance of a permit by majority vote. 53 Pa. Cons. Stat. Ann. § 10621(b). However, this ability of municipalities to waive the statutory ban in no way alters the fact that 53 Pa. Cons. Stat. Ann. § 10621 facially singles out methadone clinics, and thereby methadone patients, for different treatment, thereby rendering the statute facially discriminatory.

We agree with the [N]inth Circuit[ ] that a law that singles out methadone clinics for different zoning procedures is facially discriminatory under the ADA and the Rehabilitation Act. We also agree that it is inappropriate to apply the "reasonable modification" test to facially discriminatory laws. The only way to modify a facially discriminatory statute is to remove the discriminatory language. However, amending 53 Pa. Cons. Stat. Ann. § 10621 to remove the facial discrimination against methadone clinics would "fundamentally alter" the statute.

Having concluded that 53 Pa. Cons. Stat. Ann. § 10621 is facially discriminatory and that the reasonable modification test does not apply, we proceed to inquire whether NDTS's clients pose a significant risk. [T]he Supreme Court emphasized in *Bragdon v. Abbott* that the significant risk test requires a rigorous objective inquiry. In *Bragdon*, a dentist refused to fill a cavity for an asymptomatic AIDS patient. The Court held that:

> The existence, or nonexistence, of a significant risk must be determined from the standpoint of the person who refuses the treatment or accommodation, and the risk of assessment must be based on medical or other objective evidence. . . . As a health care professional, petitioner had the duty to assess the risk of infection based on the objective, scientific information available to him and others in his profession. His belief that a significant risk existed, even if maintained in good faith, would not relieve him of liability.

Accordingly, we cannot base our decision on the subjective judgments of the people purportedly at risk, the Reading residents, City Council, or even Pennsylvania citizens, but must look to objective evidence in the record of any dangers posed by methadone clinics and patients. The purported risk must be substantial, not speculative or remote.

The record contains ample evidence that NDTS's clients, and methadone patients as a class, do not pose a significant risk. Neither the City nor its *amicus*, the Commonwealth, have offered any evidence to the contrary. The City refers to the deposition of Glen Cooper, the Executive Director of NDTS, in which he estimated that 20 to 30 percent of the clinic's patients would test positive for illegal drugs. However, NDTS also submitted the results of drug screens at its West Reading and Bethlehem clinics showing that only patients enrolled for less than six months test positive at the 30 percent rate, whereas less than six percent of patients enrolled for more than six months test positive for illegal drugs.

More importantly, the record demonstrates no link between methadone clinics and increased crime. Cooper testified that there had been no criminal incidents at NDTS's West Reading facility. The Commonwealth offered no evidence to support its contrary assertion that there is a "frequent association" between methadone clinics and criminal activity. In depositions, City Council members expressed concerns about heavy traffic, loitering, noise pollution, littering, double parking, and jaywalking. However, the City offered no evidence to support an association between these concerns and methadone clinics. Even if such connections existed, we are skeptical that they would qualify as the substantial harms contemplated by the *Arline* and *Bragdon* Courts.

The brief legislative history of 53 Pa. Cons. Stat. Ann. § 10621 provides no further evidence that methadone patients pose a significant risk. Representative Platts, the bill's principal sponsor, stated that the legislation would protect "children from the high crime rates associated with heroin addicts," that, "[o]n average heroin addicts before treatment commit a crime on average 200 days of the year," and that "[e]ven after 6 months of methadone treatment, they still average once a month committing a crime." Representative Platts offered no source for this statistic. We find it difficult to place much weight on this unsupported statistic given Cooper's unrebutted testimony that other NDTS facilities had experienced no criminal incidents and the extremely positive reports of the National Institute on Drug Abuse and the Office of National Drug Control Policy. In addition, the statement of Representative Serafini betrays [g]eneralized prejudice and fear[ ]:

> It is unfortunate that we have to have methadone treatment facilities at all, but to locate them in areas that are residential or close to where young people might congregate or the community might meet and gather is a definite mistake, and these facilities, in my opinion, do not benefit anyone but the heroin addict, and they should be located either in a community that welcomes this kind of facility or out in an area away from people who have kept themselves clean and free of drugs and should not be confronted by this kind of a pollution in their community.

[W]e have no doubt that some methadone patients are inclined to criminal or otherwise dangerous behavior. However, in the words of the [*School Board of Nassau County v.*] *Arline*[, 480 U.S. 273 (1987),] Court:

> The fact that some persons who have contagious diseases may pose a serious health threat to others under certain circumstances does not justify excluding from the coverage of the Act all persons with actual or perceived contagious diseases. Such exclusion would mean that those accused of being contagious would never have the opportunity to have their condition evaluated in light of medical evidence and a determination made as to whether they were "otherwise qualified." Rather, they would be vulnerable to discrimination on the basis of mythology—precisely the type of injury Congress sought to prevent.

We will reverse the order of the District Court and remand with instructions that it grant NDTS's motion for partial summary judgment because 53 Pa. Cons. Stat. Ann. § 10621 facially violates the ADA and the Rehabilitation Act.

NOTES ON ZONING AND DISABILITY DISCRIMINATION LAWS

1.   **Causation and Discrimination.** In *Wisconsin Community Services*, the Court concludes that "because the mental illness of WCS' patients is not the cause-in-fact of WCS' inability to obtain a suitable facility, the program that it seeks modified does not hurt persons with disabilities 'by reason of their handicap.' " What does it mean to say that the patients' disabilities are not the "cause-in-fact" in this context? The Seventh Circuit suggests that the problem is that "the City would have rejected similar proposals from non-profit health clinics serving the non-disabled," so there could have been no discrimination. Given the facts the court presents, are you convinced that the City would have rejected similar proposals from non-profit health clinics that did not serve people with mental illness? Even if the Seventh Circuit is right on that point, what room does its analysis leave for an accommodation claim? The court seems to say that because the City did not engage in disparate treatment, it cannot have violated the ADA or the Rehabilitation Act. But as the majority opinion explicitly recognizes—and Judge Easterbrook's concurrence specifically calls attention to—the ADA and Rehabilitation Act demand that localities do more than abstain from intentional discrimination against people with disabilities; they must also make reasonable modifications in their policies in some circumstances. Are there any circumstances where, under the Seventh Circuit's analysis, a city must modify its zoning criteria? Or does *Wisconsin Community Services* implicitly hold that a city's only obligation is to avoid intentional discrimination in its zoning practices?

In this regard, is the court persuasive in its attempt to distinguish *US Airways v. Barnett* (a principal case in Chapter 3)? As Justice Scalia emphasized in his dissent in that case, US Airways would have denied Barnett's request to stay in the mailroom position even if he didn't have a disability; any employee with his level of seniority would have seen such a request rejected. Yet the *Barnett* Court explicitly rejected Justice Scalia's argument and held that an accommodation that enabled Barnett to stay in the mailroom *might* be required, depending on the structure of the seniority system, even though he had not experienced intentional discrimination. For that matter, is *Wisconsin Community Services* consistent with *Olmstead v. L.C.* (a principal case in this chapter, *supra*)? There, at least on the analysis of Justice Ginsburg's majority opinion, it did not matter whether people without disabilities would ever receive the community placements the plaintiffs sought; so long as it imposed no fundamental alteration, community placement was required as a reasonable modification anyway.

Is *Wisconsin Community Services* consistent with *Hovsons*? The Zoning Board there would have denied a variance to any nursing home, would it not? Does it make a difference that the very conditions that prompt people to move into nursing homes, by their nature, meet the definitions of disability under the disability rights laws? There is in any event a very significant difference in tone between the Seventh and Third Circuits in these cases. The Seventh Circuit's analysis proceeds in a rather formalistic fashion; the court asks whether, but for its clients' disabilities, WCS would have gotten the zoning variance. The Third Circuit's opinion, while certainly compatible with the formalistic analysis of the Seventh

Circuit, emphasizes the importance of permitting nursing homes in residential areas as a way of achieving the substantive goal of integration of people with disabilities into the full community.

Finally, consider *New Directions Treatment*. There, as the court notes, discrimination is written on the face of the state statute. Methadone clinics—which are used only by people with opiate addictions, who fairly clearly count as people with disabilities—are singled out for a political process that offers a clear path to not-in-my-backyard-ism. And the law seems clearly to single out methadone clinics based on fear and prejudice, rather than a careful assessment of risks. Under the *Wisconsin Community Services* analysis, the state law clearly discriminates.

But the question remains: In what circumstances—aside from cases of intentional discrimination—must a locality modify its zoning practices to comply with the disability discrimination laws? Do the cases you have read offer any clues?

2. Zoning Discrimination and Integration. Is there a tension between the *Olmstead* integration principle and cases challenging zoning discrimination under the Fair Housing Act? Consider the facts of *Hovsons*, for example. There, the court applied the Fair Housing Act to require the Township to permit construction of a nursing home to house people with disabilities. The court's decision rested in part on the premise that some people with disabilities have to live in congregate settings. But much *Olmstead* litigation directly challenges that premise. And, as the discussion earlier in this chapter highlighted, many recent settlements of *Olmstead* litigation impose limits on the number of people with disabilities who can be housed together. These caps are designed precisely to ensure that people with disabilities live in settings that are as fully a part of their community as possible; they rest on the premise that too-large congregate living settings are unnecessarily segregated from the community. Would a city that denied a zoning variance to a congregate living facility for people with disabilities be entitled to defend itself on the ground that it was simply enforcing the *Olmstead* integration principle?

3. *City of Edmonds v. Oxford House.* The Fair Housing Act exempts from its prohibitions "any reasonable local, State, or Federal restrictions regarding the maximum number of occupants permitted to occupy a dwelling." 42 U.S.C. § 3607(b)(1). In CITY OF EDMONDS V. OXFORD HOUSE, 514 U.S. 725 (1995), the Court held that this exemption does not protect a city zoning provision, "governing areas zoned for single-family dwelling units, [that] defines 'family' as 'persons [without regard to number] related by genetics, adoption, or marriage, or a group of five or fewer [unrelated] persons.' " *Id.* at 728. Relying on this provision, the City of Edmonds, Washington, had issued criminal citations to a group home for 10 to 12 persons recovering from alcohol and drug addiction that was located in a single-family area. Holding that exemptions to the Fair Housing Act's broad protections should be read narrowly, the Court concluded that the zoning provisions the city had invoked "do not cap the number of people who may live in a dwelling. In plain terms, they direct that dwellings be used only to house families." *Id.* at 735–736. The Court found it "curious reasoning indeed that converts a family values preserver into a maximum occupancy restriction once a town adds to a related persons prescription 'and also two unrelated persons.' " *Id.* at 737. If the city's zoning provision were treated as an occupancy restriction, the Court explained, then "so long as the City introduces a specific number—any number (two will do)—the City can insulate its single-family zone entirely from FHA coverage," a result inconsistent with the generous construction accorded the statute. *Id.* at 737 n.11. Justice Thomas, joined by Justices Scalia and Kennedy, dissented.

5. PUBLIC BENEFITS

Henrietta D. v. Bloomberg

United States Court of Appeals for the Second Circuit, 2003.
331 F.3d 261.

■ KATZMANN, CHIEF JUDGE:

The plaintiffs in this civil rights litigation, indigent New York City residents who suffer from AIDS and other HIV-related illnesses, are clients of New York City's Division of AIDS Services and Income Support ("DASIS"), an agency whose sole function is to assist persons with HIV-related diseases in obtaining public assistance benefits and services. The plaintiffs allege that in spite of DASIS's existence (and in part due to DASIS's ineffectiveness), New York City and New York State are failing to provide them with adequate access to public benefits, and are thereby violating various federal and state statutes, regulations, and constitutional provisions.

Following a bench trial in the United States District Court for the Eastern District of New York (Johnson, *J.*), the District Court found in plaintiffs' favor[.] Because we conclude that the alleged general failure of New York City's public benefits system in this case does not excuse the city defendants from their duty under the ADA and the Rehabilitation Act to ensure that the plaintiff class-members have meaningful access to the benefits to which they are facially entitled, we affirm[.]

Background

The certified plaintiff class consists of "[a]ll DAS-eligible persons, *i.e.,* persons who are New York City residents, are Medicaid eligible and meet the medical condition of having either (1) CDC-defined AIDS, or (2) an HIV-related condition and a need for home care services." The members of the class assert that they face unique physical hurdles in attempting to access certain public assistance benefits and services. They claim that DASIS, the New York City agency charged with helping them access such benefits and services, is ineffective and systemically fails to achieve its goals. The plaintiffs seek injunctive relief ordering the defendants, various city and state officials charged with implementing New York's social services system, to provide the benefits to which the plaintiff class is entitled.

1. The Social Services Network

Before turning to the plaintiffs' specific complaints, it is necessary briefly to canvass the structure of the New York public benefits system.

Congress has authorized the grant of federal money to consenting States in exchange for promises that the States will provide to qualifying individuals certain forms of public assistance, such as food stamps, welfare benefits, and Medicaid coverage. Pursuant to such a federal-state cooperative program, New York provides eligible New Yorkers with public financial assistance benefits, Medicaid benefits, and food stamps. The New York State Department of Social Services oversees the statewide benefits system, but the programs are administered on a day-to-day basis by 58 local county districts, one of which is New York City[.]

2. DASIS

The City of New York sought in 1997 to assist its HIV-afflicted residents in their efforts to access public services and benefits by combining under one umbrella several city agencies that endeavored to assist that population. *See* N.Y. City Admin. Code § 21–126 *et seq.* ("the DASIS law"). The DASIS law aims to "provide access to [publicly subsidized benefits and services] to every person with clinical/symptomatic HIV illness . . . or with AIDS." N.Y. City Admin. Code § 21–126. The DASIS law specifically locates DASIS within the New York City Department of Social Services. *See id.* ("There shall be a division of AIDS services within the New York city department of social services.").

The DASIS law imposes procedural rules designed to facilitate access to existing federal, state, and local welfare benefits and also mandates certain benefits that can arguably be characterized as additional substantive benefits. Procedural rules include, for example, an "intensive case management" requirement with specified minimum caseworker-client ratios, *see* N.Y. City Admin. Code § 21–127, and a requirement that services or benefits be provided within twenty business days of an application where no law or regulation provides a different time frame, *see* N.Y. City Admin. Code § 21–128(c)(2). Most of the services and benefits to which DASIS helps facilitate access are programs available to non-disabled individuals in addition to the plaintiff class, and the DASIS law makes clear that "[a]ny eligible person shall receive only those benefits and services for which such person qualifies in accordance with the applicable eligibility standards established pursuant to local, state or federal statute, law, regulation or rule." *Id.* at § 21–128(b). Some of the services to which DASIS is intended to facilitate access, however, are available only to those afflicted with HIV-illness. *See, e.g.,* N.Y. Comp.Codes R. & Regs. tit. 18, § 352.3(k)(1) (providing emergency shelter allowances for the HIV-afflicted population); N.Y. City Admin. Code § 21–128(b) (providing for access to enhanced rental assistance for the HIV-afflicted population and their family members residing with them). Additionally, the DASIS law requires continued provision of "transportation and nutrition allowances" in the same amounts that they had been provided prior to enactment of the DASIS law (although the city council and the mayor retain the power to adjust the amounts in the event of a "material reduction" in the state's "funding allocation"). *See* N.Y. City Admin. Code § 21–127. As we discuss below, an issue in this litigation is whether the DASIS law represents an attempt to provide the plaintiff class with additional, substantive benefits unavailable to other members of the population (as the defendants contend) or whether (as the plaintiffs contend) the DASIS law aims merely to provide an accommodation to the plaintiff class designed to facilitate meaningful access to benefits available to other similarly situated people.

3. Factual Findings With Respect To DASIS

Against this backdrop, we turn to the District Court's findings with respect to the plaintiffs' allegations that DASIS has failed adequately to provide the services it is supposed to provide.

[A]s an initial matter, the District Court, after hearing the testimony of several individuals afflicted with HIV-related illness, agreed with the plaintiffs that the physical challenges and medical risks faced by the plaintiff class create unique barriers with respect to obtaining access to public benefits and services:

> People living with HIV and AIDS develop numerous illnesses and physical conditions not found in the general population, and experience manifestations of common illnesses that are much more aggressive, recurrent, and difficult to treat. Infections and cancers spread rapidly in a person whose immune system has been compromised, and the effectiveness of medicine is diminished by nutritional problems that limit the body's ability to absorb what is ingested. Illnesses that are not lethal to the general population can kill an HIV-infected person. For all these reasons, persons with AIDS and HIV-related disease experience serious functional limitations that make it extremely difficult, if not impossible in some cases, to negotiate the complicated City social service system on their own.

> * * * * * *

> The opportunistic infections and chronic conditions that result from a weakened immune system limit the HIV-infected person's ability to engage in regular activities of daily life such as traveling, standing in line, attending scheduled appointments, completing paper work, and otherwise negotiating medical and social service bureaucracies . . . .

> Functional limitations also develop from the primary drugs used to combat AIDS and HIV-related disease. . . . An individual receiving this common regime of prescription drugs likely will be restricted in his or her ability to walk, stand, or travel. Other side effects include enhanced neuropathy, diarrhea, nausea, and vomiting.

> * * * * * *

> The requirement that persons with AIDS and advanced HIV disease travel to and wait in infection-ridden public waiting rooms can be dangerous, and even life-threatening, for this population, all of whom suffer from severely weakened immune systems.

The District Court concluded that DASIS was designed to address these obstacles, and most of the testimony at trial dealt with the plaintiffs' allegations that DASIS generally failed to provide the services that it was mandated by law to provide. After hearing testimony from DASIS clients, DASIS employees, advocates for DASIS clients, and experts, the District Court concluded that the allegations were well-founded, finding that DASIS was "chronically and systematically failing to provide plaintiffs with meaningful access to critical subsistence benefits and services, with devastating consequences."

The District Court discussed several different aspects of the evidence in reaching this conclusion. First, it cited the testimony of various plaintiffs who had testified that they frequently had limited contact with DASIS caseworkers and often had received untimely responses or no response to requests made through DASIS. Second, the District Court noted that the testimony of two individuals who had assisted DASIS clients supported the testimony of the DASIS clients that DASIS was disorganized and often unresponsive. For example, the Director of the Legal Advocacy Program of Bronx AIDS Services testified that she had "experienced extensive problems in working with clients trying to access benefits and services through DASIS," and that "(i) there [were] problems reaching case workers, (ii) her clients' public assistance cases ha[d] been improperly terminated without notice or adequate notice, and (iii) she had experience[d] significant problems with regard to relocating clients, including having clients lose apartments or face eviction because of DASIS'[s] failure timely to assist the clients." She further testified that she had encountered "daily problems reaching case managers that include calling but the case manager's phone is off the hook, not having her calls returned or not receiving a response to written correspondence or waiting several hours at a DASIS office to speak to someone concerning one of her clients."

Third, the District Court pointed to a statistical analysis of DASIS's performance in processing thirty-one rental assistance applications, prepared by Dr. Ernest Drucker, a professor of epidemiology and social medicine at Montefiore Medical Center who specializes in examining AIDS and its effects on the New York City population. The District Court summarized the results of the report:

> In over 77% of [the cases analyzed], the City failed to meet its own mandated time frames of 20 business days or approximately 30 calendar days. For those applicants who were not acted upon with [sic] the legally mandated time frames, the median length of time was 63 days but the range for applicants was up to 132 calendar days. The considerable delays in the approval of rental assistance shown in this report provide probative evidence of delays that are typical and systemic.

The District Court concluded with respect to the Drucker study that "the foregoing facts credibly demonstrate systemic problems in DASIS' efficient and timely administration of benefits."

Fourth, the District Court noted that even a key DASIS official had acknowledged the failure of DASIS to properly monitor its caseload:

> Deputy Commissioner Caldwell testified that DASIS was not fully in compliance with the legal requirements of the DASIS Law in either December 1997 or in June 1998, and is not today fully compliant with the DASIS Law. Deputy Commissioner

Caldwell further admitted that, despite the mandates of the DASIS Law, DASIS does not track the length of time required to process requests for many benefits and services, including those administered by the State; the total number of persons placed in permanent housing; the average length of time to reopen cases closed; or the average length of time required to comply with fair hearing decisions.

4. The District Court Ruling

The District Court held that the plaintiffs had demonstrated that they required special accommodations in order to access public benefits and services, and concluded that the DASIS law, if properly complied with, would provide the necessary accommodations to the HIV-positive population, but that DASIS was not functioning as the DASIS law had intended. [B]ased on these findings and conclusions, the District Court ruled in the plaintiffs' favor, holding that New York City had failed to provide the plaintiffs with meaningful access to public assistance benefits and services in violation of Title II of the ADA and section 504 of the Rehabilitation Act. Specifically, the District Court found that the DASIS law provided the reasonable accommodations requested by the plaintiffs, and that the City's failure to comply with the DASIS law violated the ADA and the Rehabilitation Act.

[A]t the trial, the District Court had precluded the defendants from introducing evidence designed to demonstrate that the plaintiffs were in fact receiving benefits on terms no worse than other individuals qualified to receive the same public benefits. Specifically, the defendants had hoped to have Patricia Smith, the Executive Deputy Commissioner of the Family Independence Administration of the City Human Resources Administration, testify about the manner in which services are provided to the non-disabled. The District Court explained its preclusion of the evidence in its opinion, holding that "[p]laintiffs have alleged, and demonstrated, that defendants have failed to provide them with the reasonable accommodations required by the federal disability statutes, thus failing to ensure them meaningful access to the benefits to which they are entitled," and that "[a] comparison with the manner in which benefits are administered to the non-disabled is thus not required, for the question of equality of administration is irrelevant to a claim for reasonable accommodations."

[D]iscussion

[A]. Whether the Plaintiffs Have Established That They Are Entitled to a Reasonable Accommodation

[T]he defendants argue that because the plaintiffs have not demonstrated that they are receiving less access than persons without disabilities to the services they seek, they have failed to show that they are "denied the benefits of the services, programs, or activities of a public entity," 42 U.S.C. § 12132, "by reason of [their] disability," id. (emphasis added), rather than as a result of other forces (such as systemic breakdowns within the entire social services system) that affect the non-disabled as well as the plaintiffs. The plaintiffs counter that they have demonstrated the requisite causal relationship based on the District Court's findings that the plaintiff class, *because of the disabilities faced by its members,* requires special accommodations in order to obtain meaningful access to social service benefits. They argue that they therefore need only show that such accommodations are not adequately being made available, and that they are not required to demonstrate disparate impact. The question, then, is whether a Title II plaintiff, to succeed on a claim alleging failure reasonably to accommodate, must also establish an adverse disparate impact on persons with the plaintiff's kind of disabilities.

1.

We first note that the plaintiffs advance a "reasonable accommodation" claim, and, contrary to the defendants' characterization, do not expressly rely on a theory of disparate impact. Our threshold question therefore is whether a Title II plaintiff who wishes to proceed on a reasonable accommodation theory must in any event also establish disparate impact. Put another way, we must determine whether the "concept of discrimination" embraced by the ADA demands that plaintiffs identify a "comparison class" of "similarly situated individuals given preferential treatment." *Olmstead* (plurality op.). We follow our fellow circuits, and the suggestions of the *Olmstead* plurality, in concluding that it does not.

Our analysis of the requirements of a reasonable accommodation claim begins with the Supreme Court's opinion in *Choate*. There, in interpreting the scope of section 504 of the Rehabilitation Act, the Court suggested that the relevant inquiry asks not whether the benefits available to persons with disabilities and to others are actually equal, but whether those with disabilities are as a practical matter able to access benefits to which they are legally entitled. The Court explained that "an otherwise qualified handicapped individual must be provided with meaningful access to the benefit that the grantee offers .... [T]o assure meaningful access, reasonable accommodations in the grantee's program or benefit may have to be made."

[T]he Justice Department's regulations, as we understand them, do not require a showing of disparate impact in reasonable accommodation cases. The Department's ADA regulations prohibiting "discrimination" provide in relevant part that:

A public entity, in providing any aid, benefit, or service, may not, directly or through contractual, licensing, or other arrangements, on the basis of disability—

(i) Deny a qualified individual with a disability the opportunity to participate in or benefit from the aid, benefit, or service;

(ii) Afford a qualified individual with a disability an opportunity to participate in or benefit from the aid, benefit, or service that is not equal to that afforded others;

(iii) Provide a qualified individual with a disability with an aid, benefit, or service that is not as effective in affording equal opportunity to obtain the same result, to gain the same benefit, or to reach the same level of achievement as that provided to others;

(iv) Provide different or separate aids, benefits, or services to individuals with disabilities or to any class of individuals with disabilities than is provided to others unless such action is necessary to provide qualified individuals with disabilities with aids, benefits, or services that are as effective as those provided to others;

. . .

(vii) Otherwise limit a qualified individual with a disability in the enjoyment of any right, privilege, advantage, or opportunity enjoyed by others receiving the aid, benefit, or service.

28 C.F.R. § 35.130(b)(1) (2002). The logical import of the regulations is that the Department has concluded that a public entity is not only prohibited from affording to persons with disabilities services that are "not equal to that afforded others," *id.* § 35.130(b)(1)(ii), or "not as effective in affording equal opportunity," *id.* § 35.130(b)(1)(iii), but also cannot prevent a qualified individual with a disability from enjoying "any aid, benefit, or service," *id.* § 35.130(b)(1)(i), regardless of whether other individuals are granted access. Similarly, the Department's regulations implementing the Rehabilitation Act state that "a recipient *shall* make reasonable accommodation to the known physical or mental limitations of an otherwise qualified handicapped applicant or employee unless the recipient can demonstrate that the accommodation would impose an undue hardship on the operation of its program." 28 C.F.R. § 41.53 (2002) (emphasis added). This mandatory language necessarily implies that the regulation is not conditioned on the ability of the "otherwise qualified . . . applicant" to show that other applicants receive more favorable treatment. The defendants have not challenged the validity, nor directly challenged the reasonableness, of either set of regulations.

We have employed a similar understanding in our cases applying the Rehabilitation Act. That is, our cases speak simply in terms of helping individuals with disabilities access public benefits to which both they and those without disabilities are legally entitled, and to which they would have difficulty obtaining access due to disabilities; the cases do not invite comparisons to the results obtained by individuals without disabilities. We have specifically embraced the view that the Rehabilitation Act requires affirmative accommodations to ensure that facially neutral rules do not in practice discriminate against individuals with disabilities. *See Dopico v. Goldschmidt,* 687 F.2d 644, 652 (2d Cir.1982). In language that is much quoted by the District Court and by the parties, we commented that:

"denial of access cannot be lessened simply by eliminating discriminatory selection criteria; because the barriers to equal participation are physical rather than abstract, some sort of action must be taken to remove them . . . . *It is not enough to open the door for the handicapped . . . ; a ramp must be built so the door can be reached.*"

Id. (emphasis added and internal quotations and citations omitted). The *Dopico* court further explained that "where the relief requested did not modify some integral aspect of a defendant's program, courts have ruled that section 504 does require efforts to make the program available to otherwise qualified handicapped persons." *Id.* at 653 n.6. Similarly, in

Rothschild v. Grottenthaler, we found that a public school had a duty under § 504 of the Rehabilitation Act reasonably to accommodate deaf parents by providing them with a sign language interpreter at "school-initiated conferences incident to the academic and/or disciplinary aspects of their child's education." 907 F.2d 286, 292–93 (2d Cir.1990) (citation omitted). Without the interpreter, deaf parents would not have meaningful access to the service provided to non-deaf parents. We stated that " 'Section 504 of the Rehabilitation Act requires some degree of positive effort to expand the availability of federally funded programs to handicapped persons otherwise qualified to benefit from them.' " *Id.* (quoting *Dopico*, 687 F.2d at 653 n. 6). In short, our measure in both cases was whether the plaintiffs with disabilities could achieve meaningful access, and not whether the access the plaintiffs had (absent a remedy) was *less* meaningful than what was enjoyed by others.

[O]ur approach also finds support in the *Olmstead* plurality's opinion. Writing on this point for herself and three other justices, Justice Ginsburg appeared to reject the suggestion that every ADA claim must necessarily include proof of disparate impact:

> Nor were [the plaintiffs] subjected to discrimination, the State contends, because discrimination necessarily requires uneven treatment of similarly situated individuals, and [plaintiffs] had identified no comparison class, *i.e.*, no similarly situated individuals given preferential treatment. We are satisfied that Congress had a more comprehensive view of the concept of discrimination advanced in the ADA.

We acknowledge, however, that the ADA and Rehabilitation Act are addressed to "rules . . . that hurt [people with disabilities] *by reason of their handicap,* rather than that hurt them solely by virtue of what they have in common with other people." *Good Shephard Manor Found., Inc. v. City of Momence,* 323 F.3d 557, 561 (7th Cir.2003) (internal quotations and citation omitted). In other words, there must be something different about the way the plaintiff is treated "by reason of . . . disability." 42 U.S.C. § 12132. We have long recognized that the basic analytical framework of the ADA includes such a comparative component.

It does not follow, though, from this framework that a plaintiff must also demonstrate disparate impact in all cases. That other applicants fail for other reasons to obtain meaningful access to a public service does not demonstrate that applicants with disabilities were not the objects of dissimilar treatment because of their disabilities, or that they were not "subject to a more onerous condition," *Olmstead* (Kennedy, J., concurring), than those who did not have disabilities. Further, the statute itself does not literally require a showing of "discrimination." A plaintiff can prevail either by showing "discrimination" or by showing "deni[al of] the benefits" of public services. 42 U.S.C. § 12132.

Therefore, we hold that a claim of discrimination based on a failure reasonably to accommodate is distinct from a claim of discrimination based on disparate impact. Quite simply, the demonstration that a disability makes it difficult for a plaintiff to access benefits that are available to both those with and without disabilities is sufficient to sustain a claim for a reasonable accommodation.

2.

In addition to arguing that the plaintiffs bear the burden of proving disparate impact in order to show failure reasonably to accommodate, an argument we reject, the defendants contend that they should be permitted to show a lack of disparate impact in order to demonstrate that the plaintiffs have not been denied access *because of their disabilities*. The parties have identified two possible causes of the plaintiffs' low rate of obtaining benefits. The plaintiffs argue that their disabilities create obstacles to access. The District Court has made specific findings that the plaintiffs' disabilities prevent them from accessing public services insofar as the plaintiffs face challenges that make it impossible for them meaningfully to access services absent accommodation, and has further found that the current accommodative measures are unacceptably ineffective. The defendants, by contrast, purport to be able to demonstrate that the plaintiffs are no less successful in gaining access to benefits than the non-disabled. Such a showing would suggest an alternative reason for the plaintiffs' low rate of obtaining benefits: systemic problems that create obstacles to access for everyone.

[W]e think that the differing explanations offered by the parties for the plaintiffs' inability to obtain the benefits to which they are facially entitled are not mutually exclusive. Again, the District Court found, and the defendants do not dispute, that the plaintiffs are sharply limited in their ability to "travel[ ], stand[ ] in line, attend[ ] scheduled appointments, complet[e] paper work, and otherwise negotiat[e] medical and social service bureaucracies." The District Court also found that the existing DASIS accommodative regime is unacceptably dysfunctional, and fails meaningfully to remedy these problems. The defendants instead contend, in essence, that their own bureaucracy is so defective that even healthy applicants cannot "negotiate" it, such that there is no disparate impact on the plaintiffs. Even accepting that contention as true, we could still be faced with a situation where either of the two alleged causes of denial of access would independently deny meaningful access even were the other fixed.

Traditional concepts of causation suggest that under such circumstances, the existence of the "disability cause" alone is enough to sustain the plaintiffs' claims. An ADA plaintiff must demonstrate that a denial of benefits occurs "by reason of . . . disability," 42 U.S.C. § 12132, which essentially means that the plaintiff must prove that the denial is "because of" the disability. The defendants' contention, rendered in these terms, is that disability was not the cause of the difficulties experienced by the plaintiffs, because the same ultimate difficulty would have resulted in any case. The common law of torts, however, instructs that the existence of additional factors causing an injury does not necessarily negate the fact that the defendant's wrong is also the legal cause of the injury. In assessing whether one cause among many constitutes proximate cause, courts have engaged in inquiries such as whether a cause is a substantial factor in bringing about the harm, or whether the cause is "too remotely or insignificantly related to the" harm to be a legal basis for liability.

In so interpreting the "by reason of . . . disability" requirement, we are mindful of the fact that Title II seeks principally to ensure that disabilities do not prevent access to public services where the disabilities can reasonably be accommodated.

[W]e therefore hold that the District Court did not clearly err in concluding, in effect, that the plaintiffs' disabilities were a substantial cause of their inability to obtain services, or that that inability was not so remotely or insignificantly related to their disabilities as not to be "by reason" of them. The District Court has identified major failures within the existing accommodative regime. This is not a case where the evidence has demonstrated that the plaintiffs are failing to access their full benefits even with the help of a smoothly functioning DASIS, and that those without disabilities are faring no better. Here, DASIS does not function smoothly, and the plaintiffs are unable meaningfully to access benefits. Under these circumstances, where testimonial evidence has made clear that the offered accommodation is highly ineffectual, it is no defense that others are equally unsuccessful in accessing benefits. Moreover, as we noted earlier, the fact that individuals other than the class members have been unable to obtain benefits does not of itself demonstrate that the plaintiffs do not face conditions that are more onerous for them because of their particular disabilities. The absence of disparate impact would not prove that DASIS is effective enough to provide benefits under a state of affairs where the social services system functioned smoothly. Where the District Court has clearly identified disability-related challenges that make access more difficult for the plaintiff class than for those without disabilities, and has found the accommodative scheme to be "broken," we hold that the plaintiffs have demonstrated that their disabilities are a cause of the denial of access to benefits.

Of course, as noted above, there is undoubtedly a comparative element to the reasonable accommodation analysis, and a plaintiff must show that the denial of benefits was "by reason of . . . disability." However, we believe that this element is satisfied by the plaintiffs' demonstration (i) that they are facially entitled to public benefits which are also available to similarly situated persons without disabilities, and (ii) that under a state of affairs where the social services system functioned properly, their disabilities would clearly necessitate a reasonable accommodation in order for them meaningfully to access the benefits (which accommodation they are not currently receiving). As we indicate below, our decision does not preclude the use in some cases of the absence of disparate impact as a basis for a defense that an offered accommodation is in fact working.

B. Whether the Relief Granted Constitutes a Reasonable Accommodation

We now turn to whether the injunctive relief ordered by the District Court constitutes a reasonable accommodation. The injunction at its core orders DASIS to perform its statutory mandate, and imposes some procedural mechanisms designed to effectuate this goal. [W]e agree with the District Court that the DASIS law represents an attempt at reasonable accommodation and can properly form a basis for the injunctive relief granted in this case. [A]s the District Court noted, the vast majority of services created by the DASIS law are fundamentally procedural in nature. The law provides for intensive case management, for low client-caseworker ratios, and for imposition of clear deadlines. We thus share the District Court's view that the plaintiffs have established that requiring DASIS to comply with the DASIS law represents appropriate reasonable accommodation relief.

The defendants in this case have not [a]lleged that the proposed accommodation would cause them or their programs undue hardship. Perhaps that is because, at least at the time this litigation was before the District Court, in the defendants' estimation, the accommodation provided by the DASIS law was not causing such a hardship. We note that if at any time such hardship arises the defendants would undoubtedly have the ability to return to the District Court to seek a modification of its order to reflect that condition.

Instead of challenging the requested accommodations based on the burden of their implementation, the defendants argue that no accommodations are required because the plaintiffs have not demonstrated that they are suffering a negative disparate impact relative to similarly situated persons without disabilities. As we have observed, no such demonstration is necessary. Accordingly, we affirm the injunction as a reasonable accommodative measure.

We pause, however, to address two additional issues raised by the defendants in other contexts that might provide bases for challenging the scope of the accommodation ordered by the District Court. First, while the defendants frame their disparate treatment argument as an attack on the need for a reasonable accommodation itself, their point also might support an argument that the plaintiffs already are being reasonably accommodated. There would be no need for injunctive relief if the plaintiffs were already being reasonably accommodated. The defendants' disparate impact argument suggests that had the defendants been able to prove that the plaintiffs are faring no worse in accessing benefits than the non-disabled, they would have proven that the plaintiffs were already being reasonably accommodated.

We reject this argument. A "reasonable accommodation" is one that gives the otherwise qualified plaintiff with disabilities "meaningful access" to the program or services sought. *Choate.* That others cannot avail themselves of the services does not make the minimal access provided to the plaintiff "meaningful." As we have held, meaningful access must be defined with reference to the plaintiff's facial entitlement to benefits. In this case, the District Court made specific findings to the effect that qualified plaintiffs cannot obtain benefits without aid, and that the current accommodative regime is dysfunctional. That is sufficient to justify relief. The mere fact that the plaintiffs, in the current apparently broken overall social services system, might not be doing worse than persons without disabilities, does not render the dysfunctional DASIS "reasonable."

Second, the defendants assert that the DASIS law fundamentally represents a grant to the plaintiff class of substantive benefits unavailable to persons without disabilities rather than an attempt to accommodate the plaintiff class's disabilities with respect to public benefits available to all qualifying individuals. While the defendants frame this issue as an attack on the plaintiffs' right to any accommodation, it could merit consideration as a basis for questioning whether the injunctive relief granted is overbroad. Even though the plaintiffs have demonstrated that they are entitled to a reasonable accommodation, an accommodation that served as a grant of special substantive rights would not constitute appropriate relief. The DASIS law nominally provides the plaintiffs with certain additional substantive benefits, such as nutritional supplements and transportation allowances. There is language in the District Court's opinion arguably to suggest that the plaintiffs might be able to state a claim to some of these substantive benefits. *See* [district ct. op.] n.22 (commenting that even the "nutritional supplements and transportation allowances act as reasonable modifications allowing persons with AIDS and HIV access to their benefits, not as benefits additional to those received by the non-disabled public").

In spite of this footnote, we do not construe the injunction of the District Court in fact to order access to any of the additional benefits provided only to the plaintiff class. The overall discussion of the opinion and the language of the injunction make clear that the District Court's holding does not ultimately embrace so broad a theory of accommodation. The District Court recognized that the

> [p]laintiffs have made no claim under the ADA or the [Rehabilitation] Act for additional or better benefits and services than provided to the non-disabled. To the contrary, plaintiffs' ADA and [Rehabilitation] Act claims seek meaningful access to the *very same benefits and services* provided to the non-disabled. Plaintiffs seek, and this Court requires, only the modifications—such as intensive case management and low case manager-to-client ratios—required to ensure meaningful access to the same benefits and services.

The injunction itself specifically limits the "benefits and services" to which it orders access to "public assistance, Medicaid, Food Stamps, housing, and other *benefits and services available to qualifying members of the general public* comparable to public assistance and welfare benefits." (emphasis added).[11] This language restricts the injunctive relief to benefits available to both the plaintiffs and the eligible non-disabled.

Thus, while we affirm the injunctive relief ordered, we note that we do not read the injunction to require provision of extra substantive benefits unavailable to the non-disabled—including, without limitation, enhanced rental assistance, nutritional supplements, and transportation allowances—nor do we construe it to permit an action based on procedural ineffectiveness if the ineffectiveness relates solely to provision of such "additional" substantive benefits.

---

[11] We are untroubled by the fact that as a practical matter the reforms in DASIS may serve to enhance access to the additional substantive benefits such as enhanced rent assistance, nutritional benefits, and transportation assistance, or by the fact that a presentation of evidence may involve reference to these benefits (as did the evidence in the District Court here). It is not realistic in practice entirely to bifurcate the different types of services DASIS provides. We simply hold that the District Court did not find any right under the ADA to access the "additional" benefits, and that an evidentiary presentation that would be unpersuasive in the absence of reference to provision of access to additional benefits should not prevail.

Finally, we have some concern about the provision of the injunction that requires the defendants to "comply with all legally-mandated time frames for the delivery of benefits and services." The DASIS law requires that "[w]here no statute, law, regulation or rule provides a time period within which a benefit or service shall be provided . . . such benefit or service shall be provided no later than twenty business days following submission of all information or documentation required to determine eligibility." N.Y. City Admin. Code § 21–128(c)(2). It is not entirely clear to us that once a plaintiff is accommodated to the point that "all information or documentation required to determine eligibility" has been filed, a further requirement for the agency to act with greater dispatch with respect to that plaintiff than it does with respect to other applicants with other infirmities is an "accommodation" of the plaintiff's disability. The fact that a requirement is in the DASIS law does not alone conclusively determine that it is an accommodation required by federal law. Because the defendants do not challenge the timeliness requirements on this ground, however, we need not and do not decide the issue.

These observations aside, we agree, as set forth above, with the District Court that the overwhelming purpose of DASIS is to provide access to public benefits available to all, and that the plaintiffs have demonstrated, and the defendants have not rebutted, evidence that DASIS offers a reasonable accommodation to the challenges faced by the plaintiff class. Indeed, counsel for the city defendants commented in colloquy in the District Court that "DASIS itself is a reasonable modification of the public assistance programs administered by HRA to all non-DASIS clients." We are thus comfortable affirming the injunction[.]

Does 1–5 v. Chandler

United States Court of Appeals for the Ninth Circuit, 1996.
83 F.3d 1150.

■ MERHIGE, SENIOR DISTRICT JUDGE:

This case arises out of a class action lawsuit brought by Appellants, John Does 1–5 and Jane Doe, individually and on behalf of others similarly situated. Appellees are Susan M. Chandler, Director of the Hawaii Department of Human Services, and Patricia Murakami, Acting Administrator, Family and Adult Services Division.

HRS § 346–71 is the principal statutory mandate for Hawaii's General Assistance ("GA") Program. HRS § 346–71 was amended in 1995 by Act 166 of the Hawaii legislature. Appellants filed suit in the United States District Court for the District of Hawaii on June 21, 1995, alleging that Act 166 violates Title II of the Americans with Disabilities Act ("ADA"), 42 U.S.C. § 12101, et seq., and its implementing regulations, 28 C.F.R. § 35.130. [A]ppellants appeal the district court's denial of their motion for a preliminary injunction to enjoin enforcement of Act 166.

I.

Prior to 1995, HRS § 346–71, Hawaii's applicable GA statute, provided GA benefits to those persons with dependent children, able-bodied persons at least 55 years of age, and disabled persons who were unable to provide sufficient support for themselves and who were not otherwise provided for under Hawaii law or eligible for federal assistance. In 1995, the Hawaii legislature passed Act 166 amending HRS § 346–71. Act 166 has the effect of eliminating GA as an entitlement and eliminating benefits for certain persons who had previously received them.

Act 166 eliminated benefits to those able-bodied persons who had been entitled to GA because they were at least 55 years old. Act 166 also limited the receipt of benefits to those who had been entitled to GA by reason of their disability to no more than one year. Thus, after Act 166 the Hawaii GA program provides durationally unlimited benefits to persons with dependent children who are unable to provide sufficient support for themselves and who are not otherwise provided for under Hawaii law or eligible for federal assistance and benefits of up to a duration of one year to disabled persons unable to provide sufficient support for themselves and who are not otherwise provided for under Hawaii law or eligible for federal assistance.

The amendments to HRS § 346–71 contained in Act 166 became effective on July 1, 1995. Thus, if Act 166 is not found to violate federal law, persons who receive GA by reason of their disabilities will begin to be terminated from the program when their eligibility elapses a year from that date.

[T]he Appellants-plaintiff class consists of "[a]ll persons who are, have been, or will be identified as 'disabled' under Chapter 346 and its implementing regulations and who will be adversely affected by the implementation of Act 166." Shortly after filing suit, Appellants brought a motion for a preliminary injunction in the district court, seeking to enjoin the enforcement of HRS § 346–71, as amended. The district court denied this motion on November 13, 1995, determining that Appellants had failed to raise a "serious question" as to the validity of HRS 346–71, as amended.

II.

[T]he Appellants' argument that Act 166 violates Title II of the ADA runs as follows: (1) Hawaii's GA program is one program with the single purpose of providing public assistance to those who are unable to provide sufficient support for themselves or those dependent upon them and who are ineligible for federally funded assistance programs; (2) Appellants are "qualified individuals with disabilities" with respect to participation in the GA program because by virtue of their need and ineligibility for federal support the Appellants "meet[ ] the essential eligibility requirements for the . . . participation in" the GA program provided by DHS; (3) Act 166 places a durational limit on GA benefits provided to the needy eligible disabled and no durational limit on benefits provided to the needy eligible persons with children in the home; (4) there is no logical or empirical support for the conclusion that eligible persons with dependent children at home are more needy than eligible disabled persons; (5) the difference in Act 166 between the treatment of the needy disabled and that of the needy persons with dependent children is not "necessary" to the "essential nature" of the GA program and, indeed, is entirely irrational; (6) Act 166, therefore, violates Title II and the implementing regulations on its face.

[A]ppellants rely heavily on the decision of the United States District Court for the Southern District of Florida in *Concerned Parents to Save Dreher Park Center v. City of West Palm Beach*, 846 F.Supp. 986 (S.D.Fla.1994). In this decision the court held that it was a violation of Title II of the ADA for the City of West Palm Beach to shut down a recreational facility for the disabled. The *Concerned Parents* Court reasoned, first, that the disabled plaintiffs were clearly "qualified individuals with disabilities" because they met the only "essential eligibility requirement" of the City's recreational program by requesting the benefits of a recreational program. Second, the court concluded that the elimination of the Dreher Park program effectively denied the disabled the benefits of the City's recreational programs. Lastly, the Court reasoned that, "while Title II does not require any particular level of services for persons with disabilities in an absolute sense, it does require that any benefits provided to non-disabled persons be equally made available for disabled persons." The Court found that the City had been unable to provide any legitimate explanation for the extreme disparity between the budget cuts in recreation programs for the disabled and the non-disabled and that there was accordingly "strong evidence that the denial of the benefits of recreation was by reason of Plaintiffs' disabilities."

The Appellants state that it is "undisputed" that they are "qualified persons with disabilities." They assert that the "essential nature" of the GA program is to "serve the most needy" and that they meet the "essential eligibility requirement" for participation in the GA program due to their need. The Appellants further assert that, as in *Concerned Parents*, the Appellees have provided no legitimate explanation for the extreme disparity between the budget cuts for GA to the disabled and those for GA to the households with dependent children. This disparity, instead of across the board cuts, according to Appellants, plainly evidences a denial of benefits "based on disability" and does violence to the very purpose of the GA program to provide for the most needy.

We disagree with Appellants' conclusion that Act 166 denies benefits based on disability. It is undisputed that Hawaii is not required to have a GA program at all. It also is clear that Hawaii may have a benefit program aimed only at families with dependent children. Such a program would not violate the ADA as long as disabled people with children were not excluded from full participation in the program. In such a situation the disabled without children would not meet the "essential eligibility requirement" for participation in the program—having dependent children.

[T]he key issue in this case, therefore, is one of characterization. The Court concludes that the Hawaii GA program is, functionally, made up of a program of support for needy families and a separate program of support for the needy disabled. The ADA does not require equivalent benefits in different programs.

Although Appellants argue that the Hawaii GA program is essentially a single, unified program with the single essential purpose of providing income support for the needy, we conclude otherwise. The Hawaii GA program does not provide benefits to all needy residents who cannot receive federal aid—only those who are disabled or who have dependent children. Non-disabled needy without dependent children are not entitled to receive any funds. This restriction cuts against viewing the program as having the unified purpose of providing for the needy as opposed to viewing it, functionally if not formally, as two discrete forms of benefit providing for two discrete subgroups of the needy population.

III.

The Court AFFIRMS the district court's denial of the motion for a preliminary injunction[.]

Weaver v. New Mexico Human Services Department

Supreme Court of New Mexico, 1997.
945 P.2d 70.

■ BACA, JUSTICE.

Defendant–Appellant, the New Mexico Human Services Department (HSD), appeals a district court Order granting summary judgment in favor of Plaintiffs–Appellees on a claim brought under the Americans with Disabilities Act (the ADA). The Order invalidated an HSD regulation which imposed a twelve-month maximum period of eligibility for disabled adults receiving benefits under the General Assistance Program.

[HSD] is the state agency responsible for the administration of all welfare activities in New Mexico. See NMSA 1978, § 27–1–3 (1987). One welfare activity administered by HSD is the General Assistance Program. See NMSA 1978, § 27–2–7 (1973). This program provides financial assistance:

> 1) to permanently disabled adults with no minor dependents who are not eligible for [Social Security Income (SSI)] because their disability is not severe enough;

> 2) [to] temporarily disabled adults with no minor dependents;

> 3) on behalf of children under 18 years of age who would be eligible for [Aid to Families with Dependant Children (AFDC)] except that they are not living with a person within the specified degree of relationship. . . .

8 NMAC 3.010.21 (1996).

In response to budgetary shortfalls for fiscal year 1996, and pursuant to the regulatory authority provided in Section 27–1–3(D), HSD promulgated Financial Assistance Program Rule 419, 8 NMAC 3.419 (1995) (hereinafter "FAP–419"). FAP–419 restricts the period of time during which disabled adults may receive General Assistance benefits. The regulation provides that "[a] grant made to an individual eligible for GA due to disability is limited to no more than 12 months. . . . " 8 NMAC 3.419.22. HSD did not impose a twelve-month time limit on General Assistance benefits for dependent children. See 8 NMAC 3.419.21.

Plaintiffs–Appellees are disabled recipients of General Assistance benefits. Plaintiffs have already received General Assistance benefits for at least 12 months and would no longer be eligible for General Assistance benefits if FAP–419 were implemented.

Plaintiffs challenged the validity of FAP–419 in district court, contending that it violated Title II of the ADA. [P]laintiffs asserted that HSD is a public entity which implemented FAP–419 to restrict disabled adults, by reason of their disability, from receiving the benefits of the General Assistance Program, in violation of [42 U.S.C. §] 12132. HSD disagreed, contending that the time limitations of FAP–419 were motivated by budgetary considerations rather than disability, and noting authority to modify the General Assistance Program under Section 27–2–7(A)(3).

[T]he district court agreed that the HSD regulation violated Title II of the ADA as a matter of law, and granted the Motion for Summary Judgment. HSD then filed for a stay of judgment pending appeal. A stay was granted and this appeal followed.

[W]e turn now to evaluate whether, as a matter of law, FAP–419 denied Plaintiffs the benefits of HSD's General Assistance Program on the basis of their disabilities. The ADA does not permit segregation of individuals with disabilities in the provision of public services, nor does it permit the provision of benefits to individuals with disabilities different from those provided to other benefits recipients.

The undisputed facts in this case establish that disabled individuals are ineligible for General Assistance benefits after twelve months of receipt, while other recipients of General Assistance benefits are eligible to receive such benefits for an indefinite period of time. See 8 NMAC 3.419.22. Thus, there is no factual dispute as to whether Plaintiffs are denied General Assistance benefits equivalent to those available to General Assistance recipients who are not disabled.

HSD denies that the disparity in benefits available to disabled and non-disabled General Assistance recipients is the result of discrimination on the basis of disability. According to HSD, FAP–419 does not deny Plaintiffs General Assistance benefits on the basis of their disabilities because the General Assistance Program is a compilation of three distinct programs: one for dependent children; one for disabled adults ineligible for SSI; and one for other people ineligible for any federal assistance programs. HSD goes on to argue that the program serving the needs of disabled individuals can be altered without consideration of the restrictions, or lack of restrictions, placed on the program serving dependent children. Such modifications do not violate the ADA because the ADA does not require different programs to provide equivalent benefits. HSD supports its argument by pointing to the recent Ninth Circuit Court of Appeals decision, *John Does 1–5 v. Chandler*, 83 F.3d 1150 (9th Cir.1996), in which durational time restrictions placed on General Assistance benefits for disabled individuals were upheld. We conclude that *Chandler* is inapplicable to the instant case.

In *Chandler*, the Ninth Circuit Court of Appeals evaluated whether Hawaii's General Assistance Program violated the ADA by placing a twelve-month durational time restriction on the availability of benefits for disabled individuals, without placing similar restrictions on the availability of benefits for other recipients of General Assistance. The

Court found that [t]he General Assistance program was not a cohesive program serving a single needy population; rather it was two programs under the umbrella heading of General Assistance. The Court concluded that the ADA restricted the regulation-making authority of the Department of Human Services, but that the ADA did not require distinct programs to offer identical benefits to recipients. By treating the two components of General Assistance as separate programs, the Court concluded that neither program discriminated against disabled individuals on the basis of disability in violation of the ADA, and upheld the General Assistance program.

Unlike the Hawaii General Assistance Program, New Mexico's General Assistance Program is a unified program of assistance. If this Court were to adopt HSD's characterization of the General Assistance Program as a compilation of three distinct programs, we would fail in our duty to give effect to the intent of the Legislature. Legislative intent is derived through evaluation of the statutory language as well as the history of the law. We read all parts of an act together to produce a harmonious whole. The objective motivating legislation is also relevant to determining legislative intent.

In the instant case, a single purpose motivated development of the General Assistance Program. The Program was intended to provide assistance to needy people not covered by federal assistance programs. See 8 NMAC 3.010.21. Further, the statute governing the General Assistance Program, and the accompanying regulations, refer to a single General Assistance program rather than a compilation of several programs. See, *e.g.*, § 27–2–7 (referring to a general assistance program); 8 NMAC 3.010.21 (identifying General Assistance as "a limited program"). Finally, HSD requests, and the Legislature provides, funding for the General Assistance Program as a single item in the State's budget. In order to give effect to our Legislature's intent, we conclude that the General Assistance Program is a single program of public benefits. While the ADA does not require equivalent benefits in different programs, see *Chandler*, we understand the law to require equivalent benefits for disabled and non-disabled recipients of a single program. Therefore, we cannot adopt the result of *Chandler* in evaluating whether FAP–419 violates Title II of the ADA.

In the instant case, there are undisputed facts establishing that the restrictions placed on benefits for Plaintiffs is by reason of their disabilities. The regulation explicitly provides that disability is the criterion used to distinguish between recipients of General Assistance benefits who are restricted by the twelve-month time limitation and those who are not restricted by the time limitation. See 8 NMAC 3.419. We conclude that the use of disability as the determinative factor in limiting eligibility for General Assistance benefits is the denial of the benefits of a public entity by reason of an individual's disability in violation of Title II of the ADA.

Rodde v. Bonta

United States Court of Appeals for the Ninth Circuit, 2004.
357 F.3d 988.

■ PREGERSON, CIRCUIT JUDGE.

Los Angeles County and Thomas Garthwaite, Director and Chief Medical Officer of Los Angeles County's Department of Health Services, (the County) plan to reduce the County's health care spending by closing Rancho Los Amigos National Rehabilitation Center (Rancho). Rancho is a County hospital dedicated primarily to providing inpatient and outpatient rehabilitative care to disabled individuals. Plaintiffs are current and future Medi-Cal patients with special needs that require medical services offered at Rancho. They challenged the impending closure of Rancho through this action. The district court granted plaintiffs' request for a preliminary injunction that barred the County from going forward with its planned closure without providing plaintiffs with necessary medical and rehabilitative services elsewhere. The County appealed. We [a]ffirm.

[R]ancho—one of six County hospitals—is a 207-bed facility that specializes in rehabilitation and the acute care needs of patients with chronic diseases. Rancho provides care to about 2,600 inpatients and 8,600 outpatients annually. While most County hospitals predominantly treat the indigent and uninsured, Rancho has a high percentage of patients with public and private insurance. About 67 percent of Rancho's inpatients and 58 percent of Rancho's outpatients are Medi-Cal recipients.

Rancho has served Los Angeles's homeless, mentally ill, disabled and elderly populations since it opened in 1888. Important health care innovations, including the "halo" device used to support the head and neck of spinal cord injury patients, were invented at Rancho. Rancho was also the first facility to replace wood with plastic for prosthetic limbs. By the early 1930s, Rancho was becoming legendary for its occupational therapy. Later, during World War II, Rancho began providing long-term care and rehabilitation for polio patients; in 1954, the majority of the 1,865 Los Angeles area polio victims were treated at Rancho.

In 2002, in an effort to increase efficiency and reduce costs, the County consolidated its clinical services for certain severe disabilities. It did so by moving all acute inpatient rehabilitation, chronic ventilator/pulmonary services, and pediatric orthopedic surgery for selected neuromuscular disorders to Rancho. Before that time, these services were also offered at other County facilities. Because of the consolidation, currently about 60 percent of Rancho's inpatients are transferred to Rancho from the other five County hospitals.

Rancho is a unique facility; no other facility in the area currently provides many of the services it offers. Because many disabled patients will be unable to find necessary medical treatment elsewhere if Rancho closes, doctors anticipate that closing Rancho will have a devastating effect on the facility's disabled patients, including plaintiffs. Doctors are also concerned that closing Rancho will negatively impact the treatment of patients at other County facilities as well as important medical training and research.

Nevertheless, on January 28, 2003, the County decided to close Rancho because of anticipated future budget deficits. The County planned to reduce services at Rancho beginning May 1, 2003, and to fully close the hospital by June 30, 2003. The County expects to save $58.6 million annually by closing Rancho. However, the County's calculation does not take into account the cost of providing Rancho patients with care at other County facilities.

Although the County was expecting a budget deficit when it began studying cost-cutting proposals, a new infusion of Medicaid funding has helped the County's health care system end the 2002–2003 fiscal year with over $300 million in its fund balance. The County now projects that it will have almost the same amount in its fund balance for fiscal year 2003–2004 and nearly $200 million at the end of fiscal year 2004–2005. No shortfall is expected until 2006–2007.

[S]hortly after the County decided to shut down Rancho, plaintiffs filed this action to enjoin the impending closure. Plaintiffs are a certified class of Medi-Cal recipients who receive medical care at Rancho. Specifically, they include:

> All present and future recipients of the Medicaid program: (a) who reside in the County of Los Angeles; (b) who have or will have disabilities; and (c) who, because of their disabilities[,] need or will need inpatient and/or outpatient rehabilitative and other medical services that are currently provided at Rancho Los Amigos National Rehabilitation Center.

Plaintiffs asserted [a]sserted an Americans with Disabilities Act (ADA) claim against all defendants, including the County. Plaintiffs then filed a motion for a preliminary injunction, seeking to enjoin the state and the County from terminating or reducing Medi–Cal covered inpatient and outpatient services at Rancho. The district court certified the class and granted plaintiffs a temporary restraining order on the same day. [A]fter further briefing, the district court granted plaintiffs' request for a preliminary injunction.

[T]he district court did not abuse its discretion in concluding that plaintiffs established a likelihood of success on the merits of their ADA claim.

[T]he County attacks "the very premise of the district court's definition of the benefit" at issue—the notion that plaintiffs are entitled to "the specialized medical expertise" they need for adequate medical care—as contrary to Supreme Court precedent.[10] The district court considered this argument, but found the County's precedent distinguishable and its contention unpersuasive. We agree.

At the core of the County's argument is *Alexander v. Choate*, 469 U.S. 287 (1985). In *Alexander*, to save money, Tennessee proposed reducing the number of annual days of inpatient care covered by the state Medicaid program from 20 to 14 for all program participants. [T]he Supreme Court concluded that the planned reduction was not discriminatory because it did not deny the disabled the benefits of the

---

[10] The County also argues that the district court's suggestion that the public "benefit" at issue here is Medi–Cal benefits is plainly erroneous because the state rather than the County provides Medi–Cal benefits. Although the district court did observe that closing Rancho would effectively deny plaintiffs the benefits of Medi–Cal, it also commented that "the closing of Rancho can lead to denial of benefits to the disabled in that they will receive inadequate or harmful medical treatment due to the lack of access to the specialized medical expertise available at Rancho." There is no real dispute here; plaintiffs agree that the benefit at issue is County patients' access to Medi–Cal covered services from County facilities.

14 days of care the state chose to provide; rather, the plan left all patients

> with identical and effective hospital services fully available for their use, with both classes of users subject to the same durational limitation.
>
> . . .
>
> Medicaid programs do not guarantee that each recipient will receive that level of health care precisely tailored to his or her particular needs. Instead, the benefit provided through Medicaid is a particular package of health care services, such as 14 days of inpatient coverage. That package of services has the general aim of assuring that individuals will receive necessary medical care, but the benefit provided remains the individual services offered—not "adequate health care." . . .
>
> Section 504 seeks to assure evenhanded treatment and the opportunity for handicapped individuals to participate in and benefit from programs receiving federal assistance. . . . The Act does not, however, guarantee the handicapped equal results from the provision of state Medicaid.

Id.

[A]*lexander* is distinguishable from the instant case. The reduction at issue in *Alexander* was facially neutral—the maximum hospital stay for all patients was reduced to 14 days. The County's argument that its proposed cuts are similarly "across-the-board" because it also plans to reduce the beds at County-USC Hospital (and already has eliminated some clinics) is unpersuasive. Reductions analogous to the cut in Alexander might include eliminating X dollars or Y percent of funding from the budget of each of the County's six hospitals or from each medical department or type of service offered therein. Eliminating entirely the only hospital of six that focuses on the needs of disabled individuals (because the County earlier decided to consolidate such services at that hospital) and that provides services disproportionately required by the disabled and available nowhere else in the County is simply not the sort of facially neutral reduction considered in *Alexander*. *Alexander* may allow the County to step down services equally for all who rely on it for their healthcare needs, but it does not sanction the wholesale elimination of services relied upon disproportionately by the disabled because of their disabilities.

Moreover, the Court in *Alexander* specifically noted that nothing in the record suggested "that the illnesses uniquely associated with the handicapped or occurring with greater frequency among them cannot be effectively treated, at least in part, with fewer than 14 days' coverage." Here, in contrast, plaintiffs presented ample evidence that rehabilitative services and treatment for complex and disabling medical conditions, such as paralysis and conditions associated with severe diabetes, cannot currently be provided effectively anywhere in the County system but Rancho. While the proposed cutback in *Alexander* did not uniquely affect disabled individuals, the County's planned cutback specifically targets services for the disabled. Even after *Alexander*, the ADA prohibits the County from eliminating healthcare services for the disabled in this manner.

Like the district court, we find the *Dreher Park* decision persuasive; it presents an analogous fact pattern, applies *Alexander*, and reaches a fair and well-reasoned result. In both *Dreher Park* and this case, the government first consolidated services for the disabled at a single facility. Then, due to budget shortages, the government decided to close the single facility providing specialized programs for the disabled, while continuing to operate the facilities providing the same category of services to non-disabled individuals. While the disabled could theoretically seek service from the remaining facilities, the evidence suggested in *Dreher Park*, as it does here, that the services designed for the general population would not adequately serve the unique needs of the disabled, who therefore would be effectively denied services that the non-disabled continued to receive. In light of all these parallels, the district court did not abuse its discretion in adopting *Dreher Park's* conclusion that such action violates the ADA and warrants an injunction.

In sum, plaintiffs demonstrated that if the County closes Rancho, it will reduce, and in some instances eliminate, necessary medical services for disabled Medi-Cal patients while continuing to provide the medical care required and sought by Medi-Cal recipients without disabilities. The district court relied on the correct legal standards and its factual findings are supported by the record. Therefore, the district court did not abuse its discretion in concluding that closing Rancho without continuing to provide medically necessary services to disabled individuals elsewhere would constitute discrimination on the basis of disability.

[I]n light of plaintiffs' strong showing of probable irreparable harm to plaintiffs and the public at large, the district court did not abuse its discretion by concluding that the public interest favored issuance of a preliminary injunction.

AFFIRMED.

NOTES ON DISABILITY DISCRIMINATION AND PUBLIC BENEFITS

1. Levels of Generality and Discrimination. Are *Chandler* and *Weaver* any different? In both cases, the state started with a program that provided the same benefits to poor people with dependent children (whether or not they had disabilities) and poor people with disabilities who had no dependent children. In both cases, the state changed its policy by retaining full benefits to poor people with dependent children (whether or not they had disabilities) and imposing a cap on the benefits for poor people with disabilities who have no dependent children. In *Chandler*, the court looks at the matter at a low level of generality and treats each category of benefits eligibility (dependent children, disability, etc.) as a separate program. A state can get rid of (or take the lesser step of limiting) any one of these programs, the court says, so long as it does not discriminate on the basis of disability in the ones that remain. Because the dependent-children benefits program does not discriminate on the basis of disability (anyone with dependent children who meets the means test—whether or not they have a disability—is eligible), and the disability benefits program does not discriminate against people with disabilities (in fact it gives them something people without disabilities don't get), the court concludes that the state has not violated the disability discrimination laws.

One might object that the *Chandler* court's analysis does not take account of the reasonable-modification requirement. So long as the state does not engage in intentional discrimination against people with disabilities in setting up its benefits programs, the court seems to say, it has satisfied its obligations under the disability discrimination laws. But, as in *Alexander v. Choate* (a principal case in this chapter, *supra*), the alternative to the *Chandler* court's approach seems problematic as well. In *Weaver*, the court looks at the matter at a high level of generality and treats the relevant program as a general one of "provid[ing] assistance to needy people not covered by federal assistance programs." Because needy people with disabilities and no dependents fit the purpose of this program just as much as do needy people with dependents, the court holds that the state could not impose limits on the former category while leaving the latter category untouched.

Does that analysis make sense? On the one hand, one might see the role of disability discrimination law in this context as ensuring that public officials who are cutting budgets take as full account of the interests of people with disabilities as they do of the interests of the nondisabled. The *Weaver* analysis certainly serves that purpose. But under our negative Constitution a state is not generally required to provide largesse to any particular class of people. Assessing the neediness of different groups raises complex empirical and normative issues. Why can't a legislature decide, as the legislatures in Hawaii and New Mexico seemed to, that poor people with dependent children (whether or not they have disabilities) have a more powerful claim on limited public resources than do poor people with disabilities who have no dependents? Does disability rights law mandate that people with disabilities have priority in receiving welfare benefits?

2. Integration and Empowerment. In *Chandler* and *Weaver*, plaintiffs with disabilities sought to obtain public assistance benefits. In *Rodde* and *Dreher Park*, plaintiffs with disabilities sought to keep disability-specific institutions from closing. How do these claims accord with the disability rights goals of integration and empowerment? As Chapter One discussed, many (though not all) disability rights activists have urged a move from welfare to work in disability policy, and many (though not all) disability rights activists have declared integration to be their central goal. Is it better—and more conducive to equal citizenship—for people with disabilities to keep their disability-specific welfare benefits, hospitals, and recreation centers? Or is it better—and more conducive to equal citizenship—for people with disabilities to face the ups and downs of the labor market, and to make their way in mainstream institutions? These are questions, as Chapter One indicates, that have divided disability rights activists for many years.

The plaintiffs in *Chandler*, *Weaver*, *Rodde*, and *Dreher Park* take one side of this long running debate. So long as mainstream institutions do not take account of people with disabilities, this position holds, welfare benefits and separate institutions will remain necessary. The other side of the debate holds that pervasive special treatment entrenches the view that people with disabilities do not belong in mainstream institutions and thus delays the day when integration will occur. Which side of the debate (which echoes long running debates within African-American and other minority communities) do you find more plausible? For an argument that disability welfare benefits will be essential to achieving integration and empowerment for people with disabilities, see Samuel R. Bagenstos, *The Future of Disability Law*, 114 Yale L.J. 1 (2004).

6. LICENSING

Applicants v. Texas State Board of Law Examiners

United States District Court for the Western District of Texas, 1994.
1994 WL 923404.

■ SPARKS, DISTRICT JUDGE.

The plaintiffs, individually and on behalf of those similarly situated, allege that the Texas Board of Law Examiners' inquiries and investigation into the mental health history of applicants seeking to practice law in the State of Texas violate the Americans with Disabilities Act (ADA), 42 U.S.C. §§ 12101–12213. The defendants are the Texas Board of Law Examiners and Rachel Martin, its executive director, collectively referred to as the defendants or the Board.

The plaintiffs, three law students who wish to be admitted to the Texas Bar, specifically challenge Section 82.027(b)(2) of the Texas Government Code requiring applicants to verify they are not mentally ill, the Texas Rules of Court governing admission that require applicants to execute an authorization for release of psychiatric records, and the Board's inquiries concerning treatment or hospitalization for mental illness in the preceding ten years and the follow-up investigations and hearings. The plaintiffs contend the statute, rules, inquiries, and investigations violate the ADA's prohibitions of discrimination against individuals on the basis of mental disability, a history of mental disability, or perceived mental disability. For these alleged violations, the plaintiffs seek injunctive and declaratory relief.

This cause was tried before the Court, without a jury, on July 7, 1994. For the reasons set forth below, the Court finds the Board's narrowly focused inquiries and investigation into the mental fitness of applicants to the Texas Bar who have been diagnosed or treated for bipolar disorder, schizophrenia, paranoia, or any other psychotic disorder do not violate the ADA.

I.   FINDINGS OF FACT

Pursuant to Texas Government Code Section 82.022(b), the Texas Supreme Court adopted the Texas Rules of Court that "govern the administration of the [Board's] functions relating to the licensing of lawyers." Tex.Gov't Code Ann. § 82.022 (West 1988). The Texas Government Code further requires each person intending to apply for admission to the Texas Bar to file with the Board a declaration of intention to study law and, before taking the bar examination, an application for examination. §§ 82.023, 82.027.

The Board is charged with assessing each applicant's moral character and fitness to practice law based on its investigation of the character and fitness of applicants. §§ 82028(a), 82.030(a). The Board, in fulfilling its statutory duties, must recommend denial of a license if the Board finds "a clear and rational connection between the applicant's present mental or emotional condition and the likelihood that the applicant will not discharge properly the applicant's responsibilities to a client, a court, or the legal profession if the applicant is licensed to practice law." § 82.028(c)(2).

The Board's investigation is limited to areas "clearly related to the applicant's moral character and present fitness to practice law." § 82.028(d). The rules promulgated by the Texas Supreme Court that govern admission to the Texas Bar define fitness as "the assessment of mental and emotional health as it affects the competence of a prospective lawyer." The fitness requirement is designed to exclude from the practice of law in Texas those persons having a mental or emotional condition that "would prevent the person from carrying out duties to clients, courts, or the profession." The fitness requirement is limited to present fitness; "prior mental or emotional illness or conditions are relevant only so far as they indicate the existence of a present lack of fitness."

Persons intending to seek admission to the Texas Bar usually file their declarations during the first year of law school. The rules require each applicant filing a declaration to provide extensive information about his or her background, including a history of mental illness.[2] The Rules also provide that the Board may require the applicant to execute a consent form authorizing the release of records to the Board.

The questions formulated by the Board to seek information about an applicant's mental health history have been substantially revised since 1992 in efforts to comply with the ADA. Question 11, the question the Board used in the declaration before April 1992, asked whether the applicant had been treated for any mental, emotional, or nervous condition in the past ten years and if the condition had resulted in either voluntary or involuntary admission to a hospital or institution.[3] Between April 1992 and July 1993, the Board used a version of question 11 that narrowed the focus to mental illness as defined by the Texas Health and Safety Code.[4] The current version of question 11 further

---

[2]   In addition, the applicant must provide information regarding his or her history, experience, and education; criminal history; history of fraud charges in any legal proceeding; history of compliance with child or spousal support orders; repayment history for federally guaranteed student loans; history of filing and paying income tax; and any other information the Board considers reasonably related to the investigation of the applicant's moral character and fitness.

[3]   The version of question 11 the Board used before April 1992 asked:

11.   Have you, within the last ten (10) years:

a) been examined or treated for any mental, emotional or nervous conditions? (You may exclude marriage counseling.)

b) been voluntarily or involuntarily admitted to a hospital or institution as a result of mental, emotional or nervous conditions?

If you answered "YES" to 11a. or b., give details on the Supplemental Form. Include dates of treatment or confinement, name and current mailing address of the person(s) who treated you (or the facility where you received treatment), and the reason for treatment.

[4]   The version of question 11 used between April 1992 and July 1993 asked:

narrows the inquiry to the diagnosis of certain specified mental illnesses that may bear on an applicant's present fitness to practice law.[5] Dr. Richard Coons, one of the experts who testified on the Board's behalf and who is educated as a lawyer, medical doctor, and psychiatrist, was a consultant to the Board in the Board's formulation of the current version of question 11.

An affirmative answer to any part of question 11 triggers a requirement that the applicant provide a detailed description of the diagnosis or treatment and identify and provide the address of each individual that has treated the applicant. The current declaration also includes a general authorization and release for records that each applicant must sign. The current authorization limits the release of mental health records to only those pertaining to diagnosis of the conditions specified in question 11.

As part of the investigation process, each applicant must identify employers or clients and provide character references. The Board then sends forms to the identified references requesting information about the applicant. The current form sent to individuals listed in the declaration by the applicant as character references, employers, or former clients includes a question regarding the reference's knowledge about whether the applicant has been diagnosed or treated in the past ten years for bipolar disorder, schizophrenia, paranoia, or any psychotic disorder.

In addition to the declaration, each person wishing to take the Bar exam must file an application not later than 180 days before the examination. § 82.027(a). By law, the application is to consist of a verified affidavit that requires, among other statements, an assertion that the applicant is not mentally ill. This statutory requirement is implemented in the Board's current application by requiring each applicant to sign a verified affidavit stating, among other things, that

---

11.   a) Have you, within the last ten (10) years, been treated for any mental illness?

b) Have you, within the last ten (10) years, been admitted to any hospital or other facility for the treatment of any mental illness?

Section 571.033, Texas Health and Safety Code, defines mental illness, as follows:

"Mental illness" means an illness, disease, or condition other than epilepsy, senility, alcoholism, or mental deficiency, that:

(A) substantially impairs a person's thought, perception of reality, emotional process, or judgment; or

(B) grossly impairs behavior as demonstrated by recent disturbed behavior.

If you answered "YES" to any part of this question, provide details on the Supplemental Form. Include dates of treatment, name, current mailing address, and telephone number of each person who treated you, each facility where you received treatment, and the reason for each treatment.

[5]   The current version of question 11 asks:

11.   a) Within the last ten years, have you been diagnosed with or have you been treated by bi-polar disorder, schizophrenia, paranoia, or any other psychotic disorder?

b) Have you, since attaining the age of eighteen or within the last ten years, whichever period is shorter, been admitted to a hospital or other facility for the treatment of bi-polar disorder, schizophrenia, paranoia, or any other psychotic disorder?

If you answered "YES" to any part of this question, please provide details on a Supplemental Form, including date(s) of diagnosis or treatment, a description of the course of treatment, and a description of your present condition. Include the name, current mailing address, and telephone number of each person who treated you, as well as each facility where you received treatment, and the reason for treatment.

the applicant has not been diagnosed, treated, or hospitalized since the filing of the declaration for bipolar disorder, schizophrenia, or any psychotic disorder.

Bipolar disorder, schizophrenia, paranoia, and psychotic disorders are serious mental illnesses that may affect a person's ability to practice law. People suffering from these illnesses may suffer debilitating symptoms that inhibit their ability to function normally. The fact that a person may have experienced an episode of one of these mental illnesses in the past but is not currently experiencing symptoms does not mean that the person will not experience another episode in the future or that the person is currently fit to practice law. Indeed, a person suffering from one of these illnesses may have extended periods between episodes, possibly as much as ten years for bipolar disorder or schizophrenia. Although a past diagnosis of the mental illness will not necessarily predict the applicant's future behavior, the mental health history is important to provide the Board with information regarding the applicant's insight into his or her illness and degree of cooperation in controlling it through counseling and medication. In summary, inquiry into past diagnosis and treatment of the severe mental illnesses is necessary to provide the Board with the best information available with which to assess the functional capacity of the individual.

The plaintiffs are law students in ABA-approved law schools. Applicant A, a first-year law student, was hospitalized in the past five years in a psychiatric facility for the treatment of depression with psychotic features and currently takes anti-depressant medication. Applicant A has not filed a declaration, pending resolution of this lawsuit. Under the current question, applicant A would be required to answer "yes."

Applicant B, a first-year law student, received out-patient mental health services in the past ten years for the treatment of a depressive disorder and is currently involved in group therapy. Applicant B filed a declaration on November 15, 1993, in which Applicant B, who has not been treated for the mental illnesses specified in the current version of question 11, answered the question "no."

Applicant C, a second-year law student, received out-patient mental health services in the past ten years for the treatment of a depressive disorder, currently takes anti-depressant and anti-anxiety medications, and receives therapy. Applicant C completed the declaration before the Board's 1993 amendments to the questions concerning mental health treatment, answering "yes" to the preceding question used from April 92 to July 93. Applicant C has not been treated or hospitalized for bipolar disorder, schizophrenia, paranoia, or any other psychotic condition in the past ten years and, therefore, would answer the current question 11 "no."

None of the plaintiffs have a history of criminal activity, financial irresponsibility, or academic discipline. At this time, none of the applicants have filed the application to take the Bar exam.

Before the current wording of question 11, if an applicant answered any part of the question affirmatively, the staff technician screening the file generally would order the treatment records. In many cases, the technician would then forward the file and records to the director of fitness and character, Jack Marshall, or his assistant. If after his review, Marshall was concerned about the mental health history of the person, he would place the person's name on the "Potentials Hearing Report" and discuss the file with Board's executive director or a staff attorney.[9] Thus, following the conclusion of the investigation of the applicant, one of three things occurred: 1) the person's technician certified the person's present fitness; 2) if the person's name had been placed on the "Potential Hearings List," Marshall, following discussion with the executive director or staff attorney, would instruct the technician to certify the person's present fitness; or 3) Marshall, in consultation with the executive director or a staff attorney, made a preliminary determination that the applicant did not possess the present fitness to practice law, necessitating consideration of the matter by the actual Board. The Board sent persons in the third category a preliminary determination letter detailing the results of the investigation and giving them thirty days to respond to the letter. The applicant also had the right to request a hearing, unless the Board had already determined a hearing was necessary. Following the hearing, the Board could require an applicant to be evaluated by a mental health professional.

Because of the narrowed focus of the current question 11, the Board's current policy is that Marshall will review all affirmative responses to the mental health question. Marshall will determine, based on the information provided in the declaration, whether direct inquiries for additional information to mental health professionals who have treated the applicant are necessary. If Marshall deems it necessary to receive additional information, he, in consultation with the executive director and a staff attorney, will review the response. If they are not convinced the person's mental health problem is completely under control, Marshall will request complete records of treatment and send the applicant to an expert chosen by the Board for evaluation. If the expert recommends that the Board continue to investigate the person and if after that continued investigation a determination is made that the person may pose potential harm to clients, the person will be sent a preliminary determination of lack of present fitness and notice of a right to a hearing before the Board.

The Board has received only one affirmative response to the current mental health question. In that case, Marshall has requested a summary of treatment from the treating professional.

As a result of this litigation, Marshall researched the issue of the number of applicants whose files raised mental health concerns. Since August 1987, the earliest "Potential Hearings Report" Marshall could find, thirty cases involved mental health issues. Of the thirty cases, nineteen raised serious mental health concerns. In thirteen of the cases,

---

[9] Two circumstances often triggered Marshall's concern about the present mental fitness of applicants: 1) if an applicant was currently in treatment or hospitalized; and 2) if an applicant's history included numerous hospitalizations, including a recent hospitalization. If, however, the Board received a statement from an applicant's treating physician that the individual had the mental fitness to practice law, Marshall generally would not forward the file to the executive director.

In practice, very few applicants are actually placed on the "Potential Hearings Report." In fact, the treating physicians of approximately half the applicants answering question 11 affirmatively indicated comfort with the applicant's fitness to practice law.

the information provided by the applicant was the only source of mental health information. Twenty-one of the cases were set for hearing, and in ten cases, the Board required a psychiatric evaluation or psychiatric review of the record following the hearing.

Of the nineteen cases involving serious mental health concerns, one remains under investigation and two were cleared either by the staff following a review of recent psychological evaluations. The sixteen remaining cases were set for hearing with the following dispositions: one was denied admission to the Bar on mental health grounds; one was denied but not on mental health grounds; seven were approved by the Board; two had hearings set but not held, and the applicants have taken no further action; one applicant's file was terminated for failure to execute a release for mental health records; one was approved by the Board with the caveat that a mental health update may be required upon filing of the application; one file was terminated for failure to complete a Board-required examination; one was approved for a temporary license that included a condition requiring mental health counseling; and one has been required to submit to a post-hearing psychological evaluation, the results of which are pending.

Eight of these cases resulted in either denial or inconclusive results. In five of the eight cases, the Board would have been unaware of mental health concerns absent the applicant's disclosure. In the three remaining cases in this group, mental health concerns were developed as a result of the applicant's disclosure and information received from other sources.

CONCLUSIONS OF LAW

[T]he prohibition against discrimination extends to "qualified individual[s] with a disability." A person is a "qualified individual with a disability" in the context of licensing or certification if the person can meet the essential eligibility requirements for receiving a license or certification. The regulations prohibit the imposition of eligibility criteria that "screen out or tend to screen out" a disabled individual from "fully and equally" enjoying any service, program, or activity, unless such criteria can be shown to be necessary for the provision of the service, program, or activity being offered. § 35.130(b)(8). When, as in this case, questions of public safety are involved, the determination of whether an applicant meets "essential eligibility requirements" involves consideration of whether the individual with a disability poses a direct threat to the health and safety of others. 28 C.F.R. pt. 35, app. A, at 448. However, a determination that a person poses such a threat may not be based on generalizations or stereotypes about the effects of a particular disability but must be based on

> an individualized assessment, based on reasonable judgment that relies on current medical evidence or on the best available objective evidence, to determine: the nature, duration, and severity of the risk; the probability that the potential injury will actually occur; and whether reasonable modifications of policies, practices, or procedures will mitigate the risk.

Id.

The plaintiffs argue that the all the mental health questions the Board has used, including the present narrow inquiry, inquire into an individual's status as mentally ill rather than focusing on behaviors that would affect the individual's ability to practice law. They contend such inquiry is not necessary, the standard required by the ADA to justify the application of criteria that "screen out or tend to screen out," because the same information can be ascertained through other sources and means. In support of their position, the plaintiffs direct the Court's attention to recent court orders holding that mental health questions asked on other states' licensing applications violate the ADA. See *Medical Soc'y v. Jacobs*, No. 93–3670 (U.S.D.C.N.J. Oct. 5, 1993) (question whether physicians seeking renewal of licenses had ever suffered or been treated for mental illness violated ADA); *In re Applications of Plano and Underwood*, No. BAR–93–21 (Me. Dec.7, 1993) (questions regarding whether applicants had ever been diagnosed with "an emotional, nervous or mental disorder" and whether they had received treatment of the disorder in the past ten years were invalid under ADA).

The plaintiffs suggest that applicants to the Board have already been extensively screened by virtue of successfully completing college and achieving admission to law school. Further, any aberrant behavior that might bear on their present mental fitness would be apparent from a criminal, educational, or employment history. The plaintiffs presented evidence that, in fact, the current question was imperfect in that some who suffer from the specified mental illnesses may be missed by current question because they have not sought diagnosis or treatment. The plaintiffs suggest reliance on other facets of the investigatory process applied to all applicants or a series of question aimed at behavior would comply with the ADA and would be just as effective as the process the Board currently employs. Alternatively, the plaintiffs suggest asking applicants to voluntarily disclose if they suffer from any mental illness that could affect their ability to perform the functions essential to being a lawyer.

The ADA prohibits the use of licensing procedures that "screen out or tend to screen out" individuals defined as disabled under the ADA unless the screening criteria are necessary to the service being offered. The defendant's expert testified that a direct mental health inquiry like the current question 11 is necessary in the licensing process to get a full understanding of the functional capacity of the applicant's mental fitness. The defendant's expert further testified that the inquiry should go back a minimum of five years and optimally ten years because of the chronic nature of the severe mental illnesses specified in the current question 11, which often have an onset during adolescence. Although relying on past behavior in other areas may reveal behavior relevant to mental fitness, the evidence reflected that in the majority of cases already reviewed by the Board, this was not the case. Further, self-disclosure-type questions suffer, possibly to a greater degree, from some of the same defects the plaintiffs criticize in the current question—those who answer untruthfully or who do not recognize or understand the nature and extent of their illness will not be identified.

The plaintiffs further contend that because only one person has been denied admission to the bar since 1986 based on mental health concerns, the question serves no useful purpose. The Court finds this contention also to be without merit. The plaintiffs' argument ignores the fact that other applicants subjected to investigation as a result of an affirmative answer to question 11 have not pursued the process, have had their files terminated for failure to comply with requirements, and have received temporary licenses contingent upon continued counseling. Further, for those applicants answering the mental health question affirmatively, the Board engages in an individualized, case-by-case investigation. In fact, the evidence reflects that many of the applicants answering the mental health question affirmatively are ultimately cleared by the Board and certified to have the present fitness to practice law. This highlights the Board's efforts to avoid improper generalization or stereotyping of mentally disabled individuals, as defined by the ADA, and to apply objective criteria on an individualized basis to determine if an applicant poses a threat to the public if licensed. The Court, therefore, finds the Board discharges its duty in a responsible manner while making every effort not to discriminate against those who have suffered a mental illness but have the present fitness to practice law.

The inquiries courts in other states have held prohibited by the ADA were virtually identical to the previous broad-based forms of question 11 used by the Board that intruded into an applicant's mental health history without focusing on only those mental illnesses that pose a potential threat to the applicant's present fitness to practice law. The Court concurs that such a broad-based inquiry violates the ADA.

As stated above, however, the ADA does not preclude a licensing body from any inquiry and investigation related to mental illness, instead allowing for such inquiry and investigation when they are necessary to protect the integrity of the service provided and the public. The Court recognizes that no perfect question can be formulated that will ensure all individuals suffering mental illnesses affecting their fitness to practice will be detected. As the plaintiff's expert testified, some may defer treatment to avoid having to answer affirmatively and others may not recognize that they suffer from a mental illness, thereby precluding diagnosis or treatment. However, reliance on "behaviors" occurring in other facets of an individual's life as triggers to indicate a mental illness affecting present fitness may be present is a much more inexact and potentially unreliable method of ascertaining mental fitness.

The plaintiffs, seeking to vindicate the rights of the mentally disabled, fail to account for the awesome responsibility with which the Board is charged. The Board has a duty not to just the applicants, but also to the Bar and the citizens of Texas to make every effort to ensure that those individuals licensed to practice in Texas have the good moral character and present fitness to practice law and will not present a potential danger to the individuals they will represent. The Board has a limited opportunity to accomplish this task—the time of the filing of the declaration and application. The Board, therefore, must make every effort to investigate each applicant as thoroughly as possible and as efficiently as possible during this limited time.

Although a negative light is often cast upon the legal profession in the information that the general public receives and hears, in reality, lawyers serve the important role in our society of assisting people in the management of the most important of their affairs. Therefore, as a practical concern, the Board must evaluate each applicant's ability in light of the important responsibilities lawyers assume. Lawyers counsel individuals contemplating everything from divorce, bankruptcy, and the disposal of assets to the institutionalization of a loved one. Is it necessary that the Board inquire whether an applicant has been diagnosed or treated for bipolar disorder, schizophrenia, paranoia, or other psychosis before licensing the individual to assume these responsibilities? Before licensing the individual to write wills, manage trusts set up for minors and disabled individuals, or draft contracts affecting parties' rights and finances? Before licensing the individual to represent a parent in a proceeding to determine if the parent will maintain or lose custody of a child? Before licensing the individual to represent a individual charged with a crime who faces loss of liberty or even life? In each of these proceedings, the lawyer must be prepared to offer competent legal advice and representation despite the stress of understanding the responsibility the lawyer has assumed while balancing other clients' interests and time demands. The rigorous application procedure, including investigating whether an applicant has been diagnosed or treated for certain serious mental illnesses, is indeed necessary to ensure that Texas' lawyers are capable, morally and mentally, to provide these important services.

[III.]   CONCLUSION

The purpose of the ADA is to protect disabled individuals from discrimination and to promote integration of disabled individuals into the mainstream of society. It is ludicrous, however, to propose that this purpose can only be accomplished by prohibiting a state from directly investigating and assessing an applicant's emotional and mental fitness to determine if the applicant has sufficient competence to discharge the responsibilities of a lawyer before the state warrants by licensing to the citizens that the individual has the mental and emotional fitness to fulfill a lawyer's legal, ethical, and moral responsibilities. The Board would be derelict in its duty if it did not investigate the mental health of prospective lawyers. It has made every effort to do so in the least intrusive, least discriminatory manner possible, focusing on only those serious mental illnesses that experts have indicated are likely to affect present fitness to practice law. It has limited the inquiry to a specified time frame, primarily spanning late adolescence and adult life. Although affirmative answers do trigger investigation that applicants answering negatively do not have to undergo, the affirmative answer does not result in an immediate denial of a license to practice law. The ensuing investigation serves two purposes: protection of the Bar and public as well as an opportunity for the applicant to indicate present fitness. Therefore, the Court finds, by a preponderance of the evidence that the Board's use of the current question 11, a narrowly focused question, and the subsequent investigation based on an affirmative response to the question are necessary to ensure the integrity of the Board's licensing procedure, as well as to provide a practical means of striking an appropriate balance between important societal goals. The Board's process furthers the goal of the ADA to integrate those defined as mentally disabled into society while ensuring that individuals licensed to practice law in Texas are capable of practicing law in a competent and ethical manner.

Brewer v. Wisconsin Board of Bar Examiners

United States District Court for the Eastern District of Wisconsin, 2006.
2006 WL 3469598.

■ GRIESBACH, DISTRICT JUDGE.

This case raises the issue of whether a state board of bar examiners violates the Americans with Disabilities Act (ADA), 42 U.S.C. §§ 12101 *et seq.*, when it orders an applicant for admission to practice law who has a history of mental illness to undergo a psychological evaluation at her own expense as a precondition to taking action on her application. The case is presently before me on the defendants' motion for summary judgment. For the reasons that follow, the defendants' motion will be denied.

FACTUAL BACKGROUND

In December of 2002, Plaintiff Marsha Brewer applied to the Board of Bar Examiners for admission to the practice of law in State of Wisconsin. There are five qualifications for admission to the practice of law in Wisconsin. The applicant must (1) attain the age of majority; (2) satisfy the legal competence requirements; (3) satisfy the character and fitness requirements; (4) take the prescribed oath or affirmation before a justice of the supreme court or other appropriate judge; and (5) subscribe to the roll of attorneys maintained by the clerk of the supreme court.

At the time she made her application, Brewer was scheduled to graduate from the University of Wisconsin Law School in May of 2003. As a graduate of one of Wisconsin's two law schools, Brewer was entitled under the State's "diploma privilege" to have her legal competence requirement satisfied without having to take the bar examination upon certification that she had satisfactorily completed her studies. However, she was still required to establish "good moral character and fitness to practice law." The purpose of the "character and fitness" requirement is:

> to limit admission to those applicants found to have the qualities of character and fitness needed to assure to a reasonable degree of certainty the integrity and the competence of services performed for clients and the maintenance of high standards in the administration of justice.

Under Supreme Court Rules, the burden of establishing qualifications for admission is on the applicant and "failure of an applicant to furnish available information or to answer questions relating to the applicant's qualifications shall be deemed a sufficient basis for denial of certification for admission."

Brewer expected to take the oath and be admitted to the bar with her classmates at one of the large-group swearing-in ceremonies at the Wisconsin Supreme Court in June or August of 2003. However, upon review of her application, a member of the Board's staff noted that she had been certified as disabled by the Social Security Administration. The staff member then referred the application to the Board's investigator for further review and follow-up. The Board's investigator recommended that Brewer's medical records be reviewed "so that the Board could ascertain the nature of the disability or disabilities underlying the certification and whether Ms. Brewer had any physical or mental conditions that would interfere with her character and fitness to practice law." He then asked Brewer to provide a copy of her psychological records from her treating physician. Brewer responded that she had no current treating physician and was not taking any medications, although she continued to receive SSDI benefits.

According to Brewer, she was determined to be disabled and eligible for SSDI benefits in July of 1986. She states she was evaluated primarily for a psychiatric condition (chronic depression), but also has other chronic medical conditions including fibromyalgia, allergies and chemical sensitivities. In order to avoid outright rejection of her application, Brewer reluctantly signed an authorization giving the Board access to her medical and psychiatric records and her Social Security Disability Application. However, none of the physicians who had treated her at the time of her disability determination had retained his records.

In December of 2003, the Board directed Brewer to undergo a psychological evaluation by one of two selected providers at her own expense. Brewer learned that such an evaluation would cost between $1,500 and $2,000, and requested that the Board pay for the evaluation due to financial hardship. Alternatively, Brewer requested that the Board waive the psychological evaluation or permit her to provide proof of her mental health in a different manner, such as by offering correspondence from past employers or law school staff. The Board denied her requests.

Under the Board's rules, its staff is authorized to close any application for a character and fitness certification that remains incomplete for one year following the date it was filed. When the Board advised her it wanted further information concerning her condition, Brewer requested an extension to complete her application. The Board granted an extension until July 14, 2004. When she failed to submit the required psychological evaluation by that time, the Board notified her that her file was closed. Although Brewer was told she could reapply for admission, she was advised that she was no longer eligible for admission under the diploma privilege. Brewer filed this lawsuit in response.

[A]NALYSIS

[1]. Applicability of ADA to Professional Licensing Schemes

Relying principally upon dicta from *Alexander v. Margolis*, 921 F.Supp. 482 (W.D.Mich.1995), defendants first argue that Title II of the ADA may not apply to Wisconsin's attorney licensing scheme because it is not a service, program, or activity within the meaning of 42 U.S.C. § 12132. In *Alexander*, a former physician sued a State Board of Medicine under various civil rights statutes, including the ADA, for the revocation and refusal to reinstate his license to practice medicine. Addressing the ADA claim, the district court first observed:

> Considering the text of section 12132(2), it is questionable whether the Board's duty to license physicians can be characterized as a "service" being denied to plaintiff or whether the Board's refusal to reinstate his license denies him participation in "programs or activities provided" by a state

entity. The Board of Medicine is, if anything, a service, program or activity provided for the public's benefit and safety, not for the benefit of any given individual who does not meet the state's requirements for practicing medicine.

The *Alexander* court found it unnecessary to decide whether the Board's activities were covered by the ADA since it found that the plaintiff was not a "qualified individual with a disability" within the meaning of the ADA. Defendants note that most other courts addressing similar ADA claims have likewise found it unnecessary to address the applicability of Title II to professional licensing schemes since those claims, too, were disposed of on other grounds. Nevertheless, defendants argue that the same reasoning applies to this case. Wisconsin's bar admission scheme, like the medical licensing scheme in Alexander, is intended to protect the public. Defendants conclude: "It may well be, therefore, that the professional licensing scheme which Brewer challenges through her Title II ADA claims are not ones [*sic*] from [which] she could be 'excluded' since the 'services, programs or activities' were expressly set up for the protection of the public rather than for any applicant or group of applicants."

As defendants also acknowledge, however, the argument that Title II of the ADA does not apply to professional licensing schemes has been rejected as unduly narrow and "at odds with the remedial goals underlying the ADA." *Hason v. Medical Bd. of California*, 279 F.3d 1167, 1172 (9th Cir.2002), reh. on banc denied, 294 F.3d 1166 (9th Cir.2002), cert. granted in part, *Medical Bd. of Calif. v. Haso*n, 537 U.S. 1028 (2002), dismissed, 538 U.S. 958 (2003). The *Hason* court found that medical licensing is a provision of a "service" for purposes of Title II of the ADA. Indeed, no court, not even the district court in *Alexander*, has adopted the defendants' position. I decline to do so here.

I find the *Hason* court's analysis persuasive on this issue. The fact that the Wisconsin bar licensing scheme was set up to protect the courts and the public does not rule out the possibility that it also provides a service to would-be attorneys. Furthermore, the language of Title II of the ADA does not require that the benefits be shared by the public at large. Thus, the fact that a relatively small segment of the public— namely, would-be attorneys—seeks the benefits of the Board's services, does not indicate that no public service component is at work here. Finally, Brewer's claim is not just that she was excluded from, or denied access to, the Board's services, but also that she was otherwise discriminated against by the Board. The language of the statute is disjunctive; it prohibits exclusion from participation, denial of benefits, or discrimination against by reason of disability. 42 U.S.C. § 12132. Thus, even if the licensing of attorneys does not constitute providing a service, Brewer's claim that the Board, a public entity, discriminated against her by reason of disability would still fall within the proscription of Title II. For all of these reasons, I conclude that Title II of the ADA applies and proceed to consider whether Brewer has sufficient evidence to proceed with her claim.

2.   Qualified individual with a disability

Defendants next contend that Brewer cannot prove she is a "qualified individual with a disability because by her own admission she has received SSDI benefits since 1986." In order to be eligible to receive

SSDI, a person must have a disability so severe that she is "unable to do [her] previous work" and "cannot . . . engage in any other kind of substantial gainful work which exists in the national economy." 42 U.S.C. § 423(d)(2)(A). To prevail on an ADA claim, however, a plaintiff must prove that she is a "qualified individual with a disability." Noting that courts have recognized an apparent contradiction in an SSDI recipient suing for employment discrimination under the ADA, defendants contend that Brewer must at least offer some explanation as to why her receipt of SSDI benefits does not render her unqualified to practice law. Because she has failed to do so in response to their motion, defendants contend they are entitled to summary judgment on this issue.

In fact, Brewer did respond to defendants' argument that her receipt of SSDI benefits was inconsistent with her claim to be a "qualified individual with a disability." In her affidavit filed in support of her own motion for summary judgment, Brewer explained that her various impairments require accommodations on her part that she hoped to achieve in the practice of law. In addition to avoiding environments that contain chemicals and other substances to which she is sensitive or allergic, Brewer states: "I am chronically depressed and fatigued. I am 57 years old. I need sedentary work, work where I can get sufficient vacation time, sufficient income and benefits." She also reports that for twenty years beginning in 1981, she represented employers at unemployment compensation hearings on an "on-call, ad hoc basis." These facts are sufficient to reconcile Brewer's receipt of SSDI benefits with her claim that she is qualified to practice law, at least on a part-time basis. After all, there is no requirement that in order to obtain a license to practice law in Wisconsin one must be able to do so on a full-time basis.

But even aside from Brewer's response, as DRW correctly points out, defendants' argument that Brewer cannot prove she is a "qualified individual with a disability" because she receives SSDI benefits confuses employment discrimination claims under Title I of the ADA with Brewer's claim of discrimination by a state licensing agency under Title II. Receipt of SSDI benefits is a problem only in employment discrimination claims under Title I. It does not pose a problem to a claim of discrimination in licensing under Title II. This is because the term "qualified individual with a disability" is defined differently under Title I than Title II. Under Title I, the term "qualified individual with a disability" means "an individual with a disability who, with or without reasonable accommodation, can perform the essential functions of the employment position that such individual holds or desires." 42 U.S.C. § 12111(8). As the Supreme Court recognized in *Cleveland v. Policy Mgmt. Sys. Corp.*, 526 U.S. 795, 806 (1999) [a principal case in Chapter Two], there is at least an apparent contradiction between an SSDI recipient's claim that she is totally disabled and the requirement under the ADA that the plaintiff prove she "can perform the essential functions of the employment position she holds or desires." For this reason, to avoid summary judgment on an employment discrimination ADA claim, an SSDI recipient "cannot simply ignore the apparent contradiction that arises out of the earlier SSDI total disability claim. Rather, she must proffer a sufficient explanation."

No such conflict exists, however, under Title II of the ADA. Under Title II, a "qualified individual with a disability" is defined as

> an individual with a disability who, with or without reasonable modifications to rules, policies, or practices, the removal of architectural, communication, or transportation barriers, or the provision of auxiliary aids and services, meets the essential eligibility requirements for the receipt of services or the participation in programs or activities provided by a public entity.

42 U.S.C. § 12131(2). There is no requirement that an ADA plaintiff asserting a claim under Title II be able to perform the essential functions of any job. Under Title II, ADA plaintiffs must simply "meet the eligibility requirements for the receipt of services or the participation in programs or activities provided by a public entity." There is therefore no contradiction between Brewer's inability to engage in any full-time gainful activity that exists in the national economy and her desire to be admitted to the State Bar of Wisconsin. Since no contradiction exists, no explanation is required. I therefore conclude that Brewer's ongoing receipt of SSDI benefits does not preclude a finding that she is a "qualified individual with a disability" for purposes of Title II of the ADA.

3. Discrimination by reason of disability

This brings us to the crux of the case: whether there is evidence that would support a finding that in requiring her to undergo and pay for a psychological evaluation, the Board discriminated against Brewer by reason of her disability. To repeat, Title II of the ADA states: "no qualified individual with a disability shall, by reason of such disability, be excluded from participation in or be denied the benefits of the services, programs, or activities of a public entity, or be subjected to discrimination by any such entity." 42 U.S.C. § 12132. In addition to this general prohibition, regulations promulgated by the Department of Justice (DOJ) set forth more specific prohibitions against discrimination under the ADA. The DOJ regulations prohibit public agencies from administering a licensing or certification program "in a manner that subjects qualified individuals with disabilities to discrimination on the basis of disability," and from establishing requirements for programs or activities of licensees or certified entities "that subject qualified individuals with disabilities to discrimination on the basis of disability." 28 C.F.R. § 35.130(b)(6). The DOJ regulations further provide:

> A public entity shall not impose or apply eligibility criteria that screen out or tend to screen out an individual with a disability or any class of individuals with disabilities from fully and equally enjoying any service, program, or activity, unless such criteria can be shown to be necessary for the provision of the service, program, or activity being offered.

28 C.F.R. § 35.130(b)(8). Brewer contends that the Board violated these regulations by subjecting her application to heightened scrutiny and placing upon her the burden of undergoing a psychological evaluation at her own expense based solely on the fact that she is disabled.

[S]ince the enactment of the ADA in 1990, the right of bar examining committees to inquire into the mental health of applicants has been the subject of intense controversy. See, *e.g.*, Jon Bauer, *The Character of the Questions and the Fitness of the Process: Mental Health, Bar Admissions and the Americans with Disabilities Act*, 49 UCLA L.Rev. 93 (2001); Carol J. Banta, *The Impact of the Americans with Disabilities Act on State Bar Examiners' Inquiries Into the Psychological History of Bar Applicants*, 94 Mich. L.Rev. 167 (1995). Several courts have held that general inquiries into the mental health history and treatment of applicants for admission constitute discrimination on the basis of disability under the ADA and the above-cited regulations. *Clark v. Virginia Bd. of Bar Examiners*, 880 F.Supp. 430 (E.D.Va.1995); *Ellen S. v. Florida Bd. of Bar Examiners*, 859 F.Supp. 1489 (S.D.Fla.1994); *In re Underwood*, 1993 WL 649283 (Me. Dec. 8, 1993). On the other hand, a district court in Texas has upheld a more narrow mental health question inquiring whether an applicant has, within the preceding ten years, been diagnosed or hospitalized for "bi-polar disorder, schizophrenia, paranoia, or any other psychotic disorder." *Applicants v. Texas State Bd. of Law Examiners*, 1994 WL 923404 (W.D.Tex. Nov. 11, 1994). And in *McCready v. Illinois Bd. of Admissions*, 1995 WL 29609, *6 (N.D.Ill. Jan. 24, 1995), the court rejected a challenge under the ADA to the Illinois Board's practice of asking the references of each applicant whether they had knowledge of "any emotional, mental, behavioral or nervous affliction" on the part of the applicant.

In this case, however, Brewer does not challenge the questions she was asked on the application for a license to practice law. To the contrary, she expressly states in her affidavit that "[t]his lawsuit is not about the screening questions that trigger 'heightened evaluation.' It is about the heightened burdens I was subjected to after I was selected for heightened evaluation as to psychiatric fitness." The question presented here then is not whether the Board violated the ADA by asking Brewer questions concerning her mental health history; rather, the question presented here is whether, having been told by Brewer that she was receiving Social Security Disability benefits based at least in part on a diagnosis of a mental illness for which she was not currently receiving treatment, the Board could, consistent with the ADA, require her to undergo a psychological evaluation at her own expense before considering her application.

The defendants argue that the Board did not subject Brewer to discrimination on the basis of disability because, in requiring her to provide (and pay for) additional information, it treated her no differently than other applicants from whom additional information was required. They also argue that the requirement that she undergo a psychological evaluation was not imposed on the basis of Brewer's disability because the Board has required psychological examinations of other applicants who have no record of disability. Under Wisconsin's system for attorney licensing, defendants note, each bar applicant bears the burden of proof that he or she meets the qualifications for bar membership set forth in Wisconsin Supreme Court Rule 40.02. These qualifications include establishing one's "good moral character and fitness to practice law" to the satisfaction of the Board of Examiners, whose duty it is then to certify to the Wisconsin Supreme Court the character and fitness of qualifying applicants. Brewer was required to undergo a psychological evaluation because, as with many other applicants for admission, the Board needed further information before it could certify to the Supreme Court that she met the qualifications. The request was made, defendants argue, not because the Board believed Brewer was disabled, but because her application raised questions concerning her current mental health and, thus, her fitness to practice law.

According to a sworn affidavit from defendant Rankin, who was Director of the Board of Examiners while Brewer's application was pending, the Board's review of applications includes looking for any patterns of conduct that would relate to the applicant's fitness to practice law.[5] Applicants whose history shows such conduct—for example, a conviction for DWI; hospitalization for mental health issues; or problems with anger management, domestic battery, or drugs or alcohol—may be required to submit to a psychological evaluation. However, requests for psychological evaluations are not limited to people with disabilities, nor are disabled persons singled out in the process of evaluating applicants' fitness to practice law. In the year Brewer applied, over 75% of all applicants were required to submit some form of additional documentation, most of which was unrelated to any health condition or disability, such as police reports, court documents, criminal history reports, driving records, credit reports, bankruptcy files, tax records, and transcripts from undergraduate and law schools. Five other applicants, in addition to Brewer, were directed to undergo psychological evaluations.

The defendants' position, at first blush, seems reasonable. Requesting further information from an applicant with a history of mental illness about the nature and extent of her impairment does not appear to be the same as discriminating against an applicant because of a disability. The purpose of the ADA, at least in part, was to put an end to the restrictions and limitations placed on individuals with disabilities that resulted from "stereotypic assumptions not truly indicative of the individual ability of such individuals to participate in, and contribute to, society." 42 U.S.C. § 12101(a)(7). The fact that the Board requested additional information regarding the nature and extent of Brewer's mental illness demonstrates that it was unwilling to act on "stereotypic assumptions" about her abilities, but wanted to assess her fitness to practice law based upon information specific to her. The Board's attempt to obtain the kind of information needed to make an individualized decision concerning Brewer's ability to practice law, as opposed to relying on outmoded and exaggerated stereotypes, is precisely what the ADA mandates. No one disputes that a mental illness, depending upon its nature and severity, can render a person unfit to practice law. By requiring additional information from

---

[5] Under the Board's rules, the revelation or discovery of "evidence of mental or emotional impairments" is one of twelve separate categories of "relevant conduct" that are "treated as cause for further inquiry before the Board decides whether the applicant possesses the character and fitness to practice law." BA 6.02. The other categories of relevant conduct that are considered cause for further inquiry include: unlawful conduct; academic misconduct; false statements by the applicant, including concealment or nondisclosure; acts involving dishonesty or misrepresentation; abuse of legal process; neglect of financial responsibilities; neglect of professional obligations; violation of an order of a court; evidence of drug or alcohol dependency; denial of admission to the bar of another jurisdiction on character and fitness grounds; and disciplinary action by a lawyer disciplinary agency or other professional disciplinary agency of any jurisdiction.

applicants who have a history of significant mental illness so that it can make an individualized assessment of their fitness to practice law, defendants contend the Board was simply fulfilling its obligation to the public.

But while the defendants' position may seem reasonable, it is not consistent with the language of the ADA and the regulations promulgated thereunder. The ADA prohibits a public entity from discriminating on the basis of one's disability. "To discriminate means merely to make a distinction on the basis of the prohibited factor." Even if the Board were ultimately to certify that Brewer was fit to practice law, requiring that she undergo a psychological evaluation at her own expense and submit the results to the Board amounts to a burden to which the vast majority of her classmates and other applicants were not subjected. If the reason the Board required Brewer to undergo such an evaluation was because she is disabled, then it discriminated against her by reason of her disability.

The fact that the Board required psychological evaluations based on a variety of factors does not mean that the evaluation required of Brewer was not "on the basis of" her disability. The defendants seem to be arguing that because the Board requires more information from, or places more hurdles before, many applicants based on a wide variety of conduct, and because it requires these applicants to pay any expenses incurred, it is treating Brewer the same as all other applicants in requiring her to pay her own expenses in providing the information it seeks. She must pay for the psychological evaluation just as another applicant might have undergo and pay for an evaluation if he has a history of domestic violence. In other words, because Brewer is treated just like other applicants, the requirement that she undergo an evaluation does not discriminate on the basis of her disability.

There are several difficulties with the defendants' argument. The first is that Brewer was treated different from the vast majority of her classmates and the other applicants for admission. Out of the approximately 1,000 applicants for admission to the bar in 2003, only six, including Brewer, were required to undergo a psychological evaluation at their own expense to prove they met the qualifications for admission prescribed in SCR 40.02. The record does not reflect why the other five applicants were required to do so. While the defendants note that more than 75% of the applicants were required to provide some type of additional information to the Board to prove their character and fitness to practice law, the information required for the vast majority of applicants consisted of records already in existence. In other words, other applicants were required to "furnish available information" pursuant to SCR 40.07. Brewer, on the other hand, was required to pay for an evaluation in order to provide the Board information that was not previously available, presumably at substantially greater expense.

While it is true that other applicants who are not disabled can be required to undergo a psychological evaluation, that fact alone does not prove that the defendants did not discriminate against Brewer on the basis of her disability in requiring that she undergo such an evaluation. Though superficially attractive, the Board's argument is tantamount to saying that the ADA allows discrimination against the disabled so long as one discriminates against other people for other reasons as well. This is not the case. The effect, if not the intent, of legislation such as the ADA is essentially to create a protected class consisting of those to whom it applies—here, the disabled. It is perfectly lawful for the Board to "discriminate" (in the non-pejorative sense) against those who have criminal records, for example, but the fact that the Board does so does not mean that it may also use disability as the reason for requiring an evaluation. That is, in fact, exactly what the Act proscribes: it says, in effect, that one cannot make disability a basis for additional burdens, and this is true even if one imposes similar burdens on those who have criminal records, were expelled from school, filed for bankruptcy, or any of the other reasons an additional burden might be required. It would be a stronger argument if the Board required psychological evaluations of every applicant: in that case, the fact that Brewer may have been disabled would have been mere coincidence and the evaluation would not have been required due to her disability. But when the Board uses a limited set of factors (including potential mental illness) as triggers for requiring the additional examination, a fact-finder could conclude that the examination was required "on the basis of" the applicant's mental disability.

Suppose by way of analogy that a nightclub charged African-American patrons an extra $10 cover charge because they were African-American. The club also used other factors to charge higher prices: it charged male patrons an extra $10 because they were men, and it charged those under 21 an additional $15 because they were young. In this scenario, no one would claim that the club's discrimination against men and those under 21 means that it did not also discriminate against African-Americans on the basis of their race: in defending his actions, the club owner essentially would be arguing that he is not a racist because he is also a sexist and is biased against the young. The existence of several discriminatory criteria, in other words, does not somehow mean that the decision to charge African-American patrons a higher price was not made on the basis of their race.

Returning to the present case, the fact that the Board may also require psychological evaluations of those with records of criminal conduct or alcohol abuse does not mean that its decision to require an evaluation of the plaintiff was not on the basis of a disability. Ultimately, the question is why the Board required Brewer to provide an evaluation, and any reasons the Board might require evaluations of other applicants are simply irrelevant to that question. To survive summary judgment Brewer must present some evidence that the Board actually did require the evaluation on the basis of her disability. She has done so. Indeed, under the Board's own version of the facts, Brewer's application was referred for further review and follow-up after a member of its staff noted she had been certified as disabled by the Social Security Administration. This constitutes practically an admission that "the defendant[s] intentionally acted on the basis of the disability." I therefore conclude that for purposes of the instant motion there is evidence in the record that would allow a fact-finder to conclude the examination was required because Brewer had "a record" of a qualifying impairment. 42 U.S.C. § 12102(2)(B).

A further issue, not sufficiently developed in the record, is whether the Board's actions were necessary in order for it to perform its licensing function. Although the ADA does not itself contain a necessity exception, the DOJ regulations promulgated thereunder do. The regulations prohibit a public entity from using criteria that "screen out or tend to screen out an individual with a disability or any class of individuals with disabilities from fully and equally enjoying any service, program, or activity unless such criteria can be shown to be necessary for the provision of the service, program, or activity being offered." 28 C.F.R. § 35.130(b)(8). Similarly, the preamble to the DOJ's regulations provides that neutral criteria that tend to screen out individuals with disabilities are permissible "if the criteria are necessary for the safe operation of the program in question." 28 C.F.R. Pt. 35, App. A at 452 (1994). At least two of the courts that have ruled on the issue of whether mental health inquiries on attorney licensing applications violate the ADA have applied the necessity exception in the course of their analyses. See *Clark v. Virginia Bd. of Bar Examiners*, 880 F.Supp. at 442; *Applicants v. Texas Bd. of Law Examiners*, 1994 WL 776693 at *8. Moreover, in rejecting the argument that such inquiries violated the ADA, the *McCready* court strongly suggested that a necessity exception existed. The court noted:

> The purpose of the ADA is to protect disabled individuals from discrimination and to promote integration of disabled individuals into the mainstream of society. It is ludicrous, however, to propose that this purpose can only be accomplished by prohibiting a state from directly investigating and assessing an applicant's emotional and mental fitness to determine if the applicant has sufficient competence to discharge the responsibilities of a lawyer before the state warrants by licensing to the citizens that the individual has the mental and emotional fitness to fulfill a lawyer's legal, ethical, and moral responsibilities. The Illinois Board of Admissions to the Bar would be derelict in its duty if it did not investigate the mental health of prospective lawyers to the extent allowed by law.

1995 WL 29609 at *7.

If Title II of the ADA does contain such an exception, it may be applicable here. Given the fact that Brewer was considered totally disabled for Social Security purposes based, at least in part, on a chronic mental illness for which she was not receiving treatment and about which there were no available records, it may be that a psychological evaluation was necessary for the Board to assess her fitness to practice law. On the other hand, if the Board did not have the option of ordering an applicant to undergo an evaluation, it does not follow that it lacks any basis upon which to make a fitness determination. Even without a current psychological evaluation, the Board would still be able to look at Brewer's past conduct and behavior to determine her fitness to practice law, just as it does in determining the character and fitness of applicants as to whom there is no evidence of emotional or mental impairment. As the authors of one article on the subject have noted, "Illness does not effect [*sic*] a professional's fitness to practice unless his disease causes conduct harmful to clients or patients." Phyllis Coleman and Ronald Shellow, *Ask About Conduct, Not Mental Illness: A Proposal For Bar Examiners And Medical Boards*

To Comply With The ADA and Constitution, 20 Journal of Legislation 147, 154 (1994). Thus, the authors argue, "professional licensing boards should inquire about conduct, not treatment for or history of mental illness or substance abuse."

Defendants have not sought summary judgment on the ground that its requirement that Brewer undergo a psychological evaluation was necessary in order for the Board to perform its function, however. As a result, the record is not sufficiently developed either to award or deny summary judgment on that basis. Accordingly, this issue also remains for trial.

[C]ONCLUSION

[B]ecause the undisputed facts do not entitle the defendants to judgment as a matter of law, [t]he motion for summary judgment must be denied.

SO ORDERED.

7. MEDICAL DECISIONMAKING

United States v. University Hospital, State University of New York at Stony Brook

United States Court of Appeals for the Second Circuit, 1984.
729 F.2d 144.

■ PRATT, CIRCUIT JUDGE:

This expedited appeal presents the question whether Section 504 of the Rehabilitation Act of 1973, as amended, 29 U.S.C. § 794, and one of its implementing regulations, 45 C.F.R. § 84.61 (1982) (incorporating 45 C.F.R. § 80.6(c) (1982)), authorize the United States Department of Health and Human Services (HHS) to obtain access to medical records maintained by defendant University Hospital concerning a seriously deformed newborn infant, identified only as Baby Jane Doe, whose parents have refused to consent to certain surgical procedures necessary to prolong the infant's life. The United States District Court for the Eastern District of New York (Leonard D. Wexler, Judge) ruled that HHS was not entitled to the records and entered summary judgment in favor of University Hospital. For the reasons set forth below, we affirm.

I.

Baby Jane Doe was born on October 11, 1983 at St. Charles Hospital in Port Jefferson, New York. She was suffering from multiple birth defects, the most serious of which were myelomeningocele, commonly known as spina bifida, a condition in which the spinal cord and membranes that envelop it are exposed; microcephaly, an abnormally small head; and hydrocephalus, a condition characterized by an accumulation of fluid in the cranial vault. In addition, she exhibited a "weak face", which prevents the infant from closing her eyes or making a full suck with her tongue; a malformed brain stem; upper extremity spasticity; and a thumb entirely within her fist.

As a result of the spina bifida, the baby's rectal, bladder, leg, and sensory functions were impaired. Due to the combination of microcephaly and hydrocephalus, there was an extremely high risk that the child would be so severely retarded that she could never interact with her environment or with other people.

At the direction of the first pediatric neurosurgeon to examine her, the baby was immediately transferred to University Hospital for dual surgery to correct her spina bifida and hydrocephalus. Essentially, this would entail excising a sac of fluid and nerve endings on the spine and closing the opening, and implanting a shunt to relieve pressure caused by fluid build-up in the cranial cavity. The record indicates that these dual, corrective surgical procedures were likely to prolong the infant's life, but would not improve many of her handicapping conditions, including her anticipated mental retardation.

After consulting with several physicians, nurses, religious advisors, a social worker, and members of their family, the parents of the baby decided to forego the corrective surgery. Instead, they opted for a "conservative" medical treatment consisting of good nutrition, the administration of antibiotics, and the dressing of the baby's exposed spinal sac.

Litigation surrounding Baby Jane Doe began on October 16, when A. Lawrence Washburn, Jr., a Vermont attorney unrelated to the child and her family, commenced a proceeding in New York State Supreme Court seeking appointment of a guardian *ad litem* for the child and an order directing University Hospital to perform the corrective surgery. The court appointed William E. Weber as guardian *ad litem* and held an evidentiary hearing on October 19 and 20 to determine whether Baby Jane Doe was "in need of immediate surgical procedures to preserve her life." Following the hearing, at which University Hospital and the parents of the child were represented, the court concluded that surgery was necessary and ordered that it be performed.

One day later the Appellate Division of the New York Supreme Court reversed the decision of the trial court and dismissed the proceeding. The Appellate Division found that the "concededly concerned and loving parents have made an informed, intelligent, and reasonable determination based upon and supported by responsible medical authority." s the court elaborated:

> The record confirms that the failure to perform the surgery will not place the infant in imminent danger of death, although surgery might significantly reduce the risk of infection. On the other hand, successful results could also be achieved with antibiotic therapy. Further, while the mortality rate is higher where conservative medical treatment is used, in this particular case the surgical procedures also involved a great risk of depriving the infant of what little function remains in her legs, and would also result in recurring urinary tract and possibly kidney infections, skin infections and edemas of the limbs.

Thus, the Appellate Division determined that the parents' decision was in the best interest of the infant and that there was, therefore, no basis for judicial intervention.

On October 28, the New York Court of Appeals affirmed the decision of the Appellate Division, relying on different grounds. Since the petitioner had no direct interest in or relationship to any party and had failed to contact the State Department of Social Services, which has primary responsibility under New York law for initiating child neglect proceedings, and since the trial court also had failed to seek that department's investigative assistance, the Court of Appeals found "no precedent or authority" for the proceeding.

[W]hile the state court proceedings were still in progress, the federal government entered the picture. On October 19, HHS received a complaint from an unidentified "private citizen" that Baby Jane Doe was being discriminatorily denied medically indicated treatment on the basis of her handicaps. HHS referred the complaint to the New York State Child Protection Services, the state agency specifically responsible for investigating suspected incidents of child abuse, mistreatment, and neglect. On November 7, that agency concluded that there was no cause for state intervention.

Meanwhile, HHS obtained a copy of the record of the state court proceedings, which contained the child's medical records through October 19. The record was forwarded to and personally reviewed by the Surgeon General of the United States, who determined, among other things, that:

> An appropriate determination concerning whether the current care of Infant Jane Doe is within the bounds of legitimate medical judgment, rather than based solely on a handicapping condition which is not a medical contraindication to surgical treatment, cannot be made without immediate access to, and careful review of, current medical records and other sources of information within the possession or control of the hospital.

Beginning on October 22, HHS repeatedly requested University Hospital to make available for inspection all of Baby Jane Doe's medical records since October 19. HHS based its authority to conduct an investigation on section 504 of the Rehabilitation Act, which provides in pertinent part that "[n]o otherwise qualified handicapped individual * * * shall, solely by reason of his handicap, * * * be subjected to discrimination under any program or activity receiving Federal financial assistance * * *." [U]niversity Hospital refused to honor HHS's requests, basing its decision in part on the refusal of the parents to release the records and in part on "serious concerns both as to the Department's jurisdiction and the procedures the Department has employed in initiating an inquiry."

The government then brought this action on November 2, alleging that University Hospital had violated section 504 and 45 C.F.R. § 80.6(c) by refusing to allow HHS access to information concerning the medical care and hospital services being rendered to Baby Jane Doe. [T]he district court ruled that defendants were entitled to summary judgment. [N]oting that 45 C.F.R. § 80.6(c) requires recipients of federal funds to provide HHS "access to such records 'as may be pertinent to ascertain compliance with' " section 504, the district court [r]easoned that "if a recipient of federal financial assistance is clearly not violating [section 504] by discriminating against handicapped persons, the Department of Health and Human Services may not obtain access to the records of such recipient * * *." [E]mphasizing that the hospital "has at all times been willing to perform the surgical procedures in question", but "lacks the legal right to perform such procedures" in the absence of parental consent, the court concluded that the hospital "failed to perform the surgical procedures in question, not because Baby Jane Doe is handicapped, but because her parents have refused to consent to such procedures." Thus, in the court's view, "the failure of the defendant University Hospital to perform the surgical procedures cannot possibly be regarded as a violation of the Rehabilitation Act."

In any case, the court went on, "the decision of the parents to refuse consent to the surgical procedures was a reasonable one based on due consideration of the medical options available and on a genuine concern for the best interests of the child." According to the court, this precluded any possibility of liability on the part of the hospital.

II.

[W]hile the philosophical, social, and ethical implications of this case may be far-reaching, the precise issue presented for our review is one of statutory construction: Did congress intend section 504 to reach the conduct HHS seeks to investigate? If the investigation is within the scope of section 504, then HHS is entitled to access to Baby Jane Doe's medical records (unless they are protected from disclosure by some statutory or constitutional provision). On the other hand, if the investigation is beyond the scope of section 504, then the district court properly denied access.

III.

To focus more sharply on this central issue, it is first necessary to examine the theory upon which the government predicates its request for the records under section 504. The theory rests on two premises. First, the government draws a distinction between decisionmaking based on a "bona fide medical judgment," which without definition it concedes to be beyond the reach of section 504, and decisionmaking based solely on an individual's handicap, which it argues is covered by section 504. Second, the government identifies Baby Jane Doe's microcephaly, which the record indicates will result in severe mental retardation, as the handicapping condition. From these premises, the government reasons that if a newborn infant suffering from spina bifida and hydrocephalus, but not microcephaly, would receive treatment or services that differ from those provided to an infant suffering from all three defects, or alternatively, if the hospital would seek a state court order compelling surgery in the former case, but not in the latter, then a violation of section 504 would have been established. Without the requested records, the government concludes, it is impossible to determine whether any such unlawful discrimination has occurred here, at least after October 19.

[W]e hold that Baby Jane Doe falls within the definition of a "handicapped individual" in section 706(7)(B). The record indicates that Baby Jane Doe's rectal, bladder, leg, and sensory functions are all presently impaired. Further, the record suggests that, with or without corrective surgery, Baby Jane Doe will experience severe mental retardation for however long she lives. [H]aving determined that Baby Jane Doe is a "handicapped individual" under section 706(7)(B), we next consider whether she possibly can be considered an "otherwise qualified" handicapped individual or to have been "subjected to discrimination" under section 504. These two issues are intertwined.

The leading cases construing the "otherwise qualified" criterion of section 504 have involved allegedly discriminatory denials of admission to certain educational programs. *Southeastern Community College v. Davis*, 442 U.S. 397 (1979); *Doe v. New York University*, 666 F.2d 761 (2d Cir.1981). In that context, this court in *Doe v. New York University* recognized that:

> * * * it is now clear that [the phrase "otherwise qualified handicapped individual"] refers to a person who is qualified in spite of her handicap and that an institution is not required to disregard the disabilities of a handicapped applicant, provided the handicap is relevant to reasonable qualifications for acceptance, or to make substantial modifications in its reasonable standards or program to accommodate handicapped individuals but may take an applicant's handicap into consideration, along with all other relevant factors, in determining whether she is qualified for admission.

Doe establishes that section 504 prohibits discrimination against a handicapped individual only where the individual's handicap is unrelated to, and thus improper to consideration of, the services in question. As defendants here point out, however, where medical treatment is at issue, it is typically the handicap itself that gives rise to, or at least contributes to, the need for services. Defendants thus argue, and with some force, that the "otherwise qualified" criterion of section 504 cannot be meaningfully applied to a medical treatment decision. Similarly, defendants argue that it would be pointless to inquire whether a patient who was affected by a medical treatment decision was, "solely by reason of his handicap, * * * subjected to discrimination".

The government's answer to both these arguments is that Baby Jane Doe can be viewed as suffering from not one, but multiple handicaps. Indeed, the crux of the government's case is that her microcephaly is the operative handicap, and that the requested records are necessary to determine whether she has been discriminated against solely for that reason.

Despite its superficial logic, the government's theory is flawed in at least two respects. First, the government's view of "otherwise qualified" is divorced from the statutory language. As the mainstream of cases under section 504 exemplifies, the phrase "otherwise qualified" is geared toward relatively static programs or activities such as education, employment, and transportation systems. As a result, the phrase cannot be applied in the comparatively fluid context of medical treatment decisions without distorting its plain meaning. In common parlance, one would not ordinarily think of a newborn infant suffering from multiple birth defects as being "otherwise qualified" to have corrective surgery performed or to have a hospital initiate litigation seeking to override a decision against surgery by the infant's parents. If congress intended section 504 to apply in this manner, it chose strange language indeed.

Second, in arguing that Baby Jane may have been "subjected to discrimination" the government has taken an oversimplified view of the medical decisionmaking process. Where the handicapping condition is related to the condition(s) to be treated, it will rarely, if ever, be possible to say with certainty that a particular decision was "discriminatory." It is at this point that the analogy to race, relied on so heavily by the dissent, breaks down. Beyond the fact that no two cases are likely to be the same, it would invariably require lengthy litigation primarily involving conflicting expert testimony to determine whether a decision to treat, or not to treat, or to litigate or not to litigate, was based on a "bona fide medical judgment," however that phrase might be defined. Before ruling that congress intended to spawn this type of litigation under section 504, we would want more proof than is apparent from the face of the statute.

The legislative history, moreover, indicates that congress never contemplated that section 504 would apply to treatment decisions of this nature. [T]he senate committee report that introduced the provision simply stated "[t]he bill further proclaims a policy of nondiscrimination against otherwise qualified handicapped individuals with respect to participation in or access to any program which is in receipt of Federal financial assistance." S.Rep.No.1135, 92d Cong., 2d Sess. 49. Examples of programs that the provision was designed to cover that were identified on the floor of the senate included housing and employment. See 119 Cong.Rec. 5882 (remarks of Sen. Cranston).

[A]s the senate report accompanying the 1974 amendments elaborated:

> [S]ection 504 was enacted to prevent discrimination against all handicapped individuals, regardless of their need for, or ability to benefit from, vocational rehabilitation services, in relation to Federal assistance in employment, housing, transportation, education, health services, or any other Federally-aided programs. Examples of handicapped individuals who may suffer discrimination in receipt of Federally-assisted services but who may have been unintentionally excluded from the protection of section 504 by the references to enhanced employability in section 7(6) are as follows: physically or mentally handicapped children who may be denied admission to Federally-supported school systems on the basis of their handicap; handicapped persons who may be denied admission to Federally-assisted nursing homes on the basis of their handicap; those persons whose handicap is so severe that employment is not feasible but who may be denied the benefits of a wide range of Federal programs; and those persons whose vocational rehabilitation is complete but who may nevertheless be discriminated against in certain Federally-assisted activities.

This passage provides the best clue to congressional intent regarding section 504's coverage of "health services." As Judge Gesell noted in *American Academy of Pediatrics v. Heckler*, 561 F.Supp. at 401:

> The legislative history * * * [on this subject] focuses on discrimination against adults and older children and denial of access to federal programs. As far as can be determined, no

congressional committee or member of the House or Senate ever even suggested that section 504 would be used to monitor medical treatment of defective newborn infants or establish standards for preserving a particular quality of life. No medical group appeared alert to the intrusion into medical practice which some doctors apprehend from such an undertaking, nor were representatives of parents or spokesmen for religious beliefs that would be affected heard.

The post-enactment legislative history also indicates both that congress was primarily concerned with affording the handicapped access to federally-funded programs and activities, and that congress never envisioned that HEW (or HHS) would attempt to apply section 504 to treatment decisions. [T]he House Subcommittee on Select Education conducted oversight hearings on the section 504 regulations in September 1977. During these hearings, the subcommittee heard testimony covering a wide range of topics from witnesses representing the federal government, state governments, education agencies, and organizations serving handicapped people. Throughout the hearings, the issue of program accessibility was a recurrent theme. [O]n the other hand, although several witnesses echoed Secretary Califano's remark that the newly-issued regulations ushered in a "new era" of civil rights for handicapped citizens, and another observed that "many are the issues which cry out for resolution," at no point did any witness even remotely suggest that section 504 could or would be applied to treatment decisions involving defective newborn infants. Instead, those witnesses who addressed the legal, as opposed to the fiscal, issues raised by HEW's section 504 regulations, including the director of HEW's Office of Civil Rights (OCR), David S. Tatel, focused on subjects such as OCR's complaint backlog, and whether attorneys' fees should be made available in private enforcement actions.

We are aware, of course, that "[w]here the words and purpose of a statute plainly apply to a particular situation, * * * the fact that the specific application of the statute never occurred to Congress does not bar us from holding that the situation falls within the statute's coverage." Here, however, the government's theory not only strains the statutory language but also goes well beyond congress's overriding concern with guaranteeing handicapped individuals access to programs or activities receiving federal financial assistance. Further, the situation in question is dramatically different in kind, not just in degree, from the applications of section 504 discussed in the legislative history. Under these circumstances, the failure of Congress to focus on treatment decisions involving defective newborn infants strikes a telling blow to the government's position.

[T]his void in the legislative history is conspicuous for another reason. Prior to the enactment of the Rehabilitation Act, congress had passed a number of measures limiting federal involvement in medical treatment decisions. [I]n view of this consistent congressional policy against the involvement of federal personnel in medical treatment decisions, we cannot presume that congress intended to repeal its earlier announcements in the absence of clear evidence of congressional intent to do so. As has already been seen there is no such clear expression of congressional intent in either the language or legislative history of section 504.

Along the same lines, we cannot presume that by enacting section 504, congress intended the federal government to enter the field of child care, which, as HHS has recently acknowledged, has traditionally been occupied by the states. Had congress intended to displace state police power functions, it surely would have made that intention explicit.

Finally, case law construing section 504, while not directly on point, also suggests that the government's new interpretation of the statute exceeds the authority conferred by congress. In *Southeastern Community College v. Davis*, the Supreme Court emphasized that "[t]he language and structure of the Rehabilitation Act of 1973 reflect the recognition by Congress of the distinction between the evenhanded treatment of qualified handicapped persons and affirmative efforts to overcome the disabilities caused by handicaps." [I]n the present case, Baby Jane Doe has been treated in an evenhanded manner at least to the extent that the hospital has always been and remains willing to perform the dual, corrective surgeries if her parents would consent. Requiring the hospital either to undertake surgery notwithstanding the parents' decision or alternatively, to petition the state court to override the parents' decision, would impose a particularly onerous affirmative action burden upon the hospital.

IV.

[We] hold that under these circumstances it is congress, rather than an executive agency, that must weigh the competing interests at stake in this context in the first instance. Until congress has spoken, it would be an unwarranted exercise of judicial power to approve the type of investigation that has precipitated this lawsuit.

The judgment of the district court is therefore affirmed.

■ WINTER, CIRCUIT JUDGE, dissenting:

Since I believe that Section 504 applies to the provision of medical services to handicapped infants, I respectfully dissent. I would reverse and remand for further consideration of whether the kinds of federal financial assistance received by the defendant hospital subject the hospital to the commands of Section 504 in the case of the infant in question.

[S]ection 504 is no first step into a hitherto uncharted legal wilderness. As the Senate Report stated:

> Section 504 was patterned after, and is almost identical to, the antidiscrimination language of section 601 of the Civil Rights Act of 1964, 42 U.S.C. 2000d–1 (relating to race, color, or national origin), and section 901 of the Education Amendments of 1972, 42 U.S.C. 1683 (relating to sex). The section therefore constitutes the establishment of a broad government policy that programs receiving Federal financial assistance shall be operated without discrimination on the basis of handicap.

Section 504 was thus enacted against a background of well understood law which was explicitly designated as a guide to interpretation. Congress was persuaded that a handicapped condition is analogous to race and that, so far as the administration of federal financial assistance is concerned, discrimination on the basis of a handicap should be on statutory par with discrimination on the basis of race.

Once Section 504's legislative heritage is acknowledged, the "void" in the legislative history is eliminated and the many issues raised by defendants with regard to medical decisions, parental judgments and state authority simply evaporate. The government has never taken the position that it is entitled to override a medical judgment. Its position rather is that it is entitled under Section 504 to inquire whether a judgment in question is a bona fide medical judgment. While the majority professes uncertainty as to what that means, application of the analogy to race eliminates all doubt. A judgment not to perform certain surgery because a person is black is not a bona fide medical judgment. So too, a decision not to correct a life threatening digestive problem because an infant has Down's Syndrome is not a bona fide medical judgment. The issue of parental authority is also quickly disposed of. A denial of medical treatment to an infant because the infant is black is not legitimated by parental consent. Finally, once the legislative analogy to race is acknowledged, the intrusion on state authority becomes insignificant.

The logic of the government's position on these aspects of the case is thus about as flawless as a legal argument can be. Any doubt must stem not from a deficiency in the argument based on the analogy to Title VI of the Civil Rights Act but from a disagreement as to whether a handicapped condition is fully analogous to race. Whether that doubt is justified or not, however, courts are not the proper fora in which the reasonableness of the analogy to race is to be judged.

[T]he majority even implies, *inter alia*, that Section 504 may not apply at all to the provision of medical services, since such services are inseparable from treatment decisions. This is in the face of the explicit statement of the Senate Report that it "was enacted to prevent discrimination against all handicapped individuals . . . in . . . health services." If that interpretation stands, the handicapped will be deprived of a fairly won political victory and exposed to the possibility of future decisions excluding other services from coverage by Section 504. On the other hand, the majority opinion also implies that a narrower holding may be intended and that only certain kinds of handicapped persons are excluded. If that interpretation stands, then the federal courts may be forced to resolve individually each of these human tragedies and moral dilemmas. It was Judge Gesell's prediction in *American Academy of Pediatrics*, the precedent drawn upon so heavily by the majority, that Section 504 will require line-drawing in individual cases between the extremes of a failure to provide services to a mildly handicapped child and a failure to use heroic measures to prolong for a period of time the life of an infant who has no hope of achieving even minimal consciousness. Such a reading of Section 504, however, intrudes quite as profoundly upon medical decisions, parental judgments and state authority as the interpretation proffered by the government and thus undermines the reasoning of the majority.

Bowen v. American Hospital Association

Supreme Court of the United States, 1986.
476 U.S. 610.

■ JUSTICE STEVENS announced the judgment of the Court and delivered an opinion, in which JUSTICE MARSHALL, JUSTICE BLACKMUN, and JUSTICE POWELL join.

This case presents the question whether certain regulations governing the provision of health care to handicapped infants are authorized by § 504 of the Rehabilitation Act of 1973.

I

The American Medical Association, the American Hospital Association, and several other respondents challenge the validity of Final Rules promulgated on January 12, 1984, by the Secretary of the Department of Health and Human Services. These Rules establish "Procedures relating to health care for handicapped infants," and in particular require the posting of informational notices, authorize expedited access to records and expedited compliance actions, and command state child protective services agencies to "prevent instances of unlawful medical neglect of handicapped infants." 45 CFR § 84.55 (1985).

Although the Final Rules comprise six parts, only the four mandatory components are challenged here. Subsection (b) is entitled "Posting of informational notice" and requires every "recipient health care provider that provides health care services to infants in programs or activities receiving Federal financial assistance"—a group to which we refer generically as "hospitals"—to post an informational notice in one of two approved forms. 45 CFR § 84.55(b) (1985). Both forms include a statement that § 504 prohibits discrimination on the basis of handicap, and indicate that because of this prohibition "nourishment and medically beneficial treatment (as determined with respect for reasonable medical judgments) should not be withheld from handicapped infants solely on the basis of their present or anticipated mental or physical impairments." The notice's statement of the legal requirement does not distinguish between medical care for which parental consent has been obtained and that for which it has not. The notice must identify the telephone number of the appropriate child protective services agency and, in addition, a toll-free number for the Department that is available 24 hours a day. Finally, the notice must state that the "identity of callers will be kept confidential" and that federal law prohibits retaliation "against any person who provides information about possible violations."

The guidelines also describe how HHS will respond to "complaints of suspected life threatening noncompliance" with § 504 in this context, progressing from telephone inquiries to the hospital to obtain information about the condition of the infant, to requests for access to records, and finally to onsite investigations and litigation in appropriate cases. ¶ (b). The guidelines do not draw any distinction between cases in which parental consent has been withheld and those in which it has been given. Nor do they draw any distinction between cases in which hospitals have made a report of parental refusal to consent to treatment and those in which no report to a state agency has been made. They do announce that the "Department will also seek to coordinate its investigation with any related investigations by the state child protective services agency so as to minimize potential disruption," ¶ (b)(4), indicating that the Department's investigations may continue even in cases that have previously been referred to a state agency.

Subsection (c), which contains the second mandatory requirement, sets forth "Responsibilities of recipient state child protective services agencies." Subsection (c) does not mention § 504 (or any other federal statute) and does not even use the word "discriminate." It requires every designated agency to establish and maintain procedures to ensure that "the agency utilizes its full authority pursuant to state law to prevent instances of unlawful medical neglect of handicapped infants." 45 CFR § 84.55(c)(1). Mandated procedures must include (1) "[a] requirement that health care providers report on a timely basis . . . known or suspected instances of unlawful medical neglect of handicapped infants," § 84.55(c)(1)(i); (2) a method by which the state agency can receive timely reports of such cases, § 84.55(c)(1)(ii); (3) "immediate" review of those reports, including "on-site investigation," where appropriate, § 84.55(c)(1)(iii); (4) protection of "medically neglected handicapped infants" including, where appropriate, legal action to secure "timely court order[s] to compel the provision of necessary nourishment and medical treatment," § 84.55(c)(1)(iv); and (5) "[t]imely notification" to HHS of every report of "suspected unlawful medical neglect" of handicapped infants. The preamble to the Final Rules makes clear that this subsection applies "where a refusal to provide medically beneficial treatment is a result, not of decisions by a health care provider, but of decisions by parents." 49 Fed.Reg. 1627 (1984).

The two remaining mandatory regulations authorize "[e]xpedited access to records" and "[e]xpedited action to effect compliance." 45 CFR §§ 84.55(d), (e) (1985). Subsection (d) provides broadly for immediate access to patient records on a 24-hour basis, with or without parental consent, "when, in the judgment of the responsible Department official, immediate access is necessary to protect the life or health of a handicapped individual." § 84.55(d). Subsection (e) likewise dispenses with otherwise applicable requirements of notice to the hospital "when, in the judgment of the responsible Department official, immediate action to effect compliance is necessary to protect the life or health of a handicapped individual." § 84.55(e). The expedited compliance provision is intended to allow "the government [to] see[k] a temporary restraining order to sustain the life of a handicapped infant in imminent danger of death." 49 Fed.Reg. 1628 (1984). Like the provision affording expedited access to records, it applies without regard to whether parental consent to treatment has been withheld or whether the matter has already been referred to a state child protective services agency.

II

The Final Rules represent the Secretary's ultimate response to an April 9, 1982, incident in which the parents of a Bloomington, Indiana, infant with Down's syndrome and other handicaps refused consent to surgery to remove an esophageal obstruction that prevented oral feeding. [C]iting "heightened public concern" in the aftermath of the Bloomington Baby Doe incident, on May 18, 1982, the director of the

Department's Office of Civil Rights, in response to a directive from the President, "remind[ed]" health care providers receiving federal financial assistance that newborn infants with handicaps such as Down's syndrome were protected by § 504.

This notice was followed, on March 7, 1983, by an "Interim Final Rule" contemplating a "vigorous federal role." The Interim Rule required health care providers receiving federal financial assistance to post "in a conspicuous place in each delivery ward, each maternity ward, each pediatric ward, and each nursery, including each intensive care nursery" a notice advising of the applicability of § 504 and the availability of a telephone "hotline" to report suspected violations of the law to HHS. Like the Final Rules, the Interim Rule also provided for expedited compliance actions and expedited access to records and facilities when, "in the judgment of the responsible Department official," immediate action or access was "necessary to protect the life or health of a handicapped individual." The Interim Rule took effect on March 22.

On April 6, 1983, respondents American Hospital Association *et al.* filed a complaint in the Federal District Court for the Southern District of New York seeking a declaration that the Interim Final Rule was invalid and an injunction against its enforcement. Little more than a week later, on April 14, in a similar challenge brought by the American Academy of Pediatrics and other medical institutions, the Federal District Court for the District of Columbia declared the Interim Final Rule "arbitrary and capricious and promulgated in violation of the Administrative Procedure Act." *American Academy of Pediatrics v. Heckler*, 561 F.Supp. 395, 404 (1983).

On July 5, 1983, the Department issued new "Proposed Rules" on which it invited comment. Like the Interim Final Rule, the Proposed Rules required hospitals to post informational notices in conspicuous places and authorized expedited access to records to be followed, if necessary, by expedited compliance action. 48 Fed.Reg. 30851. In a departure from the Interim Final Rule, however, the Proposed Rules required federally assisted state child protective services agencies to utilize their "full authority pursuant to State law to prevent instances of medical neglect of handicapped infants." Mandated procedures mirrored those contained in the Final Rules described above. The preamble and appendix to the Proposed Rules did not acknowledge that hospitals and physicians lack authority to perform treatment to which parents have not given their consent.

In addition to its unqualified endorsement of nourishment as required by § 504, the appendix announced that "[a]ny decision not to correct intestinal atresia in a Down's Syndrome child, unless an additional complication medically warrants such decision, must be deemed a denial of services based on the handicap of Down's Syndrome. The same reasoning applies to a case of Down's Syndrome [infant] with esophogeal atresia, and the denial of surgery to correct atresia." The Department did not discuss the relevance of parental nonconsent to the hospital's treatment obligation under § 504, presumably because it was irrelevant given its understanding of the provision at that time.

After the period for notice and comment had passed, HHS, on December 30, 1983, promulgated the Final Rules and announced that they would take effect on February 13, 1984. On March 12 of that year respondents American Hospital Association *et al.* amended their complaint and respondents American Medical Association *et al.* filed suit to declare the new regulations invalid and to enjoin their enforcement. The actions were consolidated in the Federal District Court for the Southern District of New York, which awarded the requested relief on the authority of the decision of the United States Court of Appeals for the Second Circuit in *United States v. University Hospital*, 729 F.2d 144 (1984).

III

[T]he Government did not file a *certiorari* petition in *University Hospital*. It did, however, seek review of the judgment in this case. We granted *certiorari*, and we now affirm.

IV

[T]his suit is not an enforcement action, and as a consequence it is not necessary to determine whether § 504 ever applies to individual medical treatment decisions involving handicapped infants. Respondents brought this litigation to challenge the four mandatory components of the Final Rules on their face. [T]he specific question presented by this case, then, is whether the four mandatory provisions of the Final Rules are authorized by § 504.

V

[B]efore examining the Secretary's reasons for issuing the Final Rules, it is essential to understand the pre-existing state-law framework governing the provision of medical care to handicapped infants. In broad outline, state law vests decisional responsibility in the parents, in the first instance, subject to review in exceptional cases by the State acting as *parens patriae*. Prior to the regulatory activity culminating in the Final Rules, the Federal Government was not a participant in the process of making treatment decisions for newborn infants. We presume that this general framework was familiar to Congress when it enacted § 504. It therefore provides an appropriate background for evaluating the Secretary's action in this case. [T]he Secretary [c]ontends that a hospital's refusal to furnish a handicapped infant with medically beneficial treatment "solely by reason of his handicap" constitutes unlawful discrimination.

VI

In the immediate aftermath of the Bloomington Baby Doe incident, the Secretary apparently proceeded on the assumption that a hospital's statutory duty to provide treatment to handicapped infants was unaffected by the absence of parental consent. He has since abandoned that view. Thus, the preamble to the Final Rules correctly states that when "a non-treatment decision, no matter how discriminatory, is made by parents, rather than by the hospital, section 504 does not mandate that the hospital unilaterally overrule the parental decision and provide treatment notwithstanding the lack of consent." A hospital's withholding of treatment when no parental consent has been given cannot violate § 504, for without the consent of the parents or a surrogate decisionmaker the infant is neither "otherwise qualified" for treatment nor has he been denied care "solely by reason of his handicap." Indeed, it would almost certainly be a tort as a matter of state law to operate on an infant without parental consent. This analysis makes clear that the Government's heavy reliance on the analogy to race-based refusals which violate § 601 of the Civil Rights Act is misplaced. If, pursuant to its normal practice, a hospital refused to operate on a black child whose parents had withheld their consent to treatment, the hospital's refusal would not be based on the race of the child even if it were assumed that the parents based their decision entirely on a mistaken assumption that the race of the child made the operation inappropriate.

Now that the Secretary has acknowledged that a hospital has no statutory treatment obligation in the absence of parental consent, it has become clear that the Final Rules are not needed to prevent hospitals from denying treatment to handicapped infants. The Solicitor General concedes that the administrative record contains no evidence that hospitals have ever refused treatment authorized either by the infant's parents or by a court order. Tr. of Oral Arg. 8. Even the Secretary never seriously maintained that posted notices, "hotlines," and emergency on-site investigations were necessary to process complaints against hospitals that might refuse treatment requested by parents. The parental interest in calling such a refusal to the attention of the appropriate authorities adequately vindicates the interest in enforcement of § 504 in such cases, just as that interest obviates the need for a special regulation to deal with refusals to provide treatment on the basis of race which may violate § 601 of the Civil Rights Act.

The Secretary's belated recognition of the effect of parental nonconsent is important, because the supposed need for federal monitoring of hospitals' treatment decisions rests entirely on instances in which parents have refused their consent. Thus, in the Bloomington, Indiana, case that precipitated the Secretary's enforcement efforts in this area, as well as in the *University Hospital* case that provided the basis for the summary affirmance in the case now before us, the hospital's failure to perform the treatment at issue rested on the lack of parental consent.

[T]he Secretary's initial failure to recognize that withholding of consent by parents does not equate with discriminatory denial of treatment by hospitals likewise undermines the Secretary's findings in the preamble to his proposed rulemaking. In that statement, the Secretary cited four sources in support of the claim that "Section 504 [is] not being uniformly followed." None of the cited examples, however, suggests that recipients of federal financial assistance, as opposed to parents, had withheld medical care on the basis of handicap.[18]

---

[18] The Secretary first cited a 1973 survey by Raymond Duff and A.G.M. Campbell calculating that 14% of deaths in the special nursery of the Yale–New Haven hospital "were related to withholding treatment." The Secretary's solitary quotation from this study, accurately illustrating the locus of the treatment decisions reviewed by the authors, involved refusal of parental consent: " 'An infant with Down's syndrome and intestinal atresia, like the much publicized one at Johns Hopkins Hospital, was not treated because his parents thought the surgery was wrong for their baby and themselves. He died several days after birth.' " (quoting Duff & Campbell, *Moral and Ethical Dilemmas in the Special–Care Nursery*, 289 New Eng. J.Med. 890, 891 (1973)).The Secretary next referred to an incident at Johns Hopkins Hospital which, as the above quotation intimates, also concerned parental refusal of consent. Then followed brief mention of the "Bloomington Baby Doe" incident, in which the parents, as the Secretary now admits, refused consent to treatment despite the hospital's insistence that it be provided. The Secretary's fourth and final example involved "a 1979 death of an infant

Notwithstanding the ostensible recognition in the preamble of the effect of parental nonconsent on a hospital's obligation to provide care, in promulgating the Final Rules the Secretary persisted in relying on instances in which parents had refused consent to support his claim that, regardless of its "magnitude," there is sufficient evidence of "illegality" to justify "establishing basic mechanisms to allow for effective enforcement of a clearly applicable statute." We have already discussed one source of this evidence—"the several specific cases cited in the preamble to the proposed rule." Contrary to the Secretary's belief, these cases do not "support the proposition that handicapped infants may be subjected to unlawful discrimination." In addition to the evidence relied on in prior notices, the Secretary included a summary of the 49 "Infant Doe cases" that the Department had processed before December 1, 1983. Curiously, however, by the Secretary's own admission none of the 49 cases had "resulted in a finding of discriminatory withholding of medical care." In fact, in the entire list of 49 cases there is no finding that a hospital failed or refused to provide treatment to a handicapped infant for which parental consent had been given.

[VIII]

Even according the greatest respect to the Secretary's action, [d]eference cannot fill the lack of an evidentiary foundation on which the Final Rules must rest. The Secretary's basis for federal intervention is perceived discrimination against handicapped infants in violation of § 504, and yet the Secretary has pointed to no evidence that such discrimination occurs. Neither the fact that regulators generally may rely on generic information in a particular field or comparable experience gained in other fields, nor the fact that regulations may be imposed for preventative or prophylactic reasons, can substitute for evidence supporting the Secretary's own chosen rationale. For the principle of agency accountability [m]eans that "an agency's action must be upheld, if at all, on the basis articulated by the agency itself."

The need for a proper evidentiary basis for agency action is especially acute in this case because Congress has failed to indicate, either in the statute or in the legislative history, that it envisioned federal superintendence of treatment decisions traditionally entrusted to state governance. [T]he administrative record does not contain the reasoning and evidence that is necessary to sustain federal intervention into a historically state-administered decisional process that appears—for lack of any evidence to the contrary—to be functioning in full compliance with § 504.

The history of these regulations exposes the inappropriateness of the extraordinary deference—virtually a *carte blanche*—requested by the Government. The Secretary's present reading of § 504 has evolved only after previous, patently erroneous interpretations had been found wanting. The checkered history of these regulations began in 1982,

---

with Down's syndrome and an intestinal obstruction at the Kapiolani–Children's Medical Center in Honolulu, Hawaii," which again appears to have resulted from "a lack of parental consent." Generalizing from these examples, the Secretary reported the results of a survey of physician attitudes. He faulted "[t]heir acquiescence in nontreatment of Down's children" which he surmised was "apparently because of the handicap represented by Down's syndrome."

when the Department notified hospitals that they would violate § 504 if they "allow[ed] an infant" to remain in their care after "the infant's parents or guardian [had withheld consent to] treatment or nourishment discriminatorily." By the time the Proposed Rules were announced one year later, the Secretary had abandoned that construction. But the Department substituted the equally untenable view that "the basic provision of nourishment, fluids, and routine nursing care" was "not an option for medical judgment" and that "[t]he decision to forego medical treatment of a correctable life-threatening defect because an infant also suffers from a permanent irremediable handicap that is not life-threatening, such as mental retardation, is a violation of Section 504," insinuating by omission that lack of parental consent did not alter the hospital's obligation to provide corrective surgery. Although the preamble to the Final Rules corrects the prior erroneous signals from the Department that § 504 authorizes it to override parental decisions and to save the lives of handicapped infants, it persists in advocating federal regulation on the basis of treatment denials precipitated by refusals of parental consent and on the ground that its experience with the Baby Doe hotline has demonstrated that "the assumption that handicapped infants will receive medically beneficial treatment is not always justified."

This response, together with its previous remarks, makes irresistible the inference that the Department regards its mission as one principally concerned with the quality of medical care for handicapped infants rather than with the implementation of § 504. [T]he administrative record demonstrates that the Secretary has asserted the authority to conduct on-site investigations, to inspect hospital records, and to participate in the decisional process in emergency cases in which there was no colorable basis for believing that a violation of § 504 had occurred or was about to occur. The District Court and the Court of Appeals correctly held that these investigative actions were not authorized by the statute and that the regulations which purport to authorize a continuation of them are invalid.

The judgment of the Court of Appeals is affirmed.

It is so ordered.

■ CHIEF JUSTICE BURGER concurs in the judgment.

■ JUSTICE REHNQUIST took no part in the consideration or decision of this case.

■ JUSTICE WHITE, with whom JUSTICE BRENNAN joins and with whom JUSTICE O'CONNOR joins [in part], dissenting.

[W]e should resolve the threshold statutory question that this case and *University Hospital* clearly pose—namely, whether the Secretary has any authority at all under the Act to regulate medical care decisions with respect to the handicapped newborn.

[L]ooking first at the language of the statute, I agree with the Court of Appeals' preliminary conclusion that handicapped newborns are handicapped individuals covered by the Act. [T]his leaves the critical question whether a handicapped infant can ever be "otherwise qualified" for medical treatment and hence possibly subjected to unlawful discrimination when he or she is denied such treatment.[7]

[E]ven under the Court of Appeals' interpretation of "otherwise qualified," [i]t does not follow that § 504 may never apply to medical treatment decisions for the newborn. An esophageal obstruction, for example, would not be part and parcel of the handicap of a baby suffering from Down's syndrome, and the infant would benefit from and is thus otherwise qualified for having the obstruction removed in spite of the handicap. In this case, the treatment is completely unrelated to the baby's handicapping condition. If an otherwise normal child would be given the identical treatment, so should the handicapped child if discrimination on the basis of the handicap is to be avoided.

It would not be difficult to multiply examples like this. And even if it is true that in the great majority of cases the handicap itself will constitute the need for treatment, I doubt that this consideration or any other mentioned by the Court of Appeals justifies the wholesale conclusion that § 504 never applies to newborn infants with handicaps. That some or most failures to treat may not fall within § 504, that discerning which failures to treat are discriminatory may be difficult, and that applying § 504 in this area may intrude into the traditional functions of the State do not support the categorical conclusion that the section may never be applied to medical decisions about handicapped infants. And surely the absence in the legislative history of any consideration of handicapped newborns does not itself narrow the reach of the statutory language. Furthermore, the broad remedial purpose of the section would be undermined by excluding handicapped infants from its coverage; and if, as the plurality indicates, the Secretary has substantial leeway to explore areas in which discrimination against the handicapped poses serious problems and to devise regulations to prohibit the discrimination, it is appropriate to take note of the

---

    [7] [F]or the purposes of addressing the Court of Appeals' *University Hospital* analysis, the most straightforward fact situation to consider is one in which the benefit provided is the medical treatment itself and in which a hospital refuses treatment in the face of parental consent. In this context, the Court of Appeals' conclusion that the nature of the decisions themselves precludes application of § 504 may be addressed with maximum simplicity. I note, however, that it may well be that the benefits provided by hospitals and doctors and covered by § 504 extend beyond treatment itself. For example, one benefit provided by hospitals and doctors to patients who cannot make their own medical treatment decisions may be medical advice in those patients' best interest to those who must ultimately make the relevant medical treatment decisions. To the extent that the provision of this benefit is a program or activity covered by the statute, I would think that the statute requires that the same advice be given to parents of a handicapped baby as to the parents of a similarly situated nonhandicapped baby. Another benefit provided may be the reporting of nontreatment to the relevant state agency in the case of a parental decision not to treat. Again, to the extent that the provision of this benefit is a program or activity covered by the statute, I would think that § 504 requires that the hospital or doctor report nontreatment of a handicapped baby when it would report the denial of the same treatment for a nonhandicapped baby. My conclusions in this regard are buttressed by my view of § 504's coverage in the case of a medical treatment decision regarding a black baby. If a hospital or doctor advised different or less efficacious treatment for a black baby than for a white baby, I believe that this would be discrimination under the statute. Similarly, a failure to report a parental decision not to treat because of race would seem to me to be illegally discriminatory—assuming that this decision otherwise came within the statute. In sum, although these additional situations present the same issue as to when a handicapped baby is otherwise qualified and when such a baby is subjected to discrimination as does the direct example of a refusal to treat and although it may well be that it would be in these contexts that the statute would most likely be given effect, for simplicity's sake I have centered my discussion of *University Hospital* on the refusal-to-treat example.

Secretary's present view that § 504 properly extends to the subject matter at issue here. Thus, I believe that the Court of Appeals in *University Hospital* incorrectly concluded that § 504 may never apply to medical treatment decisions concerning handicapped newborn infants. Where a decision regarding medical treatment for a handicapped newborn properly falls within the statutory provision, it should be subject to the constraints set forth in § 504. Consequently, I would reverse the judgment below.

[T]he plurality concludes that the four mandatory provisions of the final regulations are invalid because there is no " 'rational connection between the facts found and the choice made.' " The basis for this conclusion is the plurality's perception that two and only two wholly discrete categories of decisions are the object of the final regulations: (1) decisions made by hospitals to treat or not treat where parental consent has been given and (2) decisions made by hospitals to refer or not to refer a case to the state child protective services agency where parental consent has been withheld. Since the Secretary has not specifically pointed to discriminatory actions that provably resulted from either of these two specific types of decisions, the plurality finds that the Secretary's conclusion that discrimination is occurring is unsupported factually. The plurality's characterization of the Secretary's rationale, however, oversimplifies both the complexity of the situations to which the regulations are addressed and the reasoning of the Secretary.

First, the Secretary's proof that treatment is in fact being withheld from handicapped infants is unquestioned by the plurality. It is therefore obvious that whoever is making them, decisions to withhold treatment from such infants are in fact being made. This basic understanding is critical to the Secretary's further reasoning, and the discussion accompanying the proposed regulations clearly indicates that this was the Secretary's starting point. Proceeding with this factual understanding, the next question is whether such withholding of treatment constitutes prohibited discrimination under § 504 in some or all situations. It is at this point that the plurality errs. In the plurality's view, only two narrow paradigmatic types of decisions were contemplated by the Secretary as potentially constituting discrimination in violation of the statute. The plurality does not explain, however, precisely what in the Secretary's discussion gives rise to this distillation, and my reading of the explanation accompanying the regulations does not leave me with so limited a view of the Secretary's concerns.

The studies cited by the Secretary in support of the regulations and other literature concerning medical treatment in this area generally portray a decisionmaking process in which the parents and the doctors and often other concerned persons as well are involved—although the parental decision to consent or not is obviously the critical one.[11] Thus, the parental consent decision does not occur in a vacuum. In fact, the doctors (directly) and the hospital (indirectly) in most cases participate in the formulation of the final parental decision and in many cases

---

[11] See, *e.g.*, Duff & Campbell, *Moral and Ethical Dilemmas in the Special–Care Nursery*, 289 N. Eng. J. Med. 890 (1973). See also Gross, Cox, Tatyrek, Pollay, & Barnes, *Early Management and Decision Making for the Treatment of Myelomeningocele*, 72 Pediatrics 450 (1983).

substantially influence that decision. Consequently, discrimination against a handicapped infant may assume guises other than the outright refusal to treat once parental consent has been given. Discrimination may occur when a doctor encourages or fails to discourage a parental decision to refuse consent to treatment for a handicapped child when the doctor would discourage or actually oppose a parental decision to refuse consent to the same treatment for a nonhandicapped child. Or discrimination may occur when a doctor makes a discriminatory treatment recommendation that the parents simply follow. Alternatively, discrimination may result from a hospital's explicit laissez-faire attitude about this type of discrimination on the part of doctors.

Contrary to the plurality's constrained view of the Secretary's justification for the regulations, the stated basis for those regulations reveals that the Secretary was cognizant of this more elusive discrimination. For example, the evidence cited most extensively by the Secretary in his initial proposal of these regulations was a study of attitudes of practicing and teaching pediatricians and pediatric surgeons. See 48 Fed. Reg. 30848 (1983) (citing Shaw, Randolph, & Manard, *Ethical Issues in Pediatric Surgery: A National Survey of Pediatricians and Pediatric Surgeons*, 60 Pediatrics 588 (1977)). This study indicated that a substantial number of these doctors (76.8% of pediatric surgeons and 49.5% of pediatricians) would "acquiesce in parents' decision to refuse consent for surgery in a newborn with intestinal atresia if the infant also had . . . Down's syndrome." It also indicated that a substantial minority (23.6% of pediatric surgeons and 13.2% of pediatricians) would in fact encourage parents to refuse consent to surgery in this situation and that only a small minority (3.4% of pediatric surgeons and 15.8% of pediatricians) would attempt to get a court order mandating surgery if the parents refused consent. In comparison, only a small minority (7.9% of pediatric surgeons and 2.6% of pediatricians) would acquiesce in parental refusal to treat intestinal atresia in an infant with no other anomaly. And a large majority (78.3% of pediatric surgeons and 88.4% of pediatricians) would try to get a court order directing surgery if parental consent were withheld for treatment of a treatable malignant tumor. The Secretary thus recognized that there was evidence that doctors would act differently in terms of attempts to affect or override parental decisions depending on whether the infant was handicapped.

Based on this evidence, the Secretary conceded that "[t]he full extent of discriminatory and life-threatening practices toward handicapped infants is not yet known" but concluded "that for even a single infant to die due to lack of an adequate notice and complaint procedure is unacceptable." Thus, the Secretary promulgated the regulations at issue here. These regulations, in relevant part, require that a notice of the federal policies against discrimination on the basis of handicap be posted in a place where a hospital's health care professionals will see it. This requirement is, as the Secretary concluded, "[c]onsistent with the Department's intent to target the notice to nurses and other health care professionals." The notice requirement, therefore, may reasonably be read as aimed at fostering an awareness by health care professionals of their responsibility not to act in a discriminatory manner with respect to medical treatment decisions for handicapped infants. The second requirement of the regulations, that state agencies provide mechanisms for requiring and reporting medical neglect of handicapped children, is also consistent with the Secretary's focus on discrimination in the form of discriminatory reporting.

I therefore perceive a rational connection between the facts found by the Secretary and the regulatory choice made. The Secretary identified an existing practice that there was reason to believe resulted from discrimination on the basis of handicap. Given this finding, the amorphous nature of much of the possible discrimination, the Secretary's profession that the regulations are appropriate no matter how limited the problem, and the focus of the regulations on loci where unlawful discrimination seems most likely to occur and on persons likely to be responsible for it, I conclude that these regulations are not arbitrary and capricious and that the Court errs in striking them down on that basis.

■ JUSTICE O'CONNOR, dissenting.

[omitted]

Johnson v. Thompson

United States Court of Appeals for the Tenth Circuit, 1992.
971 F.2d 1487.

■ EBEL, CIRCUIT JUDGE.

This appeal requires us to confront a variety of issues regarding the medical treatment provided to certain infants born with spina bifida. [T]he district court entered judgment for the defendants. We affirm.

I. Background

Plaintiffs–Appellants Carlton Johnson, Melissa Camp, and Stonewall Jackson Smith were all born with myelomeningocele ("MM"), a type of spina bifida, at Oklahoma Children's Memorial Hospital ("OCMH"). The appellants allege that they received discriminatory treatment based on their handicap and on their socioeconomic status. The parties sharply dispute many of the facts in this case. However, the record supports the following factual background.

Defendant-appellee Dr. Richard H. Gross led a team of doctors and other health professionals ("the MM team") at OCMH who treated newborn infants with myelomeningocele. This treatment, which includes surgery and the administering of antibiotics, must take place soon after birth. In some cases, however, the infant will not survive even with treatment. In such cases, treating the infant merely prolongs his or her suffering.

In conjunction with his work at the hospital, Dr. Gross performed a study and published an article, entitled *Early Management and Decision Making for the Treatment of Myelomeningocele*, 72 Pediatrics 450 (1983). This study covered the period 1977 through 1982, during which time the MM team evaluated sixty-nine infants born with myelomeningocele. The MM team recommended "vigorous treatment," *i.e.*, surgery and antibiotics, for thirty-six of the infants. One of these infants later died of unrelated causes; the rest survived. The team recommended "supportive care," *i.e.*, no treatment other than making the infants as comfortable as possible, for the remaining thirty-three infants. The parents of five infants in the latter group rejected the recommendations, and three of these infants survived. Several other infants survived without treatment for several months and were subsequently treated. The remaining twenty-four infants receiving supportive care died.

The appellants allege that when the MM team made its recommendations, it considered both medical and nonmedical criteria, the latter including the parents' socioeconomic status. The appellants allege that the MM team discriminated against infants who came from families that the team believed lacked the intellectual and financial resources to provide the appropriate continuing care for a child with MM. According to the appellants, the MM team was more likely to recommend only supportive care for infants from such families. The appellants further allege that the MM team did not inform parents of its consideration of such factors when it made its recommendation. Although the appellees argue that the parents made the ultimate treatment decision, parents of sixty-four of the sixty-nine infants followed the MM team's recommendation. Thus, the appellants argue, the MM team was the true decisionmaker.

Melissa Camp and Stonewall Jackson Smith were participants in the study. The team recommended, and each infant received, only supportive care; both died. Carlton Johnson was born after completion of the study, but while the team allegedly continued to use the study's criteria to make its recommendation. The MM team recommended and Johnson received only supportive care. He survived without treatment for seventeen months, when surgery was finally performed. He was still alive at the time of trial, but suffered a severe mental handicap allegedly due, in part, to the team's failure to treat him immediately.

The hospital changed its practice in 1984. Since then, all infants born with spina bifida have received vigorous treatment, with the exception of one infant for whom treatment clearly would have been futile.

The parents of Camp, Smith, and Johnson, on behalf of their children, together with the Spina Bifida Association of America ("SBAA") and the Association for Persons with Severe Handicaps ("the plaintiffs"), filed suit against the members of the MM team, various other physicians, and a number of state officials. The plaintiffs sought class certification on behalf of 156 potential members, all infants born with MM at OCMH during the pendency of the study and all those born afterward while OCMH allegedly continued to use the study criteria. In their complaint, the plaintiffs asserted causes of action from violations of rights arising under, among other sources, [s]ection 504 of the Rehabilitation Act of 1973 ("section 504"). [T]he plaintiffs sought compensatory and punitive damages along with declaratory and injunctive relief.

The district court denied the plaintiff's application for class certification. In addition, the court dismissed [t]he cause of action brought under section 504.

II. Section 504

[W]hether section 504 applies to "individual medical treatment decisions involving handicapped infants" is a controversial issue that the Supreme Court has expressly left open. See *Bowen*. [T]he appellants argue that the MM team "used the anticipated degree of handicap as a basis for recommending that beneficial medical treatment not be provided" and in so doing violated section 504. We reject this argument because the appellants fail to [show] that they were "otherwise qualified" for the treatment they did not receive.

The "otherwise qualified" language, when considered in conjunction with the "solely" language, [p]oses a formidable obstacle for anyone alleging discrimination in violation of section 504 based upon the failure to receive medical treatment for a birth defect. Such a plaintiff must prove that he or she was discriminatorily denied medical treatment because of the birth defect and, at the same time, must prove that, in spite of the birth defect, he or she was "otherwise qualified" to receive the denied medical treatment. Ordinarily, however, if such a person were not so handicapped, he or she would not need the medical treatment and thus would not "otherwise qualify" for the treatment.

We agree, therefore, with the Second Circuit's analysis in *University Hospital*. In that case, the court considered the application of section 504, and its second requirement in particular, to infants born with multiple birth defects. The court stated that the term otherwise qualified cannot ordinarily be applied "in the comparatively fluid context of medical treatment decisions without distorting its plain meaning. In common parlance, one would not ordinarily think of a newborn infant suffering from multiple birth defects as being 'otherwise qualified' to have corrective surgery performed." The court reasoned, "[w]here the handicapping condition is related to the condition(s) to be treated, it will rarely, if ever, be possible to say . . . that a particular decision was 'discriminatory.' "[3]

[T]he SBAA argues that the team discriminated against all infants with MM by designating them as subjects of a medical research project without their parents' knowledge or consent. Because all infants with MM were part of the study during its pendency, the SBAA contends the discrimination was "solely" due to the handicap, thereby meeting the third condition.

Under this argument, the appellants still fail to satisfy the second condition. The infants required the medical treatment sought only because they were born with MM. Thus, they were not "otherwise

---

[3] Several jurists have hypothesized situations in which the handicap that forms the basis of the section 504 discrimination bears no relation to the medical treatment sought but denied. For example, Justice White stated in *Bowen*:

> An esophageal obstruction, for example, would not be part and parcel of the handicap of a baby suffering from Down's syndrome, and the infant would benefit from and is thus otherwise qualified for having the obstruction removed in spite of the handicap. In this case, the treatment is completely unrelated to the baby's handicapping condition. If an otherwise normal child would be given the identical treatment, so should the handicapped child if discrimination on the basis of the handicap is to be avoided.

We do not decide whether section 504 might apply in such a situation, but it would seem that the "otherwise qualified" condition might be satisfied under such a scenario. We do not find such a situation here.

qualified" to receive the medical treatment denied to them because of the alleged discrimination.

Section 504 proscribes discrimination between the nonhandicapped and the "otherwise qualified" handicapped. It does not create any absolute substantive right to treatment. [W]ithout a showing that the nonhandicapped received the treatment denied to the "otherwise qualified" handicapped, the appellants cannot assert that a violation of section 504 has occurred.

In sum, we hold that the appellants failed to state a claim for violation of section 504 and that the district court therefore did not err in dismissing the claim brought under this section.

[B]ecause we hold that the district court committed no reversible error, we AFFIRM its judgment.

NOTES ON THE BABY DOE CASES

1. Do the Disability Discrimination Laws Apply to Medical Treatment Decisions? Both *University Hospital* and *Johnson* suggest that the disability discrimination laws cannot (at least ordinarily) be applied to disability-based medical treatment decisions. The Second Circuit's decision in *University Hospital* offers two basic reasons for that conclusion: (1) the text and legislative history of Section 504 seem to be "geared toward relatively static programs or activities such as education, employment, and transportation systems," and nobody contemplated the statute's application to medical treatment decisions; and (2) "[w]here the handicapping condition is related to the condition(s) to be treated, it will rarely, if ever, be possible to say with certainty that a particular decision was 'discriminatory.'" Are these arguments persuasive?

Subsequent precedent casts substantial doubt on each of the arguments of the *University Hospital* majority. First, the Supreme Court's decision in *Yeskey* (a principal case above) rejects the notion that the disability discrimination laws apply only to those contexts expressly anticipated by Congress. The plain terms of the ADA and Section 504 reach *any* disability-based discrimination by a covered entity, and state facilities and hospitals receiving federal funds are covered under each respective statute. *Yeskey* accords the ADA a sweep as broad as its language.

Second, the Supreme Court's decision in *Olmstead* (also a principal case above) necessarily rejects the notion that the ADA does not apply "where the handicapping condition is related to the condition(s) to be treated." Recall that in *Olmstead* the Court held that discrimination on the basis of disability includes the unnecessary placement of individuals who receive state mental health care in institutional rather than community settings. The state contended that it could not be "discrimination" to refuse to provide community placements for those individuals, because those placements are specifically designed for people with mental disabilities, and it accordingly did not provide community placements for individuals *without* disabilities. The Court rejected that argument and concluded that "Congress had a more comprehensive view of the concept of discrimination advanced in the ADA." Does it make a difference that *Olmstead* was a case in which the plaintiffs sought to enforce the ADA's "integration mandate," while the Baby Doe cases alleged the existence of straightforward discrimination? If so, which way does that difference cut?

In any event, why isn't it perfectly coherent to argue that the baby in *University Hospital* experienced disability-based discrimination? Based on the facts the Court presents, the baby needed surgery for spina bifida, but surgery was not performed because she also had microcephaly and hydrocephalus. The government's argument, as Judge Winter explains in dissent, was that other children with spina bifida would have received surgery, and that the reason Jane Doe did not receive that surgery was because of her other disabilities. What is wrong with that argument?

Consider the case of Amelia Rivera, a three-year-old whose parents alleged that the Children's Hospital of Philadelphia denied her a kidney transplant because she has a developmental disability. See *N.J. Girl, 3, Is Being Denied Kidney Transplant Because of Mental Abilities, Parents Claim*, Assoc. Press, Jan. 18, 2012. Later in 2012, the parents of Paul Corby, a 23-year-old man with autism, alleged that Penn Medical denied him a heart transplant because of his autism. See Rehana Murray, *23-Year-Old Pennsylvania Man with Autism Denied Heart Transplant by Hospital*, N.Y. Daily News, Aug. 16, 2012. If the allegations proved true, would the hospital's conduct in either case violate the ADA or Rehabilitation Act under the *University Hospital* and *Johnson* approach? (In the Rivera case, the hospital apologized to the family after a public outcry.)

Data reported by the Autistic Self Advocacy Network suggests that discrimination against people with intellectual and developmental disabilities in transplant decisions is far from uncommon:

> A 2008 survey of 88 transplant centers conducted by researchers at Stanford University found that 85% of pediatric transplant centers consider neurodevelopmental status as a factor in their determinations of transplant eligibility at least some of the time, with heart transplant centers being more restrictive in their decisions than kidney or liver programs. For example, 46% of heart programs indicated that even mild or moderate cognitive impairment would be a relative contraindication to eligibility, whereas no liver or kidney programs considered such levels of impairment to be a relative contraindication. 71% of heart programs surveyed always or usually utilized neurodevelopmental status in determinations of eligibility for transplantation, while only 30% and 33% of kidney and liver programs utilized such factors. Evidence suggests that insofar as progress in addressing discriminatory practice has been made, it has been weakest in the context of heart transplantation. The International Society for Heart and Lung Transplantation's heart transplantation criteria specifically states, "Mental retardation or dementia may be regarded as a relative contraindication to transplantation."

Autistic Self Advocacy Network, Organ Transplantation and People with I/DD: A Review of Research, Policy and Next Steps 3 (2013).

Some medical ethicists argue that it is entirely appropriate to discriminate against people with intellectual and developmental disabilities in the allocation of scarce organs for transplantation. They make two essential points. The first relates to the quality of life. Julian Savulescu argues that "quality and length of life and probability of benefit (and cost of treatment) *are* relevant in determining who should receive treatment" and that therefore "[s]evere disability in some circumstances should disqualify a person from access to scarce resources." Julian Savulescu, *Resources, Down's Syndrome, and Cardiac Surgery: Do We Really Want "Equality of Access"?*, 322 Brit. Med. J. 875 (2001). "Whether disability such as Down's syndrome should be considered relevant in allocating a scarce resource," he contends, "turns on how much the disability associated with it detracts from a good life." *Id.* Savulescu argues that "Down's syndrome is associated with intellectual disability, infertility, reduced opportunities for independent living and employment, shorter life, and early onset Alzheimer's disease"—all consequences that "make those lives worse"—but that "considerable variation exists in the quality of life of people with disability, particularly those with Down's syndrome," so it is "essential to judge every case for heart transplantation on its merits, assessing all the factors." *Id.* The second point relates to the ability of individuals with disability to comply with post-surgical instructions necessary to make transplant surgery successful. As bioethicist Arthur Caplan explained in an article about the Corby case, "Some centers worry a person with autism can't follow directions." Murray, *supra.*

What do you make of those points? Arguments that suggest that people with disabilities experience a lesser quality of life often reflect bias against and a failure to appreciate the internal perspectives of people with disabilities. See Samuel R. Bagenstos, *The Americans with Disabilities Act as Risk Regulation*, 101 Colum. L. Rev. 1479, 1507-1508 (2001); Samuel R. Bagenstos & Margo Schlanger, *Hedonic Damages, Hedonic Adaptation, and Disability*, 60 Vand. L. Rev. 745, 760–773 (2007); Elizabeth F. Emens, *Framing Disability*, 2012 U. Ill. L. Rev. 1383, 1389–1407. In part for this reason, a number of bioethics scholars have argued that any quality-of-life calculus employed to allocate health care resources should ignore the quality-of-life effects of disabilities other than those being treated. See Einer Elhauge, *Allocating Health Care Morally*, 82 Cal. L. Rev. 1449, 1515 (1994) (arguing that, if "we must choose between unblocking the esophagus of a person with a healthy leg and another person with a limp, and that, if unblocked, both would have the same expected lifespan," there is no quality-of-life basis for choosing the person without a limp, even if a limp does reduce an individual's quality of life); Arti Kaur Rai, *Rationing Through Choice: A New Approach to Cost-Effectiveness Analysis in Health Care*, 72 Ind. L.J. 1015, 1080 (1997) (similarly arguing that people who walk unassisted should not be preferred for liver transplants over people who walk with canes). Does that suggest that *University Hospital* and *Johnson* got it wrong? Or do the clinical and normative complexities of medical decisionmaking—which necessarily take account of health status and often take place in the context of scarce resources—suggest the wisdom of *University Hospital*'s refusal to apply ordinary disability discrimination rules "in the comparatively fluid context of medical treatment decisions"?

2. The Role of Parental Consent. Justice Stevens's plurality opinion in *Bowen* rests on more narrow grounds than the *University Hospital* and *Johnson* decisions. Justice Stevens contends that Section 504 can be violated in this context only when a hospital overrides parental consent and refuses to treat a newborn because of the child's disability. Because hospitals typically cannot provide treatment without consent, Justice Stevens contends that there can be no violation of Section 504 when a parent refuses to provide consent; the hospital is neutrally applying a generally enforced consent requirement. Because the Secretary had not identified any cases where a hospital refused to treat a disabled newborn in the face of parental consent, Justice Stevens concluded that the regulation was not an appropriate means of enforcing the statute.

Is Justice Stevens's argument persuasive? Consider, in light of the evidence presented in Justice White's dissent, the following passage from an *amicus* brief filed with the Court in *Bowen*:

The tendency of some biased physicians to suggest their own sociological judgments to parents is well documented. The President's Commission [for the Study of Ethical Problems in Medicine and Biomedical and Behavioral Research] reported that some physicians actually make decisions to withhold treatment and others manipulate the situation to ensure that parents will accept their "recommendation." It reported further, that "parents may be excluded from the decisions entirely or presented with a narrower range of choices than is appropriate" and concluded that, as a result of these actions by physicians, "the child loses the protection of its surrogates." If the responsible physician believes that death (*i.e.*, withholding of beneficial treatment) is preferable to life, the physician can and often does present the options to parents in a manner which results in the direct imposition of the physician's judgment [citing the Duff & Campbell article discussed by the *Bowen* opinions]. Physicians responding to survey questions regarding "acquiescence in parents' decisions" commented that physicians are always either directly involved in forming the decision with the parents or are in a position of directly influencing the decisions parents make through the presentation of the treatment/no-treatment question. During a five year experiment 24 infants with spina bifida were denied life-saving treatment by a team of medical professionals, who, after applying a "quality-of-life" scheme, informed the parents that "we do not consider them obligated to have the baby treated" [citing the facts of *Johnson*, which was then being litigated].

In 1981 another prominent neonatologist reported that it might take physicians seeking to instill a "death wish" in parents of handicapped infants as long as three days to succeed in breaking down their resistance. The frequency with which these judgments are likely to be recommended to parents is revealed by a 1977 survey of Massachusetts pediatricians which disclosed that 51% believed that a child with Down's syndrome and duodenal atresia (blockage) should not receive surgery and 67% of the pediatricians would recommend no surgery for a child with severe myelomeningocele (spina bifida). A 1980 summary of four major surveys of physician attitudes reported that social variables are the critical perceived determinants of the preference to withhold treatment.

Studies have revealed that information provided to parents by physicians may be constrained by the physician's judgments or views concerning the social class and race ethnicity of the infant's family, the perceived emotional stability of the parents, and the physician's lack of accurate information regarding the availability of support services to assist handicapped infants and their parents. The lack of knowledge of pediatricians about handicapping conditions has been both reported to the American Academy of Pediatrics and identified by it as one of the "under-emphasized areas in pediatric residencies" and as a subject "in which education content is inadequate." Indeed, studies have even reported that the medical prognosis provided by physicians to parents consistently underestimates the infant's actual chances of survival.

Compounding the lack of information available to parents is the vulnerability of the parents' mental and emotional state. After the birth of a sick and handicapped infant, families are often in "a severe psychological crisis" in which they are foreclosed, as a result of psychological and emotional trauma that generally surrounds the birth of a handicapped infant, from either assimilating properly the information which is provided about the infant's condition or exercising clear and rational judgment concerning a no-treatment decision presented by a physician. In addition, time pressures, often artificial and unnecessary, imposed on parents to consent or acquiesce in the physician's recommendation affect both the capacity of the parents for rational judgment and the quality of the information upon which to base a judgment. This, of course, is the same period of time during which the mother is recuperating from the physical demands of childbirth and may be receiving medication or other medical treatment. The President's Commission has cautioned against "undue haste in decision-making" and observed that "[t]he longer some of the babies survive, the more reliable the prognosis for the infant becomes and the clearer parents and professionals can be on whether further treatment is warranted or futile." Both research and experience have shown that, after a period of time, parents' attitudes towards the infant they might once have hoped would die may well change, as a relationship of love and affection is allowed to develop. In fact, one medical commentator, concerned that time and the opportunity for bonding it creates may well cause parents to make a "selfish" decision to save the infant's life, actually recommends that parents not be encouraged to nurture their newborn infant.

Brief for the Association for Retarded Citizens of the United States, *et al.*, as *Amici Curiae, Heckler v. American Hospital Assn.*, 472 U.S. 1016 (1985).

As Professor Martha Field explains, concerns that a child with a disability will have poor quality of life often "are based upon prejudice against the handicapped" that results from "[t]he isolation of most of the population from the community of persons with disabilities." Martha A. Field, *Killing "the Handicapped"—Before and After Birth*, 16 Harv. Women's L.J. 79, 87–88 (1993). She argues that "There is a societal cult of 'normalcy' that leads to the devaluation of persons with retardation and other handicaps or unusual conditions, especially by people who have little experience with the populations they devalue. Such persons may truly believe that a child with a serious disability will be 'better off dead,' because it seems to them so terrible to have a handicap." *Id.*

Do these arguments suggest that Justice Stevens was wrong? Or is letting parents, notwithstanding the pressures on them, decide whether their children will receive treatment the least-bad option?

When thinking about these questions, consider the case of the "Ashley Treatment," so named for the case of

> a six-year-old child with developmental and physical disabilities, Ashley, [who] was given growth attenuation treatment via estrogen and had her uterus and breast buds removed. The intent of the treatment was to keep her permanently small. The child's parents and doctors claimed that this set of procedures was in her best interest for numerous reasons, including that it would make it easier to care for her at home.

Nat'l Disability Rights Network, Devaluing People with Disabilities: Medical Procedures that Violate Civil Rights 9 (2012). Since Ashley's case became public in 2007, "her parents report that they have been contacted by thousands of families interested in the treatment and they believe that at least a hundred children have undergone the same treatment." *Id.* at 10. Defenders of the Ashley Treatment argue "that this is the most personal of family decisions and there is no need for external judicial review of the decisions made by the family. *Id.* at 9. Opponents argue "that all individuals, regardless of their disability status, have individual rights that cannot be ignored" and that "[d]ecisions like those made in this case are the most personal of 'personal rights,' not 'family rights.' " *Id.* Which side of this dispute do you find more persuasive? How does the Ashley Treatment affect your view of the Baby Doe cases?

3. The Politics of the Baby Doe Cases. The Reagan Administration was not generally known for its aggressive readings of civil rights laws, yet its position in the Baby Doe cases was undeniably aggressive. One explanation surely is that the nontreatment of infants with disabilities aroused the intense concern not just of disability rights groups but also of anti-abortion activists. And the alignment of the justices in *Bowen* certainly suggests that the Court saw the case through the lens of abortion politics rather than antidiscrimination law. The justices in the plurality—Justices Stevens, Marshall, Blackmun, and Powell—all were strong supporters of the right to choose abortion recognized in *Roe v. Wade*, 410 U.S. 113 (1973), and all but Justice Powell tended to read civil rights statutes broadly. Justice White dissented in *Roe*, and Justice O'Connor had at the time expressed doubts about *Roe*, but both tended to read civil rights statutes relatively narrowly. Only Justice Brennan, a strong supporter of both *Roe v. Wade* and broad construction of civil rights laws, appears to have seen the case as an antidiscrimination, rather than an abortion-related, case.

The tactical alliance between (typically politically liberal) disability rights activists and (typically politically conservative) anti-abortion activists continued in a series of cases involving assertions of a constitutional right to terminate one's own life:

> As in the "Baby Doe" cases, opponents of abortion object to assisted suicide because it is inconsistent with their understanding of the sanctity of human life. But disability rights activists have again articulated a critique that is distinct from the arguments of the right-to-life movement. In an argument that parallels their position on the "Baby Doe" cases, disability rights activists like those affiliated with Not Dead Yet contend that the practice of assisted suicide reflects a discriminatory belief that life with a disability is not worth living. They further argue that if the law recognizes a "right to die"—no matter how stringently regulated—people with disabilities will be pressured into exercising it.
>
> Disability rights activists argue that if a person without a disability chooses to commit suicide, society treats that choice as the product of an irrational decisionmaking process that should not be given effect. But "when a person 'chooses' death over an 'undignified' life with a disability, the system sympathizes with that individual's plight and supports his right to die, assuming his disability is the root of his supreme despair." That difference, disability rights advocates argue, reflects biases about the "quality of life" experienced by individuals with disabilities. Both medical professionals and nondisabled members of the lay public believe that disability has a more negative effect on life quality than people with disabilities themselves report. People without disabilities thus "readily conclude that the disabled person's wish to die is reasonable because it agrees with their own preconception that the primary problem for such individuals is the unbearable experience of a permanent disability." Their biases can be seen in the "intensely stigmatized language" in which the right-to-die debate proceeds, where "disabled people are defective, damaged, debilitated, deformed, distressed, afflicted, anomalous, helpless and/or infirm," while "nonhandicapped persons are 'normal.'"

Samuel R. Bagenstos, *Disability, Life, Death, and Choice*, 29 HARV. J. L. & GENDER 427, 434–435 (2006). The position of those disability rights activists is quite contested within the movement, though:

> [Another] group—which probably constitutes a minority of disability rights activists but a majority of people with disabilities—supports the right to assisted suicide. The most prominent exponents of this position are the individuals affiliated with Autonomy, Inc., which is an organization of people with disabilities who oppose the position of Not Dead Yet. The late

Andrew Batavia, who had quadriplegia and played a key role in the passage of the ADA, was the central figure in the organization's founding. Batavia explained his views in an *amicus* brief he filed in the 1996 Term Supreme Court assisted suicide cases on behalf of a number of prominent individuals with disabilities—including the distinguished historian Hugh Gregory Gallagher and Michael Stein, who today is one of the leading disability-law scholars in the world. The Autonomy brief argued in explicitly disability rights terms for a right to assisted suicide. The brief noted poll results indicating that a majority of people with disabilities support such a right, and it contended that those results are consistent with the core disability rights principles of independence and antipaternalism: "Where for generations, almost every aspect of their existence was defined by a paternalistic society that labeled them inferior and relegated them to institutions, [people with disabilities] are unwilling to relinquish their autonomy."

The brief had harsh words for disability rights activists, like those associated with Not Dead Yet, who oppose a right to assisted suicide: "In essence," the brief contended, those advocates "appear to be saying that the individual with a disability should have control over every decision in his or her life, except for the decision of whether to live in the face of a terminal illness. This blatant contradiction is glaring and unacceptable to a substantial majority of people with disabilities."

Samuel R. Bagenstos, Law and the Contradictions of the Disability Rights Movement 112 (2009). The intersections between disability rights and abortion advocacy—and the tensions within the disability rights movement—were much on display in 2005 in the Theresa Schiavo case. For a discussion of that case from a number of different perspectives, see Symposium, *The Schiavo Case: A Symposium*, 22 CONST. COMMENT. 383 (2005).

D. REMEDIES

Barnes v. Gorman

Supreme Court of the United States, 2002.
536 U.S. 181.

■ JUSTICE SCALIA delivered the opinion of the Court.

We must decide whether punitive damages may be awarded in a private cause of action brought under § 202 of the Americans with Disabilities Act of 1990 (ADA), 104 Stat. 337, 42 U.S.C. § 12132, and § 504 of the Rehabilitation Act of 1973, 87 Stat. 394, 29 U.S.C. § 794(a).

I

Respondent Jeffrey Gorman, a paraplegic, is confined to a wheelchair and lacks voluntary control over his lower torso, including his bladder, forcing him to wear a catheter attached to a urine bag around his waist. In May 1992, he was arrested for trespass after fighting with a bouncer at a Kansas City, Missouri, nightclub. While waiting for a police van to transport him to the station, he was denied permission to use a restroom to empty his urine bag. When the van arrived, it was not equipped to receive respondent's wheelchair. Over respondent's objection, the officers removed him from his wheelchair and used a seatbelt and his own belt to strap him to a narrow bench in the rear of the van. During the ride to the police station, respondent released his seatbelt, fearing it placed excessive pressure on his urine bag. Eventually, the other belt came loose and respondent fell to the floor, rupturing his urine bag and injuring his shoulder and back. The driver, the only officer in the van, finding it impossible to lift respondent, fastened him to a support for the remainder of the trip. Upon arriving at the station, respondent was booked, processed, and released; later he was convicted of misdemeanor trespass. After these events, respondent suffered serious medical problems—including a bladder infection, serious lower back pain, and uncontrollable spasms in his paralyzed areas—that left him unable to work full time.

Respondent brought suit against petitioners—members of the Kansas City Board of Police Commissioners, the chief of police, and the officer who drove the van—in the United States District Court for the Western District of Missouri. The suit claimed petitioners had discriminated against respondent on the basis of his disability, in violation of § 202 of the ADA and § 504 of the Rehabilitation Act, by failing to maintain appropriate policies for the arrest and transportation of persons with spinal cord injuries.

A jury found petitioners liable and awarded over $1 million in compensatory damages and $1.2 million in punitive damages. The District Court vacated the punitive damages award, holding that punitive damages are unavailable in suits under § 202 of the ADA and § 504 of the Rehabilitation Act. The Court of Appeals for the Eighth Circuit reversed, relying on this Court's decision in *Franklin v. Gwinnett County Public Schools*, 503 U.S. 60, 70–71 (1992), which stated the "general rule" that "absent clear direction to the contrary by Congress, the federal courts have the power to award any appropriate relief in a cognizable cause of action brought pursuant to a federal statute." Punitive damages are appropriate relief, the Eighth Circuit held, because they are "an integral part of the common law tradition and the judicial arsenal," and Congress did nothing to disturb this tradition in enacting or amending the relevant statutes. We granted *certiorari*.

II

Section 202 of the ADA prohibits discrimination against the disabled by public entities; § 504 of the Rehabilitation Act prohibits discrimination against the disabled by recipients of federal funding, including private organizations, 29 U.S.C. § 794(b)(3). Both provisions are enforceable through private causes of action. Section 203 of the ADA declares that the "remedies, procedures, and rights set forth in [§ 505(a)(2) of the Rehabilitation Act] shall be the remedies, procedures, and rights this subchapter provides" for violations of § 202. 42 U.S.C. § 12133. Section 505(a)(2) of the Rehabilitation Act, in turn, declares that the "remedies, procedures, and rights set forth in title VI of the Civil Rights Act of 1964 . . . shall be available" for violations of § 504, as added, 92 Stat. 2983, 29 U.S.C. § 794a(a)(2). Thus, the remedies for violations of § 202 of the ADA and § 504 of the Rehabilitation Act are coextensive with the remedies available in a private cause of action brought under Title VI of the Civil Rights Act of 1964, 42 U.S.C. § 2000d *et seq.*, which prohibits racial discrimination in federally funded programs and activities.

Although Title VI does not mention a private right of action, our prior decisions have found an implied right of action, *e.g., Cannon v. University of Chicago*, 441 U.S. 677, 703 (1979), and Congress has acknowledged this right in amendments to the statute, leaving it "beyond dispute that private individuals may sue to enforce" Title VI, *Alexander v. Sandoval*, 532 U.S. 275, 280 (2001). It is less clear what remedies are available in such a suit. In *Franklin*, we recognized "the traditional presumption in favor of any appropriate relief for violation of a federal right," and held that since this presumption applies to suits under Title IX of the Education Amendments of 1972, 20 U.S.C. §§ 1681–1688, monetary damages were available. And the Court has interpreted Title IX consistently with Title VI. *Franklin*, however, did not describe the scope of "appropriate relief." We take up this question today.

Title VI invokes Congress's power under the Spending Clause, U.S. Const., Art. I, § 8, cl. 1, to place conditions on the grant of federal funds. We have repeatedly characterized this statute and other Spending Clause legislation as "much in the nature of a contract: in return for federal funds, the [recipients] agree to comply with federally imposed conditions." Just as a valid contract requires offer and acceptance of its terms, "[t]he legitimacy of Congress' power to legislate under the spending power . . . rests on whether the [recipient] voluntarily and knowingly accepts the terms of the 'contract.' . . . Accordingly, if Congress intends to impose a condition on the grant of federal moneys, it must do so unambiguously." Although we have been careful not to imply that all contract-law rules apply to Spending Clause legislation, we have regularly applied the contract-law analogy in cases defining the scope of conduct for which funding recipients may be held liable for money damages. Thus, a recipient may be held liable to third-party beneficiaries for intentional conduct that violates the clear terms of the relevant statute, but not for its failure to comply with vague language describing the objectives of the statute; and, if the statute implies that only violations brought to the attention of an official with power to correct them are actionable, not for conduct unknown to any such official. We have also applied the contract-law analogy in finding a damages remedy available in private suits under Spending Clause legislation.

The same analogy applies, we think, in determining the scope of damages remedies. We said as much in *Gebser [v. Lago Vista School Dist.]*: "Title IX's contractual nature has implications for our construction of the scope of available remedies." One of these implications, we believe, is that a remedy is "appropriate relief," Franklin, only if the funding recipient is on notice that, by accepting federal funding, it exposes itself to liability of that nature. A funding recipient is generally on notice that it is subject not only to those remedies explicitly provided in the relevant legislation, but also to those remedies traditionally available in suits for breach of contract. Thus we have held that under Title IX, which contains no express remedies, a recipient of federal funds is nevertheless subject to suit for compensatory damages and injunction, forms of relief traditionally available in suits for breach of contract. See, e.g., Restatement (Second) of Contracts § 357 (1981); 3 S. Williston, Law of Contracts §§ 1445–1450 (1920); J. Pomeroy, A Treatise on the Specific Performance of Contracts 1–5 (1879). Like Title IX, Title VI mentions no remedies—indeed, it fails to mention even a private right of action (hence this Court's decision finding an implied right of action in *Cannon*). But punitive damages, unlike compensatory damages and injunction, are generally not available for breach of contract, see 3 E. Farnsworth, Contracts § 12.8, pp. 192–201 (2d ed.1998); Restatement (Second) of Contracts § 355; 1 T. Sedgwick, Measure of Damages § 370 (8th ed. 1891).

Nor (if such an interpretive technique were available) could an implied punitive damages provision reasonably be found in Title VI. Some authorities say that reasonably implied contractual terms are those that the parties would have agreed to if they had adverted to the matters in question. See 2 Farnsworth, *supra*, § 7.16, at 335, and authorities cited. More recent commentary suggests that reasonably implied contractual terms are simply those that "compor[t] with community standards of fairness," Restatement (Second) of Contracts, supra, § 204, Comment d; see also 2 Farnsworth, *supra*, § 7.16, at 334–336. Neither approach would support the implication here of a remedy that is not normally available for contract actions and that is of indeterminate magnitude. We have acknowledged that compensatory damages alone "might well exceed a recipient's level of federal funding," *Gebser*; punitive damages on top of that could well be disastrous. Not only is it doubtful that funding recipients would have agreed to exposure to such unorthodox and indeterminate liability; it is doubtful whether they would even have accepted the funding if punitive damages liability was a required condition. "Without doubt, the scope of potential damages liability is one of the most significant factors a school would consider in deciding whether to receive federal funds." And for the same reason of unusual and disproportionate exposure, it can hardly be said that community standards of fairness support such an implication. In sum, it must be concluded that Title VI funding recipients have not, merely by accepting funds, implicitly consented to liability for punitive damages.

Our conclusion is consistent with the "well settled" rule that "where legal rights have been invaded, and a federal statute provides for a general right to sue for such invasion, federal courts may use any available remedy to make good the wrong done." [*Bell v. Hood*]. When a federal-funds recipient violates conditions of Spending Clause legislation, the wrong done is the failure to provide what the contractual obligation requires; and that wrong is "made good" when the recipient compensates the Federal Government or a third-party beneficiary (as in this case) for the loss caused by that failure. Punitive damages are not compensatory, and are therefore not embraced within the rule described in *Bell*.

Because punitive damages may not be awarded in private suits brought under Title VI of the 1964 Civil Rights Act, it follows that they may not be awarded in suits brought under § 202 of the ADA and § 504 of the Rehabilitation Act. [T]he judgment of the Court of Appeals is reversed.

It is so ordered.

■ JUSTICE SOUTER, with whom JUSTICE O'CONNOR joins, concurring.

I join the Court's opinion because I agree that analogy to the common law of contract is appropriate in this instance, with the conclusion that punitive damages are not available under the statute. Punitive damages, as the Court points out, may range in orders of "indeterminate magnitude," untethered to compensable harm, and would thus pose a concern that recipients of federal funding could not reasonably have anticipated. I realize, however, and read the Court's opinion as acknowledging, that the contract-law analogy may fail to give such helpfully clear answers to other questions that may be raised by actions for private recovery under Spending Clause legislation, such as the proper measure of compensatory damages.

■ JUSTICE STEVENS, with whom JUSTICE GINSBURG and JUSTICE BREYER join, concurring in the judgment.

[Justice Stevens argued that the judgment should be reversed based on the longstanding principle that municipalities are not subject to punitive damages liability, without reaching any Spending Clause issue.] Accordingly, I do not join the Court's opinion, although I do concur in its judgment in this case.

NOTES ON REMEDIES

1. **Under the ADA and Rehabilitation Act.** As *Barnes* explains, Title II of the ADA incorporates by reference the remedies that are available for violations of Section 504 of the Rehabilitation Act. Section 504, in turn, incorporates by reference the remedies that are available under Title VI of the Civil Rights Act of 1964, 42 U.S.C. § 2000d *et seq.* (Title IX of the Education Amendments of 1972, 20 U.S.C. §§ 1681–1688, like Section 504, was patterned on Title VI and has been interpreted as having the same remedies.) Although Title VI contains no express private right of action, the Supreme Court held, in *Cannon v. University of Chicago*, 441 U.S. 677, 703 (1979) (a Title IX case), that such a right was implicit in the statute, a holding Congress later confirmed in statutory amendments. The Court held in *Franklin v. Gwinnett County Public Schools*, 503 U.S. 60 (1992) (also a Title IX case), that a private plaintiff who establishes a violation of one of these statutes can recover compensatory damages in addition to injunctive relief. *Barnes* holds that punitive damages are not available, however.

As *Barnes* makes clear, Congress's decision to frame Section 504 (like Title VI and Title IX) as Spending Clause legislation has several important remedial consequences. See generally Samuel R. Bagenstos, *Spending Clause Litigation in the Roberts Court*, 58 Duke L.J. 345 (2008). The Supreme Court has held that funding recipients may not be liable under Spending Clause legislation unless they had clear notice of the requirements imposed by the statute at issue. See *Pennhurst State Sch. & Hosp. v. Halderman*, 451 U.S. 1, 17 (1981). And the Court has extended this notice requirement to hold (under Title IX) that, in cases "that do not involve official policy of the recipient entity," a government entity that receives federal funds will not be liable for *damages* "unless an official who at a minimum has authority to address the alleged discrimination and to institute corrective measures on the recipient's behalf has actual knowledge of discrimination in the recipient's programs and fails adequately to respond." *Gebser v. Lago Vista Indep. Sch. Dist.*, 524 U.S. 274, 290 (1998); see also, *e.g.*, *Duvall v. County of Kitsap*, 260 F.3d 1124, 1138–1139 (9th Cir.2001) (collecting cases applying this principle to Title II cases). (This principle does not limit the availability of injunctive relief.)

Because Title II of the ADA (aside from its transportation provisions) and Section 504 of the Rehabilitation Act contain only very general prohibitions of discrimination that have been fleshed out by quite detailed regulations, the Supreme Court's decision in *Alexander v. Sandoval*, 532 U.S. 275 (2001), raised important questions about the scope of the private right of action under those statutes. The *Sandoval* Court held that private parties could not enforce the Title VI regulations prohibiting disparate-impact discrimination, because Title VI itself prohibited nothing more than intentional discrimination, and the statute did not "display an intent to create a freestanding private right of action to enforce [its] regulations." *Id.* at 293. Neither Section 504 nor Title II appear to create a freestanding private right of action to enforce their regulations, either. But the *Sandoval* Court made clear that regulations that "apply[ ]" the statutory prohibition on discrimination are privately enforceable, because they "authoritatively construe the statute itself": "A Congress that intends the statute to be enforced through a private cause of action intends the authoritative interpretation of the statute to be so enforced as well." *Id.* at 284.

The courts of appeals have accordingly held that substantive regulations fleshing out the reasonable accommodation requirement of Section 504 and Title II *are* privately enforceable under *Sandoval*. See, *e.g.*, *Mark H. v. Lemahieu*, 513 F.3d 922, 939 (9th Cir.2008) (to the extent that Section 504 regulations flesh out *Alexander v. Choate*'s "meaningful access" standard, they are privately enforceable); *Dillery v. City of Sandusky*, 398 F.3d 562, 567 (6th Cir.2005) (Title II physical accessibility regulations are privately enforceable); *Ability Center of Greater Toledo v. City of Sandusky*, 385 F.3d 901, 907–913 (6th Cir.2004) (same); *Chaffin v. Kansas State Fair Bd.*, 348 F.3d 850, 858–861 (10th Cir.2003) (same). But they have generally held that regulations that are more procedural in nature—such as those requiring self-assessment and a transition plan by regulated entities—are not privately enforceable. See, *e.g.*, *Lonberg v. City of Riverside*, 571 F.3d 846 (9th Cir.2009) (regulation requiring the creation of a transition plan for barrier removal are not privately enforceable); *Iverson v. City of Boston*, 452 F.3d 94, 101 (1st Cir.2006) (same); *Ability Center*, 385 F.3d at 913–915 (same). But see *Chaffin*, 348 F.3d at 857–858 (transition plan regulation is privately enforceable). These holdings address only the power of private parties to bring suits—they say nothing about the unquestioned power of the federal government to sue. See 42 U.S.C. § 2000d–1(federal government may enforce Title VI by withholding federal funds or "by any other means authorized by law").

2.   Under the Fair Housing Act. The Fair Housing Act contains specific provisions governing enforcement. An individual who is aggrieved by a discriminatory housing practice may file a complaint with the Secretary of Housing and Urban Development, 42 U.S.C. § 3610. If the Secretary finds reasonable cause after an investigation, the complainant may choose to pursue judicial relief (in which case the Department of Justice will bring a lawsuit) or administrative relief (through an administrative law judge), *id.* § 3612. Private parties also can choose to bypass the administrative process and file their own lawsuits for injunctive relief and compensatory or punitive damages, *id.* § 3613, and the Department of Justice can file its own lawsuits for the same relief plus civil penalties, *id.* § 3614.

3. Sovereign Immunity Issues. The Supreme Court has interpreted the Eleventh Amendment as reflecting a constitutional principle of sovereign immunity that generally prohibits private parties from suing states in their own name, or from seeking money damages that will be paid from the state treasury. See *Edelman v. Jordan*, 415 U.S. 651 (1974). However, this immunity does not limit suits by the federal government. See *Alden v. Maine*, 527 U.S. 706, 755–756 (1999). Nor does it limit suits against *municipalities*, as opposed to *states* themselves (though the rules on when a municipality counts as an "arm of the state" are complicated). *Lincoln County v. Luning*, 133 U.S. 529 (1890). And private parties can obtain a forward-looking injunction that binds the state by suing the relevant state official in her official capacity. See *Ex parte Young*, 209 U.S. 123 (1908). Moreover, states can waive their sovereign immunity— Congress can, indeed, demand such a waiver in exchange for the grant of federal funds, *College Savings Bank v. Florida Prepaid Postsecondary Educ. Expense Bd.*, 527 U.S. 666, 686–687 (1999)—and when properly exercising its power to enforce the Reconstruction Amendments, Congress may abrogate state sovereign immunity, see *Fitzpatrick v. Bitzer*, 427 U.S. 445 (1976).

These rules have important implications for litigation by private parties against states under the disability rights statutes. Private plaintiffs can presumably obtain an injunction under *Ex parte Young* to enforce all of these statutes. And private plaintiffs can fairly clearly recover damages against states for violation of Section 504 of the Rehabilitation Act. Congress specifically provided that a "State shall not be immune under the Eleventh Amendment of the Constitution of the United States from suit in Federal court for a violation of section 504 of the Rehabilitation Act of 1973." 42 U.S.C. § 2000d–7(a)(1). Because Section 504 was enacted under Congress's spending power, the courts of appeals have held that this provision attaches a condition on the receipt of federal funds: If a state accepts federal funds, it has *waived* its sovereign immunity against suits to enforce the statute. See Bagenstos, *Spending Clause Litigation*, *supra*, at 349 & n.21 (collecting cases). The Supreme Court's recent decision to give some teeth to the Spending Clause coercion doctrine in *National Federation of Independent Business v. Sebelius*, 132 S.Ct. 2566 (2012) (*NFIB*), might call those holdings into some question, though it is too soon to tell. See Samuel R. Bagenstos, *The Anti-leveraging Principle and the Spending Clause After* NFIB, 101 Geo. L.J. 861, 912-916 (2013) (arguing that, under the best reading of *NFIB*, Section 504's waiver of sovereign immunity remains constitutional).

Title II of the ADA, by contrast, is not Spending Clause legislation. The ADA attempts to *abrogate* state sovereign immunity against suits for its violation, see 42 U.S.C. § 12202 ("A State shall not be immune under the eleventh amendment to the Constitution of the United States from an action in [a] Federal or State court of competent jurisdiction for a violation of this chapter."). But that abrogation is valid—and private plaintiffs can obtain money damages against states—only to the extent that Title II is valid legislation to enforce the Fourteenth Amendment. As the cases and materials in Section D.2 below demonstrate, determining the circumstances in which Title II is valid Fourteenth Amendment legislation is not a simple task.

Finally, the Fair Housing Act contains no language purporting to abrogate, or demand a waiver of, state sovereign immunity. Accordingly, private parties cannot obtain damages against states for violation of that statute—though they can, of course obtain injunctions against states and damages against most municipalities.

E. CONSTITUTIONAL QUESTIONS

1. CONSTITUTIONALITY OF DISABILITY-SPECIFIC GOVERNMENT DECISIONS

a. GENERAL PRINCIPLES

Buck v. Bell

Supreme Court of the United States, 1927.
274 U.S. 200.

■ MR. JUSTICE HOLMES delivered the opinion of the Court.

This is a writ of error to review a judgment of the Supreme Court of Appeals of the State of Virginia, affirming a judgment of the Circuit Court of Amherst County, by which the defendant in error, the superintendent of the State Colony for Epileptics and Feeble Minded, was ordered to perform the operation of salpingectomy upon Carrie Buck, the plaintiff in error, for the purpose of making her sterile. The case comes here upon the contention that the statute authorizing the judgment is void under the Fourteenth Amendment as denying to the plaintiff in error due process of law and the equal protection of the laws.

Carrie Buck is a feeble-minded white woman who was committed to the State Colony above mentioned in due form. She is the daughter of a feeble-minded mother in the same institution, and the mother of an illegitimate feeble-minded child. She was eighteen years old at the time of the trial of her case in the Circuit Court in the latter part of 1924. An Act of Virginia approved March 20, 1924 (Laws 1924, c.394) recites that the health of the patient and the welfare of society may be promoted in certain cases by the sterilization of mental defectives, under careful safeguard, etc.; that the sterilization may be effected in males by vasectomy and in females by salpingectomy, without serious pain or substantial danger to life; that the Commonwealth is supporting in various institutions many defective persons who if now discharged would become a menace but if incapable of procreating might be discharged with safety and become self-supporting with benefit to themselves and to society; and that experience has shown that heredity plays an important part in the transmission of insanity, imbecility, etc. The statute then enacts that whenever the superintendent of certain institutions including the abovenamed State Colony shall be of opinion that it is for the best interest of the patients and of society that an inmate under his care should be sexually sterilized, he may have the operation performed upon any patient afflicted with hereditary forms of insanity, imbecility, etc., on complying with the very careful provisions by which the act protects the patients from possible abuse.

The superintendent first presents a petition to the special board of directors of his hospital or colony, stating the facts and the grounds for his opinion, verified by affidavit. Notice of the petition and of the time and place of the hearing in the institution is to be served upon the inmate, and also upon his guardian, and if there is no guardian the superintendent is to apply to the Circuit Court of the County to appoint one. If the inmate is a minor notice also is to be given to his parents, if any, with a copy of the petition. The board is to see to it that the inmate may attend the hearings if desired by him or his guardian. The evidence is all to be reduced to writing, and after the board has made its order for or against the operation, the superintendent, or the inmate, or his guardian, may appeal to the Circuit Court of the County. The Circuit Court may consider the record of the board and the evidence before it and such other admissible evidence as may be offered, and may affirm, revise, or reverse the order of the board and enter such order as it deems just. Finally any party may apply to the Supreme Court of Appeals, which, if it grants the appeal, is to hear the case upon the record of the trial in the Circuit Court and may enter such order as it thinks the Circuit Court should have entered. There can be no doubt that so far as procedure is concerned the rights of the patient are most carefully considered, and as every step in this case was taken in scrupulous compliance with the statute and after months of observation, there is no doubt that in that respect the plaintiff in error has had due process at law.

The attack is not upon the procedure but upon the substantive law. It seems to be contended that in no circumstances could such an order be justified. It certainly is contended that the order cannot be justified upon the existing grounds. The judgment finds the facts that have been recited and that Carrie Buck "is the probable potential parent of socially inadequate offspring, likewise afflicted, that she may be sexually sterilized without detriment to her general health and that her welfare and that of society will be promoted by her sterilization," and thereupon makes the order. In view of the general declarations of the Legislature and the specific findings of the Court obviously we cannot say as matter of law that the grounds do not exist, and if they exist they justify the result. We have seen more than once that the public welfare may call upon the best citizens for their lives. It would be strange if it could not call upon those who already sap the strength of the State for these lesser sacrifices, often not felt to be such by those concerned, in order to prevent our being swamped with incompetence. It is better for all the world, if instead of waiting to execute degenerate offspring for crime, or to let them starve for their imbecility, society can prevent those who are manifestly unfit from continuing their kind. The principle that sustains compulsory vaccination is broad enough to cover cutting the Fallopian tubes. *Jacobson v. Massachusetts*, 197 U.S. 11. Three generations of imbeciles are enough.

But, it is said, however it might be if this reasoning were applied generally, it fails when it is confined to the small number who are in the institutions named and is not applied to the multitudes outside. It is the usual last resort of constitutional arguments to point out shortcomings of this sort. But the answer is that the law does all that is needed when it does all that it can, indicates a policy, applies it to all within the lines, and seeks to bring within the lines all similarly situated so far and so fast as its means allow. Of course so far as the operations enable those who otherwise must be kept confined to be returned to the world, and thus open the asylum to others, the equality aimed at will be more nearly reached.

Judgment affirmed.

■ MR. JUSTICE BUTLER dissents.

NOTES ON BUCK V. BELL

1. **The Collusive Nature of the Litigation.** In *Three Generations, No Imbeciles: New Light on Buck v. Bell*, 60 N.Y.U. L. Rev. 30 (1985), Paul Lombardo shows that the *Buck* case was a carefully orchestrated test case for the new Virginia sterilization law, in which the attorneys for both sides were close friends and strong supporters of the law. Carrie Buck's attorney "called no witnesses to dispute the specific allegations against Carrie or to cast doubt on the 'scientific' theories about which [the state's] four 'experts' had testified," and his "cross-examination of the witnesses for the State was so weak that it was often unclear which side he was representing." On the crucial question whether Buck was "feebleminded," Lombardo shows that most of the witnesses had never met Carrie Buck, and that "the year before she left school, her teacher entered the comment 'very good-deportment and lessons' and recommended her for promotion." The evidence that Buck's "feeblemindedness" was hereditary was perhaps even weaker: "To show this hereditary link, [the state] elicited testimony that Carrie's mother, Emma, was a feeble-minded patient at the Colony, that Carrie had exhibited 'peculiarities' since childhood, that supposed members of Carrie's family were 'peculiar,' and that Carrie's child was slow." Lombardo argues that the original commitment petition for Carrie Buck (signed by her foster parents) "was a desperate attempt to remove the embarrassment of a pregnant but unwed girl from their home"—a girl who became pregnant after she was raped by the nephew of her foster mother.

Buck's attorney did not present evidence of any of these facts, Lombardo argues, because he and the attorney for the state "had orchestrated a judicial charade. They were careful to fulfill every procedural provision of the law, while simultaneously creating a trial record so one-sided, that little, if any, evidence appeared to support a reversal. Carrie Buck was deceived into believing that her rights would be protected. In fact, her attorney had undermined her case at every stage and was arrogant enough to appear before his long-time colleagues to boast of his confidence that Carrie Buck's challenge of the law would fail."

Buck v. Bell arose as a result of the eugenics movement—an effort to use the professions of medicine and law to discourage or prevent reproduction among those groups considered "weak" or "feebleminded." Justice Holmes's opinion in *Buck* "gave a shaky eugenics movement a strong stamp of legitimacy." Mary L. Dudziak, *Oliver Wendell Holmes as a Eugenic Reformer: Rhetoric in the Writing of Constitutional Law*, 71 Iowa L. Rev. 833 (1986). Justice Holmes, himself, was a strong supporter of eugenics. Professor Dudziak argues that Justice Holmes's *Buck* opinion is "a well-crafted rhetorical statement: it arouses the emotions, it angers nonbelievers, it fortifies believers through its intrinsic sense of rightness and purpose. To the extent the opinion is convincing, it is not because the logic is compelling, but because it strikes an emotional chord with the reader and appeals to preexisting sentiment. *Buck v. Bell* appealed directly to those who were predisposed to agree." *Id.*

2. The Vitality of the *Buck* Precedent. The Supreme Court has never formally overruled *Buck*. But in SKINNER V. OKLAHOMA, 316 U.S. 535 (1942), the Court invalidated (on equal protection grounds) a statute that provided for the compulsory sterilization of certain habitual criminal offenders. *Skinner* expressly distinguished *Buck*, but its analysis seems quite inconsistent with that of *Buck*:

> But the instant legislation runs afoul of the equal protection clause, though we give Oklahoma that large deference which the rule of the foregoing cases requires. We are dealing here with legislation which involves one of the basic civil rights of man. Marriage and procreation are fundamental to the very existence and survival of the race. The power to sterilize, if exercised, may have subtle, farreaching and devastating effects. In evil or reckless hands it can cause races or types which are inimical to the dominant group to wither and disappear. There is no redemption for the individual whom the law touches. Any experiment which the State conducts is to his irreparable injury. He is forever deprived of a basic liberty. We mention these matters not to reexamine the scope of the police power of the States. We advert to them merely in emphasis of our view that strict scrutiny of the classification which a State makes in a sterilization law is essential, lest unwittingly or otherwise invidious discriminations are made against groups or types of individuals in violation of the constitutional guaranty of just and equal laws. The guaranty of "equal protection of the laws is a pledge of the protection of equal laws." *Yick Wo v. Hopkins*, 118 U.S. 356, 369. When the law lays an unequal hand on those who have committed intrinsically the same quality of offense and sterilizes one and not the other, it has made as an invidious a discrimination as if it had selected a particular race or nationality for oppressive treatment.

City of Cleburne v. Cleburne Living Center, Inc.

Supreme Court of the United States, 1985.

473 U.S. 432.

■ JUSTICE WHITE delivered the opinion of the Court.

A Texas city denied a special use permit for the operation of a group home for the mentally retarded, acting pursuant to a municipal zoning ordinance requiring permits for such homes. The Court of Appeals for the Fifth Circuit held that mental retardation is a "quasi-suspect" classification and that the ordinance violated the Equal Protection Clause because it did not substantially further an important governmental purpose. We hold that a lesser standard of scrutiny is appropriate, but conclude that under that standard the ordinance is invalid as applied in this case.

I

In July 1980, respondent Jan Hannah purchased a building at 201 Featherston Street in the city of Cleburne, Texas, with the intention of leasing it to Cleburne Living Center, Inc. (CLC), for the operation of a group home for the mentally retarded. It was anticipated that the home would house 13 retarded men and women, who would be under the constant supervision of CLC staff members. The house had four bedrooms and two baths, with a half bath to be added. CLC planned to comply with all applicable state and federal regulations.

The city informed CLC that a special use permit would be required for the operation of a group home at the site, and CLC accordingly submitted a permit application. In response to a subsequent inquiry from CLC, the city explained that under the zoning regulations applicable to the site, a special use permit, renewable annually, was required for the construction of "[h]ospitals for the insane or feeble-minded, or alcoholic [sic] or drug addicts, or penal or correctional institutions." The city had determined that the proposed group home should be classified as a "hospital for the feebleminded." After holding a public hearing on CLC's application, the City Council voted 3 to 1 to deny a special use permit.

CLC then filed suit in Federal District Court against the city and a number of its officials, alleging, inter alia, that the zoning ordinance was invalid on its face and as applied because it discriminated against the mentally retarded in violation of the equal protection rights of CLC and its potential residents. The District Court found that "[i]f the potential residents of the Featherston Street home were not mentally retarded, but the home was the same in all other respects, its use would be permitted under the city's zoning ordinance," and that the City Council's decision "was motivated primarily by the fact that the residents of the home would be persons who are mentally retarded." Even so, the District Court held the ordinance and its application constitutional. Concluding that no fundamental right was implicated and that mental retardation was neither a suspect nor a quasi-suspect classification, the court employed the minimum level of judicial scrutiny applicable to equal protection claims. The court deemed the ordinance, as written and applied, to be rationally related to the city's legitimate interests in "the legal responsibility of CLC and its residents, . . . the safety and fears of residents in the adjoining neighborhood," and the number of people to be housed in the home.

The Court of Appeals for the Fifth Circuit reversed, determining that mental retardation was a quasi-suspect classification and that it should assess the validity of the ordinance under intermediate-level scrutiny. Because mental retardation was in fact relevant to many legislative actions, strict scrutiny was not appropriate. But in light of the history of "unfair and often grotesque mistreatment" of the retarded, discrimination against them was "likely to reflect deep-seated prejudice." In addition, the mentally retarded lacked political power, and their condition was immutable. The court considered heightened scrutiny to be particularly appropriate in this case, because the city's ordinance withheld a benefit which, although not fundamental, was very important to the mentally retarded. Without group homes, the court stated, the retarded could never hope to integrate themselves into the community. Applying the test that it considered appropriate, the court held that the ordinance was invalid on its face because it did not substantially further any important governmental interests. The Court of Appeals went on to hold that the ordinance was also invalid as applied.

II

The Equal Protection Clause of the Fourteenth Amendment commands that no State shall "deny to any person within its jurisdiction the equal protection of the laws," which is essentially a direction that all persons similarly situated should be treated alike. Section 5 of the Amendment empowers Congress to enforce this mandate, but absent controlling congressional direction, the courts have themselves devised standards for determining the validity of state legislation or other official action that is challenged as denying equal protection. The general rule is that legislation is presumed to be valid and will be sustained if the classification drawn by the statute is rationally related to a legitimate state interest. When social or economic legislation is at issue, the Equal Protection Clause allows the States wide latitude, and the Constitution presumes that even improvident decisions will eventually be rectified by the democratic processes.

The general rule gives way, however, when a statute classifies by race, alienage, or national origin. These factors are so seldom relevant to the achievement of any legitimate state interest that laws grounded in such considerations are deemed to reflect prejudice and antipathy—a view that those in the burdened class are not as worthy or deserving as others. For these reasons and because such discrimination is unlikely to be soon rectified by legislative means, these laws are subjected to strict scrutiny and will be sustained only if they are suitably tailored to serve a compelling state interest. Similar oversight by the courts is due when state laws impinge on personal rights protected by the Constitution.

Legislative classifications based on gender also call for a heightened standard of review. That factor generally provides no sensible ground for differential treatment. "[W]hat differentiates sex from such nonsuspect statuses as intelligence or physical disability . . . is that the sex characteristic frequently bears no relation to ability to perform or contribute to society." *Frontiero v. Richardson*, 411 U.S. 677, 686 (1973) (plurality opinion). Rather than resting on meaningful considerations, statutes distributing benefits and burdens between the sexes in different ways very likely reflect outmoded notions of the relative capabilities of men and women. A gender classification fails unless it is substantially related to a sufficiently important governmental interest. Because illegitimacy is beyond the individual's control and bears "no relation to the individual's ability to participate in and contribute to society," official discriminations resting on that characteristic are also subject to somewhat heightened review. Those restrictions "will survive equal protection scrutiny to the extent they are substantially related to a legitimate state interest."

We have declined, however, to extend heightened review to differential treatment based on age:

> "While the treatment of the aged in this Nation has not been wholly free of discrimination, such persons, unlike, say, those who have been discriminated against on the basis of race or national origin, have not experienced a 'history of purposeful unequal treatment' or been subjected to unique disabilities on the basis of stereotyped characteristics not truly indicative of their abilities." *Massachusetts Board of Retirement v. Murgia*, 427 U.S. 307, 313 (1976).

The lesson of *Murgia* is that where individuals in the group affected by a law have distinguishing characteristics relevant to interests the State has the authority to implement, the courts have been very reluctant, as they should be in our federal system and with our respect for the separation of powers, to closely scrutinize legislative choices as to whether, how, and to what extent those interests should be pursued. In such cases, the Equal Protection Clause requires only a rational means to serve a legitimate end.

III

Against this background, we conclude for several reasons that the Court of Appeals erred in holding mental retardation a quasi-suspect classification calling for a more exacting standard of judicial review than is normally accorded economic and social legislation. First, it is undeniable, and it is not argued otherwise here, that those who are mentally retarded have a reduced ability to cope with and function in the everyday world. Nor are they all cut from the same pattern: as the testimony in this record indicates, they range from those whose disability is not immediately evident to those who must be constantly cared for. They are thus different, immutably so, in relevant respects, and the States' interest in dealing with and providing for them is plainly a legitimate one. How this large and diversified group is to be treated under the law is a difficult and often a technical matter, very much a task for legislators guided by qualified professionals and not by the perhaps ill-informed opinions of the judiciary. Heightened scrutiny inevitably involves substantive judgments about legislative decisions, and we doubt that the predicate for such judicial oversight is present where the classification deals with mental retardation.

Second, the distinctive legislative response, both national and state, to the plight of those who are mentally retarded demonstrates not only that they have unique problems, but also that the lawmakers have been addressing their difficulties in a manner that belies a continuing antipathy or prejudice and a corresponding need for more intrusive oversight by the judiciary. Thus, the Federal Government has not only outlawed discrimination against the mentally retarded in federally funded programs, see § 504 of the Rehabilitation Act of 1973, 29 U.S.C. § 794, but it has also provided the retarded with the right to receive "appropriate treatment, services, and habilitation" in a setting that is "least restrictive of [their] personal liberty." Developmental Disabilities Assistance and Bill of Rights Act, 42 U.S.C. §§ 6010(1), (2). In addition, the Government has conditioned federal education funds on a State's assurance that retarded children will enjoy an education that, "to the maximum extent appropriate," is integrated with that of nonmentally retarded children. Education of the Handicapped Act, 20 U.S.C. § 1412(5)(B). The Government has also facilitated the hiring of the mentally retarded into the federal civil service by exempting them from the requirement of competitive examination. See 5 CFR § 213.3102(t) (1984). The State of Texas has similarly enacted legislation that acknowledges the special status of the mentally retarded by conferring certain rights upon them, such as "the right to live in the least restrictive setting appropriate to [their] individual needs and abilities," including "the right to live . . . in a group home." Mentally Retarded Persons Act of 1977, Tex.Rev.Civ.Stat.Ann., Art. 5547–300, § 7 (Vernon Supp.1985).

Such legislation thus singling out the retarded for special treatment reflects the real and undeniable differences between the retarded and others. That a civilized and decent society expects and approves such legislation indicates that governmental consideration of those differences in the vast majority of situations is not only legitimate but also desirable. It may be, as CLC contends, that legislation designed to benefit, rather than disadvantage, the retarded would generally withstand examination under a test of heightened scrutiny. The relevant inquiry, however, is whether heightened scrutiny is constitutionally mandated in the first instance. Even assuming that many of these laws could be shown to be substantially related to an important governmental purpose, merely requiring the legislature to justify its efforts in these terms may lead it to refrain from acting at all. Much recent legislation intended to benefit the retarded also assumes the need for measures that might be perceived to disadvantage them. The Education of the Handicapped Act, for example, requires an "appropriate" education, not one that is equal in all respects to the education of nonretarded children; clearly, admission to a class that exceeded the abilities of a retarded child would not be appropriate. Similarly, the Developmental Disabilities Assistance Act and the Texas Act give the retarded the right to live only in the "least restrictive setting" appropriate to their abilities, implicitly assuming the need for at least some restrictions that would not be imposed on others. Especially given the wide variation in the abilities and needs of the retarded themselves, governmental bodies must have a certain amount of flexibility and freedom from judicial oversight in shaping and limiting their remedial efforts.

Third, the legislative response, which could hardly have occurred and survived without public support, negates any claim that the mentally retarded are politically powerless in the sense that they have no ability to attract the attention of the lawmakers. Any minority can be said to be powerless to assert direct control over the legislature, but if that were a criterion for higher level scrutiny by the courts, much economic and social legislation would now be suspect.

Fourth, if the large and amorphous class of the mentally retarded were deemed quasi-suspect for the reasons given by the Court of Appeals, it would be difficult to find a principled way to distinguish a variety of other groups who have perhaps immutable disabilities setting them off from others, who cannot themselves mandate the desired legislative responses, and who can claim some degree of prejudice from at least part of the public at large. One need mention in this respect only the aging, the disabled, the mentally ill, and the infirm. We are reluctant to set out on that course, and we decline to do so.

Doubtless, there have been and there will continue to be instances of discrimination against the retarded that are in fact invidious, and that are properly subject to judicial correction under constitutional norms. But the appropriate method of reaching such instances is not to create a new quasi-suspect classification and subject all governmental action based on that classification to more searching evaluation. Rather, we should look to the likelihood that governmental action premised on a particular classification is valid as a general matter, not merely to the specifics of the case before us. Because mental retardation is a characteristic that the government may legitimately take into account in a wide range of decisions, and because both State and Federal Governments have recently committed themselves to assisting the retarded, we will not presume that any given legislative action, even one that disadvantages retarded individuals, is rooted in considerations that the Constitution will not tolerate.

Our refusal to recognize the retarded as a quasi-suspect class does not leave them entirely unprotected from invidious discrimination. To withstand equal protection review, legislation that distinguishes between the mentally retarded and others must be rationally related to a legitimate governmental purpose. This standard, we believe, affords government the latitude necessary both to pursue policies designed to assist the retarded in realizing their full potential, and to freely and efficiently engage in activities that burden the retarded in what is essentially an incidental manner. The State may not rely on a classification whose relationship to an asserted goal is so attenuated as to render the distinction arbitrary or irrational. Furthermore, some objectives—such as "a bare . . . desire to harm a politically unpopular group"—are not legitimate state interests. Beyond that, the mentally retarded, like others, have and retain their substantive constitutional rights in addition to the right to be treated equally by the law.

IV

We turn to the issue of the validity of the zoning ordinance insofar as it requires a special use permit for homes for the mentally retarded. We inquire first whether requiring a special use permit for the Featherston home in the circumstances here deprives respondents of the equal protection of the laws. If it does, there will be no occasion to decide whether the special use permit provision is facially invalid where the mentally retarded are involved, or to put it another way, whether the city may never insist on a special use permit for a home for the mentally retarded in an R-3 zone. This is the preferred course of adjudication since it enables courts to avoid making unnecessarily broad constitutional judgments.

The constitutional issue is clearly posed. The city does not require a special use permit in an R-3 zone for apartment houses, multiple dwellings, boarding and lodging houses, fraternity or sorority houses, dormitories, apartment hotels, hospitals, sanitariums, nursing homes for convalescents or the aged (other than for the insane or feebleminded or alcoholics or drug addicts), private clubs or fraternal orders, and other specified uses. It does, however, insist on a special permit for the Featherston home, and it does so, as the District Court found, because it would be a facility for the mentally retarded. May the city require the permit for this facility when other care and multiple-dwelling facilities are freely permitted?

It is true, as already pointed out, that the mentally retarded as a group are indeed different from others not sharing their misfortune, and in this respect they may be different from those who would occupy other facilities that would be permitted in an R-3 zone without a special permit. But this difference is largely irrelevant unless the Featherston home and those who would occupy it would threaten legitimate interests of the city in a way that other permitted uses such as boarding houses and hospitals would not. Because in our view the record does not reveal any rational basis for believing that the Featherston home would pose any special threat to the city's legitimate interests, we affirm the judgment below insofar as it holds the ordinance invalid as applied in this case.

The District Court found that the City Council's insistence on the permit rested on several factors. First, the Council was concerned with the negative attitude of the majority of property owners located within 200 feet of the Featherston facility, as well as with the fears of elderly residents of the neighborhood. But mere negative attitudes, or fear, unsubstantiated by factors which are properly cognizable in a zoning proceeding, are not permissible bases for treating a home for the mentally retarded differently from apartment houses, multiple dwellings, and the like. It is plain that the electorate as a whole, whether by referendum or otherwise, could not order city action violative of the Equal Protection Clause, and the City may not avoid the strictures of that Clause by deferring to the wishes or objections of some fraction of the body politic. "Private biases may be outside the reach of the law, but the law cannot, directly or indirectly, give them effect." *Palmore v. Sidoti*, 466 U.S. 429, 433 (1984).

Second, the Council had two objections to the location of the facility. It was concerned that the facility was across the street from a junior high school, and it feared that the students might harass the occupants of the Featherston home. But the school itself is attended by about 30 mentally retarded students, and denying a permit based on such vague, undifferentiated fears is again permitting some portion of the community to validate what would otherwise be an equal protection violation. The other objection to the home's location was that it was located on "a five hundred year flood plain." This concern with the possibility of a flood, however, can hardly be based on a distinction between the Featherston home and, for example, nursing homes, homes for convalescents or the aged, or sanitariums or hospitals, any of which could be located on the Featherston site without obtaining a special use permit. The same may be said of another concern of the Council— doubts about the legal responsibility for actions which the mentally retarded might take. If there is no concern about legal responsibility with respect to other uses that would be permitted in the area, such as boarding and fraternity houses, it is difficult to believe that the groups of mildly or moderately mentally retarded individuals who would live at 201 Featherston would present any different or special hazard.

Fourth, the Council was concerned with the size of the home and the number of people that would occupy it. The District Court found, and the Court of Appeals repeated, that "[i]f the potential residents of the Featherston Street home were not mentally retarded, but the home was the same in all other respects, its use would be permitted under the city's zoning ordinance." Given this finding, there would be no restrictions on the number of people who could occupy this home as a boarding house, nursing home, family dwelling, fraternity house, or dormitory. The question is whether it is rational to treat the mentally retarded differently. It is true that they suffer disability not shared by others; but why this difference warrants a density regulation that others need not observe is not at all apparent. At least this record does not clarify how, in this connection, the characteristics of the intended occupants of the Featherston home rationally justify denying to those occupants what would be permitted to groups occupying the same site for different purposes. Those who would live in the Featherston home are the type of individuals who, with supporting staff, satisfy federal and state standards for group housing in the community; and there is no dispute that the home would meet the federal square-footage-per-resident requirement for facilities of this type. See 42 CFR § 442.447 (1984). In the words of the Court of Appeals, "[t]he City never justifies its apparent view that other people can live under such 'crowded' conditions when mentally retarded persons cannot."

In the courts below the city also urged that the ordinance is aimed at avoiding concentration of population and at lessening congestion of the streets. These concerns obviously fail to explain why apartment houses, fraternity and sorority houses, hospitals and the like, may freely locate in the area without a permit. So, too, the expressed worry about fire hazards, the serenity of the neighborhood, and the avoidance of danger to other residents fail rationally to justify singling out a home such as 201 Featherston for the special use permit, yet imposing no such restrictions on the many other uses freely permitted in the neighborhood.

The short of it is that requiring the permit in this case appears to us to rest on an irrational prejudice against the mentally retarded, including those who would occupy the Featherston facility and who would live under the closely supervised and highly regulated conditions expressly provided for by state and federal law.

The judgment of the Court of Appeals is affirmed insofar as it invalidates the zoning ordinance as applied to the Featherston home. The judgment is otherwise vacated, and the case is remanded.

It is so ordered.

■ JUSTICE STEVENS, with whom THE CHIEF JUSTICE joins, concurring.

[T]he discrimination against the mentally retarded that is at issue in this case is the city's decision to require an annual special use permit before property in an apartment house district may be used as a group home for persons who are mildly retarded. The record convinces me that this permit was required because of the irrational fears of neighboring property owners, rather than for the protection of the mentally retarded persons who would reside in respondent's home.

Although the city argued in the Court of Appeals that legitimate interests of the neighbors justified the restriction, the court unambiguously rejected that argument. In this Court, the city has argued that the discrimination was really motivated by a desire to protect the mentally retarded from the hazards presented by the neighborhood. Zoning ordinances are not usually justified on any such basis, and in this case, for the reasons explained by the Court, I find that justification wholly unconvincing. I cannot believe that a rational member of this disadvantaged class could ever approve of the discriminatory application of the city's ordinance in this case.

Accordingly, I join the opinion of the Court.

■ JUSTICE MARSHALL, with whom JUSTICE BRENNAN and JUSTICE BLACKMUN join, concurring in the judgment in part and dissenting in part.

The Court holds that all retarded individuals cannot be grouped together as the "feebleminded" and deemed presumptively unfit to live in a community. Underlying this holding is the principle that mental retardation *per se* cannot be a proxy for depriving retarded people of their rights and interests without regard to variations in individual ability. With this holding and principle I agree. The Equal Protection Clause requires attention to the capacities and needs of retarded people as individuals.

I cannot agree, however, with the way in which the Court reaches its result or with the narrow, as-applied remedy it provides for the city of Cleburne's equal protection violation. The Court holds the ordinance invalid on rational-basis grounds and disclaims that anything special, in the form of heightened scrutiny, is taking place. Yet Cleburne's ordinance surely would be valid under the traditional rational-basis test applicable to economic and commercial regulation. In my view, it is important to articulate, as the Court does not, the facts and principles that justify subjecting this zoning ordinance to the searching review— the heightened scrutiny—that actually leads to its invalidation. Moreover, in invalidating Cleburne's exclusion of the "feebleminded" only as applied to respondents, rather than on its face, the Court radically departs from our equal protection precedents. Because I dissent from this novel and truncated remedy, and because I cannot accept the Court's disclaimer that no "more exacting standard" than ordinary rational-basis review is being applied, I write separately.

[T]o be sure, the Court does not label its handiwork heightened scrutiny, and perhaps the method employed must hereafter be called "second order" rational-basis review rather than "heightened scrutiny." But however labeled, the rational basis test invoked today is most assuredly not the rational-basis test of *Williamson v. Lee Optical of*

Oklahoma, Inc., 348 U.S. 483(1955), *Allied Stores of Ohio, Inc. v. Bowers*, 358 U.S. 522 (1959), and their progeny.

The Court, for example, concludes that legitimate concerns for fire hazards or the serenity of the neighborhood do not justify singling out respondents to bear the burdens of these concerns, for analogous permitted uses appear to pose similar threats. Yet under the traditional and most minimal version of the rational-basis test, "reform may take one step at a time, addressing itself to the phase of the problem which seems most acute to the legislative mind." *Williamson v. Lee Optical of Oklahoma, Inc., supra*, 348 U.S., at 489. The "record" is said not to support the ordinance's classifications, but under the traditional standard we do not sift through the record to determine whether policy decisions are squarely supported by a firm factual foundation. Finally, the Court further finds it "difficult to believe" that the retarded present different or special hazards inapplicable to other groups. In normal circumstances, the burden is not on the legislature to convince the Court that the lines it has drawn are sensible; legislation is presumptively constitutional, and a State "is not required to resort to close distinctions or to maintain a precise, scientific uniformity with reference" to its goals.

I share the Court's criticisms of the overly broad lines that Cleburne's zoning ordinance has drawn. But if the ordinance is to be invalidated for its imprecise classifications, it must be pursuant to more powerful scrutiny than the minimal rational-basis test used to review classifications affecting only economic and commercial matters. The same imprecision in a similar ordinance that required opticians but not optometrists to be licensed to practice, see *Williamson v. Lee Optical of Oklahoma, Inc.*, supra, or that excluded new but not old businesses from parts of a community, see *New Orleans v. Dukes*, would hardly be fatal to the statutory scheme.

[I] have long believed the level of scrutiny employed in an equal protection case should vary with "the constitutional and societal importance of the interest adversely affected and the recognized invidiousness of the basis upon which the particular classification is drawn." *San Antonio Independent School District v. Rodriguez*, 411 U.S. 1, 99 (1973) (MARSHALL, J., dissenting). When a zoning ordinance works to exclude the retarded from all residential districts in a community, these two considerations require that the ordinance be convincingly justified as substantially furthering legitimate and important purposes.

First, the interest of the retarded in establishing group homes is substantial. The right to "establish a home" has long been cherished as one of the fundamental liberties embraced by the Due Process Clause. For retarded adults, this right means living together in group homes, for as deinstitutionalization has progressed, group homes have become the primary means by which retarded adults can enter life in the community. Excluding group homes deprives the retarded of much of what makes for human freedom and fulfillment—the ability to form bonds and take part in the life of a community.

Second, the mentally retarded have been subject to a "lengthy and tragic history," of segregation and discrimination that can only be called grotesque. During much of the 19th century, mental retardation was viewed as neither curable nor dangerous and the retarded were largely left to their own devices. By the latter part of the century and during the first decades of the new one, however, social views of the retarded underwent a radical transformation. Fueled by the rising tide of Social Darwinism, the "science" of eugenics, and the extreme xenophobia of those years, leading medical authorities and others began to portray the "feeble-minded" as a "menace to society and civilization . . . responsible in a large degree for many, if not all, of our social problems."[8] A regime of state-mandated segregation and degradation soon emerged that in its virulence and bigotry rivaled, and indeed paralleled, the worst excesses of Jim Crow. Massive custodial institutions were built to warehouse the retarded for life; the aim was to halt reproduction of the retarded and "nearly extinguish their race."[9] Retarded children were categorically excluded from public schools, based on the false stereotype that all were ineducable and on the purported need to protect nonretarded children from them. State laws deemed the retarded "unfit for citizenship."

Segregation was accompanied by eugenic marriage and sterilization laws that extinguished for the retarded one of the "basic civil rights of man"—the right to marry and procreate. *Skinner v. Oklahoma ex rel. Williamson*, 316 U.S. 535, 541 (1942). Marriages of the retarded were made, and in some States continue to be, not only voidable but also often a criminal offense. The purpose of such limitations, which frequently applied only to women of child-bearing age, was unabashedly eugenic: to prevent the retarded from propagating. To assure this end, 29 States enacted compulsory eugenic sterilization laws between 1907 and 1931. J. Landman, Human Sterilization 302–303 (1932). See *Buck v. Bell*, 274 U.S. 200, 207 (1927) (Holmes, J.); cf. *Plessy v. Ferguson*, 163 U.S. 537 (1896); *Bradwell v. Illinois*, 16 Wall. 130, 141 (1873) (Bradley, J., concurring in judgment).

Prejudice, once let loose, is not easily cabined. As of 1979, most States still categorically disqualified "idiots" from voting, without regard to individual capacity and with discretion to exclude left in the hands of low-level election officials. Not until Congress enacted the

---

[8] H. Goddard, *The Possibilities of Research as Applied to the Prevention of Feeblemindedness*, Proceedings of the National Conference of Charities and Correction 307 (1915), cited in A. Deutsch, The Mentally Ill in America 360 (2d ed.1949). See also Fernald, *The Burden of Feeblemindedness*, 17 J. Psycho–Asthenics 87, 90 (1913) (the retarded "cause unutterable sorrow at home and are a menace and danger to the community"); Terman, *Feeble–Minded Children in the Public Schools of California*, 5 Schools & Society 161 (1917) ("[O]nly recently have we begun to recognize how serious a menace [feeblemindedness] is to the social, economic and moral welfare of the state. . . . [I]t is responsible . . . for the majority of cases of chronic and semi-chronic pauperism, and for much of our alcoholism, prostitution, and venereal diseases"). Books with titles such as "The Menace of the Feeble Minded in Connecticut" (1915), issued by the Connecticut School for Imbeciles, became commonplace. See C. Frazier, (Chairman, Executive Committee of Public Charities Assn. of Pennsylvania), The Menace of the Feeble–Minded In Pennsylvania (1913); W. Fernald, The Burden of Feeble–Mindedness (1912) (Mass.); Juvenile Protection Association of Cincinnati, The Feeble–Minded, Or the Hub to Our Wheel of Vice (1915) (Ohio). The resemblance to such works as R. Shufeldt, The Negro: A Menace to American Civilization (1907), is striking, and not coincidental.

[9] A. Moore, The Feeble–Minded in New York 3 (1911). This book was sponsored by the State Charities Aid Association. See also P. Tyor & L. Bell, Caring for the Retarded in America 71–104 (1984). The segregationist purpose of these laws was clear. See, e.g., Act of Mar. 22, 1915, ch. 90, 1915 Tex.Gen.Laws 143 (repealed 1955) (Act designed to relieve society of "the heavy economic and moral losses arising from the existence at large of these unfortunate persons").

Education of the Handicapped Act, 84 Stat. 175, as amended, 20 U.S.C. § 1400 *et seq.*, were "the door[s] of public education" opened wide to handicapped children. But most important, lengthy and continuing isolation of the retarded has perpetuated the ignorance, irrational fears, and stereotyping that long have plagued them.

In light of the importance of the interest at stake and the history of discrimination the retarded have suffered, the Equal Protection Clause requires us to do more than review the distinctions drawn by Cleburne's zoning ordinance as if they appeared in a taxing statute or in economic or commercial legislation.[17] The searching scrutiny I would give to restrictions on the ability of the retarded to establish community group homes leads me to conclude that Cleburne's vague generalizations for classifying the "feeble-minded" with drug addicts, alcoholics, and the insane, and excluding them where the elderly, the ill, the boarder, and the transient are allowed, are not substantial or important enough to overcome the suspicion that the ordinance rests on impermissible assumptions or outmoded and perhaps invidious stereotypes.

[T]he Court downplays the lengthy "history of purposeful unequal treatment" of the retarded by pointing to recent legislative action that is said to "beli[e] a continuing antipathy or prejudice." Building on this point, the Court similarly concludes that the retarded are not "politically powerless" and deserve no greater judicial protection than "[a]ny minority" that wins some political battles and loses others. The import of these conclusions, it seems, is that the only discrimination courts may remedy is the discrimination they alone are perspicacious enough to see. Once society begins to recognize certain practices as discriminatory, in part because previously stigmatized groups have mobilized politically to lift this stigma, the Court would refrain from approaching such practices with the added skepticism of heightened scrutiny.

Courts, however, do not sit or act in a social vacuum. Moral philosophers may debate whether certain inequalities are absolute wrongs, but history makes clear that constitutional principles of equality, like constitutional principles of liberty, property, and due process, evolve over time; what once was a "natural" and "self-evident" ordering later comes to be seen as an artificial and invidious constraint on human potential and freedom. Shifting cultural, political, and social patterns at times come to make past practices appear inconsistent with fundamental principles upon which American society rests, an inconsistency legally cognizable under the Equal Protection Clause. It is

---

[17] This history of discrimination may well be directly relevant to the issue before the Court. Cleburne's current exclusion of the "feeble-minded" in its 1965 zoning ordinance appeared as a similar exclusion of the "feeble-minded" in the city's 1947 ordinance, see Act of Sept. 26, 1947, § 5; the latter tracked word for word a similar exclusion in the 1929 comprehensive zoning ordinance for the nearby city of Dallas. See Dallas Ordinance, No. 2052, § 4, passed Sept. 11, 1929. Although we have been presented with no legislative history for Cleburne's zoning ordinances, this genealogy strongly suggests that Cleburne's current exclusion of the "feeble-minded" was written in the darkest days of segregation and stigmatization of the retarded and simply carried over to the current ordinance. Recently we held that extant laws originally motivated by a discriminatory purpose continue to violate the Equal Protection Clause, even if they would be permissible were they reenacted without a discriminatory motive. But in any event, the roots of a law that by its terms excludes from a community the "feebleminded" are clear. As the examples above attest, "feebleminded" was the defining term for all retarded people in the era of overt and pervasive discrimination.

natural that evolving standards of equality come to be embodied in legislation. When that occurs, courts should look to the fact of such change as a source of guidance on evolving principles of equality.

[F]or the retarded, just as for Negroes and women, much has changed in recent years, but much remains the same; out-dated statutes are still on the books, and irrational fears or ignorance, traceable to the prolonged social and cultural isolation of the retarded, continue to stymie recognition of the dignity and individuality of retarded people. Heightened judicial scrutiny of action appearing to impose unnecessary barriers to the retarded is required in light of increasing recognition that such barriers are inconsistent with evolving principles of equality embedded in the Fourteenth Amendment.

[T]he fact that retardation may be deemed a constitutional irrelevancy in some circumstances is enough, given the history of discrimination the retarded have suffered, to require careful judicial review of classifications singling out the retarded for special burdens. Although the Court acknowledges that many instances of invidious discrimination against the retarded still exist, the Court boldly asserts that "in the vast majority of situations" special treatment of the retarded is "not only legitimate but also desirable." That assertion suggests the Court would somehow have us calculate the percentage of "situations" in which a characteristic is validly and invalidly invoked before determining whether heightened scrutiny is appropriate. But heightened scrutiny has not been "triggered" in our past cases only after some undefined numerical threshold of invalid "situations" has been crossed. An inquiry into constitutional principle, not mathematics, determines whether heightened scrutiny is appropriate. Whenever evolving principles of equality, rooted in the Equal Protection Clause, require that certain classifications be viewed as potentially discriminatory, and when history reveals systemic unequal treatment, more searching judicial inquiry than minimum rationality becomes relevant.

[I] would affirm the judgment of the Court of Appeals in its entirety and would strike down on its face the provision at issue. I therefore concur in the judgment in part and dissent in part.

NOTES ON CITY OF CLEBURNE V. CLEBURNE LIVING CENTER

1. **What is the Holding of *Cleburne*?** The bottom-line holding in *Cleburne* is clear enough: The city violated the Equal Protection Clause by insisting on (and denying) a special use permit for the plaintiff's group home. But what is the Court's rationale? The Court explicitly rejects the Fifth Circuit's holding that mental retardation is a quasi-suspect classification for which any discrimination triggers heightened constitutional scrutiny. Instead, the Court holds that rational-basis scrutiny—the lowest level of constitutional scrutiny—applies. But as Justice Marshall explains in his dissent on this point, the city's justifications for its decision would seem to satisfy ordinary rational-basis scrutiny. Under ordinary rational-basis scrutiny, a defendant may rely on *post hoc* justifications for its actions, and it need not respond to all instances of a problem in the same way—indeed, it need not respond to all instances of a problem at all. (Reform can take "one step at a time.") In

short, the same reasons why the city (says it) objected to the plaintiff's group home might well apply to other group living facilities that the city allowed to operate in the area—but that fact, in ordinary rational-basis review, is irrelevant.

In the end, the crux of the Court's opinion seems to be this statement: "The short of it is that requiring the permit in this case appears to us to rest on an irrational prejudice against the mentally retarded, including those who would occupy the Featherston facility and who would live under the closely supervised and highly regulated conditions expressly provided for by state and federal law." See William R. Eskridge, Jr., *Some Effects of Identity-Based Social Movements on Constitutional Law in the Twentieth Century*, 110 Mich. L. Rev. 2062, 2264 (2002) ("The review in *Cleburne* was not nearly as forgiving as standard rational basis review. Had the zoning regulation only involved a business that wanted to open up in the neighborhood, the concerns of fearful neighbors would have been enough to satisfy any judge. Clearly, the Justices were responding to the dreadful history of invidious discrimination and the survival of stereotypes about and prejudice against disabled people in their tougher look at the local decision."). Professor Cass Sunstein argues that *Cleburne* "reflect[s] the possible use of rationality review as a kind of magical trump card, or perhaps joker, hidden in the pack and used on special occasions. [There,] rationality review, traditionally little more than a rubber stamp, is used to invalidate badly motivated laws without refining a new kind of scrutiny." Cass R. Sunstein, *The Supreme Court, 1995 Term—Foreword: Leaving Things Undecided*, 110 Harv. L. Rev. 4, 61 (1996). He contends that the crucial fact in *Cleburne* was that the city seemed to be acting on a "desire to isolate and seal off members of a despised group whose characteristics are thought to be in some sense contaminating or corrosive. In its most virulent forms, this desire is rooted in a belief that members of the relevant group are not fully human." *Id.* at 62–63.

The upshot of the case seems to be that the rational basis standard at least nominally applies to discrimination against people with mental retardation, but, at least some of the time, that discrimination will be unconstitutional because rooted in prejudice—even when it would be upheld under ordinary rational-basis review. Perhaps the holding is so unclear precisely because the Court is uncomfortable drawing clear lines dividing the disability discrimination that is constitutional from the disability discrimination that is unconstitutional. Justice White's opinion for the Court emphasizes the limits of judicial competence in making the complex distinctions that are necessary to determine whether "special" treatment for people with disabilities is invidious and unequal: "How this large and diversified group is to be treated under the law is a difficult and often a technical matter, very much a task for legislators guided by qualified professionals and not by the perhaps ill-informed opinions of the judiciary." And, indeed, he seems to say that Congress itself is constitutionally empowered to adopt a standard of scrutiny under the Equal Protection Clause that best responds to these complex questions: "Section 5 of the Amendment empowers Congress to enforce this mandate, but absent controlling congressional direction, the courts have themselves devised standards for determining the validity of state legislation or other official action that is challenged as denying equal protection."

One might see the Americans with Disabilities Act as Congress's response to (what seems like) Justice White's invitation. But the Court did not see it that way in the *Garrett* case (a principal case in subsection 2 of this section).

2. Should Disability Discrimination Trigger Heightened Scrutiny? As the separate opinions of Justices Stevens and Marshall illustrate, the tiers-of-scrutiny model of equal protection law has been the subject of very cogent descriptive and normative critique. For the moment, however, take as a given that equal protection law applies three tiers of scrutiny: (1) strict scrutiny, which paradigmatically applies to race-based classifications; (2) intermediate scrutiny, which paradigmatically applies to sex-based classifications; and (3) rational-basis scrutiny, which is the presumptive level of scrutiny, and applies (among other things) to age-based classifications. Where ought disability to fit in this three-tier structure? Or, to put it another way, is disability more like race, sex, or age?

Is disability like race? As Justice Marshall shows, there is a long and virulent history of prejudice and discrimination against people with mental retardation, and the same might be shown for other disabilities. And people with various disabilities have often been treated as, in Erving Goffman's words, "not quite human." Erving Goffman, Stigma: Notes on the Management of Spoiled Identity 5 (1963). But to a far greater extent than in the race context, disability discrimination has stemmed from paternalistic impulses—the desire to "protect," rather than to disparage. Although, as disability rights advocates have emphasized, paternalistic motives may be worthy of condemnation as well, there is a moral difference. Moreover, unlike race, which can be understood for these purposes as nothing more than a social construct, disability implicates "real" differences between people. Even once we accept the insight of the social model of disability—that it is societal choices and attitudes that make some physical and mental conditions disabling—we cannot ignore that the physical and mental conditions are there, and may make it more difficult to do a variety of tasks. (It is hard, for example, to envision a world in which blind people are traffic cops, or people with significant intellectual disabilities are theoretical physicists.)

Perhaps sex is a better analogy. Like disability discrimination, sex discrimination has often been rooted in paternalism. Indeed, perhaps the key concept underlying constitutional sex discrimination law is the metaphor of the pedestal as cage—that paternalistic policies deny full citizenship. See *Frontiero v. Richardson*, 411 U.S. 677, 684 (1973) (plurality opinion) (noting that sex discrimination was traditionally "rationalized by an attitude of 'romantic paternalism' which, in practical effect, put women, not on a pedestal, but in a cage"). And sex, like disability, implicates "real" and not just "socially constructed" differences between people. The constitutional law of sex discrimination permits states to recognize those differences but prohibits states from making them engines of inequality. See *United States v. Virginia*, 518 U.S. 515, 533 (1996) (" 'Inherent differences' between men and women, we have come to appreciate, remain cause for celebration, but not for denigration of the members of either sex or for artificial constraints on an individual's opportunity."). But disability might seem different in kind. The "inherent differences" between men and women are very few; the "inherent differences" between people with and without disabilities might be thought to be much greater. Distinguishing unjustified paternalism from proper recognition of difference, one might think, will frequently be significantly more difficult in the disability context.

What about age? Disability and old age have a lot in common. Indeed, much age discrimination might really be understood as disability discrimination—it is discrimination based on a fear that old age implies infirmity. Age discrimination frequently stems from paternalism and from an anxiety about growing old oneself. In these ways, age is quite similar to disability. See Paul Steven Miller, *The Impact of Assisted Suicide on Persons with Disabilities—Is It a Right Without Freedom?*, 9 Issues L. & Med. 47, 53 (1993) ("The root of prejudice against people with disabilities comes from several sources. Foremost is that of fear: fear of the loss of autonomy and the 'there but for the grace of God go I' realization that disability can 'afflict' any person."); Harlan Hahn, *The Politics of Physical Differences: Disability and Discrimination*, 44 J. Soc. Iss. 39, 42–45 (1988) (labeling this phenomenon "existential anxiety"). But the two are not entirely the same. Nearly every younger person recognizes that she will eventually grow old if she is lucky enough, but far fewer nondisabled people understand that the same thing is true of disability. Nondisabled, nonelderly people may *fear* old age and disability in the same way, but their recognition that they will one day grow old can generate a countervailing solidarity with old people that they do not experience with people with disabilities. Accordingly, we might want the law to be more skeptical of disability-based discrimination than of age-based discrimination.

Is this even a useful exercise? Cf. Janet E. Halley, *Gay Rights and Identity Imitation: Issues in the Ethics of Representation, in* The Politics of Law: A Progressive Critique 121 (David Kairys ed., 3d ed. 1998) (arguing that analogizing sexual orientation to race, while perhaps inevitable in American legal culture, may misrepresent and distract attention from the unique nature of sexual orientation discrimination and oppression).

b.   INSTITUTIONALIZATION

Youngberg v. Romeo

Supreme Court of the United States, 1982.
457 U.S. 307.

■ JUSTICE POWELL delivered the opinion of the Court.

The question presented is whether respondent, involuntarily committed to a state institution for the mentally retarded, has substantive rights under the Due Process Clause of the Fourteenth Amendment to (i) safe conditions of confinement; (ii) freedom from bodily restraints; and (iii) training or "habilitation."[1] Respondent sued under 42 U.S.C. § 1983 three administrators of the institution, claiming damages for the alleged breach of his constitutional rights.

I

Respondent Nicholas Romeo is profoundly retarded. Although 33 years old, he has the mental capacity of an 18-month-old child, with an I.Q. between 8 and 10. He cannot talk and lacks the most basic self-care skills. Until he was 26, respondent lived with his parents in Philadelphia. But after the death of his father in May 1974, his mother was unable to care for him. Within two weeks of the father's death, respondent's mother sought his temporary admission to a nearby Pennsylvania hospital.

Shortly thereafter, she asked the Philadelphia County Court of Common Pleas to admit Romeo to a state facility on a permanent basis. Her petition to the court explained that she was unable to care for Romeo or control his violence. As part of the commitment process, Romeo was examined by a physician and a psychologist. They both certified that respondent was severely retarded and unable to care for himself. On June 11, 1974, the Court of Common Pleas committed respondent to the Pennhurst State School and Hospital, pursuant to the applicable involuntary commitment provision of the Pennsylvania Mental Health and Mental Retardation Act.

At Pennhurst, Romeo was injured on numerous occasions, both by his own violence and by the reactions of other residents to him. Respondent's mother became concerned about these injuries. After objecting to respondent's treatment several times, she filed this complaint on November 4, 1976, in the United States District Court for the Eastern District of Pennsylvania as his next friend. The complaint alleged that "[d]uring the period July, 1974 to the present, plaintiff has suffered injuries on at least sixty-three occasions." The complaint originally sought damages and injunctive relief from Pennhurst's director and two supervisors; it alleged that these officials knew, or should have known, that Romeo was suffering injuries and that they failed to institute appropriate preventive procedures, thus violating his rights under the Eighth and Fourteenth Amendments.

Thereafter, in late 1976, Romeo was transferred from his ward to the hospital for treatment of a broken arm. While in the infirmary, and by order of a doctor, he was physically restrained during portions of each day. These restraints were ordered by Dr. Gabroy, not a defendant here, to protect Romeo and others in the hospital, some of whom were in traction or were being treated intravenously. Although respondent normally would have returned to his ward when his arm healed, the parties to this litigation agreed that he should remain in the hospital due to the pending lawsuit. Nevertheless, in December 1977, a second amended complaint was filed alleging that the defendants were restraining respondent for prolonged periods on a routine basis. The second amended complaint also added a claim for damages to

---

[1] The American Psychiatric Association explains: "The word 'habilitation,' . . . is commonly used to refer to programs for the mentally-retarded because mental retardation is . . . a learning disability and training impairment rather than an illness. [T]he principal focus of habilitation is upon training and development of needed skills."

compensate Romeo for the defendants' failure to provide him with appropriate "treatment or programs for his mental retardation." All claims for injunctive relief were dropped prior to trial because respondent is a member of the class seeking such relief in another action.[6]

An 8-day jury trial was held in April 1978. Petitioners introduced evidence that respondent participated in several programs teaching basic self-care skills.[7] A comprehensive behavior-modification program was designed by staff members to reduce Romeo's aggressive behavior,[8] but that program was never implemented because of his mother's objections. Respondent introduced evidence of his injuries and of conditions in his unit.

At the close of the trial, the court instructed the jury that "if any or all of the defendants were aware of and failed to take all reasonable steps to prevent repeated attacks upon Nicholas Romeo," such failure deprived him of constitutional rights. The jury also was instructed that if the defendants shackled Romeo or denied him treatment "as a punishment for filing this lawsuit," his constitutional rights were violated under the Eighth Amendment. Finally, the jury was instructed that only if they found the defendants "deliberate[ly] indifferen[t] to the serious medical [and psychological] needs" of Romeo could they find that his Eighth and Fourteenth Amendment rights had been violated.[11] The jury returned a verdict for the defendants, on which judgment was entered.

The Court of Appeals for the Third Circuit, sitting *en banc*, reversed and remanded for a new trial. The court held that the Eighth Amendment, prohibiting cruel and unusual punishment of those convicted of crimes, was not an appropriate source for determining the rights of the involuntarily committed. Rather, the Fourteenth Amendment and the liberty interest protected by that Amendment provided the proper constitutional basis for these rights. In applying the Fourteenth Amendment, the court found that the involuntarily committed retain liberty interests in freedom of movement and in personal security. These were "fundamental liberties" that can be limited only by an "overriding, non-punitive" state interest. It further found that the involuntarily committed have a liberty interest in habilitation designed to "treat" their mental retardation.

---

[6] *Pennhurst State School and Hospital v. Halderman*, 451 U.S. 1 (1981) (remanded for further proceedings).

[7] Prior to his transfer to Pennhurst's hospital ward, Romeo participated in programs dealing with feeding, showering, drying, dressing, self-control, and toilet training, as well as a program providing interaction with staff members. Some programs continued while respondent was in the hospital, and they reduced respondent's aggressive behavior to some extent.

[8] The program called for short periods of separation from other residents and for use of "muffs" on plaintiff's hands for short periods of time, *i.e.*, five minutes, to prevent him from harming himself or others.

[11] The "deliberate indifference" standard was adopted by this Court in *Estelle v. Gamble*, 429 U.S. 97, 104 a case dealing with prisoners' rights to punishment that is not "cruel and unusual" under the Eighth Amendment. Although the District Court did not refer to *Estelle v. Gamble* in charging the jury, it erroneously used the deliberate-indifference standard articulated in that case.

The *en banc* court did not, however, agree on the relevant standard to be used in determining whether Romeo's rights had been violated. [W]e granted the petition for *certiorari* because of the importance of the question presented to the administration of state institutions for the mentally retarded.

II

[T]he mere fact that Romeo has been committed under proper procedures does not deprive him of all substantive liberty interests under the Fourteenth Amendment. Indeed, the state concedes that respondent has a right to adequate food, shelter, clothing, and medical care. We must decide whether liberty interests also exist in safety, freedom of movement, and training. If such interests do exist, we must further decide whether they have been infringed in this case.

A

Respondent's first two claims involve liberty interests recognized by prior decisions of this Court, interests that involuntary commitment proceedings do not extinguish. The first is a claim to safe conditions. In the past, this Court has noted that the right to personal security constitutes a "historic liberty interest" protected substantively by the Due Process Clause. And that right is not extinguished by lawful confinement, even for penal purposes. If it is cruel and unusual punishment to hold convicted criminals in unsafe conditions, it must be unconstitutional to confine the involuntarily committed—who may not be punished at all—in unsafe conditions.

Next, respondent claims a right to freedom from bodily restraint. In other contexts, the existence of such an interest is clear in the prior decisions of this Court. Indeed, "[l]iberty from bodily restraint always has been recognized as the core of the liberty protected by the Due Process Clause from arbitrary governmental action." This interest survives criminal conviction and incarceration. Similarly, it must also survive involuntary commitment.

B

Respondent's remaining claim is more troubling. In his words, he asserts a "constitutional right to minimally adequate habilitation." This is a substantive due process claim that is said to be grounded in the liberty component of the Due Process Clause of the Fourteenth Amendment. The term "habilitation," used in psychiatry, is not defined precisely or consistently in the opinions below or in the briefs of the parties or the *amici*.[20] As noted previously in n.1, *supra*, the term refers to "training and development of needed skills." Respondent emphasizes that the right he asserts is for "minimal" training, and he would leave the type and extent of training to be determined on a case-by-case basis "in light of present medical or other scientific knowledge."

---

[20] Professionals in the habilitation of the mentally retarded disagree strongly on the question whether effective training of all severely or profoundly retarded individuals is even possible. See, *e.g.*, Favell, Risley, Wolfe, Riddle, & Rasmussen, *The Limits of Habilitation: How Can We Identify Them and How Can We Change Them?*, 1 Analysis and Intervention in Developmental Disabilities 37 (1981); Bailey, *Wanted: A Rational Search for the Limiting Conditions of Habilitation in the Retarded*, 1 Analysis and Intervention in Developmental Disabilities 45 (1981); Kauffman & Krouse, *The Cult of Educability: Searching for the Substance of Things Hoped For; The Evidence of Things Not Seen*, 1 Analysis and Intervention in Developmental Disabilities 53 (1981).

In addressing the asserted right to training, we start from established principles. As a general matter, a State is under no constitutional duty to provide substantive services for those within its border. See *Harris v. McRae*, 448 U.S. 297, 318 (1980) (publicly funded abortions); *Maher v. Roe*, 432 U.S. 464, 469 (1977) (medical treatment). When a person is institutionalized—and wholly dependent on the State—it is conceded by petitioners that a duty to provide certain services and care does exist, although even then a State necessarily has considerable discretion in determining the nature and scope of its responsibilities. Nor must a State "choose between attacking every aspect of a problem or not attacking the problem at all."

Respondent, in light of the severe character of his retardation, concedes that no amount of training will make possible his release. And he does not argue that if he were still at home, the State would have an obligation to provide training at its expense. The record reveals that respondent's primary needs are bodily safety and a minimum of physical restraint, and respondent clearly claims training related to these needs. As we have recognized that there is a constitutionally protected liberty interest in safety and freedom from restraint, training may be necessary to avoid unconstitutional infringement of those rights. On the basis of the record before us, it is quite uncertain whether respondent seeks any "habilitation" or training unrelated to safety and freedom from bodily restraints. In his brief to this Court, Romeo indicates that even the self-care programs he seeks are needed to reduce his aggressive behavior. And in his offer of proof to the trial court, respondent repeatedly indicated that, if allowed to testify, his experts would show that additional training programs, including self-care programs, were needed to reduce his aggressive behavior. If, as seems the case, respondent seeks only training related to safety and freedom from restraints, this case does not present the difficult question whether a mentally retarded person, involuntarily committed to a state institution, has some general constitutional right to training *per se*, even when no type or amount of training would lead to freedom.[23]

Chief Judge Seitz, in language apparently adopted by respondent, observed:

> "I believe that the plaintiff has a constitutional right to minimally adequate care and treatment. The existence of a constitutional right to care and treatment is no longer a novel legal proposition."

Chief Judge Seitz did not identify or otherwise define—beyond the right to reasonable safety and freedom from physical restraint—the "minimally adequate care and treatment" that appropriately may be required for this respondent. In the circumstances presented by this case, and on the basis of the record developed to date, we agree with his view and conclude that respondent's liberty interests require the State

---

[23] In the trial court, respondent asserted that "state officials at a state mental hospital have a duty to provide residents . . . with such treatment as will afford them a reasonable opportunity to acquire and maintain those life skills necessary to cope as effectively as their capacities permit." But this claim to a sweeping *per se* right was dropped thereafter. In his brief to this Court, respondent does not repeat it and, at oral argument, respondent's counsel explicitly disavowed any claim that respondent is constitutionally entitled to such treatment as would enable him "to achieve his maximum potential."

to provide minimally adequate or reasonable training to ensure safety and freedom from undue restraint. In view of the kinds of treatment sought by respondent and the evidence of record, we need go no further in this case.[25]

III

A

We have established that Romeo retains liberty interests in safety and freedom from bodily restraint. Yet these interests are not absolute; indeed to some extent they are in conflict. In operating an institution such as Pennhurst, there are occasions in which it is necessary for the State to restrain the movement of residents—for example, to protect them as well as others from violence. Similar restraints may also be appropriate in a training program. And an institution cannot protect its residents from all danger of violence if it is to permit them to have any freedom of movement. The question then is not simply whether a liberty interest has been infringed but whether the extent or nature of the restraint or lack of absolute safety is such as to violate due process.

In determining whether a substantive right protected by the Due Process Clause has been violated, it is necessary to balance "the liberty of the individual" and "the demands of an organized society." *Poe v. Ullman*, 367 U.S. 497, 542 (1961) (Harlan, J., dissenting). In seeking this balance in other cases, the Court has weighed the individual's interest in liberty against the State's asserted reasons for restraining individual liberty. [A]ccordingly, whether respondent's constitutional rights have been violated must be determined by balancing his liberty interests against the relevant state interests. If there is to be any uniformity in protecting these interests, this balancing cannot be left to the unguided discretion of a judge or jury. We therefore turn to consider the proper standard for determining whether a State adequately has protected the rights of the involuntarily committed mentally retarded.

B

We think the standard articulated by Chief Judge Seitz affords the necessary guidance and reflects the proper balance between the legitimate interests of the State and the rights of the involuntarily committed to reasonable conditions of safety and freedom from unreasonable restraints. He would have held that "the Constitution only requires that the courts make certain that professional judgment in fact was exercised. It is not appropriate for the courts to specify which of several professionally acceptable choices should have been made." Persons who have been involuntarily committed are entitled to more considerate treatment and conditions of confinement than criminals whose conditions of confinement are designed to punish. Cf. *Estelle v. Gamble*, 429 U.S. 97, 104 (1976). At the same time, this

---

[25] It is not feasible, as is evident from the variety of language and formulations in the opinions below and the various briefs here, to define or identify the type of training that may be required in every case. A court properly may start with the generalization that there is a right to minimally adequate training. The basic requirement of adequacy, in terms more familiar to courts, may be stated as that training which is reasonable in light of identifiable liberty interests and the circumstances of the case. A federal court, of course, must identify a constitutional predicate for the imposition of any affirmative duty on a State. Because the facts in cases of confinement of mentally retarded patients vary widely, it is essential to focus on the facts and circumstances of the case before a court[.]

standard is lower than the "compelling" or "substantial" necessity tests the Court of Appeals would require a State to meet to justify use of restraints or conditions of less than absolute safety. We think this requirement would place an undue burden on the administration of institutions such as Pennhurst and also would restrict unnecessarily the exercise of professional judgment as to the needs of residents.

Moreover, we agree that respondent is entitled to minimally adequate training. In this case, the minimally adequate training required by the Constitution is such training as may be reasonable in light of respondent's liberty interests in safety and freedom from unreasonable restraints. In determining what is "reasonable"—in this and in any case presenting a claim for training by a State—we emphasize that courts must show deference to the judgment exercised by a qualified professional. By so limiting judicial review of challenges to conditions in state institutions, interference by the federal judiciary with the internal operations of these institutions should be minimized. Moreover, there certainly is no reason to think judges or juries are better qualified than appropriate professionals in making such decisions. For these reasons, the decision, if made by a professional,[30] is presumptively valid; liability may be imposed only when the decision by the professional is such a substantial departure from accepted professional judgment, practice, or standards as to demonstrate that the person responsible actually did not base the decision on such a judgment. In an action for damages against a professional in his individual capacity, however, the professional will not be liable if he was unable to satisfy his normal professional standards because of budgetary constraints; in such a situation, good-faith immunity would bar liability.

IV

In deciding this case, we have weighed those postcommitment interests cognizable as liberty interests under the Due Process Clause of the Fourteenth Amendment against legitimate state interests and in light of the constraints under which most state institutions necessarily operate. We repeat that the State concedes a duty to provide adequate food, shelter, clothing, and medical care. These are the essentials of the care that the State must provide. The State also has the unquestioned duty to provide reasonable safety for all residents and personnel within the institution. And it may not restrain residents except when and to the extent professional judgment deems this necessary to assure such safety or to provide needed training. In this case, therefore, the State is under a duty to provide respondent with such training as an appropriate professional would consider reasonable to ensure his safety and to facilitate his ability to function free from bodily restraints. It may well be unreasonable not to provide training when training could significantly reduce the need for restraints or the likelihood of violence.

---

[30] By "professional" decisionmaker, we mean a person competent, whether by education, training or experience, to make the particular decision at issue. Long-term treatment decisions normally should be made by persons with degrees in medicine or nursing, or with appropriate training in areas such as psychology, physical therapy, or the care and training of the retarded. Of course, day-to-day decisions regarding care—including decisions that must be made without delay—necessarily will be made in many instances by employees without formal training but who are subject to the supervision of qualified persons.

Respondent thus enjoys constitutionally protected interests in conditions of reasonable care and safety, reasonably nonrestrictive confinement conditions, and such training as may be required by these interests. Such conditions of confinement would comport fully with the purpose of respondent's commitment. In determining whether the State has met its obligations in these respects, decisions made by the appropriate professional are entitled to a presumption of correctness. Such a presumption is necessary to enable institutions of this type—often, unfortunately, overcrowded and understaffed—to continue to function. A single professional may have to make decisions with respect to a number of residents with widely varying needs and problems in the course of a normal day. The administrators, and particularly professional personnel, should not be required to make each decision in the shadow of an action for damages.

In this case, we conclude that the jury was erroneously instructed on the assumption that the proper standard of liability was that of the Eighth Amendment. We vacate the decision of the Court of Appeals and remand for further proceedings consistent with this decision.

So ordered.

■ JUSTICE BLACKMUN, with whom JUSTICE BRENNAN and JUSTICE O'CONNOR join, concurring.

I join the Court's opinion. I write separately, however, to make clear why I believe that opinion properly leaves unresolved two difficult and important issues.

The first is whether the Commonwealth of Pennsylvania could accept respondent for "care and treatment," as it did under the Pennsylvania Mental Health and Mental Retardation Act of 1966, and then constitutionally refuse to provide him any "treatment," as that term is defined by state law. Were that question properly before us, in my view there would be a serious issue whether, as a matter of due process, the State could so refuse. I therefore do not find that issue to be a "frivolous" one, as THE CHIEF JUSTICE does.

In *Jackson v. Indiana*, 406 U.S. 715 (1972), this Court, by a unanimous vote of all participating Justices, suggested a constitutional standard for evaluating the conditions of a civilly committed person's confinement: "At the least, due process requires that the nature and duration of commitment bear some reasonable relation to the purpose for which the individual is committed." Under this standard, a State could accept a person for "safekeeping," then constitutionally refuse to provide him treatment. In such a case, commitment without treatment would bear a reasonable relation to the goal for which the person was confined.

If a state court orders a mentally retarded person committed for "care and treatment," however, I believe that due process might well bind the State to ensure that the conditions of his commitment bear some reasonable relation to each of those goals. In such a case, commitment without any "treatment" whatsoever would not bear a reasonable relation to the purposes of the person's confinement.

In respondent's case, the majority and principal concurring opinions in the Court of Appeals agreed that "[b]y basing [respondent's] deprivation of liberty at least partially upon a promise of treatment, the state ineluctably has committed the community's resources to providing minimal treatment." Neither opinion clarified, however, whether respondent in fact had been totally denied "treatment," as that term is defined under Pennsylvania law. To the extent that the majority addressed the question, it found that "the evidence in the record, although somewhat contradictory, suggests not so much a total failure to treat as an inadequacy of treatment."

This Court's reading of the record supports that conclusion. Moreover, the Court today finds that respondent's entitlement to "treatment" under Pennsylvania law was not properly raised below. Given this uncertainty in the record, I am in accord with the Court's decision not to address the constitutionality of a State's total failure to provide "treatment" to an individual committed under state law for "care and treatment."

The second difficult question left open today is whether respondent has an independent constitutional claim, grounded in the Due Process Clause of the Fourteenth Amendment, to that "habilitation" or training necessary to preserve those basic self-care skills he possessed when he first entered Pennhurst—for example, the ability to dress himself and care for his personal hygiene. In my view, it would be consistent with the Court's reasoning today to include within the "minimally adequate training required by the Constitution" such training as is reasonably necessary to prevent a person's pre-existing self-care skills from deteriorating because of his commitment.

The Court makes clear, ante that even after a person is committed to a state institution, he is entitled to such training as is necessary to prevent unreasonable losses of additional liberty as a result of his confinement—for example, unreasonable bodily restraints or unsafe institutional conditions. If a person could demonstrate that he entered a state institution with minimal self-care skills, but lost those skills after commitment because of the State's unreasonable refusal to provide him training, then, it seems to me, he has alleged a loss of liberty quite distinct from—and as serious as—the loss of safety and freedom from unreasonable restraints. For many mentally retarded people, the difference between the capacity to do things for themselves within an institution and total dependence on the institution for all of their needs is as much liberty as they ever will know.

Although respondent asserts a claim of this kind, I agree with the Court that "[o]n the basis of the record before us, it is quite uncertain whether respondent [in fact] seeks any 'habilitation' or training unrelated to safety and freedom from bodily restraints." Since the Court finds respondent constitutionally entitled at least to "such training as may be reasonable in light of [his] liberty interests in safety and freedom from unreasonable restraints," I accept its decision not to address respondent's additional claim.

If respondent actually seeks habilitation in self-care skills not merely to reduce his aggressive tendencies, but also to maintain those basic self-care skills necessary to his personal autonomy within Pennhurst, I believe he is free on remand to assert that claim. Like the Court, I would be willing to defer to the judgment of professionals as to whether or not, and to what extent, institutional training would preserve respondent's pre-existing skills. As the Court properly notes, "[p]rofessionals in the habilitation of the mentally retarded disagree strongly on the question whether effective training of all severely or profoundly retarded individuals is even possible."

If expert testimony reveals that respondent was so retarded when he entered the institution that he had no basic self-care skills to preserve, or that institutional training would not have preserved whatever skills he did have, then I would agree that he suffered no additional loss of liberty even if petitioners failed to provide him training. But if the testimony establishes that respondent possessed certain basic self-care skills when he entered the institution, and was sufficiently educable that he could have maintained those skills with a certain degree of training, then I would be prepared to listen seriously to an argument that petitioners were constitutionally required to provide that training, even if respondent's safety and mobility were not imminently threatened by their failure to do so.

The Court finds it premature to resolve this constitutional question on this less than fully developed record. Because I agree with that conclusion, I concur in the Court's opinion.

■ CHIEF JUSTICE BURGER, concurring in the judgment.

I agree with much of the Court's opinion. However, I would hold flatly that respondent has no constitutional right to training, or "habilitation," *per se*. The parties, and the Court, acknowledge that respondent cannot function outside the state institution, even with the assistance of relatives. Indeed, even now neither respondent nor his family seeks his discharge from state care. Under these circumstances, the State's provision of food, shelter, medical care, and living conditions as safe as the inherent nature of the institutional environment reasonably allows, serves to justify the State's custody of respondent. The State did not seek custody of respondent; his family understandably sought the State's aid to meet a serious need.

I agree with the Court that some amount of self-care instruction may be necessary to avoid unreasonable infringement of a mentally retarded person's interests in safety and freedom from restraint; but it seems clear to me that the Constitution does not otherwise place an affirmative duty on the State to provide any particular kind of training or habilitation—even such as might be encompassed under the essentially standardless rubric "minimally adequate training," to which the Court refers. Since respondent asserts a right to "minimally adequate" habilitation "[q]uite apart from its relationship to decent care," Brief for Respondent 23, unlike the Court I see no way to avoid the issue.*

I also point out that, under the Court's own standards, it is largely irrelevant whether respondent's experts were of the opinion that "additional training programs, including self-care programs, were

---

* Indeed, in the trial court respondent asserted a broad claim to such "treatment as [would] afford [him] a reasonable opportunity to acquire and maintain those life skills necessary to cope as effectively as [his] capacities permit." Respondent also maintains that, because state law purportedly creates a right to "care and treatment," he has a federal substantive right under the Due Process Clause to enforcement of this state right. This contention is obviously frivolous; were every substantive right created by state law enforceable under the Due Process Clause, the distinction between state and federal law would quickly be obliterated.

needed to reduce [respondent's] aggressive behavior"—a prescription far easier for "spectators" to give than for an institution to implement. The training program devised for respondent by petitioners and other professionals at Pennhurst was, according to the Court's opinion, "presumptively valid"; and "liability may be imposed only when the decision by the professional is such a substantial departure from accepted professional judgment, practice, or standards as to demonstrate that the person responsible actually did not base the decision on such a judgment." Thus, even if respondent could demonstrate that the training programs at Pennhurst were inconsistent with generally accepted or prevailing professional practice—if indeed there be such—this would not avail him so long as his training regimen was actually prescribed by the institution's professional staff.

Heller v. Doe

Supreme Court of the United States, 1993.
509 U.S. 312.

■ JUSTICE KENNEDY delivered the opinion of the Court.

In the Commonwealth of Kentucky, involuntary civil commitments of those alleged to be mentally retarded and of those alleged to be mentally ill are governed by separate statutory procedures. Two differences between these commitment proceedings are at issue in this case. First, at a final commitment hearing, the applicable burden of proof for involuntary commitment based on mental retardation is clear and convincing evidence, Ky.Rev.Stat.Ann. § 202B.160(2) (Michie 1991), while the standard for involuntary commitment based on mental illness is beyond a reasonable doubt, § 202A.076(2). Second, in commitment proceedings for mental retardation, unlike for mental illness, "[g]uardians and immediate family members" of the subject of the proceedings "may participate . . . as if a party to the proceedings," with all attendant rights, including the right to present evidence and to appeal. § 202B.160(3). Respondents are a class of mentally retarded persons committed involuntarily to Kentucky institutions. They argue that these distinctions are irrational and violate the Equal Protection Clause of the Fourteenth Amendment. They claim also that granting close family members and guardians the status of parties violates the Due Process Clause. We reject these contentions and hold the Kentucky statutes constitutional.

I

This case has a long and complicated history. It began in 1982 when respondents filed suit against petitioner, the Kentucky Secretary of the Cabinet for Human Resources, claiming that Kentucky's failure to provide certain procedural protections before institutionalizing people on the basis of mental retardation violated the Constitution. Kentucky has amended its civil commitment statutes several times since 1982, with each new statute being attacked in court by respondents. As the previous incarnations of this lawsuit have little effect on the issues currently before this Court, we limit our discussion to the current round of the litigation. See *Doe v. Cowherd*, 770 F.Supp. 354, 355–356 (WD Ky.1991) (recounting the procedural history).

At issue here are elements of Kentucky's statutory procedures, enacted in 1990, for the involuntary commitment of the mentally retarded. In many respects the procedures governing commitment of the mentally retarded and the mentally ill are parallel. The statutes recognize a large class of persons who can petition for an individual's involuntary commitment, whether on grounds of mental retardation or mental illness. Ky.Rev.Stat.Ann. § 202B.100(3) (Michie 1991) (mental retardation); § 202A.051 (mental illness). Upon filing of the petition, the trial court must appoint counsel to represent the individual in question, unless he retains private counsel. § 202B.210 (mental retardation); § 202A.121 (mental illness). The trial court also must examine the person who filed the petition and, if there is probable cause to believe that the individual who is the subject of the petition should be involuntarily committed, the court must order his examination by two qualified professionals. §§ 202B.100(5), (6)(c) (mental retardation); §§ 202A.051(5), (6)(c) (mental illness). The subject of the proceeding has the right to retain a professional of his own choosing, who may "witness and participate in any examination" of him. § 202B.140 (mental retardation); § 202A.066 (mental illness). In cases of commitment for mental retardation, a professional retained by the subject's "parent or guardian" also must be permitted to witness and participate in any examination. § 202B.140.

If both qualified professionals certify that the individual meets the criteria for involuntary commitment, the trial court must conduct a preliminary hearing. § 202B.130 (mental retardation); § 202A.061 (mental illness). At the hearing, the court must receive as evidence the reports of these two professionals and any other professional retained under the statute. § 202B.160(1) (mental retardation); § 202A.076(1) (mental illness). The individual whose commitment is sought may testify and may call and cross-examine witnesses. § 202B.160(1) (mental retardation); § 202A.076(1) (mental illness). In cases of mental retardation, at both the preliminary hearing and, if there is one, the final hearing, Kentucky law provides particular rights to guardians and immediate family members:

> "Guardians and immediate family members of the respondent shall be allowed to attend all hearings, conferences or similar proceedings; may be represented by private counsel, if desired; may participate in the hearings or conferences as if a party to the proceedings; may cross-examine witnesses if desired; and shall have standing to appeal any adverse decision." § 202B.160(3)

See also § 202B.230. If the trial court determines that there is probable cause to believe that the subject should be involuntarily committed, it proceeds to a final hearing. § 202B.100(8) (mental retardation); § 202A.051(9) (mental illness).

At the final hearing, the State, through the county attorney for the county in which the person subject to the proceeding lives, prosecutes the petition, § 202B.019 (mental retardation); § 202A.016 (mental illness), and counsel for the person defends against institutionalization. At this hearing, "[t]he manner of proceeding and the rules of evidence shall be the same as those in any criminal proceeding." § 202B.160(2) (mental retardation); § 202A.076(2) (mental illness). As in the preliminary hearing, the subject of the proceedings may testify and call and cross-examine witnesses. § 202B.160(2) (mental retardation); § 202A.076(2) (mental illness). In proceedings for commitment based on mental retardation, the standard of proof is clear and convincing evidence, § 202B.160(2); for mental illness, the standard is proof beyond a reasonable doubt, § 202A.076(2). For commitment of the mentally retarded, four propositions must be proved by clear and convincing evidence: "(1) The person is a mentally retarded person; (2) The person presents a danger or a threat of danger to self, family, or others; (3) The least restrictive alternative mode of treatment presently available requires placement in [a residential treatment center]; and (4) Treatment that can reasonably benefit the person is available in [a residential treatment center]." § 202B.040. The criteria for commitment of the mentally ill are in substance identical, requiring proof beyond a reasonable doubt that an individual "is a mentally ill person: (1) Who presents a danger or threat of danger to self, family or others as a result of the mental illness; (2) Who can reasonably benefit from treatment; and (3) For whom hospitalization is the least restrictive alternative mode of treatment presently available." § 202A.026. Appeals from involuntary commitment proceedings are taken in the same manner as other appeals from the trial court. § 202B.230 (mental retardation); § 202A.141 (mental illness).

After enactment of the 1990 modifications, respondents moved for summary judgment in their pending lawsuit against petitioner. They argued, among other things, that the differences in treatment between the mentally retarded and the mentally ill—the different standards of proof and the right of immediate family members and guardians to participate as parties in commitment proceedings for the mentally retarded but not the mentally ill—violated the Equal Protection Clause's prohibition of distinctions that lack a rational basis, and that participation by family members and guardians violated the Due Process Clause. The District Court for the Western District of Kentucky accepted these arguments and granted summary judgment to respondents on these and other grounds not at issue here, and the Court of Appeals for the Sixth Circuit affirmed. We granted Kentucky's petition for *certiorari* and now reverse.

[III]

We many times have said, and but weeks ago repeated, that rational-basis review in equal protection analysis "is not a license for courts to judge the wisdom, fairness, or logic of legislative choices." Nor does it authorize "the judiciary [to] sit as a superlegislature to judge the wisdom or desirability of legislative policy determinations made in areas that neither affect fundamental rights nor proceed along suspect lines." For these reasons, a classification neither involving fundamental rights nor proceeding along suspect lines is accorded a strong presumption of validity. Such a classification cannot run afoul of the Equal Protection Clause if there is a rational relationship between the disparity of treatment and some legitimate governmental purpose. Further, a legislature that creates these categories need not "actually articulate at any time the purpose or rationale supporting its classification." Instead, a classification "must be upheld against equal protection challenge if there is any reasonably conceivable state of facts that could provide a rational basis for the classification."

A State, moreover, has no obligation to produce evidence to sustain the rationality of a statutory classification. "[A] legislative choice is not subject to courtroom factfinding and may be based on rational speculation unsupported by evidence or empirical data." A statute is presumed constitutional, and "[t]he burden is on the one attacking the legislative arrangement to negative every conceivable basis which might support it," whether or not the basis has a foundation in the record. Finally, courts are compelled under rational-basis review to accept a legislature's generalizations even when there is an imperfect fit between means and ends. A classification does not fail rational-basis review because it " 'is not made with mathematical nicety or because in practice it results in some inequality.' " "The problems of government are practical ones and may justify, if they do not require, rough accommodations—illogical, it may be, and unscientific." We have applied rational-basis review in previous cases involving the mentally retarded and the mentally ill. See *Cleburne.* In neither case did we purport to apply a different standard of rational-basis review from that just described.

True, even the standard of rationality as we so often have defined it must find some footing in the realities of the subject addressed by the legislation. That requirement is satisfied here. Kentucky has proffered more than adequate justifications for the differences in treatment between the mentally retarded and the mentally ill.

A

Kentucky argues that a lower standard of proof in commitments for mental retardation follows from the fact that mental retardation is easier to diagnose than is mental illness. That general proposition should cause little surprise, for mental retardation is a developmental disability that becomes apparent before adulthood. See American Psychiatric Assn., Diagnostic and Statistical Manual of Mental Disorders 29 (3d rev. ed. 1987) (hereinafter Manual of Mental Disorders); American Assn. on Mental Retardation, Mental Retardation: Definition, Classification, and Systems of Support 5, 16–18 (9th ed. 1992) (hereinafter Mental Retardation); S. Brakel, J. Parry, & B. Weiner, The Mentally Disabled and the Law 16–17, 37 (3d ed. 1985) (hereinafter Mentally Disabled); Ky.Rev.Stat.Ann. § 202B.010(9) (Michie 1991). By the time the person reaches 18 years of age the documentation and other evidence of the condition have been accumulated for years. Mental illness, on the other hand, may be sudden and may not occur, or at least manifest itself, until adulthood. See, *e.g.*, Manual of Mental Disorders 190 (onset of schizophrenia may occur any time during adulthood); *id.*, at 220, 229 (onset of depression usually is during adulthood). Furthermore, as we recognized in an earlier case, diagnosis of mental illness is difficult. See *Addington v. Texas*, 441 U.S. 418, 430 (1979). See also Mentally Disabled 18. Kentucky's basic premise that mental retardation is easier to diagnose than is mental illness has a sufficient basis in fact. See, e.g., *id.*, at 16; Ellis & Luckasson, *Mentally Retarded Criminal Defendants*, 53 Geo.Wash.L.Rev. 414, 438–439 (1985).

This difference between the two conditions justifies Kentucky's decision to assign a lower standard of proof in commitment proceedings involving the mentally retarded. In assigning the burden of proof, Kentucky was determining the "risk of error" faced by the subject of the proceedings. *Addington v. Texas, supra,* at 423. If diagnosis is more difficult in cases of mental illness than in instances of mental retardation, a higher burden of proof for the former tends to equalize the risks of an erroneous determination that the subject of a commitment proceeding has the condition in question.[1] See G. Keppel, Design and Analysis 65–68 (1973). From the diagnostic standpoint alone, Kentucky's differential burdens of proof (as well as the other statutory distinction at issue) are rational.

There is, moreover, a "reasonably conceivable state of facts" from which Kentucky could conclude that the second prerequisite to commitment—that "[t]he person presents a danger or a threat of danger to self, family, or others," Ky.Rev.Stat.Ann. § 202B.040 (Michie 1991)— is established more easily, as a general rule, in the case of the mentally retarded. Previous instances of violent behavior are an important indicator of future violent tendencies. See, e.g., J. Monahan, The Clinical Prediction of Violent Behavior 71–72 (1981) (hereinafter Monahan); Kozol, Boucher, & Garofalo, *The Diagnosis and Treatment of Dangerousness,* 18 Crime & Delinquency 371, 384 (1972). Mental retardation is a permanent, relatively static condition, see Mentally Disabled 37, so a determination of dangerousness may be made with some accuracy based on previous behavior. We deal here with adults only, so almost by definition in the case of the retarded there is an 18-year record upon which to rely.

This is not so with the mentally ill. Manifestations of mental illness may be sudden, and past behavior may not be an adequate predictor of future actions. Prediction of future behavior is complicated as well by the difficulties inherent in diagnosis of mental illness. *Developments in the Law—Civil Commitment of the Mentally Ill,* 87 Harv.L.Rev. 1190, 1242–1243 (1974). It is thus no surprise that many psychiatric predictions of future violent behavior by the mentally ill are inaccurate. See, *e.g.,* Steadman, *Employing Psychiatric Predictions of Dangerous Behavior: Policy vs. Fact,* in Dangerous Behavior: A Problem in Law and Mental Health 123, 125–128 (C. Frederick ed. 1978); Monahan 47– 49. For these reasons, it would have been plausible for Kentucky to conclude that the dangerousness determination was more accurate as to the mentally retarded than the mentally ill.

A statutory classification fails rational-basis review only when it " 'rests on grounds wholly irrelevant to the achievement of the State's

---

[1]   JUSTICE SOUTER suggests that this description of the function of burdens of proof is inconsistent with *Addington v. Texas.* His reasoning, however, would impose the due process conception of burdens of proof on a State's policy decision as to which standard is most appropriate in the circumstances. The Due Process Clause sets the minimum standard of proof required in particular contexts, based on consideration both of the respective interests of the State and individual and of the risk of erroneous decisions. A State is free to adopt any burden of proof that meets or exceeds the constitutional minimum required by due process, and a State may select a standard of proof based on any rational policy of its choice. It may seek, as JUSTICE SOUTER would require, to balance the respective interests of the affected parties. But it may also calibrate its standard of proof in an effort to establish the risk of error at a certain level.

objective.' " Because ease of diagnosis is relevant to two of the four inquiries, it is not "wholly irrelevant" to the achievement of Kentucky's objective, and thus the statutory difference in the applicable burden of proof survives rational-basis review. In any event, it is plausible for Kentucky to have found that, for purposes of determining the acceptable risk of error, diagnosis and dangerousness are the most critical factors in the commitment decision, so the appropriate burden of proof should be tied to them.

There is a further, more far-reaching rationale justifying the different burdens of proof: The prevailing methods of treatment for the mentally retarded, as a general rule, are much less invasive than are those given the mentally ill. The mentally ill are subjected to medical and psychiatric treatment which may involve intrusive inquiries into the patient's innermost thoughts, see Meissner & Nicholi, The Psychotherapies: Individual, Family, and Group, in The Harvard Guide to Modern Psychiatry 357–385 (A. Nicholi ed. 1978) (hereinafter Harvard Guide), and use of psychotropic drugs, see Baldessarini, Chemotherapy, in Harvard Guide 387–431; Berger, *Medical Treatment of Mental Illness*, 200 Science 974 (1978); Mentally Disabled 327–330; Brief for American Psychological Association as *Amicus Curiae* in *Washington v. Harper*, O.T. 1988, No. 88–599, pp. 10–11. By contrast, the mentally retarded in general are not subjected to these medical treatments. Rather, " 'because mental retardation is . . . a learning disability and training impairment rather than an illness,' " *Youngberg v. Romeo*, 457 U.S. 307, 309, n.1 (1982), quoting Brief for American Psychiatric Association as *Amicus Curiae* in *Youngberg v. Romeo*, O.T. 1981, No. 80–1429, p. 4, n.1, the mentally retarded are provided "habilitation," which consists of education and training aimed at improving self-care and self-sufficiency skills. See *Youngberg, supra*, at 309, n.1; M. Rosen, G. Clark, & M. Kivitz, Habilitation of the Handicapped 47–59 (1977); Mentally Disabled 332.

It is true that the loss of liberty following commitment for mental illness and mental retardation may be similar in many respects; but the different treatment to which a committed individual is subjected provides a rational basis for Kentucky to decide that a greater burden of proof is needed before a person may be committed for mental illness. The procedures required before the government acts often depend on the nature and extent of the burden or deprivation to be imposed. For example, because confinement in prison is punitive and hence more onerous than confinement in a mental hospital, the Due Process Clause subjects the former to proof beyond a reasonable doubt, whereas it requires in the latter case only clear and convincing evidence, *Addington v. Texas, supra*. It may also be true that some persons committed for mental retardation are subjected to more intrusive treatments while confined. Nonetheless, it would have been plausible for the Kentucky Legislature to believe that most mentally retarded individuals who are committed receive treatment that is different from, and less invasive than, that to which the mentally ill are subjected. [T]hus, since " 'the question is at least debatable,' " rational-basis review permits a legislature to use just this sort of generalization.

These distinctions may explain, too, the differences in treatment between the mentally retarded and the mentally ill that have long existed in Anglo-American law. At English common law there was a "marked distinction" in the treatment accorded "idiots" (the mentally retarded) and "lunatics" (the mentally ill). 1 F. Pollock & F. Maitland, The History of English Law 481 (2d ed.1909) (hereinafter Pollack and Maitland). As Blackstone explained, a retarded person became a ward of the King, who had a duty to preserve the individual's estate and provide him with "necessaries," but the King could profit from the wardship. In contrast, the King was required to "provide for the custody and sustentation of [the mentally ill], and preserve their lands and the profits of them," but the King was prohibited from profiting thereby. 1 W. Blackstone, Commentaries *302–*304. See Pollack and Maitland 481; S. Herr, Rights and Advocacy for Retarded People 9–10 (1983).

Ancient lineage of a legal concept does not give it immunity from attack for lacking a rational basis. That the law has long treated the classes as distinct, however, suggests that there is a commonsense distinction between the mentally retarded and the mentally ill. The differentiation continues to the present day. A large majority of States have separate involuntary commitment laws for the two groups, and many States as well have separate agencies for addressing their needs.

Kentucky's burden of proof scheme, then, can be explained by differences in the ease of diagnosis and the accuracy of the prediction of future dangerousness and by the nature of the treatment received after commitment. Each of these rationales, standing on its own, would suffice to establish a rational basis for the distinction in question.

B

There is a rational basis also for the other distinction challenged by respondents: that Kentucky allows close relatives and guardians to participate as parties in proceedings to commit the mentally retarded but not the mentally ill. As we have noted, by definition, mental retardation has its onset during a person's developmental period. Mental retardation, furthermore, results in "deficits or impairments in adaptive functioning," that is to say, "the person's effectiveness in areas such as social skills, communication, and daily living skills, and how well the person meets the standards of personal independence and social responsibility expected of his or her age by his or her cultural group." Manual of Mental Disorders 28–29. See also Mental Retardation 5–6, 15–16, 38–41. Based on these facts, Kentucky may have concluded that close relatives and guardians, both of whom likely have intimate knowledge of a mentally retarded person's abilities and experiences, have valuable insights that should be considered during the involuntary commitment process.

Mental illness, by contrast, may arise or manifest itself with suddenness only after minority, when the afflicted person's immediate family members have no knowledge of the medical condition and have long ceased to provide care and support. Further, determining the proper course of treatment may be far less dependent upon observations made in a household setting. Indeed, we have noted the severe difficulties inherent in psychiatric diagnosis conducted by experts in the field. *Addington v. Texas*, 441 U.S., at 430. See also Mentally Disabled 18. In addition, adults previously of sound mental health who are diagnosed as mentally ill may have a need for privacy that justifies the State in confining a commitment proceeding to the smallest group compatible with due process. Based on these facts, Kentucky may have concluded that participation as parties by relatives and guardians of the mentally ill would not in most cases have been of sufficient help to the trier of fact to justify the additional burden and complications of granting party status. To be sure, Kentucky could have provided relatives and guardians of the mentally retarded some participation in commitment proceedings by methods short of providing them status as parties. That, however, is irrelevant in rational-basis review. We do not require Kentucky to have chosen the least restrictive means of achieving its legislative end.

[V]

In sum, there are plausible rationales for each of the statutory distinctions challenged by respondents in this case. It could be that "[t]he assumptions underlying these rationales [are] erroneous, but the very fact that they are 'arguable' is sufficient, on rational-basis review, to 'immunize' the [legislative] choice from constitutional challenge."[4]

The judgment of the Court of Appeals for the Sixth Circuit is

Reversed.

■ JUSTICE O'CONNOR, concurring in the judgment in part and dissenting in part.

I agree with JUSTICE SOUTER that Kentucky's differential standard of proof for committing the mentally ill and the mentally retarded is irrational and therefore join Part II of his opinion. I conclude, however, that there is a rational basis for permitting close relatives and guardians to participate as parties in proceedings to commit the mentally retarded but not the mentally ill. As the Court points out, there are sufficiently plausible and legitimate reasons for the legislative determination in this area. [L]ike my colleagues, I would not reach the question whether heightened equal protection scrutiny should be applied to the Kentucky scheme.

■ JUSTICE BLACKMUN, dissenting.

I join JUSTICE SOUTER's dissenting opinion, for I agree with him that this statute is not even rational. I write separately only to note my continuing adherence to the view that laws that discriminate against individuals with mental retardation, or infringe upon fundamental rights, are subject to heightened review.

■ JUSTICE SOUTER, with whom JUSTICE BLACKMUN and JUSTICE STEVENS join, and with whom JUSTICE O'CONNOR joins [in part], dissenting.

---

[4] Under a previous version of Kentucky's laws relating to the commitment of the mentally retarded, application by the parents or guardian of a mentally retarded person for placement in a mental retardation treatment center was treated as a voluntary commitment to which the procedural requirements of involuntary commitments were inapplicable. In a previous decision, the Court of Appeals held that persons committed upon application of parents or guardians must be considered to have been admitted involuntarily. *Doe v. Austin*, 848 F.2d 1386, 1391–1392 (CA6 1988). We denied Kentucky's petition for *certiorari* from this decision, and Kentucky subsequently amended its statutes to remove this provision. In its brief, however, Kentucky again attacks this prior holding of the Court of Appeals. Even were this issue not mooted by the repeal of the provision at issue, it is not "fairly included" within the questions on which we granted *certiorari*, this Court's Rule 14.1(a).

Because I conclude that Kentucky's provision of different procedures for the institutionalization of the mentally retarded and the mentally ill is not supported by any rational justification, I respectfully dissent.

[O]bviously there are differences between mental retardation and mental illness. They are distinct conditions, they have different manifestations, they require different forms of care or treatment, and the course of each differs. It is without doubt permissible for the State to treat those who are mentally retarded differently in some respects from those who are mentally ill. The question here, however, is whether some difference between the two conditions rationally can justify the particular disparate treatment accorded under this Kentucky statute.

The first distinction wrought by the statute is the imposition of a lesser standard of proof for involuntary institutionalization where the alleged basis of a need for confinement is mental retardation rather than mental illness. As the Court observes, four specific propositions must be proven before a person may be involuntarily institutionalized on the basis of mental retardation: "that: (1) [t]he person is a mentally retarded person; (2) [t]he person presents a danger or a threat of danger to self, family, or others; (3) [t]he least restrictive alternative mode of treatment presently available requires placement in [a state-run institution]; and (4) [t]reatment that can reasonably benefit the person is available in [a state-run institution]." Ky.Rev.Stat.Ann. § 202B.040 (Michie 1991). At issue in this case is only the application of this provision to adults who have not been shown to be mentally retarded, but who are simply alleged to be. The subject of such a proceeding retains as full an interest in liberty as anyone else. The State of Kentucky has deemed this liberty interest so precious that, before one may be institutionalized on the basis of mental illness, the statutory prerequisites must be shown "beyond a reasonable doubt." § 202A.076(2). However, when the allegation against the individual is one of mental retardation, he is deprived of the protection of that high burden of proof. The first question here, then, is whether, in light of the State's decision to provide that high burden of proof in involuntary commitment proceedings where illness is alleged, there is something about mental retardation that can rationally justify provision of less protection.

[I]n concluding [t]hat the demands of minimal rationality are satisfied if burdens of proof rise simply with difficulties of proof, the Court misunderstands the principal object in setting burdens. [B]urdens of proof are assigned and risks of error are allocated not to reflect the mere difficulty of avoiding error, but the importance of avoiding it as judged after a thorough consideration of those respective interests of the parties that will be affected by the allocation.

[T]he question whether a lower burden of proof is rationally justified, then, turns not only on whether ease of diagnosis and proof of dangerousness differ as between cases of illness and retardation, but also on whether there are differences in the respective interests of the public and the subjects of the commitment proceedings, such that the two groups subject to commitment can rationally be treated differently by imposing a lower standard of proof for commitment of the retarded. The answer is clearly that they can not. While difficulty of proof, and of interpretation of evidence, could legitimately counsel against setting the standard so high that the State may be unable to satisfy it (thereby effectively thwarting efforts to satisfy legitimate interests in protection, care, and treatment), that would at most justify a lower standard in the allegedly more difficult cases of illness, not in the easier cases of retardation. We do not lower burdens of proof merely because it is easy to prove the proposition at issue, nor do we raise them merely because it is difficult.[5] Nor do any other reasonably conceivable facts cut in favor of the distinction in treatment drawn by the Kentucky statute. Both the ill and the retarded may be dangerous, each may require care, and the State's interest is seemingly of equal strength in each category of cases. No one has or would argue that the value of liberty varies somehow depending on whether one is alleged to be ill or retarded, and a mentally retarded person has as much to lose by civil commitment to an institution as a mentally ill counterpart, including loss of liberty to "choos[e] his own friends and companions, selec[t] daily activities, decid[e] what to eat, and retai[n] a level of personal privacy," among other things. Brief for American Association on Mental Retardation (AAMR) *et al.* as *Amici Curiae* 12 (AAMR Br.). [E]ven assuming, then, that the assertion of different degrees of difficulty of proof both of mental illness and mental retardation and of the dangerousness inherent in each condition is true (an assertion for which there is no support in the record), it lends not a shred of rational support to the decision to discriminate against the retarded in allocating the risk of erroneous curtailment of liberty.

The Court also rests its conclusion on the view that "it would have been plausible for the Kentucky Legislature to believe that most mentally retarded individuals who are committed receive treatment that is . . . less invasive tha[n] that to which the mentally ill are subjected." Nothing cited by the Court, however, demonstrates that such a belief would have been plausible for the Kentucky Legislature, nor does the Court's discussion render it plausible now. One example of the invasiveness to which the Court refers is the use of (and the results of the administration of) psychotropic drugs. I take no exception to the proposition that they are extensively used in treating mental illness. Nor do I except to the proposition that the appropriate and perhaps characteristic response to mental retardation, but not to mental illness, is that kind of training in the necessities of self-sufficiency known as "habilitation."

Neither of these propositions tells us, however, that the same invasive mind-altering medication prescribed for mental illness is not also used in responding to mental retardation. And in fact, any apparent plausibility in the Court's suggestion that "the mentally retarded in general are not subjected to th[is] medical treatmen[t]," dissipates the moment we examine readily available material on the subject, including studies of institutional practices affecting the

---

[5] And indeed, to the extent *Addington v. Texas*, 441 U.S. 418 (1979), does discuss the difficulty of diagnosing mental illness, it supports use only of a lesser standard of proof because of the practical problems created by a supposed "serious question as to whether a state could ever prove beyond a reasonable doubt that an individual is both mentally ill and likely to be dangerous." Of course, in this case Kentucky has determined that the liberty of those alleged to be mentally ill is sufficiently precious that the State should assume the risk inherent in use of that higher standard.

retarded comparable to those studies concerning the treatment of mental illness cited by the Court. One recent examination of institutions for the mentally retarded in Kentucky's neighboring State of Missouri, for example, found that 76% of the institutionalized retarded receive some type of psychoactive drug and that fully 54% receive psychotropic drugs. See Intagliata & Rinck, *Psychoactive Drug Use in Public and Community Residential Facilities for Mentally Retarded Persons*, 21 Psychopharmacology Bull. 268, 272–273 (1985). Another study, this one national in scope, found that 38% of the residents of institutions for the mentally retarded receive psychotropic drugs. See Hill, Balow, & Bruininks, *A National Study of Prescribed Drugs in Institutions and Community Residential Facilities for Mentally Retarded People*, 21 Psychopharmacology Bull. 279, 283 (1985). "Surveys conducted within institutions [for the mentally retarded] have generally shown prevalences in the range of 30% to 50% of residents receiving psychotropic drugs at any given time." Aman & Singh, *Pharmacological Intervention*, in Handbook of Mental Retardation 347, 348 (J. Matson & J. Mulick eds., 2d ed.1991) (hereinafter Handbook of Mental Retardation).

Psychotropic drugs, according to the available material, are not only used to treat the institutionalized retarded, but are often misused. Indeed, the findings of fact by a United States District Court in North Carolina, another State nearby Kentucky, show that in three hospitals, 73% of persons committed as mentally retarded were receiving antipsychotic drugs. Less than half of these individuals had been diagnosed as mentally ill as well as mentally retarded following their commitment on the latter ground. See *Thomas S. v. Flaherty*, 699 F.Supp. 1178, 1187 (WDNC 1988), aff'd, 902 F.2d 250 (CA4), cert. denied, 498 U.S. 951–952 (1990). The District Court found that the institutionalized retarded plaintiffs "have been seriously endangered and injured by the inappropriate use of antipsychotic drugs." Flaherty, *supra*, at 1186. See also *Halderman v. Pennhurst State School Hospital*, 446 F.Supp. 1295, 1307–1308 (EDPa.1977), aff'd, 612 F.2d 84 (CA3 1979), rev'd on other grounds, 451 U.S. 1 (1981) (discussing evidence that 51% of the residents of a state institution for the mentally retarded received psychotropic drugs though less than one-third of those who received the drugs were monitored to determine the effectiveness of the treatment); Bates, Smeltzer, & Arnoczky, *Appropriate and Inappropriate Use of Psychotherapeutic Medications for Institutionalized Mentally Retarded Persons*, 90 Am.J. Mental Deficiency 363 (1986) (finding that between 39% and 54% of medications prescribed to mentally retarded persons are inappropriate for the conditions diagnosed).

These facts are consistent with a law review study of drugs employed in treating retardation, which observed that the reduction in the need for institutional staff resulting from the use of sedating drugs has promoted drug use in responding to retardation despite "frightening adverse effects [including the suppression of] learning and intellectual development." Plotkin & Gill, *Invisible Manacles: Drugging Mentally Retarded People*, 31 Stan.L.Rev. 637, 638 (1979). There being nothing in the record to suggest that Kentucky's institutions are free from these practices, and no reason whatever to assume so, there simply is no plausible basis for the Court's assumption that the institutional response to mental retardation is in the main less intrusive in this way than treatment of mental illness.

The Court also suggests that medical treatment for the mentally retarded is less invasive than in the case of the mentally ill because the mentally ill are subjected to psychiatric treatment that may involve intrusive enquiries into the patient's innermost thoughts. Again, I do not disagree that the mentally ill are often subject to intrusive psychiatric therapy. But the mentally retarded too are subject to intrusive therapy, as the available material on the medical treatment of the mentally retarded demonstrates. The mentally retarded are often subjected to behavior modification therapy to correct, among other things, anxiety disorders, phobias, hyperactivity, and antisocial behavior, therapy that may include aversive conditioning as well as forced exposure to objects that trigger severe anxiety reactions. See McNally, *Anxiety and Phobias*, in Handbook of Mental Retardation 413–423; Mulick, Hammer, & Dura, *Assessment and Management of Antisocial and Hyperactive Behavior*, in Handbook of Mental Retardation 397–412; Gardner, *Use of Behavior Therapy with the Mentally Retarded*, in Psychiatric Approaches to Mental Retardation 250–275 (F. Menolascino ed. 1970). Like drug therapy, psychiatric therapy for the mentally retarded can be, and has been misused. In one recent case, a Federal District Court found that "aversive procedures [including seclusion and physical restraints were] being inappropriately used with no evidence for their effectiveness and no relationship between the choice of the procedure and the analysis of the cause of the problem[,] . . . plac[ing] clients at extreme risk for maltreatment." *Lelsz v. Kavanagh*, 673 F.Supp. 828, 850 (NDTex.) (internal quotation marks and citation omitted), rev'd on unrelated grounds, 824 F.2d 372 (CA5 1987). Invasive behavior therapy for the mentally retarded, finally, is often employed together with drug therapy. See McNally, supra, at 413–423; Mulick, Hammer, & Dura, supra, at 397–412.

The same sorts of published authorities on which the Court relies, in sum, refute the contention that "[t]he prevailing methods of treatment for the mentally retarded, as a general rule, are much less invasive than are those given the mentally ill."[6] The available literature indicates that psychotropic drugs and invasive therapy are routinely administered to the retarded as well as the [mentally] ill, and there are no apparent differences of therapeutic regimes that would plausibly explain less rigorous commitment standards for those alleged to be mentally retarded than for those alleged to be mentally ill.

[W]ith respect to the involvement of family members and guardians in the commitment proceeding, the Court holds it to be justified by the fact that mental retardation "has its onset during a person's

---

[6] I also see little point in the Court's excursion into the historical difference in treatment between so-called "idiots," and so-called "lunatics." Surely the Court does not intend to suggest that the irrational and scientifically unsupported beliefs of pre–19th–century England can support any distinction in treatment between the mentally ill and the mentally retarded today. At that time, "lunatics" were "[s]een as demonically possessed or the products of parental sin [and] were often punished or left to perish." See S. Herr, Rights and Advocacy for Retarded People 9 (1983). The primary purpose of an adjudication of "idiocy" appears to have been to "depriv[e] [an individual] of [his] property and its profits." Id., at 10. Those without wealth "were dealt with like other destitute or vagrant persons through workhouses and houses of correction." Id., at 11.

developmental period," while mental illness "may arise or manifest itself with suddenness only after minority." The Court suggests that a mentally ill person's parents may have "ceased to provide care and support" for him well before the onset of illness, whereas parents are more likely to have retained connection with a retarded son or daughter, whose "proper course of treatment" may depend on matters related to "observations made in a household setting."

These suggested distinctions, if true, would apparently not apply to guardians, whose legal obligations to protect the persons and estates of their wards would seem to require as much connection to the one class of people as to the other. In any event, although these differences might justify a scheme in which immediate relatives and guardians were automatically called as witnesses in cases seeking institutionalization on the basis of mental retardation, they are completely unrelated to those aspects of the statute to which *Doe* objects: permitting these immediate relatives and guardians to be involved "as parties" so as to give them, among other things, the right to appeal as "adverse" a decision not to institutionalize the individual who is subject to the proceedings. Where the third party supports commitment, someone who is alleged to be retarded is faced not only with a second advocate for institutionalization, but with a second prosecutor with the capacity to call and cross-examine witnesses, to obtain expert testimony and to raise an appeal that might not otherwise be taken, whereas a person said to require commitment on the basis of mental illness is not. This is no mere theoretical difference, and my suggestion that relatives or guardians may support curtailment of liberty finds support in the record in this case. It indicates that of the 431 commitments to Kentucky's state-run institutions for the mentally retarded during a period between 1982 and the middle of 1985, all but one were achieved through the application or consent of family members or guardians.

The Court simply points to no characteristic of mental retardation that could rationally justify imposing this burden of a second prosecutor on those alleged to be mentally retarded where the State has decided not to impose it upon those alleged to be mentally ill. Even if we assumed a generally more regular connection between the relatives and guardians of those alleged to be retarded than those said to be mentally ill, it would not explain why the former should be subject to a second prosecutor when the latter are not.

The same may be said about the Court's second suggested justification, that the mentally ill may have a need for privacy not shown by the retarded. Even assuming the ill need some additional privacy, and that participation of others in the commitment proceeding should therefore be limited "to the smallest group compatible with due process," why should the retarded be subject to a second prosecutor? The Court provides no answer.

Without plausible justification, Kentucky is being allowed to draw a distinction that is difficult to see as resting on anything other than the stereotypical assumption that the retarded are "perpetual children," an assumption that has historically been taken to justify the disrespect and "grotesque mistreatment" to which the retarded have been subjected. See *Cleburne* (STEVENS, J., concurring) (internal quotation marks and citation omitted). As we said in *Cleburne*, the mentally retarded are not "all cut from the same pattern: . . . they range from those whose disability is not immediately evident to those who must be constantly cared for."

[I]n the absence of any rational justification for the disparate treatment here either with respect to the burdens of proof or the participation of third parties in institutionalization proceedings, I would affirm the judgment of the Court of Appeals[.]

NOTES ON YOUNGBERG AND HELLER

1. The Constitutional Law of Institutionalization. The constitutional law governing the institutionalization of people with disabilities is too extensive and complex to be treated fully in a general disability rights law casebook. For a fuller treatment, see Michael L. Perlin, Mental Disability Law: Cases and Materials (2005). In O'CONNOR V. DONALDSON, 422 U.S. 563 (1975), a case involving the institutionalization of a plaintiff with a psychiatric disability (rather than an intellectual disability as in *Youngberg*), the Court held that a state could not involuntarily commit such an individual unless he is dangerous to himself or others or it provides him treatment:

A finding of "mental illness" alone cannot justify a State's locking a person up against his will and keeping him indefinitely in simple custodial confinement. Assuming that that term can be given a reasonably precise content and that the "mentally ill" can be identified with reasonable accuracy, there is still no constitutional basis for confining such persons involuntarily if they are dangerous to no one and can live safely in freedom.

May the State confine the mentally ill merely to ensure them a living standard superior to that they enjoy in the private community? That the State has a proper interest in providing care and assistance to the unfortunate goes without saying. But the mere presence of mental illness does not disqualify a person from preferring his home to the comforts of an institution. Moreover, while the State may arguably confine a person to save him from harm, incarceration is rarely if ever a necessary condition for raising the living standards of those capable of surviving safely in freedom, on their own or with the help of family or friends.

May the State fence in the harmless mentally ill solely to save its citizens from exposure to those whose ways are different? One might as well ask if the State, to avoid public unease, could incarcerate all who are physically unattractive or socially eccentric. Mere public intolerance or animosity cannot constitutionally justify the deprivation of a person's physical liberty.

In short, a State cannot constitutionally confine without more a nondangerous individual who is capable of surviving safely in freedom by himself or with the help of willing and responsible family members or friends. Since the jury found, upon ample evidence, that O'Connor, as an agent of the State, knowingly did so confine Donaldson, it properly concluded that O'Connor violated Donaldson's constitutional right to freedom.

Relying on the jury's findings "that Donaldson was neither dangerous to himself nor dangerous to others" and "that, if mentally ill, Donaldson had not received treatment," the Court held that Donaldson had been unconstitutionally confined.

In JACKSON V. INDIANA, 406 U.S. 715, 738 (1972), the Court held that "due process requires that the nature and duration of commitment bear some reasonable relation to the purpose for which the individual is committed." Accordingly, it ruled that a person institutionalized because of his incompetence to stand trial on a criminal charge "cannot be held more than the reasonable period of time necessary to determine whether there is a substantial probability that he will attain that capacity in the foreseeable future. If it is determined that this is not the case, then the State must either institute the customary civil commitment proceeding that would be required to commit indefinitely any other citizen, or release the defendant." *Id.* See also *Foucha v. Louisiana*, 504 U.S. 71 (1992) (reaffirming *Jackson*).

Do *O'Connor* and *Jackson*, taken together, impose on states a *constitutional* obligation to provide treatment (or "habilitation") to individuals whom they institutionalize? *O'Connor* says that a state may not confine an individual unless she is a danger to herself or others or she needs treatment. If care and treatment was the basis for the commitment, *O'Connor* requires that the care and treatment be provided, doesn't it? And for individuals committed based on danger to self or others, *Jackson*'s holding that that the nature and duration of the commitment must reasonably follow the purposes of the commitment clearly requires that, once an individual no longer poses a danger to self or others, she must be released. If treatment is available that would reduce an individual's danger to self or others, and thus potentially make confinement unnecessary, is it "reasonably related" to the purpose of the commitment to confine the individual for years without providing that treatment?

The *Youngberg* Court addresses this question by holding that an institutionalized person is entitled to "minimally adequate training," which the Court defines as "such training as may be reasonable in light of respondent's liberty interests in safety and freedom from unreasonable restraints." Because Nicholas Romeo sought training that would reduce his aggressive and self-injurious behavior—even if, like training in self-care skills, it might achieve that result only indirectly—the Court holds that he had a constitutional interest in receiving the training. (That interest, however, is subject to the "professional judgment" standard, which is discussed in the next note.)

Note that it is uncontroversial among the justices that a state has affirmative constitutional obligations to those it institutionalizes. Under the general run of constitutional doctrine, the state does not owe individuals food, clothing, shelter, or protection from private depredations. See, *e.g.*, *DeShaney v. Winnebago County Dept. of Social Services*, 489 U.S. 189, 196–198 (1989).* But when a state confines an individual and

---

* For a critique of this principle, see, for example, Susan Bandes, *The Negative Constitution: A Critique*, 88 Mich. L. Rev. 2271 (1990).

necessarily limits her ability to provide for her own interests—as in incarceration or, as *Youngberg* makes clear, civil commitment—the state assumes affirmative obligations to provide for those basic necessities. See *id.* at 200 ("The rationale for this principle is simple enough: when the State by the affirmative exercise of its power so restrains an individual's liberty that it renders him unable to care for himself, and at the same time fails to provide for his basic human needs—*e.g.*, food, clothing, shelter, medical care, and reasonable safety—it transgresses the substantive limits on state action set by the Eighth Amendment and the Due Process Clause.").

2.   The Professional Judgment Standard. Adopting the position Chief Judge Seitz took in his separate opinion in the Third Circuit, the Court holds that the state's affirmative obligations are limited by a professional judgment standard: "[T]he Constitution only requires that the courts make certain that professional judgment in fact was exercised. It is not appropriate for the courts to specify which of several professionally acceptable choices should have been made." The Court elaborates that "the decision, if made by a professional, is presumptively valid; liability may be imposed only when the decision by the professional is such a substantial departure from accepted professional judgment, practice, or standards as to demonstrate that the person responsible actually did not base the decision on such a judgment."

Susan Stefan argues that [a]lthough the professional judgment standard may be appropriate to measure the level of services that a state is constitutionally bound to provide to individuals in its custody, the standard is inappropriate to justify the imposition of unwanted government "services" that restrict constitutional liberty, such as forcible medication, prolonged restraint, and prohibitions on patients' family visitation. Susan Stefan, *Leaving Civil Rights to the "Experts": From Deference to Abdication Under the Professional Judgment Standard*, 102 Yale L.J. 639, 642 (1992). She argues that courts "regard the professional-client relationship as befitting protection from state interference because they envision it as an intimate partnership dedicated to the client's benefit and furtherance of the client's goals," but that "neither the idealized values attributed to medical professionals nor their actual perspectives and priorities have much in common with the ideals of autonomy, self-determination, and individualism embodied in the Constitution." *Id.* at 644. Moreover, she argues, [t]he Court's image of "freely chosen professional-client interaction" is especially inapposite in "institutional settings where the professionals are state actors, the professional-client relationship is permeated with state concerns and conflicts of interest, and the clients are an indigent and captive population." *Id.* See also Richard H. Fallon, Jr., *Individual Rights and the Powers of Government*, 27 Ga. L. Rev. 343, 382 (1993) ("[T]hough experts on the scene may know more than courts about the interests supporting claims of government power and discretion, those officials may be less sensitive to the interests underlying claims of constitutional rights. Human nature being as it is, officials are likely to prefer that things be done in a way that promotes order and preserves routines that the officials find comfortable because a central function of rights is to preserve spheres of privacy and autonomy against the order-imposing impulses of officialdom.").

Do you agree with these critiques? Granting that professional judgment will often give short shrift to important interests, isn't Justice Powell nonetheless right that judges and jurors face severe limitations on their ability to comprehend the complex choices and tradeoffs that are inherent in the day-to-day operations of an institution? Consider what other legal standard the Court could have adopted.

3. **Nicholas Romeo.** Note that all of the justices, accepting the concession of Nicholas Romeo's counsel, presumed that Romeo could never live outside of an institution. But

> "ten months after the Court's decision, Nicholas Romeo moved to a community residence in Philadelphia." Timothy M. Cook, *The Americans with Disabilities Act: The Move to Integration*, 64 Temp. L. Rev. 393, 443 (1991). Eight years later, Cook observed that "[s]ince April 1983, Romeo has been living, receiving services, and working part-time in his neighborhood." *Id.* Nicholas Romeo's experience was typical of those released from Pennhurst, the institution where he had been confined. See James W. (discussing three separate case studies of Pennhurst residents and their improvements in quality of life and ability after moving into community living arrangements after Pennhurst's closing).

Samuel R. Bagenstos & Margo Schlanger, *Hedonic Damages, Hedonic Adaptation, and Disability*, 60 Vand. L. Rev. 745, 782 n.177 (2007). As Cook reports, "[n]umerous studies have now demonstrated that persons with disabilities can live successfully in integrated settings. This is true even though they may possess low skill levels, exhibit severe aberrant behavior difficulties, or live in sparsely populated rural areas with lesser services available. Research shows that practically all people with disabilities can live and work in community settings, so long as they receive appropriate supports. All of the resources in institutional settings can be replicated in community settings." Cook, *supra*, at 444. Given the research Cook reports, and the experience of the former Pennhurst residents, ought disability rights advocates bring cases to improve institutional conditions, as in *Youngberg*, or to seek deinstitutionalization, as in *Olmstead* (a principal case above). What about the concerns Justice Kennedy raised in his *Olmstead* concurrence?

4. **Whither *Cleburne*?** Is *Heller* consistent with *Cleburne*? Justice Kennedy certainly takes pains in his *Heller* majority opinion to insist that the cases are consistent: "We have applied rational-basis review in previous cases involving the mentally retarded and the mentally ill. See *Cleburne*. In neither case did we purport to apply a different standard of rational-basis review from that just described." But although the *Cleburne* Court did not "purport" to apply a different standard than ordinary, minimal rational-basis review, its holding disregarded all of the normal rules governing that level of scrutiny: the permissibility of *post hoc* rationalizations, the notion that reform can take one step at a time, and so forth. The *Cleburne* Court carefully interrogated the reasons for treating the plaintiff's group home differently from other land uses; it did not engage in the sort of deference

that Justice Kennedy rightly describes as the hallmark of rational-basis review. Given the arguments and data presented in Justice Souter's dissent, could the Kentucky distinction between psychiatric and intellectual disabilities have survived under the sort of scrutiny the *Cleburne* Court actually applied?

2. CONSTITUTIONALITY OF FEDERAL DISABILITY RIGHTS STATUTES

INTRODUCTORY NOTE

As applied to private parties, the federal disability discrimination laws are rather clearly valid exercises of Congress's power, under the Commerce Clause, to regulate economic activity that, in the aggregate, substantially affects interstate commerce. See *Gonzales v. Raich*, 545 U.S. 1 (2005); *United States v. Morrison*, 529 U.S. 598 (2000). As applied to state and local government entities (the subject of this chapter) the federal disability discrimination laws are also rather clearly valid exercises of the commerce power—in *most* circumstances. The Fair Housing Act certainly is valid Commerce Clause legislation, because it regulates economic transactions, as is Title I (the employment title) and most if not all applications of Title II (the public services title) of the ADA. Section 504, as discussed in Section C, *supra*, has been uniformly upheld as a valid exercise of Congress's spending power. See Samuel R. Bagenstos, *The Anti-leveraging Principle and the Spending Clause After NFIB*, 101 Geo. L.J. 861, 912-916 (2013) (arguing that the Supreme Court's decision in *National Federation of Independent Business v. Sebelius*, 132 S.Ct. 2566 (2012), ought not to threaten the constitutionality of Section 504).

But the ADA has faced a number of serious constitutional challenges from states. Those states have not, by and large, challenged the *substance* of the requirements the ADA imposes on them. What they have challenged is the statute's *abrogation of state sovereign immunity* and concomitant authorization of a money damages remedy against the states. As explained in Section C, *supra*, Congress may not abrogate state sovereign immunity unless it is acting pursuant to its authority to enforce the Fourteenth Amendment. See *Seminole Tribe v. Florida*, 517 U.S. 44, 59–73 (1996). In *City of Boerne v. Flores*, 521 U.S. 507, 520 (1997), the Court held that a statute is not a valid exercise of Congress's Fourteenth Amendment enforcement authority unless there is a "congruence and proportionality" between the statute and a history or threat of constitutional violations. In a series of cases, states have argued that various provisions of the ADA lack the required congruence and proportionality, and that the statute therefore does not validly abrogate their sovereign immunity.

Board of Trustees of the University of Alabama v. Garrett

Supreme Court of the United States, 2001.
531 U.S. 356.

■ CHIEF JUSTICE REHNQUIST delivered the opinion of the Court.

We decide here whether employees of the State of Alabama may recover money damages by reason of the State's failure to comply with the provisions of Title I of the Americans with Disabilities Act of 1990 (ADA or Act), 104 Stat. 330, 42 U.S.C. §§ 12111–12117.[1] We hold that such suits are barred by the Eleventh Amendment.

The ADA prohibits certain employers, including the States, from "discriminat[ing] against a qualified individual with a disability because of the disability of such individual in regard to job application procedures, the hiring, advancement, or discharge of employees, employee compensation, job training, and other terms, conditions, and privileges of employment." §§ 12112(a), 12111(2), (5), (7). To this end, the Act requires employers to "mak[e] reasonable accommodations to the known physical or mental limitations of an otherwise qualified individual with a disability who is an applicant or employee, unless [the employer] can demonstrate that the accommodation would impose an undue hardship on the operation of the [employer's] business." § 12112(b)(5)(A). [T]he Act also prohibits employers from "utilizing standards, criteria, or methods of administration . . . that have the effect of discrimination on the basis of disability." § 12112(b)(3)(A).

[R]espondent Patricia Garrett, a registered nurse, was employed as the Director of Nursing, OB/Gyn/Neonatal Services, for the University of Alabama in Birmingham Hospital. In 1994, Garrett was diagnosed with breast cancer and subsequently underwent a lumpectomy, radiation treatment, and chemotherapy. Garrett's treatments required her to take substantial leave from work. Upon returning to work in July 1995, Garrett's supervisor informed Garrett that she would have to give up her Director position. Garrett then applied for and received a transfer to another, lower paying position as a nurse manager.

Respondent Milton Ash worked as a security officer for the Alabama Department of Youth Services (Department). Upon commencing this employment, Ash informed the Department that he suffered from chronic asthma and that his doctor recommended he avoid carbon monoxide and cigarette smoke, and Ash requested that the Department modify his duties to minimize his exposure to these substances. Ash was later diagnosed with sleep apnea and requested, again pursuant to his doctor's recommendation, that he be reassigned to daytime shifts to accommodate his condition. Ultimately, the Department granted none of the requested relief. Shortly after Ash filed a discrimination claim with the Equal Employment Opportunity Commission, he noticed that his performance evaluations were lower than those he had received on previous occasions.

Garrett and Ash filed separate lawsuits in the District Court, both seeking money damages under the ADA. Petitioners moved for

---

[1] Respondents' complaints in the United States District Court alleged violations of both Title I and Title II of the ADA, and petitioners' "Question Presented" can be read to apply to both sections. See Brief for Petitioners i; Brief for United States I. Though the briefs of the parties discuss both sections in their constitutional arguments, no party has briefed the question whether Title II of the ADA, dealing with the "services, programs, or activities of a public entity," 42 U.S.C. § 12132, is available for claims of employment discrimination when Title I of the ADA expressly deals with that subject. We are not disposed to decide the constitutional issue whether Title II, which has somewhat different remedial provisions from Title I, is appropriate legislation under § 5 of the Fourteenth Amendment when the parties have not favored us with briefing on the statutory question.

summary judgment, claiming that the ADA exceeds Congress' authority to abrogate the State's Eleventh Amendment immunity. In a single opinion disposing of both cases, the District Court agreed with petitioners' position and granted their motions for summary judgment. The cases were consolidated on appeal to the Eleventh Circuit. The Court of Appeals reversed.

[W]e granted *certiorari* to resolve a split among the Courts of Appeals on the question whether an individual may sue a State for money damages in federal court under the ADA.

I

The Eleventh Amendment provides:

"The Judicial power of the United States shall not be construed to extend to any suit in law or equity, commenced or prosecuted against one of the United States by Citizens of another State, or by Citizens or Subjects of any Foreign State."

Although by its terms the Amendment applies only to suits against a State by citizens of another State, our cases have extended the Amendment's applicability to suits by citizens against their own States. The ultimate guarantee of the Eleventh Amendment is that nonconsenting States may not be sued by private individuals in federal court.

We have recognized, however, that Congress may abrogate the States' Eleventh Amendment immunity when it both unequivocally intends to do so and "act[s] pursuant to a valid grant of constitutional authority." The first of these requirements is not in dispute here. See 42 U.S.C. § 12202 ("A State shall not be immune under the eleventh amendment to the Constitution of the United States from an action in [a] Federal or State court of competent jurisdiction for a violation of this chapter"). The question, then, is whether Congress acted within its constitutional authority by subjecting the States to suits in federal court for money damages under the ADA.

Congress may not, of course, base its abrogation of the States' Eleventh Amendment immunity upon the powers enumerated in Article I. *Seminole Tribe v. Florida* ("The Eleventh Amendment restricts the judicial power under Article III, and Article I cannot be used to circumvent the constitutional limitations placed upon federal jurisdiction"). In *Fitzpatrick v. Bitzer*, 427 U.S. 445 (1976), however, we held that "the Eleventh Amendment, and the principle of state sovereignty which it embodies, are necessarily limited by the enforcement provisions of § 5 of the Fourteenth Amendment." As a result, we concluded, Congress may subject nonconsenting States to suit in federal court when it does so pursuant to a valid exercise of its § 5 power. Our cases have adhered to this proposition. Accordingly, the ADA can apply to the States only to the extent that the statute is appropriate § 5 legislation.

[S]ection 5 of the Fourteenth Amendment grants Congress the power to enforce the substantive guarantees contained in [the Amendment] by enacting "appropriate legislation." See *City of Boerne v. Flores*, 521 U.S. 507, 536 (1997). Congress is not limited to mere legislative repetition of this Court's constitutional jurisprudence. "Rather, Congress' power 'to enforce' the Amendment includes the authority both to remedy and to deter violation of rights guaranteed thereunder by prohibiting a somewhat broader swath of conduct, including that which is not itself forbidden by the Amendment's text."

City of Boerne also confirmed, however, the long-settled principle that it is the responsibility of this Court, not Congress, to define the substance of constitutional guarantees. Accordingly, § 5 legislation reaching beyond the scope of § 1's actual guarantees must exhibit "congruence and proportionality between the injury to be prevented or remedied and the means adopted to that end."

II

The first step in applying these now familiar principles is to identify with some precision the scope of the constitutional right at issue. Here, that inquiry requires us to examine the limitations § 1 of the Fourteenth Amendment places upon States' treatment of the disabled.

[In *Cleburne*,] we considered an equal protection challenge to a city ordinance requiring a special use permit for the operation of a group home for the mentally retarded. The specific question before us was whether the Court of Appeals had erred by holding that mental retardation qualified as a "quasi-suspect" classification under our equal protection jurisprudence. We answered that question in the affirmative, concluding instead that such legislation incurs only the minimum "rational-basis" review applicable to general social and economic legislation.[4] In a statement that today seems quite prescient, we explained that

> "if the large and amorphous class of the mentally retarded were deemed quasi-suspect for the reasons given by the Court of Appeals, it would be difficult to find a principled way to distinguish a variety of other groups who have perhaps immutable disabilities setting them off from others, who cannot themselves mandate the desired legislative responses, and who can claim some degree of prejudice from at least part of the public at large. One need mention in this respect only the aging, the disabled, the mentally ill, and the infirm. We are reluctant to set out on that course, and we decline to do so."

Under rational-basis review, where a group possesses "distinguishing characteristics relevant to interests the State has the authority to implement," a State's decision to act on the basis of those differences does not give rise to a constitutional violation. "Such a classification cannot run afoul of the Equal Protection Clause if there is a rational relationship between the disparity of treatment and some legitimate governmental purpose." Moreover, the State need not articulate its reasoning at the moment a particular decision is made. Rather, the burden is upon the challenging party to negative " 'any

---

[4] Applying the basic principles of rationality review, *Cleburne* struck down the city ordinance in question. The Court's reasoning was that the city's purported justifications for the ordinance made no sense in light of how the city treated other groups similarly situated in relevant respects. Although the group home for the mentally retarded was required to obtain a special use permit, apartment houses, other multiple-family dwellings, retirement homes, nursing homes, sanitariums, hospitals, boarding houses, fraternity and sorority houses, and dormitories were not subject to the ordinance.

reasonably conceivable state of facts that could provide a rational basis for the classification.' "

JUSTICE BREYER suggests that Cleburne stands for the broad proposition that state decisionmaking reflecting "negative attitudes" or "fear" necessarily runs afoul of the Fourteenth Amendment. See (dissenting opinion) (quoting *Cleburne*). Although such biases may often accompany irrational (and therefore unconstitutional) discrimination, their presence alone does not a constitutional violation make. As we noted in *Cleburne*: "*[M]ere* negative attitudes, or fear, *unsubstantiated by factors which are properly cognizable in a zoning proceeding*, are not permissible bases for treating a home for the mentally retarded differently. . . . " (emphases added). This language, read in context, simply states the unremarkable and widely acknowledged tenet of this Court's equal protection jurisprudence that state action subject to rational-basis scrutiny does not violate the Fourteenth Amendment when it "rationally furthers the purpose identified by the State."

Thus, the result of *Cleburne* is that States are not required by the Fourteenth Amendment to make special accommodations for the disabled, so long as their actions toward such individuals are rational. They could quite hardheadedly—and perhaps hardheartedly—hold to job-qualification requirements which do not make allowance for the disabled. If special accommodations for the disabled are to be required, they have to come from positive law and not through the Equal Protection Clause.

III

Once we have determined the metes and bounds of the constitutional right in question, we examine whether Congress identified a history and pattern of unconstitutional employment discrimination by the States against the disabled. Just as § 1 of the Fourteenth Amendment applies only to actions committed "under color of state law," Congress' § 5 authority is appropriately exercised only in response to state transgressions. The legislative record of the ADA, however, simply fails to show that Congress did in fact identify a pattern of irrational state discrimination in employment against the disabled.

Respondents contend that the inquiry as to unconstitutional discrimination should extend not only to States themselves, but to units of local governments, such as cities and counties. All of these, they say, are "state actors" for purposes of the Fourteenth Amendment. This is quite true, but the Eleventh Amendment does not extend its immunity to units of local government. See *Lincoln County v. Luning*, 133 U.S. 529, 530 (1890). These entities are subject to private claims for damages under the ADA without Congress' ever having to rely on § 5 of the Fourteenth Amendment to render them so. It would make no sense to consider constitutional violations on their part, as well as by the States themselves, when only the States are the beneficiaries of the Eleventh Amendment.

Congress made a general finding in the ADA that "historically, society has tended to isolate and segregate individuals with disabilities, and, despite some improvements, such forms of discrimination against individuals with disabilities continue to be a serious and pervasive social problem." 42 U.S.C. § 12101(a)(2). The record assembled by Congress includes many instances to support such a finding. But the great majority of these incidents do not deal with the activities of States.

Respondents in their brief cite half a dozen examples from the record that did involve States. A department head at the University of North Carolina refused to hire an applicant for the position of health administrator because he was blind; similarly, a student at a state university in South Dakota was denied an opportunity to practice teach because the dean at that time was convinced that blind people could not teach in public schools. A microfilmer at the Kansas Department of Transportation was fired because he had epilepsy; deaf workers at the University of Oklahoma were paid a lower salary than those who could hear. The Indiana State Personnel Office informed a woman with a concealed disability that she should not disclose it if she wished to obtain employment.[6]

Several of these incidents undoubtedly evidence an unwillingness on the part of state officials to make the sort of accommodations for the disabled required by the ADA. Whether they were irrational under our decision in *Cleburne* is more debatable, particularly when the incident is described out of context. But even if it were to be determined that each incident upon fuller examination showed unconstitutional action on the part of the State, these incidents taken together fall far short of even suggesting the pattern of unconstitutional discrimination on which § 5 legislation must be based. Congress, in enacting the ADA, found that "some 43,000,000 Americans have one or more physical or mental disabilities." 42 U.S.C. § 12101(a)(1). In 1990, the States alone employed more than 4.5 million people. It is telling, we think, that given these large numbers, Congress assembled only such minimal evidence of unconstitutional state discrimination in employment against the disabled.

JUSTICE BREYER maintains that Congress applied Title I of the ADA to the States in response to a host of incidents representing unconstitutional state discrimination in employment against persons with disabilities. A close review of the relevant materials, however, undercuts that conclusion. JUSTICE BREYER's Appendix C consists not of legislative findings, but of unexamined, anecdotal accounts of "adverse, disparate treatment by state officials." Of course, as we have already explained, "adverse, disparate treatment" often does not amount to a constitutional violation where rational-basis scrutiny applies. These accounts, moreover, were submitted not directly to Congress but to the Task Force on the Rights and Empowerment of Americans with Disabilities, which made no findings on the subject of state discrimination in employment.[7] See the Task Force's Report entitled

---

[6] The record does show that some States, adopting the tenets of the eugenics movement of the early part of this century, required extreme measures such as sterilization of persons suffering from hereditary mental disease. These laws were upheld against constitutional attack 70 years ago in *Buck v. Bell*, 274 U.S. 200 (1927). But there is no indication that any State had persisted in requiring such harsh measures as of 1990 when the ADA was adopted.

[7] Only a small fraction of the anecdotes JUSTICE BREYER identifies in his Appendix C relate to state discrimination against the disabled in employment. At most, somewhere around 50 of these allegations describe conduct that could conceivably amount to constitutional violations by the States, and most of them are so general and brief that no firm conclusion can

From ADA to Empowerment (Oct. 12, 1990). And, had Congress truly understood this information as reflecting a pattern of unconstitutional behavior by the States, one would expect some mention of that conclusion in the Act's legislative findings. There is none. See 42 U.S.C. § 12101. Although JUSTICE BREYER would infer from Congress' general conclusions regarding societal discrimination against the disabled that the States had likewise participated in such action, the House and Senate committee reports on the ADA flatly contradict this assertion. After describing the evidence presented to the Senate Committee on Labor and Human Resources and its subcommittee (including the Task Force Report upon which the dissent relies), the Committee's Report reached, among others, the following conclusion: "Discrimination still persists in such critical areas as employment *in the private sector*, public accommodations, public services, transportation, and telecommunications." S.Rep.No.101–116, p. 6 (1989) (emphasis added). The House Committee on Education and Labor, addressing the ADA's employment provisions, reached the same conclusion: "[A]fter extensive review and analysis over a number of Congressional sessions, . . . there exists a compelling need to establish a clear and comprehensive Federal prohibition of discrimination on the basis of disability in the areas of employment *in the private sector*, public accommodations, public services, transportation, and telecommunications." H.R.Rep.No.101–485, pt. 2, p. 28 (1990) (emphasis added). Thus, not only is the inference JUSTICE BREYER draws unwarranted, but there is also strong evidence that Congress' failure to mention States in its legislative findings addressing discrimination in employment reflects that body's judgment that no pattern of unconstitutional state action had been documented.

Even were it possible to squeeze out of these examples a pattern of unconstitutional discrimination by the States, the rights and remedies created by the ADA against the States would raise the same sort of concerns as to congruence and proportionality as were found in *City of Boerne, supra*. For example, whereas it would be entirely rational (and therefore constitutional) for a state employer to conserve scarce financial resources by hiring employees who are able to use existing facilities, the ADA requires employers to "mak[e] existing facilities used by employees readily accessible to and usable by individuals with disabilities." 42 U.S.C. §§ 12112(5)(B), 12111(9). The ADA does except employers from the "reasonable accommodatio[n]" requirement where the employer "can demonstrate that the accommodation would impose an undue hardship on the operation of the business of such covered entity." § 12112(b)(5)(A). However, even with this exception, the accommodation duty far exceeds what is constitutionally required in that it makes unlawful a range of alternative responses that would be reasonable but would fall short of imposing an "undue burden" upon the employer. The Act also makes it the employer's duty to prove that it would suffer such a burden, instead of requiring (as the Constitution does) that the complaining party negate reasonable bases for the employer's decision.

---

be drawn. The overwhelming majority of these accounts pertain to alleged discrimination by the States in the provision of public services and public accommodations, which areas are addressed in Titles II and III of the ADA.

The ADA also forbids "utilizing standards, criteria, or methods of administration" that disparately impact the disabled, without regard to whether such conduct has a rational basis. § 12112(b)(3)(A). Although disparate impact may be relevant evidence of racial discrimination, see *Washington v. Davis*, 426 U.S. 229, 239 (1976), such evidence alone is insufficient even where the Fourteenth Amendment subjects state action to strict scrutiny. See, *e.g.*, *ibid.* ("[O]ur cases have not embraced the proposition that a law or other official act, without regard to whether it reflects a racially discriminatory purpose, is unconstitutional solely because it has a racially disproportionate impact").

[C]ongressional enactment of the ADA represents its judgment that there should be a "comprehensive national mandate for the elimination of discrimination against individuals with disabilities." 42 U.S.C. § 12101(b)(1). Congress is the final authority as to desirable public policy, but in order to authorize private individuals to recover money damages against the States, there must be a pattern of discrimination by the States which violates the Fourteenth Amendment, and the remedy imposed by Congress must be congruent and proportional to the targeted violation. Those requirements are not met here, and to uphold the Act's application to the States would allow Congress to rewrite the Fourteenth Amendment law laid down by this Court in *Cleburne*.[9] Section 5 does not so broadly enlarge congressional authority. The judgment of the Court of Appeals is therefore

Reversed.

■ JUSTICE KENNEDY, with whom JUSTICE O'CONNOR joins, concurring.

Prejudice, we are beginning to understand, rises not from malice or hostile animus alone. It may result as well from insensitivity caused by simple want of careful, rational reflection or from some instinctive mechanism to guard against people who appear to be different in some respects from ourselves. Quite apart from any historical documentation, knowledge of our own human instincts teaches that persons who find it difficult to perform routine functions by reason of some mental or physical impairment might at first seem unsettling to us, unless we are guided by the better angels of our nature. There can be little doubt, then, that persons with mental or physical impairments are confronted with prejudice which can stem from indifference or insecurity as well as from malicious ill will.

One of the undoubted achievements of statutes designed to assist those with impairments is that citizens have an incentive, flowing from a legal duty, to develop a better understanding, a more decent perspective, for accepting persons with impairments or disabilities into the larger society. The law works this way because the law can be a teacher. So I do not doubt that the Americans with Disabilities Act of

---

[9] Our holding here that Congress did not validly abrogate the States' sovereign immunity from suit by private individuals for money damages under Title I does not mean that persons with disabilities have no federal recourse against discrimination. Title I of the ADA still prescribes standards applicable to the States. Those standards can be enforced by the United States in actions for money damages, as well as by private individuals in actions for injunctive relief under *Ex parte Young*, 209 U.S. 123 (1908). In addition, state laws protecting the rights of persons with disabilities in employment and other aspects of life provide independent avenues of redress.

1990 will be a milestone on the path to a more decent, tolerant, progressive society.

It is a question of quite a different order, however, to say that the States in their official capacities, the States as governmental entities, must be held in violation of the Constitution on the assumption that they embody the misconceived or malicious perceptions of some of their citizens. It is a most serious charge to say a State has engaged in a pattern or practice designed to deny its citizens the equal protection of the laws, particularly where the accusation is based not on hostility but instead on the failure to act or the omission to remedy. States can, and do, stand apart from the citizenry. States act as neutral entities, ready to take instruction and to enact laws when their citizens so demand. The failure of a State to revise policies now seen as incorrect under a new understanding of proper policy does not always constitute the purposeful and intentional action required to make out a violation of the Equal Protection Clause. See *Washington v. Davis*, 426 U.S. 229 (1976).

For the reasons explained by the Court, an equal protection violation has not been shown with respect to the several States in this case. If the States had been transgressing the Fourteenth Amendment by their mistreatment or lack of concern for those with impairments, one would have expected to find in decisions of the courts of the States and also the courts of the United States extensive litigation and discussion of the constitutional violations. This confirming judicial documentation does not exist. That there is a new awareness, a new consciousness, a new commitment to better treatment of those disadvantaged by mental or physical impairments does not establish that an absence of state statutory correctives was a constitutional violation.

■ JUSTICE BREYER, with whom JUSTICE STEVENS, JUSTICE SOUTER, and JUSTICE GINSBURG join, dissenting.

Reviewing the congressional record as if it were an administrative agency record, the Court holds the statutory provision before us, 42 U.S.C. § 12202, unconstitutional. The Court concludes that Congress assembled insufficient evidence of unconstitutional discrimination, that Congress improperly attempted to "rewrite" the law we established in *Cleburne v. Cleburne Living Center, Inc.*, 473 U.S. 432 (1985), and that the law is not sufficiently tailored to address unconstitutional discrimination.

[T]he Court says that its primary problem with this statutory provision is one of legislative evidence. It says that "Congress assembled only . . . minimal evidence of unconstitutional state discrimination in employment." In fact, Congress compiled a vast legislative record documenting " 'massive, society-wide discrimination' " against persons with disabilities. S.Rep.No.101–116, pp. 8–9 (1989) (quoting testimony of Justin Dart, chairperson of the Task Force on the Rights and Empowerment of Americans with Disabilities). In addition to the information presented at 13 congressional hearings (see Appendix A, *infra* [omitted]), and its own prior experience gathered over 40 years during which it contemplated and enacted considerable similar legislation (see Appendix B, *infra* [omitted]), Congress created a special task force to assess the need for comprehensive legislation. That task force held hearings in every State, attended by more than 30,000 people, including thousands who had experienced discrimination first hand. See From ADA to Empowerment, Task Force on the Rights and Empowerment of Americans with Disabilities 16 (Oct. 12, 1990) (hereinafter Task Force Report). The task force hearings, Congress' own hearings, and an analysis of "census data, national polls, and other studies" led Congress to conclude that "people with disabilities, as a group, occupy an inferior status in our society, and are severely disadvantaged socially, vocationally, economically, and educationally." 42 U.S.C. § 12101(a)(6). As to employment, Congress found that "[t]wo-thirds of all disabled Americans between the age of 16 and 64 [were] not working at all," even though a large majority wanted to, and were able to, work productively. S.Rep.No.101–116, at 9. And Congress found that this discrimination flowed in significant part from "stereotypic assumptions" as well as "purposeful unequal treatment." 42 U.S.C. § 12101(a)(7).

The powerful evidence of discriminatory treatment throughout society in general, including discrimination by private persons and local governments, implicates state governments as well, for state agencies form part of that same larger society. There is no particular reason to believe that they are immune from the "stereotypic assumptions" and pattern of "purposeful unequal treatment" that Congress found prevalent. The Court claims that it "make[s] no sense" to take into consideration constitutional violations committed by local governments. But the substantive obligation that the Equal Protection Clause creates applies to state and local governmental entities alike. Local governments often work closely with, and under the supervision of, state officials, and in general, state and local government employers are similarly situated. Nor is determining whether an apparently "local" entity is entitled to Eleventh Amendment immunity as simple as the majority suggests—it often requires a " 'detailed examination of the relevant provisions of [state] law.' "

In any event, there is no need to rest solely upon evidence of discrimination by local governments or general societal discrimination. There are roughly 300 examples of discrimination by state governments themselves in the legislative record. See, e.g., Appendix C, *infra*. I fail to see how this evidence "fall[s] far short of even suggesting the pattern of unconstitutional discrimination on which § 5 legislation must be based."

The congressionally appointed task force collected numerous specific examples, provided by persons with disabilities themselves, of adverse, disparate treatment by state officials. They reveal, not what the Court describes as "half a dozen" instances of discrimination, but hundreds of instances of adverse treatment at the hands of state officials—instances in which a person with a disability found it impossible to obtain a state job, to retain state employment, to use the public transportation that was readily available to others in order to get to work, or to obtain a public education, which is often a prerequisite to obtaining employment. State-imposed barriers also frequently made it difficult or impossible for people to vote, to enter a public building, to access important government services, such as calling for emergency assistance, and to find a place to live due to a pattern of irrational zoning decisions similar to the discrimination that we held unconstitutional in Cleburne, 473 U.S., at 448. See Appendix C, *infra*.

As the Court notes, those who presented instances of discrimination rarely provided additional, independent evidence sufficient to prove in court that, in each instance, the discrimination they suffered lacked justification from a judicial standpoint. Perhaps this explains the Court's view that there is "minimal evidence of unconstitutional state discrimination." But a legislature is not a court of law. And Congress, unlike courts, must, and does, routinely draw general conclusions—for example, of likely motive or of likely relationship to legitimate need—from anecdotal and opinion-based evidence of this kind, particularly when the evidence lacks strong refutation. See Task Force Report 16, 20 (task force "met many times with significant representatives of groups opposed to [the] ADA," and as to the general public, although the task force received "about 2,000 letters" in support of the ADA, there was only "one letter in opposition"); S. Rep. No. 101–116, at 10 (summarizing testimony that many reasonable accommodations cost "less than $50," and the expense of others, such as hiring employees who can interpret for the deaf, is "frequently exaggerated"). In reviewing § 5 legislation, we have never required the sort of extensive investigation of each piece of evidence that the Court appears to contemplate. Nor has the Court traditionally required Congress to make findings as to state discrimination, or to break down the record evidence, category by category.

Regardless, Congress expressly found substantial unjustified discrimination against persons with disabilities. 42 U.S.C. § 12101(9) (finding a pattern of "unnecessary discrimination and prejudice" that "costs the United States billions of dollars in unnecessary expenses resulting from dependency and nonproductivity"). See also 2 Legislative History of the Americans with Disabilities Act (Leg.Hist.) (Committee Print compiled for the House Committee on Education and Labor), Ser. No. 102–B, p. 1620 (1990) (testimony of Arlene B. Mayerson) (describing "unjustifiable and discriminatory loss of job opportunities"); *id.*, at 1623 (citing study showing " 'strong evidence that employers' fears of low performance among disabled workers are unjustified"). Moreover, it found that such discrimination typically reflects "stereotypic assumptions" or "purposeful unequal treatment." 42 U.S.C. § 12101(7). See also 2 Leg. Hist. 1622 (testimony of Arlene B. Mayerson) ("Outmoded stereotypes whether manifested in medical or other job 'requirements' that are unrelated to the successful performance of the job, or in decisions based on the generalized perceptions of supervisors and hiring personnel, have excluded many disabled people from jobs for which they are qualified"). In making these findings, Congress followed our decision in *Cleburne*, which established that not only discrimination against persons with disabilities that rests upon "a bare . . . desire to harm a politically unpopular group," violates the Fourteenth Amendment, but also discrimination that rests solely upon "negative attitude[s]," "fea[r]," or "irrational prejudice." Adverse treatment that rests upon such motives is unjustified discrimination in *Cleburne*'s terms.

The evidence in the legislative record bears out Congress' finding that the adverse treatment of persons with disabilities was often arbitrary or invidious in this sense, and thus unjustified. For example, one study that was before Congress revealed that "most . . . governmental agencies in [one State] discriminated in hiring against job applicants for an average period of five years after treatment for cancer," based in part on coworkers' misguided belief that "cancer is contagious." A school inexplicably refused to exempt a deaf teacher, who taught at a school for the deaf, from a "listening skills" requirement. A State refused to hire a blind employee as director of an agency for the blind—even though he was the most qualified applicant. Certain state agencies apparently had general policies against hiring or promoting persons with disabilities. A zoo turned away children with Downs Syndrome "because [the zookeeper] feared they would upset the chimpanzees." S.Rep.No.101–116, at 7. There were reports of numerous zoning decisions based upon "negative attitudes" or "fear," *Cleburne*, such as a zoning board that denied a permit for an obviously pretextual reason after hearing arguments that a facility would house " 'deviants' " who needed " 'room to roam.' " A complete listing of the hundreds of examples of discrimination by state and local governments that were submitted to the task force is set forth in Appendix C, *infra* [omitted]. Congress could have reasonably believed that these examples represented signs of a widespread problem of unconstitutional discrimination.

II

[T]he problem with the Court's approach is that neither the "burden of proof" that favors States nor any other rule of restraint applicable to judges applies to Congress when it exercises its § 5 power. "Limitations stemming from the nature of the judicial process . . . have no application to Congress." [I]ndeed, the Court in *Cleburne* drew this very institutional distinction. We emphasized that "courts have been very reluctant, as they should be in our federal system and with our respect for the separation of powers, to closely scrutinize legislative choices." Our invocation of judicial deference and respect for Congress was based on the fact that "[§]5 of the [Fourteenth] Amendment empowers Congress to enforce [the equal protection] mandate." Indeed, we made clear that the absence of a contrary congressional finding was critical to our decision to apply mere rational-basis review to disability discrimination claims—a "congressional direction" to apply a more stringent standard would have been "controlling." In short, the Court's claim that "to uphold the Act's application to the States would allow Congress to rewrite the Fourteenth Amendment law laid down by this Court in *Cleburne*" is repudiated by *Cleburne* itself.

III

[T]he Court argues in the alternative that the statute's damages remedy is not "congruent" with and "proportional" to the equal protection problem that Congress found. The Court suggests that the Act's "reasonable accommodation" requirement, 42 U.S.C. § 12112(b)(5)(A), and disparate-impact standard, § 12112(b)(3)(A), "far excee[d] what is constitutionally required." [W]hat is wrong with a remedy that, in response to unreasonable employer behavior, requires an employer to make accommodations that are reasonable? Of course, what is "reasonable" in the statutory sense and what is "unreasonable" in the constitutional sense might differ. In other words, the requirement may exceed what is necessary to avoid a constitutional violation. But it is just that power—the power to require more than the minimum that § 5 grants to Congress, as this Court has repeatedly confirmed.

IV

[F]or the reasons stated, I respectfully dissent.

NOTES ON *BOARD OF TRUSTEES V. GARRETT*

1. Whither *Cleburne*? The majority concludes that "to uphold the Act's application to the States would allow Congress to rewrite the Fourteenth Amendment law laid down by this Court in *Cleburne*." Is that really correct? Although *Cleburne* purported to apply the rational basis test, isn't it a stretch to say that the Court's decision to strike down the zoning decision "[a]ppl[ied] the basic principles of rationality review"? More important, as Justice Breyer suggests in his dissent, the majority ignores the strong overtones of judicial restraint that pervaded Justice White's opinion for the Court in *Cleburne*. Justice White suggested that "congressional direction" of the appropriate standard of review would be "controlling," and he also said that the Court was refraining from adopting a more stringent standard of review precisely because the legislature, not the judiciary, was competent to make the complex distinctions necessary to determine when disability discrimination is invidious. By adopting the ADA, with its complex definition of disability and its intricate rules governing prohibited discrimination and required accommodation, Congress was taking up the *Cleburne* Court's invitation, no? Or does *City of Boerne* simply reject *Cleburne*'s suggestion that Congress has some power to elaborate the standards of review that courts apply to determine whether discrimination is unconstitutional? And if one grants its premise that disability discrimination is unconstitutional only when it fails minimal rational basis scrutiny, isn't the majority right that the ADA extends far beyond that constitutional prohibition?

2. Hardheaded if Hardhearted. Chief Justice Rehnquist seems to suggest that a refusal to make "special accommodations" for people with disabilities is, *ipso facto*, rational: A state can "quite hardheadedly—and perhaps hardheartedly—hold to job-qualification requirements which do not make allowance for the disabled." Is a refusal to make accommodations always rational? Recall the discussion of the justifications for the accommodation requirement in Chapter Three. As defenders of the ADA's reasonable accommodation often mandate insist, accommodations for workers with disabilities often entail little or no direct cost. But the ADA requires employers to make accommodations that are reasonable and do not cause undue hardship, even if they impose well more than a *de minimis* direct cost. And monitoring, responding to, and carrying out accommodations requests will necessarily impose some additional, indirect cost on an employer. Is it rational, in the constitutional sense, for a state to seek to avoid these costs? Under ordinary rational-basis analysis, avoiding those costs may well be rational. And to the extent that the accommodation mandate is understood as a form of pure redistribution, it is almost certainly rational, under standard Fourteenth Amendment doctrine, for a state to choose not to incur the costs involved. See *Dandridge v. Williams*, 397 U.S. 471, 487 (1970).

What, however, about the argument that reasonable accommodation is necessary to rectify discrimination? If, as Professors Harlan Hahn and Robert Burgdorf have argued, employers accommodate the particular needs of workers without disabilities all the time, then the accommodation mandate does not demand "special" accommodations so much as "equal accommodations." See Harlan Hahn, *Accommodations and the ADA: Unreasonable Bias or Biased Reasoning?*, 21 Berkeley J. Emp. & Lab. L. 166, 178 n.61 (2000); Robert L. Burgdorf Jr., "Substantially Limited" Protection from Disability Discrimination: The Special Treatment Model and Misconstructions of the Definition of Disability, 42 Vill. L. Rev. 409, 530–531 (1997). See generally Peter J. Rubin, *Equal Rights, Special Rights, and the Nature of Antidiscrimination Law*, 97 Mich. L. Rev. 564 (1998) (arguing that antidiscrimination protections can always be characterized as guaranteeing "equal rights" or "special rights"). Chief Justice Rehnquist stacks the deck a bit in characterizing the ADA as demanding "special" accommodations—particularly because only one of the two plaintiffs before the Court (Milton Ash) invoked the statute to demand an accommodation. The other plaintiff, Patricia Garrett, was challenging straightforward discrimination.

Of course, if one grants the Court's premise that only minimal rational-basis review applies, it may well still be true as a doctrinal matter that the refusal to provide "equal" accommodations to employees with disabilities is constitutional. Under the standard rational-basis doctrine, the government need not treat everybody who seems to be similarly situated in the same way. See, *e.g.*, *Nordlinger v. Hahn*, 505 U.S. 1 (1992) (upholding California law under which the property of new owners is assessed at a much higher value for tax purposes than is the property of old owners). The characterization of *Cleburne* as an ordinary rational basis case seems to do all of the analytic work in Chief Justice Rehnquist's majority opinion.

Garrett addressed the Fourteenth Amendment basis for Title I of the ADA, which addresses employment discrimination. What about Title II of the ADA, which extends broadly to everything a state or local government does? On the one hand, Title II seems to be on firmer Fourteenth Amendment ground, as it prohibits discrimination in core areas of civic life (voting and jury service, for example) where citizens have a constitutional right against exclusion that goes beyond the rational-basis requirement that applies in the employment context. On the other hand, Title II also extends to a wide array of state activities (licensing and the operation of state-owned sports arenas, for example) that involve nothing more than the basic rational-basis right. Is such a statute "congruent and proportional"? The Supreme Court addressed that question in the two cases that follow.

Tennessee v. Lane

Supreme Court of the United States, 2004.
541 U.S. 509.

■ JUSTICE STEVENS delivered the opinion of the Court.

[T]he question presented in this case is whether Title II [of the Americans with Disabilities Act] exceeds Congress' power under § 5 of the Fourteenth Amendment.

I

In August 1998, respondents George Lane and Beverly Jones filed this action against the State of Tennessee and a number of Tennessee counties, alleging past and ongoing violations of Title II. Respondents, both of whom are paraplegics who use wheelchairs for mobility, claimed that they were denied access to, and the services of, the state court system by reason of their disabilities. Lane alleged that he was compelled to appear to answer a set of criminal charges on the second floor of a county courthouse that had no elevator. At his first appearance, Lane crawled up two flights of stairs to get to the courtroom. When Lane returned to the courthouse for a hearing, he refused to crawl again or to be carried by officers to the courtroom; he consequently was arrested and jailed for failure to appear. Jones, a certified court reporter, alleged that she has not been able to gain access to a number of county courthouses, and, as a result, has lost both work and an opportunity to participate in the judicial process. Respondents sought damages and equitable relief.

The State moved to dismiss the suit on the ground that it was barred by the Eleventh Amendment. The District Court denied the motion without opinion, and the State appealed. The [court of appeals affirmed]. We granted *certiorari* and now affirm.

II

The ADA was passed by large majorities in both Houses of Congress after decades of deliberation and investigation into the need for comprehensive legislation to address discrimination against persons with disabilities. In the years immediately preceding the ADA's enactment, Congress held 13 hearings and created a special task force that gathered evidence from every State in the Union. The conclusions Congress drew from this evidence are set forth in the task force and Committee Reports, described in lengthy legislative hearings, and summarized in the preamble to the statute. Central among these conclusions was Congress' finding that

> "individuals with disabilities are a discrete and insular minority who have been faced with restrictions and limitations, subjected to a history of purposeful unequal treatment, and relegated to a position of political powerlessness in our society, based on characteristics that are beyond the control of such individuals and resulting from stereotypic assumptions not truly indicative of the individual ability of such individuals to participate in, and contribute to, society." 42 U.S.C. § 12101(a)(7).

Invoking "the sweep of congressional authority, including the power to enforce the fourteenth amendment and to regulate commerce," the ADA is designed "to provide a clear and comprehensive national mandate for the elimination of discrimination against individuals with disabilities." §§ 12101(b)(1), (b)(4). It forbids discrimination against persons with disabilities in three major areas of public life: employment, which is covered by Title I of the statute; public services, programs, and activities, which are the subject of Title II; and public accommodations, which are covered by Title III.

Title II, §§ 12131–12134, prohibits any public entity from discriminating against "qualified" persons with disabilities in the provision or operation of public services, programs, or activities. The Act defines the term "public entity" to include state and local governments, as well as their agencies and instrumentalities. § 12131(1). Persons with disabilities are "qualified" if they, "with or without reasonable modifications to rules, policies, or practices, the removal of architectural, communication, or transportation barriers, or the provision of auxiliary aids and services, mee[t] the essential eligibility requirements for the receipt of services or the participation in programs or activities provided by a public entity." § 12131(2).

III

[T]he Act specifically provides: "A State shall not be immune under the eleventh amendment to the Constitution of the United States from an action in Federal or State court of competent jurisdiction for a violation of this chapter." 42 U.S.C. § 12202. As in *Garrett*, no party disputes the adequacy of that expression of Congress' intent to abrogate the States' Eleventh Amendment immunity. The question, then, is whether Congress had the power to give effect to its intent.

[W]e have [r]epeatedly affirmed that "Congress may enact so-called prophylactic legislation that proscribes facially constitutional conduct, in order to prevent and deter unconstitutional conduct." *Nevada Dept. of Human Resources v. Hibbs*, 538 U.S. 721, 727–728 (2003). The most recent affirmation of the breadth of Congress' § 5 power came in *Hibbs*, in which we considered whether a male state employee could recover money damages against the State for its failure to comply with the family-care leave provision of the Family and Medical Leave Act of 1993 (FMLA), 107 Stat. 6, 29 U.S.C. § 2601 *et seq.* We upheld the FMLA as a valid exercise of Congress' § 5 power to combat unconstitutional sex discrimination, even though there was no suggestion that the State's leave policy was adopted or applied with a discriminatory purpose that would render it unconstitutional under the rule of *Personnel Administrator of Mass. v. Feeney*, 442 U.S. 256 (1979). When Congress seeks to remedy or prevent unconstitutional discrimination, § 5 authorizes it to enact prophylactic legislation proscribing practices that are discriminatory in effect, if not in intent, to carry out the basic objectives of the Equal Protection Clause.

[A]pplying the *Boerne* test in *Garrett*, we concluded that Title I of the ADA was not a valid exercise of Congress' § 5 power to enforce the Fourteenth Amendment's prohibition on unconstitutional disability discrimination in public employment. [W]e concluded Congress' exercise of its prophylactic § 5 power was unsupported by a relevant history and pattern of constitutional violations. Although the dissent pointed out that Congress had before it a great deal of evidence of discrimination by the States against persons with disabilities (opinion of BREYER, J.), the

Court's opinion noted that the "overwhelming majority" of that evidence related to "the provision of public services and public accommodations, which areas are addressed in Titles II and III," rather than Title I. We also noted that neither the ADA's legislative findings nor its legislative history reflected a concern that the States had been engaging in a pattern of unconstitutional employment discrimination. We emphasized that the House and Senate Committee Reports on the ADA focused on " '[d]iscrimination [in] . . . employment in the private sector,' " and made no mention of discrimination in public employment. Finally, we concluded that Title I's broad remedial scheme was insufficiently targeted to remedy or prevent unconstitutional discrimination in public employment. Taken together, the historical record and the broad sweep of the statute suggested that Title I's true aim was not so much to enforce the Fourteenth Amendment's prohibitions against disability discrimination in public employment as it was to "rewrite" this Court's Fourteenth Amendment jurisprudence.

In view of the significant differences between Titles I and II, however, *Garrett* left open the question whether Title II is a valid exercise of Congress' § 5 enforcement power. It is to that question that we now turn.

IV

[T]itle II, like Title I, seeks to enforce [*Cleburne's*] prohibition on irrational disability discrimination. But it also seeks to enforce a variety of other basic constitutional guarantees, infringements of which are subject to more searching judicial review. These rights include some, like the right of access to the courts at issue in this case, that are protected by the Due Process Clause of the Fourteenth Amendment. The Due Process Clause and the Confrontation Clause of the Sixth Amendment, as applied to the States via the Fourteenth Amendment, both guarantee to a criminal defendant such as respondent Lane the "right to be present at all stages of the trial where his absence might frustrate the fairness of the proceedings." *Faretta v. California*, 422 U.S. 806, 819, n. 15 (1975). The Due Process Clause also requires the States to afford certain civil litigants a "meaningful opportunity to be heard" by removing obstacles to their full participation in judicial proceedings. *Boddie v. Connecticut*, 401 U.S. 371, 379 (1971); *M.L.B. v. S.L. J.*, 519 U.S. 102 (1996). We have held that the Sixth Amendment guarantees to criminal defendants the right to trial by a jury composed of a fair cross section of the community, noting that the exclusion of "identifiable segments playing major roles in the community cannot be squared with the constitutional concept of jury trial." *Taylor v. Louisiana*, 419 U.S. 522, 530 (1975). And, finally, we have recognized that members of the public have a right of access to criminal proceedings secured by the First Amendment. *Press-Enterprise Co. v. Superior Court of Cal., County of Riverside*, 478 U.S. 1, 8–15 (1986).

[I]t is not difficult to perceive the harm that Title II is designed to address. Congress enacted Title II against a backdrop of pervasive unequal treatment in the administration of state services and programs, including systematic deprivations of fundamental rights. For example, "[a]s of 1979, most States . . . categorically disqualified 'idiots' from voting, without regard to individual capacity." The majority of these laws remain on the books, and have been the subject of legal challenge as recently as 2001. Similarly, a number of States have prohibited and continue to prohibit persons with disabilities from engaging in activities such as marrying and serving as jurors. The historical experience that Title II reflects is also documented in this Court's cases, which have identified unconstitutional treatment of disabled persons by state agencies in a variety of settings, including unjustified commitment, e.g., *Jackson v. Indiana*, 406 U.S. 715 (1972); the abuse and neglect of persons committed to state mental health hospitals, *Youngberg v. Romeo*, 457 U.S. 307 (1982); and irrational discrimination in zoning decisions, *Cleburne v. Cleburne Living Center, Inc.*, 473 U.S. 432 (1985). The decisions of other courts, too, document a pattern of unequal treatment in the administration of a wide range of public services, programs, and activities, including the penal system, public education, and voting. Notably, these decisions also demonstrate a pattern of unconstitutional treatment in the administration of justice.[14]

This pattern of disability discrimination persisted despite several federal and state legislative efforts to address it. In the deliberations that led up to the enactment of the ADA, Congress identified important shortcomings in existing laws that rendered them "inadequate to address the pervasive problems of discrimination that people with disabilities are facing." S.Rep.No.101–116, at 18. It also uncovered further evidence of those shortcomings, in the form of hundreds of examples of unequal treatment of persons with disabilities by States and their political subdivisions. *See Garrett*, 531 U.S., at 379 (BREYER, J., dissenting). As the Court's opinion in *Garrett* observed, the "overwhelming majority" of these examples concerned discrimination in the administration of public programs and services.

With respect to the particular services at issue in this case, Congress learned that many individuals, in many States across the country, were being excluded from courthouses and court proceedings by reason of their disabilities. A report before Congress showed that some 76% of public services and programs housed in state-owned buildings were inaccessible to and unusable by persons with disabilities, even taking into account the possibility that the services and programs might be restructured or relocated to other parts of the buildings. U.S. Commission on Civil Rights, Accommodating the Spectrum of Individual Abilities 39 (1983). Congress itself heard testimony from persons with disabilities who described the physical

---

[14] *E.g., Ferrell v. Estelle*, 568 F.2d 1128, 1132–1133 (C.A.5) (deaf criminal defendant denied interpretive services), opinion withdrawn as moot, 573 F.2d 867 (C.A.5 1978); *State v. Schaim*, 65 Ohio St.3d 51, 64, 600 N.E.2d 661, 672 (1992) (same); *People v. Rivera*, 125 Misc.2d 516, 528, 480 N.Y.S.2d 426, 434 (Sup.Ct.1984) (same). See also, *e.g., Layton v. Elder*, 143 F.3d 469, 470–472 (C.A.8 1998) (mobility-impaired litigant excluded from a county quorum court session held on the second floor of an inaccessible courthouse); *Matthews v. Jefferson*, 29 F.Supp.2d 525, 533–534 (W.D.Ark.1998) (wheelchair-bound litigant had to be carried to the second floor of an inaccessible courthouse, from which he was unable to leave to use restroom facilities or obtain a meal, and no arrangements were made to carry him downstairs at the end of the day); *Pomerantz v. County of Los Angeles*, 674 F.2d 1288, 1289 (C.A.9 1982) (blind persons categorically excluded from jury service); *Galloway v. Superior Court of District of Columbia*, 816 F.Supp. 12 (D.D.C. 1993) (same); *DeLong v. Brumbaugh*, 703 F.Supp. 399, 405 (W.D.Pa.1989) (deaf individual excluded from jury service); *People v. Green*, 148 Misc.2d 666, 669, 561 N.Y.S.2d 130, 133 (Cty.Ct.1990) (prosecutor exercised peremptory strike against prospective juror solely because she was hearing impaired).

inaccessibility of local courthouses. Oversight Hearing on H.R. 4498 before the House Subcommittee on Select Education of the Committee on Education and Labor, 100th Cong., 2d Sess., 40–41, 48 (1988). And its appointed task force heard numerous examples of the exclusion of persons with disabilities from state judicial services and programs, including exclusion of persons with visual impairments and hearing impairments from jury service, failure of state and local governments to provide interpretive services for the hearing impaired, failure to permit the testimony of adults with developmental disabilities in abuse cases, and failure to make courtrooms accessible to witnesses with physical disabilities. Government's Lodging in *Garrett*, O.T.2000, No. 99–1240. See also Task Force on the Rights and Empowerment of Americans with Disabilities, From ADA to Empowerment (Oct. 12, 1990).[16]

[T]he conclusion that Congress drew from this body of evidence is set forth in the text of the ADA itself: "[D]iscrimination against individuals with disabilities persists in such critical areas as . . . education, transportation, communication, recreation, institutionalization, health services, voting, and access to public services." 42 U.S.C. § 12101(a)(3). This finding, together with the extensive record of disability discrimination that underlies it, makes clear beyond peradventure that inadequate provision of public services and access to public facilities was an appropriate subject for prophylactic legislation.

V

The only question that remains is whether Title II is an appropriate response to this history and pattern of unequal treatment. At the outset, we must determine the scope of that inquiry. Title II— unlike [t]he other statutes we have reviewed for validity under § 5— reaches a wide array of official conduct in an effort to enforce an equally wide array of constitutional guarantees. Petitioner urges us both to examine the broad range of Title II's applications all at once, and to treat that breadth as a mark of the law's invalidity. According to petitioner, the fact that Title II applies not only to public education and voting-booth access but also to seating at state-owned hockey rinks indicates that Title II is not appropriately tailored to serve its objectives. But nothing in our case law requires us to consider Title II, with its wide variety of applications, as an undifferentiated whole. Whatever might be said about Title II's other applications, the question presented in this case is not whether Congress can validly subject the States to private suits for money damages for failing to provide reasonable access to hockey rinks, or even to voting booths, but whether Congress had the power under § 5 to enforce the constitutional right of

---

[16] THE CHIEF JUSTICE dismisses as "irrelevant" the portions of this evidence that concern the conduct of nonstate governments. This argument rests on the mistaken premise that a valid exercise of Congress' § 5 power must always be predicated solely on evidence of constitutional violations by the States themselves. To operate on that premise in this case would be particularly inappropriate because this case concerns the provision of judicial services, an area in which local governments are typically treated as "arm[s] of the State" for Eleventh Amendment purposes, and thus enjoy precisely the same immunity from unconsented suit as the States. See, *e.g.*, *Callahan v. Philadelphia*, 207 F.3d 668, 670–674 (C.A.3 2000) (municipal court is an "arm of the State" entitled to Eleventh Amendment immunity); *Kelly v. Municipal Courts*, 97 F.3d 902, 907–908 (C.A.7 1996) (same); *Franceschi v. Schwartz*, 57 F.3d 828, 831 (C.A.9 1995) (same).

access to the courts. Because we find that Title II unquestionably is valid § 5 legislation as it applies to the class of cases implicating the accessibility of judicial services, we need go no further.

Congress' chosen remedy for the pattern of exclusion and discrimination described above, Title II's requirement of program accessibility, is congruent and proportional to its object of enforcing the right of access to the courts. The unequal treatment of disabled persons in the administration of judicial services has a long history, and has persisted despite several legislative efforts to remedy the problem of disability discrimination. Faced with considerable evidence of the shortcomings of previous legislative responses, Congress was justified in concluding that this "difficult and intractable proble[m]" warranted "added prophylactic measures in response."

The remedy Congress chose is nevertheless a limited one. Recognizing that failure to accommodate persons with disabilities will often have the same practical effect as outright exclusion, Congress required the States to take reasonable measures to remove architectural and other barriers to accessibility. 42 U.S.C. § 12131(2). But Title II does not require States to employ any and all means to make judicial services accessible to persons with disabilities, and it does not require States to compromise their essential eligibility criteria for public programs. It requires only "reasonable modifications" that would not fundamentally alter the nature of the service provided, and only when the individual seeking modification is otherwise eligible for the service. As Title II's implementing regulations make clear, the reasonable modification requirement can be satisfied in a number of ways. In the case of facilities built or altered after 1992, the regulations require compliance with specific architectural accessibility standards. 28 CFR § 35.151 (2003). But in the case of older facilities, for which structural change is likely to be more difficult, a public entity may comply with Title II by adopting a variety of less costly measures, including relocating services to alternative, accessible sites and assigning aides to assist persons with disabilities in accessing services. § 35.150(b)(1). Only if these measures are ineffective in achieving accessibility is the public entity required to make reasonable structural changes. And in no event is the entity required to undertake measures that would impose an undue financial or administrative burden, threaten historic preservation interests, or effect a fundamental alteration in the nature of the service. §§ 35.150(a)(2), (a)(3).

This duty to accommodate is perfectly consistent with the well-established due process principle that, "within the limits of practicability, a State must afford to all individuals a meaningful opportunity to be heard" in its courts. *Boddie*.[20] Our cases have recognized a number of affirmative obligations that flow from this principle: the duty to waive filing fees in certain family-law and criminal cases, the duty to provide transcripts to criminal defendants seeking review of their convictions, and the duty to provide counsel to certain criminal defendants. Each of these cases makes clear that ordinary considerations of cost and convenience alone cannot justify a

---

[20] Because this case implicates the right of access to the courts, we need not consider whether Title II's duty to accommodate exceeds what the Constitution requires in the class of cases that implicate only *Cleburne*'s prohibition on irrational discrimination.

State's failure to provide individuals with a meaningful right of access to the courts. Judged against this backdrop, Title II's affirmative obligation to accommodate persons with disabilities in the administration of justice cannot be said to be "so out of proportion to a supposed remedial or preventive object that it cannot be understood as responsive to, or designed to prevent, unconstitutional behavior." *Boerne.* It is, rather, a reasonable prophylactic measure, reasonably targeted to a legitimate end.

For these reasons, we conclude that Title II, as it applies to the class of cases implicating the fundamental right of access to the courts, constitutes a valid exercise of Congress' § 5 authority to enforce the guarantees of the Fourteenth Amendment. The judgment of the Court of Appeals is therefore affirmed.

It is so ordered.

■ JUSTICE SOUTER, with whom JUSTICE GINSBURG joins, concurring.

[A]lthough I concur in the Court's approach applying the congruence-and-proportionality criteria to Title II of the Americans with Disabilities Act of 1990 as a guarantee of access to courts and related rights, I note that if the Court engaged in a more expansive enquiry as THE CHIEF JUSTICE suggests (dissenting opinion), the evidence to be considered would underscore the appropriateness of action under § 5 to address the situation of disabled individuals before the courts, for that evidence would show that the judiciary itself has endorsed the basis for some of the very discrimination subject to congressional remedy under § 5. *Buck v. Bell*, 274 U.S. 200 (1927), was not grudging in sustaining the constitutionality of the once-pervasive practice of involuntarily sterilizing those with mental disabilities. See *id.*, at 207 ("It is better for all the world, if instead of waiting to execute degenerate offspring for crime, or to let them starve for their imbecility, society can prevent those who are manifestly unfit from continuing their kind. . . . Three generations of imbeciles are enough"). Laws compelling sterilization were often accompanied by others indiscriminately requiring institutionalization, and prohibiting certain individuals with disabilities from marrying, from voting, from attending public schools, and even from appearing in public. One administrative action along these lines was judicially sustained in part as a justified precaution against the very sight of a child with cerebral palsy, lest he "produc[e] a depressing and nauseating effect" upon others. *State ex rel. Beattie v. Board of Ed. of Antigo*, 169 Wis. 231, 232, 172 N.W. 153 (1919) (approving his exclusion from public school).

Many of these laws were enacted to implement the quondam science of eugenics, which peaked in the 1920's, yet the statutes and their judicial vindications sat on the books long after eugenics lapsed into discredit. Quite apart from the fateful inspiration behind them, one pervasive fault of these provisions was their failure to reflect the "amount of flexibility and freedom" required to deal with "the wide variation in the abilities and needs" of people with disabilities. Instead, like other invidious discrimination, they classified people without regard to individual capacities, and by that lack of regard did great harm. In sustaining the application of Title II today, the Court takes a welcome step away from the judiciary's prior endorsement of blunt instruments imposing legal handicaps.

■ JUSTICE GINSBURG, with whom JUSTICE SOUTER and JUSTICE BREYER join, concurring.

For the reasons stated by the Court, and mindful of Congress' objective in enacting the Americans with Disabilities Act—the elimination or reduction of physical and social structures that impede people with some present, past, or perceived impairments from contributing, according to their talents, to our Nation's social, economic, and civic life—I join the Court's opinion.

The Americans with Disabilities Act of 1990 (ADA or Act), 42 U.S.C. §§ 12101–12213, is a measure expected to advance equal-citizenship stature for persons with disabilities. See Bagenstos, *Subordination, Stigma, and "Disability,"* 86 Va. L. Rev. 397, 471 (2000) (ADA aims both to "guarante[e] a baseline of equal citizenship by protecting against stigma and systematic exclusion from public and private opportunities, and [to] protec[t] society against the loss of valuable talents"). [I]ncluding individuals with disabilities among people who count in composing "We the People," Congress understood in shaping the ADA, would sometimes require not blindfolded equality, but responsiveness to difference; not indifference, but accommodation. Central to the Act's primary objective, Congress extended the statute's range to reach all government activities, § 12132 (Title II), and required "reasonable modifications to [public actors'] rules, policies, or practices," §§ 12131(2)–12132 (Title II). See also § 12112(b)(5) (defining discrimination to include the failure to provide "reasonable accommodations") (Title I); § 12182(b)(2)(A)(ii) (requiring "reasonable modifications in [public accommodations'] policies, practices, or procedures") (Title III); Bagenstos, supra, at 435 (ADA supporters sought "to eliminate the practices that combine with physical and mental conditions to create what we call 'disability.' The society-wide universal access rules serve this function on the macro level, and the requirements of individualized accommodation and modification fill in the gaps on the micro level." (footnote omitted)).

In *Olmstead v. L. C.*, 527 U.S. 581 (1999), this Court responded with fidelity to the ADA's accommodation theme when it held a State accountable for failing to provide community residential placements for people with disabilities. The State argued in *Olmstead* that it had acted impartially, for it provided no community placements for individuals without disabilities. Congress, the Court observed, advanced in the ADA "a more comprehensive view of the concept of discrimination," one that embraced failures to provide "reasonable accommodations." The Court today is similarly faithful to the Act's demand for reasonable accommodation to secure access and avoid exclusion.

[A]s the Court's opinion documents, Congress considered a body of evidence showing that in diverse parts of our Nation, and at various levels of government, persons with disabilities encounter access barriers to public facilities and services. That record, the Court rightly holds, at least as it bears on access to courts, sufficed to warrant the barrier-lowering, dignity-respecting national solution the People's representatives in Congress elected to order.

■ CHIEF JUSTICE REHNQUIST, with whom JUSTICE KENNEDY and JUSTICE THOMAS join, dissenting.

In *Garrett*, we held that Congress did not validly abrogate States' Eleventh Amendment immunity when it enacted Title I of the Americans with Disabilities Act of 1990 (ADA or Act), 42 U.S.C. §§ 12111–12117. Today, the Court concludes that Title II of that Act, §§ 12131–12165, does validly abrogate that immunity, at least insofar "as it applies to the class of cases implicating the fundamental right of access to the courts." Because today's decision is irreconcilable with *Garrett* and the well-established principles it embodies, I dissent.

[I]n this case, the task of identifying the scope of the relevant constitutional protection is more difficult because Title II purports to enforce a panoply of constitutional rights of disabled persons: not only the equal protection right against irrational discrimination, but also certain rights protected by the Due Process Clause. However, because the Court ultimately upholds Title II "as it applies to the class of cases implicating the fundamental right of access to the courts," the proper inquiry focuses on the scope of those due process rights. The Court cites four access-to-the-courts rights that Title II purportedly enforces: (1) the right of the criminal defendant to be present at all critical stages of the trial; (2) the right of litigants to have a "meaningful opportunity to be heard" in judicial proceedings; (3) the right of the criminal defendant to trial by a jury composed of a fair cross section of the community; and (4) the public right of access to criminal proceedings. [B]ut the majority identifies nothing in the legislative record that shows Congress was responding to widespread violations of the due process rights of disabled persons.

Rather than limiting its discussion of constitutional violations to the due process rights on which it ultimately relies, the majority sets out on a wide-ranging account of societal discrimination against the disabled. This digression recounts historical discrimination against the disabled through institutionalization laws, restrictions on marriage, voting, and public education, conditions in mental hospitals, and various other forms of unequal treatment in the administration of public programs and services. Some of this evidence would be relevant if the Court were considering the constitutionality of the statute as a whole; but the Court rejects that approach in favor of a narrower "as-applied" inquiry. We discounted much the same type of outdated, generalized evidence in *Garrett* as unsupportive of Title I's ban on employment discrimination. The evidence here is likewise irrelevant to Title II's purported enforcement of due process access-to-the-courts rights.

[W]ith respect to the due process "access to the courts" rights on which the Court ultimately relies, Congress' failure to identify a pattern of actual constitutional violations by the States is even more striking. Indeed, there is nothing in the legislative record or statutory findings to indicate that disabled persons were systematically denied the right to be present at criminal trials, denied the meaningful opportunity to be heard in civil cases, unconstitutionally excluded from jury service, or denied the right to attend criminal trials.[4]

---

[4] Certainly, respondents Lane and Jones were not denied these constitutional rights. The majority admits that Lane was able to attend the initial hearing of his criminal trial. Lane was arrested for failing to appear at his second hearing only after he refused assistance from officers dispatched by the court to help him to the courtroom. The court conducted a

[L]acking any real evidence that Congress was responding to actual due process violations, the majority relies primarily on three items to justify its decision: (1) a 1983 U.S. Civil Rights Commission Report showing that 76% of "public services and programs housed in state-owned buildings were inaccessible" to persons with disabilities, ante, at 1990; (2) testimony before a House subcommittee regarding the "physical inaccessibility" of local courthouses; and (3) evidence submitted to Congress' designated ADA task force that purportedly contains "numerous examples of the exclusion of persons with disabilities from state judicial services and programs."

On closer examination, however, the Civil Rights Commission's finding consists of a single conclusory sentence in its report, and it is far from clear that its finding even includes courthouses. The House subcommittee report, for its part, contains the testimony of two witnesses, neither of whom reported being denied the right to be present at constitutionally protected court proceedings. Indeed, the witnesses' testimony, like the U.S. Commission on Civil Rights Report, concerns only physical barriers to access, and does not address whether States either provided means to overcome those barriers or alternative locations for proceedings involving disabled persons.

Based on the majority's description, the report of the ADA Task Force on the Rights and Empowerment of Americans with Disabilities sounds promising. But the report itself says nothing about any disabled person being denied access to court. The Court thus apparently relies solely on a general citation to the Government's Lodging in Garrett, O.T.2000, No. 99–1240, which, amidst thousands of pages, contains only a few anecdotal handwritten reports of physically inaccessible courthouses, again with no mention of whether States provided alternative means of access. This evidence, moreover, was submitted not to Congress, but only to the task force, which itself made no findings regarding disabled persons' access to judicial proceedings.

[E]ven if the anecdotal evidence and conclusory statements relied on by the majority could be properly considered, the mere existence of an architecturally "inaccessible" courthouse—i.e., one a disabled person cannot utilize without assistance—does not state a constitutional violation. A violation of due process occurs only when a person is actually denied the constitutional right to access a given judicial proceeding. We have never held that a person has a constitutional right to make his way into a courtroom without any external assistance.

[T]he near-total lack of actual constitutional violations in the congressional record is reminiscent of Garrett, wherein we found that the same type of minimal anecdotal evidence "f[e]ll far short of even suggesting the pattern of unconstitutional [state action] on which § 5 legislation must be based."

[T]itle II requires, on pain of money damages, special accommodations for disabled persons in virtually every interaction they

---

preliminary hearing in the first-floor library to accommodate Lane's disability, and later offered to move all further proceedings in the case to a handicapped-accessible courthouse in a nearby town. In light of these facts, it can hardly be said that the State violated Lane's right to be present at his trial; indeed, it made affirmative attempts to secure that right. Respondent Jones, a disabled court reporter, does not seriously contend that she suffered a constitutional injury.

have with the State. "Despite subjecting States to this expansive liability," the broad terms of Title II "d[o] nothing to limit the coverage of the Act to cases involving arguable constitutional violations." By requiring special accommodation and the elimination of programs that have a disparate impact on the disabled, Title II prohibits far more state conduct than does the equal protection ban on irrational discrimination. We invalidated Title I's similar requirements in *Garrett*, observing that "[i]f special accommodations for the disabled are to be required, they have to come from positive law and not through the Equal Protection Clause." Title II fails for the same reason. Like Title I, Title II may be laudable public policy, but it cannot be seriously disputed that it is also an attempt to legislatively "redefine the States' legal obligations" under the Fourteenth Amendment.

The majority, however, claims that Title II also vindicates fundamental rights protected by the Due Process Clause—in addition to access to the courts—that are subject to heightened Fourteenth Amendment scrutiny. But Title II is not tailored to provide prophylactic protection of these rights; instead, it applies to any service, program, or activity provided by any entity. Its provisions affect transportation, health, education, and recreation programs, among many others, all of which are accorded only rational-basis scrutiny under the Equal Protection Clause. A requirement of accommodation for the disabled at a state-owned amusement park or sports stadium, for example, bears no permissible prophylactic relationship to enabling disabled persons to exercise their fundamental constitutional rights. Thus, as with Title I in *Garrett*, [I]t is unlikely "that many of the [state actions] affected by [Title II] have [any] likelihood of being unconstitutional." Viewed as a whole, then, there is little doubt that Title II of the ADA does not validly abrogate state sovereign immunity.

The majority concludes that Title II's massive overbreadth can be cured by considering the statute only "as it applies to the class of cases implicating the accessibility of judicial services." I have grave doubts about importing an "as applied" approach into the § 5 context. While the majority is of course correct that this Court normally only considers the application of a statute to a particular case, the proper inquiry under *City of Boerne* and its progeny is somewhat different. In applying the congruence-and-proportionality test, we ask whether Congress has attempted to statutorily redefine the constitutional rights protected by the Fourteenth Amendment. This question can only be answered by measuring the breadth of a statute's coverage against the scope of the constitutional rights it purports to enforce and the record of violations it purports to remedy.

[F]or the foregoing reasons, I respectfully dissent.

■ JUSTICE SCALIA, dissenting.

[I] joined the Court's opinion in Boerne with some misgiving. I have generally rejected tests based on such malleable standards as "proportionality," because they have a way of turning into vehicles for the implementation of individual judges' policy preferences. [I] yield to the lessons of experience. The "congruence and proportionality" standard, like all such flabby tests, is a standing invitation to judicial arbitrariness and policy-driven decisionmaking.

I would replace "congruence and proportionality" with another test—one that provides a clear, enforceable limitation supported by the text of § 5. Section 5 grants Congress the power "to enforce, by appropriate legislation," the other provisions of the Fourteenth Amendment. U.S. Const., Amdt. 14 (emphasis added). [O]ne does not, within any normal meaning of the term, "enforce" a prohibition by issuing a still broader prohibition directed to the same end. One does not, for example, "enforce" a 55-mile-per-hour speed limit by imposing a 45-mile-per-hour speed limit—even though that is indeed directed to the same end of automotive safety and will undoubtedly result in many fewer violations of the 55-mile-per-hour limit. And one does not "enforce" the right of access to the courts at issue in this case by requiring that disabled persons be provided access to all of the "services, programs, or activities" furnished or conducted by the State, 42 U.S.C. § 12132. That is simply not what the power to enforce means—or ever meant. The 1860 edition of Noah Webster's American Dictionary of the English Language, current when the Fourteenth Amendment was adopted, defined "enforce" as: "To put in execution; to cause to take effect; as, to enforce the laws." Id., at 396. See also J. Worcester, Dictionary of the English Language 484 (1860) ("To put in force; to cause to be applied or executed; as, 'To enforce a law' "). Nothing in § 5 allows Congress to go beyond the provisions of the Fourteenth Amendment to proscribe, prevent, or "remedy" conduct that does not itself violate any provision of the Fourteenth Amendment. So-called "prophylactic legislation" is reinforcement rather than enforcement.

[O]ne of the first pieces of legislation passed under Congress's § 5 power was the Ku Klux Klan Act of April 20, 1871, 17 Stat. 13, entitled "An Act to enforce the Provisions of the Fourteenth Amendment to the Constitution of the United States, and for other Purposes." Section 1 of that Act, later codified as Rev. Stat. § 1979, 42 U.S.C. § 1983, authorized a cause of action against "any person who, under color of any law, statute, ordinance, regulation, custom, or usage of any State, shall subject, or cause to be subjected, any person within the jurisdiction of the United States to the deprivation of any rights, privileges, or immunities secured by the Constitution of the United States." 17 Stat. 13. Section 5 would also authorize measures that do not restrict the States' substantive scope of action but impose requirements directly related to the facilitation of "enforcement"—for example, reporting requirements that would enable violations of the Fourteenth Amendment to be identified. But what § 5 does not authorize is so-called "prophylactic" measures, prohibiting primary conduct that is itself not forbidden by the Fourteenth Amendment.

[P]rincipally for reasons of stare decisis, I shall henceforth apply the permissive McCulloch standard to congressional measures designed to remedy racial discrimination by the States. [I] shall also not subject to "congruence and proportionality" analysis congressional action under § 5 that is not directed to racial discrimination. Rather, I shall give full effect to that action when it consists of "enforcement" of the provisions of the Fourteenth Amendment, within the broad but not unlimited meaning of that term I have described above. When it goes beyond enforcement to prophylaxis, however, I shall consider it ultra vires. The present legislation is plainly of the latter sort.

■ JUSTICE THOMAS, dissenting.

[omitted]

United States v. Georgia

Supreme Court of the United States, 2006.
546 U.S. 151.

■ JUSTICE SCALIA delivered the opinion of the Court.

We consider whether a disabled inmate in a state prison may sue the State for money damages under Title II of the Americans with Disabilities Act of 1990 (ADA).

I

[P]etitioner in No. 04–1236, Tony Goodman, is a paraplegic inmate in the Georgia prison system who, at all relevant times, was housed at the Georgia State Prison in Reidsville. After filing numerous administrative grievances in the state prison system, Goodman filed a pro se complaint in the United States District Court for the Southern District of Georgia challenging the conditions of his confinement. He named as defendants the State of Georgia and the Georgia Department of Corrections (state defendants) and several individual prison officials. He brought claims under Rev. Stat. § 1979, 42 U.S.C. § 1983, Title II of the ADA, and other provisions not relevant here, seeking both injunctive relief and money damages against all defendants.

Goodman's pro se complaint and subsequent filings in the District Court included many allegations, both grave and trivial, regarding the conditions of his confinement in the Reidsville prison. Among his more serious allegations, he claimed that he was confined for 23–to–24 hours per day in a 12-by-3-foot cell in which he could not turn his wheelchair around. He alleged that the lack of accessible facilities rendered him unable to use the toilet and shower without assistance, which was often denied. On multiple occasions, he asserted, he had injured himself in attempting to transfer from his wheelchair to the shower or toilet on his own, and, on several other occasions, he had been forced to sit in his own feces and urine while prison officials refused to assist him in cleaning up the waste. He also claimed that he had been denied physical therapy and medical treatment, and denied access to virtually all prison programs and services on account of his disability.

The District Court adopted the Magistrate Judge's recommendation that the allegations in the complaint were vague and constituted insufficient notice pleading as to Goodman's § 1983 claims. It therefore dismissed the § 1983 claims against all defendants without providing Goodman an opportunity to amend his complaint. The District Court also dismissed his Title II claims against all individual defendants. Later, after our decision in Garrett, the District Court granted summary judgment to the state defendants on Goodman's Title II claims for money damages, holding that those claims were barred by state sovereign immunity.

Goodman appealed to the United States Court of Appeals for the Eleventh Circuit. The United States, petitioner in No. 04–1203, intervened to defend the constitutionality of Title II's abrogation of state sovereign immunity. The Eleventh Circuit determined that the

District Court had erred in dismissing all of Goodman's § 1983 claims, because Goodman's multiple pro se filings in the District Court alleged facts sufficient to support "a limited number of Eighth-Amendment claims under § 1983" against certain individual defendants. The Court of Appeals held that the District Court should have given Goodman leave to amend his complaint to develop three Eighth Amendment claims relating to his conditions of confinement:

> "First, Goodman alleges that he is not able to move his wheelchair in his cell. If Goodman is to be believed, this effectively amounts to some form of total restraint twenty-three to twenty-four hours-a-day without penal justification. Second, Goodman has alleged several instances in which he was forced to sit in his own bodily waste because prison officials refused to provide assistance. Third, Goodman has alleged sufficient conduct to proceed with a § 1983 claim based on the prison staff's supposed 'deliberate indifference' to his serious medical condition of being partially paraplegic. . . . "

The Court remanded the suit to the District Court to permit Goodman to amend his complaint, while cautioning Goodman not to reassert all the § 1983 claims included in his initial complaint, "some of which [we]re obviously frivolous."

The Eleventh Circuit did not address the sufficiency of Goodman's allegations under Title II. Instead, relying on its prior decision in *Miller v. King*, 384 F.3d 1248 (2004), the Court of Appeals affirmed the District Court's holding that Goodman's Title II claims for money damages against the State were barred by sovereign immunity. We granted *certiorari* to consider whether Title II of the ADA validly abrogates state sovereign immunity with respect to the claims at issue here.

II

[I]n reversing the dismissal of Goodman's § 1983 claims, the Eleventh Circuit held that Goodman had alleged actual violations of the Eighth Amendment by state agents on the grounds set forth above. The State does not contest this holding, and we did not grant *certiorari* to consider the merits of Goodman's Eighth Amendment claims; we assume without deciding, therefore, that the Eleventh Circuit's treatment of these claims was correct. Moreover, Goodman urges, and the State does not dispute, that this same conduct that violated the Eighth Amendment also violated Title II of the ADA. In fact, it is quite plausible that the alleged deliberate refusal of prison officials to accommodate Goodman's disability-related needs in such fundamentals as mobility, hygiene, medical care, and virtually all other prison programs constituted "exclu[sion] from participation in or . . . den[ial of] the benefits of" the prison's "services, programs, or activities." 42 U.S.C. § 12132; see also *Yeskey* (noting that the phrase "services, programs, or activities" in § 12132 includes recreational, medical, educational, and vocational prison programs). Therefore, Goodman's claims for money damages against the State under Title II were evidently based, at least in large part, on conduct that independently violated the provisions of § 1 of the Fourteenth Amendment. See *Louisiana ex rel. Francis v. Resweber*, 329 U.S. 459, 463 (1947), (plurality opinion) (the Due Process Clause of the Fourteenth Amendment incorporates the Eighth Amendment's guarantee against cruel and unusual punishment). In this respect, Goodman differs from the claimants in our other cases addressing Congress's ability to abrogate sovereign immunity pursuant to its § 5 powers. See *Tennessee v. Lane*, 541 U.S. 509, 543, n.4 (2004) (Rehnquist, C.J., dissenting) (respondents were not actually denied constitutional rights); *Nevada Dept. of Human Resources v. Hibbs*, 538 U.S. 721, 752, 755 (2003) (KENNEDY, J., dissenting) (Nevada provided family leave "on a gender-neutral basis"—"a practice which no one contends suffers from a constitutional infirmity"); *Garrett*, 531 U.S., at 362, 367–368 (failure to make the special accommodations requested by disabled respondents was not unconstitutional); *Kimel v. Florida Bd. of Regents*, 528 U.S. 62, 69–70, 83–84 (2000) (most petitioners raised nonconstitutional disparate-impact challenges to the State's age-related policies); *Florida Prepaid Postsecondary Ed. Expense Bd. v. College Savings Bank*, 527 U.S. 627, 643–644, and n.9 (1999) (Florida satisfied due process by providing remedies for patent infringement by state actors); *City of Boerne v. Flores*, 521 U.S. 507, 512 (1997) (church building permit denied under neutral law of general applicability).

While the Members of this Court have disagreed regarding the scope of Congress's "prophylactic" enforcement powers under § 5 of the Fourteenth Amendment, see, *e.g.*, Lane, 541 U.S., at 513 (majority opinion of STEVENS, J.); *id.*, at 538 (REHNQUIST, C.J., dissenting); *id.*, at 554 (SCALIA, J., dissenting), no one doubts that § 5 grants Congress the power to "enforce . . . the provisions" of the Amendment by creating private remedies against the States for actual violations of those provisions. "Section 5 authorizes Congress to create a cause of action through which the citizen may vindicate his Fourteenth Amendment rights." *Id.*, at 559–560 (SCALIA, J., dissenting). This enforcement power includes the power to abrogate state sovereign immunity by authorizing private suits for damages against the States. Thus, insofar as Title II creates a private cause of action for damages against the States for conduct that actually violates the Fourteenth Amendment, Title II validly abrogates state sovereign immunity. The Eleventh Circuit erred in dismissing those of Goodman's Title II claims that were based on such unconstitutional conduct.

From the many allegations in Goodman's *pro se* complaint and his subsequent filings in the District Court, it is not clear precisely what conduct he intended to allege in support of his Title II claims. Because the Eleventh Circuit did not address the issue, it is likewise unclear to what extent the conduct underlying Goodman's constitutional claims also violated Title II. Moreover, the Eleventh Circuit ordered that the suit be remanded to the District Court to permit Goodman to amend his complaint, but instructed him to revise his factual allegations to exclude his "frivolous" claims—some of which are quite far afield from actual constitutional violations (under either the Eighth Amendment or some other constitutional provision), or even from Title II violations. See, *e.g.*, App. 50 (demanding a "steam table" for Goodman's housing unit). It is therefore unclear whether Goodman's amended complaint will assert Title II claims premised on conduct that does not independently violate the Fourteenth Amendment. Once Goodman's complaint is amended, the lower courts will be best situated to determine in the first instance, on a claim-by-claim basis, (1) which aspects of the State's alleged conduct violated Title II; (2) to what extent such misconduct also violated the Fourteenth Amendment; and (3) insofar as such misconduct violated Title II but did not violate the Fourteenth Amendment, whether Congress's purported abrogation of sovereign immunity as to that class of conduct is nevertheless valid.

* * *

The judgment of the Eleventh Circuit is reversed, and the suit is remanded for further proceedings consistent with this opinion.

It is so ordered.

■ JUSTICE STEVENS, with whom JUSTICE GINSBURG joins, concurring.

[R]ather than attempting to define the outer limits of Title II's valid abrogation of state sovereign immunity on the basis of the present record, the Court's opinion wisely permits the parties, guided by *Tennessee v. Lane*, to create a factual record that will inform that decision. I therefore join the opinion.

It is important to emphasize that although petitioner Goodman's Eighth Amendment claims provide a sufficient basis for reversal, our opinion does not suggest that this is the only constitutional right applicable in the prison context and therefore relevant to the abrogation issue. As we explain, when the District Court and the Court of Appeals revisit that issue, they should analyze Goodman's claims to see whether they state "actual constitutional violations (under either the Eighth Amendment or some other constitutional provision)," and to evaluate whether "Congress's purported abrogation of sovereign immunity in such contexts is nevertheless valid." This approach mirrors that taken in *Lane*, which identified a constellation of "basic constitutional guarantees" that Title II seeks to enforce and ultimately evaluated whether Title II was an appropriate response to the "class of cases" at hand. The Court's focus on Goodman's Eighth Amendment claims arises simply from the fact that those are the only constitutional violations the Eleventh Circuit found him to have alleged properly.

Moreover, our approach today is fully consistent with our recognition that the history of mistreatment leading to Congress' decision to extend Title II's protections to prison inmates was not limited to violations of the Eighth Amendment. In fact, as the Solicitor General points out in his brief arguing that Title II's damages remedy constitutes appropriate prophylactic legislation in the prison context, the record of mistreatment of prison inmates that Congress reviewed in its deliberations preceding the enactment of Title II was comparable in all relevant respects to the record that we recently held sufficient to uphold the application of that title to the entire class of cases implicating the fundamental right of access to the courts. And while it is true that cases involving inadequate medical care and inhumane conditions of confinement have perhaps been most numerous, courts have also reviewed myriad other types of claims by disabled prisoners, such as allegations of the abridgment of religious liberties, undue censorship, interference with access to the judicial process, and procedural due process violations. See, *e.g.*, *Vitek v. Jones*, 445 U.S. 480 (1980) (procedural due process); *May v. Sheahan*, 226 F.3d 876 (C.A.7

2000) (access to judicial process, lawyers, legal materials, and reading materials); *Littlefield v. Deland*, 641 F.2d 729 (C.A.10 1981) (access to reading and writing materials); *Nolley v. County of Erie*, 776 F.Supp. 715 (W.D.N.Y.1991) (access to law library and religious services).

NOTES ON LANE AND GEORGIA

1. **Is *Lane* Consistent with *Garrett*?** In his *Lane* dissent, Chief Justice Rehnquist (the author of *Garrett*) argues that the majority has disregarded *Garrett*'s holding. And, indeed, eight of the nine justices take the same position in *Lane* on the constitutionality of Title II's abrogation of sovereign immunity as they took in *Garrett* on the constitutionality of Title I's abrogation of sovereign immunity. Justice O'Connor joined the four *Garrett* dissenters to make a majority for Lane. And the *Lane* majority does clearly fail to heed some of the *statements* in the *Garrett* opinion. *Garrett* said that evidence of discrimination by municipalities is irrelevant in a case involving state sovereign, but *Lane* specifically considers evidence of inaccessible municipal courthouses. (As the *Lane* Court explains, municipal courthouses have a direct connection with the state government in a way municipal employment may not, however.) And *Garrett* seemed to say that the evidence before and the report of the congressionally appointed Task Force was irrelevant because the Task Force was not Congress itself; the *Lane* Court freely relied on both the evidence and the report.

What was the difference between *Lane* and *Georgia* that justified such different treatment? As Justice Stevens explains in his opinion for the Court in *Lane*, inaccessible courthouses threaten the fundamental right of access to the courts—really a bundle of rights, which trigger more than rational-basis scrutiny when they are denied by a state. Indeed, as Justice Stevens explains at the end of his opinion, the Court has held outside of the disability context that states have an affirmative constitutional obligation to make various accommodations to enable people of limited means to access court proceedings. Given this legal backdrop, the application of Title II of the ADA to the "class of cases implicating the fundamental right of access to the courts" was far more proportionate to the states' preexisting constitutional obligations than was the application of Title I to state employment.

2. **The As-Applied Analysis.** In *Garrett*, the Court did not ask whether Title I was valid Fourteenth Amendment enforcement legislation as applied to the two plaintiffs before it. Instead, it considered Title I in its full sweep and asked whether Congress could validly prohibit disability discrimination and require disability accommodation by states *in general*. In *Lane*, the Court did not consider Title II in its full sweep. Instead, it asked whether Congress had power under the Fourteenth Amendment to apply the statute to the "class of cases" involving access to the courts. In *Georgia*, the Court did not even ask whether Title II was valid Fourteenth Amendment legislation as applied to a "class of cases." Instead, the Court held that, to the extent that the facts the plaintiff alleged violated the Fourteenth Amendment as well as the statute, Title II was valid enforcement legislation *as applied to those facts*. In both *Lane* and *Georgia*, the Court reserved the question whether Title II is valid Fourteenth Amendment legislation across its entire sweep.

The upshot seems to be this: When a plaintiff alleges that the state violated Title II in a way that also violated her Fourteenth Amendment rights (including her rights under Bill of Rights provisions incorporated into the Fourteenth Amendment), the statute will be valid enforcement legislation as applied to her case. *Georgia.* When a plaintiff alleges that the state violated Title II in a way that posed a threat to rights that trigger heightened constitutional scrutiny, even if the state might not actually have violated her own constitutional rights, the statute will also likely be valid enforcement legislation as applied to her case. *Lane.* When the plaintiff alleges that the state violated Title II in a way that neither violated her own constitutional rights nor posed a threat to rights that trigger heightened constitutional scrutiny, the statute will not be valid enforcement legislation unless the courts uphold Title II as a whole as valid enforcement legislation (something the Court carefully avoided doing in *Lane* and *Georgia*). The notes that follow show how these principles have played out in post-*Lane* and post-*Georgia* litigation.

3.   Education. A number of courts of appeals have held, after *Lane* and *Georgia*, that Title II is valid Fourteenth Amendment enforcement legislation in the "class of cases" involving public education (including public higher education). These courts have acknowledged the Supreme Court's holding that "public education is not a fundamental right" triggering heightened scrutiny. *Toledo v. Sanchez*, 454 F.3d 24, 33 (1st Cir.2006) (citing *San Antonio Indep. Sch. Dist. v. Rodriguez*, 411 U.S. 1, 35 (1973)). But, these courts have noted, the Court has treated public education as triggering more significant constitutional protections than ordinary legislation. See *id.* ("[N]either is education 'merely some governmental "benefit" indistinguishable from other forms of social welfare legislation.' ") (quoting *Plyler v. Doe*, 457 U.S. 202, 221 (1982)). Indeed, the Court struck down a law excluding the children of illegal immigrants from public school based on something that seemed to be more than ordinary rational basis scrutiny. See *id.* (citing Plyler, 457 U.S. at 230).

These courts have also pointed to an extensive record of state exclusion of children with disabilities from schools and discriminating against children with disabilities who are in school. See, *e.g.*, *id.* at 37–38 (noting that "[n]umerous lower court decisions demonstrate that the states were violating the Due Process and Equal Protection rights of disabled children by completely denying them educational opportunities" prior to the adoption of the Rehabilitation Act and the IDEA; "[c]ongressional studies in the early 1970s revealed that of the roughly eight million handicapped children in the United States, one million were 'excluded entirely from the public school system' and more than half were not receiving appropriate educational services"; "[a] report before Congress in 1983 indicated that tens of thousands of disabled children continued to be excluded from public schools or placed in inappropriate programs"; and "[t]estimony before the House Committee on Education and Labor and the Senate Subcommittee on Disability Policy included statements by numerous disabled individuals who had been excluded from participation or faced irrational prejudice at all levels of public education").

Are these arguments sufficient under *Lane* to uphold the abrogation of sovereign immunity in cases alleging: (possibly animus-based) failure to excuse a graduate student's tardiness in class, extend deadlines for written work, or reschedule a course to the afternoon, *Toledo*, 454 F.3d at 34; refusal to give a college scholarship to a student whose learning disability prevented him from taking the required number of core classes in high school, *Bowers v. National Collegiate Athletic Assn.*, 475 F.3d 524, 553 (3d Cir.2007); refusal to grant extra time to a law student who experienced a migraine headache during her Constitutional Law final, *Constantine v. Rectors and Visitors of George Mason Univ.*, 411 F.3d 474, 478 (4th Cir.2005); or failure to provide sign language interpreters, note takers, and physical access to university students with disabilities, *Association for Disabled Americans, Inc. v. Florida Intern. Univ.*, 405 F.3d 954, 956 (11th Cir.2005)? In each of these cases, the court held that Title II validly abrogated the defendant's sovereign immunity.

4. Parking Placards. In *Klingler v. Director, Dept. of Revenue*, 455 F.3d 888 (8th Cir.2006), the Eighth Circuit applied *Lane* and *Georgia* to hold that Title II did not validly abrogate state sovereign immunity insofar as the statute applied to the plaintiffs' challenge to Missouri's $2.00 annual fee for the use of a disabled parking placard. The court recognized that the fee was discriminatory: "Because non-disabled people are not required to purchase a placard in order to park at public facilities, the fee discriminates against some disabled people who require the use of accessible parking spaces." *Id.* at 894. But the $2.00 fee did not itself violate the Constitution—thus bringing the case outside the scope of *Georgia*. *Id.* And, "[u]nlike the situation in *Lane*," disability-based discrimination in parking fees triggers nothing more than rational basis review. *Id.* The court did, however, hold that the fee violated Title II. It awarded injunctive relief to the plaintiffs (holding the statute valid for these purposes under the commerce power). But because the statute was not valid Fourteenth Amendment legislation as applied to parking placards, the court held that the plaintiffs' damages claim was barred by sovereign immunity. *Id.*

5. Voting. Is Title II valid Fourteenth Amendment enforcement legislation in cases challenging discrimination in voting? Professor Michael Waterstone argues that the answer is yes, because the Supreme Court has characterized voting as a fundamental right. See Michael E. Waterstone, Lane, *Fundamental Rights, and Voting*, 56 Ala. L. Rev. 793 (2005). The issue has not been the subject of significant litigation.

6. Deinstitutionalization. Is Title II, as applied to cases enforcing the *Olmstead* case (a principal case above), valid Fourteenth Amendment legislation? One might argue that *Olmstead* enforces *Youngberg*'s principle that an individual is entitled to the exercise of professional judgment in the interest of freedom from restraint—including the overarching restraint of the institution. One might also look to the history of abuses and constitutional violations within institutions (as illustrated by the facts of *Youngberg*) and argue that moving people out of institutions is a remedy for confinement in unconstitutional institutions. Are these arguments persuasive?

CHAPTER 5

PRIVATE HOUSING AND PUBLIC ACCOMMODATIONS

A. COVERAGE

PGA Tour, Inc. v. Martin

Supreme Court of the United States, 2001.
532 U.S. 661.

■ JUSTICE STEVENS delivered the opinion of the Court.

This case raises two questions concerning the application of the Americans with Disabilities Act of 1990 to a gifted athlete: first, whether the Act protects access to professional golf tournaments by a qualified entrant with a disability; and second, whether a disabled contestant may be denied the use of a golf cart because it would "fundamentally alter the nature" of the tournaments, [42 U.S.C.] § 12182(b)(2)(A)(ii), to allow him to ride when all other contestants must walk.

I

Petitioner PGA TOUR, Inc., a nonprofit entity formed in 1968, sponsors and cosponsors professional golf tournaments conducted on three annual tours. About 200 golfers participate in the PGA TOUR; about 170 in the NIKE TOUR; and about 100 in the SENIOR PGA TOUR. PGA TOUR and NIKE TOUR tournaments typically are 4-day events, played on courses leased and operated by petitioner. The entire field usually competes in two 18-hole rounds played on Thursday and Friday; those who survive the "cut" play on Saturday and Sunday and receive prize money in amounts determined by their aggregate scores for all four rounds. The revenues generated by television, admissions, concessions, and contributions from cosponsors amount to about $300 million a year, much of which is distributed in prize money.

There are various ways of gaining entry into particular tours. For example, a player who wins three NIKE TOUR events in the same year, or is among the top-15 money winners on that tour, earns the right to play in the PGA TOUR. Additionally, a golfer may obtain a spot in an official tournament through successfully competing in "open" qualifying rounds, which are conducted the week before each tournament. Most participants, however, earn playing privileges in the PGA TOUR or NIKE TOUR by way of a three-stage qualifying tournament known as the "Q-School."

Any member of the public may enter the Q-School by paying a $3,000 entry fee and submitting two letters of reference from, among others, PGA TOUR or NIKE TOUR members. The $3,000 entry fee covers the players' greens fees and the cost of golf carts, which are permitted during the first two stages, but which have been prohibited during the third stage since 1997. Each year, over a thousand contestants compete in the first stage, which consists of four 18-hole rounds at different locations. Approximately half of them make it to the second stage, which also includes 72 holes. Around 168 players survive the second stage and advance to the final one, where they compete over 108 holes. Of those finalists, about a fourth qualify for membership in the PGA TOUR, and the rest gain membership in the NIKE TOUR. The significance of making it into either tour is illuminated by the fact that there are about 25 million golfers in the country.

Three sets of rules govern competition in tour events. First, the "Rules of Golf," jointly written by the United States Golf Association (USGA) and the Royal and Ancient Golf Club of Scotland, apply to the game as it is played, not only by millions of amateurs on public courses and in private country clubs throughout the United States and worldwide, but also by the professionals in the tournaments conducted by petitioner, the USGA, the Ladies' Professional Golf Association, and the Senior Women's Golf Association. Those rules do not prohibit the use of golf carts at any time.[3]

Second, the "Conditions of Competition and Local Rules," often described as the "hard card," apply specifically to petitioner's professional tours. The hard cards for the PGA TOUR and NIKE TOUR require players to walk the golf course during tournaments, but not during open qualifying rounds.[4] On the SENIOR PGA TOUR, which is limited to golfers age 50 and older, the contestants may use golf carts. Most seniors, however, prefer to walk.

Third, "Notices to Competitors" are issued for particular tournaments and cover conditions for that specific event. Such a notice may, for example, explain how the Rules of Golf should be applied to a particular water hazard or manmade obstruction. It might also authorize the use of carts to speed up play when there is an unusual distance between one green and the next tee.[6]

The basic Rules of Golf, the hard cards, and the weekly notices apply equally to all players in tour competitions. As one of petitioner's witnesses explained with reference to "the Masters Tournament, which is golf at its very highest level, . . . the key is to have everyone tee off on the first hole under exactly the same conditions and all of them be tested over that 72-hole event under the conditions that exist during those four days of the event."

II

Casey Martin is a talented golfer. As an amateur, he won 17 Oregon Golf Association junior events before he was 15, and won the

---

[3]   Instead, Appendix I to the Rules of Golf lists a number of "optional" conditions, among them one related to transportation:

If it is desired to require players to walk in a competition, the following condition is suggested: "Players shall walk at all times during a stipulated round."

[4]   The PGA TOUR hard card provides: "Players shall walk at all times during a stipulated round unless permitted to ride by the PGA TOUR Rules Committee." The NIKE TOUR hard card similarly requires walking unless otherwise permitted. Additionally, as noted, golf carts have not been permitted during the third stage of the Q–School since 1997. Petitioner added this recent prohibition in order to "approximat[e] a PGA TOUR event as closely as possible."

[6]   See, *e.g.*, App. 156–160 (Notices to Competitors for 1997 Bob Hope Chrysler Classic, 1997 AT & T Pebble Beach National Pro–Am, and 1997 Quad City Classic).

state championship as a high school senior. He played on the Stanford University golf team that won the 1994 National Collegiate Athletic Association (NCAA) championship. As a professional, Martin qualified for the NIKE TOUR in 1998 and 1999, and based on his 1999 performance, qualified for the PGA TOUR in 2000. In the 1999 season, he entered 24 events, made the cut 13 times, and had 6 top-10 finishes, coming in second twice and third once.

Martin is also an individual with a disability as defined in the Americans with Disabilities Act of 1990 (ADA or Act). Since birth he has been afflicted with Klippel-Trenaunay-Weber Syndrome, a degenerative circulatory disorder that obstructs the flow of blood from his right leg back to his heart. The disease is progressive; it causes severe pain and has atrophied his right leg. During the latter part of his college career, because of the progress of the disease, Martin could no longer walk an 18-hole golf course. Walking not only caused him pain, fatigue, and anxiety, but also created a significant risk of hemorrhaging, developing blood clots, and fracturing his tibia so badly that an amputation might be required. For these reasons, Stanford made written requests to the Pacific 10 Conference and the NCAA to waive for Martin their rules requiring players to walk and carry their own clubs. The requests were granted.

When Martin turned pro and entered petitioner's Q-School, the hard card permitted him to use a cart during his successful progress through the first two stages. He made a request, supported by detailed medical records, for permission to use a golf cart during the third stage. Petitioner refused to review those records or to waive its walking rule for the third stage. Martin therefore filed this action. A preliminary injunction entered by the District Court made it possible for him to use a cart in the final stage of the Q-School and as a competitor in the NIKE TOUR and PGA TOUR. Although not bound by the injunction, and despite its support for petitioner's position in this litigation, the USGA voluntarily granted Martin a similar waiver in events that it sponsors, including the U.S. Open.

III

In the District Court, petitioner moved for summary judgment on the ground that [t]he play areas of its tour competitions do not constitute places of "public accommodation" within the scope of that Title.[11] [A]fter noting that the statutory definition of public accommodation included a "golf course,"[12] [the Magistrate Judge] rejected petitioner's argument that its competitions are only places of public accommodation in the areas open to spectators. The operator of a public accommodation could not, in his view, "create private enclaves within the facility . . . and thus relegate the ADA to hop-scotch areas." Accordingly, he denied petitioner's motion for summary judgment.

At trial, petitioner did not contest the conclusion that Martin has a disability covered by the ADA, or the fact "that his disability prevents him from walking the course during a round of golf." Rather, petitioner asserted that the condition of walking is a substantive rule of

---

[11]   See § 12181(7).

[12]   § 12181(7)(L).

competition, and that waiving it as to any individual for any reason would fundamentally alter the nature of the competition. Petitioner's evidence included the testimony of a number of experts, among them some of the greatest golfers in history. Arnold Palmer,[13] Jack Nicklaus,[14] and Ken Venturi[15] explained that fatigue can be a critical factor in a tournament, particularly on the last day when psychological pressure is at a maximum. Their testimony makes it clear that, in their view, permission to use a cart might well give some players a competitive advantage over other players who must walk. They did not, however, express any opinion on whether a cart would give Martin such an advantage.

Rejecting petitioner's argument that an individualized inquiry into the necessity of the walking rule in Martin's case would be inappropriate, the District Court stated that it had "the independent duty to inquire into the purpose of the rule at issue, and to ascertain whether there can be a reasonable modification made to accommodate plaintiff without frustrating the purpose of the rule" and thereby fundamentally altering the nature of petitioner's tournaments. The judge found that the purpose of the rule was to inject fatigue into the skill of shotmaking, but that the fatigue injected "by walking the course cannot be deemed significant under normal circumstances." Furthermore, Martin presented evidence, and the judge found, that even with the use of a cart, Martin must walk over a mile during an 18-hole round,[17] and that the fatigue he suffers from coping with his disability is "undeniably greater" than the fatigue his able-bodied competitors endure from walking the course. As the judge observed:

> "[P]laintiff is in significant pain when he walks, and even when he is getting in and out of the cart. With each step, he is at risk of fracturing his tibia and hemorrhaging. The other golfers have to endure the psychological stress of competition as part of their fatigue; Martin has the same stress plus the added stress of pain and risk of serious injury. As he put it, he would gladly trade the cart for a good leg. To perceive that the

---

[13] "Q. And fatigue is one of the factors that can cause a golfer at the PGA Tour level to lose one stroke or more?

"A. Oh, it is. And it has happened.

"Q. And can one stroke be the difference between winning and not winning a tournament at the PGA Tour level?

"A. As I said, I've lost a few national opens by one stroke."

[14] "Q. Mr. Nicklaus, what is your understanding of the reason why in these competitive events . . . that competitors are required to walk the course?

"A. Well, in my opinion, physical fitness and fatigue are part of the game of golf."

[15] "Q. So are you telling the court that this fatigue factor tends to accumulate over the course of the four days of the tournament?

"A. Oh definitely. There's no doubt.

"Q. Does this fatigue factor that you've talked about, Mr. Venturi, affect the manner in which you—you perform as a professional out on the golf course?

"A. Oh, there's no doubt, again, but that, that fatigue does play a big part. It will influence your game. It will influence your shot-making. It will influence your decisions."

[17] "In the first place, he does walk while on the course—even with a cart, he must move from cart to shot and back to the cart. In essence, he still must walk approximately 25% of the course. On a course roughly five miles in length, Martin will walk 1 1/4 miles."

cart puts him—with his condition—at a competitive advantage is a gross distortion of reality."

As a result, the judge concluded that it would "not fundamentally alter the nature of the PGA Tour's game to accommodate him with a cart." The judge accordingly entered a permanent injunction requiring petitioner to permit Martin to use a cart in tour and qualifying events.

[The Ninth Circuit affirmed.] The day after the Ninth Circuit ruled in Martin's favor, the Seventh Circuit came to a contrary conclusion in a case brought against the USGA by a disabled golfer who failed to qualify for "America's greatest—and most democratic—golf tournament, the United States Open." The Seventh Circuit endorsed the conclusion of the District Court in that case that "the nature of the competition would be fundamentally altered if the walking rule were eliminated because it would remove stamina (at least a particular type of stamina) from the set of qualities designed to be tested in this competition." In the Seventh Circuit's opinion, the physical ordeals endured by Ken Venturi and Ben Hogan when they walked to their Open victories in 1964 and 1950 amply demonstrated the importance of stamina in such a tournament. As an alternative basis for its holding, the court also concluded that the ADA does not require the USGA to bear "the administrative burdens of evaluating requests to waive the walking rule and permit the use of a golf cart."

Although the Seventh Circuit merely assumed that the ADA applies to professional golf tournaments, and therefore did not disagree with the Ninth on the threshold coverage issue, our grant of certiorari encompasses that question as well as the conflict between those courts.

IV

Congress enacted the ADA in 1990 to remedy widespread discrimination against disabled individuals. In studying the need for such legislation, Congress found that "historically, society has tended to isolate and segregate individuals with disabilities, and, despite some improvements, such forms of discrimination against individuals with disabilities continue to be a serious and pervasive social problem." 42 U.S.C. § 12101(a)(2); see § 12101(a)(3) ("[D]iscrimination against individuals with disabilities persists in such critical areas as employment, housing, public accommodations, education, transportation, communication, recreation, institutionalization, health services, voting, and access to public services"). Congress noted that the many forms such discrimination takes include "outright intentional exclusion" as well as the "failure to make modifications to existing facilities and practices." § 12101(a)(5). After thoroughly investigating the problem, Congress concluded that there was a "compelling need" for a "clear and comprehensive national mandate" to eliminate discrimination against disabled individuals, and to integrate them "into the economic and social mainstream of American life." S.Rep.No.101–116, p. 20 (1989).

In the ADA, Congress provided that broad mandate. See 42 U.S.C. § 12101(b). In fact, one of the Act's "most impressive strengths" has been identified as its "comprehensive character," Hearings on S. 933 before the Senate Committee on Labor and Human Resources and the Subcommittee on the Handicapped, 101st Cong., 1st Sess., 197 (1989) (statement of Attorney General Thornburgh), and accordingly the Act has been described as "a milestone on the path to a more decent, tolerant, progressive society," *Board of Trustees of Univ. of Ala. v. Garrett* (KENNEDY, J., concurring). To effectuate its sweeping purpose, the ADA forbids discrimination against disabled individuals in major areas of public life, among them employment (Title I of the Act), public services (Title II), and public accommodations (Title III). At issue now, as a threshold matter, is the applicability of Title III to petitioner's golf tours and qualifying rounds, in particular to petitioner's treatment of a qualified disabled golfer wishing to compete in those events.

Title III of the ADA prescribes, as a "[g]eneral rule":

"No individual shall be discriminated against on the basis of disability in the full and equal enjoyment of the goods, services, facilities, privileges, advantages, or accommodations of any place of public accommodation by any person who owns, leases (or leases to), or operates a place of public accommodation." 42 U.S.C. § 12182(a).

The phrase "public accommodation" is defined in terms of 12 extensive categories,[24] which the legislative history indicates "should be construed liberally" to afford people with disabilities "equal access" to the wide variety of establishments available to the nondisabled.

It seems apparent, from both the general rule and the comprehensive definition of "public accommodation," that petitioner's golf tours and their qualifying rounds fit comfortably within the coverage of Title III, and Martin within its protection. The events occur on "golf course[s]," a type of place specifically identified by the Act as a public accommodation. § 12181(7)(L). In addition, at all relevant times, petitioner "leases" and "operates" golf courses to conduct its Q-School and tours. § 12182(a). As a lessor and operator of golf courses, then, petitioner must not discriminate against any "individual" in the "full and equal enjoyment of the goods, services, facilities, privileges, advantages, or accommodations" of those courses. Certainly, among the

---

[24] "(A) an inn, hotel, motel, or other place of lodging, except for an establishment located within a building that contains not more than five rooms for rent or hire and that is actually occupied by the proprietor of such establishment as the residence of such proprietor;

"(B) a restaurant, bar, or other establishment serving food or drink;

"(C) a motion picture house, theater, concert hall, stadium, or other place of exhibition or entertainment;

"(D) an auditorium, convention center, lecture hall, or other place of public gathering;

"(E) a bakery, grocery store, clothing store, hardware store, shopping center, or other sales or rental establishment;

"(F) a laundromat, dry-cleaner, bank, barber shop, beauty shop, travel service, shoe repair service, funeral parlor, gas station, office of an accountant or lawyer, pharmacy, insurance office, professional office of a health care provider, hospital, or other service establishment;

"(G) a terminal, depot, or other station used for specified public transportation;

"(H) a museum, library, gallery, or other place of display or collection;

"(I) a park, zoo, amusement park, or other place of recreation;

"(J) a nursery, elementary, secondary, undergraduate, or postgraduate private school, or other place of education;

"(K) a day care center, senior citizen center, homeless shelter, food bank, adoption agency, or other social service center establishment; and

"(L) a gymnasium, health spa, bowling alley, *golf course*, or other place of exercise or recreation." § 12181(7) (emphasis added).

"privileges" offered by petitioner on the courses are those of competing in the Q-School and playing in the tours; indeed, the former is a privilege for which thousands of individuals from the general public pay, and the latter is one for which they vie. Martin, of course, is one of those individuals. It would therefore appear that Title III of the ADA, by its plain terms, prohibits petitioner from denying Martin equal access to its tours on the basis of his disability.

Petitioner argues otherwise. To be clear about its position, it does not assert (as it did in the District Court) that it is a private club altogether exempt from Title III's coverage. In fact, petitioner admits that its tournaments are conducted at places of public accommodation. Nor does petitioner contend (as it did in both the District Court and the Court of Appeals) that the competitors' area "behind the ropes" is not a public accommodation, notwithstanding the status of the rest of the golf course. Rather, petitioner reframes the coverage issue by arguing that the competing golfers are not members of the class protected by Title III of the ADA.

According to petitioner, Title III is concerned with discrimination against "clients and customers" seeking to obtain "goods and services" at places of public accommodation, whereas it is Title I that protects persons who work at such places. As the argument goes, petitioner operates not a "golf course" during its tournaments but a "place of exhibition or entertainment," 42 U.S.C. § 12181(7)(C), and a professional golfer such as Martin, like an actor in a theater production, is a provider rather than a consumer of the entertainment that petitioner sells to the public. Martin therefore cannot bring a claim under Title III because he is not one of the " 'clients or customers of the covered public accommodation.' " Rather, Martin's claim of discrimination is "job-related" and could only be brought under Title I— but that Title does not apply because he is an independent contractor (as the District Court found) rather than an employee.

The reference to "clients or customers" that petitioner quotes appears in 42 U.S.C. § 12182(b)(1)(A)(iv), which states: "For purposes of clauses (i) through (iii) of this subparagraph, the term 'individual or class of individuals' refers to the clients or customers of the covered public accommodation that enters into the contractual, licensing or other arrangement." Clauses (i) through (iii) of the subparagraph prohibit public accommodations from discriminating against a disabled "individual or class of individuals" in certain ways either directly or indirectly through contractual arrangements with other entities. Those clauses make clear on the one hand that their prohibitions cannot be avoided by means of contract, while clause (iv) makes clear on the other hand that contractual relationships will not expand a public accommodation's obligations under the subparagraph beyond its own clients or customers.

As petitioner recognizes, clause (iv) is not literally applicable to Title III's general rule prohibiting discrimination against disabled individuals. Title III's broad general rule contains no express "clients or customers" limitation, § 12182(a), and § 12182(b)(1)(A)(iv) provides that its limitation is only "[f]or purposes of" the clauses in that separate subparagraph. Nevertheless, petitioner contends that clause (iv)'s restriction of the subparagraph's coverage to the clients or customers of public accommodations fairly describes the scope of Title III's protection as a whole.

We need not decide whether petitioner's construction of the statute is correct, because petitioner's argument falters even on its own terms. If Title III's protected class were limited to "clients or customers," it would be entirely appropriate to classify the golfers who pay petitioner $3,000 for the chance to compete in the Q-School and, if successful, in the subsequent tour events, as petitioner's clients or customers. In our view, petitioner's tournaments (whether situated at a "golf course" or at a "place of exhibition or entertainment") simultaneously offer at least two "privileges" to the public—that of watching the golf competition and that of competing in it. Although the latter is more difficult and more expensive to obtain than the former, it is nonetheless a privilege that petitioner makes available to members of the general public. In consideration of the entry fee, any golfer with the requisite letters of recommendation acquires the opportunity to qualify for and compete in petitioner's tours. Additionally, any golfer who succeeds in the open qualifying rounds for a tournament may play in the event. That petitioner identifies one set of clients or customers that it serves (spectators at tournaments) does not preclude it from having another set (players in tournaments) against whom it may not discriminate. It would be inconsistent with the literal text of the statute as well as its expansive purpose to read Title III's coverage, even given petitioner's suggested limitation, any less broadly.[33]

Our conclusion is consistent with case law in the analogous context of Title II of the Civil Rights Act of 1964, 78 Stat. 243, 42 U.S.C. § 2000a *et seq.* Title II of that Act prohibits public accommodations from discriminating on the basis of race, color, religion, or national origin. § 2000a(a). In *Daniel v. Paul*, 395 U.S. 298 (1969), applying Title II to the Lake Nixon Club in Little Rock, Arkansas, we held that the definition of a "place of exhibition or entertainment," as a public accommodation, covered participants "in some sport or activity" as well as "spectators or listeners." We find equally persuasive two lower court opinions applying Title II specifically to golfers and golf tournaments. In *Evans v. Laurel Links, Inc.*, 261 F.Supp. 474, 477 (E.D.Va.1966), a class action brought to require a commercial golf establishment to permit black golfers to play on its course, the District Court held that Title II "is not limited to spectators if the place of exhibition or entertainment provides facilities for the public to participate in the

---

[33] Contrary to the dissent's suggestion, our view of the Q–School does not make "everyone who seeks a job" at a public accommodation, through "an open tryout" or otherwise, "a customer." *Post* (opinion of SCALIA, J.). Unlike those who successfully apply for a job at a place of public accommodation, or those who successfully bid for a contract, the golfers who qualify for petitioner's tours play at their own pleasure (perhaps, but not necessarily, for prize money), and although they commit to playing in at least 15 tournaments, they are not bound by any obligations typically associated with employment. See, e.g., App. 260 (trial testimony of PGA commissioner Timothy Finchem) (petitioner lacks control over when and where tour members compete, and over their manner of performance outside the rules of competition). Furthermore, unlike athletes in "other professional sports, such as baseball," *post*, in which players are employed by their clubs, the golfers on tour are not employed by petitioner or any related organizations. The record does not support the proposition that the purpose of the Q–School "is to hire," *ibid.*, rather than to narrow the field of participants in the sporting events that petitioner sponsors at places of public accommodation.

entertainment."[34] And in *Wesley v. Savannah*, 294 F.Supp. 698 (S.D.Ga. 1969), the District Court found that a private association violated Title II when it limited entry in a golf tournament on a municipal course to its own members but permitted all (and only) white golfers who paid the membership and entry fees to compete.[35] These cases support our conclusion that, as a public accommodation during its tours and qualifying rounds, petitioner may not discriminate against either spectators or competitors on the basis of disability.

V

[Part V of Justice Stevens's opinion discusses the "reasonable modification" question; it is excerpted in Section C, *infra*.]

■ JUSTICE SCALIA, with whom JUSTICE THOMAS joins, dissenting.

In my view today's opinion exercises a benevolent compassion that the law does not place it within our power to impose. The judgment distorts the text of Title III, the structure of the ADA, and common sense. I respectfully dissent.

I

The Court holds that a professional sport is a place of public accommodation and that respondent is a "custome[r]" of "competition" when he practices his profession. It finds that this strange conclusion is compelled by the "literal text" of Title III of the Americans with Disabilities Act of 1990(ADA), 42 U.S.C. § 12101 *et seq.*, by the "expansive purpose" of the ADA, and by the fact that Title II of the Civil Rights Act of 1964, 42 U.S.C. § 2000a(a), has been applied to an amusement park and public golf courses. I disagree.

The ADA has three separate titles: Title I covers employment discrimination, Title II covers discrimination by government entities, and Title III covers discrimination by places of public accommodation. Title II is irrelevant to this case. Title I protects only "employees" of employers who have 15 or more employees, §§ 12112(a), 12111(5)(A). It does not protect independent contractors. Respondent claimed employment discrimination under Title I, but the District Court found him to be an independent contractor rather than an employee.

Respondent also claimed protection under § 12182 of Title III. That section applies only to particular places and persons. The place must be a "place of public accommodation," and the person must be an "individual" seeking "enjoyment of the goods, services, facilities, privileges, advantages, or accommodations" of the covered place. § 12182(a). Of course a court indiscriminately invoking the "sweeping" and "expansive" purposes of the ADA could argue that when a place of public accommodation denied any "individual," on the basis of his disability, anything that might be called a "privileg[e]," the individual has a valid Title III claim. On such an interpretation, the employees and independent contractors of every place of public accommodation

---

[34] Title II of the Civil Rights Act of 1964 includes in its definition of "public accommodation" a "place of exhibition or entertainment" but does not specifically list a "golf course" as an example. See 42 U.S.C. § 2000a(b).

[35] Under petitioner's theory, Title II would not preclude it from discriminating against golfers on racial grounds. App. 197; Tr. of Oral Arg. 11–12.

come within Title III: The employee enjoys the "privilege" of employment, the contractor the "privilege" of the contract.

For many reasons, Title III will not bear such an interpretation. The provision of Title III at issue here (§ 12182, its principal provision) is a public-accommodation law, and it is the traditional understanding of public-accommodation laws that they provide rights for customers. "At common law, innkeepers, smiths, and others who made profession of a public employment, were prohibited from refusing, without good reason, to serve a customer." This understanding is clearly reflected in the text of Title III itself. Section 12181(7) lists 12 specific types of entities that qualify as "public accommodations," with a follow-on expansion that makes it clear what the "enjoyment of the goods, services, etc.," of those entities consists of—and it plainly envisions that the person "enjoying" the "public accommodation" will be a customer. For example, Title III is said to cover an "auditorium" or "other place of public gathering," § 12181(7)(D). Thus, "gathering" is the distinctive enjoyment derived from an auditorium; the persons "gathering" at an auditorium are presumably covered by Title III, but those contracting to clean the auditorium are not. Title III is said to cover a "zoo" or "other place of recreation," § 12181(7)(I). The persons "recreat[ing]" at a "zoo" are presumably covered, but the animal handlers bringing in the latest panda are not. The one place where Title III specifically addresses discrimination by places of public accommodation through "contractual" arrangements, it makes clear that discrimination against the other party to the contract is not covered, but only discrimination against "clients or customers of the covered public accommodation that enters into the contractual, licensing or other arrangement." § 12182(b)(1)(A)(iv). And finally, the regulations promulgated by the Department of Justice reinforce the conclusion that Title III's protections extend only to customers. "The purpose of the ADA's public accommodations requirements," they say, "is to ensure accessibility to the goods offered by a public accommodation." 28 CFR, ch. 1, pt. 36, App. B, p. 650 (2000). Surely this has nothing to do with employees and independent contractors.

If there were any doubt left that § 12182 covers only clients and customers of places of public accommodation, it is eliminated by the fact that a contrary interpretation would make a muddle of the ADA as a whole. The words of Title III must be read "in their context and with a view to their place in the overall statutory scheme." Congress expressly excluded employers of fewer than 15 employees from Title I. The mom-and-pop grocery store or laundromat need not worry about altering the nonpublic areas of its place of business to accommodate handicapped employees—or about the litigation that failure to do so will invite. Similarly, since independent contractors are not covered by Title I, the small business (or the large one, for that matter) need not worry about making special accommodations for the painters, electricians, and other independent workers whose services are contracted for from time to time. It is an entirely unreasonable interpretation of the statute to say that these exemptions so carefully crafted in Title I are entirely eliminated by Title III (for the many businesses that are places of public accommodation) because employees and independent contractors "enjoy" the employment and contracting that such places provide. The only distinctive feature of places of public accommodation is that they accommodate the public, and Congress could have no conceivable reason for according the employees and independent contractors of such businesses protections that employees and independent contractors of other businesses do not enjoy.

The United States apparently agrees that employee claims are not cognizable under Title III, but despite the implications of its own regulations, see 28 CFR, ch. 1, pt. 36, App.B, at 650, appears to believe (though it does not explicitly state) that claims of independent contractors are cognizable. In a discussion littered with entirely vague statements from the legislative history, the United States argues that Congress presumably wanted independent contractors with private entities covered under Title III because independent contractors with governmental entities are covered by Title II—a line of reasoning that does not commend itself to the untutored intellect. But since the United States does not provide (and I cannot conceive of) any possible construction of the terms of Title III that will exclude employees while simultaneously covering independent contractors, its concession regarding employees effectively concedes independent contractors as well. Title III applies only to customers.

The Court, for its part, assumes that conclusion for the sake of argument, but pronounces respondent to be a "customer" of the PGA TOUR or of the golf courses on which it is played. That seems to me quite incredible. The PGA TOUR is a professional sporting event, staged for the entertainment of a live and TV audience, the receipts from whom (the TV audience's admission price is paid by advertisers) pay the expenses of the tour, including the cash prizes for the winning golfers. The professional golfers on the tour are no more "enjoying" (the statutory term) the entertainment that the tour provides, or the facilities of the golf courses on which it is held, than professional baseball players "enjoy" the baseball games in which they play or the facilities of Yankee Stadium. To be sure, professional ballplayers participate in the games, and use the ballfields, but no one in his right mind would think that they are customers of the American League or of Yankee Stadium. They are themselves the entertainment that the customers pay to watch. And professional golfers are no different. It makes not a bit of difference, insofar as their "customer" status is concerned, that the remuneration for their performance (unlike most of the remuneration for ballplayers) is not fixed but contingent—*viz.*, the purses for the winners in the various events, and the compensation from product endorsements that consistent winners are assured. The compensation of many independent contractors is contingent upon their success—real estate brokers, for example, or insurance salesmen.

As the Court points out, the ADA specifically identifies golf courses as one of the covered places of public accommodation. See § 12181(7)(L) ("a gymnasium, health spa, bowling alley, golf course, or other place of exercise or recreation"); and the distinctive "goo[d], servic[e], facilit[y], privileg [e], advantag[e], or accommodatio[n]" identified by that provision as distinctive to that category of place of public accommodation is "exercise or recreation." Respondent did not seek to "exercise" or "recreate" at the PGA TOUR events; he sought to make money (which is why he is called a professional golfer). He was not a customer buying recreation or entertainment; he was a professional athlete selling it. That is the reason (among others) the Court's reliance upon Civil Rights Act cases like *Daniel v. Paul*, 395 U.S. 298 (1969), is misplaced. A professional golfer's practicing his profession is not comparable to John Q. Public's frequenting "a 232-acre amusement area with swimming, boating, sun bathing, picnicking, miniature golf, dancing facilities, and a snack bar." *Daniel*, *supra*, at 301.

The Court relies heavily upon the Q-School. It says that petitioner offers the golfing public the "privilege" of "competing in the Q-School and playing in the tours; indeed, the former is a privilege for which thousands of individuals from the general public pay, and the latter is one for which they vie." But the Q-School is no more a "privilege" offered for the general public's "enjoyment" than is the California Bar Exam. It is a competition for entry into the PGA TOUR—an open tryout, no different in principle from open casting for a movie or stage production, or walk-on tryouts for other professional sports, such as baseball. See, *e.g.*, *Amateurs Join Pros for New Season of HBO's "Sopranos,"* Detroit News, Dec. 22, 2000, p. 2 (20,000 attend open casting for "The Sopranos"); Bill Zack, *Atlanta Braves*, Sporting News, Feb. 6, 1995 (1,300 would-be players attended an open tryout for the Atlanta Braves). It may well be that some amateur golfers enjoy trying to make the grade, just as some amateur actors may enjoy auditions, and amateur baseball players may enjoy open tryouts (I hesitate to say that amateur lawyers may enjoy taking the California Bar Exam). But the purpose of holding those tryouts is not to provide entertainment; it is to hire. At bottom, open tryouts for performances to be held at a place of public accommodation are no different from open bidding on contracts to cut the grass at a place of public accommodation, or open applications for any job at a place of public accommodation. Those bidding, those applying—and those trying out—are not converted into customers. By the Court's reasoning, a business exists not only to sell goods and services to the public, but to provide the "privilege" of employment to the public; wherefore it follows, like night the day, that everyone who seeks a job is a customer.[2]

II

[Part II of Justice Scalia's opinion addresses the reasonable modification question. It is excerpted in Section C, *infra*.]

NOTE ON ADA TITLE III AND FAIR HOUSING ACT COVERAGE

1. "Places of Public Accommodation." Title III prohibits discrimination by "place[s] of public accommodation." 42 U.S.C § 12182(a). Must a plaintiff be discriminated against at, or denied access to, the physical "place" where the defendant does business in order to bring a

---

[2] The Court suggests that respondent is not an independent contractor because he "play[s] at [his] own pleasure," and is not subject to PGA TOUR control "over [his] manner of performance." But many independent contractors—composers of movie music, portrait artists, script writers, and even (some would say) plumbers—retain at least as much control over when and how they work as does respondent, who agrees to play in a minimum of 15 of the designated PGA TOUR events, and to play by the rules that the PGA TOUR specifies. Moreover, although, as the Court suggests in the same footnote, in rare cases a PGA TOUR winner will choose to forgo the prize money (in order, for example, to preserve amateur status necessary for continuing participation in college play) he is contractually entitled to the prize money if he demands it, which is all that a contractual relationship requires.

claim under this provision? In a case decided soon after the ADA became effective, the First Circuit held that "establishments of 'public accommodation' " under the statute are not "limited to actual physical structures." *Carparts Distribution Center, Inc. v. Automotive Wholesaler's Assn. of New England*, 37 F.3d 12, 19 (1st Cir.1994). The court noted that the statutory definition of public accommodation expressly includes "travel service[s]," 42 U.S.C. § 12181(7)(F), and "[m]any travel services conduct business by telephone or correspondence without requiring their customers to enter an office in order to obtain their services." *Id.* "It would be irrational," the court held, "to conclude that persons who enter an office to purchase services are protected by the ADA, but persons who purchase the same services over the telephone or by mail are not." *Id.* See also *Pallozzi v. Allstate Life Ins. Co.*, 198 F.3d 28, 33 (2d Cir.1999) (permitting the plaintiff to sue an insurance company for refusing to sell him life insurance, even though he never sought access to the company's place of business).

But a number of courts of appeals have disagreed and held that a plaintiff may not maintain a lawsuit under Title III unless she was denied access to, or discriminated against at, the defendant's physical place of business. In *Ford v. Schering-Plough Corp.*, 145 F.3d 601, 614 (3d Cir.1998), the court relied on the canon of *noscitur a sociis* and noted that the overwhelming majority of the "public accommodations" enumerated in the statute "refer to places with resources utilized by physical access." Accordingly, the court held that the plaintiff could not sue her insurance company for discriminatory plan terms, because she never went to her insurer's physical facilities. *Id.* See also *Parker v. Metropolitan Life Ins. Co.*, 121 F.3d 1006 (6th Cir.1997) (*en banc*) (same). Which side do you think has the better of this argument? The issue has obvious implications for Title III's coverage of goods and services provided over the internet, the subject of the note immediately below.

2. Independent Contractors. Does *PGA Tour* imply that Title III of the ADA applies to businesses' decisions to hire and fire independent contractors? Justice Scalia certainly thinks so. In *Menkowitz v. Pottstown Memorial Medical Center*, 154 F.3d 113 (3d Cir.1998), the defendant hospital suspended the staff privileges of the plaintiff doctor (an independent contractor) after he was diagnosed with Attention Deficit Disorder. The Third Circuit concluded that the plaintiff had stated a claim under Title III, because he had been denied the "full and equal enjoyment of the goods, services, facilities, privileges, advantages, or accommodations," 42 U.S.C. § 12182(a), of the hospital—a place of public accommodation. *Menkowitz*, 154 F.3d at 121–123. Does this holding make sense? Was Dr. Menkowitz's situation any different from Casey Martin's? Does it make a difference, in this regard, that the PGA Tour holds open tryouts, while hospitals presumably do not?

3. Commercial Facilities. Title III applies its requirements of accessible construction (see Section B, *infra*) to all "commercial facilities," even if they do not constitute "public accommodations." See 42 U.S.C. § 12183. But the remainder of Title III's requirements apply only to those facilities that constitute "public accommodations." See *id.* § 12182. Unlike its coverage of "public accommodations," the statute's coverage of "commercial facilities" aims to protect employees rather than customers.

See, *e.g.*, H.R.Rep.No.101–485, Part 2, at 117 (1990) ("To the extent that new facilities are built in a manner that make them accessible to all individuals, including potential employees, there will be less of a need for individual employers to engage in reasonable accommodations for particular employees.").

4.   Cruise Ships. In *Spector v. Norwegian Cruise Line Ltd.*, 545 U.S. 119 (2005), the Supreme Court held that foreign-flagged cruise ships in United States waters are "public accommodations."

5.   The Fair Housing Act. As the remaining sections in the chapter will show, the Fair Housing Act imposes accessibility and accommodation requirements that largely parallel those of ADA Title III. See 42 U.S.C. § 3604(f). Those requirements apply to any multifamily dwelling except those in which the owner and no more than three other families live. See *id.* § 3603(b)(2) (the "Mrs. Murphy" exception).

NOTE ON INTERNET COVERAGE

A number of cases have addressed the application of Title III to claims that businesses' internet sites do not contain features that make them accessible to people with visual impairments who are using screen readers. Perhaps the two most significant cases are *National Federation of the Blind v. Target Corp.*, 452 F.Supp.2d 946 (N.D.Cal.2006), and *Access Now v. Southwest Airlines*, 227 F.Supp.2d 1312 (S.D.Fla. 2002). In *National Federation of the Blind*, the court held that, even if the plaintiffs were not denied physical access to Target's stores, they stated a claim that Target's inaccessible website denied them "full enjoyment," 42 U.S.C. § 12182(a), of the goods and services offered at the company's brick-and-mortar stores. *National Federation of the Blind*, 452 F.Supp.2d at 954–955. In *Access Now*, the court held that Southwest Airlines' website was not a place of public accommodation, and its alleged inaccessibility did not deny plaintiffs the enjoyment of the goods and services of a place of public accommodation. *Access Now*, 227 F.Supp.2d at 1318–1321. (Note one complication for the *Access Now* plaintiffs: Title III does not list airports or airlines as "public accommodations." Disability discrimination by airlines is covered by the Air Carrier Access Act, 49 U.S.C. § 41705, which has no private right of action.)

In NATIONAL ASSOCIATION OF THE DEAF V. NETFLIX, INC., 869 F.Supp.2d 196 (D.Mass.2012), a deaf person and two organizations of people who are deaf or hard of hearing alleged that Netflix's on-demand online streaming videos were inaccessible to people with hearing impairments because, among other things, captioning was available for only a small proportion of them. The plaintiffs contended that the lack of captioning denied them full and equal enjoyment of Netflix's services in violation of Title III. Netflix moved for judgment on the pleadings. The company argued that its video-streaming website was not a "place of public accommodation." The court rejected that argument and denied the motion:

> The ADA lists twelve categories of entities that qualify as places of public accommodation. 42 U.S.C. § 12181(7). Plaintiffs argue that the Watch Instantly web site falls within the scope of four of these categories: "place of exhibition and entertainment," "place of recreation," "sales or rental establishment," and "service

establishment." *Id.* According to Plaintiffs, Defendant is a business that provides a subscription service of internet-based streaming video through the Watch Instantly web site and, as such, is analogous to a brick-and-mortar store or other venue that provides similar services, such as a video rental store.

Plaintiffs' interpretation of the statute as applying to web-based businesses is supported by the First Circuit's decision in *Carparts* [discussed in the previous note], which held that "places of public accommodation" are not limited to "actual physical structures." The First Circuit explained that

> [i]t would be irrational to conclude that persons who enter an office to purchase services are protected by the ADA, but persons who purchase the same services over the telephone or by mail are not. Congress could not have intended such an absurd result.

Carparts's reasoning applies with equal force to services purchased over the Internet, such as video programming offered through the Watch Instantly web site. In a society in which business is increasingly conducted online, excluding businesses that sell services through the Internet from the ADA would

> run afoul of the purposes of the ADA and would severely frustrate Congress's intent that individuals with disabilities fully enjoy the goods, services, privileges and advantages, available indiscriminately to other members of the general public.

Defendant argues that *Carparts* is irrelevant because the issue here is not whether the ADA applies to non-physical structures, but whether the list of public accommodations in the statute includes entities like web sites or services such as streaming video programming. Because it does not, according to Defendant, the Watch Instantly web site does not fall within the scope of the ADA.

This argument fails because the fact that the ADA does not include web-based services as a specific example of a public accommodation is irrelevant. First, while such web-based services did not exist when the ADA was passed in 1990 and, thus, could not have been explicitly included in the Act, the legislative history of the ADA makes clear that Congress intended the ADA to adapt to changes in technology. See, e.g., H.R. Rep. 101–485(II), at 108 (1990), 1990 U.S.C.C.A.N. 303, 391 ("[T]he Committee intends that the types of accommodation and services provided to individuals with disabilities, under all of the titles of this bill, should keep pace with the rapidly changing technology of the times.").

Second, and more importantly, Congress did not intend to limit the ADA to the specific examples listed in each category of public accommodations. Plaintiffs must show only that the web site falls within a general category listed under the ADA. See, e.g., S.Rep.

No. 116, at 59 (1990) ("[W]ithin each of these categories, the legislation only lists a few examples and then, in most cases, adds the phrase 'other similar' entities. The Committee intends that the 'other similar' terminology should be construed liberally consistent with the intent of the legislation . . . ."); H.R.Rep. No. 485 (III), at 54 (1990), 1990 U.S.C.C.A.N. 445, 477 ("A person alleging discrimination does not have to prove that the entity being charged with discrimination is similar to the examples listed in the definition. Rather, the person must show that the entity falls within the overall category.").

Plaintiffs convincingly argue that the Watch Instantly web site falls within at least one, if not more, of the enumerated ADA categories. The web site may qualify as: a "service establishment" in that it provides customers with the ability to stream video programming through the internet; a "place of exhibition or entertainment" in that it displays movies, television programming, and other content; and a "rental establishment" in that it engages customers to pay for the rental of video programming. 42 U.S.C. § 12181(7).

Defendant next argues that the Watch Instantly web site cannot be a place of public accommodation because it is accessed only in private residences, not in public spaces. According to Defendant, every specific example of a public accommodation in the ADA refers to a public arena that involves people outside of the home (e.g., motion picture house, bakery, laundromat, zoo, and the like). Under the doctrine of ejusdem generis—which provides that "where general words . . . follow the enumeration of particular classes of things . . . , the general words will be construed as applying only to things of the same general class as those enumerated"—Defendant argues that all "public accommodations" must be accessed outside of a private residence.

Again, this argument is unpersuasive. The ADA covers the services "of" a public accommodation, not services "at" or "in" a public accommodation. 42 U.S.C. § 12182(a). This distinction is crucial. Consequently, while the home is not itself a place of public accommodation, entities that provide services in the home may qualify as places of public accommodation.

Under Defendant's reading of the statute, many businesses that provide services to a customer's home—such as plumbers, pizza delivery services, or moving companies—would be exempt from the ADA. The First Circuit held in *Carparts* that such an interpretation is absurd. 37 F.3d at 19 (extending the ADA to businesses that offers services to customers in their homes through the telephone or mail). Under the *Carparts* decision, the Watch Instantly web site is a place of public accommodation and Defendant may not discriminate in the provision of the services of that public accommodation—streaming video—even if those services are accessed exclusively in the home.

Does the court's analysis in *Netflix* persuade you? For a highly critical reaction to that decision, see Eric Goldman, *Will the Americans with Disabilities Act Tear a Hole in Internet Law?*, Ars Technica, June 27, 2012, http://arstechnica.com/tech-policy/2012/06/will-the-americans-with-disabilities-act-tear-a-hole-in-internet-law/ ("If websites must comply with the ADA, all hell will break loose. Could YouTube be obligated to close-caption videos on the site? (This case seems to leave that door open.) Could every website using Flash have to redesign their sites for browsers that read the screen?"). Following the denial of Netflix's motion for judgment on the pleadings, the parties entered into a consent decree, in which Netflix agreed to ensure that closed captioning was available for all of its streaming video content within two years. See *National Association of the Deaf v. Netflix, Inc.*, No. 11-30168-MAP (consent decree entered October 9, 2012).

In 2010, the Department of Justice issued an Advance Notice of Proposed Rulemaking regarding website accessibility. The notice stated that the Department was "considering revising the regulations implementing title III * * * in order to establish requirements for making the goods, services, facilities, privileges, accommodations, or advantages offered by public accommodations via the Internet, specifically at sites on the World Wide Web (Web), accessible to individuals with disabilities." The Department described at some length the importance of web access for people with disabilities:

> Being unable to access websites puts individuals at a great disadvantage in today's society, which is driven by a dynamic electronic marketplace and unprecedented access to information. On the economic front, electronic commerce, or "e-commerce," often offers consumers a wider selection and lower prices than traditional, "brick-and-mortar" storefronts, with the added convenience of not having to leave one's home to obtain goods and services. For individuals with disabilities who experience barriers to their ability to travel or to leave their homes, the Internet may be their only way to access certain goods and services.

> [The] Internet also is changing the way individuals socialize and seek entertainment. Social networks and other online meeting places provide a unique way for individuals to meet and fraternize. These networks allow individuals to meet others with similar interests and connect with friends, business colleagues, elected officials, and businesses. They also provide an effective networking opportunity for entrepreneurs, artists, and others seeking to put their skills and talents to use. Websites also bring a myriad of entertainment and information options for Internet users—from games and music to news and videos. With the Internet, individuals can find countless ways to entertain themselves without ever leaving home.

> More and more, individuals are also turning to the Internet to obtain healthcare information. Individuals use the Internet to research diagnoses they have received or symptoms that they are experiencing. There are a myriad of websites that provide

information about causes, risk factors, complications, test and diagnosis, treatment and drugs, prevention, and alternative therapies for just about any disease or illness. Moreover, healthcare and insurance providers are increasingly offering patients the ability to access their healthcare records electronically via websites. As use of the Internet to provide and obtain healthcare information increases, the inability of individuals with disabilities to also access this information can potentially have a significant adverse effect on their health.

The Department described a number of the barriers to web access that people with a variety of disabilities confront. For example, "individuals who are deaf are unable to access information in Web videos and other multimedia presentations that do not have captions"; "[i]ndividuals with low vision may be unable to read websites that do not allow the font size or the color contrast of the site's page to be modified"; and "many websites provide information visually without features that allow screen readers or other assistive technology to retrieve information on the site so it can be presented in an accessible manner."

The notice reaffirmed the Department's longstanding position, expressed as early as 1999, that Title III applies even to the websites of businesses that operate solely over the internet. See Brief for the United States as Amicus Curiae in Support of Appellant, *Hooks v. OKbridge, Inc.*, 232 F.3d 208 (5th Cir.2000) (No. 99-50891), 1999 WL 33806215, available at www.justice.gov/crt/briefs/hooks.htm; Brief for the United States as Amicus Curiae in Support of Appellant, *Rendon v. Valleycrest Productions, Inc.*, 294 F.3d 1279 (11th Cir.2002) (No. 01-11197), 2001 WL 34094038, available at www.justice.gov/crt/briefs/rendon.htm. Despite that longstanding position, the Department had never issued regulations adopting specific web accessibility requirements to implement Title III's general nondiscrimination and reasonable modification rules. Accordingly, the notice sought public input on what sorts of web accessibility requirements the Department should issue. The Department has not yet issued proposed regulations reflecting that input.

B. PHYSICAL ACCESSIBILITY

1. PHYSICAL ACCESSIBILITY UNDER TITLE III

INTRODUCTORY NOTE

Title III of the ADA requires the facilities it covers to be physically accessible to people with disabilities. The statute employs an old-new distinction: Facilities constructed (or renovated) *after* the effective date of the statute must generally meet full accessibility standards, see 42 U.S.C. § 12183. But facilities constructed *before* the effective date of the statute face a lighter burden. Title III requires older facilities to remove architectural and communications barriers "where such removal is readily achievable." *Id.* § 12182(b)(2)(A)(iv). "Readily achievable," in turn, "means easily accomplishable and able to be carried out without much difficulty or expense." *Id.* § 12181(9). (You may recall from Chapter Four that ADA Title II, with its "program accessibility" requirement for existing facilities, employs a similar old-new distinction.)

This statutory old-new distinction reflects the difference in cost between retrofitting existing facilities to make them accessible and building new facilities with accessible features in the first place. "[R]etrofitting to full accessibility can be costly—'an average of 3 percent of a building's value.' The costs of including accessible features in the initial design of a facility, by contrast, are relatively tiny—'an estimated one-tenth to one-half of 1 percent of construction costs.' " Samuel R. Bagenstos, *"Rational Discrimination," Accommodation, and the Politics of (Disability) Civil Rights*, 89 Va. L. Rev. 825, 869 n.140 (2003) (quoting U.S. Comm'n on Civil Rights, Accommodating the Spectrum of Individual Abilities 81 (1983)). See also Mark Kelman, Strategy or Principle? The Choice Between Regulation and Taxation 7–8 (1999) ("At least insofar as the issue is prospective design decisions rather than retrofitting, though, public accommodation owners often bear no cost at all in these cases. Instead, they must simply rethink the way in which buildings are designed.").

The Title III requirement of "readily achievable" barrier removal in existing facilities mitigates the burden on the owners of those facilities, but it does not eliminate it. And the burden may well turn on how wealthy or profitable the facility's owner is. See 42 U.S.C. § 12181(9) (in determining whether an action is readily achievable, courts should consider the cost of the barrier removal as well as, *inter alia*, "the overall financial resources of the facility or facilities involved in the action" and "the overall financial resources of the covered entity"). Is it problematic to impose a heavier barrier removal burden on an entity just because that entity has more money? Professor Kelman suggests that this differential burden is, indeed, problematic. He notes that "owners' wealth or capacity to increase accessibility do not affect the degree to which those with disabilities are *harmed* by the failure to provide certain sorts of access." Kelman, Strategy or Principle, *supra*, at 56 (emphasis added). And, as Professor Samuel Issacharoff notes, when only *some* businesses serving a given product market must make certain accessibility expenditures, they will be unable to pass those costs along fully to their consumers (lest they lose market share to businesses that need not make those expenditures). See Samuel Issacharoff, *Bearing the Costs*, 53 Stan. L. Rev. 519, 534 (2000).

Is this a major problem? As the previous section shows, Title III sweeps broadly to reach nearly all providers of goods and services to the public (except, perhaps, internet-only businesses). Unlike Title I's requirement of reasonable accommodation in employment—or even Title III's own requirement to make reasonable modifications at the behest of customers with disabilities—Title III's physical accessibility requirements apply to *all* businesses covered by the statute's broad terms, not just those that perhaps fortuitously encounter a person with a disability. See *id.* (making this point). Perhaps Title III's barrier-removal requirements can be understood as a sort of progressive tax on businesses. Is that normatively problematic? Professor Kelman suggests that it is, at least to the extent that the implicit tax on richer businesses takes away social resources that could be used for more important public purposes. See Kelman, Strategy or Principle, *supra*, at 114.

There are two possible answers to Professor Kelman's objection—one moralistic, one economistic. The moralistic answer is that people with disabilities deserve to be treated as "equal members of the community"; the stores, restaurants, places of recreation, and other entities covered by Title III, in this view are key areas of community life from which people with disabilities should not be excluded. Robert L. Burgdorf Jr., *"Equal Members of the Community: The Public Accommodations Provisions of the Americans with Disabilities Act"*, 64 Temp. L. Rev. 551 (1991). Professor Burgdorf points to pre-ADA statistics that showed people with disabilities attending movies, the theater, sporting events, restaurants, and grocery stores at a far lower rate than the nondisabled. See *id.* at 554. He argues that architectural barriers are a "significant obstacle to the full participation of Americans with disabilities in mainstream society. The presence of physical barriers not only effectively bars people with certain disabilities from visiting social, commercial, and recreational establishments, but also enhances the population with disabilities' perception that they are unwelcome." *Id.* Does this denial of equal participation in community life give people with disabilities a claim in justice for barrier removal? Cf. Kelman, Strategy or Principle, *supra* (contending that such an argument improperly cloaks a redistributive claim in the trumping language of rights).

The economistic answer goes something like this: It may cost businesses money to make their facilities accessible, but they will realize a countervailing benefit by opening themselves up to a new market of customers with disabilities. Business owners may not appreciate the (low) costs and (high) benefits of making their facilities accessible, because they lack information about these costs and benefits, or because their assessment is skewed (perhaps unconsciously) by prejudice and stigma. See Michael Ashley Stein, *The Law and Economics of Disability Accommodations*, 53 Duke L.J. 79, 124–27 (2003). Moreover, business accessibility is characterized by what economists call network externalities: The value of making any given business accessible increases as other businesses become accessible (at least up to a point), because people with disabilities are more likely to shop in person when they can visit many stores on the same trip. See Samuel R. Bagenstos, *The Perversity of Limited Civil Rights Remedies: The Case of "Abusive" ADA Litigation*, 54 UCLA L. Rev. 1, 8 (2006). Because any given business cannot capture all of the value of its decision to make its facilities accessible, businesses will produce a socially inefficient level of accessibility unless we require *all* businesses to become accessible.

Is this more economistic argument sufficient to justify Title III's accessibility requirements? Even if business owners do underestimate the benefits they will achieve from making their premises accessible, surely there are some businesses for which the costs of barrier removal outweigh their individual benefits. See *id.* (acknowledging that point). And even granting that accessibility carries network externalities, what reason do we have to believe that Title III's barrier removal requirements impose the most efficient level of accessibility?

As you read the cases in this section, consider whether there is an adequate normative justification for the burdens the courts read the ADA as imposing on businesses.

a. ACCESSIBILITY IN NEW CONSTRUCTION AND MODIFICATIONS

Oregon Paralyzed Veterans of America v. Regal Cinemas, Inc.

United States Court of Appeals for the Ninth Circuit, 2003.
339 F.3d 1126.

■ BETTY B. FLETCHER, CIRCUIT JUDGE:

This appeal concerns the validity of the Department of Justice's ("DOJ") interpretation of its own regulation requiring that movie theaters, pursuant to Title III of the ADA, provide comparable lines of sight for wheelchair-bound and non-wheelchair-bound moviegoers. Three individual, disabled plaintiffs and the Oregon Paralyzed Veterans of America ("OPVA") sued two companies that own and operate movie theaters in Oregon. The theaters at issue located all wheelchair-accessible seats in the front rows, where the vertical viewing angle was significantly sharper than in the rest of the theater.

The plaintiffs [a]lleged that the "stadium seating" plans in six of the defendants' movie theaters violate Title III of the Americans with Disabilities Act ("ADA"), 42 U.S.C. § 12182, and DOJ's regulations promulgated thereunder. [T]hey sought declaratory and injunctive relief, compensatory and punitive damages under the Oregon statute, and damages for negligence (in an amount to be proved at trial), in addition to attorneys' fees and costs.

The district court granted summary judgment to the defendants. [T]he three individual plaintiffs now appeal the district court's decision as to the ADA claim only. We [r]everse.

I. FACTS

[T]he plaintiffs-appellants in this case are three disabled, wheelchair-bound individuals living in Oregon. The defendants are Regal Cinemas, Inc. and Eastgate Theatre, Inc., two companies that own and/or operate six movie theaters in Oregon.[2] All six theaters utilize a design incorporating "stadium-riser seating," which places most of the theater seats on stepped risers rather than on a sloped floor. The purpose of the stadium design is to maximize unobstructed views for theater patrons. In most cases, the first few rows at the front of the theater are set on a sloped floor; there is an aisle at the entry level of the theater separating the sloped portion of the seating from the riser section, and the stadium seats (approximately 6–13 rows) then rise behind the aisle, with each row raised 15–18" above the one in front of it.

In order to get to the seats in the stadium riser section, patrons must walk up stairs on either side of the seating section. The riser seats

---

[2] [A]ll six were designed and constructed for first occupancy after January 26, 1993, and are thus subject to the requirements of Title III of the A.D.A. for "new construction." 42 U.S.C. § 12183(a)(1).

are not wheelchair-accessible. In all six theaters, seating for disabled patrons is located only in the first five rows; in five of the six theaters,[3] wheelchair-accessible seating is located only on the sloped portion of the floor, not in the aisle or in the stadium seating, with over half of the accessible seats in the very front row. The result is that all patrons who require wheelchairs have no choice but to sit in the first few rows of the theater.

As the appellants point out, locating all of the wheelchair-accessible seating in the first few rows of the theaters creates significant disadvantages for wheelchair-bound patrons. Plaintiffs' experts, who visited the theaters and conducted research there, found that the vertical lines of sight for the wheelchair seating locations ranged from 24 to 60 degrees, with an average of approximately 42 degrees, as compared with the average median line of sight of 20 degrees in the non-wheelchair seating—a difference the experts termed a "tremendous disparity." In reality, however, the disparity is even greater, because wheelchair-bound patrons cannot slump in their seats and recline their bodies in order to adjust for the unfavorable viewing angle, as can able-bodied patrons sitting in the same part of the theater.

In its engineering guideline for movie theaters, the Society of Motion Picture and Television Engineers ("SMPTE") concluded that, for most viewers, physical discomfort occurs when the vertical viewing angle to the top of the screen exceeds 35 degrees, and when the horizontal line of sight measured between a perpendicular to the viewer's seat and the centerline of the screen exceeds 15 degrees. Soc'y of Motion Picture & Television Eng'rs, SMPTE Engineering Guideline: Design of Effective Cine Theaters 5 (1994) (hereinafter SMPTE Guideline). Thus, not only do the wheelchair seats themselves have, on average, highly unfavorable viewing angles relative to the rest of the theater, but the patrons sitting in them will be less able than other patrons to adjust for those angles by shifting position in their seats.

The experts' conclusions were also borne out by the individual plaintiffs' own experiences in the theaters, as recounted in their affidavits and deposition testimony. Kathy Stewmon, who has multiple sclerosis and has been wheelchair-bound since 1989, related:

> Sitting in [the front row], so close to the screen, the screen was so huge that I couldn't focus on it; it made me dizzy trying to focus. I had to keep moving my head and neck back and forth to look at the whole movie screen. I found myself losing the story because I was working so hard to watch the screen; I couldn't concentrate on the movie.

> I only lasted about 15 minutes in the front row—I couldn't tolerate it. My family members dragged my wheelchair up the stairs, which was [a] very dangerous and precarious thing to do, so I could watch the movie.

Plaintiffs Tina Smith and Kathleen Braddy related similar experiences: sitting in the front row of the theater made Smith nauseous and gave her a headache, and Braddy testified that she was unable to watch a movie with her grandson from the wheelchair-accessible rows of the

---

[3] The only exception is the Sherwood Theater, in which four of the auditoriums have wheelchair-accessible seating located in the stadium riser areas.

theater because she would have had to bend her neck back to the point where her vision would have been blurry, and because the sound was "not comfortable that close."

In the district court, both the plaintiffs and the defendants moved for summary judgment. The district court denied the plaintiffs' motion for summary judgment and granted the defendants' motion for summary judgment. The district court recognized that the defendants' movie theaters are public accommodations subject to Title III of the ADA, which provides generally:

> No individual shall be discriminated against on the basis of disability in the full and equal enjoyment of the goods, services, facilities, privileges, advantages, or accommodations of any place of public accommodation by any person who owns, leases (or leases to), or operates a place of public accommodation.

42 U.S.C. § 12182(a). As the district court went on to note, Congress directed the Department of Justice ("DOJ") to issue regulations that provide substantive standards applicable to facilities covered under Title III. 42 U.S.C. § 12186(b). DOJ, in turn, adopted as regulations a set of guidelines promulgated by the Architectural and Transportation Barriers Compliance Board ("Access Board"), a body charged with "establish[ing] and maintain[ing] minimum guidelines and requirements for the standards issued pursuant to" Title III of the A.D.A. 29 U.S.C. § 792(b)(3)(B). These regulations, known as the Americans with Disabilities Act Accessibility Guidelines ("ADAAG"), provide, in relevant part, as follows:

> Wheelchair areas shall be an integral part of any fixed seating plan and shall be provided so as to provide people with physical disabilities a choice of admission prices and lines of sight comparable to those for members of the general public.

28 C.F.R. Pt. 36, App.A, § 4.33.3.

In granting the defendants' motion for summary judgment, the district court held that the language about "lines of sight comparable to those for members of the general public" in § 4.33.3 does not require that wheelchair-accessible seating afford patrons comparable viewing angles to those in non-accessible seating. The district court followed what was, at the time, the only federal appellate decision in the nation addressing the viewing-angle issue directly: *Lara v. Cinemark USA, Inc.*, 207 F.3d 783 (5th Cir.2000). [DOJ] had filed an *amicus* brief in the *Lara* case in which it interpreted § 4.33.3 to require that, in stadium-style theaters, "wheelchair locations must be provided lines of sight in the stadium seating seats within the range of viewing angles as those offered to most of the general public in the stadium style seats, adjusted for seat tilt."[5] [T]he district court granted summary judgment to the defendants on the plaintiffs' ADA claim, holding that DOJ's interpretation of § 4.33.3 was inconsistent with the regulation and therefore not entitled to deference. This appeal followed.

---

[5] This continues to be DOJ's interpretation, as explained in its *amicus* brief in this case.

II. DISCUSSION

[I]n this case, the district court concluded that DOJ's interpretation of § 4.33.3 is so inconsistent with the regulation as to preclude deference—that is to say, that DOJ's interpretation is unreasonable. That conclusion is unwarranted. The language at issue is § 4.33.3's reference to "lines of sight comparable to those for members of the general public." Webster's Third New International Dictionary defines "line of sight," in relevant part, as "a line from an observer's eye to a distant point (as on the celestial sphere) toward which he is looking or directing an observing instrument." In the context of a movie theater, this means a line extending from the viewer's eye to the points on the screen where the film is projected, taking into account the angle from the viewer's eye to those points. In its engineering guideline, promulgated in 1994, the SMPTE explained:

> In addition to ensuring that everyone will see well, seating in the effective cine theater must avoid physical discomfort, which occurs when the vertical viewing angle to the top of the screen image is excessive or the lateral viewing angle to the centerline of the screen requires uncomfortable head and/or body position. Since the normal line of sight is 12 to 15 below the horizontal, seat backs should be tilted to elevate the normal line of sight approximately the same amount. For most viewers, physical discomfort occurs when the vertical viewing angle to the top of the screen exceeds 35, and when the horizontal line of sight measured between a perpendicular to his seat and the centerline of the screen exceeds 15.

SMPTE Engineering Guideline at 4–5. Indeed, the National Association of Theatre Owners ("NATO"), participating in this case as *amicus curiae* on behalf of the appellees, has advanced a similar conception of "viewing angle." Steven John Fellman, NATO Position Paper on Wheelchair Seating in Motion Picture Theatre Auditoriums 6 (1994) ("NATO explained that lines of sight are measured in degrees. . . . ").[7]

The question here, then, is whether it is unreasonable for DOJ to interpret "comparable line of sight" to encompass factors in addition to physical obstructions, such as viewing angle. The answer, in light of the plain meaning of the regulation both in general and as understood in the movie theater industry, is "no." We do not accept the *Lara* court's suggestion that the legislative and administrative history of § 4.33.3 compels a different answer. We agree that stadium-style movie theaters were rare in this country until the mid-1990s, and the older theaters,

---

[7]   We disagree with the Fifth Circuit's suggestion in *Lara*, 207 F.3d at 789, that it is impossible to parse "comparability" without embarking on subjective judgments of where each individual prefers to sit in a movie theater. The point is this: Able-bodied movie theater patrons in a stadium-style theater may choose from a wide range of viewing angles, most of which are objectively comfortable according to SMPTE standards, regardless of what personal viewing preferences individuals may have within that comfortable range. As it currently stands in the theaters at issue, however, wheelchair-bound patrons may sit only in the first few rows, where uncontroverted evidence demonstrates that, not only is the viewing angle objectively uncomfortable for all viewers, but the discomfort is exacerbated for wheelchair-bound viewers relative to able-bodied viewers sitting in the same row. Note that the SMPTE has determined that physical discomfort occurs "for most viewers" when the viewing angle exceeds 35 degrees; the average vertical viewing angle for disabled patrons in the subject theaters is 42 degrees. Thus, there is objective evidence that disabled patrons would likely experience discomfort in the theaters in question.

which were built on sloping floors, did not generally create the same kinds of dramatic disparities in vertical viewing angles that stadium-style theaters do. But the fact that DOJ may not have been contemplating viewing-angle issues in the context of stadium-style seating at the time when § 4.33.3 was promulgated is not dispositive. Rather, the issue is whether a broadly-drafted regulation—with a broad purpose—may be applied to a particular factual scenario not expressly anticipated at the time the regulation was promulgated—a question that the Supreme Court has answered in the affirmative. See *Pennsylvania Dep't of Corr. v. Yeskey*, 524 U.S. 206, 212 (1998) (holding that, where statutory text is unambiguous, "the fact that a statute can be applied in situations not expressly anticipated by Congress does not demonstrate ambiguity. It demonstrates breadth." (internal quotation marks omitted)). We see no reason to treat regulations differently.

III. CONCLUSION

One of the central goals of Title III of the ADA is to ensure that people with disabilities have access to "the full and equal enjoyment of the goods, services, facilities, privileges, advantages, or accommodations of any place of public accommodation." 42 U.S.C. § 12182(a). In the theaters at issue in this case, wheelchair-bound movie theater patrons must sit in seats that are objectively uncomfortable, requiring them to crane their necks and twist their bodies in order to see the screen, while non-disabled patrons have a wide range of comfortable viewing locations from which to choose. We find it simply inconceivable that this arrangement could constitute "full and equal enjoyment" of movie theater services by disabled patrons. [A]ccordingly, the judgment of the district court is reversed, and the case is remanded with instructions to enter summary judgment in favor of the plaintiffs on their ADA claim.

REVERSED AND REMANDED.

■ KLEINFELD, CIRCUIT JUDGE, dissenting.

[E]vidently the Justice Department has been unable to sell its litigation position within the executive branch, so it has come to the Ninth Circuit. The statute requires that "[s]tandards included in regulations . . . shall be consistent with the minimum guidelines and requirements issued by the Architectural and Transportation Barriers Compliance Board,"[2] called the "Access Board." The Access Board published a Notice of Proposed Rulemaking in 1999 that it was considering promulgating new regulations for "stadium-style motion picture theaters" because of the frequent placement of wheelchair spaces in the first few rows.[3]

The Access Board notes that "DOJ has asserted in attempting to settle particular cases" that the usual wheelchair placement should be changed to give wheelchair patrons sight lines "equivalent to or better than the viewing angles provided by 50 percent of the seats in the auditorium," by elevating the wheelchair seats to the stadium section.[4] Far from announcing that DOJ was right about what the existing regulation meant, the Access Board announced that "the Board is considering whether to include specific requirements in the final rule

---

[2]   42 U.S.C. § 12186(c).

[3]   64 Fed.Reg. 62,248 62,278 (Nov. 16, 1999).

[4]   *Id.*

that are consistent with DOJ's interpretation."[5] The Board notes the desirability of affording better sight lines to wheelchair patrons, but also notes that "design professionals have expressed some uncertainty about how to measure their compliance."[6] Balancing these concerns, "the Board is proposing to amend the guidelines to include specific technical provisions" governing sight lines.[7]

It is striking to contrast the just approach of the Access Board with the unjust approach of the majority decision. When and if the Access Board promulgates a regulation, architects will know before a movie theater is built how they must design it, and owners of existing theaters will know what reconstruction they must perform. By contrast, under today's decision, retroactive as judicial decisions generally are, thousands of movie theaters will discover that they are out of compliance with the law, and must destroy facilities built in compliance with the law according to the best knowledge of design professionals at the time. They must rebuild them to satisfy the architectural inferences design professionals will have to draw from today's opinion. Those inferences are obscure and debatable. Though I could come up with a scheme that I think could satisfy the implications of the majority opinion, I am not sure that it would satisfy the majority, and I am entirely unable to say what is the least expensive design that would satisfy the majority. If a judge on the panel cannot say just what is required, how can a movie theater owner? It is irresponsible to impose on the country a decision that will require of an industry so much reconstruction, without clear guidance on what must be done.

We ought to leave the Access Board process alone. If the Access Board adopts the Justice Department's position or something like it, the requirements will be clear, precise and prospective. Though any result might be subject to substantive objections (it is hard to justify a gloss on the statute that requires wheelchair users to have a better view than half or more of the seats), at least the result would be obtained after a fair process. Regulating movie theater architecture retroactively by vague judicial fiat is unjust.

[T]he "accessibility guidelines" surrounding § 4.33.3—the one covering lines of sight—are written with great precision, e.g., telephone cord length must be at least 29",[8] and wheelchair seating knee clearance at tables and counters must be "at least 27 in (685 mm) high, 30 in (760 mm) wide, and 19 in (485 mm) deep."[9] Where a regulation tells movie architects and owners to the millimeter how they must construct knee space, the use of the vague term "comparable" must be looser by intent. It is unreasonable to infer from the regulation on the next page, "lines of sight comparable to those for members of the general public,"[10] something like the "better than 50%" of the seats rule that the Justice Department has suggested.

---

[5]   *Id.*

[6]   *Id.* at 62,277.

[7]   *Id.*

[8]   28 C.F.R. Part 36, App.A, § 4.31.8.

[9]   *Id.* at § 4.32.3.

[10]   *Id.* at § 4.33.3.

The majority is rightly troubled by the notion of a wheelchair ghetto in one part of the movie theater with sight lines worse than those of the other patrons. But that concern is a chimera, because the regulation already speaks to that issue. It says that "[w]hen the seating capacity exceeds 300, wheelchair spaces shall be provided in more than one location,"[11] and in all theaters, the wheelchair seating has to be an "integral part" of the seating with "lines of sight comparable to those for members of the general public." That means that in the smaller theaters, it is permissible to group the wheelchair seating rather than to distribute it throughout the theater, but that it has to be part of the general seating footprint rather than separated, and the lines of sight cannot be substantially different from those of seats available for the general public. Under the existing regulations, there cannot be a wheelchair ghetto out of the way, behind a post, or off to the side.

The regulation at issue, in contrast with the highly specific (to the millimeter) requirements of the surrounding regulations, requires that wheelchair areas be "an integral part" of the fixed seating plan, that they "adjoin an accessible route" that also serves as an emergency exit, that they be adjacent to "companion" seating, and that they have "lines of sight comparable to those for members of the general public."[12] The majority opinion disregards all the other requirements that give context to the lines of sight requirement, such as the access and emergency exit requirements. These other requirements complicate any construction plans.

[V]iewing angles differ for every seat in the house. As the Fifth Circuit noted, preferences are highly subjective, and people's preferences differ. Some people like to sit in front, for maximum size of picture and stereo effect of the sound, and to avoid distractions from people in front of them. Some people like to sit in back, for the greater height and sense of separation from the picture. Some like the aisles, so they can get out easily to go to the bathroom or the popcorn stand. Some like the center, so they won't be distracted by the people who get up during the movie to go the bathroom or the popcorn stand. The lines of sight for the wheelchair seats cannot be comparable to all of these, without requiring the scattering of wheelchair seating that the 300-seat provision expressly avoids requiring in small theaters. The wheelchair seats up front are comparable (though as a matter of geometry a line of sight will not be identical to any particular other seat) to the other seats up front, preferred by those patrons who like to sit up front. If the seats up front, or in the back, were uniformly considered undesirable, theaters would have to charge less for them. They don't.

The Fifth Circuit solves this problem by interpreting the line of sight requirement as requiring an unobstructed view. Whether we adopt precisely that reading or not, the regulation plainly does not mean what the Justice Department says it means (and what the majority opinion may or may not imply that it means): "equal to or better than 50 percent of the seats," whatever "better" may mean.

[A]ll the majority tells us with any clarity is that it is not satisfied with the existing state of affairs, where wheelchair patrons sit in the

---

[11] *Id.*

[12] 28 C.F.R. Part 36, App.A, § 4.33.3.

front rows. But architects and theater owners need to know, not only what the Ninth Circuit rejects, but what construction and reconstruction will be acceptable. That is why the regulations delimit knee space to the millimeter. Judicial opinions cannot be written that way, which is a good reason why we should not try to rewrite the regulations as the majority does. The majority admits that stadium seating was a "factual scenario not expressly anticipated at the time the regulation was promulgated," yet construes the regulation to address it. If the regulation did not contemplate stadium seating, the only fair inference is that it did not provide specially for it. Obviously, there was wheelchair seating before stadium seating, and if the regulations did not prohibit a wheelchair section in the front of the theater before, it is impossible to justify a construction that the very same regulation prohibits the very same wheelchair seating, with identical angles of view, after stadium seating came into use.

NOTES ON REGAL CINEMAS

1.   **Subsequent Regulatory History.** In 2010, the Department of Justice issued revised Title III regulations, along with new ADA Standards for Accessible Design (which incorporate and supplant the ADA Accessibility Guidelines as amended in 2004).   The new standards for assembly areas provide that "[w]heelchair spaces shall be dispersed vertically at varying distances from the screen, performance area, or playing field," but they also provide that "[v]ertical dispersion shall not be required in assembly areas with 300 or fewer seats if the wheelchair spaces provide viewing angles that are equivalent to, or better than, the average viewing angle provided in the facility."   ADA Standards for Accessible Design § 221.2.3.2.   In addition, the 2010 regulations specifically provide that stadium-style movie theaters must "locate wheelchair spaces and companion seats on a riser or cross-aisle in the stadium section" that is either (i) "located within the rear 60% of the seats provided in an auditorium"; or (ii) "located within the area of an auditorium in which the vertical viewing angles (as measured to the top of the screen) are from the 40th to the 100th percentile of vertical viewing angles for all seats as ranked from the seats in the first row (1st percentile) to seats in the back row (100th percentile)."   28   C.F.R. § 35.151(g)(4) (2010). These requirements are quite similar to the *Regal Cinemas* majority's interpretation of the former Section 4.33.3. Does that suggest that the majority got it right? Or does it suggest that Judge Kleinfeld was correct that the Access Board process should have been allowed to run its course? In answering these questions, does it matter to you that the 2010 rules singled out stadium-style movie theaters for specific provisions that do not apply to assembly areas generally?

2.   **The Burden of Remedy.** Even though it is generally quite inexpensive to incorporate accessible features in new construction, it can be extremely expensive to go back and undo that construction if it failed to incorporate accessible features. When, as in *Regal Cinemas*, the owner of a place of public accommodation fails to comply with the ADA's requirements for new construction, how ought a court to respond? Should the court order the owner to retrofit the building so that it complies with the new-construction requirements, no matter what the cost? Note that a court

cannot award damages under Title III, as discussed in Section E, *infra*, so anything less than an injunction requiring full accessibility will, in some ways, give the owner a windfall. But what if the costs of retrofitting would bankrupt (or nearly bankrupt) the defendant? Does your answer depend on whether the defendant acted in good faith or violated a clear accessibility requirement?

Colorado Cross-Disability Coalition v. Abercrombie & Fitch Co.

United States District Court for the District of Colorado, 2011.
835 F.Supp.2d 1077.

■ WILEY Y. DANIEL, CHIEF JUDGE.

[P]laintiffs' Motion for Partial Summary Judgment requests summary judgment on the issue of whether the entrances to Defendants' Hollister clothing stores located at the Park Meadows and Orchard Town Center malls in suburban Denver violate Title III of the Americans with Disabilities Act ("ADA") 42 U.S.C. § 12181 *et seq.*

[T]he parties agree on some of the material facts regarding this motion. The Hollister stores at issue were both built after the passage of the ADA. Although one store is in an enclosed, "indoor" mall (Park Meadows) and the other is in an "outdoor mall" (Orchard Town Center), the design of the front of the stores is the same, at least for purposes of this motion.

Each store has a raised porch-like platform that is two steps above ground level. It is not accessible to people in wheelchairs. The platform is covered by a roof and contains a door leading into the store. Inside the door are two steps down into either the half of the store with goods for males or the other half with goods for females. On each side of the 'porch structure,' are two doors at ground level. The stores adjacent to the Hollister stores at both malls have ground level entrances. Consequently the steps at the Hollister stores are purely ornamental. The porch structure creates an aesthetic which is a valuable part of Defendant Hollister's branding efforts.

[P]laintiffs' arguments start with the policy statements regarding the aims of the ADA and the timing for the requirements that new buildings be "readily accessible to and usable by individuals with disabilities." 42 U.S.C. § 12183(a)(1). As mentioned, the parties agree that the Hollister stores were built after this ADA requirement went into effect. They also agree that no exceptions apply to these stores. There is no 'feasability' issue in this case.

In particular, Plaintiffs allege that those stores violate the ADA regulation that requires that accessible entrances, where feasible, shall be the entrances used by the majority of people visiting or working in the building. 28 C.F.R. § 36.406 Appendix A-1991 Standard for Accessible Design 4.1.3(8)(a) [hereinafter "Design Standard—.—"]. Plaintiffs go on to note that the ADA encourages that facilities be provided in the "most integrated setting appropriate." 42 U.S.C. § 12182(b)(1)(B). A discussion of the statutory aim of ending the segregation of handicapped individuals and allowing them, whenever possible, to use the same facilities as individuals who are not disabled is also discussed by Plaintiffs. It is their view that the two entrances that frame the porch-like structure of the central door are 'separate' and 'different' entrances that are an important part of what the statutory plan was attempting to preclude.

It is Defendants' contention that the Hollister stores do not violate the ADA, its regulations or standards. Their briefs contain several arguments in support of this position. The first is that the words in the Design Standard quoted above including the words "where feasible," are an aspirational standard that essentially can be ignored when adequate accessible entrances are provided. This argument must be rejected in light of the use of the mandatory "shall" in that sentence.

As an alternative, Defendants argue that even if the three doors at the front of Hollister stores comprise three separate entrances, the feasability standard set forth in Design Standard 4.1.3(8)(a), by its own terms, refers only to entrances used by the majority of people entering the facility. Only for those 'majority use' doors does the Design Standard relied upon by Plaintiffs express that they should be accessible if feasible. Defendants argue that Plaintiffs have presented no evidence to show that the center door is the majority use door and it would be improper for the Court to assume this 'crucial' fact. Furthermore, they contend that as the center door involves a 'more arduous and less direct route,' it would make no sense for the Court to assume the center door is used by a majority of customers.

Defendants rely on another subsection of the same Design Standard to argue that the doors at the Hollister stores meet the requirement that "[a]t least 50% of all public entrances . . . must be accessible." Design Standard 4.1.3(8)(a)(i).

Defendants' main argument appears to be that all three doors at the Hollister stores are part of the same 'entrance.' In support, Defendants point out that the three doors are on the same side of the building and constitute a continuous series along the wall. They all lead from the general mall area to inside the store. Defendants note that the ADA Design Standards define entrance as possibly including more than a single door. Design Standard 3.5. They go on to note another Design Standard provides that "[a]t each accessible entrance to a building or facility, at least one door shall comply with 4.13." Design Standard 4.1.3(7)(a). Since both side doors must be considered accessible in light of the parties' stipulation for this motion, the entrances to the two Hollister stores comply with both Design Standards 4.1.3(8)(a)(I) and 4.1.3(7)(a). In fact, not only 50%, but in excess of 66% of the front doors at the entrance to the stores are accessible.

To strengthen their argument, and because the Design Standards do not include a provision that deals exactly with the configuration at issue in this case, Defendants have searched the Design Standards for analogous situations. They point out that one subsection provides that an inaccessible revolving door and an accessible door are considered a single accessible entrance if the accessible door is adjacent to the revolving door and allows the same use pattern. Design Standard 4.13.2. As the regulations do not define 'adjacent,' Defendants cite dictionary definitions to demonstrate that adjacent generally means close but not necessary adjoining.

Plaintiffs disagree strongly with Defendants' single entrance argument. In particular they reject Defendants' reliance on Design Standard 4.13.2. It is Plaintiffs' position that just because that particular Design Standard permits turnstiles or revolving doors if there is an adjacent accessible door, does not mean that the Department of Justice (DOJ) is articulating a general standard that is encouraging non-accessible doors if an accessible door is close by. Plaintiffs dispute that anything about the allowance of turnstiles or revolving doors gives any indications that the DOJ has separate rules for single entrances that include multiple doors.

[T]he United States has also filed a Statement of Interest ("SOI") with regard to this motion. [T]he United States takes the position that because the stores at issue were built after the ADA took effect, both the design and the construction of the entrances 'violate the purpose and the letter of the ADA by unnecessarily relegating people who use wheelchairs to separate and objectively different entrances than those available for other people.'

As something built after the effective date of the statute, newly constructed facilities must comply with Design Standard 4.1.3(8) regarding feasibility. The implementing regulations require compliance unless it is "structurally impractical to do so." 42 U.S.C.A. § 12183(a)(1). Regulations explain that the exception refers to "unique characteristics of terrain" that preclude application of some accessibility features. 28 C.F.R. § 36.401(c)(1). [D]efendants acknowledge the exception does not apply to either of the stores at issue. Consequently, the United States argues, Defendants must make the stores accessible unless it is not feasible for them to do so. Defendants have conceded that they could easily make the applicable doors accessible.

Although the United States does not accept Defendants' argument that the three doors comprise a single entrance, it argues that whether it is one entrance or three, that does not change the fact that the two 'accessible' doors are qualitatively different from the raised center door. It points to the lack of roof, plants, pictures and other features that the center door has but the side doors do not have. It further notes that Defendants' argument about a single entrance would be more convincing if some of the features like the roof and decorations were expanded to include all three doors.

Defendants' response to the SOI strongly disputes the position of the United States ("DOJ"). Defendants [a]rgue that [i]t is essentially illogical to assume that they have created 'second class, segregated side entrances' that would discourage shoppers who use wheelchairs. Like all retailers, they say, they strive to increase the number of customers, not the contrary. They reiterate that the raised porch is part of a brand design to convey a certain ambiance and appearance that makes the store inviting as a whole. In this vein, they continue that the "fully compliant" side doors "permit the same pattern of use as the raised entry door and equal access to all merchandise."

[D]efendants use a variety of arguments to attempt to make the point that their center door which, at the very least, includes a porch and roof and access to the male or female side of the store, is not preferable to the side doors which, even if they are assumed to be accessible, lead to either the male- or female-oriented side of the store and therefore necessitate additional travel through a possibly crowded store if one needs to reach the side devoted to the other gender.

To say that the issue of which door is used by a majority of customers is a genuine issue of fact ignores the obvious. Looking at the photographs attached to Plaintiffs' motion, it was not even clear that there are doors on either side of the porch. This was particularly true when the 'shutter' portion of the door was closed, although it seems doubtful whether the electronic door opener would work in those circumstances anyway. And while I tend to agree that the door opener would be readily visible to someone in front of the side doors, for anyone who was drawn to the decorated entrance, the door button would appear small and far away.

Defendants argue that by a variety of other measures, their present design is adequate. They note that it does allow entrance to people using wheelchairs if those people find the side doors and the doors are actually accessible; i.e. they are not locked, the electronic opener works and the path into the store is not blocked by tables or merchandise. However, it is not a preferable entrance by any means because there do not appear to be any signs outside the store explaining which side has goods for males or for females. While it is possible that a wheelchair-bound customer might be able to make that determination by looking through the glass in the doors, it is just as likely that close to 50% of the side door entrants would need to make their way through the store to the other side. Obviously this is easier said than done for individuals in wheelchairs. Clearly the side doors do not "permit the same pattern of use as the raised entry door and equal access to all merchandise" as argued by Defendants.

Defendant has strongly objected to the DOJ's characterization of their treatment of customers who must use their side doors as second class because they cannot use the main door. By citing one of the many small subsections with which they have complied, Defendants contend "[t]he Standards thus recognize that accessible and inaccessible entrances may be 'different or separate' as long as the other standards are met."

Once again Defendants are missing the big picture. Compliance with numerous precise design standards does not protect them from violating the broad statutory requirements.

> **It shall be discriminatory to provide** an individual or class of individuals, on the basis of a disability or disabilities of such individual or class, directly, or through contractual, licensing, or other arrangements with a good, service, facility, privilege, advantage, or **accommodation that is different or separate** from that provided to other individuals, **unless such action is necessary** to provide the individual or class of individuals with a good, service, facility, privilege, advantage, or accommodation, or other opportunity that is as effective as that provided to others.

42 U.S.C.A. § 12182(b)(1)(A)(iii) (emphasis added).

It is precisely this sort of language, as well as similar provisions such as "Goods, services, facilities, privileges, advantages, and accommodations shall be afforded to an individual with a disability in the **most integrated setting appropriate** to the needs of the individual" that provide support for the general position that the ADA seeks to eliminate unequal access for people with disabilities. 42 U.S.C.A. § 12182(b)(1)(B) (emphasis added).

It appears that Defendants would prefer to take the micro view that allows them to comply with the details in the regulations without taking the aims of the ADA to heart and fulfilling its overarching aims. This is where Plaintiffs' seminal provision comes in: "Where feasible, accessible entrances shall be the entrances used by the majority of the people visiting or working in the building." Design Standard 4.1.3(8)(a). Unlike the specific provisions with which Defendants apparently do not have trouble complying, this one is more general and is likely meant further emphasize that one aim of the ADA is that new buildings be "readily accessible to and usable by individuals with disabilities." 42 U.S.C. § 12183(a)(1). Defendants have unnecessarily created a design for their brand that excludes people using wheelchairs from full enjoyment of the aesthetic for that brand. The steps to the center entrance are a legally unacceptable piece of that branding and violate Title III of the ADA.

Colorado Cross-Disability Coalition v. Abercrombie & Fitch Co.

United States District Court for the District of Colorado, 2013.
__ F.Supp.2d __.

■ WILEY Y. DANIEL, CHIEF JUDGE.

THIS MATTER comes before the Court on Plaintiffs' Motion for Summary Judgment, Entry of Injunction, and Entry of Judgment, filed April 27, 2012, and Defendants' Motion for Summary Judgment or, In the Alternative, To Vacate August 31, 2011 Order. The motions have been fully briefed by the parties and the United States Department of Justice ("DOJ") has filed its Statement of Interest On the Parties' Motions for Summary Judgment ("Statement of Interest"). Based on these briefs and oral argument to the Court on January 24, 2013, I grant Plaintiffs motion and deny Defendants' motion as more fully set forth below.

Plaintiffs, a class of individuals who use wheelchairs or scooters for mobility, challenge the raised porch entrances at approximately 248 Hollister brand stores operated by Defendant Abercrombie & Fitch Stores LLC. On August 31, 2011, this Court held that the raised porch entrances at two stores in Colorado were in violation of section 4.1.3(8) of the 1991 Department of Justice Standards for Accessible Design ("1991 Standards"), 28 C.F.R. pt. 36, app. D (2012), and therefore of Title III of the Americans with Disabilities Act ("ADA"), 42 U.S.C. § 12183(a)(1). On April 20, 2012, this Court certified a class defined as follows:

> all people with disabilities who use wheelchairs for mobility who, during the two years prior to the filing of the Complaint in this case, were denied the full and equal enjoyment of the goods, services, facilities, privileges, advantages, or accommodations of any Hollister Co. Store in the United States

on the basis of disability because of the presence of an Elevated Entrance.

Following certification of the class, Plaintiffs moved to extend the summary judgment holding to the remainder of the Hollister stores with Raised Porch Entrances. Defendants simultaneously moved for summary judgment and/or to vacate the Court's August 31, 2011 order on the grounds that they had made modifications to the remaining open store visited by the Representative Plaintiffs, and that the stores in question were in compliance with the 2010 DOJ Standards for Accessible Design ("2010 Standards").[1] It is these motions that are currently before the Court.

[T]he front areas of approximately 248 of the Hollister stores around the country are configured similarly. They contain a raised front porch that leads to two possible store entrances: one to the "Dudes" side, containing men's clothing, and the other to the "Bettys" side, containing women's. Steps lead up to the porch from the mall floor and then down from the porch into the two sides of the store. These porches, which will be referred to herein as "Raised Porch Entrances," are accessible only by steps, and are therefore inaccessible to people who use wheelchairs.

[T]he purpose of this Raised Porch Entrance "is to give the stores the aesthetic appearance of a Southern California surf shack . . . ." As such, the Raised Porch Entrance "is a significant aspect of the stores' branding and marketing efforts." The Raised Porch Entrance was included in the design "to create . . . an entry to a house in southern California that you would walk up onto the porch or walk down into the porch, to enter like you would do at a beach house."

[T]he Raised Porch Entrances at Hollister stores have upholstered chairs, a marketing image, and mannequins displaying merchandise. While the furniture is not intended as seating, customers are permitted to sit there. Where the porch is raised, *i.e.,* at the approximately 248 Hollister stores at issue here, customers in wheelchairs do not "have the ability to touch or feel the clothes" on display there or otherwise take part in this Hollister experience.

[S]hoppers who use wheelchairs are not able to enter the stores through the Raised Porch Entrances. Rather, they enter through accessible doors—on the same level as the mall floor—to each side of the Raised Porch Entrance. The accessible side entrances are designed to look like French doors similar to the inoperable French doors farther to the left and right of the accessible side entrances.

[O]verall, the visual impression is of a main, decorated, primary but inaccessible entrance in the center, with smaller, inferior, undecorated accessible entrances to each side.

[A]ll of the Hollister stores at issue were constructed after January 26, 1993 but before September 15, 2010.

[ANALYSIS]

---

[1] The 2010 Standards consist of the 2004 ADAAG, 36 C.F.R. pt. 1191, apps. B & D, and subpart D of 28 C.F.R. pt. 36. See 28 C.F.R. § 36.104 (definitions). The 2010 Standards and the DOJ's guidance thereto are published on the Department's website. http://www.ada.gov/2010ADAstandards_index.htm

[T]itle III of the ADA prohibits discrimination on the basis of disability by those who own or operate places of public accommodation. 42 U.S.C. § 12182(a). In enacting the ADA, Congress found that "historically, society has tended to isolate and segregate individuals with disabilities." 42 U.S.C. § 12101(a)(2). The ADA's legislative history states that "[i]ntegration is fundamental to the purposes of the ADA. Provision of segregated accommodations and services relegate persons with disabilities to second-class citizen status." H. Rep. 101–485(III), 101st Cong., 2d Sess, at 56, *reprinted in* 1990 U.S.C.C.A.N. 445, 479. [T]he ADA provides a "broad mandate" to "eliminate discrimination against disabled individuals, and to integrate them 'into the economic and social mainstream of American life.'" *PGA Tour, Inc. v. Martin,* 532 U.S. 661, 675, 121 S.Ct. 1879, 149 L.Ed.2d 904 (2001) (quoting H.R.Rep. No. 101–485, pt. 2, p. 50 (1990), *reprinted in* 1991 U.S.C.C.A.N. 303, 332).

This integration mandate is found in two sections of the statute. Title III makes it discriminatory to provide individuals with disabilities "with a good, service, facility, privilege, advantage, or accommodation that is different or separate from that provided to other individuals, unless such action is necessary" to provide facilities, accommodations and the like that are as effective as those provided others. 42 U.S.C. § 12182(b)(1)(A)(iii). It also requires that "[g]oods, services, facilities, privileges, advantages, and accommodations shall be afforded to an individual with a disability in the most integrated setting appropriate to the needs of the individual." *Id.,* § 12182(b)(1)(B).

Section 303 of the ADA required that all facilities designed and constructed after January 26, 1993 must be "readily accessible to and useable by" individuals with disabilities. 42 U.S.C. § 12183(a)(1). The statute further instructed the DOJ to adopt implementing standards and regulations. 42 U.S.C. § 12186(b). On July 26, 1991, the DOJ adopted the Americans with Disabilities Act Accessibility Guidelines as the 1991 Standards. 28 C.F.R. § 36.406(a) (1991). The 1991 Standards are now published as Appendix D to title 28, part 36 of the Code of Federal Regulations. On September 15, 2010, the DOJ amended its regulations and adopted the 2010 Standards. *See supra* n. 1.

Because the stores at issue in this case were constructed after January 26, 1993 but before September 15, 2010, they are required to comply with the 1991 Standards. 28 C.F.R. § 36.406(a)(1) (2012). The only exception to this requirement is that, if the 2010 Standards "reduce the technical requirements or the number of required accessible elements below the number required by the 1991 Standards," the newer standards apply. 28 C.F.R. § 36.211(c) (2012).

1. *The 1991 Standards*

The 1991 Standards required that at least 50% of all public entrances be accessible and that, "[w]here feasible, accessible entrances shall be the entrances used by the majority of people visiting or working in the building." *Id.* § 4.1.3(8)(a). This Court has previously held that, by requiring individuals with disabilities to enter through the side entrances, the Raised Porch Entrances violated this provision and therefore Title III of the ADA. The combination of the inaccessible Raised Porch Entrance and the side accessible entrances also violates sections 12182(b)(1)(A)(iii) and 12182(b)(1)(B), because it provides separate facilities and does not provide an integrated setting for people with disabilities.

2. The 2010 Standards

The 2010 Standards require that 60% of all public entrances be accessible. *Id.* § 206.4.1. This section—unlike the 1991 Standards' section governing the percentage of entrances required to be accessible—does not contain the "majority of the people" language. Defendants argue that this therefore "reduce [s] the technical requirements" of the 1991 Standards so that, by operation of 28 C.F.R. § 36.211(c), Hollister stores need only comply with the 2010 Standards. Defendants further argue that they comply with the 2010 Standards. The Court will examine each of those arguments in turn.

a. The 1991 and 2010 Standards Governing Entrances

While Defendants are correct that the "majority of the people" language from section 4.1.3(8)(a) of the 1991 Standards is not present in the 2010 Standards, *see id.* § 206.4.1, that difference does not thereby "reduce the technical requirements" of the 1991 Standards governing entrances. The DOJ commentary to section 206.4.1 states that that section was designed to clarify the number of required accessible entrances, and was "intended to achieve the same result as the 1991 Standards." Analysis and Commentary on the 2010 ADA Standards for Accessible Design, 28 C.F.R. pt. 36, app. B at 824 (2012). As the DOJ explained in its Statement of Interest:

> Defendants' argument [that their raised porches comply with the 2010 Standards] is misplaced. Many changes were made in the 2010 Standards after a section by section review of the 1991 Standards. The changes clarified and simplified the 2010 Standards as compared to the 1991 Standards. One of the significant goals of the changes was to eliminate duplication or overlap in Federal accessibility guidelines, as well as to harmonize the 2010 Standards with model codes that are the basis of many State and local building codes. See Nondiscrimination on the Basis of Disability by Public Accommodations and in Commercial Facilities, 75 Fed.Reg. 56,236, 56,245-46 (Sept. 15, 2010).

> The Department of Justice's interpretive guidance accompanying the 2010 Standards specifically states that the revision regarding accessible public entrances is intended to achieve the same result as the 1991 Standards. Consequently, this Court's holding that the raised porches failed to comply with the 1991 Standards compels the conclusion that they also violate the 2010 Standards.

This guidance is entitled to deference because it represents the DOJ's authoritative interpretation of its own regulations. As the Supreme Court has held, an agency's interpretation of its own regulation is controlling unless "plainly erroneous or inconsistent with the regulation." *Auer v. Robbins,* 519 U.S. 452, 461 (1997) (citation omitted).

The Raised Porch Entrances continue to violate the 2010 Standards governing entrances. This interpretation is not only consistent with the agency's interpretation of its own regulations, it is consistent with the fundamental purpose and explicit language of the ADA requiring integration and prohibiting separate-but-equal facilities. *See* 42 U.S.C. §§ 12101(a)(2); 12182(b)(1)(A)(iii), (b)(1)(B). "[A] regulation must be interpreted in such a way as to not conflict with the objective of its organic statute." *Time Warner Entm't Co. v. Everest Midwest Licensee, LLC,* 381 F.3d 1039, 1050 (10th Cir.2004).

Defendants also argue, with respect to both the 1991 and 2010 Standards, that the Raised Porch Entrances and the accessible entrances to each side constitute a single entrance. Defendants further argue that the entrances—construed as a single entrance—comply with section 206.5.1 of the 2010 Standards, which requires that "[e]ach entrance to a building or facility required to comply with 206.4 shall have at least one [accessible] door." While this might permit, say, a bank of nearly identical doors to contain only one accessible door, the language and purpose of the statute do not permit an interpretation that allows a door that is qualitatively different or superior to remain inaccessible while inferior side doors are the only accessible entrances. Furthermore, as noted in this Court's order granting partial summary judgment, it is the position of the DOJ that, because the doors at Defendants' stores are on different elevations, the definition of "entrance" in section 3.5 of the 1991 Standards precludes them from being considered a single entrance. The definition of "entrance" in the 2010 Standards is materially identical to that of the 1991 Standards, *compare* 1991 Standards § 3.5 *with* 2010 Standards § 106.5. The Court agrees with the DOJ's reasoning: the Raised Porch Entrances and the accessible side entrances cannot be considered a single entrance.

b. *The 2010 Standards Governing Accessible Spaces*

As the DOJ points out, "where a space contains more than one use, 'each portion shall comply with the applicable requirements for that use.'" Here, the Raised Porch Entrances must comply with the standards governing entrances, which, as explained above, they do not. In addition, because each Raised Porch Entrance is also a space in the Hollister store that Defendants make available to individuals who do not require wheelchairs for mobility, they must comply with regulations governing circulation paths and accessible routes to accessible spaces. Again, they fail to comply with these regulations.

The 2010 Standards require that—unless covered by an exception—if nondisabled customers can get to a space, customers who use wheelchairs have to be able to get to that space as well. "At least one accessible route shall connect accessible building or facility entrances with all accessible spaces and elements within the building or facility which are otherwise connected by a circulation path," unless exempted by an applicable exception. A circulation path is defined as "way of passage provided for pedestrian travel, including . . . stairways, and landings." *Id.* § 106.5. Because the porches are connected to mall and store entrances by a circulation path—the steps—pursuant to section 206.2.4, they must be on an accessible route. This is in keeping with the broad scoping requirement of the 2010 Standards, which mandates that "[a]ll areas of newly designed and newly constructed buildings and facilities and altered portions of existing buildings and facilities shall comply with these requirements." *Id.* § 201.1. The upshot of section 206.2.4 is that—unless covered by an exception—if you can walk to a space, you must be able to roll to it.

The exceptions to 206.2.4 are narrow and specific, including, for example, certain areas of detention facilities, residential facilities, transient lodging, and air traffic control towers, as well as areas of courtrooms, portions of assembly areas that do not include accessible seating, and mezzanines in single-story buildings. §§ 206.2.3, Exceptions 3–6; 206.2.4, Exceptions 1–3. There is no exception for porches or raised areas of retail spaces. Indeed, the Advisory to section 206.2.4 states, "[a]ccessible routes must connect all spaces and elements required to be accessible including, but not limited to, raised areas and speaker platforms." And although the 2010 Standards specifically except certain "raised areas," this exception does not include a raised portion of a retail store. *Id.* § 203.3 ("[a]reas raised primarily for purposes of security, life safety, or fire safety, including but not limited to, observation or lookout galleries, prison guard towers, fire towers, or life guard stands shall not be required to comply with these requirements or to be on an accessible route.") Hollister's Raised Porch Entrances are not covered by any applicable exception and therefore, pursuant to section 206.2.4, must be on an accessible route.

The DOJ's Statement of Interest summarizes the situation:

> [T]he raised porches at issue in this case function not only as entrances; they also are part of the public retail space of the store. As such, they are required to be accessible, under both the 1991 and 2010 Standards. Throughout this litigation, Defendants have emphasized the importance of the "in-store experience" for the Hollister brand. Defendants have indicated that the unique Hollister store design—including its raised porches, which are covered by a roof, feature a wooden floor, and include furniture and "props" such as lamps, plants, and oars—is at the core of creating this experience. Because the raised porches including these special features and attributes are used as both public retail spaces and public entrances, they must meet the requirements under the ADA for both uses.

Defendant argues that the Raised Porch Entrances "are designed to provide a *visual experience* to shoppers, and plaintiffs have not been deprived of that experience." This argument overlooks the reality that shoppers without mobility impairments may step up onto the Raised Porch Entrance, examine the displayed merchandise from all angles, sit in the chairs, and generally have the intended experience of entering a California beach shack by walking up onto the porch. Because these uses of the space are denied to shoppers who use wheelchairs, the Raised Porch Entrances are in violation of section 206.2.4.

[F]or the reasons set forth above, the Raised Porch Entrances at those Hollister stores that contain them violate both the 1991 and 2010 Standards. Because all of the Hollister stores at issue were built after January 26, 1993, these stores thus violate the new construction provisions of Title III of the ADA, 42 U.S.C. § 12183(a)(1).

NOTES ON ABERCROMBIE & FITCH

Assume that wheelchair users could enter Hollister stores freely through the side doors. If that were the case, would the court's holding make sense? On the one hand, wheelchair users would be able to access the same goods, in nearly all the same spaces, as everyone else. It may therefore seem like an overreach to demand that the company spend *any* money to ensure that wheelchair users can enter through all of the same entrances. (Recall Judge Posner's discussion of the plaintiff's use of the bathroom sink in the *Vande Zande* case in Chapter Three.)

On the other hand, the decision to build a front step on a flat shopping mall floor, and to therefore relegate wheelchair users to a secondary side entrance, might be thought to send a powerful message of exclusion. That message would certainly resonate with the history of race-based public accommodations discrimination in the United States prior to the Civil Rights Act of 1964. And the recipients of that message would have strong reason to suspect that the message was intentional. Abercrombie and Fitch places a substantial emphasis on projecting brand identity. See Susan Greene, *Denver Judge: Abercrombie Brand Hollister Violates Disabilities Act*, Colo. Independent, May 16, 2013 (quoting a shareholder report describing Hollister as "a 'fantasy of Southern California'" that is " 'all about hot lifeguards and beautiful beaches' "; noting that "[i]n 2006, Abercrombie CEO Mike Jeffries told Salon that his stores specifically don't market to teens who are overweight, unattractive or outliers among their peers"; and describing a case in which an Abercrombie "employee said she was moved from a sales position on the floor to one behind the scenes in the stockroom because her prosthetic arm didn't comply with the company's aesthetic standards"). Is it proper to use the law to forbid the sending of such a message of exclusion?

b. BARRIER REMOVAL IN EXISTING FACILITIES

Colorado Cross Disability Coalition v. Hermanson Family Ltd. Partnership I

United States Court of Appeals for the Tenth Circuit, 2001.
264 F.3d 999.

■ BALDOCK, CIRCUIT JUDGE.

Defendant Hermanson Family Limited Partnership I owns certain commercial buildings in Larimer Square, an historic block of shops and restaurants located in downtown Denver, Colorado. Plaintiff Kevin W. Williams is a Denver attorney who, as a result of a spinal cord injury, is paralyzed from the chest down and uses a power wheel chair for mobility. Since he moved to Denver around 1990, Plaintiff Williams has visited Larimer Square frequently. On his trips to Larimer Square, Plaintiff Williams noticed that architectural barriers prevented him from accessing many of the stores. Specifically, a 5.5 inch iron stoop at the entrance to the Crawford Building, owned by Defendant, prevents wheelchair access. In addition, the door to the store is recessed from the storefront and adds another barrier to wheelchair access of one to three inches.

In 1996, Plaintiff Williams and his employer, the Colorado Cross Disability Coalition, filed four separate lawsuits in the federal district court against Defendants under Title III of the Americans with Disabilities Act (ADA), 42 U.S.C. §§ 12181 thru 12189. [I]n their suits, Plaintiffs asked the district court to compel Defendants to install ramps at four locations in Larimer Square.[1] The district court consolidated the cases for both discovery and trial.

The consolidated cases proceeded to a bench trial. At the close of Plaintiff's case, the district court granted Defendants' motions for judgment as a matter of law, concluding that Plaintiff failed to establish that removal of architectural barriers at the four locations was readily achievable. Plaintiff appeals the district court's ruling as to only one of the four locations, the Crawford Building. [W]e affirm.

I.

[U]nder Title III of the ADA, "discrimination" specifically includes "failure to remove architectural barriers . . . in existing facilities . . . where such removal is readily achievable." *Id.* § 12182(b)(2)(A)(iv).

The ADA defines "readily achievable" as "easily accomplishable and able to be carried out without much difficulty or expense." *Id.* § 12181(9). The ADA further sets out several factors to be considered in determining whether removal of architectural barriers is readily achievable: (1) nature and cost of the action; (2) overall financial resources of the facility or facilities involved; (3) number of persons employed at such facility; (4) effect on expenses and resources; (5) impact of such action upon the operation of the facility; (6) overall financial resources of the covered entity; (7) overall size of the business of a covered entity with respect to the number of its employees; (8) the number, type, and location of its facilities; (9) type of operation or operations of the covered entity, including composition, structure, and functions of the workforce of such entity; and (10) geographic separateness, administrative or fiscal relationship of the facility or facilities in question to the covered entity. *Id.* § 12181(9)(A)–(D).

[S]ubsection (v) states that discrimination includes, "*where an entity can demonstrate* that the removal of a barrier under clause (iv) is not readily achievable, a failure to make such goods, services, facilities, privileges, advantages, or accommodations available through alternative methods if such methods are readily achievable." 42 U.S.C. § 12182(b)(2)(A)(v) (emphasis added). Subsection (v) clearly contemplates that the entity, rather than the plaintiff, bears the burden to demonstrate that barrier removal under subsection (iv) is not readily achievable. Read together, subsections (iv) and (v) provide an affirmative defense for an entity. Accordingly, we conclude Plaintiff must initially present evidence tending to show that the suggested method of barrier removal is readily achievable under the particular circumstances. If Plaintiff does so, Defendant then bears the ultimate burden of persuasion that barrier removal is not readily achievable under subsection (iv).

[T]he Department of Justice (DOJ) Regulations regarding Title III [s]upport our conclusion that "readily achievable" is an affirmative

---

[1]   Colorado Cross Disability Coalition, originally a plaintiff in this case, was dismissed on its own motion before trial.

defense. The regulations specifically refer to the "readily achievable defense." 28 C.F.R. Pt. 36, App.B. at 647 (2000). Furthermore, the regulations compare the "readily achievable defense" to the "undue burden defense" of § 12182(b)(2)(A)(iii), which limits a public accommodation's obligation to provide auxiliary aids, and the "undue hardship defense" of § 12112(b)(5)(A), which limits an employer's obligation to make reasonable accommodations in the employment context. *Id.* While the regulations state the readily achievable defense is less demanding than the undue burden or undue hardship defenses, they nevertheless explicitly place the burden of persuasion on the entity. *Id.*

[A]ccording to the plain language of Title III and the allocation of burdens we have adopted, Plaintiff must initially introduce evidence tending to establish that the proposed method of architectural barrier removal is "readily achievable," *i.e.*, "easily accomplishable and able to be carried out without much difficulty or expense" under the particular circumstances. 42 U.S.C. § 12181(9). Only if Plaintiff satisfies this initial burden does the burden of persuasion shift to Defendant to prove that the requested barrier removal method is not readily achievable.

II.

We now turn to the question of whether Plaintiff in this case produced sufficient evidence to satisfy his burden that his suggested method of barrier removal is readily achievable. At trial, Plaintiff introduced evidence regarding the installation of a ramp at the entrance to the Crawford Building. Plaintiff called Nore Winter, an expert in historical preservation in architecture and urban design. Winter owns a company called Winter & Company, which provides consultation to property owners, architects, and municipalities in developing preservation policies and design concepts. Winter testified that the front entrance to the Crawford Building could be made accessible without threatening or destroying the historic significance of the building or the district.

Winter prepared a sketch for a concept of a warped-plane sidewalk to provide access to the Crawford Building. He testified that did not intend for the sketch to be a construction drawing, but rather to illustrate an approach for achieving accessibility that would be compatible with the historic character of the building. Winter acknowledged that his sketch was "conceptual." Further, he stated that "[w]hen you start talking about real building design, et cetera, it's going to take a team of collaboration of all the parties involved with all the different viewpoints and interests to come up with the solutions that are going to best meet everyone's needs." Winter did not provide precise cost estimates. Instead, he estimated probable costs associated with the ramps of $10,750 based on his experience with similar projects. Winter testified that he reviewed a report by John Salmen, Defendant's consultant. According to Winter, Salmen's report suggested that Winter's approach would be valid, but Salmen would recommend extending the ramp out the full width of the sidewalk.

On cross-examination, Winter appeared to be unaware that the rise of the threshold of the building was three inches, bringing the total rise from the sidewalk elevation into the building to nine inches. To address the nine-inch rise, Winter suggested extending the elevation out for the full width of the sidewalk. When cross-examined about designing the ramp to accommodate both wheelchair access and people with vision impairments who could fail to discern the change in grade and trip on such a ramp, Winter responded that—

> you're getting beyond what my focus has been, which is on the historic impacts on these properties. As I stated earlier, I would work in collaboration with the design team to help solve these kinds of problems and these kinds of questions. I can't give you the design for that altering of the ramp right here.

Winter also suggested slanting the stoop to address the nine-inch rise. He acknowledged, however, that "I haven't really inspected this, but only to say I believe it could be possible."

Plaintiff next presented the testimony of expert accountant Robert Aucone regarding Defendant's financial resources. Aucone concluded that the financial impacts of installing ramps would be relatively immaterial and easily accomplishable. Aucone testified that in his opinion, even if the actual cost of a ramp was twice as much as estimated, his opinion would not change.

Plaintiff further introduced testimony and documentary evidence that Defendant and its predecessor had received estimates to ramp the Crawford Building. Plaintiff called Susan Spencer, the general manager of Larimer Square from 1986 until 1995. Spencer acted as general manager when Defendant purchased the Crawford Building in 1993. As general manager of Larimer Square, Spencer's duties included property management and leasing responsibilities. In addition, Spencer's responsibilities included discerning costs and making recommendations concerning whether ramps would be installed at buildings in Larimer Square. In July 1992, Rich Langston, a contractor, sent Spencer an estimate for a ramp at the Crawford building in the amount of $2,195.00. In the memo, Langston recommended against the ramp because it would require cutting the iron stoop. In November 1992, Langston sent Spencer an estimate in the amount of $2,272.00 to ramp the Crawford Building.

Spencer testified that she considered ramping the Crawford Building, but decided against it. According to Spencer, a ramp extending to the side of the building would have extended into the doorway or into the neighboring property. Further, Spencer expressed concern that a ramp extending straight out from the building would have created a trip hazard for persons with visual impairments.

Finally, Plaintiff introduced Title III DOJ regulations and commentary concerning whether a method of architectural barrier removal is readily achievable under subsection (iv). The regulations specifically list "[i]nstalling ramps" as an example of barrier removal under § 12182(b)(2)(A)(iv). 28 C.F.R. § 36.304(b)(1). The commentary points out, however, that

> the inclusion of a measure on this list does not mean that it is readily achievable in all cases. Whether or not any of these measures is readily achievable is to be determined on a case-by-case basis in light of the particular circumstances presented and the factors listed in the definition of readily achievable (§ 36.104).

28 C.F.R. Pt. 36, App.B at 647 (2000). The commentary further explains when ramping steps may be required:

> A public accommodation generally would not be required to remove a barrier to physical access posed by a flight of steps, if removal would require extensive ramping or an elevator. Ramping a single step, however, will likely be readily achievable, and ramping several steps will in many circumstances also be readily achievable.

Id. The DOJ regulations also urge public accommodations—

> to comply with the barrier removal requirements of this section in accordance with the following order of priorities.
>
> (1) First, a public accommodation should take measures to provide access to a place of public accommodation from public sidewalks, parking, or public transportation. These measures include, for example, installing an entrance ramp. . . .

28 C.F.R. § 36.304(c)(1).

While the regulations specifically mention ramping a single step as a top priority and likely to be readily achievable, the regulations also state that whether removal of a barrier is readily achievable is subject to a case by case inquiry. 28 C.F.R. Pt. 36, App.B at 647. Accordingly, Plaintiff must show that installation of a ramp at the Crawford Building is readily achievable in light of the particular circumstances.

While this is a close case, we conclude Plaintiff introduced evidence regarding only speculative concepts of ramp installation, rather than evidence that a specific design was readily achievable. For instance, Plaintiff failed to present any evidence to establish the likelihood that the City of Denver would approve a proposed modification to the historical building. Plaintiff also failed to provide any precise cost estimates regarding the proposed modification. Perhaps most importantly, Plaintiff's expert testimony failed to demonstrate that under the particular circumstances installing a ramp would be readily achievable. Instead, expert Winter provided speculative conceptual ideas, rather than a specific design which would be easily accomplishable and able to be carried out without much difficulty or expense. Winter acknowledged that his sketch was conceptual and that he did not intend the sketch to be a construction drawing. Notably, Winters appeared unaware of the exact height of the architectural barrier.

While the regulations state that ramping a single step will likely be readily achievable, such an inquiry must be based on a case by case basis under the particular circumstances and factors listed in the definition of readily achievable. Because Plaintiff failed to present sufficient evidence that removal of the architectural barrier is readily achievable, the district court properly granted Defendant's motion for judgment as a matter of law.

The judgment of the district court is AFFIRMED.

■ LUCERO, CIRCUIT JUDGE, concurring and dissenting.

I concur in the majority's Section I analysis concerning the burden of proof in cases brought to remove architectural barriers under 42 U.S.C. § 12182(b)(2)(A)(iv). [H]owever, I dissent from the resolution of this case in Section II of the majority opinion. In my judgment, the majority demands too much of ADA Title III plaintiffs. Moreover, in simply premising its holding on a negative—that Williams presented too little evidence showing his proposal was readily achievable—the majority provides inadequate guidance to trial courts in this undeveloped area of ADA law.

[T]he majority opinion does not clarify the type and quantum of evidence a plaintiff must present to show that removal of an architectural barrier is "readily achievable" pursuant to 42 U.S.C. § 12182(b)(2)(A)(iv). As to the type of evidence, an obvious starting place is the language of the ADA itself, which defines "readily achievable" as "easily accomplishable and able to be carried out without much difficulty or expense." 42 U.S.C. § 12181(9). A clear reading of that definition is that it requires a plaintiff to show two things related to the removal of an architectural barrier: (1) that it can be done with ease and (2) that it can be done inexpensively.

The first requirement addresses non-monetary qualitative issues such as feasibility, engineering/structural concerns, historic preservation, and so forth. These concerns will vary with the design of the building, the character of the neighborhood, local laws and regulations, and other variables. In most cases, plaintiffs should provide expert testimony presenting a plan and assuring its feasibility, keeping in mind any applicable engineering, structural, and historic preservation concerns.

The second requirement addresses quantitative, monetary issues and includes such considerations as "cost," 42 U.S.C. § 12181(9)(A), "overall financial resources," § 12181(9)(B), (C), and "the effect on expenses and resources," § 12181(9)(B). Plaintiffs can satisfy their burden through the testimony of a financial expert who can relate the estimated costs of the proposal to the defendant's financial position and ability to pay those costs.

It is the quantum of evidence—the amount of detail and precision— as to which the majority requires too much. In the vast majority of cases, there will be an information imbalance between plaintiffs and defendants. Defendants, who possess the practical experience and knowledge gained by owning and operating the building containing the architectural barrier, will have a much better sense of the true impact and feasibility of a barrier removal proposal. As a result, while plaintiffs bear the burden of advancing a reasonable plan, defendants ultimately are in a better position to produce—as part of their affirmative defense—the detailed evidence the majority apparently wishes to see in these types of cases. I find it unreasonable to require ADA Title III plaintiffs to anticipate and counter any and all potential objections as part of their prima facie case. Placing too high a burden on ADA plaintiffs risks ignoring Congressional intent and gutting the ADA's private right of action. If plaintiffs must all but present the court with a pre-approved construction contract for a sum certain which includes detailed plans, impact statements, engineering studies, and permits to meet their threshold burden, virtually no plaintiff could afford to bring an architectural barrier removal claim under 42 U.S.C. § 12182(b)(2)(A)(iv). Plaintiffs should present some evidence as to cost and feasibility that recognizes and addresses these considerations but should not be required to have final, detailed answers as to any of them.

[T]he majority's criticisms of the "speculative" nature of the proposed barrier removal plan, which appear to critique Williams's evidence addressing the qualitative prong of the "readily achievable" standard, are undermined by the fact that both Winter and Hermanson's expert, John Salmen, approved the same approach to removing the challenged architectural barrier: warping and raising the sidewalk gradually from the curb to the entrance of the Crawford Building. At the very least, this demonstrates that the basic approach advocated by Winter was sound. That is enough, in my view, to satisfy Williams's burden. Hermanson would have ample opportunity to demonstrate whatever flaws exist in Winter's plan during Hermanson's presentation of his affirmative defense.

There is no need for "precise" cost estimates in this case because there was no uncertainty surrounding Hermanson's ability to pay for the proposed barrier removal plan. Aucone testified that "even if the actual cost of a ramp was twice as much as estimated, his opinion" that Hermanson could easily afford to install the ramp "would not change." In fact, Aucone testified that Hermanson could well afford, by a factor of six, the estimated cost of Salmen's Crawford Building proposal. Perhaps precise estimates would be necessary if the cost of the barrier removal plan were at the margin of Hermanson's ability to pay for it, but that was not the situation. The issue is "could Hermanson easily afford to remove the barrier?" The clear answer, even assuming a six-fold error by Winter in estimating the cost of the proposal, is "yes."

I do not believe Williams should be required to present evidence demonstrating the likelihood of approval by the City of Denver as part of his prima facie case. No reason is advanced to suspect that the City of Denver would not approve the proposed plan—the only evidence on this subject indicated that the City of Denver had approved other barrier removal projects in the Larimer Square area. We are not presented with a complicated and expensive project such as incorporating an elevator into an antiquated building, and absent such evidence or a similar reason—such as unusually large scope or novelty—we should not presume significant hurdles to planning approval. Moreover, given the character of Larimer Square, the most likely obstacle to the City of Denver's approval of the barrier removal plan would be historic preservation concerns. However, that was exactly the area of Winter's expertise and the area he most thoroughly addressed in his testimony.

Molski v. Foley Estates Vineyard and Winery, LLC

United States Court of Appeals for the Ninth Circuit, 2008.
531 F.3d 1043.

■ D.W. NELSON, SENIOR CIRCUIT JUDGE.

This case involves a paraplegic who encountered discriminatory barriers to access when he visited a winery with his grandmother. Unwilling to remove barriers to the historic wine-tasting room, Foley Estates Vineyard and Winery ("Foley") began providing services on a gazebo with a "big bell" where individuals barred from the wine-tasting room could ring for service. Jarek Molski and Disability Rights

Enforcement, Education, Services ("DREES") sued Foley for injunctive relief and damages to redress physical barriers to wheelchair accessibility. The district court ordered barrier removal within the building, but determined that it would not be readily achievable to make an accessible ramp to the entrance. We affirm the injunction requiring barrier removal within the building and we remand for the district court to apply 28 C.F.R. § 36.405 and the Americans with Disabilities Act Accessibility Guidelines for Buildings and Facilities, 28 C.F.R. § 36 app. A § 4.1.7 ("ADAAG § 4.1.7" or "§ 4.1.7") when evaluating whether an accessible ramp would be readily achievable.

FACTUAL AND PROCEDURAL BACKGROUND

On January 18, 2003, Jarek Molski visited the Foley Estates Winery with his grandmother. While attending a wine-tasting, Molski encountered multiple physical barriers to entry with his wheelchair. An accessibility expert, Rick Sarantschin, conducted a sub rosa investigation of the property on October 12, 2003. Sarantschin confirmed the existence of barriers to entry including a ramp with a slope that varies between 6% and 20%; a raised threshold measuring 4.5"; a round door knob; a rear door width of only 30"; another door width of 31.25"; and a wine-tasting counter height of 42". Jarek Molski and DREES filed suit against Foley on December 22, 2003.

Prior to the commencement of litigation, Foley undertook $23,994 in renovations to provide all services on a wheelchair-accessible gazebo. Renovations included an accessible ramp from the parking lot and a "big bell" to summon for service. Nearly two years into the court proceedings, the Santa Barbara County Historic Landmarks Advisory Commission declared Foley Estates a "Place of Historical Merit" by way of resolution No. 2005-01.

At trial, the court heard expert testimony regarding proposed methods of barrier removal and associated costs. The court also heard testimony from Foley's architectural historian, who opined that an access ramp would have a severe impact on the historical nature of the cottage. The judge determined that it would cost $34,074 to construct an access ramp to the rear of the building, and it would cost $5,130 to remove all physical access barriers inside the building. The judge found that removal of interior barriers would be readily achievable, but removal of exterior barriers would not be readily achievable because it would threaten the architectural significance of the property. In reaching this finding, the judge held that 28 C.F.R. § 36.405 and ADAAG § 4.1.7 do not apply to barrier removal for existing facilities. Thus, the judge allocated the burden of production to the plaintiff to show that the proposed alteration would not threaten the historic significance of the building. The trial judge issued a permanent injunction requiring barrier removal inside the cottage.

DREES timely appeals the district court's findings regarding the applicability of 28 C.F.R. § 36.405 and ADAAG § 4.1.7, and the ready achievability of constructing an accessible ramp. Foley cross-appeals and challenges the permanent injunction requiring removal of interior physical barriers.

[D]ISCUSSION
I. EXTERIOR RAMP
A. APPLICABLE REGULATIONS

On appeal, we are asked to decide whether 28 C.F.R. § 36.405 and ADAAG § 4.1.7 apply to barrier removal in existing facilities. By their terms, these regulations apply to "alterations;" however, 28 C.F.R. § 36.304(d)(1) extends their application to readily achievable barrier removal in existing facilities. Despite this regulatory directive, the district court declined to apply § 36.405 and § 4.1.7. We reverse and remand.

Our analysis begins with 28 C.F.R. § 36.304, which regulates barrier removal in existing facilities of public accommodation. That section requires "[a] public accommodation [to] remove architectural barriers in existing facilities ... where such removal is readily achievable." 28 C.F.R. § 36.304(a). The regulation goes on to specify that, "measures taken to comply with the barrier removal requirements of this section shall comply with the applicable requirements for *alterations* in § 36.402 and §§ 36.404-36.406 ...." 28 C.F.R. § 36.304(d)(1) (emphasis added). If compliance under those additional regulations would not be readily achievable, "a public accommodation may take other readily achievable measures to remove the barrier that do not fully comply with the specified requirements." 28 C.F.R. § 36.304(d)(2).

In this case, we look to the regulations governing historic buildings because the Santa Barbara County Historic Landmarks Advisory Commission designated the building as a place of local historic merit. Through its plain language, 28 C.F.R. § 36.304(d)(1) directs vendors to comply with 28 C.F.R. § 36.405 when making readily achievable accommodations. Section 36.405 requires qualified historic buildings to "comply to the maximum extent feasible with [ADAAG § 4.1.7]." 28 C.F.R. § 36.405(a). Under § 4.1.7, "if the entity undertaking the alterations believes that compliance with the requirements ... would threaten or destroy the historic significance of the building ... the entity should consult with the State Historic Preservation Officer." ADAAG § 4.1.7(2)(b). "If the State Historic Preservation Officer agrees that compliance with the accessibility requirements for accessible routes (exterior and interior), ramps, entrances or toilets would threaten or destroy the historical significance of the building or facility, the alternative requirements in 4.1.7(3) may be used." *Id.* Under our reading, 28 C.F.R. § 36.304(d)(1) requires compliance with § 36.405, which incorporates § 4.1.7(2)(b) and provides a procedure for businesses to seek alternative requirements for historic properties.

Our reading of 28 C.F.R. § 36.304 preserves the leniency allocated to existing facilities under Title III of the Americans with Disabilities Act. The ADA only requires barrier removal in existing facilities "where such removal is readily achievable." 42 U.S.C. § 12182(b)(2)(A)(iv). Section 36.304 integrates the "readily achievable" standard into both § 36.304(a) and § 36.304(d)(2). Section 36.304(a) ensures that only readily achievable barrier removal triggers the incorporation of § 36.405 and § 4.1.7, and § 36.304(d)(2) allows for partial compliance if full compliance with those regulations would not be readily achievable.

Thus 28 C.F.R. § 36.304 incorporates § 36.405 and § 4.1.7 into the ready achievability framework, and retains the flexible standard reserved for existing facilities.

Additionally, § 4.1.7 establishes a procedure for determining whether barrier removal in existing facilities will be readily achievable. According to the ADA Title III Technical Assistance Manual ("ADA Manual") § III-4.4200, "[b]arrier removal would not be considered 'readily achievable' if it would threaten or destroy the historic significance of a building or facility that is . . . designated as historic under State or local law." The standard set in § 4.1.7 is identical to the standard of ready achievability proffered by the ADA Manual. This similarity between the language suggests that application of § 4.1.7 is consistent with the standard for existing historic facilities. Therefore, the procedure set forth in § 4.1.7 may be used to determine what is readily achievable in existing historic facilities.

For the foregoing reasons, we find that the district court erred when it refused to apply § 36.405 and § 4.1.7 to readily achievable barrier removal in existing facilities. We acknowledge that three courts have considered historical significance as a factor for determining ready achievability without invoking 28 C.F.R. § 36.405 or ADAAG § 4.1.7.[4] However, we find the explicit regulatory language to be more persuasive than the absence of discussion of these regulations in our sister circuits. Therefore, we remand to the district court to apply § 36.405 and § 4.1.7 when determining whether an exterior ramp would be readily achievable.

B. BURDEN OF PRODUCTION

At trial, the judge relied on *Colorado Cross Disability Coalition v. Hermanson Family Ltd.* to find that DREES bore the initial burden of production for the question of ready achievability. As noted above, *Colorado Cross* failed to address § 36.405 and § 4.1.7. This omission tainted the inquiry into who bears the burden of production for the ready achievability of barrier removal in historic facilities. We reverse and remand because we find that § 4.1.7 counsels in favor of placing the burden of production on the defendant.

We begin by looking to § 36.405 and § 4.1.7 to allocate the burden of production. Under § 4.1.7(2)(b), "if the entity undertaking alterations believes that compliance with the requirements . . . would threaten or destroy the historic significance of the building . . . the entity should consult with the State Historic Preservation Officer." Although this clause uses permissive language, it calls upon the party who believes that compliance would threaten the historical significance of the building to consult the appropriate agency. It does not place that burden on the party advocating for remedial measures. Thus, the language of § 4.1.7(2)(b) counsels in favor of placing the burden of production upon the defendant.

---

[4] In, *Gathright-Dietrich v. Atlanta Landmarks, Inc.*, 452 F.3d 1269, 1275 (11th Cir.2006), *Colorado Cross Disability Coalition v. Hermanson Family Ltd.*, 264 F.3d 999, 1007 (10th Cir.2001), and *Speciner v. NationsBank, N.A.*, 215 F.Supp.2d 622, 631 (D.Md.2002), courts have considered historical significance as a factor for determining ready achievability without invoking 28 C.F.R. § 36.405 or ADAAG § 4.1.7. Notably, none of these cases rejects the application of 28 C.F.R. § 36.405 and ADAAG § 4.1.7; they simply proceed without analyzing those authorities.

By placing the burden of production on the defendant, we place the burden on the party with the best access to information regarding the historical significance of the building. The defendant sought the historical designation in this case. Thus, the defendant possesses the best understanding of the circumstances under which that designation might be threatened. The defendant is also in the best position to discuss the matter with the Santa Barbara County Historic Landmarks Advisory Commission and to request an opinion on proposed methods of barrier removal. As a result, the defendant is in a better position to introduce, as part of its affirmative defense, detailed evidence and expert testimony concerning whether the historic significance of a structure would be threatened or destroyed by the proposed barrier removal plan.

As the dissent reasoned in *Colorado Cross*, "[i]f plaintiffs must all but present the court with a pre-approved construction contract for a sum certain which includes detailed plans, impact statements, engineering studies, and permits to meet their threshold burden, virtually no plaintiff could afford to bring an architectural barrier removal claim under 42 U.S.C. § 12182(b)(2)(A)(iv)." Colorado Cross (Lucero, J., dissenting). We need not require an ADA plaintiff to undertake such heroic measures. Congress relies on private actors, i.e., disabled individuals, to enforce the ADA by filing lawsuits. Thus plaintiffs should not be deterred from filing meritorious claims by an inappropriate allocation of the burden of production.

We find that the language of § 4.1.7, the access to information, and the congressional intent behind the ADA support placing the burden of production on the defendant. Thus, we reverse and remand for the district court to assign the burden of production to the defendant on the issue of whether barrier removal would threaten the historical significance of the building.

II. DUTY TO REMOVE INTERIOR BARRIERS

When the district court ordered removal of interior barriers to the building, the court arguably enhanced the probability that persons with disabilities would attempt to traverse the non-compliant ramp to access the building. Foley argues that we should absolve the winery of its responsibility to remove interior barriers because the only existing ramp is non-compliant. We reject this argument and affirm the district court's injunction requiring barrier removal inside the building.

Both parties find support for their positions in 28 C.F.R. § 36.304(d)(2). According to this regulation:

> If . . . the measures required to remove a barrier would not be readily achievable, a public accommodation may take other readily achievable measures to remove the barrier that do not fully comply with the specified requirements. Such measures include, for example, providing a ramp with a steeper slope . . . . No measure shall be taken, however, that poses a significant risk to the health or safety of individuals with disabilities or others.

28 C.F.R. § 36.304(d)(2). DREES relies on the provision for partial accommodation wherever complete accommodation is not readily achievable. Foley relies on the caution against partial accommodations

where they pose a significant risk to health and safety. We find that partial accommodation was appropriate in this case.

First, § 36.304(d)(2) expressly contemplates that a venue may provide a ramp with a steeper slope. The provision of such a ramp does not excuse the facility from otherwise making readily achievable accommodations to the maximum extent feasible. Therefore, the fact that there is an *existing* ramp with a steeper slope also does not excuse the facility from making readily achievable accommodations to the maximum extent feasible. Second, the inaccessibility of entry to one group of individuals does not justify retaining barriers to access inside the building for all others who may safely gain entry. Where readily achievable, the interior of the building must be made accessible for all who may enter.

Foley argues that removing barriers to the interior of the building might tempt people with disabilities to traverse a ramp that is nearly twelve percent steeper at points than ADA Guidelines recommend. According to Foley, this temptation implicates 28 C.F.R. § 36.304(d)(2) because it "poses a significant risk to the health or safety of individuals with disabilities." When weighing this consideration, we recognize the diversity in the population of persons with disabilities who might seek to use this ramp. People using canes, walkers, braces, and powered chairs can often navigate a steeper ramp than people using manual chairs, so safety risks vary with the nature of the disability and adaptive equipment. Notably, the only evidence that Foley cites to support its theory of a health and safety risk is the pleading of a manual wheelchair user who complained of trauma to his upper extremities. Although the ramp allegedly caused injury to Jarek Molski, the ramp might not cause injury to people using different adaptive equipment. Because safe access is possible for many persons who might need or use the ramp, the district court did not abuse its discretion by ordering readily achievable accommodations to the interior of the wine-tasting room.

III. ALTERNATIVE GAZEBO

Foley argues that the provision of all relevant services on the wheelchair-accessible gazebo was legally adequate as a means of barrier removal. We reject this argument and affirm the district court's imposition of readily achievable barrier removal inside the building.

As a threshold matter, a facility may only substitute alternatives to barrier removal where "as a result of compliance with the alterations requirements specified in paragraph (d)(1) of this section, the measures required to remove a barrier would not be readily achievable." 28 C.F.R. § 36.304(d)(2). As noted above, the district court did not abuse its discretion in determining that barrier removal inside the building was readily achievable. In light of this holding, no alternative accommodations can supplant the legally required barrier removal.

Although we find the gazebo inadequate for those who could otherwise access the wine-tasting room, the gazebo provides an important avenue of participation for those who cannot traverse the steps or ramp to the wine-tasting room. We acknowledge Foley's efforts to serve this community; however, these efforts do not change Foley's obligation to make readily available changes to enable the maximum participation possible for those who are able to access the interior of the wine-tasting room. The gazebo places those who could otherwise access the wine-tasting room at a disadvantage that the ADA seeks to remove. Thus, the Gazebo is not an appropriate alternative accommodation.

CONCLUSION

We REVERSE and REMAND for the district court to apply § 36.405 and § 4.1.7 and place the burden of production on the defendant. Additionally, we AFFIRM the district court's permanent injunction requiring removal of interior barriers to wheelchair access.

REVERSED AND REMANDED IN PART AND AFFIRMED IN PART.

■ FERNANDEZ, CIRCUIT JUDGE, CONCURRING AND DISSENTING:

I concur in the majority's determination that the district court did not err when it required Foley Estates Vineyard and Winery, LLC, to make changes to the interior of its building pursuant to the Americans with Disabilities Act, 42 U.S.C. § 12181-12189 ("ADA"). However, I dissent from the majority's reversal of the district court's order denying a demand that Foley make the proposed exterior changes.

It is important to note that this is not a case where Foley sought to construct a new facility. *See* 42 U.S.C. § 12183(a)(1). Nor is it a case where Foley sought to alter an old facility. *See id.* § 12183(a)(2). It is, instead, a case where Foley was not seeking to make any change, but Disability Rights Enforcement Education Services: Helping You Help Others (hereafter "Disability Rights") demanded that changes be made because the failure to do so would be discriminatory. *See id.* § 12182(b)(2)(A)(iv). However, a mere failure to remove an architectural barrier is discriminatory only "where such removal is readily achievable." *Id.* In other words, the mere existence of the barrier does not bespeak wrongdoing; it only becomes wrongful if removal can be readily achieved.

Barrier removal is readily achievable when it is "easily accomplishable and able to be carried out without much difficulty or expense." *Id.* § 12181(9). That definition is extremely important. It imposes a much less stringent standard upon owners of existing properties than that imposed upon owners who undertake new construction and are required to show structural impracticability in order to avoid violating the ADA. *See id.* § 12183(a)(1). It is also less stringent than the "maximum extent feasible" standard imposed upon owners who seek to alter their facilities. *See id.* § 12183(a)(2).

In determining ready achievability, "the nature and cost of the action needed" must be taken into account. *Id.* § 12181(9)(A). Furthermore, because it was never intended that the nation's architectural heritage be destroyed under the banner of readily achievable accessibility, special consideration is given to buildings that "are designated as historic under State or local law." 28 C.F.R. § 36.405(a). As to those, it is important to avoid changes that would "threaten or destroy the historic significance of the building. . . ." *Id.* § 36.405(b). As the Department of Justice puts it: "Barrier removal would not be considered 'readily achievable' if it would threaten or destroy the historic significance of a building or facility that is . . . designated as historic under State or local law." Dep't of Justice, ADA

Title III Technical Assistance Manual: Covering Pub. Accommodations & Commercial Facilities, § III-4.4200; *see also* 16 U.S.C. § 470f; Nondiscrimination on the Basis of Disability by Pub. Accommodations & in Commercial Facilities, 56 Fed.Reg. 35,544, 35,568-69 (July 26, 1991). It is through that lens that we must review the district court's decision in this case because the Foley building in question is a Craftsman house which has been designated as a Place of Historic Merit by the Santa Barbara County Historic Landmark Commission. Nobody doubts that.

When that proper method of examining the district court's determination is used, it is apparent that the district court did not clearly err when, based on the record before it, the court determined that the changes suggested by Disability Rights would, in fact, severely impact or destroy the historic significance of Foley's building. In reaching that conclusion, the court relied upon the unrebutted evidence from an expert architectural historian, Dr. Pamela Post, who testified to that effect and added that if the suggested changes had been made previously, they would have made the designation of the house as a Place of Historic Merit problematic. She, by the way, is the person who presented the initial report that supported the designation of the property in the first place.

But, argues Disability Rights, the district court was not permitted to make that finding. Why? Well, Disability Rights points to the fact that the regulation on removal of barriers states that when measures *are* taken to comply with readily achievable barrier removal requirements, any alterations made are to comply with 28 C.F.R. § 36.405(a) "for the element being altered." 28 C.F.R. § 36.304(d)(1). Of course, that is no surprise because if a change is made, it becomes an alteration and ought to then make the property accessible. But, to state that the intent of the regulation is to make barrier removal essentially the same as voluntary alteration is to conflate those two different concepts by making the very threshold for removability the same as the standard for alteration. That cannot have been the intent of the regulation.

Leaving that objection aside, however, Disability Rights' second step is even more problematic. Having been referred to 28 C.F.R. § 36.405, we should, says Disability Rights, then note that § 36.405 further refers to 28 C.F.R. Pt. 36, app. A (hereafter "Appendix A"). And, notes Disability Rights, § 4.17(2)(b) of Appendix A states that when making alterations to historic buildings the entity (here Foley) "should consult with the State Historic Preservation Officer." What Disability Rights bypasses is the clear definition of "should" as used in Appendix A. As opposed to "may" and "shall," the word "should" by definition "[d]enotes an advisory specification or recommendation." *See* Appendix A § 3.4. I fail to see how or why the existence of that recommendation of a possible course of action would preclude a district court from taking direct expert testimony and making a finding on the effect of a proposed change on the historic significance of the property in question. Thus, the claim that the district court could not make a finding on the issue must fail.

Disability Rights also raises questions about whether it had any burden to propound a prima facie case that included an element regarding the effect of its proposed changes on the historic significance of the property. Other courts have indicated that plaintiffs, like Disability Rights, do have that obligation. *See, e.g., Gathright-Dietrich; Colorado Cross; Speciner.* However, I see no need to resolve that issue in this case. The district court decided the question of ready achievability after a trial. Thus, any shifting burdens of production are of no import. Here the district court received all evidence that the parties chose to put forward, and made a finding that there would be a deleterious impact upon the historic significance of the property. No more was needed, and the fact that Disability Rights did not put forth any historic significance evidence of its own, expert or otherwise, is fatal to its position.

In short, as I see it, the district court's perspicacity and care led it to the correct result in this case. Its decision should be affirmed.

Thus, I concur in part and respectfully dissent in part.

NOTES ON BARRIER REMOVAL IN EXISTING FACILITIES

Hermanson and *Molski* raise a number of connected issues regarding Title III's requirement of readily achievable barrier removal. The most basic question concerns how difficult or expensive a barrier-removal effort must be before it is no longer readily achievable. See 42 U.S.C. § 12181(9) ("The term 'readily achievable' means easily accomplishable and able to be carried out without much difficulty or expense."). What guidance do the cases give you on that question? A subsidiary question concerns the role of historic preservation interests in the readily achievable inquiry. Do you agree with how the courts addressed that question? And, even if we know what legally counts as readily achievable, we face the question of which party bears what burden to establish the existence of ready achievability in a particular case. Which analysis of the burden of proof question do you find persuasive, *Hermanson*'s or *Molski*'s?

2. PHYSICAL ACCESSIBILITY UNDER THE FAIR HOUSING ACT

United States v. Edward Rose & Sons

United States Court of Appeals for the Sixth Circuit, 2004.
384 F.3d 258.

■ SILER, CIRCUIT JUDGE.

This housing discrimination case turns on what doors must be accessible to the handicapped. At issue are two sets of apartment complexes, designed with an inaccessible front door, but an accessible back patio door. The district court granted the U.S. Justice Department ("government") a preliminary injunction halting the construction and occupancy of the buildings. The main defendant, the builder and owner, Edward Rose & Sons ("Rose"), appeals, arguing that court erred (1) by misconstruing the requirements of the Fair Housing Act, 42 U.S.C. § 3601 *et seq.* ("FHA"), and (2) by incorrectly weighing the relative preliminary injunction interests and harms. We AFFIRM the district court's grant of the preliminary injunction.

[D]efendant Rose constructed and owns the nineteen apartment buildings, located in Michigan and Ohio, at issue. These buildings are at various stages of construction, but all have the same basic design. The ground floor apartments at issue have two exterior entrances—a front door and rear patio door. The front door is closer to the parking lot, but is handicapped inaccessible because it can only be reached by descending stairs. At the bottom of the stairs is a landing shared by two front doors leading into two different apartments. The rear patio entrance is accessible, but is located farther from the parking lot.

The government alleged that the apartments violated the disability portions of the FHA. The district court granted a preliminary injunction, adopting the government's position that the front door was the "primary entrance" used by the public and guests, and as such, it was a "public" or "common area" that the FHA mandates be accessible. See 42 U.S.C. 3604(f)(3)(C)(i). In reaching this conclusion, the court relied on the Housing and Urban Development ("HUD") regulations, guidelines, and design manual. The preliminary injunction halts construction on the "covered dwellings" and restrains the defendants from occupying "covered dwellings" not yet leased. In this case, "covered dwellings" means simply the ground floor. See 42 U.S.C. § 3604(f)(7) (stating if building has no elevator, only the ground floor is a covered dwelling subject to the FHA). Rose appeals.

[T]he basic question of this litigation is whether the space outside the front door is a public or common use area that must be handicapped accessible. We are the first circuit to consider the issue. The statute reads:

C) in connection with the design and construction of covered multifamily dwellings for first occupancy after the date that is 30 months after September 13, 1988, a failure to design and construct those dwellings in such a manner that—

(i) *the public use and common use portions of such dwellings are readily accessible to and usable by handicapped persons*;

(ii) all the doors designed to allow passage into and within all premises within such dwellings are sufficiently wide to allow passage by handicapped persons in wheelchairs; and

(iii) *all premises within such dwellings contain the following features of adaptive design*:

(I) *an accessible route into and through the dwelling*;

(II) light switches, electrical outlets, thermostats, and other environmental controls in accessible locations;

(III) reinforcements in bathroom walls to allow later installation of grab bars; and

(IV) usable kitchens and bathrooms such that an individual in a wheelchair can maneuver about the space.

42 U.S.C. § 3604(f)(3) (emphasis added).

The government asserts that because the landing at the bottom of the stairs is a "common area," § 3604(f)(3)(C)(i) mandates that the landing must be accessible. The landing in front of the entrances is not accessible because it can only be reached by the stairs. The government argues that this entrance is the "primary" door because it is in the front and closest to the parking lot. As such, it is the entrance most visitors will use, and thus the space or landing in front of the door is a public or common area. Additionally, the stair landing is shared by two entrances to two different apartment units, and thus a common area used by two tenants.

Rose correctly points out that neither the statute nor any possibly binding regulations make any reference or distinction between "primary," "front," or "back" doors. Rose argues that the government's interpretation requires almost every entrance to a unit be accessible. If the space in front of an entrance becomes a common use area, simply because people use the entrance, then the statute would require virtually every entrance to be accessible.

Rose asserts that if the space in front of virtually every entrance is a "common" or "public" area, § 3604(f)(3)(C)(iii)(I) becomes superfluous. Section 3604(f)(3)(C)(iii)(I) mandates all premises must have "*an* accessible route into and through the dwelling." (Emphasis added.). Rose contends that the indefinite article "an" indicates that the statute only requires one accessible route into each unit. As such, the space in front of every door to a private unit cannot be a common area, or all doors would have to be accessible, and there would be no need for § 3604(f)(3)(C)(iii)(I) to separately mandate "an accessible route" into the unit. Moreover, even if there were such a thing as a single "primary" entrance, whose anterior space must be accessible as a common area, there would still be no need for § 3604(f)(3)(C)(iii)(I) to redundantly mandate "an accessible route." An accessible route would already be mandated by the common area in front of the primary entrance of every unit.

We find that, in this particular case, the stair landing in front of the entrance is a common area that the statute mandates be accessible. The fact that two apartment units share the stair landing makes the space a common area. The plain meaning of "common use" unambiguously covers the entrance under dispute. At the time of the statute's enactment, dictionaries generally defined "common" as belonging to or shared by two or more individuals. See The Oxford English Dictionary 565 (J.A. Simpson & E.S.C. Weiner eds., Clarendon Press 2d ed.1989) (defining common as "[b]elonging equally to more than one" and "possessed or shared alike by both or all."); Webster's Third New International Dictionary 458 (Philip Babcock Gove ed., Merriam-Webster 1986) ("held, enjoyed, experienced, or participated in equally by a number of individuals; possessed or manifested by more than one individual"); Funk & Wagnalls New International Dictionary (Publishers International Press Comprehensive ed.1984) ("Pertaining to, connected with, or participated in by two or more persons or things; joint."). Here, the stair landing belongs to, and is shared by, two apartments, and exists for their "common use."[4]

---

[4]   While our finding that the plain meaning of "common use" unambiguously covers the stair landing at issue, even if we found the statute ambiguous, the space in front of the two

Our ruling is narrow; we simply hold in this case that because the two apartments share the stair landing, the stair landing qualifies as a "common area" that must be accessible. We express no opinion on what the FHA would require if the stairs only led to one apartment unit entrance and decline to delve into the parties' "primary entrance" arguments because we find them unnecessary for the resolution of this case. Assuming arguendo that, as Rose submits, not every entrance constitutes a "common area" because otherwise § 3604(f)(3)(C)(iii)(I)'s mandate that all premises have "*an* accessible route" is superfluous, we still would find that the shared landing is a common area. Section § 3604(f)(3)(C)(iii)(I) would not be superfluous because that section would ensure that apartment units that share no entrance with another apartment unit would still have "an accessible" entrance.

[T]he stair landing shared by two apartments qualifies as a "common area" that the FHA mandates be handicapped accessible. This strong finding of a likelihood of success on the merits coupled with the public's interest in eradicating housing discrimination overcomes any weakness in the irreparable injury and harm to others factors.

AFFIRMED.

United States v. Freer

United States District Court for the Western District of New York, 1994.
864 F.Supp. 324.

■ Telesca, Chief Judge.

[T]he United States of America brings this action for declaratory and injunctive relief, on behalf of the complainant Ann Soper, under the Fair Housing Act, 42 U.S.C. § 3602, *et seq.* Ms. Soper is a disabled individual who resides in a trailer park owned by the defendants Jack and Beverly Freer. The Government alleges that the defendants failed to make a reasonable accommodation for Ms. Soper's disability by refusing to allow her to install a wheelchair ramp to gain access to her trailer.

The Government seeks a preliminary injunction enjoining the defendants from continuing to withhold their approval of Ms. Soper's request to install a wheelchair ramp. Although the Government also seeks declaratory relief and monetary damages in this action, those issues are not before the Court at this time. For the following reasons, the Government's motion for a preliminary injunction is granted.

[M]s. Soper is a disabled individual who is confined to a wheelchair. Ms. Soper has a trailer home which is located in the defendants' trailer park. In order to enter the trailer, Ms. Soper must climb five steps. Without a wheelchair ramp, Ms. Soper needs to be carried (or otherwise

---

entrances would fall under the HUD regulations defining "common use area." The regulation defines "common use areas" as "rooms, spaces or elements inside or outside of a building that are made available for the use of residents of a building or the guests thereof . . . includ[ing] hallways, lounges, lobbies, laundry rooms, refuse rooms, mail rooms, recreational areas and passageways among and between buildings." 24 C.F.R. § 100.201. In the instant case, the shared landing is like a common "hallway" shared by the two apartments. Thus, even if we found "common area" ambiguous, Rose still would lose under the regulations.

attended) up the steps and into her home. Recently, while being assisted into her home, Ms. Soper fell and was injured.

Prior to her accident, Ms. Soper had asked the defendants for permission to install, at her own cost, a wheelchair ramp which wrapped around the side and front of her trailer and partially protruded into her driveway. The defendants refused to allow installation of a ramp with that configuration, claiming that it would impede trailer removal and would so shorten Ms. Soper's driveway that parked cars would obstruct the trailer park's access road. The defendants proposed an alternative ramp design which Ms. Soper has rejected as unsuitable to her needs.

[T]he Fair Housing Act (the "Act"), 42 U.S.C. § 3604(f)(2), prohibits discrimination against handicapped individuals in the terms, conditions or privileges of rental of a dwelling or in the provision of services or facilities in connection with such a dwelling. Under the statute, unlawful discrimination includes,

> a refusal to permit, at the expense of the handicapped person, reasonable modifications of existing premises occupied or to be occupied by such person if such modifications may be necessary to afford such person full enjoyment of the premises except that, in the case of a rental, the landlord may where is it reasonable to do so condition permission for a modification on the renter agreeing to restore the interior of the premises to the condition that existed before the modification, reasonable wear and tear excepted.

§ 3604(f)(3)(A).

[T]he Government has established a prima facie case of discrimination under the Act. There is no dispute that Ms. Soper qualifies as a handicapped person under the Act or that the defendants knew of her handicap and refused to allow her to install a wheelchair ramp at her home. Unquestionably, the defendants' refusal to permit installation of the ramp has effectively denied Ms. Soper an equal opportunity to use and enjoy her home.

The defendants have failed to rebut the presumption of discrimination by demonstrating that Ms. Soper's proposed modification is unreasonable, i.e., imposes upon them an undue financial or administrative burden. The defendants claim that Ms. Soper's "wrap around" ramp proposal will make trailer removal and driveway parking difficult, thereby obstructing traffic using the access road. Instead, they propose an alternative design which meets all applicable laws and codes, does not block the driveway and costs no more than Ms. Soper's proposed ramp.

[T]he Government has clearly demonstrated a possibility of success on the merits of its claim. There is no dispute that the defendants have refused to accommodate Ms. Soper's disability by not allowing her to build the "wrap around" wheelchair ramp. Pursuant to the Act, the defendants are obligated to approve Ms. Soper's ramp proposal unless it is proven that the proposal is unreasonable. The defendants cannot accomplish this by simply tossing Ms. Soper's proposal aside and pressing for acceptance of their alternative design.

This Court is unconvinced that Ms. Soper's ramp proposal is unreasonable.[1] Installation of the ramp will not impose an undue financial burden on the defendants because Ms. Soper is assuming the construction costs. In addition, the defendants will not suffer undue administrative burdens should the ramp be built. The Government has stated that Ms. Soper's proposed ramp can be disassembled within three hours and will not impede removal of the trailer. This Court has also reviewed a photograph of the Soper driveway which sheds substantial doubt on the defendants' claim that installation of Ms. Soper's ramp design will impede traffic in the driveway and on the access road. In short, the defendants have submitted insufficient evidence to rebut the inference of discrimination under the Act.

WHEREFORE, the Government's motion for a preliminary injunction is granted. The defendants shall allow Ms. Soper to install her proposed "wrap around" wheelchair ramp. The issue of damages is deferred to a future date.

NOTES ON ACCESSIBILITY UNDER THE FAIR HOUSING ACT

The Fair Housing Act's physical accessibility requirements incorporate the same sort of old-new distinction as appears in Title III's accessibility requirements. But there is one significant difference: Unlike Title III, which requires the covered business to pay for barrier removal in older facilities, the Fair Housing Act requires only that older facilities "permit, *at the expense of the handicapped person*, reasonable modifications of existing premises occupied or to be occupied by such person if such modifications may be necessary to afford such person full enjoyment of the premises." 42 U.S.C. § 3604(f)(3)(A) (emphasis added).

Why does the Fair Housing Act require the individual with a disability to pay for barrier removal, while Title III requires the business owner to pay? Is the reason simply one of administrative efficiency—that it is easier to charge the resident with a disability who specifically requests barrier removal than it is to charge the customers with disabilities who may benefit from barrier removal months or years later? Or does the distinction reflect a normative judgment—that people with disabilities should bear the costs of accessibility in the places where they live, but not in the businesses they patronize? What arguments might justify this sort of public-private distinction? (Note that the distinction parallels the job-related rule in the employment context, which holds that employers need not pay for accommodations that assist a worker with a disability outside of the workplace.)

The requirement to pay for one's own barrier removal might have countervailing benefits for people with disabilities, however. In *Freer*, the court holds that the trailer park owner must permit Ms. Soper to make the reasonable modifications of her choice. Even if the trailer park would prefer that she build her ramp in another way, and even if the trailer park's preferred ramp design would be reasonable, the park must nonetheless permit Ms. Soper to build according to whatever reasonable design *she*

---

[1]   The plan proposed by Ms. Soper allows for a manageable graduated incline albeit over a longer ramp. The Freer proposal would allow for a much more severe incline (thus less manageable) over a shorter span of ramp.

prefers. In the employment context, as Chapter Three demonstrates, the rule is the opposite—even if the preferred accommodation of an employee with a disability is reasonable, she must nonetheless accept whatever reasonable accommodation the employer chooses. (You might think of this rule as the "who pays the piper" rule.) And, presumably because the person with a disability is paying, the Fair Housing Act requires housing providers to permit more extensive barrier-removal efforts than are required under the ADA—"reasonable modifications of existing premises," as opposed to "readily achievable" barrier removal.

C. REASONABLE MODIFICATIONS

PGA Tour, Inc. v. Martin

Supreme Court of the United States, 2001.
532 U.S. 661.

■ JUSTICE STEVENS delivered the opinion of the Court.*

[A]s we have noted, 42 U.S.C. § 12182(a) sets forth Title III's general rule prohibiting public accommodations from discriminating against individuals because of their disabilities. The question whether petitioner has violated that rule depends on a proper construction of the term "discrimination," which is defined by Title III to include

"a failure to make reasonable modifications in policies, practices, or procedures, when such modifications are necessary to afford such goods, services, facilities, privileges, advantages, or accommodations to individuals with disabilities, unless the entity can demonstrate that making such modifications would fundamentally alter the nature of such goods, services, facilities, privileges, advantages, or accommodations." § 12182(b)(2)(A)(ii).

Petitioner does not contest that a golf cart is a reasonable modification that is necessary if Martin is to play in its tournaments. Martin's claim thus differs from one that might be asserted by players with less serious afflictions that make walking the course uncomfortable or difficult, but not beyond their capacity. In such cases, an accommodation might be reasonable but not necessary. In this case, however, the narrow dispute is whether allowing Martin to use a golf cart, despite the walking requirement that applies to the PGA TOUR, the NIKE TOUR, and the third stage of the Q-School, is a modification that would "fundamentally alter the nature" of those events.

In theory, a modification of petitioner's golf tournaments might constitute a fundamental alteration in two different ways. It might alter such an essential aspect of the game of golf that it would be unacceptable even if it affected all competitors equally; changing the diameter of the hole from three to six inches might be such a modification. Alternatively, a less significant change that has only a

---

* [This excerpt of the justices' opinions in *PGA Tour* addresses the question whether waiving the walking rule was a reasonable modification. The portion of the justices' opinions that addresses the question whether the PGA Tour was covered by Title III appears in Section A, *supra*.—ed.]

peripheral impact on the game itself might nevertheless give a disabled player, in addition to access to the competition as required by Title III, an advantage over others and, for that reason, fundamentally alter the character of the competition. We are not persuaded that a waiver of the walking rule for Martin would work a fundamental alteration in either sense.

As an initial matter, we observe that the use of carts is not itself inconsistent with the fundamental character of the game of golf. From early on, the essence of the game has been shotmaking—using clubs to cause a ball to progress from the teeing ground to a hole some distance away with as few strokes as possible.[39] That essential aspect of the game is still reflected in the very first of the Rules of Golf, which declares: "The Game of Golf consists in playing a ball from the teeing ground into the hole by a stroke or successive strokes in accordance with the rules." Rule 1-1, Rules of Golf. Over the years, there have been many changes in the players' equipment, in golf course design, in the Rules of Golf, and in the method of transporting clubs from hole to hole. Originally, so few clubs were used that each player could carry them without a bag. Then came golf bags, caddies, carts that were pulled by hand, and eventually motorized carts that carried players as well as clubs. "Golf carts started appearing with increasing regularity on American golf courses in the 1950's. Today they are everywhere. And they are encouraged. For one thing, they often speed up play, and for another, they are great revenue producers." There is nothing in the Rules of Golf that either forbids the use of carts or penalizes a player for

---

[39] Golf is an ancient game, tracing its ancestry to Scotland, and played by such notables as Mary Queen of Scots and her son James. That shot-making has been the essence of golf since early in its history is reflected in the first recorded rules of golf, published in 1744 for a tournament on the Leith Links in Edinburgh:

"Articles & Laws in Playing at Golf

"1. You must Tee your Ball, within a Club's length of the [previous] Hole.

"2. Your Tee must be upon the Ground.

"3. You are not to change the Ball which you Strike off the Tee.

"4. You are not to remove, Stones, Bones or any Break Club for the sake of playing your Ball, Except upon the fair Green/ & that only/ within a Club's length of your Ball.

"5. If your Ball comes among Water, or any Watery Filth, you are at liberty to take out your Ball & bringing it behind the hazard and Teeing it, you may play it with any Club and allow your Adversary a Stroke for so getting out your Ball.

"6. If your Balls be found anywhere touching one another, You are to lift the first Ball, till you play the last.

"7. At Holling, you are to play your Ball honestly for the Hole, and, not to play upon your Adversary's Ball, not lying in your way to the Hole.

"8. If you should lose your Ball, by its being taken up, or any other way, you are to go back to the Spot, where you struck last & drop another Ball, And allow your Adversary a Stroke for the misfortune.

"9. No man at Holling his Ball, is to be allowed, to mark his way to the Hole with his Club or, any thing else.

"10. If a Ball be stopp'd by any person, Horse, Dog, or any thing else, The Ball so stop'd must be play'd where it lyes.

"11. If you draw your Club, in order to Strike & proceed so far in the Stroke, as to be bringing down your Club; If then, your Club shall break, in, any way, it is to be Accounted a Stroke.

"12. He, whose Ball lyes farthest from the Hole is obliged to play first.

"13. Neither Trench, Ditch, or Dyke, made for the preservation of the Links, nor the Scholar's Holes or the Soldier's Lines, Shall be accounted a Hazard; But the Ball is to be taken out/Teed/and play'd with any Iron Club." K. Chapman, Rules of the Green 14–15 (1997).

using a cart. That set of rules, as we have observed, is widely accepted in both the amateur and professional golf world as the rules of the game. The walking rule that is contained in petitioner's hard cards, based on an optional condition buried in an appendix to the Rules of Golf, is not an essential attribute of the game itself.

Indeed, the walking rule is not an indispensable feature of tournament golf either. As already mentioned, petitioner permits golf carts to be used in the SENIOR PGA TOUR, the open qualifying events for petitioner's tournaments, the first two stages of the Q-School, and, until 1997, the third stage of the Q-School as well. Moreover, petitioner allows the use of carts during certain tournament rounds in both the PGA TOUR and the NIKE TOUR. In addition, although the USGA enforces a walking rule in most of the tournaments that it sponsors, it permits carts in the Senior Amateur and the Senior Women's Amateur championships.[44]

Petitioner, however, distinguishes the game of golf as it is generally played from the game that it sponsors in the PGA TOUR, NIKE TOUR, and (at least recently) the last stage of the Q-School—golf at the "highest level." According to petitioner, "[t]he goal of the highest-level competitive athletics is to assess and compare the performance of different competitors, a task that is meaningful only if the competitors are subject to identical substantive rules." The waiver of any possibly "outcome-affecting" rule for a contestant would violate this principle and therefore, in petitioner's view, fundamentally alter the nature of the highest level athletic event. The walking rule is one such rule, petitioner submits, because its purpose is "to inject the element of fatigue into the skill of shot-making," and thus its effect may be the critical loss of a stroke. As a consequence, the reasonable modification Martin seeks would fundamentally alter the nature of petitioner's highest level tournaments even if he were the only person in the world who has both the talent to compete in those elite events and a disability sufficiently serious that he cannot do so without using a cart.

The force of petitioner's argument is, first of all, mitigated by the fact that golf is a game in which it is impossible to guarantee that all competitors will play under exactly the same conditions or that an individual's ability will be the sole determinant of the outcome. For example, changes in the weather may produce harder greens and more head winds for the tournament leader than for his closest pursuers. A lucky bounce may save a shot or two. Whether such happenstance events are more or less probable than the likelihood that a golfer afflicted with Klippel-Trenaunay-Weber Syndrome would one day qualify for the NIKE TOUR and PGA TOUR, they at least demonstrate that pure chance may have a greater impact on the outcome of elite golf tournaments than the fatigue resulting from the enforcement of the walking rule.

---

[44] Furthermore, the USGA's handicap system, used by over 4 million amateur golfers playing on courses rated by the USGA, does not consider whether a player walks or rides in a cart, or whether she uses a caddy or carries her own clubs. Rather, a player's handicap is determined by a formula that takes into account the average score in the 10 best of her 20 most recent rounds, the difficulty of the different courses played, and whether or not a round was a "tournament" event.

Further, the factual basis of petitioner's argument is undermined by the District Court's finding that the fatigue from walking during one of petitioner's 4-day tournaments cannot be deemed significant. The District Court credited the testimony of a professor in physiology and expert on fatigue, who calculated the calories expended in walking a golf course (about five miles) to be approximately 500 calories— "'nutritionally . . . less than a Big Mac.'" What is more, that energy is expended over a 5-hour period, during which golfers have numerous intervals for rest and refreshment. In fact, the expert concluded, because golf is a low intensity activity, fatigue from the game is primarily a psychological phenomenon in which stress and motivation are the key ingredients. And even under conditions of severe heat and humidity, the critical factor in fatigue is fluid loss rather than exercise from walking.

Moreover, when given the option of using a cart, the majority of golfers in petitioner's tournaments have chosen to walk, often to relieve stress or for other strategic reasons.[49] As NIKE TOUR member Eric Johnson testified, walking allows him to keep in rhythm, stay warmer when it is chilly, and develop a better sense of the elements and the course than riding a cart.

Even if we accept the factual predicate for petitioner's argument— that the walking rule is "outcome affecting" because fatigue may adversely affect performance—its legal position is fatally flawed. Petitioner's refusal to consider Martin's personal circumstances in deciding whether to accommodate his disability runs counter to the clear language and purpose of the ADA. As previously stated, the ADA was enacted to eliminate discrimination against "individuals" with disabilities, 42 U.S.C. § 12101(b)(1), and to that end Title III of the Act requires without exception that any "policies, practices, or procedures" of a public accommodation be reasonably modified for disabled "individuals" as necessary to afford access unless doing so would fundamentally alter what is offered, § 12182(b)(2)(A)(ii). To comply with this command, an individualized inquiry must be made to determine whether a specific modification for a particular person's disability would be reasonable under the circumstances as well as necessary for that person, and yet at the same time not work a fundamental alteration. See S.Rep. No. 101–116, at 61 (public accommodations "are required to make decisions based on facts applicable to individuals"). Cf. *Sutton v. United Air Lines, Inc.*, 527 U.S. 471, 483 (1999) ("[W]hether a person has a disability under the ADA is an individualized inquiry").

To be sure, the waiver of an essential rule of competition for anyone would fundamentally alter the nature of petitioner's tournaments. As we have demonstrated, however, the walking rule is at best peripheral to the nature of petitioner's athletic events, and thus it might be waived in individual cases without working a fundamental alteration. Therefore, petitioner's claim that all the substantive rules for its "highest-level" competitions are sacrosanct and cannot be modified under any circumstances is effectively a contention that it is exempt

---

[49] That has been so not only in the SENIOR PGA TOUR and the first two stages of the Q–School, but also, as Martin himself noticed, in the third stage of the Q–School after petitioner permitted everyone to ride rather than just waiving the walking rule for Martin as required by the District Court's injunction.

from Title III's reasonable modification requirement. But that provision carves out no exemption for elite athletics, and given Title III's coverage not only of places of "exhibition or entertainment" but also of "golf course[s]," 42 U.S.C. §§ 12181(7)(C), (L), its application to petitioner's tournaments cannot be said to be unintended or unexpected, see §§ 12101(a)(1), (5). Even if it were, "the fact that a statute can be applied in situations not expressly anticipated by Congress does not demonstrate ambiguity. It demonstrates breadth." *Pennsylvania Dept. of Corrections v. Yeskey*, 524 U.S., at 212 (internal quotation marks omitted).[51]

Under the ADA's basic requirement that the need of a disabled person be evaluated on an individual basis, we have no doubt that allowing Martin to use a golf cart would not fundamentally alter the nature of petitioner's tournaments. As we have discussed, the purpose of the walking rule is to subject players to fatigue, which in turn may influence the outcome of tournaments. Even if the rule does serve that purpose, it is an uncontested finding of the District Court that Martin "easily endures greater fatigue even with a cart than his able-bodied competitors do by walking." The purpose of the walking rule is therefore not compromised in the slightest by allowing Martin to use a cart. A modification that provides an exception to a peripheral tournament rule without impairing its purpose cannot be said to "fundamentally alter" the tournament. What it can be said to do, on the other hand, is to allow Martin the chance to qualify for, and compete in, the athletic events petitioner offers to those members of the public who have the skill and desire to enter. That is exactly what the ADA requires. As a result, Martin's request for a waiver of the walking rule should have been granted.

The ADA admittedly imposes some administrative burdens on the operators of places of public accommodation that could be avoided by strictly adhering to general rules and policies that are entirely fair with respect to the able-bodied but that may indiscriminately preclude access by qualified persons with disabilities. But surely, in a case of this kind, Congress intended that an entity like the PGA not only give individualized attention to the handful of requests that it might receive from talented but disabled athletes for a modification or waiver of a rule to allow them access to the competition, but also carefully weigh the purpose, as well as the letter, of the rule before determining that no accommodation would be tolerable.

---

[51] Hence, petitioner's questioning of the ability of courts to apply the reasonable modification requirement to athletic competition is a complaint more properly directed to Congress, which drafted the ADA's coverage broadly, than to us. Even more misguided is JUSTICE SCALIA's suggestion that Congress did not place that inquiry into the hands of the courts at all. According to the dissent, the game of golf as sponsored by petitioner is, like all sports games, the sum of its "arbitrary rules," and no one, including courts, "can pronounce one or another of them to be 'nonessential' if the rulemaker (here the PGA TOUR) deems it to be essential." Whatever the merit of JUSTICE SCALIA's postmodern view of "What Is [Sport]," it is clear that Congress did not enshrine it in Title III of the ADA. While Congress expressly exempted "private clubs or establishments" and "religious organizations or entities" from Title III's coverage, 42 U.S.C. § 12187, Congress made no such exception for athletic competitions, much less did it give sports organizations carte blanche authority to exempt themselves from the fundamental alteration inquiry by deeming any rule, no matter how peripheral to the competition, to be essential. In short, JUSTICE SCALIA's reading of the statute renders the word "fundamentally" largely superfluous, because it treats the alteration of any rule governing an event at a public accommodation to be a fundamental alteration.

The judgment of the Court of Appeals is affirmed.

■ JUSTICE SCALIA, with whom JUSTICE THOMAS joins, dissenting.

[H]aving erroneously held that Title III applies to the "customers" of professional golf who consist of its practitioners, the Court then erroneously answers—or to be accurate simply ignores—a second question. The ADA requires covered businesses to make such reasonable modifications of "policies, practices, or procedures" as are necessary to "afford" goods, services, and privileges to individuals with disabilities; but it explicitly does not require "modifications [that] would fundamentally alter the nature" of the goods, services, and privileges. § 12182(b)(2)(A)(ii). In other words, disabled individuals must be given access to the same goods, services, and privileges that others enjoy. The regulations state that Title III "does not require a public accommodation to alter its inventory to include accessible or special goods with accessibility features that are designed for, or facilitate use by, individuals with disabilities." 28 CFR § 36.307 (2000); see also 28 CFR, ch. 1, pt. 36, App.B, at 650. As one Court of Appeals has explained:

> "The common sense of the statute is that the content of the goods or services offered by a place of public accommodation is not regulated. A camera store may not refuse to sell cameras to a disabled person, but it is not required to stock cameras specially designed for such persons. Had Congress purposed to impose so enormous a burden on the retail sector of the economy and so vast a supervisory responsibility on the federal courts, we think it would have made its intention clearer and would at least have imposed some standards. It is hardly a feasible judicial function to decide whether shoestores should sell single shoes to one-legged persons and if so at what price, or how many Braille books the Borders or Barnes and Noble bookstore chains should stock in each of their stores." *Doe v. Mutual of Omaha Ins. Co.*, 179 F.3d 557, 560 (C.A.7 1999).

Since this is so, even if respondent here is a consumer of the "privilege" of the PGA TOUR competition, I see no basis for considering whether the rules of that competition must be altered. It is as irrelevant to the PGA TOUR's compliance with the statute whether walking is essential to the game of golf as it is to the shoe store's compliance whether "pairness" is essential to the nature of shoes. If a shoe store wishes to sell shoes only in pairs it may; and if a golf tour (or a golf course) wishes to provide only walk-around golf, it may. The PGA TOUR cannot deny respondent access to that game because of his disability, but it need not provide him a game different (whether in its essentials or in its details) from that offered to everyone else.

Since it has held (or assumed) professional golfers to be customers "enjoying" the "privilege" that consists of PGA TOUR golf; and since it inexplicably regards the rules of PGA TOUR golf as merely "policies, practices, or procedures" by which access to PGA TOUR golf is provided, the Court must then confront the question whether respondent's requested modification of the supposed policy, practice, or procedure of walking would "fundamentally alter the nature" of the PGA TOUR game, § 12182(b)(2)(A)(ii). The Court attacks this "fundamental alteration" analysis by asking two questions: first, whether the "essence" or an "essential aspect" of the sport of golf has been altered; and second, whether the change, even if not essential to the game, would give the disabled player an advantage over others and thereby "fundamentally alter the character of the competition." It answers no to both.

Before considering the Court's answer to the first question, it is worth pointing out that the assumption which underlies that question is false. Nowhere is it writ that PGA TOUR golf must be classic "essential" golf. Why cannot the PGA TOUR, if it wishes, promote a new game, with distinctive rules (much as the American League promotes a game of baseball in which the pitcher's turn at the plate can be taken by a "designated hitter")? If members of the public do not like the new rules—if they feel that these rules do not truly test the individual's skill at "real golf" (or the team's skill at "real baseball")—they can withdraw their patronage. But the rules are the rules. They are (as in all games) entirely arbitrary, and there is no basis on which anyone—not even the Supreme Court of the United States—can pronounce one or another of them to be "nonessential" if the rulemaker (here the PGA TOUR) deems it to be essential.

If one assumes, however, that the PGA TOUR has some legal obligation to play classic, Platonic golf—and if one assumes the correctness of all the other wrong turns the Court has made to get to this point—then we Justices must confront what is indeed an awesome responsibility. It has been rendered the solemn duty of the Supreme Court of the United States, laid upon it by Congress in pursuance of the Federal Government's power "[t]o regulate Commerce with foreign Nations, and among the several States," U.S. Const., Art.I, § 8, cl.3, to decide What Is Golf. I am sure that the Framers of the Constitution, aware of the 1457 edict of King James II of Scotland prohibiting golf because it interfered with the practice of archery, fully expected that sooner or later the paths of golf and government, the law and the links, would once again cross, and that the judges of this august Court would some day have to wrestle with that age-old jurisprudential question, for which their years of study in the law have so well prepared them: Is someone riding around a golf course from shot to shot really a golfer? The answer, we learn, is yes. The Court ultimately concludes, and it will henceforth be the Law of the Land, that walking is not a "fundamental" aspect of golf.

Either out of humility or out of self-respect (one or the other) the Court should decline to answer this incredibly difficult and incredibly silly question. To say that something is "essential" is ordinarily to say that it is necessary to the achievement of a certain object. But since it is the very nature of a game to have no object except amusement (that is what distinguishes games from productive activity), it is quite impossible to say that any of a game's arbitrary rules is "essential." Eighteen-hole golf courses, 10-foot-high basketball hoops, 90-foot baselines, 100-yard football fields—all are arbitrary and none is essential. The only support for any of them is tradition and (in more modern times) insistence by what has come to be regarded as the ruling body of the sport—both of which factors support the PGA TOUR's position in the present case. (Many, indeed, consider walking to be the central feature of the game of golf—hence Mark Twain's classic criticism of the sport: "a good walk spoiled.") I suppose there is some point at which the rules of a well-known game are changed to such a degree that no reasonable person would call it the same game. If the PGA TOUR competitors were required to dribble a large, inflated ball and put it through a round hoop, the game could no longer reasonably be called golf. But this criterion—destroying recognizability as the same generic game—is surely not the test of "essentialness" or "fundamentalness" that the Court applies, since it apparently thinks that merely changing the diameter of the *cup* might "fundamentally alter" the game of golf.

Having concluded that dispensing with the walking rule would not violate federal-Platonic "golf" (and, implicitly, that it is federal-Platonic golf, and no other, that the PGA TOUR can insist upon), the Court moves on to the second part of its test: the competitive effects of waiving this nonessential rule. In this part of its analysis, the Court first finds that the effects of the change are "mitigated" by the fact that in the game of golf weather, a "lucky bounce," and "pure chance" provide different conditions for each competitor and individual ability may not "be the sole determinant of the outcome." I guess that is why those who follow professional golfing consider Jack Nicklaus the luckiest golfer of all time, only to be challenged of late by the phenomenal luck of Tiger Woods. The Court's empiricism is unpersuasive. "Pure chance" is randomly distributed among the players, but allowing respondent to use a cart gives him a "lucky" break every time he plays. Pure chance also only matters at the margin—a stroke here or there; the cart substantially improves this respondent's competitive prospects beyond a couple of strokes. But even granting that there are significant nonhuman variables affecting competition, that fact does not justify adding another variable that always favors one player.

In an apparent effort to make its opinion as narrow as possible, the Court relies upon the District Court's finding that even with a cart, respondent will be at least as fatigued as everyone else. This, the Court says, proves that competition will not be affected. Far from thinking that reliance on this finding cabins the effect of today's opinion, I think it will prove to be its most expansive and destructive feature. Because step one of the Court's two-part inquiry into whether a requested change in a sport will "fundamentally alter [its] nature," § 12182(b)(2)(A)(ii), consists of an utterly unprincipled ontology of sports (pursuant to which the Court is not even sure whether golf's "essence" requires a 3-inch hole), there is every reason to think that in future cases involving requests for special treatment by would-be athletes the second step of the analysis will be determinative. In resolving that second step—determining whether waiver of the "nonessential" rule will have an impermissible "competitive effect"—by measuring the athletic capacity of the requesting individual, and asking whether the special dispensation would do no more than place him on a par (so to speak) with other competitors, the Court guarantees that future cases of this sort will have to be decided on the basis of individualized factual findings. Which means that future cases of this sort will be numerous, and a rich source of lucrative litigation. One can envision the parents of a Little League player with attention deficit disorder trying to convince a judge that their son's disability makes it at least 25% more difficult to hit a pitched ball. (If they are successful, the only thing that could prevent a court order giving the kid four strikes would be a judicial determination that, in baseball, three strikes are metaphysically necessary, which is quite absurd.)

The statute, of course, provides no basis for this individualized analysis that is the Court's last step on a long and misguided journey. The statute seeks to assure that a disabled person's disability will not deny him equal access to (among other things) competitive sporting events—not that his disability will not deny him an equal chance to win competitive sporting events. The latter is quite impossible, since the very nature of competitive sport is the measurement, by uniform rules, of unevenly distributed excellence. This unequal distribution is precisely what determines the winners and losers—and artificially to "even out" that distribution, by giving one or another player exemption from a rule that emphasizes his particular weakness, is to destroy the game. That is why the "handicaps" that are customary in social games of golf—which, by adding strokes to the scores of the good players and subtracting them from scores of the bad ones, "even out" the varying abilities—are not used in professional golf. In the Court's world, there is one set of rules that is "fair with respect to the able-bodied" but "individualized" rules, mandated by the ADA, for "talented but disabled athletes." The ADA mandates no such ridiculous thing. Agility, strength, speed, balance, quickness of mind, steadiness of nerves, intensity of concentration—these talents are not evenly distributed. No wild-eyed dreamer has ever suggested that the managing bodies of the competitive sports that test precisely these qualities should try to take account of the uneven distribution of God-given gifts when writing and enforcing the rules of competition. And I have no doubt Congress did not authorize misty-eyed judicial supervision of such a revolution.

My belief that today's judgment is clearly in error should not be mistaken for a belief that the PGA TOUR clearly ought not allow respondent to use a golf cart. *That* is a close question, on which even those who compete in the PGA TOUR are apparently divided; but it is a different question from the one before the Court. Just as it is a different question whether the Little League ought to give disabled youngsters a fourth strike, or some other waiver from the rules that makes up for their disabilities. In both cases, whether they ought to do so depends upon (1) how central to the game that they have organized (and over whose rules they are the master) they deem the waived provision to be, and (2) how competitive—how strict a test of raw athletic ability in all aspects of the competition—they want their game to be. But whether Congress has said they must do so depends upon the answers to the legal questions I have discussed above—not upon what this Court sententiously decrees to be " 'decent, tolerant, [and] progressive.' "

And it should not be assumed that today's decent, tolerant, and progressive judgment will, in the long run, accrue to the benefit of sports competitors with disabilities. Now that it is clear courts will review the rules of sports for "fundamentalness," organizations that value their autonomy have every incentive to defend vigorously the necessity of every regulation. They may still be second-guessed in the end as to the Platonic requirements of the sport, but they will assuredly lose if they have at all wavered in their enforcement. The lesson the PGA TOUR and other sports organizations should take from this case is to make sure that the same written rules are set forth for all levels of play, and never voluntarily to grant any modifications. The second lesson is to end open tryouts. I doubt that, in the long run, even disabled athletes will be well served by these incentives that the Court has created.

Complaints about this case are not "properly directed to Congress." They are properly directed to this Court's Kafkaesque determination that professional sports organizations, and the fields they rent for their exhibitions, are "places of public accommodation" to the competing athletes, and the athletes themselves "customers" of the organization that pays them; its Alice in Wonderland determination that there are such things as judicially determinable "essential" and "nonessential" rules of a made-up game; and its Animal Farm determination that fairness and the ADA mean that everyone gets to play by individualized rules which will assure that no one's lack of ability (or at least no one's lack of ability so pronounced that it amounts to a disability) will be a handicap. The year was 2001, and "everybody was finally equal." K. Vonnegut, Harrison Bergeron, in Animal Farm and Related Readings 129 (1997).

NOTES ON REASONABLE MODIFICATIONS

1.   **The Casey Martin Case.** Justice Scalia says that "since it is the very nature of a game to have no object except amusement (that is what distinguishes games from productive activity), it is quite impossible to say that any of a game's arbitrary rules is 'essential.' " What should we make of this point? One might think that Justice Scalia's point actually supports the Court's decision to require a waiver of the walking rule. If all of the rules of a game are arbitrary—none essential—why isn't *any* modification to those rules reasonable? But Justice Scalia seems to mean almost the opposite—that precisely because the rules of a game are arbitrary, any modification to those rules *fundamentally alters* the game: "But the rules are the rules. They are (as in all games) entirely arbitrary, and there is no basis on which anyone—not even the Supreme Court of the United States—can pronounce one or another of them to be 'nonessential' if the rulemaker (here the PGA TOUR) deems it to be essential." Isn't Justice Stevens right that Justice Scalia's position would insulate athletic leagues from Title III's "reasonable modification" requirement?

Perhaps a better way to put Justice Scalia's point is this: The rules of a game may be arbitrary, and no particular rule might be essential, but what is essential (at least in high-level athletic competition) is that every contestant must compete under the *same* rules. Top-level athletes bring different strengths and weaknesses to the game, and they seek to make the most of their strengths and avoid their weaknesses to defeat their competition. Does Justice Stevens adequately answer that point? He says that even if the walking rule *does* serve the purpose of injecting fatigue into the game, "it is an uncontested finding of the District Court that Martin 'easily endures greater fatigue even with a cart than his able-bodied competitors do by walking.' " Thus, Justice Stevens says, the "purpose of the walking rule" is not "compromised in the slightest by allowing Martin to use a cart." But is that really right? If the walking rule does inject fatigue into the game, presumably it affects different players differently.

Those who get more fatigued by walking are at a disadvantage, while those who get less fatigued by walking are at an advantage. That is the nature of an athletic competition. How can a court calibrate just how much fatigue Casey Martin would have experienced if he did not have a disability and walked the course? And why should a person with a *disability* have the right to obtain an exemption from the rule, when a person without a disability, who perhaps experiences an unusual degree of fatigue, does not?

A possible answer to these objections has two parts. First, one should note that Casey Martin's problem is *not* that walking the course makes him so fatigued that it affects his shotmaking. If that were his problem, and the function of the walking rule was to create fatigue, it would be very difficult to defend excusing him from the rule—it would be serving its purpose by suppressing the performance of those who, for whatever reason, get unusually fatigued by walking. His problem, rather, was that walking for the entire round of golf would cause such pain and damage to his leg that he simply could not participate. The walking rule *totally excluded* him from the competition. Second, the evidence that the walking rule actually did inject fatigue into the competition was quite weak. The PGA's evidence on the point consisted of first-person testimonials by famous golfers, while Martin's evidence consisted of testimony from a physiology professor that walking five miles in a five-hour period, while a caddy carries one's bag, with "numerous intervals for rest and refreshment," did not inject any meaningful fatigue into the game. In light of these two points, one could plausibly argue that the walking rule was maintained out of nothing more than a sense of tradition, and that it gratuitously excluded golfers like Casey Martin. Is that argument persuasive?

Note that Justice Scalia applies an access/content distinction, just like the one courts have applied to cases involving government services under Title II of the ADA and Section 504 of the Rehabilitation Act. Does Justice Stevens's majority opinion disagree that the access/content distinction governs, or does it conclude that Casey Martin was asking only for access, not a change to the content of the service that was provided?

2.   *Johnson v. Gambrinus.* As in the employment context, the number of possible "reasonable modifications" in the public accommodations context is essentially infinite; what modification is necessary, and whether it is reasonable is necessarily a fact-intensive question. In JOHNSON V. GAMBRINUS COMPANY/SPOETZL BREWERY, 116 F.3d 1052 (5th Cir.1997), the Fifth Circuit adopted an influential formulation of the burdens of proof in a Title III reasonable modification action (a formulation that parallels the Supreme Court's formulation of the burdens of proof under Title I in *US Airways v. Barnett*, a principal case in Chapter Three):

> The plaintiff has the burden of proving that a modification was requested and that the requested modification is reasonable. The plaintiff meets this burden by introducing evidence that the requested modification is reasonable in the general sense, that is, reasonable in the run of cases. While the defendant may introduce evidence indicating that the plaintiff's requested modification is not reasonable in the run of cases, the plaintiff bears the ultimate burden of proof on the issue. If the plaintiff meets this burden, the defendant must make

the requested modification unless the defendant pleads and meets its burden of proving that the requested modification would fundamentally alter the nature of the public accommodation. The type of evidence that satisfies this burden focuses on the specifics of the plaintiff's or defendant's circumstances and not on the general nature of the accommodation. Under the statutory framework, such evidence is relevant only to a fundamental alteration defense and not relevant to the plaintiff's burden to show that the requested modification is reasonable in the run of cases.

The court held that the defendant brewery violated Title III by refusing to modify its blanket no-animals policy to allow the plaintiff to bring his guide dog on a brewery tour. The court concluded that the plaintiff had established his burden of showing that the modification was reasonable in the run of cases, based on a Department of Justice regulation that stated: "Generally, a public accommodation shall modify policies, practices, or procedures to permit the use of a service animal by an individual with a disability." 28 C.F.R. § 36.302(c)(1). And the court went on to hold that the brewery had not carried its burden of establishing a fundamental alteration, based on the district court's finding that there were "many areas of the tour where a guide dog could be present without a likelihood of contamination."

Consider the application of the reasonable modification standard in the following cases.

Baughman v. Walt Disney World Co.

United States Court of Appeals for the Ninth Circuit, 2012.
685 F.3d 1131.

■ KOZINSKI, CHIEF JUDGE.

Segways at Disneyland? Could happen.

Facts

Tina Baughman suffers from limb girdle muscular dystrophy, which makes it difficult for her to walk or stand from a seated position. Baughman nevertheless hoped to fulfill her daughter's eighth-birthday wish: a visit to the happiest place on earth. She contacted Disneyland to explain her physical limitations and request permission to use a Segway, a two-wheeled mobility device operated while standing. Disney's policy is to allow wheelchairs and motorized scooters; "two-wheeled vehicles or devices," like bicycles and Segways, are prohibited. Disney refused to make an exception for Baughman.

Baughman sued Disney under the Americans with Disabilities Act ("ADA"), claiming that Disney denied her full and equal access to Disneyland. The district court [g]ranted summary judgment for Disney.

Discussion

[C]ongress enacted the ADA "to remedy widespread discrimination against disabled individuals." PGA Tour, Inc. v. Martin. Title III of the ADA provides that "[n]o individual shall be discriminated against on the basis of disability in the *full and equal enjoyment* of the goods, services, facilities, privileges, advantages, or accommodations of any place of public accommodation ....” 42 U.S.C. § 12182(a) (emphasis added). Discrimination is defined, in part, as “a failure to make reasonable modifications in policies, practices, or procedures, when such modifications are *necessary* to afford such goods, services, facilities, privileges, advantages, or accommodations to individuals with disabilities ....” § 12182(b)(2)(A)(ii) (emphasis added); *see also Martin,* 532 U.S. at 683 n. 38, 121 S.Ct. 1879.

The district court held that Disney is not required to modify its policy because it permits motorized wheelchairs or scooters. Disney argues vigorously in support of the district court's judgment that “necessary” means only one thing: can't do without. Because Baughman *can* access Disneyland by using a wheelchair or scooter, a Segway isn't “necessary” for her to use the park. QED.

Read as Disney suggests, the ADA would require very few accommodations indeed. After all, a paraplegic *can* enter a courthouse by dragging himself up the front steps, *see Tennessee v. Lane,* 541 U.S. 509, 513–14 (2004), so lifts and ramps would not be “necessary” under Disney's reading of the term. And no facility would be required to provide wheelchair-accessible doors or bathrooms, because disabled individuals could be carried in litters or on the backs of their friends. That's not the world we live in, and we are disappointed to see such a retrograde position taken by a company whose reputation is built on service to the public.

Disney's (and the district court's) error lies in fixating on a single word in the statute rather than reading all of the relevant words together. The ADA guarantees the disabled more than mere access to public facilities; it guarantees them “full and equal enjoyment.” 42 U.S.C. § 12182(a). What this means is illustrated by cases such as *Fortyune v. American Multi-Cinema, Inc.,* 364 F.3d 1075, 1085 (9th Cir.2004), where we held that a theater was required to provide wheelchair seating for the disabled individual *and* an adjacent seat for his wife. The attendant seat was obviously not necessary for Fortyune to see the movie, but moviegoers expect to sit with their friends and family during the show; their enjoyment is diminished if they are forced to sit apart. “Because Fortyune require[d] an attendant to *enjoy* the viewing of a film, the modification that he requested, *i.e.,* that [the theater] ensure that his companion could be seated next to him, was necessary.” *Id.* at 1083 (emphasis added).

Public accommodations must start by considering how their facilities are used by non-disabled guests and then take reasonable steps to provide disabled guests with a like experience. For example, the movie theaters in *Oregon Paralyzed Veterans of America v. Regal Cinemas, Inc.,* 339 F.3d 1126, 1127–28 (9th Cir.2003), provided seating for wheelchair-bound patrons only in the front rows of the theater. We found it “simply inconceivable that this arrangement could constitute ‘full and equal enjoyment’ of movie theater services by disabled patrons” because it required them “to crane their necks and twist their bodies in order to see the screen, while non-disabled patrons [had] a wide range of comfortable viewing locations from which to choose.” *Id.* at 1133. We rejected the notion that "[n]o matter where in the theater the seats are, and no matter how sharp the viewing angle, so long as there is no physical object standing between the disabled patron and the screen" the theaters satisfied the ADA. *Id.* We held that theaters had to provide disabled patrons an experience comparable to that of able-bodied patrons. *Id.*

Facilities are not required to make any and all possible accommodations that would provide full and equal access to disabled patrons; they need only make accommodations that are reasonable. In deciding what's reasonable, facilities may consider the costs of such accommodations, disruption of their business and safety. But they must also take into account evolving technology that might make it cheaper and easier to ameliorate the plight of the disabled. In the past, it might have been enough for a theme park to permit only non-powered wheelchairs. As technology made motorized wheelchairs and scooters cheaper, safer and more reliable, our expectations of what is reasonable changed—as Disney recognizes. But technological advances didn't end with the powered wheelchair. As new devices become available, public accommodations must consider using or adapting them to help disabled guests have an experience more akin to that of non-disabled guests.

The modification Baughman seeks is entirely consistent with our caselaw. She claims that she has difficulty standing up from a seated position, so the Segway—which allows her to remain standing—makes it easier for her to visit Disneyland's many attractions, concessions and facilities. She also claims that using a Segway allows her to be at eye-level with other guests and staff, rather than having everyone look down at her. Disney doesn't dispute Baughman's claim that using a motorized wheelchair or scooter would require her to stand and sit many times during her visit, or that doing so would be painful for her. Nor does Disney dispute that Baughman would feel more comfortable and dignified using a Segway. Disney simply takes the position that, even if Baughman's access is made "uncomfortable or difficult" by its policies, any discomfort or difficulty she may suffer is too darn bad. Disney is obviously mistaken. If it can make Baughman's experience less onerous and more akin to that enjoyed by its able-bodied patrons, it must take reasonable steps to do so.

Our conclusion is supported by regulations recently promulgated by the Department of Justice ("DOJ"), which is charged with administering the ADA. *See Bragdon v. Abbott,* 524 U.S. 624, 646 (1998); 28 C.F.R. § 36.311. The regulations identify two classes of mobility devices: (1) wheelchairs and manually powered mobility aids and (2) other power-driven mobility devices. § 36.311. According to the DOJ, Segways fall into the second category. § 36, app. A, at 726.

When faced with an individual who uses a device from the second category, the public accommodation must "make reasonable modifications" to permit the device unless it can demonstrate that the device can't be operated "in accordance with legitimate safety requirements." § 36.311(b)(1). The regulation discusses Segways at length, concluding "that in the vast majority of circumstances" public accommodations will have to admit them. § 36, app. A, at 726.

"As the agency directed by Congress to issue implementing regulations, to render technical assistance explaining the responsibilities of covered individuals and institutions, and to enforce Title III in court, the Department's views are entitled to deference." Bragdon; *see also* 42 U.S.C. § 12186(b). Where Congress has given "express delegation of authority to [an] agency to elucidate a specific provision of [a] statute by regulation," such regulation is "given controlling weight unless [it's] arbitrary, capricious, or manifestly contrary to the statute." *Chevron, U.S.A., Inc. v. Natural Res. Def. Council, Inc.*, 467 U.S. 837, 843–44 (1984).

Disney scoffs at the regulation, claiming it conflicts with precedent. It argues that in Martin the Supreme Court adopted Disney's strict meaning of "necessary," precluding the Justice Department from adopting a broader definition by way of regulation. According to Disney, the *Martin* Court held that a requested modification under Title III of the ADA isn't necessary, "even when access to the public accommodation may be 'uncomfortable or difficult' for the plaintiffs without it, so long as access is not ' *beyond their capacity*. In such cases, an accommodation might be reasonable but not necessary.' "

But the issue presented in *Martin* was whether the requested modification—using a golf cart—fundamentally altered the nature of the PGA Tour, which required golfers to walk. The Court had no occasion to rule on whether the requested modification was necessary "[g]iven the concession by [the public accommodation] that the modification sought [was] reasonable and necessary." *Martin* offers Disney no help, and Disney's other arguments that the regulation is invalid border on the absurd.

We do not hold that Disney must permit Segways at its theme parks. It might be able to exclude them if it can prove that Segways can't be operated safely in its parks. Section 36.311(b) lists several factors to consider in determining whether a device can be used in a particular facility, including the size, weight and speed of the device; the volume of pedestrian traffic in the facility; and whether legitimate safety requirements can be established to ensure safe operation of the device. § 36.311(b)(2). Disney might, for example, permissibly require Segways to travel only as fast as motorized wheelchairs. But any safety requirements Disney imposes "must be based on actual risks and not on mere speculation, stereotypes, or generalizations about individuals with disabilities." 28 C.F.R. § 36.301(b).

New technology presents risks as well as opportunities; we must not allow fear of the former to deprive us of the latter. We have every confidence that the organization that, half a century ago, brought us the Carousel of Progress and Great Moments with Mr. Lincoln can lead the way in using new technology to make its parks more welcoming to disabled guests. As the man who started it all said, "Disneyland will never be completed as long as there is imagination left in the world." *Walt Disney, 65, Dies on Coast; Founded an Empire on a Mouse,* N.Y. Times, Dec. 16, 1966, at 40.

REVERSED AND REMANDED.

Argenyi v. Creighton University

United States Court of Appeals for the Eighth Circuit, 2013.
703 F.3d 441.

■ MURPHY, CIRCUIT JUDGE.

Michael Argenyi, a young man with a serious hearing impairment, moved from Seattle to Omaha, Nebraska to attend medical school at Creighton University. Before enrolling Argenyi requested specific accommodations from Creighton for his hearing impairment. They were denied, but Argenyi repeatedly renewed them during his first two years at Creighton Medical School. He explained that without these accommodations he was unable to follow lectures, participate in labs, or communicate with patients.

Because Creighton failed to provide what he considered necessary and reasonable accommodations, Argenyi brought this action under Title III of the Americans with Disabilities Act (ADA), 42 U.S.C. § 12182, and § 504 of the Rehabilitation Act, 29 U.S.C. § 794. The district court decided that Argenyi had not shown his requested accommodations were necessary and granted summary judgment to Creighton. [W]e reverse and remand.

I.

Argenyi began using hearing aids before he was one year old, but his parents primarily communicated with him through spoken language. To distinguish between sounds that appear the same on a speaker's lips Argenyi relied on "cued speech," which uses hand signals to represent sounds. He does not know sign language. In eighth grade Argenyi began using Communication Access Real-time Transcription (CART), a system which transcribes spoken words into text on a computer screen. Argenyi received a cochlear implant in his right ear in September 2004 before he began undergraduate studies at Seattle University. That university provided CART for Argenyi's lectures and a cued speech interpreter for his lab courses, and Argenyi graduated from Seattle in 2008 with a 3.87 grade point average.

Argenyi stated in his application to Creighton University Medical School in 2009 that he was "hearing-impaired." Upon his admission Argenyi explained to Michael Kavan, Creighton's associate dean for student affairs, that he would require accommodation "similar to what [he] had used in the past . . . primarily interpretation or captioning services during lectures and teaching sessions." Dean Kavan asked for more information about the nature of his hearing disability and a more specific request for the type of accommodation he needed.

Argenyi's otolaryngologist, Dr. Douglas Backous, responded that Argenyi "would benefit from closed captioning" and an FM system which transmits sound directly into cochlear implants. Argenyi also renewed his requests that Creighton supply CART for his lectures, a cued speech interpreter for labs, and an FM system for small learning groups of eight students or fewer. Kavan replied that the written requests submitted by Dr. Backous and Argenyi were inadequate because they differed and the doctor had not made a "direct request."

Before starting medical school Argenyi received a bilateral cochlear implant, and his implant audiologist and Dr. Backous both recommended that to succeed in his studies he would also need CART, a cued speech interpreter, and the FM system. Dr. Backous wrote to Creighton that Argenyi "remains . . . deaf regardless of if he is or is not using his cochlear implants . . . . [He] has a bilateral profound sensorineural hearing loss." Before Argenyi's enrollment, Creighton's medical education management team met to review his requests for accommodation. Dean Kavan then informed Argenyi that Creighton would provide him with an FM system for lectures, small groups, and labs. Argenyi agreed to give the FM system "a wholehearted try."

Shortly before classes began on August 16, 2009, Argenyi renewed his original requests for accommodations. Creighton denied them. After trying the FM system for two weeks, Argenyi informed Dean Kavan that he needed to obtain CART for himself. He wrote the dean that "[t]he [university's] accommodations are inadequate as evidenced by the level of stress and fatigue I am experiencing, as well as the amount of information I am missing . . . . [They] do not provide for meaningful participation nor independence as a student, and also put me at a significant disadvantage academically." Dr. Backous wrote to Creighton in support of Argenyi's needs, urging that

> It is *imperative* that [Argenyi] have access to visual cues for everyday communication and education. Visual cues include, but are not limited to closed captioning on videos and films, real time captioning for lectures and discussions, and speech reading cues for one-on-one interactions.

The dean responded by offering Argenyi only enhanced note taking services.

In late September 2009 Argenyi brought this action against Creighton, alleging violations of Title III of the ADA and § 504 of the Rehabilitation Act by the university's failure to provide "auxiliary aids and services to ensure effective communication and an equal opportunity to participate in and benefit from the School of Medicine." Argenyi sought a declaratory judgment compelling Creighton to provide him with "auxiliary aids and services to ensure effective communication," as well as compensatory damages and attorney fees.

Argenyi continued to attend class and pursue his medical education. In February 2010 he consulted ear specialist Dr. Britt Thedinger as an expert witness. Dr. Thedinger tested the Creighton FM system and found that with the background noise that Argenyi had only 38 percent speech perception. Dr. Thedinger determined that "the FM system does not provide any significant benefit and . . . actually reduces [Argenyi's] discrimination ability."

Creighton provided no further auxiliary support or services during Argenyi's first year of medical school, and Argenyi borrowed approximately $53,000 to pay for CART and interpreters himself. In a document publicly available on its website, Creighton estimates that the first year of its medical school costs approximately $71,000 for an average student before financial aid. After paying for his accommodations, the effective cost to

Argenyi for his first year of medical school was therefore more than $120,000.

Argenyi renewed his request for accommodation before his second year of medical school. In response Creighton offered to provide an interpreter for lectures and a seat next to the instructor for small group discussions. Argenyi found the interpreter not sufficient to convey complex new vocabulary and again took out approximately $61,000 in loans to pay for CART.

The second year curriculum included clinical courses in which students interviewed and cared for patients. For those courses Creighton refused to allow Argenyi to use an interpreter even if he paid for one himself. Argenyi tried the clinical courses without an interpreter for approximately two weeks and then renewed his request for one. As he explained on September 21, 2010,

> I met with patients . . . and found that I could not understand all of what patients and others at the clinic said. With some patients I understood very little . . . . I know you said I only have to show up to pass, but I want to learn how to be a doctor and I think it is important to understand what the patients are saying to me.

Argenyi and Creighton entered into settlement negotiations in January 2011, and the university temporarily provided him with an interpreter in his clinical courses. Settlement talks ended the following month, however, and Argenyi was again prohibited from using an interpreter. Argenyi nevertheless succeeded in passing his clinical and other courses, but after his second year he took a leave of absence pending the resolution of his claims under the ADA and the Rehabilitation Act.

In July 2011 Argenyi and Creighton both moved for summary judgment. The district court granted summary judgment to Creighton[.]

II.

A.

[I]n granting summary judgment to Creighton the district court disregarded Argenyi's affidavit, termed it "self-serving," and concluded that "there [was] an absence of evidence to support [his] claim." There was, however, a variety of supporting evidence in the record. Argenyi's affidavit must be considered, and its particular factual allegations scrutinized for "independent documentary evidence" to support them. In a case such as this it is especially important to consider the complainant's testimony carefully because "the individual with a disability is most familiar with his or her disability and is in the best position to determine what type of aid or service will be effective." U.S. Dep't of Justice, The Americans with Disabilities Act Title II Technical Assistance Manual, at II–7.1100 (1993).

Argenyi testified in his affidavit that without CART and interpreters he was "unable to follow class lectures and classroom dialogue" or "the rapid pace of dialogue in the clinical setting." He stated that he "began experiencing debilitating headaches and extreme fatigue" from his "fruitless attempts" to follow lectures, even though he had "utilized all of

[his] time outside of the classroom trying to obtain the information the other students obtained in the classroom."

In clinical courses Argenyi and his patients frequently failed to communicate effectively. He described in his affidavit a "consult with the parents of a two month old, with communication limited such that [he] did not know ... why the infant was hospitalized," as well as his struggle to communicate with "emotional family members, patients with accents, and ... a patient with a history of a broken jaw." Argenyi stated that Creighton had done "nothing to remedy [his] inability to understand what was happening in the clinic" and eventually advised him to "refrain from making requests for additional auxiliary aids and services."

After a careful review of the record, we cannot agree with the district court's conclusion that Argenyi's allegations were "unsupported." The record contains five letters from Argenyi's doctors to Creighton confirming his need for additional auxiliary aids and services. [A]rgenyi's affidavit, corroborated by evidence from Dr. Backous and Dr. Thedinger and his own need to obtain private loans for CART and interpreters, provides strong evidence that Creighton's accommodations were inadequate and that the university was not entitled to summary judgment. We conclude that the district court erred by disregarding Argenyi's affidavit, the "independent documentary evidence" offered in its support, and all aspects of the record before it.

B.

[T]he key question is whether Creighton discriminated against Argenyi by failing to provide necessary auxiliary aids and services during his first year of medical school and by refusing to permit Argenyi to use an interpreter during his second year clinic.

1.

Congress recognized in enacting the ADA that "individuals with disabilities continually encounter various forms of discrimination, including ... communication barriers." 42 U.S.C. § 12101(a)(5). The purpose of the ADA was to "provide clear, strong, consistent, enforceable standards" to remedy discrimination in employment (Title I), in the services of public entities (Title II), and in places of public accommodation (Title III). *Id.* § 12101(b)(2). Under Title III of the ADA, places of public accommodation include "undergraduate[ ] or postgraduate private schools" like Creighton. 28 C.F.R. § 36.104.

Discrimination is defined by the ADA as a failure to "make reasonable modifications in policies, practices, or procedures" that are "necessary to afford ... privileges, advantages, or accommodations to individuals with disabilities" or a failure to "take such steps as may be necessary to ensure that no individual with a disability is ... treated differently than other individuals because of the absence of auxiliary aids and services." *Id.* § 12182(b)(2)(A)(ii), (iii). In furtherance of the congressional purpose, Title III of the ADA prohibits places of public accommodation such as Creighton from discriminating against individuals with disabilities "in the full and equal enjoyment" of the "privileges, advantages, or accommodations" they offer. 42 U.S.C. § 12182(a).

Congress specifically intended the ADA to remedy "the discriminatory effects of . . . communication barriers" for individuals with hearing disabilities. 42 U.S.C. § 12101(a)(5). Regulations promulgated under Title III of the ADA require the provision of "appropriate auxiliary aids and services where necessary to ensure effective communication with individuals with disabilities," 28 C.F.R. § 36.303(c)(1), and instruct places of public accommodation to "consult with individuals with disabilities whenever possible to determine what type of auxiliary aid is needed to ensure effective communication," *id.* § 36.303(c)(1)(ii). The regulations specifically provide that appropriate aids and services for deaf individuals include interpreters and CART. *Id.* § 36.303(b)(1).

The Rehabilitation Act is similar to the ADA. Congress enacted the Rehabilitation Act as a "comprehensive federal program," to ensure that individuals with disabilities would not "be denied the benefits of [ ] or be subjected to discrimination under any program or activity" receiving federal funding, 29 U.S.C. § 794(a). To achieve that purpose the Rehabilitation Act requires entities receiving federal funding to furnish auxiliary aids which "afford handicapped persons equal opportunity to obtain the same result, to gain the same benefit, or to reach the same level of achievement" as others. 45 C.F.R. § 84.4(b)(2). Creighton receives financial assistance from federal agencies including the Department of Education, so it must comply with § 504 of the Rehabilitation Act.

Both the ADA and the Rehabilitation Act are intentionally broad in scope, but they do not require institutions to provide all requested auxiliary aids and services. Instead, each statute requires the responsible parties to provide "necessary" auxiliary aids and services to individuals with disabilities. 42 U.S.C. § 12182(b)(2)(A)(ii) (ADA); 34 C.F.R. § 104.44(d)(1) (Rehabilitation Act). Since the ADA and the Rehabilitation Act are "similar in substance," we treat the case law interpreting them as "interchangeable." Our court has never determined the definition of "necessary" under Title III of the ADA so we must consult the Rehabilitation Act standards as we consider Argenyi's claims under that statute and under Title III of the ADA.

2.

The Supreme Court has held that § 504 of the Rehabilitation Act requires that "an otherwise qualified handicapped individual must be provided with meaningful access to the benefit that the grantee offers." Alexander v. Choate [a principal case in Chapter Four]. In applying *Alexander,* our court has concluded that the Rehabilitation Act requires a private medical school to provide "reasonable accommodations . . . when a disabled student would otherwise be denied meaningful access to a university." *Stern v. Univ. of Osteopathic Med. & Health Sciences,* 220 F.3d 906, 908 (8th Cir.2000). In that case, a dyslexic student at a private medical university sued the university under § 504 of the Rehabilitation Act for failing to provide reasonable accommodations in testing. We affirmed the district court's grant of summary judgment to the university after concluding that the student had "failed to establish a nexus between his requested testing scheme and his dyslexia."

We also applied a "meaningful access" standard to a Rehabilitation Act claim brought by a hearing impaired prisoner against the Missouri Department of Corrections for having denied him an interpreter during internal disciplinary proceedings. *Randolph v. Rodgers,* 170 F.3d 850, 858 (8th Cir.1999). The district court in that case had granted the prisoner summary judgment after determining that "[t]he undisputed evidence . . . show[ed] that although he ha[d] been provided with some . . . benefits, he ha[d] not received the full benefits solely because of his disability." We affirmed on appeal, concluding that the record did not "contain credible evidence to support a finding that [the prisoner] enjoyed meaningful access to the prison's internal disciplinary process."

Under a "meaningful access" standard, we have decided that aids and services "are not required to produce the identical result or level of achievement for handicapped and nonhandicapped persons," but they nevertheless "must afford handicapped persons equal opportunity to . . . gain the same benefit." The Eleventh Circuit has similarly concluded that the "proper inquiry" under the Rehabilitation Act to determine if a hospital had provided "necessary" auxiliary aids to a hearing impaired patient was whether the proffered aids "gave that patient an equal opportunity to benefit from the hospital's treatment." *Liese v. Indian River Cnty. Hosp. Dist.,* 701 F.3d 334, 343 (11th Cir.2012). As the court observed in *Liese,* that inquiry "is inherently fact-intensive" and "largely depends on context."

The meaningful access standard to ensure an equal opportunity is consistent with the purpose of Title III of the ADA, which is to ensure that all people have "full and equal enjoyment" of public accommodations regardless of disability. 42 U.S.C. § 12182(a). We conclude that § 504 of the Rehabilitation Act and Title III of the ADA each require Creighton to provide reasonable auxiliary aids and services to afford Argenyi "meaningful access" or an equal opportunity to gain the same benefit as his nondisabled peers.

The Ninth Circuit applied a similar standard to a claim arising under Title III of the ADA. *See* Baughman. There, the district court had granted summary judgment to the defendant after concluding that Baughman had failed to show that it was "necessary" for her to use a Segway to visit Disneyland because she would not have been "effectively excluded" without it. The Ninth Circuit reversed, reasoning that the ADA "guarantees the disabled more than mere access to public facilities; it guarantees them 'full and equal enjoyment.'" (quoting 42 U.S.C. § 12182(a)). The appellate court instructed the Disney company to "start by considering how their facilities are used by non-disabled guests and then take reasonable steps to provide disabled guests with a like experience."

Considering Argenyi's Rehabilitation Act and ADA claims together, the district court granted summary judgment to Creighton after concluding that Argenyi had failed to show that his requested accommodations were necessary as required under the ADA. The district court looked to guidance from the Supreme Court's decision in *Martin,* a quite different case from the one brought by Argenyi. In *Martin,* a professional golfer with a degenerative circulatory disorder sought to travel in a golf cart between the eighteen holes at tournaments. The Court distinguished that golfer from "players with less serious afflictions that make walking the course uncomfortable or difficult, but not beyond their capacity. *In such cases, an accommodation might be reasonable but not necessary*" (emphasis added).

Here, the district court compared Argenyi's situation not with the golfer with the degenerative disorder who obtained relief in *Martin* but with those "players with less serious afflictions" for whom walking the course was "not beyond their capacity." With this faulty analogy the court reasoned that by use of the auxiliary aids and services Creighton did supply, Argenyi's medical school experience, although "uncomfortable or difficult," was not "beyond [his] capacity." Since Argenyi had not been "effectively excluded" from Creighton, his requested additional aids and services were not "necessary" under the ADA. Overlooking Argenyi's evidence which showed that aspects of his medical education at Creighton were beyond his capacity without the accommodations he requested, the court failed to make the appropriate comparison with the golfer with the degenerative disorder in *Martin*.

[T]o the extent that the district court interpreted *Martin* to mean that the word "necessary" in the ADA requires a showing that the claimant has been effectively excluded from a place of public accommodation, it would be inconsistent with the congressional purpose of the ADA and the Rehabilitation Act. In Title III of the ADA and § 504 of the Rehabilitation Act, Congress required public accommodations and entities which receive public funding to furnish reasonable auxiliary aids and services so that all individuals have an equal opportunity to gain "a like" or "equal" benefit. Rather than merely ensure that Argenyi is not "effectively excluded" from its medical school, the ADA and the Rehabilitation Act require Creighton to "start by considering how [its educational programs] are used by non-disabled [medical school students] and then take reasonable steps to provide [Argenyi] with a like experience." *Baughman*.

We conclude that the evidence produced in this case created a genuine issue of material fact as to whether Creighton denied Argenyi an equal opportunity to gain the same benefit from medical school as his nondisabled peers by refusing to provide his requested accommodations. At this stage the record supports Argenyi's claim that he was unable to follow lectures and classroom dialogue or successfully communicate with clinical patients. From such evidence a reasonable factfinder could determine that Argenyi was denied an opportunity to benefit from medical school equal to that of his nondisabled classmates. The district court's grant of summary judgment to Creighton should therefore be reversed and the case remanded.[3]

NOTE ON COMMUNICATIONS BARRIERS AND AUXILIARY AIDS

Title III specifically requires public accommodations to "to take such steps as may be necessary to ensure that no individual with a disability is excluded, denied services, segregated or otherwise treated differently than

---

[3] On remand Creighton may also submit evidence of the cost of Argenyi's requested auxiliary aids and services for a determination of whether providing them would impose an undue burden on the university. *See* 42 U.S.C. § 12182(b)(2)(A)(iii) (ADA); 29 U.S.C. § 794a(a)(1) (Rehabilitation Act).

other individuals because of the absence of auxiliary aids and services, unless the entity can demonstrate that taking such steps would fundamentally alter the nature of the good, service, facility, privilege, advantage, or accommodation being offered or would result in an undue burden." 42 U.S.C. § 12182(b)(2)(A)(iii). The statute defines "auxiliary aids" as "qualified interpreters or other effective methods of making aurally delivered materials available to individuals with hearing impairments"; "qualified readers, taped texts, or other effective methods of making visually delivered materials available to individuals with visual impairments"; "acquisition or modification of equipment or devices"; and "other similar services and actions." *Id.* § 12103(1). The Department of Justice has issued regulations interpreting these provisions to require that public accommodations "furnish appropriate auxiliary aids and services where necessary to ensure effective communication with individuals with disabilities." 28 C.F.R. § 36.303(c).

The 2010 ADA regulations add a number of provisions elaborating on the "effective communication" requirement. One such provision emphasizes that the requirement "includes an obligation to provide effective communication to companions who are individuals with disabilities." *Id.* Another makes clear that the requirement is necessarily fact-intensive: "The type of auxiliary aid or service necessary to ensure effective communication will vary in accordance with the method of communication used by the individual; the nature, length, and complexity of the communication involved; and the context in which the communication is taking place." *Id.* § 36.303(c)(1)(ii). But "[t]o be effective, auxiliary aids and services must be provided in accessible formats, in a timely manner, and in such a way as to protect the privacy and independence of the individual with a disability." *Id.* The 2010 regulations also provide that a public accommodation shall not: (a) "require an individual with a disability to bring another individual to interpret for him or her"; (b) "rely on an adult accompanying an individual with a disability to interpret or facilitate communication" (except in an emergency or where the individual with a disability requests that the adult interpret, the adult agrees, and "reliance on that adult for assistance is appropriate under the circumstances"); or (c) "rely on a minor child to interpret or facilitate communication," except in an emergency. *Id.* §36.303(c)(2)–(4).

One key question, addressed in *Argenyi*, is whether the public accommodation must defer to the preference of a person with a disability for a particular communications aid. The 2010 regulations, reflecting the Department of Justice's longstanding enforcement position, resolve this question in favor of requiring consultation but not absolute deference: "A public accommodation should consult with individuals with disabilities whenever possible to determine what type of auxiliary aid is needed to ensure effective communication, but the ultimate decision as to what measures to take rests with the public accommodation, provided that the method chosen results in effective communication." *Id.* The preamble to the 2010 regulations explained why the Department rejected a standard that would have "require[d] public accommodations to give primary consideration to the expressed choice of an individual with a disability":

[A]s the Department explained when it initially promulgated the 1991 title III regulation, the Department believes that Congress did not intend under title III to impose upon a public accommodation the requirement that it give primary consideration to the request of the individual with a disability. The legislative history does, however, demonstrate congressional intent to strongly encourage consulting with persons with disabilities.

[T]he commenters who urged that primary consideration be given to the individual with a disability noted, for example, that a public accommodation would not provide effective communication by using written notes where the individual requiring an auxiliary aid is in severe pain, or by providing a qualified ASL interpreter when an individual needs an oral interpreter instead. Both examples illustrate the importance of consulting with the individual with a disability in order to ensure that the communication provided is effective. When a public accommodation ignores the communication needs of the individual requiring an auxiliary aid or service, it does so at its peril, for if the communication provided is not effective, the public accommodation will have violated title III of the ADA.

Consequently, the regulation strongly encourages the public accommodation to engage in a dialogue with the individual with a disability to determine what auxiliary aids and services are appropriate under the circumstances. This dialogue should include a communication assessment of the individual with a disability initially, regularly, and as needed, because the auxiliary aids and services necessary to provide effective communication to the individual may fluctuate. For example, a deaf individual may go to a private community health center with what is at first believed to be a minor medical emergency, such as a sore knee, and the individual with a disability and the community health center both may believe that exchanging written notes will be effective; however, during that individual's visit, it may be determined that the individual is, in fact, suffering from an anterior cruciate ligament tear and must have surgery to repair the torn ligament. As the situation develops and the diagnosis and recommended course of action evolve into surgery, an interpreter likely will be necessary. The community health center has a continuing obligation to assess the auxiliary aids and services it is providing, and should consult with individuals with disabilities on a continuing basis to assess what measures are required to ensure effective communication.

Similarly, the Department strongly encourages public accommodations to keep individuals with disabilities apprised of the status of the expected arrival of an interpreter or the delivery of other requested or anticipated auxiliary aids and services. Also, when the public accommodation decides not to provide the auxiliary aids and services requested by an individual with a disability, the public accommodation should provide that individual with the reason for its decision.

75 Fed. Reg. 56,282. Does the Department's resolution of this problem persuade you? The individual with the disability is far more likely than any given business to know what communications aids work best for her. Why shouldn't the business have to use the aids that she knows to be effective? On the other hand, why should an individual with a disability be able to force a business to use her preferred communications aid when other, perhaps more convenient and less expensive, aids will do the job nearly as well?

Even when a particular communications aid is necessary for effective communication, it may be quite costly. Does the regulation require that a public accommodation owner pay for a sign-language interpreter, where that is necessary for effective communication, even if the cost of the interpreter means that the owner will necessarily lose money? As *Argenyi* makes clear in its final footnote, a public accommodation can defeat the obligation to provide particular communications aids if it "can demonstrate that taking those steps would fundamentally alter the nature of the goods, services, facilities, privileges, advantages, or accommodations being offered or would result in an undue burden, i.e., significant difficulty or expense." 28 C.F.R. § 36.303(a). See *Mayberry v. Von Valtier*, 843 F.Supp. 1160 (E.D.Mich.1994) (denying defendant's motion for summary judgment where defendant doctor refused to pay for an interpreter for plaintiff patient; defendant netted $13.94 per visit, but was then required to pay $28.00 for the interpreter). Is it fair to impose that burden on a the owner simply because of the fortuity that a person with a disability chose to patronize her business rather than the business next door? (Note that the $5,000 disabled access tax credit, 26 U.S.C. § 44, applies to such services as sign language interpreters, whether for employees or customers and clients.)

NOTE ON REASONABLE ACCOMMODATION AND THE FAIR HOUSING ACT

The Fair Housing Act requires covered entities "to make reasonable accommodations in rules, policies, practices, or services, when such accommodations may be necessary to afford such person equal opportunity to use and enjoy a dwelling." 42 U.S.C. § 3604(f)(3)(B). As with Title III's reasonable modification requirement, application of the Fair Housing Act's reasonable accommodation requirement is fact-intensive.

An important category of cases involves requests for alterations to rules distributing parking spaces. In *Shapiro v. Cadman Towers, Inc.*, 51 F.3d 328 (2d Cir.1995), the court upheld a preliminary injunction that required the defendant landlord to give the plaintiff a parking space at her apartment complex, thereby allowing her to jump ahead of the other residents on the waiting list. The complex had more apartments than parking spaces, but the court explained that the plaintiff's disability—which made it difficult and dangerous to walk long distances—rendered the parking space necessary for her equal use and enjoyment of her apartment. The court noted "that Shapiro could be accommodated without displacing any existing tenants, because three parking spots are reserved for building personnel and these workers could park in a commercial garage," and that "one parking space was used by a person that did not live in the building." Are these facts sufficient to warrant allowing Ms. Shapiro to obtain a parking space ahead of her fellow tenants who have been waiting longer than she has?

Another significant set of cases involves requests that landlords or homeowners' associations waive various fees at the instance of residents with disabilities. In *United States v. California Mobile Home Park Management Co.*, 29 F.3d 1413 (9th Cir.1994), a resident with a disability asked the management of her mobile home park to waive its guest fee ($1.50 per day, plus $25.00 per month for parking). The district court dismissed the plaintiff's complaint on the ground that the Fair Housing Act does not bar the imposition of generally applicable fees. The Ninth Circuit reversed and remanded for consideration of whether the particular fee at issue denied equal opportunity to use and enjoy the mobile home park:

> In order to trigger review under § 3604(f)(3)(B), the challenged fee rule must [h]ave the potential to deny persons an "equal opportunity to use and enjoy a dwelling" because of their handicap. There are, of course, many types of residential fees that affect handicapped and non-handicapped residents equally; such fees are clearly proper. Fees that merit closer scrutiny are those with unequal impact, imposed in return for permission to engage in conduct that, under the FHAA, a landlord is required to permit.

> Some generally applicable fees might be too small to have any exclusionary effect. Other fees might be sustained because to require their waiver would extend a preference to handicapped residents, as opposed to affording them equal opportunity. The waiver of others might impose an undue financial burden on the landlord. The reasonable accommodation inquiry is highly fact-specific, requiring case-by-case determination. In a case such as this one, a reviewing court should examine, among other things, the amount of fees imposed, the relationship between the amount of fees and the overall housing cost, the proportion of other tenants paying such fees, the importance of the fees to the landlord's overall revenues, and the importance of the fee waiver to the handicapped tenant.

On remand, the district court concluded that the challenged fee did *not* deny equal use and enjoyment, and the court of appeals affirmed. See *United States v. California Mobile Home Park Management Co.*, 107 F.3d 1374 (9th Cir.1997) ("In this case, plaintiff asks for a reasonable accommodation not for herself, but for a caregiver, Ms. Dawson. Plaintiff failed to show why Dawson's convenience is necessary for her own use and enjoyment of her home. Plaintiff submitted no evidence explaining why Dawson could not have parked outside of the mobile home park and still have provided caregiver services to Cohen-Strong's daughter.").

In *Giebeler v. M & B Associates*, 343 F.3d 1143 (9th Cir.2003), the Ninth Circuit ruled that the landlord was required to waive its no-cosigners policy for a tenant who, because of his advanced AIDS, was unable to work—and thus unable to satisfy the landlord's financial requirements:

Here, the causal link between Branham's failure to accommodate and Giebeler's disability is obvious. Giebeler was unemployed because of his disability and therefore had insufficient income to qualify for the apartment. Once Branham refused to allow Anne Giebeler to rent an apartment for her son to live in, Giebeler could not show financial ability to pay the rent and therefore could not live in the housing complex. Allowing Anne Giebeler to rent an apartment on her son's behalf, or in some other manner accommodating his inability to prove financial responsibility in the usual way, was necessary to enable Giebeler to live in an apartment at Branham.

In addition to causation, equal opportunity is a key component of the necessity analysis; an accommodation must be possibly necessary to afford the plaintiff equal opportunity to use and enjoy a dwelling. M & B's refusal to allow Anne Giebeler to rent an apartment for her son denies him an opportunity for which he would otherwise be qualified. With Anne Giebeler as renter, Giebeler could satisfy Branham's minimum income requirement and ensure that Branham receives its monthly rent. Giebeler is similarly situated to other tenants at Branham in terms of the financial resources he can bring to a tenancy at Branham. It is his way of demonstrating and deploying these resources that is different. So defendants' relaxation of their no cosigner policy "may be necessary" to afford Giebeler equal opportunity to use and enjoy a dwelling at Branham.

The court further explained that the plaintiff's requested accommodation was reasonable:

The rental arrangement requested by Giebeler would not require Branham to accept less rent, would not otherwise alter the essential obligations of tenancy at Branham (such as appropriate behavior and care of the premises), and would provide a lessee with the proper financial qualifications and credit history. As the official renter of the apartment, Anne Giebeler would be primarily responsible for the rent, thereby obviating the need for M & B to first go to her son to collect rent before pursuing her for unpaid rent. Rentals by parents for children are not unusual in most rental markets.

Is this a sensible decision? Cf. *Salute v. Stratford Greens Garden Apartments*, 136 F.3d 293 (2d Cir.1998) (rejecting plaintiffs' claim that defendant landlord should be required to accept Section 8 housing vouchers as an accommodation to people whose disabilities prevent them from working: "The 'opportunity to use and enjoy' language of the FHAA reinforces the ability of people with handicaps to have the same opportunity as similarly situated persons who have no evident handicaps. What stands between these plaintiffs and the apartments at Stratford Greens is a shortage of money, and nothing else. In this respect, impecunious people with disabilities stand on the same footing as everyone else. Thus, the accommodation sought by plaintiffs is not 'necessary' to afford handicapped persons 'equal opportunity' to use and enjoy a dwelling.").

D. INSURANCE

INTRODUCTORY NOTE

"[F]ar and away the most significant barrier to employment for people with disabilities is the current structure of our health insurance system." Samuel R. Bagenstos, Law and the Contradictions of the Disability Rights Movement 129 (2009). The limitations on private health insurance coverage often force people with disabilities to enroll in public health insurance programs like Medicare and Medicaid—programs that make it difficult to stay in the workforce. (See the discussion in Chapter Three.) The limitations of private health insurance take two major forms:

> Largely in response to perceived problems of adverse selection, private health insurance often places severe limitations on coverage for disabling conditions. Insurers frequently offer policies that are subject to "exclusion waivers," which bar reimbursement for any treatment for particular named conditions. When they do not exclude coverage altogether, insurers often impose annual or lifetime caps on the permitted reimbursement for specific conditions or classes of conditions. These caps frequently are set far below the amount that would be necessary to pay for even minimally sufficient care for the targeted conditions.

> [A]lthough the exclusion and capping of coverage for particular conditions is a major problem for individuals with disabilities, it may not be the most important way in which private health insurance policies fail to meet their needs. For even when private health insurance contains no limitations on the conditions for which individuals may be treated, it typically imposes strict limitations on the specific treatments and other interventions for which it will pay. Those treatment-specific limitations formally affect all policyholders—disabled and nondisabled alike. But they often fall most heavily in practice on individuals with disabilities. Two aspects of private insurance largely account for this effect: (1) the tilt of insurance policies toward acute, as opposed to chronic, care; and (2) the typical requirement that covered treatments be "medically necessary." These aspects are intertwined, because insurance policies' definitions of medical necessity often incorporate an acute-care bias by "requir[ing] evidence that a service will significantly improve a person's health status" and not merely "maintain [that person's] functional capacity."

> The acute-care orientation of private health insurance creates a number of gaps in coverage that have a significant effect on individuals with disabilities. Individuals who experience disabling injuries or strokes, for example, typically find that their insurance does not cover the rehabilitative therapy they need. Individuals with disabilities who need other forms of

ongoing therapy—such as those with hearing impairments who need speech therapy—have a similar experience. Private insurers will pay for such therapy when it is a short-term response to an acute condition, but not when it is a continuing response to a chronic condition.

Similarly, private insurers often do not cover, or do not adequately cover, durable medical equipment and assistive technologies. The failure of private insurers to cover the costs of hearing aids is widely documented. Individuals with limb amputations also frequently have difficulty obtaining coverage for their prostheses. Insurers often invoke the "medical necessity" concept to refuse to pay for more advanced (and more functional) prostheses where less expensive (and less functional) prostheses are available. The same "medical necessity" issue often arises when individuals with mobility impairments seek reimbursements for wheelchairs.

Samuel R. Bagenstos, *The Future of Disability Law*, 114 Yale L.J. 1, 27–32 (2004) (citations omitted).

The Patient Protection and Affordable Care Act (ACA) will address some, though not all, of these problems for people with disabilities. The statute prohibits preexisting conditions exclusions in health insurance policies, 42 U.S.C. § 300gg-3; it bans health insurers from establishing rules for eligibility based on an individual's health status or disability, 42 U.S.C. § 300gg-4; and it prohibits lifetime and annual caps on health insurance benefits, 42 U.S.C. § 300gg-11. As noted in Chapter Three, the ACA also will enable people with disabilities who cannot obtain health insurance through employers to obtain their coverage through an exchange or through the Medicaid expansion. For a general discussion of the effect of these reforms on people with disabilities, see Jessica L. Roberts, *Health Law as Disability Rights Law*, 97 Minn. L. Rev. 1963 (2013).

The ACA's reforms respond to much of the discrimination against people with disabilities in health insurance. But the ADA will retain a role in regulating insurance, both in and out of the health insurance context. Both ADA Title I (in its prohibition of discrimination in employee benefits) and ADA Title III (in its prohibition of discrimination by, for example, "insurance office[s]," 42 U.S.C. § 12181(7)(F)) might plausibly be read to reach disability-related distinctions in insurance coverage. (Recall, however, the discussion in Section A regarding whether Title III covers insurance contracts that an individual does not obtain by visiting the insurer's office.) But the ADA contains a specific safe harbor provision for certain insurance decisions. That provision states that the statute "shall not be construed to prohibit or restrict":

(1) an insurer, hospital or medical service company, health maintenance organization, or any agent, or entity that administers benefit plans, or similar organizations from underwriting risks, classifying risks, or administering such risks that are based on or not inconsistent with State law; or

(2) a person or organization covered by this chapter from establishing, sponsoring, observing or administering the terms

of a bona fide benefit plan that are based on underwriting risks, classifying risks, or administering such risks that are based on or not inconsistent with State law; or

(3) a person or organization covered by this chapter from establishing, sponsoring, observing or administering the terms of a bona fide benefit plan that is not subject to State laws that regulate insurance.

42 U.S.C. § 12201(c). But that safe harbor, in turn, is limited by the proviso that "[p]aragraphs (1), (2), and (3) shall not be used as a subterfuge to evade the purposes of" Titles I and III. *Id.* The safe harbor provision was inserted at the insistence of insurance companies during Congress's consideration of the ADA. See Chai R. Feldblum, *The Employment Sector, in* Implementing the Americans with Disabilities Act 81, 111–18 (Jane West ed., 1996).

Why, other than the political power of insurance companies, might Congress have wanted to give insurance arrangements special protection in the ADA? There is a strong tradition in the United States, ratified by the McCarran-Ferguson Act, 15 U.S.C. § 1011 *et seq.,* of state regulation of the insurance industry. State insurance laws, in turn, have adopted the principle of "fair discrimination," which holds that insurance companies may distinguish among classes of people based on actuarial differences between the classes. See, *e.g.,* Mary Crossley, *Discrimination Against the Unhealthy in Health Insurance,* 54 U. Kan. L. Rev. 73, 109–110 (2005). The endorsement of "fair discrimination" in the culture of insurance is not grudging, as the words of one mainstream insurance-law scholar demonstrate:

"Fair" discrimination has never been illegal; it was and is not only permissible but also required as the essence of good ratemaking techniques in insurance; the goal of the ratemaking process is to discriminate fairly—to measure as accurately as is practicable the burden shifted to the insurance fund by the policy holder and to charge exactly for it, no more and no less. To do so is "fair" discrimination in the seventy year old tradition of insurance rate law and the much older practice of the insurance business. Not to do so is unfair discrimination.

Spencer L. Kimball, *Reverse Sex Discrimination:* Manhart, 1979 Am. Bar. Found. Res. J. 83, 105.

The "fair discrimination" principle responds, in part, to problems economists have labeled "moral hazard" and "adverse selection." The term "moral hazard" refers "to the tendency for insurance against loss to reduce incentives to prevent or minimize the cost of loss." Tom Baker, *On the Genealogy of Moral Hazard,* 75 Tex. L. Rev. 237, 239 (1996). The insight is straightforward: If one is insured, then, up to the level that insurance compensates, one will be indifferent to the costs he or she incurs, because "someone else" is paying for them. (For a critical examination of the moral hazard concept, see *id..*) The term "adverse selection" refers to a difficulty in pricing insurance—and even continuing to offer insurance—when the insured knows something important about her insurability that the insurer does not know. The difficulty, in stylized form, goes like this: If an insurer cannot assess any individual's health needs, it will set health insurance premiums so that each insured person pays the costs of an average person's health needs, plus a normal profit. If it sets insurance premiums at that level, people with more extensive health needs than average will rush to get insurance, because they will pay less in premiums than they otherwise would in health care costs. But people with less extensive health care needs than average will have no reason to buy health insurance—they will pay more in premiums than they would pay in health care costs if they had no insurance at all. But if the only people who buy health insurance are those who incur higher-than-average health care costs, the insurer will have to raise its premiums so that each insured person pays the average costs of this costlier group, plus a normal profit, which, many analysts argue, will start the (vicious) cycle over again. For the basic theory, see Michael Rothschild & Joseph Stiglitz, *Equilibrium in Competitive Insurance Markets: An Essay on the Economics of Imperfect Information*, 90 Q.J. Econ. 629 (1976). For a critique, see Peter Siegelman, *Adverse Selection in Insurance Markets: An Exaggerated Threat*, 113 Yale L.J. 1223 (2004).

It is easy to see how the condition- and treatment-specific limitations on insurance for people with disabilities might respond to moral hazard and adverse selection problems. An insurer thus might cap reimbursements for particular treatments, or limit reimbursements only to those treatments that meet a restrictive definition of medical necessity, to keep people from making inefficiently large expenditures on their treatments—expenditures that they might make only because someone else is paying for them. And an insurance company might cap coverage for a particular costly condition in order to avoid adverse selection: People with that condition can buy coverage, or more extensive coverage, for it by spending extra money; but the cap keeps them from driving up insurance costs for people who do not have the condition. See Siegelman, *supra*, at 1237–1238 (noting that this is the standard suggestion for avoiding adverse selection problems).

Given the moral hazard and adverse selection concerns, is there any justification for prohibiting insurers from making disability-based distinctions in insurance? Professor Deborah Stone argues for a solidaristic understanding of insurance. She contends that insurance is best understood as "a form of mutual aid and collective responsibility. To participate in a risk-pooling scheme is to agree to tax yourself not only for your own benefit should you incur a loss, but also for the benefit of others who might suffer from loss when you do not." Deborah A. Stone, *Beyond Moral Hazard: Insurance as Moral Opportunity*, 6 Conn. Ins. L.J. 11, 15 (1999); see also Deborah A. Stone, *The Struggle for the Soul of Health Insurance*, 18 J. Health Pol. Pol'y & L. 287 (1993). Does that argument suggest that insurers should not be permitted to divide their customers into different risk groups and charge riskier people more? If less risky customers could opt out (as they could unless the government mandated participation or collected the premiums as taxes), how would insurers avoid the adverse selection problem? Professor Peter Siegelman argues that, given modest risk aversion, healthier individuals may actually find insurance *more* valuable than do less healthy individuals—which would lead to propitious, rather than adverse, selection. He points to a variety of anecdotal evidence in support of the propitious selection theory. Siegelman, *supra*.

Even if moral hazard and adverse selection are problems, can we expect insurance companies to precisely calibrate the proper costs of particular treatments or the risks attendant to particular disabilities? Insurance companies are in the business of assessing risk, so one might be inclined to trust them to make correct judgments in this area. But stigma and (perhaps unconscious) prejudice can lead risk assessors to overestimate the risks attendant to disability and to fail to appreciate the harm a restrictive "medical necessity" standard for reimbursement causes to people with disabilities. And, indeed, companies may use socially salient disability-based categories when other ways of categorizing people would be as good or better at classifying risk. See Regina Austin, *The Insurance Classification Controversy*, 131 U. Pa. L. Rev. 517, 534 (1983) ("In order to assess risk it is necessary to focus upon the behavior of some existing group of individuals possessing a common trait. The companies utilize commonly recognized social status groups."). Does disability discrimination law have a role in ensuring that insurers' risk assessments are rational and evidence-based?

As you read the cases below, consider the role they give the ADA in policing insurers' risk classifications? Is it the right role? Is it too intrusive into the affairs of insurance companies—or not intrusive enough?

Doe v. Mutual of Omaha Ins. Co.

United States Court of Appeals for the Seventh Circuit, 1999.
179 F.3d 557.

■ POSNER, CHIEF JUDGE.

Mutual of Omaha appeals from a judgment that the AIDS caps in two of its health insurance policies violate the public accommodations provision of the Americans with Disabilities Act. One policy limits lifetime benefits for AIDS or AIDS-related conditions (ARC) to $25,000, the other limits them to $100,000, while for other conditions the limit in both policies is $1 million. Mutual of Omaha has stipulated that it "has not shown and cannot show that its AIDS Caps are or ever have been consistent with sound actuarial principles, actual or reasonably anticipated experience, *bona fide* risk classification, or state law." It also concedes that AIDS is a disabling condition within the meaning of the Americans with Disabilities Act. Since the Supreme Court held in *Bragdon* that infection with the AIDS virus (HIV) is a disabling condition from the onset of the infection, before any symptoms appear, it is apparent that both ARC and AIDS are disabilities. Mutual of Omaha does not question this, but argues only that the Americans with Disabilities Act does not regulate the content of insurance policies.

Title III of the Act, in section 302(a), provides that "no individual shall be discriminated against on the basis of disability in the full and equal enjoyment of the goods, services, facilities, privileges, advantages, or accommodations of any place of public accommodation" by the owner, lessee, or operator of such a place. 42 U.S.C. § 12182(a). The core meaning of this provision, plainly enough, is that the owner or operator of a store, hotel, restaurant, dentist's office, travel agency, theater, Web site, or other facility (whether in physical space or in electronic space) that is open to the public cannot exclude disabled persons from entering the facility and, once in, from using the facility in the same way that the nondisabled do. The owner or operator of, say, a camera store can neither bar the door to the disabled nor let them in but then refuse to sell its cameras to them on the same terms as to other customers. To come closer to home, a dentist cannot refuse to fill a cavity of a person with AIDS unless he demonstrates a direct threat to safety or health, *Bragdon*, and an insurance company cannot (at least without pleading a special defense, discussed below) refuse to sell an insurance policy to a person with AIDS. 28 C.F.R. § 36.104 Place of Public Accommodation (6). Mutual of Omaha does not refuse to sell insurance policies to such persons—it was happy to sell health insurance policies to the two plaintiffs. But because of the AIDS caps, the policies have less value to persons with AIDS than they would have to persons with other, equally expensive diseases or disabilities. This does not make the offer to sell illusory, for people with AIDS have medical needs unrelated to AIDS, and the policies give such people as much coverage for those needs as the policies give people who don't have AIDS. If all the medical needs of people with AIDS were AIDS-related and thus excluded by the policies, this might support an inference that Mutual of Omaha was trying to exclude such people, and such exclusion, as we shall see, might violate the Act. But that is not argued.

Since most health-insurance policies contain caps, the position urged by the plaintiffs would discriminate among diseases. Diseases that happened to be classified as disabilities could not be capped, but equally or more serious diseases that are generally not disabling, such as heart disease, could be. Moreover, the plaintiffs acknowledge the right of an insurance company to exclude coverage for an applicant's pre-existing medical conditions. If the applicant is already HIV-positive when he applies for a health-insurance policy, the insurer can in effect cap his AIDS-related coverage at $0. This "discrimination" is not limited to AIDS or for that matter to disabilities, which is why the plaintiffs do not challenge it; but it suggests that the rule for which they contend is at once arbitrary and unlikely to do much for people with AIDS.

The insurance company asks us to compare this case to one in which a person with one leg complains of a shoestore's refusal to sell shoes other than by the pair, or in which a blind person complains of a bookstore's refusal to stock books printed in Braille. We do not understand the plaintiffs to be contending that such complaints are actionable under section 302(a), even though there is a sense in which the disabled individual would be denied the full and equal enjoyment of the services that the store offers. In fact, it is apparent that a store is not required to alter its inventory in order to stock goods such as Braille books that are especially designed for disabled people. But it is apparent as a matter of interpretation rather than compelled by a simple reading which would place the present case on the other side of the line; and so the case cannot be resolved by reference simply to the language of section 302(a).

The common sense of the statute is that the content of the goods or services offered by a place of public accommodation is not regulated. A camera store may not refuse to sell cameras to a disabled person, but it is not required to stock cameras specially designed for such persons. Had Congress purposed to impose so enormous a burden on the retail sector of the economy and so vast a supervisory responsibility on the federal courts, we think it would have made its intention clearer and would at least have imposed some standards. It is hardly a feasible judicial function to decide whether shoestores should sell single shoes to one-legged persons and if so at what price, or how many Braille books the Borders or Barnes and Noble bookstore chains should stock in each of their stores. There are defenses to a prima facie case of public-accommodation discrimination, but they would do little to alleviate the judicial burden of making standardless decisions about the composition of retail inventories. The only defense that might apply to the Braille case or the pair of shoes case is that the modification of a seller's existing practices that is necessary to provide equal access to the disabled "would fundamentally alter the nature of . . . [the seller's] services," 42 U.S.C. § 12182(b)(2)(A)(ii), and it probably would not apply to either case and certainly not to the Braille one.

The plaintiffs might be able to distinguish the shoestore hypothetical by pointing out that a nondisabled person might be in the market for one shoe simply because he had lost a shoe; in refusing to sell single shoes the store thus would not be refusing to adapt its service to a class of customers limited to disabled people. But the Braille case, and many others that we can imagine (such as a furniture store's decision not to stock wheelchairs, or a psychiatrist's refusal to treat schizophrenia, as distinct from his refusing to treat schizophrenics for the psychiatric disorders in which he specializes, or a movie theater's refusal to provide a running translation into sign language of the movie's soundtrack), cannot be so distinguished, although some of them might find shelter in the "fundamental alteration" defense. All are cases of refusing to configure a service to make it as valuable to a disabled as to a nondisabled customer.

That the plaintiffs are asking that a limitation be removed rather than that a physical product be added or altered cannot distinguish these cases. For the same thing is true in our example of the psychiatrist who refuses to treat schizophrenia. More important, since section 302(a) is not limited to physical products, but includes contracts and other intangibles, such as an insurance policy, a limitation upon the duty to serve cannot be confined to physical changes. An insurance policy is a product, and a policy with a $25,000 limit is a different product from one with a $1 million limit, just as a wheelchair is a different product from an armchair. A furniture store that does not stock wheelchairs knows that it is making its services less valuable to disabled than to nondisabled people, but the Americans with Disabilities Act has not been understood to require furniture stores to stock wheelchairs.

It might seem that the AIDS caps could be distinguished from the "refusal to stock" cases because the caps include complications of AIDS. If being infected by HIV leads one to contract pneumonia, the cost of treating the pneumonia is subject to the AIDS cap; if a person not infected by HIV contracts pneumonia, the costs of treating his pneumonia are fully covered. It looks, therefore, like a difference in treatment referable solely to the fact that one person is disabled and the other not.

But this is not correct. The essential point to understand is that HIV doesn't cause illness directly. What it does is weaken and eventually destroy the body's immune system. As the immune system falters, the body becomes prey to diseases that the system protects us against. These "opportunistic" diseases that HIV allows, as it were, to ravage the body are exotic cancers and rare forms of pneumonia and other infectious diseases. Anthony S. Fauci & H. Clifford Lane, *"Human Immunodeficiency Virus (HIV) Disease: AIDS and Related Disorders," in* 2 Harrison's Principles of Internal Medicine 1791, 1824–45 (Anthony S. Fauci *et al.* eds., 14th ed.1998). To refer to them as "complications" of HIV or AIDS is not incorrect, but it is misleading, because they are the chief worry of anyone who has the misfortune to be afflicted with AIDS. An AIDS cap would be meaningless if it excluded the opportunistic diseases that are the most harmful consequences of being infected by the AIDS virus.

What the AIDS caps in the challenged insurance policies cover, therefore, is the cost of fighting the AIDS virus itself and trying to keep the immune system intact plus the cost of treating the opportunistic diseases to which the body becomes prey when the immune system has eroded to the point at which one is classified as having AIDS. The principal opportunistic diseases of AIDS, such as Kaposi's sarcoma, Pneumocystis carinii pneumonia, AIDS wasting, and esophageal candidiasis, are rarely encountered among people who are not infected by HIV—so rarely as to be described frequently as "AIDS-defining opportunistic infections." *Id.* at 1818. The frequency of Pneumocystis carinii pneumonia, for example, "among patients infected with human immunodeficiency virus (HIV) far exceeds that among other immuno-compromised hosts" and is "a leading cause of opportunistic infection and death among AIDS patients in industrialized countries." Peter D. Walzer, *"Pneumocystis Carinii Infection,"* in 1 Harrison's, *supra,* at 1161. It is these distinctive diseases that are the target (along with the costs of directly treating infection by HIV) of the AIDS caps. This is not a case of refusing, for example, to provide the same coverage for a broken leg, or other afflictions not peculiar to people with AIDS, to such people, which would be a good example of discrimination by reason of disability.

It is true that as the immune system collapses because of infection by HIV, the patient becomes subject to opportunistic infection not only by the distinctive AIDS-defining diseases but also by a host of diseases to which people not infected with HIV are subject. Even when they are the same disease, however, they are far more lethal when they hit a person who does not have an immune system to fight back with. Which means they are not really the same disease. This is not a point that is peculiar to AIDS. The end stage of many diseases is an illness different from the one that brought the patient to that stage; nowadays when a person dies of pneumonia, it is usually because his body has been gravely weakened by some other ailment. If a health insurance policy that excluded coverage for cancer was interpreted not to cover the pneumonia that killed a patient terminally ill with cancer, this would not be "discrimination" against cancer.

To summarize the discussion to this point, we cannot find anything in the Americans with Disabilities Act or its background, or the nature of AIDS and AIDS caps, to justify so radically expansive an interpretation as would be required to bring these cases under section 302(a) without making an unprincipled distinction between AIDS caps and other product alterations—unless it is section 501(c)(1) of the Act. That section provides that Title I (employment discrimination against the disabled) and Title III (public accommodations, the title involved in this case) "shall not be construed to prohibit or restrict an insurer . . . from underwriting risks, classifying risks, or administering such risks that are based on or not inconsistent with State law," 42 U.S.C. § 12201(c)(1), unless the prohibition or restriction is "a subterfuge to evade the purposes" of either title. § 12201(c). Even with the "subterfuge" qualification, section 501(c) is obviously intended for the benefit of insurance companies rather than plaintiffs and it may seem odd therefore to find the plaintiffs placing such heavy weight on what is in effect a defense to liability. But a defense can cast light on what is to be defended against, that is, what the prima facie case of a violation is. Suppose, for example, that a statute regulated the sale of "animals" but it was unclear whether the legislature had meant to include fish. Were there a statutory exclusion for goldfish, it would be pretty clear that "animals" included fish, since otherwise there would be no occasion for such an exclusion. And, with that clarified, the advocate of regulating the sale of a particular goldfish would have to show only that the exclusion was somehow inapplicable to him. That is the plaintiffs' strategy here. They use the insurance provision to show that section 302(a) regulates content, then argue that the excluding provision is narrow enough to allow them to challenge the coverage limits in Mutual of Omaha's policies. There is even some legislative history, which the plaintiffs hopefully call "definitive," to section 501(c) that suggests that an insurance company can limit coverage on the basis of a disability only if the limitation is based either on claims experience or on sound actuarial methods for classifying risks. H.R.Rep.No.485, 101st Cong., 2d Sess. 136–37 (1990); S.Rep.No.116, 101st Cong., 1st Sess. 84–86 (1989). And Mutual of Omaha conceded itself out of relying on section 501(c)'s safe harbor by stipulating that it cannot show that its AIDS caps are based on sound actuarial principles or claims experience or are consistent with state law.

The plaintiffs argue, consistent with our goldfish example, that the insurance exemption has no function if section 302(a) does not regulate the content of insurance policies, and so we should infer that the section does regulate that content. But this reasoning is not correct. If it were, it would imply that section 302(a) regulates the content not only of insurance policies but also of all other products and services, since the section is not limited to insurance. The insurance industry may have worried that the section would be given just the expansive interpretation that the district court gave it in this case, and so the industry may have obtained the rule of construction in section 501(c) just to backstop its argument that section 302(a) regulates only access and not content. Or it may have worried about being sued under section 302(a) for refusing to sell an insurance policy to a disabled person. Remember that the right of full and equal enjoyment as we interpret it includes the right to buy on equal terms and not just the right to enter the store. For Mutual of Omaha to take the position that people with AIDS are so unhealthy that it won't sell them health insurance would be a prima facie violation of section 302(a). But the insurance company just might be able to steer into the safe harbor provided by section 501(c), provided it didn't run afoul of the "subterfuge" limitation, as it would do if, for example, it had adopted the AIDS caps to deter people who know they are HIV positive from buying the policies at all.

The legislative history is consistent with this interpretation. Both committee reports on which the plaintiffs rely give the example of refusing to sell an insurance policy to a blind person, as does the gloss placed on section 501(c) by the Department of Justice. 28 C.F.R. Pt. 36, App.B § 36.212, p. 601 (1998). A refusal to sell insurance to a blind person is not the same thing as a provision in the policy that if the insured becomes blind, the insurer will not pay the expense of his learning Braille. We find nothing in the language or history of the statute to suggest that the latter refusal would be unlawful. The Department's Technical Assistance Manual, supra, § III–3.11000, contains somewhat broader language than either the statute or the regulation or the committee reports, language about insurers' being forbidden to discriminate on the basis of disability in the sale, terms, or conditions of insurance contracts; but basically this just parrots the statute and the regulation and does not indicate a focused attention to coverage limits. There is, as we have pointed out, a difference between refusing to sell a health-insurance policy at all to a person with AIDS, or charging him a higher price for such a policy, or attaching a condition obviously designed to deter people with AIDS from buying the policy (such as refusing to cover such a person for a broken leg), on the one hand, and, on the other, offering insurance policies that contain caps for various diseases some of which may also be disabilities within the meaning of the Americans with Disabilities Act.

[W]e conclude that section 302(a) does not require a seller to alter his product to make it equally valuable to the disabled and to the nondisabled, even if the product is insurance. This conclusion is consistent with all the appellate cases to consider this or cognate issues.

[R]eversed.

■ TERENCE T. EVANS, CIRCUIT JUDGE, dissenting.

The Americans with Disabilities Act is a broad, sweeping, protective statute requiring the elimination of discrimination against individuals with disabilities. Because I believe the insurance policies challenged in this case discriminate against people with AIDS in violation of the ADA, I dissent.

The majority believes we are being asked to regulate the content of insurance policies—something we should not do under the ADA. But as I see it we are not being asked to regulate content; we are being asked to decide whether an insurer can discriminate against people with AIDS, refusing to pay for them the same expenses it would pay if they did not have AIDS. The ADA assigns to courts the task of passing judgment on such conduct. And to me, the Mutual of Omaha policies at issue violate the Act.

Chief Judge Posner's opinion likens the insurance company here to a camera store forced to stock cameras specially designed for disabled persons. While I agree that the ADA would not require a store owner to alter its inventory, I think the analogy misses the mark. The better analogy would be that of a store which lets disabled customers in the door, but then refuses to sell them anything but inferior cameras. To pick up on another analogy raised at oral argument, we are not being asked to force a restaurant to alter its menu to accommodate disabled diners; we are being asked to stop a restaurant that is offering to its nondisabled diners a menu containing a variety of entrees while offering a menu with only limited selections to its disabled patrons. Section 501(c)'s "safe harbor" would allow Mutual of Omaha to treat insureds with AIDS differently than those without AIDS if the discrimination were consistent with Illinois law or could be justified by actuarial principles or claims experience. But Mutual of Omaha conceded that its AIDS and ARC caps do not fall under the ADA's safe harbor protection.

The parties stipulated that the very same affliction (e.g., pneumonia) may be both AIDS-related and not AIDS-related and that, in such cases, coverage depends solely on whether the patient has AIDS. In my view that is more than enough to trigger an ADA violation. Chief Judge Posner reasons that, although the policies appear to discriminate solely based on an insured's HIV status, they really don't, when you consider the nature of AIDS. He suggests that the phrase "AIDS related conditions" embodies a unique set of symptoms and afflictions that would make it easy for the insurance company to determine with certainty whether an expense incurred for a particular illness is "AIDS-related" and therefore subject to the cap. His analysis—charitable to Mutual of Omaha to be sure—may very well be medically sound. But it doesn't come from the insurance policies. The policies don't even hint at what illnesses or afflictions might fall within the ARC exclusion. Nor has the medical community embraced an accepted definition for what "conditions" are "AIDS-related." The practical effect of all this, as Mutual of Omaha concedes, is that coverage for certain expenses would be approved or denied based solely on whether the insured had AIDS. Given that the ADA is supposed to signal a "clear and comprehensive national mandate for the elimination of discrimination against individuals with disabilities," see 42 U.S.C. § 12101(b)(1), I would use the statute to right the wrong committed by Mutual of Omaha[.]

Leonard F. v. Israel Discount Bank

United States Court of Appeal for the Second Circuit, 1999.
199 F.3d 99.

■ LEVAL, CIRCUIT JUDGE:

Plaintiff Leonard F. appeals from the judgment of the United States District Court for the Southern District of New York (Charles L. Brieant, Jr., J.) dismissing his complaint against Defendant The Metropolitan Life Insurance Company ("MetLife") for failure to state a claim under Fed. R. Civ. P. 12(b)(6). The complaint alleged (*inter alia*) that MetLife discriminated against Plaintiff on the basis of his mental disability in violation of Title III of the Americans with Disabilities Act (the "ADA" or "Act"), 42 U.S.C. §§ 12181–12189, by contracting with his employer, Defendant Israel Discount Bank of New York (the "Bank"), to provide him with a health insurance policy that limited coverage for mental disabilities to two years while providing coverage for physical disabilities that was not so limited. The district court dismissed the complaint, finding that because MetLife's policy is consistent with state law and does not constitute a subterfuge to evade the purposes of the Act, MetLife is exempt from Plaintiff's Title III claim under the "safe harbor" provision of Section 501(c) of the ADA, 42 U.S.C. § 12201(c). We agree with the district court's reasoning. However, we believe it erred in dismissing the complaint under Fed.R.Civ.P. 12(b)(6) based on a finding that relied on matter outside the pleadings without converting the motion to one for summary judgment and affording Plaintiff an opportunity to take discovery and contest the finding. We accordingly vacate and remand so that Plaintiff may have such an opportunity.

Background

[I]n 1987, the Bank hired Plaintiff as an Assistant Vice President. As a fringe benefit of employment, it furnished him short-term and long-term disability insurance coverage issued by MetLife. For persons with "mental" disabilities, the long-term disability ("LTD") plan limits benefits to two years. For persons with "physical" disabilities, the plan provides benefits up to age 65.

In April 1994, Plaintiff became disabled as a result of depression. After receiving benefits under the Bank's short-term disability plan, he applied for LTD benefits. MetLife approved his claim retroactive to October 1994.

In August 1995, Plaintiff filed this lawsuit in the United States District Court for the Southern District of New York. His original complaint named only his employer, the Bank, as a defendant. The complaint alleged that the Bank discriminated against him on the basis of his mental disability in violation of Title I of the ADA by imposing a two-year limit on benefits for mental disabilities, while imposing no such limit for physical disabilities.

In October 1996, MetLife terminated Plaintiff's benefits pursuant to the two-year cap on coverage for mental disabilities. Plaintiff was at that time, and continues to be, unable to work.

In November 1996, Plaintiff amended his complaint to add MetLife as a defendant, and to assert that both MetLife and the Bank violated Title III of the ADA by virtue of the shorter duration of coverage provided for mental, than for physical, disabilities. The complaint also alleged that the shorter benefits limitation for mental disabilities constituted a "subterfuge to evade the purposes of the ADA" under Section 501(c) of Title V. Plaintiff sought a declaration that the Bank and MetLife were in violation of the ADA, and an injunction prohibiting MetLife "from continuing to provide long-term disability insurance in a manner that limits benefits for mental disorders to Leonard F."

In March 1997, the EEOC moved to intervene in Plaintiff's suit. In April 1997, the district court granted the motion, and in May, the EEOC filed its complaint-in-intervention, alleging principally that the LTD policy furnished by the Bank and issued by MetLife violated Title I of the ADA.

[T]he district court dismissed the claim against MetLife, [h]olding that MetLife is protected by the safe harbor provision of Section 501(c). The court reasoned that the safe harbor exempts insurance underwriters from the ADA's regulatory scope so long as their conduct complies with state law, and does not constitute a "subterfuge to evade the purposes of the [Act]." Applying this standard to MetLife's LTD policy in the instant dispute, the court first found that "[p]roviding a time limitation on benefits for persons with mental disorders while not doing so for persons with physical disorders is consistent with state insurance law." The court then found that MetLife's policy does not constitute a subterfuge to evade the purposes of the Act. The court noted that in *Public Employees Retirement Sys. v. Betts*, 492 U.S. 158 (1989), a case involving the Age Discrimination in Employment Act ("ADEA"), the Supreme Court had ruled that a benefit plan adopted before the Act was passed could not be a subterfuge to evade the purposes of the Act. Finding that Congress intended that the ADA's subterfuge clause have the same meaning as the analogous clause in the ADEA, the district court determined that MetLife's LTD policy could not be a subterfuge, as it existed in its present form before the ADA was enacted in 1990.

Plaintiff, having in the meantime settled his claims against the Bank, now appeals from the judgment in favor of MetLife.

Discussion

Plaintiff advances two main arguments. (1) He contends that Congress, in enacting the ADA, intended to reject the *Betts* interpretation of "subterfuge," and included the subterfuge clause in Section 501(c) to require that insurance underwriters base their decisions with respect to disabled individuals on "sound actuarial principles." (2) He contends that the district court improperly reached beyond the pleadings to determine that (i) MetLife's LTD policy is consistent with state law, and (ii) the policy existed in its present form prior to the ADA's enactment.

[S]ection 501(c) of Title V mandates in relevant part that Titles I through III of the ADA shall not prevent insurers from "underwriting risks, classifying risks, or administering such risks that are based on or not inconsistent with State law," provided that this safe harbor "shall not be used as a subterfuge to evade the purposes of [Titles] I and III of [the Act]." 42 U.S.C. § 12201(c). The plain meaning of Section 501(c) is that insurers are exempt from regulation under the ADA so long as (i) their actions conform to state law, and (ii) they do not use the exemption as a "subterfuge to evade the purposes of [the Act]."

In *United Air Lines, Inc. v. McMann*, 434 U.S. 192 (1977), and then in *Betts*, the Supreme Court construed an analogous subterfuge clause in Section 4(f)(2) of the ADEA. This provision, before Congress amended it in 1990, exempted any *bona fide* employee benefit plan from the ADEA's general prohibition of age discrimination so long as the plan was not a " 'subterfuge to evade the purposes of [the Act]' " (and met certain other criteria). *McMann*, 434 U.S. at 195–96 (quoting 29 U.S.C. § 623(f)(2) (1988) (amended 1990)); *Betts*, 492 U.S. at 165–66 (same).

The plaintiff in *McMann* challenged a retirement income plan established 26 years prior to the passage of the ADEA that called for compulsory retirement at age 60. The plaintiff argued, and the Fourth Circuit held, that the age-60 retirement provision was a "subterfuge to evade the purposes of the [ADEA]" unless the employer could show that this provision had some other economic or business purpose.

In *Betts*, the plaintiff challenged a plan that rendered employees ineligible for disability retirement benefits once they reached age 60. She maintained that, because her employer had not shown that the plan's age-based limitation was justified by age-related cost considerations, the plan constituted a "subterfuge to evade the purposes of the ADEA." In support of her claim, the plaintiff cited Equal Employment Opportunity Commission (EEOC) interpretive regulations and legislative history consonant with her construction of the subterfuge clause. See id. The Sixth Circuit embraced her interpretation of the clause and ruled in her favor.

In both cases, the Supreme Court rejected the plaintiffs' arguments and reversed the courts of appeals. Construing the term "subterfuge" to have its ordinary meaning, including the necessary element of intent to evade, the Court held in *McMann*, and reaffirmed in *Betts*, that a benefit plan adopted prior to enactment of the ADEA could not be a "subterfuge to evade the purposes of the Act." This conclusion followed because a plan adopted prior to the Act could not have been conceived in order to circumvent it.

The *Betts* Court, beyond reaffirming the Court's ruling in *McMann*, also held invalid the EEOC regulations construing the ADEA's subterfuge clause to require actuarial justification for age-based differences in plan benefits. Noting that no deference is due to agency interpretations at odds with the statutory text, the *Betts* Court found that the EEOC regulations "cannot be squared with the plain language of the statute." For the same reason, the *Betts* Court was unswayed by the plaintiff's appeal to the ADEA's legislative history. Plaintiff argued that this history, like the regulations, supported her view that the subterfuge clause should be interpreted to require actuarial justification for age-based differences; the Court reasoned that if Congress had intended to require such justification, it would have said so in the statutory text.

In construing the subterfuge clause in Section 501(c) of the ADA, all three of our sister circuits that have adjudicated the issue have adopted *Betts*'s interpretation of the analogous subterfuge clause in the ADEA. See *Ford v. Schering-Plough Corp.*, 145 F.3d 601, 611 (3d Cir.1998); *Krauel v. Iowa Methodist Med. Ctr.*, 95 F.3d 674, 678–79 (8th Cir.1996); *Modderno v. King*, 82 F.3d 1059, 1064–65 (D.C.Cir.1996). The D.C. Circuit in *Modderno* explained:

> *Betts* had been decided . . . before Congress adopted the "subterfuge" language of § 501(c) of the ADA. Thus when Congress chose the term "subterfuge" for the insurance safe-harbor of the ADA, it was on full alert as to what the Court understood the word to mean and possessed (obviously) a full grasp of the linguistic devices available to avoid that meaning.

82 F.3d at 1065; see also *Ford*, 145 F.3d at 611 ("Congress enacted section 501(c) of the ADA in 1990, . . . while the Supreme Court decided *Betts* in 1989. Congress therefore is presumed to have adopted the Supreme Court's interpretation of 'subterfuge' in the ADEA context when Congress enacted the ADA."); *Krauel*, 95 F.3d at 679 ("Had

Congress intended to reject the Betts interpretation of subterfuge when it enacted the ADA, it could have done so expressly by incorporating language for that purpose into the bill that Congress voted on and the President signed.").

We find the reasoning of our sister circuits persuasive. Accordingly, we hold that the subterfuge clause in Section 501(c) of the ADA should be construed, as in *Betts*, to require an intent to evade, making it inapplicable to a plan formulated prior to the passage of the Act regardless whether the plan relies on sound actuarial principles. When "judicial interpretations have settled the meaning of an existing statutory provision, repetition of the same language in a new statute indicates, as a general matter, the intent to incorporate its . . . judicial interpretations as well." Furthermore, we believe that applying *Betts*'s interpretation of a "subterfuge to evade the purposes of the Act" to Section 501(c) of the ADA is particularly appropriate because the *Betts* Court gave the clause its "ordinary meaning."

Plaintiff, urging us not to rely on Congress's apparent adoption of the *Betts* interpretation or on the ordinary meaning of the subterfuge clause, maintains that we should instead construe the clause to require that underwriters base their decisions with respect to disabled individuals on "sound actuarial principles." In support of this contention, Plaintiff points to portions of the ADA's legislative history suggesting that Congress intended to reject the *Betts* interpretation, and that it included the subterfuge clause in Section 501(c) so as to prohibit underwriters from treating disabled persons differently except where actuarially justified.[1] That legislative history, Plaintiff contends, finds corroboration in interpretive guidelines promulgated by the Department of Justice (DOJ) and the EEOC, which endorse a similar construction of the subterfuge clause.[2]

We are not persuaded by Plaintiff's argument, principally because we believe that his interpretation of the subterfuge clause in Section 501(c) "cannot be squared with the plain language of the statute." *Betts*. Neither the subterfuge clause nor the safe harbor provision to which it belongs makes reference to "sound actuarial principles." See 42 U.S.C. 12201(c). Furthermore, the term "subterfuge" has a well-understood meaning that does not lend support to Plaintiff's construction. Merriam

---

[1] In support of his contention that Congress intended to reject the *Betts* definition, Plaintiff cites several statements from the floor debates concerning the ADA's adoption. See, *e.g.*, 136 Cong.Rec. S9697 (daily ed. July 12, 1990) (statement of Sen. Kennedy); 136 Cong.Rec. H4624 (daily ed. July 12, 1990) (statement of Rep. Edwards). He also cites Committee Reports indicating that Congress intended to prohibit use of the safe harbor provision as a subterfuge "regardless of the date the insurance plan or employer benefit plan was adopted." S.Rep.No.101–116, at 85 (1989); see also H.R.Rep.No.101–485, pt. 2, at 137 (1990). In support of his contention that Congress included the subterfuge clause in Section 501(c) so as to require underwriters to base their decisions on "sound actuarial principles," Plaintiff cites several Committee Reports. See, *e.g.*, S.Rep.No.101–116, at 85; H.R.Rep.No.101–485, pt. 3., at 71 (1990).

[2] In particular, Plaintiff cites DOJ's Preamble to Regulation on Nondiscrimination on the Basis of Disability by Public Accommodations and in Commercial Facilities (July 26, 1991), reprinted at 28 C.F.R. Ch. 1, pt. 36, App.B, at 629 (1997); DOJ's Americans with Disabilities Act Title III Technical Assistance Manual § III–3.11000 at 18 (1992); and the EEOC's Interim Enforcement Guidance on the Application of the Americans with Disabilities Act of 1990 to Disability–Based Distinctions in Employer Provided Health Insurance 11 (1993).

Webster's New Third International Dictionary defines a "subterfuge" as "a deception by artifice or a stratagem to conceal, escape, avoid or evade." The Supreme Court in *McMann* and *Betts* observed that the term refers in ordinary parlance to "a scheme, plan, stratagem, or artifice of evasion." In the context of the subterfuge clause of Section 501(c) of the ADA, neither the dictionary definition nor the Supreme Court's reasonably suggests that absence of actuarial justification for differential insurance benefits is sufficient to demonstrate a "subterfuge" to evade the purposes of an Act, at least where the insurance policy was adopted prior to the Act's passage.

Assuming arguendo that we were to find that the legislative history supported Plaintiff's view, we would decline to accord it primacy over incompatible language in the Act.[4] For a similar reason, we do not defer to the DOJ and EEOC interpretive guidelines. While an agency's reasonable interpretation of an ambiguous provision in a statute that it administers is entitled to judicial deference, see *Chevron, U.S.A., Inc. v. Natural Resources Defense Council, Inc.*, 467 U.S. 837, 843–44 (1984), "no deference is due to agency interpretations at odds with the plain language of the statute itself." *Betts*.

For the foregoing reasons, we agree with the district court that, if MetLife's LTD policy is consistent with state law and was adopted prior to the passage of the ADA, it is exempt from regulation under the Act pursuant to the safe harbor provision of Section 501(c), regardless whether it was based on actuarial experience.

[P]laintiff contends that, even if we reject his interpretation of the subterfuge clause in Section 501(c), we should nonetheless reverse the district court's judgment because the court improperly reached beyond the pleadings to make adverse factual determinations in dismissing his complaint under Fed.R.Civ.P. 12(b)(6). Specifically, he maintains that the court improperly found that MetLife's policy [w]as adopted prior to the enactment of the ADA in 1990.

[W]e agree with Plaintiff that the court's finding with respect to MetLife's prior adoption of the policy was improper in the context of a

---

[4] In any event, we believe that this legislative history is far less conclusive than Plaintiff contends, and provides only equivocal support for his reading of Section 501(c). For example, one of the key Committee Reports on which Plaintiff relies, S.Rep.No.101–116 (1989), states in part that

the Committee added Section 501(c) to make it clear that this legislation will not disrupt the current nature of insurance underwriting or the current regulatory structure for self-insured employers or of the insurance industry in sales, underwriting, pricing, administrative and other services, claims and similar insurance activities based on classification of risks as regulated by the States.

Id. at 84. We are not the first federal court of appeals to observe that construing Section 501(c) to require insurers to base their underwriting decisions on "sound actuarial principles" in all cases involving persons with disabilities would dramatically expand the federal role in the regulation of insurance and thereby "disrupt . . . the current regulatory structure . . . of the insurance industry." See, *e.g.*, *Doe v. Mutual of Omaha*, 179 F.3d 557, 564 (7th Cir.1999) (Posner, C.J.) ("It is one thing to say that an insurance company may not refuse to deal with disabled persons; the prohibition of such refusals can probably be administered with relatively little interference with state insurance regulation. . . . It is another thing to require federal courts to determine whether limitations on coverage are actuarially sound. . . . ") (internal citations omitted); *Ford*, 145 F.3d at 612 (construing Section 501(c) to mandate underwriting based on sound actuarial principles would "requir[e] insurers to justify their coverage plans in [federal] court after a mere allegation by a plaintiff," thereby effecting "a seismic shift in the insurance business").

motion to dismiss for failure to state a claim under Rule 12(b)(6). [T]he complaint included no information as to the date that MetLife designed the policy. MetLife's moving papers asserted that the policy predated the Act. Before the district court could credit this assertion and rule on that basis, it was required to convert Defendant's Rule 12(b)(6) motion into a motion for summary judgment and give Plaintiff an opportunity to contest the asserted fact.

We accordingly vacate the judgment and remand the case so that Plaintiff may have an opportunity, with appropriate discovery, to contest whether the policy was adopted prior to the enactment of the ADA[.]

Seff v. Broward County, Fla.

United States Court of Appeal for the Eleventh Circuit, 2012.
691 F.3d 1221.

■ BLACK, CIRCUIT JUDGE:

Appellant Bradley Seff filed this class action lawsuit, alleging that Appellee Broward County's (Broward's) employee wellness program violated the Americans with Disabilities Act of 1990 (ADA), 42 U.S.C. § 12101 *et seq*. The district court granted Broward's motion for summary judgment, finding the employee wellness program fell within the ADA's safe harbor provision for insurance plans. We affirm.

[B]roward offers its employees a group health insurance plan. In 2009, employees enrolling in Broward's group plan became eligible to participate in a new employee wellness program sponsored by Broward's group health insurer, Coventry Healthcare (formerly known as VISTA).

The employee wellness program consisted of two components: a biometric screening, which entailed a "finger stick for glucose and cholesterol," and an "online Health Risk Assessment questionnaire." Coventry Healthcare used information gathered from the screening and questionnaire to identify Broward employees who had one of five disease states: asthma, hypertension, diabetes, congestive heart failure, or kidney disease. Employees suffering from any of the five disease states received the opportunity to participate in a disease management coaching program, after which they became eligible to receive co-pay waivers for certain medications.

Participation in the employee wellness program was not a condition for enrollment in Broward's group health plan. To increase participation in the employee wellness program, however, Broward imposed a $20 charge beginning in April 2010 on each biweekly paycheck issued to employees who enrolled in the group health insurance plan but refused to participate in the employee wellness program. Broward suspended the charges on January 1, 2011.

Seff, a former Broward employee who incurred the $20 charges on his paychecks from June 2010 until January 1, 2011, filed this class action, alleging that the employee wellness program's biometric screening and online Health Risk Assessment questionnaire violated the ADA's prohibition on non-voluntary medical examinations and disability-related inquiries. On the parties' cross-motions for summary judgment, the district court granted Broward's motion, finding that the ADA's safe harbor provision for insurance plans exempted the employee wellness program from any potentially relevant ADA prohibitions. Because it found that the employee wellness program fell within the ADA's safe harbor provision, the district court declined to address whether the program imposed non-voluntary examinations or inquiries that would have otherwise been prohibited under the ADA.

[U]nder the ADA, a "covered entity" is prohibited from "requir[ing] a medical examination" and "mak[ing] inquiries of an employee as to whether such employee is an individual with a disability or as to the nature or severity of the disability, unless such examination or inquiry is shown to be job-related and consistent with business necessity." 42 U.S.C. § 12112(d)(4)(A).

The ADA, however, contains a safe harbor provision that exempts certain insurance plans from the ADA's general prohibitions, including the prohibition on "required" medical examinations and disability-related inquiries. 42 U.S.C. § 12201(c)(2). The safe harbor provision states that the ADA "shall not be construed" as prohibiting a covered entity "from establishing, sponsoring, observing or administering the terms of a bona fide benefit plan that are based on underwriting risks, classifying risks, or administering such risks that are based on or not inconsistent with State law." *Id.*

The district court granted summary judgment in Broward's favor based on its conclusion that the employee wellness program fell within the ADA's safe harbor provision. In reaching its conclusion, the district court found that the employee wellness program qualified as a "term[ ] of a bona fide benefit plan" within the meaning of the safe harbor provision because the employee wellness program constituted a "term" of Broward's group health plan. Seff's only argument on appeal is that the district court improperly ignored the deposition testimony of Lisa Morrison, which he claims gave rise to a dispute of material fact regarding the employee wellness program's status as a "term[ ] of a bona fide benefit plan" under the safe harbor provision.

Morrison, who was Broward's corporate representative and acting benefits manager, testified that the employee wellness program was not a term of Broward's benefit plan and that the employee wellness program was not a term contained in Broward's health and pharmacy plans. Her testimony is subject to two interpretations. First, the testimony may be read as expressing Morrison's opinion that the employee wellness program was not a "term[ ] of a bona fide benefit plan" within the meaning of the ADA's safe harbor provision. Understood this way, the testimony would constitute a conclusion of law.

Second, Morrison's testimony may be understood as asserting that the physical plan documents for Broward's group health plan do not contain a written term providing for the employee wellness program. This alternative reading construes Morrison's testimony as addressing an issue of fact regarding the contents of Broward's plan documents. Read this way, Seff's argument would nonetheless fail because he presents no substantive argument that the issue of whether the employee wellness program was a written term contained within the physical plan documents for Broward's group health plan is material to the determination of the safe harbor provision's applicability. The parties do not cite, nor are we independently aware of, any authority suggesting that an employee wellness program must be explicitly identified in a benefit plan's written documents to qualify as a "term" of the benefit plan within the meaning of the ADA's safe harbor provision.

The record establishes that Coventry Healthcare sponsored the employee wellness program as part of the contract to provide Broward with a group health plan, the program was only available to group plan enrollees, and Broward presented the program as part of its group plan in at least two employee handouts. In light of these facts, the district court did not err in finding as a matter of law that the employee wellness program was a "term" of Broward's group health insurance plan, such that the employee wellness program fell within the ADA's safe harbor provision. We affirm the district court's grant of summary judgment.

NOTES ON INSURANCE AND THE ADA

1.   **The Access/Content Distinction.** Judge Posner's majority opinion in *Doe* employs an access/content distinction. As in the public services context (see Chapter Four, *supra*), application of the access/content distinction turns crucially on the level of generality at which the relevant good or service is defined. Judge Posner argues that the plaintiff was not denied access to Mutual of Omaha's goods and services, because the company offered to sell him the same insurance policy, on the same terms, as it would offer to people without AIDS. And under that contract, he contends, people *without* AIDS are not entitled to any service that is denied to people *with* AIDS. But, as in *Alexander v. Choate* (a principal case in Chapter Four), when the matter is considered at a higher level of generality, it certainly appears discriminatory: The company offers to cover all of the health needs of people without AIDS, but it will not cover all of the health needs of people with AIDS. Indeed, as Judge Evans explains in his dissent, the policy at issue might be understood to be discriminatory even when we consider the question at a low level of generality: When a person without AIDS gets pneumonia, the policy covers it, but when a person with AIDS gets pneumonia, the policy does not necessarily. Does Judge Posner have an adequate answer to that objection? Is the access/content aspect of the *Doe* opinion still good law after *PGA Tour v. Martin*? Note that the insurance policy at issue in *Doe*, with its lifetime cap, would now violate the ACA, 42 U.S.C. § 300gg-11. (The long-term disability policy at issue in *Leonard F.*, which merely replaces lost income, is not a health insurance policy for purposes of the ACA and therefore is not subject to its prohibition on lifetime caps.)

2.   **The Safe Harbor.** In *Doe*, Judge Posner rules for the insurance company without relying on the safe harbor provision. As his majority opinion notes, the company conceded that the safe harbor did not apply. The company presumably made the concession so that it could tee up the broader access/content argument that the Seventh Circuit adopted—an argument that will shield insurance companies from liability for plan terms in many cases. In *Leonard F.* and *Boots*, however, the courts reached the

safe harbor question. What, exactly, does the ADA's safe harbor provision cover?

By its terms, the safe harbor provision protects risk classification decisions that are "based on or not inconsistent with State law," so long as those decisions are not a "subterfuge to evade the purposes" of the ADA. 42 U.S.C. § 12201(c). To enter the safe harbor, then, an insurance company must comply with state-law prohibitions on "unfair discrimination," which generally requires an actuarial basis (though precisely how much is a matter of some dispute). But even if the risk classification complies with state law, the insurance company will still be liable if the classification is a "subterfuge." *Id.* What does "subterfuge" mean in this context? In *Doe*, Judge Posner suggests a subterfuge would exist if Mutual of Omaha "had adopted the AIDS caps to deter people who know they are HIV positive from buying the policies at all." In *Leonard F.*, Judge Leval reads the subterfuge proviso as reaching only those classifications that were adopted in an effort to evade the purposes of *the ADA* specifically. Under his interpretation, a risk classification that a company instituted prior to the adoption of the ADA necessarily could not be a subterfuge—because there was no ADA at the time. What do you find to be the best interpretation of the subterfuge provision, and why?

3. Employee Wellness Programs. Workplace wellness programs have become an increasingly popular tool among employers who seek to control their health care costs. See Jill R. Horwitz, Brenna D. Kelly & John E. DiNardo, *Wellness Incentives in the Workplace: Cost Savings Through Cost Shifting to Unhealthy Workers*, 32 Health Aff. 468, 468-469 (2013). These programs can take two general forms: (1) health-contingent wellness programs, which reward (or penalize) employees who satisfy (or fail to satisfy) specified health standards; and (2) participatory wellness programs, which incentivize employees to participate in health-promoting activities, whether through rewards or penalties (as in the program at issue in *Seff*) or through subsidizing those activities through discounted gym memberships and the like. Whether these programs in fact save health care costs is controversial. Compare Katherine Baicker, David Cutler & Zirui Song, *Workplace Wellness Programs Can Generate Savings*, 29 Health Aff. 304 (2010) (finding that medical costs fall by $3.27 for each dollar spent on wellness programs), with Horwitz *et al.*, *supra* (reviewing evidence suggesting that savings from health-contingent programs "may not, in fact, derive from health improvements" but rather may derive from "making workers with health risks pay more for their health care than workers without health risks do").

Despite the controversy, the Affordable Care Act loosens various pre-existing restrictions on workplace wellness programs. See 42 U.S.C. § 300gg-4(j); John E. McDonough, Inside National Health Reform 192-194 (2011). The Departments of Treasury, Labor, and Health and Human Services implemented these provisions of the ACA in a joint regulation. See 26 C.F.R. § 54.9802-1(f) (Treasury); 29 C.F.R. § 2590.702(f) (Labor); 45 C.F.R. § 146.121(f) (HHS). The regulation continues to impose significant restrictions on wellness programs. For *participatory* wellness programs, the regulation requires that any program must be "made available to all similarly situated individuals, regardless of health status." 45 C.F.R.

§ 146.121(f)(2). For *health-contingent* wellness programs, the regulation requires that:

- eligible individuals must have the opportunity to qualify for the program at least once per year;

- the monetary reward for compliance with the program is no more than 30% of the cost of health insurance (an amount that can rise to 50% to the extent that the program is designed to reduce or prevent tobacco use);

- the program is "reasonably designed to promote health or prevent disease"—which the regulations define to mean that the program, "based on all the relevant facts and circumstances," "has a reasonable chance of improving the health of, or preventing disease in, participating individuals, and it is not overly burdensome, is not a subterfuge for discriminating based on a health factor, and is not highly suspect in the method chosen to promote health or prevent disease"; and

- the full reward is "available to all similarly situated individuals."

45 C.F.R. § 146.121(f)(3), (4). To satisfy the last criterion, the program must "allow[ ] a reasonable alternative standard (or waiver of the otherwise applicable standard) for obtaining the reward" for those persons for whom "it is unreasonably difficult due to a medical condition" or "medically inadvisable" to satisfy or attempt to satisfy the program's normal criteria. *Id.* For those health-contingent programs that are "outcome-based" (which the regulation defines as those that "require[ ] an individual to attain or maintain a specific health outcome (such as not smoking or attaining certain results on biometric screenings) in order to obtain a reward," *id.* § 146.121(f)(1)(v)), the regulation additionally provides that "a reasonable alternative standard to qualify for the reward must be provided to any individual who does not meet the initial standard based on a measurement, test, or screening that is related to a health factor." *Id.* § 146.121(f)(4)(iii). These "reasonable alternative standard" requirements obviously have some—though not perfect—overlap with the ADA concept of reasonable accommodation.

Even if a wellness program complies with these ACA requirements, it still must comply with the ADA. See 45 C.F.R. § 146.121(h) ("Compliance with this section is not determinative of compliance with * * * any other State or Federal law, such as the Americans with Disabilities Act."). Wellness programs might raise a number of questions under the ADA.

One set of questions concerns the requirement of reasonable accommodation in employment, 42 U.S.C. § 12112(b)(5)(A). If an employer offers a wellness program that subsidizes membership in a gym, but the gym the employer has chosen does not provide accessible exercise equipment, must the employer accommodate an employee with a disability by providing her with a subsidized opportunity to participate in accessible fitness activities? If an employee has a disability that makes her incapable of participating in a participatory wellness program or of meeting the standards of a health-contingent wellness program, how must the employer modify the terms of the program to accommodate her disability? See 29 C.F.R. § 1635.8(b)(2)(iv) (EEOC GINA regulation) ("[I]f an employer offers a financial inducement for participation in disease management programs or other programs that promote healthy lifestyles and/or require individuals to meet particular health goals, the employer must make reasonable accommodations to the extent required by the ADA, that is, the employer must make 'modifications or adjustments that enable a covered entity's employee with a disability to enjoy equal benefits and privileges of employment as are enjoyed by its other similarly situated employees without disabilities' unless 'such covered entity can demonstrate that the accommodation would impose an undue hardship on the operation of its business.' ") (quoting 29 C.F.R. § 1630.2(o)(1)(iii); 29 C.F.R. § 1630.9(a)).

A second set of questions concerns the ADA's regulation of post-employment medical examinations and inquiries. Recall that Title I of the ADA prohibits employers from "requir[ing] a medical examination" or "mak[ing] inquiries of an employee as to whether such employee is an individual with a disability or as to the nature or severity of the disability, unless such examination or inquiry is shown to be job-related and consistent with business necessity." 42 U.S.C. § 12112(d)(4)(A). The statute makes an exception to this prohibition for "voluntary medical examinations, including voluntary medical histories, which are part of an employee health program available to employees at that work site." *Id.* § 12112(d)(4)(B). The EEOC has said that a "wellness program is 'voluntary' as long as an employer neither requires participation nor penalizes employees who do not participate." EEOC, Enforcement Guidance: Disability-Related Inquiries and Medical Examinations of Employees under the Americans With Disabilities Act (ADA), available at http://www.eeoc.gov/policy/docs/guidance-inquiries.html. But what constitutes a "penal[ty]?" When, as in *Seff*, employers give their workers a financial incentive to provide health information, are the employers' medical examinations and inquiries properly understood as "voluntary"? Does it matter how large is the financial incentive? Is $10 deducted from an employee's pay each week, as in *Seff*, sufficient to render the examinations involuntary?

A final set of questions concerns the application of the insurance safe harbor. *Seff* holds that the medical inquiries involved in Broward's wellness plan were entitled to the benefit of the safe harbor, because the wellness plan was provided as part of Broward's contract with its health insurance carrier, participation in the plan was limited to individuals who received health insurance from that carrier, and Broward's documents described the wellness program as part of its health insurance plan. Accordingly, the Eleventh Circuit concluded, the wellness plan was a "term[ ] of a bona fide benefit plan" protected by the safe harbor, 42 U.S.C. § 12201(c)(2). Is this a proper reading of the safe harbor? Does a wellness program like Broward's "underwrit[e] risks, classify[ ] risks, or administer[ ] * * * risks," *id.*? It certainly does not assign people to different coverage or rates based on their actuarial risks—the sort of conduct that the safe harbor seems designed to protect. Does *Seff* mean that an employer can avoid ADA review of a wellness program simply by declaring that program to be part of its health insurance benefits plan? Would the "subterfuge" limitation on the safe harbor limit that sort of evasive conduct?

E. REMEDIES

INTRODUCTORY NOTE

Title III of the ADA may be enforced in two ways. Any "person aggrieved" by a violation of the statute may file a suit for injunctive—but not monetary—relief. See 42 U.S.C. 12188(a) (incorporating procedures for enforcement of Title II of the Civil Rights Act of 1964, 42 U.S.C. § 2000a–3(a), by reference). In cases in which the defendant "is engaged in a pattern or practice of discrimination" in violation of Title III, or in which the claimed discrimination "raises an issue of general public importance," the Attorney General may file an enforcement suit as well. Id. § 12188(b)(1)(B). Unlike a private party, the Attorney General may seek compensatory "monetary damages to persons aggrieved" and civil penalties not exceeding $50,000 for the first violation and $100,000 for each subsequent violation, as well as injunctive relief. Id. § 12188(b)(2). Because the Department of Justice has limited resources with which to enforce Title III, private attorneys account for the bulk of enforcement. See generally Samuel R. Bagenstos, *The Perversity of Limited Civil Rights Remedies: The Case of "Abusive" ADA Litigation*, 54 UCLA L. Rev. 1 (2006). Under the Fair Housing Act, by contrast, private plaintiffs can recover actual and punitive damages, as well as obtaining injunctive relief. See 42 U.S.C. § 3613(c). For an argument that Congress should apply the Fair Housing Act scheme to Title III of the ADA as well, see Ruth Colker, *ADA Title III: A Fragile Compromise*, 21 Berkeley J. Emp. & Lab. L. 377 (2000).

1. STANDING AND PLEADING REQUIREMENTS

Naiman v. New York Univ.

United States District Court for the Southern District of New York, 1997.
1997 WL 249970, 6 A.D. Cases 1345, 10 NDLR P 39.

■ MCKENNA, D.J.

Plaintiff Alec Naiman, who is deaf, was a patient at New York University Medical Center ("NYUMC"), a medical facility operated by defendant New York University ("NYU"), on four occasions between February 9, 1993, and October 18, 1995. Naiman alleges that NYU effectively excluded him from its medical facility because it failed to provide him sufficient sign language interpreting services during his visits. He seeks monetary and injunctive relief under the Americans with Disabilities Act ("ADA"), 42 U.S.C. § 12182, the Rehabilitation Act ("RA") of 1973, as amended, 29 U.S.C. § 794, and state law. [N]YU moves to dismiss Naiman's First Amended Complaint pursuant to Rule 12(b)(6) of the Federal Rules of Civil Procedure on the grounds that [N]aiman does not have standing to seek injunctive relief[.]

[O]n February 9, 1993, and again on November 16, 1993, Naiman was seen at NYUMC for "an excruciatingly painful kidney stone attack." (Compl.¶¶ 10–11.) Despite Naiman's requests, NYUMC failed to provide Naiman with a qualified sign language interpreter. On the November 16, 1993, visit, after Naiman had been at NYUMC most of the day, NYUMC eventually presented a person with minimal ability to communicate in basic sign. This person was, in large part, unable to understand Naiman. (Compl.¶¶ 12–13.) On October 3, 1995, when Naiman was again a patient, NYUMC failed to provide him with any sign language interpreting services. During the fourth visit, on October 18, 1995, NYUMC failed to provide such services "in a timely manner." (Compl.¶¶ 18–19.)

Naiman claims that he requires a sign language interpreter to "meaningfully participate[ ] in his own medical care." (Compl.¶ 12.) Naiman also claims that NYUMC's failure to provide a qualified interpreter denied him the "effective communication" necessary to allow him to communicate with NYUMC doctors and staff. (Compl.¶ 14.) Naiman allegedly continues to suffer as a result of never knowing whether NYUMC, when rendering medical services to him, will be capable of effectively communicating with him.

[T]o establish that he has standing, Naiman bears the burden to establish three elements:

> First, the plaintiff must have suffered an "injury in fact"—an invasion of a legally protected interest which is (a) concrete and particularized, and (b) "actual or imminent, not 'conjectural' or 'hypothetical.' Second, there must be a causal connection between the injury and the conduct complained of. Third, it must be 'likely,' as opposed to merely 'speculative,' that the injury will be 'redressed by a favorable decision.' "

Lujan v. Defenders of Wildlife, 504 U.S. 555, 560–61 (1992). Regarding the "injury in fact" requirement, which is the only element of standing at issue on NYU's motion, "[p]ast exposure to illegal conduct does not in itself show a present case or controversy regarding injunctive relief . . . if unaccompanied by any continuing, present adverse effects." *City of Los Angeles v. Lyons*, 461 U.S. 95, 102 (1983) (quoting *O'Shea v. Littleton*, 414 U.S. 488, 495–96 (1974)). Thus, in order for Naiman to have standing to seek injunctive relief against NYU, he must allege facts sufficient to demonstrate a "real or immediate threat that [he] will be wronged again." *Id.* at 111.

NYU argues that the four incidents alleged in the complaint, which NYU describes as "intermittent visits to the emergency room over a period of years," are insufficient to demonstrate a real or immediate threat that Naiman will be wronged again. NYU contends that Naiman has failed to set forth sufficient facts in his complaint to show that "the bouts of pain he has suffered are very likely to be repeated and to necessitate emergency attention at NYU Medical Center."

The instant case is distinguishable from the cases NYU cites in favor of dismissal. In the majority of those cases there was but a single allegedly discriminatory incident, and thus the plaintiffs failed to show that they were likely to be harmed again. See *Lyons*, 461 U.S. at 111–12 (plaintiff did not have standing to seek injunctive relief against city for allegedly illegal choke-hold performed by arresting officer); *O'Brien v. Werner Bus Lines, Inc.*, 1996 WL 82484 (E.D.Pa.1996) (blind plaintiff did not have standing to seek injunctive relief against bus company that refused to allow plaintiff's guide dog onto bus, where company, among other things, issued public apology, provided plaintiff with free bus tickets, and directed its bus drivers to admit guide dogs onto buses); *Atakpa v. Perimeter Ob-Gyn Assoc., P.C.*, 912 F.Supp. 1566 (N.D.Ga.1994) (pregnant plaintiff did not have standing to seek injunctive relief against clinic that required HIV screening, where plaintiff sought treatment elsewhere); *Hoepfl v. Barlow*, 906 F.Supp. 317 (E.D.Va.1995) (prospective surgical patient with AIDS did not have standing to seek injunctive relief against doctor who said that he would not touch AIDS patient with ten-foot pole, where doctor later said he would conduct the surgery and plaintiff received surgery from different doctor); *Aikins v. St. Helena Hosp.*, 843 F.Supp. 1329 (N.D.Cal.1994) (deaf plaintiff did not have standing to seek injunctive relief against hospital, which failed to provide effective communication to plaintiff, who arrived in emergency room because of husband's fatal cardiac arrest); *Farmland Dairies v. McGuire*, 789 F.Supp. 1243, 1254 (S.D.N.Y.1992) (plaintiffs failed to show that Commissioner would again issue orders, which court declared unconstitutional).

[N]aiman's allegation of four visits to NYUMC in which NYUMC failed to provide him with effective communication are sufficient, for pleading purposes, to demonstrate that, if Naiman were to go to NYUMC again, it would again fail to provide him with effective communication. However, this is not enough to satisfy Naiman's burden to demonstrate standing to seek injunctive relief. Naiman must also show a "real or immediate threat" that he will require the services of NYUMC in the future.[4] Although the Court concludes that Naiman's First Amended Complaint fails to allege facts sufficient to demonstrate standing to seek injunctive relief against NYU, the Court grants Naiman leave to amend the complaint within thirty days of the date of this Memorandum and Order to satisfy his pleading burden.

Chapman v. Pier 1 Imports

United States Court of Appeals for the Ninth Circuit, *en banc*, 2011.
631 F.3d 939.

■ WARDLAW, CIRCUIT JUDGE:

Byron Chapman is unable to walk unassisted, and he requires the use of a motorized wheelchair when traveling in public. In July 2004, Chapman sued a Pier 1 Imports store ("Pier One" or "Store") in Vacaville, California, alleging that some of the Store's architectural features denied him full and equal enjoyment of the premises in violation of the Americans with Disabilities Act ("ADA"). Chapman requested an injunction requiring the Store to remove the barriers he personally encountered during his visits to the Store that deprived him of full and equal enjoyment because of his wheelchair confinement, as

---

[4] Although not exhaustive nor necessarily dispositive, such allegations (if they can be made on the facts) might include whether Naiman suffers from a recurring medical condition and the reasons why NYUMC, as opposed to some other hospital, is the facility which Naiman would go to in an emergency.

well as barriers that he did not personally encounter but that might impede his access during future visits due to his disability. Chapman also requested monetary damages pursuant to provisions of California law. During discovery, Chapman testified that he was not deterred by the alleged ADA violations; rather, Chapman freely acknowledged that he actually intends to return to the Store, which is located near his home and offers products he finds desirable.

Chapman's complaint provided a list of the architectural barriers existing at the Store, "to the extent known" to him, some of which he alleged that he had personally encountered. More than one year after the complaint was filed, and two months before the close of discovery, Chapman submitted an additional report compiled by his expert, Joe Card. The Card Report identified thirty alleged ADA and CBC violations at the Store, some of which were listed in the complaint, others of which were new. The parties cross-moved for summary judgment. Chapman's motion papers sought judgment as to only eleven of the alleged barriers, some of which had been listed in his complaint and some of which were identified only in the Card Report. The Store moved for summary judgment on the grounds that Chapman lacks standing and that the asserted barriers were not barriers as a matter of law or had been remedied.

The district court granted Pier One's motion as to numerous challenged barriers, concluding either that Chapman had failed to cite any applicable ADA regulation or that the barrier Chapman identified no longer existed. The court considered each of Chapman's eleven claims, including some that were raised only in the Card Report, finding that Chapman disclosed the violations in sufficient time to permit Pier One to address them in the context of its summary judgment motion. The court granted summary judgment to Chapman as to seven of the barriers listed solely in the Card Report. The parties later jointly stipulated to entry of final judgment, subject to Pier One's reservation of the right to appeal the grant of summary judgment to Chapman and the denial of its motion to strike the Card Report.

Pier One timely appealed, challenging, among other things, the district court's conclusion that Chapman had standing to seek an injunction as to barriers he did not personally encounter. A three-judge panel of our court agreed with Pier One, concluding that Chapman lacked Article III standing as to barriers he had not personally encountered, because they did not deter him from returning to the Store. We vacated the panel's decision after a majority of our court's non-recused active judges voted to rehear the appeal *en banc* to examine the Article III standing doctrine in the context of actions for injunctive relief under the ADA.

We now clarify that when an ADA plaintiff has suffered an injury-in-fact by encountering a barrier that deprives him of full and equal enjoyment of the facility due to his particular disability, he has standing to sue for injunctive relief as to that barrier and other barriers related to his disability, even if he is not deterred from returning to the public accommodation at issue. First, we hold that an ADA plaintiff can establish standing to sue for injunctive relief either by demonstrating deterrence, or by demonstrating injury-in-fact coupled with an intent to return to a noncompliant facility. Second, we hold that an ADA plaintiff who establishes standing as to encountered barriers may also sue for injunctive relief as to unencountered barriers related to his disability. Here, however, Chapman has failed to allege and prove the required elements of Article III standing to support his claim for injunctive relief under the ADA. Specifically, he has not alleged or proven that he personally suffered discrimination as defined by the ADA as to encountered barriers on account of his disability. We therefore vacate the district court's grant of summary judgment, and remand with instructions to dismiss Chapman's ADA claim for lack of jurisdiction and for further proceedings consistent with this opinion.

I.

The ADA was enacted "to provide clear, strong, consistent, enforceable standards addressing discrimination against individuals with disabilities." 42 U.S.C. § 12101(b)(2). Its passage was premised on Congress's finding that discrimination against the disabled is "most often the product, not of invidious animus, but rather of thoughtlessness and indifference," of "benign neglect," and of "apathetic attitudes rather than affirmative animus." *Alexander v. Choate*, 469 U.S. 287, 295–96 (1985). The concept of "discrimination" under the ADA does not extend only to obviously exclusionary conduct—such as a sign stating that persons with disabilities are unwelcome or an obstacle course leading to a store's entrance. Rather, the ADA proscribes more subtle forms of discrimination—such as difficult-to-navigate restrooms and hard-to-open doors—that interfere with disabled individuals' "full and equal enjoyment" of places of public accommodation. 42 U.S.C. § 12182(a).

As defined by the ADA, unlawful "discrimination" occurs when features of an accommodation

> subject an individual or class of individuals on the basis of a disability or disabilities of such individual or class, directly, or through contractual, licensing, or other arrangements, to a denial of the opportunity of the individual or class to participate in or benefit from the goods, services, facilities, privileges, advantages, or accommodations of an entity.

42 U.S.C. § 12182(b)(1)(A)(i). In the context of existing facilities, discrimination includes "a failure to remove architectural barriers . . . where such removal is readily achievable." *Id.* § 12182(b)(2)(A)(iv). In the case of newly constructed facilities, compliance with the ADA's antidiscrimination mandate requires that facilities be "readily accessible to and usable by individuals with disabilities." *Id.* § 12183(a)(1).

Whether a facility is "readily accessible" is defined, in part, by the ADA Accessibility Guidelines ("ADAAG"). *See* 28 C.F.R. § 36.406(a); 28 C.F.R. pt. 36, app. A. Promulgated by the Attorney General to "carry out the provisions" of the ADA, 42 U.S.C. § 12186(b), these guidelines "lay out the technical structural requirements of places of public accommodation." *Fortyune v. Am. Multi-Cinema, Inc.*, 364 F.3d 1075, 1080–81 (9th Cir.2004). The ADAAG provides the objective contours of the standard that architectural features must not impede disabled individuals' full and equal enjoyment of accommodations. We have held that "obedience to the spirit of the ADA" does not excuse noncompliance with the ADAAG's requirements. The ADAAG's requirements are as precise as they are thorough, and the difference between compliance and noncompliance with the standard of full and equal enjoyment established by the ADA is often a matter of inches. *E.g.,* ADAAG § 4.16.4 (requiring grab bar behind water closets to be at least thirty-six inches long); *id.* § 4.19.6 ("Mirrors shall be mounted with the bottom edge of the reflecting surface no higher than 40 in (1015 mm) above the finish floor . . . .").

Though its purpose is "sweeping," PGA Tour, and its mandate "comprehensive," 42 U.S.C. § 12101(b)(1), the ADA's reach is not unlimited. Rather, as with other civil rights statutes, to invoke the jurisdiction of the federal courts, a disabled individual claiming discrimination must satisfy the case or controversy requirement of Article III by demonstrating his standing to sue at each stage of the litigation. *See* U.S. Const. art. III, § 2; *Lujan v. Defenders of Wildlife,* 504 U.S. 555, 560 (1992); *Fortyune,* 364 F.3d at 1081 (citing *City of Los Angeles v. Lyons,* 461 U.S. 95, 101 (1983)). As the Supreme Court has stated, "It goes without saying that those who seek to invoke the jurisdiction of the federal courts must satisfy the threshold requirements imposed by Article III of the Constitution by alleging an actual case or controversy." *Lyons,* 461 U.S. at 101. Given these principles, we are also mindful that the "Supreme Court has instructed us to take a broad view of constitutional standing in civil rights cases, especially where, as under the ADA, private enforcement suits 'are the primary method of obtaining compliance with the Act.'" *Doran v. 7-Eleven, Inc.,* 524 F.3d 1034, 1039 (9th Cir.2008) (quoting *Trafficante v. Metro. Life Ins. Co.,* 409 U.S. 205, 209 (1972)).

II.

Under the oft-repeated standing formulation, Chapman must demonstrate that he has suffered an injury-in-fact, that the injury is traceable to the Store's actions, and that the injury can be redressed by a favorable decision. In addition, to establish standing to pursue injunctive relief, which is the only relief available to private plaintiffs under the ADA, he must demonstrate a "real and immediate threat of repeated injury" in the future. As the three-judge panel observed, the causation and redressability elements of standing are not at issue in this appeal. Therefore, our standing inquiry focuses on the legal standards governing whether Chapman has suffered an injury-in-fact and whether he has demonstrated a likelihood of future injury sufficient to support injunctive relief. The original panel concluded that Chapman did not suffer an injury-in-fact as to unencountered accessibility barriers because the barriers he did encounter did not deter him from returning to the Store. This conclusion was a misapplication of the deterrent effect doctrine and reflected a misapprehension of its relationship to fundamental standing principles.

A.

[U]nder the ADA, when a disabled person encounters an accessibility barrier violating its provisions, it is not necessary for standing purposes that the barrier completely preclude the plaintiff from entering or from using a facility in any way. *See Doran,* 524 F.3d at 1041 n.4 (stating that the ADA "does not limit its antidiscrimination mandate to barriers that completely prohibit access"). Rather, the barrier need only interfere with the plaintiff's "full and equal enjoyment" of the facility. 42 U.S.C. § 12182(a). As we stated in *Doran,*

> Once a disabled individual has encountered or become aware of alleged ADA violations that deter his patronage of or otherwise interfere with his access to a place of public accommodation, he has already suffered an injury in fact traceable to the defendant's conduct and capable of being redressed by the courts, and so he possesses standing under Article III . . . .

Doran, 524 F.3d at 1042 n.5.

Of course, a "barrier" will only amount to such interference if it affects the plaintiff's full and equal enjoyment of the facility on account of his particular disability. Because the ADAAG establishes the technical standards required for "full and equal enjoyment," if a barrier violating these standards relates to a plaintiff's disability, it will impair the plaintiff's full and equal access, which constitutes "discrimination" under the ADA. That discrimination satisfies the "injury-in-fact" element of *Lujan.* As we have held, once a disabled plaintiff has encountered a barrier violating the ADA, "that plaintiff will have a 'personal stake in the outcome of the controversy' so long as his or her suit is limited to barriers related to that person's particular disability."[4] *Id.* at 1044.

Following this principle, the original three-judge panel recognized that Chapman's initial encounter with accessibility barriers at the Store constituted an injury-in-fact. The now withdrawn panel opinion stated, "It is clear that Chapman had standing to sue Pier 1 Imports for not complying with the ADA with respect to the . . . barriers he claimed to have encountered." Although encounters with the noncompliant barriers related to one's disability are sufficient to demonstrate an injury-in-fact for standing purposes, a plaintiff seeking injunctive relief must additionally demonstrate "a sufficient likelihood that he will again be wronged in a similar way." *Lyons.* That is, he must establish a "real and immediate threat of repeated injury." Id. For instance, in *Fortyune,* a quadriplegic plaintiff sued to enjoin a movie theater's ongoing seating policy that failed to ensure that wheelchair-bound patrons could sit next to their companions or aides during sold-out shows.

Fortyune required both a wheelchair and an aide to attend movies at the theater. Thus, to have full and equal access to the movie theater he needed to have available a "companion seat" for his aide (in his case, his wife) next to which he could situate his wheelchair. He suffered an injury-in-fact when he and his wife attempted to see an AMC movie, but were prevented from doing so, because the companion seats were

---

[4] The concurrence fails to recognize that a plaintiff's standing to claim an ADA violation is necessarily linked to the nature of his disability. We recognize that an encountered barrier must interfere with the particular plaintiff's full and equal enjoyment of the facility, making his use of the facility more difficult than a nondisabled individual's, to constitute an injury-in-fact, and that he is required to allege and prove that injury. Thus, a blind person would have standing to assert an ADA violation where a newly constructed multi-story facility has elevators lacking floor buttons in Braille, while Chapman, who we assume can see and press the floor buttons, would not. *See, e.g.,* ADAAG § 4.10.12(2) (requiring that "[a]ll control buttons shall be designated by Braille and by raised standard alphabet characters for letters, arabic characters for numerals, or standard symbols"). Where the barrier is related to the particular plaintiff's disability, however, an encounter with the barrier necessarily injures the plaintiff by depriving him of full and equal enjoyment of the facility.

occupied by nondisabled patrons whom the manager refused to move on the basis of a company-wide policy governing the use of wheelchair companion seats at sold-out screenings. We noted that, while "past wrongs do not in themselves amount to [a] real and immediate threat of injury necessary to make out a case or controversy, past wrongs are evidence bearing on whether there is a real and immediate threat of repeated injury." Because Fortyune attended three or four movies per week with a companion, and the theater's discriminatory seating policy was ongoing, we concluded that Fortyune established "a 'real and immediate threat' that the injury will be repeated" sufficient to permit him to pursue injunctive relief.

[That holding reflects] first principles: It is well settled that a plaintiff need not "await the consummation of threatened injury to obtain prospective relief." Rather than contending with discriminatory barriers due to his related disability when he returns to a public accommodation, a plaintiff may seek a judicial order requiring their removal. Article III, however, requires a sufficient showing of likely injury in the future related to the plaintiff's disability to ensure that injunctive relief will vindicate the rights of the particular plaintiff rather than the rights of third parties.

B.

Demonstrating an intent to return to a noncompliant accommodation is but one way for an injured plaintiff to establish Article III standing to pursue injunctive relief. A disabled individual also suffers a cognizable injury if he is deterred from visiting a noncompliant public accommodation because he has encountered barriers related to his disability there.

[T]hus, an ADA plaintiff can show a likelihood of future injury when he intends to return to a noncompliant accommodation and is therefore likely to reencounter a discriminatory architectural barrier. Alternatively, a plaintiff can demonstrate sufficient injury to pursue injunctive relief when discriminatory architectural barriers deter him from returning to a noncompliant accommodation. Just as a disabled individual who intends to return to a noncompliant facility suffers an imminent injury from the facility's "existing or imminently threatened noncompliance with the ADA," a plaintiff who is deterred from patronizing a store suffers the ongoing "actual injury" of lack of access to the store. That is, an ADA plaintiff suffers an injury-in-fact either because discriminatory architectural barriers deter him from returning to a facility or because they "otherwise interfere with his access to" the facility. Thus, we have Article III jurisdiction to entertain requests for injunctive relief both to halt the deterrent effect of a noncompliant accommodation and to prevent imminent "discrimination," as defined by the ADA, against a disabled individual who plans to visit a noncompliant accommodation in the future.

III.

Once a plaintiff establishes Article III standing, there remains the question of the scope of his standing. [W]e have held that "[a]n ADA plaintiff who has Article III standing as a result of at least one barrier at a place of public accommodation may, in one suit, permissibly challenge all barriers in that public accommodation that are related to his or her specific disability." [*Doran.*] Under *Doran,* Chapman need not have personally encountered all the barriers that impede his access to the Store in order to seek an injunction to remove those barriers. If Chapman has standing to pursue injunctive relief as to some of the barriers that he actually encountered, then he has standing to seek an order requiring the removal of all barriers at the Store that are related to his disability and that he is likely to encounter on future visits.

The rule in *Doran* is a direct application of the statute. The ADA's remedial scheme is not limited to orders for the removal of encountered barriers, but instead dictates that "injunctive relief shall include an order to alter facilities to make such facilities readily accessible to and usable by individuals with disabilities." 42 U.S.C. § 12188(a)(2). The ability to pursue this relief extends to "any person who is being subjected to discrimination on the basis of disability in violation of this subchapter or who has reasonable grounds for believing that such person is about to be subjected to discrimination." 42 U.S.C. § 12188(a)(1). The statute provides that "[n]othing in this section shall require a person with a disability to engage in a futile gesture if such person has actual notice that a person or organization covered by this subchapter does not intend to comply with its provisions." *Id.* Thus, the ADA specifically does not require that the disabled individual personally encounter each architectural barrier as a predicate to seeking its removal.

[A]n ADA challenge to unencountered barriers does not implicate the prohibition on generalized grievances, or violate prudential standing principles, by raising the rights of third parties rather than the rights of the individual plaintiff. We stated in *Doran* that "[e]ven if a disabled plaintiff did not know about certain barriers when the plaintiff first filed suit, that plaintiff will have a 'personal stake in the outcome of the controversy' so long as his or her suit is limited to barriers related to that person's particular disability." We recognized that "it is ultimately misleading to conceptualize each separate architectural barrier inhibiting a disabled person's access to a public accommodation as a separate injury that must satisfy the requirements of Article III." Rather, the injury suffered by disabled plaintiffs is the "discrimination" under the ADA that results from an accommodation's "failure to remove architectural barriers." In *Doran,* this injury was suffered "the first time [the plaintiff] encountered architectural barriers," and it continued even after some of the barriers were corrected because "others remained in place that would have interfered with his access as a wheelchair user." We held that "a constricted reading of the ADA," such as requiring an encounter with each alleged barrier, "could render the benefits [the ADA] promises largely illusory."

Moreover, "a rule limiting a plaintiff to challenging the barriers he or she had encountered . . . would burden businesses and other places of public accommodation with more ADA litigation, encourage piecemeal compliance with the ADA, and ultimately thwart the ADA's remedial goals of eliminating widespread discrimination against the disabled and integrating the disabled into the mainstream of American life." Noting the "broad view" of standing that applies in the context of remedial civil rights legislation, as well as the scope of injunctive relief provided by the ADA, we held that an ADA plaintiff who has standing to sue because he has been discriminated against in one aspect of a public accommodation may, in one lawsuit, obtain an injunction to prevent impending discrimination throughout the accommodation.

The Store asks us to overturn our precedent on this point, arguing that each architectural barrier in a public accommodation be treated as a separate injury in the standing inquiry. We decline to do so. The Store's conception of a cognizable "injury" under the ADA mistakes the statute's forest for its trees by focusing on individual barriers instead of access to places of public accommodation. An ADA plaintiff suffers a legally cognizable injury under the ADA if he is "discriminated against on the basis of disability in the full and equal enjoyment of the goods, services, [or] facilities . . . of any place of public accommodation." 42 U.S.C. § 12182(a). This experience of discrimination confers standing to seek the remedy provided by the ADA—an injunction to correct the other, albeit unencountered, barriers that will subject a wheelchair-bound individual like Chapman to future discrimination, provided that the threat of such discrimination is real and immediate.

[T]his conclusion does not transform the ADA into an open-ended private attorney general statute, because the scope of such an injunction is limited. First, our holding in no way relieves plaintiffs from the constitutionally imposed burden of demonstrating an injury-in-fact and a sufficient likelihood of repeated harm. An ADA plaintiff must show at each stage of the proceedings either that he is deterred from returning to the facility or that he intends to return to the facility and is therefore likely to suffer repeated injury. He lacks standing if he is indifferent to returning to the store or if his alleged intent to return is not genuine, or if the barriers he seeks to enjoin do not pose a real and immediate threat to him due to his particular disability. Injunctions do not extend to barriers not affecting persons with the plaintiff's particular disability; barriers that the plaintiff is not reasonably likely to encounter, such as those in areas off limits to customers; or barriers in areas he is unlikely to enter, such as ladies' restrooms or employee work areas.

Second, in declining to overturn *Doran,* we do not expand or otherwise modify Congress's considered choice as to the rights or remedies available to the disabled. As noted above, our precedent is anchored in Congress's decision to authorize courts to issue "order[s] to alter facilities to make such facilities readily accessible to and usable by individuals with disabilities." 42 U.S.C. § 12188(a)(2).

Finally, we are not persuaded by Pier One's warning that *Doran* opens the floodgates to "potentially vexatious lawsuits." Instead, our precedent facilitates ADA compliance by eliminating the piecemeal litigation that would result from the contrary rule Pier One urges. As we have previously observed, "It makes no sense to require a disabled plaintiff to challenge, in separate cases, multiple barriers in the same facility, controlled by the same entity, all related to the plaintiff's specific disability."

[IV.]

Throughout this litigation Chapman has failed to allege and prove the elements of standing in the ADA context that we describe above. Chapman's complaint itself is jurisdictionally defective. [C]hapman's complaint fails to sufficiently allege the essential elements of Article III standing. Although Chapman alleges that he is "physically disabled," and that he "visited the Store" and "encountered architectural barriers that denied him full and equal access," he never alleges what those barriers were and how his disability was affected by them so as to deny him the "full and equal" access that would satisfy the injury-in-fact requirement (*i.e.,* that he personally suffered discrimination under the ADA on account of his disability).

Instead, Chapman attached to his complaint an "Accessibility Survey," which listed barriers known to him that he claims "denied him access to the Store, *or* which he seeks to remove on behalf of others under related state statutes." The Accessibility Survey simply identifies alleged ADA and CBC violations without connecting the alleged violations to Chapman's disability, or indicating whether or not he encountered any one of them in such a way as to impair his full and equal enjoyment of the Store. [T]his list of alleged CBC and ADAAG violations cannot substitute for the factual allegations required in the complaint to satisfy Article III's requirement of an injury-in-fact. Chapman does not even attempt to relate the alleged violations to his disability.[9]

Unlike in other cases where we have found Article III standing, Chapman leaves the federal court to guess which, if any, of the alleged violations deprived him of the same full and equal access that a person who is not wheelchair bound would enjoy when shopping at Pier One. Nor does he identify how any of the alleged violations threatens to deprive him of full and equal access due to his disability if he were to return to the Store, or how any of them deter him from visiting the Store due to his disability. Although Chapman may establish standing as to unencountered barriers related to his disability, the list of barriers incorporated into his complaint does nothing more than "perform a wholesale audit of the defendant's premises."[10]

Because Chapman lacked standing at the outset of this litigation to assert the ADA claims, the district court should have dismissed them. We therefore vacate the district court's grant of summary judgment, and remand with instructions to dismiss Chapman's ADA claim for lack of jurisdiction and for further proceedings consistent with this opinion.

VACATED, DISMISSED and REMANDED.

■ N.R. SMITH, CIRCUIT JUDGE, CONCURRING IN THE JUDGMENT, JOINED BY RAWLINSON, CIRCUIT JUDGE:

I concur in the majority's conclusion that Chapman failed procedurally to demonstrate standing to maintain this action. However, I disagree with the majority's analysis in reaching its conclusion and

---

[9] The Supreme Court's recent decision in Ashcroft v. Iqbal, 556 U.S. 662 (2009), supports this conclusion. Chapman's allegation that the barriers at the Store "denied him full and equal enjoyment" is precisely the "formulaic recitation" of the elements of a claim that the Supreme Court has deemed insufficient under Rule 8. To sufficiently allege standing, Chapman must do more than offer "labels and conclusions" that parrot the language of the ADA.

[10] It is for the same reason that the Card Report does not supply the "injury-in-fact" element, even if it had been properly filed as part of an amended complaint. It, too, does nothing more than to list additional CBC and ADAAG provisions that the Store allegedly violated.

believe it expands standing for ADA plaintiffs beyond the constitutional confines of Article III.

[T]o the extent the majority's analysis would have allowed Chapman to simply allege a specific encounter with an ADAAG barrier related to his disability to satisfy the injury in fact requirement for standing, it fails to meet the requirement that the encounter "affect[s] the plaintiff in a personal and individual way," *Lujan*, and is no different than allowing standing for barriers not related to the plaintiff's disability. An encounter with an ADAAG defined barrier that a disabled person does not notice (or that does not affect the individual) is not a "distinct and palpable" injury.

The majority correctly points out that a barrier need not "completely preclude the plaintiff from entering or from any use of the facility" to give standing to the plaintiff. However, it is important that the encounter with the barrier adversely affect the plaintiff in some way to satisfy the particularized injury requirement for injury in fact.

An abstract injury (as suggested by the majority) is not enough. *Lyons*. "[C]laims of injury that are purely abstract, even if they might be understood to lead to 'the psychological consequence presumably produced by observation of conduct with which one disagrees,' do not provide the kind of particular, direct, and concrete injury that is necessary to confer standing . . . ." *ASARCO, Inc. v. Kadish,* 490 U.S. 605, 616 (1989) (internal citation omitted).

Rather than merely pointing to a violation of the ADAAG, a plaintiff must also point to some type of personalized injury, whether the injury is objective (physical or economic) or subjective (emotional or aesthetic). This requirement is consistent with precedent. For example, in *Fortyune,* the plaintiff who planned to return to the movie theater nevertheless was adversely affected, because he worried about his ability to sit with his wife, as was his right. Given the language in *Fortyune,* a barrier's adverse effect on a plaintiff may encompass frustration, embarrassment, or physical difficulty with a barrier in addition to actually being deterred from entering a facility. Another example of a subjective adverse affect is the aesthetic injury relied upon by environmental plaintiffs to maintain standing.

[L]astly, to satisfy the requirement for a "real and immediate" threat of repeated injury required by Article III for injunctive relief, a plaintiff must also show an "actual or imminent" injury. An actual or imminent injury occurs when a plaintiff has a concrete intent to return to a facility with a barrier which will continue to adversely affect his ability to benefit from or participate in the facility. As an alternative basis for an actual injury, this circuit has held that a plaintiff, who does not intend to return to a non-ADA compliant store because he is deterred by a barrier at the store, suffers an ongoing injury, redressable by injunctive relief. [T]o the extent that the majority would allow a simple encounter with an ADAAG barrier that does not "deprive" a plaintiff "of the same full and equal access" that a non-disabled person would enjoy at a facility to confer standing, it exceeds the confines of Article III and impermissibly allows plaintiffs to sue on behalf of others, rather then themselves.

[O]nce standing based on encountering one barrier is established, "[t]here remains a question . . . about the scope of barriers that [a plaintiff] may challenge." *Doran.* Expanding on the "deterrent effect" doctrine, *Doran* held that, once a plaintiff establishes that he encountered a barrier which deterred him from use and enjoyment of the facility, that plaintiff could then send an expert into the store to discover other ADA violations. The plaintiff was then deemed to have standing to challenge all discovered violations affecting his or her disability.

[B]y not requiring deterrence before a plaintiff can conduct discovery to find barriers, the majority seeks to allow an ADA plaintiff to represent similarly situated plaintiffs, *regardless* of whether he would be injured (adversely affected) by the challenged barrier. Because Chapman repeatedly disavowed any deterrence resulted from the barriers he encountered, he experienced no unified injury and had no basis to challenge all unencountered barriers at Pier 1.

Not only does such an expansion of standing violate the constitutional aspects of standing, as discussed above, but it also violates the prudential aspects of standing. In *Doran,* we recognized the "question regarding the breadth of [an ADA plaintiff's] right to sue also implicates the prudential aspects of the standing doctrine." Prudential standing limits federal jurisdiction, including "the general prohibition on a litigant's raising another person's legal rights, the rule barring adjudication of generalized grievances more appropriately addressed in the representative branches, and the requirement that a plaintiff's complaint fall within the zone of interests protected by the law invoked." Allowing a plaintiff to challenge barriers which never affected him in the past, which he had never considered at the time of filing the complaint, and of which he could easily learn by returning to a store (that he is not deterred from frequenting), runs afoul of the prudential principles against generalized grievances.

[T]herefore, as the prior panel outlined, Chapman did not have standing as to unencountered barriers, because he was not deterred from returning to Pier 1. The lack of deterrence defeats *Doran's* justification for allowing unencountered barriers to be considered as one injury and allows Chapman to bring what amounts to generalized grievances against Pier 1.

Oliver v. Ralphs Grocery Co.

United States Court of Appeals for the Ninth Circuit, 2011.
654 F.3d 903.

■ IKUTA, CIRCUIT JUDGE:

A.J. Oliver is a disabled individual who requires the use of a motorized wheelchair to get around. On December 7, 2007, Oliver filed a lawsuit against Ralphs Grocery Company ("Ralphs") and Cypress Creek Company ("Cypress Creek") alleging that a Food 4 Less grocery store in Chula Vista, California did not comply with the Americans with Disabilities Act of 1990 (ADA), 42 U.S.C. §§ 12101 12213, and certain state laws. The district court granted summary judgment to the defendants on Oliver's ADA claim and dismissed his state law claims without prejudice. We affirm.

I

A

In order to address Oliver's arguments, it is first necessary to understand the requirements imposed by the ADA. Title III of the ADA prohibits discrimination on the basis of disability in the "full and equal enjoyment of the goods, services, facilities, privileges, advantages, or accommodations of any place of public accommodation" with a nexus in interstate commerce. 42 U.S.C. §§ 2000a(b), 12182(a). Compliance with the ADA requires that new facilities be "readily accessible to and usable by individuals with disabilities," unless this would be "structurally impracticable." § 12183(a)(1).

In general, a facility is "readily accessible to and usable by individuals with disabilities" if it meets the requirements promulgated by the Attorney General in the "ADA Accessibility Guidelines" or the "ADAAG," which is essentially an encyclopedia of design standards. If a particular architectural feature of a place of public accommodation is inconsistent with the ADAAG, a plaintiff can bring a civil action claiming that the feature constitutes a barrier that denies the plaintiff full and equal enjoyment of the premises in violation of the ADA. *See* §§ 2000a–3(a), 12188(a)(2). Because a private plaintiff can sue only for injunctive relief (i.e., for removal of the barrier) under the ADA, *see id.,* a defendant's voluntary removal of alleged barriers prior to trial can have the effect of mooting a plaintiff's ADA claim. The ADA provides for attorneys' fees and costs for prevailing plaintiffs, however, *see* § 12205, and ADA plaintiffs frequently seek damages by bringing parallel claims under applicable state civil rights laws.

B

On December 7, 2007, Oliver filed a complaint in federal district court alleging that he had visited the Chula Vista Food 4 Less store and "encountered barriers (both physical and intangible) that interfered with—if not outright denied—his ability to use and enjoy the goods, services, privileges, and accommodations offered" at the facility. The complaint also stated that, "[t]o the extent known by Oliver, the barriers at the Food 4 Less included, but [we]re not limited to" 18 separate architectural features.[5] Claiming that the existence of these

---

[5] The 18 architectural features listed in the complaint were:

• The tow away signage provided at the facility is incorrect;

• The signage in the van accessible stall is incorrect;

• There is no stop sign painted on the pavement where the accessible route crosses the vehicular way;

• There are no detectable warnings where the accessible route crosses the vehicular way;

• The pay point machine is mounted too high and out of reach;

• There is no directional signage leading to the accessible restrooms;

• The signage at the men's restroom's entrance door is incorrect;

• The door into the men's restroom requires too much force to operate and does not completely close;

• The stall door is not self closing;

• The handle and lock on the stall door requires pinching and twisting to operate;

• The side grab bar is mounted more than 12 inches from the back wall;

• The side grab bar does not extend 24 inches beyond the toilet tissue dispenser;

• The toilet tissue dispenser protrudes into the clear floor space needed at the water closet;

barriers amounted to discrimination against him on the basis of his disability, Oliver sought injunctive relief, attorneys' fees, and legal expenses under the ADA, as well as money damages through two parallel state law claims.[6]

Shortly after receiving Oliver's complaint, Ralphs began renovations at the store. During this process, Ralphs removed several of the barriers Oliver had identified in his complaint. At a pre-trial scheduling conference on May 14, 2008, Oliver stated his intention to amend his complaint to allege the existence of additional architectural features at the store which violated the ADA. The parties agreed on June 13, 2008 as the deadline for filing amended pleadings, and the magistrate judge issued a scheduling order to that effect.

Oliver did not file an amended complaint by the June 13, 2008 deadline. Rather, on June 30, 2008, after the deadline for filing amended pleadings had passed, Oliver filed a motion to modify the scheduling order and a motion to amend his complaint to identify six additional architectural features at the store that allegedly violated the ADA. The district court determined that Oliver had failed to show good cause to modify the scheduling order, *see* Fed.R.Civ.P. 16(b), and denied Oliver's motion. A little over four months later, Oliver filed an expert report identifying approximately 20 "architectural barriers" at the Food 4 Less store. This expert report provided additional detail concerning some of the barriers already identified in Oliver's complaint, but also added several additional barriers that had not been listed in the complaint (e.g., telephone and transaction counter accessibility issues).[7]

The parties subsequently filed cross-motions for summary judgment, and the district court granted summary judgment to Ralphs and Cypress Creek. In doing so, the court ruled that it would not consider the barriers listed in Oliver's expert report, because they were not properly before the court. The court then reviewed each of the 18 architectural barriers listed in the complaint and ruled against Oliver on all of them. Specifically, the court: (1) ruled that Oliver had conceded summary judgment as to some of the barriers, (2) granted summary judgment to the defendants as to others, and (3) found that others were moot because they had already been remedied. Finally, the district court declined to exercise supplemental jurisdiction over Oliver's state law claims and dismissed them without prejudice.

• The trash receptacle protrudes into the clear floor space needed at the water closet;

• The pipes underneath the lavatory are not wrapped to prevent burns;

• The handles to operate the lavatory controls require twisting and grasping;

• The soap dispenser's operable part is mounted at more than 40 inches from the floor; and,

• The operable part of the hand dryer is mounted at more than 40 inches from the floor.

Cypress Creek asserts that only the first four features listed in the complaint relate to areas under its control.

[6] Oliver's complaint alleged violations of the Disabled Persons Act, see Cal. Civil Code § 54, and the Unruh Civil Rights Act, *see* Cal. Civil Code § 51.

[7] Oliver's counsel later explained that his delays in identifying the barriers at the facility were part of his legal strategy: he purposely "forces the defense to wait until expert disclosures (or discovery) before revealing a complete list of barriers," because otherwise a defendant could remove all the barriers prior to trial and moot the entire case.

II

On appeal, Oliver [c]ontends that the district court erred in refusing to consider the allegations in his expert report.

[A]

Before we can reach th[at] issue[ ], however, we must address a threshold question: whether in light of our recent decision in *Chapman v. Pier 1 Imports,* Oliver adequately established his standing to bring this action. Although neither Ralphs nor Cypress Creek raised the issue of standing before the district court or on appeal, we "must[ ] resolve any doubts about this constitutional issue *sua sponte.*"

The "irreducible constitutional minimum of standing" includes three elements: (1) injury in fact; (2) causation; and (3) redressability. *See Lujan.* In *Chapman,* we explained that a disabled person suffers an injury in fact when he "encounter[s] a barrier" at a place of public accommodation "that deprives him of full and equal enjoyment of the facility due to his particular disability." Chapman's complaint did not adequately allege such an injury in fact, however, because it merely included a lengthy list of alleged barriers without identifying which barriers Chapman had encountered or establishing how they had affected his specific disability. Because Chapman did not cure this jurisdictional defect later in the litigation, we vacated the judgment and remanded with instructions for the district court to dismiss the case for lack of jurisdiction.

The jurisdictional allegations in Oliver's complaint are almost identical to those we found deficient in *Chapman.* Although Oliver's complaint stated that he had encountered barriers at the store and provided a list of alleged barriers, it did not specify which (if any) Oliver had personally encountered or explain "how his disability was affected by [any of] them so as to deny him . . . 'full and equal' access" to the store. Thus, Oliver's complaint, like the complaint in *Chapman,* was "jurisdictionally defective." *Id.*

Nevertheless, we need not dismiss Oliver's action. *In Chapman,* not only were Chapman's jurisdictional allegations insufficient, but the necessary jurisdictional facts were absent from the record. In this case, by contrast, there is sufficient evidence in the record to establish that Oliver suffered an injury in fact. In support of his cross-motion for summary judgment, for example, Oliver filed a sworn declaration stating that he had visited the Food 4 Less in question at least ten times between October 2007 and August 2008, and that on one of these visits, he discovered that it was difficult to use the accessible stall in the men's restroom because the door lacked the proper hardware, the position of the grab bar behind the toilet made it difficult to transfer from his wheelchair to the toilet, and the soap dispenser and hand dryer were mounted too high for him to reach. These undisputed facts demonstrate that Oliver personally encountered barriers at the Food 4 Less store that impaired his full and equal enjoyment of the facility due to his particular disability. Therefore, under the standard we articulated in *Chapman,* Oliver had standing to sue as to those barriers as well as all "other barriers related to his disability." Considering that Oliver filed his defective complaint before we issued our decision in *Chapman,* we see little value in vacating the district court's judgment and remanding this case for dismissal. We therefore exercise our discretion under 28 U.S.C. § 1653 to deem the complaint's defective allegations of jurisdiction amended and the jurisdictional defect cured, and proceed to consider the merits of Oliver's appeal.

B

We now turn to Oliver's argument that the district court erred in refusing to consider the barriers that were identified in his expert report but not alleged in his complaint.

[R]ule 8 states that a civil complaint "must contain . . . a short and plain statement of the claim showing that the pleader is entitled to relief." Fed.R.Civ.P. 8(a)(2). The Supreme Court has interpreted the "short and plain statement" requirement to mean that the complaint must provide "the defendant [with] fair notice of what the . . . claim is and the grounds upon which it rests." *Bell Atlantic Corp. v. Twombly,* 550 U.S. 544, 555 (2007) (quoting *Conley v. Gibson,* 355 U.S. 41, 47 (1957)). Where the claim is one of discrimination under the ADA due to the presence of architectural barriers at a place of public accommodation, we have held that the relevant "grounds" are the allegedly non-compliant architectural features at the facility. *Pickern v. Pier 1 Imports (U.S.), Inc.,* 457 F.3d 963, 968 (9th Cir.2006). Thus, in order for the complaint to provide fair notice to the defendant, each such feature must be alleged in the complaint. *See id.*

In *Pickern,* for example, the plaintiff's complaint listed a number of barriers that were "illustrative of the kinds of barriers a disabled person may confront," but did not allege that any of those barriers existed at the facility in question. We held that such a complaint does not provide a defendant with fair notice concerning the grounds upon which the plaintiff bases the claim of discrimination because it does not identify the specific barriers for which the plaintiff seeks injunctive relief. Nor was the plaintiff's expert report identifying the barriers at the facility sufficient to constitute "fair notice" under Rule 8 because it did not specify "what allegations [the plaintiff] was including in the suit" and was "not filed and served until after the discovery deadline."

Applying the principles of *Pickern* to this case, Oliver did not give the defendants fair notice that the barriers listed for the first time in the expert report were grounds for his claim of discrimination under the ADA. Oliver attempts to distinguish *Pickern* on the basis that Oliver filed his expert report before the close of discovery, unlike the plaintiff in *Pickern.* This distinction is unavailing. The issue underlying *Pickern,* as in this case, is whether the defendant had fair notice as required by Rule 8. In general, only disclosures of barriers in a properly pleaded complaint can provide such notice; a disclosure made during discovery, including in an expert report, would rarely be an adequate substitute. Here, for example, Oliver's expert report included the allegation that the exterior public telephone at the Food 4 Less store lacked an International Symbol of Accessibility, but Oliver did not seek summary judgment regarding this alleged barrier. Thus, Ralphs and Cypress Creek would have had to guess which of the items listed in the expert report were grounds for Oliver's claim, and which, like the exterior public phone, were not. Further, an expert report is typically filed later in the litigation process, after the defendant has already taken steps to investigate and defend against the claims in the complaint.

Notwithstanding *Pickern,* Oliver argues that the complaint need not give the defendant notice of every barrier for which the plaintiff seeks relief, because a disabled plaintiff who has encountered at least one barrier at a facility can sue to remove all the barriers at the facility related to his specific disability. *See Doran v. 7-Eleven,* 524 F.3d 1034, 1047 (9th Cir.2008). But *Doran* does not help Oliver, because it speaks only to constitutional standing; it sheds no light on what a plaintiff's complaint must include to comply with the fair notice requirement of Rule 8.

In sum, for purposes of Rule 8, a plaintiff must identify the barriers that constitute the grounds for a claim of discrimination under the ADA in the complaint itself; a defendant is not deemed to have fair notice of barriers identified elsewhere. Therefore, the district court did not err in refusing to consider the barriers that Oliver identified only in his expert report.

[A]FFIRMED.

NOTES ON STANDING AND PLEADING REQUIREMENTS

1. What is the Nature of the Injury? Because private Title III plaintiffs are limited to seeking forward-looking injunctive relief, questions of constitutional standing frequently arise in their cases. In particular, as *Naiman* and *Chapman* illustrate, Title III defendants often challenge the plaintiffs' injury-in-fact. Under the Supreme Court's *Lyons* line of cases (discussed in *Naiman* and *Chapman*), past injury is not sufficient for a plaintiff to have standing to obtain injunctive relief; the plaintiff must experience an actual or imminent threat of future injury resulting from the defendant's conduct. How can a person with a disability show that a barrier at a particular business, which injured her when she patronized that business in the past, will impose an injury in the future?

In this regard, the easy cases are those in which the plaintiff has definite and provable plans to return to the business with the barrier— or, perhaps even better, has been a frequent patron of that business over time, thereby establishing a pattern that can be expected to continue in the future. Do you believe that Naiman's four visits to the defendant hospital over two and a half years are sufficient to show an actual or imminent threat that he will experience the defendant's denial of effective communication in the future? What additional information would be helpful in resolving this question?

Cases in which the plaintiff has not returned to the defendant business, and has no specific plans to return, are harder. If the plaintiff can show that she *would* return if the barriers were removed, all of the judges in *Chapman* agree, the plaintiff will satisfy the injury-in-fact test. How can a plaintiff prove that the barriers at a business have deterred her from returning? Would the plaintiff's bare testimony about what she would do if the barriers were removed be enough?

In many cases, of course, it will be difficult for a plaintiff to show that she would patronize any specific business in the future. Perhaps the plaintiff encountered an inaccessible gas station while passing through town. Perhaps an inaccessible fast food restaurant is located close to other, accessible, fast food restaurants, so the plaintiff has no particular desire to return to the inaccessible one, even if it removes its barriers. If private plaintiffs do not have standing to challenge barriers in these sorts of situations, many violations of Title III will go unremedied. (Note that bringing a suit as a class action will not avoid this problem, because the named plaintiff must have standing at the commencement of the suit.) Consider the following argument for finding standing in those situations (an argument the author concludes is "an uphill one under current doctrine"):

> It is certainly plausible to argue that an individual with a disability experiences current "injury in fact" whenever a place of public accommodation is inaccessible, whether or not that individual intends to patronize the business again. The statute guarantees people with disabilities the right to choose stores and restaurants from the same array of options as people without disabilities, and one business's violation deprives a person with a disability of that opportunity to choose, even if at the end of the day she would not have decided to patronize that store.

> The argument for Article III standing in such circumstances would start with the proposition that "Congress may create a statutory right or entitlement the alleged deprivation of which can confer standing to sue even where the plaintiff would have suffered no judicially cognizable injury in the absence of statute." [*Warth v. Seldin*, 422 U.S. 490, 514 (1975).] As Justice Kennedy explained in his concurring opinion in *Lujan v. Defenders of Wildlife,* that principle gives Congress "the power to define injuries and articulate chains of causation that will give rise to a case or controversy where none existed before." Here, the statutory right is a right to choose from the same (or close to the same) array of goods and services providers as can anyone else—the right not to have some choices foreclosed because of disability. The denial of that statutory right is an injury. And it is not an injury to every person in the world; it is an injury to the narrowly drawn class of individuals with disabilities, as defined by the ADA. In the ADA's public accommodations title, then, Congress has clearly "identif[ied] the injury it seeks to vindicate and relate[d] the injury to the class of persons entitled to bring suit." [*Lujan,* 504 U.S. at 580 (Kennedy, J., concurring).]

Bagenstos, *Perversity of Limited Civil Rights Remedies, supra,* at 28-29. Does that argument persuade you?

Even if the plaintiff can satisfy the "actual or imminent" requirement, there remains the question of what constitutes an "injury" in this context. Much of the discussion in *Chapman* focuses on that question. Under Judge Smith's view in his concurrence, a barrier does not injure the plaintiff unless it either deters her from patronizing the business or causes her some specific objective or subjective harm. Accordingly, the concurrence would hold that a plaintiff cannot challenge barriers that she did not personally encounter, unless other barriers deterred her patronage and thereby prevented her from encountering those barriers. That rule, Judge Smith argued, is necessary to comply with the constitutional requirement that the plaintiff experience some personal injury.

The *Chapman* majority rejected Judge Smith's position, however. The majority concluded that a plaintiff experiences an injury whenever she encounters a barrier that violates some accessibility requirement under the ADA—so long as the accessibility requirement is designed to respond to the sort of disability that the plaintiff has. Under that holding, a plaintiff with quadriplegia who was not blind could not challenge a business's failure to include Braille signage, but she could challenge the excessive slope of a ramp at the business—even if, in fact, the ramp's slope did not prevent or deter her from accessing the business or cause her any psychological harm. And having encountered one such barrier, the plaintiff may challenge any other barriers at the business that similarly relate to her disability—even if she did not encounter those other barriers, and even if the barriers that she did encounter did not deter her from encountering those other barriers.

Which of these positions do you find persuasive, the majority's or the concurrence's?

2. What Must a Plaintiff Plead? In *Chapman*, quoting its earlier decision in *Doran*, the court explained

> that "it is ultimately misleading to conceptualize each separate architectural barrier inhibiting a disabled person's access to a public accommodation as a separate injury that must satisfy the requirements of Article III." Rather, the injury suffered by disabled plaintiffs is the "discrimination" under the ADA that results from an accommodation's "failure to remove architectural barriers."

Quoting *Doran* again, the *Chapman* court thus concluded that standing exists under Title III " '[e]ven if a disabled plaintiff did not know about certain barriers when the plaintiff first filed suit.' " Yet in its subsequent decision in *Oliver*, the same court held that "each ["allegedly non-compliant architectural feature"] must be alleged in the complaint." Are the *Chapman* and *Oliver* holdings consistent with each other? Is it enough of a distinction that *Chapman* involved the question of constitutional standing while *Oliver* involved the pleading requirements under Fed.R.Civ.P. 8? If a Title III plaintiff sues a business to challenge some barriers, and then later finds other barriers at the same business, how can she challenge those other barriers? Must she file a new lawsuit? See *Morales v. Ralphs Grocery Co.*, 2012 WL 6087699 (E.D.Cal., Dec. 6, 2012) (permitting plaintiff to file amended complaint adding allegations related to barriers discovered after filing the lawsuit).

2. NOTICE AND SERIAL LITIGATION

Botosan v. Paul McNally Realty

United States Court of Appeals for the Ninth Circuit, 2000.
216 F.3d 827.

■ KING, DISTRICT JUDGE:

Plaintiff-Appellee Kornel Botosan ("Appellee") filed a private action against Defendants-Appellants Chuck and Judith Ruston (the

"Rustons") and Paul McNally Realty, Inc., dba Realty World ("Realty World"; collectively, "Appellants"), alleging violations of the Americans With Disabilities Act ("ADA" or the "Act"), 42 U.S.C. § 12101 *et seq.* [A]ppellee claims he was denied access to Realty World's real estate office due to a lack of handicapped parking. Appellants argue, *inter alia*, that Appellee is not entitled to recovery because [h]e did not provide notice of his ADA claim to a state or local agency charged with administering the relevant civil rights laws before filing suit. [T]he district court ruled in favor of Appellee on all arguments. We affirm.

[A]ppellee is a paraplegic who requires the use of a wheelchair at all times. In December 1997, he visited Realty World, a real estate office, and discovered that the office did not provide handicapped parking. Due to the lack of a designated parking space for disabled persons, he was prevented from entering the office and becoming a customer. He made no other attempt to patronize Realty World after that single incident. On February 18, 1998, he filed a complaint alleging violations of the public accommodations provisions of the ADA (Title III). [H]e did not notify any state or local authorities about the violations he alleged in the complaint before filing suit.

The Rustons are trustees of the trust that owns the property on which Realty World is situated. Realty World leases the property from the Rustons. The lease contains several provisions that allocate responsibility for maintenance of the property and compliance with the law, as between the landlord and tenant.

[O]n September 2, 1998, Appellants filed a motion to dismiss arguing that Appellee failed to provide notice to a state or local agency charged with enforcing civil rights laws before filing suit pursuant to 42 U.S.C. § 2000a–3(c), thereby depriving the district court of subject matter jurisdiction. The district court denied this motion on November 24, 1998. [The district court granted Botosan's motion for summary judgment, and the defendants appealed.]

[C]ongress patterned Title III of the ADA ("Title III") after Title VII of the Civil Rights Act of 1964 ("Title VII").* Specifically, Title III provides that "[t]he remedies and procedures set forth in section 2000a–3(a) of [Title VII] are the remedies and procedures this subchapter provides to any person who is being subjected to discrimination on the basis of disability. . . . " 42 U.S.C. § 12188(a)(1). In turn, 42 U.S.C. § 2000a–3(a) provides that an aggrieved individual may bring "a civil action for preventive relief, including an application for a permanent or temporary injunction, restraining order, or other order. . . . " 42 U.S.C. § 2000a–3(a). Appellants suggest that the remedies and procedures applicable to Title III and those applicable to Title VII are completely identical—that is, that suits brought under Title III are subject to all limitations imposed on suits maintained pursuant to Title VII. The limitation relevant in this case is found in § 2000a–3(c):

---

*   [Title 42 U.S.C. 2000a–3 is actually a part of Title II, not Title VII, of the Civil Rights Act of 1964.—ed.]

> [N]o civil action may be brought under subsection (a) of
> [§ 2000a–3] before the expiration of thirty days after written
> notice of such alleged act or practice has been given to the
> appropriate State or local authority by registered mail or in
> person, provided that the court may stay proceedings in such
> civil action pending the termination of State or local
> enforcement proceedings.

42 U.S.C. § 2000a–3(c). The question before us is whether actions for violations of Title III are subject to this limitation. Section 12188(a)(1) of the ADA makes no explicit reference to § 2000a–3(c), thus leaving uncertain whether notice to an appropriate state or local agency is a prerequisite to filing suit under Title III.

[T]he plain language of § 12188(a)(1) is clear and unambiguous, and it can be understood without reference to any other statutory provision. Section 12188(a)(1) is devoid of any reference to § 2000a–3(c). Yet, Congress explicitly incorporated subsection (a) of § 2000a–3 into § 12188(a)(1). The incorporation of one statutory provision to the exclusion of another must be presumed intentional under the statutory canon of *expressio unius*. Surely, "Congress obviously knew how to adopt provisions of Title VII because it expressly adopted subsection (a) . . . [and it is] unlikely that Congress would absentmindedly forget to adopt a provision that appears a mere two paragraphs below the subsection it adopted." Even if incorporation of all subsections of § 2000a–3 into § 12188(a)(1) did not render the explicit reference to § 2000a–3(a) superfluous or redundant, the statute's legislative history, the Code of Federal Regulations, see 28 C.F.R. § 26.501(a), and the Department of Justice's Technical Assistance Manual generally support the conclusion that Title III actions do not require state notification. Thus, we hold that § 12188(a)(1) does not implicitly incorporate § 2000a–3(c). A plaintiff in a private Title III action is not required to provide notice to any state or local agency as a prerequisite to filing suit.

Accordingly, Appellee was not required to give notice to any state or local agency before filing his Title III action.

Molski v. M.J. Cable, Inc.

United States Court of Appeals for the Ninth Circuit, 2007.
481 F.3d 724.

■ FERGUSON, CIRCUIT JUDGE.

Jarek Molski ("Molski") appeals the District Court's denial of his motion for a new trial following a jury verdict in favor of M.J. Cable Inc., owner of Cable's Restaurant ("Cable's"). Molski, who is paraplegic, sued Cable's for violations of the Americans with Disabilities Act ("ADA") and California's Unruh Civil Rights Act ("Unruh Act"), alleging that Cable's failed to accommodate the disabled. Although Molski provided uncontradicted evidence that Cable's did not identify and remove architectural barriers, the jury returned a verdict for the restaurant. The District Court denied Molski's motion for a new trial, speculating that the jury could have reasonably concluded that because of Molski's record of litigiousness, he was a "business" and not an "individual" entitled to the ADA's protections. We reverse.

FACTUAL AND PROCEDURAL BACKGROUND

Molski is a paraplegic who has been confined to a wheelchair since a motorcycle accident paralyzed him at the age of 18. Considered by some to be a controversial figure, Molski has brought hundreds of lawsuits against inaccessible public accommodations throughout California. Molski considers himself a civil rights activist who uses litigation to force compliance with the ADA; California businesses and a federal district court consider him a vexatious litigant who exploits the ADA and its state law counterpart for pecuniary gain.[1]

On January 26, 2003, Molski took his grandmother to church, then to lunch at Cable's Restaurant in Woodland Hills, California, where he spent thirty-five dollars on their meal. After eating lunch, Molski excused himself to use the restaurant's public restroom.

Upon entering the restroom, Molski noticed numerous architectural barriers to his accessing the facilities. The door pressure on the bathroom door was too heavy, and the door lacked a handicap accessible sign. Inside, the stall doors could not close with Molski's wheelchair in the stall. The stall lacked grab bars on both the rear wall and side wall, which prevented Molski from maneuvering from his wheelchair to the toilet. The toilet seat cover dispenser was unreachable. The pipes underneath the sink were not insulated, and therefore, according to Molski, posed a special risk to those without feeling in their legs, as hot pipes could burn them without their realization. The sink also lacked levered hardware, a type of fixture that is easily moveable without strong grip strength. Molski was unable to reach at least one of the paper towel dispensers. Molski testified that the hygienic violations were especially important in his case because, due to his chest-down paralysis, he uses a catheter and a urine bag that must be emptied frequently. He explained that failure to empty the urine bag can cause autonomic dysreflexia, a condition that can result in whole body spasms and even cardiac arrest. Handling the bag with unwashed hands can also lead to bladder infections.

On March 7, 2003, Rick Sarantschin ("Sarantschin"), the principal of Access Investigation Monitoring, conducted an inspection of Cable's and confirmed Molski's observations using the ADA Accessibility Guidelines for Buildings and Facilities ("ADAAG"). See 28 C.F.R. § 36 App.A. Four months later, Molski brought a lawsuit against Cable's in the Central District of California, alleging violations of the ADA and state laws. The District Court held a three-day trial.

At trial, Molski, Sarantschin, and construction expert Michael Beall ("Beall") testified on behalf of Molski, and Cable's vice president Anthony Dalkas ("Dalkas") testified as an adverse witness. Molski testified primarily about his experience at Cable's, his prior lawsuits,

---

[1]   *Molski v. Mandarin Touch Restaurant*, 347 F.Supp.2d 860 (C.D.Cal.2004) (declaring Molski a vexatious litigant and requiring court approval prior to his filing future lawsuits); see also Samuel R. Bagenstos, *The Perversity of Limited Civil Rights Remedies: The Case of "Abusive" ADA Litigation*, 54 UCLA L. Rev. 1, 7, 34 (2006) (defending serial ADA litigation as "essential" but identifying prior allegations of ethical violations by Molski's attorney); Carri Becker, *Private Enforcement of the Americans with Disabilities Act via Serial Litigation: Abusive or Commendable?*, 17 Hastings Women's L.J. 93 (2006) (using Molski as case study of serial litigation under Title III of the ADA).

and his views on disability access discrimination. Sarantschin testified about his investigation of Cable's and the ADA violations he observed.

Beall testified about the construction costs of making Cable's compliant with the ADA. He estimated that the approximate total cost to remodel both the men's and women's bathrooms would be $8,600, or $6,000 for just the men's bathroom. Beall noted that incremental steps were even cheaper: lowering the toilet seat cover dispenser would cost $20 and take about 15 minutes; insulating the pipes would cost under $20 and take "about a minute and a half to do." Other repairs were as inexpensive as $30.

In his testimony, Dalkas acknowledged that the company had not attempted to identify barriers to the disabled. He admitted that Cable's had not made the renovations because "[w]e weren't compelled to do it." Dalkas testified that Cable's could afford each of the repairs but stated, "once you start down that path[,] you're opening a can of worms that will cost a lot of money." Dalkas described issues with Cable's landlord, as well as the economic costs of remodeling, such as the need to close the restaurant during renovations. Dalkas said he had received estimates of $40,000 to "bring the two bathrooms up to the current [c]ode," although Cable's had not disclosed any such remodeling bids during discovery.

The defendant did not call any witnesses, but relied primarily on its cross-examination of Molski and Dalkas. In essence, the defendant's strategy was to discredit Molski by exposing an ulterior motive for bringing suit: Molski and his lawyer Thomas Frankovich ("Frankovich") were purportedly in the business of tracking down public accommodations with ADA violations and extorting settlements out of them. On cross examination, Molski acknowledged that: he did not complain to any of Cable's employees about his access problems; he had filed 374 similar ADA lawsuits as of October 8, 2004; Frankovich had filed 232 of the 374 lawsuits; even more lawsuits had been filed since that date; Molski and Frankovich averaged $4,000 for each case that settled; Molski did not pay any fees to Frankovich; Molski maintained no employment besides prosecuting ADA cases, despite his possession of a law degree; Molski's projected annual income from settlements was $800,000;[2] Molski executed blank verification forms for Frankovich to submit with responses to interrogatories; they had also filed lawsuits against two other restaurants owned by Cable's; they had filed a lawsuit against a nearby restaurant; and Sarantschin obtained up to 95% of his income from Frankovich's firm for performing investigations for ADA lawsuits.[3]

During closing arguments, Molski focused primarily on the ADA violations, and Cable's focused primarily on Molski. The Court

---

[2]   The method used to calculate this number was questionable. It assumed that Molski had no litigation expenses, that he obtained a $4,000 settlement from each case filed (rather than each case settled), that Molski would settle two hundred cases every year, and that all proceeds went to Molski.

[3]   It is unclear why this evidence was admitted by the trial court under Fed. R. Evid. 401. The narrow issue in the case was whether Cable's failed to identify and remove architectural barriers. Although some of the above facts may be admissible witness impeachment evidence, most appear to be irrelevant or at least far more prejudicial than probative. See Fed. R. Evid. 403. However, because these evidentiary questions are not before us on appeal, we do not address them here.

instructed the jury on, inter alia, the elements of an ADA claim, and gave it a Special Verdict Form. The jury returned a verdict for Cable's, responding "No" to the threshold question: "Do you find that the defendant failed to identify and remove architectural barriers at Cable's restaurant?"

Pursuant to Rule 59(a) of the Federal Rules of Civil Procedure, Molski moved for a new trial on the grounds that the verdict was against the weight of the evidence. The District Court denied the motion. Molski timely appealed.

DISCUSSION

[C]ongress passed the ADA, 42 U.S.C. § 12101 *et seq.*, in 1990 "to provide clear, strong, consistent, enforceable standards addressing discrimination against individuals with disabilities." § 12101(b)(2). Title III of the ADA prohibits discrimination by public accommodations. § 12181 *et seq.* Title III provides, "No individual shall be discriminated against on the basis of disability in the full and equal enjoyment of the goods, services, facilities, privileges, advantages, or accommodations of any place of public accommodation by any person who owns, leases (or leases to), or operates a place of public accommodation." § 12182(a). Discrimination includes "a failure to remove architectural barriers . . . in existing facilities . . . where such removal is readily achievable." § 12182(b)(2)(A)(iv). Readily achievable means "easily accomplishable and able to be carried out without much difficulty or expense." § 12181(9).

Federal regulations clarify which barrier removals are likely to be readily achievable and provide examples in 28 C.F.R. § 36.304. They include installing grab bars in toilet stalls, rearranging toilet partitions to increase maneuvering space, insulating lavatory pipes under sinks to prevent burns, installing raised toilet seats, installing full-length bathroom mirrors, and repositioning paper towel dispensers. 28 C.F.R. § 36.304(b)(12)–(17). The Department of Justice has referred to these examples as "the types of modest measures that may be taken to remove barriers and that are likely to be readily achievable." Appendix B to Part 36—Preamble to Regulation on Nondiscrimination on the Basis of Disability by Public Accommodations and in Commercial Facilities, 56 Fed.Reg. 35,546 (July 26, 1991); see also 28 C.F.R. § 36 App.A.

[A]ggrieved individuals or the Attorney General may enforce the ADA. 42 U.S.C. § 12188. Private parties may utilize the remedies and procedures made available by the Civil Rights Act of 1964. § 12188(a)(1) (citing § 2000a–3(a)). In particular, they may obtain injunctive relief against public accommodations with architectural barriers, including "an order to alter facilities to make such facilities readily accessible to and usable by individuals with disabilities." § 12188(a)(2). In suits brought by the Attorney General, courts may grant both equitable relief and monetary damages. § 12188(b)(2). Monetary damages are not available in private suits under Title III of the ADA, but the ADA gives courts the discretion to award attorney's fees to prevailing parties. 42 U.S.C. § 12205.

[I]n the disability context, California's Unruh Civil Rights Act operates virtually identically to the ADA. It states,

All persons within the jurisdiction of this state are free and equal, and no matter what their sex, race, color, religion, ancestry, national origin, disability, medical condition, marital status, or sexual orientation are entitled to the full and equal accommodations, advantages, facilities, privileges, or services in all business establishments of every kind whatsoever.

Cal.Civ.Code § 51(b). Any violation of the ADA necessarily constitutes a violation of the Unruh Act. § 51(f).

The Unruh Act, however, does allow for monetary damages. Victims of discrimination may obtain actual damages, as well as "any amount that may be determined by a jury . . . up to a maximum of three times the amount of actual damage but in no case less than four thousand dollars." § 52(a). The litigant need not prove she suffered actual damages to recover the independent statutory damages of $4,000. The Unruh Act also allows for attorney's fees. Cal.Civ.Code § 52(a).

Because the Unruh Act is coextensive with the ADA and allows for monetary damages, litigants in federal court in California often pair state Unruh Act claims with federal ADA claims. *Molski v. Mandarin Touch Restaurant*, 347 F.Supp.2d at 862–63.

[T]he issue in this case is whether the District Court abused its discretion when it denied Molski's motion for a new trial. The first question is whether there was an absence of evidence to support the jury's conclusion that "defendant[s did not] fail[ ] to identify and remove architectural barriers at Cable's Restaurant." The second question is whether the District Court's explanation of the verdict, that Molski was a business and not an individual, somehow justifies the jury's conclusion.

[T]he District Court structured the Special Verdict Form to track the elements of a Title III claim. First, as a threshold question, it asked, "Do you find that the defendant failed to identify and remove architectural barriers at Cable's Restaurant?" The form then instructed the jury, if it answered "yes," to answer three questions for each of the purported violations: "(1) Did this barrier exist at the Cable's Restaurant on January 26, 2003? (2) If 'yes,' did defendant M.J. Cable fail to identify and remove the barrier? (3) If 'yes,' was it readily achievable to remove?" After these questions, the form asked, "Should plaintiff be awarded statutory damages in the sum of $4,000?" The jury answered "no" to the first question and therefore did not go on to answer any of the subsequent questions.

Reviewing the trial transcript, "the record contains no evidence in support of the verdict." The testimony of Molski and Sarantschin established a laundry list of architectural barriers, including: the absence of accessibility signage, excessive door pressure, stalls that were neither wide enough nor long enough, the absence of side and rear grab bars, the absence of looped handles for opening or closing the stall door, no sliding lock, no automatic door opener, a toilet seat cover dispenser that was too high, a paper towel dispenser that was too high, a height-compliant paper towel dispenser that was blocked by a sink, sinks without levered hardware, no insulation on the pipes, urinals that were too close and too high, stall doors that were too narrow, and toilets that were too short.[5]

Dalkas, the vice president of Cable's, acknowledged the continued existence of these violations and flatly admitted that neither he nor anyone else at Cable's had attempted to identify or remove architectural barriers.

The only issue about which there was any disagreement was whether or not the removal of the barriers was "readily achievable."[6] 42 U.S.C. § 12182(b)(2)(A)(iv). This issue is separate from whether Cable's identified and removed the barriers. The Special Verdict Form specifically distinguished those questions, allowing the jury to find initially that Cable's had failed to identify or remove the barriers, but then that removal was not readily achievable. It did not do so.

The jury's determination, in response to the threshold question, that Cable's had not failed to identify and remove barriers was against the clear weight of the evidence, given the undisputed testimony from both Molski and Dalkas. Accordingly, the District Court abused its discretion in denying Molski's motion for a new trial.

[I]n denying Molski's motion, the District Court accepted the defendant's "reasonable explanation for the jury's verdict: the jury determined that Molski was not an 'individual' under the ADA, and therefore could not recover against Defendants." This conclusion is unreasonable and legally flawed.

First, the District Court's explanation is inconsistent with the plain language, structure, and spirit of the ADA. Neither the District Court nor the defendant provide any support for concluding that a person may be considered a business and not an individual because of a history of litigiousness.

Title III of the ADA protects "individuals" who are disabled. 42 U.S.C. § 12182(a). It is clear that Molski, who is paraplegic, falls within that term. "Statutory interpretation begins with the plain meaning of the statute's language. Where the statutory language is clear and consistent with the statutory scheme at issue, the plain language of the statute is conclusive and the judicial inquiry is at an end." *Botosan*, 216 F.3d at 831 (citations omitted).

The defendant, citing 42 U.S.C. § 12182(b)(1)(A)(iv), contends that the ADA defines individuals as referring only "to the clients and customers of the covered public accommodation." This argument is unavailing for two reasons: first, it misinterprets the relevant provision of the ADA; second, even if its interpretation of the statute were correct, as a factual matter, it does not exclude Molski.

---

[5] "The issues involved [in ADA accessibility cases] are, to be frank, mind-numbingly boring; the ADA Accessibility Guidelines regulate design elements down to the minutest detail. . . . [But, a]lthough the ADA's requirements are highly technical, they are essential to serve a core function of all civil rights laws: ensuring that the arenas of civic life are open to everyone." Bagenstos, supra, at 23–24.

[6] Federal regulations provide examples of removals of barriers that are readily achievable. 28 C.F.R. § 36.304(b)(12)–(17). We express no opinion as to whether, given these regulations, the "readily achievable" dispute raises a genuine issue of material fact on remand. See Fed. R. Civ. P. 56(c).

First, § 12182(b)(1)(A)(iv), which defines "individuals" as "clients or customers," applies only "[f]or purposes of clauses (i) through (iii) of . . . subparagraph[(b)(1)(A)]." § 12182(b)(1)(A)(iv); see also *PGA Tour v. Martin*, 532 U.S. 661, 678–79 (2001). Sections (i) through (iii) of subparagraph (b)(1)(A) generally prohibit public accommodations from denying participation to the disabled, providing disabled participants an unequal benefit, or providing disabled participants a separate benefit. § 12182(b)(1)(A)(i)–(iii). However, it is subsection (a), not subsection (b), that provides the general prohibition against discrimination on the basis of disability. § 12182(a). As the Supreme Court has pointed out, "clause (iv) [of subparagraph (b)(1)(A)] is not literally applicable to Title III's general rule [in subsection (a)] prohibiting discrimination against disabled individuals. Title III's broad general rule contains no express 'clients or customers' limitation. . . . " *Martin*, 532 U.S. at 679. Aside from being inapplicable to subsection (a)'s general prohibition, the limited definition of "individual" in § 12182(b)(1)(A)(iv) is also inapplicable to § 12182(b)(2)(A)(iv), which defines discrimination to include the failure to remove architectural barriers.

[A]ccordingly, Molski did not need to have been a client or customer of Cable's to be an "individual" entitled to the protections of Title III. One need not be a client or customer of a public accommodation to feel the sting of its discrimination.[7]

But even if the defendant's reading of the ADA were proper, it would not exclude Molski. Molski was plainly a "customer" of Cable's Restaurant. He brought a guest to the restaurant, ordered food, ate it, paid thirty-five dollars for it, tried to use the restroom, and left. He even returned the day before the trial for some ice cream. In *Martin*, the Supreme Court held that a one-time payment is sufficient to make a disabled person a client or customer of a public accommodation. 532 U.S. at 679–80 (holding that professional golfer was a client or customer of a golf tour because he paid a one-time qualifying fee).

Even assuming it would have been a viable legal theory for Molski to have been a business and not an individual, the jury instructions provide no basis for making such a finding. Cable's did not put forth any evidence that Molski was incorporated, paid salaries, advertised, held himself out as a business, or conducted any activities that could make him a business as a matter of law. In fact, the Joint Pre-Trial Conference Order identifies the plaintiff as "JAREK MOLSKI, an individual" and states as an "admitted fact" that "Plaintiff Jarek Molski is a person with disabilities as defined by the ADA." The jury could not have then come to the opposite conclusion.

The jury instructions do not give any support to the District Court's explanation of the verdict, either. The jury was never instructed on the Molski-as-business theory. Although the District Court gave the jury definitions for "disability," "major life activities," "public accommodation," "denial of access," "architectural barrier," and "readily achievable," it never discussed the possibility that Molski was not an

---

[7]   See, e.g., Bagenstos, *supra*, at 26–27 ("The [ADA] guarantees people with disabilities the right to choose stores and restaurants from the same array of options as people without disabilities, and one business's violation deprives a person with a disability of that opportunity to choose, even if at the end of the day she would not have decided to patronize that store.")

"individual" under the ADA, nor did it provide any definition of that term.

Finally, the test provided in the jury instructions stated only the following requirements for finding an ADA violation: (1) that Molski be disabled, (2) that Cable's be a public accommodation, and (3) that "Plaintiff was denied access to elements of the Defendants' public accommodation due to Defendants' failure to remove architectural barriers." The parties stipulated to the first two elements, and Molski unequivocally proved the third. The jury instructions therefore provide no support for the District Court's speculation that the jury concluded that Molski was not an individual.

CONCLUSION

We conclude that the record provides no evidence whatsoever for the jury's verdict. The District Court abused its discretion in denying Molski's motion for a new trial. Accordingly, we reverse the District Court's denial of the motion, vacate the judgment against Molski, including that for incurred costs, and remand for a new trial. Costs on appeal are awarded to appellant.

REVERSED; VACATED and REMANDED.

Molski v. Evergreen Dynasty Corp.

United States Court of Appeals for the Ninth Circuit, 2007.
500 F.3d 1047,reh'g en banc denied, 521 F.3d 1215 (9th Cir.), cert. denied, 555 U.S.
1031, 129 S.Ct. 594 (2008).

■ PER CURIAM:

This appeal presents two orders of the district court for our review. The first order declared Jarek Molski a vexatious litigant and ordered that Molski obtain leave of the court before filing any claims under Title III of the Americans With Disabilities Act ("ADA") in the United States District Court for the Central District of California. The second order sanctioned the law firm representing Molski, Thomas E. Frankovich, a Professional Law Corporation ("the Frankovich Group"), by requiring it to obtain leave of the court before filing any claims under Title III of the ADA in the Central District of California. We [h]old that the district court acted within its sound discretion in entering the pre-filing orders against Molski and against the Frankovich Group, and we affirm the orders of the district court.

I

Molski, who is paralyzed from the chest down, needs a wheelchair to get around. He has filed about 400 lawsuits in the federal courts within the districts in California. Molski lives in Woodland Hills, California, but frequently travels. According to Molski's amended complaint in this case, during his travels, he stopped at the Mandarin Touch Restaurant in Solvang, California on January 25, 2003. After finishing his meal, Molski decided to use the restroom. Molski was able to pass through the narrow restroom door, but there was not enough clear space to permit him to access the toilet from his wheelchair. Molski then exited the restroom, and in the course of doing so, got his hand caught in the restroom door, "causing trauma" to his hand.

Molski's amended complaint also alleged that Mandarin Touch contained other accessibility barriers "too numerous to list."

Asserting claims under the ADA and California law, Molski, along with co-plaintiff Disability Rights Enforcement, Education Services: Helping You Help Others ("DREES"), a non-profit corporation, sought injunctive relief, attorneys' fees and costs, and damages. Specifically, the complaint sought "daily damages of not less than $4,000/day . . . for each day after [Molski's] visit until such time as the restaurant is made fully accessible" as well as punitive damages and pre-judgment interest. The amended complaint named as defendants Mandarin Touch Restaurant, Evergreen Dynasty Corp., and Brian and Kathy McInerney.

Shortly after the defendants answered the complaint, Mandarin Touch and Evergreen Dynasty filed a motion for an order (1) declaring Molski a vexatious litigant; (2) requiring Molski to obtain the court's permission before filing any more complaints under the ADA; and (3) imposing monetary sanctions against Molski and his counsel, Thomas E. Frankovich. [I]n a published order, the district court granted the motion in part, declaring Molski a vexatious litigant and granting the defendants' request for a pre-filing order.

[T]he district court first noted that Molski had an extensive history of litigation. While acknowledging that the fact that a plaintiff has filed a large number of suits, standing alone, does not warrant a pre-filing order, the district court noted that a large volume of suits might indicate an intent to harass defendants into agreeing to cash settlements. The district court also noted that Molski's complaints were all textually and factually similar. While again not entirely dispositive, the district court surmised that boilerplate complaints might indicate an intent to harass defendants.

Against this background, the district court's reasoning made clear that the most important consideration was its specific finding that the allegations in Molski's numerous and similar complaints were "contrived and not credible." The court stressed that Molski often filed multiple complaints against separate establishments asserting that Molski had suffered identical injuries at each establishment on the same day. The district court pointed out that Molski had filed thirteen separate complaints for essentially identical injuries allegedly sustained during one five-day period in May 2003. In particular, Molski had alleged that, at each establishment, he injured his "upper extremities" while transferring himself to a non-ADA-compliant toilet. The district court explicitly found that, in making these duplicitous injury claims, Molski had "plainly lied" in his filings to the court because the district court "simply [did] not believe that Molski suffered 13 nearly identical injuries, generally to the same part of his body, in the course of performing the same activity, over a five-day period."

[T]he district court [also] concluded that Molski's motivation in bringing numerous suits alleging both violations of the ADA and California state civil rights laws was to extract cash settlements from defendants. Although the ADA grants private plaintiffs like Molski only the rights to seek injunctive relief, attorneys' fees, and costs, the California state civil rights laws amplify the scope of relief available under federal law by also permitting the recovery of money damages.

Compare 42 U.S.C. §§ 2000a–3(a), 12188(a)(1), with Cal.Civ.Code §§ 51(f), 52(a), 54(c), 54.3(a). The district court acknowledged that raising multiple claims in one suit is, in and of itself, not vexatious. However, because Molski had tried on the merits only one of his approximately 400 suits and had settled all the others, the district court concluded that Molski's consistent approach was to use the threat of money damages under California law to extract cash settlements and move on to his next case.

Finally, [t]he district court found that the only effective way to protect the courts and other parties from future vexatious litigation by Molski was by entering a pre-filing order. Accordingly, the district court held that, "[b]efore filing any new litigation alleging violations of Title III of the ADA in the United States District Court for the Central District of California, Molski [must] file a motion for leave to file a complaint." The court required that Molski "submit a copy of this order and a copy of the proposed filing with every motion for leave."

In the same order, the district court denied the motion of Evergreen Dynasty and Mandarin Touch for sanctions as pre-mature. Finally, the district court issued an order to show cause why it should not impose a pre-filing sanction on Molski's attorneys, the Frankovich Group.

About three months later, the district court issued a published memorandum decision regarding that order to show cause. The district court imposed a pre-filing order on the Frankovich Group similar to the order that it had imposed on Molski. In its decision, the district court first observed that in 2004 the Frankovich Group filed at least 223 nearly identical lawsuits in the Northern and Central Districts of California, that the complaints all stated an ADA claim and the same four claims under California state law, that the damages requested in each case were identical and that, other than superficial alteration of the names and facts, the complaints were textually identical down to the typos. The district court also noted that plaintiffs represented by the Frankovich Group would often file multiple complaints regarding similar or identical injuries sustained at multiple establishments on a single day. The district court noted that one-third of the suits were against ethnic restaurants and commented that "such establishments are seen as easy prey for coercive claims."

Supplementing its findings from its decision accompanying the pre-filing order entered against Molski, the district court found that the Frankovich Group had filed sixteen lawsuits on Molski's behalf alleging injuries sustained over a four-day period from May 20, 2003 to May 23, 2003, all alleging that Molski suffered injuries to his upper extremities as a result of transfers or negotiating barriers. The district court also noted that, on thirty-seven occasions in 2004 alone, Molski alleged that he had been injured two or more times on the same day. On nineteen occasions, Molski alleged that he had been injured three or more times in one day. And, on nine occasions in 2004, Molski alleged that he suffered four or more injuries in one day.

Additionally, the district court discussed what it characterized as an "astonishing" letter the Frankovich Group had sent to defendants in at least two cases after suing them. The letter described itself as "friendly advice" and counseled the unrepresented defendant against hiring a lawyer. The letter warned that a defense attorney would embark on a "billing expedition" and that the defendant's money would be best spent on settlement and remediation of the ADA violations, rather than hiring a defense attorney. The letter also advised the defendant that its insurance policy might cover the claim. Finally, the letter advised the defendant that it had no bona fide defense to the lawsuit.

Relying on its inherent power to levy sanctions, the district court ordered

> that The Frankovich Group, as presently constituted, and as it may hereafter be constituted, including shareholders, associates and employees, is required to file a motion requesting leave of court before filing any new complaints alleging violations of Title III of the Americans with Disabilities Act in the United States District Court for the Central District of California. Such a motion must include a copy of this order.

As the basis for its sanction, the court first emphasized the ethics rules violations contained in the letter discussed above. For example, the letter offered legal advice to an unrepresented party whose interests conflicted with the interests of the Frankovich Group's clients. (citing Model Rules of Prof'l Conduct R.4.3).

Next, the district court found that many of the claims of bodily injury in complaints filed by the Frankovich Group were "contrived." The court found in particular that "the rate of physical injury defies common sense," noting that the plaintiffs alleged similar injuries sustained in a similar fashion at different businesses on the same day. The court noted that the similar injuries did not excuse the existence of accessibility barriers, but that its finding that the injury claims were contrived was "merely a recognition of the fact that reasonable people, once injured, tend to take affirmative steps to avoid similar physical injuries, rather than repeat that same activity 400 times (or five times in the same day)."

The district court also criticized the practice of the Frankovich Group of waiting one year before filing their complaints, in order to maximize the damages threatened and to intimidate the small businesses against whom the Frankovich Group frequently filed its suits.

Finally, the district court found that the high settlement rate in cases brought by the Frankovich Group, coupled with the volume of cases filed, showed a pattern of extortion.

In addition to imposing a pre-filing order on the Frankovich Group, the district court requested that the California state bar investigate the Frankovich Group's practices and consider disciplinary action. In the same order, the district court dismissed the plaintiffs' state law claims, declining to exercise supplemental jurisdiction over them.

On August 31, 2005, the district court, in a third published order, granted the defendants summary judgment on Molski's ADA claim for lack of standing. Because Molski's ADA claim was the final claim remaining in the case, the district court also entered an order dismissing with prejudice the plaintiffs' case in its entirety. (The district court had already dismissed DREES's ADA claim for lack of standing in an unpublished order filed on February 9, 2005.)

On September 13, 2005, Molski and DREES filed their notice of appeal. The notice provided that the plaintiffs were appealing four rulings of the district court: (1) the December 2004 order declaring Molski a vexatious litigant; (2) the February 2005 order dismissing DREES's ADA claim for lack of standing; (3) the March 2005 order sanctioning the Frankovich Group; and (4) the August 2005 order granting the defendants summary judgment on Molski's ADA claim for lack of standing and dismissing the case.

[IV]

[T]wo district courts in our circuit disagree about whether Molski's frequent litigation is vexatious. In this case, the Central District of California deemed Molski a vexatious litigant. However, the Northern District of California has denied a motion to declare Molski a vexatious litigant in that district. See *Molski v. Rapazzini Winery*, 400 F.Supp.2d 1208, 1212 (N.D.Cal.2005). We review a pre-filing order entered against a vexatious litigant for abuse of discretion. A district court abuses its discretion when it bases its decision on an incorrect view of the law or a clearly erroneous finding of fact.

The All Writs Act, 28 U.S.C. § 1651(a), provides district courts with the inherent power to enter pre-filing orders against vexatious litigants. However, such pre-filing orders are an extreme remedy that should rarely be used. Courts should not enter pre-filing orders with undue haste because such sanctions can tread on a litigant's due process right of access to the courts. A court should enter a pre-filing order constraining a litigant's scope of actions in future cases only after a cautious review of the pertinent circumstances. [N]evertheless, "[f]lagrant abuse of the judicial process cannot be tolerated because it enables one person to preempt the use of judicial time that properly could be used to consider the meritorious claims of other litigants."

The first factor under [our case law] is whether Molksi was given notice and an opportunity to be heard before the district court entered the pre-filing order. This is a core requirement of due process. In this case, Molski had fair notice of the possibility that he might be declared a vexatious litigant and have a pre-filing order entered against him because the district court's order was prompted by a motion filed by the defendants and served on Molski's counsel. Also, Molski had the opportunity to oppose the motion, both in writing and at a hearing.

The second factor [i]s whether the district court created an adequate record for review. "An adequate record for review should include a listing of all the cases and motions that led the district court to conclude that a vexatious litigant order was needed." The record before the district court contained a complete list of the cases filed by Molski in the Central District of California, along with the complaints from many of those cases. Although the district court's decision entering the pre-filing order did not list every case filed by Molski, it did outline and discuss many of them. The district court supplemented its findings in [its first order] with a further discussion of Molski's litigation history in [its second order]. The district court compiled a record adequate for review of its order.

The third factor [g]ets to the heart of the vexatious litigant analysis, inquiring whether the district court made " 'substantive findings as to the frivolous or harassing nature of the litigant's actions.' " To decide whether the litigant's actions are frivolous or harassing, the district court must "look at 'both the number and content of the filings as indicia' of the frivolousness of the litigant's claims." "An injunction cannot issue merely upon a showing of litigiousness. The plaintiff's claims must not only be numerous, but also be patently without merit."

Molski concedes that he has filed numerous claims. However, Molski contends that his suits were not vexatious because they had merit. As the district court observed, it is likely that many of the businesses Molski sued were not in compliance with the ADA. However, while Molski's complaints may have stated a legitimate claim for relief, it was not clearly erroneous for the district court to find that the claims of injury contained in those complaints were patently without merit. Because many of the violations Molski challenged were similar, it would have been reasonable for Molski's complaints to contain similar allegations of barriers to entry, inadequate signage, and so on. However, it is very unlikely that Molski suffered the same injuries, often multiple times in one day, performing the same activities— transferring himself from his wheelchair to the toilet or negotiating accessibility obstacles. Common sense dictates that Molski would have figured out some way to avoid repetitive injury-causing activity; even a young child who touches a hot stove quickly learns to avoid pain by not repeating the conduct. The district court's conclusion that Molski "plainly lied" in making his injury allegations was not clearly erroneous.

In light of the district court's finding that Molski did not suffer the injuries he claimed, it was not clearly erroneous for the district court to conclude that the large number of complaints filed by Molski containing false or exaggerated allegations of injury were vexatious.

The district court's determination that Molski harassed defendants into cash settlements was justified by its findings regarding Molski's litigation strategy. California law provides that a plaintiff who suffers discrimination based on his or her disability may recover up to three times the amount of actual damages for each offense, and that, at a minimum, the plaintiff must recover damages of not less than $4000. Cal.Civ.Code § 52(a). Thus, Molski usually sought damages of not less than $4000 for each day that a facility did not comply with the ADA. Because Molski would often wait to file suit until a full year elapsed since his visit to the defendants' establishments, defendants often faced claims for statutory damages of over one million dollars. While Molski's claim for daily damages might have been legally justified, it was not clearly erroneous for the district court to find that Molski's litigation strategy evidenced an intent to harass businesses into cash settlements.[6]

---

[6] We note that there was a substantial disconnect between the magnitude of injuries Molski suffered and the amount of damages he sought to recover. For example, in this case, in a declaration submitted to the district court, Molski admitted that the injury he suffered at Mandarin Touch—scraping his hand on the door frame—was "not a big injury." Nonetheless, Molski claimed damages of "not less than $4,000" for each of the 363 days that elapsed between when he visited Mandarin Touch on January 25, 2003, and when he filed his

The district court also did not err when it inferred an intent to harass defendants into settlement from the fact that Molski had tried on the merits only one of his roughly 400 ADA cases and the fact that Molski and the Frankovich Group targeted ethnic restaurants viewed as easy prey for coercive claims.

Frivolous litigation is not limited to cases in which a legal claim is entirely without merit. It is also frivolous for a claimant who has some measure of a legitimate claim to make false factual assertions. Just as bringing a completely baseless claim is frivolous, so too a person with a measured legitimate claim may cross the line into frivolous litigation by asserting facts that are grossly exaggerated or totally false. In an adversary system, we do not fault counsel or client for putting their best arguments forward, and it is likely the unusual case in which a finding of frivolous litigation follows in the train of a legitimate legal claim. It is a question of degree where the line falls between aggressive advocacy of legitimate claims and the frivolous assertion of false allegations. In this case, the district court, looking at the allegations of hundreds of lawsuits, made a decision that Molski's baseless and exaggerated claims of injuries exceeded any legitimacy and were made for the purpose of coercing settlement. We cannot on this record conclude that the district court's factual determinations were clearly erroneous or that the district court erroneously reached the legal conclusion that Molski's litigation was vexatious.

The fourth and final factor [i]s that the pre-filing order must be narrowly tailored to the vexatious litigant's wrongful behavior. [H]ere, [t]he district court's order is much narrower [than in cases in which we rejected pre-filing orders as overbroad]—it only prevents Molski from filing actions under Title III of the ADA in the Central District of California. The order thus appropriately covers only the type of claims Molski had been filing vexatiously—ADA claims. The order also does not prevent Molski from filing any ADA complaints, it merely subjects Molski's complaints to an initial screening review by a district judge. The order is narrowly tailored because it will not deny Molski access to courts on any ADA claim that is not frivolous, yet it adds a valuable layer of protection, which we think was warranted, for the courts and those targeted by Molski's claims.

In summary, we reemphasize that the simple fact that a plaintiff has filed a large number of complaints, standing alone, is not a basis for designating a litigant as "vexatious." We also emphasize that the textual and factual similarity of a plaintiff's complaints, standing alone,

---

complaint on January 23, 2004. Molski thus made a damage claim of no less than $1,452,000 on the day he filed his complaint, with that amount growing by the day. Even if Molski could claim statutory minimum damages in an amount far greater than any actual injury he suffered, Molski's claims of damages far in excess of the injuries he suffered are not entirely irrelevant to determining whether his litigation was vexatious. By seeking damages of not less than $4000 per day, Molski would claim actual damages beyond those to which he was arguably entitled under the California statutes. See Cal.Civ.Code §§ 52(a), 54.3(a) (permitting the recovery of actual damages). Also, there existed a possibility that the district court would reject the notion that Molski could recover daily damages, and that Molski would be forced to seek, for the most part, actual damages. Additionally, Molski's complaints usually sought punitive damages. In all of those situations, to recover actual or punitive damages, Molski would need to prove a corresponding injury. Because he claimed damages far in excess of his actual injuries, his exaggerated claims of damages support a pre-filing order to the extent that he sought to recover more than the statutory minimum of damages.

is not a basis for finding a party to be a vexatious litigant. Accessibility barriers can be, and often are, similar in different places of public accommodation, and there is nothing inherently vexatious about using prior complaints as a template.

As we discussed above, the ADA does not permit private plaintiffs to seek damages, and limits the relief they may seek to injunctions and attorneys' fees. We recognize that the unavailability of damages reduces or removes the incentive for most disabled persons who are injured by inaccessible places of public accommodation to bring suit under the ADA. See Samuel R. Bagenstos, *The Perversity of Limited Civil Rights Remedies: The Case of "Abusive" ADA Litigation,* 54 U.C.L.A. L.Rev. 1, 5 (2006). As a result, most ADA suits are brought by a small number of private plaintiffs who view themselves as champions of the disabled. District courts should not condemn such serial litigation as vexatious as a matter of course. For the ADA to yield its promise of equal access for the disabled, it may indeed be necessary and desirable for committed individuals to bring serial litigation advancing the time when public accommodations will be compliant with the ADA. But as important as this goal is to disabled individuals and to the public, serial litigation can become vexatious when, as here, a large number of nearly-identical complaints contain factual allegations that are contrived, exaggerated, and defy common sense. False or grossly exaggerated claims of injury, especially when made with the intent to coerce settlement, are at odds with our system of justice, and Molski's history of litigation warrants the need for a pre-filing review of his claims.

We acknowledge that Molski's numerous suits were probably meritorious in part—many of the establishments he sued were likely not in compliance with the ADA. On the other hand, the district court had ample basis to conclude that Molski trumped up his claims of injury. The district court could permissibly conclude that Molski used these lawsuits and their false and exaggerated allegations as a harassing device to extract cash settlements from the targeted defendants because of their noncompliance with the ADA. In light of these conflicting considerations and the relevant standard of review, we cannot say that the district court abused its discretion in declaring Molski a vexatious litigant and in imposing a pre-filing order against him.

V

The final issue in this case is whether the district court erred in imposing a pre-filing order against the Frankovich Group. [I]n this case, the district court afforded the Frankovich Group notice and an opportunity to be heard before imposing its sanction. [T]he district court also did not abuse its discretion in making the substantive determination that a pre-filing order was justified based on the conduct of the Frankovich Group. As discussed above, Molski's complaints repeatedly alleged injuries that the district court found to be contrived and untrue. Also, the claims of injuries often were inconsistent with the barriers alleged. For example, complaints filed by the Frankovich Group would allege bodily injury suffered as a result of inadequate signage or the lack of an accessible parking space.

In light of the similarity and exaggerated nature of the frequent injuries Molski alleged, we concluded above that the district court's findings regarding the lack of veracity in Molski's complaints were not clearly erroneous and that the district court was within its discretion in imposing a pre-filing order on Molski. When a client stumbles so far off the trail, we naturally should wonder whether the attorney for the client gave inadequate or improper advice. That the Frankovich Group filed numerous complaints containing false factual allegations, thereby enabling Molski's vexatious litigation, provided the district court with sufficient grounds on which to base its discretionary imposition of sanctions.

The district court also emphasized that the letter that the Frankovich Group sent to the defendants in at least two cases may have violated multiple ethics rules. While we do not rely on the possible ethical violations as a ground for affirming the sanction imposed on the Frankovich Group, we note that Frankovich Group's decision to send letters that many might view as intimidating to unrepresented defendants was, at best, a questionable exercise of professional judgment. The letters gave legal advice to unrepresented parties whose interests conflicted with the interests of the Frankovich Group, and this advice quite possibly ran afoul of relevant ethical rules. See Model Rules of Prof'l Conduct R.4.3 ("The lawyer shall not give legal advice to an unrepresented person, other than the advice to secure counsel, if the lawyer knows or reasonably should know that the interests of such a person are or have a reasonable possibility of being in conflict with the interests of the client."); Model Code of Prof'l Responsibility DR 7–104(A)(2) (providing that "a lawyer shall not . . . [g]ive advice to a person who is not represented by a lawyer, other than the advice to secure counsel, if the interests of such person are or have a reasonable possibility of being in conflict with the interests of his client").

Additionally, the letters advised the defendant that it had no bona fide defense to the ADA action, when in fact this might not be true in a particular case. For example, the ADA requires the removal of barriers in certain structures only when "such removal is readily achievable." 42 U.S.C. § 12182(b)(2)(A)(iv). This possibly false statement of law may have violated ethics provisions regarding a lawyer's candor to third parties. See Model Rules of Prof'l Conduct R.4.1(a) (providing that "[i]n the course of representing a client a lawyer shall not knowingly . . . make a false statement of material fact or law to a third person"); Model Code of Prof'l Responsibility DR 7–102(A)(5). [B]ut because the district court was within its discretion in sanctioning the Frankovich Group based on the questionable allegations of physical injury in the complaints they filed, we need not rely on the possible ethics rules violations as a ground for affirming the district court's sanction.

Finally, we hold that the district court's pre-filing sanction is sufficiently tailored to combat the Frankovich Group's practice of repetitive litigation based on false allegations of injury. The sanction requires the Frankovich Group to seek leave of the court before filing any more ADA complaints in the Central District of California, and requires that the district court's order in this case accompany the Frankovich Group's motion for leave. Functionally, the sanction ensures that a judge will initially determine whether the factual allegations in future complaints are colorable. The order will protect against the extracting of possibly unjustified settlements from uncounseled small-business defendants intimidated by the spectre of a federal complaint coupled with a coercive and misleading communication from a law firm. However, the order does not make it impossible for the Frankovich Group to pursue meritorious ADA litigation in the district court. Moreover, as far as the evidence before the district court showed, the Frankovich Group only used abusive litigation tactics in connection with litigation under the ADA. The pre-filing order rightly applies only to complaints asserting claims for relief under the ADA. For these reasons, we hold that the pre-filing order imposed in this case is adequately tailored to punish the past sanctionable conduct of the Frankovich Group, and, more importantly, to protect the courts and the public from any future misconduct by that law firm. Lawyers are required to give their clients' interests zealous advocacy, and while the pre-filing order in this case will not stand in the way of advocacy for legitimate claims, it will help to ensure that the services of the Frankovich Group are used in support of valid claims and not as a device to encourage settlement of unwarranted or exaggerated claims. We affirm the district court's order imposing sanctions on the Frankovich Group.

ORDER

All judges on the panel have voted to deny Plaintiff/ Appellant's Petition for Panel Rehearing, and so that petition is DENIED.

The full court has been advised of Plaintiff/Appellant's Petition for Rehearing *En Banc*, and a judge of this court requested a vote on whether this case should be reheard *en banc*; however, a majority of the non-recused active judges of the court did not vote in favor of *en banc* consideration. Fed. R. App. P. 35. Accordingly, the Petition for Rehearing *En Banc* is also DENIED. No further petitions for rehearing or rehearing *en banc* shall be considered.

Judges Graber and Fisher were recused from considering the *en banc* issues in this case and did not participate in the court's decision.

■ BERZON, CIRCUIT JUDGE, with whom KOZINSKI, CHIEF JUDGE, and PREGERSON, REINHARDT, HAWKINS, MCKEOWN, WARDLAW, W. FLETCHER, and PAEZ, CIRCUIT JUDGES, join, dissenting from the denial of rehearing en banc:

Pre-filing orders infringe the fundamental right to access the courts. They are properly reserved for extreme situations where there is absolutely no possibility that the allegations could support judicial relief and filing the suit is a burden on both the court and the opposing party—a costly exercise in futility. Under those circumstances, less draconian sanctions will not suffice. Because, by any measure, this is not such a case, I respectfully dissent from the denial of rehearing en banc.

I.

The First Amendment right to "petition the Government for a redress of grievances"—which includes the filing of lawsuits—is "one of 'the most precious of the liberties safeguarded by the Bill of Rights.'" *BE & K Constr. Co. v. NLRB*, 536 U.S. 516, 524 (2002) (quoting *United Mine Workers v. Illinois Bar Assn.*, 389 U.S. 217, 222 (1967)). Consequently, a determination that a litigant has repeatedly filed frivolous and harassing lawsuits itself implicates his First Amendment interest in access to the courts. Indeed, where an individual's use of the courts is declared abusive or baseless, "the threat of reputational harm[,] . . . different and additional to any burden posed by other penalties," is alone sufficient to trigger First Amendment concerns. See *id.* at 530.

Because the right to access the courts implicates due process and First Amendment rights, courts have been exceedingly reluctant to restrict such access. We have noted that because a pre-filing order "restricts an individual's access to the court system, it is an extraordinary remedy that should be narrowly tailored and rarely used." *Moy v. United States*, 906 F.2d 467, 470 (9th Cir.1990). This is so even though litigants and lawyers covered by a pre-filing order are not entirely enjoined from filing suits covered by the order, but must obtain the court's approval first. This pre-clearance requirement is in itself a serious imposition on the right to access the courts: "Among all other citizens, he is to be restricted in his right of access to the courts. As far as he is concerned, his future filings run the risk of delay and even possible rejection before he can call upon defendants to respond to those filings. . . . We cannot predict what harm might come to him as a result, and he should not be forced to predict it either. What he does know is that a Sword of Damocles hangs over his hopes for federal access for the foreseeable future." *Id.*

Because it interferes with the basic right of court access, "[a]n injunction cannot issue merely upon a showing of litigiousness." *Id.* Rather, "[t]he plaintiff's claims must not only be numerous, but also be patently without merit." *Id.* Other circuits have similarly emphasized the extreme caution to be used in imposing such orders. See, e.g., *In re Powell*, 851 F.2d 427, 434 (D.C.Cir.1988) ("[M]ere litigiousness alone does not support the issuance of an injunction. Both the number and content of the filings bear on a determination of frivolousness or harassment." (citation and footnote omitted)); *In re Oliver*, 682 F.2d 443, 446 (3d Cir.1982) ("Oliver's litigiousness alone would not support an injunction restricting his filing activities. . . . [L]egitimate claims should receive a full and fair hearing no matter how litigious the plaintiff may be.").

II.

[T]he panel opinion pays lip service to the long-standing and constitutionally-based principle that "[a]n injunction cannot issue merely upon a showing of litigiousness. The plaintiff's claims must not only be numerous, but also be patently without merit." Yet, neither the panel nor the district court contend that all or most of Molski's hundreds of ADA claims actually lack merit. In fact, both expressly concede that they are probably meritorious. [See panel op.:] ("We acknowledge that Molski's numerous suits were probably meritorious in part—many of the establishments he sued were likely not in compliance with the ADA."); [district court op.:] ("It is possible, even likely, that many of the businesses sued[by Molski] were not in full compliance with the ADA."). Instead, the panel relies on the district court's finding that Molski's "claims of injury . . . were patently without merit," and concludes this is enough to make the litigation frivolous.

As an initial matter, the district court's conclusion that Molski fabricated many allegations of injury, which was affirmed by the panel, simply cannot meet our standard for factual frivolousness. To be frivolous, factual allegations must be "wholly fanciful" or "conflicting with facts of which the district court may take judicial notice." *Franklin v. Murphy*, 745 F.2d 1221, 1228 (9th Cir.1984) (internal quotation marks omitted).

The district court and the panel relied solely upon the similarity and multitude of Molski's injuries: Numerous complaints alleged that he incurred physical injuries while attempting to overcome non-ADA-compliant public accommodations. The panel asserts that "it is very unlikely that Molski suffered the same injuries, often multiple times in one day, performing the same activities—transferring himself from his wheelchair to the toilet or negotiating accessibility obstacles. Common sense dictates that Molski would have figured out some way to avoid repetitive injury-causing activity; even a young child who touches a hot stove quickly learns to avoid pain by not repeating the conduct." On this reasoning, the panel concludes that the district court's finding that Molski "plainly lied" in his injury allegations was not clearly erroneous.

But the similarity of these injuries alone does not lead to the conclusion that the allegations are patently false. First, as the panel concedes, "[b]ecause many of the violations Molski challenged were similar, it would have been reasonable for Molski's complaints to contain similar allegations of barriers to entry, inadequate signage, and so on." In addition, Molski provided a reasonable explanation for the similarity of his injuries and the injurious nature of seemingly small acts. As another district court explained, in rejecting the district court's analysis here and declining to find Molski a vexatious litigant:

> Molski explains that, as a paraplegic, he relies entirely on his upper extremities and the strain of the improper transfers to the toilet are real injuries to him. Even though the pain might be short-lived, the cumulative effect of the multiple injuries is to wear down his upper extremities, joints, and shoulders. Molski also frequently injures his buttocks when forced to transfer to a toilet that is not configured in compliance with the ADA. Molski explains that, because he sits on his buttocks all day, bruises on his buttocks do not heal quickly or easily. . . .
>
> Molski supports the veracity of his claims of injury with a declaration from his treating physician, Dr. Thomas Lyle Hedge. . . . Dr. Hedge declares that Molksi [sic] has suffered "repetitive, continuous and cumulative" trauma/physical injury to the upper extremities from confronting architectural barriers such as unpaved pathways and toilets without proper grab bars or at an improper height.

Molski v. Rapazzini Winery, 400 F.Supp.2d 1208, 1210–11 (N.D.Cal.2005) (record citations omitted). Given this explanation,[1] the factual allegations of injury here were simply not "wholly fanciful," *Franklin*, 745 F.2d at 1228, even if the incremental nature of the alleged injury was not spelled out.

---

[1] Molski and Dr. Hedge both submitted declarations in the instant case providing the same explanations accepted in Rapazinni Winery.

But even if Molski's allegations of injury were meritless, the pre-filing order would not be justified: The allegations of injury are entirely irrelevant to Molski's ADA causes of action; past actual injury is not necessary to bring a claim under Title III of the ADA. *Molski v. M.J. Cable, Inc.*, 481 F.3d 724, 730 (9th Cir.2007). Allegations of injury are not necessary either to sue for statutory damages under California's Unruh Act. The panel appears to so recognize, but suggests that there are some scenarios under which Molski might want to pursue actual rather than statutory damages under state law, so the allegations of physical injury "are not entirely irrelevant." That may be. But the tangential connection of the physical injury allegation to the potential for success in the cases certainly makes it difficult to characterize the complaints as a whole as frivolous in any ordinary sense of that term.

The panel's other complaints similarly fail to justify a prefiling order. The panel complains that Molski sought daily statutory damages under California law, yet recognizes that these claims "might have been legally justified" because of a split among district courts on the issue. The panel also relies upon the fact that Molski often waited a year before filing suit, which greatly increased the statutory dam ages claim. But this conduct is permitted under the statute; if there is a problem created by the statutory scheme, the appropriate fix is legislative, not judicial.

In sum: The panel justifies its ruling by relying on assertedly false claims of injury that would be relevant only under California law and on permissible litigation strategies that increase Molski's damages claim under California law. Not only do these reasons entirely fail to justify the extreme sanction of a pre-filing order, they are also exclusively concerned with Molski's claims under state law. Yet the prefiling order enjoins Molski from filing only federal ADA claims. "If we are to permit pre-filing restrictive orders, these orders must be narrowly tailored to closely fit the specific vice encountered." At the very least, the pre-filing order should restrict Molski's ability to file access claims only under California law. What we have here, in other words, is not a "close[ ] fit" but a grotesquely oversized pre-filing order, going far beyond the only "vice[s] encountered" in the complaints, none of which have anything at all to do with the allegations of ADA violations.

III.

I recognize that some of the tactics used by Molski and the Frankovich Group are cause for concern. But there are ample avenues for addressing any concerns raised by this case—avenues that do not involve one judge, acting alone, imposing a pre-filing order that covers an entire district.

Let me emphasize the impact of the district court's decision: One judge has determined that Molski and the Frankovich Group are forbidden to file ADA complaints without prior approval in the entire Central District. That judge has not in any way specified what standards will be used in deciding which cases may be filed and which may not. Other judges in that district may disagree with the imposition of the pre-filing order—in fact, a majority may. Yet, they have no say at all in the matter. The likelihood of internal disagreement is highlighted by the fact that a judge in the Northern District has determined, on a similar record, that Molski should not be subjected to a pre-filing order. *Molski v. Rapazzini Winery*, 400 F.Supp.2d at 1209–12. So Molski can now bring ADA suits in the Northern District seeking to assure access in places of public accommodation, but cannot do so in the Central District without subjecting himself to prescreening by a single judge.

There are alternative mechanisms for addressing the perception that a litigant or lawyer is engaged in widespread litigation abuse— mechanisms that do not allow one judge, acting alone, to bar the courthouse door in perpetuity. The Central District, like most districts, has detailed procedures to investigate and sanction attorney misconduct. See C.D.Cal. Local R. 83–3. This process permits the involvement of multiple judges and members of the bar, rather than the one-judge disciplinary committee presented here. Or, if the conduct of ADA litigation concerns the entire Central District judiciary, the court as a whole can issue a general order setting forth particular guidelines for ADA access cases, as the Northern District has. See N.D.Cal.Gen.Order 56.

Moreover, Rule 11 is designed to deal on a case-by-case basis with the precise abuse found here: false factual allegations. See Fed.R.Civ.P. 11(b)(3), (c)(1) (requiring an attorney or unrepresented party to certify that "the factual contentions [contained in a pleading or motion] have evidentiary support" and permitting sanctions on "any attorney, law firm, or party that violated the rule or is responsible for the violation"). As far as I can tell, Rule 11 sanctions have never been imposed on either Molski or the Frankovich Group for their ADA litigation. Surely a lesser sanction in an individual case should first be attempted to cure any offending conduct before a broad pre-filing order covering all future cases is imposed.

IV.

At bottom, the panel may be uncomfortable with ADA litigation that it suspects is being brought to induce settlement.[3] This concern with serial access litigation is shared by many, rightly or wrongly. But the phenomenon is a creature of our federal and state statutes and cannot justify the issuing of prefiling orders that enjoin meritorious lawsuits. Moreover, while self-interest surely drives serial access litigation in part, the reason there can be so many lawsuits about access to public accommodations is that there are so many violations of the laws that seek to assure access, and so many disabled people are thwarted from participating equally in the activities of everyday life. I fear that the panel's opinion may be widely used to restrict critical private enforcement of civil rights laws by other litigants and lawyers. This case should have been heard en banc to prevent that result.

■ KOZINSKI, CHIEF JUDGE, with whom JUDGES REINHARDT, W. FLETCHER and PAEZ join, dissenting from the order denying the petition for rehearing en banc:

I agree with Judge Berzon that neither the district court nor our panel had an adequate basis for finding that Molski "plainly lied" about

---

[3] It is not clear why the settlements are so troubling. Judging by the dozens of settlement agreements in the record, the vast majority of these settlements include provisions for remedying barriers to access—precisely the goal sought by the ADA—as well as small amounts of monetary relief and payment of attorney's fees.

his injuries, or that his "claims of injury . . . were patently without merit." But I do so on an additional ground: The district court had no power to make such findings, nor a record to base them on, because it never held an evidentiary hearing.

Oh, sure, the docket indicates (somewhat misleadingly) that a "hearing" was held on the vexatious litigant motion, but it plainly was not an evidentiary hearing. What happened instead is this: The judge spent the first half of the hearing berating Molski and his lawyers, in pretty much the same terms as his subsequent order—which suggests that his views were cast in cement by the time of the "hearing." Compare Excerpts of Record (ER) 1094 ("After examining plaintiff's extensive collection of lawsuits. . . . "), and ER 1097 ("The Court simply does not believe that Molski suffered 13 identical injuries generally to the same part of his body, in the course of performing the same activity, over a five-day period."), with [the district court's order:] ("After examining Plaintiff's extensive collection of law suits. . . . "), and *id.* ("The Court simply does not believe that Molski suffered 13 nearly identical injuries, generally to the same part of his body, in the course of performing the same activity, over a five-day period."). After the judge was done, Molski's counsel was allowed to address the court, ER 1102–06, but no witnesses testified, no evidence was presented, there was no cross-examination and there were no evidentiary rulings— in short there was no trial. Molski, whose veracity the district court impugned, was not even present.

How then did the judge manage to make factual findings, and how does this panel affirm those findings on appeal? It's bad enough that the panel relies on its own armchair wisdom about plaintiff's supposed ability to avoid repetitive injuries, rather than looking to whether the record supports the findings of the district court. Worse still is that there is no record the panel could consult if it were of a mind to do so. There is no statement at all from Molski himself, as the complaint is not verified. The panel does not find the absence of an evidentiary record remarkable, perhaps laboring under the mistaken impression that there must be an evidentiary record somewhere under all that paper. Still and all, those of us unfamiliar with the alchemy of making findings based on no evidence—and affirming them based on no record—would dearly love to know why the absence of an evidentiary record is not an insuperable obstacle to affirming a district court's factual finding.

The bottom line is this: The district court made, and the panel affirms, a finding that Molski is a liar and a bit of a thief, without any evidence at all. The district court and the panel also manage to find that plaintiff just couldn't have suffered the injuries he alleges, without the benefit of an expert or any other proof. But does the district court have authority to make findings that severely curtail access to the federal court, not only for plaintiff but also for his lawyers and their other clients (present and future), without swearing in a single witness? Without giving notice and an opportunity to present evidence? Without cross-examination? Without any of the other rudiments of due process? Isn't Molski at least entitled to get on the stand, look the judge in the eye and tell his story?

Fortunately, there's a cure. The lawyers and judges of the Central District don't have to put up with this kind of tyranny by one judge acting entirely on his own. A member of a multi-judge court should not be able to single-handedly cut off one party or law firm's access to all the other judges of the court. The Central District judges can and should adopt a local rule or general order that any judge wishing to bar a litigant or a law firm from accessing the court must obtain the concurrence of a committee of his colleagues. Enforcement of the order, too, should not be entrusted to the judge who entered it, as he may take an unduly broad view as to its scope. Far wiser, and fairer, to have other judges, drawn at random, enforce the order in future cases.

By adopting such measures, the court would ensure that draconian orders such as this one will not be the handiwork of a single judge, subject only to cursory supervision by the court of appeals, but a shared responsibility of the court's judges, as such orders should be. And the new local rule or general order should be applied retroactively to Molski's case.

Like Judge Berzon, I'm very sorry that such an order was ever entered, and on such a non-existent record. I'm even sorrier that our panel has seen fit to affirm it, and that our full court has chosen to look the other way. But ultimately, it's up to the judges of the Central District to ensure that due process is upheld and that an injustice is avoided. I have every confidence that they will be equal to the task.

NOTES ON SERIAL LITIGATION

As the various *Molski* cases illustrate, a large proportion of ADA public accommodations litigation is brought by serial litigants—individuals with disabilities, like Jarek Molski, who go from town to town, suing dozens of stores, hotels, or restaurants in each for violations of the statute's physical accessibility requirements. A handful of individuals with disabilities (represented by a handful of lawyers) have brought hundreds of cases each to challenge the inaccessibility of businesses. See, *e.g.*, Bagenstos, *supra*, at 4 n.14 (listing examples). As in most of Molski's cases, these suits are typically meritorious in the sense that the defendant businesses are actually in violation of the ADA. Yet, perhaps not surprisingly, they have provoked significant resistance from businesses, courts, and legislators. Consider the following discussion of the major arguments against serial ADA litigation:

A.   The Notice Argument

Perhaps the most prominent argument against serial ADA litigation focuses not on the decision to bring large numbers of suits per se but on the refusal of many lawyers who bring such suits to give defendants prior notice and an opportunity to make their premises accessible without litigation. A number of judges have argued that this failure to provide notice is unethical and counterproductive. Rather than "rush[ing] to file suit," one federal district judge asserted in a typical formulation, "conciliation and voluntary compliance" would "[o]f course" be "a more rational solution" to inaccessibility. [T]he "ADA Notification Act," which has been introduced in four successive Congresses, would [b]ar a state or federal court from exercising jurisdiction over an ADA public accommodations suit unless the plaintiff provides the defendant written notice of "the specific facts that constitute the alleged violation" by registered mail, and ninety days elapses without the defendant correcting the violation. Echoing the comments of the federal judges who have denied attorneys' fees [to successful plaintiffs who fail to provide notice], the ADA Notification Act's proponents emphasize that notice would often make a lawsuit unnecessary by alerting businesses of the need to make changes.

Proponents of the notice argument fail to appreciate one salient fact: [T]he failure of many attorneys to provide presuit notice in accessibility cases is a direct result of the remedial limitations of the ADA's public accommodations title. If the plaintiff provides notice, the defendant will often be able to fix the problem in time to render any lawsuit nonjusticiable. Suing without notice will thus be the only way plaintiff's counsel can recover her fees.

To the extent that they attribute the lack of notice to the desire for attorneys' fees, then, critics of serial ADA litigation are correct. They go astray, however, in assuming that there is something wrong with plaintiffs' counsel wanting to recover their fees. [T]he ADA has been on the books for over fifteen years. If a business continually violated that law until the moment a plaintiff's lawyer came into the picture, the lawyer plainly deserves credit for making the business accessible. And the defendant business is poorly positioned to complain about the lack of notice. The ADA has been widely publicized. Though the statute's accessibility requirements are complex, the federal government offers businesses a number of free technical assistance resources to help them comply. And, as in other technical regulatory areas (workplace safety and environmental law come readily to mind), businesses can always hire their own lawyers or consultants to assess their current compliance with the law and to make plans to come into compliance. As between a lawyer whose efforts were necessary to make a facility accessible and a business that has not yet taken the steps to comply with the ADA more than fifteen years after its enactment, fairness dictates that it is the defendant business, and not the plaintiff's lawyer, who should bear the costs of enforcement.

B.   The Burdensome Litigation Argument

[A] second argument against serial ADA litigation focuses on the large numbers of accessibility suits plaintiffs have brought and on the burden those suits place on the courts. Not surprisingly, businesses that are sued by serial litigants complain that "firms filing lawsuits to force compliance have tied up federal court dockets." But it is not just defendants; federal judges have made the same charge. In a newspaper article published in September 2004, Judge Dickran Tevrizian of the United States District Court for the Central District of California was described as "troubled by the flood of litigation: 'There are roughly 40 ADA lawsuits on his docket,' he said. 'Multiply that by all the federal judges in the country. It's causing a lot of court congestion.' " And in decisions dismissing on other grounds ADA accessibility suits brought by serial plaintiffs, courts have gone out of their way to decry the burden imposed by the large numbers of lawsuits filed by such litigants. Complaints about a "blizzard of lawsuits" filed in an "alarming" volume that "clutter up our courts and make it tough on everyone" also received attention at the hearings on the proposed ADA Notification Act.

[S]trikingly, the opponents of serial ADA litigation have essentially acknowledged that the bulk of the lawsuits about which they complain have targeted business conduct that in fact violated the law. In the hearings on the proposed ADA Notification Act, Representative Mark Foley, the bill's primary sponsor, explained that state bar discipline could not be relied upon to regulate serial ADA litigation because "it is hard to prove the lawsuits are frivolous if violations do exist." Joseph Fields, an attorney who represents businesses that have been sued by serial ADA litigants, similarly explained that his clients need legislative protection because they have no adequate defense: When his clients are sued, Fields has "to tell them, no, you are not in compliance." As one federal judge recently noted, engaging in only a bit of hyperbole, "[I]t would be difficult to find any restaurant, specialty store, service station, or other public accommodation between Chico and Sacramento which does not have some barrier to disabled access under the Americans with Disabilities Act Accessibility Guidelines."

C.   The Outside Agitator Argument

[A] third frequent argument against serial ADA litigation asserts that the plaintiffs in such cases are not connected to the communities in which they bring suits, and that they challenge barriers about which local residents with disabilities have never complained. In media coverage of serial ADA litigation, this argument has taken on some of the overtones of Southern criticism of "outside agitators" during the African American civil rights movement. Thus, one editorial that criticized serial litigator Jarek Molski for "traveling throughout Southern California, finding violations of requirements in the Americans With Disabilities Act" asserted that in "many" of Molski's cases "other disabled folks found no fault and used the facilities with ease." And Walter Olson, in his attack on what he called the "ADA Shakedown Racket," prominently featured the claim of recently sued businesses that no person with a disability had "ever complained before about their facilities."

So too in the ADA Notification Act hearings, where Clint Eastwood set the tone by calling serial ADA plaintiffs' lawyers "self-appointed vigilantes." One witness, criticizing a series of suits against inaccessible businesses in Palm Beach, Florida, emphasized that "[t]he lawsuits were not filed by a Palm Beach County resident who would likely be seeking the services of these businesses, but by a Broward County resident." Another witness criticized an attorney for "develop[ing] a cottage industry based upon a single client who went door-to-door in Hawaii suing public accommodations" and subsequently "moved to the San Francisco area [where he] is doing the same thing."

The outside agitator argument has not been confined to the media or the political arena. Courts have frequently invoked the argument in the course of dismissing ADA public accommodations suits for lack of standing. [I]n a large number of cases brought by serial ADA litigants, courts have relied on the distance between the plaintiff's home and the defendant's business as grounds for concluding that there is no "real and immediate threat" that the plaintiff will visit the defendant's business again.

[W]orse, some courts (particularly in the Middle District of Florida) have considered it a factor weighing against the plaintiff's standing that, though the defendant's business is not accessible, other similar businesses in the area are accessible. These rulings directly contradict the statute's purposes. Congress specifically highlighted the "isolat[ion] and segregat[ion of] individuals with disabilities" as a principal target of the ADA. The statute's public accommodations title further emphasizes the antisegregation purpose by prohibiting businesses from providing "different or separate" accommodations to individuals with disabilities except where "necessary" to provide accommodations that are "as effective as [those] provided to others." To say that an individual with a disability is less likely to have standing to challenge inaccessible facilities at one hotel because other hotels are accessible is to disregard the essential principle that all places of public accommodation must comply with the statute.

Id. at 16–30 (footnotes omitted). Are these points well taken? Or do they overlook the serious problems posed to businesses and the legal system by serial ADA litigation? In particular, what is the justification for permitting plaintiffs to file suit under Title III without providing presuit notice? If plaintiffs really want access, not attorneys' fees, why don't they provide notice before bringing suit? Or is allowing plaintiffs' lawyers to recover fees in these cases necessary to get them to do the work to figure out whether a public accommodation is accessible in the first place?

The laws in some states provide broader remedies than does the ADA for plaintiffs challenging inaccessible public accommodations. California law, for example, authorizes the award of damages—including minimum statutory damages—for violations of its disability-access laws (laws that themselves incorporate the ADA). See Cal. Civil Code §§ 51-55. Do these laws provide a necessary incentive for public accommodations enforcement? Do they simply exacerbate the problem of burdensome litigation?

3. STATUTE OF LIMITATIONS

Pickern v. Holiday Quality Foods

United States Court of Appeals for the Ninth Circuit, 2002.
293 F.3d 1133.

■ WILLIAM A. FLETCHER, CIRCUIT JUDGE.

Plaintiff Jerry Doran appeals the district court's dismissal of his suit seeking injunctive relief for an alleged violation of Title III of the Americans with Disabilities Act, 42 U.S.C. § 12181 *et seq.* ("ADA" or

"Title III"). Doran, a paraplegic who uses a wheelchair, alleges that because defendant Holiday Quality Foods' ("Holiday") grocery stores are "public accommodations" within the meaning of the ADA, 42 U.S.C. § 12181(7)(E), Holiday is required to remove architectural barriers that make it difficult for Doran to gain access to one of Holiday's stores. On motion for summary judgment, the district court held that because Doran had not attempted to enter the store during the limitations period, and thus had not actually encountered any barriers during that period, his claim was time-barred and he did not have standing.

We hold that when a plaintiff who is disabled within the meaning of the ADA has actual knowledge of illegal barriers at a public accommodation to which he or she desires access, that plaintiff need not engage in the "futile gesture" of attempting to gain access in order to show actual injury during the limitations period. When such a plaintiff seeks injunctive relief against an ongoing violation, he or she is not barred from seeking relief either by the statute of limitations or by lack of standing.

We therefore reverse and remand.

[D]oran has patronized a number of Holiday stores and is a regular customer of the Holiday store in his hometown of Cottonwood, California. He states in a declaration: "My favorite grocery store chain is the Holiday Foods grocery stores. When I need to buy groceries, I look first to Holiday Foods grocery stores." Doran's complaint does not allege ADA violations by the Cottonwood store; rather, he alleges a failure to comply with the ADA at the Holiday store in Paradise, California, which is about 70 miles from Cottonwood. Doran's grandmother lives in Paradise, and Doran visits Paradise frequently to see her. He states in his deposition that "I try to go every Sunday to see my grandmother. She lives there [in Paradise], so I go up all the time." At some time prior to 1998, Doran visited the Paradise store and encountered the architectural barriers of which he now complains. He states that he would like to patronize the Paradise store when he visits his grandmother, but is deterred from doing so by the store's allegedly unlawful barriers.

Title III of the ADA provides that "[n]o individual shall be discriminated against on the basis of disability" in places of public accommodation. 42 U.S.C. § 12182(a). Title III defines "discrimination" as, among other things, a failure to remove "barriers . . . where such removal is readily achievable." 42 U.S.C. § 12182(b)(2)(A)(iv). If removal of a barrier is not "readily achievable," a public accommodation must make its facilities available through "alternative methods if such methods are readily available." 42 U.S.C. § 12182(b)(2)(A)(v).

Doran alleges that the Paradise store has inadequate access to and from the parking lot; inadequate checkstand access; inadequate signs; and inadequate access to the restroom and to vending machines. After visiting the store prior to 1998, he visited it again only once before filing his complaint on March 1, 1999. On that second visit, in late 1998, he was obliged, because of the barriers, to wait in the parking lot while his companion went into the store on his behalf. Because Doran delayed for more than a year in filing his complaint after he first became aware of the barriers at the Paradise store, the district court dismissed his complaint. Doran timely appealed from the dismissal.

[T]he enforcement provisions of Title III provide only for injunctive relief. Damages are not available to individuals. See 42 U.S.C. § 12188(a) (providing that the remedies available to individuals shall be those set forth in 42 U.S.C. § 2000a–3(a), which allows only injunctive relief for violations of Title II of the Civil Rights Act of 1964, Pub.L.88–352, codified as amended at 42 U.S.C. § 2000a *et seq.*); *Newman v. Piggie Park Enterprises, Inc.*, 390 U.S. 400, 402 (1968) (Title II allows injunctive relief only). Injunctive relief is available to "any person who is being subjected to discrimination on the basis of disability" or who has "reasonable grounds for believing that such person is about to be subjected to discrimination." 42 U.S.C. § 12188(a)(1) (emphases added). By employing the phrases "is being subjected to" and "is about to be subjected to," the statute makes clear that either a continuing or a threatened violation of the ADA is an injury within the meaning of the Act. A plaintiff is therefore entitled to injunctive relief to stop or to prevent such injury.

Seeking to avoid unreasonable burdens on ADA plaintiffs, Title III explicitly provides that it does not require "a person with a disability to engage in a futile gesture if such person has actual notice that a person or organization . . . does not intend to comply" with the ADA. *Id.* The "futile gesture" language of Title III is taken from *Teamsters v. United States*, 431 U.S. 324, 366 (1977). In *Teamsters*, the Court held that plaintiffs who did not actually apply for promotions could nevertheless challenge the employer's racially discriminatory seniority system under Title VII of the Civil Rights Act of 1964, Pub.L.88–352, codified as amended at 42 U.S.C. § 2000e *et seq.*, if they could show that they would have applied for the job if not for the employer's discriminatory practices. See *Teamsters*, 431 U.S. at 367–68. The Court reasoned that "[w]hen a person's desire for a job is not translated into a formal application solely because of his unwillingness to engage in a futile gesture he is as much a victim of discrimination as is he who goes through the motions of submitting an application." *Id.* at 365–66.

Congress specifically intended that *Teamsters'* "futile gesture" reasoning be applied to ADA claims. See H.Rep.No.101–485(II) at 82–83 (1990) ("The Committee intends for this doctrine to apply to this title"); S.Rep.No.101–116 at 43 (1989). Thus, under the ADA, once a plaintiff has actually become aware of discriminatory conditions existing at a public accommodation, and is thereby deterred from visiting or patronizing that accommodation, the plaintiff has suffered an injury. So long as the discriminatory conditions continue, and so long as a plaintiff is aware of them and remains deterred, the injury under the ADA continues.

A plaintiff has no cause of action under the ADA for an injury that occurred outside the limitations period.[2] But he or she has a cause of

---

[2]   The parties agree that a one-year limitations period applies. Because the ADA does not contain a statute of limitations, the court must apply the statute of limitations of the most analogous state law. See *Goodman v. Lukens Steel Co.*, 482 U.S. 656, 660; *Addisu v. Fred Meyer, Inc.*, 198 F.3d 1130, 1140 (9th Cir.2000). Most district courts have applied California's one-year limit for personal injury actions to federal disability discrimination claims brought in California. See *Daviton v. Columbia/HCA Healthcare Corp.*, 241 F.3d 1131, 1136 n.8 (9th Cir.2001) (citing cases, but not deciding the issue of whether a one-year limitations period applied to a disability claim brought under § 1983). Because the parties agree that the

action, and is entitled to injunctive relief, for an injury that is occurring within the limitations period, as well as for threatened future injury. Doran states that he is currently aware of barriers to access that now exist at the Paradise store, and that these barriers currently deter him. Indeed, he states that the barriers deterred him from entering the store just before filing suit, when he needed something from the store and was obliged to remain in the parking lot. Doran's suit for injunctive relief is therefore not time-barred.

[R]EVERSED AND REMANDED.

Garcia v. Brockway

United States Court of Appeals for the Ninth Circuit, *en banc*, 2008.
526 F.3d 456.

■ KOZINSKI, CHIEF JUDGE:

We consider when the statute of limitations begins to run in a design-and-construction claim under the Fair Housing Act (FHA).

Facts

In these consolidated cases, plaintiffs appeal the district court's determination that their FHA design-and-construction claim was time-barred by the two-year statute of limitations. The fact patterns in these cases (at summary judgment) differ in several significant respects:

Garcia v. Brockway, No. 05–35647: In 1993, Dennis Brockway built the South Pond Apartments in Boise, Idaho, and sold the last unit in 1994. In 1998, the Idaho Fair Housing Council filed an administrative complaint with the U.S. Department of Housing and Urban Development (HUD), and in 2001 Brockway entered into a conciliation agreement with HUD and the Idaho Fair Housing Council that resolved the complaint and provided a fund to pay for accessibility modifications to any unit for any resident with a disability.

In 2001, plaintiff Noll Garcia rented a unit at South Pond and resided there until 2003. Because of a disability Garcia uses a wheelchair for mobility. While at South Pond, his apartment did not comply with the design-and-construction requirements of the FHA. It lacked curb cuts from the parking lot to the sidewalk, it didn't have a ramp to the front entrance door and the doorways were too narrow to allow clear passage of a wheelchair. Garcia's requests that management make accessibility improvements were ignored, as was his request that management build a ramp to his door or that he be relocated to a more accessible unit. Within two years of leasing the apartment, Garcia sued the original builder and architect (Brockway and Robert Stewart, respectively), and the current owners and management (the Zavoshy defendants). The district court granted summary judgment in favor of Brockway and Stewart because Garcia's design-and-construction claim was not filed within the limitations period. The court denied the Zavoshy defendants' summary judgment on the accommodations and interference claims, and they subsequently settled. Garcia appeals the summary judgment in favor of Brockway and Stewart.

---

applicable limitations period is one year and do not argue the point to us, we assume without deciding that they are correct.

Thompson v. Gohres Construction Co., No. 06–15042: In 1997, Gohres Construction built the Villas at Rancho del Norte in North Las Vegas, Nevada. Shortly thereafter, the Villas were issued a final certificate of occupancy, and the property was sold through foreclosure in 2001. Defendant Michael Turk is an officer of Rancho del Norte Villas, Inc., and of Gohres Construction. In 1997, the Disabled Rights Action Committee (DRAC) filed a complaint with HUD, and HUD terminated the complaint in 2001 because the complainants, as "testers," lacked standing. We subsequently held that testers have standing to sue under the FHA. See *Smith v. Pac. Props. & Dev. Corp.*, 358 F.3d 1097, 1104 (9th Cir.2004).

In 2004, plaintiff Tamara Thompson, a member of DRAC, "tested" the Villas and found discriminatory conditions—including an inaccessible building entrance, no curb cuts for the handicapped parking spaces and inadequate access to the pool. Within a year of Thompson's inspection, plaintiffs Thompson and DRAC sued Turk, Marc Gohres and Gohres Construction, asserting an FHA design-and-construction claim. The district court granted defendants' motion to dismiss because the claim was time-barred. We granted plaintiffs' motion to voluntarily dismiss the appeal as to Gohres and Gohres Construction. Plaintiffs thus only appeal the district court's order with respect to Turk.

Analysis

The FHA prohibits the design and construction of multifamily dwellings that do not have certain listed accessibility features. 42 U.S.C. § 3604(f)(3)(C). The statute provides three enforcement mechanisms. First, an administrative complaint may be initiated with HUD, see *id.* §§ 3610–3612, and remedies include actual damages to the aggrieved person, civil penalties and injunctive relief. See 24 C.F.R. § 180.670(b)(3). An aggrieved person—*i.e.*, any person who "claims to have been injured by a discriminatory housing practice," 42 U.S.C. § 3602(i)(1)—must file the complaint "not later than one year after an alleged discriminatory housing practice has occurred or terminated." Id. § 3610(a)(1)(A)(i). HUD may also file a complaint *sua sponte*; it's unclear whether HUD is subject to the same limitations period. See *id.*

Second, the Attorney General may bring a civil action if a defendant has "engaged in a pattern or practice of resistance" to FHA rights, or if a "group of persons has been denied any [FHA] rights . . . and such denial raises an issue of general public importance." *Id.* § 3614(a). The FHA does not provide a statute of limitations for these actions, and other courts have held that such actions seeking equitable relief are not subject to any time limit. Actions seeking damages are subject to the general three-year statute of limitations, see 28 U.S.C. § 2415(b), and those for civil penalties must be "commenced within five years from the date when the claim first accrued." *Id.* § 2462.

The third enforcement mechanism—the one at issue here—is a private civil action. The FHA provides that "[a]n aggrieved person may commence a civil action in an appropriate United States district court or State court not later than 2 years after the occurrence or the termination of an alleged discriminatory housing practice." 42 U.S.C. § 3613(a)(1)(A). In other words, an aggrieved person must bring the lawsuit within two years of either "the occurrence . . . of an alleged discriminatory housing practice" or "the termination of an alleged discriminatory housing practice." Here, the practice is the "failure to design and construct" a multifamily dwelling according to FHA standards.[1] *Id.* § 3604(f)(3)(C). The statute of limitations is thus triggered at the conclusion of the design-and-construction phase, which occurs on the date the last certificate of occupancy is issued. In both cases, this triggering event occurred long before plaintiffs brought suit.[2]

Plaintiffs advance three theories that would extend the limitations period to cover their lawsuits. We address each in turn.

1. Plaintiffs contend that an FHA design-and-construction violation is a continuing one that does not terminate until the building defects are cured. The Supreme Court has held that "where a plaintiff, pursuant to the Fair Housing Act, challenges not just one incident of conduct violative of the Act, but an unlawful practice that continues into the limitations period, the complaint is timely when it is filed within [the statutory period, running from] the last asserted occurrence of that practice." *Havens Realty Corp. v. Coleman*, 455 U.S. 363, 380–81 (1982) (footnote omitted). Congress has since codified this continuing violation doctrine by amending the FHA to include both "the occurrence [and] the termination of an alleged discriminatory housing practice" as events triggering the two-year statute of limitations. 42 U.S.C. § 3613(a)(1)(A).

---

[1] The dissent concedes that our reading of the statute is "not entirely implausible," but insists that the practice at issue is the sale or rental of an FHA-noncompliant unit, rather than design and construction of the building. Therefore, according to the dissent, the statute of limitations begins to run when a party "first attempts to buy or rent or tests a FHA-noncompliant unit." The dissent reaches this conclusion by distinguishing section (f)(3)(C) from sections (f)(1) and (f)(2) on the grounds that (f)(3)(C) is a definitional provision, whereas (f)(1) and (f)(2) provide causes of action. However, (f)(3)(C) is a coordinate section, not a subordinate section within (f)(1) or (f)(2), so treating (f)(3)(C) as subordinate makes no structural sense.

Additionally, under the dissent's interpretation, only the party that actually does the selling or renting would be liable, not the party that designed or constructed an FHA-noncompliant unit, because section (f)(1) prohibits only discrimination "in the sale or rental . . . [of] a dwelling," while section (f)(2) prohibits discrimination "in the terms, conditions, or privileges of sale or rental of a dwelling." Thus, if (f)(3)(C) does not operate as an independent prohibition, but merely defines the meaning of "discriminate" under (f)(1) or (f)(2), Garcia wouldn't have a private cause of action under the FHA against Brockway and Stewart (the builders) because they sold or rented no individual units.

The fundamental problem with the dissent's interpretation is that isolating (f)(1) and (f)(2) from (f)(3)(C) alters both the starting point for the statute of limitations and who is liable under the FHA. Were we to adopt the dissent's interpretation, we would make it impossible, or at least more difficult, for the Attorney General to bring a design-and-construction claim against builders under 42 U.S.C. § 3614(a), because design and construction of an FHA-noncompliant building alone would not, under the dissent's interpretation, be actionable under the FHA. The dissent's interpretation therefore may help a few FHA plaintiffs today, but it could harm many more people living in FHA-noncompliant units in the future.

[2] This does not leave plaintiffs without any recourse. They can still report the violation to the Attorney General, and—long after construction is complete—he can seek to enforce defendants' legal duty to design and construct if there's "a pattern or practice of resistance," or if "any group of persons has been denied any [FHA] rights . . . and such denial raises an issue of general public importance." 42 U.S.C. § 3614(a). They can also request accommodations, for which they bear the costs, to remedy an impediment. See *id.* § 3604(f)(3)(A)–(B). Garcia's case is a good example. Despite the fact that his claims against Stewart and Brockway were time-barred, Garcia was able to obtain relief by settling with the current owners and management of South Pond with respect to his accommodations claim.

Plaintiffs claim Congress's insertion of "termination" would be meaningless if it weren't read as termination of the design-and-construction defect. HUD's Fair Housing Act Design Manual supports this reading: "With respect to the design and construction requirements, complaints could be filed at any time that the building continues to be in noncompliance, because the discriminatory housing practice—failure to design and construct the building in compliance—does not terminate." U.S. Dep't of Hous. & Urban Dev., Fair Housing Act Design Manual: A Manual to Assist Designers and Builders in Meeting the Accessibility Requirements of the Fair Housing Act 22 (rev. 1998).

Plaintiffs and HUD confuse a continuing violation with the continuing effects of a past violation. "Termination" refers to "the termination of an alleged discriminatory housing practice." The Supreme Court has "stressed the need to identify with care the specific [discriminatory] practice that is at issue." *Ledbetter v. Goodyear Tire & Rubber Co.*, 550 U.S. 618 (2007). Here, the practice is "a failure to design and construct," which is not an indefinitely continuing practice, but a discrete instance of discrimination that terminates at the conclusion of the design-and-construction phase. This violation differs from the one Congress codified as "continuing" in light of *Havens*, where the claims were "based not solely on isolated incidents . . . , but a continuing violation manifested in a number of incidents—including at least one . . . that [wa]s asserted to have occurred within the [limitations] period." 455 U.S. at 381.

Put differently, "[a] continuing violation is occasioned by continual unlawful acts, not by continual ill effects from an original violation."[4] The Supreme Court last Term reiterated the distinction between a continuing violation and continual effects when it held that "current effects alone cannot breathe life into prior, unchanged discrimination; as we held in *Evans*, such effects in themselves have 'no present legal consequences.' " *Ledbetter*, 127 S.Ct. at 2169 (quoting *United Air Lines, Inc. v. Evans*, 431 U.S. 553, 558 (1977)). Although the ill effects of a failure to properly design and construct may continue to be felt decades after construction is complete, failing to design and construct is a single instance of unlawful conduct. Here, this occurred long before plaintiffs brought suit. Were we to now hold the contrary, the FHA's statute of limitations would provide little finality for developers, who would be required to repurchase and modify (or destroy) buildings containing inaccessible features in order to avoid design-and-construction liability for every aggrieved person who solicits tenancy from subsequent owners and managers. Indeed, now that we have recognized tester standing, an aggrieved person wouldn't even need to solicit tenancy, but merely observe the violation. This is not what Congress provided in erecting a

---

[4] The dissent maintains we're making a "crucial error" by defining the alleged discriminatory housing practice as the failure to design or construct an FHA-compliant unit. The dissent seems to define the act of selling or leasing an FHA-noncompliant unit as the discriminatory housing practice. However, this confuses the "discrete act of alleged . . . discrimination" with the "date when the effects of this practice were felt." *Ledbetter*, 127 S. Ct. at 2168. The failure to design and construct the unit according to FHA standards is the "underlying" discrete act of discrimination. *Id.* (quoting *Lorance v. AT & T Techs., Inc.*, 490 U.S. 900, 911 (1989)). And the date of this underlying act "governs the limitations period." *Id.* at 2169 (quoting *Lorance*, 490 U.S. at 911).

two-year statute of limitations for FHA design-and-construction claims. If Congress wanted to leave developers on the hook years after they cease having any association with a building, it could have phrased the statute to say so explicitly.

Nor may we ignore the statute of limitations to help an aggrieved person who suffers from the effects of such violation decades after construction. As the Supreme Court has held, "[t]he limitations periods, while guaranteeing the protection of the civil rights laws to those who promptly assert their rights, also protect [defendants] from the burden of defending claims arising from . . . decisions that are long past." *Del. State Coll. v. Ricks*, 449 U.S. 250, 256–57 (1980). "A discriminatory act which is not made the basis for a timely charge . . . is merely an unfortunate event in history which has no present legal consequences." *Ledbetter*, 127 S. Ct. at 2168 (quoting *Evans*, 431 U.S. at 558).

2. Plaintiffs also argue that the statute of limitations should not begin to run until the aggrieved person encounters the design-and-construction defect. This novel legal theory was first articulated in a law review article. See Robert G. Schwemm, *Barriers to Accessible Housing: Enforcement Issues in "Design and Construction" Cases Under the Fair Housing Act*, 40 U. Rich. L. Rev. 753, 849–55 (2006).

There's some support for this "encounter" theory: "A damages action under the [FHA] sounds basically in tort—the statute merely defines a new legal duty, and authorizes the courts to compensate a plaintiff for the injury caused by the defendant's wrongful breach." *Curtis v. Loether*, 415 U.S. 189, 195 (1974). Because an FHA damages action "sounds basically in tort," plaintiffs claim the statute of limitations is not triggered until a disabled person is actually damaged by the practice. Plaintiffs contend that, upon completion of construction, no injury has yet occurred, and "the standard rule [for tort purposes is] that the limitations period commences when the plaintiff has a complete and present cause of action." *Bay Area Laundry & Dry Cleaning Pension Tr. Fund v. Ferbar Corp. of Cal.*, 522 U.S. 192, 201 (1997) (internal quotation marks omitted). Under this theory, the statute of limitations did not begin to run until Thompson tested the Villas, which occurred within two years of filing suit.

Plaintiffs make too much of the Supreme Court's observation that the FHA "sounds basically in tort." The Court was not dealing with the statute of limitations but with the very different question of whether FHA plaintiffs are entitled to a jury trial. This passing reference to tort law cannot be read to trump statutory provisions that deal expressly with the statute of limitations. The FHA's limitations period does not start when a particular disabled person is injured by a housing practice, but by "the occurrence or the termination of an alleged discriminatory housing practice." 42 U.S.C. § 3613(a)(1)(A). Under the FHA, the ability to privately enforce the "new legal duty" thus only lasts for two years from the time of the violation, and the violation here is "a failure to design and construct." *Id.* § 3604(f)(3)(C). Plaintiff's injury only comes into play in determining whether she has standing to bring suit. See *id.* §§ 3602(i)(1), 3604(f)(2). Some aggrieved persons may not encounter this violation until decades after the limitations period has run and thus will be unable to file a civil action, even though they have standing to raise the claim. However, "[i]t goes without saying that statutes of limitations often make it impossible to enforce what were otherwise perfectly valid claims. But that is their very purpose, and they remain as ubiquitous as the statutory rights or other rights to which they are attached or are applicable." *United States v. Kubrick*, 444 U.S. 111, 125 (1979).

Plaintiffs' theory is further undercut by our decision in *Smith*, in which we held that the harm of the violation occurs when a design-and-construction defect is observed. 358 F.3d at 1104. Under plaintiffs' theory post-*Smith*, any individual with a disability who merely observes the design-and-construction defect could bring suit—even if the limitations period had long run for every tenant and/or owner. The author of plaintiffs' encounter theory concedes that Smith creates serious problems for his theory: "[If] testers do have standing based on injury to their § (f)(1)–(2) rights caused by encountering such a building, they could presumably generate an endless series of such injuries by repeated visits to the building. . . . Eventually, the limitations periods would run on the claims based on the earlier encounters, but the tester could always start a new clock by returning to the building." Schwemm, 40 U. Rich. L. Rev. at 859 (footnote omitted). The encounter theory thus "raise[s] serious equitable issues with respect to timeliness," *id.*, because it strips the statute of limitations of all meaning.

3.   Garcia argues that the limitations period does not begin to run until the aggrieved person discovers the design-and-construction defect. Garcia advances this theory as both the discovery rule and the equitable tolling doctrine, but neither helps him.

The discovery rule serves to extend the time from which the limitations period starts to run until "the plaintiff knows both the existence and the cause of his injury." *Kubrick*, 444 U.S. at 113. Garcia thus contends that the limitations period shouldn't have started to run until he first visited South Pond in 2001. The discovery rule is strikingly similar to plaintiffs' encounter theory, and thus fails for the same reasons. Holding that each individual plaintiff has a claim until two years after he discovers the failure to design and construct would contradict the text of the FHA, as the statute of limitations for private civil actions begins to run when the discriminatory act occurs—not when it's encountered or discovered. See 42 U.S.C. § 3613(a)(1)(A).

"Equitable tolling may be applied if, despite all due diligence, a plaintiff is unable to obtain vital information bearing on the existence of his claim." This doctrine "focuses on a plaintiff's excusable ignorance and lack of prejudice to the defendant." As Judge Posner has explained, "[e]quitable tolling is frequently confused . . . with the discovery rule. . . . It differs from the [discovery rule] in that the plaintiff is assumed to know that he has been injured, so that the statute of limitations has begun to run; but he cannot obtain information necessary to decide whether the injury is due to wrongdoing and, if so, wrongdoing by the defendant."

Here, Garcia doesn't claim he was injured within the limitations period but was unable to obtain vital information concerning the existence of his claim until the period expired. Instead, he basically contends that it would be inequitable not to allow him to bring a civil lawsuit. Fairness, without more, is not sufficient justification to invoke equitable tolling, and the district court properly refused to apply it. In his plea for a fairer outcome, Garcia fails to mention the extreme prejudice defendants would suffer if plaintiffs could indefinitely bring civil damages actions for buildings defendants no longer own and cannot fix without the cooperation of the current owners. This is hardly a situation where there is a "lack of prejudice to the defendant."

In sum, application of the discovery rule or the equitable tolling doctrine, as the district court noted in *Garcia*, "would render the clear language of the statute meaningless and superfluous." Both doctrines would have the same effect as the continuing violation doctrine by tolling the statute of limitations indefinitely and thus stripping it of all meaning. Even if we thought this interpretation were more equitable, we don't have the authority to "interpret a provision in a manner that renders other provisions of the same statute inconsistent, meaningless or superfluous."

As both district courts held, an aggrieved person must bring a private civil action under the FHA for a failure to properly design and construct within two years of the completion of the construction phase, which concludes on the date that the last certificate of occupancy is issued. Because neither plaintiff brought a timely suit, their cases were properly dismissed.

AFFIRMED.

■ PREGERSON and REINHARDT, CIRCUIT JUDGES, dissenting:

We adopt in full Judge Fisher's dissent to the three-judge panel's decision, *Garcia v. Brockway*, 503 F.3d 1092, 1101–11 (9th Cir.2007) (Fisher, Circuit Judge, dissenting), which also appears immediately below, as the dissenting opinion of the en banc minority. We write additionally only to emphasize the extent to which the majority's holding perverts the purpose and intent of the statute. Indeed, the majority's decision well illustrates how statutes of limitations have been twisted by courts to limit the scope and thrust of civil rights laws.

The majority takes an Act that was designed to protect disabled persons by mandating that multifamily housing be made accessible to them and construes its statute of limitations in a way that solely benefits the housing construction industry and renders the statute of far less use to disabled individuals than Congress intended. The Fair Housing Act ("FHA") contains a 30 month grace period that gave developers building new multifamily housing clear notice of what was required to satisfy the statute's accessibility standards. See 42 U.S.C. § 3604(f)(3)(C). There is no reason that a developer who fails to comply with these requirements should not be held accountable for such violations. Nevertheless, the majority holds that unless a disabled person happens to become aware of the developer's failure to comply within two years after the certificate of completion is issued, the developer is home-free—completely immune from suit. Thus, a disabled person who seeks to acquire an FHA non-compliant unit in a housing development more than two years after the development is certified for occupancy cannot sue the developer even if no person familiar with the needs of disabled persons had previously seen the property and no disabled person had been aware of or injured by the violation until the would-be plaintiff attempted to buy or lease the unit. It seems apparent to us that Congress intended the statute of limitations to have the opposite result: that the disabled person who is injured by the developer's violation of the FHA should be able to sue that developer if he institutes his action within two years of the injury. It did not intend to invite the developer to assume the risk of non-compliance, in order to save construction costs, by taking the chance that his violation of the law would remain undiscovered by the disabled community for a period of two years.

The purpose of the FHA's design and construction requirements was to protect an important civil right. It was to help provide disabled individuals equal access to multifamily housing and to eliminate the de facto segregation to which handicap-inaccessible housing gives rise. See H.R.Rep.No.100–711, at 27–28 (1988) ("The Committee believes that these basic features of adaptability are essential for equal access and to avoid future de facto exclusion of persons with handicaps, as well as being easy to incorporate in housing design and construction. Compliance with these minimal standards will eliminate many of the barriers which discriminate against persons with disabilities in their attempts to obtain equal housing opportunities."). The Act, including its statute of limitations provision, is to be construed in a manner that accomplishes this purpose. This the majority has not done. Instead, it construes the FHA's statute of limitations so as to offer the least benefit to disabled persons and the most to developers of multifamily housing. Because we cannot condone a construction so wholly at odds with the purpose of the statute, and the manner in which we are to construe it, we respectfully dissent.

■ FISHER, CIRCUIT JUDGE, dissenting:

I respectfully dissent. The majority erroneously treats a building's improper design and construction as the event that triggers the Fair Housing Act's (FHA) two-year statute of limitations. It does so by finding an ambiguity in the statute and then resolving that ambiguity contrary to the overall purpose and structure of the FHA and its legislative and judicial history.

I believe instead that the most plausible reading of the statute is that the limitations period begins (at the earliest) when a disabled person actually experiences discrimination—either in attempting to buy or rent a noncompliant housing unit, in "testing" such a unit or upon moving in as a tenant. The majority contravenes the general rule that statutes of limitations are triggered by the accrual of a plaintiff's cause of action. Under the majority's approach, a real estate developer or landlord of a noncompliant building will often be immunized from suit long before a particular disabled individual has been injured and able to challenge the noncompliant features. Importantly, the majority's position is at odds with the FHA's legislative history, with Supreme Court precedent regarding the statute's construction and with the longstanding interpretation of the government agency charged with administering the FHA.

As a result of the majority's reading, disabled persons—the statute's actual intended beneficiaries—will be stripped of their ability to enforce the FHA's most important protection and instead will be relegated to "reasonable modifications" at their own expense. In contrast, real estate developers and landlords who ignore the FHA's design requirements will receive a free pass once two years have elapsed since a defective building's construction. Ironically, by invoking provisions Congress inserted into the FHA to expand disabled persons' access to the courts and to facilitate private enforcement, the majority transforms a statute of limitations into a highly unusual statute of repose for the benefit of real estate developers and landlords.

I would hold that Appellants' claims are not time-barred. Noll Garcia filed suit within two years of moving into the South Pond Apartments, and Tamara Thompson sued less than a year after finding discriminatory conditions at the Villas at Rancho del Norte. Accordingly, I would reverse the district courts' rulings and remand so that Appellants may proceed with their cases.

I.

The majority begins its analysis of private civil actions under the FHA by correctly quoting the applicable statute of limitations. See 42 U.S.C. § 3613(a)(1)(A) ("An aggrieved person may commence a civil action . . . not later than 2 years after the occurrence or the termination of an alleged discriminatory housing practice . . . whichever occurs last. . . . "). But the majority then commits a crucial error that underlies the rest of its decision. "Here," the majority states, "the [discriminatory housing] practice is the 'failure to design and construct' a multifamily dwelling according to FHA standards." Having conceived of Appellants' claims as being limited to the design and construction of the South Pond Apartments and the Villas at Rancho del Norte, the majority leaps to the conclusion that those claims are time-barred. "In both cases, th[e] triggering event," *i.e.*, "the conclusion of the design-and-construction phase," "occurred long before plaintiffs brought suit."

The problem with the majority's analysis is that a "failure to design and construct" is not itself an event that can trigger the FHA's statute of limitations. Under § 3613(a)(1)(A), an "aggrieved person" must file suit within two years of "the occurrence or the termination of an alleged discriminatory housing practice." Section 3602(f) defines a discriminatory housing practice, in relevant part, as "an act that is unlawful under section 3604 . . . of this title." Section 3604, in turn, states that "it shall be unlawful," among other things, "[t]o discriminate in the sale or rental, or to otherwise make unavailable or deny, a dwelling to any buyer or renter because of a handicap," § 3604(f)(1), and "[t]o discriminate against any person in the terms, conditions, or privileges of sale or rental of a dwelling, or in the provision of services or facilities in connection such dwelling, because of a handicap," § 3604(f)(2). Section 3604 separately states that "[f]or purposes of this subsection, discrimination includes—. . . a failure to design and construct [covered multifamily] dwellings" in accordance with various requirements concerning accessibility to and use by disabled persons. § 3604(f)(3)(C).

The most natural reading of these provisions is that the FHA's statute of limitations is triggered when someone is aggrieved by one of the unlawful actions specified by § 3604(f)(1) or § 3604(f)(2), with the two-year period running from the occurrence or termination of the offending practice. The limitations period for a disabled would-be buyer or renter or tester thus begins (at the earliest) when that individual first attempts to buy or rent or tests a FHA-noncompliant unit. At that point—but not previously—it can be said that a real estate developer or landlord has "discriminate[d] in the sale or rental, or [has] otherwise ma[d]e unavailable or den[ied] a dwelling to [the individual] because of a handicap," § 3604(f)(1), or has "discriminate[d] against [the individual] in the terms, conditions, or privileges of sale or rental of a dwelling . . . because of a handicap," § 3604(f)(2). Until then, the disabled person has not been subjected to any discriminatory action. Analogously, the limitations period for an actual tenant begins (at the earliest) when the individual first moves into a FHA-noncompliant unit. Only at that point is it fair to say that a real estate developer or landlord has "discriminate[d] against [the individual] . . . in the provision of services or facilities . . . because of a handicap." § 3604(f)(2). Because real estate developers, like landlords, engage in the "provision of services or facilities" and "make unavailable or deny[ ] a dwelling" to a handicapped individual, they can be liable under (f)(2) and (f)(1).

This reading is consistent with the understanding of other courts, commentators and, as discussed below, the Department of Housing and Urban Development (HUD), the agency charged with enforcing the FHA. See, *e.g.*, *Fair Housing Council, Inc. v. Village of Olde St. Andrews, Inc.*, 210 Fed.Appx. 469, 481 (6th Cir.2006) (unpublished) (FHA limitations period "begin [s] to run from the date that the individual attempted to buy the unit and discovered the nonconforming conditions"); *id.* at 480 (referring to the "overwhelming majority of . . . federal courts that have . . . rejected the position advanced" here by the majority); *Montana Fair Housing, Inc. v. Am. Capital Dev., Inc.*, 81 F.Supp.2d 1057, 1063 (D.Mont.1999); Robert G. Schwemm, *Barriers to Accessible Housing: Enforcement Issues in "Design and Construction" Cases Under the Fair Housing Act*, 40 U. Rich L. Rev. 753, 851 (2006) ("If a disabled homeseeker's § (f)(1)–(2) rights are not violated until his first encounter with the defendant's building, then a complaint filed promptly thereafter is timely, regardless of how old the building is."). The majority, however, goes down a different path, contending that it is the actions described by § 3604(f)(3)(C)—namely the faulty design and construction of a covered dwelling—that trigger the FHA's statute of limitations. The majority's construction, while not entirely implausible, ultimately fails for the simple reason that § 3604(f)(3)(C) is crucially different from § 3604(f)(1) and § 3604(f)(2).

The activities specified by § 3604(f)(1) and § 3604(f)(2)—all of which involve taking action against a disabled person "because of" that person's "handicap"—are clearly "unlawful" "discriminatory housing practices" that begin the FHA's limitations period. In contrast, § 3604(f)(3)(C) is best read as a specific example of the discrimination that in fact becomes actionable under § 3604(f)(1) and § 3604(f)(2)— when that discrimination takes place "in the sale or rental . . . to any buyer or renter," § 3604(f)(1), or "against any person in the terms, conditions, or privileges of sale or rental . . . or in the provision of services or facilities," § 3604(f)(2). Section § 3604(f)(3)(C) is a definitional provision, stating that "discrimination includes . . . the [faulty] design and construction of covered multifamily dwellings," rather than a provision that actually sets forth a cause of action.[4] The construction of a FHA-noncompliant building thus no more triggers the FHA's statute of limitations than the creation of any other latent discriminatory condition or policy (*e.g.*, a landlord's policy—as yet unenforced—not to rent to disabled people). It is only when that latent condition or policy results in an action prohibited by § 3604(f)(1) or § 3604(f)(2) that the limitations period begins. Beforehand, the improperly designed building (and the landlord's unimplemented rental policy) are much like a potentially dangerous ditch into which no one has yet fallen—capable of inflicting harm and violating the law, but not yet actually doing either. See *Village of Olde St. Andrews, Inc.*, 210 Fed.Appx. at 480 ("[F]rom a purely textual standpoint a violation of the relevant Fair Housing Act provision here requires more than the mere design and construction of a noncompliant housing unit. Recall, the text of the Fair Housing Act itself focuses on housing discrimination in the sale or rental of housing units.").

Applying this analysis to the cases at hand, Appellants' suits were plainly timely. While both the South Pond Apartments and the Villas at Rancho del Norte were built more than two years before Garcia and Thompson sued, this fact is irrelevant since their rights under § 3604(f)(1) and § 3604(f)(2) were not violated until they came into contact with the defective buildings. Garcia's limitations period thus began no earlier than when he moved into South Pond (less than two years before he filed suit), and Thompson's limitations period began no earlier than when she tested the Villas (less than one year before she brought her claims). It is on those dates—not when South Pond and the Villas were constructed—that Garcia and Thompson were the victims of discriminatory housing practices that triggered the FHA's statute of limitations.

My conclusion that Appellants' suits are not time-barred is thus based directly on the statutory text, and does not depend on the statute's codification of the continuing violations doctrine. Nevertheless, it is worth noting that the majority's analysis of that doctrine, suffers from the same defect as its analysis of the rest of the statutory text. Appellants "confuse a continuing violation with the continuing effects of a past violation" only if the relevant violation is defined (incorrectly) as a failure to design and construct FHA-compliant dwellings. If the violation is properly characterized as a practice of carrying out the actions prohibited by § 3604(f)(1) and § 3604(f)(2), then it is plain that Appellees' unlawful conduct itself—as opposed to merely its consequences—continues until that practice is halted. See Schwemm, *supra*, at 848 ("[A] nonconforming building amounts to an ongoing discriminatory denial of 'privileges' or 'facilities' to disabled tenants and homeseekers regardless of how many years have passed since the building was completed."); cf. *Havens Realty Corp. v. Coleman*, 455 U.S. 363, 380–81 (1982) (holding that FHA suit is timely if allegedly unlawful policy continues into the limitations period).

---

[4] The majority reads far too much into § 3604(f)(3)(C)'s placement as coordinate with subsections (f)(1) and (f)(2). Section (f)(3) is framed very differently from (f)(1) and (f)(2), indicating that it is a definitional provision, not a coordinate one. Section 3604 states that it is "unlawful" to do the actions described in (f)(1) and (f)(2), but does not state that the actions in (f)(3) are similarly unlawful.

II.

The majority's interpretation not only disconnects "design and construction" from § 3604(f)(1) and § 3604(f)(2), but it is also flawed because it triggers the limitations period before a particular plaintiff has been "aggrieved"—*i.e.*, injured. This reading conflicts with the statutory text as well as the presumption that statutes of limitations are not triggered at least until the plaintiff's cause of action has accrued. In effect, the majority converts what is plainly a statute of limitations into a statute of repose.

Subsection 3613(a)(1)(A) states that only "[a]n aggrieved person" may file suit under the FHA. Under § 3602(i), " '[a]ggrieved person' includes any person who—(1) claims to have been injured by a discriminatory housing practice; or (2) believes that such person will be injured by a discriminatory housing practice that is about to occur." Accordingly, until a plaintiff has become "aggrieved," he cannot "commence a civil action"; and until he can legally initiate his action, there is no reason even to consider the further requirement that FHA suits be filed "not later than 2 years after the occurrence or the termination of an alleged discriminatory housing practice." § 3613(a)(1)(A); see *Havens*, 455 U.S. at 381 (linking start of FHA's limitations period to plaintiffs' assertions that they were "deprived . . . of the benefits of interracial association" and suffered "injury to [their] counseling and referral services"); *Village of Olde St. Andrews*, 210 Fed.Appx. at 481.

The majority asserts, however, that the "aggrieved person" terminology pertains only to potential plaintiffs' standing to file suit. But this is not how very similar language in other statutes of limitations has been interpreted. Title VII of the Civil Rights Act of 1964, for example, refers to "person[s] aggrieved" and states that the limitations period begins "after the alleged unlawful employment practice occurred." 42 U.S.C. § 2000e–5(e)(1). In its recent decision interpreting this provision, the Supreme Court never so much as hinted that Title VII's limitations period would commence before a plaintiff was injured. Indeed, the Court declared that if "an employer forms an illegal discriminatory intent towards an employee but does not act on it until 181 days later," "[t]he charging period would not begin to run until the employment practice was executed on day 181 because until that point the employee had no cause of action. The act and intent had not yet been joined." *Ledbetter v. Goodyear Tire & Rubber Co.*, 550 U.S. 618, ___ n. 3, 127 S.Ct. 2162, 2171 n. 3 (2007).[6]

Ledbetter [is an] illustration[ ] of the general rule that statutes of limitations are not triggered at least until a plaintiff's cause of action has accrued. This general rule—which the majority fails to acknowledge, let alone rebut—has been explicitly articulated by the Supreme Court. "While it is theoretically possible for a statute to create

---

[6] The majority misreads *Ledbetter* as standing for the proposition that an individual's first experience of discrimination can nonetheless constitute the mere "effects" of a past discriminatory decision for statute of limitations purposes. As *Ledbetter* makes clear, however, the statute of limitations does not begin to run until the individual actually experiences the discrimination herself—*i.e.*, when a discriminatory decision "was made and communicated to [the plaintiff]"—not when the defendant adopted a policy that might someday impact a particular plaintiff. See *Ledbetter*, 127 S.Ct. at 2169.

a cause of action that accrues at one time for the purpose of calculating when the statute of limitations begins to run, but at another time for the purpose of bringing suit, we will not infer such an odd result in the absence of any such indication in the statute." *Reiter v. Cooper*, 507 U.S. 258, 267 (1993); see also *Bay Area Laundry & Dry Cleaning Pension Trust Fund v. Ferbar Corp.*, 522 U.S. 192, 201 (1997) ("Unless Congress has told us otherwise in the legislation at issue, a cause of action does not become 'complete and present' for limitations purposes until the plaintiff can file suit and obtain relief."). Under the majority's reading, the "odd result" discussed in *Reiter* becomes the law of this circuit. The FHA's two-year limitations period begins to run as soon as a covered building's construction has been completed, even though no plaintiff has yet been injured or can yet sue. Such an unusual rule should follow only if it were unambiguously compelled by the statutory text—which it is not.

[IV].

The majority argues that my interpretation of the statute—under which the limitations period for private suits brought under the FHA begins no earlier than when a plaintiff is first injured by a discriminatory housing practice—would "eviscerate[ ]" the FHA's statute of limitations and have adverse consequences for real estate developers. This contention is meritless. First, the FHA's limitations period would not be obviated by my reading of the statute. In fact, plaintiffs would be barred from bringing suit under § 3604(f)(1) and § 3604(f)(2) once two years have elapsed since their injuries, and potential defendants would be immunized from suit two years after remedying the statutory violations of covered dwellings. It is also hard to see how an interpretation that follows the accrual rule presumption can be more radical than one that flouts it.

Second, the legislative history demonstrates that Congress did not share the majority's solicitude for real estate developers. In passing the FHA, and then in amending it in 1988, Congress intended to issue "a clear pronouncement of a national commitment to end the unnecessary exclusion of persons with handicaps from the American mainstream." House Report at 18. Congress notably did not express any concern about builders who failed to comply with the relatively modest requirements of § 3604(f)(3)(C) being held to account for their failures more than two years after the offending dwellings were constructed. Indeed, in 1999, Congress rejected a proposed bill that would have barred the FHA's application to housing that was FHA-noncompliant but that had "received a building permit or other similar approval . . . as meeting the requirements of the applicable building code." Justice in Fair Housing Enforcement Act of 1999, H.R. 2437, 106th Cong. § 2(2). Congress was unpersuaded by the bill's proponents that it should "provide relief from prosecution to those in the building community who may have committed building design violations" since the FHA was amended 11 years earlier. Justice in Fair Housing Enforcement Act of 1999: Hearing on H.R. 2437 Before the Subcomm. on the Constitution of the H. Comm. on the Judiciary, 1999 WL 983520 (statement of Chairman Charles T. Canady). Ironically, the majority now creates for real estate developers the time-bar they were denied by Congress.

Third, to the extent policy considerations are relevant here, they cut against the majority's position. Under its reading of the statute, the intended beneficiaries of the FHA—disabled persons—are barred from enforcing their right to accessible housing (other than through reasonable modifications at their own expense) as soon as two years have elapsed since the completion of a dwelling's construction. A builder could even construct a FHA-noncompliant dwelling and insulate himself altogether from suit simply by waiting two years to look for tenants. See *Village of Olde St. Andrews*, 210 Fed.Appx. at 480 ("Often, housing units go unsold or unlet for some time after they are built. If the statute of limitations were to begin running immediately upon completion of the building, potential buyers may not even look at the property until after the statute of limitations has run. Such a result would run counter to . . . the broad remedial intent of Congress embodied in the Act.") (internal quotation marks omitted). Moreover, the judicial interest in having cases brought while relevant evidence is still available is at a low ebb here. As one district court has observed, "as the FHA requires no showing of intent, defendant's architectural plans and apartment complexes can themselves speak to the alleged construction violations." *Silver State Fair Housing Council, Inc. v. ERGS, Inc.*, 362 F.Supp.2d 1218, 1222 n.1 (D.Nev.2005).

V.

The majority's reading of the FHA's statute of limitations is inconsistent with the statutory text, the presumption in favor of an accrual rule, the relevant legislative history, the generous construction that the FHA must be accorded and HUD's reading of the provision. In accordance with both the statute's language itself and these non-textual considerations, I would hold that the limitations period for claims brought under § 3604(f)(1) and § 3604(f)(2) commences at the earliest when a plaintiff is first injured by a discriminatory housing practice. Applying that approach, I would reverse the district courts' rulings because both Garcia and Thompson were first injured less than two years before they filed suit, and remand for further proceedings. Therefore, I respectfully dissent.

Disabled in Action v. SEPTA

United States Court of Appeals for the Third Circuit, 2008.
539 F.3d 199.

■ HARDIMAN, CIRCUIT JUDGE.

In this statutory interpretation case, we must decide when the statute of limitations begins to run in a case arising under the Americans With Disabilities Act (ADA) and the Rehabilitation Act (RA). Appellant Disabled in Action of Pennsylvania (DIA) argues that under the plain language of the statute, its claims accrued "upon the completion" of alterations to two Philadelphia subway stations. Appellee Southeastern Pennsylvania Transportation Authority (SEPTA) argues, and the District Court held, that DIA's claims accrued prior to the completion of the alterations when DIA discovered that the planned alterations would not include elevators.

I.

[D]IA is a nonprofit corporation that seeks to eliminate discrimination against disabled individuals in all aspects of community life. To achieve this goal, DIA employs a variety of methods including: government monitoring, political activism, direct involvement in municipal planning, and, as a last resort, litigation. Many of DIA's approximately 450 members use wheelchairs and rely on SEPTA for their public transportation needs.

SEPTA is an agency of the Commonwealth of Pennsylvania responsible for providing public transportation in Southeastern Pennsylvania. In Philadelphia, SEPTA's City Transit Division operates a vast network of subway and subway-elevated rapid rails, regional rails, light rails, trackless trolleys, and buses that provide over 850,000 passenger trips per day. SEPTA receives federal funding for many of its activities, including its recent remodeling of an entrance to the 15th Street Station.

A.   15th Street Station and Courtyard

The bustling 15th Street Station is located underground near 15th and Market Streets in downtown Philadelphia. Passengers can access the station in two ways. First, using the stairway at the southwest side of 15th and Market Streets, passengers can descend directly to the platform for the Market-Frankford subway line. Second, using the stairway or escalator at the northwest side of the same block, passengers can descend to the "15th Street Courtyard." From there, they can turn northward toward the Suburban Regional Rail Line Station (Suburban Station), or southward, toward the Market-Frankford platform. SEPTA's renovations to this latter entrance gave rise to the present dispute.

Prior to SEPTA's renovations, the 15th Street Courtyard included a set of stairs and two escalators enclosed within a headhouse. On September 27, 1999, SEPTA received a $700,000 grant from the Economic Development Administration of the United States Department of Commerce for a project entitled "Renovation of 15th and Market Streets Headhouse at Suburban Station." According to the grant, the project was to involve "various renovations to the 15th and Market Streets entrances and related areas" including "renovation of entrances to the underground train station concourse; demolition of existing facilities; the construction/installation of new stairs, landscaping, lighting, signage, finishes, canopies; and all appurtenances."

In accepting the Commerce Department funding, SEPTA agreed to "pursue diligently the development of the Project so as to ensure completion . . . within [the] time schedule." Specifically, the grant required SEPTA to begin construction within 18 months of its receipt of the funds and to limit the total construction period to 29 months. In addition, the grant was to expire "five (5) years from the fiscal year of the Grant Award," requiring that the project be "physically and financially completed by September 30, 2004."

Having secured funding, SEPTA applied to the City of Philadelphia for a variance from certain provisions of the Building Code. Among the provisions from which SEPTA sought a variance was Section B–

1110.2.2(9), which requires that "[w]here building entrances are altered, or when plans are presented to relocate and provide a new primary entrance, the entrance shall be made accessible." For obvious reasons, SEPTA's variance application caught the attention of DIA's legal counsel, Stephen F. Gold.

Fearful that SEPTA's renovations would not include an elevator, Gold wrote to Edward McLaughlin, City Commissioner for the Department of Licenses and Inspections. In his letter of August 3, 2000, Gold expressed concern "that the City would allow SEPTA to apply for such a variance on its behalf for such a major public access point." Gold insisted that "[i]n addition to ensuring that renovations . . . are carried out in compliance with the Building Code, the City also has an obligation to ensure that such renovations are . . . carried out in compliance with the [Americans With Disabilities Act]." He asked McLaughlin to keep him informed "as to how the City plans to proceed with [SEPTA's] variance request."

Gold received no response from McLaughlin and consequently discussed his concerns with Pete Winebrake, an attorney in the City Solicitor's Office. Gold summarized the discussion in a letter dated September 28, 2000: "As I stated on the phone yesterday, this problem should be resolved before construction commences, or you leave me with very few options. I am very concerned that the City's train has already left the station and I must act sooner than later [sic]. I am available to meet with you at your earliest convenience."

Gold heard nothing more from Winebrake, but received a letter dated November 14, 2000 from Assistant City Solicitor Fredrick K. Pasour regarding the "15th Street Courtyard Portion of the Suburban Station Project." In pertinent part, Pasour's letter stated:

> I represent the City of Philadelphia with respect to the above-referenced project. I understand that you believe that the ADA, its regulations and the Accessibility Guidelines require an elevator in the 15th Street courtyard. I also understand that you are considering bringing a lawsuit to enjoin the 15th Street courtyard portion of the project if the City issues a building permit based on plans that do not include an elevator in the 15th Street courtyard.

> This letter is to advise you that the City doe [sic] not share your view that an elevator is required in the 15th Street courtyard and has issued a building permit for the project. Please remember that the 15th Street courtyard will be readily accessible to and usable by individuals with disabilities. As you are aware, elevators are planned for other locations near the 15th Street courtyard.

> The current bids for the portion of the project that includes the 15th Street courtyard renovations are only good through December 30, 2000. If, therefore, you plan to bring an action challenging the 15th Street courtyard portion of the project, please do so in an expeditious manner.

> I understand that you had one meeting with representatives of the City and SEPTA at the 15th Street courtyard to discuss the project. I believe that another meeting this week may be

useful in order to discuss the project in more detail and to determine if we can reach an agreement that is satisfactory to you, the disabled community, the City and SEPTA.

Despite Pasour's letter, Gold did not immediately file a lawsuit, and the City issued SEPTA a building permit on or about February 14, 2001, describing the 15th Street Courtyard project as follows:

Demolition incorporates head house, stair, railings, limited wall, veneer, pavement, and lighting systems. Also to be removed are planters, fountain and ceilings. Construction scope consists of glass head house, stair, (2) retail spaces, railings, storefront sys., planters, lighting and paving installed, as well as new ceiling.

SEPTA commenced construction a few days later.

The record suggests several explanations for DIA's decision not to file suit prior to this juncture. First, Gold testified that in 2000, he met with representatives of SEPTA and the City because "they were really anxious to get a commitment from [him] that there would not be a lawsuit regarding 15th Street." According to Gold, Frances Egan, Assistant to SEPTA's General Manager for Government and Public Affairs, and Deborah Russo, a representative of the City, assured him that in lieu of an elevator at 15th Street, SEPTA "would put in the elevator at City Hall and begin construction in 02 with the completion date of 04."

Gold discussed the proposed compromise with DIA, and DIA agreed that it was acceptable. Gold informed Egan of his client's assent, but neither party memorialized the deal. Assuaged nonetheless, DIA took no further action until late 2002 when it appeared that SEPTA was not installing an elevator at City Hall.

Gold's explanation for DIA's decision not to file a pre-construction lawsuit is supported by a Settlement Agreement in which DIA voluntarily dismissed its claims against the City, and the City affirmed that it "only granted permits for [the 15th Street Courtyard] renovation because [it] believed SEPTA had agreed to construct elevators in the City Hall Courtyard in lieu of the required elevator at 15th and Market."

Alternatively, the record suggests that at some point, DIA's strategy shifted from obtaining a pre-construction injunction to pursuing post-construction remedies based on Gold's belief that even though "[SEPTA] had started construction or even completed [construction]," the ADA enabled DIA to force SEPTA to install an elevator. Gold admitted that he gave Pasour's admonition to file suit in an expeditious manner "[v]ery, very, very much consideration" but determined that he could "optimize representing [DIA] [by] letting [SEPTA] move the stairs and begin[ ] the construction because [DIA] could always get the elevator and make [SEPTA] put it [in] if necessary along 15th Street." For reasons that are not clear from the record, Gold concluded that if construction did not proceed, "there would be no elevator." Accordingly, he "decided . . . to let [SEPTA and the City] sit in their own petard [*sic*]."

Whatever the reasons for waiting, DIA filed its initial Complaint on March 14, 2003, approximately eight months after the newly renovated

15th Street Courtyard entrance was opened on August 8, 2002 without an elevator. DIA requested "permanent injunctive relief to enjoin [SEPTA] to begin construction immediately of a[n] elevator at the 15th and Market Street entrance . . . to assure access for persons with disabilities."

B.   City Hall Station and Courtyard

The second subject of the present dispute is SEPTA's replacement of an escalator that carried passengers from the concourse above the City Hall Station platform to City Hall Courtyard. Located near the 15th Street Station, City Hall Station is one of the busiest stops on the Broad Street subway line and serves as a transfer point between the Broad Street Line, the Market-Frankford Line, and Regional Rail Lines. For instance, from the concourse below City Hall Courtyard, passengers can access the 11th and 13th Street Market-Frankford Line platforms without using stairs.

The City Hall Courtyard project was part of SEPTA's Escalator Replacement Program, launched in 1999 to improve the safety of escalators throughout the system. SEPTA included funding for the program in its FY 2001 Capital Budget after holding a public meeting to discuss the improvements on May 22, 2000. Although no representative of DIA attended the meeting, DIA's Executive Director testified that DIA reviews SEPTA's Capital Budget each year and was aware of the project.

By August 17, 2001, SEPTA had barricaded the area around the City Hall Courtyard escalator and posted signs that read "Project of the Pennsylvania Public Transportation Assistance Fund; Escalator Replacement at Erie, Spring Garden, City Hall & 30th Street Stations; Southeastern Pennsylvania Transportation Authority." SEPTA removed the existing escalator, extended the wellway and relocated the truss upon which it sat, and installed a new escalator. Construction was completed and the escalator was opened to the public on or about August 24, 2003. The finished project did not include an elevator. On February 15, 2005, DIA filed its Fourth Amended Complaint, adding allegations regarding this project.

C.   The District Court Proceedings

DIA filed its initial Complaint on March 14, 2003, alleging that SEPTA's renovations to the 15th Street Station entrance violated the ADA and the RA. The District Court dismissed the complaint because DIA failed to name the City of Philadelphia, the owner of the real property upon which the entrance is located, as a defendant. After the Court granted DIA relief from the dismissal, DIA added the City as a defendant in its First Amended Complaint. On October 10, 2003, DIA filed a Second Amended Complaint, which included allegations about a deal between DIA, SEPTA, and the City to install an elevator at the City Hall Courtyard instead of the 15th Street Courtyard.

After an unsuccessful settlement attempt, DIA filed a Third Amended Complaint, adding an ADA "key station" claim. See 42 U.S.C. § 12147(b); 29 C.F.R. § 37.47. SEPTA moved to dismiss the key station claim and argued that portions of the Third Amended Complaint should be stricken pursuant to a stipulation between DIA and SEPTA. The District Court refused to dismiss the key station claim, but DIA agreed to strike its allegations that SEPTA had agreed to install an elevator at City Hall in lieu of 15th Street.

On August 16, 2004, DIA reached a settlement agreement with the City. Therein, the City stipulated that "[i]t is the City's legal opinion that SEPTA is legally obligated under the ADA and accompanying Regulations to construct an elevator at the 15th and Market Street Courtyard entrance, which SEPTA renovated." Moreover, the City asserted that it "only granted permits for [the 15th Street] renovation because [it] believed SEPTA had agreed to construct elevators in the City Hall Courtyard." Based on this agreement, the District Court dismissed the City from the case.

On February 15, 2005, DIA filed a Fourth Amended Complaint in which it added a second claim under § 12147(a) based on SEPTA's renovations to the City Hall Courtyard. DIA alleged that SEPTA's renovations to both the 15th Street and City Hall Courtyards constituted "alterations" that triggered ADA and RA accessibility obligations. 42 U.S.C. § 12147(a); 29 U.S.C. § 794(a). DIA also alleged that both 15th Street and City Hall are "key stations" that SEPTA must make accessible. 42 U.S.C. § 12147(b); 29 U.S.C. § 794(a). DIA requested, inter alia, an injunction compelling SEPTA to construct elevators at both locations. After completing discovery, the parties filed cross motions for summary judgment.

The District Court granted SEPTA's motion for summary judgment on all counts. As to DIA's § 12147(a) claims, the court reasoned that "[t]o determine the accrual date of a discrimination claim, a court must focus on when the discriminatory act occurred, not when the effect of that act became painful." The District Court rejected DIA's argument that SEPTA's discriminatory acts occurred "upon completion of [the] alterations" to the 15th Street and City Hall Courtyards. Rather, the District Court held that the claims accrued when DIA knew, or had reason to know, that SEPTA's renovations would not include elevators. According to the District Court, DIA had such knowledge regarding the 15th Street Courtyard "no later than November 1, 2000, when DIA was informed that SEPTA would proceed with the planned construction at the 15th and Market Street Courtyard without installing an elevator," and regarding the City Hall Courtyard, "at least as early as August 17, 2001," when a sign was posted "in the City Hall Courtyard on the outside of the boarded-off construction area where the escalator was being replaced." Because DIA filed its § 12147(a) claims more than two years after these dates, the District Court dismissed them as barred by the statute of limitations, id., and DIA appealed.

[III.]

Neither Title II of the ADA nor Section 504 of the RA includes an express statute of limitations. As both statutes were enacted prior to the effective date of the default four-year statute of limitations for federal statutes, see 28 U.S.C. § 1658, we borrow the statute of limitations of the most analogous state law cause of action. The District Court concluded, and the parties do not dispute, that Pennsylvania's two-year statute of limitations for personal injury claims should apply to claims under § 12147(a). [T]he more difficult question—and the crux of the dispute between DIA and SEPTA—is when this two year statute of limitations begins to run.

A.

Ordinarily, a statute of limitations begins to run from the moment the potential plaintiff has a "complete and present cause of action." *Bay Area Laundry & Dry Cleaning Pension Trust Fund v. Ferbar Corp.*, 522 U.S. 192, 195 (1997). [W]here Congress has specified an accrual date by "explicit command" or "by implication from the structure and text of the statute," we defer to its directive. "[I]n the absence of a contrary directive from Congress," we apply the "federal discovery rule," which dictates that a federal cause of action accrues "when the plaintiff discovers, or with due diligence should have discovered, the injury that forms the basis for the claim." [F]or the reasons that follow, we hold that the "structure and text of the statute" evince Congress's intention that claims under § 12147(a) accrue "upon the completion of . . . alterations" to public transportation facilities.

1.

The portion of § 12147(a) at issue in this appeal provides:

> With respect to alterations of an existing facility or part thereof used in the provision of designated public transportation services that affect or could affect the usability of the facility or part thereof, it shall be considered discrimination, for purposes of section 12132 of this title and section 794 of Title 29, for a public entity to fail to make such alterations (or to ensure that the alterations are made) in such a manner that, to the maximum extent feasible, the altered portions of the facility are readily accessible to and usable by individuals with disabilities, including individuals who use wheelchairs, upon the completion of such alterations.

[L]ike the parties and the District Court, we believe § 12147(a)'s concluding phrase—"upon the completion of such alterations"—is of fundamental importance in answering this question.

DIA argues that the phrase modifies the entire definition of what "shall be considered discrimination" because "only when . . . alterations are completed and the inaccessible facility is re-opened will people with mobility disabilities be subject to discrimination." Therefore, DIA concludes, claims under § 12147(a) do not accrue until alterations are completed.

SEPTA invokes the rule of the last antecedent, arguing that the "upon the completion" phrase only modifies the phrase "the altered portions of the facility are readily accessible to and usable by individuals with disabilities" and not "the entire definition of what constitutes discrimination." Under this interpretation, which the District Court adopted, the function of the "upon the completion" phrase is "merely [to] suggest that accessibility for disabled individuals must be in place at the time the alterations are completed." In other words, the phrase merely acknowledges that while renovations are in progress, facilities will necessarily be inaccessible to everyone, including "individuals with disabilities," and that this temporary inaccessibility is not what § 12147(a) prohibits.

[W]e find DIA's interpretation of the "upon the completion" phrase more persuasive. The language appears in the "specific context" of a single sentence that defines activities that "shall be considered discrimination"; and in the "broader context" of Title II, which assures that no "individual with a disability" is "subjected to discrimination." 42 U.S.C. §§ 12147(a) and 12132. "Discrimination," as it is ordinarily defined, is the denial of "privileges to a certain class because of race, age, sex, nationality, religion, or handicap." Black's Law Dictionary 500 (8th ed.2004). The privileges at stake in § 12147(a) are access to, and use of, public transportation facilities. It is difficult to understand how these privileges are denied to individuals with disabilities by the mere promulgation or approval of renovation plans that do not include accessibility features. Instead, as Congress recognized, it is only when renovations are completed that individuals with disabilities will be excluded from accessing and using such facilities while others will not. This is the time at which disabled individuals are subjected to the disparate treatment that § 12147(a) was enacted to prevent.

SEPTA's argument that the "upon the completion" language merely clarifies that § 12147(a) imposes no duty upon public entities to ensure accessibility while transportation facilities are under construction is specious. We are confident that Congress would not have felt compelled to make such an obvious clarification. Faced with a choice between SEPTA's interpretation, which essentially renders the phrase surplusage, and DIA's interpretation, which gives it substantial effect, we choose the latter.

We thus interpret the "upon the completion" clause as modifying the statutory definition of discrimination such that claims under § 12147(a) arise "upon the completion" of inaccessible "alterations."

2.

Our interpretation of this seminal clause in dispute on appeal is bolstered by the remainder of the statute. In fact, even if the "upon the completion" clause was absent from the statute, we would conclude that a claim under § 12147(a) does not accrue until alterations are completed.

As the District Court stated, "[t]o determine the accrual date of a discrimination claim, a court must focus on when the discriminatory act occurred." Section 12147(a) defines two closely related discriminatory acts: the failure (1) "to make" alterations, and (2) the failure "to ensure that . . . alterations are made," in such a manner that the altered portions of transportation facilities are accessible and usable.

Regarding the first act, we agree with the *amicus curiae* submission of the U.S. Department of Justice that as a matter of logic, there can be no "fail[ure] to make" the "altered portions" of a facility accessible until the alterations are completed. The relevant act is "to make"—"to cause (something) to exist." Black's Law Dictionary 975 (8th ed.2004). Merely funding, designing, approving, or even commencing construction of alterations that will not provide accessibility does not "cause" such alterations "to exist," especially in light of the notoriously contingent nature of construction plans. Therefore, an individual cannot suffer discrimination under this portion of the statute until the alterations are completed.

Unlike the first discriminatory act, the second act can logically occur before, during, or after construction. For example, a public entity arguably fails "to ensure that . . . alterations are made" when it fails to insist that construction drawings include certain features. Although rational *in vacuo*, this reading is unfaithful to the structure of the statute. The phrase "or to ensure that the alterations are made" appears in parentheses immediately following the phrase "to fail to make such alterations," indicating that the meaning of the former phrase is related to, or dependent upon, the latter. Furthermore, both phrases center around a form of the verb "to make," an additional indication that they are, in DIA's words, "two sides of the same coin." Given this context, we hesitate to ascribe to the phrase "ensure that the alterations are made" the broad and independent meaning SEPTA urges.

It is more probable that Congress included the parenthetical and used the passive verb form "are made" because it recognized that a public entity is rarely the entity that "make[s]" the alterations. Instead, alterations "are made" by sundry contractors and subcontractors. Without the parenthetical, a public entity could immunize itself from § 12147(a) liability by delegating renovation projects to private entities that are not subject to ADA liability. 42 U.S.C. § 12132. The parenthetical closes this loophole by placing the onus on the public entity, as opposed to its agents, "to ensure" that alterations "are made" in an accessible and usable manner.

3.

[F]inally, to establish whether a public entity committed the discriminatory acts of "fail[ing] to make" alterations, or "fail[ing] . . . to ensure that . . . alterations are made" in an accessible manner, the statute directs us to determine whether "the altered portions of the facility are readily accessible"—not whether the portions to be altered will be readily accessible. 42 U.S.C. § 12147(a). The verb tenses employed by Congress in this phrase (*i.e.* "altered," past tense, and "are," present tense) further clarify that the time for passing upon a public entity's success or failure in complying with the statute is upon completion of the alterations.

In short, despite the District Court's repeated emphasis on SEPTA's construction plans, the word "plan" is absent from the statute while the phrase "completion of . . . alterations" is present. Consistent with this language, as well as the structure and purpose of the statute, we hold that the discriminatory acts defined by § 12147(a) occur, and the statute of limitations begins to run, "upon the completion of . . . alterations" to public transportation facilities.

B.

[B]ecause a potential plaintiff cannot discover his injury before it has occurred, the discovery rule only postpones the accrual date of a claim "where the [plaintiff] is unaware of the injury." It does not accelerate the accrual date "when the [plaintiff] becomes aware that he will suffer injury in the future." [A]ccordingly, the first step in applying the discovery rule in a situation like the present is to establish when the injurious discriminatory act defined by the statute actually occurred. The second step is to determine whether that injury was immediately discoverable, or whether the accrual date will be postponed until it is reasonable to expect the plaintiff to discover the injury. Having skipped step one, the District Court's application of the discovery rule resulted in an accrual date that preceded the occurrence of DIA's alleged injuries.

Because DIA was not injured before SEPTA completed its alterations, the discovery rule would not have rendered DIA's claims untimely.

C.

We conclude by reviewing the policy considerations underlying our holding. In particular, we appreciate the District Court's concern that:

> [I]t would be impractical to impose upon a defendant the requirement that it fully complete a facility modification before having to address any assertion that modifications that can be clearly understood from design drawings and specifications amount to alterations triggering an obligation under the ADA that might require significant and material modifications that surely would have been more easily, efficiently and economically incorporated well prior to the completion of the work.

This concern—that public entities will incur unnecessary expense if potential plaintiffs can wait until "the last nail is hammered into place" to bring suit—is assuaged by a number of mitigating and countervailing considerations.

First, our interpretation of § 12147(a) does not prevent a public entity like SEPTA from obtaining preliminary declaratory relief to ensure ADA compliance prior to commencing alterations. [A]lthough SEPTA's activities did not ripen into actual violations of § 12147(a) until SEPTA completed its alterations to the 15th Street and City Hall Courtyards, a substantial, immediate, and real controversy existed between SEPTA and DIA regarding these activities much earlier. On August 3, 2000, DIA's attorney, Stephen Gold, wrote to City Commissioner Edward McLaughlin expressing DIA's concern that the 15th Street Courtyard project would not comply with the ADA. Gold relayed the same concerns to SEPTA throughout 2000 in a series of meetings with SEPTA and the City. In these meetings, Gold also discussed SEPTA's ADA obligations regarding the City Hall Courtyard project. Because of these interactions, SEPTA was "anxious" to get a commitment from DIA "that there would not be a lawsuit" and was undeniably aware that a substantial controversy existed. Accordingly, to the extent that SEPTA's planned "modifications [could be] clearly understood from design drawings and specifications," SEPTA could have obtained a declaratory judgment to assuage its anxieties before proceeding with construction.

Conversely, our interpretation of § 12147(a) does not prevent an entity like DIA from seeking an injunction prior to the commencement of construction to prevent threatened ADA violations. [T]here is little doubt that it would have been better for all if DIA or SEPTA had sought declaratory or injunctive relief before construction began. It does not follow, however, that a claim for relief on the merits under § 12147(a) accrues as soon as claims for declaratory and injunctive relief accrue.

[I]n light of the availability of preliminary relief to parties facing the dilemma that confronted DIA and SEPTA, we believe the District Court's concern that public entities will be forced to "re-engineer" completed projects "to add the ADA-compliance features" is overstated.

That may be the unfortunate consequence of our decision in this instance, however.

Second, the District Court's desire to give public entities repose from § 12147(a) liability is not advanced by an interpretation of the statute that incorporates the discovery rule. The discovery rule dictates that a cause of action accrues when a potential claimant discovers, or should have discovered, the injury that forms the basis of his claim. As DIA argues, it is easy to imagine a situation where an individual with a disability relocates to Philadelphia many years from now and attempts to use the 15th Street or City Hall Courtyard for the first time. A court might fairly conclude that this individual neither discovered, nor, having moved from some distant locale, should have discovered, the inaccessibility of these stations until his arrival there. Perhaps recognizing this danger, Congress rejected a variable accrual date in favor of a bright-line rule: § 12147(a) claims accrues "upon the completion of . . . alterations." We find nothing "implausible," much less imprudent, about this decision.

[S]EPTA's proffered rule also encourages claimants to bring unripe lawsuits that rely on "contingent future events that may not occur as anticipated, or indeed may not occur at all." Here, for example, SEPTA could have decided to install elevators before completing its renovations, thus making DIA's ADA and RA claims unnecessary.

Third, the facts of this case belie the District Court's suggestion that applying the discovery rule to § 12147(a) will assure that accessibility concerns will be addressed "well prior to completion of the work." In fact, under the District Court's accrual theory, DIA could have filed a timely claim after SEPTA completed the 15th Street Station renovations. The District Court concluded that DIA had notice of SEPTA's allegedly injurious alterations to the 15th Street Courtyard "no later than November 1, 2000." Accepting the District Court's conclusion that DIA's cause of action accrued on this date, DIA would have had until November 1, 2002 to bring suit. SEPTA completed construction on the 15th Street Courtyard on August 8, 2002, three months before November 1, 2002. Thus, it is apparent that the rule of law established by the District Court is ineffectual in preventing cases from being brought after construction is completed.

V.

[I]t is undisputed that DIA's § 12147(a) claims were timely if the statute of limitations began to run from the date the alterations to the 15th Street and City Hall Stations were completed. Because we have so held, we reverse the District Court's grant of summary judgment in favor of SEPTA and remand for further proceedings consistent with the opinion.

NOTES ON STATUTES OF LIMITATIONS

[**Rewrite and add discussion of CA7 in Scherr and CA5 in Frame**] What is the justification, in *Garcia*, for holding that the statute of limitations for the Fair Housing Act's new-construction provisions begins to run before a plaintiff even has a chance to learn about whether the construction complies with the statute or not? As a practical matter, the court's decision is likely to make it extremely hard to enforce the new-construction provisions. Unless a person with a disability happens to find out about inaccessible new construction in a timely manner, or the federal government gets involved, violations of those provisions will be unchallengeable. Are you persuaded by the majority's statutory and policy arguments in favor of that result?

In *Pickern* and *DIA*, by contrast, the courts allow the plaintiffs to proceed with their suits even though more time than the limitations period elapsed between the time they first learned of the violations and the time they filed suit. See also *Scherr v. Marriott Intern., Inc.*, 703 F.3d 1069 (7th Cir.2013) (following *Pickern* and applying continuing violation theory to Title III accessibility suit); *Frame v. City of Arlington*, 657 F.3d 215 (5th Cir.2011) (*en banc*) (holding, in *Title II* suit regarding new construction and alterations, that statute of limitations did not begin to run until the plaintiff knew or should have known of the inaccessibility of the facilities at issue). Do the courts' statutory and policy arguments in favor of that result persuade you?

CHAPTER 6

EDUCATION

A. PRIMARY/SECONDARY EDUCATION AND THE INDIVIDUALS WITH DISABILITIES EDUCATION ACT

1. THE FREE APPROPRIATE PUBLIC EDUCATION AND THE LEAST RESTRICTIVE ENVIRONMENT

Board of Educ. v. Rowley

Supreme Court of the United States, 1982.
458 U.S. 176.

■ JUSTICE REHNQUIST delivered the opinion of the Court.

This case presents a question of statutory interpretation. Petitioners contend that the Court of Appeals and the District Court misconstrued the requirements imposed by Congress upon States which receive federal funds under the Education of the Handicapped Act. We agree and reverse the judgment of the Court of Appeals.

I

The Education of the Handicapped Act (Act), 84 Stat. 175, as amended, 20 U.S.C. § 1401 *et seq.*, provides federal money to assist state and local agencies in educating handicapped children, and conditions such funding upon a State's compliance with extensive goals and procedures.* The Act represents an ambitious federal effort to promote the education of handicapped children, and was passed in response to Congress' perception that a majority of handicapped children in the United States "were either totally excluded from schools or [were] sitting idly in regular classrooms awaiting the time when they were old enough to 'drop out.' " H.R.Rep.No.94–332, p. 2 (1975) (H.R.Rep.). The Act's evolution and major provisions shed light on the question of statutory interpretation which is at the heart of this case.

Congress first addressed the problem of educating the handicapped in 1966 when it amended the Elementary and Secondary Education Act of 1965 to establish a grant program "for the purpose of assisting the States in the initiation, expansion, and improvement of programs and projects . . . for the education of handicapped children." Pub.L.89–750, § 161, 80 Stat. 1204. That program was repealed in 1970 by the Education of the Handicapped Act, Pub.L.91–230, 84 Stat. 175, Part B of which established a grant program similar in purpose to the repealed legislation. Neither the 1966 nor the 1970 legislation contained specific guidelines for state use of the grant money; both were aimed primarily at stimulating the States to develop educational resources and to train personnel for educating the handicapped.

---

* [In 1990, the Education of the Handicapped Act was renamed the Individuals with Disabilities Education Act.—ed.]

Dissatisfied with the progress being made under these earlier enactments, and spurred by two District Court decisions holding that handicapped children should be given access to a public education,[2] Congress in 1974 greatly increased federal funding for education of the handicapped and for the first time required recipient States to adopt "a goal of providing full educational opportunities to all handicapped children." Pub.L.93–380, 88 Stat. 579, 583 (1974 statute). The 1974 statute was recognized as an interim measure only, adopted "in order to give the Congress an additional year in which to study what if any additional Federal assistance [was] required to enable the States to meet the needs of handicapped children." H.R.Rep., at 4. The ensuing year of study produced the Education for All Handicapped Children Act of 1975.

In order to qualify for federal financial assistance under the Act, a State must demonstrate that it "has in effect a policy that assures all handicapped children the right to a free appropriate public education." 20 U.S.C. § 1412(1). That policy must be reflected in a state plan submitted to and approved by the Secretary of Education, § 1413, which describes in detail the goals, programs, and timetables under which the State intends to educate handicapped children within its borders. §§ 1412, 1413. States receiving money under the Act must provide education to the handicapped by priority, first "to handicapped children who are not receiving an education" and second "to handicapped children . . . with the most severe handicaps who are receiving an inadequate education," § 1412(3), and "to the maximum extent appropriate" must educate handicapped children "with children who are not handicapped." § 1412(5).[4] The Act broadly defines "handicapped children" to include "mentally retarded, hard of hearing, deaf, speech impaired, visually handicapped, seriously emotionally disturbed, orthopedically impaired, [and] other health impaired children, [and] children with specific learning disabilities." § 1401(1).

The "free appropriate public education" required by the Act is tailored to the unique needs of the handicapped child by means of an "individualized educational program" (IEP). § 1401(18). The IEP, which is prepared at a meeting between a qualified representative of the local educational agency, the child's teacher, the child's parents or guardian, and, where appropriate, the child, consists of a written document containing

> "(A) a statement of the present levels of educational performance of such child, (B) a statement of annual goals, including short-term instructional objectives, (C) a statement

---

[2] Two cases, *Mills v. Board of Education of District of Columbia*, 348 F.Supp. 866 (D.C.1972), and *Pennsylvania Assn. for Retarded Children v. Commonwealth*, 334 F.Supp. 1257 (ED Pa.1971) and 343 F.Supp. 279 (1972), were later identified as the most prominent of the cases contributing to Congress' enactment of the Act and the statutes which preceded it. H.R.Rep., at 3–4. Both decisions are discussed in Part III of this opinion.

[4] Despite this preference for "mainstreaming" handicapped children—educating them with nonhandicapped children—Congress recognized that regular classrooms simply would not be a suitable setting for the education of many handicapped children. The Act expressly acknowledges that "the nature or severity of the handicap [may be] such that education in regular classes with the use of supplementary aids and services cannot be achieved satisfactorily." § 1412(5). The Act thus provides for the education of some handicapped children in separate classes or institutional settings. See *ibid.*; § 1413(a)(4).

of the specific educational services to be provided to such child, and the extent to which such child will be able to participate in regular educational programs, (D) the projected date for initiation and anticipated duration of such services, and (E) appropriate objective criteria and evaluation procedures and schedules for determining, on at least an annual basis, whether instructional objectives are being achieved." § 1401(19).

Local or regional educational agencies must review, and where appropriate revise, each child's IEP at least annually. § 1414(a)(5). See also § 1413(a)(11).

In addition to the state plan and the IEP already described, the Act imposes extensive procedural requirements upon States receiving federal funds under its provisions. Parents or guardians of handicapped children must be notified of any proposed change in "the identification, evaluation, or educational placement of the child or the provision of a free appropriate public education to such child," and must be permitted to bring a complaint about "any matter relating to" such evaluation and education. §§ 1415(b)(1)(D) and (E).[6] Complaints brought by parents or guardians must be resolved at "an impartial due process hearing," and appeal to the state educational agency must be provided if the initial hearing is held at the local or regional level. §§ 1415(b)(2) and (c). Thereafter, "[a]ny party aggrieved by the findings and decision" of the state administrative hearing has "the right to bring a civil action with respect to the complaint . . . in any State court of competent jurisdiction or in a district court of the United States without regard to the amount in controversy." § 1415(e)(2).

Thus, although the Act leaves to the States the primary responsibility for developing and executing educational programs for handicapped children, it imposes significant requirements to be followed in the discharge of that responsibility. Compliance is assured by provisions permitting the withholding of federal funds upon determination that a participating state or local agency has failed to satisfy the requirements of the Act, §§ 1414(b)(2)(A), 1416, and by the provision for judicial review. At present, all States except New Mexico receive federal funds under the portions of the Act at issue today.

---

[6]   The requirements that parents be permitted to file complaints regarding their child's education, and be present when the child's IEP is formulated, represent only two examples of Congress' effort to maximize parental involvement in the education of each handicapped child. In addition, the Act requires that parents be permitted "to examine all relevant records with respect to the identification, evaluation, and educational placement of the child, and . . . to obtain an independent educational evaluation of the child." § 1415(b)(1)(A). See also §§ 1412(4), 1414(a)(4). State educational policies and the state plan submitted to the Secretary of Education must be formulated in "consultation with individuals involved in or concerned with the education of handicapped children, including handicapped individuals and parents or guardians of handicapped children." § 1412(7). See also § 1412(2)(E). Local agencies, which receive funds under the Act by applying to the state agency, must submit applications which assure that they have developed procedures for "the participation and consultation of the parents or guardian[s] of [handicapped] children" in local educational programs, § 1414(a)(1)(C)(iii), and the application itself, along with "all pertinent documents related to such application," must be made "available to parents, guardians, and other members of the general public." § 1414(a)(4).

II

This case arose in connection with the education of Amy Rowley, a deaf student at the Furnace Woods School in the Hendrick Hudson Central School District, Peekskill, N.Y. Amy has minimal residual hearing and is an excellent lipreader. During the year before she began attending Furnace Woods, a meeting between her parents and school administrators resulted in a decision to place her in a regular kindergarten class in order to determine what supplemental services would be necessary to her education. Several members of the school administration prepared for Amy's arrival by attending a course in sign-language interpretation, and a teletype machine was installed in the principal's office to facilitate communication with her parents who are also deaf. At the end of the trial period it was determined that Amy should remain in the kindergarten class, but that she should be provided with an FM hearing aid which would amplify words spoken into a wireless receiver by the teacher or fellow students during certain classroom activities. Amy successfully completed her kindergarten year.

As required by the Act, an IEP was prepared for Amy during the fall of her first-grade year. The IEP provided that Amy should be educated in a regular classroom at Furnace Woods, should continue to use the FM hearing aid, and should receive instruction from a tutor for the deaf for one hour each day and from a speech therapist for three hours each week. The Rowleys agreed with parts of the IEP, but insisted that Amy also be provided a qualified sign-language interpreter in all her academic classes in lieu of the assistance proposed in other parts of the IEP. Such an interpreter had been placed in Amy's kindergarten class for a 2-week experimental period, but the interpreter had reported that Amy did not need his services at that time. The school administrators likewise concluded that Amy did not need such an interpreter in her first-grade classroom. They reached this conclusion after consulting the school district's Committee on the Handicapped, which had received expert evidence from Amy's parents on the importance of a sign-language interpreter, received testimony from Amy's teacher and other persons familiar with her academic and social progress, and visited a class for the deaf.

When their request for an interpreter was denied, the Rowleys demanded and received a hearing before an independent examiner. After receiving evidence from both sides, the examiner agreed with the administrators' determination that an interpreter was not necessary because "Amy was achieving educationally, academically, and socially" without such assistance. The examiner's decision was affirmed on appeal by the New York Commissioner of Education on the basis of substantial evidence in the record. Pursuant to the Act's provision for judicial review, the Rowleys then brought an action in the United States District Court for the Southern District of New York, claiming that the administrators' denial of the sign-language interpreter constituted a denial of the "free appropriate public education" guaranteed by the Act.

The District Court found that Amy "is a remarkably well-adjusted child" who interacts and communicates well with her classmates and has "developed an extraordinary rapport" with her teachers. It also found that "she performs better than the average child in her class and is advancing easily from grade to grade," but "that she understands considerably less of what goes on in class than she could if she were not deaf" and thus "is not learning as much, or performing as well academically, as she would without her handicap." This disparity between Amy's achievement and her potential led the court to decide that she was not receiving a "free appropriate public education," which the court defined as "an opportunity to achieve [her] full potential commensurate with the opportunity provided to other children." According to the District Court, such a standard "requires that the potential of the handicapped child be measured and compared to his or her performance, and that the resulting differential or 'shortfall' be compared to the shortfall experienced by nonhandicapped children." The District Court's definition arose from its assumption that the responsibility for "giv[ing] content to the requirement of an 'appropriate education' " had "been left entirely to the [federal] courts and the hearing officers."

A divided panel of the United States Court of Appeals for the Second Circuit affirmed. [W]e granted *certiorari* to review the lower courts' interpretation of the Act. Such review requires us to consider two questions: What is meant by the Act's requirement of a "free appropriate public education"? And what is the role of state and federal courts in exercising the review granted by 20 U.S.C. § 1415? We consider these questions separately.

III

A

This is the first case in which this Court has been called upon to interpret any provision of the Act. [T]he District Court and the Court of Appeals concluded that "[t]he Act itself does not define 'appropriate education,' " but leaves "to the courts and the hearing officers" the responsibility of "giv[ing] content to the requirement of an 'appropriate education.' " Petitioners contend that the definition of the phrase "free appropriate public education" used by the courts below overlooks the definition of that phrase actually found in the Act. Respondents agree that the Act defines "free appropriate public education," but contend that the statutory definition is not "functional" and thus "offers judges no guidance in their consideration of controversies involving 'the identification, evaluation, or educational placement of the child or the provision of a free appropriate public education.' " The United States, appearing as *amicus curiae* on behalf of respondents, states that "[a]lthough the Act includes definitions of a 'free appropriate public education' and other related terms, the statutory definitions do not adequately explain what is meant by 'appropriate.' "

We are loath to conclude that Congress failed to offer any assistance in defining the meaning of the principal substantive phrase used in the Act. It is beyond dispute that, contrary to the conclusions of the courts below, the Act does expressly define "free appropriate public education":

> "The term 'free appropriate public education' means special education and related services which (A) have been provided at public expense, under public supervision and direction, and without charge, (B) meet the standards of the State

educational agency, (C) include an appropriate preschool, elementary, or secondary school education in the State involved, and (D) are provided in conformity with the individualized education program required under section 1414(a)(5) of this title." § 1401(18).

"Special education," as referred to in this definition, means "specially designed instruction, at no cost to parents or guardians, to meet the unique needs of a handicapped child, including classroom instruction, instruction in physical education, home instruction, and instruction in hospitals and institutions." § 1401(16). "Related services" are defined as "transportation, and such developmental, corrective, and other supportive services . . . as may be required to assist a handicapped child to benefit from special education." § 1401(17).[10]

Like many statutory definitions, this one tends toward the cryptic rather than the comprehensive, but that is scarcely a reason for abandoning the quest for legislative intent. Whether or not the definition is a "functional" one, as respondents contend it is not, it is the principal tool which Congress has given us for parsing the critical phrase of the Act. We think more must be made of it than either respondents or the United States seems willing to admit.

According to the definitions contained in the Act, a "free appropriate public education" consists of educational instruction specially designed to meet the unique needs of the handicapped child, supported by such services as are necessary to permit the child "to benefit" from the instruction. Almost as a checklist for adequacy under the Act, the definition also requires that such instruction and services be provided at public expense and under public supervision, meet the State's educational standards, approximate the grade levels used in the State's regular education, and comport with the child's IEP. Thus, if personalized instruction is being provided with sufficient supportive services to permit the child to benefit from the instruction, and the other items on the definitional checklist are satisfied, the child is receiving a "free appropriate public education" as defined by the Act.

Other portions of the statute also shed light upon congressional intent. Congress found that of the roughly eight million handicapped children in the United States at the time of enactment, one million were "excluded entirely from the public school system" and more than half were receiving an inappropriate education. 89 Stat. 774, note following § 1401. In addition, as mentioned in Part I, the Act requires States to extend educational services first to those children who are receiving no education and second to those children who are receiving an "inadequate education." § 1412(3). When these express statutory findings and priorities are read together with the Act's extensive procedural requirements and its definition of "free appropriate public education," the face of the statute evinces a congressional intent to bring previously excluded handicapped children into the public education systems of the States and to require the States to adopt

---

[10] Examples of "related services" identified in the Act are "speech pathology and audiology, psychological services, physical and occupational therapy, recreation, and medical and counseling services, except that such medical services shall be for diagnostic and evaluation purposes only." § 1401(17).

procedures which would result in individualized consideration of and instruction for each child.

Noticeably absent from the language of the statute is any substantive standard prescribing the level of education to be accorded handicapped children. Certainly the language of the statute contains no requirement like the one imposed by the lower courts—that States maximize the potential of handicapped children "commensurate with the opportunity provided to other children." That standard was expounded by the District Court without reference to the statutory definitions or even to the legislative history of the Act. Although we find the statutory definition of "free appropriate public education" to be helpful in our interpretation of the Act, there remains the question of whether the legislative history indicates a congressional intent that such education meet some additional substantive standard. For an answer, we turn to that history.

B

(i)

As suggested in Part I, federal support for education of the handicapped is a fairly recent development. Before passage of the Act some States had passed laws to improve the educational services afforded handicapped children, but many of these children were excluded completely from any form of public education or were left to fend for themselves in classrooms designed for education of their nonhandicapped peers. As previously noted, the House Report begins by emphasizing this exclusion and misplacement, noting that millions of handicapped children "were either totally excluded from schools or [were] sitting idly in regular classrooms awaiting the time when they were old enough to 'drop out.'" H.R.Rep., at 2. See also S.Rep., at 8. One of the Act's two principal sponsors in the Senate urged its passage in similar terms:

> "While much progress has been made in the last few years, we can take no solace in that progress until all handicapped children are, in fact, receiving an education. The most recent statistics provided by the Bureau of Education for the Handicapped estimate that . . . 1.75 million handicapped children do not receive any educational services, and 2.5 million handicapped children are not receiving an appropriate education." 121 Cong.Rec. 19486 (1975) (remarks of Sen. Williams).

This concern, stressed repeatedly throughout the legislative history, confirms the impression conveyed by the language of the statute: By passing the Act, Congress sought primarily to make public education available to handicapped children. But in seeking to provide such access to public education, Congress did not impose upon the States any greater substantive educational standard than would be necessary to make such access meaningful. Indeed, Congress expressly "recognize[d] that in many instances the process of providing special education and related services to handicapped children is not guaranteed to produce any particular outcome." S.Rep., at 11. Thus, the intent of the Act was more to open the door of public education to handicapped children on appropriate terms than to guarantee any particular level of education once inside.

Both the House and the Senate Reports attribute the impetus for the Act and its predecessors to two federal-court judgments rendered in 1971 and 1972. As the Senate Report states, passage of the Act "followed a series of landmark court cases establishing in law the right to education for all handicapped children." S.Rep., at 6. The first case, *Pennsylvania Assn. for Retarded Children v. Commonwealth*, 334 F.Supp. 1257 (ED Pa.1971) and 343 F.Supp. 279 (1972) (*PARC*), was a suit on behalf of retarded children challenging the constitutionality of a Pennsylvania statute which acted to exclude them from public education and training. The case ended in a consent decree which enjoined the State from "deny[ing] to any mentally retarded child access to a free public program of education and training."

PARC was followed by *Mills v. Board of Education of District of Columbia*, 348 F.Supp. 866 (D.C.1972), a case in which the plaintiff handicapped children had been excluded from the District of Columbia public schools. The court's judgment, quoted in S.Rep., at 6, provided that

> "no [handicapped] child eligible for a publicly supported education in the District of Columbia public schools shall be excluded from a regular school assignment by a Rule, policy, or practice of the Board of Education of the District of Columbia or its agents unless such child is provided (a) adequate alternative educational services suited to the child's needs, which may include special education or tuition grants, and (b) a constitutionally adequate prior hearing and periodic review of the child's status, progress, and the adequacy of any educational alternative."

Mills and *PARC* both held that handicapped children must be given access to an adequate, publicly supported education. Neither case purports to require any particular substantive level of education. Rather, like the language of the Act, the cases set forth extensive procedures to be followed in formulating personalized educational programs for handicapped children. The fact that both *PARC* and *Mills* are discussed at length in the legislative Reports suggests that the principles which they established are the principles which, to a significant extent, guided the drafters of the Act. Indeed, immediately after discussing these cases the Senate Report describes the 1974 statute as having "incorporated the major principles of the right to education cases." S.Rep., at 8. Those principles in turn became the basis of the Act, which itself was designed to effectuate the purposes of the 1974 statute. H.R.Rep., at 5.

That the Act imposes no clear obligation upon recipient States beyond the requirement that handicapped children receive some form of specialized education is perhaps best demonstrated by the fact that Congress, in explaining the need for the Act, equated an "appropriate education" to the receipt of some specialized educational services. The Senate Report states: "[T]he most recent statistics provided by the Bureau of Education for the Handicapped estimate that of the more than 8 million children . . . with handicapping conditions requiring special education and related services, only 3.9 million such children are receiving an appropriate education." S.Rep., at 8. This statement, which reveals Congress' view that 3.9 million handicapped children were "receiving an appropriate education" in 1975, is followed immediately in the Senate Report by a table showing that 3.9 million handicapped children were "served" in 1975 and a slightly larger number were "unserved." A similar statement and table appear in the House Report. H.R.Rep., at 11–12.

It is evident from the legislative history that the characterization of handicapped children as "served" referred to children who were receiving some form of specialized educational services from the States, and that the characterization of children as "unserved" referred to those who were receiving no specialized educational services. For example, a letter sent to the United States Commissioner of Education by the House Committee on Education and Labor, signed by two key sponsors of the Act in the House, asked the Commissioner to identify the number of handicapped "children served" in each State. The letter asked for statistics on the number of children "being served" in various types of "special education program[s]" and the number of children who were not "receiving educational services." Similarly, Senator Randolph, one of the Act's principal sponsors in the Senate, noted that roughly one-half of the handicapped children in the United States "are receiving special educational services." By characterizing the 3.9 million handicapped children who were "served" as children who were "receiving an appropriate education," the Senate and House Reports unmistakably disclose Congress' perception of the type of education required by the Act: an "appropriate education" is provided when personalized educational services are provided.

The use of "appropriate" in the language of the Act, although by no means definitive, suggests that Congress used the word as much to describe the settings in which handicapped children should be educated as to prescribe the substantive content or supportive services of their education. For example, § 1412(5) requires that handicapped children be educated in classrooms with nonhandicapped children "to the maximum extent appropriate." Similarly, § 1401(19) provides that, "whenever appropriate," handicapped children should attend and participate in the meeting at which their IEP is drafted. In addition, the definition of "free appropriate public education" itself states that instruction given handicapped children should be at an "appropriate preschool, elementary, or secondary school" level. § 1401(18)(C). The Act's use of the word "appropriate" thus seems to reflect Congress' recognition that some settings simply are not suitable environments for the participation of some handicapped children. At the very least, these statutory uses of the word refute the contention that Congress used "appropriate" as a term of art which concisely expresses the standard found by the lower courts.

(ii)

Respondents contend that "the goal of the Act is to provide each handicapped child with an equal educational opportunity." We think, however, that the requirement that a State provide specialized educational services to handicapped children generates no additional requirement that the services so provided be sufficient to maximize each child's potential "commensurate with the opportunity provided other children." Respondents and the United States correctly note that Congress sought "to provide assistance to the States in carrying out their responsibilities under . . . the Constitution of the United States to provide equal protection of the laws." S.Rep., at 13. But we do not think that such statements imply a congressional intent to achieve strict equality of opportunity or services.

The educational opportunities provided by our public school systems undoubtedly differ from student to student, depending upon a myriad of factors that might affect a particular student's ability to assimilate information presented in the classroom. The requirement that States provide "equal" educational opportunities would thus seem to present an entirely unworkable standard requiring impossible measurements and comparisons. Similarly, furnishing handicapped children with only such services as are available to nonhandicapped children would in all probability fall short of the statutory requirement of "free appropriate public education"; to require, on the other hand, the furnishing of every special service necessary to maximize each handicapped child's potential is, we think, further than Congress intended to go. Thus to speak in terms of "equal" services in one instance gives less than what is required by the Act and in another instance more. The theme of the Act is "free appropriate public education," a phrase which is too complex to be captured by the word "equal" whether one is speaking of opportunities or services.

The legislative conception of the requirements of equal protection was undoubtedly informed by the two District Court decisions referred to above. But cases such as *Mills* and *PARC* held simply that handicapped children may not be excluded entirely from public education. [T]he right of access to free public education enunciated by these cases is significantly different from any notion of absolute equality of opportunity regardless of capacity. To the extent that Congress might have looked further than these cases which are mentioned in the legislative history, at the time of enactment of the Act this Court had held at least twice that the Equal Protection Clause of the Fourteenth Amendment does not require States to expend equal financial resources on the education of each child.

In explaining the need for federal legislation, the House Report noted that "no congressional legislation has required a precise guarantee for handicapped children, *i.e.* a basic floor of opportunity that would bring into compliance all school districts with the constitutional right of equal protection with respect to handicapped children." H.R.Rep., at 14. Assuming that the Act was designed to fill the need identified in the House Report—that is, to provide a "basic floor of opportunity" consistent with equal protection—neither the Act nor its history persuasively demonstrates that Congress thought that equal protection required anything more than equal access. Therefore, Congress' desire to provide specialized educational services, even in furtherance of "equality," cannot be read as imposing any particular substantive educational standard upon the States.

The District Court and the Court of Appeals thus erred when they held that the Act requires New York to maximize the potential of each handicapped child commensurate with the opportunity provided nonhandicapped children. Desirable though that goal might be, it is not the standard that Congress imposed upon States which receive funding under the Act. Rather, Congress sought primarily to identify and evaluate handicapped children, and to provide them with access to a free public education.

(iii)

Implicit in the congressional purpose of providing access to a "free appropriate public education" is the requirement that the education to which access is provided be sufficient to confer some educational benefit upon the handicapped child. It would do little good for Congress to spend millions of dollars in providing access to a public education only to have the handicapped child receive no benefit from that education. The statutory definition of "free appropriate public education," in addition to requiring that States provide each child with "specially designed instruction," expressly requires the provision of "such . . . supportive services . . . as may be required to assist a handicapped child to benefit from special education." § 1401(17). We therefore conclude that the "basic floor of opportunity" provided by the Act consists of access to specialized instruction and related services which are individually designed to provide educational benefit to the handicapped child.

The determination of when handicapped children are receiving sufficient educational benefits to satisfy the requirements of the Act presents a more difficult problem. The Act requires participating States to educate a wide spectrum of handicapped children, from the marginally hearing-impaired to the profoundly retarded and palsied. It is clear that the benefits obtainable by children at one end of the spectrum will differ dramatically from those obtainable by children at the other end, with infinite variations in between. One child may have little difficulty competing successfully in an academic setting with nonhandicapped children while another child may encounter great difficulty in acquiring even the most basic of self-maintenance skills. We do not attempt today to establish any one test for determining the adequacy of educational benefits conferred upon all children covered by the Act. Because in this case we are presented with a handicapped child who is receiving substantial specialized instruction and related services, and who is performing above average in the regular classrooms of a public school system, we confine our analysis to that situation.

The Act requires participating States to educate handicapped children with nonhandicapped children whenever possible.[24] When that "mainstreaming" preference of the Act has been met and a child is being educated in the regular classrooms of a public school system, the system itself monitors the educational progress of the child. Regular examinations are administered, grades are awarded, and yearly advancement to higher grade levels is permitted for those children who

---

[24] Title 20 U.S.C. § 1412(5) requires that participating States establish "procedures to assure that, to the maximum extent appropriate, handicapped children, including children in public or private institutions or other care facilities, are educated with children who are not handicapped, and that special classes, separate schooling, or other removal of handicapped children from the regular educational environment occurs only when the nature or severity of the handicap is such that education in regular classes with the use of supplementary aids and services cannot be achieved satisfactorily."

attain an adequate knowledge of the course material. The grading and advancement system thus constitutes an important factor in determining educational benefit. Children who graduate from our public school systems are considered by our society to have been "educated" at least to the grade level they have completed, and access to an "education" for handicapped children is precisely what Congress sought to provide in the Act.

C

When the language of the Act and its legislative history are considered together, the requirements imposed by Congress become tolerably clear. Insofar as a State is required to provide a handicapped child with a "free appropriate public education," we hold that it satisfies this requirement by providing personalized instruction with sufficient support services to permit the child to benefit educationally from that instruction. Such instruction and services must be provided at public expense, must meet the State's educational standards, must approximate the grade levels used in the State's regular education, and must comport with the child's IEP. In addition, the IEP, and therefore the personalized instruction, should be formulated in accordance with the requirements of the Act and, if the child is being educated in the regular classrooms of the public education system, should be reasonably calculated to enable the child to achieve passing marks and advance from grade to grade.

IV

A

As mentioned in Part I, the Act permits "[a]ny party aggrieved by the findings and decision" of the state administrative hearings "to bring a civil action" in "any State court of competent jurisdiction or in a district court of the United States without regard to the amount in controversy." § 1415(e)(2). The complaint, and therefore the civil action, may concern "any matter relating to the identification, evaluation, or educational placement of the child, or the provision of a free appropriate public education to such child." § 1415(b)(1)(E). In reviewing the complaint, the Act provides that a court "shall receive the record of the [state] administrative proceedings, shall hear additional evidence at the request of a party, and, basing its decision on the preponderance of the evidence, shall grant such relief as the court determines is appropriate." § 1415(e)(2).

The parties disagree sharply over the meaning of these provisions, petitioners contending that courts are given only limited authority to review for state compliance with the Act's procedural requirements and no power to review the substance of the state program, and respondents contending that the Act requires courts to exercise *de novo* review over state educational decisions and policies. We find petitioners' contention unpersuasive, for Congress expressly rejected provisions that would have so severely restricted the role of reviewing courts. In substituting the current language of the statute for language that would have made state administrative findings conclusive if supported by substantial evidence, the Conference Committee explained that courts were to make "independent decision[s] based on a preponderance of the evidence." S.Conf.Rep.No.94–455, p. 50 (1975).

But although we find that this grant of authority is broader than claimed by petitioners, we think the fact that it is found in § 1415, which is entitled "Procedural safeguards," is not without significance. When the elaborate and highly specific procedural safeguards embodied in § 1415 are contrasted with the general and somewhat imprecise substantive admonitions contained in the Act, we think that the importance Congress attached to these procedural safeguards cannot be gainsaid. It seems to us no exaggeration to say that Congress placed every bit as much emphasis upon compliance with procedures giving parents and guardians a large measure of participation at every stage of the administrative process, see, e.g., §§ 1415(a)–(d), as it did upon the measurement of the resulting IEP against a substantive standard. We think that the congressional emphasis upon full participation of concerned parties throughout the development of the IEP, as well as the requirements that state and local plans be submitted to the Secretary for approval, demonstrates the legislative conviction that adequate compliance with the procedures prescribed would in most cases assure much if not all of what Congress wished in the way of substantive content in an IEP.

Thus the provision that a reviewing court base its decision on the "preponderance of the evidence" is by no means an invitation to the courts to substitute their own notions of sound educational policy for those of the school authorities which they review. The very importance which Congress has attached to compliance with certain procedures in the preparation of an IEP would be frustrated if a court were permitted simply to set state decisions at nought. The fact that § 1415(e) requires that the reviewing court "receive the records of the [state] administrative proceedings" carries with it the implied requirement that due weight shall be given to these proceedings. And we find nothing in the Act to suggest that merely because Congress was rather sketchy in establishing substantive requirements, as opposed to procedural requirements for the preparation of an IEP, it intended that reviewing courts should have a free hand to impose substantive standards of review which cannot be derived from the Act itself. In short, the statutory authorization to grant "such relief as the court determines is appropriate" cannot be read without reference to the obligations, largely procedural in nature, which are imposed upon recipient States by Congress.

Therefore, a court's inquiry in suits brought under § 1415(e)(2) is twofold. First, has the State complied with the procedures set forth in the Act? And second, is the individualized educational program developed through the Act's procedures reasonably calculated to enable the child to receive educational benefits? If these requirements are met, the State has complied with the obligations imposed by Congress and the courts can require no more.

B

In assuring that the requirements of the Act have been met, courts must be careful to avoid imposing their view of preferable educational methods upon the States.[29] The primary responsibility for formulating

---

[29] In this case, for example, both the state hearing officer and the District Court were presented with evidence as to the best method for educating the deaf, a question long debated among scholars. See Large, *Special Problems of the Deaf Under the Education for All*

the education to be accorded a handicapped child, and for choosing the educational method most suitable to the child's needs, was left by the Act to state and local educational agencies in cooperation with the parents or guardian of the child. The Act expressly charges States with the responsibility of "acquiring and disseminating to teachers and administrators of programs for handicapped children significant information derived from educational research, demonstration, and similar projects, and [of] adopting, where appropriate, promising educational practices and materials." § 1413(a)(3). In the face of such a clear statutory directive, it seems highly unlikely that Congress intended courts to overturn a State's choice of appropriate educational theories in a proceeding conducted pursuant to § 1415(e)(2).

We previously have cautioned that courts lack the "specialized knowledge and experience" necessary to resolve "persistent and difficult questions of educational policy." We think that Congress shared that view when it passed the Act. As already demonstrated, Congress' intention was not that the Act displace the primacy of States in the field of education, but that States receive funds to assist them in extending their educational systems to the handicapped. Therefore, once a court determines that the requirements of the Act have been met, questions of methodology are for resolution by the States.

V

Entrusting a child's education to state and local agencies does not leave the child without protection. Congress sought to protect individual children by providing for parental involvement in the development of state plans and policies, and in the formulation of the child's individual educational program. As the Senate Report states:

> "The Committee recognizes that in many instances the process of providing special education and related services to handicapped children is not guaranteed to produce any particular outcome. By changing the language [of the provision relating to individualized educational programs] to emphasize the process of parent and child involvement and to provide a written record of reasonable expectations, the Committee intends to clarify that such individualized planning conferences are a way to provide parent involvement and protection to assure that appropriate services are provided to a handicapped child." S.Rep., at 11–12.

See also S.Conf.Rep.No.94–445, p. 30 (1975); 34 CFR § 300.345 (1981). As this very case demonstrates, parents and guardians will not lack ardor in seeking to ensure that handicapped children receive all of the benefits to which they are entitled by the Act.

VI

Applying these principles to the facts of this case, we conclude that the Court of Appeals erred in affirming the decision of the District Court. Neither the District Court nor the Court of Appeals found that petitioners had failed to comply with the procedures of the Act, and the

---

Handicapped Children Act of 1975, 58 Wash. U. L.Q. 213, 229 (1980). The District Court accepted the testimony of respondents' experts that there was "a trend supported by studies showing the greater degree of success of students brought up in deaf households using [the method of communication used by the Rowleys]."

findings of neither court would support a conclusion that Amy's educational program failed to comply with the substantive requirements of the Act. On the contrary, the District Court found that the "evidence firmly establishes that Amy is receiving an 'adequate' education, since she performs better than the average child in her class and is advancing easily from grade to grade." In light of this finding, and of the fact that Amy was receiving personalized instruction and related services calculated by the Furnace Woods school administrators to meet her educational needs, the lower courts should not have concluded that the Act requires the provision of a sign-language interpreter. Accordingly, the decision of the Court of Appeals is reversed, and the case is remanded for further proceedings consistent with this opinion.

So ordered.

■ JUSTICE BLACKMUN, concurring in the judgment.

Although I reach the same result as the Court does today, I read the legislative history and goals of the Education of the Handicapped Act differently. Congress unambiguously stated that it intended to "take a more active role under its responsibility for equal protection of the laws to guarantee that handicapped children are provided equal educational opportunity." S.Rep.No.94–168, p. 9 (1975). See also 20 U.S.C. § 1412(2)(A)(i) (requiring States to establish plans with the "goal of providing full educational opportunity to all handicapped children").

As I have observed before, "[i]t seems plain to me that Congress, in enacting [this statute], intended to do more than merely set out politically self-serving but essentially meaningless language about what the [handicapped] deserve at the hands of state . . . authorities." The clarity of the legislative intent convinces me that the relevant question here is not, as the Court says, whether Amy Rowley's individualized education program was "reasonably calculated to enable [her] to receive educational benefits," measured in part by whether or not she "achieve[s] passing marks and advance[s] from grade to grade." Rather, the question is whether Amy's program, viewed as a whole, offered her an opportunity to understand and participate in the classroom that was substantially equal to that given her nonhandicapped classmates. This is a standard predicated on equal educational opportunity and equal access to the educational process, rather than upon Amy's achievement of any particular educational outcome.

In answering this question, I believe that the District Court and the Court of Appeals should have given greater deference than they did to the findings of the School District's impartial hearing officer and the State's Commissioner of Education, both of whom sustained petitioners' refusal to add a sign-language interpreter to Amy's individualized education program. Cf. 20 U.S.C. § 1415(e)(2) (requiring reviewing court to "receive the records of the administrative proceedings" before granting relief). I would suggest further that those courts focused too narrowly on the presence or absence of a particular service—a sign-language interpreter—rather than on the total package of services furnished to Amy by the School Board.

As the Court demonstrates, petitioner Board has provided Amy Rowley considerably more than "a teacher with a loud voice." By concentrating on whether Amy was "learning as much, or performing as well academically, as she would without her handicap," the District Court and the Court of Appeals paid too little attention to whether, on the entire record, respondent's individualized education program offered her an educational opportunity substantially equal to that provided her nonhandicapped classmates. Because I believe that standard has been satisfied here, I agree that the judgment of the Court of Appeals should be reversed.

■ JUSTICE WHITE, with whom JUSTICE BRENNAN and JUSTICE MARSHALL join, dissenting.

In order to reach its result in this case, the majority opinion contradicts itself, the language of the statute, and the legislative history. Both the majority's standard for a "free appropriate education" and its standard for judicial review disregard congressional intent.

[I] agree that the language of the Act does not contain a substantive standard beyond requiring that the education offered must be "appropriate." However, if there are limits not evident from the face of the statute on what may be considered an "appropriate education," they must be found in the purpose of the statute or its legislative history. The Act itself announces it will provide a "full educational opportunity to all handicapped children." 20 U.S.C. § 1412(2)(A). This goal is repeated throughout the legislative history, in statements too frequent to be " 'passing references and isolated phrases.' " These statements elucidate the meaning of "appropriate." According to the Senate Report, for example, the Act does "guarantee that handicapped children are provided equal educational opportunity." S.Rep.No.94–168, p. 9 (1975). This promise appears throughout the legislative history. Indeed, at times the purpose of the Act was described as tailoring each handicapped child's educational plan to enable the child "to achieve his or her maximum potential." H.R.Rep.No.94–332, pp. 13, 19 (1975). Senator Stafford, one of the sponsors of the Act, declared: "We can all agree that education [given a handicapped child] should be equivalent, at least, to the one those children who are not handicapped receive." The legislative history thus directly supports the conclusion that the Act intends to give handicapped children an educational opportunity commensurate with that given other children.

The majority opinion announces a different substantive standard, that "Congress did not impose upon the States any greater substantive educational standard than would be necessary to make such access meaningful." While "meaningful" is no more enlightening than "appropriate," the Court purports to clarify itself. Because Amy was provided with some specialized instruction from which she obtained some benefit and because she passed from grade to grade, she was receiving a meaningful and therefore appropriate education.

This falls far short of what the Act intended. The Act details as specifically as possible the kind of specialized education each handicapped child must receive. It would apparently satisfy the Court's standard of "access to specialized instruction and related services which are individually designed to provide educational benefit to the handicapped child," for a deaf child such as Amy to be given a teacher with a loud voice, for she would benefit from that service. The Act requires more. It defines "special education" to mean "specifically designed instruction, at no cost to parents or guardians, to meet the unique needs of a handicapped child. . . . " § 1401(16). Providing a teacher with a loud voice would not meet Amy's needs and would not satisfy the Act. The basic floor of opportunity is instead, as the courts below recognized, intended to eliminate the effects of the handicap, at least to the extent that the child will be given an equal opportunity to learn if that is reasonably possible. Amy Rowley, without a sign-language interpreter, comprehends less than half of what is said in the classroom—less than half of what normal children comprehend. This is hardly an equal opportunity to learn, even if Amy makes passing grades.

Despite its reliance on the use of "appropriate" in the definition of the Act, the majority opinion speculates that "Congress used the word as much to describe the settings in which handicapped children should be educated as to prescribe the substantive content or supportive services of their education." Of course, the word "appropriate" can be applied in many ways; at times in the Act, Congress used it to recommend mainstreaming handicapped children; at other points, it used the word to refer to the content of the individualized education. The issue before us is what standard the word "appropriate" incorporates when it is used to modify "education." The answer given by the Court is not a satisfactory one.

[T]he Court's discussion of the standard for judicial review is as flawed as its discussion of a "free appropriate public education." According to the Court, a court can ask only whether the State has "complied with the procedures set forth in the Act" and whether the individualized education program is "reasonably calculated to enable the child to receive educational benefits." Both the language of the Act and the legislative history, however, demonstrate that Congress intended the courts to conduct a far more searching inquiry.

[U]nder the judicial review provisions of the Act, neither the District Court nor the Court of Appeals was bound by the State's construction of what an "appropriate" education means in general or by what the state authorities considered to be an appropriate education for Amy Rowley. Because the standard of the courts below seems to me to reflect the congressional purpose and because their factual findings are not clearly erroneous, I respectfully dissent.

NOTES ON ROWLEY

1. **What is an "Appropriate" Education?** Justice Rehnquist's opinion for the Court adopts a standard that focuses largely on access and process. So long as a child with a disability is served in the mainstream classroom, obtains passing marks, and is promoted from grade to grade, and the school district satisfies the procedural requirements for creating an IEP, the child has received the "free appropriate public education" required by the statute. In general, he says, courts should ask, first, whether the school district complied with the statutory procedures, and, second, whether the IEP is "reasonably calculated to enable the child to receive educational benefits." Justice White, in dissent, agrees with the lower courts that an "appropriate" education is one that gives the child with a disability an equal opportunity to learn as that provided to children without disabilities.

What is wrong with Justice White's argument? As Justice White points out, without a sign language interpreter Amy Rowley was unable to make out more than half of the words spoken in her classroom. Could the statutory guarantee of an "appropriate" education really mean an education that places a child with a disability at such a disadvantage? The fact that Amy Rowley was able to fight through the disadvantage to obtain passing grades hardly suggests her education was "appropriate," does it?

In ruling that the IDEA does not require an equal opportunity, Justice Rehnquist looks to the legislative history, which shows Congress was responding to the complete exclusion from school of many children with disabilities. He also suggests that, because the statute covers such a wide range of different children with different needs, any equality standard would be unworkable. Are these arguments persuasive? Is it fair to say that the *Rowley* majority treats the IDEA not as a civil rights law but instead as a public benefits law?

Consider the Fifth Circuit's recent application of *Rowley* in KLEIN INDEPENDENT SCHOOL DISTRICT V. HOVEM, 690 F.3d 390 (2012). The case involved Per Hovem, a very intelligent teenager with a learning disability that affected his writing abilities. Hovem got very good grades in high school and passed readily from grade to grade. He achieved these results with certain accommodations, which included "extra time to complete written assignments, the opportunity to respond orally to assignments, printed copies of class notes, and the * * * use of his portable speller in class and at home." (Apparently, Hovem never used the portable speller in class, because he found it stigmatizing; his teachers never saw him use it, but they assumed that he was using it, and he told them that he had been using it when asked.)

On the statewide Texas Assessment of Knowledge and Skills (TAKS) administered at the end of his junior year, Hovem "achieved Commended scores in Social Studies and Science, but he failed the written composition sections, which comprised a portion of the exit level English test." To address this problem, the school assigned him to a "practical writing course" for his senior year. When he took the SAT that fall, he received a 650 in Critical Reading and a 640 in Math, but only a 340 in Writing. The Fifth Circuit concluded that Hovem received a FAPE under the standards established in *Rowley*:

> Nowhere in *Rowley* is the educational benefit defined exclusively or even primarily in terms of correcting the child's disability. Certainly, given the wide range of disabilities covered by IDEA, remediation may often be part of an IEP. Behavioral modifications, for instance, immediately come to mind as an example of an IEP strategy that may remediate a disability while also being necessary to confer educational benefits. But the whole educational experience, and its adaptation to confer "benefits" on the child, is the ultimate statutory goal.

> [T]he fundamental issue as seen by the district court is whether Per's program, fully acquiesced in by his parents until his senior high school year, was not sufficiently individualized because it failed to enable him to write and spell better. On the facts before

us, *Rowley* is decisive. As has been noted, overall educational
benefit, not solely disability remediation, is IDEA's statutory goal.
Per's IEPs were sufficient because they were "reasonably
calculated to enable [Per] to achieve passing marks and advance
from grade to grade" in mainstream classes. *Rowley.* Moreover, an
IEP is not required to maximize a child's potential, but to provide
"a basic floor of opportunity." Finally, *Rowley* emphasizes that
courts should not lightly disregard educators' decisions on the
appropriate educational methods to achieve a FAPE. Whether
KISD could have remediated Per's disability more effectively is
debatable, but the school district did far more, and offered him far
more, than robotic IDEA form-checking to assist his performance
in school. And, to say nothing of his generally admirable academic
career, the record shows that he made progress in his written
expression over the course of high school. His IEPs were
sufficiently individualized.

In dissent, Judge Stewart argued that the school district does not
satisfy its obligations under the IDEA simply because the student does well
in the areas not affected by his disability; the district also has to provide the
student with services that will address the limitations imposed by the
disability. He found "numerous flaws with the majority's reasoning":

> The majority disregards the nuance of the *Rowley* opinion, and
> instead treats Rowley as a blanket permission slip for federally-
> funded school districts to ignore the special needs of disabled
> students by affording them passing grades and advancement in
> the regular classroom. [P]romotion from grade to grade is less
> indicative of a disabled student's receipt of a FAPE where it
> appears that the student was promoted pursuant to a school
> policy rather than his achievement, where good grades are
> traceable to exemptions from standard expectations intended to
> circumvent rather than address his area of disability, and when
> independent evaluations contradict the amount of progress
> otherwise to be inferred from class promotion.

> In this case, there is plentiful evidence that Per's promotion in
> classes in which his disability affected his performance was due in
> large part to the school's policy of excepting his full participation
> rather than tailoring his instruction to address his disability. As
> expressed above, Per was in a posture to graduate only upon the
> school's waiver, on the basis of his disability, of the requirement
> that he pass the written component of the TAKS. Moreover, the
> battery of tests Per undertook as part of his application to the
> Landmark School provided measurable data that he was
> performing significantly below grade level in areas affected by his
> disability. Accordingly, Per's passing grades and presumptive
> graduation are insufficient to establish that KISD had provided
> him a FAPE.

> Acquiescence to a disabled student's weaknesses, even if well-
> meaning, cannot obviate the requirements of the IDEA. Put
> otherwise, the fulfillment of a school district's obligations under

the IDEA is not a matter of intention. It is entirely reasonable to assume, as the majority apparently does, that KISD's employees believed that they were doing Per a favor by excusing his failure to complete written assignments legibly, timely, or even at all; by emphasizing his many strengths when grading his performance, yet ignoring his core weaknesses; by matriculating and promoting him through the general education curriculum toward graduation, in spite of the fact that, though he possesses an impressive intellect, he plainly displayed severe difficulty in producing even the most basic forms of written communication, such as words, sentences, and paragraphs, which average students produce with ease.

Is Judge Stewart's analysis consistent with *Rowley*? Does it point out a flaw in that decision?

2.   Educational Policy Judgments. Justice Rehnquist's opinion for the Court also discusses the standard of review to be applied by courts in IDEA proceedings. He acknowledges that Congress directed courts to make independent determinations, based on the preponderance of the evidence, but his opinion limits the power of reviewing courts in a significant way: They may not "substitute their own notions of sound educational policy for those of the school authorities which they review." This rule of deference to school districts' policy choices might rest on two grounds: (1) expertise—school officials might be more up to date on the current research into what educational techniques work than are federal judges; and (2) federalism and democratic accountability—in our federalist system, states and local school districts are the primary makers of education policy, because they are understood to be closer, and thus more accountable, to the people affected. Are these adequate justifications for Justice Rehnquist's rule of deference? Perhaps more important, how can a court tell when a disagreement between parents and a school district reflects a disagreement about *policy*—in which the school district is entitled to some deference—or instead reflects a disagreement about the best way of serving the particular needs of the particular child—in which case the court presumably must independently review the record on a preponderance standard? Nearly all disputes between parents and school district can be characterized either way, can't they?

In *Rowley* itself, the dispute between the parties reflected a longstanding dispute among educators regarding the best way to teach deaf children. One camp has advocated oralism—teaching and learning in an oral language, with a focus on lipreading. The other camp—often associated in recent years with politically active, culturally Deaf people—advocates teaching deaf children in sign language. The Hendrick Hudson School District took the side of oralism, the Rowleys took the side of teaching in sign language. Given the long-running policy debate, perhaps it is not surprising that the Court deferred to the school district's choice of approach. See R.C. Smith, A Case About Amy (1996) (making this point).

3.   Amy Rowley. As Smith, *supra*, recounts, the Rowleys moved to Mountain Lakes, New Jersey, where the school district provided sign language interpreters. When this book went to press, she was serving as an

Assistant Professor of Modern Languages and Literature, and Coordinator of the American Sign Language Program, at California State University-East Bay.

4. No Child Left Behind. Does the No Child Left Behind Act of 2001, 20 U.S.C. § 6301 *et seq.*, change the *Rowley* standard? As one advocate noted, the NCLB law "sets high achievement standards for all students, including those with a physical or mental impairment," and it "requir[es] that the same grade-level academic content standards apply to all students." Stephen A. Rosenbaum, *Aligning or Maligning? Getting Inside a New IDEA, Getting Behind No Child Left Behind and Getting Outside of it All*, 15 Hastings Women's L.J. 1, 27–28 (2004). As Professor Daniel explains, the principles of the standards-and-accountability movement—which No Child Left Behind incorporates to a large extent—seem quite inconsistent with *Rowley*'s process orientation:

> The standards movement assumes that all students can achieve high levels of learning if they receive high expectations, clearly defined standards, and effective teaching to support achievement. These high expectations in state education standards, however, are at odds with the core holding in Rowley that school districts only need to meet the minimalist "some educational benefit" standard. The shift from process to outcome, which is at the heart of the standards-based movement, also contradicts the Rowley finding that the purpose of the IDEA is to provide access to education. The movement's emphasis on content and proficiency focuses on what students actually learn, not necessarily the process by which they learn.

Philip T.K. Daniel, *"Some Benefit" or "Maximum Benefit": Does the No Child Left Behind Act Render Greater Educational Entitlement to Students with Disabilities*, 37 J.L. & Educ. 347, 353 (2008). As Professor Daniel explains, however, courts have not read NCLB as overturning the access-plus-process holding of *Rowley*. See *id.*

Sacramento City Unified Sch. Dist. v. Rachel H.

United States Court of Appeals for the Ninth Circuit, 1994.
14 F.3d 1398.

■ SNEED, CIRCUIT JUDGE:

The Sacramento Unified School District ("the District") timely appeals the district court's judgment in favor of Rachel Holland ("Rachel") and the California State Department of Education. The court found that the appropriate placement for Rachel under the Individuals with Disabilities Act ("IDEA") was full-time in a regular second grade classroom with some supplemental services. The District contends that the appropriate placement for Rachel is half-time in special education classes and half-time in a regular class. We affirm the judgment of the district court.

[R]achel Holland is now 11 years old and is mentally retarded. She was tested with an I.Q. of 44. She attended a variety of special education programs in the District from 1985–89. Her parents sought to increase the time Rachel spent in a regular classroom, and in the fall of

1989, they requested that Rachel be placed full-time in a regular classroom for the 1989–90 school year. The District rejected their request and proposed a placement that would have divided Rachel's time between a special education class for academic subjects and a regular class for non-academic activities such as art, music, lunch, and recess. The district court found that this plan would have required moving Rachel at least six times each day between the two classrooms. The Hollands instead enrolled Rachel in a regular kindergarten class at the Shalom School, a private school. Rachel remained at the Shalom School in regular classes and at the time the district court rendered its opinion was in the second grade.

The Hollands and the District were able to agree on an Individualized Education Program ("IEP") for Rachel. Although the IEP is required to be reviewed annually, see 20 U.S.C. § 1401a(20)(B), because of the dispute between the parties, Rachel's IEP has not been reviewed since January 1990.[3]

The Hollands appealed the District's placement decision to a state hearing officer pursuant to 20 U.S.C. § 1415(b)(2). They maintained that Rachel best learned social and academic skills in a regular classroom and would not benefit from being in a special education class. The District contended Rachel was too severely disabled to benefit from full-time placement in a regular class. The hearing officer concluded that the District had failed to make an adequate effort to educate Rachel in a regular class pursuant to the IDEA. The officer found that (1) Rachel had benefitted from her regular kindergarten class—that she was motivated to learn and learned by imitation and modeling; (2) Rachel was not disruptive in a regular classroom; and (3) the District had overstated the cost of putting Rachel in regular education—that the cost would not be so great that it weighed against placing her in a regular classroom. The hearing officer ordered the District to place Rachel in a regular classroom with support services, including a special education consultant and a part-time aide.

The District appealed this determination to the district court. Pursuant to 20 U.S.C. § 1415(e)(2), the parties presented additional evidence at an evidentiary hearing. The court affirmed the decision of the hearing officer that Rachel should be placed full-time in a regular classroom.

In considering whether the District proposed an appropriate placement for Rachel, the district court examined the following factors: (1) the educational benefits available to Rachel in a regular classroom, supplemented with appropriate aids and services, as compared with the educational benefits of a special education classroom; (2) the non-academic benefits of interaction with children who were not disabled; (3) the effect of Rachel's presence on the teacher and other children in the classroom; and (4) the cost of mainstreaming Rachel in a regular classroom.

---

[3] The 1990 IEP objectives include: speaking in 4– or 5–word sentences; repeating instructions of complex tasks; initiating and terminating conversations; stating her name, address and phone number; participating in a safety program with classmates; developing a 24–word sight vocabulary; counting to 25; printing her first and last names and the alphabet; playing cooperatively; participating in lunch without supervision; and identifying upper and lower case letters and the sounds associated with them.

1. Educational Benefits

The district court found the first factor, educational benefits to Rachel, weighed in favor of placing her in a regular classroom. Each side presented expert testimony. [T]he court noted that the District's evidence focused on Rachel's limitations but did not establish that the educational opportunities available through special education were better or equal to those available in a regular classroom. Moreover, the court found that the testimony of the Hollands' experts was more credible because they had more background in evaluating children with disabilities placed in regular classrooms and that they had a greater opportunity to observe Rachel over an extended period of time in normal circumstances. The district court also gave great weight to the testimony of Rachel's current teacher, Nina Crone, whom the court found to be an experienced, skillful teacher. Ms. Crone stated that Rachel was a full member of the class and participated in all activities. Ms. Crone testified that Rachel was making progress on her IEP goals: She was learning one-to-one correspondence in counting, was able to recite the English and Hebrew alphabets, and was improving her communication abilities and sentence lengths.

The district court found that Rachel received substantial benefits in regular education and that all of her IEP goals could be implemented in a regular classroom with some modification to the curriculum and with the assistance of a part-time aide.

2. Non-academic Benefits

The district court next found that the second factor, non-academic benefits to Rachel, also weighed in favor of placing her in a regular classroom. The court noted that the Hollands' evidence indicated that Rachel had developed her social and communications skills as well as her self-confidence from placement in a regular class, while the District's evidence tended to show that Rachel was not learning from exposure to other children and that she was isolated from her classmates. The court concluded that the differing evaluations in large part reflected the predisposition of the evaluators. The court found the testimony of Rachel's mother and her current teacher to be the most credible. These witnesses testified regarding Rachel's excitement about school, learning, and her new friendships and Rachel's improved self-confidence.

3. Effect on the Teacher and Children in the Regular Class

The district court next addressed the issue of whether Rachel had a detrimental effect on others in her regular classroom. The court looked at two aspects: (1) whether there was detriment because the child was disruptive, distracting or unruly, and (2) whether the child would take up so much of the teacher's time that the other students would suffer from lack of attention. The witnesses of both parties agreed that Rachel followed directions and was well-behaved and not a distraction in class. The court found the most germane evidence on the second aspect came from Rachel's second grade teacher, Nina Crone, who testified that Rachel did not interfere with her ability to teach the other children and in the future would require only a part-time aide. Accordingly, the district court determined that the third factor, the effect of Rachel's presence on the teacher and other children in the classroom weighed in favor of placing her in a regular classroom.

4.   Cost

Finally, the district court found that the District had not offered any persuasive or credible evidence to support its claim that educating Rachel in a regular classroom with appropriate services would be significantly more expensive than educating her in the District's proposed setting.

The District contended that it would cost $109,000 to educate Rachel full-time in a regular classroom. This figure was based on the cost of providing a full-time aide for Rachel plus an estimated $80,000 for school-wide sensitivity training. The court found that the District did not establish that such training was necessary. Further, the court noted that even if such training were necessary, there was evidence from the California Department of Education that the training could be had at no cost. Moreover, the court found it would be inappropriate to assign the total cost of the training to Rachel when other children with disabilities would benefit. In addition, the court concluded that the evidence did not suggest that Rachel required a full-time aide.

In addition, the court found that the District should have compared the cost of placing Rachel in a special class of approximately 12 students with a full-time special education teacher and two full-time aides and the cost of placing her in a regular class with a part-time aide. The District provided no evidence of this cost comparison.

The court also was not persuaded by the District's argument that it would lose significant funding if Rachel did not spend at least 51% of her time in a special education class. The court noted that a witness from the California Department of Education testified that waivers were available if a school district sought to adopt a program that did not fit neatly within the funding guidelines. The District had not applied for a waiver.

By inflating the cost estimates and failing to address the true comparison, the District did not meet its burden of proving that regular placement would burden the District's funds or adversely affect services available to other children. Therefore, the court found that the cost factor did not weigh against mainstreaming Rachel.

The district court concluded that the appropriate placement for Rachel was full-time in a regular second grade classroom with some supplemental services and affirmed the decision of the hearing officer.

[T]he IDEA provides that each state must establish:

> [P]rocedures to assure that, to the maximum extent appropriate, children with disabilities . . . are educated with children who are not disabled, and that special classes, separate schooling, or other removal of children with disabilities from the regular educational environment occurs only when the nature or severity of the disability is such that education in regular classes with the use of supplementary aids and services cannot be achieved satisfactorily. . . .

20 U.S.C. § 1412(5)(B).

[T]his provision sets forth Congress's preference for educating children with disabilities in regular classrooms with their peers.

[W]e have not adopted or devised a standard for determining the presence of compliance with 20 U.S.C. § 1412(5)(B). The Third, Fifth and Eleventh Circuits use what is known as the *Daniel R.R.* test.[5] The Fourth, Sixth and Eighth Circuits apply the *Roncker* test.[6]

Although the district court relied principally on *Daniel R.R.*, [i]t did not specifically adopt the *Daniel R.R.* test over the *Roncker* test. Rather, it employed factors found in both lines of cases in its analysis. The result was a four-factor balancing test in which the court considered (1) the educational benefits of placement full-time in a regular class; (2) the non-academic benefits of such placement; (3) the effect Rachel had on the teacher and children in the regular class; and (4) the costs of mainstreaming Rachel. This analysis directly addresses the issue of the appropriate placement for a child with disabilities under the requirements of 20 U.S.C. § 1412(5)(B). Accordingly, we approve and adopt the test employed by the district court.

[T]he District strenuously disagrees with the district court's findings that Rachel was receiving academic and non-academic benefits in a regular class and did not have a detrimental effect on the teacher or other students. It argues that the court's findings were contrary to the evidence of the state Diagnostic Center and that the court should not have been persuaded by the testimony of Rachel's teacher, particularly her testimony that Rachel would need only a part-time aide in the future. The district court, however, conducted a full evidentiary hearing and made a thorough analysis. The court found the Hollands' evidence to be more persuasive. Moreover, the court asked Rachel's teacher extensive questions regarding Rachel's need for a part-time aide. We will not disturb the findings of the district court.

The District is also not persuasive on the issue of cost. The District now claims that it will lose up to $190,764 in state special education funding if Rachel is not enrolled in a special education class at least 51% of the day. However, the District has not sought a waiver pursuant

---

[5]   First, the court must determine "whether education in the regular classroom, with the use of supplemental aids and services, can be achieved satisfactorily. . . . " If the court finds that education cannot be achieved satisfactorily in the regular classroom, then it must decide "whether the school has mainstreamed the child to the maximum extent appropriate." Factors the courts consider in applying the first prong of this test are (1) the steps the school district has taken to accommodate the child in a regular classroom; (2) whether the child will receive an educational benefit from regular education; (3) the child's overall educational experience in regular education; and (4) the effect the disabled child's presence has on the regular classroom. In [one case] the court added the factor of cost, stating that "if the cost of educating a handicapped child in a regular classroom is so great that it would significantly impact upon the education of other children in the district, then education in a regular classroom is not appropriate."

Regarding the second factor, [at least two] courts compared the educational benefits received in a regular classroom with the benefits received in a special education class.

[6]   According to the court in *Roncker*: "[W]here the segregated facility is considered superior, the court should determine whether the services which make that placement superior could be feasibly provided in a non-segregated setting. If they can, the placement in the segregated school would be inappropriate under the Act." Courts are to (1) compare the benefits the child would receive in special education with those she would receive in regular education; (2) consider whether the child would be disruptive in the non-segregated setting; and (3) consider the cost of mainstreaming.

to California Education Code § 56101. This section provides that (1) any school district may request a waiver of any provision of the Education Code if the waiver is necessary or beneficial to the student's IEP, and (2) the Board may grant the waiver when failure to do so would hinder compliance with federal mandates for a free appropriate education for children with disabilities. Cal.Educ.Code § 56101(a) & (b) (Deering 1992).

[W]e affirm the judgment of the district court. While we cannot determine what the appropriate placement is for Rachel at the present time, we hold that the determination of the present and future appropriate placement for Rachel should be based on the principles set forth in this opinion and the opinion of the district court.

AFFIRMED.

Hartmann v. Loudoun County Bd. of Educ.

United States Court of Appeals for the Fourth Circuit, 1997.
118 F.3d 996.

■ WILKINSON, CHIEF JUDGE:

Roxanna and Joseph Hartmann brought suit on behalf of their disabled son Mark against the Loudoun County Board of Education under the Individuals With Disabilities Education Act (IDEA), 20 U.S.C. § 1400 *et seq.* The Hartmanns alleged that the Board had failed to ensure that Mark was educated with non-handicapped children "to the maximum extent appropriate" as required by the IDEA's mainstreaming provision, 20 U.S.C. § 1412(5)(B). The district court agreed, rejecting the findings of both the local hearing officer and the state review officer. The Board appeals, contending that the court's decision is contrary to the law and the evidence in the record. We agree. As Supreme Court precedent makes clear, the IDEA does not grant federal courts a license to substitute their own notions of sound educational policy for those of local school authorities, or to disregard the findings developed in state administrative proceedings. Upon careful review of the record, however, we are forced to conclude that this is precisely what has occurred in this case. Accordingly, we reverse and remand with directions to dismiss.

I.

Mark Hartmann is an eleven-year-old autistic child. Autism is a developmental disorder characterized by significant deficiencies in communication skills, social interaction, and motor control. Mark is unable to speak and suffers severe problems with fine motor coordination. Mark's writing ability is extremely limited; he does not write by hand and can consistently type only a few words such as "is" and "at" by himself on a keyboard device known as a Canon communicator. The parties agree that Mark's greatest need is to develop communication skills.

Mark spent his pre-school years in various programs for disabled children. In kindergarten, he spent half his time in a self-contained program for autistic children and half in a regular education classroom at Butterfield Elementary in Lombard, Illinois. Upon entering first grade, Mark received speech and occupational therapy one-on-one, but was otherwise included in the regular classroom at Butterfield full-time with an aide to assist him.

After Mark's first-grade year, the Hartmanns moved to Loudoun County, Virginia, where they enrolled Mark at Ashburn Elementary for the 1993–1994 school year. Based on Mark's individualized education program (IEP) from Illinois, the school placed Mark in a regular education classroom. To facilitate Mark's inclusion, Loudoun officials carefully selected his teacher, hired a full-time aide to assist him, and put him in a smaller class with more independent children. Mark's teacher, Diane Johnson, read extensively about autism, and both Johnson and Mark's aide, Suz Leitner, received training in facilitated communication, a special communication technique used with autistic children. Mark received five hours per week of speech and language therapy with a qualified specialist, Carolyn Clement. Halfway through the year, Virginia McCullough, a special education teacher, was assigned to provide Mark with three hours of instruction a week and to advise Mark's teacher and aide.

Mary Kearney, the Loudoun County Director of Special Education, personally worked with Mark's IEP team, which consisted of Johnson, Leitner, Clement, and Laurie McDonald, the principal of Ashburn. Kearney provided in-service training for the Ashburn staff on autism and inclusion of disabled children in the regular classroom. Johnson, Leitner, Clement, and McDonald also attended a seminar on inclusion held by the Virginia Council for Administrators of Special Education. Mark's IEP team also received assistance from educational consultants Jamie Ruppmann and Gail Mayfield, and Johnson conferred with additional specialists whose names were provided to her by the Hartmanns and the school. Mark's curriculum was continually modified to ensure that it was properly adapted to his needs and abilities.

Frank Johnson, supervisor of the county's program for autistic children, formally joined the IEP team in January, but provided assistance throughout the year in managing Mark's behavior. Mark engaged in daily episodes of loud screeching and other disruptive conduct such as hitting, pinching, kicking, biting, and removing his clothing. These outbursts not only required Diane Johnson and Leitner to calm Mark and redirect him, but also consumed the additional time necessary to get the rest of the children back on task after the distraction.

Despite these efforts, by the end of the year Mark's IEP team concluded that he was making no academic progress in the regular classroom. In Mark's May 1994 IEP, the team therefore proposed to place Mark in a class specifically structured for autistic children at Leesburg Elementary. Leesburg is a regular elementary school which houses the autism class in order to facilitate interaction between the autistic children and students who are not handicapped. The Leesburg class would have included five autistic students working with a special education teacher and at least one full-time aide. Under the May IEP, Mark would have received only academic instruction and speech in the self-contained classroom, while joining a regular class for art, music, physical education, library, and recess. The Leesburg program also would have permitted Mark to increase the portion of his instruction received in a regular education setting as he demonstrated an improved ability to handle it.

The Hartmanns refused to approve the IEP, claiming that it failed to comply with the mainstreaming provision of the IDEA, which states that "to the maximum extent appropriate," disabled children should be educated with children who are not handicapped. 20 U.S.C. § 1412(5)(B). The county initiated due process proceedings, see 20 U.S.C. § 1415(b), and on December 14, 1994, the local hearing officer upheld the May 1994 IEP. She found that Mark's behavior was disruptive and that despite the "enthusiastic" efforts of the county, he had obtained no academic benefit from the regular education classroom. On May 3, 1995, the state review officer affirmed the decision, adopting both the hearing officer's findings and her legal analysis. The Hartmanns then challenged the hearing officer's decision in federal court.

While the administrative process continued, Mark entered third grade in the regular education classroom at Ashburn. In December of that year, the Hartmanns withdrew Mark from Ashburn. Mark and his mother moved to Montgomery County, Virginia, to permit the Hartmanns to enroll Mark in public school there. Mark was placed in the regular third-grade classroom for the remainder of that year as well as the next

The district court reversed the hearing officer's decision. The court rejected the administrative findings and concluded that Mark could receive significant educational benefit in a regular classroom and that "the Board simply did not take enough appropriate steps to try to include Mark in a regular class." The court made little of the testimony of Mark's Loudoun County instructors, and instead relied heavily on its reading of Mark's experience in Illinois and Montgomery County. While the hearing officer had addressed Mark's conduct in detail, the court stated that "[g]iven the strong presumption for inclusion under the IDEA, disruptive behavior should not be a significant factor in determining the appropriate educational placement for a disabled child." Loudoun County now appeals.

II.

The IDEA embodies important principles governing the relationship between local school authorities and a reviewing district court. Although section 1415(e)(2) provides district courts with authority to grant "appropriate" relief based on a preponderance of the evidence, 20 U.S.C. § 1415(e)(2), that section "is by no means an invitation to the courts to substitute their own notions of sound educational policy for those of the school authorities which they review." *Board of Education of Hendrick Hudson Central Sch. Dist. v. Rowley*, 458 U.S. 176, 206 (1982). Absent some statutory infraction, the task of education belongs to the educators who have been charged by society with that critical task. Likewise, federal courts must accord "due weight" to state administrative proceedings. Id. Administrative findings in an IDEA case "are entitled to be considered prima facie correct," and "the district court, if it is not going to follow them, is required to explain why it does not."

These principles reflect the IDEA's recognition that federal courts cannot run local schools. Local educators deserve latitude in determining the individualized education program most appropriate for a disabled child. The IDEA does not deprive these educators of the right to apply their professional judgment. Rather it establishes a "basic floor of opportunity" for every handicapped child. *Rowley*, 458 U.S. at 201. States must provide specialized instruction and related services "sufficient to confer some educational benefit upon the handicapped child," *id.* at 200, but the Act does not require "the furnishing of every special service necessary to maximize each handicapped child's potential," *id.* at 199.

In this same vein, the IDEA's mainstreaming provision establishes a presumption, not an inflexible federal mandate. Under its terms, disabled children are to be educated with children who are not handicapped only "to the maximum extent appropriate." 20 U.S.C. § 1412(5)(B). Section 1412(5)(B) explicitly states that mainstreaming is not appropriate "when the nature or severity of the disability is such that education in regular classes with the use of supplementary aids and services cannot be achieved satisfactorily." 20 U.S.C. § 1412(5)(B); see also *Rowley*, 458 U.S. at 181 n.4.

III.

The district court's ruling strayed generally from the aforementioned principles. [A]fter careful examination of the record, [w]e are forced to conclude that the district court's decision fails to account for the administrative findings and is not supported by the evidence based on a correct application of the law. In effect, the court simply substituted its own judgment regarding Mark's proper educational program for that of local school officials.

A.

In finding that Mark could receive an educational benefit in a regular classroom, the district court disregarded both the hearing officer's finding and the overwhelming evidence that Mark made no academic progress in the regular second grade classroom at Ashburn. Mark's teacher testified, for example, that he was unable to retain skills: "once we thought he mastered [a math skill] and we left it alone and went onto another concept, if we went back to review, it seemed that he had forgotten." She confessed, "I felt like he lost a year in my classroom." Other Loudoun County personnel testified to the same effect. His speech therapist, for instance, stated that "[t]he only gain that I saw him make was in the one to one setting." The supervisor for the county's program for autistic students likewise concluded, "I think there has been no progress academically in the inclusive settings;" "I think we're wasting his time." The hearing officer accordingly found that "Mark made no measurable academic progress attributable to his placement in the regular classroom."

[T]he district court acknowledged the testimony of Mark's second grade teacher regarding his lack of progress, but asserted that the hearing officer's conclusions were erroneous because the officer failed to give due weight to the testimony of Cathy Thornton, Mark's private tutor during second grade, and to Mark's first grade experience in Illinois. To the contrary, the administrative decisions took careful note of both. The hearing officer fully credited Thornton's testimony, finding that Mark made progress with both her and his speech therapist. The officer went further, however, and observed that both the tutoring and speech instruction occurred in a one-to-one setting outside of the regular class. In light of Mark's failure to progress in the regular classroom, the officer drew the only reasonable inference from this evidence, namely that separate instruction was precisely what Mark needed to make educational progress. As to Mark's experience in Illinois, the state review officer explained that the Illinois assessment of Mark's capabilities was flawed:

> [I]t became clear during the course of the second grade that Mark's academic skills were not as advanced as the Illinois school system thought. Mark cannot read and cannot add, yet the Illinois teachers thought he was reading at first grade level and progressing in the first grade math workbook. . . .

[W]hile the district court opinion references the hearing officer's decision, its failure to address the administrative findings noted above simply does not reflect the teaching[ ] of *Rowley* [t]hat state proceedings must command considerable deference in federal courts.

The district court also relied heavily on Mark's subsequent performance in the Montgomery County schools during fourth grade. While Montgomery County personnel did make some conclusory statements asserting that Mark made progress, the evidence is inconclusive at best. The district court pointed to math skills Mark demonstrated at the end of fourth grade, for example, but Mark was pulled out of the regular class for math instruction, just as Loudoun County had recommended. Any progress he made in math therefore simply supports the conclusion that separate, one-on-one instruction is appropriate for Mark. Mark also continued to receive speech therapy one-on-one, and his special education teacher in Montgomery County admitted that the county had no reliable method for assessing Mark's reading ability.

Finally, the district court pointed to perceived improvement in Mark's social skills due to interaction with his non-disabled peers. Any such benefits, however, cannot outweigh his failure to progress academically in the regular classroom. The mainstreaming provision represents recognition of the value of having disabled children interact with non-handicapped students. The fact that the provision only creates a presumption, however, reflects a congressional judgment that receipt of such social benefits is ultimately a goal subordinate to the requirement that disabled children receive educational benefit. Here the evidence clearly supports the judgment of the local education officials and the administrative hearing officers that Mark's educational progress required significant instruction outside of the regular classroom setting.

B.

The district court attributed Mark's lack of progress in Loudoun County to the county's alleged failure to make reasonable efforts to accommodate him in the regular classroom. We interpret this as a ruling that the county failed to provide the supplementary aids and services contemplated by the IDEA's mainstreaming provision. 20 U.S.C. § 1412(5)(B).

The district court's conclusion is remarkable in light of the extensive measures taken on Mark's behalf. The hearing officer found that Loudoun personnel were "enthusiastic" about including Mark at Ashburn, a description fully supported by the record. The Ashburn principal deliberately reduced the size of Mark's class and ensured that it was composed of students who were more independent and had higher level skills. Mark's teacher was selected because of her excellent teaching abilities, and the county hired a full-time, one-on-one aide for Mark. Mark received a full hour of speech and language instruction daily. Frank Johnson, the supervisor of the county's program for autistic children, provided assistance in behavior management throughout the year. Halfway through the year, the school's efforts increased when Virginia McCullough began providing special education services directly to Mark as well as advising Mark's teacher and aide. Inclusion specialists Gail Mayfield and Jamie Ruppmann consulted with the school during the fall, and Mark's teacher sought advice from other experts whose names were provided to her by the school or the Hartmanns. The teacher testified that she met constantly with Mark's aide, his speech therapist, the IEP team, and others to work on Mark's program—daily at the beginning of the year and at least twice a week throughout.

The district court nonetheless found the county's efforts insufficient. The court relied primarily on its conclusion that the Loudoun educators involved with Mark had inadequate training and experience to work with an autistic child. The court found the credentials of two groups to be lacking. Neither the special education professionals nor the regular education instructors were deemed properly qualified. The conclusion that Mark had inadequately trained personnel developing and implementing his program, however, is irreconcilable with either the law or the record.

As to special education personnel, the district court concedes that the individuals working with Mark during the first half of the year, Mary Kearney and Jamie Ruppmann, were fully competent to assist him. Kearney led Mark's IEP team, while Ruppmann provided consultation services. In addition to serving as the county Director of Special Education, Kearney had participated in the Virginia Systems Change Project, a two-year state program on mainstreaming which involved selected schools from across the state. Ruppmann is an experienced, highly qualified consultant.

During the second half of the year, Frank Johnson led the IEP team, and Virginia McCullough provided Mark with special education services. The district court rejected their qualifications, asserting, for example, that Johnson's credentials were clearly inadequate because they were inferior to those of Kearney and Ruppmann. However, in addition to serving as the supervisor of Loudoun County's program for autistic children, Johnson had a special education masters degree, did graduate work with an autistic child, worked directly with approximately ten autistic children as a teacher, and had attended special education courses and seminars relating to autism throughout his professional career. Both McCullough's early childhood degree program and her work in Loudoun County focused specifically on integrating children with disabilities into the regular classroom.

To dismiss Johnson's and McCullough's qualifications is to adopt exactly the sort of potential-maximizing standard rejected by the Supreme Court in *Rowley*. [N]ot all school systems will have the resources to hire top-notch consultants, nor will every school have the good fortune to have personnel who were involved in a major state program related to the needs of every disabled child. We note that in Virginia, there is no certification for autism. Furthermore, at the time of the trial, Loudoun County had eleven autistic children in a total school population of approximately 20,000 students. In this light, Johnson's experience teaching ten autistic children was substantial. Johnson and McCullough were clearly qualified to work with Mark as special educators, even accepting the district court's assertion that Ruppmann and Kearney had better credentials.

The suggestion that the regular education instructors, Mark's teacher and aide, were not adequately qualified also does not survive close scrutiny. Diane Johnson was an experienced professional properly certified under state law, and Virginia law does not require teaching assistants to be certified. Furthermore, Johnson and Leitner both obtained special training to work with Mark. Both received in-service instruction and attended an outside seminar on inclusion of disabled children in the regular classroom. They also were trained in facilitated communication, a special communication method used with Mark in Illinois.

To demand more than this from regular education personnel would essentially require them to become special education teachers trained in the full panoply of disabilities that their students might have. Virginia law does not require this, nor does the IDEA. [W]e can think of few steps that would do more to usurp state educational standards and policy than to have federal courts re-write state teaching certification requirements in the guise of applying the IDEA.

C.

The district court also gave little or no weight to the disruptive effects of Mark's behavior in the classroom, stating that "[g]iven the strong presumption for inclusion under the IDEA, disruptive behavior should not be a significant factor in determining the appropriate educational placement for a disabled child." This statement simply ignores [our prior holding] that mainstreaming is inappropriate when "the handicapped child is a disruptive force in the non-segregated setting." In this case, disruptive behavior was clearly an issue. The hearing officer summarized:

> [Mark's] misbehaviors include continual vocalization, especially whining, screeching and crying when unhappy or frustrated, hitting, pinching, kicking, biting, sucking the leg of a chair, rolling on the floor, and removing his shoes and clothing. Mark is a big strong child who cannot be easily restrained when he engages in injurious behaviors such as hitting, kicking, pinching and biting. His continual vocalizations are distracting and make it difficult for other children to stay on task. When Jamie Ruppmann observed

Mark in his classroom, she observed two instances of significant disruption, in which he threw himself on the floor. She noted that in each instance it took about five to eight minutes to get Mark settled down. His loud screeching outbursts, which occur daily, take the attention of the teacher and the aide to redirect him; these outbursts also take the other children off task and they then have to be redirected. Mark hits and pinches others several times a day.

While the hearing officer did not find Mark's disruptive behavior by itself to be dispositive, the attention she gave to Mark's conduct was entirely appropriate, indeed required, under [our case law].

D.

The district court also found that Leesburg would not have been an appropriate placement. This conclusion generally derived from the same analysis that led to the court's determination that Mark should remain in the regular classroom. To the contrary, we hold that the proposed Leesburg placement was carefully tailored to ensure that he was mainstreamed "to the maximum extent appropriate." 20 U.S.C. § 1412(5)(B). Leesburg was a regular elementary school. Responding to Mark's lack of academic progress in the regular classroom, the May IEP would have placed Mark in the self-contained class for his academic subjects, while including him with his non-disabled peers for all other school activities such as art, music, and physical education. To promote the success of this partial mainstreaming, the hearing officer required the school to have an aide or teacher accompany Mark whenever he was in the regular classroom environment and to place Mark with the same regular education class for all his nonacademic activities.

IV.

This is not a case which either the local educational authorities or the reviewing administrative officers took lightly. We have sketched in great detail the efforts that Loudoun County made to provide Mark Hartmann with a suitable education. Furthermore, the administrative review process could not have been more thorough. The hearing officer heard testimony from eighteen witnesses over a two month period and made detailed factual findings regarding all aspects of Mark's educational experience. The officer's analysis carefully incorporated those findings and specifically addressed the evidence the Hartmanns presented in support of their position. The district court, however, set all this extensive effort and review at nought. The court failed to mention, let alone discuss, critical administrative findings inconsistent with its conclusions. While making much of the credentials and credibility of witnesses endorsing full inclusion, the court gave little or no attention to the testimony of Loudoun professionals. In some instances the court, without listening to local educators, discounted their views despite the fact that the hearing officer had found them credible. One Loudoun official was dismissed outright as "a philosophical opponent of inclusion" for daring to state that he saw no evidence that Mark had progressed in the regular classroom.

The IDEA encourages mainstreaming, but only to the extent that it does not prevent a child from receiving educational benefit. The evidence in this case demonstrates that Mark Hartmann was not making academic progress in a regular education classroom despite the provision of adequate supplementary aids and services. Loudoun County properly proposed to place Mark in a partially mainstreamed program which would have addressed the academic deficiencies of his full inclusion program while permitting him to interact with nonhandicapped students to the greatest extent possible. This professional judgment by local educators was deserving of respect. The approval of this educational approach by the local and state administrative officers likewise deserved a deference from the district court which it failed to receive. In rejecting reasonable pedagogical choices and disregarding well-supported administrative findings, the district court assumed an educational mantle which the IDEA did not confer. Accordingly, the judgment must be reversed, and the case remanded with directions to dismiss it.

REVERSED AND REMANDED.

NOTES ON THE INTEGRATION PRESUMPTION

1.   Relationship to the FAPE Standard. What is the relationship between the free appropriate public education standard (FAPE) of *Rowley* and the integration presumption discussed in *Rachel H.* and *Hartmann*? In many if not all cases, it will be just as easy to characterize the facts as involving placement in an unnecessarily restrictive environment as it will be to characterize the facts as involving the denial of an appropriate education. Consider the facts of *Rowley*. Rowley's parents framed the case as a challenge to the school district's denial of an appropriate education. But they could just have easily framed the case as one involving a violation of the integration presumption: If the school district had provided an interpreter, they could have argued, it would have been unnecessary for them to pull Rowley out of the classroom eight hour each week for special instruction.

As *Rachel H.* indicates, many courts (particularly in the first 15 years after *Rowley* was decided) have viewed cases invoking the integration presumption as not presenting the same sorts of challenge to local educational policy decisions as do cases invoking the right to an "appropriate" education. Until the last ten years or so, cases addressing integration claims under the IDEA typically did not apply *Rowley*-style deference to school districts' policy decisions. See Anne Proffitt Dupre, *Disability, Deference, and the Integrity of the Academic Enterprise*, 32 Ga. L. Rev. 393, 429–439 (1998). Because appropriate-education cases can easily be redescribed as integration cases, the lack of deference in integration cases blunted *Rowley*'s impact significantly. See generally Mark C. Weber, *The Transformation of the Education of the Handicapped Act: A Study in the Interpretation of Radical Statutes*, 24 U.C. Davis L. Rev. 349 (1990). In *Hartmann*, by contrast, the court treated integration cases as implicating school districts' policy decisions just as surely as do appropriate-education cases. In this respect, *Hartmann* is probably more typical of the recent case law. Which approach do you find more persuasive?

2.   Critiques of the Integration Presumption. Professor Ruth Colker argues that the integration presumption "causes school districts and courts to prefer a more mainstream education for a child even if the available evidence suggests that the child would attain more educational benefit from a more segregated environment." Ruth Colker, When is Separate Unequal? A Disability Perspective 79 (2009). She argues that the presumption served an important function in ending the "warehousing" of children with disabilities in disability-only institutions, but that evidence suggests that the most integrated setting is not necessarily the best educational setting for many individuals with disabilities. See *id.* at 78–140. Professor Anne Proffitt Dupre similarly argues that the integration presumption has been used to support "full inclusion"—the practice of including children with disabilities in mainstream classrooms for the entire school day—and that full inclusion often fails to serve the needs of children with disabilities at the same time that it disrupts the learning community for nondisabled children. See Anne Proffitt Dupre, *Disability and the Public Schools: The Case Against "Inclusion,"* 72 Wash. L. Rev. 775 (1997).

Are these arguments persuasive? Professor Mark Weber observes that a number of "experts in the field [have] survey[ed] the literature and come to conclusions contrary to Professor Colker's." Mark C. Weber, *A Nuanced Approach to the Disability Integration Presumption*, 156 U. Pa. L. Rev. PENNumbra 174, 180 (2007). He argues that the integration presumption "should be applied in a nuanced fashion" that does not necessarily require "total" integration but instead focuses "on the intensity of services provided to facilitate success in the mainstream." *Id.* at 186. And he argues that courts should be more receptive to parents', rather than school districts', requests for a more segregated setting. See *id.* For an argument that the integration presumption, as currently applied, has *not* placed undue pressure on school districts to move children with disabilities into (inappropriate) integrated settings, see Samuel R. Bagenstos, *Abolish the Integration Presumption? Not Yet*, 156 U. Pa. L. Rev. PENNumbra 157, 158 (2007) ("[T]he individualized integration presumption does not prevent a school district from providing a separate placement to a child with a disability when that is truly the best option for her. It merely requires the school district to demonstrate that its chosen course is, in fact, the best option. That burden, it seems to me, is fully justified. Teachers and school officials too often simply find it easier to deal with people who are different by putting them aside in 'special' settings rather than implementing the changes necessary to make the regular settings more accessible.").

Do the professional disputes regarding the value of integrated settings suggest that courts should defer to school districts' resolution of those disputes? Or are there good reasons for judicial intervention to place a thumb on the scale on the side of integration?

3. **Balancing the Interests of Students with and Without Disabilities.** If a student with a disability is placed in an integrated setting and exhibits disruptive behavior, how ought a school district to respond? Do school administrators have any "substantive reason" to "weigh the welfare of disabled children more highly than the welfare of regular ed children" in this context? Mark Kelman & Gillian Lester, Jumping the Queue: An Inquiry into the Legal Treatment of Students with Learning Disabilities 96 (1997). Both *Rachel H.* and *Hartmann* treat some degree of disruption as a legitimate reason—if backed up by the evidence—for

placing a child with a disability in a more restrictive setting. But how much disruption is enough? And is it appropriate to place an already disruptive student into a more restrictive setting even if that placement will make the disruption worse? Cf. *id.* at 96–97 (noting the views of some school administrators that placing disruptive students in self-contained settings with other disruptive students makes things worse because "they just feed off each other").

2. RELATED SERVICES

Cedar Rapids Community Sch. Dist. v. Garret F.

Supreme Court of the United States, 1999.

526 U.S. 66.

■ JUSTICE STEVENS delivered the opinion of the Court.

The Individuals with Disabilities Education Act (IDEA), 84 Stat. 175, as amended, was enacted, in part, "to assure that all children with disabilities have available to them . . . a free appropriate public education which emphasizes special education and related services designed to meet their unique needs." 20 U.S.C. § 1400(c). Consistent with this purpose, the IDEA authorizes federal financial assistance to States that agree to provide disabled children with special education and "related services." See §§ 1401(a)(18), 1412(1). The question presented in this case is whether the definition of "related services" in § 1401(a)(17)[1] requires a public school district in a participating State to provide a ventilator-dependent student with certain nursing services during school hours.

Originally, the statute was enacted without a definition of "related services." See Education of the Handicapped Act, 84 Stat. 175. In 1975, Congress added the definition at issue in this case. Education for All Handicapped Children Act of 1975, § 4(a)(4), 89 Stat. 775. Aside from nonsubstantive changes and added examples of included services, see, e.g., Individuals with Disabilities Education Act Amendments of 1997, § 101, 111 Stat. 45; Individuals with Disabilities Education Act Amendments of 1991, § 25(a)(1)(B), 105 Stat. 605; Education of the Handicapped Act Amendments of 1990, § 101(c), 104 Stat. 1103, the relevant language in § 1401(a)(17) has not been amended since 1975. All references to the IDEA herein are to the 1994 version as codified in Title 20 of the United States Code—the version of the statute in effect when this dispute arose.

I

Respondent Garret F. is a friendly, creative, and intelligent young man. When Garret was four years old, his spinal column was severed in

---

[1] "The term 'related services' means transportation, and such developmental, corrective, and other supportive services (including speech pathology and audiology, psychological services, physical and occupational therapy, recreation, including therapeutic recreation, social work services, counseling services, including rehabilitation counseling, and medical services, except that such medical services shall be for diagnostic and evaluation purposes only) as may be required to assist a child with a disability to benefit from special education, and includes the early identification and assessment of disabling conditions in children." 20 U.S.C. § 1401(a)(17).

a motorcycle accident. Though paralyzed from the neck down, his mental capacities were unaffected. He is able to speak, to control his motorized wheelchair through use of a puff and suck straw, and to operate a computer with a device that responds to head movements. Garret is currently a student in the Cedar Rapids Community School District (District), he attends regular classes in a typical school program, and his academic performance has been a success. Garret is, however, ventilator dependent,[2] and therefore requires a responsible individual nearby to attend to certain physical needs while he is in school.[3]

During Garret's early years at school his family provided for his physical care during the schoolday. When he was in kindergarten, his 18-year-old aunt attended him; in the next four years, his family used settlement proceeds they received after the accident, their insurance, and other resources to employ a licensed practical nurse. In 1993, Garret's mother requested the District to accept financial responsibility for the health care services that Garret requires during the schoolday. The District denied the request, believing that it was not legally obligated to provide continuous one-on-one nursing services.

Relying on both the IDEA and Iowa law, Garret's mother requested a hearing before the Iowa Department of Education. An Administrative Law Judge (ALJ) received extensive evidence concerning Garret's special needs, the District's treatment of other disabled students, and the assistance provided to other ventilator-dependent children in other parts of the country. In his 47-page report, the ALJ found that the District has about 17,500 students, of whom approximately 2,200 need some form of special education or special services. Although Garret is the only ventilator-dependent student in the District, most of the health care services that he needs are already provided for some other students.[4] "The primary difference between Garret's situation and that of other students is his dependency on his ventilator for life support." The ALJ noted that the parties disagreed over the training or licensure required for the care and supervision of such students, and that those providing such care in other parts of the country ranged from nonlicensed personnel to registered nurses. However, the District did

---

[2] In his report in this case, the Administrative Law Judge explained: "Being ventilator dependent means that [Garret] breathes only with external aids, usually an electric ventilator, and occasionally by someone else's manual pumping of an air bag attached to his tracheotomy tube when the ventilator is being maintained. This later procedure is called ambu bagging."

[3] "He needs assistance with urinary bladder catheterization once a day, the suctioning of his tracheotomy tube as needed, but at least once every six hours, with food and drink at lunchtime, in getting into a reclining position for five minutes of each hour, and ambu bagging occasionally as needed when the ventilator is checked for proper functioning. He also needs assistance from someone familiar with his ventilator in the event there is a malfunction or electrical problem, and someone who can perform emergency procedures in the event he experiences autonomic hyperreflexia. Autonomic hyperreflexia is an uncontrolled visceral reaction to anxiety or a full bladder. Blood pressure increases, heart rate increases, and flushing and sweating may occur. Garret has not experienced autonomic hyperreflexia frequently in recent years, and it has usually been alleviated by catheterization. He has not ever experienced autonomic hyperreflexia at school. Garret is capable of communicating his needs orally or in another fashion so long as he has not been rendered unable to do so by an extended lack of oxygen."

[4] "Included are such services as care for students who need urinary catheterization, food and drink, oxygen supplement positioning, and suctioning."

not contend that only a licensed physician could provide the services in question.

The ALJ explained that federal law requires that children with a variety of health impairments be provided with "special education and related services" when their disabilities adversely affect their academic performance, and that such children should be educated to the maximum extent appropriate with children who are not disabled. In addition, the ALJ explained that applicable federal regulations distinguish between "school health services," which are provided by a "qualified school nurse or other qualified person," and "medical services," which are provided by a licensed physician. See 34 C.F.R. §§ 300.16(a), (b)(4), (b)(11) (1998). The District must provide the former, but need not provide the latter (except, of course, those "medical services" that are for diagnostic or evaluation purposes, 20 U.S.C. § 1401(a)(17)). According to the ALJ, the distinction in the regulations does not just depend on "the title of the person providing the service"; instead, the "medical services" exclusion is limited to services that are "in the special training, knowledge, and judgment of a physician to carry out." The ALJ thus concluded that the IDEA required the District to bear financial responsibility for all of the services in dispute, including continuous nursing services.

The District challenged the ALJ's decision in Federal District Court, but that court approved the ALJ's IDEA ruling and granted summary judgment against the District. The Court of Appeals affirmed. It noted that, as a recipient of federal funds under the IDEA, Iowa has a statutory duty to provide all disabled children a "free appropriate public education," which includes "related services." The Court of Appeals read our opinion in *Irving Independent School Dist. v. Tatro*, 468 U.S. 883 (1984), to provide a two-step analysis of the "related services" definition in § 1401(a)(17)—asking first, whether the requested services are included within the phrase "supportive services"; and second, whether the services are excluded as "medical services." The Court of Appeals succinctly answered both questions in Garret's favor. The Court found the first step plainly satisfied, since Garret cannot attend school unless the requested services are available during the schoolday. As to the second step, the court reasoned that *Tatro* "established a bright-line test: the services of a physician (other than for diagnostic and evaluation purposes) are subject to the medical services exclusion, but services that can be provided in the school setting by a nurse or qualified layperson are not."

In its petition for *certiorari*, the District challenged only the second step of the Court of Appeals' analysis. The District pointed out that some federal courts have not asked whether the requested health services must be delivered by a physician, but instead have applied a multifactor test that considers, generally speaking, the nature and extent of the services at issue. We granted the District's petition to resolve this conflict.

II

The District contends that § 1401(a)(17) does not require it to provide Garret with "continuous one-on-one nursing services" during the schoolday, even though Garret cannot remain in school without such care. However, the IDEA's definition of "related services," our decision in *Irving Independent School Dist. v. Tatro*, 468 U.S. 883 (1984), and the overall statutory scheme all support the decision of the Court of Appeals.

The text of the "related services" definition, see n.1, *supra*, broadly encompasses those supportive services that "may be required to assist a child with a disability to benefit from special education." As we have already noted, the District does not challenge the Court of Appeals' conclusion that the in-school services at issue are within the covered category of "supportive services." As a general matter, services that enable a disabled child to remain in school during the day provide the student with "the meaningful access to education that Congress envisioned." *Tatro*, 468 U.S., at 891 (" 'Congress sought primarily to make public education available to handicapped children' and 'to make such access meaningful' " (quoting *Rowley*)).

This general definition of "related services" is illuminated by a parenthetical phrase listing examples of particular services that are included within the statute's coverage. § 1401(a)(17). "[M]edical services" are enumerated in this list, but such services are limited to those that are "for diagnostic and evaluation purposes." *Ibid.* The statute does not contain a more specific definition of the "medical services" that are excepted from the coverage of § 1401(a)(17).

The scope of the "medical services" exclusion is not a matter of first impression in this Court. In *Tatro* we concluded that the Secretary of Education had reasonably determined that the term "medical services" referred only to services that must be performed by a physician, and not to school health services. 468 U.S., at 892–894. Accordingly, we held that a specific form of health care (clean intermittent catheterization) that is often, though not always, performed by a nurse is not an excluded medical service. We referenced the likely cost of the services and the competence of school staff as justifications for drawing a line between physician and other services, but our endorsement of that line was unmistakable.[6] It is thus settled that the phrase "medical services" in § 1401(a)(17) does not embrace all forms of care that might loosely be

---

[6] "The regulations define 'related services' for handicapped children to include 'school health services,' 34 C.F.R. § 300.13(a) (1983), which are defined in turn as 'services provided by a qualified school nurse or other qualified person,' § 300.13(b)(10). 'Medical services' are defined as 'services provided by a licensed physician.' § 300.13(b)(4). Thus, the Secretary has [reasonably] determined that the services of a school nurse otherwise qualifying as a 'related service' are not subject to exclusion as a 'medical service,' but that the services of a physician are excludable as such.

". . . By limiting the 'medical services' exclusion to the services of a physician or hospital, both far more expensive, the Secretary has given a permissible construction to the provision." 468 U.S., at 892–893 (footnote omitted); see also *id.*, at 894 ("[T]he regulations state that school nursing services must be provided only if they can be performed by a nurse or other qualified person, not if they must be performed by a physician").

Based on certain policy letters issued by the Department of Education, it seems that the Secretary's post-*Tatro* view of the statute has not been entirely clear. We may assume that the Secretary has authority under the IDEA to adopt regulations that define the "medical services" exclusion by more explicitly taking into account the nature and extent of the requested services; and the Secretary surely has the authority to enumerate the services that are, and are not, fairly included within the scope of § 1407(a)(17). But the Secretary has done neither; and, in this Court, she advocates affirming the judgment of the Court of Appeals. We obviously have no authority to rewrite the regulations, and we see no sufficient reason to revise *Tatro*, either.

described as "medical" in other contexts, such as a claim for an income tax deduction. See 26 U.S.C. § 213(d)(1) (defining "medical care").

The District does not ask us to define the term so broadly. Indeed, the District does not argue that any of the items of care that Garret needs, considered individually, could be excluded from the scope of 20 U.S.C. § 1401(a)(17). It could not make such an argument, considering that one of the services Garret needs (catheterization) was at issue in *Tatro*, and the others may be provided competently by a school nurse or other trained personnel. As the ALJ concluded, most of the requested services are already provided by the District to other students, and the in-school care necessitated by Garret's ventilator dependency does not demand the training, knowledge, and judgment of a licensed physician. While more extensive, the in-school services Garret needs are no more "medical" than was the care sought in *Tatro*.

Instead, the District points to the combined and continuous character of the required care, and proposes a test under which the outcome in any particular case would "depend upon a series of factors, such as [1] whether the care is continuous or intermittent, [2] whether existing school health personnel can provide the service, [3] the cost of the service, and [4] the potential consequences if the service is not properly performed."

The District's multifactor test is not supported by any recognized source of legal authority. The proposed factors can be found in neither the text of the statute nor the regulations that we upheld in *Tatro*. Moreover, the District offers no explanation why these characteristics make one service any more "medical" than another. The continuous character of certain services associated with Garret's ventilator dependency has no apparent relationship to "medical" services, much less a relationship of equivalence. Continuous services may be more costly and may require additional school personnel, but they are not thereby more "medical." Whatever its imperfections, a rule that limits the medical services exemption to physician services is unquestionably a reasonable and generally workable interpretation of the statute. Absent an elaboration of the statutory terms plainly more convincing than that which we reviewed in *Tatro*, there is no good reason to depart from settled law.

Finally, the District raises broader concerns about the financial burden that it must bear to provide the services that Garret needs to stay in school. The problem for the District in providing these services is not that its staff cannot be trained to deliver them; the problem, the District contends, is that the existing school health staff cannot meet all of their responsibilities and provide for Garret at the same time.[9] Through its multifactor test, the District seeks to establish a kind of undue-burden exemption primarily based on the cost of the requested

---

[9]   See Tr. of Oral Arg. 4–5, 13; Brief for Petitioner 6–7, 9. The District, however, will not necessarily need to hire an additional employee to meet Garret's needs. The District already employs a one-on-one teacher associate (TA) who assists Garret during the schoolday. At one time, Garret's TA was a licensed practical nurse (LPN). In light of the state Board of Nursing's recent ruling that the District's registered nurses may decide to delegate Garret's care to an LPN, the dissent's future-cost estimate is speculative. See App. to Pet. for Cert. 28a, 58a–60a (if the District could assign Garret's care to a TA who is also an LPN, there would be "a minimum of additional expense").

services. The first two factors can be seen as examples of cost-based distinctions: Intermittent care is often less expensive than continuous care, and the use of existing personnel is cheaper than hiring additional employees. The third factor—the cost of the service—would then encompass the first two. The relevance of the fourth factor is likewise related to cost because extra care may be necessary if potential consequences are especially serious.

The District may have legitimate financial concerns, but our role in this dispute is to interpret existing law. Defining "related services" in a manner that accommodates the cost concerns Congress may have had, cf. *Tatro*, 468 U.S., at 892, is altogether different from using cost itself as the definition. Given that § 1401(a)(17) does not employ cost in its definition of "related services" or excluded "medical services," accepting the District's cost-based standard as the sole test for determining the scope of the provision would require us to engage in judicial lawmaking without any guidance from Congress. It would also create some tension with the purposes of the IDEA. The statute may not require public schools to maximize the potential of disabled students commensurate with the opportunities provided to other children, see *Rowley*, 458 U.S., at 200; and the potential financial burdens imposed on participating States may be relevant to arriving at a sensible construction of the IDEA, see *Tatro*, 468 U.S., at 892. But Congress intended "to open the door of public education" to all qualified children and "require[d] participating States to educate handicapped children with nonhandicapped children whenever possible." *Rowley*, 458 U.S., at 192.[10]

This case is about whether meaningful access to the public schools will be assured, not the level of education that a school must finance once access is attained. It is undisputed that the services at issue must be provided if Garret is to remain in school. Under the statute, our precedent, and the purposes of the IDEA, the District must fund such "related services" in order to help guarantee that students like Garret are integrated into the public schools.

The judgment of the Court of Appeals is accordingly

Affirmed.

■ JUSTICE THOMAS, with whom JUSTICE KENNEDY joins, dissenting.

The majority, relying heavily on our decision in *Irving Independent School Dist. v. Tatro*, 468 U.S. 883 (1984), concludes that the Individuals with Disabilities Education Act (IDEA), 20 U.S.C. § 1400 *et seq.*, requires a public school district to fund continuous, one-on-one nursing care for disabled children. Because *Tatro* cannot be squared with the text of IDEA, the Court should not adhere to it in this case. Even assuming that *Tatro* was correct in the first instance, the

---

[10] The dissent's approach, which seems to be even broader than the District's, is unconvincing. The dissent's rejection of our unanimous decision in *Tatro* comes 15 years too late, see *Patterson v. McLean Credit Union*, 491 U.S. 164, 172–173 (1989) (*stare decisis* has "special force" in statutory interpretation), and it offers nothing constructive in its place. Aside from rejecting a "provider-specific approach," the dissent cites unrelated statutes and offers a circular definition of "medical services." (opinion of THOMAS, J.) (" 'services' that are 'medical' in 'nature' "). Moreover, the dissent's approach apparently would exclude most ordinary school nursing services of the kind routinely provided to nondisabled children; that anomalous result is not easily attributable to congressional intent[.]

majority's extension of it is unwarranted and ignores the constitutionally mandated rules of construction applicable to legislation enacted pursuant to Congress' spending power.

I

As the majority recounts, IDEA authorizes the provision of federal financial assistance to States that agree to provide, inter alia, "special education and related services" for disabled children. § 1401(a)(18). In *Tatro*, supra, we held that this provision of IDEA required a school district to provide clean intermittent catheterization to a disabled child several times a day. In so holding, we relied on Department of Education regulations, which we concluded had reasonably interpreted IDEA's definition of "related services" to require school districts in participating States to provide "school nursing services" (of which we assumed catheterization was a subcategory) but not "services of a physician." This holding is contrary to the plain text of IDEA, and its reliance on the Department of Education's regulations was misplaced.

A

Before we consider whether deference to an agency regulation is appropriate, "we first ask whether Congress has 'directly spoken to the precise question at issue. If the intent of Congress is clear, that is the end of the matter; for the court, as well as the agency, must give effect to the unambiguously expressed intent of Congress.' " [U]nfortunately, the Court in *Tatro* failed to consider this necessary antecedent question before turning to the Department of Education's regulations implementing IDEA's related services provision. The Court instead began "with the regulations of the Department of Education, which," it said, "are entitled to deference." *Tatro*, *supra*, at 891–892. The Court need not have looked beyond the text of IDEA, which expressly indicates that school districts are not required to provide medical services, except for diagnostic and evaluation purposes. 20 U.S.C. § 1401(a)(17). The majority asserts that *Tatro* precludes reading the term "medical services" to include "all forms of care that might loosely be described as 'medical.' " The majority does not explain, however, why "services" that are "medical" in nature are not "medical services." Not only is the definition that the majority rejects consistent with other uses of the term in federal law,[2] it also avoids the anomalous result of holding that the services at issue in *Tatro* (as well as in this case), while not "medical services," would nonetheless qualify as medical care for federal income tax purposes.

The primary problem with *Tatro*, and the majority's reliance on it today, is that the Court focused on the provider of the services rather than the services themselves. We do not typically think that automotive services are limited to those provided by a mechanic, for example. Rather, anything done to repair or service a car, no matter who does the

---

[2] See, e.g., 38 U.S.C. § 1701(6) ("The term 'medical services' includes, in addition to medical examination, treatment, and rehabilitative services—. . . surgical services, dental services . . . , optometric and podiatric services, . . . preventive health services, . . . [and] such consultation, professional counseling, training, and mental health services as are necessary in connection with the treatment"); § 101(28) ("The term 'nursing home care' means the accommodation of convalescents . . . who require nursing care and related medical services"); 26 U.S.C. § 213(d)(1) ("The term 'medical care' means amounts paid—. . . for the diagnosis, cure, mitigation, treatment, or prevention of disease").

work, is thought to fall into that category. Similarly, the term "food service" is not generally thought to be limited to work performed by a chef. The term "medical" similarly does not support *Tatro*'s provider-specific approach, but encompasses services that are "of, relating to, or concerned with physicians or with the practice of medicine." See Webster's Third New International Dictionary 1402 (1986); see also *id.*, at 1551 (defining "nurse" as "a person skilled in caring for and waiting on the infirm, the injured, or the sick; specif: one esp. trained to carry out such duties under the supervision of a physician").

IDEA's structure and purpose reinforce this textual interpretation. Congress enacted IDEA to increase the educational opportunities available to disabled children, not to provide medical care for them. See 20 U.S.C. § 1400(c) ("It is the purpose of this chapter to assure that all children with disabilities have . . . a free appropriate public education"); see also § 1412 ("In order to qualify for assistance . . . a State shall demonstrate . . . [that it] has in effect a policy that assures all children with disabilities the right to a free appropriate public education"); *Board of Ed. of Hendrick Hudson Central School Dist., Westchester Cty. v. Rowley*, 458 U.S. 176, 179 (1982) ("The Act represents an ambitious federal effort to promote the education of handicapped children"). As such, where Congress decided to require a supportive service—including speech pathology, occupational therapy, and audiology—that appears "medical" in nature, it took care to do so explicitly. See § 1401(a)(17). Congress specified these services precisely because it recognized that they would otherwise fall under the broad "medical services" exclusion. Indeed, when it crafted the definition of related services, Congress could have, but chose not to, include "nursing services" in this list.

B

Tatro was wrongly decided even if the phrase "medical services" was subject to multiple constructions, and therefore, deference to any reasonable Department of Education regulation was appropriate. The Department of Education has never promulgated regulations defining the scope of IDEA's "medical services" exclusion. One year before *Tatro* was decided, the Secretary of Education issued proposed regulations that defined excluded medical services as "services relating to the practice of medicine." 47 Fed. Reg. 33838 (1982). These regulations, which represent the Department's only attempt to define the disputed term, were never adopted. Instead, "[t]he regulations actually define only those 'medical services' that are owed to handicapped children," *Tatro*, 468 U.S., at 892, n.10, not those that are not. Now, as when *Tatro* was decided, the regulations require districts to provide services performed " 'by a licensed physician to determine a child's medically related handicapping condition which results in the child's need for special education and related services.' " *Ibid.* (quoting 34 C.F.R. § 300.13(b)(4) (1983), recodified and amended as 34 C.F.R. § 300.16(b)(4) (1998)).

Extrapolating from this regulation, the *Tatro* Court presumed that this meant that " 'medical services' not owed under the statute are those 'services by a licensed physician' that serve other purposes." *Tatro, supra,* at 892, n.10 (emphasis deleted). The Court, therefore, did not defer to the regulation itself, but rather relied on an inference drawn from it to speculate about how a regulation might read if the Department of Education promulgated one. Deference in those circumstances is impermissible. We cannot defer to a regulation that does not exist.

II

Assuming that *Tatro* was correctly decided in the first instance, it does not control the outcome of this case. Because IDEA was enacted pursuant to Congress' spending power, our analysis of the statute in this case is governed by special rules of construction. We have repeatedly emphasized that, when Congress places conditions on the receipt of federal funds, "it must do so unambiguously." *Pennhurst State School and Hospital v. Halderman*, 451 U.S. 1, 17 (1981). This is because a law that "condition[s] an offer of federal funding on a promise by the recipient . . . amounts essentially to a contract between the Government and the recipient of funds." *Gebser v. Lago Vista Independent School Dist.*, 524 U.S. 274, 286 (1998). As such, "[t]he legitimacy of Congress' power to legislate under the spending power . . . rests on whether the State voluntarily and knowingly accepts the terms of the 'contract.' There can, of course, be no knowing acceptance if a State is unaware of the conditions or is unable to ascertain what is expected of it." *Pennhurst, supra*, at 17 (citations omitted). It follows that we must interpret Spending Clause legislation narrowly, in order to avoid saddling the States with obligations that they did not anticipate.

The majority's approach in this case turns this Spending Clause presumption on its head. We have held that, in enacting IDEA, Congress wished to require "States to educate handicapped children with nonhandicapped children whenever possible," *Rowley, supra*, at 202. Congress, however, also took steps to limit the fiscal burdens that States must bear in attempting to achieve this laudable goal. These steps include requiring States to provide an education that is only "appropriate" rather than requiring them to maximize the potential of disabled students, see 20 U.S.C. § 1400(c); *Rowley, supra*, at 200, recognizing that integration into the public school environment is not always possible, see § 1412(5), and clarifying that, with a few exceptions, public schools need not provide "medical services" for disabled students, §§ 1401(a)(17) and (18).

For this reason, we have previously recognized that Congress did not intend to "impos[e] upon the States a burden of unspecified proportions and weight" in enacting IDEA. *Rowley, supra*, at 190, n.11. These federalism concerns require us to interpret IDEA's related services provision, consistent with *Tatro*, as follows: Department of Education regulations require districts to provide disabled children with health-related services that school nurses can perform as part of their normal duties. This reading of *Tatro*, although less broad than the majority's, is equally plausible and certainly more consistent with our obligation to interpret Spending Clause legislation narrowly. Before concluding that the district was required to provide clean intermittent catheterization for Amber Tatro, we observed that school nurses in the district were authorized to perform services that were "difficult to distinguish from the provision of [clean intermittent catheterization] to the handicapped." *Tatro*, 468 U.S., at 893. We concluded that "[i]t would be strange indeed if Congress, in attempting to extend special services to handicapped children, were unwilling to guarantee them services of a kind that are routinely provided to the nonhandicapped." *Id.*, at 893–894.

Unlike clean intermittent catheterization, however, a school nurse cannot provide the services that respondent requires and continue to perform her normal duties. To the contrary, because respondent requires continuous, one-on-one care throughout the entire schoolday, all agree that the district must hire an additional employee to attend solely to respondent. This will cost a minimum of $18,000 per year. Although the majority recognizes this fact, it nonetheless concludes that the "more extensive" nature of the services that respondent needs is irrelevant to the question whether those services fall under the medical services exclusion. This approach disregards the constitutionally mandated principles of construction applicable to Spending Clause legislation and blindsides unwary States with fiscal obligations that they could not have anticipated.

*   *   *

For the foregoing reasons, I respectfully dissent.

NOTE ON CEDAR RAPIDS V. GARRET F.

As Justice Thomas emphasizes in his dissent, the IDEA is Spending Clause legislation. In exchange for accepting federal special-education funds, states agree to comply with the IDEA's requirements. But the federal special-education funds account for only a small portion of the excess costs of educating students covered by the IDEA. In the 2008 federal fiscal year, for example, federal IDEA funds "covered 17.1 percent of the estimated excess cost of educating children with disabilities." Federal Education Budget Project, New America Foundation, Individuals with Disabilities Education Act—Funding Distribution (2009), available at http://febp.newamerica.net/background-analysis/individuals-disabilities-education-act-funding-distribution. Given the lack of federal funding, what is the justification for imposing on states a requirement that they provide "related services" like catheterization and nursing, regardless of their cost? Local education budgets can be extremely tight, and the money that goes to pay for those services must come from somewhere—most likely from services that would be provided to other students. (Interjurisdictional competition constrains, to some extent, the practical ability of school districts to raise taxes. See Advisory Commission on Intergovernmental Relations, Interjurisdictional Tax and Policy Competition: Good or Bad for the Federal System? 31–44 (1991).)

Is it fair to require a school district to devote a disproportionate share of its resources to students who have been identified as having disabilities, even if it comes at the expense of all of the other students who could benefit from those resources? For a sense of the difficult normative questions here, see Kelman & Lester, *supra*, at 116–160. An argument for the "related services" duty might run like this: First, the point of related services is not to give students with disabilities an extra increment of education over and above what they would otherwise have gotten; the point is to enable students with disabilities to get in the schoolhouse door and get an education. In the terms that have been central to other areas of disability discrimination law, related services do not change the "content" of the education a student receives. Rather, they merely guarantee that students with disabilities have "access" to schooling—a guarantee that responds directly to the history of exclusion that prompted enactment of the statute. Second, the statute cushions the financial blow of the related services provision by limiting the required services to those that are not "medical" in nature. As *Tatro* explains, medical services are the ones that are most likely to be extremely costly. Is this argument for the related services obligation persuasive?

3. DISCIPLINE, THE STAY-PUT REQUIREMENT, AND RESTRAINT AND SECLUSION

Honig v. Doe

Supreme Court of the United States, 1988.
484 U.S. 305.

■ JUSTICE BRENNAN delivered the opinion of the Court.

As a condition of federal financial assistance, the Education of the Handicapped Act requires States to ensure a "free appropriate public education" for all disabled children within their jurisdictions. In aid of this goal, the Act establishes a comprehensive system of procedural safeguards designed to ensure parental participation in decisions concerning the education of their disabled children and to provide administrative and judicial review of any decisions with which those parents disagree. Among these safeguards is the so-called "stay-put" provision, which directs that a disabled child "shall remain in [his or her] then current educational placement" pending completion of any review proceedings, unless the parents and state or local educational agencies otherwise agree. 20 U.S.C. § 1415(e)(3). Today we must decide whether, in the face of this statutory proscription, state or local school authorities may nevertheless unilaterally exclude disabled children from the classroom for dangerous or disruptive conduct growing out of their disabilities. In addition, we are called upon to decide whether a district court may, in the exercise of its equitable powers, order a State to provide educational services directly to a disabled child when the local agency fails to do so.

I

In the Education of the Handicapped Act (EHA or the Act), 84 Stat. 175, as amended, 20 U.S.C. § 1400 *et seq.*, Congress sought "to assure that all handicapped children have available to them . . . a free appropriate public education which emphasizes special education and related services designed to meet their unique needs, [and] to assure that the rights of handicapped children and their parents or guardians are protected." § 1400(c). When the law was passed in 1975, Congress had before it ample evidence that such legislative assurances were sorely needed: 21 years after this Court declared education to be "perhaps the most important function of state and local governments," *Brown v. Board of Education*, 347 U.S. 483, 493 (1954), congressional studies revealed that better than half of the Nation's 8 million disabled children were not receiving appropriate educational services. § 1400(b)(3). Indeed, one out of every eight of these children was excluded from the public school system altogether, § 1400(b)(4); many others were simply "warehoused" in special classes or were neglectfully shepherded through the system until they were old enough to drop out. See H.R.Rep.No.94–332, p. 2 (1975). Among the most poorly served of disabled students were emotionally disturbed children: Congressional statistics revealed that for the school year immediately preceding passage of the Act, the educational needs of 82 percent of all children with emotional disabilities went unmet. See S.Rep.No.94–168, p. 8 (1975) (hereinafter S.Rep.).

Although these educational failings resulted in part from funding constraints, Congress recognized that the problem reflected more than a lack of financial resources at the state and local levels. Two federal-court decisions, which the Senate Report characterized as "landmark," see *id.*, at 6, demonstrated that many disabled children were excluded pursuant to state statutes or local rules and policies, typically without any consultation with, or even notice to, their parents. See *Mills v. Board of Education of District of Columbia*, 348 F.Supp. 866 (DC 1972); *Pennsylvania Assn. for Retarded Children v. Pennsylvania*, 334 F.Supp. 1257 (ED Pa.1971), and 343 F. Supp. 279 (1972) (*PARC*). Indeed, by the time of the EHA's enactment, parents had brought legal challenges to similar exclusionary practices in 27 other States. See S.Rep., at 6.

In responding to these problems, Congress did not content itself with passage of a simple funding statute. Rather, the EHA confers upon disabled students an enforceable substantive right to public education in participating States, see *Rowley*, and conditions federal financial assistance upon a State's compliance with the substantive and procedural goals of the Act. Accordingly, States seeking to qualify for federal funds must develop policies assuring all disabled children the "right to a free appropriate public education," and must file with the Secretary of Education formal plans mapping out in detail the programs, procedures, and timetables under which they will effectuate these policies. 20 U.S.C. §§ 1412(1), 1413(a). Such plans must assure that, "to the maximum extent appropriate," States will "mainstream" disabled children, *i.e.*, that they will educate them with children who are not disabled, and that they will segregate or otherwise remove such children from the regular classroom setting "only when the nature or severity of the handicap is such that education in regular classes . . . cannot be achieved satisfactorily." § 1412(5).

The primary vehicle for implementing these congressional goals is the "individualized educational program" (IEP), which the EHA mandates for each disabled child. Prepared at meetings between a representative of the local school district, the child's teacher, the parents or guardians, and, whenever appropriate, the disabled child, the IEP sets out the child's present educational performance, establishes annual and short-term objectives for improvements in that performance, and describes the specially designed instruction and services that will enable the child to meet those objectives. § 1401(19). The IEP must be reviewed and, where necessary, revised at least once a year in order to ensure that local agencies tailor the statutorily required "free appropriate public education" to each child's unique needs. § 1414(a)(5).

Envisioning the IEP as the centerpiece of the statute's education delivery system for disabled children, and aware that schools had all too often denied such children appropriate educations without in any way consulting their parents, Congress repeatedly emphasized throughout the Act the importance and indeed the necessity of parental participation in both the development of the IEP and any subsequent assessments of its effectiveness. See §§ 1400(c), 1401(19), 1412(7), 1415(b)(1)(A), (C), (D), (E), and 1415(b)(2). Accordingly, the Act establishes various procedural safeguards that guarantee parents both an opportunity for meaningful input into all decisions affecting their child's education and the right to seek review of any decisions they think inappropriate. These safeguards include the right to examine all relevant records pertaining to the identification, evaluation, and educational placement of their child; prior written notice whenever the responsible educational agency proposes (or refuses) to change the child's placement or program; an opportunity to present complaints concerning any aspect of the local agency's provision of a free appropriate public education; and an opportunity for "an impartial due process hearing" with respect to any such complaints. §§ 1415(b)(1), (2).

At the conclusion of any such hearing, both the parents and the local educational agency may seek further administrative review and, where that proves unsatisfactory, may file a civil action in any state or federal court. §§ 1415(c), (e)(2). In addition to reviewing the administrative record, courts are empowered to take additional evidence at the request of either party and to "grant such relief as [they] determine[ ] is appropriate." § 1415(e)(2). The "stay-put" provision at issue in this case governs the placement of a child while these often lengthy review procedures run their course. It directs that:

> "During the pendency of any proceedings conducted pursuant to [§ 1415], unless the State or local educational agency and the parents or guardian otherwise agree, the child shall remain in the then current educational placement of such child. . . . " § 1415(e)(3).

The present dispute grows out of the efforts of certain officials of the San Francisco Unified School District (SFUSD) to expel two emotionally disturbed children from school indefinitely for violent and disruptive conduct related to their disabilities. In November 1980, respondent John Doe assaulted another student at the Louise Lombard School, a developmental center for disabled children. Doe's April 1980 IEP identified him as a socially and physically awkward 17-year-old who experienced considerable difficulty controlling his impulses and anger. Among the goals set out in his IEP was "[i]mprovement in [his] ability to relate to [his] peers [and to] cope with frustrating situations without resorting to aggressive acts." Frustrating situations, however, were an unfortunately prominent feature of Doe's school career: physical abnormalities, speech difficulties, and poor grooming habits had made him the target of teasing and ridicule as early as the first grade; his 1980 IEP reflected his continuing difficulties with peers, noting that his social skills had deteriorated and that he could tolerate only minor frustration before exploding.

On November 6, 1980, Doe responded to the taunts of a fellow student in precisely the explosive manner anticipated by his IEP: he choked the student with sufficient force to leave abrasions on the child's neck, and kicked out a school window while being escorted to the principal's office afterwards. Doe admitted his misconduct and the school subsequently suspended him for five days. Thereafter, his principal referred the matter to the SFUSD Student Placement Committee (SPC or Committee) with the recommendation that Doe be expelled. On the day the suspension was to end, the SPC notified Doe's mother that it was proposing to exclude her child permanently from SFUSD and was therefore extending his suspension until such time as the expulsion proceedings were completed. The Committee further advised her that she was entitled to attend the November 25 hearing at which it planned to discuss the proposed expulsion.

After unsuccessfully protesting these actions by letter, Doe brought this suit against a host of local school officials and the State Superintendent of Public Instructions. Alleging that the suspension and proposed expulsion violated the EHA, he sought a temporary restraining order canceling the SPC hearing and requiring school officials to convene an IEP meeting. The District Judge granted the requested injunctive relief and further ordered defendants to provide home tutoring for Doe on an interim basis; shortly thereafter, she issued a preliminary injunction directing defendants to return Doe to his then current educational placement at Louise Lombard School pending completion of the IEP review process. Doe reentered school on December 15, 5 1/2 weeks, and 24 school-days, after his initial suspension.

Respondent Jack Smith was identified as an emotionally disturbed child by the time he entered the second grade in 1976. School records prepared that year indicated that he was unable "to control verbal or physical outburst[s]" and exhibited a "[s]evere disturbance in relationships with peers and adults." Further evaluations subsequently revealed that he had been physically and emotionally abused as an infant and young child and that, despite above average intelligence, he experienced academic and social difficulties as a result of extreme hyperactivity and low self-esteem. Of particular concern was Smith's propensity for verbal hostility; one evaluator noted that the child reacted to stress by "attempt[ing] to cover his feelings of low self worth through aggressive behavior[,] . . . primarily verbal provocations."

Based on these evaluations, SFUSD placed Smith in a learning center for emotionally disturbed children. His grandparents, however, believed that his needs would be better served in the public school setting and, in September 1979, the school district acceded to their requests and enrolled him at A.P. Giannini Middle School. His February 1980 IEP recommended placement in a Learning Disability Group, stressing the need for close supervision and a highly structured environment. Like earlier evaluations, the February 1980 IEP noted that Smith was easily distracted, impulsive, and anxious; it therefore proposed a half-day schedule and suggested that the placement be undertaken on a trial basis.

At the beginning of the next school year, Smith was assigned to a full-day program; almost immediately thereafter he began misbehaving.

School officials met twice with his grandparents in October 1980 to discuss returning him to a half-day program; although the grandparents agreed to the reduction, they apparently were never apprised of their right to challenge the decision through EHA procedures. The school officials also warned them that if the child continued his disruptive behavior—which included stealing, extorting money from fellow students, and making sexual comments to female classmates—they would seek to expel him. On November 14, they made good on this threat, suspending Smith for five days after he made further lewd comments. His principal referred the matter to the SPC, which recommended exclusion from SFUSD. As it did in John Doe's case, the Committee scheduled a hearing and extended the suspension indefinitely pending a final disposition in the matter. On November 28, Smith's counsel protested these actions on grounds essentially identical to those raised by Doe, and the SPC agreed to cancel the hearing and to return Smith to a half-day program at A.P. Giannini or to provide home tutoring. Smith's grandparents chose the latter option and the school began home instruction on December 10; on January 6, 1981, an IEP team convened to discuss alternative placements.

After learning of Doe's action, Smith sought and obtained leave to intervene in the suit. The District Court subsequently entered summary judgment in favor of respondents on their EHA claims and issued a permanent injunction. In a series of decisions, the District Judge found that the proposed expulsions and indefinite suspensions of respondents for conduct attributable to their disabilities deprived them of their congressionally mandated right to a free appropriate public education, as well as their right to have that education provided in accordance with the procedures set out in the EHA. The District Judge therefore permanently enjoined the school district from taking any disciplinary action other than a 2- or 5-day suspension against any disabled child for disability-related misconduct, or from effecting any other change in the educational placement of any such child without parental consent pending completion of any EHA proceedings. In addition, the judge barred the State from authorizing unilateral placement changes and directed it to establish an EHA compliance-monitoring system or, alternatively, to enact guidelines governing local school responses to disability-related misconduct. Finally, the judge ordered the State to provide services directly to disabled children when, in any individual case, the State determined that the local educational agency was unable or unwilling to do so.

On appeal, the Court of Appeals for the Ninth Circuit affirmed the orders with slight modifications. Agreeing with the District Court that an indefinite suspension in aid of expulsion constitutes a prohibited "change in placement" under § 1415(e)(3), the Court of Appeals held that the stay-put provision admitted of no "dangerousness" exception and that the statute therefore rendered invalid those provisions of the California Education Code permitting the indefinite suspension or expulsion of disabled children for misconduct arising out of their disabilities. The court concluded, however, that fixed suspensions of up to 30 schooldays did not fall within the reach of § 1415(e)(3), and therefore upheld recent amendments to the state Education Code authorizing such suspensions. Lastly, the court affirmed that portion of the injunction requiring the State to provide services directly to a disabled child when the local educational agency fails to do so.

Petitioner Bill Honig, California Superintendent of Public Instruction, sought review in this Court, claiming that the Court of Appeals' construction of the stay-put provision conflicted with that of several other Courts of Appeals which had recognized a dangerousness exception, and that the direct services ruling placed an intolerable burden on the State. We granted *certiorari* to resolve these questions, and now affirm.

[III]

The language of § 1415(e)(3) is unequivocal. It states plainly that during the pendency of any proceedings initiated under the Act, unless the state or local educational agency and the parents or guardian of a disabled child otherwise agree, "the child shall remain in the then current educational placement." § 1415(e)(3). Faced with this clear directive, petitioner asks us to read a "dangerousness" exception into the stay-put provision on the basis of either of two essentially inconsistent assumptions: first, that Congress thought the residual authority of school officials to exclude dangerous students from the classroom too obvious for comment; or second, that Congress inadvertently failed to provide such authority and this Court must therefore remedy the oversight. Because we cannot accept either premise, we decline petitioner's invitation to rewrite the statute.

Petitioner's arguments proceed, he suggests, from a simple, commonsense proposition: Congress could not have intended the stay-put provision to be read literally, for such a construction leads to the clearly unintended, and untenable, result that school districts must return violent or dangerous students to school while the often lengthy EHA proceedings run their course. We think it clear, however, that Congress very much meant to strip schools of the unilateral authority they had traditionally employed to exclude disabled students, particularly emotionally disturbed students, from school. In so doing, Congress did not leave school administrators powerless to deal with dangerous students; it did, however, deny school officials their former right to "self-help," and directed that in the future the removal of disabled students could be accomplished only with the permission of the parents or, as a last resort, the courts.

As noted above, Congress passed the EHA after finding that school systems across the country had excluded one out of every eight disabled children from classes. In drafting the law, Congress was largely guided by the recent decisions in *Mills* and *PARC*, both of which involved the exclusion of hard-to-handle disabled students. *Mills* in particular demonstrated the extent to which schools used disciplinary measures to bar children from the classroom. There, school officials had labeled four of the seven minor plaintiffs "behavioral problems," and had excluded them from classes without providing any alternative education to them or any notice to their parents. 348 F.Supp., at 869–870. After finding that this practice was not limited to the named plaintiffs but affected in one way or another an estimated class of 12,000 to 18,000 disabled students, *id.*, at 868–869, 875, the District Court enjoined future exclusions, suspensions, or expulsions "on grounds of discipline." *Id.*, at 880.

Congress attacked such exclusionary practices in a variety of ways. It required participating States to educate all disabled children, regardless of the severity of their disabilities, 20 U.S.C. § 1412(2)(C), and included within the definition of "handicapped" those children with serious emotional disturbances. § 1401(1). It further provided for meaningful parental participation in all aspects of a child's educational placement, and barred schools, through the stay-put provision, from changing that placement over the parent's objection until all review proceedings were completed. Recognizing that those proceedings might prove long and tedious, the Act's drafters did not intend § 1415(e)(3) to operate inflexibly, see 121 Cong.Rec. 37412 (1975) (remarks of Sen. Stafford), and they therefore allowed for interim placements where parents and school officials are able to agree on one. Conspicuously absent from § 1415(e)(3), however, is any emergency exception for dangerous students. This absence is all the more telling in light of the injunctive decree issued in *PARC*, which permitted school officials unilaterally to remove students in " 'extraordinary circumstances.' " 343 F.Supp., at 301. Given the lack of any similar exception in *Mills*, and the close attention Congress devoted to these "landmark" decisions, see S.Rep., at 6, we can only conclude that the omission was intentional; we are therefore not at liberty to engraft onto the statute an exception Congress chose not to create.

Our conclusion that § 1415(e)(3) means what it says does not leave educators hamstrung. The Department of Education has observed that, "[w]hile the [child's] placement may not be changed [during any complaint proceeding], this does not preclude the agency from using its normal procedures for dealing with children who are endangering themselves or others." Comment following 34 CFR § 300.513 (1987). Such procedures may include the use of study carrels, timeouts, detention, or the restriction of privileges. More drastically, where a student poses an immediate threat to the safety of others, officials may temporarily suspend him or her for up to 10 schooldays.[8] This authority, which respondent in no way disputes, not only ensures that school administrators can protect the safety of others by promptly removing the most dangerous of students, it also provides a "cooling down" period during which officials can initiate IEP review and seek to persuade the child's parents to agree to an interim placement. And in

---

[8] The Department of Education has adopted the position first espoused in 1980 by its Office of Civil Rights that a suspension of up to 10 school-days does not amount to a "change in placement" prohibited by § 1415(e)(3). U.S. Dept. of Education, Office of Special Education Programs, Policy Letter (Feb. 26, 1987). The EHA nowhere defines the phrase "change in placement," nor does the statute's structure or legislative history provide any guidance as to how the term applies to fixed suspensions. Given this ambiguity, we defer to the construction adopted by the agency charged with monitoring and enforcing the statute. Moreover, the agency's position comports fully with the purposes of the statute: Congress sought to prevent schools from permanently and unilaterally excluding disabled children by means of indefinite suspensions and expulsions; the power to impose fixed suspensions of short duration does not carry the potential for total exclusion that Congress found so objectionable. Indeed, despite its broad injunction, the District Court in *Mills* recognized that school officials could suspend disabled children on a short-term, temporary basis. Cf. *Goss v. Lopez*, 419 U.S. 565, 574–576 (1975) (suspension of 10 schooldays or more works a sufficient deprivation of property and liberty interests to trigger the protections of the Due Process Clause). Because we believe the agency correctly determined that a suspension in excess of 10 days does constitute a prohibited "change in placement," we conclude that the Court of Appeals erred to the extent it approved suspensions of 20 and 30 days' duration.

those cases in which the parents of a truly dangerous child adamantly refuse to permit any change in placement, the 10-day respite gives school officials an opportunity to invoke the aid of the courts under § 1415(e)(2), which empowers courts to grant any appropriate relief.

Petitioner contends, however, that the availability of judicial relief is more illusory than real, because a party seeking review under § 1415(e)(2) must exhaust time-consuming administrative remedies, and because under the Court of Appeals' construction of § 1415(e)(3), courts are as bound by the stay-put provision's "automatic injunction," as are schools. It is true that judicial review is normally not available under § 1415(e)(2) until all administrative proceedings are completed, but as we have previously noted, parents may bypass the administrative process where exhaustion would be futile or inadequate. While many of the EHA's procedural safeguards protect the rights of parents and children, schools can and do seek redress through the administrative review process, and we have no reason to believe that Congress meant to require schools alone to exhaust in all cases, no matter how exigent the circumstances. The burden in such cases, of course, rests with the school to demonstrate the futility or inadequacy of administrative review, but nothing in § 1415(e)(2) suggests that schools are completely barred from attempting to make such a showing. Nor do we think that § 1415(e)(3) operates to limit the equitable powers of district courts such that they cannot, in appropriate cases, temporarily enjoin a dangerous disabled child from attending school. As the EHA's legislative history makes clear, one of the evils Congress sought to remedy was the unilateral exclusion of disabled children by schools, not courts, and one of the purposes of § 1415(e)(3), therefore, was "to prevent school officials from removing a child from the regular public school classroom over the parents' objection pending completion of the review proceedings." The stay-put provision in no way purports to limit or pre-empt the authority conferred on courts by § 1415(e)(2); indeed, it says nothing whatever about judicial power.

In short, then, we believe that school officials are entitled to seek injunctive relief under § 1415(e)(2) in appropriate cases. In any such action, § 1415(e)(3) effectively creates a presumption in favor of the child's current educational placement which school officials can overcome only by showing that maintaining the child in his or her current placement is substantially likely to result in injury either to himself or herself, or to others. In the present case, we are satisfied that the District Court, in enjoining the state and local defendants from indefinitely suspending respondent or otherwise unilaterally altering his then current placement, properly balanced respondent's interest in receiving a free appropriate public education in accordance with the procedures and requirements of the EHA against the interests of the state and local school officials in maintaining a safe learning environment for all their students.

IV

We believe the courts below properly construed and applied § 1415(e)(3), except insofar as the Court of Appeals held that a suspension in excess of 10 schooldays does not constitute a "change in placement." We therefore affirm the Court of Appeals' judgment on this issue as modified herein. Because we are equally divided on the question whether a court may order a State to provide services directly to a disabled child where the local agency has failed to do so, we affirm the Court of Appeals' judgment on this issue as well.

Affirmed.

■ CHIEF JUSTICE REHNQUIST, concurring.

[omitted]

■ JUSTICE SCALIA, with whom JUSTICE O'CONNOR joins, dissenting.

Without expressing any views on the merits of this case, I respectfully dissent because in my opinion we have no authority to decide it. I think the controversy is moot. [The remainder of this dissent is omitted.]

NOTES ON DISCIPLINE AND THE IDEA

Subsequent to the Supreme Court's decision in *Honig*, Congress amended and reauthorized the IDEA three times, in 1990, 1997, and 2004. The 1997 and 2004 amendments adopted specific provisions governing the discipline of students with disabilities. The statute now provides:

(k) Placement in alternative educational setting

(1) Authority of school personnel

(A) Case-by-case determination

School personnel may consider any unique circumstances on a case-by-case basis when determining whether to order a change in placement for a child with a disability who violates a code of student conduct.

(B) Authority

School personnel under this subsection may remove a child with a disability who violates a code of student conduct from their current placement to an appropriate interim alternative educational setting, another setting, or suspension, for not more than 10 school days (to the extent such alternatives are applied to children without disabilities).

(C) Additional authority

If school personnel seek to order a change in placement that would exceed 10 school days and the behavior that gave rise to the violation of the school code is determined not to be a manifestation of the child's disability pursuant to subparagraph (E), the relevant disciplinary procedures applicable to children without disabilities may be applied to the child in the same manner and for the same duration in which the procedures would be applied to children without disabilities, except as provided in section 1412(a)(1) of this title although it may be provided in an interim alternative educational setting.

(D) Services

A child with a disability who is removed from the child's current placement under subparagraph (G) (irrespective of whether the behavior is determined to be a manifestation of the child's disability) or subparagraph (C) shall—

(i) continue to receive educational services, as provided in section 1412(a)(1) of this title, so as to enable the child to continue to participate in the general education curriculum, although in another setting, and to progress toward meeting the goals set out in the child's IEP; and

(ii) receive, as appropriate, a functional behavioral assessment, behavioral intervention services and modifications, that are designed to address the behavior violation so that it does not recur.

(E) Manifestation determination

(i) In general

Except as provided in subparagraph (B), within 10 school days of any decision to change the placement of a child with a disability because of a violation of a code of student conduct, the local educational agency, the parent, and relevant members of the IEP Team (as determined by the parent and the local educational agency) shall review all relevant information in the student's file, including the child's IEP, any teacher observations, and any relevant information provided by the parents to determine—

(I) if the conduct in question was caused by, or had a direct and substantial relationship to, the child's disability; or

(II) if the conduct in question was the direct result of the local educational agency's failure to implement the IEP.

(ii) Manifestation

If the local educational agency, the parent, and relevant members of the IEP Team determine that either subclause (I) or (II) of clause (i) is applicable for the child, the conduct shall be determined to be a manifestation of the child's disability.

(F) Determination that behavior was a manifestation

If the local educational agency, the parent, and relevant members of the IEP Team make the determination that the conduct was a manifestation of the child's disability, the IEP Team shall—

(i) conduct a functional behavioral assessment, and implement a behavioral intervention plan for such child, provided that the local educational agency had not conducted such assessment prior to such determination before the behavior that resulted in a change in placement described in subparagraph (C) or (G);

(ii) in the situation where a behavioral intervention plan has been developed, review the behavioral intervention plan if the child already has such a behavioral intervention plan, and modify it, as necessary, to address the behavior; and

(iii) except as provided in subparagraph (G), return the child to the placement from which the child was removed, unless the parent and the local educational agency agree to a change of placement as part of the modification of the behavioral intervention plan.

(G) Special circumstances

School personnel may remove a student to an interim alternative educational setting for not more than 45 school days without regard to whether the behavior is determined to be a manifestation of the child's disability, in cases where a child—

(i) carries or possesses a weapon to or at school, on school premises, or to or at a school function under the jurisdiction of a State or local educational agency;

(ii) knowingly possesses or uses illegal drugs, or sells or solicits the sale of a controlled substance, while at school, on school premises, or at a school function under the jurisdiction of a State or local educational agency; or

(iii) has inflicted serious bodily injury upon another person while at school, on school premises, or at a school function under the jurisdiction of a State or local educational agency.

(H) Notification

Not later than the date on which the decision to take disciplinary action is made, the local educational agency shall notify the parents of that decision, and of all procedural safeguards accorded under this section.

(2) Determination of setting

The interim alternative educational setting in subparagraphs (C) and (G) of paragraph (1) shall be determined by the IEP Team.

(3) Appeal

(A) In general

The parent of a child with a disability who disagrees with any decision regarding placement, or the manifestation determination under this subsection, or a local educational agency that believes that maintaining the current placement of the child is substantially likely to result in injury to the child or to others, may request a hearing.

(B) Authority of hearing officer

(i) In general

A hearing officer shall hear, and make a determination regarding, an appeal requested under subparagraph (A).

(ii) Change of placement order

In making the determination under clause (i), the hearing officer may order a change in placement of a child with a disability. In such situations, the hearing officer may—

(I) return a child with a disability to the placement from which the child was removed; or

(II) order a change in placement of a child with a disability to an appropriate interim alternative educational setting for not more than 45 school days if the hearing officer determines that maintaining the current placement of such child is substantially likely to result in injury to the child or to others.

(4) Placement during appeals

When an appeal under paragraph (3) has been requested by either the parent or the local educational agency—

(A) the child shall remain in the interim alternative educational setting pending the decision of the hearing officer or until the expiration of the time period provided for in paragraph (1)(C), whichever occurs first, unless the parent and the State or local educational agency agree otherwise; and

(B) the State or local educational agency shall arrange for an expedited hearing, which shall occur within 20 school days of the date the hearing is requested and shall result in a determination within 10 school days after the hearing.

(5) Protections for children not yet eligible for special education and related services

(A) In general

A child who has not been determined to be eligible for special education and related services under this subchapter and who has engaged in behavior that violates a code of student conduct, may assert any of the protections provided for in this subchapter if the local educational agency had knowledge (as determined in accordance with this paragraph) that the child was a child with a disability before the behavior that precipitated the disciplinary action occurred.

(B) Basis of knowledge

A local educational agency shall be deemed to have knowledge that a child is a child with a disability if, before the behavior that precipitated the disciplinary action occurred—

(i) the parent of the child has expressed concern in writing to supervisory or administrative personnel of the appropriate educational agency, or a teacher of the child, that the child is in need of special education and related services;

(ii) the parent of the child has requested an evaluation of the child pursuant to section 1414(a)(1)(B) of this title; or

(iii) the teacher of the child, or other personnel of the local educational agency, has expressed specific concerns about a pattern of behavior demonstrated by the child, directly to the director of special education of such agency or to other supervisory personnel of the agency.

(C) Exception

A local educational agency shall not be deemed to have knowledge that the child is a child with a disability if the parent of the child has not allowed an evaluation of the child pursuant to section 1414 of this title or has refused services under this subchapter or the child has been evaluated and it was determined that the child was not a child with a disability under this subchapter.

(D) Conditions that apply if no basis of knowledge

(i) In general

If a local educational agency does not have knowledge that a child is a child with a disability (in accordance with subparagraph (B) or (C)) prior to taking disciplinary measures against the child, the child may be subjected to disciplinary measures applied to children without disabilities who engaged in comparable behaviors consistent with clause (ii).

(ii) Limitations

If a request is made for an evaluation of a child during the time period in which the child is subjected to disciplinary measures under this subsection, the evaluation shall be conducted in an expedited manner. If the child is determined to be a child with a disability, taking into consideration information from the evaluation conducted by the agency and information provided by the parents, the agency shall provide special education and related services in accordance with this subchapter, except that, pending the results of the evaluation, the child shall remain in the educational placement determined by school authorities.

(6) Referral to and action by law enforcement and judicial authorities

(A) Rule of construction

Nothing in this subchapter shall be construed to prohibit an agency from reporting a crime committed by a child with a disability to appropriate authorities or to prevent State law enforcement and judicial authorities from exercising their responsibilities with regard to the application of Federal and State law to crimes committed by a child with a disability.

(B) Transmittal of records

An agency reporting a crime committed by a child with a disability shall ensure that copies of the special education and disciplinary records of the child are transmitted for consideration by the appropriate authorities to whom the agency reports the crime.

20 U.S.C. § 1415(k)(1)–(6).

Is it right to give students with disabilities a form of immunity from discipline if their school misconduct is a manifestation of their disability? Consider three possible critiques of the IDEA's discipline provisions. One critique might raise issues of fairness: Why should students with disabilities, and only students with disabilities, be protected against harsh discipline? See Kelman & Lester, *supra*, at 105 ("[I]f the federal government wishes to ban 'severe discipline,' it ought to do so outright, without any regard to 'disability.'"). A second critique might assert that school districts will be less willing to identify students as having disabilities—and thus less willing to give them the special education and related services they need—if doing so will give those students a form of disciplinary immunity. See *id.* at 110 (stating that school districts that "[a]nticipat[e] that a child may ultimately be someone the district might want to expel" may "be loath to place him in special ed"). And a third critique might look to the effects on the overall educational environment. Professor Dupre, for example, argues that the IDEA's discipline provisions cause serious harm to the educational environment by hamstringing schools from dealing with disruptive and violent students with disabilities. Invoking the "broken windows" theory of criminology, she argues that the IDEA's discipline provisions undermine the moral authority of teachers and promote general disorder in the schools. See Anne Proffitt Dupre, *A Study in Double Standards, Discipline, and the Disabled Student*, 75 Wash. L. Rev. 1 (2000). See also Richard Arum, Judging School Discipline: The Crisis of Moral Authority (2005) (arguing that litigation over school discipline outside of the disability context has the same effect).

Advocates of the discipline provisions argue, by contrast, that disciplinary infractions have frequently been invoked by school districts as a pretext to exclude or segregate students whose disabilities place them outside the norm. (See, for example, Justice Brennan's discussion in *Honig* of the history of the stay-put provision.) Which of these arguments do you find persuasive? Do the IDEA's discipline provisions strike the appropriate balance between the interests of students with and without disabilities? Do they make much difference as a practical matter? Cf. Kelman & Lester, *supra*, at 116 (finding, in their empirical examination of school district practices, a "widespread refusal to pay a great deal of heed to federal discipline law").

For a discussion of the changes the 2004 amendments made to the discipline provisions, see Mark C. Weber, *Reflections on the New Individuals with Disabilities Education Improvement Act*, 58 Fla. L. Rev. 7, 34–39 (2006).

CJN v. Minneapolis Public Schools
United States Court of Appeals for the Eighth Circuit, 2003.
323 F.3d 630.

■ MORRIS SHEPPARD ARNOLD, CIRCUIT JUDGE.

This case raises the question, among others, of whether a disabled student, whom we shall call CJN, received a free, appropriate public education (FAPE) in his third-grade year as required by the Individuals with Disabilities Education Act (IDEA), 20 U.S.C. §§ 1400-1487. The district court held that he did, focusing on CJN's academic progress and the continuous efforts to tailor his individualized education plan (IEP) to his behavioral challenges. Because we agree with the district court that CJN received a FAPE, and agree as well with its assessment of related issues, we affirm.

I.

As part of providing a FAPE under the IDEA, a school must formulate an IEP tailored to the disabled child's unique needs. 20 U.S.C. § 1412. For an IEP to pass substantive muster, it must be "reasonably calculated to enable the child to receive educational benefits." *Rowley.*

CJN is an eleven-year-old boy with lesions in his brain and a long history of psychiatric illness. A special education student in the Minneapolis Public Schools, Special School District No. 1 (District) since kindergarten, CJN has consistently had behavioral difficulties while nonetheless progressing academically at an average rate.

At the beginning of his third-grade year in September, 2000, CJN was placed in a special program for elementary needs (SPEN) classroom at Keewaydin Elementary School (moving with a teacher from his prior school) while he awaited the results of a functional behavior assessment and an occupational therapy evaluation. Within a few weeks, he had transferred to Elana Schroeder's SPEN classroom, because it provided more structure and because her students functioned at a higher academic level. In light of CJN's educational needs, Ms. Schroeder offered him reduced homework assignments, more time to complete assignments, positive reinforcement for meeting minimal requirements, and a so-called token economy system for reinforcing good behavior.

CJN nevertheless misbehaved in Ms. Schroeder's classroom many times, leading to him being given "time-outs" and even to being physically restrained. Most episodes of restraint were for less than a minute, but there were six days on which CJN was restrained for five or more minutes: Restraint was used after CJN began kicking others, hitting staff with pencils, or banging his head against the wall. On one occasion in December, a behavioral outburst led to police intervention and a period of hospitalization for CJN. This was his last day at Keewaydin.

CJN's IEP team convened in October, 2000, to discuss his evaluation results and recent misbehavior and again in November to discuss his behavioral goals and the procedures to be followed if CJN required restraint. Immediately after the holiday break, CJN's IEP team decided that he would divide his time between Whittier Elementary School and a day treatment program. At Whittier, CJN was to receive the help of a one-to-one paraprofessional and was to participate in a point reward system to reinforce good behavior. CJN attended Whittier for only seven half-days, however, because an episode occurred that required him to be taken to a local crisis center. The District and his mother then agreed to instruction at home, but, a day after that instruction began, his mother unilaterally decided to enroll CJN in Calvin Academy, a private school that serves disabled and "at-risk" students.

CJN's mother then filed a complaint with the Minnesota Department of Children, Families and Learning, seeking, among other things, a declaration that the District had not provided CJN with a FAPE and asking for reimbursement for his private school tuition. As part of this proceeding, several independent evaluators analyzed CJN, the principal evaluation being provided by Dr. Richard Ziegler. In March, the IEP team reviewed Dr. Ziegler's summary and proposed that CJN be placed in a "Public Separate Day School setting" which could provide more mental health services than Whittier. CJN has continued to have significant behavioral difficulties at Calvin Academy.

Based on 290 "findings of fact," an independent hearing officer (HO) found that although CJN had received a FAPE through the second grade, he had not received one from September 2000 to February 2001, mainly because of the lack of sufficient positive behavioral interventions during the latter period and the amount of physical restraint that he was subjected to. In addition to granting other relief, the HO ordered the District to reimburse CJN's mother for his private school tuition and placed him at Calvin through the 2002-2003 academic school year. On appeal, a state hearing review officer (HRO) reversed the HO's decision that CJN did not receive a FAPE from September 2000 to February 2001, adopting 286 of the HO's "findings of fact" and making thirty-five more of his own. The district court affirmed the HRO's decision, giving due weight to the HRO's conclusions and focusing on CJN's academic progress and his IEP team's continuous efforts to refine his IEPs to account for his behavioral challenges in its eight IEP team meetings between August 29, 2000, and March 2, 2001.

[III.]

[CJN] maintains that the district court erred in holding that the District provided him with a FAPE in his third-grade year based on academic progress alone. CJN contends that evidence of academic progress is particularly irrelevant here "because his disability does not adversely affect his ability to learn" academically. CJN points to the amount of physical restraint to which he was subject and the high number of "time-outs" imposed on him, arguing that they are fundamentally inconsistent with the existence of a FAPE. CJN maintains that Minnesota law requires more positive behavioral reinforcement and more analysis of CJN's behavioral problems than CJN received before he can be said to have received a FAPE.

The District responds by stating that CJN's IEPs need to be analyzed at the time of their adoption. It asserts that his IEP team consistently focused on CJN's behavioral problems using the information that they had available, including a functional behavior assessment and an occupational therapy evaluation. It contends that CJN received positive behavioral interventions in the form of the token economy system and point rewards system as well as sufficient personalized services, such as the attention of a one-to-one paraprofessional. And it points to the fact that CJN was progressing at an average rate academically.

At the outset, we reject CJN's characterization of the district court's holding as based on academic progress alone. Although the district court does state that "CJN was learning within the average range in his academic subjects, thus demonstrating educational progress," this statement came only after the court's observations that "[w]ith CJN's behavioral challenges in mind, the team tailored the IEP to his needs" and that "[a]t numerous meetings, CJN's IEP team was continually making efforts to refine his instruction programs." We view the district court's acknowledgment of CJN's academic progress to mean only that his IEP was managing CJN's behavioral problems in a way that allowed him to learn. Academic progress, the Supreme Court has stated, is an "important factor" in ascertaining whether a disabled student's IEP was reasonably calculated to provide educational benefit. *Rowley.*

We also reject CJN's contention that because academic progress "has not been identified as among C.J.N.'s educational needs," evidence of academic progress is particularly irrelevant in CJN's case. As we recently noted[,] "at least in Congress's judgment, social and emotional problems are not *ipso facto* separable from the learning process." Behavioral difficulties might impede learning ability even if the individual is not learning disabled. The record squarely supports the conclusion that that is the situation here. For instance, Dr. Ziegler's report explains how frontal lobe activity is responsible for an individual's ability to plan and affects his or her "flexibility, generation of information, inhibition of impulses, and working memory." In relation to CJN, Dr. Ziegler states that "[w]hile some skills associated with frontal lobe functioning are intact, it is clear that his behavioral and emotional dysregulation and disinhibition associated with his frontal striatal lesion can overwhelm these adequately developed skills to [the] point where he is unable to utilize them in his school environment." [CJN] has always progressed academically at an average rate. That his behavioral difficulties are severe, as CJN contends, makes his academic progress even more relevant to the educational benefit inquiry, because it demonstrates that his IEPs were not only reasonably calculated to provide educational benefit, but, at least in part, did so as well.

When a disabled student has failed to achieve some major goals, it is difficult to look back at the many roads not taken and ascertain exactly how reasonable his IEPs were at the time of their adoption. But this difficulty is precisely why we have recognized that "[a]s long as a student is benefiting from his education, it is up to the educators to determine the appropriate educational methodology." Specific results are not required, 34 C.F.R. § 300.350(b), and an IEP need not be designed to maximize a student's potential "commensurate with the opportunity provided to other children," *see Rowley.* Thus, even assuming *arguendo* that more positive behavior interventions could have been employed, that fact is largely irrelevant. The record reveals that the District made a "good faith effort" to assist CJN in achieving his educational goals. *See* 34 C.F.R. § 300.350(a)(2). Although it is true, as CJN contends, that the District "offered only services available within its standardized programs for students with emotional and behavioral disorders," one can reasonably conclude from this record that more did not appear necessary at the time to help him progress behaviorally. Indeed, at the January IEP meeting, undisputed testimony indicates that the District suggested a more structured setting as an alternative to Whittier, but CJN's mother chose Whittier instead.

We of course very much regret that CJN was subject to an increased amount of restraint in his third-grade year, but that fact alone does not make his education inappropriate within the meaning of the IDEA. In response to his difficulties, the District made its suspension policy more lenient, suspending him only in the case of physical aggression to adults, children, or property. We believe that this demonstrates a good faith effort and comports, moreover, with a previous observation of ours that schools' suspension policies toward disabled students must be "appropriate in the context of the IEP." Because the appropriate use of restraint may help prevent bad behavior from escalating to a level where a suspension is required, we refuse to create a rule prohibiting its use, even if its frequency is increasing.

CJN contends that restraints and "time-outs" were used inappropriately here, pointing to four purported violations of Minnesota rules governing behavioral interventions. In analyzing these purported deficiencies, we note that minor "procedural and technical deficiencies in the IEPs" cannot support a claim that a FAPE has been denied.

As CJN correctly notes, under the IDEA a disabled student's IEP must "meet the standards of the State educational agency." 20 U.S.C. § 1401(8)(B). Thus, "[w]hen a state provides for educational benefits exceeding the minimum federal standards set forth under *Rowley,* the state standards are . . . enforceable through the IDEA."

First, CJN contends that his IEP was inappropriate because CJN was constantly being restrained in emergency situations and his team failed to develop a behavioral intervention program (BIP) that focused on skill acquisition. CJN argues that such a BIP was required because Minnesota has chosen to exceed the federal requirements.

Under the IDEA, IEP teams are required to consider positive behavioral interventions where appropriate. 20 U.S.C. § 1414(d)(3)(B)(i). Under Minnesota law, "[t]he objective of any behavioral intervention must be that pupils acquire appropriate behaviors and skills. It is critical that [BIPs] focus on skills acquisition rather than merely behavior reduction or elimination." Minn. R. 3525.0850. [A]t the October IEP meeting, Ms. Schroeder had proposed a BIP that included both positive reinforcement mechanisms as well as what is called conditional procedures (*e.g.,* time-outs and physical restraint). No BIP was adopted, however, because of CJN's mother's disagreement with the proposal. They discussed the matter again in November, at which time CJN's mother dismissed the team's suggestions as counterproductive. In January, CJN's teacher at Whittier was in the process of developing a plan, but CJN was withdrawn from her classroom before she finished it. Heeding *Rowley*'s warning that "courts must be careful to avoid imposing their view of preferable educational methods upon the States," and giving "due weight" to the HRO's implicit decision of sufficiency, we do not believe that the failure to develop a BIP could fairly be said to constitute a denial of a FAPE in these circumstances.

CJN also contends that the number of IEP team meetings was insufficient in view of a Minnesota rule providing that when conditional procedures are used in an emergency situation "twice in a month or [when] a pupil's pattern of behavior is emerging . . . a team meeting must be called to determine if the pupil's IEP is adequate . . . no later than five school days after emergency procedures have commenced." Minn. R. 3525.2900, subp. 5C. The district court did not discuss this rule.

This rule was violated if one views the five-day requirement as restarting with every two emergency interventions. For instance, conditional procedures were used on October 10, 11, and 12, but the only IEP meetings were on October 10 and November 14. We need not, however, resolve the nuances of the rule's interpretation, because the record reveals that any potential violation was immaterial. As we have already noted, CJN's IEP team consistently addressed the use of conditional procedures in their IEP meetings, but a BIP was not adopted because of his mother's disagreement. We believe that the purpose of the relevant rule is to guarantee that the IEP team is aware that conditional procedures have been employed and to allow the IEP team to develop a BIP, because under Minnesota law conditional procedures can be used either in an emergency situation *or* pursuant to a BIP (as part of an IEP), *see id.* subp. 5A(1). That requisite awareness and the attempt to develop a BIP already existed here. Failure to hold more meetings is immaterial.

CJN points, in addition, to a state requirement that IEP teams identify "the frequency and severity of target behaviors for which the conditional procedure is being considered" before using conditional procedures. *Id.* This provision, however, does not apply here, as it pertains only to conditional procedures resorted to as part of a BIP and not to emergency situations like the ones in the instant case.

CJN argues finally that "time-outs" of more than an hour violate state standards *per se,* citing a state administrative decision that holds that "[s]eclusion for brief periods may be defensible, but not confinement for one to six hours forcing a student into discomfort, making [the action at issue] a punitive, negative intervention" under Minn. R. 3525.0850. *Complaint File # 1408,* p.16 (State Educ. Agency Minn. March 29, 2002). But close analysis of the Minnesota Department of Children, Families and Learning's statement in this file reveals that its conclusion was based both on the duration of the "time-out" and the fact that the "time-out" room had no place for the child to sit, which is not the situation here. Furthermore, the only time-outs of more than an hour occurred in the seven half-days at Whittier. Any violation of the State's rule would therefore be immaterial to a larger determination of whether reimbursement was required.

[VI.]

Judge Bye contends that we are holding that any school district necessarily satisfies its duties to provide a student with a FAPE when a student with a behavioral disability makes academic progress. That is not the case. As we said, academic progress is an "important factor" among others in ascertaining whether the student's IEP was reasonably calculated to provide educational benefit. *Rowley.* We believe, as the district court did, that the student's IEP must be responsive to the student's specific disabilities, whether academic or behavioral.

Academic and behavioral matters, however, are not always independent of each other. [W]here, as here, the record indicates that a student's behavioral problems, if unattended, might significantly curtail his ability to learn, the fact that he is learning is significant evidence that his behavioral problems have, at least in part, been attended to. Of course, we wish that CJN had made more behavioral progress, but the IDEA does not require that schools attempt to maximize a child's potential, or, as a matter of fact, guarantee that the student actually make any progress at all. It requires only that the student be provided with an IEP that is reasonably calculated to provide educational benefit and we conclude that that happened here.

Neosho R-V Sch. Dist. v. Clark, 315 F.3d 1022 (8th Cir.2003), does not cut against our conclusion. In fact, it supports it. In that case, both the state administrative panel and the district court held that the disabled student did not receive a FAPE because his IEPs did not appropriately address his behavioral problems. On appeal, the school district argued that the panel and district court had improperly discounted evidence that some academic progress had been made. We noted that while there was "evidence of some slight academic progress," the evidence was "contradicted by other evidence in the record." For instance, we observed that every time the student's "special education teacher advanced his work to [his current grade level], the stress engendered resulted in behavioral problems that forced the teacher to readjust his work [downward] to afford [the student] a measure of success." We were therefore convinced that the administrative panel had not improperly discounted "the evidence of de minimis academic and social progress where the panel pointed to specific evidence in the record contradicting such a benefit and noted that any slight benefit obtained was lost due to behavior problems that went unchecked and interfered with his ability to obtain a benefit from his education." *Id.* This is in stark contrast to the circumstances in the instant case where there is undisputed evidence that CJN is progressing academically at an average rate, thus indicating, at the very least, that his behavioral problems are being sufficiently controlled for him to receive some educational benefit.

VII.

Accordingly, we affirm the judgment of the district court.

■ BYE, CIRCUIT JUDGE, DISSENTING.

The record in this case portrays a clear contrast. When the District adapted its approach to meet CJN's unique needs, he made some progress on his behavioral disabilities. But when the District expected CJN's behavior to conform to its structured and inflexible approach, he began to self-destruct. Because the IDEA requires the District to adapt to a child's "unique needs," 20 U.S.C. § 1400(d)(1), rather than the child to the District's "normal" approach, I respectfully dissent.

I

I start with a more-detailed explanation of this case's background, based upon the findings of the independent hearing officer (HO).

CJN was born on December 28, 1991. Between the ages of two and four, he suffered from chronic upper respiratory infections and consistent high fevers. During the 1994-95 winter season he experienced four seizures as a result of high fevers. In 1999 he began experiencing headaches. An MRI performed in February 2000 revealed lesions and atrophy in the right frontal lobe of his brain. CJN's brain injury was most likely due to the previous infections, demyelination (nerve damage), or possibly a stroke.

The frontal lobe of the brain is associated with self-regulation skills, such as the capacity to inhibit inappropriate behavior, and to control emotions.

CJN's emotional problems began at an early age. When he started kindergarten in February 1998 at Parkview Elementary School, he already had a history of explosive outbursts at home, at pre-school, and at day care, where his behavior would escalate to the point of threats and violence. His mother requested the District to evaluate him for placement in special education, and he eventually was placed in special education.

CJN's behavior problems continued while at Parkview. Gary Berg, a District employee identified as a "Behavior Person," worked with CJN through kindergarten and first grade. In the beginning of his first grade year, CJN spent a great deal of time in time-outs, which were unsuccessful in regulating his behavior. He was transferred to another teacher and responded more favorably to a behavior program initiated by Berg that utilized replacement behaviors and role-play instead of time-outs. In part, Berg's system allowed CJN to signal when he felt he needed to be out of the classroom. CJN would remove himself from the classroom, and sometimes go visit with Berg, until CJN felt he was ready to return to the classroom.

During the summer between first and second grade, CJN received an occupational therapy (OT) evaluation. The evaluation found CJN had excessive tactile sensitivities (e.g., irritated by labels on clothing), was averse to grooming activities, was overly active, had a moderate to high degree of sensory defensiveness in his reactions to touch, sound, smell, and visual stimuli, and sometimes engaged in self-injurious behavior. The evaluation recommended "calming activities" to minimize CJN's chances of becoming over-stimulated and leading to an outburst. These calming activities included heavy work to use the large muscles of his body, such as carrying objects, moving furniture, or doing push-ups. The evaluation also recommended oral activities, such as sucking thick substances through a straw, or chewing gum.

At the start of second grade (the 1999-2000 school year) CJN's condition deteriorated. In October 1999 he was removed from school in mid-November while his psychiatric medication was more aggressively introduced, and eventually hospitalized for psychiatric care for nine days, followed by a three-week day-treatment program. When he returned to school in March 2000, Berg suggested that CJN attend a Special Elementary Needs (SPEN) classroom taught by Mary Thompson at Marcy School. CJN spent March, April and May 2000 in Thompson's room, prior to being hospitalized again in May. Ms. Thompson had some success with CJN, describing him as "a beautiful child, very intelligent, very sensitive" but with "very severe needs with lots of sensory issues, and some neurological processing issues." CJN's placement with Thompson was followed by a successful summer program at Washburn Child Guidance Center, which his mother initiated. She privately hired Joseph Brown, a school district employee who worked with CJN in Ms. Thompson's classroom, to be CJN's one-on-one aide during the summer program.

In third grade (2000-2001 school year), the Marcy School programs taught by Ms. Thompson moved to Keewaydin School. CJN moved with Ms. Thompson to Keewaydin, and started third grade in her classroom. But after a few weeks, CJN transferred to a special education classroom taught by Elana Schroeder. The District gave two reasons for the transfer. First, the students in Ms. Thompson's classroom were at a lower academic level than CJN (whose academic abilities were average but impeded by his behavioral problems), and the students in Ms. Schroeder's classroom were a closer fit academically for CJN. Second, after a successful spring and summer, CJN's Individualized Education Plan (IEP) team believed he was ready for more responsibility and structure.

His condition quickly deteriorated in Ms. Schroeder's classroom. Despite the prior failures of a time-out approach with CJN, Ms. Schroeder used only a time-out system to handle CJN's behavioral problems. The District failed to implement the mother's recommendations to use the calming techniques recommended in the OT evaluation. The District failed to implement a system with immediate rewards/consequences for appropriate/inappropriate behavior, or the successful approach used by Berg while CJN was in second grade. The District failed to implement the mother's request for the one-on-one assistance that proved successful during the summer of 2000. Essentially, Ms. Schroeder expected CJN to adapt himself to her structured approach, rather than Schroeder adapting her approach to meet CJN's special needs. The HO concluded "the Student was expected to fit into the program and the program was not adjusted to meet the needs of the Student."

Ms. Schroeder apparently did not believe CJN was disabled, but, instead, a manipulative and controlling child. In a phone call during the time CJN was in Ms. Schroeder's classroom, Schroeder told CJN's mother that her claim of frontal lobe brain injury was simply an excuse for allowing CJN to do what he wanted to do.

The results of this combination (an educator who discredited the child's disability *and* expected the child to conform his behavior to the teacher's "normal" approach rather than adjusting her approach to meet the child's unique behavioral needs) were disastrous. CJN's outbursts worsened as a result of the use of time-outs, and the seclusion he experienced. During a fourteen day period in September 2000, CJN spent a part of seven days in seclusion after having been restrained. From October 9 to November 13, CJN was restrained on more than half of all days, at a rate eleven times greater than other students in Ms. Schroeder's class. CJN would verbally abuse, kick, and spit at District personnel who restrained him. He would threaten his teacher and other students by claiming he would bring a gun or knife to school the following day. The District reached the point where they advised CJN's mother it would resort to police intervention to deal with CJN's outbursts.

On November 16, 2000, that is exactly what happened. With as much time as CJN was spending at school in restraints or seclusion, he understandably would not get off the bus the morning of November 16. He pushed and kicked staff and threatened to kill them. He yelled and threatened peers, and wiped his mucus on them. He continued his outburst after he got to Ms. Schroeder's classroom. Finally, the police were called and removed this third grader from school.

On December 6, 2000, CJN punched a District staff member in the lip. That same day, Ms. Schroeder told CJN's mother that CJN was the problem, that Schroeder had not wanted him in her classroom, and that she would continue to initiate police intervention at every opportunity. The next day, CJN's mother requested an independent evaluation of CJN, objected to police intervention to address his disability-related behaviors while in school, and asked for a transfer to another classroom. The district finally enrolled CJN in another SPEN classroom at Whittier Elementary on January 16, 2001.

CJN fared no better at Whittier. Whittier also utilized the ineffective time-out system to address CJN's outbursts, with even more serious consequences. CJN attended just seven days at Whittier. On four of those days he was locked in seclusion for excessive periods of time without any criteria for his release, without his mother's consent or authority, and in direct opposition to the opinion of his current mental health provider. Finally, on January 24, 2001, while in the locked seclusion room, CJN attempted suicide by wrapping his shirtsleeve around his neck. The police were summoned again, and removed this third grader from the school in handcuffs. Thus, in five months, while the school used a time-out approach already shown to be unsuccessful during CJN's first and second grades, all the behavioral progress CJN made during the previous spring and summer had been replaced by suicidal ideations. Frustrated with the District's failures, CJN's mother found a private school that could, and did, meet her child's unique behavioral needs. By the time the HO held its hearings in March and April of 2001, CJN had made significant progress at the Calvin Academy. The Calvin Academy educators had not resorted to locked seclusion or police intervention, the need for even short periods (less than five minutes) of any restraint had substantially subsided, and CJN had less behavioral outbursts at home and an increased interest in learning, friends, and school.

II

[N]otwithstanding its assertion to the contrary, I believe the majority decision essentially holds the District can satisfy its duty to provide a FAPE so long as a student with a *behavioral* disability makes *academic* progress. Such reflects a myopic view of the purpose of the IDEA. The educational benefits of an IEP must be reasonably calculated to address more than academic ability or disability.

[W]e recently decided *Neosho R-V Sch. Dist. v. Clark,* 315 F.3d 1022 (8th Cir.2003), which addressed whether FAPE was provided to Robert Clark, a child with behavioral *and* learning disabilities. We concluded that "because the IEPs did not appropriately address his *behavior problem,* Robert was denied a free appropriate public education." We also addressed whether the administrative hearing panel erred in discounting the slight academic progress Robert had made. We concluded it had not:

> Our review of the record convinces us that the panel did not err in discounting the evidence of de minimis academic and social progress where the panel pointed to specific evidence in the record contradicting such a benefit and noted that any slight benefit obtained was lost *due to behavior problems that went unchecked*

and interfered with his ability to obtain a benefit from his education.

As the majority correctly notes, academic progress may be an "important factor" in ascertaining whether an IEP provides educational benefit, but it is clearly not the only factor. The Supreme Court noted the limited nature of its holding in *Rowley,* stating:

> One child may have little difficulty competing successfully in an academic setting with nonhandicapped children while another child may encounter great difficulty in acquiring even the most basic of self-maintenance skills. We do not attempt today to establish any one test for determining the adequacy of educational benefits conferred upon all children covered by the Act . . . . We do not hold today that every handicapped child who is advancing from grade to grade in a regular public school is automatically receiving a "free appropriate public education."

Rowley also explained that Congress passed the IDEA, in part, so that handicapped children could "achieve a reasonable degree of self-sufficiency" and "become a contributing part of our society." CJN has a behavioral disability that qualifies him for individualized education under the IDEA, not a learning disability. Thus, behavioral deficiencies, not learning deficiencies, are and will be his obstacle to achieving a reasonable degree of self-sufficiency and contributing to society as an adult. His current ability to read, write, or multiply simply is not the only issue. Therefore, the success of CJN's IEP cannot be measured solely by the maintenance of his academic proficiency, but must include some reference to progress in teaching him to control his behavior.

If a child has a speech impediment that qualifies him for special education services, we do not measure the educational benefit he derives from attending speech therapy solely by his progress in math class. Or if a child qualifies for special education because of a reading impairment, we do not measure the educational benefit she derives from a remedial reading course by how well-behaved she is. And if the student was well-behaved prior to receiving special education services, but her IEP failed abysmally to address her reading impairment, we would not conclude the child received an educational benefit because she is still well-behaved.

Likewise, we cannot address the propriety of CJN's IEP, or the District's provision of a FAPE in this instance, solely by CJN's performance in math or English or Geography. Rather, in determining whether the District provided a FAPE, we must also determine whether CJN received any benefit from the District in learning to control his behavior. Unlike Amy Rowley's IEPs, which were not and could not be directed towards improving her hearing but merely ensuring that her deafness did not stand in the way of an "adequate" education, the goals and directives of CJN's IEPs were all directed towards teaching emotional, behavioral, and social skills, not academics. The record is replete with evidence that the District's use of a time-out system to restrain and control CJN's behavior failed. The District's approach to CJN's unique disability was counter-productive and actually exacerbated his behavior problems. There is no evidence the time-out system and use of restraints taught CJN to control his behavior. Nor is there evidence the District's ultimate resort to police intervention would ever teach CJN how to become a productive member of society.

[F]inally, I fear we allow Minnesota's education system to take a step backward with our tacit approval of the District's use of restraint to cope with CJN's behavioral outbursts. The HO concluded the District failed to comply with certain state standards governing the use of punitive and aversive deprivation procedures. Specifically, the HO found the District failed to comply with Minn. R. 3525.0850, which requires that the "objective of any behavioral intervention must be that pupils acquire appropriate behavior and skills. It is critical that behavioral intervention programs focus on skills acquisition rather than merely behavior reduction or elimination."

The HO also found the District failed to comply with Minn. R. 3525.1400, which requires that pupils receive education in "an atmosphere that is conducive to learning; and meet the child's special physical, sensory, and emotional needs." These administrative rules were adopted pursuant to Minn.Stat. § 121A.67, which requires the rules to "promote the use of positive approaches and must not encourage or require the use of aversive or deprivation procedures."

[T]he HO concluded that CJN "was trapped in an increasingly punitive approach to disciplining, which resulted in increasing the levels of isolation, time-out and locked seclusion." Neither the district court or the HRO addressed the HO's conclusion that the district violated Minn. R. 3525.0850 & 3525.1400 with its "increasingly punitive approach to disciplining." Furthermore, I find most disconcerting this court's attempt to explain away the District's violations by suggesting that CJN's mother was the obstacle to the adoption of an appropriate behavioral intervention program (BIP). My review of the record indicates that CJN's mother opposed the BIPs suggested by the District precisely because they violated Minnesota law.

I am discouraged by this court's tacit approval of the use of counter-productive and punitive disciplinary measures. We are essentially telling school districts that it's copacetic to deal with students with behavioral disabilities by punishing them for their disability, rather than finding an approach that addresses the problem. We also tacitly approve the District's resort to police intervention for the behavioral problems it helped create by failing to address CJN's unique behavioral disorder. That is clearly not a message this court should dispatch.

I commend CJN's mother for her wisdom in removing CJN from the destructive downward spiral created by the District's inability to address her son's unique educational, behavioral needs. She should now be reimbursed under the IDEA, pursuant to 20 U.S.C. § 1412(10)(C)(ii), for her decision to enroll her son in a private school capable of providing her son with an appropriate education.

Bryant v. New York State Education Dept.

United States Court of Appeals for the Second Circuit, 2012.
692 F.3d 202.

■ DENNIS JACOBS, CHIEF JUDGE:

Plaintiffs—the parents and/or legal guardians of seven children with disabilities, who bring this suit on behalf of themselves and the children—appeal a judgment of the United States District Court for the Northern District of New York (Sharpe, *J.*), dismissing their suit for failure to state a claim upon which relief can be granted, and denying their motion for a preliminary injunction. Plaintiffs seek equitable relief preventing the New York Board of Regents ("Board of Regents"), the New York State Education Department ("Education Department"), and the Commissioner of the Education Department (David M. Steiner, in his official capacity) from enforcing a prohibition on the use of aversive interventions. Aversive interventions are negative consequences or stimuli administered to children who exhibit problematic and disruptive behavior that impedes their education.

Plaintiffs contend that New York's prohibition of aversive interventions undermines their children's right to a free and appropriate public education ("FAPE"), which is guaranteed by federal law. We conclude that the State's prohibition of one possible method of reducing the consequences of a child's behavioral disability does not undermine the child's right to a FAPE or prevent administrators from enacting an individualized plan for the child's education.

[B]ACKGROUND

[II]

[P]laintiffs are the parents or legal guardians of seven children, each of whom has a long history of severe behavior problems, including aggressive, self-injurious, destructive, and non-compliant behavior. These behavioral disabilities cause the children to engage in behaviors such as: yanking out their own teeth, attempting to stab themselves, tying ropes around their necks, scratching themselves, banging their heads on walls and other things, and assaulting teachers and staff members. These behaviors have impeded their education and development.

Plaintiffs have tried a number of measures to treat and educate these children, including: special education, day and residential programs, psychiatric hospitalization, counseling, physical restraints, paraprofessional support, home instruction, sensory tents, positive-only programs of behavioral modification, and anti-psychotic and other psychotropic medications. None has been successful, and the children continue to pose physical risks to themselves and others. As a result, they have been foreclosed from public schools and private institutions or confined in psychiatric wards and detention centers. Each child's IEP now suggests they receive residential special-education services. Accordingly, each child is enrolled at the Judge Rotenb[e]rg Educational Center, Inc. ("JRC") in Massachusetts.

JRC provides residential, educational, and behavioral services to individuals with severe behavioral disorders, and is often a placement of last resort for those who have proven resistant to other forms of psychological and psychiatric treatment. Although JRC is out of state, the children are permitted to attend under a New York law that allows New York students with disabilities who are unable to obtain an appropriate education in-state to attend an out-of-state facility that, in the judgment of the Education Department, can meet the needs of the child. N.Y. Educ. Law §§ 4407(1)(a), 4401(2)(f), (h).

At JRC, each student starts with a non-intrusive, positive-only, treatment program in which students receive rewards (*e.g.,* treats, video games, music, field trips) for maintaining positive behaviors, including learning. The complaint alleges that these positive-only measures are effective for most of JRC's school-age students. For other students, JRC may also employ negative-consequence interventions known as aversives or aversive interventions.

According to the complaint, aversive interventions have been used to deal with behaviors that pose significant dangers to the student or others, or significantly interfere with a student's education, development, or appropriate behavior. The techniques aim to stop the behavior and thereby enable the student to receive an appropriate education, to enjoy safety and well-being, and to develop basic skills for learning and daily living. The complaint alleges that aversive interventions have helped many JRC students to participate in activities with peers and helped some to attend college, join the armed forces, obtain employment, and go on extended family visits.

The types of aversive interventions used by JRC include helmets with safeguards that prevent removal, manual and mechanical restraints, and food-control programs. But, according to the complaint, JRC's "principal form" of aversive intervention is electric skin shock, in which a low-level electrical current is applied to a small area of the student's skin (usually an arm or a leg). The shock lasts approximately two seconds, and is administered, on average, less than once a week. The complaint alleges that severe problematic behavior decreases with this regime, thus alleviating an impediment to academic progress. Possible side effects include temporary redness or marking, which clears up within a few minutes (or a few days at most), and a rare occurrence of blistering.

Clinicians have opined that it is necessary to supplement these children's ongoing educational and treatment programs with aversives. However, none of the children has yet received an IEP that authorizes such interventions.

III

The Education Department, which is governed by the Board of Regents, regulates educational services and programs for New York residents. [I]n 2006, the Board of Regents promulgated a regulation prohibiting schools, including "approved out-of-state day or residential schools" (such as JRC), from using aversive interventions. N.Y. Comp.Codes R. & Regs. tit. 8, § 19.5(b)(1) (2012). The regulation defines an "aversive intervention" as an intervention "intended to induce pain or discomfort to a student for the purpose of eliminating or reducing maladaptive behaviors," such as the contingent application of painful, intrusive, or similar stimuli or activity. *Id.* § 19.5(b)(2).

A child-specific exemption allows pre-approved aversives to be administered in exceptional cases in the three school years following the enactment of the prohibition (2006–2007, 2007–2008, 2008–2009), and a grandfather clause provides "that a student whose IEP includes the use of aversive interventions as of June 30, 2009"—three years after the enactment of the prohibition—"may be granted a child-specific exception in each subsequent school year . . . ." N.Y. Comp.Codes R. & Regs. tit. 8, § 200.22(e).

Neither exception applies to the children in the instant case because the initial three years of limited aversive interventions has now ended, and none of these children had an IEP that authorized aversives prior to June 30, 2009.

DISCUSSION

[II]

Two types of claims lie under the IDEA: [1] a procedural claim challenging the State's compliance with the procedures set forth in the IDEA, and [2] a substantive claim challenging whether the IEP is reasonably calculated to enable the student to receive educational benefits. Plaintiffs assert both kinds of claim.

A

Plaintiffs' procedural claim is that prohibiting aversive interventions prevents these children from obtaining a truly *individualized* education program because they are categorically barred from getting an IEP that includes aversive interventions without regard to their individual needs.

Nothing in New York's regulation prevents individualized assessment or precludes educators from considering a wide range of possible treatments. The regulation prohibits consideration of a single method of treatment without foreclosing other options. In so doing, the regulation follows the goals and emphasis of the IDEA. *See* 20 U.S.C. § 1400(c)(5)(F) ("Almost 30 years of research and experience has demonstrated that the education of children with disabilities can be made more effective by . . . positive behavioral interventions and supports"); 64 Fed. Reg. 12406, 12589 (Mar. 12, 1999) ("[T]he primary focus must be on ensuring that the behavioral management strategies in the child's IEP reflect the [IDEA's] requirement for the use of positive behavioral interventions and strategies to address the behavior that impedes the learning of the child or that of other children.").[6] Although the IDEA does not prohibit alternatives such

---

[6] *See also* 20 U.S.C. § 1411(e)(2)(C)(iii) (allowing states to reserve federal funding "[t]o assist local education agencies in providing positive behavior interventions and supports"); *id.* § 1414(d)(3)(B)(i) (providing that the IEP team should "consider the use of positive behavioral interventions and supports, and other strategies, to address" "behavior [that] impedes the child's learning or that of others"); *id.* § 1454(a)(3)(B)(iii)(I) (allowing states to use federal grants to train educators in methods of "positive behavioral interventions and supports to improve student behavior in the classroom"); *id.* § 1462(a)(6)(D) (authorizing the Secretary of Education to enter into contracts with entities to ensure training in "positive behavioral supports."); *id.* § 1465(b)(1)(B)–(C) (permitting the Secretary of Education to support effective,

as aversives, *see* 20 U.S.C. § 1414(d)(3)(B)(i), it cannot be said that a policy that relies on positive behavioral interventions only is incompatible with the IDEA.

Plaintiffs argue that, because the regulation eliminates one possible method from the students' IEP, it amounts to a predetermination that violates the procedural guarantees of the IDEA, as explained in *Deal v. Hamilton Cnty. Bd. of Educ.*, 392 F.3d 840 (6th Cir.2004). However, there is a distinction between a policy that affects individual cases on a categorical basis (such as the policy at issue here) and a local predetermination that rejects preemptively a measure that is permitted as a matter of state law.

In *Deal,* a school district refused to consider a particular teaching approach. The Sixth Circuit concluded that foreclosure of a program without regard for its effectiveness was a procedural violation of the IDEA because it deprived the parents of meaningful participation in the IEP process. We need not pass on the reasoning of *Deal* because unlike the instant challenge to a statewide prohibition enacted by a state government, *Deal* involved a challenge to an unofficial district policy involving a particular child's specific IEP as to which the parents had a statutory right of input, 20 U.S.C. § 1414(d)(1)(B).

The distinction is significant. [P]laintiffs' interpretation of the IDEA would effectively strip state governments of the ability to adopt statewide policy because it is impossible to consider each student's circumstances before adopting statewide policy. For this reason, New York collects input—by parents, professionals, and the public—when the Education Department publishes a proposed regulation and an opportunity is afforded for notice and comment.

In this case, New York adopted the ban of aversives only after the Education Department made site visits, reviewed reports, and considered complaints from parents as well as school districts and others raising concerns about aversive techniques. It concluded that aversive interventions are dangerous and may backfire and that positive behavioral interventions are sufficiently effective to provide a FAPE.

The prohibition therefore represents a considered judgment; one that conforms to the IDEA's preference for positive behavioral intervention. *See, e.g.,* 20 U.S.C. § 1400(c)(5)(F). (Another such New York policy is the long-standing bar on corporal punishment. *See* N.Y. Comp.Codes R. & Regs. tit. 8, § 19.5(a).) The IDEA does not categorically bar such statewide regulations that resolve problems in special education; otherwise, the IDEA would be transformed from a legislative scheme that preserves the states' fundamental role in education to one that usurps the role of the states. *Cf. Rowley,* 458 U.S. at 208, 102 S.Ct. 3034 (explaining that "Congress' intention was not that the [IDEA] displace the primacy of States in the field of education, but that States receive funds to assist them in extending their educational systems to the handicapped").

---

research-based practices through training educators in "positive behavioral interventions and supports" and "effective strategies for positive behavioral interventions").

In sum, New York's regulation prohibits only consideration of a single method of treatment without foreclosing other options. Nothing in the regulation prevents individualized assessment, predetermines the children's course of education, or precludes educators from considering a wide range of possible treatments. Therefore, the district court correctly dismissed the procedural IDEA claim.

B

Plaintiffs contend that the prohibition on aversive interventions is a substantive violation of the IDEA because aversives are necessary to control the severe behavioral disorders that undermine the children's education. Plaintiffs allege that a positive-only program is effective with 70% of students but that each of these children fall within the 30% who are not sufficiently treated with positive-only interventions.

For many of the reasons discussed above, Plaintiffs cannot state a substantive IDEA claim. The prohibition on aversive interventions does not prevent these students from obtaining an IEP specifically aimed at providing them an appropriate education. Moreover, the Education Department has decided to focus its special-education programs on positive-only behavioral interventions, which is the clear (although not exclusive) methodology favored by the IDEA.

Even if we assumed that permitting these children to receive aversive interventions would help them fulfill their potential, Plaintiffs' substantive claim would still fail. The "IDEA does not require states to develop IEPs that 'maximize the potential of handicapped children.'" The IDEA "guarantees" only that students with disabilities are provided an "'appropriate' education, not one that provides everything that might be thought desirable by loving parents." A state satisfies its obligation to provide a free *appropriate* public education if it "provide[s] a disabled child with meaningful access to an education" even if the state "cannot guarantee totally successful results." *[A]ccord Rowley* (explaining that the IDEA "imposes no clear obligation upon recipient States beyond the requirement that handicapped children receive some form of specialized education").

Defendants provide these students with meaningful access to education opportunities by authorizing and funding their specialized education and behavioral modification treatment at an out-of-state residential facility that has expertise in treating children with severe behavioral disorders. Aversive interventions may help maximize the children's potential, but the IDEA does not require such measures.

Moreover, we decline Plaintiffs' invitation to review and second guess New York's education policy. Although the IDEA provides for some judicial review, "the Supreme Court has cautioned[ ] . . . that this 'independent' review 'is by no means an invitation to the courts to substitute their own notions of sound educational policy for those of the school authorities they review.'" [citing an earlier Second Circuit case quoting *Rowley*]. We will not "simply rubber stamp" the decisions of the states and locals, but we must be "mindful that the judiciary generally lacks the specialized knowledge and experience necessary to resolve persistent and difficult questions of educational policy."

There is an ongoing debate among the experts regarding the advantages and disadvantages of aversive interventions and positive-only methods of behavioral modification. The judiciary is ill-suited to decide the winner of that debate.

Our deference to the Education Department's decision is further justified in this instance because New York adopted the regulation after the Education Department obtained information raising concerns regarding the potential health and safety implications of aversives. The Education Department was concerned that aversive interventions can result in "aggressive and/or escape behaviors" and can foster the development of "negative attitudes toward [one's] self and school programs"—concerns raised by reports and complaints by parents, school districts, and others. One such source of concern was a lawsuit alleging abuse at JRC, *see Nicholson v. New York,* 23 Misc.3d 313, 872 N.Y.S.2d 846 (Ct.Cl.2008), which prompted a site visit on which the Education Department "identified significant concerns for the potential impact on the health and safety of New York students." This Court is not institutionally suited to now second guess the policy decision made by experts charged with formulating education policy in New York.

Because Plaintiffs have not and cannot allege that these children have been deprived of a FAPE, they cannot prevail on their substantive IDEA claim

[C]ONCLUSION

Accordingly, the judgment of the district court is affirmed.

■ RICHARD J. SULLIVAN, DISTRICT JUDGE, [D]ISSENTING IN PART:

[I] respectfully dissent insofar as the Court's opinion relates to the dismissal of Appellants' IDEA claims because I believe that Appellants' complaint alleged sufficient facts to survive a motion to dismiss.

[I]n dismissing Appellants' complaint, the district court held that "the allegations demonstrate that the NYSED and the Board of Regents explored the available data, studies, and literature before making a reasoned decision that aversives should be generally prohibited." However, nowhere in the opinion did the district court actually cite from the pleadings to support this conclusion. Instead, the district court merely observed that "plaintiffs do not allege that [d]efendants did not *consider* the use of aversive interventions before adopting § 200.22" and then concluded that "[t]he [c]ourt is not willing to second guess that policy decision."

While it is of course true that courts are not to second guess state authorities in matters relating to educational policy, the law is equally clear that federal courts may not merely "rubber stamp administrative decisions" of this kind. Indeed, this Court has recognized that, notwithstanding "our deferential position with respect to state educational authorities crafting educational policy," "our review must be searching, and we must recognize that even when educational authorities act with the best intentions they may sometimes fall short of their obligations under the IDEA, and courts must then act to ensure compliance with Congress's directives." Here, the district court's conclusion that the prohibition of aversive interventions was reasonable is particularly problematic, because

Appellants alleged in their complaint that the scientific literature, which the district court mentioned (but did not cite) in its opinion, actually "supports the use of aversive interventions and their vital role in providing a FAPE to students with severe behavior disorders."

The majority affirms the district court's dismissal of Appellants' suit, finding that the prohibition of aversive interventions reflects "a considered judgment by the State of New York regarding the education and safety of its children that is consistent with federal education policy and the United States Constitution." In reaching this conclusion, the majority relies not on the pleadings or on the district court's opinion, but rather on four pages from the Education Department's *Notice of Emergency Adoption and Proposed Rule Making,* of which it has taken judicial notice. While the Court can certainly take judicial notice of facts, these four pages, standing alone, are insufficient to justify the district court's dismissal of Appellants' claims at this early stage of the litigation. Indeed, the first two of those pages simply note the Department's "concerns" with aversive interventions based on "site visits, reports and complaints filed by parents, school districts and others"; the latter two merely catalog scientific studies that purportedly support the proposed rule.

Importantly, the scientific studies summarized in the *Notice of Emergency Adoption and Proposed Rule Making* do not directly call for the prohibition of aversive interventions. To the contrary, these studies presuppose the use and utility of aversive interventions at least in certain contexts and merely set forth "standards" and "strategies to improve an ABI's [aversive behavioral intervention's] effectiveness and acceptability." It is worth noting that of the several studies cited in the *Notice of Emergency Adoption and Proposed Rule Making,* the two included in full in the record actually describe the *need* for aversive interventions in certain instances. *See* Dorothy C. Lerman & Christina M. Vondram, *On the Status of Knowledge for Using Punishment: Implications for Behavior Disorders,* 35 J. APPL. BEHAV. ANAL. 431, 456 (2002) (noting that "punishment is still sometimes needed to reduce destructive behavior to acceptable levels"); Sarah-Jeanne Salvy et al., *Contingent Electric Shock (SIBIS) and a Conditioned Punisher Eliminate Severe Head Banging in a Preschool Child,* 19 BEHAV. INTERVENT. 59 (2004) (noting that ABIs "can sometime be necessary, although not sufficient, to eliminate severe and harmful [self-injurious behavior] in the natural environment"). Consequently, I am unpersuaded that the *Notice of Emergency Adoption and Proposed Rule Making* cited by the majority provides a sufficient basis for upholding the district court's dismissal.

Of course, like the majority, I am "mindful that the judiciary generally lacks the specialized knowledge and experience necessary to resolve persistent and difficult questions of educational policy." However, it seems to me that the appropriate course would be to return this action to the district court, which could then review a fuller record, beyond the pleadings, to assess the regulation and its compliance with the IDEA. If my cursory review of the literature in the field is any indication, it seems likely that Appellees will be able to demonstrate that "the regulations represent an informed, rational choice between two opposing schools of thought on the use of aversives," and that Appellants will therefore have difficulty overcoming the "substantial deference" accorded to the review of state policy-making agencies. Nevertheless, while the outcome may ultimately be the same, it is important that the result be based on a careful assessment of the merits, founded on a well-developed record. In my view, the district court's dismissal—and the majority's affirmance—takes an unnecessary short cut to reach an outcome that cannot be justified at this stage of the proceedings. For these reasons, I respectfully dissent.

NOTES ON RESTRAINT AND SECLUSION

1. **The *CJN* and *Bryant* Holdings.** Is Judge Bye correct to say in his *CJN* dissent that "the majority decision essentially holds the District can satisfy its duty to provide a FAPE so long as a student with a *behavioral* disability makes *academic* progress"? Even if Judge Bye's characterization is not correct, do you agree with the majority that the school district complied with the IDEA in its response to CJN's behavioral issues? What more could the school district have done? Is it reasonable to expect a school district, with many competing demands on its resources and attention, to provide children with behavioral disabilities the sort of highly individualized treatment that Judge Bye demands? What are the implications of *Rowley* for that question? Is *Bryant* a faithful application of *Rowley*?

2. **How Does the Law Limit Restraint and Seclusion?** In a 2009 report, the Government Accountability Office found that "thousands of public and private school students were restrained or secluded during the last academic year." Gov't Accountability Off., Seclusions and Restraints: Selected Cases of Death and Abuse at Public and Private Schools and Treatment Centers 7 (May 19, 2009). In particular, "Texas public school officials stated they restrained 4,202 students 18,741 times during the September 2007 through June 2008 academic year," and "California officials reported 14,354 instances of students' being subjected to restraint, seclusion or other undefined 'emergency interventions' in public and private schools" during that period. *Id.* The GAO also found "hundreds" of "allegations of death and abuse" from restraint and seclusion in schools between 1990 and 2009, "[a]lmost all" of which "involved children with disabilities." *Id.* at 5. It reported a number of common themes to the cases it examined:

> (1) children with disabilities were sometimes restrained and secluded even when they did not appear to be physically aggressive and their parents did not give consent; (2) facedown or other restraints that block air to the lungs can be deadly; (3) teachers and staff in these cases were often not trained in the use of restraints and techniques; and (4) teachers and staff from these cases continue to be employed as educators.

Id. at 7. Allegations of restraint and seclusion of students with disabilities included the following:

> The children in these cases were diagnosed with autism or other conditions, including post traumatic stress disorder and attention deficit hyperactivity disorder. Although we did not evaluate whether the seclusion and restraint used by the staff in our cases

was proper under applicable state laws, we did observe that the
children in the cases were restrained or secluded as disciplinary
measures, even when their behavior did not appear to be
physically aggressive. For example, teachers restrained a 4 year
old with cerebral palsy in a device that resembled a miniature
electric chair because she was reportedly being "uncooperative."
In other cases, we found that teachers and other staff did not have
parental consent prior to using restraints and seclusions. For
example, an IEP for a 9 year old with learning disabilities
specified that placement in a timeout room could be used to
correct inappropriate behavior, but only as a last resort. However,
teachers confined this child to a small, dirty room 75 times over
the course of 6 months for offenses such as whistling, slouching,
and hand waving. Parents in another case gave a teacher explicit
instructions to stop restraining their 7-year-old child and
secluding her for prolonged periods of time. Despite these
instructions, the restraints and seclusions continued. In another
case, a residential day school implemented a behavior plan,
without parental consent, that included confining an 11-year-old
autistic child to his room for extended periods of time, restricting
his food, and using physical restraints. The child was diagnosed
with post traumatic stress disorder as a result of this treatment.

Id. at 8.

Do allegations like these state a violation of the law? The GAO found
wide variation in the state laws governing restraint and seclusion in
schools. It found that: "nineteen states have no laws or regulations" on the
topic; "seven states place some restrictions of the use of restraints, but do
not regulate seclusions"; seventeen states require certain staff training;
thirteen states require parental consent before "using foreseeable or non-
emergency physical restraints"; nineteen states require *ex post* parental
notification of restraint use; two states require annual reporting of
restraint use; and eight states prohibit prone restraints. *Id.* at 4.

What about federal law? *CJN* highlights both the promise and limits
of the IDEA as a response to improper restraint and seclusion of students
with disabilities. Parents have also brought challenges in this area under
the Fourteenth and Fourth Amendments to the Constitution. These cases
tend to succeed, if at all, only when the facts are particularly egregious.
See, for example, ORANGE V. COUNTY OF GRUNDY, 950 F.Supp. 1365
(E.D.Tenn.1996), in which the district court denied the defendants' motion
for summary judgment on a substantive Due Process claim that was based
on the following facts:

Plaintiff Robin Orange has suffered with a bladder disorder since
she was in elementary school. During the eight years of
elementary school, she was allowed by Principal Ronnie Fults to
use a private restroom where she could catheterize herself to
avoid risking embarrassment and ridicule by other students.
Fults later became Superintendent of the school system.

When plaintiff began high school in 1989, her mother discussed
her bladder condition with the assistant principal, Ms. Pickett,

and provided her with a doctor's statement regarding plaintiff's medical condition. Plaintiff's mother requested the same accommodation for privacy that had been made at the elementary school, but this was denied. However, Ms. Pickett did accommodate plaintiff's parents' request that plaintiff be excused from class to go to the restroom as necessary. Defendants contend that Ms. Pickett advised the teachers of plaintiff's urological condition and she was allowed to leave class as necessary. During the 1992–93 school year, plaintiff, because of her medical needs, was permitted to sign herself out to go home to change clothes and catheterize herself when necessary.

Plaintiff returned to Grundy County High School during the 1993–94 academic year to enroll in a few courses to complete her senior year. In early November, 1993, she requested to sign herself out because she had involuntarily wet her clothes. Plaintiff claims that her request to leave school was refused by the office staff, even though they were reminded that her parents had given her permission to leave school when needed. Plaintiff contends that she was then faced with an emergency situation and she decided to leave school to change into clean, dry clothes.

On November 15, 1993, Ms. Pickett instructed plaintiff to come to the office and instructed her that she would be placed in detention for leaving school without permission. When asked whether she agreed that she left school without permission of school personnel, plaintiff responded in the affirmative and claims that she was asked no further questions. Plaintiff's claim that no attempt was made by Ms. Pickett or other school personnel to advise plaintiff's parents that the in-school isolation was about to take place.

As punishment for leaving school without permission, Ms. Pickett instructed the plaintiff to report to Coach Ray's classroom. Plaintiff contends that the coach instructed her to go into a small, dirty, cluttered closet located in his classroom which contained a desk, a light bulb hanging from the ceiling, a mop and a bucket, dust, dirt, and discarded food on the floor. Plaintiff claims that during her first day of isolation in the storage closet her request to be allowed to use the restroom was refused by the coach. She claims that she was told she could not use the restroom and to go back in the closet and not come out. She contends that she was told to stay in there all day, where she sat shivering in wet clothes.

Plaintiff Orange claims that she had no prior notice that she would be confined to the storage closet for the entire school day and thus did not bring any lunch with her. She claims that the school made no arrangements for her to use the restroom or to be provided lunch. She further claims that during the first day of isolation in the storage closet not one teacher or school official supervised or checked on her. Plaintiff alleges that she was afraid to come out after Coach Ray would not allow her to go to the restroom and told her to stay in the closet.

Plaintiff contends that her urological condition caused her clothes to become wet, and she sat shivering in the storage closet for two days. On the second day, plaintiff contends that the coach would allow her to use the restroom only when students were in classes and the halls were empty. She claims that she requested to be allowed to use the restroom while there were no students present in the coach's classroom to avoid embarrassment upon exiting the storage closet, but apparently that request was denied. At some point during the second day, defendant Fults did check on her and she seemed to be "O.K."

Ms. Orange claims that she became distressed about returning to school and being ridiculed by other students. She says that, when she returned to school and was subjected to ridicule, she eventually left Grundy County to complete her high school education in an adjacent county.

Id. at 1369-1370.

Consider the Keeping All Students Safe Act, H.R. 1893, 113th Cong., 1st Sess. (2013), recently introduced in the House of Representatives. That bill would require the Secretary of Education to issue regulations limiting restraint and seclusion, which states would incorporate into their own policies as a condition of receiving federal funding. The Secretary's regulations would be required to "establish[ ] the following minimum standards":

(1) School personnel shall be prohibited from imposing on any student the following:

(A) Mechanical restraints.

(B) Chemical restraints.

(C) Physical restraint or physical escort that restricts breathing.

(D) Aversive behavioral interventions that compromise health and safety.

(2) School personnel shall be prohibited from imposing physical restraint or seclusion on a student unless—

(A) the student's behavior poses an imminent danger of physical injury to the student, school personnel, or others;

(B) less restrictive interventions would be ineffective in stopping such imminent danger of physical injury;

(C) such physical restraint or seclusion is imposed by school personnel who—

(i) continuously monitor the student face-to-face; or

(ii) if school personnel safety is significantly compromised by such face-to-face monitoring, are in continuous direct visual contact with the student;

(D) such physical restraint or seclusion is imposed by—

(i) school personnel trained and certified by a State-approved crisis intervention training program (as defined in section 4(16)); or

(ii) other school personnel in the case of a rare and clearly unavoidable emergency circumstance when school personnel trained and certified as described in clause (i) are not immediately available due to the unforeseeable nature of the emergency circumstance; and

(E) such physical restraint or seclusion ends immediately upon the cessation of the conditions described in subparagraphs (A) and (B).

(3) States, in consultation with local educational agencies and private school officials, shall ensure that a sufficient number of personnel are trained and certified by a State-approved crisis intervention training program * * * to meet the needs of the specific student population in each school.

(4) The use of physical restraint or seclusion as a planned intervention shall not be written into a student's education plan, individual safety plan, behavioral plan, or individualized education program (as defined in section 602 of the Individuals with Disabilities Education Act (20 U.S.C. 1401)). Local educational agencies or schools may establish policies and procedures for use of physical restraint or seclusion in school safety or crisis plans, provided that such school plans are not specific to any individual student.

(5) Schools shall establish procedures to be followed after each incident involving the imposition of physical restraint or seclusion upon a student, including—

(A) procedures to provide to the parent of the student, with respect to each such incident—

(i) an immediate verbal or electronic communication on the same day as the incident; and

(ii) written notification within 24 hours of the incident; and

(B) any other procedures the Secretary determines appropriate.

Id. § 5(a). Would this law solve the problem of improper use of restraint and seclusion? Would it give teachers and school administrators sufficient tools to maintain order and a safe and appropriate learning environment for all students?

4. PRIVATE SCHOOL REIMBURSEMENT

Florence County Sch. Dist. Four v. Carter

Supreme Court of the United States, 1993.
510 U.S. 7.

■ JUSTICE O'CONNOR delivered the opinion of the Court.

[T]his case presents the question whether a court may order reimbursement for parents who unilaterally withdraw their child from a public school that provides an inappropriate education under IDEA and put the child in a private school that provides an education that is otherwise proper under IDEA, but does not meet all the requirements of § 1401(a)(18). We hold that the court may order such reimbursement, and therefore affirm the judgment of the Court of Appeals.

I

Respondent Shannon Carter was classified as learning disabled in 1985, while a ninth grade student in a school operated by petitioner Florence County School District Four. School officials met with Shannon's parents to formulate an individualized education program (IEP) for Shannon, as required under IDEA. 20 U.S.C. §§ 1401(a)(18) and (20), 1414(a)(5) (1988 ed. and Supp. IV). The IEP provided that Shannon would stay in regular classes except for three periods of individualized instruction per week, and established specific goals in reading and mathematics of four months' progress for the entire school year. Shannon's parents were dissatisfied, and requested a hearing to challenge the appropriateness of the IEP. See § 1415(b)(2). Both the local educational officer and the state educational agency hearing officer rejected Shannon's parents' claim and concluded that the IEP was adequate. In the meantime, Shannon's parents had placed her in Trident Academy, a private school specializing in educating children with disabilities. Shannon began at Trident in September 1985 and graduated in the spring of 1988.

Shannon's parents filed this suit in July 1986, claiming that the school district had breached its duty under IDEA to provide Shannon with a "free appropriate public education," § 1401(a)(18), and seeking reimbursement for tuition and other costs incurred at Trident. After a bench trial, the District Court ruled in the parents' favor. The court held that the school district's proposed educational program and the achievement goals of the IEP "were wholly inadequate" and failed to satisfy the requirements of the Act. The court further held that "[a]lthough [Trident Academy] did not comply with all of the procedures outlined in [IDEA]," the school "provided Shannon an excellent education in substantial compliance with all the substantive requirements" of the statute. The court found that Trident "evaluated Shannon quarterly, not yearly as mandated in [IDEA], it provided Shannon with low teacher-student ratios, and it developed a plan which allowed Shannon to receive passing marks and progress from grade to grade." The court also credited the findings of its own expert, who determined that Shannon had made "significant progress" at Trident and that her reading comprehension had risen three grade levels in her three years at the school. The District Court concluded that Shannon's education was "appropriate" under IDEA, and that Shannon's parents were entitled to reimbursement of tuition and other costs.

The Court of Appeals for the Fourth Circuit affirmed. The court agreed that the IEP proposed by the school district was inappropriate under IDEA. It also rejected the school district's argument that reimbursement is never proper when the parents choose a private school that is not approved by the State or that does not comply with all the terms of IDEA. According to the Court of Appeals, neither the text of the Act nor its legislative history imposes a "requirement that the private school be approved by the state in parent-placement reimbursement cases." To the contrary, the Court of Appeals concluded, IDEA's state-approval requirement applies only when a child is placed in a private school by public school officials. Accordingly, "when a public school system has defaulted on its obligations under the Act, a private school placement is 'proper under the Act' if the education provided by the private school is 'reasonably calculated to enable the child to receive educational benefits.' "

II

[I]n *School Comm. of Burlington v. Department of Ed. of Mass.*, 471 U.S. 359, 369 (1985), we held that IDEA's grant of equitable authority empowers a court "to order school authorities to reimburse parents for their expenditures on private special education for a child if the court ultimately determines that such placement, rather than a proposed IEP, is proper under the Act." Congress intended that IDEA's promise of a "free appropriate public education" for disabled children would normally be met by an IEP's provision for education in the regular public schools or in private schools chosen jointly by school officials and parents. In cases where cooperation fails, however, "parents who disagree with the proposed IEP are faced with a choice: go along with the IEP to the detriment of their child if it turns out to be inappropriate or pay for what they consider to be the appropriate placement." For parents willing and able to make the latter choice, "it would be an empty victory to have a court tell them several years later that they were right but that these expenditures could not in a proper case be reimbursed by the school officials." Because such a result would be contrary to IDEA's guarantee of a "free appropriate public education," we held that "Congress meant to include retroactive reimbursement to parents as an available remedy in a proper case."

As this case comes to us, two issues are settled: (1) the school district's proposed IEP was inappropriate under IDEA, and (2) although Trident did not meet the § 1401(a)(18) requirements, it provided an education otherwise proper under IDEA. This case presents the narrow question whether Shannon's parents are barred from reimbursement because the private school in which Shannon enrolled did not meet the § 1401(a)(18) definition of a "free appropriate public education." We hold that they are not, because § 1401(a)(18)'s requirements cannot be read as applying to parental placements.

Section 1401(a)(18)(A) requires that the education be "provided at public expense, under public supervision and direction." Similarly, § 1401(a)(18)(D) requires schools to provide an IEP, which must be designed by "a representative of the local educational agency," 20 U.S.C. § 1401(a)(20), and must be "establish[ed]," "revise[d]," and "review[ed]" by the agency, § 1414(a)(5). These requirements do not make sense in the context of a parental placement. In this case, as in all *Burlington* reimbursement cases, the parents' rejection of the school district's proposed IEP is the very reason for the parents' decision to put their child in a private school. In such cases, where the private placement has necessarily been made over the school district's objection, the private school education will not be under "public supervision and direction." Accordingly, to read the § 1401(a)(18) requirements as applying to parental placements would effectively eliminate the right of unilateral withdrawal recognized in *Burlington*. Moreover, IDEA was intended to ensure that children with disabilities receive an education that is both appropriate and free. To read the provisions of § 1401(a)(18) to bar reimbursement in the circumstances of this case would defeat this statutory purpose.

Nor do we believe that reimbursement is necessarily barred by a private school's failure to meet state education standards. Trident's deficiencies, according to the school district, were that it employed at least two faculty members who were not state-certified and that it did not develop IEP's. As we have noted, however, the § 1401(a)(18) requirements—including the requirement that the school meet the standards of the state educational agency, § 1401(a)(18)(B)—do not apply to private parental placements. Indeed, the school district's emphasis on state standards is somewhat ironic. As the Court of Appeals noted, "it hardly seems consistent with the Act's goals to forbid parents from educating their child at a school that provides an appropriate education simply because that school lacks the stamp of approval of the same public school system that failed to meet the child's needs in the first place." Accordingly, we disagree with the Second Circuit's theory that "a parent may not obtain reimbursement for a unilateral placement if that placement was in a school that was not on [the State's] approved list of private" schools. Parents' failure to select a program known to be approved by the State in favor of an unapproved option is not itself a bar to reimbursement.

Furthermore, although the absence of an approved list of private schools is not essential to our holding, we note that parents in the position of Shannon's have no way of knowing at the time they select a private school whether the school meets state standards. South Carolina keeps no publicly available list of approved private schools, but instead approves private school placements on a case-by-case basis. In fact, although public school officials had previously placed three children with disabilities at Trident, Trident had not received blanket approval from the State. South Carolina's case-by-case approval system meant that Shannon's parents needed the cooperation of state officials before they could know whether Trident was state-approved. As we recognized in *Burlington*, such cooperation is unlikely in cases where the school officials disagree with the need for the private placement.

III

The school district also claims that allowing reimbursement for parents such as Shannon's puts an unreasonable burden on financially strapped local educational authorities. The school district argues that requiring parents to choose a state approved private school if they want reimbursement is the only meaningful way to allow States to control costs; otherwise States will have to reimburse dissatisfied parents for any private school that provides an education that is proper under the Act, no matter how expensive it may be.

There is no doubt that Congress has imposed a significant financial burden on States and school districts that participate in IDEA. Yet public educational authorities who want to avoid reimbursing parents for the private education of a disabled child can do one of two things: give the child a free appropriate public education in a public setting, or place the child in an appropriate private setting of the State's choice. This is IDEA's mandate, and school officials who conform to it need not worry about reimbursement claims.

Moreover, parents who, like Shannon's, "unilaterally change their child's placement during the pendency of review proceedings, without the consent of state or local school officials, do so at their own financial risk." They are entitled to reimbursement only if a federal court concludes both that the public placement violated IDEA and that the private school placement was proper under the Act.

Finally, we note that once a court holds that the public placement violated IDEA, it is authorized to "grant such relief as the court determines is appropriate." 20 U.S.C. § 1415(e)(2). Under this provision, "equitable considerations are relevant in fashioning relief," *Burlington*, and the court enjoys "broad discretion" in so doing, *id.*. Courts fashioning discretionary equitable relief under IDEA must consider all relevant factors, including the appropriate and reasonable level of reimbursement that should be required. Total reimbursement will not be appropriate if the court determines that the cost of the private education was unreasonable.

Accordingly, we affirm the judgment of the Court of Appeals.

So ordered.

NOTES ON PRIVATE SCHOOL REIMBURSEMENT

1.   The Reimbursement Rule. Three sorts of criticisms have been leveled against the reimbursement rule of *Burlington* and *Florence County*. One involves the high cost of private school tuition. Private school is costly—a single student's tuition will typically be significantly more expensive than a district's average per-pupil expenditure—so requiring a school district to reimburse the cost of private school tuition can impose substantial burdens on the district's budget. To be sure, serving a student in a public special education program often costs more than a district's average per-pupil expenditure, but private school tuition typically costs substantially more than public special education services. An analysis of data compiled by the Special Education Expenditure Project concluded that, in 2000, the average cost of a private placement under IDEA was $25,580, while "the average privately placed student would have cost $15,517 if he had instead been served in a public school"—so that "private placement cost an additional $10,463 per student." Jay P. Greene & Marcus A. Winters, *Debunking a Special Education* Myth, Education Next, Vol. 7, No. 2, at 67–71 (Spring 2007). Those burdens will necessarily be borne by some combination of the district's taxpayers and other students and their families. With the number of private placements under IDEA growing at about twice the rate of the number of IDEA-served students overall by some estimates, school districts are understandably concerned about the costs the reimbursement rule imposes. See generally Brief for the National School Boards Assn. and American Assn. of School Administrators as *Amici Curiae, Board of Education v. Tom F.*, 552 U.S. 1 (2007).

Yet the aggregate costs of private-school placements under IDEA are not exceptionally high. Greene and Winters conclude:

> Given the conservative estimate of $10,463 per pupil as the additional cost of private placement and given 88,156 privately placed students, the total additional cost of placing disabled students in private schools may be as high as $922 million. This sounds like a lot of money, but to public schools it is almost a rounding error. In the school year ending in 2000, the same year as our cost estimates, public schools spent $382 billion. The $922 million for private placement amounts to just 0.24 percent of the total budget. The cost of family-driven private placement is certainly less.

Greene & Winters, *supra.* Greene and Winters do acknowledge that in some jurisdictions—especially the District of Columbia, where in 2004 "the cost of private placements represent[ed] 15 percent of the school district's budget"—the cost is more significant, though. *Id.*

A second criticism implicates questions of equity. Because the parent bears the burden of finding the appropriate private school and then must front the tuition pending the resolution of reimbursement proceedings (and risk not obtaining reimbursement if the hearing officer or court concludes that the school was providing adequate services to the child), the beneficiaries of the reimbursement rule are likely to be disproportionately wealthy and educated. An extreme example is Tom Freston, the former CEO of Viacom, who received an $85 million severance package from his company and then (successfully) litigated all the way to the Supreme Court to demand that the New York City schools reimburse his child's $38,000 annual private school tuition. See *Board of Education v. Tom F.*, 552 U.S. 1 (2007) (*per curiam*). Freston explained, quite plausibly, that he cared not about the money but about the principle. See Joseph Berger, *Fighting Over When Public Should Pay Private Tuition for Disabled*, N.Y. Times, Mar. 21, 2007. Are less well-to-do parents in a position to front private school tuition for their children in the hope that (someday, perhaps at the end of a long administrative and judicial process) the school district will reimburse them?

One might respond to the equity criticism in several ways. One might argue, for example, that what matters is the welfare of each individual student with a disability; the fact that not all students with disabilities will be able to take advantage of private school reimbursement may be an argument for trying to *extend* the reimbursement program, in this view, but is not an argument for taking it away from those who can now take advantage of it. Or one might argue that the better-off parents who can credibly threaten to place their children in private school will give public school systems a strong financial incentive to create adequate special education programs of their own, and that those programs will benefit the children with disabilities whose parents could not credibly threaten to leave as well. Or, if one favors school vouchers generally, one might argue that private school reimbursement under IDEA is a step along the way to a broader voucher program

A third objection would look to the core principle of integration. Will paying the private-school tuition of students with disabilities increase or decrease the likelihood that children with and without disabilities will attend school together? The fact patterns of decided cases suggest that parents will frequently use the reimbursement rule to finance the placement of their children in schools that specialize in dealing with children with disabilities. The rule is therefore likely to have a segregative rather than an integrative effect.

One might respond, following Professor Colker, that integration ought not to be the overriding principle in this context. See Ruth Colker, When is Separate Unequal: A Disability Perspective 78–140 (2008) (arguing that educational quality, not integration, ought to be the overriding principle, and that the two will often be in conflict). Will parents be good judges of when a segregated placement is educationally preferable to an integrated one? Or will parents view their children with disabilities as defined by their "special needs" and choose segregated placements even when they are unnecessary?

In light of these arguments, do you think the private school reimbursement rule is a good or bad one? Does your answer depend on whether you think private-school vouchers are a good policy tool generally?

2.   The *Florence County* Holding. One can understand why the *Florence County* Court was hesitant to allow state authorities a veto power over what schools' tuition would be reimbursed under IDEA. But doesn't the Court's holding create the opposite problem—that school districts will be forced to reimburse the tuition of schools that do not meet basic educational standards and do not even provide the sort of appropriately tailored education that the statute requires? The Court seemed to take the view that, as between the parents of a child with a disability and a school district that has failed to provide an appropriate education to the child, the parents can best be trusted to look after the child's welfare and select an appropriate private school. Are parents really capable of monitoring the quality of their children's education? Cf. Dupre, *A Study in Double Standards*, *supra*, at 76 (stating that "even those parents who intend to act in their disabled child's best interests may nonetheless be influenced by forces that conflict with the actual best interest of the child," because, among other things, "parents dealing with a child's disability often suffer from emotional stress that may hinder their ability to make decisions that prompt the best interest of their children"). Note that, even under *Florence County*, courts need not always defer to the parents' choice of alternative placement. See, *e.g.*, *T.B. v. St. Joseph School Dist.*, 677 F.3d 844 (8th Cir.2012) (denying reimbursement for "home-based" program that primarily taught social, behavioral, and self-care skills, on the ground that the program was not reasonably calculated to enable the child to receive educational benefits); *C.L. v. Scarsdale Union Free School Dist.*, 2012 WL 6646958 (S.D.N.Y., Dec. 21, 2012) (denying reimbursement for private school that exclusively served students with learning disabilities, on the ground that school was an unnecessarily segregated setting).

3. *Forest Grove School District v. T.A.* In the 1997 reauthorization of the IDEA, Congress added a provision that specifically addressed private school reimbursement:

Payment for education of children enrolled in private schools without consent of or referral by the public agency

(i) In general

Subject to subparagraph (A), this subchapter does not require a local educational agency to pay for the cost of education, including special education and related services, of a child with a disability at a private school or facility if that agency made a free appropriate public education available to the child and the parents elected to place the child in such private school or facility.

(ii) Reimbursement for private school placement

If the parents of a child with a disability, who previously received special education and related services under the authority of a public agency, enroll the child in a private elementary school or secondary school without the consent of or referral by the public agency, a court or a hearing officer may require the agency to reimburse the parents for the cost of that enrollment if the court or hearing officer finds that the agency had not made a free appropriate public education available to the child in a timely manner prior to that enrollment.

(iii) Limitation on reimbursement

The cost of reimbursement described in clause (ii) may be reduced or denied—

(I) if—

(aa) at the most recent IEP meeting that the parents attended prior to removal of the child from the public school, the parents did not inform the IEP Team that they were rejecting the placement proposed by the public agency to provide a free appropriate public education to their child, including stating their concerns and their intent to enroll their child in a private school at public expense; or

(bb) 10 business days (including any holidays that occur on a business day) prior to the removal of the child from the public school, the parents did not give written notice to the public agency of the information described in item (aa);

(II) if, prior to the parents' removal of the child from the public school, the public agency informed the parents, through the notice requirements described in section 1415(b)(3) of this title, of its intent to evaluate the child (including a statement of the purpose of the evaluation that was appropriate and reasonable), but the parents did not make the child available for such evaluation; or

(III) upon a judicial finding of unreasonableness with respect to actions taken by the parents.

(iv) Exception

Notwithstanding the notice requirement in clause (iii)(I), the cost of reimbursement—

(I) shall not be reduced or denied for failure to provide such notice if—

(aa) the school prevented the parent from providing such notice;

(bb) the parents had not received notice, pursuant to section 1415 of this title, of the notice requirement in clause (iii)(I); or

(cc) compliance with clause (iii)(I) would likely result in physical harm to the child; and

(II) may, in the discretion of a court or a hearing officer, not be reduced or denied for failure to provide such notice if—

(aa) the parent is illiterate or cannot write in English; or

(bb) compliance with clause (iii)(I) would likely result in serious emotional harm to the child.

20 U.S.C. § 1412(a)(10)(C). This provision specifically authorizes reimbursement for parents of children "who previously received special education and related services under the authority of a public agency." 20 U.S.C. § 1412(a)(10)(C)(ii). Does it implicitly preclude reimbursement for parents of a child who were denied a free appropriate public education by their public school system but were sent to private school before they actually received special education in a public school? The Supreme Court considered that question in the following case.

Forest Grove Sch. Dist. v. T.A.

Supreme Court of the United States, 2009.
129 S.Ct. 2484.

■ JUSTICE STEVENS delivered the opinion of the Court.

The Individuals with Disabilities Education Act (IDEA or Act), 84 Stat. 175, as amended, 20 U.S.C. § 1400 *et seq.*, requires States receiving federal funding to make a "free appropriate public education" (FAPE) available to all children with disabilities residing in the State, § 1412(a)(1)(A). We have previously held that when a public school fails to provide a FAPE and a child's parents place the child in an appropriate private school without the school district's consent, a court may require the district to reimburse the parents for the cost of the private education. *Burlington.* The question presented in this case is whether the IDEA Amendments of 1997 (Amendments), 111 Stat. 37, categorically prohibit reimbursement for private-education costs if a child has not "previously received special education and related services under the authority of a public agency." § 1412(a)(10)(C)(ii). We hold that the Amendments impose no such categorical bar.

I

Respondent T.A. attended public schools in the Forest Grove School District (School District or District) from the time he was in kindergarten through the winter of his junior year of high school. From kindergarten through eighth grade, respondent's teachers observed that he had trouble paying attention in class and completing his assignments. When respondent entered high school, his difficulties increased.

In December 2000, during respondent's freshman year, his mother contacted the school counselor to discuss respondent's problems with his schoolwork. At the end of the school year, respondent was evaluated by a school psychologist. After interviewing him, examining his school records, and administering cognitive ability tests, the psychologist concluded that respondent did not need further testing for any learning disabilities or other health impairments, including attention deficit hyperactivity disorder (ADHD). The psychologist and two other school officials discussed the evaluation results with respondent's mother in June 2001, and all agreed that respondent did not qualify for special-education services. Respondent's parents did not seek review of that decision, although the hearing examiner later found that the School District's evaluation was legally inadequate because it failed to address all areas of suspected disability, including ADHD.

With extensive help from his family, respondent completed his sophomore year at Forest Grove High School, but his problems worsened during his junior year. In February 2003, respondent's parents discussed with the School District the possibility of respondent completing high school through a partnership program with the local community college. They also sought private professional advice, and in March 2003 respondent was diagnosed with ADHD and a number of disabilities related to learning and memory. Advised by the private specialist that respondent would do best in a structured, residential learning environment, respondent's parents enrolled him at a private academy that focuses on educating children with special needs.

Four days after enrolling him in private school, respondent's parents hired a lawyer to ascertain their rights and to give the School District written notice of respondent's private placement. A few weeks later, in April 2003, respondent's parents requested an administrative due process hearing regarding respondent's eligibility for special-education services. In June 2003, the District engaged a school psychologist to assist in determining whether respondent had a disability that significantly interfered with his educational performance. Respondent's parents cooperated with the District during the evaluation process. In July 2003, a multidisciplinary team met to discuss whether respondent satisfied IDEA's disability criteria and concluded that he did not because his ADHD did not have a sufficiently significant adverse impact on his educational performance. Because the School District maintained that respondent was not eligible for special-education services and therefore declined to provide an individualized education program (IEP), respondent's parents left him enrolled at the private academy for his senior year.

The administrative review process resumed in September 2003. After considering the parties' evidence, including the testimony of numerous experts, the hearing officer issued a decision in January 2004 finding that respondent's ADHD adversely affected his educational performance and that the School District failed to meet its obligations under IDEA in not identifying respondent as a student eligible for special-education services. Because the District did not offer respondent a FAPE and his private-school placement was appropriate under IDEA, the hearing officer ordered the District to reimburse respondent's parents for the cost of the private-school tuition.

The School District sought judicial review pursuant to § 1415(i)(2), arguing that the hearing officer erred in granting reimbursement. The District Court accepted the hearing officer's findings of fact but set aside the reimbursement award after finding that the 1997 Amendments categorically bar reimbursement of private-school tuition for students who have not "previously received special education and related services under the authority of a public agency." § 612(a)(10)(C)(ii), 111 Stat. 63, 20 U.S.C. § 1412(a)(10)(C)(ii). The District Court further held that, "[e]ven assuming that tuition reimbursement may be ordered in an extreme case for a student not receiving special education services, under general principles of equity where the need for special education was obvious to school authorities," the facts of this case do not support equitable relief.

The Court of Appeals for the Ninth Circuit reversed and remanded for further proceedings. [B]ecause the Courts of Appeals that have considered this question have reached inconsistent results, we granted *certiorari* to determine whether § 1412(a)(10)(C) establishes a categorical bar to tuition reimbursement for students who have not previously received special-education services under the authority of a public education agency.

II

[W]e granted *certiorari* in *Burlington* to determine whether IDEA authorizes reimbursement for the cost of private education when a parent or guardian unilaterally enrolls a child in private school because the public school has proposed an inadequate IEP and thus failed to provide a FAPE. The Act at that time made no express reference to the possibility of reimbursement, but it authorized a court to "grant such relief as the court determines is appropriate." § 1415(i)(2)(C)(iii). In determining the scope of the relief authorized, we noted that "the ordinary meaning of these words confers broad discretion on the court" and that, absent any indication to the contrary, what relief is "appropriate" must be determined in light of the Act's broad purpose of providing children with disabilities a FAPE, including through publicly funded private-school placements when necessary. Accordingly, we held that the provision's grant of authority includes "the power to order school authorities to reimburse parents for their expenditures on private special-education services if the court ultimately determines that such placement, rather than a proposed IEP, is proper under the Act."

Our decision rested in part on the fact that administrative and judicial review of a parent's complaint often takes years. We concluded that, having mandated that participating States provide a FAPE for every student, Congress could not have intended to require parents to either accept an inadequate public-school education pending adjudication of their claim or bear the cost of a private education if the court ultimately determined that the private placement was proper under the Act. Eight years later, we unanimously reaffirmed the availability of reimbursement in *Florence County v. Carter.*

The dispute giving rise to the present litigation differs from those in *Burlington* and *Carter* in that it concerns not the adequacy of a proposed IEP but the School District's failure to provide an IEP at all. And, unlike respondent, the children in those cases had previously received public special-education services. These differences are insignificant, however, because our analysis in the earlier cases depended on the language and purpose of the Act and not the particular facts involved. Moreover, when a child requires special-education services, a school district's failure to propose an IEP of any kind is at least as serious a violation of its responsibilities under IDEA as a failure to provide an adequate IEP. It is thus clear that the reasoning of *Burlington* and *Carter* applies equally to this case. The only question is whether the 1997 Amendments require a different result.

III

[A]fter examining the States' progress under IDEA, Congress found in 1997 that substantial gains had been made in the area of special education but that more needed to be done to guarantee children with disabilities adequate access to appropriate services. See S.Rep.No.105–17, p. 5 (1997). The 1997 Amendments were intended "to place greater emphasis on improving student performance and ensuring that children with disabilities receive a quality public education." Id., at 3.

Consistent with that goal, the Amendments preserved the Act's purpose of providing a FAPE to all children with disabilities. And they did not change the text of the provision we considered in *Burlington*, § 1415(i)(2)(C)(iii), which gives courts broad authority to grant "appropriate" relief, including reimbursement for the cost of private special education when a school district fails to provide a FAPE. [A]bsent a clear expression elsewhere in the Amendments of Congress' intent to repeal some portion of that provision or to abrogate our decisions in *Burlington* and *Carter*, we will continue to read § 1415(i)(2)(C)(iii) to authorize the relief respondent seeks.

The School District and the dissent argue that one of the provisions enacted by the Amendments, § 1412(a)(10)(C), effects such a repeal. Section 1412(a)(10)(C) is entitled "Payment for education of children enrolled in private schools without consent of or referral by the public agency," and it sets forth a number of principles applicable to public reimbursement for the costs of unilateral private-school placements. Section 1412(a)(10)(C)(i) states that IDEA "does not require a local educational agency to pay for the cost of education . . . of a child with a disability at a private school or facility if that agency made a free appropriate public education available to the child" and his parents nevertheless elected to place him in a private school. Section 1412(a)(10)(C)(ii) then provides that a "court or hearing officer may require [a public] agency to reimburse the parents for the cost of [private-school] enrollment if the court or hearing officer finds that the agency had not made a free appropriate public education available" and the child has "previously received special education and related services under the authority of [the] agency." Finally, § 1412(a)(10)(C)(iii) discusses circumstances under which the "cost of reimbursement described in clause (ii) may be reduced or denied," as when a parent fails to give 10 days' notice before removing a child from public school or refuses to make a child available for evaluation, and § 1412(a)(10)(C)(iv) lists circumstances in which a parent's failure to give notice may or must be excused.

Looking primarily to clauses (i) and (ii), the School District argues that Congress intended § 1412(a)(10)(C) to provide the exclusive source of authority for courts to order reimbursement when parents unilaterally enroll a child in private school. According to the District, clause (i) provides a safe harbor for school districts that provide a FAPE by foreclosing reimbursement in those circumstances. Clause (ii) then sets forth the circumstance in which reimbursement is appropriate— namely, when a school district fails to provide a FAPE to a child who has previously received special-education services through the public school. The District contends that because § 1412(a)(10)(C) only discusses reimbursement for children who have previously received special-education services through the public school, IDEA only authorizes reimbursement in that circumstance. The dissent agrees.

For several reasons, we find this argument unpersuasive. First, the School District's reading of the Act is not supported by its text and context, as the 1997 Amendments do not expressly prohibit reimbursement under the circumstances of this case, and the District offers no evidence that Congress intended to supersede our decisions in *Burlington* and Carter. Clause (i)'s safe harbor explicitly bars reimbursement only when a school district makes a FAPE available by correctly identifying a child as having a disability and proposing an IEP adequate to meet the child's needs. The clause says nothing about the availability of reimbursement when a school district fails to provide a FAPE. Indeed, its statement that reimbursement is not authorized when a school district provides a FAPE could be read to indicate that reimbursement is authorized when a school district does not fulfill that obligation.

Clause (ii) likewise does not support the District's position. Because that clause is phrased permissively, stating only that courts "may require" reimbursement in those circumstances, it does not foreclose reimbursement awards in other circumstances. Together with clauses (iii) and (iv), clause (ii) is best read as elaborating on the general rule that courts may order reimbursement when a school district fails to provide a FAPE by listing factors that may affect a reimbursement award in the common situation in which a school district has provided a child with some special-education services and the child's parents believe those services are inadequate. Referring as they do to students who have previously received special-education services through a public school, clauses (ii) through (iv) are premised on a history of cooperation and together encourage school districts and parents to continue to cooperate in developing and implementing an appropriate IEP before resorting to a unilateral private placement. The clauses of § 1412(a)(10)(C) are thus best read as elucidative rather than exhaustive. Cf. *United States v. Atlantic Research Corp.*, 551 U.S. 128, 137 (2007) (noting that statutory language may "perfor[m] a significant function simply by clarifying" a provision's meaning).

This reading of § 1412(a)(10)(C) is necessary to avoid the conclusion that Congress abrogated *sub silentio* our decisions in *Burlington* and *Carter*. In those cases, we construed § 1415(i)(2)(C)(iii) to authorize reimbursement when a school district fails to provide a FAPE and a child's private-school placement is appropriate, without regard to the child's prior receipt of services. It would take more than Congress' failure to comment on the category of cases in which a child has not previously received special-education services for us to conclude that the Amendments substantially superseded our decisions and in large part repealed § 1415(i)(2)(C)(iii).

The School District's reading of § 1412(a)(10)(C) is also at odds with the general remedial purpose underlying IDEA and the 1997 Amendments. The express purpose of the Act is to "ensure that all children with disabilities have available to them a free appropriate public education that emphasizes special education and related services designed to meet their unique needs," § 1400(d)(1)(A)—a factor we took into account in construing the scope of § 1415(i)(2)(C)(iii), see *Burlington*. Without the remedy respondent seeks, a "child's right to a free appropriate education . . . would be less than complete." The District's position similarly conflicts with IDEA's "child find" requirement, pursuant to which States are obligated to "identif[y], locat[e], and evaluat[e]" "[a]ll children with disabilities residing in the State" to ensure that they receive needed special-education services. § 1412(a)(3)(A); see § 1412(a)(10)(A)(ii). A reading of the Act that left parents without an adequate remedy when a school district unreasonably failed to identify a child with disabilities would not comport with Congress' acknowledgment of the paramount importance of properly identifying each child eligible for services.

Indeed, by immunizing a school district's refusal to find a child eligible for special-education services no matter how compelling the child's need, the School District's interpretation of § 1412(a)(10)(C) would produce a rule bordering on the irrational. It would be particularly strange for the Act to provide a remedy, as all agree it does, when a school district offers a child inadequate special-education services but to leave parents without relief in the more egregious situation in which the school district unreasonably denies a child access to such services altogether. That IDEA affords parents substantial procedural safeguards, including the right to challenge a school district's eligibility determination and obtain prospective relief, see [Justice Souter's dissent], is no answer. We roundly rejected that argument in *Burlington*, observing that the "review process is ponderous" and therefore inadequate to ensure that a school's failure to provide a FAPE is remedied with the speed necessary to avoid detriment to the child's education. Like *Burlington*, this case vividly demonstrates the problem of delay, as respondent's parents first sought a due process hearing in April 2003, and the District Court issued its decision in May 2005—almost a year after respondent graduated from high school. The dissent all but ignores these shortcomings of IDEA's procedural safeguards.

IV

The School District advances two additional arguments for reading the Act to foreclose reimbursement in this case. First, the District contends that because IDEA was an exercise of Congress' authority under the Spending Clause, U.S. Const., Art. I, § 8, cl. 1, any conditions attached to a State's acceptance of funds must be stated unambiguously. Applying that principle, we held in *Arlington Central School Dist. Bd. of Ed. v. Murphy*, 548 U.S. 291, 304 (2006) [set forth as a principal case below], that IDEA's fee-shifting provision, § 1415(i)(3)(B), does not authorize courts to award expert-services fees to prevailing parents in IDEA actions because the Act does not put States on notice of the possibility of such awards. But Arlington is readily distinguishable from this case. In accepting IDEA funding, States expressly agree to provide a FAPE to all children with disabilities. See § 1412(a)(1)(A). An order awarding reimbursement of private-education costs when a school district fails to provide a FAPE merely requires the district "to belatedly pay expenses that it should have paid all along." *Burlington*. And States have in any event been on notice at least since our decision in *Burlington* that IDEA authorizes courts to order reimbursement of the costs of private special-education services in appropriate circumstances.

[F]inally, the District urges that respondent's reading of the Act will impose a substantial financial burden on public school districts and encourage parents to immediately enroll their children in private school without first endeavoring to cooperate with the school district. The dissent echoes this concern. For several reasons, those fears are unfounded. Parents "are entitled to reimbursement only if a federal court concludes both that the public placement violated IDEA and the private school placement was proper under the Act." *Carter*. And even then courts retain discretion to reduce the amount of a reimbursement award if the equities so warrant—for instance, if the parents failed to give the school district adequate notice of their intent to enroll the child in private school. In considering the equities, courts should generally presume that public-school officials are properly performing their obligations under IDEA. As a result of these criteria and the fact that parents who " 'unilaterally change their child's placement during the pendency of review proceedings, without the consent of state or local school officials, do so at their own financial risk,' " *Carter*, the incidence of private-school placement at public expense is quite small, see Brief for National Disability Rights Network *et al.* as *Amici Curiae* 13–14.

V

The IDEA Amendments of 1997 did not modify the text of § 1415(i)(2)(C)(iii), and we do not read § 1412(a)(10)(C) to alter that provision's meaning. Consistent with our decisions in *Burlington* and *Carter*, we conclude that IDEA authorizes reimbursement for the cost of private special-education services when a school district fails to provide a FAPE and the private-school placement is appropriate, regardless of whether the child previously received special education or related services through the public school.

When a court or hearing officer concludes that a school district failed to provide a FAPE and the private placement was suitable, it must consider all relevant factors, including the notice provided by the parents and the school district's opportunities for evaluating the child, in determining whether reimbursement for some or all of the cost of the child's private education is warranted. As the Court of Appeals noted, the District Court did not properly consider the equities in this case and will need to undertake that analysis on remand. Accordingly, the judgment of the Court of Appeals is affirmed.

It is so ordered.

■ JUSTICE SOUTER, with whom JUSTICE SCALIA and JUSTICE THOMAS join, dissenting.

[In *Burlington*, we] said that, for want of any specific limitation, this remedy was within the general authorization for courts to award "such relief as [they] determin[e] is appropriate." § 1415(e)(2) (1982 ed.) (now codified at § 1415(i)(2)(C)(iii) (2006 ed.)). In 1997, however, Congress amended the IDEA with a number of provisions explicitly addressing the issue of "[p]ayment for education of children enrolled in private schools without consent of or referral by the public agency." § 1412(a)(10)(C). These amendments generally prohibit reimbursement if the school district made a "free appropriate public education" (FAPE) available, § 1412(a)(10)(C)(i), and if they are to have any effect, there is no exception except by agreement, § 1412(a)(10)(B), or for a student who previously received special education services that were inadequate, § 1412(a)(10)(C)(ii).

The majority says otherwise and holds that § 1412(a)(10)(C)(ii) places no limit on reimbursements for private tuition. The Court does not find the provision clear enough to affect the rule in *Burlington*, and it does not believe Congress meant to limit public reimbursement for unilaterally incurred private school tuition. But there is no authority for a heightened standard before Congress can alter a prior judicial interpretation of a statute, and the assessment of congressional policy aims falls short of trumping what seems to me to be the clear limitation imposed by § 1412(a)(10)(C)(ii).

I

In *Burlington*, [w]e emphasized that the Act did not speak specifically to the issue of reimbursement, and held that "[a]bsent other reference," reimbursement for private tuition and expenses would be an " 'appropriate' " remedy in light of the purposes of the Act. In short, we read the general provision for ordering equitable remedies in § 1415(i)(2)(C)(iii) as authorizing a reimbursement order, in large part because Congress had not spoken more specifically to the issue.

But Congress did speak explicitly when it amended the IDEA in 1997. It first said that whenever the State or a local educational agency refers a student to private special education, the bill is a public expense. See 20 U.S.C. § 1412(a)(10)(B). It then included several clauses addressing "[p]ayment for education of children enrolled in private schools without consent of or referral by the public agency." § 1412(a)(10)(C). The first contrasts with the provision covering an agency referral:

"(i) In general

". . . this subchapter does not require a local educational agency to pay for the cost of education . . . of a child with a disability at a private school or facility if that agency made a free appropriate public education available to the child and the parents elected to place the child in such private school or facility." § 1412(a)(10)(C).

The second clause covers the case in which the school authority failed to make a FAPE available in its schools. It does not, however, provide simply that the authority must pay in this case, no matter what. Instead it provides this:

"(ii) Reimbursement for private school placement

"If the parents of a child with a disability, who previously received special education and related services under the authority of a public agency, enroll the child in a private elementary school or secondary school without the consent of or referral by the public agency, a court or a hearing officer may require the agency to reimburse the parents for the cost of that enrollment if the court or hearing officer finds that the agency had not made a free appropriate public education available to the child in a timely manner prior to that enrollment." § 1412(a)(10)(C).

Two additional clauses spell out in some detail various facts upon which the reimbursement described in clause (ii) may be "reduced or denied." See §§ 1412(a)(10)(C)(iii) and (iv).

As a purely semantic matter, these provisions are ambiguous in their silence about the case with no previous special education services and no FAPE available. As the majority suggests, clause (i) could theoretically be understood to imply that reimbursement may be ordered whenever a school district fails to provide a FAPE, and clause (ii) could be read as merely taking care to mention one of a variety of circumstances in which such reimbursement is permitted. But this is overstretching. When permissive language covers a special case, the natural sense of it is taken to prohibit what it fails to authorize. When a mother tells a boy that he may go out and play after his homework is done, he knows what she means.

So does anyone who reads the authorization of a reimbursement order in the case of "a child with a disability, who previously received special education and related services under the authority of a public agency." § 1412(a)(10)(C)(ii). If the mother did not mean that the homework had to be done, why did she mention it at all, and if Congress did not mean to restrict reimbursement authority by reference to previous receipt of services, why did it even raise the subject? "[O]ne of the most basic interpretive canons [is] that [a] statute should be construed so that effect is given to all its provisions, so that no part will be inoperative or superfluous, void or insignificant." But not on the Court's reading, under which clause (ii) does nothing but describe a particular subset of cases subject to remedial authority already given to courts by § 1415(i)(2)(C)(iii) and recognized in *Burlington*: a court may order reimbursement for a child who previously received special education related services, but it may do this for any other child, too. But this is just not plausible, the notion that Congress added a new provision to the IDEA entitled "Reimbursement for private school placement" that had no effect whatsoever on reimbursement for private school placement. I would read clause (i) as written on the assumption that the school authorities can be expected to honor their obligations and as stating the general rule that unilateral placement cannot be reimbursed. See § 1412(a)(10)(C)(i) ("In general . . . "). And I would read clause (ii) as imposing a receipt of prior services limit on any exceptions to that general rule when school officials fall short of providing a FAPE. See § 1412(a)(10)(C)(ii) ("Reimbursement for private school placement . . . ").

This reading can claim the virtue of avoiding a further anomaly. Section 1412(a)(10)(C)(iii), which limits otherwise available reimbursement, is expressly directed to "[t]he cost of reimbursement described in clause (ii)." This makes perfect sense under my reading. Since clause (ii) is now the exclusive source of authority to order reimbursement, it is natural to refer to it in the clause setting out the conditions for reducing or even denying reimbursement otherwise authorized. Yet, as T.A. and the Government concede, Brief for Respondent 22; Brief for United States as *Amicus Curiae* 4, 17, under the majority's reading, Congress has called for reducing reimbursement only for the most deserving (parents described in clause (ii) who consult with the school district and give public special education services a try before demanding payment for private education), but provided no mechanism to reduce reimbursement to the least deserving (parents who have not given public placement a chance).

[B]ecause any other interpretation would render clause (ii) pointless and clause (iii) either pointless or perverse, § 1412(a)(10)(C)(ii) must be read to allow reimbursement only for "parents of a child with a disability, who previously received special education and related services under the authority of a public agency."

II

Neither the majority's clear statement rule nor its policy considerations prevail over the better view of the 1997 Amendments.

[S]ection 1412(a)(10)(C) in no way repealed the provision we considered in Burlington. The relief that "is appropriate" under § 1415(i)(2)(C)(iii) depends on the substantive provisions of the IDEA as surely as if the provision authorized equitable relief "consistent with the provisions of this statute." When we applied § 1415(i)(2)(C)(iii) in Burlington, we expressly referred to those provisions and concluded that, in the absence of a specific rule, "appropriate" relief included the reimbursement sought. By introducing new restrictions on reimbursement, the 1997 Amendments produce a different conclusion about what relief is "appropriate." But § 1415(i)(2)(C)(iii) remains in effect, just as it would remain in effect if Congress had explicitly amended the IDEA to prohibit reimbursement absent prior receipt of services.

As for the rule that reenactment incorporates prior interpretation, the Court's reliance on it to preserve *Burlington*'s reading of § 1415(i)(2)(C)(iii) faces two hurdles. First, so far as I can tell, this maxim has never been used to impose a clear statement rule. If Congress does not suggest otherwise, reenacted statutory language retains its old meaning; but when a new enactment includes language undermining the prior reading, there is no presumption favoring the old, and the only course open is simply to read the revised statute as a whole. This is so because there is no reason to distinguish between amendments that occur in a single clause (as if Congress had placed all the changes in § 1415(i)(2)(C)(iii)), and those that take the form of a separate section (here, § 1412(a)(10)(C)). If Congress had added a caveat within § 1415(i)(2)(C)(iii), or in an immediately neighboring provision, I assume the majority would not approach it with skepticism on the ground that it purported to modify a prior judicial interpretation.

Second, nothing in my reading of § 1412(a)(10)(C)(ii) is inconsistent with the holdings of *Burlington* and the other prior decision on the subject, *Carter*. Our opinion in *Burlington* was expressly premised on there being no "other reference" that would govern reimbursement for private tuition, and this all but invited Congress to provide one. Congress's provision of such a reference in 1997 is, to say the very least, no reason for skepticism that Congress wished to alter the law on reimbursement. The 1997 legislation, read my way, would not, however, alter the result in either *Burlington* or *Carter*. In each case, the school district had agreed that the child was disabled, the parents had cooperated with the district and tried out an IEP, and the only question was whether parents who later resorted to a private school could be reimbursed " 'if the court ultimately determines that such placement, rather than a proposed IEP, is proper under the Act.' " *Carter* (quoting *Burlington*). In ordering reimbursement, the Court in both *Burlington* and *Carter* emphasized that the parents took part in devising an IEP, 471 U.S., at 368, 510 U.S., at 12, and expressed concern for parents who had sought an IEP before placing their child in private school, but received one that was inadequate, 471 U.S., at 370, 510 U.S., at 12. The result in each case would have been the same under my reading of the amended Act, both sets of parents being "parents of a child with a disability, who previously received special education and related services under the authority of a public agency." § 1412(a)(10)(C)(ii). It is therefore too much to suggest that my reading of § 1412(a)(10)(C)(ii) would "abrogat[e] *sub silentio* our decisions in *Burlington* and *Carter*," [majority opinion].

The majority argues that the policy concerns vindicated in *Burlington* and *Carter* justify reading those cases to authorize a reimbursement authority going beyond their facts, and would hold reimbursement possible even for parents who, like those here, unilaterally resort to a private school without first establishing at the administrative or appellate level that the child is disabled, or engaging in a collaborative process with the school officials. But how broadly one should read *Burlington* and *Carter* is beside the point, Congress having explicitly addressed the subject with statutory language that precludes the Court's result today.

B

The Court also rejects the natural sense of § 1412(a)(10)(C) as an interpretation that would be "at odds with the general remedial purpose underlying IDEA and the 1997 Amendments." The majority thinks my reading would place the school authorities in total control of parents' eligibility for reimbursement: just refuse any request for special education or services in the public school, and the prior service condition for eligibility under clause (ii) can never be satisfied. Thus, as the majority puts it, it would "borde[r] on the irrational" to "immuniz[e] a school district's refusal to find a child eligible for special-education services no matter how compelling the child's need." I agree that any such scheme would be pretty absurd, but there is no absurdity here. The majority's suggestion overlooks the terms of the IDEA process, the substantial procedures protecting a child's substantive rights under the IDEA, and the significant costs of its rule.

To start with the costs, special education can be immensely expensive, amounting to tens of billions of dollars annually and as much as 20% of public schools' general operating budgets. See Brief for Council of the Great City Schools as *Amicus Curiae* 22–23. The more private placement there is, the higher the special education bill, a fact that lends urgency to the IDEA's mandate of a collaborative process in which an IEP is "developed jointly by a school official qualified in special education, the child's teacher, the parents or guardian, and, where appropriate, the child." *Burlington.*

The Act's repeated emphasis on the need for cooperative joint action by school and parent does not, however, leave the school in control if officials should wish to block effective (and expensive) action for the child's benefit, for if the collaborative approach breaks down, the IDEA provides for quick review in a "due process hearing" of the parents' claim that more services are needed to provide a FAPE than the school is willing to give. See § 1415(c)(2) (district must respond to due process hearing complaint within 10 days and hearing officer must assess facial validity of complaint within 5 days); § 1415(e) (mediation is available, provided it does not delay due process hearing); § 1415(f)(1)(B) (district must convene a meeting with parents within 15 days to attempt to resolve complaint); 34 CFR §§ 300.510(b)(1)–(2) (2008) (if complaint is not resolved, a hearing must be held within 30 days of complaint and a decision must be issued within 75 days of complaint). Parents who remain dissatisfied after these first two levels of process may have a right of appeal to the state educational agency and in any case may bring a court action in federal district court. See 20 U.S.C. § 1415(i)(2). This scheme of administrative and judicial review is the answer to the Court's claim that reading the prior services condition as restrictive, not illustrative, immunizes a school district's intransigence, giving it an effective veto on reimbursement for private placement.

That said, the Court of course has a fair point that the prior services condition qualifies the remedial objective of the statute, and pursuing appeals to get a satisfactory IEP with special services worth accepting could be discouraging. The child who needs help does not stop needing it, or stop growing, while schools and parents argue back and forth. But we have to decide this case on the premise that most such arguments will be carried on in good faith, and even on the assumption that disagreements about the adequacy of IEPs will impose some burdens on the Act's intended beneficiaries, there is still a persuasive reason for Congress to have written the statute to mandate just what my interpretation requires. Given the burden of private school placement, it makes good sense to require parents to try to devise a satisfactory alternative within the public schools, by taking part in the collaborative process of developing an IEP that is the "modus operandi" of the IDEA. *Burlington.* And if some time, and some educational opportunity, is lost in consequence, this only shows what we have realized before, that no policy is ever pursued to the ultimate, single-minded limit, and that "[t]he IDEA obviously does not seek to promote

[its] goals at the expense of all considerations, including fiscal considerations."

NOTES ON *FOREST GROVE V. T.A.*

Which of the opinions in *Forest Grove* do you find persuasive? Is the statutory-interpretation analysis in Justice Souter's dissent consistent with the statutory analysis in Justice Souter's opinion for the Court in *Chevron v. Echazabal* (a principal case in Chapter Three)?

5. PROCEDURE AND REMEDIES

Schaffer v. Weast

Supreme Court of the United States, 2005.
546 U.S. 49.

■ JUSTICE O'CONNOR delivered the opinion of the Court.

The Individuals with Disabilities Education Act (IDEA or Act), 84 Stat. 175, as amended, 20 U.S.C. § 1400 *et seq.*, is a Spending Clause statute that seeks to ensure that "all children with disabilities have available to them a free appropriate public education," § 1400(d)(1)(A). Under IDEA, school districts must create an "individualized education program" (IEP) for each disabled child. § 1414(d). If parents believe their child's IEP is inappropriate, they may request an "impartial due process hearing." § 1415(f). The Act is silent, however, as to which party bears the burden of persuasion at such a hearing. We hold that the burden lies, as it typically does, on the party seeking relief.

I

A

[I]DEA is "frequently described as a model of 'cooperative federalism.' " It "leaves to the States the primary responsibility for developing and executing educational programs for handicapped children, [but] imposes significant requirements to be followed in the discharge of that responsibility." *Rowley.* For example, the Act mandates cooperation and reporting between state and federal educational authorities. Participating States must certify to the Secretary of Education that they have "policies and procedures" that will effectively meet the Act's conditions. 20 U.S.C. § 1412(a). (Unless otherwise noted, all citations to the Act are to the pre-2004 version of the statute because this is the version that was in effect during the proceedings below. We note, however, that nothing in the recent 2004 amendments, 118 Stat. 2674, appears to materially affect the rule announced here.) State educational agencies, in turn, must ensure that local schools and teachers are meeting the State's educational standards. §§ 1412(a)(11), 1412(a)(15)(A). Local educational agencies (school boards or other administrative bodies) can receive IDEA funds only if they certify to a state educational agency that they are acting in accordance with the State's policies and procedures. § 1413(a)(1).

The core of the statute, however, is the cooperative process that it establishes between parents and schools. The central vehicle for this collaboration is the IEP process. State educational authorities must identify and evaluate disabled children, §§ 1414(a)–(c), develop an IEP for each one, § 1414(d)(2), and review every IEP at least once a year, § 1414(d)(4). Each IEP must include an assessment of the child's current educational performance, must articulate measurable educational goals, and must specify the nature of the special services that the school will provide. § 1414(d)(1)(A).

Parents and guardians play a significant role in the IEP process. They must be informed about and consent to evaluations of their child under the Act. § 1414(c)(3). Parents are included as members of "IEP teams." § 1414(d)(1)(B). They have the right to examine any records relating to their child, and to obtain an "independent educational evaluation of the[ir] child." § 1415(b)(1). They must be given written prior notice of any changes in an IEP, § 1415(b)(3), and be notified in writing of the procedural safeguards available to them under the Act, § 1415(d)(1). If parents believe that an IEP is not appropriate, they may seek an administrative "impartial due process hearing." § 1415(f). School districts may also seek such hearings, as Congress clarified in the 2004 amendments. See S.Rep.No.108–185, p. 37 (2003). They may do so, for example, if they wish to change an existing IEP but the parents do not consent, or if parents refuse to allow their child to be evaluated. As a practical matter, it appears that most hearing requests come from parents rather than schools. Brief for Petitioners 7.

Although state authorities have limited discretion to determine who conducts the hearings, § 1415(f)(1), and responsibility generally for establishing fair hearing procedures, § 1415(a), Congress has chosen to legislate the central components of due process hearings. It has imposed minimal pleading standards, requiring parties to file complaints setting forth "a description of the nature of the problem," § 1415(b)(7)(B)(ii), and "a proposed resolution of the problem to the extent known and available . . . at the time," § 1415(b)(7)(B)(iii). At the hearing, all parties may be accompanied by counsel, and may "present evidence and confront, cross-examine, and compel the attendance of witnesses." §§ 1415(h)(1)–(2). After the hearing, any aggrieved party may bring a civil action in state or federal court. § 1415(i)(2). Prevailing parents may also recover attorney's fees. § 1415(i)(3)(B). Congress has never explicitly stated, however, which party should bear the burden of proof at IDEA hearings.

B

This case concerns the educational services that were due, under IDEA, to petitioner Brian Schaffer. Brian suffers from learning disabilities and speech-language impairments. From prekindergarten through seventh grade he attended a private school and struggled academically. In 1997, school officials informed Brian's mother that he needed a school that could better accommodate his needs. Brian's parents contacted respondent Montgomery County Public Schools System (MCPS) seeking a placement for him for the following school year.

MCPS evaluated Brian and convened an IEP team. The committee generated an initial IEP offering Brian a place in either of two MCPS middle schools. Brian's parents were not satisfied with the arrangement, believing that Brian needed smaller classes and more intensive services. The Schaffers thus enrolled Brian in another private school, and initiated a due process hearing challenging the IEP and seeking compensation for the cost of Brian's subsequent private education.

In Maryland, IEP hearings are conducted by administrative law judges (ALJs). [T]he ALJ [d]eemed the evidence truly in "equipoise" and ruled in favor of the parents. [T]he District Court [ruled] that the school district has the burden of proof. On appeal, a divided panel of the Fourth Circuit reversed. Judge Michael, writing for the majority, concluded that petitioners offered no persuasive reason to "depart from the normal rule of allocating the burden to the party seeking relief." We granted *certiorari* to resolve the following question: At an administrative hearing assessing the appropriateness of an IEP, which party bears the burden of persuasion?

II

[W]hen we are determining the burden of proof under a statutory cause of action, the touchstone of our inquiry is, of course, the statute. The plain text of IDEA is silent on the allocation of the burden of persuasion. We therefore begin with the ordinary default rule that plaintiffs bear the risk of failing to prove their claims. [T]he ordinary default rule, of course, admits of exceptions. For example, the burden of persuasion as to certain elements of a plaintiff's claim may be shifted to defendants, when such elements can fairly be characterized as affirmative defenses or exemptions. Under some circumstances this Court has even placed the burden of persuasion over an entire claim on the defendant. But while the normal default rule does not solve all cases, it certainly solves most of them. Decisions that place the entire burden of persuasion on the opposing party at the outset of a proceeding—as petitioners urge us to do here—are extremely rare. Absent some reason to believe that Congress intended otherwise, therefore, we will conclude that the burden of persuasion lies where it usually falls, upon the party seeking relief.

[P]etitioners [c]ontend that we should take instruction from the lower court opinions of *Mills v. Board of Education*, 348 F.Supp. 866 (D.D.C.1972), and *Pennsylvania Association for Retarded Children v. Pennsylvania*, 334 F.Supp. 1257 (E.D.Pa.1971) (hereinafter *PARC*). IDEA's drafters were admittedly guided "to a significant extent" by these two landmark cases. *Rowley*. As the court below noted, however, the fact that Congress "took a number of the procedural safeguards from *PARC* and *Mills* and wrote them directly into the Act" does not allow us to "conclude . . . that Congress intended to adopt the ideas that it failed to write into the text of the statute."

Petitioners also urge that putting the burden of persuasion on school districts will further IDEA's purposes because it will help ensure that children receive a free appropriate public education. In truth, however, very few cases will be in evidentiary equipoise. Assigning the burden of persuasion to school districts might encourage schools to put more resources into preparing IEPs and presenting their evidence. But IDEA is silent about whether marginal dollars should be allocated to litigation and administrative expenditures or to educational services. Moreover, there is reason to believe that a great deal is already spent on the administration of the Act. Litigating a due process complaint is an expensive affair, costing schools approximately $8,000–to–$12,000 per hearing. See Department of Education, J. Chambers, J. Harr, & A. Dhanani, What Are We Spending on Procedural Safeguards in Special Education 1999–2000, p. 8 (May 2003) (prepared under contract by American Institutes for Research, Special Education Expenditure Project). Congress has also repeatedly amended the Act in order to reduce its administrative and litigation-related costs. For example, in 1997 Congress mandated that States offer mediation for IDEA disputes. § 615(e) of IDEA, as added by § 101 of the Individuals with Disabilities Education Act Amendments of 1997, Pub.L.105–17, 111 Stat. 90, 20 U.S.C. § 1415(e). In 2004, Congress added a mandatory "resolution session" prior to any due process hearing. § 615(f)(1)(B) of IDEA, as added by § 101 of the Individuals with Disabilities Education Improvement Act of 2004, Pub.L.108–446, 118 Stat. 2720, 20 U.S.C.A. § 1415(f)(1)(B) (Supp.2005). It also made new findings that "[p]arents and schools should be given expanded opportunities to resolve their disagreements in positive and constructive ways," and that "[t]eachers, schools, local educational agencies, and States should be relieved of irrelevant and unnecessary paperwork burdens that do not lead to improved educational outcomes." §§ 1400(c)(8)–(9).

Petitioners in effect ask this Court to assume that every IEP is invalid until the school district demonstrates that it is not. The Act does not support this conclusion. IDEA relies heavily upon the expertise of school districts to meet its goals. It also includes a so-called "stay-put" provision, which requires a child to remain in his or her "then-current educational placement" during the pendency of an IDEA hearing. § 1415(j). Congress could have required that a child be given the educational placement that a parent requested during a dispute, but it did no such thing. Congress appears to have presumed instead that, if the Act's procedural requirements are respected, parents will prevail when they have legitimate grievances. See *Rowley* (noting the "legislative conviction that adequate compliance with the procedures prescribed would in most cases assure much if not all of what Congress wished in the way of substantive content in an IEP").

Petitioners' most plausible argument is that "[t]he ordinary rule, based on considerations of fairness, does not place the burden upon a litigant of establishing facts peculiarly within the knowledge of his adversary." But this "rule is far from being universal, and has many qualifications upon its application." School districts have a "natural advantage" in information and expertise, but Congress addressed this when it obliged schools to safeguard the procedural rights of parents and to share information with them. As noted above, parents have the right to review all records that the school possesses in relation to their child. § 1415(b)(1). They also have the right to an "independent educational evaluation of the[ir] child." Ibid. The regulations clarify this entitlement by providing that a "parent has the right to an independent educational evaluation at public expense if the parent disagrees with an evaluation obtained by the public agency." 34 CFR § 300.502(b)(1) (2005). IDEA thus ensures parents access to an expert who can evaluate all the materials that the school must make available, and who can give an independent opinion. They are not left to challenge the government without a realistic opportunity to access the necessary evidence, or without an expert with the firepower to match the opposition.

Additionally, in 2004, Congress added provisions requiring school districts to answer the subject matter of a complaint in writing, and to provide parents with the reasoning behind the disputed action, details about the other options considered and rejected by the IEP team, and a description of all evaluations, reports, and other factors that the school used in coming to its decision. § 615(c)(2)(B)(i)(I) of IDEA, as added by § 101 of Pub.L. 108–446, 118 Stat. 2718, 20 U.S.C. § 1415(c)(2)(B)(i)(I). Prior to a hearing, the parties must disclose evaluations and recommendations that they intend to rely upon. 20 U.S.C. § 1415(f)(2). IDEA hearings are deliberately informal and intended to give ALJs the flexibility that they need to ensure that each side can fairly present its evidence. IDEA, in fact, requires state authorities to organize hearings in a way that guarantees parents and children the procedural protections of the Act. See § 1415(a). Finally, and perhaps most importantly, parents may recover attorney's fees if they prevail. § 1415(i)(3)(B). These protections ensure that the school bears no unique informational advantage.

III

Finally, respondents and several States urge us to decide that States may, if they wish, override the default rule and put the burden always on the school district. Several States have laws or regulations purporting to do so, at least under some circumstances. See, e.g., Minn.Stat. § 125A.091, subd. 16 (2004); Ala. Admin. Code Rule 290–8–9–.08(8)(c)(6) (Supp.2004); Alaska Admin. Code, tit. 4, § 52.550(e)(9) (2003); Del.Code Ann., Tit. 14, § 3140 (1999). Because no such law or regulation exists in Maryland, we need not decide this issue today. JUSTICE BREYER contends that the allocation of the burden ought to be left entirely up to the States. But neither party made this argument before this Court or the courts below. We therefore decline to address it.

We hold no more than we must to resolve the case at hand: The burden of proof in an administrative hearing challenging an IEP is properly placed upon the party seeking relief. In this case, that party is Brian, as represented by his parents. But the rule applies with equal effect to school districts: If they seek to challenge an IEP, they will in turn bear the burden of persuasion before an ALJ. The judgment of the United States Court of Appeals for the Fourth Circuit is, therefore, affirmed.

It is so ordered.

■ THE CHIEF JUSTICE took no part in the consideration or decision of this case.

■ JUSTICE STEVENS, concurring.

It is common ground that no single principle or rule solves all cases by setting forth a general test for ascertaining the incidence of proof burdens when both a statute and its legislative history are silent on the question. Accordingly, I do not understand the majority to disagree with the proposition that a court, taking into account " 'policy considerations, convenience, and fairness' " (GINSBURG, J., dissenting), could conclude that the purpose of a statute is best effectuated by placing the burden of persuasion on the defendant. Moreover, I agree with much of what JUSTICE GINSBURG has written about the special aspects of this statute. I have, however, decided to join the Court's disposition of this case, not only for the reasons set forth in JUSTICE O'CONNOR's opinion, but also because I believe that we should presume that public school officials are properly performing their difficult responsibilities under this important statute.

■ JUSTICE GINSBURG, dissenting.

When the legislature is silent on the burden of proof, courts ordinarily allocate the burden to the party initiating the proceeding and seeking relief. As the Fourth Circuit recognized, however, "other factors," prime among them "policy considerations, convenience, and fairness," may warrant a different allocation. The Court has followed the same counsel. For reasons well stated by Circuit Judge Luttig, dissenting in the Court of Appeals, I am persuaded that "policy considerations, convenience, and fairness" call for assigning the burden of proof to the school district in this case.

The Individuals with Disabilities Education Act (IDEA), 20 U.S.C. § 1400 *et seq.*, was designed to overcome the pattern of disregard and neglect disabled children historically encountered in seeking access to public education. The IDEA is atypical in this respect: It casts an affirmative, beneficiary-specific obligation on providers of public education. School districts are charged with responsibility to offer to each disabled child an individualized education program (IEP) suitable to the child's special needs. 20 U.S.C. §§ 1400(d)(1), 1412(a)(4), 1414(d). The proponent of the IEP, it seems to me, is properly called upon to demonstrate its adequacy.

Familiar with the full range of education facilities in the area, and informed by "their experiences with other, similarly-disabled children," "the school district is . . . in a far better position to demonstrate that it has fulfilled [its statutory] obligation than the disabled student's parents are in to show that the school district has failed to do so." [U]nderstandably, school districts striving to balance their budgets, if "[l]eft to [their] own devices," will favor educational options that enable them to conserve resources. Saddled with a proof burden in administrative "due process" hearings, parents are likely to find a district-proposed IEP "resistant to challenge." Placing the burden on the district to show that its plan measures up to the statutorily mandated "free appropriate public education," 20 U.S.C. § 1400(d)(1)(A), will strengthen school officials' resolve to choose a course genuinely tailored to the child's individual needs.

[T]his case is illustrative. Not until the District Court ruled that the school district had the burden of persuasion did the school design an IEP that met Brian Schaffer's special educational needs. Had the school district, in the first instance, offered Brian a public or private school placement equivalent to the one the district ultimately provided, this entire litigation and its attendant costs could have been avoided.

Notably, nine States, as friends of the Court, have urged that placement of the burden of persuasion on the school district best comports with the IDEA's aim. See Brief for Commonwealth of Virginia *et al.* as *Amici Curiae.* If allocating the burden to school districts would saddle school systems with inordinate costs, it is doubtful that these States would have filed in favor of petitioners.

[I]t bears emphasis that "the vast majority of parents whose children require the benefits and protections provided in the IDEA" lack "knowledg[e] about the educational resources available to their [child]" and the "sophisticat[ion]" to mount an effective case against a district-proposed IEP. [quoting Judge Luttig's dissent below]; cf. 20 U.S.C. § 1400(c)(7)–(10). See generally Department of Education, M. Wagner, C. Marder, J. Blackorby, & D. Cardoso, The Children We Serve: The Demographic Characteristics of Elementary and Middle School Students with Disabilities and their Households (Sept.2002) (prepared under contract by SRI International, Special Education Elementary Longitudinal Study), http://www.seels.net/designdocs/SEELS_Children_ We_Serve_Report.pdf (as visited Nov. 8, 2005, and available in Clerk of Court's case file). In this setting, "the party with the 'bigger guns' also has better access to information, greater expertise, and an affirmative obligation to provide the contested services." Policy considerations, convenience, and fairness, I think it plain, point in the same direction. Their collective weight warrants a rule requiring a school district, in "due process" hearings, to explain persuasively why its proposed IEP satisfies the IDEA's standards. I would therefore reverse the judgment of the Fourth Circuit.

■ JUSTICE BREYER, dissenting.

[T]he statute's silence suggests that Congress did not think about the matter of the burden of persuasion. It is, after all, a relatively minor issue that should not often arise. That is because the parties will ordinarily introduce considerable evidence (as in this case where the initial 3-day hearing included testimony from 10 witnesses, 6 qualified as experts, and more than 50 exhibits). And judges rarely hesitate to weigh evidence, even highly technical evidence, and to decide a matter on the merits, even when the case is a close one. Thus, cases in which an administrative law judge (ALJ) finds the evidence in precise equipoise should be few and far between.

Nonetheless, the hearing officer held that before him was that *rara avis*—a case of perfect evidentiary equipoise. Hence we must infer from Congress' silence (and from the rest of the statutory scheme) which party—the parents or the school district—bears the burden of persuasion.

One can reasonably argue, as the Court holds, that the risk of nonpersuasion should fall upon the "individual desiring change." That, after all, is the rule courts ordinarily apply when an individual complains about the lawfulness of a government action. On the other hand, one can reasonably argue to the contrary, that, given the technical nature of the subject matter, its human importance, the school district's superior resources, and the district's superior access to relevant information, the risk of nonpersuasion ought to fall upon the district. My own view is that Congress took neither approach. It did not decide the "burden of persuasion" question; instead it left the matter to the States for decision.

The Act says that the "establish[ment]" of "procedures" is a matter for the "State" and its agencies. § 1415(a). It adds that the hearing in question, an administrative hearing, is to be conducted by the "State" or "local educational agency." 20 U.S.C. § 1415(f)(1)(A). And the statute as a whole foresees state implementation of federal standards. The minimum federal procedural standards that the Act specifies are unrelated to the "burden of persuasion" question. And different States, consequently and not surprisingly, have resolved it in different ways. See, e.g., Alaska Admin. Code, tit. 4, § 52.550(e)(9) (2003) (school district bears burden); Ala.Admin. Code Rule 290–8–9–.08(8)(c)(6)(ii)(I) (Supp.2004) (same); Conn.Agencies Regs. § 10–76h–14 (2005) (same); Del.Code Ann., Tit. 14, § 3140 (1999) (same); 1 D.C.Mun.Regs., tit. 5, § 3030.3 (2003) (same); W.Va.Code Rules § 126–16–8.1.11(c) (2005) (same); Ind.Admin.Code, tit. 511, Rule 7–30–3 (2003) (incorporating by reference Ind.Code § 4–21.5–3–14 (West 2002)) (moving party bears burden); 7 Ky.Admin.Regs., tit. 707, ch. 1:340, § 7(4) (2004) (incorporating by reference Ky.Rev.Stat.Ann. § 13B.090(7) (Lexis 2003)) (same); Ga.Comp.Rules & Regs., Rule 160–4–7–.18(1)(g)(8) (2002) (burden varies depending upon remedy sought); Minn.Stat.Ann. § 125A.091, subd. 16 (West Supp.2005) (same). There is no indication that this lack of uniformity has proved harmful.

Nothing in the Act suggests a need to fill every interstice of the Act's remedial scheme with a uniform federal rule. And should some such need arise—*i.e.*, if nonuniformity or a particular state approach were to prove problematic—the Federal Department of Education, expert in the area, might promulgate a uniform federal standard, thereby limiting state choice. 20 U.S.C. § 1406(a). [M]ost importantly, Congress has made clear that the Act itself represents an exercise in "cooperative federalism." Respecting the States' right to decide this procedural matter here, where education is at issue, where expertise matters, and where costs are shared, is consistent with that cooperative approach. And judicial respect for such congressional determinations is important. Indeed, in today's technologically and legally complex world, whether court decisions embody that kind of judicial respect may represent the true test of federalist principle.

Maryland has no special state law or regulation setting forth a special IEP-related burden of persuasion standard. But it does have rules of state administrative procedure and a body of state administrative law. The state ALJ should determine how those rules, or other state law, applies to this case. Because the state ALJ did not do this (*i.e.*, he looked for a federal, not a state, burden of persuasion rule), I would remand this case.

Arlington Central Sch. Dist. v. Murphy

Supreme Court of the United States, 2006.
548 U.S. 291.

■ JUSTICE ALITO delivered the opinion of the Court.

The Individuals with Disabilities Education Act (IDEA or Act) provides that a court "may award reasonable attorneys' fees as part of the costs" to parents who prevail in an action brought under the Act. 111 Stat. 92, 20 U.S.C. § 1415(i)(3)(B). We granted *certiorari* to decide whether this fee-shifting provision authorizes prevailing parents to recover fees for services rendered by experts in IDEA actions. We hold that it does not.

I

Respondents Pearl and Theodore Murphy filed an action under the IDEA on behalf of their son, Joseph Murphy, seeking to require petitioner Arlington Central School District Board of Education to pay for their son's private school tuition for specified school years. Respondents prevailed in the District Court, and the Court of Appeals for the Second Circuit affirmed.

As prevailing parents, respondents then sought $29,350 in fees for the services of an educational consultant, Marilyn Arons, who assisted respondents throughout the IDEA proceedings. The District Court granted respondents' request in part. It held that only the value of Arons' time spent between the hearing request and the ruling in respondents' favor could properly be considered charges incurred in an "action or proceeding brought" under the Act, see 20 U.S.C. § 1415(i)(3)(B). This reduced the maximum recovery to $8,650. The District Court also held that Arons, a nonlawyer, could be compensated only for time spent on expert consulting services, not for time spent on legal representation, but it concluded that all the relevant time could be characterized as falling within the compensable category, and thus allowed compensation for the full $8,650.

The Court of Appeals for the Second Circuit affirmed. [W]e granted *certiorari*, to resolve the conflict among the Circuits with respect to whether Congress authorized the compensation of expert fees to prevailing parents in IDEA actions. We now reverse.

II

Our resolution of the question presented in this case is guided by the fact that Congress enacted the IDEA pursuant to the Spending Clause. U.S. Const., Art. I, § 8, cl. 1; see *Schaffer*. Like its statutory predecessor, the IDEA provides federal funds to assist state and local agencies in educating children with disabilities "and conditions such funding upon a State's compliance with extensive goals and procedures." *Rowley*.

Congress has broad power to set the terms on which it disburses federal money to the States, but when Congress attaches conditions to a State's acceptance of federal funds, the conditions must be set out "unambiguously," see *Pennhurst State School and Hospital v. Halderman,* 451 U.S. 1, 17 (1981); *Rowley*. "[L]egislation enacted pursuant to the spending power is much in the nature of a contract," and therefore, to be bound by "federally imposed conditions," recipients of federal funds must accept them "voluntarily and knowingly." *Pennhurst*. States cannot knowingly accept conditions of which they are "unaware" or which they are "unable to ascertain." Thus, in the present case, we must view the IDEA from the perspective of a state official who is engaged in the process of deciding whether the State should accept IDEA funds and the obligations that go with those funds. We must ask whether such a state official would clearly understand that one of the obligations of the Act is the obligation to compensate prevailing parents for expert fees. In other words, we must ask whether the IDEA furnishes clear notice regarding the liability at issue in this case.

III

A

In considering whether the IDEA provides clear notice, we begin with the text. We have "stated time and again that courts must presume that a legislature says in a statute what it means and means in a statute what it says there." [T]he governing provision of the IDEA, 20 U.S.C. § 1415(i)(3)(B), provides that "[i]n any action or proceeding brought under this section, the court, in its discretion, may award reasonable attorneys' fees as part of the costs" to the parents of "a child with a disability" who is the "prevailing party." While this provision provides for an award of "reasonable attorneys' fees," this provision does not even hint that acceptance of IDEA funds makes a State responsible for reimbursing prevailing parents for services rendered by experts.

Respondents contend that we should interpret the term "costs" in accordance with its meaning in ordinary usage and that § 1415(i)(3)(B) should therefore be read to "authorize reimbursement of all costs parents incur in IDEA proceedings, including expert costs." [T]his argument has multiple flaws. For one thing, as the Court of Appeals in this case acknowledged, " 'costs' is a term of art that generally does not include expert fees." The use of this term of art, rather than a term such as "expenses," strongly suggests that § 1415(i)(3)(B) was not meant to be an open-ended provision that makes participating States liable for all expenses incurred by prevailing parents in connection with an IDEA case—for example, travel and lodging expenses or lost wages due to time taken off from work. Moreover, contrary to respondents' suggestion, § 1415(i)(3)(B) does not say that a court may award "costs" to prevailing parents; rather, it says that a court may award reasonable attorney's fees "as part of the costs" to prevailing parents. This language simply adds reasonable attorney's fees incurred by prevailing parents to the list of costs that prevailing parents are otherwise entitled to recover. This list of otherwise recoverable costs is obviously the list set out in 28 U.S.C. § 1920, the general statute governing the taxation of costs in federal court, and the recovery of witness fees under § 1920 is strictly limited by § 1821, which authorizes travel reimbursement and a $40 per diem. Thus, the text of 20 U.S.C. § 1415(i)(3)(B) does not authorize an award of any additional expert fees, and it certainly fails to provide the clear notice that is required under the Spending Clause.

Other provisions of the IDEA point strongly in the same direction. While authorizing the award of reasonable attorney's fees, the Act contains detailed provisions that are designed to ensure that such awards are indeed reasonable. See §§ 1415(i)(3)(C)–(G). The absence of any comparable provisions relating to expert fees strongly suggests that recovery of expert fees is not authorized. Moreover, the lack of any reference to expert fees in § 1415(d)(2) gives rise to a similar inference. This provision, which generally requires that parents receive "a full explanation of the procedural safeguards" available under § 1415 and refers expressly to "attorneys' fees," makes no mention of expert fees.

B

Respondents contend that their interpretation of § 1415(i)(3)(B) is supported by a provision of the Handicapped Children's Protection Act of 1986 that required the General Accounting Office (GAO) to collect certain data, § 4(b)(3), 100 Stat. 797 (hereinafter GAO study provision), but this provision is of little significance for present purposes. The GAO study provision directed the Comptroller General, acting through the GAO, to compile data on, among other things: "(A) the specific amount of attorneys' fees, costs, and expenses awarded to the prevailing party" in IDEA cases for a particular period of time, and (B) "the number of hours spent by personnel, including attorneys and consultants, involved in the action or proceeding, and expenses incurred by the parents and the State educational agency and local educational agency." Id., at 797–798.

Subparagraph (A) would provide some support for respondents' position if it directed the GAO to compile data on awards to prevailing parties of the expense of hiring consultants, but that is not what subparagraph (A) says. Subparagraph (A) makes no mention of consultants or experts or their fees.

Subparagraph (B) similarly does not help respondents. Subparagraph (B), which directs the GAO to study "the number of hours spent [in IDEA cases] by personnel, including . . . consultants," says nothing about the award of fees to such consultants. Just because Congress directed the GAO to compile statistics on the hours spent by consultants in IDEA cases, it does not follow that Congress meant for States to compensate prevailing parties for the fees billed by these consultants.

Respondents maintain that "Congress' direction to the GAO would be inexplicable if Congress did not anticipate that the expenses for 'consultants' would be recoverable," but this is incorrect. There are many reasons why Congress might have wanted the GAO to gather data on expenses that were not to be taxed as costs. Knowing the costs incurred by IDEA litigants might be useful in considering future procedural amendments (which might affect these costs) or a future amendment regarding fee shifting. And, in fact, it is apparent that the GAO study provision covered expenses that could not be taxed as costs. For example, the GAO was instructed to compile statistics on the hours spent by all attorneys involved in an IDEA action or proceeding, even though the Act did not provide for the recovery of attorney's fees by a prevailing state or local educational agency.[2] Similarly, the GAO was directed TO compile data on "expenses incurred by the parents," not just those parents who prevail and are thus eligible to recover taxed costs.

In sum, the terms of the IDEA overwhelmingly support the conclusion that prevailing parents may not recover the costs of experts or consultants. Certainly the terms of the IDEA fail to provide the clear notice that would be needed to attach such a condition to a State's receipt of IDEA funds.

---

[2] In 2000, the attorneys' fees provision provided only an award to prevailing parents. See 20 U.S.C. § 1415(i)(3)(B). In 2004, Congress amended § 1415(i)(3)(B) to include two additional awards. See § 101, 118 Stat. 2724. The amendments provided awards "to a prevailing party who is a State educational agency or local educational agency" where the complaint filed is frivolous or presented for an improper purpose, such as to harass, delay, or increase the cost of litigation. See 20 U.S.C.A. §§ 1415(i)(3)(B)(i)(II)–(III) (Supp.2006).

IV

Thus far, we have considered only the text of the IDEA, but perhaps the strongest support for our interpretation of the IDEA is supplied by our decisions and reasoning in *Crawford Fitting [Co. v. J.T. Gibbons, Inc.,]* 482 U.S. 437 [(1987)], and *[West Virginia Hospitals, Inc. v.] Casey*, 499 U.S. 83 [(1991)]. In light of those decisions, we do not see how it can be said that the IDEA gives a State unambiguous notice regarding liability for expert fees.

In *Crawford Fitting*, the Court rejected an argument very similar to respondents' argument that the term "costs" in § 1415(i)(3)(B) should be construed as an open-ended reference to prevailing parents' expenses. It was argued in *Crawford Fitting* that Federal Rule of Civil Procedure 54(d), which provides for the award of "costs" to a prevailing party, authorizes the award of costs not listed in 28 U.S.C. § 1821. The Court held, however, that Rule 54(d) does not give a district judge "discretion to tax whatever costs may seem appropriate"; rather, the term "costs" in Rule 54(d) is defined by the list set out in § 1920. Because the recovery of witness fees, see § 1920(3), is strictly limited by § 1821, the Court observed, a broader interpretation of Rule 54(d) would mean that the Rule implicitly effected a partial repeal of those provisions. But, the Court warned, "[w]e will not lightly infer that Congress has repealed §§ 1920 and 1821, either through Rule 54(d) or any other provision not referring explicitly to witness fees."

The reasoning of *Crawford Fitting* strongly supports the conclusion that the term "costs" in 20 U.S.C. § 1415(i)(3)(B), like the same term in Rule 54(d), is defined by the categories of expenses enumerated in 28 U.S.C. § 1920. This conclusion is buttressed by the principle, recognized in *Crawford Fitting*, that no statute will be construed as authorizing the taxation of witness fees as costs unless the statute "refer[s] explicitly to witness fees."

Our decision in *Casey* confirms even more dramatically that the IDEA does not authorize an award of expert fees. In *Casey*, [w]e interpreted a fee-shifting provision, 42 U.S.C. § 1988, the relevant wording of which was virtually identical to the wording of 20 U.S.C. § 1415(i)(3)(B). Compare *ibid.* (authorizing the award of "reasonable attorneys' fees as part of the costs" to prevailing parents) with 42 U.S.C. § 1988(b) (1988 ed.) (permitting prevailing parties in certain civil rights actions to be awarded "a reasonable attorney's fee as part of the costs"). We held that § 1988 did not empower a district court to award expert fees to a prevailing party. To decide in favor of respondents here, we would have to interpret the virtually identical language in 20 U.S.C. § 1415 as having exactly the opposite meaning. Indeed, we would have to go further and hold that the relevant language in the IDEA unambiguously means exactly the opposite of what the nearly identical language in 42 U.S.C. § 1988 was held to mean in *Casey*.

V

Respondents make several arguments that are not based on the text of the IDEA, but these arguments do not show that the IDEA provides clear notice regarding the award of expert fees.

Respondents argue that their interpretation of the IDEA furthers the Act's overarching goal of "ensur[ing] that all children with disabilities have available to them a free appropriate public education," 20 U.S.C. § 1400(d)(1)(A) as well as the goal of "safeguard[ing] the rights of parents to challenge school decisions that adversely affect their child." Brief for Respondents 20. These goals, however, are too general to provide much support for respondents' reading of the terms of the IDEA. The IDEA obviously does not seek to promote these goals at the expense of all other considerations, including fiscal considerations. Because the IDEA is not intended in all instances to further the broad goals identified by the respondents at the expense of fiscal considerations, the goals cited by respondents do little to bolster their argument on the narrow question presented here.

Finally, respondents vigorously argue that Congress clearly intended for prevailing parents to be compensated for expert fees. They rely on the legislative history of § 1415 and in particular on the following statement in the Conference Committee Report, discussed above: "The conferees intend that the term 'attorneys' fees as part of the costs' include reasonable expenses and fees of expert witnesses and the reasonable costs of any test or evaluation which is found to be necessary for the preparation of the . . . case." H.R.Conf.Rep.No.99–687, at 5, U.S.Code Cong. & Admin.News, 1986, pp. 1807, 1808.

Whatever weight this legislative history would merit in another context, it is not sufficient here. Putting the legislative history aside, we see virtually no support for respondents' position. Under these circumstances, where everything other than the legislative history overwhelming suggests that expert fees may not be recovered, the legislative history is simply not enough. In a Spending Clause case, the key is not what a majority of the Members of both Houses intend but what the States are clearly told regarding the conditions that go along with the acceptance of those funds. Here, in the face of the unambiguous text of the IDEA and the reasoning in *Crawford Fitting* and *Casey*, we cannot say that the legislative history on which respondents rely is sufficient to provide the requisite fair notice.

We reverse the judgment of the Court of Appeals for the Second Circuit and remand the case for further proceedings consistent with this opinion.

It is so ordered.

■ JUSTICE GINSBURG, concurring in part and concurring in the judgment.

I agree, in the main, with the Court's resolution of this case, but part ways with the Court's opinion in one respect. The Court extracts from *Pennhurst State School and Hospital v. Halderman*, 451 U.S. 1, 17 (1981), a "clear notice" requirement, and deems it applicable in this case because Congress enacted the Individuals with Disabilities Education Act (IDEA), as it did the legislation at issue in *Pennhurst*, pursuant to the Spending Clause. That extraction, in my judgment, is unwarranted. *Pennhurst*'s "clear notice" requirement should not be unmoored from its context. The Court there confronted a plea to impose "an unexpected condition for compliance—a new [programmatic] obligation for participating States." The controversy here is lower key: It concerns not the educational programs IDEA directs school districts to provide, but "the remedies available against a noncomplying [district]."

The Court's repeated references to a Spending Clause derived "clear notice" requirement, are questionable on other grounds as well. For one thing, IDEA was enacted not only pursuant to Congress' Spending Clause authority, but also pursuant to § 5 of the Fourteenth Amendment. Furthermore, no "clear notice" prop is needed in this case given the twin pillars on which the Court's judgment securely rests. First, as the Court explains, the specific, attorneys'-fees-oriented, provisions of IDEA, *i.e.*, 20 U.S.C. § 1415(i)(3)(B)–(G); § 1415(d)(2)(L), "overwhelmingly support the conclusion that prevailing parents may not recover the costs of experts or consultants." Those provisions place controls on fees recoverable for attorneys' services, without mentioning costs parents might incur for other professional services and controls geared to those costs. Second, as the Court develops, prior decisions closely in point "strongly suppor[t]," even "confir[m] . . . dramatically," today's holding that IDEA trains on attorneys' fees and does not authorize an award covering amounts paid or payable for the services of an educational consultant.

For the contrary conclusion, Justice BREYER's dissent relies dominantly on a Conference Report stating the conferees' view that the term "attorneys' fees as part of the costs" includes "expenses and fees of expert witnesses" and payments for tests necessary for the preparation of a case. H.R.Conf.Rep.No.99–687, p. 5 (1986) (internal quotation marks omitted). Including costs of consultants and tests in § 1415(i)(3)(B) would make good sense in light of IDEA's overarching goal, i.e., to provide a "free appropriate public education" to children with disabilities, § 1400(d)(1)(A). But Congress did not compose § 1415(i)(3)(B)'s text,[2] as it did the texts of other statutes too numerous and varied to ignore, to alter the common import of the terms "attorneys' fees" and "costs" in the context of expense-allocation legislation. See, e.g., 42 U.S.C. § 1988(c) (2000 ed. and Supp. III) (added in 1991 specifically to "include expert fees as part of the attorney's fee"); *Casey*, 499 U.S., at 88–92, and n.4 (citing variously composed statutes that "explicitly shift expert . . . fees as well as attorney's fees"). Given the constant meaning of the formulation "attorneys' fees as part of the costs" in federal legislation, we are not at liberty to rewrite "the statutory text adopted by both Houses of Congress and submitted to the President," to add several words Congress wisely might have included. The ball, I conclude, is properly left in Congress' court to provide, if it so elects, for consultant fees and testing expenses beyond those IDEA and

---

[2] At the time the Conference Report was submitted to the Senate and House, sponsors of the legislation did not mention anything on the floor about expert or consultant fees. They were altogether clear, however, that the purpose of the legislation was to "reverse" this Court's decision in *Smith v. Robinson*, 468 U.S. 992 (1984). In Smith, the Court held that, under the statute as then designed, prevailing parents were not entitled to attorneys' fees. See 132 Cong.Rec. 16823 (1986) (remarks of Sen. Weicker) ("In adopting this legislation, we are rejecting the reasoning of the Supreme Court in Smith versus Robinson."); *id.*, at 16824 (remarks of Sen. Kerry) ("This vital legislation reverses a U.S. Supreme Court decision Smith versus Robinson [.]"); *id.*, at 17608–17609 (remarks of Rep. Bartlett) ("I support those provisions in the conference agreement that, in response to the Supreme Court decision in . . . Smith versus Robinson, authoriz[e] the awarding of reasonable attorneys' fees to parents who prevail in special education court cases."); *id.*, at 17609 (remarks of Rep. Biaggi) ("This legislation clearly supports the intent of Congress back in 1975 and corrects what I believe was a gross misinterpretation of the law. Attorneys' fees should be provided to those individuals who are being denied access to the educational system.").

its implementing regulations already authorize,[3] along with any specifications, conditions, or limitations geared to those fees and expenses Congress may deem appropriate. Cf. § 1415(i)(3)(B)–(G); § 1415(d)(2)(L) (listing only attorneys' fees, not expert or consulting fees, among the procedural safeguards about which school districts must inform parents).

In sum, although I disagree with the Court's rationale to the extent that it invokes a "clear notice" requirement tied to the Spending Clause, I agree with the Court's discussion of IDEA's terms, and of our decisions in *Crawford* and *Casey*. Accordingly, I concur in part in the Court's opinion, and join the Court's judgment.

■ JUSTICE SOUTER, dissenting.

I join JUSTICE BREYER's dissent and add this word only to say outright what would otherwise be implicit, that I agree with the distinction he draws between this case and *Barnes v. Gorman*, 536 U.S. 181 (2002). Beyond that, I emphasize the importance for me of § 4 of the Handicapped Children's Protection Act of 1986, 100 Stat. 797, as amended, 20 U.S.C.A. § 1415 note, which mandated the study by what is now known as the Government Accountability Office. That section, of equal dignity with the fee-shifting provision enacted by the same statute, makes JUSTICE BREYER's resort to the related Conference Report the reasonable course.

■ JUSTICE BREYER, with whom JUSTICE STEVENS and JUSTICE SOUTER join, dissenting.

The Individuals with Disabilities Education Act (IDEA or Act), 20 U.S.C.A. § 1400 *et seq.*, (Supp.2006), says that a court may "award reasonable attorneys' fees as part of the costs to the parents" who are prevailing parties. § 1415(i)(3)(B). Unlike the Court, I believe that the word "costs" includes, and authorizes payment of, the costs of experts. The word "costs" does not define its own scope. Neither does the phrase "attorneys' fees as part of costs." But Members of Congress did make clear their intent by, among other things, approving a Conference Report that specified that "the term 'attorneys' fees as part of the costs' include[s] reasonable expenses of expert witnesses and reasonable costs of any test or evaluation which is found to be necessary for the preparation of the parent or guardian's case in the action or proceeding." H.R.Conf.Rep.No. 99–687, p. 5 (1986), U.S.Code Cong. & Admin.News, 1986, pp. 1807, 1808. No Senator or Representative voiced any opposition to this statement in the discussion preceding the vote on the Conference Report—the last vote on the bill before it was sent to the President. I can find no good reason for this Court to interpret the language of this statute as meaning the precise opposite of what Congress told us it intended.

I

There are two strong reasons for interpreting the statutory phrase to include the award of expert fees. First, that is what Congress said it

---

[3]   Under 34 C.F.R. § 300.502(b)(1) (2005), a "parent has the right to an independent educational evaluation at public expense if the parent disagrees with an evaluation obtained by the public agency."

intended by the phrase. Second, that interpretation furthers the IDEA's statutorily defined purposes.

A

Congress added the IDEA's cost-shifting provision when it enacted the Handicapped Children's Protection Act of 1986 (HCPA), 100 Stat. 796. Senator Lowell Weicker introduced the relevant bill in 1985. 131 Cong.Rec. 1979–1980 (1985). As introduced, it sought to overturn this Court's determination that the then-current version of the IDEA (and other civil rights statutes) did not authorize courts to award attorneys' fees to prevailing parents in IDEA cases. See *Smith v. Robinson*, 468 U.S. 992 (1984). The bill provided that "[i]n any action or proceeding brought under this subsection, the court, in its discretion, may award a reasonable attorney's fee as part of the costs to a parent or legal representative of a handicapped child or youth who is the prevailing party." 131 Cong.Rec.1980; see S.Rep.No.99–112, p. 2 (1985).

After hearings and debate, several Senators introduced a new bill in the Senate that would have put a cap on attorneys' fees for legal services lawyers, but at the same time would have explicitly authorized the award of "a reasonable attorney's fee, reasonable witness fees, and other reasonable expenses of the civil action, in addition to the costs to a parent . . . who is the prevailing party." While no Senator objected to the latter provision, some objected to the cap. A bipartisan group of Senators, led by Senators Hatch and Weicker, proposed an alternative bill that authorized courts to award "a reasonable attorney's fee in addition to the costs to a parent" who prevailed.

Senator Weicker explained that the bill:

"will enable courts to compensate parents for whatever reasonable costs they had to incur to fully secure what was guaranteed to them by the EHA. As in other fee shifting statutes, it is our intent that such awards will include, at the discretion of the court, reasonable attorney's fees, necessary expert witness fees, and other reasonable expenses which were necessary for parents to vindicate their claim to a free appropriate public education for their handicapped child."

Not a word of opposition to this statement (or the provision) was voiced on the Senate floor, and S. 415 passed without a recorded vote. Id., at 21393.

The House version of the bill also reflected an intention to authorize recovery of expert costs. Following the House hearings, the Committee on Education and Labor produced a substitute bill that authorized courts to "award reasonable attorneys' fees, expenses and costs" to prevailing parents. H.R.Rep.No.99–296, pp. 1, 5 (1985). The House Report stated that

"The phrase 'expenses and costs' includes expenses of expert witnesses; the reasonable costs of any study, report, test, or project which is found to be necessary for the preparation of the parents' or guardian's due process hearing, state administrative review or civil action; as well as traditional costs and expenses incurred in the course of litigating a case (e.g., depositions and interrogatories)."

No one objected to this statement. By the time H.R. 1523 reached the floor, another substitute bill was introduced. 131 Cong.Rec. 31369 (1985). This new bill did not change in any respect the text of the authorization of expenses and costs. It did add a provision, however, that directed the General Accounting Office (GAO)—now known as the Government Accountability Office, see 31 U.S.C.A. § 731 note (Supp.2006)—to study and report to Congress on the fiscal impact of the cost-shifting provision. The newly substituted bill passed the House without a recorded vote.

Members of the House and Senate (including all of the primary sponsors of the HCPA) then met in conference to work out certain differences. At the conclusion of those negotiations, they produced a Conference Report, which contained the text of the agreed-upon bill and a "Joint Explanatory Statement of the Committee of the Conference." See H.R.Conf.Rep.No.99–687 (1986), U.S.Code Cong. & Admin.News, 1986, pp. 1807. The Conference accepted the House bill's GAO provision with "an amendment expanding the data collection requirements of the GAO study to include information regarding the amount of funds expended by local educational agencies and state educational agencies on civil actions and administrative proceedings." And it accepted (with minor changes) the cost-shifting provisions provided in both the Senate and House versions. The conferees explained:

> "With slightly different wording, both the Senate bill and the House amendment provide for the awarding of attorneys' fees in addition to costs. The Senate recedes to the House and the House recedes to the Senate with an amendment clarifying that 'the court, in its discretion, may award reasonable attorneys' fees as part of the costs . . . ' This change in wording incorporates the Supreme Court['s] *Marek v. Chesny* decision [473 U.S. 1 (1985)]. The conferees intend that the term 'attorneys' fees as part of the costs' include reasonable expenses and fees of expert witnesses and the reasonable costs of any test or evaluation which is found to be necessary for the preparation of the parent or guardian's case in the action or proceeding, as well as traditional costs incurred in the course of litigating a case."

The Conference Report was returned to the Senate and the House. A motion was put to each to adopt the Conference Report, and both the Senate and the House agreed to the Conference Report by voice votes. No objection was raised to the Conference Report's statement that the cost-shifting provision was intended to authorize expert costs. I concede that "sponsors of the legislation did not mention anything on the floor about expert or consultant fees" at the time the Conference Report was submitted. But I do not believe that silence is significant in light of the fact that every Senator and three of the five Representatives who spoke on the floor had previously signed his name to the Conference Report— a Report that made Congress' intent clear on the first page of its explanation. And every Senator and Representative that took the floor preceding the votes voiced his strong support for the Conference Report. The upshot is that Members of both Houses of Congress voted to adopt both the statutory text before us and the Conference Report that made clear that the statute's words include the expert costs here in question.

B

The Act's basic purpose further supports interpreting the provision's language to include expert costs. The IDEA guarantees a "free" and "appropriate" public education for "all" children with disabilities. 20 U.S.C.A. § 1400(d)(1)(A). [P]arents have every right to become involved in the Act's efforts to provide that education; indeed, the Act encourages their participation. § 1400(c)(5)(B) (IDEA "ensur[es] that families of [disabled] children have meaningful opportunities to participate in the education of their children at school"). It assures parents that they may question a school district's decisions about what is "appropriate" for their child. And in doing so, they may secure the help of experts. § 1415(h)(1) (parents have "the right to be accompanied and advised by counsel and by individuals with special knowledge or training with respect to the problems of children with disabilities").

The practical significance of the Act's participatory rights and procedural protections may be seriously diminished if parents are unable to obtain reimbursement for the costs of their experts. In IDEA cases, experts are necessary. See *Is Mediation a Fair Way to Resolve Special Education Disputes? First Empirical Findings*, 2 Harv. Negotiation L.Rev. 35, 40 (1997) (detailing findings of study showing high correlation between use of experts and success of parents in challenging school district's plan); Kuriloff, *Is Justice Served by Due Process?: Affecting the Outcome of Special Education Hearings in Pennsylvania*, 48 Law & Contemp. Prob. 89, 100–101, 109 (1985) (same); see also Brief for National Disability Rights Network *et al.* as *Amici Curiae* 6–15 (collecting sources); cf. *Schaffer* (GINSBURG, J., dissenting) ("[T]he vast majority of parents whose children require the benefits and protections provided in the IDEA lack knowledge about the educational resources available to their child and the sophistication to mount an effective case against a district-proposed IEP").

Experts are also expensive. See Brief for Respondents 28, n. 17 (collecting District Court decisions awarding expert costs ranging from $200 to $7,600, and noting three reported cases in which expert awards exceeded $10,000). The costs of experts may not make much of a dent in a school district's budget, as many of the experts they use in IDEA proceedings are already on the staff. But to parents, the award of costs may matter enormously. Without potential reimbursement, parents may well lack the services of experts entirely. See Department of Education, M. Wagner *et al.*, The Individual and Household Characteristics of Youth With Disabilities: A Report from the National Longitudinal Transition Study-2 (NLTS-2), pp. 3–5 (Aug.2003) (finding that 25% of disabled children live in poverty and 65% live in households with incomes less than $50,000); see Department of Education, M. Wagner *et al.*, The Children We Serve: The Demographic Characteristics of Elementary and Middle School Students with Disabilities and Their Households, p. 28 (Sept.2002), available at http://www.seels.net/designdocs/SEELS_Children_We_Serve_Report.pdf (as visited June 23, 2006, and available in Clerk of Court's case file) (finding that 36% of disabled children live in households with incomes of $25,000 or less).

In a word, the Act's statutory right to a "free" and "appropriate" education may mean little to those who must pay hundreds of dollars to obtain it. That is why this Court has previously avoided interpretations that would bring about this kind of result. See *Burlington; Carter*. [I]n *Carter*, we explained: "IDEA was intended to ensure that children with disabilities receive an education that is both appropriate and free. To read the provisions of § 1401(a)(18) to bar reimbursement in the circumstances of this case would defeat this statutory purpose."

To read the word "costs" as requiring successful parents to bear their own expenses for experts suffers from the same problem. Today's result will leave many parents and guardians "without an expert with the firepower to match the opposition," a far cry from the level playing field that Congress envisioned.

II

The majority makes essentially three arguments against this interpretation. It says that the statute's purpose and "legislative history is simply not enough" to overcome: (1) the fact that this is a Spending Clause case; (2) the text of the statute; and (3) our prior cases which hold that the term "costs" does not include expert costs. I do not find these arguments convincing.

A

[I] agree that the statute on its face does not clearly tell the States that they must pay expert fees to prevailing parents. But I do not agree that the majority has posed the right question. For one thing, we have repeatedly examined the nature and extent of the financial burdens that the IDEA imposes without reference to the Spending Clause or any "clear-statement rule." See, e.g., *Burlington*; (private school fees); *Carter* (same); *Smith*, (attorneys' fees); *Garret F.* (continuous nursing service). Those cases did not ask whether the statute "furnishes clear notice" to the affirmative obligation or liability at issue.

For another thing, neither *Pennhurst* nor any other case suggests that every spending detail of a Spending Clause statute must be spelled out with unusual clarity. To the contrary, we have held that Pennhurst's requirement that Congress "unambiguously" set out "a condition on the grant of federal money" does not necessarily apply to legislation setting forth "the *remedies* available against a noncomplying State." *Bell v. New Jersey*, 461 U.S. 773, 790, n.17 (1983) (emphasis added). We have added that Pennhurst does not require Congress "specifically" to "identify" and "proscribe each condition in [Spending Clause] legislation." *Jackson v. Birmingham Bd. of Ed.*, 544 U.S. 167, 183 (2005). And we have denied any implication that "suits under Spending Clause legislation are suits in contract, or that contract-law principles apply to all issues that they raise." *Barnes v. Gorman*, 536 U.S. 181, 188–189, n.2 (2002).

[P]ermitting parents to recover expert fees will not lead to awards of "indeterminate magnitude, untethered to compensable harm" and consequently will not "pose a concern that recipients of federal funding could not reasonably have anticipated." *Barnes* (SOUTER, J., joined by O'CONNOR, J., concurring) (citation and internal quotation marks omitted). Unlike, say, punitive damages, an award of costs to expert parties is neither "unorthodox" nor "indeterminate," and thus does not throw into doubt whether the States would have entered into the program. If determinations as to whether the IDEA requires States to provide continuing nursing services, *Cedar Rapids*, *supra*, or reimbursement for private school tuition, *Burlington*, *supra*, do not call for linguistic clarity, then the precise content of recoverable "costs" does not call for such clarity here *a fortiori*.

B

If the Court believes that the statute's language is unambiguous, I must disagree. The provision at issue says that a court "may award reasonable attorneys' fees as part of the costs" to parents who prevail in an action brought under the Act. 20 U.S.C.A. § 1415(i)(3)(B) (Supp.2006). The statute neither defines the word "costs" nor points to any other source of law for a definition. And the word "costs," alone, says nothing at all about which costs falls within its scope.

C

The majority's most persuasive argument does not focus on either the Spending Clause or lack of statutory ambiguity. Rather, the majority says that "costs" is a term of art. In light of the law's long practice of excluding expert fees from the scope of the word "costs," along with this Court's cases interpreting the word similarly in other statutes, the "legislative history is simply not enough."

I am perfectly willing to assume that the majority is correct about the traditional scope of the word "costs." In two cases this Court has held that the word "costs" is limited to the list set forth in 28 U.S.C. § 1920 and does not include fees paid to experts. See *Crawford Fitting*; *Casey*. But Congress is free to redefine terms of art. And we have suggested that it might well do so through a statutory provision worded in a manner similar to the statute here—indeed, we cited the Conference Report language here at issue.

Regardless, here the statute itself indicates that Congress did not intend to use the word "costs" as a term of art. The HCPA, which added the cost-shifting provision (in § 2) to the IDEA, also added another provision (in § 4) directing the GAO to "conduct a study of the impact of the amendments to the [IDEA] made by section 2" over a 3 1/2 year period following the Act's effective date. § 4(a), 100 Stat. 797. To determine the fiscal impact of § 2 (the cost-shifting provision), § 4 ordered the GAO to submit a report to Congress containing, among other things, the following information:

> "Data, for a geographically representative select sample of States, indicating (A) the specific amount of attorneys' fees, costs, and expenses awarded to the prevailing party, in each action and proceeding under [§ 2] from the date of the enactment of this Act through fiscal year 1988, and the range of such fees, costs and expenses awarded in the actions and proceedings under such section, categorized by type of complaint and (B) for the same sample as in (A) the number of hours spent by personnel, including attorneys and consultants, involved in the action or proceeding, and expenses incurred by the parents and the State educational agency and local educational agency." § 4(b)(3), id., at 797–798.

If Congress intended the word "costs" in § 2 to authorize an award of only those costs listed in the federal cost statute, why did it use the word "expenses" in § 4(b)(3)(A) as part of the "amount awarded to the prevailing party"? When used as a term of art, after all, "costs" does not cover expenses. Nor does the federal costs statute cover any expenses—at least not any that Congress could have wanted the GAO to study. Cf. 28 U.S.C. § 1920 (referring only once to "expenses," and doing so solely to refer to special interpretation services provided in actions initiated by the United States).

Further, why did Congress, when asking the GAO (in the statute itself) to study the "numbers of hours spent by personnel" include among those personnel both attorneys "and consultants"? Who but experts could those consultants be? Why would Congress want the GAO to study the hours that those experts "spent," unless it thought that it would help keep track of the "costs" that the statute imposed?

[F]or these reasons, I respectfully dissent.

NOTES ON *SCHAFFER* AND *ARLINGTON CENTRAL*

It is too soon to know what the effects of *Schaffer* and *Arlington Central* will be. But one could safely predict that the two cases will make it significantly harder for parents to challenge schools' IEP decisions. Because school officials presumably have expertise in educational decisions, frequently the only way for parents to carry their *Schaffer* burden and prove that the school's educational decisions are incorrect will be to introduce expert testimony of their own. Indeed, the *Rowley* deference principle makes challenging a school district's educational decisions especially hard. But, because *Arlington Central* requires parents to finance expert witness fees out of their own pockets, it will be very difficult to obtain the necessary expert testimony. See Kelly D. Thomason, Note, *The Costs of a "Free" Education: The Impact of Schaffer v. Weast and Arlington v. Murphy on Litigation Under the IDEA*, 57 Duke L.J. 457 (2007).

Payne v. Peninsula School Dist.

United States Court of Appeals for the Ninth Circuit, *en banc*, 2011.
653 F.3d 863.

■ BYBEE, CIRCUIT JUDGE.

We agreed to rehear this case en banc to clarify under what circumstances the IDEA's exhaustion requirement bars non-IDEA federal or state law claims.

Appellant Windy Payne, on behalf of herself and her son, D.P., appeals the district court's grant of summary judgment to the defendants. The district court dismissed her claim for lack of subject matter jurisdiction because Payne did not initially seek relief in a due process hearing and therefore failed to comply with one of the exhaustion-of-remedies requirement of the Individuals with Disabilities Education Act ("IDEA"), 20 U.S.C. § 1415(*l*). We hold that (1) the IDEA's exhaustion requirement is not jurisdictional, and (2) Payne's non-IDEA federal and state-law claims are not subject to the IDEA's exhaustion requirement. We therefore reverse.

I

The facts in this case, and the inferences to be drawn from them, are vigorously contested by the parties. Because Payne is appealing an adverse grant of summary judgment, we review this case de novo and state the facts in the light most favorable to her case, although we outline only the facts material to our decision.

D.P. is a minor who was diagnosed with oral motor apraxia and autism when he was five years old. During the 2003–04 school year, when D.P. was seven, he was placed in a contained special education classroom within Artondale Elementary School, part of the Peninsula School District. Defendant Jodi Coy was his teacher that year. Coy employed a small room about the size of a closet as a time-out room or "safe room" for students who became "overly stimulated."

At a meeting to discuss D.P.'s Individual Education Program ("IEP") and Behavior Assessment Plan, Coy requested permission to use the time-out room while the IEP paperwork was pending. The Paynes initially objected, claiming that their son was unable to perceive a difference between positive and negative reinforcement. They eventually gave limited consent to the time-out room, specifying that they would agree to allow Coy to use the room for time-out periods only (and not punishment), but that the door had to remain open and that D.P. was not to be left alone inside the room. According to Payne, Coy nonetheless used the room to punish D.P. and locked him in the closet a number of times without supervision. In some instances, D.P. responded by removing his clothing and urinating or defecating on himself. Although the Paynes repeatedly requested that Coy stop using her "aversive therapy" techniques, Coy continued. Eventually, in January 2004, Coy refused to allow the Paynes to visit her classroom or pick up their son directly from the classroom, insisting that the Paynes might misinterpret what they observed.

The Paynes and the school district underwent mediation, and they agreed that D.P. would transfer to another school in the district. Later, the Paynes removed D.P. from the public school system and began home schooling him. They never underwent a formal due process hearing with the school district.

In 2005, Windy Payne filed the current complaint on behalf of herself and her son, seeking relief under 42 U.S.C. § 1983 by alleging violations of the Fourth, Eighth, and Fourteenth Amendments, and the IDEA. The complaint also advanced negligence and outrage claims under Washington law. The defendants moved for summary judgment, claiming that Payne had failed to exhaust her remedies as required by 20 U.S.C. § 1415(*l*) by failing to go through the informal due process hearing and appeal process established by 20 U.S.C. § 1415(f), (g). The district court dismissed Payne's entire case, citing our decision in *Robb v. Bethel School District # 403,* 308 F.3d 1047 (9th Cir.2002), where we held that the IDEA's exhaustion requirement applied to any case in which "a plaintiff has alleged injuries that could be redressed to any degree by the IDEA's administrative procedures and remedies."

Payne timely appealed. In a divided decision, a panel of this court affirmed the district court's grant of summary judgment. [O]n a vote of the majority of nonrecused active judges on our court, we vacated the panel opinion and agreed to rehear this case en banc.

II

We begin by clarifying the nature of the IDEA's exhaustion requirement. Adhering to this circuit's precedent, the original panel treated the requirement as a jurisdictional one, but questioned the soundness of this conclusion. Indeed, the conclusion it reached was consistent with our precedent. In light of a spate of Supreme Court cases clarifying the difference between provisions limiting our subject matter jurisdiction, which cannot be waived and must be pled in the complaint, and "claims processing provisions," which must be pled as an affirmative defense or forfeited, we now overrule our previous treatment of § 1415(*l*) and hold that the IDEA's exhaustion requirement is a claims processing provision that IDEA defendants may offer as an affirmative defense.

[T]he IDEA's exhaustion requirement provides:

> Nothing in this chapter shall be construed to restrict or limit the rights, procedures, and remedies available under the Constitution, the Americans with Disabilities Act of 1990 [42 U.S.C. § 12101 et seq.], title V of the Rehabilitation Act of 1973 [29 U.S.C. § 791 et seq.], or other Federal laws protecting the rights of children with disabilities, *except that before the filing of a civil action under such laws seeking relief that is also available under this subchapter, the procedures under subsections (f) and (g) shall be exhausted to the same extent as would be required had the action been brought under this subchapter.*

20 U.S.C. § 1415(*l*) (emphasis added). The Fourth and Eighth Circuits share our earlier assumption that this language creates a jurisdictional limitation. *See, e.g., MM ex rel. DM v. Sch. Dist. of Greenville Cnty.,* 303 F.3d 523, 536 (4th Cir.2002) ("The failure of the Parents to exhaust their administrative remedies . . . deprives us of subject matter jurisdiction over those claims . . . ."); *Urban by Urban v. Jefferson Cnty. Sch. Dist. R-1,* 89 F.3d 720, 725 (10th Cir.1996) ("We conclude that the district court correctly dismissed the [unexhausted] claims for lack of jurisdiction."). By contrast, the Seventh and Eleventh Circuits have treated the exhaustion requirement as an affirmative defense, rather than a jurisdictional requirement. *See, e.g., Mosely v. Bd. of Educ.,* 434 F.3d 527, 533 (7th Cir.2006) ("A failure to exhaust is normally considered to be an affirmative defense, and we see no reason to treat it differently here." (citation omitted)); *N.B. by D.G. v. Alachua Cnty. Sch. Bd.,* 84 F.3d 1376, 1379 (11th Cir.1996) (per curiam) ("The exhaustion requirement . . . is not jurisdictional . . . .").

Last Term, the Supreme Court reminded us that "the word 'jurisdiction' has been used by courts . . . to convey 'many, too many, meanings'" and "cautioned . . . against profligate use of the term." *Union Pac. R.R. Co. v. Bhd. of Locomotive Eng'rs & Trainmen Gen. Comm. of Adjustment, Cent. Region,* 558 U.S. 67, 130 S.Ct. 584, 596 (2009) (quoting *Steel Co. v. Citizens for a Better Env't,* 523 U.S. 83, 90 (1998)). "Accordingly, the term 'jurisdictional' properly applies only to 'prescriptions delineating the classes of cases (subject-matter jurisdiction) and the persons (personal jurisdiction)' implicating [the court's adjudicatory] authority." The Court confessed that "[w]hile perhaps clear in theory, the distinction between jurisdictional conditions and claim-processing rules can be confusing in practice," that we should "us[e] the term 'jurisdictional' only when it is apposite," and that we should "curtail . . . 'drive-by jurisdictional rulings.'"

Two cases recently decided by the Court are instructive. In *Reed Elsevier*[, Inc. v. Muchnick, 559 U.S. 154 (2010)], the Court examined a provision of the Copyright Act providing that copyright holders must register their works before bringing suit for copyright infringement. Section 41(a) of the Copyright Act provides that "no civil action for infringement of the copyright in any United States work shall be instituted until preregistration or registration of the copyright claim has been made in accordance with this title." 17 U.S.C. § 411(a). Holding that § 411(a) is not jurisdictional, the Court pointed to three factors. First, the Court pointed out that § 411(a) does not " 'clearly state[ ]' that its registration requirement is 'jurisdictional.'" Second, the Court noted that § 411(a) was separate from other statutes that grant subject matter jurisdiction and that neither 28 U.S.C. § 1331 nor 28 U.S.C. § 1338—which is specific to copyright—mentions the registration requirement. Finally, the Court could not find "any other factor [that] suggest[s] that 17 U.S.C. § 411(a)'s registration requirement can be read to 'speak in jurisdictional terms or refer in any way to the jurisdiction of the district courts.'"

In *Jones v. Bock,* 549 U.S. 199 (2007), the Court addressed whether the Prison Litigation Reform Act's ("PLRA") exhaustion requirement[2] was a pleading requirement that the prisoner must include in his complaint or an affirmative defense that the defendant must raise. The Court held that "failure to exhaust is an affirmative defense under the PLRA, and that inmates are not required to specially plead or demonstrate exhaustion in their complaints." Although the Court did not treat a heightened pleading requirement as going to the jurisdiction of the federal courts, the Court's conclusion—that PLRA defendants have the burden of pleading non-exhaustion, and that PLRA plaintiffs need not specifically plead exhaustion in their initial complaints—is consonant with our discussion of jurisdictional versus claim-processing requirements. If a requirement is jurisdictional, then a federal plaintiff has the burden of pleading in her initial complaint (however briefly) how that requirement has been met. *See* Fed.R.Civ.P. 8(a)(1). In other words, even though the Court did not state its result in such terms, it follows from *Jones* that the PLRA's exhaustion requirement is non-jurisdictional.

With that background we return to the IDEA's exhaustion requirement in § 1415(*l*) and to our prior statement that "[i]f a plaintiff is required to exhaust administrative remedies, but fails to, federal courts are without jurisdiction to hear the plaintiff's claim." First, we observe that nothing in § 1415 mentions the jurisdiction of the federal courts. In fact,

---

[2] The PLRA exhaustion provision reads:

No action shall be brought with respect to prison conditions under section 1983 of this title, or any other Federal law, by a prisoner confined in any jail, prison, or other correctional facility until such administrative remedies as are available are exhausted.

42 U.S.C. § 1997e(a).

neither the word "courts" nor the word "jurisdiction" appears in § 1415(*l*). Section 1415 is written as a restriction on the rights of plaintiffs to bring suit, rather than as a limitation on the power of the federal courts to hear the suit. That textual choice strongly suggests that the restriction may be enforced by defendants but that the exhaustion requirement may be waived or forfeited.

Second, nothing in the relevant jurisdictional statutes requires exhaustion under the IDEA. Section 1415(*l*) provides that if the plaintiff is "seeking relief that is also available under [the IDEA], the procedures under [20 U.S.C. § 1415(f), (g)] shall be exhausted to the same extent as would be required had the action been brought under this subchapter." Section 1415(i) describes the actions that can be brought under the IDEA. A party who is "aggrieved by the findings and decision" made under the IDEA's procedures has "the right to bring a civil action . . . in any State court of competent jurisdiction or in a district court of the United States, without regard to the amount in controversy." 20 U.S.C. § 1415(i)(2)(A). There is no restriction in this section on the subject matter jurisdiction of the federal courts. The only provision that arguably affects federal subject matter jurisdiction is the provision specifying that there is no amount-in-controversy requirement, and it appears to expand, rather than contract, federal jurisdiction. More to the point, the section expressly provides that suit may be brought in state or federal courts. As state courts are courts of general subject matter jurisdiction, it is hard to think that Congress would permit IDEA suits to be brought in state court but at the same time restrict the subject matter jurisdiction of the federal courts. Without clearer instruction from Congress, we are reluctant to infer such a restriction where Congress has not made it explicit.

Finally, we can find no reason why § 1415(*l*) should be read to make exhaustion a prerequisite to the exercise of federal subject matter jurisdiction. We can think of many good reasons why it should not. As we discuss in the next section, the exhaustion requirement in § 1415(*l*) is not a check-the-box kind of exercise. [I]n other words, the exhaustion requirement appears more flexible than a rigid jurisdictional limitation—questions about whether administrative proceedings would be futile, or whether dismissal of a suit would be consistent with the "general purposes" of exhaustion, are better addressed through a fact-specific assessment of the affirmative defense than through an inquiry about whether the court has the power to decide the case at all. If we were to hold that exhaustion was jurisdictional, the question of exhaustion *vel non* would haunt the entire proceeding, including any appeals. We would have the obligation to raise the issue *sua sponte,* a particularly frustrating exercise for parties and courts when Congress has authorized the parties to file suit in state court in the first place. Congress may, of course, override our concerns and make the IDEA's exhaustion requirement jurisdictional, but we would need a clearer statement of its intent before we will impose such a requirement.

In sum, we hold that the exhaustion requirement in § 1415(*l*) is not jurisdictional.

[III]

We now turn to the merits. We hold that the IDEA's exhaustion provision applies only in cases where the relief sought by a plaintiff in the pleadings is available under the IDEA. Non-IDEA claims that do not seek relief available under the IDEA are not subject to the exhaustion requirement, even if they allege injuries that could conceivably have been redressed by the IDEA. We overrule our previous cases to the extent that they state otherwise and conclude that, although the district court properly dismissed Payne's IDEA-based § 1983 claim, it should not have dismissed her non-IDEA claims on exhaustion grounds.

A

The IDEA was enacted to protect children with disabilities and their parents by requiring participating states to provide "a free appropriate public education [('FAPE')] that emphasizes special education and related services designed to meet [disabled students'] unique needs and prepare them for further education, employment, and independent living." 20 U.S.C. § 1400(d)(1)(A). Participating states must provide eligible students with a "free appropriate public education," *id.* § 1412(a)(1)(A), that, among other things, conforms to a proper IEP, *see id.* §§ 1412(a)(4), 1436(d), and ensures that disabled students "[t]o the maximum extent appropriate, . . . are educated with children who are not disabled," *id.* § 1412(a)(5)(A). Children with disabilities and their parents are provided with the extensive procedural protections set out in 20 U.S.C. § 1415. In particular, the statute requires states to provide aggrieved parties with the opportunity to mediate their disputes, *id.* § 1415(e), to secure an impartial due process hearing to resolve certain differences with state agencies, *id.* § 1415(f), and to appeal any decision and findings to the state educational agency, *id.* § 1415(g). As we have stated above, the exhaustion provision requires parties to avail themselves of these procedures (and the corresponding local appeals process) before resorting to the courts whenever they "seek[ ] relief that is also available under [the IDEA]." *Id.* § 1415(*l*).

The exhaustion requirement is found in § 1415(*l*). [W]e begin with a few observations. First, this provision is titled "Rule of construction." It thus provides us with a rule for harmonizing the IDEA with overlapping "rights, procedures, and remedies" found in other laws. Second, the rule of construction tells us in very plain terms that the IDEA must be construed to coexist with other remedies, including remedies available under the Constitution, the Americans with Disabilities Act ("ADA"), the Rehabilitation Act, and "other Federal laws." The principal remedy available for violations of the Constitution is 42 U.S.C. § 1983, which creates an action in law or suit in equity against any person who, acting under color of state law, deprives the plaintiff of "any rights, privileges, or immunities secured by the Constitution and laws." Like the IDEA, the ADA and the Rehabilitation Act create their own private causes of action to enforce those acts, *see* 42 U.S.C. § 12117; 29 U.S.C. § 794a, although all three acts have been enforced under § 1983 as well. *See, e.g., Marie O. v. Edgar,* 131 F.3d 610, 622 (7th Cir.1997); *K.M. ex rel. D.G. v. Hyde Park Cent. Sch. Dist.,* 381 F.Supp.2d 343, 361–63 (S.D.N.Y.2005); *BD v. DeBuono,* 130 F.Supp.2d 401, 427–29 (S.D.N.Y.2000). *But see Blanchard v. Morton Sch. Dist.,* 509 F.3d 934, 938 (9th Cir.2007) (holding that

§ 1983 does not authorize actions predicated on violations of the IDEA). Third, the exhaustion provision in § 1415(*l*) is framed as an exception to the general rule of construction that "[n]othing in [the IDEA] shall be construed to restrict" the rights, procedures, and remedies available under § 1983, the ADA, or the Rehabilitation Act. In other words, remedies available under the IDEA, by rule, are in addition to the remedies parents and students have under other laws. Indeed, § 1415 makes it clear that Congress understood that parents and students affected by the IDEA would likely have issues with schools and school personnel that could be addressed—and perhaps could only be addressed—through a suit under § 1983 or other federal laws. Finally, we observe that § 1415(*l*) requires exhaustion of IDEA remedies only when the civil action brought under § 1983, the ADA, the Rehabilitation Act, or other federal laws "seek[s] *relief that is also available*" under the IDEA. Thus, the "except" clause requires that parents and students exhaust the remedies available to them under the IDEA before they seek *the same relief* under other laws.

Our decision in Witte [*v. Clark County School Dist.*, 197 F.3d 1271 (9th Cir.1999),] is consistent with these principles. There, we recognized that the IDEA's exhaustion provision does not encompass every challenge concerning a school's treatment of a disabled student. The Wittes complained that school officials forced their disabled child to eat oatmeal (to which he was allergic) occasionally mixed with his own vomit, choked him, and subjected him to "take-downs" and other physical abuses. These actions were punitive responses to the child's bodily tics that resulted from Tourette's Syndrome. The Wittes eventually agreed with the school district to transfer their son to another school in the same district and then sued for compensatory and punitive damages under 42 U.S.C. § 1983, the Rehabilitation Act, the ADA, and state tort law. The district court granted the defendants summary judgment on the ground that the Wittes had failed to exhaust their administrative remedies under the IDEA.

We reversed. We held that the IDEA's exhaustion provision did not apply to plaintiffs who claimed that school officials had inflicted physical and emotional abuse on their child, when their complaint sought only retrospective damages because the parties had already resolved their educational issues through "the remedies that are available under the IDEA." We emphasized that because monetary damages were ordinarily unavailable under the IDEA, the plaintiffs were "not seeking relief that is also available under the IDEA." Accordingly, "under the plain words of the statute, exhaustion of administrative remedies is not required."

We subsequently took a more muscular view of § 1415(*l*) in *Robb [v. Bethel School Dist. #403*, 308 F.3d 1047 (9th Cir.2002)]*, holding "that when a plaintiff has alleged injuries that could be redressed to any degree by the IDEA's administrative procedures and remedies, exhaustion of those remedies is required." *Robb* involved a student who was diagnosed with cerebral palsy and was regularly removed from her classroom "for extended 'peer-tutoring' by junior high school and high school students without the supervision of a certified teacher." This tutoring took place on the floor of a dim hallway without a chair or desk. No additional abuse was alleged. Taking guidance from *Witte,* the Robbs limited their prayer for relief to money damages, but specified that they were for "lost educational opportunities and emotional distress, humiliation, embarrassment, and psychological injury." The district court held that the Robbs had not exhausted their administrative remedies.

We affirmed in a divided decision. The panel majority expressed concern that parents might "be permitted to opt out of the IDEA simply by making a demand for money or services the IDEA does not provide." [W]e held "that a plaintiff cannot avoid the IDEA's exhaustion requirement merely by limiting a prayer for relief to money damages." We then adopted the rule that the IDEA's exhaustion requirement applied to any case in which a plaintiff "alleged injuries that could be redressed *to any degree* by the IDEA's administrative procedures and remedies." In a number of subsequent cases, we have reaffirmed *Robb*'s "injury-centered" approach.

Furthermore, the Seventh and Tenth Circuits have adopted "injury-centered" tests similar to the one we adopted in *Robb*. [O]ther circuits have generally agreed that plaintiffs cannot evade the exhaustion requirement simply by limiting their prayer for relief to a request for damages. However, these courts have not articulated a comprehensive standard for determining when exactly the exhaustion requirement applies.

B

We now clarify and restate the proper method for resolving IDEA exhaustion cases, and we overrule *Robb* to the extent it is inconsistent with our decision. The IDEA's exhaustion requirement applies to claims only to the extent that the relief actually sought by the plaintiff could have been provided by the IDEA. In other words, we reject the "injury-centered" approach developed by *Robb* and hold that a "relief-centered" approach more aptly reflects the meaning of the IDEA's exhaustion requirement.

1

[I]n a way, our approach in *Robb* treated § 1415(*l*) as a quasi-preemption provision, requiring administrative exhaustion for any case that falls within the general "field" of educating disabled students.

For reasons we have explained, this approach is inconsistent with the IDEA's exhaustion provision. The statute specifies that exhaustion is required "before the filing of a civil action . . . seeking *relief* that is also available under [the IDEA]." 20 U.S.C. § 1415(*l*) (emphasis added). This suggests that whether a plaintiff *could have* sought relief available under the IDEA is irrelevant—what matters is whether the plaintiff *actually* sought relief available under the IDEA. In other words, when determining whether the IDEA requires a plaintiff to exhaust, courts should start by looking at a complaint's prayer for relief and determine whether the relief sought is also available under the IDEA. If it is not, then it is likely that § 1415(*l*) does not require exhaustion in that case.

We agree with much of the approach proposed by amicus United States Department of Justice. Under a relief-centered approach, § 1415(*l*) requires exhaustion in three situations. First, exhaustion is clearly required when a plaintiff seeks an IDEA remedy or its functional equivalent. For example, if a disabled student files suit under the ADA and challenges the school district's failure to accommodate his special needs and seeks damages for the costs of a private school education, the IDEA requires exhaustion regardless of whether such a remedy is available under the ADA, or whether the IDEA is mentioned in the prayer for relief. Again, in that case the "relief . . . is also available" under the IDEA, *see* 20 U.S.C. § 1412(a)(10), and the student must exhaust his IDEA remedies before seeking parallel relief under the ADA. Second, the IDEA requires exhaustion in cases where a plaintiff seeks prospective injunctive relief to alter an IEP or the educational placement of a disabled student. As with the previous point, § 1415(*l*) bars plaintiffs from seeking relief that is available to them under the IDEA, even if the plaintiffs have urged the court to craft the remedy from a different federal statute. Third, exhaustion is required in cases where a plaintiff is seeking to enforce rights that arise as a result of a denial of a free appropriate public education, whether pled as an IDEA claim or any other claim that relies on the denial of a FAPE to provide the basis for the cause of action (for instance, a claim for damages under § 504 of the Rehabilitation Act of 1973, 29 U.S.C. § 794, premised on a denial of a FAPE). Such claims arise under either the IDEA (if the IDEA violation is alleged directly) or its substantive standards (if a § 504 claim is premised on a violation of the IDEA), so the relief follows directly from the IDEA and is therefore "available under this subchapter." 20 U.S.C. § 1415(*l*). We think that these situations encompass cases in which "[b]oth the genesis and the manifestations of the problem are educational."

This approach is consistent with our understanding that the exhaustion provision is designed to "allow[ ] for the exercise of discretion and educational expertise by state and local agencies, afford[ ] full exploration of technical educational issues, further[ ] development of a complete factual record, and promote[ ] judicial efficiency by giving . . . agencies the first opportunity to correct shortcomings in their educational programs for disabled children." The exhaustion requirement is intended to prevent courts from acting as ersatz school administrators and making what should be expert determinations about the best way to educate disabled students. At the same time, it is not intended to temporarily shield school officials from all liability for conduct that violates constitutional and statutory rights that exist *independent* of the IDEA and entitles a plaintiff to relief *different* from what is available under the IDEA. Our decision reflects this limited purpose of the IDEA's exhaustion requirement.

2

The legislative history of 20 U.S.C. § 1415(*l*) supports our understanding of its meaning. The exhaustion provision was included as part of the Handicapped Children's Protection Act of 1986, Pub.L. No. 99–372, § 3, and followed the Supreme Court's decision in *Smith v. Robinson,* 468 U.S. 992 (1984). *See* S.Rep. No. 99–112, at 2 (1985). In *Smith,* the Court held that the Education of the Handicapped Act ("EHA")—the IDEA's predecessor statute—served as "the exclusive avenue through which a plaintiff may assert an equal protection claim to a publicly financed special education." In doing so, the Court held that Congress intended to eliminate a plaintiff's ability to seek relief for that injury under 42 U.S.C. § 1983. The language now codified in § 1415(*l*) was enacted in response to that decision. *See* Pub.L. No. 99–372, § 3 (1986). Congress specifically sought to "make[ ] it clear that when parents choose to file suit under another law that protects the rights of handicapped children . . . , *if that suit could have been filed under the EHA,* then parents are required to exhaust EHA administrative remedies." S.Rep. No. 99–112, at 15 (1985) (emphasis added). Indeed, a number of cases decided shortly after § 1415(*l*) was enacted understood it to implement Congress's will that the provision "reaffirm ... the viability of ... other statutes as separate vehicles for ensuring the rights of handicapped children." *Digre v. Roseville Schs. Indep. Dist. No. 623,* 841 F.2d 245, 250 (8th Cir.1988); *see also Mrs. W. v. Tirozzi,* 832 F.2d 748, 754 (2d Cir.1987) (characterizing § 1415(*l*) as a "nonexclusivity provision").

3

The approach we have adopted yields a number of implications. First, because our approach emphasizes the relief sought rather than the types of injuries alleged, we find no merit to the distinction we have previously drawn between physical and non-physical injuries. *See Robb.* Although physical injuries might bolster a plaintiff's likelihood of success in a case, there is no reason to treat constitutional violations that do not result in physical injuries differently under the exhaustion provision.

We also hold that in cases where a plaintiff is seeking money damages, courts should not engage in the depth of speculation we conducted in *Robb.* In that case, we inferred that the Robbs sought money "[p]resumably at least in part to pay for services (such as counseling and tutoring) that will assist their daughter's recovery of self-esteem and promote her progress in school. Damages could be measured by the cost of these services. Yet the school district may be able ... to provide these services *in kind* under the IDEA." We no longer think that such speculation is appropriate. Although we agree with the proposition that "a plaintiff cannot avoid the IDEA's exhaustion requirement merely by limiting a prayer for relief to money damages," we do not think, especially in the context of motions to dismiss or summary judgment motions, that it is proper for courts to assume that money damages will be directed toward forms of relief that would be available under the IDEA.

At the same time, plaintiffs cannot avoid exhaustion through artful pleading. If the measure of a plaintiff's damages is the cost of counseling, tutoring, or private schooling—relief available under the IDEA—then the IDEA requires exhaustion. In such a case, the plaintiffs are seeking the same relief, even if they are willing to accept cash in lieu of services in kind. Accordingly, the exhaustion requirement would also apply in cases where a plaintiff is arguing that a state's failure to provide specialized programs for disabled students violates the Equal Protection Clause of the Fourteenth Amendment and seeks damages to fund a private education (without mentioning the IDEA). It would also apply to cases in which the plaintiff requests damages to compensate for costs associated with unilaterally altering a disabled student's educational placement, since such a request would also be "seeking relief that is also available under" the IDEA. 20 U.S.C. § 1415(*l*). In other words, to the extent that a request for money damages functions as a substitute for relief under the IDEA, a plaintiff cannot escape the exhaustion requirement simply by limiting her prayer for relief to such damages. However, to the extent that a plaintiff has laid out a plausible claim for damages unrelated to the deprivation of a

FAPE, the IDEA does not require her to exhaust administrative remedies before seeking them in court.

Finally, we do not believe that the exhaustion requirement is triggered simply because the challenged conduct constitutes "at least . . . an attempt at an educational program." *See* [panel op.]. As amicus Department of Justice points out, whether a school official's action is a reasonable "attempt at an educational program" may comprise the very heart of a dispute about the constitutionality of that action. Thus, for example, if a student alleges a Fourth Amendment violation, the school may answer that any search or seizure was reasonably related to the school's educational programs; but the student is not deprived of a § 1983 remedy merely because the conduct took place in the context of educating the disabled. Particularly in contexts where courts are expected to draw inferences in favor of plaintiffs, we do not think it is appropriate to make what are essentially merits determinations in the context of evaluating the need for exhaustion. Nothing in the IDEA protects a school from non-IDEA liability simply because it was making a good-faith attempt to educate its disabled students. If the school's conduct constituted a violation of laws other than the IDEA, a plaintiff is entitled to hold the school responsible under those other laws.

4

The National School Boards Association ("NSBA"), as amicus, [a]ppeals to the inevitability of parent-school disputes and argues that "[r]elaxing the IDEA's administrative exhaustion requirement does violence" to Congress's goal of expediting the resolution of these disputes. We are mindful of "the general rule that parties exhaust prescribed administrative remedies before seeking relief from the federal courts." *McCarthy v. Madigan,* 503 U.S. 140, 144–45 (1992). The general rule is a salutary one allowing agencies to exercise their expertise, to correct their own errors, and to provide relief that may be both swifter and more satisfactory than relief available through more formal litigation. Even where the parties ultimately file suit in federal court after exhausting their administrative remedies, we may benefit from a process that has developed the factual record and narrowed the issues contested by the parties.

The reasons for administrative exhaustion do not change the fact that the IDEA's exhaustion requirement is not as broad as the NSBA urges. Moreover, the NSBA's reading would actually place disabled students in a disadvantaged position relative to students without special needs. As Payne accurately notes, a student who had no disability—and therefore had no need for an IEP—would be able to challenge the constitutionality of his teacher's confinement procedures without first resorting to administrative procedures. The student could simply advance a § 1983 claim alleging violations of his constitutional rights. No exhaustion would be required. If a disabled student would be able to make out a similarly meritorious constitutional claim—one that need not reference his disability at all—it is odd to suggest that the IDEA would impose additional qualifications to sue, simply because he had a disability.

C

We have carefully examined the criticism raised by the dissent and, with respect, do not think such criticism alters our views.

1

The dissent argues that our approach "largely nullifies § 1415(*l*) by providing plaintiffs with an easy end-run around the exhaustion requirement," because exhaustion would not be required "[s]o long as a complaint which seeks monetary damages does not mention a specific provision of the IDEA, or demand a remedy specifically provided by it." Nothing in our analysis "nullifies" § 1415(*l*). If a plaintiff does not seek relief based on an IDEA right, and does not seek a remedy provided by the IDEA, then she is not bound by the IDEA's prerequisites for litigation. This does not "nullif[y] § 1415(*l*)"—it simply limits the provision to its intended scope.

Indeed, the dissent seems particularly concerned with the fact that our approach "elevates the form of plaintiffs' pleadings over their substance," and facilitates "gamesmanship." But this worry is misplaced. In each case where a defendant raises § 1415(*l*) as a complete or partial defense, two possibilities arise. First, a court might decide that a complaint states a facially meritorious claim that does not either rely on rights created by the IDEA or seek remedies available under the IDEA. If a complaint can stand on its own without reference to the IDEA, it is difficult to see why the IDEA should compel its dismissal. It is hardly an "nullification of the congressionally mandated exhaustion requirement," to say that a complaint that presents sound claims wholly apart from the IDEA need not comport with the IDEA's requirements. Even though such a case might "subject school districts to civil liability for money damages, without first giving school districts the opportunity to remedy the plaintiff's injuries under the IDEA," this will only be because some other governing law *authorizes* such liability. The dissent's suggestion that this constitutes "gamesmanship" is puzzling. The fact that the plaintiff *could have* added IDEA claims to an otherwise sound complaint (and thus subjected themselves to the exhaustion requirement), but chose not to, should not detract from the viability of that complaint.

Of course, a plaintiff might try to evade the exhaustion requirement by relying on "artful" allegations. This is the situation the dissent appears to worry most about. But our approach still requires exhaustion in these cases. For example, the dissent provides the example of "a disabled child who seeks monetary damages because a school district's implementation of some educational program resulted in a claimed failure to adequately instruct him in reading." The dissent interprets our opinion as allowing such a claim to proceed without exhaustion so long as the complaint "does not mention a specific provision of the IDEA." But where the claim arises only as a result of a denial of a FAPE, whether under the IDEA or the Rehabilitation Act, exhaustion is clearly required no matter how the claim is pled. To use the dissent's example, a claim for failure to adequately instruct a student in reading can arise only under the IDEA because there is no other federal cause of action for such a claim. The claim asserted here—for knowing and intentional infliction of excessive force—is cognizable under the Fourth Amendment and exists separate and apart from the denial of a FAPE, irrespective of the fact that the alleged excessive punishment took place in a special education classroom. Although we would not doubt, for example, that an unconstitutional beating might interfere with a student enjoying the fruits of a FAPE, the resulting excessive force claim is not, for that reason alone, a claim that must be brought under the IDEA.

2

The dissent nonetheless contends that § 1415(*l*) requires exhaustion whenever the IDEA's administrative procedures "may lead to the provision of curative or palliative 'related services.'" Here, for example, the dissent suggests that the school district could have provided "intensive individualized tutoring" or "[p]sychological counseling" to correct both the past and ongoing aftereffects suffered by D.P. as a result of Coy's use of the isolation room. The dissent therefore concludes that because Payne is seeking damages "for the past and ongoing academic and psychological aftereffects of D.P.'s claimed mistreatment of the school district," exhaustion is required.

This approach misreads § 1415(*l*) and is at odds with *Witte*. First, it is not clear that the IDEA actually authorizes relief designed to correct the effects of misconduct by the school. The dissent suggests that "the 'related services' provided under the IDEA—academic services, psychological counseling and therapy—may cure, alleviate, or mitigate [injuries caused by a school district's wrongful act or omission]." But the IDEA defines "related services" to include "transportation, and such developmental, corrective, and other supportive services . . . as may be required to assist a child with a disability *to benefit from special education,* and includes the early identification and assessment of disabling conditions in children." 20 U.S.C. § 1401(26)(A) (emphasis added). In other words, it is far from clear that the IDEA authorizes the provision of services designed to correct injuries caused by the school's past violation of other laws.

Furthermore, even if such services *are* available under the IDEA, the dissent's proposal is plainly too broad. For example, the student in *Witte* could plausibly have received *some* psychological counseling and therapy that *might* have corrected or mitigated some of the harms resulting from the abuse he suffered at school. Under the dissent's view, the fact that Witte sought remedies only for physical injuries without seeking relief under the IDEA could easily be characterized as "gamesmanship" that should be set aside in favor of the exhaustion requirement. The dissent's approach would necessarily require such speculation, even in fact patterns identical to the one in *Witte*. The dissent would hold that if psychological counseling *could* correct a student's injuries, then exhaustion is required even if the injuries were caused by a non-IDEA violation for which federal law authorizes remedies apart from the IDEA.

We think such an approach would be mistaken. If a plaintiff can identify a school district's violation of federal laws other than the IDEA and can point to an authorized remedy for that violation unavailable under the IDEA, then there is no reason to require exhaustion under § 1415(*l*). The dissent's approach would effectively refashion § 1415(*l*) from a provision designed to facilitate the coexistence of the IDEA with other forms of relief into one designed to preempt all cases involving the mistreatment of disabled students by a school. We do not think that the IDEA's exhaustion requirement was intended to penalize disabled students for their disability. This is not what § 1415(l) says, and we think it is not what Congress intended.

IV

A

We now apply our approach to Payne's case and supply instructions for the district court. Payne alleged several § 1983 claims, as well as Washington state tort actions for negligence and outrage. The district court did not specifically address each claim and explain why exhaustion was required for each. Relying on *Robb,* it simply stated that "because plaintiffs' injuries could be remedie[d] to some degree by the IDEA's administrative procedures and remedies, the plaintiffs must exhaust those administrative remedies before filing suit." However, in light of the new standards announced in this decision, the district court on remand should permit Payne to amend her complaint in order to flesh out her specific claims and enable the court to determine which claims require IDEA exhaustion and which do not.

The district court should then provide the defendants with an opportunity to seek dismissal of some or all of Payne's claims on the ground that they require administrative exhaustion. The district court need not wait to consider the applicability of the exhaustion requirement until the record is complete and a motion for summary judgment has been filed.

[B]ecause § 1415(l) focuses on the "relief" sought in an action, it is conceivable that a district court, in entertaining a motion to dismiss, might not *initially* conclude that exhaustion is required for certain claims, but might recognize subsequently that, in fact, the remedies being sought by a plaintiff could have been provided by the IDEA. In such a case, we think the defendants should be permitted to provide evidence showing that the relief being sought by that plaintiff was, in fact, available under the IDEA. Because the line between damages available under other remedial sources and relief available under the IDEA is less than clear, the finder of fact should, in assessing remedies, be permitted to assess the evidence and withhold those that are unexhausted and available under the IDEA.

We recognize that this approach to exhaustion is somewhat unconventional—it is anomalous to permit a party to raise failure to exhaust as a defense in both a motion to dismiss and at the fact-finding stage of a proceeding. But as we have noted, § 1415(l) is itself an anomalous provision, since it does not categorically preclude claims and instead requires a court to examine the relief being sought by those claims and to compare it to the relief available under the IDEA. Ultimately, § 1415(l) is designed to channel requests for a FAPE (and its incidents) through IDEA-prescribed procedures. The procedure we have outlined, while somewhat unusual, faithfully executes Congress's design.

B

After Payne is given the opportunity to amend her complaint, the district court should examine each of Payne's requests for relief and determine whether the exhaustion requirement applies to each. It may then dismiss any claims that are governed by the exhaustion requirement, but it should not dismiss any remaining claims. To provide additional guidance concerning the new approach we have adopted, we briefly discuss some of Payne's federal claims in her current complaint and the relief sought. We reiterate, of course, that the district court should permit Payne to amend her complaint before determining which aspects are barred by the exhaustion requirement.

The easiest claim to address is Payne's claim that the defendants violated D.P.'s "statutory rights under the IDEA." This claim is plainly barred by § 1415(*l*) because any relief that Payne could obtain for violations of the IDEA is "relief that is also available under [the IDEA]" itself. Section 1415(*l*) is explicit that Payne must exhaust her IDEA remedies "to the same extent as would be required had the action been brought under [the IDEA]."

With respect to the remaining § 1983 claims—alleged violations of the Fourth, Eighth, and Fourteenth Amendments—the complaint does not explicitly link each constitutional claim to a form of requested relief. Rather, the complaint seeks declaratory relief and general, special, and punitive damages. Accordingly, it will be the task of the district court on remand to determine whether the relief being sought is "also available under" the IDEA. For example, Payne's request for "general damages for extreme mental suffering and emotional distress" would not fall within the purview of § 1415(*l*) if such damages are intended to compensate Payne for injuries resulting from Fourth or Eighth Amendment violations committed by school officials. If, however, the "emotional distress" stems from Payne's concern that D.P. was not receiving an adequate education, then exhaustion is required.

To take a second example, the complaint alleges violations of "procedural and substantive due process" under the Fourteenth Amendment. If Payne seeks damages for the school district's failure to provide procedural due process for rights conferred by the IDEA, the claims must be exhausted because the IDEA provides procedural due process rights, 20 U.S.C. § 1415(f)–(g), and Payne cannot simply claim damages in place of the process available to her. Similarly, we cannot discern the contours of Payne's current substantive due process claim, but if, for example, the claim is for deprivation of a "free and appropriate education," see 20 U.S.C. § 1412(a)(1)(A), then Payne seeks relief that is also available under the IDEA, and she must exhaust her statutory remedies.

Finally, we emphasize that our holding only removes certain procedural barriers preventing Payne from litigating her non-IDEA claims. We have not been asked to, and do not, decide whether any of these claims are meritorious.

V

We hold that 20 U.S.C. § 1415(*l*) gives IDEA defendants an opportunity to plead non-exhaustion as an affirmative defense without limiting federal jurisdiction. We affirm the district court's dismissal of Payne's IDEA-based claim under 42 U.S.C. § 1983. We reverse its dismissal of her other § 1983 claims and remand for reconsideration under the standards we have articulated.

Costs on appeal are awarded to Payne.

AFFIRMED IN PART, REVERSED IN PART, AND REMANDED.

■ CALLAHAN, CIRCUIT JUDGE, CONCURRING:

I concur in the opinion, but write separately because I share the concern expressed by Judge Bea in his separate concurrence and dissent that our clarification of IDEA's exhaustion requirement, 20 U.S.C. § 1415(*l*), may be used to circumvent the requirement. Even under the "relief-centered" approach we adopt, it is not always possible to determine whether the alleged damages are separate and distinct from those covered by the IDEA. The solution to this dilemma may not lie solely in the dismissal of an ambiguous complaint or cause of action for failure to exhaust, but may be complemented by allowing a defendant school district to assert, even at trial, that an aspect of plaintiff's claim of damages would have been addressed in the administrative proceedings. Then, to the extent that the defendant meets its burden of demonstrating that the administrative processes would have addressed an aspect of the alleged damages, plaintiff would be denied any recovery for that aspect because that portion of his claim is unexhausted.

This approach differs in its critical aspects from the concept of mitigation. Although the statute states that an action may not be filed until administrative proceedings have been exhausted, it may not always be possible to determine, either at the pleadings stage or on a motion for summary judgment, whether some aspect of the alleged damages would have been addressed, in whole or in part, in administrative proceedings. Accordingly, lest the purpose of the exhaustion requirement be evaded, we should recognize that the scope of the unexhausted administrative proceedings may only become clear at trial. Of course, at that point in time it is impossible to literally enforce the exhaustion requirement. The lawsuit has been filed and presumably some aspects of the alleged damages would not have been addressed in the available administrative proceedings (otherwise the court would have already dismissed the action). In such a situation, the intent of the statute is best served by denying the plaintiff any recovery for any aspect of the alleged damages that the defendant school district shows would have been addressed in the administrative proceedings.

The school district has the burden of making the requisite factual showing that an aspect of a damage claim would have been addressed in the administrative proceedings, but it need not show that the administrative proceedings would have produced a solution. Rather, if the school district shows, to the requisite degree of certainty, that the administrative proceedings would have addressed an aspect of the plaintiff's alleged damages, the plaintiff may not recover for that aspect. In essence, if the factfinder determines that an aspect of plaintiff's claim for damages would have been addressed by the administrative proceedings, the plaintiff has failed to exhaust the administrative procedures for that aspect. Accordingly, to enforce the exhaustion provision, the plaintiff should be barred from seeking damages for that aspect of his or her claim. This is not mitigation in the sense of reducing damages based on a plaintiff's failure to prevent the harm, rather it enforces a statutory prerequisite to the entitlement to collect the damages—engaging in the requisite pre-suit administrative proceedings.

The allegations in this case allow for an illustration of this approach. D.P.'s confinement to the "safe room" arose out of the parties['] relationship based on the IDEA. However, his confinement was also arguably a violation of D.P.'s constitutional rights irrespective of the parties' relationship under the IDEA. Our focus, however, is not on whether the alleged injury resulted from a violation of the IDEA or of the child's constitutional rights, but whether the "relief sought is also available under the IDEA."

The difficulty in measuring damages, is implicitly admitted in our direction to the district court to allow Payne "to amend her complaint in order to flesh out her specific claims and enable the court to determine which claims require IDEA exhaustion and which do not." For example, we recognize that Payne's request for "general damages for extreme mental suffering and emotional distress" might not fall "within the purview of § 1415(*l*)," but will if "the 'emotional distress' stems from Payne's concern that D.P. was not receiving an adequate education." It is not clear to what extent long term academic, psychological or emotional harms, must be addressed in the administrative proceedings. The majority holds that "[t]he IDEA's exhaustion requirement applies to claims only to the extent that the relief actually sought could have been provided by the IDEA." It further holds that "exhaustion is required in cases where a plaintiff is seeking to enforce rights that arise as a result of a denial of a free appropriate public education." Thus, although it may be "far from clear that the IDEA authorizes the provision of services designed to correct injuries caused by the school's past violation of other laws," the line between those aspects of damages which would have been addressed in administrative proceedings, and those which would not, may be a factual issue that will have to be determined on a case by case basis.

Here, as noted by Judge Bea, much of the relief or damages Payne sought was arguably available under the IDEA. On the other hand, as all admit, to the extent that plaintiffs seek monetary damages for compensation for past pain and suffering, such relief is not available under the IDEA. Furthermore, as the majority notes, the complaint "does not explicitly link each constitutional claim to a form of requested relief." Although we direct the district court to scrutinize the complaint, we implicitly admit that the line between damages that are and are not addressable in IDEA administrative proceedings may not be clear. It follows that the district court may be able to use the IDEA's exhaustion requirement to narrow the complaint at the pleading stage, but may not be able to dispose of the case.

The danger is, as Judge Bea notes, that artful pleading may enable plaintiffs to circumvent the exhaustion requirement. However, much of the incentive to do so will be dissipated if, at trial, the defendant may present evidence showing that the administrative proceedings under the IDEA, if utilized, would have addressed certain aspects of the claimed damages. This also recognizes the exhaustion requirement is akin to an affirmative defense, rather than a jurisdictional bar to the lawsuit.

Such an approach is consistent with the intent of the IDEA to encourage the parties to take advantage of the administrative proceedings. At the same time, it recognizes that just because a student is subject to the IDEA, he or she does not forfeit his or her other constitutional and statutory rights. Nonetheless, where (1) the alleged damages arise in the context of a relationship under the IDEA, (2) plaintiff did not exhaust the administrative proceedings under the IDEA, and (3) the measure of damages includes aspects that would have been addressed in the administrative proceedings, then the exhaustion requirement should be construed as denying plaintiff any recovery for those aspects of the claim that it is determined—under the applicable standard of proof and by the appropriate factfinder—would have been addressed by the administrative proceedings.

■ BEA, CIRCUIT JUDGE, JOINED BY SILVERMAN AND RAWLINSON, CIRCUIT JUDGES, CONCURRING IN PART AND DISSENTING IN PART:

I respectfully dissent from what the majority calls its "clarification" of the "proper method for resolving IDEA exhaustion cases." Rather than a clarification, I see it as a nullification of the congressionally mandated exhaustion requirement. The majority opinion clashes with the clear language of the IDEA, which requires administrative exhaustion "*before* the filing of a civil action . . . seeking relief that is *also available* under [the IDEA]." 20 U.S.C. § 1415(*l*) (emphasis added). The majority's approach is also inconsistent with the core purposes of IDEA exhaustion: allowing state and local agencies "the exercise of discretion and education expertise," giving agencies "the first opportunity to correct shortcomings in their educational programs for disabled children," and allowing "full exploration of technical educational issues." *Hoeft v. Tucson Unified Sch. Dist.*, 967 F.2d 1298, 1303 (9th Cir.1992). Finally, the newly-restricted exhaustion requirement will allow plaintiffs—through gamesmanship and cleverly-crafted pleadings—to subject school districts to civil liability for money damages, without first giving school districts the opportunity to remedy the plaintiff's injuries under the IDEA.

[I.]

With respect, the majority opinion begins by misreading the IDEA's exhaustion provision, codified at 20 U.S.C. § 1415(*l*). The majority reads § 1415(*l*)—which requires a plaintiff to exhaust administrative remedies if the plaintiff is "seeking relief that is also available under" the IDEA—to mean that exhaustion is required only if a plaintiff *specifically* alleges violations of substantive IDEA rights, or their "functional equivalent." According to the majority, "whether a plaintiff *could have* sought relief available under the IDEA is irrelevant—what matters is whether the plaintiff *actually* sought relief available under the IDEA." Therefore, according to the majority, courts charged with "determining whether the IDEA requires a plaintiff to exhaust ... should start by looking at a complaint's prayer for relief and determine whether the relief sought is also available under the IDEA. If it is not, then it is likely that § 1415(*l*) does not require exhaustion." The majority sees "relief that is available" under the IDEA as restricted to three situations: 1) when a claim is based upon alleged violations of a plaintiff's substantive IDEA right to a Free Appropriate Public Education (FAPE); 2) when a plaintiff seeks an IDEA remedy, or the "functional equivalent of an IDEA remedy under a different law" (for example, when a plaintiff seeks recompense for a private school education under the Americans with Disabilities Act, or explicitly measures its calculation of damages as the cost of academic tutoring or psychological counseling); and 3) when a plaintiff seeks injunctive relief to alter a child's individualized education program (IEP) or educational placement.

As an initial matter, the majority's limited exhaustion requirement is inconsistent with the plain text of § 1415(*l*). Section 1415(*l*) does not state that exhaustion is required only for relief that is premised upon an alleged violation of the plaintiff's substantive IDEA rights, seeks the functional equivalent of an IDEA remedy, or seeks injunctive relief after IDEA remedies have been effected. Rather, § 1415(*l*) simply and broadly states that exhaustion is required if a plaintiff seeks relief that is "also available" under the IDEA. The IDEA requires public schools to provide disabled students with a "free appropriate public education." A "free appropriate public education" includes not just "an appropriate pre-school, elementary school, or secondary school education," but also "related services" which include counseling and psychological services. *See* 20 USC § 1401(26). Thus, if a disabled student brings suit seeking monetary damages to compensate him for his academic regression or psychological injuries which he claims persist after the completion of a school district's claimed wrongful act or omission, relief for those injuries is "also available" *in kind* under the IDEA, because the "related services" provided under the IDEA—academic services, psychological counseling and therapy—may cure, alleviate, or mitigate such injuries. In such a case, the plain text of § 1415(*l*) requires a plaintiff to exhaust the IDEA's administrative procedures which may lead to the provision of curative or palliative "related services" *before* filing a civil suit.

The majority's skepticism that the "IDEA actually authorizes relief designed to correct the effects of misconduct by the school" is misplaced. The majority notes that the IDEA defines "related services" as services which "may be required to assist a child with a disability *to benefit from special education*," and posits that the IDEA does not require schools to alleviate academic and psychological damage *to a child which is caused* by the school. But this reading of the IDEA makes little sense. The statute plainly holds that if a child requires "related services" to benefit from special education, those services must be provided. Nothing in the statute requires any inquiry as to *why* those services are required. Thus, if a child suffers from crippling anxiety at school, and that anxiety must be alleviated before he can learn (or, in the words of the statute, "benefit from special education"), the IDEA plainly requires psychological services be provided. It makes no difference whether that anxiety was caused by the school or whether it was caused by some external factor.

Of course, § 1415(*l*) does not require IDEA exhaustion for *all* lawsuits brought by disabled students who allege academic or psychological injuries—only for those lawsuits seeking relief for those injuries which may be cured or alleviated by the "related services" provided through IDEA's administrative process. As we held in *Witte v. Clark County School District,* 197 F.3d 1271 (9th Cir.1999), plaintiffs need not exhaust IDEA remedies if they seek damages for "retrospective" psychological injuries. For example, had the Paynes sought monetary damages for the claimed past and temporary emotional and psychological trauma D.P. suffered while locked in the isolation room, IDEA exhaustion would not have been required. This is so because when the damages sought are for purely retrospective injuries, relief is not "also available" under the IDEA: no amount of academic or counseling services could possibly alleviate the past, but temporary, fright D.P. might claim he felt inside the isolation room. Neither could IDEA's "related services" cure or alleviate the pain and suffering D.P. might have suffered in the "isolation room" and for a few days thereafter, had he sprained his ankle while locked inside. As this court held in *Witte,* the "remedies available under the IDEA would not appear to be well suited to addressing past physical injuries adequately."

On the other hand, when a plaintiff seeks monetary damages to compensate for the academic and psychological *after-effects* of a school district's wrongful act or omission in the provision of education, relief is necessarily available under the IDEA. Here, for example, intensive individualized tutoring might well have alleviated D.P.'s claimed academic regression. Psychological counseling might also have eliminated the nightmares from which the Paynes contend D.P. suffered as a result of the district's use of the "isolation room" in which it placed D.P. And relief for such academic regression and nightmares is "also available" under the IDEA if the regression and nightmares are likely to continue.[3] Here—as discussed in further detail below—the Paynes sought damages for the past and ongoing academic and psychological *after-effects* of D.P.'s claimed mistreatment by the school district. In such cases, the plain text of § 1415(*l*) requires a plaintiff to exhaust the IDEA's administrative procedures before filing a civil suit.

The majority expresses concern that this "muscular" view of § 1415(*l*) "penalize[s] disabled students for their disability," "preempt[s] all cases involving the mistreatment of disabled students by a school," and "temporarily *shield[s]* " school officials from liability for violations of constitutional and statutory rights. Not at all. First, my reading of § 1415(*l*) does not preempt all cases involving disabled students harmed by a school. Contrary to the majority's assertion, I embrace *Witte,* which eschews preemption in cases where plaintiffs seek compensation only for physical or

---

[3] Plaintiffs can also avoid the IDEA's exhaustion requirement if they can prove that recourse to the IDEA's administrative procedures would have been futile or inadequate. For example, parents who seek monetary damages as compensation for the out-of-pocket expenses they paid for a specialized form of private tutoring or private psychological counseling could avoid the IDEA's exhaustion requirement if they prove that such tutoring or counseling was 1) necessary, and 2) could not have been provided by the school district[.]

retrospective injuries. Moreover, any shield imposed by the exhaustion requirement is of very limited duration. Due process complaints under the IDEA must be heard and decided within 45 days. 34 C.F.R. § 300.515(a). And so long as plaintiffs exhaust their IDEA remedies, nothing prevents them from subsequently bringing civil claims based upon violations of constitutional or statutory rights. Thus, § 1415(*l*) does not absolve school districts of civil liability for injuries which could not be remedied or palliated by IDEA's "related services." Instead, it codifies a recognition that the education of disabled children is a complex endeavor, calling for much individual attention, and that a misjudgment in a child's IEP—or a mistake in execution of that plan—can result in unexpected academic and psychological injuries. For that reason, in cases where "both the genesis and the manifestations of the problem are educational," § 1415(*l*) requires potential plaintiffs first to give school districts the opportunity to correct the effects of their claimed educational mistakes under the IDEA's administrative process, before recasting claims arising from acts or omissions related to educational efforts as violations of constitutional and statutory rights, with compensation sought in money damages. Far from *penalizing* disabled students, § 1415(*l*) provides a fast, efficient way to redress such students' academic and psychological injuries, as an alternative to civil litigation which may drag on for years.

In contrast, the eviscerated exhaustion requirement articulated by the majority elevates the form of plaintiffs' pleadings over their substance. Consider, for example, a disabled child who seeks monetary damages because a school district's implementation of some educational program resulted in a claimed failure adequately to instruct him in reading. Such a child could allege either: 1) the school district failed to provide a "free appropriate public education" as required by the IDEA, 20 U.S.C. § 1401(9), or, as the plaintiffs here claim, 2) the school district's actions caused the child's "academic prowess and abilities" to be diminished, entitling the child to general and special damages for his emotional and psychological pain and suffering. Although the facts underlying both of these claims would be identical, the majority holds that the IDEA requires exhaustion of administrative remedies *only* if the plaintiff styles his complaint as a failure to provide a "free appropriate public education" under the IDEA, or explicitly measures damages as the cost of counseling, tutoring, or private schooling. Only *then,* according to the majority, is the claim based upon "either the IDEA . . . or its substantive standards." The majority opinion thus effectively serves as a roadmap for plaintiffs who wish to avoid § 1415(*l*)'s exhaustion requirement and any curative or palliative services the school district could offer to eliminate or reduce damages, but would rather obtain a money award in a federal court. So long as a complaint which seeks monetary damages does not mention a specific provision of the IDEA, demand a remedy specifically provided by it, or seek injunctive relief to modify an implemented IEP, the majority holds there is no need to exhaust administrative remedies which could remedy the harm done to a disabled child through the school's mistakes in implementing the child's education. Thus, the majority largely nullifies § 1415(*l*) by providing plaintiffs with an easy end-run around the exhaustion requirement. It does not take a crystal ball to foresee the result. Would a plaintiff's attorney rather 1) state a claim for the provision of in-kind services under the IDEA, and if successful, be paid in court-supervised attorney'[s] fees, *see* 20 U.S.C. § 1415(i)(3)(B), or 2) seek monetary damages under a contingent fee contract with the parents?

The majority incorrectly insists that our previous "injury-centered" approach to exhaustion was inconsistent with § 1415(*l*)'s requirement that plaintiffs exhaust administrative remedies if a plaintiff is "*seeking* relief that is also available under [the IDEA]." 20 U.S.C. § 1415(*l*) (emphasis added). According to the majority, the phrase "seeking relief" suggests that "whether a plaintiff *could have* sought relief available under the IDEA is irrelevant—what matters is whether the plaintiff *actually* sought relief available under the IDEA." But this interpretation of the phrase "seeking relief" is inconsistent with this court's prior determination that a plaintiff cannot circumvent the IDEA's exhaustion requirement by seeking only monetary damages. Although monetary damages are not ordinarily available under the IDEA, we have joined at least five sister circuits to hold that a prayer for monetary damages does not automatically excuse the IDEA's exhaustion requirement. Thus—because a plaintiff who includes an education-related prayer for monetary damages necessarily does not "actually" seek relief available under the IDEA—we, and our sister circuits, have held that what "matters" for exhaustion purposes is *precisely* whether a plaintiff "could have" sought relief for the claimed injuries, which relief is also available under the IDEA through in-kind services. The majority opinion does not overturn this aspect of our IDEA jurisprudence; this leaves us with a puzzling inconsistency. On the one hand, as the majority holds today, the phrase "seeking relief" requires courts to look *solely* at what form of relief the plaintiff "actually sought." On the other hand, courts will look necessarily to what sort of relief a plaintiff "could have" sought in complaints which seek damages measured in the cost of services available in-kind under the IDEA, or which seek monetary damages for claims which are explicitly based upon alleged violations of a plaintiff's substantive IDEA rights.

Finally, the majority opinion undermines the sound principles behind the exhaustion requirement. We have previously held that the IDEA's exhaustion requirement "recognizes the traditionally strong state and local interest in education, allows for the exercise of discretion and educational expertise by state agencies, affords full exploration of technical educational issues, furthers development of a factual record and promotes judicial efficiency by giving state and local agencies the first opportunity to correct shortcomings." In addition, because due process complaints under the IDEA must be heard and decided within 45 days, 34 C.F.R. § 300.515(a), the IDEA's expedited timetable encourages quick and efficient resolution of disputes. Yet the majority's curtailment of the exhaustion requirement promotes none of these goals. On the contrary, the weakened exhaustion requirement will bode to flood federal courts with IDEA cases, before a local agency has had an opportunity to resolve the dispute. Federal judges and juries—not education experts—will be asked to serve as "ersatz school administrators," and make determinations about what money damage awards are necessary to prevent or alleviate academic, psychological, or emotional harm. And disabled children whose academic and psychological injuries might have been quickly cured or mitigated by in-kind services supplied by a school district under the IDEA may have to wait until the resolution of a potentially lengthy civil lawsuit to receive a monetary balm.

II.

Recognizing, perhaps, that its reading § 1415(*l*) could financially burden school districts by requiring them to reimburse plaintiffs for palliative services the school districts could have cost-effectively provided in-kind, the majority rewrites § 1415(*l*)—an exhaustion statute—as a mitigation statute. The majority concludes that after a court determines exhaustion was not required, a defendant subsequently should "be permitted to provide evidence showing that the relief being sought by that plaintiff was, in fact, available under the IDEA" and "withhold [remedies] that are unexhausted and available under the IDEA." I am puzzled as to how the majority can so interpret § 1415(*l*). Section 1415(*l*) is not a "collateral source" doctrine which would permit defendant school districts to submit evidence proving a plaintiff's monetary damages would have been reduced had plaintiffs availed themselves of remedies also available under the IDEA. It is thus distinguishable from, for example, the collateral source provision of California's Medical Injury Compensation Reform Act (MICRA), Cal. Civ.Code § 3333.1. MICRA permits health care providers who are sued for personal injuries allegedly caused by medical malpractice to mitigate damages by "introduc[ing] evidence of any amount payable to the plaintiff as a result of the personal injury" from outside sources, including the Social Security Act, worker's compensation schemes, and private insurance plans. Cal. Civ.Code § 3333.1(a). In contrast, § 1415(*l*) does not provide for the introduction of mitigating evidence at a hearing to assess damages. To the contrary, § 1415(*l*) very clearly states:

> "*before the filing of a civil action* under such laws seeking relief that is also available under [the IDEA], the [administrative] procedures . . . *shall be exhausted* to the same extent as would be required had the action been brought under [the IDEA]."

20 U.S.C. § 1415(*l*) (emphasis added).

The majority's attempt to turn § 1415(*l*) into a mitigation statute is thus belied by the plain text of the law. If the defendant is permitted *at trial* to "provide evidence showing that the relief being sought by that plaintiff was, in fact, available under the IDEA," then such evidence was "also available" before the action was filed. After all, evidence that the school district could have provided palliative academic or psychological services under the IDEA is relevant—for mitigation purposes—only if those services could have reduced plaintiffs' damages. To reduce plaintiffs' damages, such services must have been "also available" to the plaintiff. And *if* relief is "also available" to a plaintiff under the IDEA, § 1415(*l*) requires a plaintiff to *exhaust* his remedies under the IDEA "*before the filing of a civil action.*" 20 U.S.C. § 1415(*l*) (emphasis added). There is not a word in § 1415(*l*) about mitigation, nor anything which permits a school district to introduce evidence that relief was "also available" under the IDEA at trial for the purpose of reducing a monetary award to plaintiffs at trial.

[IV.]

Before bringing this suit in federal court—and sparking this protracted litigation which has now dragged on for six years—the Paynes should first have exhausted their administrative remedies and sought relief that was "also available" under the IDEA, as required by the plain text of § 1415(*l*). Indeed, even under the majority's narrow reading of § 1415(*l*), the evidence submitted by the parties supported the district court's grant of summary judgment to the school district. The majority holds that "[i]f the measure of a plaintiff's damages is the cost of counseling, tutoring, or private schooling—relief available under the IDEA—then the IDEA requires exhaustion." Here, Windy Payne has explicitly stated in her deposition that she sought reimbursement for the cost of the counseling and psychological services needed to make D.P. a "happy boy again." The Paynes submitted no evidence to suggest this was not *a* measure of the damages they sought. Thus, even under the majority's newly-articulated exhaustion requirement, the district court's grant of summary judgment should be affirmed.

Therefore, I would affirm the district court's grant of summary judgment to the school district in its entirety.

NOTES ON REMEDIES UNDER THE IDEA

1.   May Non-Lawyer Parents Bring IDEA Actions? In Winkelman v. Parma City Sch. Dist., 550 U.S. 516 (2007), the Supreme Court, per Justice Kennedy, held that the IDEA grants parents substantial rights relating to the education of their children, "including the one most fundamental to the Act: the provision of a free appropriate public education to a child with a disability." The Court thus held that parents, even those who are not lawyers, may sue *pro se* to enforce the rights the IDEA grants. The school district, invoking *Arlington Central*, argued that it lacked notice that parents would have independent rights under the statute, but the court rejected that argument: "Our determination that IDEA grants to parents independent, enforceable rights does not impose any substantive condition or obligation on States they would not otherwise be required by law to observe." Justice Scalia, joined by Justice Thomas, concurred only in part. They "would hold that parents have the right to proceed *pro se* under the Individuals with Disabilities Education Act when they seek reimbursement for private school expenses or redress for violations of their own procedural rights, but not when they seek a judicial determination that their child's free appropriate public education (or FAPE) is substantively inadequate."

2.   Section 1983. May children with disabilities or their parents sue under 42 U.S.C. § 1983 to seek damages for violations of the IDEA? The Supreme Court has not addressed the question, and the lower courts have reached differing conclusions. Compare *A.W. v. Jersey City Public Schools*, 486 F.3d 791 (3d Cir.2007) (*en banc*) (holding that the IDEA's incorporation of its own complex remedial scheme indicates congressional intent to foreclose a Section 1983 remedy pursuant to *City of Rancho Palos Verdes v. Abrams*, 544 U.S. 113 (2005), and citing cases from other circuits that have taken the same view), with *Marie O. v. Edgar*, 131 F.3d 610 (7th Cir.1997) (pre-*Rancho Palos Verdes* decision holding that IDEA could be enforced through Section 1983).

3. Class Actions. May children with disabilities or their parents challenge a school district's systemic violations of the IDEA by bringing a class action? The Supreme Court's decision in *Wal-Mart Stores, Inc. v. Dukes*, 131 S.Ct. 2541 (2011), combined with the exhaustion requirement and the individualized nature of a school's obligations under the IDEA, has made class certification difficult in such cases. In JAMIE S. V. MILWAUKEE PUBLIC SCHOOLS, 668 F.3d 481 (7th Cir.2012), the Seventh Circuit vacated class certification in a case challenging alleged systemic IDEA violations in the Milwaukee schools:

> We begin with the terms of the class definition, something over which the parties and the judge struggled mightily. The plaintiffs initially sought to represent a class so broad that it effectively included all students eligible for special education and related services from MPS. The original proposed class thus joined together all Milwaukee-area disabled students, regardless of differences in their disabilities or educational situations, whose procedural or substantive rights under the IDEA were violated in any way. The district court properly rejected this sweeping class definition, but not for the obvious reason that it sought to lump together thousands of disparate plaintiffs with widely varying individual claims. Rather, the court rejected the plaintiffs' proposed class definition based on difficulties associated with the IDEA's requirement that administrative remedies be exhausted before filing suit.

> The district court was justifiably concerned about the administrative-exhaustion requirement. But the court's effort to resolve the problem was misguided. The court *sua sponte* divided the class into two categories: those with "pre-determination claims" and those with "post-determination claims." These designations were apparently meant to categorize individual violations of the IDEA, separating those that occurred prior to an IEP meeting from those that occurred after an IEP meeting. The judge thought this categorization made it possible to excuse the exhaustion requirement for "pre-determination claims" and allow these alleged IDEA violations to be litigated on a class-wide basis, while enforcing the exhaustion requirement for "post-determination claims," excluding them from class-action treatment.

> There is reason to doubt the propriety of this approach, but for present purposes we will address it on its own terms. Ordinarily, a plaintiff may not file an IDEA lawsuit without first exhausting available administrative remedies. However, exhaustion may be excused if administrative review would be futile or inadequate. *Honig*. The district court applied this exception to all pre-determination claims, reasoning that the parents of disabled students might not be fully aware of the right to administrative remedies prior to a properly constructed IEP

meeting, making exhaustion an exercise in futility. Once an IEP meeting is convened, however, the court thought that parents would sufficiently understand their rights, making administrative review adequate and keeping the IDEA's exhaustion requirement intact for post-determination claims. On this rationale the court was willing to certify a class defined to include only pre-determination claims, for which it excused the plaintiffs' failure to exhaust administrative remedies.

The court thus certified a class of its own creation:

> Those students eligible for special education services from the Milwaukee Public School System who are, have been or will be either denied or delayed entry or participation in the processes which result in a properly constituted meeting between the IEP team and the parents or guardians of the student.

In other words, the certified class combined all disabled students eligible for special education from MPS who were not identified as potentially eligible for services, not timely referred for evaluation after identification, not timely evaluated after referral, not evaluated in a properly constituted IEP meeting, or whose parents did not (for whatever reason) attend an otherwise proper IEP meeting. The court made it clear that students who suffered a pre-determination violation but have since received a proper IEP meeting—for example, students who received a late IEP meeting—are also included in the class.

One immediately obvious defect in this class is its indefiniteness. A significant segment of the class (of unknown and unknowable size) comprises disabled students who may have been eligible for special education but were *not identified* and *remain unidentified.* There is no question that MPS has a legal obligation under the IDEA to seek out disabled students and refer for evaluation those it reasonably believes are disabled and in need of special education. The failure to properly identify a disabled student can itself be a violation of the IDEA *if* the failure results in the denial of a free appropriate public education to a qualifying child with a disability. The problem with a class of potentially eligible but unidentified students is not that their rights might not been violated but that the relevant criteria for class membership are unknown. By what standard is class membership to be determined? How is the court to decide whether there was reason to believe *in 2000–2005* that a presently unidentified child was *potentially eligible* for special-education services from MPS? It's not hard to see how this class lacks the definiteness required for class certification; there is no way to know or readily ascertain who is a member of the class.

Of course, unidentified but potentially eligible disabled students are defined not only by having not been identified but also by having a disability. If we could easily identify all Milwaukee students with disabilities during the relevant time period, perhaps we could crosscheck that list against a list of known disabled students to determine which students MPS failed to identify and refer for an IEP evaluation. But identifying disabled students who might be eligible for special-education services is a complex, highly individualized task, and cannot be reduced to the application of a set of simple, objective criteria. Every step of the child-find inquiry and IEP process under the IDEA is child specific and requires the application of trained and particularized professional educational judgment. In short, a class of unidentified but potentially IDEA-eligible disabled students is inherently too indefinite to be certified.

[B]eyond its inherent indefiniteness, the class certified here fails to satisfy Rule 23(a)(2)'s commonality prerequisite, which requires that the class claims involve "questions of law or fact common to the class." FED.R.CIV.P. 23(a)(2). It's true that " '[e]ven a single [common] question' will do." Wal-Mart (quoting Richard A. Nagareda, *The Preexistence Principle and the Structure of the Class Action*, 103 Colum. L. Rev. 149, 176, n.110 (2003)) (alteration in original). But the Supreme Court explained in *Wal-Mart* that superficial common questions—like whether each class member is an MPS student or whether each class member "suffered a violation of the same provision of law"—are not enough. Rather, "[c]ommonality requires the plaintiffs to demonstrate that the class members 'have suffered the same injury.'" The class "claims must depend upon a common contention," and "[t]hat common contention, moreover, must be of such a nature that it is capable of classwide resolution—which means that determination of its truth or falsity will resolve an issue that is central to the validity of each one of the claims in one stroke."

The plaintiffs identify the following common issue: "[A]ll potential class members have suffered as a result of MPS' failure to ensure their Child Find rights under IDEA and Wisconsin law." This completely misunderstands Rule 23(a)(2). Whether MPS failed in its obligations under the IDEA and thereby deprived an eligible disabled child of a free appropriate public education is the bottom-line liability question in any individual plaintiff's IDEA claim. To bring individual IDEA claims together to litigate as a class, the plaintiffs must show that they share some question of law or fact that can be answered *all at once* and that the *single answer* to that question will resolve a central issue in all class members' claims. That all the class members have "suffered" as a result of disparate individual IDEA child-find violations is not enough; it does not establish that the individual claims have any question of law or fact in common. The plaintiffs have identified no common factual or legal question that satisfies the Rule 23(a)(2) standard, and it is their burden to do so.

[T]hat the court narrowed its focus to child-find violations (what the court called "pre-determination claims") is not enough. Child-find inquiries, like other aspects of the IDEA, are necessarily child specific. There is no such thing as a "systemic" failure to find and refer individual disabled children for IEP evaluation—except perhaps if there was "significant proof" that MPS operated under child-find *policies* that violated the IDEA. *See id.* at 2553. As the Supreme Court noted in *Wal-Mart,* an illegal *policy* might provide the "glue" necessary to litigate otherwise highly individualized claims as a class. But again, as in *Wal-Mart,* proof of an illegal policy "is entirely absent here." Lacking any common questions, the class fails to satisfy Rule 23(a)(2) and should not have been certified.

Finally, it should be clear from our discussion thus far that the district court also erred when it certified an injunction class under Rule 23(b)(2). Rule 23(b)(2) permits the court to certify a case for class-action treatment if "the party opposing the class has acted or refused to act on grounds that apply generally to the class, so that final injunctive relief or corresponding declaratory relief is appropriate respecting the class as a whole." FED.R.CIV.P. 23(b)(2). The final clause is important: The injunctive or declaratory relief sought must be "final" to "the class as a whole." In other words, "claims for *individualized* relief . . . do not satisfy [Rule 23(b)(2)]." *Wal-Mart.* To the contrary, "Rule 23(b)(2) applies only when a single injunction or declaratory judgment would provide relief to each member of the class. It does not authorize class certification when each individual class member would be entitled to a *different* injunction or declaratory judgment against the defendant." *Id.*

That the plaintiffs have superficially structured their case around a claim for class-wide injunctive and declaratory relief does not satisfy Rule 23(b)(2) if as a substantive matter the relief sought would merely initiate a process through which highly individualized determinations of liability and remedy are made; this kind of relief would be class-wide in name only, and it would certainly not be final.

The relief sought here does not come close to satisfying Rule 23(b)(2)'s standard. That much is clear from the intricate remedial scheme ordered by the district court, which requires thousands of individual determinations of class membership, liability, and appropriate remedies. While the compensatory-education remedies will often or always be injunctive in nature, there can be no single injunction that provides final relief to the class as a whole. It is no answer to say that the June 9 remedial order affects the entire class; that order merely establishes a system for eventually providing individualized relief. It does not, on its own, provide "final" relief to any class member.

Under the court's analysis, will a class action ever be possible in an IDEA case? Consider the argument in Judge Rovner's partial concurrence:

I am mindful that the parties and the court, from the time that the class was certified forward, appear to have developed an understanding that the class would include the four sets of individuals that the court later expressly identified in its liability decision: (1) students with suspected disabilities who were never referred for an evaluation; (2) students who were referred for evaluation, but whose evaluations were not completed within the requisite 90-day limit; (3) students who were suspended in such a way as to frustrate their evaluation; and (4) students whose IEP meetings took place in the absence of their parents. Moreover, the court's liability decision was limited to the time period commencing in September 2000 and ending in June 2005.

[B]ut even as confined to these four groups of students and this roughly five-year period, the class includes unknown numbers of variations. To cite one example: When, in her 2004 report, Dr. Rogers-Adkinson addressed MPS's failure to meet statutory deadlines during the assessment process, she identified at least four different patterns of delays: (1) delays occasioned by the initial mis-categorization of a student's suspected disability; (2) delays caused by extensions of time routinely requested for disability assessments solicited during the spring semester; (3) delays triggered by the need for additional medical records; and (4) delays for reasons not revealed in the files she reviewed. Each of these four scenarios might be a manifestation of MPS's failure to timely identify students with disabilities and to convene IEP meetings to address those disabilities, but it is difficult to discern a common, wrongful policy or practice that might account for them all. Instead, this looks more like an effort to sweep many individual plaintiffs and sets of facts into one class on the premise that all reflect illegal conduct by the defendant in practice and culture if not in policy. As the majority points out, that is precisely the sort of class that the Supreme Court recently rejected in *Wal-Mart*. Like my colleagues, I am not convinced that the certified class in this case is united by common legal or factual issues.

Nonetheless, I do not rule out the possibility that a class properly could be certified in this case or one like it, and it is to this limited extent that I dissent. [I] believe that notwithstanding the inherently child specific nature of child-find inquiries, a class action based on a truly systemic child-find failure may be viable. And the fact that it may not be possible to identify individual class members until the remedial phase of the litigation, when prospective members of the class are invited to come forward and establish that they were among those injured by this systemic failure, should not preclude a class action, which may be the only realistic avenue of relief for those injured by systemic violations of their rights.

Systemic violations of the IDEA are cognizable. The problem here is that the plaintiffs' claims appear to be based on multiple, disparate failures to comply with the school district's statutory child-find obligations rather than a truly systemic policy or practice which affects them all. But my colleagues go so far as to state that "[t]here is no such thing as a 'systemic' failure to find and refer individual disabled children for IEP evaluation—except perhaps if there was 'significant proof' that MPS operated under child-find *policies* that violated the IDEA." Certainly I agree that an illegal policy would support a claim for a systemic violation of the IDEA's child-find mandate. But I also think that widespread practices might also support such a claim. Suppose, for example, that MPS ignored and did not refer for evaluation students with a particular type of potential disability—e.g., dyslexia—and as a result, large numbers of students with that disability went unidentified and were deprived of the educational services to which they were entitled under the IDEA. To my mind, this would be a genuinely systemic violation of the district's child-find obligations that would be amenable to recognition and remediation in a class action: Notwithstanding the fact that each student is unique and is entitled to his own, individualized IEP, all members of the class would suffer a common injury resulting from the school district's failure to have appropriate systems in place to identify students with that particular disability. Insisting instead that each student exhaust his administrative remedies and/or sue independently would surely mean that many such students would remain unidentified and denied their right to free appropriate public education (if only because they would be unaware of their rights) and likely would mean that the systemic violation underlying their claims to relief would persist, as any individual proceedings would result in individual rather than structural relief.

B. THE AMERICANS WITH DISABILITIES ACT AND THE REHABILITATION ACT

1. IN PRIMARY/SECONDARY EDUCATION

K.M. v. Tustin Unified School Dist.

United States Court of Appeals for the Ninth Circuit, 2013.
___ F.3d ___, 2013 WL 3988677.

■ BERZON, CIRCUIT JUDGE.

These two cases, consolidated for oral argument, raise questions about the obligations of public schools under federal law to students who are deaf or hard-of-hearing. The plaintiffs' central claim is that their school districts have an obligation under the Americans with Disabilities Act ("ADA") to provide them with a word-for-word transcription service so that they can fully understand the teacher and fellow students without undue strain and consequent stress.

K.M., a high schooler in the Tustin Unified School District ("Tustin") in Orange County, California, and D.H., a high schooler in the Poway Unified School District ("Poway") in San Diego County, California, both have hearing disabilities. Each student, through her parents, requested that, to help her follow classroom discussions, her school district provide her with Communication Access Realtime Translation ("CART") in the classroom. CART is a word-for-word transcription service, similar to court reporting, in which a trained stenographer provides real-time captioning that appears on a computer monitor. In both cases, the school district denied the request for CART but offered other accommodations. Also in both cases, the student first unsuccessfully challenged the denial of CART in state administrative proceedings and then filed a lawsuit in federal district court.

In the district court, both K.M. and D.H. claimed that the denial of CART violated both the Individuals with Disabilities Education Act ("IDEA") and Title II of the ADA. In each case, the district court granted summary judgment for the school district, holding that the district had fully complied with the IDEA and that the plaintiff's ADA claim was foreclosed by the failure of her IDEA claim. On appeal, both K.M. and D.H. do not contest the conclusion that their respective school districts complied with the IDEA. They challenge, however, the district courts' grants of summary judgment on their ADA claims, because they maintain that Title II imposes effective communication obligations upon public schools independent of, not coextensive with, schools' obligations under the IDEA.

In light of this litigation history, these appeals present this court with a narrow question: whether a school district's compliance with its obligations to a deaf or hard-of-hearing child under the IDEA also necessarily establishes compliance with its effective communication obligations to that child under Title II of the ADA. For the reasons explained below, we hold that it does not. We do not find in either statute an indication that Congress intended the statutes to interact in a mechanical fashion in the schools context, automatically pretermitting any Title II claim where a school's IDEA obligation is satisfied. Moreover, in one of these cases, *K.M. v. Tustin,* the Department of Justice ("DOJ") has filed an amicus brief in support of the plaintiff that includes an interpretation of the relevant Title II regulations, to which we accord deference under *Auer v. Robbins,* 519 U.S. 452 (1997), and which bolsters our conclusion.

FACTUAL AND PROCEDURAL BACKGROUND

K.M.

Because of her hearing loss, K.M. is eligible for special education services under the IDEA. Her eligibility means that Tustin must provide K.M. with a "free appropriate public education" ("FAPE") suited to her individual needs. *See* 20 U.S.C. § 1412(a)(1). As required by the statute, Tustin has convened regular meetings to develop an annual "individualized education plan" ("IEP") identifying K.M.'s educational goals and laying out which special services Tustin will provide to address those goals in the upcoming academic year. *See id.* § 1412(a)(4).

In spring 2009, when K.M. was completing the eighth grade, Tustin and her parents began to prepare for her upcoming transition to high school. At a June 2009 meeting of K.M.'s IEP team, K.M.'s mother requested that Tustin provide her with CART beginning the first day of ninth grade, in Fall 2009. K.M.'s long-time auditory-visual therapist recommended that K.M. receive CART in high school. The IEP team deferred a decision on the CART request, instead developing an IEP that offered K.M. other accommodations.

Shortly thereafter, K.M. filed an administrative complaint challenging the June 2009 IEP. During the course of K.M.'s ninth grade year, her parents and Tustin officials met for several IEP meetings but were unable to come to an agreement that would resolve the complaint. After providing K.M. with trials of both CART and an alternative transcription technology called TypeWell, her IEP team concluded that she did not require transcription services to receive a FAPE under the IDEA, *see* 20 U.S.C. § 1412(a)(1), and reaffirmed the June 2009 IEP.

K.M.'s challenge to the June 2009 IEP proceeded to a seven-day hearing before a California administrative law judge ("ALJ"). K.M. testified that she could usually hear her teachers but had trouble hearing her classmates and classroom videos. Several of K.M.'s teachers testified that, in their opinion, K.M. could hear and follow classroom discussion well.

Applying the relevant legal standards, the ALJ concluded that Tustin had complied with both its procedural and substantive obligations under the IDEA and had provided K.M. with a FAPE. The ALJ observed that K.M.'s mother was requesting CART so that K.M. could "maximize her potential," but the IDEA, as interpreted by the Supreme Court in *Board of Education of Hendrick Hudson Central School District, Westchester County v. Rowley,* 458 U.S. 176 (1982), does not require schools to provide "a potential-maximizing education."

Dissatisfied, K.M. filed a complaint in district court challenging the ALJ decision on her IDEA claim. She also asserted disability discrimination claims under Section 504 of the Rehabilitation Act [and] Title II of the ADA. [W]ith respect to her ADA claim, she sought, in addition to other relief, "an Order compelling Defendants to provide CART." The complaint alleges that CART "is commonly paid for by other Southern California public school districts," including the Los Angeles Unified School District and the Santa Monica Malibu School District, and "is also commonly provided at the college level under the ADA."

In declarations submitted to the district court, K.M.'s teachers declared that she participated in classroom discussions comparably to other students. K.M. saw her situation quiet differently, emphasizing that she could only follow along in the classroom with intense concentration, leaving her exhausted at the end of each day.

The district court granted summary judgment for Tustin. First, as to K.M.'s IDEA claim, the district court stated that it was "reluctant to adopt fully teacher and administrator conclusions about K.M.'s comprehension levels over the testimony of K.M. herself," and found "that K.M.'s testimony reveals that her difficulty following discussions may have been greater than her teachers perceived." Nevertheless, the district court agreed with the ALJ that, under the relevant legal standards, K.M. had been afforded a FAPE compliant with the IDEA. Second, the district court held that "K.M.'s claims under the ADA and the Rehabilitation Act fail on the merits for the same reason that her claim under [the] IDEA failed."

[D.H.]

Like K.M., D.H. is eligible for and receives special education services under the IDEA, pursuant to an annual IEP. At an IEP meeting held towards the end of D.H.'s seventh-grade year, D.H.'s parents "agreed . . . that [D.H.] was making progress," but said that they "believed that [she] needed CART in order to have equal access in the classroom." The IEP team decided that CART was not necessary to provide D.H. with a FAPE, noting that D.H. was making good academic progress.

D.H. filed an administrative complaint challenging her April 2009 IEP. During the ensuing hearing, D.H. testified that she sometimes had trouble following class discussions and teacher instructions. The ALJ concluded, however, that Poway had provided D.H. with a FAPE under the IDEA, finding that D.H. "hears enough of what her teachers and fellow pupils say in class to allow her to access the general education curriculum" and "did not need CART services to gain educational benefit."

D.H. challenged the ALJ decision on her IDEA claim in district court, and also alleged disability discrimination claims under Section 504 of the Rehabilitation Act and Title II of the ADA, seeking, in addition to other relief, "an Order compelling Defendants to provide CART." Like K.M.'s complaint, D.H.'s complaint alleges that CART is commonly provided by other Southern California school districts and at the college level.

D.H. entered high school in Fall 2010. Before the district court, D.H. submitted a declaration in support of her motion for summary judgment which she declared that she has continued to have difficulty hearing in her classes. Although D.H. can use visual cues to follow conversations, "[u]se of these strategies requires a lot of mental energy and focus," leaving her "drained" at the end of the school day. D.H.'s declaration questioned whether her teachers understood the extra effort it required for her to do well in school.

The district court initially granted partial summary judgment for Poway on D.H.'s IDEA claim, holding that the April 2009 IEP provided a FAPE under the IDEA. Although noting that it was "sympathetic to the parents' view that the CART service would make it easier for [D.H.] to follow the lectures and class discussions," the district court denied the request to order the service, on the ground that "the IDEA does not require States to 'maximize each child's potential . . . .' " Later, the district court granted summary judgment for defendants on D.H.'s remaining—ADA and Section 504—claims. Relying in part on the earlier district court decision in *K.M. v. Tustin*, the district court held that "a plaintiff's failure to show a deprivation of a FAPE under the IDEA dooms a claim under [Section] 504, and, accordingly, under the ADA."

This appeal, in which D.H. challenges only the district court's ruling on her ADA claim, followed.

DISCUSSION

I. General Statutory Background

Before discussing K.M. and D.H.'s specific claims, we provide some necessary context concerning the three statutes primarily implicated by these appeals, the IDEA, Title II of the ADA, and Section 504 of the Rehabilitation Act, especially as they apply to accommodation of students with communication difficulties.

A.

The IDEA requires schools to make available to children with disabilities a "free appropriate public education," or "FAPE," tailored to their individual needs. 20 U.S.C. § 1400(d)(1)(A). States receiving federal funds under the IDEA must show that they have implemented "policies and procedures" to provide disabled children with a FAPE, including procedures to develop an IEP for each eligible child. *Id.* § 1412(a), (a)(1), (a)(4).

The IDEA enumerates several general factors that a child's IEP team must consider in developing her IEP. These are "the strengths of the child," "the concerns of the parents for enhancing the education of their child," "the results of the initial evaluation or most recent evaluation of the child," and "the academic, developmental, and functional needs of the child." *Id.* § 1414(d)(3)(A). In addition, the IDEA enumerates "special factors" that must be considered if a child has a particular type of disability. For a child who is deaf or hard-of-hearing, the IEP team is required to

consider the child's language and communication needs, opportunities for direct communications with peers and professional personnel in the child's language and communication mode, academic level, and full range of needs, including opportunities for direct instruction in the child's language and communication mode[.]

Id. § 1414(d)(3)(B)(iv). The IEP team is also required to "consider whether the child needs assistive technology devices and services." *Id.* § 1414(d)(3)(B)(v).

The IDEA does not, however, specify "any substantive standard prescribing the level of education to be accorded handicapped children." *Rowley,* 458 U.S. at 189. Rather, the IDEA primarily provides parents with various procedural safeguards, including the right to participate in IEP meetings and the right to challenge an IEP in state administrative proceedings and, ultimately, in state or federal court. *Rowley* saw the statute as resting on the premise "that adequate compliance with the procedures prescribed would in most cases assure much if not all of what Congress wished in the way of substantive content in an IEP."

[T]he IDEA does have a substantive component, but a fairly modest one: The IEP developed through the required procedures must be "reasonably calculated to enable the child to receive educational benefits." *Rowley.* The IDEA does not require states to provide disabled children with "a potential-maximizing education." This access-centered standard means that, for a child being educated in mainstream classrooms, an IEP is substantively valid so long as it is "reasonably calculated to enable the child to achieve passing marks and advance from grade to grade."

B.

In contrast to the more process-oriented IDEA, the ADA imposes less elaborate procedural requirements. It also establishes different substantive requirements that public entities must meet.

Title II of the ADA, the title applicable to public services, provides that "no qualified individual with a disability shall, by reason of such disability, be excluded from participation in or be denied the benefits of the services, programs, or activities of a public entity, *or be subjected to discrimination by any such entity,*" and requires that the DOJ promulgate regulations to implement this provision. 42 U.S.C. §§ 12132, 12134 (emphasis added). We have recognized that, under the principles of deference established in *Chevron U.S.A. Inc. v. Natural Resources Defense Council, Inc.,* 467 U.S. 837 (1984), the DOJ's Title II-implementing regulations "should be given controlling weight unless they are arbitrary, capricious, or manifestly contrary to the statute."

Among the DOJ's Title II-implementing regulations, and at the core of these appeals, is the so-called "effective communications regulation," which spells out public entities' communications-related duties towards those with disabilities. *See* 28 C.F.R. § 35.160 (2010). The Title II effective communications regulation states two requirements: First, public entities must "take appropriate steps to ensure that communications with applicants, participants, and members of the public with disabilities are as effective as communications with others." *Id.* § 35.160(a). Second, public entities must "furnish appropriate auxiliary aids and services where necessary to afford an individual with a disability an equal opportunity to participate in, and enjoy the benefits of, a service, program, or activity conducted by a public entity." *Id.* § 35.160(b)(1). The Title II regulations define the phrase "auxiliary aids and services" for purposes of § 35.160 as including, *inter alia,* "real-time computer-aided transcription services" and "videotext displays." *Id.* § 35.104. "In determining what type of auxiliary aid and service is necessary, a public entity shall give primary consideration to the requests of the individual with disabilities." *Id.* § 35.160(b)(2).

A separate, more general Title II regulation limits the application of these requirements: Notwithstanding any other requirements in the regulations, a public entity need not, under Title II, "take any action that it can demonstrate would result in a fundamental alteration in the nature of a service, program, or activity or in undue financial and administrative burdens." *Id.* § 35.164. The public entity has the burden to prove that a proposed action would result in undue burden or fundamental alteration, and the decision "must be made by the head of the public entity or his or her designee after considering all resources available for use in the funding and operation of the service, program, or activity and must be accompanied by a written statement of the reasons for reaching that conclusion." *Id.* The public entity must "take any other action that would not result in such an alteration or such burdens but would nevertheless ensure that, to the maximum extent possible, individuals with disabilities receive the benefits or services provided by the public entity." *Id.*

As should be apparent, the IDEA and Title II differ in both ends and means. Substantively, the IDEA sets only a floor of access to education for children with communications disabilities, but requires school districts to provide the individualized services necessary to get a child to that floor, regardless of the costs, administrative burdens, or program alterations required. Title II and its implementing regulations, taken together, require public entities to take steps towards making existing services not just accessible, but *equally* accessible to people with communication disabilities, but only insofar as doing so does not pose an undue burden or require a fundamental alteration of their programs.

C.

Finally, at least as a general matter, public schools must comply with both the IDEA and the ADA. The IDEA obviously governs public schools. There is also no question that public schools are among the public entities governed by Title II. *See* 42 U.S.C. § 12101(a)(3) (listing "education" in the ADA congressional findings section as one of "critical areas" in which disability discrimination exists); *Tennessee v. Lane,* 541 U.S. 509, 525 (2004) (listing "public education" among the sites of discrimination that Congress intended to reach with Title II).

Moreover, Congress has specifically and clearly provided that the IDEA coexists with the ADA and other federal statutes, rather than swallowing the others. *See Payne v. Peninsula Sch. Dist.,* 653 F.3d 863, 872 (9th Cir.2011) (en banc). After the Supreme Court interpreted an earlier version of the IDEA to provide the "exclusive avenue" for pursuing "an equal protection claim to a publicly financed special education," Congress enacted legislation to overturn that ruling. An amendment to the IDEA, enacted in 1986, clarified that the IDEA does not foreclose any additional constitutional or federal statutory claims that children with disabilities may have, so long as they first exhaust their IDEA claims through the IDEA administrative process. In its current version, the IDEA non-exclusivity provision reads:

> Nothing in this chapter shall be construed to restrict or limit the rights, procedures, and remedies available under the Constitution, the Americans with Disabilities Act of 1990 [42 U.S.C. § 12101 *et seq.*], title V of the Rehabilitation Act of 1973 [29 U.S.C. § 791 *et seq.*], or other Federal laws protecting the rights of children with disabilities, except that before the filing of a civil action under such laws seeking relief that is also available under this subchapter, the procedures under subsections (f) and (g) shall be exhausted to the same extent as would be required had the action been brought under this subchapter.

20 U.S.C. § 1415(l) (alterations in original).

D.

It is against this statutory background that we shall consider how the IDEA and Title II interact with respect to school districts' obligations to IDEA-eligible students, like K.M. and D.H., who are deaf or hard-of-hearing. First, however, we must clarify one way in which the statutes do not interact.

In the district court's analysis in *K.M.,* relied upon by the district court in *D.H.,* the plaintiffs' ADA claims were tethered to their IDEA claims through the connective thread of a third federal statute, Section 504 of the Rehabilitation Act. Section 504 bars the exclusion of individuals with disabilities from any program or activity receiving federal funds. *See* 29 U.S.C. § 794(a). The district court in *K.M.* reasoned that "the fact that K.M. has failed to show a deprivation of a FAPE under IDEA . . . dooms her claim under Section 504, and, *accordingly,* her ADA claim" (emphasis added). Similarly, the district court in *D.H.* reasoned that "a plaintiff's failure to show a deprivation of a FAPE under the IDEA dooms a claim under [Section] 504, and, *accordingly,* under the ADA" (emphasis added).

The district courts arrived at this reasoning by combining two lines of our case law. In the first line of cases, we have identified a partial overlap between the statutory FAPE provision under the IDEA and a similar provision within the Section 504 regulations promulgated by the Department of Education, requiring schools receiving federal funds to provide "a free appropriate public education to each qualified handicapped person who is in the recipient's jurisdiction." 34 C.F.R. § 104.33(a). Although both the IDEA and the Section 504 regulation use the locution "free appropriate public education," or "FAPE," we have concluded that the two FAPE requirements are "overlapping but different." At the same time, we have noted that, as provided by the Section 504 FAPE regulation, "adopting a valid IDEA IEP is sufficient but not necessary to satisfy the [Section] 504 FAPE requirements."

In the second line of cases, we have discussed the close relationship between Section 504 and Title II of the ADA. Congress used the earlier-enacted Section 504 as a model when drafting Title II. We have observed on occasion that "there is no significant difference in the analysis of rights and obligations created by the two Acts."

Combining these two lines of cases, the district courts reasoned that (1) a valid IDEA IEP satisfies the Section 504 FAPE regulation; (2) Section 504 and Title II are substantially similar statutes; (3) therefore, a valid IDEA IEP also satisfies Title II. This syllogism overstates the connections both between the IDEA and Section 504, and between Section 504 and Title II.

First, we have never held that compliance with the IDEA dooms *all* Section 504 claims. [We have] held only that "adopting a valid IDEA IEP is sufficient . . . to satisfy the [Section] 504 *FAPE requirements.*" We so held because the Section 504 FAPE regulation itself provides that provision of a FAPE under the IDEA "is one means of meeting *the standard established in paragraph (b)(1)(i) of this section,*" 34 C.F.R. § 104.33(b)(2) (emphasis added), i.e., the Section 504 FAPE standard. Because a school district's provision of a FAPE under the IDEA meets Section 504 FAPE requirements, a claim predicated on finding a violation of the Section 504 FAPE standard will fail if the IDEA FAPE requirement has been met. Section 504 claims predicated on other theories of liability under that statute and its implementing regulations, however, are not precluded by a determination that the student has been provided an IDEA FAPE.

Second, the connection between Title II and Section 504 is nuanced. [C]ongress [m]andated that the federal regulations implementing Title II be consistent with certain, but not all, of the regulations enforcing Section 504. *See id.* § 12134(b). Specifically, Congress mandated that the Title II regulations as to all topics "[e]xcept for 'program accessibility, existing facilities,' and 'communications'" be consistent with the Section 504 regulations codified at 28 C.F.R. part 41, and that the Title II regulations as to "'program accessibility, existing facilities,' and 'communications'" be consistent with the Section 504 regulations codified at 28 C.F.R. part 39. *Id.* Congress did not, however, mandate that Title II regulations be consistent with the Section 504 *FAPE* regulation, which is codified at 34 C.F.R. part 104.

Neither K.M. nor D.H.'s theory of Title II liability is predicated on a denial of FAPE under any definition of that term; indeed, Title II does not impose any FAPE requirement. Rather, both K.M. and D.H. ground their claims in the Title II effective communications regulation, which they argue establishes independent obligations on the part of public schools to students who are deaf or hard-of-hearing. Insofar as the Title II effective communications regulation has a Section 504 analog, it is not the Section 504 FAPE regulation at 34 C.F.R. § 104.33. [R]ather, it is the Section 504 communications regulation at 28 C.F.R. § 39.160, as that is the regulation with which Congress has specified that Title II communications regulations must be consistent. *See* 42 U.S.C. § 12134(b).

II. The IDEA and ADA Communications Provisions

A.

The question whether a school meets the ADA's requirements for accommodating deaf or hard-of-hearing students as long as it provides a FAPE for such students in accord with the IDEA is therefore one that cannot be answered through any general principles concerning the overall relationship between the two statutes. Instead, we must address the question by comparing the *particular* provisions of the ADA and the IDEA covering students who are deaf or hard-of-hearing, as well as the implementing regulations for those provisions. If the ADA requirements are sufficiently different from, and in some relevant respect more stringent than, those imposed by the IDEA, then compliance with the IDEA FAPE requirement would not preclude an ADA claim. Because we have no cases addressing the parallelism between the IDEA and either the Title II effective communications regulation or its analogous Section 504 regulation, we must construe the relevant statutes and regulations as a question of first impression.

In doing so, "[w]e afford . . . considerable respect" to the DOJ's interpretation of the ADA effective communication regulation, as expressed in its amicus brief to this court. *M.R. v. Dreyfus,* 697 F.3d 706, 735 (9th Cir.2012). "An agency's interpretation of its own regulation is 'controlling unless plainly erroneous or inconsistent with the regulation.'" *Id.* (quoting *Auer,* 519 U.S. at 461). Applying that standard, we conclude from our comparison of the relevant statutory and regulatory texts that the IDEA FAPE requirement and the Title II communication requirements are significantly different. The result is that in some situations, but not others, schools may be required under the ADA to provide services to deaf or hard-of-hearing students that are different than the services required by the IDEA.

First, the factors that the public entity must consider in deciding what accommodations to provide deaf or hard-of-hearing children are different. The key variables in the IDEA framework are the child's "needs" and "opportunities." When developing a deaf or hard-of-hearing child's IEP for IDEA purposes, the IEP team is required to consider, among other factors, "the child's language and communication *needs,"* "*opportunities* for direct communications with peers and professional personnel in the child's language and communication mode," and "whether the child needs assistive technology devices and services." 20 U.S.C. § 1414(d)(3)(B)(iv) & (v) (emphases added). Under the ADA effective communications regulation, a public entity is also required to "furnish appropriate auxiliary aids and services *where necessary.*" 28 C.F.R. § 35.160(b)(1) (emphasis added). But the ADA adds another variable: In determining how it will meet the child's needs, the ADA regulations require that the public entity "give primary consideration to the *requests* of the individual with disabilities." *Id.* § 35.160(b)(2) (emphasis added). That provision has no direct counterpart in the IDEA. Although the IDEA requires schools to consult with parents and to include the child in IEP meetings "whenever appropriate," 20 U.S.C. § 1414(d)(1)(B)(vii), it does not require that parental or child requests be assigned "primary" weight.

Second, Title II provides the public entity with defenses unavailable under the IDEA. Specifically, Title II "does not require a public entity to take any action that it can demonstrate would result in a fundamental alteration in the nature of a service, program, or activity or in undue financial and administrative burdens." 28 C.F.R. § 35.164. In particular, as the DOJ explained in its amicus brief to this court, the ADA effective communication obligation "is limited to the provision of services for *existing programs;* the ADA does not require a school to provide new programs or new curricula" (emphasis in original). The IDEA does not provide schools with any analog to Title II's fundamental alteration and undue burden defenses.

Third, the specific regulation at issue here, the Title II effective communications regulation, requires public schools to communicate "as effective[ly]" with disabled students as with other students, and to provide disabled students the "auxiliary aids . . . necessary to afford . . . an *equal opportunity* to participate in, and enjoy the benefits of," the school program. 28 C.F.R. §§ 35.160(a)(1) & (b)(1) (emphasis added). That requirement is not relevant to IDEA claims, as the IDEA does not require schools to "provide 'equal' educational opportunities" to all students. *Rowley.*

Given these differences between the two statutes, we are unable to articulate any unified theory for how they will interact in particular cases. Precisely because we are unable to do so, we must reject the argument that the success or failure of a student's IDEA claim dictates, as a matter of law, the success or failure of her Title II claim. As a result, courts evaluating claims under the IDEA and Title II must analyze each claim separately under the relevant statutory and regulatory framework. We note, however, that nothing in our holding should be understood to bar district courts from applying ordinary principles of issue and claim preclusion in cases raising both IDEA and Title II claims where the IDEA administrative appeals process has functionally adjudicated some or all questions relevant to a Title II claim in a way that precludes relitigation.

B.

Both school districts make one final argument that requires a brief response. They argue that, even if analyzed independently under Title II, K.M. and D.H.'s claims must fail because ADA liability requires plaintiffs to show that they were denied "meaningful access" to school services, programs, or activities, and that they cannot make this showing. The phrase "meaningful access" derives not from the text of the ADA or its implementing regulations, but from the Supreme Court's opinion in *Alexander v. Choate,* 469 U.S. 287 (1985).

Choate involved a class-action lawsuit brought by individuals with disabilities who argued that cost-saving measures to Tennessee's Medicaid program would disproportionately affect them and therefore amounted to impermissible discrimination under Section 504. Rejecting both the contention that Section 504 reaches only purposeful discrimination and "the boundless notion that all disparate-impact showings constitute prima facie cases under [Section] 504," the Court construed Section 504 as including a "meaningful access" standard that identified which disparate-impact showings rise to the level of actionable discrimination. In construing Section 504 in this manner, the Court considered and relied on the regulations applicable to Section 504.

We have relied on *Choate*'s construction of Section 504 in ADA Title II cases, and have held that to challenge a facially neutral government policy on the ground that it has a disparate impact on people with disabilities, the policy must have the effect of denying meaningful access to public services. As in *Choate,* in considering Title II's "meaningful access" requirement, we are guided by the relevant regulations interpreting Title II. Consequently, in determining whether K.M. and D.H. were denied meaningful access to the school's benefits and services, we are guided by the specific standards of the Title II effective communications regulation.

In other words, the "meaningful access" standard incorporates rather than supersedes applicable interpretive regulations, and so does not preclude K.M. and D.H. from litigating their claims under those regulations. The school districts' suggestion to the contrary therefore fails.

III. Application to This Case

Finally, we return to the specifics of the cases before us in this appeal. Here, in both cases, the district court held that the plaintiff's Title II claim was foreclosed as a matter of law by the failure of her IDEA claim. For the reasons explained above, the district courts legally erred in granting summary judgment on that basis. The failure of an IDEA claim does not automatically foreclose a Title II claim grounded in the Title II effective communications regulation.

[P]rudence counsels in favor of returning these cases to the district court for further proceedings. Having granted summary judgment on legal grounds, neither district court considered whether there was a genuine issue of material fact as to the school districts' compliance with Title II. Moreover, the school districts have litigated these cases thus far from the position that the plaintiffs' IDEA and Title II claims were coextensive. Now that we have clarified that the school districts' position is not correct, we expect that the parties may wish to further develop the factual record and, if necessary, revise their legal positions to address the specifics of a Title II as opposed to an IDEA claim.

To give the district courts an opportunity to consider the merits of K.M. and D.H.'s Title II claims in the first instance, we reverse the grants of summary judgment on the ADA claims in both cases, [a]nd remand for further proceedings consistent with this opinion, without prejudice to whether the school districts may renew their motions for summary judgment on other grounds.

R.K. ex rel. J.K. v. Board of Educ. of Scott County

United States Court of Appeals for the Sixth Circuit, 2012.
494 Fed.Appx. 589.

■ BOGGS, CIRCUIT JUDGE.

R.K. is a child with Type 1 diabetes. R.K. was not permitted to attend the neighborhood school, Eastern Elementary School, which lacked a full-time nurse, and was assigned to Anne Mason Elementary, another school in Scott County, which had a full-time nurse on duty. R.K., by his next friends, J.K. and R.K., brought suit in federal court, alleging that the decision to assign R.K. to the non-neighborhood school constituted discrimination in violation of § 504 of the Rehabilitation Act, the Americans with Disabilities Act, the Fourteenth Amendment's due-process and equal-protection clauses, and K.R.S. § 344.130. The district court granted summary judgment in favor of the defendants on all counts.

[W]e vacate the judgment of the district court [i]n part, and remand for further proceedings not inconsistent with this opinion[.]

I

A

The facts, as stated by the district court, can be summarized as follows. On June 23, 2008, R.K.—then four years old—was diagnosed with Type 1 diabetes. R.K. requires insulin injections in order to control glucose levels. In March 2009, at an open enrollment, the child's parents enrolled R.K. at the neighborhood school, Eastern Elementary School (EES), located at 3407 Newtown Pike. R.K.'s parents informed the administration of Eastern Elementary School that R.K. would need insulin injections during the school day. The Board of Education of Scott County Schools told R.K.'s parents that there was not a full-time school nurse on the premises of Eastern Elementary School to give R.K. injections during the day. On August 6, 2009, the Board informed R.K.'s parents that their child would have to attend Anne Mason Elementary School (AMES), located at 350 Champion Way, and denied R.K. enrollment at Eastern Elementary School.[1] At the time the complaint was filed on October 20, 2009—about a month into R.K.'s kindergarten year—the Board had not put forth a plan that would allow him to attend Eastern Elementary School. In December 2009, two months after the complaint was filed and four months after the decision was made, R.K.'s parents informed the Board that R.K. had an insulin pump that eliminated the need for him to receive daily injections. R.K.'s parents argued that the Board should allow R.K. to attend Eastern Elementary and that someone other than a nurse could be trained to assist the student in monitoring the pump and counting carbohydrates (carbs). The Board continued to deny the parents' request to transfer R.K. to Eastern Elementary School, asserting that under Kentucky law, only a nurse or other qualified medical official can monitor R.K.'s insulin pump and assist with counting carbs.

Both parties agree that R.K. is not able to use the pump without assistance. The Board believes that this requires him to attend a school

---

[1] Eastern Elementary and Anne Mason Elementary are approximately six miles apart.

with a nurse on site. R.K. argues that he should be allowed to attend the neighborhood school despite the lack of a nurse on duty. The district court granted summary judgment in favor of the Board, finding that R.K. "fails to assert that Defendants' accommodations for the Child have prevented him from receiving an adequate and beneficial education, participating in extra-curricular activities, field trips, or advancing to the next grade. The only distinction between the two schools, based upon Plaintiff's arguments, is that EES is his neighborhood school and AMES is not."

B

The factual record in this case is quite underdeveloped, and ultimately unhelpful to resolve the significant legal issues presented. No discovery was undertaken by the parties. On appeal, both parties, as well as amici, have varying accounts of the facts with respect to how the decision was made to assign R.K. to Anne Mason Elementary. R.K.'s fact section has *no* references to the record as required by Federal Rules of Appellate Procedure 28(a)(7) and 28(e). Further, R.K. attached materials and excerpts from expert reports and publications to his brief that are not part of the record—including expert reports submitted to *other* courts that were never considered below.

Likewise, the district court based its opinion on a number of factual statements made in the briefs of R.K. and the Board—facts that were not to be found in any evidence. There were no citations to any exhibits in the district court's opinion to support its account of the facts, and it did not mention some of the few facts that were available. This is reversible error, especially because the paucity of facts in the record shows that genuine issues of material fact are in dispute with respect to how the Board decided to assign R.K. to Anne Mason Elementary, rather than Eastern Elementary, his neighborhood school, and why it denied a subsequent request to transfer him.

The only facts in the record are found in three affidavits and a letter. There are no depositions. First, an affidavit by James A. (Tony) Harrison, a Registered Nurse (RN) and the District Services Manager for the Scott County Schools. Second, an affidavit by J.K., R.K.'s father, along with a letter from the Scott County Schools. Third, an affidavit from Leslie Scott, an Assistant Professor of Nursing at the University of Kentucky.

1

Harrison is a "member of the School District's § 504 Committee." He stated that he "reviewed all [of R.K.'s] glucose readings obtained during school hours from September 21, 2009 through December 14, 2009." It is unclear if he was involved in the review of R.K.'s case during the summer of 2009 or if he was involved in the initial decision to assign him to Anne Mason Elementary, which is the only stated subject of R.K.'s complaint. Harrison acknowledged that as of September 21, 2009, R.K.'s insulin was injected through an insulin pump. Harrison discussed the procedures that Rose Lewis, the full-time RN at Anne Mason Elementary, had to go through to monitor R.K.'s pump and help him count carbs.

Based on a review of R.K.'s glucose readings, Harrison observed that R.K.'s readings were "outside [R.K.'s physician's] requested glucose range 48% of the time." "Low glucose readings (hypoglycemia) occurred 12% of the time and high glucose readings (hyperglycemia) were obtained 36% of the time." Harrison found that these spikes and drops in his glucose level "require decision-making to determine if treatment is necessary, and what type of treatment to use." Upon reviewing how the nurse handled these events, Harrison observed "that there also is an element of prevention in the treatments provided by Mrs. Lewis upon the occurrences of hypoglycemia and hyperglycemia, precluding a more severe health care event."

Harrison acknowledged that there are other elementary school students with diabetes who attend Scott County schools where full-time nurses are not on duty. "School District decisions pertaining to whether a student with special health care needs may require full time care and over-site [*sic*] by medically trained staff are individualized. Two factors weigh heavily in this decision: 1) whether a student has medical orders that specify self-treatment; and, 2) the stability of the student's health condition indicating the degree of risk for the student."

This admission, which was known to R.K. when he filed his motion for relief of judgment, undercuts the relevance of the affidavit that another diabetic student was permitted to attend a Scott County school that did not have a full-time nurse. Further, Harrison's admission supports the Board's contention—contrary to R.K. and the United States's claim—that it undertakes an individualized approach to accommodating students with disabilities. It does not have a blanket policy of sending *all* diabetic students to schools with a nurse on duty. Indeed, Harrison lists eighteen different "factors [that] are considered in deciding the intensity and frequency of care for each individual student with special health care needs." He states that "both General and individual factors are considered and analyzed to evaluate health care needs for each individual student."

It was Harrison's "professional opinion . . . that R.K.'s glucose readings are erratic and are best served by a school nurse to accommodate his health care needs, ensure his safety and well being, and minimize any detrimental effects on his learning." He made this decision in light of the fact that he had "been determined by his treating physician to be unable to give his own insulin injections, and requires assistance with all aspects of the management of his medical condition while at school, including with the operation of the insulin pump." Therefore, "as part of the School District's § 504 Committee, [Harrison] recommended that R.K. remain at the school where he is attended throughout his day by an RN [at Anne Mason Elementary], to ensure a trained and licensed professional is monitoring and providing for his health care needs."

Harrison based this specific decision on five factors. First, "R.K.'s glucose levels were out of [the] acceptable range 48% of the time during school hours." Second, "R.K. continues to receive subcutaneous injections of insulin." Third, "[i]t is the professional opinion of the Affiant, consistent with advisory opinions of the Kentucky Board of Nursing, that the administration of medication via any injectable route should not be delegated to unlicensed personnel unless for immediate intervention in a life threatening situation." Fourth, "[t]eachers, paraprofessionals, bus drivers and other educational personnel are not trained nor qualified in medical care." Fifth, Harrison "would not recommend the delegation of duties to these other school employees regarding administration of medication to R.K." Harrison does not mention who else participated on the § 504 Committee, nor does he explain how anyone else on the Committee reached a decision.

The district court did not once cite Harrison's affidavit, nor did R.K. acknowledge its existence other than to argue that Harrison should not have relied on advisory opinions of the Kentucky Board of Nursing. None of these facts were mentioned by the United States or the American Diabetes Association in their amicus briefs. This case seems somewhat schizophrenic—there is on one hand the actual case, and on the other, the case that R.K. and amici present for this court to resolve. We decline the latter invitation.

However, we do not think that the Harrison affidavit allows this court to affirm on alternate grounds. Harrison's analysis only focused on R.K.'s condition *after* Scott County knew he had the insulin pump, sometime between September and December of 2009. We can assume, but cannot know for certain, that the same factors were considered by the Board in its decision in August 2009 to assign R.K. to Anne Mason Elementary—that is, before R.K. filed suit in federal court. And it is this decision that is the subject of R.K.'s complaint, which was never amended. Such questions would be appropriate questions during a deposition of Harrison or others involved in the § 504 Committee after remand.

2

The other primary piece of evidence in the spotty record is an affidavit of J.K., R.K.'s father. J.K. stated that he informed the Board that R.K. had diabetes when he registered the child in March 2009. J.K. "received a call from Jan Sharp, Director of Child and Family Services for Scott County Board in April 2009," who told J.K. that "R.K. should attend Western Elementary or Anne Mason Elementary." J.K. informed Ms. Sharp that he wanted R.K. to attend Eastern Elementary. "After several calls and many meetings Scott County Board of Education told us that R.K. would only be able to attend Anne Mason Elementary or Western Elementary." J.K. provided no information about what transpired at these meetings, where they occurred, whether they were § 504 meetings, or who attended these meetings. J.K. stated that "[a]t the beginning of the 2009–2010 school year my wife and I were informed that our son could not attend Eastern Elementary due to the fact there was not a school nurse assigned to Eastern Elementary. Due to the fact that my son may need insulin injections during the day Scott County Board of Education assigned him to Anne Mason Elementary School which had a school nurse." J.K. recounted that he was "told by Scott County Board of Education that the *only reason* our son was being assigned to Anne Mason was due to his diabetes." (emphasis added). J.K. stated that he was told that if "R.K. did not need injections he could be transferred to his neighborhood school Eastern Elementary."

On December 14, 2009, J.K. informed the "director of 504 compliance . . . that our [child] was now using an insulin pump and would not need insulin injections during the day." The Board denied his transfer to Eastern Elementary, based on a letter dated January 5, 2010. The letter states:

The Scott County School District Review Team met December 17, 2009 to review your request that [R.K.], attend [the] home school, Eastern Elementary. The review team read and discussed the amended Section 504 Accommodation Plan and minutes taken during the December 14, 2009 meeting. The minutes reflect concerns noted by District nurses Rose Lewis and Tony Harrison in allowing untrained staff to be responsible for the implementation of the Accommodation Plan. Mr. Harrison stated there is a risk allowing an unlicensed medical person to carry out the plan. Further, Mrs. Lewis noted that although R.K. is not receiving an injection, the use of the insulin pump is infusion and she does not recommend delegating this responsibility to another person.

The review team has considered all information and supports the opinions of Mr. Harrison and Mrs. Lewis. R.K. will continue to attend a Scott County School where a nurse is stationed full time. The team makes this decision putting the safety and well-being of R.K. first. The two schools that meet this requirement are Anne Mason Elementary School and Western Elementary School. Transportation will be provided to either school.

The letter was signed by Superintendent Patricia Putty, Section 504 Coordinator Martin Hendrix, Director of Child and Family Services Jan Sharpe, Director of Elementary Curriculum Matthew Thompson, and District Nurse Tony Harrison. The letter is entirely consistent with Harrison's affidavit.

J.K. also talks about events that transpired after R.K.'s kindergarten year—that he attended a YMCA day camp where there was no nurse on duty, that he was denied a transfer during the following school year, that the school stated that R.K.'s attendance at Eastern Elementary "would expose Scott County to liability if [R.K.] became ill or injured," and that R.K. attended a Taekwondo Academy that lacks a nurse. All of these events relate to facts that occurred after, and are unrelated to, the filing of the unamended complaint. The time frame of this appeal is limited to R.K.'s kindergarten year, the 2009–2010 school year.

[3]

The final affidavit is from Leslie Scott, an Assistant Professor at the University of Kentucky College of Nursing. In this affidavit, she offers opinion testimony that "[i]t is not difficult nor time consuming to train a lay person to administer to a child's needs in the school setting." Further Scott stated that it was her "opinion that unlicensed school personnel properly trained can safely and accurately administer and/or monitor insulin in the school setting." The American Diabetes Association makes similar arguments in its amicus brief. Finally, Scott concludes that it "is my opinion that in the absence of a school nurse insulin and carbohydrate counting can be administered/performed by a trained non-licensed person safely and effectively in the school setting." Scott was never qualified as an expert witness, nor was she involved in the decision to assign R.K. to Anne Mason Elementary. [H]ad this evidence been submitted as an expert report, it may have been probative, but as an affidavit, it is simply inadmissible opinion testimony.

C

There seems to be a conflict between the affidavit accounts of Harrison and J.K. Harrison attested, as confirmed by the letter, that an individualized assessment was made based on R.K.'s glucose levels and other factors specific to him. R.K.'s father disputes this conclusion and claims that no individualized assessment was made—the child was simply discriminated against based on the fact that he had diabetes.[7] Further, R.K.'s claim is undermined by the Board's position that it considered multiple factors when reassigning R.K. and not simply whether a nurse was available. Because there are no depositions in the record, there is no way to assess their accounts through the adversarial lens.

The factual record is too incomplete to assess, under the ADA and § 504, whether the decisions made by the Board—both during the summer of 2009 and during R.K.'s kindergarten year—constituted any form of discrimination There is a genuine issue of material fact in dispute as to whether individualized factors were considered by the Board in making these decisions. Summary judgment in favor of the Board was not appropriate.

[III]

A

On remand, the parties should engage in discovery to assess precisely how the decision was made to assign R.K. to Anne Mason Elementary. The minutes of the December 14, 2009 meeting would seem to be particularly appropriate. Without such facts, resolution of the complicated, fact-intensive inquiries involved in an ADA or § 504 case would be impossible. Also, giving R.K. an opportunity to amend the complaint may clarify the scope of the issues before the court and allow an assessment of how R.K.'s ability to manage his diabetes has progressed. As it stands now, the events are limited to the kindergarten year. This fall, R.K. will likely be entering the third grade. A complete factual record would permit the district court to apply the correct legal standards.

B

As the United States and the National School Board Association point out in their helpful amicus briefs, the district court did not consider a wealth of law in this area and failed to apply the correct standards in analyzing whether the Board complied with § 504 of the Rehabilitation Act.

Students with diabetes will generally be protected by § 504 of the Rehabilitation Act, which provides that "[n]o otherwise qualified individual with a disability . . . shall, solely by reason of her or his disability, be excluded from the participation in, be denied the benefits of, or be subjected to discrimination under any program or activity receiving Federal financial assistance." 29 U.S.C. § 794(a). The district

---

[7] The United States alludes to a claim that the Board had a blanket policy where all students with diabetes would be reassigned to schools with a nurse regardless of any individualized analysis. This claim does not seem to be supported by any admissible evidence.

court did not mention any of a number of § 504 regulations promulgated by the Department of Education. *See, e.g.,* 34 C.F.R. § 104.10(a) ("The obligation to comply with [those regulations] is not obviated or alleviated by the existence of any state or local law or other requirement that, on the basis of handicap, imposes prohibitions or limits upon the eligibility of qualified handicapped persons to receive services . . . ."); *id.* § 104.4(b)(iv) ("[Covered entities may not p]rovide different or separate aid, benefits, or services to handicapped persons or to any class of handicapped persons unless such action is necessary to provide qualified handicapped persons with aid, benefits, or services that are as effective as those provided to others."); *id.* § 104.33(a) (requiring that elementary schools provide a "free appropriate public education" (FAPE) to students with disabilities "regardless of the nature or severity" of the students' disabilities).[9] Without considering these rules, the court failed to develop an appropriate factual record in light of any of these standards and the circumstances of the case.

A key regulation not addressed below is that the schools must conduct an individualized assessment of the student's needs before making a school placement decision. 34 C.F.R. § 104.35. Schools must consider a variety of information, including the student's "aptitude and achievement tests, teacher recommendations, physical condition, social or cultural background, and adaptive behavior." *Id.* § 104.35(c).

Based on the record, it is unclear if such an individualized assessment occurred when assigning R.K. to Anne Mason Elementary and denying a later transfer request. Harrison's affidavit suggests that, at least with respect to the denial of R.K.'s transfer request during the school year, the school may have considered many of these factors. J.K. argues that none of these factors were considered. Further, we know nothing about what factors went into the decision to initially assign R.K. to Anne Mason Elementary. The record is not sufficient to allow an assessment of whether the Board complied with these regulations.

C

Finally, the United States raises an important issue with respect to whether the Supremacy Clause trumps possible concerns by the Board about avoiding tort liability under Kentucky law. "Even if Kentucky law barred a lay person from administering insulin in public schools, such a state law requirement must yield to federal obligations." United States Br. at 24. This issue was not addressed below. Bundled up in this issue is whether it would have been feasible for the Board to delegate to a non-professional the responsibility of monitoring R.K.'s blood sugar and carb count. Harrison suggested in his affidavit that this would not have been safe. On remand, briefing on this point would be instructive, as the issue of field preemption may be more complicated than the United States suggests. *See* Nat'l Sch. Bds. Ass'n Br. at 12–18.

IV

The judgment of the district court with respect to the Board is VACATED, and REMANDED for further proceedings not inconsistent with this order[.]

---

[9] The district court mentioned the FAPE requirements in the context of the Individuals with Disabilities Education Act (IDEA), 20 U.S.C. § 1415, not in the context of the Rehabilitation Act. The IDEA was not at issue in this case.

NOTES ON ELEMENTARY AND SECONDARY SCHOOLS

1.   The Relationship Between the IDEA and the ADA and Rehabilitation Act.   As *K.M.* and *R.K.* make clear, Title II of the ADA and Section 504 of the Rehabilitation Act impose duties on public elementary and secondary schools that are formally separate from the duties imposed by the IDEA. (In the case of *private* elementary and secondary schools, ADA Title III imposes similar duties to those imposed by ADA Title II in the public-school context.)   In some instances, like the discrimination claim considered in *Ellenberg*, the ADA and Rehabilitation Act impose requirements that are also *substantively* distinct from those imposed by the IDEA.   But as *R.K.* shows, the Department of Education regulations implementing the Rehabilitation Act parallel the requirements of the IDEA in a number of respects—including, most notably, a requirement that school districts provide students with disabilities a "free appropriate public education."   34 C.F.R. § 104.33(a).   Because the ADA specifically incorporates the standards applied by the Rehabilitation Act regulations, see 42 U.S.C. § 12201(a), those regulations provide the baseline for determining ADA Title II's requirements as well.

As the materials in the earlier part of this chapter make clear, the IDEA is enforced through a process that is very different from the process used to enforce the ADA and the Rehabilitation Act.   The existence of parallel obligations under the IDEA and the latter statutes thus raises significant questions about exhaustion of remedies (a matter discussed in the previous section).   But that parallelism also raises significant questions about how school districts order their affairs.   In their empirical examination of school district practices, Professors Kelman and Lester found that districts often were able as a practical matter to channel challenges to their education of students with disabilities through the IDEA process—a process the districts found to be far more tractable than the administrative and judicial process under Section 504. See Kelman & Lester, *supra*, at 112 ("[IDEA] is perceived by administrators as playing a particular role in managing special education and the demands of pupils with disabilities. IDEA not only is perceived to establish a set of minimum substantive and procedural standards for students with disabilities, it also appears to be seen as serving both to limit the claims tat can be made and to leave more control over the administration of special education programs in the hands of local directors."). School administrators expressed great fear that students with disabilities and their parents would invoke (what they perceived to be) the open-ended obligations of Section 504. See *id.* at 112–115. Obviously, schools cannot prevent students and parents from invoking Section 504 and the ADA (though the exhaustion doctrine can at least channel ADA and Rehabilitation Act claims into the IDEA dispute resolution process in the first instance). Why might parents choose to pursue their remedies through the IDEA instead?

2.   The Preemption Question.   *R.K.* remands the question whether the ADA and Rehabilitation Act preempt a state law that bars lay persons from administering insulin injections.   The same question is currently pending before the state courts in California.   In AMERICAN NURSES ASS'N V. O'CONNELL, 110 Cal.Rptr.3d 305 (Cal.App. 3 Dist.), *rev'd*, ___ P.3d ___, 2013 WL 4046566 (Cal.2013), the Court of Appeal held, in a subsequently reversed decision, that California's Nursing Practice Act prohibited school personnel who were not licensed nurses from administering insulin injections to students with diabetes who required the injections under IEPs or Section 504 education plans. The court rejected the argument that, so interpreted, the Nursing Practice Act was preempted by the IDEA and the Rehabilitation Act:

> Appellants argue the record establishes there are a large number of diabetic students in California, that some of those students must take insulin several times a day in order to survive, that such students may require their insulin shots not only while they are at school, but on school field trips or when they are participating in extracurricular school activities, that California has a significant shortage of registered nurses, in particular school nurses, and that California is currently gripped by fiscal crisis. As a result of these facts, appellants contend substantial numbers of students will not receive their required insulin if unlicensed school personnel are not authorized to administer prescribed insulin injections.

> We do not believe the facts submitted by appellant warrant their dramatic conclusion. Appellants have not provided any specific facts showing what number of schools have a diabetic student with a Section 504 Plan or IEP that requires insulin administration during the school day or at school-related activities who are unable to self-administer their medication and who do not have a parent or guardian who elects to administer their insulin or designate another family member or friend to administer the child's insulin. We, therefore, have no idea how many children may actually require the services of a licensed nurse provided by the school district. The fact that there is generally a shortage of registered nurses in California and that there is a particular shortage of school nurses does not establish that a school needing to provide diabetic care to a student pursuant to a Section 504 Plan or IEP plan will be unable to locate and contract for the services of a licensed nurse, including as necessary a licensed vocational nurse, in any particular case. We find it particularly telling that we have not been directed to any data in the record regarding the availability of licensed vocational nurses. Finally, while we can guess that funding of the required services may be difficult for schools in these economic times, we have no evidence that such difficulties cannot be overcome in order to meet the requirements of federal law.

> Appellants rely heavily on the case of *Crowder v. Kitagawa,* (9th Cir.1996) 81 F.3d 1480, as illustrating what they suggest is an analogous situation of conflict preemption. We find *Crowder* to be materially distinguishable from the situation present in this case. In *Crowder,* the Ninth Circuit Court of Appeals held the application, without reasonable modifications, of Hawaii's 120-day quarantine requirement for carnivorous animals entering the state to guide dogs needed by visually-impaired individuals effectively prevented such persons from enjoying the benefits of

state services and activities in violation of the Americans with Disabilities Act (ADA). The court reasoned that: "Although Hawaii's quarantine requirement applies equally to all persons entering the state with a dog, its enforcement burdens visually-impaired persons in a manner different and greater than it burdens others. Because of the unique dependence upon guide dogs among many of the visually-impaired, Hawaii's quarantine effectively denies these persons—the plaintiffs in this case— meaningful access to state services, programs, and activities while such services, programs, and activities remain open and easily accessible by others. The quarantine, therefore, discriminates against the plaintiffs by reason of their disability." It acknowledged "the general principle that courts will not second-guess the public health and safety decisions of state legislatures acting within their traditional police powers." "However, when Congress has passed antidiscrimination laws such as the ADA which require reasonable modifications to public health and safety policies, it is incumbent upon the courts to insure that the mandate of federal law is achieved."

In contrast here, appellants have not met their burden to show it is necessary for unlicensed school personnel to administer insulin to diabetic students in order "to insure that the mandate of federal law is achieved." A showing that there may be tension or potential conflict between California law and the federal law is not enough. California law does not frustrate or stand as an obstacle to the purposes of the federal law in assuring students with disabilities free appropriate public education because schools can comply with both the federal law and the California law.

The California Supreme Court reversed the Court of Appeal's decision on state-law grounds without reaching the federal preemption question. See *American Nurses Ass'n v. Torlakson*, ___ P.3d ___, 2013 WL 4046566 (Cal.2013).

2. IN POSTSECONDARY EDUCATION

Pushkin v. Regents of Univ. of Colorado

United States Court of Appeals for the Tenth Circuit, 1981.
658 F.2d 1372.

■ DOYLE, CIRCUIT JUDGE.

This is an appeal by the defendants-appellants consisting of the Regents of the University of Colorado; the University of Colorado Hospital, also known as University of Colorado Health Science Center; the University of Colorado Psychiatric Hospital; and Douglas Carter, M. D. The action was brought by Joshua R. Pushkin, M. D., the plaintiff-appellee in this court, pursuant to § 504 of the Rehabilitation Act of 1973, 29 U.S.C. § 794. [T]he decree in question is an injunction directing that plaintiff-appellee be admitted to the next class at the University of Colorado Psychiatric Residency Program; the judgment awarded plaintiff attorneys fees and costs.

[D]r. Pushkin is a medical doctor who alleges that the University of Colorado wrongfully denied him admittance to the Psychiatric Residency Program because he suffers from multiple sclerosis. As a result of this disease Dr. Pushkin is confined to a wheelchair, and is disabled in his abilities to walk and to write. The court found that Dr. Pushkin was an otherwise qualified handicapped individual who had been excluded from a program receiving federal financial assistance solely by reason of his handicap, and that the University was in violation of § 504 of the Rehabilitation Act. [T]he district court [r]uled that the statute was violated because the plaintiff was excluded from participation in or denied the benefits of or subjected to discrimination under a program receiving such funds within the meaning of the statute. The court also held that Dr. Pushkin was an otherwise qualified individual in spite of his handicap [a]nd thus was entitled to admittance to the program. Pursuant to the injunction, Dr. Pushkin was admitted to the residency program on July 1, 1981 and he is actually taking part in the program at the present time. We have expedited the appeal in an effort to reach an early resolution of the controversy. [D]efendants have not disputed that Dr. Pushkin is handicapped within the meaning of the statute [or] that the Psychiatric Residency Program is a program or activity receiving federal financial assistance within the meaning of the statute. [D]efendants [m]aintain that [t]he trial court erroneously decided the merits of the case.

[S]UMMARY OF THE TRIAL COURT'S FINDINGS.

The memorandum opinion of the trial court included far reaching and extensive findings of fact. The essence of the court's ruling was that the judge had weighed all of the defendants' allegations at trial that Dr. Pushkin was not qualified for the program apart from his handicap and found that the evidence intended to show that the plaintiff was rejected as being unqualified due to his handicap was more persuasive. The testimony of the University's own witnesses was conflicting, and the after the fact allegations given at trial that Dr. Pushkin was not of the caliber of applicants usually interviewed for the residency program are not supported by the record, including the interviewers' reports. Also they are contrary to comments made by the Chairman, Dr. Carter, to both Dr. and Mrs. Pushkin concerning the reasons for Dr. Pushkin's rejection, which emphasized the fact of the handicap. The trial court specifically noted:

> What is clear, however, is that when informing Dr. Pushkin of his rejection, Dr. Carter discussed the rejection only in terms of the handicap and gave no other reason; that when subsequently discussing the rejection with Dr. Pushkin's wife Dr. Carter again explained the decision only in terms of Dr. Pushkin's handicap; and that the interviewers' reports document assumptions of inability based upon the handicap.

The trial court further stated that its conclusions that the reason for plaintiff's exclusion from the program was his handicap were based on:

> The interview sheets which refer to assumed disabilities occasioned by his multiple sclerosis . . . and additional testimony which shows after the fact articulation of concern about his alleged emotional instability which was not

manifested in the interview sheets or in Dr. Carter's conversations with Dr. and Mrs. Pushkin.

The trial court weighed the credibility of the conflicting evidence and rejected the after the fact testimony that Dr. Pushkin was not qualified for the program apart from his handicap. This evidence of non-qualification came to the surface, of course, after the interviews. The record supports the findings that the trial court made that the reason for rejecting Dr. Pushkin was entirely his affliction. Having found that Dr. Pushkin was rejected from the residency program on the basis that his multiple sclerosis would preclude him from performing well in the duties of the program, the trial court applied the proper test in determining whether defendants' articulated reasons for finding Dr. Pushkin unqualified in spite of his handicap were legitimate, or whether those reasons were based upon incorrect assumptions or inadequate factual grounds. In any event, after weighing all of the evidence the trial court held that the latter was applicable, that is that the reasons were based on incorrect assumptions or inadequate factual grounds. Since the decision so reached is supported by the record, this court is not at liberty to reach an independent factual conclusion and determine otherwise. We do however consider further the applicable test or standard.

WHAT IS THE PROPER STANDARD OF REVIEW?

The standards for determining the merits of a case under § 504 are contained in the statute. [F]irst, the individual is required to show that he is otherwise qualified for the position sought; second, the individual must show that even though he is otherwise qualified, he was rejected for the position solely on the basis of his handicap. The two factors are interrelated, since if the individual is not otherwise qualified he cannot be said to have been rejected solely because of his handicap.

In *Southeastern Community College v. Davis*, [t]he first test applied was whether the individual in question was qualified for the position sought in spite of his handicap. If the plaintiff's handicap would preclude him from doing the job in question, the plaintiff cannot be found to be otherwise qualified. If the handicap would not preclude the individual from performing the job in question, however, and the plaintiff has met all other qualifications for the position in question, the plaintiff cannot be rejected from the program solely on the basis of his handicap. The record is clear that Dr. Pushkin established that he had the necessary ability despite his handicap. The examining committee, however, focused on the handicap continuously in connection with determining whether to admit him to the residency program. It emphasized factors such as the effect of the handicap on patients and the resulting effect on Dr. Pushkin. Thus, the issue is not merely whether the handicap played a prominent part in his rejection, as in cases dealing with alleged discrimination on the basis of race, for example (where race is never expressly mentioned as a consideration), the issue is whether rejecting Dr. Pushkin after expressly weighing the implication of his handicap was justified. The question is whether Dr. Pushkin was qualified for admission to the residency program in spite of his handicap, so that he was wrongfully rejected from the program on the basis of that handicap, or whether Dr. Pushkin's handicap would preclude him from carrying out the responsibilities involved in the residency program and future patient care, so that the University rightfully excluded him from the program after weighing the implications of his disability.

The trial judge quotes in his findings that an interrogatory was submitted by counsel for Dr. Pushkin requesting the defendants to state every reason why the application of plaintiff for the position of psychiatric resident in any defendant institution was rejected and every reason why he was not appointed to said position. The response to that interrogatory was "the plaintiff was not admitted into the 'psychiatric resident, R II program,' because plaintiff's interview mean ratings, based upon plaintiff's four interviews with faculty members of the University of Colorado Psychiatric Hospital, was far below the level of any other person accepted into the program."

The trial court's findings go on to say that the mean interview ratings as a general practice are not necessarily controlling in the selection process. Moreover, in a specific reference to Dr. Pushkin, Dr. Carter stated that "the numbers," *i.e.* the mean interview ratings, did not dispose of his application. Dr. Pushkin was never told that his mean interview rating was the reason for his rejection. However, even if the mean interview ratings were the reason for his rejection, that is like saying that he was rejected because he was rejected. In other words the interrogatories should have detailed his insufficiencies in specific terms at the very least. The court also found that the

> narrative contained on each interviewer's report, explains the reasons for the rating on the prediction scale. Each instance shows that the interviewer's rating was inextricably involved with Dr. Pushkin's handicap and by the interviewer's perception of the problems the handicap would create. It is not possible to extricate ratings from the reactions to the handicap itself.

The court finally noted that neither Pushkin nor his wife were ever given a reason for his rejection from the program other than that specified by Dr. Carter that Pushkin was rejected because of his handicap. They were left to draw inferences in their conversations with Dr. Carter and the only inference to be drawn by each from the statements made and the absence of other statements being made was that the handicap itself was the reason for the rejection.

The record is replete with testimony dealing with the inability of Dr. Pushkin to serve in the residency program based upon his handicap. These observations of the members of the panel are not predicated on any known deficiency of Dr. Pushkin himself, but rather these are reasons that are based upon the examiners' general knowledge of multiple sclerosis and their concern for psychologic reactions of the patient and in turn the doctor, as a result of his being in a wheelchair. The trial court concluded that the evidence in the case clearly established that these general reasons did not apply with regard to Dr. Pushkin, but that Dr. Pushkin was an otherwise qualified handicapped individual who was wrongfully, by sole reason of his handicap, excluded from participation in or denied the benefits of or subjected to discrimination under a program or activity receiving federal financial assistance.

[T]HE FINAL ANALYSIS

Unquestionably plaintiff has established a prima facie case by showing that he is a handicapped person who is qualified for the residency program apart from his handicap and that he was rejected from the program under circumstances which support a finding that his rejection was based solely on his handicap. As to his qualifications, plaintiff met the requisite academic standards of the program in that he held an M.D. degree and had obtained a satisfactory "dean's letter." Plaintiff also presented a letter from Dr. Wong, his supervisor during one year of residency in psychiatry at the Menninger Foundation in Topeka, Kansas. In this letter Dr. Wong stated:

> Doctor Pushkin is a hard-working, thorough, reliable and efficient physician, showing remarkable patience and perserverence and more than the average understanding for his patients. His supervisors did not feel that his medical illness presented any emotional impairment in his work in the field of psychiatry and felt that he had great potential for a future in psychiatry. He has a pleasing personality, works well with his colleagues and is able to handle the most difficult case in a satisfactory manner. He was an inspiration to his colleagues, to faculty and staff.

Furthermore, plaintiff had been practicing medicine with an emphasis on psychiatry at the time that he applied for the program in question.

The position of the University is that Dr. Pushkin was denied admittance to the residency program on the basis of the interview reports of four members of the program faculty: Drs. Carter, Weissberg, Scully and Barchilon. Dr. Pushkin's mean interview ratings, when computed by scores granted by the four interviewers, were held to be too low. In addition to the grades given by the interviewers each made comments expressing their views about Pushkin's capabilities. Dr. Carter stated that Dr. Pushkin "is teachable, but to face the devastation, guilt, pity and rage that can be stirred up in his patients by his physical condition appears to be too much to ask of his patients or of him."

Dr. Weissberg's report noted that while Dr. Pushkin is bright and has terrific drive, that it was doubtful that Dr. Pushkin would be able to work full time.

Dr. Scully's report noted that Pushkin had multiple sclerosis with significant physical defects, that prognosis is unclear, and that Dr. Pushkin has a lot of anger due to his multiple sclerosis that he is "either unaware of or cannot deal with at this time." Dr. Scully stated in his report that Dr. Pushkin is "able to talk about how his illness might be an issue in psychotherapy," that the effect on his classmates is unclear, and that, clearly, Dr. Pushkin "is a risk."

Dr. Barchilon's report indicates concern that the emotional stress of treating patients may be too much for Dr. Pushkin, and that he might not be able to stand the stress and strain of on call duty due to his disease.

With the possible exception of Dr. Weissberg, all of the reports appear to focus on his handicap. At trial, as will appear below, the interviewers testified that Dr. Pushkin's physical limitations were not the reason he was not accepted into the program, but they indicated that Dr. Pushkin's mental status, as interrelated with his MS, was a controlling factor in that decision. Unquestionably the evidence was sufficient to establish a prima facie case of a violation of § 504.

We next consider the reasons articulated by the University at trial for the plaintiff's rejection.

Dr. Barchilon testified that he viewed Pushkin as an ill person, rather than a handicapped one, since a handicapped person is "stabilized" in that his defect is predictable and can be accounted for, while a sick person is not stabilized. Dr. Pushkin was said by him to be ill, barely in equilibrium, and taking large doses of Prednisone which leads to unpredictable results because of its accumulative effect. Side effects cited by Dr. Barchilon were said to be highs and lows of emotions and outbursts of anger, both of which symptoms Dr. Barchilon claimed to have observed in Dr. Pushkin. Dr. Barchilon felt that Dr. Pushkin had emotional problems from which he was unable to achieve enough distance to enable him to empathize with his patients and their problems. Dr. Barchilon seemed equally concerned with the effect on Dr. Pushkin if he were accepted in the program (i.e., that Dr. Pushkin's work would make him unhappy) as with the effect of Dr. Pushkin's treatment on the patients.

Dr. Carter's testimony was that Dr. Pushkin "elicits strong feelings in people. Whether it's pity, whether it's concern, whether it's 'My God, I'm glad it's not me,' it stirs up a lot of things and it seems very clear that many things would be stirred up in his patients with that problem." Dr. Carter also testified that he was not sure that Dr. Pushkin could handle either the emotional strain of caring for the patients, or the physical load. He added that he was not Dr. Pushkin's psychiatrist, "but I had a sense that he is very angry underneath."

Dr. Weissberg's testimony was that "as a regular person Dr. Pushkin was doing fine," in that "he used a fair amount of pushing away of feelings" about his illness, but that this "would not have been appropriate in a psychiatrist."

Dr. Scully testified that the issue was not the wheelchair, "the issue is what does the MS mean?" Dr. Scully testified that Dr. Pushkin was very angry. He also testified that he and Dr. Pushkin talked about how patients might react to his illness.

Dr. Bernstein, head of the psychiatric liaison division of the Department of Psychiatry at the University Medical School, who participated in a post-interview conference about Dr. Pushkin, testified that he and Dr. Scully discussed the latter's observations of Dr. Pushkin. Dr. Bernstein said that Dr. Scully felt that he could "never meet Dr. Pushkin head on," and that "there was some organicity here that impaired Dr. Pushkin being able to engage with him." He said that he and Dr. Scully discussed the fact that when a person has MS "there is some difficulty in mentation. There is some delirium," and that the fact that Dr. Pushkin was on steroids could "very seriously disturb (his) sensorium," that is, difficulty in orientation, judgment and memory. Dr. Bernstein stated that Dr. Scully felt that Pushkin exhibited problems in both areas. He also testified that in his own mind the determinative factor for Pushkin's rejection was the latter's difficulties in mentation, delirium and disturbed sensorium. He stated that from what Dr. Scully and Weissberg had told him, he felt that Dr. Pushkin "has not worked his own condition through to the extent that he can be open and receptive, not only to his patients' reactions to him, but to whatever their own problems are. . . . "

The Pushkins, husband and wife, testified as to what Dr. Carter had told them, which was that Dr. Pushkin had been rejected from the program because of his handicap. According to Dr. and Mrs. Pushkin, Dr. Carter had told them that Pushkin's multiple sclerosis would prevent him from relating well with his patients, and would prevent the patients from relating well to Dr. Pushkin. Mrs. Pushkin also stated that Dr. Carter had told her that Dr. Pushkin might miss work due to hospitalization for his illness, and that would leave his patients without a doctor. Regarding this, both Doctor and Mrs. Pushkin testified that Dr. Pushkin's multiple sclerosis allowed his episodes of hospitalization to be planned in advance, similar to the way vacations were planned in advance by other doctors, and that Dr. Pushkin had always arranged for other doctors to care for his patients when he was hospitalized, just as most doctors arrange for others to care for their patients when they are on vacation. Dr. and Mrs. Pushkin further noted that Dr. Pushkin did not tell his patients he would be hospitalized, any more than other doctors told their patients where they were going on vacation, so that the patients would not be unduly burdened by such information.

There was testimony also from Dr. Gordon Farley, Dr. Pushkin's psychiatrist and a psychiatrist at the University of Colorado Health Center. Dr. Farley expressed anxiety about being subpoenaed as a witness since his patient was suing his employer. He was apprehensive about testifying in opposition to his employers. Also to be noted is that Dr. Farley participates as an interviewer of potential residents at the University of Colorado, but that he was not one of Dr. Pushkin's interviewers. Farley testified that Dr. Pushkin's emotional responses were "within the range of normal," and that from Dr. Pushkin's discussions of his work with his patients, Dr. Pushkin had "treated those patients appropriately," "has had good emotional accessibility" to his patients, and has "reasonably well understood their feelings toward him." Dr. Farley said that Dr. Pushkin is "quick mentally," that he "exercises good judgment in his care of patients," and that he is a "responsible, reasonable, reasoned and conscientious physician." Dr. Farley said that Dr. Pushkin's mentation had not been affected by either the medications that he was taking or by the disease itself. He testified that having observed Dr. Pushkin for four years he had never observed any delirium in him, any disabled sensorium, or any noticeable effect from either the steroids or from the disease. Dr. Farley further testified that Dr. Pushkin "does as well as he can with his illness as any human being could," and that he is "well within the norm of emotional control and behavior." According to Dr. Farley, Dr. Pushkin would make an "exceptional" psychiatrist.

The reports of the interviewers and the testimony of the other witnesses indicates that on the basis of 45 minute interviews and discussions by some of the interviewers with Dr. Bernstein, the admissions committee made certain assumptions regarding his handicap, such as:

1) That Dr. Pushkin was angry and so emotionally upset due to his MS that he would be unable to do an effective job as a psychiatrist; and

2) That Dr. Pushkin's MS and use of steroids had led to difficulties with mentation, delirium and disturbed sensorium; and

3) That Dr. Pushkin would be unable to handle the work involved in the residency because of his MS; and

4) That Dr. Pushkin would miss too much time away from his patients whereby they would suffer.

The testimony of the Pushkins and Dr. Farley and the letter from Dr. Wong rebut all these assumptions. Dr. Farley, who actually counseled Dr. Pushkin, and has done so for over a long period of time and was not merely reaching conclusions on the basis of his observations in the interview, stated that after four years of observing Pushkin closely he could not agree that any of the assumptions made by the admissions committee regarding MS applied to Dr. Pushkin.

It is within the power of the trier of the facts, here the trial court, to weigh the evidence and to determine the credibility of the witnesses. The trial judge found that the assumptions made by the admissions committee were rebutted by other evidence, and thus Dr. Pushkin could not be held to be unqualified due to his handicap. When the trial court's decision is supported by substantial evidence in the record, we are not free to reverse that decision. It boils down to that factor. We fully understand also why the trial court would find that the evidence on behalf of Pushkin was the more persuasive.

[T]he trial court weighed the credibility of the conflicting evidence and rejected the after the fact testimony that Dr. Pushkin was not qualified for the program apart from his handicap. We are disinclined to substitute our judgment for that of the trial court, since that court's conclusion is supported by the record. We have evaluated the evidence and considered the findings and have approved the trial court's action. The conclusions of the examining board rest on psychologic theory. Our reaction is that these are weak and inadequate threads where, as here, the entire future of the plaintiff is at stake. We also hold that he applied the proper tests in determining whether defendants' articulated reasons for finding Dr. Pushkin unqualified on the basis of his handicap were legitimate or whether those reasons were based upon incorrect assumptions or inadequate factual grounds. Based upon the weighing of all the evidence the trial court held that the latter applied and since the decision is supported by the record, this court cannot reach its own factual conclusion and determine otherwise.

Viewing the record as a whole we conclude that the judgment of the district court is affirmed.

Guckenberger v. Boston Univ.

United States District Court for the District of Massachusetts, 1997.
974 F.Supp. 106.

■ SARIS, DISTRICT JUDGE.

This is a class action brought by students with Attention Deficit Hyperactivity Disorder ("ADHD"), Attention Deficit Disorder ("ADD"), and learning disorders (collectively "learning disabilities") against Boston University ("BU") under the Americans with Disabilities Act ("ADA"), 42 U.S.C.A. § 12101 *et seq.*. [and] the Rehabilitation Act, 29 U.S.C.A. § 794. The class claims that BU discriminates against the learning-disabled by: (1) establishing unreasonable, overly-burdensome eligibility criteria for qualifying as a disabled student; (2) failing to provide reasonable procedures for evaluation and review of a student's request for accommodations; and (3) instituting an across-the-board policy precluding course substitutions in foreign language and mathematics. BU contends that its eligibility criteria are reasonably designed to ensure that a student is entitled to the requested accommodations, that its review procedures are adequate, and that it has the right to require that a student meet certain levels of proficiency in math and foreign language before it confers a liberal arts degree.

Particularly with respect to the issue of course substitution, this class action concerns the interplay between the rights of learning-disabled students to reasonable accommodation and the rights of institutions of higher education to establish and enforce academic standards.

The plaintiff class now seeks injunctive and declaratory relief against the continued implementation of BU's accommodations policy. [A]fter a two-week bench trial, and an evaluation of the witnesses and evidence in this case, I have made numerous findings of fact and conclusions of law. To assist the reader, the Court's fundamental conclusions are summarized as follows:

1.   Federal law prohibits private and public universities, colleges and post-secondary educational institutions from discriminating against students with specific learning disabilities.

2.   In the fall of 1995, BU imposed new documentation requirements that required students with learning disabilities to be retested every three years, and that provided that evaluations by persons who were not physicians, clinical psychologists, or licensed psychologists were unacceptable. These new documentation requirements, as initially framed, violated the ADA and the Rehabilitation Act because they were "eligibility criteria" that "screen[ed] out or tended to screen out" students with specific learning disabilities, and because BU did not demonstrate that the requirements were necessary to the provision of educational services or reasonable accommodations.

3.   The documentation policies have changed, however, since the start of this litigation. Because BU now permits a student to obtain a waiver of the three-year currency retesting requirement where medically unnecessary, I conclude that the retesting requirement, as currently framed, does not screen out or tend to screen out learning disabled students.

4.   BU has also restructured its policy with respect to the qualifications of evaluators by permitting evaluators with doctorates in education (and in "other appropriate specialties") to document students' learning disabilities. Nevertheless, by precluding any evaluations by

persons with masters degrees, BU's present policy still unnecessarily screens out or tends to screen out some students with specific learning disorders who have been evaluated by adequately trained professionals. BU has not demonstrated that an evaluator with a masters degree and appropriate training and experience cannot perform the testing for an assessment of learning disability as well as an evaluator with a doctorate. Accordingly, BU has not proven that a doctorate-level of qualification is necessary to the provision of reasonable accommodations with respect to students with learning disorders.

5.   However, with respect to students with ADD and ADHD, BU has demonstrated that its "bright line" policy of requiring current evaluation by a person with a doctorate is necessary because ADD/ADHD is often accompanied by co-existing physical and psychological conditions, is frequently treated by medications, and is a rapidly changing condition that usually remits over the period from adolescence through early adulthood.

6.   The administration of BU's new accommodations policy during the 1995–1996 school year violated the ADA and the Rehabilitation Act because it was implemented without any advance warning to eligible students, in such a way as to have the effect of delaying or denying reasonable accommodations. Moreover, BU President Jon Westling and his staff administered the program on the basis of uninformed stereotypes about the learning disabled.

7.   However, because BU has recently hired an experienced clinical psychologist to review student accommodation requests, and because President Westling and his assistant Craig Klafter now review recommended accommodations primarily to ensure that they meet academic standards, the university's current procedure for evaluating requests for accommodation submitted by students with learning disabilities does not violate federal law.

8.   The plaintiff class has no private right of action to challenge BU's violation of Rehabilitation Act regulations that require a university to adopt grievance procedures that incorporate appropriate due process standards.

9.   In general, federal law does not require a university to modify degree requirements that it determines are a fundamental part of its academic program by providing learning disabled students with course substitutions.

10. Here, BU's refusal to modify its degree requirements in order to provide course substitutions, particularly in the area of foreign languages, was motivated in substantial part by uninformed stereotypes by the President and his staff that many students with learning disabilities (like the infamous, nonexistent "Somnolent Samantha") are lazy fakers, and that many evaluators are "snake oil salesmen" who overdiagnose the disability.

11. BU failed to demonstrate that it met its duty of seeking appropriate reasonable accommodations for learning disabled students with difficulty in learning foreign languages by considering alternative means and coming to a rationally justifiable conclusion that the available alternative (*i.e.*, a course substitution) would lower academic standards or require substantial program alteration. Rather, the

university simply relied on the status quo as the rationale for refusing to consider seriously a reasonable request for modification of its century-old degree requirements.

12. Plaintiffs have failed to demonstrate that a request to modify the degree requirement in mathematics is reasonable in light of the dearth of scientific evidence that any specific learning disability in mathematics (i.e. dyscalculia) is sufficiently severe to preclude any student from achieving sufficient proficiency in mathematics to meet BU's degree requirements with appropriate accommodations.

[F]INDINGS OF FACT

I. BU's Recruitment of the Learning Disabled

BU is one of the largest private universities in the United States, with 20,000 students, 2,000 faculty members, and fifteen undergraduate and graduate colleges that offer 150 separate degree-granting programs. The College of Arts and Sciences is the largest college in the university. It has longstanding course requirements, including one semester of mathematics and four semesters of a foreign language. Degree requirements at all of BU's colleges are approved by the Provost, the President, and the Board of Trustees.

Before 1995, BU was a leader among educational institutions in seeking to provide comprehensive services to students with diagnosed learning disabilities. The university recruited learning-disabled enrollees by establishing the Learning Disabilities Support Services ("LDSS"), a renowned accommodations program that functioned as a unit within BU's Disability Services office ("DSO"). LDSS was often described as a "model program." Through LDSS, the university declared a commitment to enabling students with learning disabilities to reach their maximum academic potential.

[B]efore 1995, not only did LDSS often authorize in-class notetakers, tape-recorded textbooks, and time and one half on final examinations for students with documented learning disabilities (the so-called "vanilla" accommodations), but LDSS staff also occasionally recommended that disabled students receive a course substitution for required mathematics and foreign language classes. For example, students who received an LDSS recommendation for a math substitution were allowed to take classes such as Anthropology 245 ("Anthropology of Money"), Economics 320 ("Economics of Less Developed Regions"), or Geography 100 ("Introduction to Environmental Science") instead of the required math curriculum. Similarly, learning-disabled students who received a foreign language exemption might opt instead for one of several foreign culture courses including Art History 226 ("Arts of Japan") or History 292 ("African Colonial History").

In developing lists of "approved" course substitutions and recommending waivers of math and foreign language requirements for certain students, LDSS worked with the heads of the various academic departments at the College of Liberal Arts ("CLA") (now called the College of Arts and Sciences) ("CAS"). However, neither LDSS nor CLA notified or sought the approval of the President, Provost, or any other member of BU's central administration. Eighty-eight students requested foreign language waivers at CLA during academic years

1992–1993 and 1993–1994. On average, BU granted approximately 10 to 15 requests for course substitutions a year.

Prior to 1995, the process of applying for accommodations, including course substitutions, from BU was relatively straightforward. A learning-disabled student submitted to LDSS a description of her need for accommodation, a statement of her accommodations history, and a current medical or psycho-educational evaluation (one that had been conducted within three years of entering the university). Once the student's documentation was filed, members of the LDSS staff determined whether accommodation was appropriate. In 1995, LDSS was permanently staffed with a full-time director, two assistant coordinators and a secretary, and it also employed several part-time learning disabilities specialists. Several of these administrators had specific training in special education and in the provision of accommodations to post-secondary students with learning disabilities.

If LDSS granted a student's request for accommodation, the student would be notified. An LDSS staff member would also write letters, referred to as "accommodations letters," to the student's faculty members and to the dean of the student's particular school explaining the student's disability and recommending that the student be provided with the listed accommodations. Students were responsible for distributing these letters to their professors, and for meeting with their instructors to arrange the provision of in-class and exam accommodations.

The results of LDSS's "marketing" to students with learning disabilities were pronounced. In academic year 1990–1991, 42 students who self-identified as learning disabled applied, 24 were accepted and two enrolled. Four years later, 348 such students applied, 233 accepted and 94 enrolled. In late 1995, 429 learning-disabled students applied to the university. As its reputation developed, BU was recommended by guidance counselors and college manuals as a desirable academic setting the learning disabled. Between 1990 and 1996, hundreds of students with learning disabilities came to BU and registered for academic accommodations and/or comprehensive services through LDSS. By the 1995–1996 school year, BU had approximately 480 learning disabled students.

II. Westling Orders Change

Current BU president Jon Westling became the university's provost (i.e., its chief academic officer) in 1985. A graduate of Reed College and a Rhodes Scholar, Westling has spent a total of 23 years at BU. He has served as both an administrator and as a teacher in the humanities core curriculum at the CLA. Westling holds no graduate degrees.

In the spring of 1995, Provost Westling discovered that LDSS and CLA had been allowing students with learning disabilities to substitute other classes for the mathematics and foreign language coursework that was otherwise a long-standing prerequisite to obtaining a baccalaureate degree in the College of Arts and Sciences. Chagrined that LDSS was facilitating alterations of the core curriculum without university approval, Westling assigned his assistant and troubleshooter, Craig Klafter, a Ph.D in Modern History, to research learning disabilities in general and LDSS's process of granting accommodations in particular. Confronting LDSS-director Loring Brinckerhoff, Klafter sought proof of the existence of a disability that prevented a student from learning a foreign language. Brinckerhoff referred Klafter to a book that he had co-authored concerning learning disabilities in post-secondary education. After reading Brinckerhoff's book and other secondary materials, Klafter determined that there was no scientific proof of the existence of a learning disability that prevents the successful study of math or foreign language.

As a result of Klafter's investigation, in June of 1995 Westling informed W. Norman Johnson, BU's Vice President and Dean of Students, and the College of Liberal Arts that the university was to cease granting course substitutions, "effective immediately." In addition, Westling told Johnson to direct LDSS to send all accommodation letters to the Provost's office for review before they were distributed to the students or faculty. Westling made the decision to end the course substitution practice without convening any committees or panels, and without speaking to any experts on learning disabilities or to any faculty members on the importance of math and foreign language to the liberal arts curriculum. With the course substitution "bee" in his academic bonnet, Westling decided to become personally involved with the accommodations evaluation process, even though he had no expertise or experience in diagnosing learning disabilities or in fashioning appropriate accommodations.

III. "Somnolent Samantha"

At around the time that Westling ordered the first changes in the accommodations practice at BU, he also began delivering speeches denouncing the zealous advocacy of "the learning disabilities movement." In addresses delivered in Australia and in Washington, D.C., Westling questioned the rapidly increasing number of children being diagnosed with learning disorders, and accused learning-disabilities advocates of fashioning "fugitive" impairments that are not supported in the scientific and medical literature. Although Westling's orations recognized a need to "endorse the profoundly humane goal of addressing the specific needs of individuals with specific impairments," his public addresses resonated with a dominant theme: that "the learning disability movement is a great mortuary for the ethics of hard work, individual responsibility, and pursuit of excellence, and also for genuinely humane social order."

At the beginning of one such speech entitled "Disabling Education: The Culture Wars Go to School," which was delivered on July 22, 1995, Westling introduced a student named Samantha, who was, he said, a freshman in one of his classes at BU. Westling recounted how Samantha approached him on the first day of class and how, "shyly yet assertively," she presented a letter addressed to him from the Disability Services office.

> The letter explained that Samantha had a learning disability "in the area of auditory processing" and would need the following accommodations: "time and one-half on all quizzes, tests, and examinations;" double-time on any mid-term or final examination; examinations in a room separate from other students; copies of my lecture notes; and a seat at the front of

the class. Samantha, I was also informed, might fall asleep in my class, and I should be particularly concerned to fill her in on any material she missed while dozing.

Westling's speech went on to name the student "Somnolent Samantha" and to label her "an unwitting casualty of the culture wars." To Westling, Samantha exemplified those students who, placated by the promise of accommodation rather than encouraged to work to achieve their fullest potential, had become "sacrificial victims to the triumph of the therapeutic." Throughout his twenty-page address, Westling reiterated the view that, by "seiz[ing] on the existence of some real disabilities and conjur[ing] up other alleged disabilities in order to promote a particular vision of human society," the learning disabilities movement cripples allegedly disabled students who could overcome their academic difficulties "with concentrated effort," demoralizes non-disabled students who recognize hoaxes performed by their peers, and "wreak [s] educational havoc." In closing, Westling remarked:

> The policies that have grown out of learning disabilities ideology leach our sense of humanity. We are taught not that mathematics is difficult for us but worth pursuing, but that we are ill. Samantha, offered the pillow of learning disability on which to slumber, was denied, perhaps forever, access to a dimension of self-understanding.

Westling fabricated the student named Samantha to illustrate his point regarding students with learning disorders. Remarkably, at trial, Westling admitted not only that such a student never existed, but that his description of her did not even represent a prototype of the learning-disabled students he had encountered. Rather, Somnolent Samantha represented Westling's belief—fuelled mostly by popular press and anecdotal accounts—that students with learning disabilities were often fakers who undercut academic rigor.

As in the speech "Disabling Education," since the spring of 1995, many of Westling's addresses, statements, and letters regarding accommodations for the learning disabled have reflected his opinion that "hundreds of thousands of children are being improperly diagnosed with learning disabilities by self-proclaimed experts who fail to accept that behavioral and performance difficulties exist." Even though Westling has referred to students with learning disabilities as "draft dodgers" and has repeatedly voiced his concern that students without established learning disorders might be faking a disability to gain an educational advantage, to date, there has not been a single documented instance at BU in which a student has been found to have fabricated a learning disorder in order to claim eligibility for accommodations.

IV. The Twenty-Eight Files

By the fall semester of the 1995–1996 academic year, BU was at a bureaucratic impasse. LDSS head Loring Brinckerhoff was ignoring Westling's directives, and LDSS was continuing the practice of approving course substitutions and granting accommodations without Westling's involvement. Although Dean Johnson had specifically conveyed Westling's orders to Brinckerhoff in a memo dated June 29, 1995, LDSS issued 58 accommodations letters (some of which allowed course substitutions) to students between July and September of 1995 without seeking Westling's approval.

Irate that his mandates were being disregarded, in October of 1995, Westling directly ordered that all of the accommodations letters that LDSS had prepared but that had not yet been picked up by the affected students be delivered to his office. At the time, LDSS held 28 such letters. Westling also requested that he be given access to the documentation files for each of the students who were the subject of the 28 letters.

After receiving the letters and files, Westling and his staff reviewed the documentation to determine if the students' evaluations actually supported LDSS's recommended accommodations. Specifically, when reviewing the files, the provost's office looked for current evaluations done by credentialed evaluators, clear diagnoses, an evaluator's recommendation listing specific accommodations, and an LDSS recommendation that was consistent with the recommendations made by the student's evaluator. None of the provost office staff members who were involved in this review had any expertise in learning disabilities.

In a letter dated November 2, 1995, Westling communicated his analysis of the letters and files to Brinckerhoff's supervisor, the director of the Office of Disability Services, William P. ("Kip") Opperman. Of the 28 files, Westling determined that, "[i]n all but a few cases, the requested accommodations [were] not supported by the attached documentation." With respect to several of the students, Westling reached the reasonable conclusion that there was actually "insufficient information" to determine whether or not students were entitled to accommodation because the documentation provided by LDSS was not current, did not support the requested accommodation, or was missing. For example, in regard to one student, Westling states that the testing psychologist "does not say [the student] is incapable of learning a foreign language," only that the student " 'has had a history of difficulty with foreign language.' "Rather than authorizing a course substitution as LDSS had done, Westling remarks that the student should be "encouraged to avail himself of the tutoring available to him through the University." With respect to other students, Westling incorrectly determined that the documentation did not support a claim of learning disability.

After describing in detail the perceived shortcomings of each file, Westling's letter to Kip Opperman concludes:

> [I]t is clear to me that the staff of the Learning Disabilities Support Services does not meet any reasonable standard of professional competence in their field. There is also considerable evidence that in addition to being incompetent, the staff has willfully and knowingly undermined University academic standards, distributed false information about University policy, and directly disobeyed University policy. I do not know whether it is possible to make Learning Disabilities Support Services perform its appropriate functions under its current management and with its current staff. While I am still considering this issue, I strongly advise you to take the corrective actions indicated in this letter.

Among the "corrective actions" Westling suggests throughout the letter are: (1) that students "be required to provide current evaluations" in light of federal guidelines stating that evaluations that are more than three years old are unreliable; (2) that the evaluations provide actual test results that support the tester's conclusions; (3) that "[i]ndividuals who provide evaluations of learning disabilities should be physicians, clinical psychologists or licensed psychologists and must have a record of reputable practice"; (4) that all requests for accommodation contain an analysis by LDSS staff, an academic history of the student, and the student's academic status at BU; and (5) that LDSS "should not misinform students that course substitutions for foreign language or mathematics requirements are available." Although Westling had no evidence that learning disabilities changed or abated after students finished high school, he mandated that BU students provide current evaluations (i.e., those that are less than three years old) on the basis of regulations promulgated by the Department of Education for grades kindergarten through twelve. In establishing standards for the credentials of evaluators, Westling relied on consultations with doctors at BU's School of Medicine that Klafter sought in late 1995.

In crafting the November 2, 1995 letter to Opperman, Westling did not intend for LDSS to deny all accommodations to the students whose files he reviewed. Rather, Westling hoped to castigate ODS officials regarding the office's method of approving accommodation requests for students who claimed to have a learning disability, and to obtain better documentation prior to granting a requested accommodation. Nonetheless, as a result of Westling's correspondence, Brinckerhoff sent a letter on behalf of LDSS to most of the 28 students whose files Westling had reviewed, denying the student's request for accommodation and informing the student of his right to appeal the decision to the Provost. For example, in a letter dated December 3, 1995, addressed to named plaintiff Scott Greeley, Brinckerhoff states that Greeley's request for accommodation "was reviewed" and that "the proposed accommodation of requiring the instructor to provide an opportunity to clarify test questions is not supported by the 'educational therapist' who evaluated you." As a further example, in the fall of 1995, plaintiff Michael Cahaly received an accommodations letter from the LDSS office authorizing him to receive up to double time on his exams and to use a notetaker in his classes. However, in December 1995, he received another letter refusing accommodation because his evaluation was not conducted within the past three years. Cahaly had never been informed that there was any problem with the qualifications of his evaluator.

LDSS staff members later told several worried students to disregard Brinckerhoff's letter denying accommodations; however, no formal letter or statement retracting the denial of accommodations was ever issued.

V. Chaos

On December 4, 1995, Brinckerhoff sent a form letter to all BU students who had previously registered with LDSS. The letter, which purported "to inform [students] of recent policy changes at LD Support Services," stated that the following requirements must be fulfilled by

January 8, 1996, if students were to remain eligible for accommodations through LDSS:

(1) Students whose documentation was more than three years old "must be reevaluated in order to continue to receive services and accommodations through the LDSS office;"

(2) Students must submit to LDSS documentation of a learning disability that has been prepared by "a licensed psychologist, clinical psychologist, neuropsychologist, or reputable physician;" and

(3) Students seeking accommodations for the spring semester of 1996 must provide LDSS with a high school transcript, a college transcript, and a current BU course schedule including course numbers, course descriptions, and the names and addresses of the professors.

Brinckerhoff distributed the letter to students just prior to final examinations for the fall semester of 1995. He did not forward a copy of the letter to Westling for his approval; nor did he check that it accurately conveyed Westling's policy directives. When Westling learned of the letter, he requested that Norm Johnson issue a statement retracting some of the requirements for accommodation that Brinckerhoff had articulated.

On December 22, 1995, approximately three weeks after Brinckerhoff's correspondence, Johnson sent a letter to the learning-disabled students at BU. Johnson's letter notified students that the university was deferring the deadline for submitting current documentation from January 8, 1996—the date set forth by Brinckerhoff—until August 31, 1996. Moreover, it sought "to correct a significant error in Dr. Brinckerhoff's letter" regarding the need for reevaluation. Although Brinckerhoff's letter stated that students with old documentation must be retested if they were to continue to receive assistance from LDSS, Johnson maintained (without explanation) that "[n]o such reevaluation will be necessary in order to continue receiving services from Learning Disability Support Services." Johnson also expressed his "regret" that students "were notified of these proposed changes during the examination period," and he apologized "for any inconvenience."

Throughout the first semester of the 1995–1996 school year, learning-disabled students, parents and professors received mixed and inconsistent messages from university administrators regarding the requirements for seeking and receiving academic accommodations at BU. As a result of the confusing and chaotic climate occasioned by BU's new accommodations policy, there was a substantial reduction in the number of students with self-identified learning disabilities who have attended BU since 1995. Whereas 94 students with self-proclaimed learning disabilities enrolled at BU in 1994, the number of such students had dropped to 71 by the 1996–1997 academic year.

VI. Resignation, Reorganization, and Restructure

Early in 1996, several members of the disability services office resigned, including Brinckerhoff and Opperman, and the Provost's office became the primary decision maker in determining whether a student was to receive an accommodation for a learning disability. In evaluating requests for reasonable accommodations, the Provost's office consulted with specialists like neuropsychologists or the remaining staff at LDSS. With the LDSS office virtually unstaffed, the university undertook to restructure the entire disability services department. Instead of having a self-contained unit within the disability services office to evaluate the accommodations requests of learning-disabled students, the new Office of Disability Services ("DS") was structured to manage accommodations for all students with disabilities, whether physical, mental, or in learning. The reconfigured DS staff consisted of a full-time director, an assistant director, a clinical director of learning disability support services, an LD coordinator, a coordinator of interpreter services, and two senior staff assistants. The office was also designed to employ several part-time learning specialists, tutors, interpreters, readers, and notetakers.

On March 25, 1996, BU hired Allan Macurdy, an adjunct assistant professor of law, as the new DS director. Macurdy, a quadriplegic, is a specialist in laws affecting the physically disabled. Soon after his arrival, in the absence of a complete staff, Macurdy personally undertook to review the accommodation requests of students with learning disabilities, even though the student files were in complete disarray (many were inaccurate, incomplete or missing), and neither he nor the other newly-hired DS staff members had any expertise in diagnosing learning disabilities or in fashioning appropriate accommodations.[10] Between March of 1996 and January of 1997, Macurdy's office reviewed over 80 student files and made recommendations about the requested accommodations. During this time, BU also retained neuropsychologists with expertise in learning disabilities to review student files and make accommodations determinations with regard to learning-disabled students. All recommendations for accommodations made by the DS staff were forwarded to the Provost's office for approval.

By May 31, 1996, the Office of the Provost at BU had reviewed DS recommendations for 77 learning-disabled students. Students whose requests for accommodation were denied by Westling's office were often told to contact the Provost in order to seek reconsideration. However, because there was no established appeal procedure, students and their parents were occasionally not given any information at all regarding further review. As a matter of informal, unwritten policy, the only appeal from the denial of a requested accommodation was to seek reconsideration by the Provost. Students with physical disabilities grieved any denials through the Section 504 procedure handled by the Office of the Dean of Students.

VII. Present Accommodations Process

In January of 1997, BU hired Dr. Lorraine Wolf as the new clinical director for learning disability support services. Before being appointed, Wolf was a practicing neuropsychologist and an assistant professor of Clinical Psychology at Columbia University. Wolf had also done consulting work for BU since November of 1996.

---

[10] BU hired Carrie Lewis, a former executive assistant to the superintendent in Chelsea, Massachusetts, as the assistant director of disability services, and Judith Zafft, a former high school special education teacher, as the coordinator of learning disability services. The new DS staff was "hand-picked" by Westling, and Zafft had expressed to Westling her belief that "there is too much abuse in the granting of accommodations" prior to her consideration for the job.

From early 1997 until the present, Wolf's responsibilities as clinical director have included reviewing the documentation submitted by learning-disabled students and making recommendations regarding the accommodations that should be provided to a student on the basis of a learning disability. [A]t present, students with documented learning disabilities at BU may request accommodations such as reduced course loads, use of special computer technology, books on tape, extra time on examinations in a distraction-free environment, and note takers. BU's eligibility requirements for receiving such accommodations are summarized as follows:

(1) Learning-disabled students must be tested for a learning disorder by a physician, licensed clinical psychologist or a person with a doctorate degree in neuropsychology, educational or child psychology, or another appropriate specialty. The evaluator must have at least three year's experience in diagnosing learning disorders.

(2) Documentation must be current, as it is recognized by BU for only three years after the date of the evaluation. A learning-disabled student whose documentation is too old at the time he matriculates, or whose documentation "expires" during his time at BU, must be reevaluated (including retesting). If retesting is deemed unnecessary by the student's evaluator, the evaluator is required to fill in a form explaining why it is not "medically necessary."

The procedure for requesting and receiving an accommodation for a learning disability at BU is as follows. First, a student requesting accommodations submits an application to the DS office. Wolf reviews the submitted documentation and makes a determination regarding the accommodations that are appropriate for the student. Then, the student's file and Wolf's recommendations are forwarded to the President's Office. Klafter reviews each student's documentation for consistency and, when necessary, discusses with university faculty and administrators how the recommended accommodation will affect a particular academic program or course of study. If the President's Office accepts Wolf's accommodation recommendations, as is mostly the case, the DS office notifies the student. Generally within two weeks of the request, the DS office also generates accommodations letters to be given to the affected faculty members.

As of April 1997, the President's office endorsed most of Wolf's recommendations for a grant or denial of a request for accommodations due to a learning disability. In several situations, Westling consulted with Wolf and with the relevant department head and denied a requested accommodation where he believed the request was inconsistent with academic standards. For example, Westling rejected a request for a notetaker by a learning-disabled ROTC student in a course on manufacturing engineering; however, he authorized the student's use of a tape-recorder. In other situations, despite initial hesitation, Westling agreed to a notetaker for a student studying social work and a calculator for a student in a math course. In the Wolf era, the interaction between the President's Office and DS in evaluating student files focuses on determining which modifications of academic requirements are appropriate for a given learning-disabled student, rather than on ascertaining the nature and extent of a student's learning disability.

BU admits that it has yet to articulate a single, specific process for students to follow if their request for accommodation is denied. In this litigation, the university takes the position that either the appeal to President Westling or the university's Section 504 grievance procedure is adequate to address student concerns.

[C]ONCLUSIONS OF LAW

[B]. Documentation Requirements

Plaintiffs argue that BU's new accommodations policy makes it unnecessarily difficult for students to document their learning disabilities when requesting accommodation. Specifically, plaintiffs allege that BU's documentation requirements violate the provision of the ADA that defines discrimination to include:

> the imposition or application of eligibility criteria that screen out or tend to screen out an individual with a disability or any class of individuals with disabilities from fully and equally enjoying any goods, services, facilities, privileges, advantages, or accommodations, unless such criteria can be shown to be necessary for the provision of the goods, services, facilities, privileges, advantages, or accommodations.

42 U.S.C. § 12182(b)(2)(i). [T]his tend-to-screen-out concept [m]akes it discriminatory to impose policies or criteria that, while not creating a direct bar to individuals with disabilities, diminish an individual's chances of such participation. Plaintiffs need not show discriminatory intent to establish a violation of the ADA's tend-to-screen-out provision

1.   BU's Eligibility Criteria

At present, students who seek reasonable accommodation from BU on the basis of a learning disability are required to document their disability by: a) being tested by a physician, or a licensed psychologist, or an evaluator who has a doctorate degree in neuropsychology, education, or another appropriate field; b) producing the results of testing conducted no more than three years prior to the accommodation request; and c) providing the results of I.Q. tests in addition to the results of the normal battery of tests designed to assess the nature and extent of a learning disability. These requirements are "eligibility criteria" within the meaning of the ADA and Section 504 because they are policies that allow the university to judge which students are eligible for the learning disability services and to tailor reasonable academic accommodations provided by BU.

2.   Screen Out

The ADA permits a university to require a student requesting a reasonable accommodation to provide current documentation from a qualified professional concerning his learning disability. [N]evertheless, a university cannot impose upon such individuals documentation criteria that unnecessarily screen out or tend to screen out the truly disabled. 42 U.S.C. § 12182(b)(2)(i). Just as a covered entity is prohibited from defining the offered benefit "in a way that effectively denies otherwise qualified handicapped individuals the meaningful access to which they are entitled," [*Alexander v. Choate*], so too is a university prevented from employing unnecessarily burdensome proof-of-disability criteria that preclude or unnecessarily discourage individuals with disabilities from establishing that they are entitled to reasonable accommodation.

In determining whether BU's documentation requirements "screen out or tend to screen out" students with learning disabilities, the Court considers separately each of the contested eligibility criteria and takes into account the changes that BU has made to its policies in response to this litigation.

a. Currency Requirement

During the 1995–1996 school year, BU's policy required that a student seeking accommodations on the basis of a learning disability submit documentation that had been completed within three years of the request for accommodation. This meant that students essentially had to be retested every three years. Based on the evidence, I easily find that this initial "currency" requirement imposed significant additional burdens on disabled students. For example, Elizabeth Guckenberger testified that her retesting process took four days and cost $800.00. Jill Cutler's retesting took four hours and cost $650.00. Dean Robert Shaw testified that the evaluations could cost up to $1,000 and involve multiple visits. Cutler's tearful testimony was particularly compelling with respect to the emotional impact of the retesting because it was a poignant reminder that she was not "normal." BU's initial requirement mandating retesting for students with learning disabilities screened out or tended to screen out the learning disabled within the meaning of the federal law.

However, BU's retesting policy at present has been changed substantially to provide for a waiver of the reevaluation requirement. A recent statement of policy provides:

> Reevaluation is required to ensure that services and accommodations are matched to the student's changing needs. Comprehensive re-testing is not required. A student need only be re-tested for his previously diagnosed learning disability. The issue of what specific re-testing is required is, in the first instance, left to the discretion of the student's physician or licensed clinical psychologist. If the student's physician or licensed psychologist believes that retesting is not necessary to reevaluate the student's learning disability, the physician or licensed clinical psychologist should write to DS to explain why. Re-testing that is not medically necessary will be waived.

This waiver process was reconfirmed in the procedural pronouncements that BU distributed in March of 1997. Thus, it is clear that the retesting can now be obviated if a qualified professional deems it not medically necessary.

I am not persuaded that BU's current retesting policy tends to screen out disabled students. The university's new waiver position appears consistent with plaintiffs' position that the need for retesting should be examined on a student-by-student basis. This policy permits a qualified professional to evaluate the noncurrent testing data, examine issues of co-morbidity (whether other psychological or physical problems are contributing to the learning problem), and talk with the student to determine whether re-testing is desirable, thereby meeting BU's goals without placing an undue burden on the students. In any event, the waiver provision is so new this Court has an insufficient record for determining how this policy is being implemented, and whether it tends to screen out students.

b.   Credentials of Evaluators

BU accepts evaluations and test results that document a learning disability only if the student's evaluator has certain qualifications. Plaintiffs appear to concede that a university can require credentialed evaluators; however, they argue that BU's policy of accepting only the evaluations of medical doctors, licensed clinical psychologists, and individuals with doctorate degrees is too restrictive. With respect to BU's narrow definition of the acceptable qualifications of the persons performing an evaluation, plaintiffs have proven that, both in its initial and current form, these eligibility criteria tend to screen out learning disabled students.

Many students (*e.g.*, Greeley) with long histories of learning disorders in elementary and high school were tested by trained, experienced professionals whose credentials do not match BU's criteria but were deemed acceptable by the student's secondary school, and are acceptable under the guidelines set forth by the Association for Higher Education and Disabilities ("AHEAD"). BU's policy raises a high hurdle because it seemingly requires students with current testing to be retested if the evaluation has not been performed by a person with credentials acceptable to BU. As initially drafted and implemented, the policy tends to screen out students because of the time, expense and anxiety of having to be completely retested, even if their documentation has been recently performed by an evaluator who specialized in learning disabilities and who had a masters degree in education or developmental psychology.

To complicate things further, BU's implementation of the credentials policy has been uneven. It has permitted some students with learning disabilities to fulfill the requirement via the much less expensive route of asking an evaluator with the requisite credentials to review and confirm the evaluator's test results, while other students have been required to undergo a complete reevaluation. For example, plaintiff Jordan Nodelman only spent $150 to obtain a review of his original ADD evaluation from a licensed clinical psychologist, and there is no evidence that he had difficulty procuring the confirmation letter. However, though Scott Greeley was offered a similar concession, BU ultimately refused to accept Greeley's confirmation correspondence. Assuming that the Nodelman review procedure is unavailable under the current policy for students who have been tested by evaluators with masters degrees, I conclude that plaintiffs have proven that BU's present eligibility criteria concerning the credentials of the evaluators tend to screen out some students with learning disabilities.

One caveat. With respect to BU students who have not been tested for a learning disability prior to matriculation at the university, there is no evidence that testing by evaluators with doctorate degrees is significantly more expensive or burdensome than testing by a person with a masters degree. Also, there is no evidence that it is more difficult to locate or to schedule an appointment with a person with credentials acceptable to BU, particularly in an academic mecca like Boston. This Court finds that BU's credentials requirement does not tend to screen out students who do not have to bear the burden of being re tested in order to satisfy BU's qualifications mandate.

c.   I.Q. Tests

Finally, plaintiffs have offered no persuasive evidence that BU's requirement that a student provide his I.Q. test scores tends to screen out any students. Indeed, under the AHEAD guidelines, the diagnostic criteria in the DSM IV, and the standards in 29 states, IQ tests are administered as part of a learning disabilities assessment.

d.   BU's Response

BU argues that neither its initial or its current documentation criteria "screen out" the learning disabled within the meaning of federal law because there is no persuasive evidence that its requirements have had the effect of actually preventing students with learning disabilities from getting accommodations from the university. The strongest evidence in support of BU's position is that all of the named plaintiffs, after much hassle, eventually received the requested accommodations (except course substitutions) from BU in spite of its new and more burdensome documentation requirements. BU also attempted to present data suggesting that roughly the same number of students are receiving accommodations under the current policy as during the prior LDSS reign.

Contrary to BU's assertions, plaintiffs have demonstrated that BU's initial eligibility criteria actually screened out students. The number of enrolled students who self-identify as learning-disabled dropped 40 percent between the 1994–1995 academic year and the 1996–1997 academic year. Moreover, as considered in detail above, plaintiffs have established that as initially implemented, the currency and qualifications requirements were burdensome and, thus, they at least tended to screen out the disabled students.

3.   Necessity

Documentation requirements that screen out or tend to screen out disabled students—in this case, the qualification criteria and the currency requirement as it was initially imposed—still do not violate the ADA and Rehabilitation Act if BU can demonstrate that the requirement is a "necessary" part of the accommodations process. Again, I consider the necessity of the criteria separately.

a.   Currency

Because every expert who testified agreed that there is no demonstrable change in a specific learning disorder, such as dyslexia, after an individual reaches age 18, BU has failed to demonstrate that the three-year retesting requirement, as initially written, was necessary for students who had been diagnosed with specific learning disorders.

Professor Shaywitz of Yale University School of Medicine, a physician and medical researcher in the area of dyslexia, has performed a comprehensive longitudinal study of the changes in a large population of dyslexic children over an extended period of time. She testified that dyslexia causes a persistent, life-long deficit in the ability to decode language at the most basic levels of intellectual functioning. This deficit persists after age 18 and does not change. Defendants have produced no peer reviewed literature or scientific testimony that provides evidence for the idea that a person's learning disability will show any change after adulthood, or that a student's test scores will show significant change during the course of their college career. Indeed, there are no peer-reviewed studies about the need for current evaluations in the post-secondary educational environment. Moreover, no other college or university in the United States or Canada requires retesting after age 18, and the AHEAD guidelines call for retesting every five years once an individual reaches adulthood.

To show that learning disabilities change over time, BU relies in part on the testimony of plaintiffs' expert Dean Shaw of Brown University. Shaw testified that approximately 25 percent of the students at Brown University who begin college with accommodations do not need them by the time they graduate. This opinion is consistent with Dr. Shaywitz's research that many so-called "compensated" dyslexics may actually learn to read, even though the decoding effort remains laborious, tiring and slow. Another defense expert, Professor Hynd, believed that retesting would provide "important insights" to a university monitoring co-morbid psychological and physiological conditions (because 30 to 40 percent of all individuals with reading disabilities have a co-morbid condition such as ADHD, depression or anxiety disorders), and that retesting even on a quarterly or semesterly basis would help an institution to make the most accurate determination of appropriate accommodations.

Nevertheless, Dr. Shaywitz testified credibly that "once a student comes to school diagnosed with a learning disability, there is no test that is currently available that can determine precisely what accommodations should be provided to a particular student." Professor Hynd's desire for retesting semesterly might be appropriate in an "ideal" world, but few would argue it is "necessary" to do the job. If there is a history of psychological problems in a student, a reevaluation may be appropriate to monitor the co-morbid conditions that Professor Hynd was fairly concerned about; however, the defendants have not proven, as they must, that retesting every three years is "necessary" in adulthood.

On the other hand, BU has presented credible evidence that reevaluation of students with ADD and ADHD is essential because the symptoms of ADD and ADHD change in different environments, are often treated with medication, and these disorders often remit from adolescence to adulthood. Professor Rachel Klein, one of the foremost authorities in this area, testified credibly about the need for current information.

b.   Qualifications Requirements

BU argues that it is necessary to set a high standard for the qualifications of evaluators in order to prevent overdiagnoses for learning disabilities like dyslexia, and to ensure proper documentation of conditions such as ADD and ADHD. To support its assertion that a master's degree does not meet its quality litmus test, it argues in its legal briefs that "[a] doctorate degree is more likely to bring an evaluator into contact with new research and changes in the field. Evaluators with lower degrees tend not to have the sophistication necessary to properly evaluate people with attention deficit disorders and learning disabilities." BU points to the research of Associate Professor Richard Sparks, who believes that overdiagnosis of learning disabilities for students seeking foreign language waivers or substitutions is a problem in the field, and to testimony that between twenty and thirty percent of college students seeking accommodations due to a learning disability provide insufficient documentation. Klafter testified that although there was a large number of potential evaluators, he wanted only the "best evaluations available."

To begin with, BU has produced no evidence that its initial policy in effect from November of 1995 through March of 1997, which required that learning disabled students could only submit evaluations prepared by physicians and licensed clinical psychologists, was necessary to ensure proper documentation and prevent overdiagnosis. Under this initial policy, two of BU's experts at trial who had doctorates in education—Professors Sparks and Hynd—would have been precluded from providing evaluations of learning disabled students. Accordingly, the initial policy flunks the necessity test because BU failed to show the need to preclude evaluators with doctorates in education from providing evaluations.

The post-March 1997 policy is a tougher question because it uses a doctorate degree as the proxy for quality. There is an intuitive appeal to this bright line because evaluators with doctorates generally do have more training and a better education than those with only a masters degree. However, BU's burden is a heavy one because it must show that the more stringent eligibility criterion is "necessary" to achieve its goal of ensuring proper documentation. The record is sparse on the point. While concerns about improving the quality of documentation of learning disabilities are valid, there is no evidence that reports or testing by those evaluators with masters degrees are worse than those by Ph.D.'s, nor is there evidence that a Ph.D. gets better training than a person with a masters in the specific standardized testing that must be conducted to diagnose learning disabilities. Indeed, the AHEAD guidelines list "educational psychologists" and "learning disabilities specialists" among the professionals who may have the experience that qualifies them to diagnose learning disabilities.

The best argument advanced in support of a doctorate requirement is that an evaluator with a lesser level of education may be too focused on learning disabilities and have insufficient training to pick up other "co-morbid" causes for poor academic performance (like medical or psychological problems). However, this myopia concern could be alleviated with a waiver policy akin to the one followed for Nodelman which required an evaluator with a doctorate to evaluate the prior testing to determine its adequacy. In short, BU bears the burden of proving a complete re-evaluation by a person with doctorate degree or a licensed psychologist is "necessary" to accomplish its goal of improving the quality of evaluations. Because it has not met its burden, the Court concludes that the blanket policy requiring students to be retested if the prior evaluator has only a masters degree violates federal law.

On the other hand, BU has met its burden of proof with respect to the credentials necessary to evaluate ADD and ADHD. These conditions are primarily identified through clinical evaluations rather than through standardized testing, and a well-trained eye is essential for proper diagnosis. Defendants' expert Professor Klein testified credibly that an evaluator with a Ph.D. or an M.D. is more likely to distinguish between ADD/ADHD and medical or psychological conditions that present comparable symptoms. The Court is persuaded that, in regard to ADD/ADHD, a doctorate level of training is "necessary" within the meaning of the federal law.

C.   BU's Evaluation Procedure

Plaintiffs contend that BU's process for evaluating accommodation requests is discriminatory because Westling and Klafter, who are actively participating in closed-door evaluations of student files, have no expertise in learning disabilities and are motivated by false stereotypes about learning disabled students. Moreover, the class contends that BU's evaluation process is insufficiently "interactive" and that students with learning disabilities have been denied the right to due process (as guaranteed by Section 504 regulations) because BU has failed to provide a neutral grievance procedure when a student's requests for accommodations has been denied.

[T]he concerns about the nitty-gritty involvement of Westling and Klafter in the accommodations process during the 1995–1996 school year are well founded. There is no dispute that Westling and Klafter, who have no expertise in learning disabilities and no training in fashioning reasonable accommodations for the learning disabled, were actively involved in the process of approving accommodation requests at that time. Worse still, during that year, these administrators expressed certain biases about the learning disabilities movement and stereotypes about learning disabled students. Westling and Klafter indicated repeatedly that many students who sought accommodations on the basis of a learning disability were lazy or fakers (*e.g.*, "Somnolent Samantha"), and Klafter labeled learning disabilities evaluators "snake oil salesmen." If not invidiousness, at the very least, these comments reflect misinformed stereotypes that, when coupled with Westling and Klafter's dominant role in the implementation of BU's accommodations policy during the 1995–1996 school year, conflicted with the university's obligation to provide a review process "based on actual risks and not on speculation, stereotypes, or generalizations about disabilities." H.R.Rep.No.101–485, pt. II, at 105 (1990).

BU's internally-contentious, multi-tiered evaluation process involving evaluators who were not only inexperienced but also biased caused the delay and denial of reasonable accommodations and much emotional distress for learning disabled students. The Court concludes that the implementation of BU's initial accommodations policy violated the ADA and Section 504 during the 1995–1996 academic year.

The issue for purposes of the requested declaratory and injunctive relief, however, is whether the current procedure is propelled by discriminatory animus or has the effect of discrimination on the basis of disability. This Court concludes that it does not.

At present, Lorraine Wolf, a highly trained professional, makes the initial evaluation as to whether the student is learning disabled and whether the requested accommodations are reasonable. Plaintiffs do not claim she is a wolf in lamb's clothing. They do not challenge her credentials or good faith. While she does forward all recommendations for accommodations to Westling's office, there is no evidence that her professional judgments have been second-guessed or that Klafter does anything other than "rubberstamp" her impartial recommendations. Although BU has occasionally refused a student's request to abrogate a substantial academic requirement since Wolf's arrival, there is no evidence to suggest that the decision not to modify that degree requirement was unreasonable or discriminatory. In sum, plaintiffs have not proven that the present method of administering the learning disability program has the effect of discrimination on the basis of disability, or is tainted by impermissible stereotypes.

The plaintiffs also make the argument that the ADA and Section 504 require BU to engage in an "interactive" process in fashioning accommodations for students with learning disabilities, and that BU's review process fails to meet that obligation. [D]uring much of the 1995–1996 academic year, the administration of the learning disability program miserably failed to achieve any measure of interactivity. The president's office did not communicate directly with LDSS and vice versa. Learning disabled students desperately seeking information concerning the status of their reasonable accommodations requests received conflicting information from university officials, wrong information, or no information at all. When accommodations were denied, inadequate explanations of the documentation deficiencies were provided, and parental inquiries were fruitless. While DS head Macurdy did his best in March of 1996 to handle the problem, he was inadequately staffed and trained.

BU's administrative methods during 1995–1996 were also not sufficiently interactive to the extent that unwary students were ambushed by the new, unwritten requirements for accommodation, and the multi-tiered process for reviewing student files was not clearly developed or disclosed. For example, by Westling's insistence that the new policy on course substitutions be implemented "effective immediately"—without giving students any notice or time to adjust— and Brinckerhoff's precipitous letter requesting retesting at exam time, BU failed to communicate effectively its new accommodation mandates. Westling and Klafter point the finger at Brinckerhoff for much of the insensitivity, delays, poor communication, and bad timing at LDSS. Even if Brinckerhoff fairly shoulders the blame, he, too, is a university official. As a result of BU's representatives' poor implementation of the policy, many students who applied for accommodations at the beginning of the fall semester were not given the requested assistance or even told of the reason for the delay so that documentation deficiencies could be remedied until some time in November-long after classes had begun. At least one student was not accommodated until the following semester.

For the purposes of prospective relief, however, the bleak picture has brightened. No doubt as a result of this litigation, the university has now formulated harmonious written statements of policy that have been authorized by the relevant academic officials. Moreover, the university has hired a professional evaluator who, at trial, promised that she will meet with students and address their concerns as she assesses their need for accommodation.

This Court finds that BU's current review process [i]s sufficiently interactive to withstand the attack under the ADA and Section 504.

Plaintiffs have submitted no evidence that students requesting personal meetings do not get them, that phone calls are not returned, that misinformation is generated, or that accommodations requests are not timely handled. Even though BU no longer works as closely with students as it did under Brinckerhoff, this Court has no evidence that, as revamped, the administration of the current learning disabilities review procedure has the effect of discriminating against students.

[D]. Course Substitutions

1.   The Competing Contentions

Plaintiffs claim that BU's blanket refusal to authorize course substitutions for students with learning disabilities amounts to a failure to modify the university's practices to prevent discrimination as required by federal law. Specifically, the class argues that, because many learning-disabled students have extreme difficulty in taking and passing courses in mathematics and foreign language, allowing course substitutions for those class members is a reasonable accommodation, and, thus, BU's refusal to authorize such a modification is discriminatory.

BU asserts that its refusal of course substitutions is consistent with the law because exemptions of this nature would amount to a fundamental alteration of its academic liberal arts program, a course of study that has been in place for over a century. Also, BU emphasizes that it provides special programs for students with foreign language and math difficulties (like an oral enhancement program and one-on-one tutoring) in addition to the classroom accommodations that are available in any other course.

2.   The Legal Framework

[T]he ADA specifically defines discrimination to include:

> a failure to make reasonable modifications in policies, practices or procedures, when such modifications are necessary to afford such goods, services, facilities, privileges, advantages, or accommodations to individuals with disabilities, unless the entity can demonstrate that making such modifications would fundamentally alter the nature of such goods, services, facilities, privileges, advantages, or accommodations.

42 U.S.C. § 12182(b)(2)(A)(ii). The regulations implementing Section 504 also require an educational institution that receives federal funding to "make such modifications to its academic requirements as are necessary to ensure that such requirements do not have the effect of discriminating, on the basis of handicap, against a qualified handicapped applicant or student." 34 C.F.R. § 104.44 (entitled "Academic Adjustments"). However, the regulations further explain that "academic requirements that the recipient can demonstrate are essential to the program of instruction being pursued by such student . . . will not be regarded as discriminatory within the meaning of this section." *Id.*

Significantly, with regard to academic institutions, the regulations interpreting Section 504 provide that reasonable modifications "may include changes in the length of time permitted for the completion of degree requirements, *substitution of specific courses* required for the completion of degree requirements, and adaptation of the manner in which specific courses are conducted." 34 C.F.R. § 104.44 (emphasis added). The appendix to the regulations elaborates:

> Paragraph (a) of § 104.44 requires that a recipient make certain adjustments to academic requirements and practices that discriminate or have the effect of discriminating on the basis of handicap. This requirement, like its predecessor in the proposed legislation, does not obligate an institution to waive course or other academic requirements. But such institutions must accommodate those requirements to the needs of individual handicapped students. For example, an institution might permit an otherwise qualified handicapped student who is deaf to substitute an art appreciation or music history course for a required course in music appreciation or could modify the manner in which the music appreciation course is conducted for the deaf student. It should be stressed that academic requirements that can be demonstrated by the recipient to be essential to its program of instruction or to particular degrees need not be changed.

34 C.F.R. § 104, app.A ¶ 31. In interpreting these regulations, the Office of Civil Rights ("OCR"), the federal agency responsible for investigating complaints of disability discrimination, has consistently maintained that, even though an educational institution must modify its academic requirements to accommodate a disabled student, an institution need not waive academic requirements that are essential to its program or course of study. See, *e.g.*, *Bennett College*, 7 Nat'l Disability L. Rep. ¶ 26 (1995); *Northern Ill. Univ.*, 7 Nat'l Disability L. Rep. ¶ 39 (1995); *City Univ. of N.Y.*, 3 Nat'l Disability L. Rep. ¶ 104 (1992); *Cabrillo College*, 2 Nat'l Disability L. Rep. ¶ 78 (1991).

[3]. The Analysis

Turning to the instant case, the Court must first consider whether plaintiffs have met their burden of establishing that course substitutions in math and foreign language are, generally, "reasonable" accommodations.

The plaintiffs are aided substantially in satisfying their initial burden by the mere fact that the administrative regulations interpreting Section 504 and the ADA specifically provide that modifying academic requirements to allow course substitutions may be a reasonable means of accommodating the disabled. See 34 C.F.R. § 104, app.A ¶ 31. In addition, plaintiffs offered evidence at trial to support their contention that a course substitution is reasonable, at least in regard to BU's foreign language requirements. Even though the experts disagreed as to whether a language disability made acquisition of a foreign language literally impossible for some students, and plaintiffs' experts conceded there are no peer-reviewed scientific studies which indicate that it is impossible for a student with a learning disability to learn a foreign language, the weight of the evidence supports plaintiffs' arguments that students with learning disorders such as dyslexia have a significantly more difficult challenge in becoming proficient in a foreign language than students without such an impairment. The only evidence to the contrary was the testimony of defendants' expert, Professor Sparks, who has recently concluded that difficulties in learning foreign languages are not necessarily attributable to learning disabilities. However, Sparks conceded that his research was "preliminary." Although another defense expert, George Hynd, testified that most students had the potential to learn with appropriate accommodations, he agreed that persons with learning disabilities may have difficulty learning a foreign language because of neurological deficits. On all of the evidence, the Court is persuaded that plaintiffs have demonstrated that requesting a course substitution in foreign language for students with demonstrated language disabilities is a reasonable modification.

With respect to math course substitutions, however, I conclude that there was no scientific evidence introduced at trial to support plaintiffs' claim that a course substitution is a plausible alternative for a learning disability in mathematics (*i.e.*, dyscalculia). Dyscalculia is specifically listed in the DSM-IV as a learning disorder; however, none of the named testifying plaintiffs had dyscalculia, and the record documents that only two students in CLA requested a course substitution in mathematics. Moreover, plaintiffs' witness, Dean Robert Shaw of Brown University, who is an Associate Professor of Education and the coordinator of the learning disability program, testified that he never met a student with a disability that prevented her from learning math. Professor Seigel, an expert called by the defense, found one student (out of the twenty-eight files) who she claimed had a severe case of "dyscalculia" entitling him to accommodations; however, Professor Seigel testified that "with the appropriate accommodations," a student should be able to fulfill BU's mathematics requirements. Moreover, with regard to the one student whose file she reviewed, Seigel never said that the condition was so severe that a course substitution was needed. Essentially, the evidence at trial concerning dyscalculia was sketchy at best. Accordingly, plaintiffs have not demonstrated that a request for a course substitution in mathematics is a reasonable modification of BU's degree requirements.

Because plaintiffs have established that the request for a course substitution in foreign language is reasonable, the burden now shifts to BU to demonstrate that the requested course substitution would fundamentally alter the nature of its liberal arts degree program.

Fortunately, in determining which modifications amount to a "fundamental alteration," the Court does not write on a clean blackboard. Two related First Circuit cases provide invaluable assistance in evaluating a university's burden of supporting its conclusion that a requested modification by a learning disabled student of an academic requirement would fundamentally alter the nature of the program. See *Wynne v. Tufts Univ. Sch. of Med.*, 932 F.2d 19 (1st Cir.1991) (*en banc*) (hereinafter "*Wynne I*"); *Wynne v. Tufts Univ. Sch. of Med.*, 976 F.2d 791 (1st Cir.1992) (hereinafter "*Wynne II*"). Both Wynne opinions, which arise out of a single student's efforts to get Tufts' Medical School to change its testing policy to accommodate his learning disability, bear discussion at length.

Stephen Wynne was admitted to Tufts Medical School in 1983. After experiencing extreme difficulty with the multiple-choice format of his first year examinations, and after failing eight out of fifteen first-year courses, Wynne underwent a neuropsychological evaluation at the expense of the medical school. The evaluation revealed that Wynne had serious processing difficulties indicative of a learning disability. It was later discovered that, in particular, Wynne had difficulty interpreting the type of multiple choice questions that were characteristic of medical school examinations.

Wynne brought suit in federal court claiming that the school's failure to offer an alternative to written multiple choice examinations violated his rights under Section 504 The *Wynne I* Court concluded that, "in determining whether an individual meets the 'otherwise qualified' requirement of section 504, it is necessary to look at more than the individual's ability to meet a program's present requirements." The Court stressed that, while deference need be given to the institutional decisionmakers in deciding whether an accommodation is possible, "there is a real obligation on the academic institution to seek suitable means of reasonably accommodating a handicapped person." Specifically, it found that

> [i]f the institution submits undisputed facts demonstrating that the relevant officials within the institution considered alternative means, their feasibility, cost and effect on the academic program, and came to a rationally justifiable conclusion that the available alternative would result either in lowering academic standards or requiring substantial program alteration, the court could rule as a matter of law that the institution had met its duty of seeking reasonable accommodation.

The *Wynne I* Court remanded the case for a determination of whether Tufts had met its burden "of demonstrating that its determination that no reasonable way existed to accommodate Wynne's inability to perform adequately on written multiple-choice examinations was a reasoned, professional academic judgment, not a mere ipse dixit."

On appeal after remand, the First Circuit decided whether, in fact, Tufts had reached "a rationally justifiable conclusion that accommodating plaintiff would lower academic standards or otherwise unduly affect its program." *Wynne II*. The Court considered voluminous documents that Tufts produced after remand which discussed, among other things, why biochemistry is important to a medical school curriculum, why multiple choice testing was the fairest means of evaluating the subject matter, "what thought [the university] had given to different methods of testing proficiency in biochemistry," and "why it eschewed alternatives to multiple-choice testing, particularly with respect to make-up examinations." The First Circuit concluded that, through evidence of this nature, Tufts had successfully "demythologized the institutional thought processes leading to its determination that it could not deviate from its wanted format to accommodate Wynne's professed disability." Tufts met its burden of proving fundamental alteration because it showed that its officials had decided "rationally, if not inevitably, that no further accommodation could be made without imposing and undue (and injurious) hardship on the academic program."

Even more than the dispute over the format of a test in the *Wynne* cases, the degree requirements that are at issue in the instant litigation go to the heart of academic freedom. Universities have long been considered to have the freedom to determine "what may be taught, how it shall be taught, and who may be admitted to study." *Sweezy v. New Hampshire*, 354 U.S. 234, 263 (1957) (Frankfurter, J., concurring).

Based on a review of the relevant cases, I conclude that a university can refuse to modify academic degree requirements—even course requirements that students with learning disabilities cannot satisfy—as long it "undertake[s] a diligent assessment of the available options," *Wynne II*, and makes "a professional, academic judgment that reasonable accommodation is simply not available." *Wynne I*. That is to say, neither the ADA nor the Rehabilitation Act require a university to provide course substitutions that the university rationally concludes would alter an essential part of its academic program. Accordingly, plaintiffs' front-line of attack against any across-the-board policy precluding course substitutions under the ADA and Rehabilitation Act fails.

4.   Westling's Ipse Dixit

As a fallback, the plaintiff class argues: (1) that in the circumstances of this case, BU's refusal to modify its liberal arts degree requirements flunks the *Wynne*-test because Westling was motivated by discriminatory animus in declining to modify the academic standards in question, and (2) that BU refused to modify its math and foreign language requirements as an accommodation for the learning disabled without making a diligent, reasoned, academic judgment.

Based on my review of the record, plaintiffs prevail on both of these arguments. A substantial motivating factor in Westling's decision not to consider degree modifications was his unfounded belief that learning disabled students who could not meet degree requirements were unmotivated (like "Somnolent Samantha") or disingenuous. Although Westling was also inspired by a genuine concern for academic standards, his course substitution prohibition was founded, in part, on uninformed stereotypes. Relying only on popular press accounts that suggested learning disabilities were being unfairly exaggerated and misdiagnosed, Westling provided no concrete evidence that any BU student faked a learning disability to get out of a course requirement.

Even though Westling may have had a good faith (even passionate) belief in the value of foreign languages to a liberal arts program, the Court finds that he did not dispassionately determine whether the benefits of attaining that proficiency are outweighed by the costs to the learning disabled student. Westling made the decision not to modify the mathematics and foreign language requirements for students with learning disabilities without consulting any experts on learning disabilities. Nor did Westling discuss the importance of foreign language to BU's liberal arts curriculum with any of the relevant BU department heads, professors or officials. Indeed, the only deliberation that took place regarding academic adjustments as accommodations for the learning disabled was Westling's consultation with Klafter about whether scientific evidence supports the existence of a learning disability that prevents foreign language proficiency. Westling's reliance on discriminatory stereotypes, together with his failure to consider carefully the effect of course substitutions on BU's liberal arts programs and to consult with academics and experts in learning disabilities, constitutes a failure of BU's obligation to make a rational judgment that course substitutions would fundamentally alter the course of study. Although BU ultimately has the right to decline to modify its degree requirements—and that decision will be given great deference—it must do so after reasoned deliberations as to whether modifications would change the essential academic standards of its liberal arts curriculum.

[O]RDER OF JUDGMENT

1. The Court orders BU to cease and desist implementing its current policy of requiring that students with learning disorders (not ADD or ADHD) who have current evaluations by trained professionals with masters degrees and sufficient experience be completely retested by professionals who have medical degrees, or doctorate degrees, or licensed clinical psychologists in order to be eligible for reasonable accommodations.

2. The Court orders BU to propose, within 30 days of the receipt of this order, a deliberative procedure for considering whether modification of its degree requirement in foreign language would fundamentally alter the nature of its liberal arts program. Such a procedure shall include a faculty committee set up by the College of Arts and Sciences to examine its degree requirements and to determine whether a course substitution in foreign languages would fundamentally alter the nature of the liberal arts program. The faculty's determination will be subject to the approval of the president, as university by-laws provide. As provided in *Wynne*, BU shall report back to the Court by the end of the semester concerning its decision and the reasons. In the meantime, the university shall process all requests for a reasonable accommodation involving a course substitution in foreign language, and shall maintain records of such students. BU is not required to grant such a course substitution in the area of foreign language until its deliberation process is complete.

Guckenberger v. Boston Univ.

United States District Court for the District of Massachusetts, 1997.
8 F.Supp.2d 82.

■ SARIS, DISTRICT JUDGE.

INTRODUCTION

In paragraph two of its [earlier] order, the Court required BU to propose and to implement a "deliberative procedure" for considering whether course substitutions for the foreign language requirement of BU's College of Arts and Sciences (the "College") would "fundamentally alter the nature" of BU's undergraduate liberal arts degree. BU, using the College's existing Dean's Advisory Committee to consider the issue, decided that course substitutions would constitute such a fundamental alteration. Plaintiffs challenge that determination. After hearing, the Court holds that BU has complied with the order.

BACKGROUND

[O]n October 6, 1997, the Court approved the use of the existing Dean's Advisory Committee (the "Committee") of the College as the mechanism for deliberating the issue of course substitutions for the foreign language requirement in accordance with the Court's order. In the course of normal business, the Committee "is charged by the by-laws of the College with advising the Dean on issues involving academic standards." During the relevant time period, the Committee was composed of eleven faculty members of the College, including professors of mathematics, English, philosophy, natural sciences, engineering and foreign languages. The Committee is normally chaired by Dennis D. Berkey, who is the Dean of the College and the Provost of BU. However, Dean Berkey removed himself as chairman of proceedings relating to course substitutions because of his role in the "central administration" of BU. In his place, Associate Professor of Mathematics Paul Blanchard assumed the role of Acting Chairman.

The Committee convened to consider the issue of course substitutions on seven occasions. In keeping with its practice for general business, the Committee meetings were closed to interested parties and the public, with two exceptions. The first meeting on this issue was attended by Attorneys Lawrence Elswit and Erika Geetter, counsel for BU, who "set out the Committee's responsibilities as outlined in the Court's decision." Also, several College students addressed the Committee at the November 14, 1997 meeting. Their involvement was directed by the Court at a October 6, 1997 hearing and was solicited through notice posted on an internet bulletin board and an advertisement published in BU's student newspaper, The Daily Free Press, on October 27, October 29 and November 3. The opportunity for student input was also reported on the second page of a front-page story in the October 24 issue of The Daily Free Press. Only current College students were permitted to address the Committee, and only five students did so. Among the students who spoke was Catherine Hays Miller, who had testified at trial. Neither President Westling nor his direct staff had any involvement with the Committee proceedings, and the Committee did not officially seek any other input from non-members.

The Committee kept minutes of four of its seven meetings. No minutes were recorded during the first two meetings, but, following the Court's order to do so at the October 6 hearing, minutes were kept for all but the last of the remaining meetings. The minutes are topical summaries of the discussions that took place at the covered meetings. They do not identify speakers. The Committee had never before kept minutes in the course of normal business.

On December 2, 1997, the Committee completed its eight-page report (plus attachments) and submitted it to President Westling in accordance with the BU by-laws. Its final recommendation was:

> After extensive review and deliberation, the [Committee's] professional and academic judgment is that the conjunction of the foregoing considerations (which we have merely summarized here) entails but one conclusion: the foreign language requirement is fundamental to the nature of the liberal arts degree at Boston University. The [Committee] therefore recommends against approving course substitutions for any student as an alternative to fulfilling the foreign language requirement.

Two days later, President Westling, in a letter to Dean Berkey, accepted the recommendation of the Committee. The completed report, along with minutes and attachments, was filed with the Court on December 5, 1997 and refiled as an attachment to an affidavit of Dean Berkey on February 19, 1998.

DISCUSSION

A. The Test

The First Circuit crafted the following test for evaluating the decision of an academic institution with respect to the availability of reasonable accommodations for the learning disabled:

> If the institution submits undisputed facts demonstrating that the relevant officials within the institution considered alternative means, their feasibility, cost and effect on the academic program, and came to a rationally justifiable conclusion that the available alternatives would result either in lowering academic standards or requiring substantial program alteration, the court could rule as a matter of law that the institution had met its duty of seeking reasonable accommodation.

Wynne I. "[T]he point is not whether a [university] is 'right' or 'wrong' in making program-related decisions. Such absolutes rarely apply in the context of subjective decisionmaking, particularly in a scholastic setting." *Wynne II.*

B. Basic Facts Showing Reasoned Deliberation

The Court's first task under this test is "to find the basic facts, giving due deference to the school. . . . " *Wynne I.* Those "basic facts" must include showings of the following: (1) an "indication of who took part in the decision [and] when it was made;" (2) a "discussion of the unique qualities" of the foreign language requirement as it now stands; and (3) "a consideration of possible alternatives" to the requirement. As these elements suggest, the required showing of undisputed facts refers to the "consideration" of the request by BU and not, as plaintiffs suggest, to a broad-ranging consensus of expert or university opinion on the value of foreign languages to a liberal arts curriculum.

The Court concludes that BU has presented sufficient undisputed essential facts, satisfying each of the three aspects of *Wynne's* requirements. First, the Committee, made up of eminent members of the College faculty, deliberated this issue over the course of two months. The eleven Committee members include four department chairmen and represent diverse disciplines beyond the foreign languages. Though it would have been better to have kept minutes of all seven meetings, the four meetings provide the Court with sufficient insight to allow the Court to review the procedure that BU followed and to "demythologize[ ] the institutional thought processes. . . . " *Wynne II.* BU took pains to insulate President Westling from the process to remove any concerns about his earlier comments which, in substantial part, necessitated this remedy. The Committee gave adequate notice to College students, both with and without learning disabilities, of the opportunity to provide input into the Committee's decision. The Committee's reliance on only its own academic judgment and the input of College students was reasonable and in keeping with the nature of the decision.

Second, the Committee had vigorous discussions of the "unique qualities" of the foreign language requirement and its importance to the liberal arts curriculum. Its members rallied around an articulated defense, highlighted throughout the Report, of the rigorous foreign language requirement of the College. In both the Minutes and the Report, the Committee mentioned technical educational gains from the learning of foreign languages, such as enhancing an ability to read foreign literature in its original form and laying a "foundation" for other areas of academic concentration. For example, some members at the October 8 meeting believed it was important to be immersed in ancient Greek and Latin to understand Greek and Roman cultures. Another Committee member waxed "that someone who can read in French would realize that Madame Bovary dies in the imperfect tense, something we don't have in the English language, and it makes for a very different understanding of the novel."

Additionally, the Committee repeatedly emphasized its view that foreign language study uniquely contributed to the College's emphasis on multiculturalism: "A mind cooped up within a single culture is not liberally educated, and knowledge of a foreign language is essential to countering parochialism of outlook and knowledge." The Committee also portrayed foreign language study as part of a broader liberal arts education which, in its view, contemplates "some competence in thinking in diverse areas of knowledge." Commenting on the specific contribution of foreign language learning to liberal arts, the Committee reported that "[e]ncountering a foreign culture in and through the complexities of its verbal structures and representations poses a unique challenge to familiar idioms, settled habits of mind, and securities of knowledge."

Third, the Committee "explained what thought it had given to different methods" of meeting the requirement and "why it eschewed alternatives" to meeting the requirement. *Wynne II.* The minutes indicate that alternatives were discussed in at least four of the Committee's meetings. The Report discusses objections to the Committee's conclusion. One dissenting member suggested an alternative proposal whereby a "student would select courses from a faculty approved list that focus on the language, culture, history, literature, and art of countries where the language is spoken." However, "[n]o other member shared this belief that the goals of foreign language study could be met by 'alternative paths' outside the foreign languages." Additionally, the objections of several students were noted at length.

As a whole, the Committee concluded that "[n]o content course taught in English can substitute fully for the insider access to other cultures—with its attendant invitation to thoroughgoing critical self-awareness—that is the hallmark of foreign language study." The Committee acknowledged that some students, both learning disabled and not, will "struggle" with the rigorous requirement, but nonetheless concluded "that no other goal could serve the same purpose within the [College] curriculum."

Furthermore, the Committee discussed the College's existing accommodations of learning disabled students attempting to fulfill the foreign language requirement, a consideration that weighs in BU's favor in this analysis. See *Wynne II* (noting with favor Tufts' accommodations of tutoring, taped lectures and untimed examinations). The College allows all its students to satisfy the foreign language requirement in a variety of ways, including a free "Foreign Language Enhancement Program" that provides one-on-one instruction to learning disabled students navigating the required sequences of language classes. Learning disabled students are allowed spelling accommodations in language classes, and student tutoring is provided by the foreign language department at no cost to students. BU provides for additional time on tests, a reading track for French and Spanish, distraction-free testing, distribution of lecture notes in advance, and replacement of written with oral exams.

C.   Professional, Academic Judgment

Having found undisputed facts of a reasoned deliberation, the Court must "evaluate whether those facts add up to a professional, academic judgment that reasonable accommodation is simply not available." *Wynne I.* In the unique context of academic curricular decision-making, the courts may not override a faculty's professional judgment "unless it is such a substantial departure from accepted academic norms as to demonstrate that the person or committee responsible did not actually exercise professional judgment."

This standard is in keeping with the policy of judicial deference to academic decision making. The Court previously indicated that BU's decision would be given "great deference" so long as it occurred "after reasoned deliberations as to whether modifications would change the essential academic standards of its liberal arts curriculum." Such deference is appropriate in this arena, because "[w]hen judges are asked to review the substance of a genuinely academic decision, . . . they should show great respect for the faculty's professional judgment." *Wynne I.* While, of course, "academic freedom does not embrace the freedom to discriminate," the First Circuit has observed that "[w]e are a society that cherishes academic freedom and recognizes that universities deserve great leeway in their operations."

Plaintiffs attack the academic judgment of the Committee in three ways. First, they argue that BU's decision does mark "a substantial departure from accepted academic norms" because a majority of other colleges and universities—including Princeton, Harvard, Yale, Columbia, Dartmouth, Cornell and Brown—either do not have a general foreign language requirement or permit course substitutions for foreign languages. They also point out that the academic program would not be substantially affected because at BU only 15 students (out of 26,000) a semester would require such course modifications and suggest that similar low numbers of students requesting accommodations in other universities inform their willingness to allow substitutions. The evidence that BU is only among a handful of schools of higher education in its decision to deny course substitutions in language requirements is relevant to an evaluation of its decision to deny a reasonable accommodation. However, a court should not determine that an academic decision is a "substantial departure from accepted academic norms" simply by conducting a head-count of other universities. This approach is particularly inappropriate in the protean area of a liberal arts education. The liberal arts curriculum cannot be fit into a cookie cutter mold, unlike the medical school curriculum in

Wynne, where no one disputed that mastery of biochemistry was necessary.

The *Wynne* decisions indicate that the appropriate question is whether BU's decision is "rationally justifiable" rather than the only possible conclusion it could have reached or other universities have reached. See *Wynne I*. In *Wynne II*, the First Circuit endorsed the professional, academic judgment of Tufts Medical School officials, who had concluded after deliberation that allowing a requested accommodation "would require substantial program alterations, result in lowering academic standards, and devalue Tufts' end product. . . . " *Wynne II*. The Court of Appeals there rejected a similar argument that at least one other medical school and a national testing service had permitted oral renderings of multiple-choice examinations. Indeed, because "Tufts decided, rationally if not inevitably, that no further accommodation could be made without imposing an undue (and injurious) hardship on the academic program," *Wynne II*, the First Circuit ruled as a matter of law that the medical school had met its burden under the ADA.

This Court concludes that so long as an academic institution rationally, without pretext, exercises its deliberate professional judgment not to permit course substitutions for an academic requirement in a liberal arts curriculum, the ADA does not authorize the courts to intervene even if a majority of other comparable academic institutions disagree.

Second, plaintiffs challenge the substance of the Committee's conclusions and analysis. Specifically, they argue that there are sixteen "material facts" in dispute, such as the following: (1) the two year (four semester) foreign language requirement is not "sufficient to permit the vast majority of students to read major works of literature in a foreign language," thus debunking the Madame Bovary line of argument as involving an imperfect logic, not an imperfect tense; (2) a "foreign language requirement does not provide students with educational benefits regarding a foreign culture;" (3) there is "no particular thinking process involved in learning a foreign language that is distinct from any other type of learning;" and (4) BU's "foreign language requirement does not address ethnocentrism among students."

In particular, Naomi S. Baron, a chair of the Department of Language and Foreign Studies at American University, criticized the foreign language "mystique" on plaintiffs' behalf. Nevertheless, even Professor Baron acknowledges that many academic and governmental institutions in recent years have espoused foreign language requirements, indicating the existence of a genuine academic dispute on this issue. For example, she cites a study commissioned by then President Carter which suggested that foreign language study was in the national interest. Many colleges and universities (like Harvard and Haverford) have required proficiency in foreign languages based on the rationale that they deepen the students' appreciation of their own language, promote mental discipline, improve understanding between languages and thought, and make students less ethnocentric. While plaintiffs have submitted affidavits of Professor Baron and other academics who strongly disagree with BU's conclusions and label them as "trite," "idealistic" or "clichés," these issues raise the kinds of academic decisions that universities—not courts—are entrusted with making.

Plaintiffs' final mode of attack is to argue that BU's report does not meet the minimum accepted standards of academic study and inquiry, especially in the Committee's not having referred to outside experts. [P]laintiffs' vigorous attacks on BU's submission generally overstate the Court's level of scrutiny at this stage of litigation. My opinion as to the value of foreign languages in a liberal arts curriculum is not material so long as the requirements of *Wynne* have been met. Despite plaintiffs' attempts to pull truly academic policy debates into the courtroom, the facts "essential" to this order are actually undisputed: BU implemented a deliberative procedure by which it considered in a timely manner both the importance of the foreign language requirement to this College and the feasibility of alternatives. Plaintiffs' argument that the procedure should have been more extensive and inclusive—effectively, more like a legal proceeding—does not have any support in the *Wynne* opinions.

BU's deliberations and conclusions pass muster under *Wynne*. The Court has no cause to doubt the academic qualifications and professionalism of the eleven members of the Committee. There is no evidence that the Committee's decision was mere lip service to the Court's order or was tainted by pretext, insincerity, or bad faith, beyond plaintiffs' unsubstantiated speculation that President Westling's bias infected the Committee. The Report is rationally premised on the Committee's conclusion that the liberal arts degree is "[i]n no sense a technical or vocational degree" like other degrees and that, in its view, the foreign language requirement "has a primarily intellectual, non-utilitarian purpose." With the justifiable belief in mind that this decision could not be made empirically, the Committee concluded that "[k]nowledge of a foreign language is one of the keys to opening the door to the classics and so to liberal learning. It is not the only key, but we do judge it as indispensable."

The Court concludes that the Committee's judgment that "a person holding a liberal arts degree from Boston University ought to have some experience studying a foreign language," is "rationally justifiable" and represents a professional judgment with which the Court should not interfere. Therefore, the Court concludes as a matter of law that BU has not violated its duty to provide reasonable accommodations to learning disabled students under the ADA by refusing to provide course substitutions.

NOTES ON HIGHER EDUCATION

1. **Three Types of Discrimination.** *Pushkin* and *Guckenberger* highlight three classes of discrimination cases that might arise in higher education. One class, exemplified by *Pushkin*, involves discrimination in *admissions* decisions. As *Pushkin* shows, the legal analysis that applies to that class of cases is not especially different from the legal analysis that applies to claims of employment discrimination. Another class, exemplified by the *Wynne* case discussed in *Guckenberger*, involves challenges to universities' means of *assessment* of success in their academic programs. Wynne sought to be assessed by means other than multiple-choice examinations. Recognizing the diversity of academic opinions on the

matter, courts have tended to defer to universities' choices of what sorts of assessment techniques to employ—so long as, as *Wynne* held, they engage in some sort of serious deliberation in formulating and explaining their choices. But where, like some of the *Guckenberger* plaintiffs, students seek extra *time* on exams, they are often successful, because it is difficult for universities to explain why speeded exams are necessary to test knowledge and aptitude. See Laura F. Rothstein, *Higher Education and the Future of Disability Policy*, 52 Ala. L. Rev. 241, 257 (2000). Note that the 2010 revisions of the Attorney General's ADA regulations specifically provide that, in responding to a request for a testing accommodation, a covered entity must "give[ ] considerable weight to documentation of past modifications, accommodations, or auxiliary aids or services received in similar testing situations, as well as such modifications, accommodations, or related aids and services provided" to the student under an IEP or a Section 504 plan. 28 C.F.R. § 36.309(b)(1)(v). How might this regulation have bolstered the plaintiffs' request for testing accommodations in *Guckenberger*? For a discussion of extra testing time as an accommodation, see Section C, below.

The third class of cases is exemplified by the major portion of *Guckenberger*—cases in which students with disabilities seek a modification of course assignments or graduation requirements. This class of cases raises much harder issues, because, unlike assessment procedures, are not necessarily means to a particularly defined end. They aim at the general goal of being an educated person—or, in the case of graduate or professional schools, being prepared for a career as a scholar or professional—but there are potentially infinite ways of achieving that goal. St. John's College in Maryland and New Mexico believes that the best way to become an educated person is to engage with the great works of the Western cultural tradition; all of its students take the same classes—which involve reading and discussing "great books"—through all four years of their college education. See Alex Beam, A Great Idea at the Time: The Rise, Fall, and Curious Afterlife of the Great Books 165–180 (2008). The University of Chicago, which once had a great books curriculum of its own, has a "core curriculum" under which "roughly one-third of an undergraduate's time is spent taking courses prescribed by the university." *Id.* at 152. Brown University, by contrast, famously has no core curriculum.

Or think of law schools. Some law schools have course requirements that occupy students well into their second year. The Yale Law School, by contrast, has only one semester of required courses. The Washington & Lee Law School recently overhauled its curriculum to require all students to spend their third year undergoing a practical, experiential course of study. Many law schools have moved to abandon or loosen grading systems, while other schools retain fine-grained numerical grading systems (*e.g.*, a scale of 100) that would have been familiar in Felix Frankfurter's day.

Given this diversity of approaches among quality schools, how can a court say that *any* particular approach is necessary or fundamental? But if universities must waive their curricular requirements whenever they exclude a person with a disability, is that result consistent with the academic freedom of a university to maintain the academic program it desires? Cf. *Regents of Univ. of California v. Bakke*, 438 U.S. 265, 312

(1978) (opinion of Powell, J.) ("It is the business of a university to provide that atmosphere which is most conducive to speculation, experiment and creation. It is an atmosphere in which there prevail 'the four essential freedoms' of a university—to determine for itself on academic grounds who may teach, what may be taught, how it shall be taught, and who may be admitted to study.") (internal quotation marks omitted). Is it any surprise that courts like the *Guckenberger* court have responded by focusing on universities' decision-making process rather than their substantive outcomes?

Note the parallels between *Guckenberger* and *PGA Tour v. Martin*, a principal case in Chapter Five, and *Alexander v. Choate*, a principal case in Chapter Four. In all of these cases, plaintiffs sought to challenge rules that were in some significant ways constitutive of the activity at issue rather than instrumental in achieving some particular goal. Did the courts analyze the problem in the same way in each of these cases?

2. **The *Guckenberger* Resolution.** In the end, the *Guckenberger* court upholds Boston University's decision to refuse to grant students with learning disabilities a waiver from the foreign-language requirement. Is the court's analysis persuasive? The members of the committee that reevaluated the requirement were all employees of the university; could they really have felt free to defy President Westling's strongly stated views, however "insulated" the committee itself was as a formal matter? And are you persuaded by the arguments the committee mustered in favor of a non-waivable foreign-language requirement? Do students who comply with that requirement learn enough French to read Madame Bovary in an untranslated version? Even if they do, is the incremental educational gain from being able to read for oneself that Madame Bovary dies in the imperfect tense—rather than having the point explained by a literature teacher, for example, or reading about it in the Federal Supplement—so important that a Boston University education just would not be the same if a person with a learning disability were excused from the requirement? In the context of President Westling's statements and actions, is Madame Bovary a post hoc rationalization for an impulsive decision made by an individual who was profoundly skeptical of learning disabilities and reasonable accommodations? Or would any attempt to justify any academic standard look like this?

One background fact might illuminate the dynamics at play here. Boston University is generally acknowledged to be the third best university on the banks of the Charles River. Perhaps BU feels a particularly strong need to emphasize its strict academic standards as a result of anxiety about comparisons with the two schools that sit across the river from it, MIT and Harvard. At colleges that are just a step below the most selective ones, it is common for students to brag about the rigor of their studies—and to compare their school's rigor favorably to the perceived lack of rigor at the most selective schools. See, *e.g.*, Beam, *supra*, at 152 (quoting a senior at the University of Chicago: "It may be harder to get into Harvard, but it's harder to get out of here, and I'm proud of that."). The fact that Harvard allows waivers of its foreign language requirement thus may not undermine what BU is trying to do—instead, it reinforces the argument that BU is more rigorous than those more "selective" schools, with their pampered, entitled students. Does that point offer an argument in favor of, or against, the court's decision in *Guckenberger*. (Note that a similar sense of anxiety might be at play in the PGA Tour's insistence that golfers walk the course. Perhaps it's especially important to the Tour to require golfers to engage in visible physical exertion precisely because many people doubt golf requires serious athletic ability, and those doubts limit the Tour's ability to be taken seriously as a professional sport.)

C. ADMISSIONS AND LICENSING EXAMINATIONS, WITH GENERAL NOTES ON TESTING

Enyart v. National Conference of Bar Examiners, Inc.

United States Court of Appeals for the Ninth Circuit, 2011.
630 F.3d 1153.

■ SILVERMAN, CIRCUIT JUDGE:

Stephanie Enyart, a legally blind law school graduate, sought to take the Multistate Professional Responsibility Exam and the Multistate Bar Exam using a computer equipped with assistive technology software known as JAWS and ZoomText. The State Bar of California had no problem with Enyart's request but the National Conference of Bar Examiners refused to grant this particular accommodation. Enyart sued NCBE under the Americans with Disabilities Act seeking injunctive relief. The district court issued preliminary injunctions requiring NCBE to allow Enyart to take the exams using the assistive software, and NCBE appealed. We hold that in granting the injunctions, the district court did not abuse its discretion. We affirm.

I. Background

Enyart suffers from Stargardt's Disease, a form of juvenile macular degeneration that causes her to experience a large blind spot in the center of her visual field and extreme sensitivity to light. Her disease has progressively worsened since she became legally blind at age fifteen. Enyart relies on assistive technology to read.

Enyart graduated from UCLA School of Law in 2009. Before she could be admitted to practice law in California, Enyart needed to pass two exams: the Multistate Professional Responsibility Exam, a 60-question, multiple-choice exam testing applicants' knowledge of the standards governing lawyers' professional conduct; and the California Bar Exam. The Bar Exam spans three days, on one of which the Multistate Bar Exam is administered. The MBE is a six-hour, 200-question, multiple-choice exam that tests applicants' knowledge of the law in a number of subject areas. NCBE develops both the MPRE and the MBE. NCBE contracts with another testing company, ACT, to administer the MPRE and licenses the MBE to the California Committee of Bar Examiners for use in the Bar Exam.

Enyart registered to take the March 2009 administration of the MPRE and wrote to ACT requesting a number of accommodations for her disability: extra time, a private room, hourly breaks, permission to bring and use her own lamp, digital clock, sunglasses, yoga mat, and migraine medication during the exam, and permission to take the exam on a laptop equipped with JAWS and ZoomText software. JAWS is an assistive screen-reader program that reads aloud text on a computer screen. ZoomText is a screen-magnification program that allows the user to adjust the font, size, and color of text and to control a high-visibility cursor.

ACT granted all of Enyart's requests with the exception of the computer equipped with JAWS and ZoomText. ACT explained that it was unable to offer this accommodation because NCBE would not make the MPRE available in electronic format. In lieu of Enyart's requested accommodation, ACT offered her a choice between a live reader or an audio CD of the exam, along with use of closed-circuit television for text magnification. Enyart sought reconsideration of ACT's denial of her request to use JAWS and ZoomText, asserting that the options offered would be ineffective because they would not allow her to synchronize the auditory and visual inputs. After ACT denied Enyart's request for reconsideration, Enyart cancelled her registration for the March 2009 MPRE.

In April 2009, Enyart applied to take the July 2009 California Bar Exam, requesting the same accommodations she asked for on the MPRE. The California Committee of Bar Examiners granted all of Enyart's requested accommodations with the exception of her request to take the MBE portion of the test using a computer equipped with ZoomText and JAWS. The Committee denied this request because NCBE would not provide the MBE in electronic format. Because of this denial, Enyart cancelled her registration for the July 2009 Bar Exam.

Enyart registered for the November 2009 MPRE and requested the same accommodations she previously sought for the March 2009 administration. NCBE again declined to allow Enyart to take the MPRE using a computer equipped with ZoomText and JAWS. Instead, they offered to provide a human reader, an audio CD of the test questions, a Braille version of the test, and/or a CCTV with a hard-copy version in large font with white letters printed on a black background. Because of NCBE's denial of her request to use a computer with ZoomText and JAWS, Enyart cancelled her registration for the November 2009 MPRE.

After these repeated denials of her requests to take the MPRE and MBE using assistive technology software, Enyart filed this action against NCBE, ACT, and the State Bar of California, alleging violations of the ADA and the Uhruh Act, California's civil rights law. Enyart sought declaratory and injunctive relief.

Enyart moved for a preliminary injunction, asking the district court to order NCBE to allow Enyart to use a computer equipped with ZoomText and JAWS on the February 2010 MBE and the March 2010 MPRE. After hearing oral argument, the court granted Enyart's motion, addressing the factors for deciding whether to issue a preliminary injunction in a well-reasoned order[.]

[M]eanwhile, while NCBE's appeal of the preliminary injunction was pending, Enyart learned that her score on the March 2010 MPRE was not high enough to allow her to qualify for admission to the

California Bar. She moved for a second preliminary injunction, asking the court to order NCBE to provide her requested accommodations on the August 2010 MPRE and "any other administration to Ms. Enyart of the California Bar Exam, the Multistate Bar Exam ('MBE') and/or the MPRE." After filing her motion, Enyart learned that she did not pass the July 2009 Bar Exam. The district court granted a second preliminary injunction ordering NCBE to allow Enyart to take the July 2010 MBE and the August 2010 MPRE on a computer equipped with ZoomText and JAWS, stating:

> The relevant question here is whether the auxiliary aids offered by NCBE make the test's "visually delivered materials available" to Enyart. As this Court has previously concluded, they do not . . . . NCBE continues to argue that Enyart is not entitled to her preferred accommodations, and in so doing continues to miss the point. She does not argue that she simply "prefers" to use JAWS and ZoomText. On the contrary, she has presented evidence that the accommodations offered by NCBE do not permit her to fully understand the test material, and that some of the offered accommodations result in serious physical discomfort. CCTV makes her nauseous and results in eye strain, and the use of human readers is not suited to the kind of test where one must re-read both questions and answers, and continually shift back and forth between different passages of text . . . . Such accommodations do not make the test accessible to Enyart, and so do not satisfy the standard under the ADA.

The court required Enyart to post an additional $5,000 injunction bond. NCBE immediately appealed, and the appeal was consolidated with NCBE's appeal of the first preliminary injunction.

Enyart has since learned that she received a high enough score on the August 2010 MPRE to qualify for admission to the California Bar but that she did not pass the July 2010 California Bar Exam.

II. Discussion

[A] plaintiff seeking a preliminary injunction must show that: (1) she is likely to succeed on the merits, (2) she is likely to suffer irreparable harm in the absence of preliminary relief, (3) the balance of equities tips in her favor, and (4) an injunction is in the public interest. *Winter v. Natural Res. Def. Council,* 555 U.S. 7 (2008) (citations omitted). The district court correctly identified the *Winter* standard as controlling in this case.

1. Likelihood of Success on the Merits

Congress enacted the ADA in order to eliminate discrimination against individuals with disabilities. *See* 42 U.S.C. § 12101(b). The ADA furthers Congress's goal regarding individuals with disabilities: "to assure equality of opportunity, full participation, independent living, and economic self-sufficiency for such individuals[.]" 42 U.S.C. § 12101(a)(8). The ADA contains four substantive titles: Title I relates to employment; Title II relates to state and local governments; Title III relates to public accommodations and services operated by private entities; and Title IV relates to telecommunications and common carriers. *See generally* Americans with Disabilities Act of 1990, 42 U.S.C. §§ 12101–12213 and 47 U.S.C. §§ 225, 611.

42 U.S.C. § 12189, which falls within Title III of the ADA, governs professional licensing examinations. This section requires entities that offer examinations "related to applications, licensing, certification, or credentialing for ... professional, or trade purposes" to "offer such examinations ... in a place and manner *accessible* to persons with disabilities or offer alternative accessible arrangements for such individuals." 42 U.S.C. § 12189 (emphasis added). The purpose of this section is "to assure that persons with disabilities are not foreclosed from educational, professional, or trade opportunities because an examination or course is conducted in an inaccessible site or without an accommodation." H.R.Rep. No. 101–485(III), at 68–69 (1990).

The Attorney General is charged with carrying out many of the provisions of the ADA and issuing such regulations as he deems necessary. Relevant here, the Attorney General is responsible for issuing regulations carrying out all non-transportation provisions of Title III, including issuing accessibility standards. 42 U.S.C. § 12186(b).

Pursuant to its authority to issue regulations carrying out the provisions of Title III, the Department of Justice has adopted a regulation interpreting § 12189. This regulation defines the obligations of testing entities:

> Any private entity offering an examination covered by this section must assure that ... [t]he examination is selected and administered so as to *best ensure* that, when the examination is administered to an individual with a disability that impairs sensory, manual, or speaking skills, the examination results accurately reflect the individual's aptitude or achievement level or whatever other factor the examination purports to measure, rather than reflecting the individual's impaired sensory, manual, or speaking skills ... [.]

28 C.F.R. § 36.309(b)(1)(i) (emphasis added). The regulation continues:

> A private entity offering an examination covered by this section shall provide appropriate auxiliary aids for persons with impaired sensory, manual, or speaking skills, unless that entity can demonstrate that offering a particular auxiliary aid would fundamentally alter the measurement of the skills or knowledge the examination is intended to test or would result in an undue burden.

Id. § 36.309(b)(3).

Enyart argues that DOJ's regulation requires NCBE to administer the MBE and MPRE "so as to best ensure" that her results on the tests accurately reflect her aptitude, rather than her disability. NCBE argues that the regulation is invalid and asks this court to apply a reasonableness standard in lieu of the regulation's "best ensure" standard. The district court declined to rule on the validity of 28 C.F.R. § 36.309, and instead held that "even assuming NCBE's more defendant-friendly standard applies," Enyart had demonstrated a likelihood of success on the merits.

We defer to an agency's interpretation of a statute it is charged with administering if the statute "is silent or ambiguous with respect to the specific issue" and the agency's interpretation is "based upon a permissible construction of the statute." *Contract Mgmt., Inc. v. Rumsfeld,* 434 F.3d 1145, 1146–47 (9th Cir.2006) (quoting *Chevron U.S.A. Inc. v. Natural Res. Def. Council, Inc.,* 467 U.S. 837, 842–43 (1984)). We hold that 28 C.F.R. § 36.309 is entitled to *Chevron* deference.

Section 12189 requires entities like NCBE to offer licensing exams in a manner "accessible" to disabled people or to offer "alternative accessible arrangements." 42 U.S.C. § 12189. Congress's use of the phrases "accessible" and "alternative accessible arrangements" is ambiguous in the context of licensing exams. Nowhere in § 12189, in Title III more broadly, or in the entire ADA did Congress define these terms. The phrase "readily accessible" appears in Titles II and III, but only with respect to physical spaces, i.e., facilities, vehicles, and rail cars. *See* 42 U.S.C. §§ 12142– 12148, 12162– 12165, 12182– 12184. The phrase is not defined; instead, the Act directs the Secretary of Transportation to issue regulations establishing accessibility standards for public transportation facilities, vehicles, and rail cars, 42 U.S.C. §§ 12149, 12163–12164, and 12186(a), and directs the Attorney General to issue regulations establishing accessibility standards for new construction and alterations in public accommodations and commercial facilities, 42 U.S.C. § 12186(b). The text of these other ADA provisions does not resolve the ambiguity in § 12189's use of term "accessible" because an examination is not equivalent to a physical space.

Because § 12189 is ambiguous with respect to its requirement that entities administer licen[s]ing exams in a manner "accessible" to individuals with disabilities, we defer to DOJ's interpretation of the statute so long as that interpretation is based upon a permissible construction of the statute. *See Contract Mgmt., Inc.,* 434 F.3d at 1146– 47. NCBE seeks to invalidate 28 C.F.R. § 36.309, arguing that the regulation imposes an obligation beyond the statutory mandate. Instead of the regulation's requirement that entities administer licensing exams in a manner "so as to best ensure" that the results reflect whatever skill or aptitude the exam purports to measure, NCBE argues that the ADA only requires such entities to provide "reasonable accommodations."

The "reasonable accommodation" standard advocated by NCBE originated in the Department of Health and Human Services' regulations implementing the Rehabilitation Act of 1973. *See* 45 C.F.R. 84.12(a) (requiring employers to make "reasonable accommodation to the known physical or mental limitations of an otherwise qualified handicapped applicant or employee unless the [employer] can demonstrate that the accommodation would impose an undue hardship on the operation of its program or activity."). When Congress enacted the ADA, it incorporated 45 C.F.R. 84.12's "reasonable accommodation" standard into Title I, which applies in the employment context. *See* H.R.Rep. No. 101–485(II), at 2 (1990) ("Title I of the ADA ... incorporates many of the standards of discrimination set out in regulations implementing section 504 of the Rehabilitation Act of 1973, including the obligation to provide reasonable accommodations unless it would result in an undue hardship on the operation of the business.").

Notably, Congress did *not* incorporate 45 C.F.R. 84.12's "reasonable accommodation" standard into § 12189. Instead, § 12189 states that entities offering licensing exams "shall offer such examinations . . . in a place and manner accessible to persons with disabilities or offer alternative arrangements for such individuals." 42 U.S.C. § 12189. One reasonable reading of § 12189's requirement that entities make licensing exams "accessible" is that such entities must provide disabled people with an equal opportunity to demonstrate their knowledge or abilities to the same degree as nondisabled people taking the exam—in other words, the entities must administer the exam "so as to best ensure" that exam results accurately reflect aptitude rather than disabilities. DOJ's regulation is not based upon an impermissible construction of § 12189, so this court affords *Chevron* deference to 28 C.F.R. § 36.309 and applies the regulation's "best ensure" standard.

Applying 28 C.F.R. § 36.309's "best ensure" standard, we conclude that the district court did not abuse its discretion by holding that Enyart demonstrated a likelihood of success on the merits. The district court found that the accommodations offered by NCBE did not make the MBE and MPRE accessible to Enyart. This finding is supported by evidence that Enyart would suffer eye fatigue, disorientation, and nausea if she used a CCTV, so CCTV does not best ensure that the exams are accessible to her; that auditory input alone is insufficient to allow Enyart to effectively comprehend and retain the language used on the exam; and that, according to Enyart's ophthalmologist, the combination of ZoomText and JAWS is the only way she can fully comprehend the material she reads.

NCBE argues that because Enyart has taken other standardized tests using accommodations comparable to those offered by NCBE, the district court erred in finding that those accommodations did not make the MPRE and MBE accessible to her. In support of this argument, NCBE points out that Enyart took the SAT college admissions test using large-print exam booklets; that she used CCTV for her Advanced Placement tests; and that she relied on a human reader and scribe during the LSAT. Although Enyart's prior experiences with the accommodations offered by NCBE may be relevant to establishing whether those accommodations make the MPRE and MBE accessible, they are not conclusive, especially as to whether those accommodations best ensure that the exams are accessible. Enyart graduated from college more than a decade ago, and took the LSAT six years ago. Enyart's disability is a progressive one, and as the district court noted, an accommodation that may or may not have been sufficient years ago is not necessarily sufficient today. Moreover, assistive technology is not frozen in time: as technology advances, testing accommodations should advance as well.

NCBE also argues that because it offered to provide auxiliary aids expressly identified in the ADA, the regulations, a DOJ settlement agreement, and a Resolution of the National Federation of the Blind, courts should not require it do more. We do not find this argument persuasive. The issue in this case is not what might or might not accommodate other people with vision impairments, but what is necessary to make the MPRE and MBE accessible to Enyart given her specific impairment and the specific nature of these exams.

As NCBE concedes, the lists of auxiliary aids contained at 42 U.S.C. § 12103 and at 28 C.F.R. § 36.309 are not exhaustive. *See* 42 U.S.C. § 12103(1) ("the term 'auxiliary aids and services' includes (A) qualified interpreters *or other effective methods* of making aurally delivered materials available to individuals with hearing impairments; (B) qualified readers, taped texts, *or other effective methods* of making visually delivered materials available to individuals with visual impairments; . . . and (D) *other similar services and actions.*") (emphases added); 28 C.F.R. § 36.309(c)(3) ("Auxiliary aids and services required by this section may include taped texts, interpreters *or other effective methods* of making orally delivered materials available to individuals with hearing impairments, Brailled or large print texts or qualified readers for individuals with visual impairments . . . *and other similar services and actions.*") (emphases added). To hold that, as a matter of law, an entity fulfills its obligation to administer an exam in an accessible manner so long as it offers some or all of the auxiliary aids enumerated in the statute or regulation would be inconsistent with Congressional intent:

> The Committee wishes to make it clear that technological advances can be expected to further enhance options for making meaningful and effective opportunities available to individuals with disabilities. Such advances may require public accommodations to provide auxiliary aids and services in the future which today they would not be required because they would be held to impose undue burdens on such entities.
>
> Indeed, the Committee intends that the types of accommodations and services provided to individuals with disabilities, under all of the titles of this bill, should keep pace with the rapidly changing technology of the times.

H.R. Rep. 101–485(II), at 108 (1990).

NCBE points next to a July 2000 settlement between DOJ and the American Association of State Social Work Boards in which the AASSWB agreed to adopt a policy allowing vision-impaired candidates to choose among a list of available accommodations for the social work licensing exam. The list included an audiotaped version of the exam, a large print test book, a Braille version of the exam, extra time, a private room, a qualified reader, and a flexible start time. NCBE argues that because it offered Enyart the accommodations listed in the AASSWB settlement, the court should conclude that the accommodations offered satisfied NCBE's obligations under § 12189 as a matter of law. We find this argument unpersuasive. There is no reason that this decade-old settlement agreement should define the maximum NCBE can be required to do in order to meet its obligation to make the MBE and MPRE accessible to Enyart.[5]

Finally, NCBE makes much of a Resolution of the National Federation of the Blind from 2000 that called upon the American Council on Education to ensure that it administered the GED exam in "the four standard media routinely used by blind persons to access standardized tests: large print, Braille, tape, and live reader." This NFB

---

[5] Moreover, a settlement is, by definition, a compromise and does not necessarily embrace the maximum reach of the statute.

Resolution appears to have been written to address a specific problem identified in the administration of the GED exam, namely the prohibition on the use of live readers. Moreover, the NFB has no power to define testing entities' obligations under the ADA. The fact that the NFB ten years ago urged the American Council on Education to allow test-takers to choose among large print, Braille, tape, and live reader accommodations does not lead to the conclusion that, as a matter of law, the accommodations offered by NCBE made the MBE and MPRE accessible to Enyart.

The sources described above—the lists of auxiliary aids contained in the statute and regulation, the AASSWB settlement agreement, and the NFB's Resolution—possibly support a conclusion that the accommodations offered by NCBE are sufficient to meet their obligations with respect to many blind people in many situations. As we have tried to make clear already, accommodations that make an exam accessible to many blind people may not make the exam accessible to Enyart, and our analysis depends on the individual circumstances of each case, requiring a "fact-specific, individualized analysis of the disabled individual's circumstances."

Enyart provided the district court with evidence that the accommodations offered by NCBE will put her at a disadvantage by making her nauseated or by preventing her from comprehending the test material. Enyart presented evidence that she used JAWS and ZoomText for all but one of her law school examinations; that a combination of JAWS and ZoomText is the only way she can effectively access the exam; and that use of a CCTV causes her to suffer nausea and eye fatigue. In a sworn statement, Enyart's ophthalmologist stated that the only way Enyart can fully comprehend the material she reads is if she is able to simultaneously listen to and see magnified test material, as JAWS and ZoomText allow.

The district court reviewed the evidence of Enyart's disability and her history of using auxiliary aids including JAWS and ZoomText, and concluded that "the accommodations offered by NCBE would either result in extreme discomfort and nausea, or would not permit Enyart to sufficiently comprehend and retain the language used on the text. This would result in Enyart's disability severely limiting her performance on the exam, which is clearly forbidden both by the statute and the corresponding regulation." The court compared Enyart's evidence to that offered by NCBE, and found that the balance "more strongly supports the conclusion that only ZoomText and JAWS make the text 'accessible' to Enyart." This is a logical conclusion, supported by the evidence, and therefore we conclude that the district court did not abuse its discretion in holding that Enyart demonstrated a likelihood of success on the merits.

2. Irreparable Harm

[T]he district court found that, in the absence of preliminary relief, Enyart would likely suffer irreparable harm in the form of (1) the loss of the chance to engage in normal life activity, i.e., pursuing her chosen profession, and (2) professional stigma. Enyart additionally argues that, as a matter of law, she faced irreparable injury from the fact of NCBE's violation of the ADA. We need not decide whether discrimination in violation of the ADA constitutes irreparable harm *per se,* or whether irreparable harm can be presumed based on such a statutory violation, because we agree with the district court's conclusion that Enyart demonstrated irreparable harm in the form of the loss of opportunity to pursue her chosen profession.

[3]. Balance of Equities

The district court compared the harm Enyart would suffer in the absence of preliminary relief to the harm an injunction would cause NCBE, and concluded that the equities weighed in Enyart's favor. The district court rejected NCBE's argument that the injunction would cause NCBE harm that cannot be undone. NCBE argues that providing Enyart's requested accommodations is expensive[6] and poses a security concern; however, as the district court noted, Enyart posted two $5,000 injunction bonds that will cover NCBE's costs in the event it prevails on the merits at trial, and the injunction minimized security risks by requiring Enyart to use NCBE's laptop rather than her own. Compared to the likelihood that Enyart would suffer irreparable harm by losing the chance to pursue her chosen profession in the absence of an injunction, the potential harm to NCBE resulting from injunctive relief was minimal. The district court did not abuse its discretion in holding that the balance of equities favored Enyart.

4. Public Interest

The district court held that "the public clearly has an interest in the enforcement of its statutes," and concluded that the public interest weighed in favor of granting the injunctions. NCBE argues that the public's interest in having statutes enforced is not sufficient to support a grant of a preliminary injunction.

In enacting the ADA, Congress demonstrated its view that the public has an interest in ensuring the eradication of discrimination on the basis of disabilities. 42 U.S.C. § 12101(a)(9) (finding that "the continuing existence of unfair and unnecessary discrimination and prejudice . . . costs the United States billions of dollars in unnecessary expenses resulting from dependency and nonproductivity"). This public interest is served by requiring entities to take steps to "assure equality of opportunity" for people with disabilities. *See id.* § 12101(a)(8). Although it is true that the public also has an interest in ensuring the integrity of licensing exams, NCBE never argued that allowing Enyart to take the MPRE and MBE using a computer equipped with JAWS and ZoomText would result in unreliable or unfair exam results. The district court did not abuse its discretion in concluding that the issuance of these preliminary injunctions served the public's interest in enforcement of the ADA and in elimination of discrimination on the basis of disability.

III. Conclusion

For the foregoing reasons, we affirm the district court's February 4, 2010 and June 22, 2010 orders issuing preliminary injunctions requiring NCBE to permit Enyart to take the MBE and MPRE using a laptop equipped with JAWS and ZoomText.

---

[6] NCBE has conceded, however, that the accommodations requested by Enyart would not cause an undue burden on NCBE.

Breimhorst v. Educational Testing Service

United States District Court for the Northern District of California, 2000.
2000 WL 34510621.

■ ORRICK, J.

In this disability rights action against the Educational Testing Service ("ETS"), plaintiffs challenge the ETS' practice of "flagging" test score reports for test takers who obtained accommodations for their disabilities to indicate that the scores were obtained under special conditions. Plaintiffs contend that this policy discriminates against disabled test takers because ETS has no basis for concluding that the scores for tests taken with accommodations are not comparable to those taken under standard conditions. Essentially, plaintiffs complain that ETS forces test takers who obtain accommodations for their disabilities to wear a "scarlet letter" that calls into question the validity of their test scores for no reason.

ETS now moves for judgment on the pleadings. For the reasons set forth hereinafter, the Court grants ETS' motion with respect to plaintiffs' claim for violation of § 302 of the Americans with Disabilities Act ("ADA"), but denies it in all other respects.

I.

The following statement of facts is summarized from the allegations of the first amended complaint.

ETS administers the Scholastic Aptitude Test ("SAT"), the Graduate Records Exam ("GRE"), the Graduate Management Admissions Test ("GMAT"), and some 500 other high stakes screening exams. ETS is responsible for preparing, administering and scoring these exams, and also for reporting the scores to school admissions offices and other interested entities.

Whenever a disabled individual receives an accommodation to take one of ETS' tests, ETS brands the test score report with the prominent mark "SCORES OBTAINED UNDER SPECIAL CONDITIONS" (hereinafter "flag" or "flagging"). ETS publishes and distributes information test bulletins in which it states that its policy is to include this flag with the score report because, when standardized tests are taken under nonstandard conditions, the scores may not accurately reflect the test taker's educational ability. Plaintiffs contend that ETS has no factual basis for its conclusion that the scores of disabled people who received test-taking accommodations are any less reliable or valid than the scores of people who took the same test without accommodations.

Plaintiffs allege that the purpose of the accommodations provided to disabled test takers is to "level the playing field" so that tests will in fact measure their abilities, rather than reflect their disabilities. Plaintiffs contend that the flag communicates a stigmatizing message that people with disabilities obtain an unfair advantage when they receive accommodations, and that their scores should be viewed with skepticism. Plaintiffs allege that this practice violates §§ 302, 309, and 503(b) of the Americans with Disabilities Act, § 504 of the Rehabilitation Act, § 54 of the California Civil Code, the California

Unruh Civil Rights Act, and constitutes an unfair business practice in violation of § 17200 of the California Business and Professions Code.

Plaintiffs in this action are Mark Breimhorst ("Breimhorst"), the International Dyslexia Association ("IDA"), and Californians for Disability Rights ("CDR").

Breimhorst wants to go to business school. He does not have hands, so he took the GMAT on a computer with a track ball and with twenty-five per cent additional test taking time to accommodate his disability. ETS branded his score report: "Scores obtained under special conditions." Breimhorst asked the ETS to remove this flag from his score reports, and to stop its flagging policy, but ETS denied Breimhorst's requests.

IDA is a nonprofit organization dedicated to the removal of social, institutional, and cultural barriers currently preventing people with learning disabilities from obtaining their potential. IDA has over 12,000 members and forty-three branches in the United States, including four branches in California, and one branch in the Northern District of California. IDA's members include people with disabilities who have allegedly been denied equal access to ETS' tests due to its policy and practice of flagging. IDA joins this action to represent the interests of its members and because the flagging policy allegedly interferes with the organization's goals and mission.

CDR is a grass roots coalition of people with disabilities that works and advocates for full compliance with the ADA. CDR has chapters throughout California. Its membership includes people with disabilities who have allegedly been denied equal access to ETS' tests due to its policy and practice of flagging. CDR joins this action to represent the interests of its members and because the flagging policy allegedly interferes with the organization's goals and mission.

II.

ETS now moves for judgment on the pleadings, pursuant to Rule 12(c) of the Federal Rules of Civil Procedure. ETS contends that accurately flagging a reported test score to indicate that it was not taken under standardized testing conditions does not violate any applicable law.

[B.]

ETS' first argument is that none of the plaintiffs have standing because they have not shown that they have been injured by ETS' flagging of their test scores.

This argument was rejected recently by the Third Circuit, in what both parties agree is the only federal appellate opinion to have consider the legality of flagging under the ADA. *Doe v. National Bd. of Med. Examiners*, 199 F.3d 146, 152–53 (3d Cir.1999). Although the court vacated a preliminary injunction because the plaintiff had not demonstrated, on the record before the Third Circuit, that he was likely to prevail on the merits, the Third Circuit did find that he had standing to raise his claims. *Id*. at 152–53, 158.

In *Doe*, the plaintiff was a medical student with multiple sclerosis. He received extra time from the National Board of Medical Examiners ("NBME") to take the United States Medical Licensing Examination, as an accommodation for his disability. The NBME followed a practice of annotating the scores of test takers who received testing accommodations if, in its judgment, the accommodations affected the comparability of the accommodated score to nonaccommodated scores. Doe sued the NBME to enjoin it from annotating his scores to reflect that he received testing accommodations.

The Third Circuit rejected the NBME's argument that Doe lacked standing. [T]he court found that Doe had established a concrete injury in that flagging his test scores identified him as a disabled person against his will. "Being so identified harms him in the sense that, because of justifiable and reasonable concern as a disabled person with how people who can affect his future and his livelihood, and whose judgment may be informed by the information, will perceive him, he has actively sought to avoid being so identified." The court also found that "[b]ecause the injury complained of is an injury fairly traceable to the NBME that would be redressed by the relief Doe seeks, we conclude that Doe has met the constitutional standing requirement."

Similarly, Breimhorst and the members of the IDA and CDR complain that ETS' flagging policy identifies and stigmatizes them as disabled, against their will, and prevents people with disabilities from competing in the application process on an equal basis with nondisabled people.

In addition, plaintiffs allege that they have been injured because the scores they receive from the ETS are less valuable than scores received by test takers who have not requested accommodations for disabilities. The scores of test takers who have received accommodations for their disabilities are flagged to indicate that they were taken under special conditions, because ETS believes that when standardized tests are taken under nonstandard conditions, the scores may not accurately reflect the test taker's educational ability. Thus, the scores of disabled test takers who received accommodations are automatically cast under a cloud of suspicion. This is also a concrete injury caused by ETS' policy, which would be entirely redressed by cessation of that policy.

C.

[P]laintiffs' first claim is that the ETS' flagging policy violates § 309 of the ADA. That section provides:

> Any person that offers examinations or courses related to applications, licensing, certification, or credentialing for secondary or post-secondary education, professional, or trade purposes shall offer such examinations or courses in a place and manner accessible to persons with disabilities or offer alternative arrangements for such individuals.

42 U.S.C. § 12189 (ADA § 309). A federal regulation adopted by the Department of Justice to implement this section of the ADA requires private entities who offer such examinations to ensure that:

> The examination is selected and administered so as to best ensure that, when the examination is administered to an individual with a disability that impairs sensory, manual, or speaking skills, the examination results accurately reflect the individual's aptitude or achievement level or whatever other

factor the examination purports to measure, rather than reflecting the individual's impaired sensory, manual, or speaking skills (except where those skills are the factors that the examination purports to measure) [.]

28 C.F.R. § 36.309(b)(1)(i).

The Third Circuit found, on the record before it, that the plaintiff had not demonstrated that flagging was barred by these provisions. *Doe*, 199 F.3d at 155–57. It found that although these provisions require testing organizations to accommodate disabled test takers, there is no "requirement that the resulting scores be declared psychometrically comparable to the scores of examinees who take the test under standard conditions." *Id.* at 156.

> The notion of accessibility, or best ensuring that examination results accurately reflect "aptitude or achievement level," see 28 C.F.R. § 36.309(b)(1)(i), does not mandate that the NBME provide examinations to the disabled that yield technically equal results; it mandates changes to the examinations— "alternative accessible arrangements," 42 U.S.C. § 12189—so that disabled people who are disadvantaged by certain features of standardized examinations may take the examinations without those features that disadvantage them.

Id.

It is true that the plain language of § 12189 of the ADA addresses the place and manner in which the test is given; it does not address the scoring of the test. Similarly, most of 28 C.F.R. § 36.309 also addresses the place and manner in which the test is given, to ensure that disabled test takers can take the test with accommodations for their disabilities. One of the key goals of the ADA, however, is to assure equality of opportunity for disabled people. 42 U.S.C. § 12101(8). Thus, the Court will not focus narrowly on the ability of disabled people to take the test. To fulfill the goals of the ADA, the test itself must allow disabled people to demonstrate their true abilities.

Section 36.309(b)(1) specifically addresses that goal. That section requires the test provider to assure that the examination "is selected and administered so as to best ensure that . . . the examination results accurately reflect" the individual's ability, rather than his or her disability. 28 C.F.R. § 36.309(b)(1)(i). Read together, 28 U.S.C. § 12189 and 28 C.F.R § 36.309 require the test provider to provide accommodations for disabled test takers and to select and administer the test to best ensure that the test results for disabled test takers reflect their actual abilities. Thus, while the Third Circuit is correct that § 36.309(b)(1) does not require that the test results be exactly psychometrically equivalent, it does require the test provider to take steps to best ensure that the tests equally measure the skills of disabled and nondisabled test takers.

This requirement is imposed regardless of the burden it causes the test provider. A different subsection of § 36.309 requires test providers to provide "appropriate auxiliary aids" for disabled test takers unless "offering a particular auxiliary aid would fundamentally alter the measurement of the skills or knowledge the examination is intended to test or would result in an undue burden." 28 C.F.R. § 36.309(b)(3). The "fundamental alteration" and "undue burden" defenses were deliberately excluded from the requirement of § 36.309(b)(1) that the tests be selected and administered so as to equally measure the abilities of disabled and nondisabled test takers. 28 C.F.R. Pt. 36, App. B at 651.

Section § 36.309(b)(1) imposes a duty on test providers to best ensure that their tests are selected and administered to equally measure the abilities of disabled and nondisabled test takers. If test providers meet this burden, then there would be no reason to flag the test results of disabled test takers who receive accommodations. It may be that there is no way to ensure that the test results are precisely equivalent. Then, even though ETS may have taken steps to best ensure that the results are equal, the results may still differ so significantly that flagging is appropriate. That is an issue of fact, however, and not a matter to be decided on a motion for judgment on the pleadings.

Even the Third Circuit expressly noted that Doe might have had a claim if he had shown "that his scores are comparable to non-accommodated scores, and thus that, by flagging, the NBME has imposed an inequality on him by treating the same thing differently." Doe, 199 F.3d at 156. That is precisely what the plaintiffs allege here. Plaintiffs allege that ETS has no legitimate grounds to conclude that the accommodations provided to Breimhorst and other disabled examinees compromised the validity or reliability of their test scores. (First Amended Compl. ¶¶ 13, 34–36.) Accordingly, the Court finds that plaintiffs have stated a claim against ETS for violation of § 309 of the ADA.

D.

Plaintiffs also allege that ETS is violating § 302 of the ADA. That section sets forth a general rule that:

> No individual shall be discriminated against on the basis of disability in the full and equal enjoyment of the goods, services, facilities, privileges, advantages, or accommodations of any place of public accommodation by any person who owns, leases (or leases to), or operates a place of public accommodation.

42 U.S.C. § 12182(a). The Third Circuit, in Doe, found this section to be inapplicable because § 309 specifically defined the duties of testing providers under the ADA. Doe, 199 F.3d at 154–55. The court based its analysis on the canon of statutory construction that "the specific governs the general." Id. at 155. " 'The law is settled that however inclusive may be the general language of a statute, it will not be held to apply to a matter specifically dealt with in another part of the same enactment.' " Id.. The Third Circuit found that "although applying section 302 would not necessarily undermine limitations created by section 309 (neither section explicitly mentions flagging), it would render 309 superfluous." Id. at 155. "If section 302 settled the question, there would have been no need to enact section 309." Id.

The Court agrees with the Third Circuit's analysis on this point. In addition, the implementing regulations for § 302 and § 309 of the ADA also support the Third Circuit's holding that only § 309 sets forth the ADA's requirements for testing providers.

The implementing regulations for Title III of the ADA, which includes §§ 302 and 309, are set forth in 28 C.F.R. Part 36 (§§ 36.101 though 36.608). Sections 36.201 and 36.202 set forth regulations that restate the requirements of § 302 of the ADA. Section 36.102(d) provides, however, that "[t]he requirements of this part applicable to private entities that offer examinations . . . are set forth in § 36.309." 28 C.F.R. § 36.102(d). Section 36.102(d) thus quite clearly suggests that the remainder of the regulations, including those that restate the general prohibitions of § 302 of the ADA, are not applicable to testing providers.

Appendix B to Part 36 also suggests that § 302 does not apply to testing providers. As the Court has already noted, § 36.309(b)(3) provides a "fundamental alteration" or "undue burden" defense to the provision of auxiliary aids for disabled test takers. Those defenses are not incorporated into § 36.309(b)(1)'s requirement that the test be selected and administered to equally measure the actual abilities of disabled and nondisabled test takers. Appendix B to Part 36 states that the "fundamental alteration" and "undue burden" defenses were imported into § 36.309(b)(3) from § 302 of the ADA. 28 C.F.R. Pt. 36, App.B at 651 (1999). It goes on to state that "[o]ne commenter argued that similar limitations should apply to all of the requirements of § 36.309, but the Department did not consider this extension appropriate." *Id.* Thus, the Department of Justice imported part of § 302 into the regulations for testing providers, but not all of it. This also strongly suggests that § 309 of the ADA and 28 C.F.R. § 36.309 define the ADA's requirements for testing providers, and that § 302 of the ADA does not apply.

Accordingly, for the reasons stated by the Third Circuit in *Doe*, and for the reasons stated above, the Court finds that plaintiffs have not stated a claim against ETS under § 302 of the ADA. ETS' motion for judgment on the pleadings is granted with respect to plaintiffs' claim for violation of § 302 of the ADA.

E.

Plaintiffs' third claim is for violation of § 503(b) of the ADA, which provides:

> It shall be unlawful to coerce, intimidate, threaten or interfere with any individual in the exercise or enjoyment of, or on account of his or her having exercised or enjoyed, or on account of his or her having aided or encouraged any other individual in the exercise or enjoyment of, any right granted or protected by this chapter.

42 U.S.C. § 12203(b) (ADA § 503(b)). Plaintiffs allege that ETS' flagging policy interferes with their right to reasonable testing accommodations by discouraging them from requesting such accommodations. Plaintiffs also allege that it interferes with their right to maintain the confidentiality of their disabilities from third parties, such as school admissions offices.

Case law interpreting § 503(b) is sparse. The plain words of the statute, however, preclude a party from intimidating or coercing another party not to exercise his rights under the ADA, as well as barring interference against a person who has exercised his rights under the ADA. [P]laintiffs assert both types of claims: ETS' flagging policies intimidate them not to request accommodations, and ETS punishes them for doing so by flagging their test results even though ETS has no reason to believe that their scores are any less valid or reliable than those of test takers who took the test without accommodations. Plaintiffs have thus stated a claim for violation of § 503(b) of the ADA, and ETS' motion for judgment on the pleadings on this claim is denied.

F.

Plaintiffs' next claim is for violation of § 504 of the Rehabilitation Act. Section 504 of the Rehabilitation Act, 29 U.S.C. § 794, provides in relevant part:

> No otherwise qualified person with a disability in the United States . . . shall, solely by reason of her or his disability, be excluded from the participation in, denied the benefits of, or be subjected to discrimination under any program or activity receiving Federal financial assistance[.]

29 U.S.C. § 794(a).

ETS argues that flagging is expressly permitted under the Department of Education's interpretation of regulations promulgated under the Rehabilitation Act. ETS' citations to authority do not support that argument. Section 104.42(b)(4) of Title 34 of the Code of Federal Regulations provides that postsecondary education programs and activities generally "may not make preadmission inquiry as to whether an applicant for admission is a handicapped person but, after admission, may make inquiries on a confidential basis as to handicaps that may require accommodation." The Department of Education Office for Civil Rights ("OCR") has stated that a postsecondary education institution does not violate this regulation by "using test scores indicating that the test was taken under nonstandard conditions, so long as the test score is not the only criterion used for admission, and a person with a disability is not denied admission because the person with a disability took the test under nonstandard testing conditions." *Duke University*, 4 Nat. Disability Law Rep. ¶ 87, Compl.No.04–91–2124 (OCR Apr. 2, 1993). The OCR has also stated that a postsecondary educational institution violates the regulation by adopting "a practice of devaluing the [test] scores of individuals with disabilities who have taken the [test] under nonstandard conditions, thereby subjecting these individuals to differential treatment on the basis of disability." *SUNY Health Science Ctr. at Brooklyn-College of Medicine* (N.Y.), 5 Nat. Disability Law Rep. ¶ 77, Compl.No.02–92–2004 (OCR Aug. 18, 1993). In other words, a university can use flagged test scores in the admission process as long as it does not deny admission to disabled applicants because they took the test under nonstandard conditions.

This regulation and the OCR's interpretation of it says nothing about whether a testing provider can be liable for discriminatorily flagging test scores. By its terms, 34 C.F.R. § 104.42 applies to postsecondary schools, not to testing providers. Underlying the OCR's interpretation of that regulation seems to be an assumption that flagged test scores are not in themselves discriminatory because they reflect a real difference between test scores taken under nonstandard conditions and those taken with accommodations. Plaintiffs expressly challenge that assumption in this action.

Testing providers are required to best ensure that "examination results accurately reflect the individual's aptitude or achievement level or whatever other factor the examination purports to measure, rather than reflecting the individual's impaired sensory, manual or speaking skills[.]" 28 C.F.R. § 36.309(b)(i). Although that regulation was enacted under the ADA, it is intended to mimic the liability for test providers under the Rehabilitation Act. 28 C.F.R. Pt. 36, App.B at 651 (1999). The notes to 28 C.F.R. § 36.309 state that § 309 of the ADA was enacted "to fill the gap that is created when licensing, certification, and other testing authorities are not covered by section 504 of the Rehabilitation Act or title II of the ADA." 28 C.F.R. Pt. 36, App.B at 651 (1999).

> Many licensing, certification, and testing authorities are not covered by section 504, because no Federal money is received; nor are they covered by title II of the ADA because they are not State or local agencies. However, States often require the licenses provided by such authorities in order for an individual to practice a particular profession or trade. Thus, the provision was included in the ADA to assure that persons with disabilities are not foreclosed from educational, professional, or trade opportunities because an examination or course is conducted in an inaccessible site or without needed modifications.

Id. This language strongly suggests that liability for testing providers is intended to be the same under the Rehabilitation Act and the ADA.

As the Court has already noted, if the testing provider complies fully with the requirement that its tests measure equally the abilities of disabled and nondisabled test takers, there would be no need for flagging. All test scores would accurately reflect the abilities of the test taker, regardless of whether the test was taken with accommodations for the test taker's disability.

On the pleadings before the Court, plaintiffs allege that ETS discriminates against disabled test takers by flagging their scores without any justification for doing so. These allegations state a claim. Whether that claim can be proven is a factual matter to be determined later in these proceedings.

ETS' motion for judgment on plaintiffs' claims for violation of the Rehabilitation Act is denied.

NOTES ON TESTING AND THE DISABILITY DISCRIMINATION LAWS

1. What Testing Accommodations Are Reasonable? Enyart requested a series of accommodations on the MPRE and the bar exam: "extra time, a private room, hourly breaks, permission to bring and use her own lamp, digital clock, sunglasses, yoga mat, and migraine medication during the exam, and permission to take the exam on a laptop equipped with JAWS and ZoomText software." Breimhorst received two accommodations when he took the GMAT: He was allowed to take the test on a computer with a track ball, and he was given 25% more time than is standard. Leave aside for the moment the test-flagging question. Were the NCBE and ETS required to provide those accommodations?

Professors Kelman & Lester argue that giving a blind student a Braille version of a law school exam is "the normatively easiest, core case[ ] for accommodation on tests." Kelman & Lester, *supra*, at 166. They offer three reasons for this conclusion: First, the examiner is not trying to test for the ability to read hard copy with one's eyes (as might be the case on an art appreciation exam, for instance); the test is written on hard copy, rather than in Braille, simply for administrative convenience, because most people read with their eyes. See *id*. Second, if the blind student must take the test in hard copy, she "will have literally *no* opportunity" to demonstrate the knowledge, understanding, and ability for which the examiner is actually trying to test. *Id*. Finally, nondisabled students would not benefit from being given a Braille test. "The exam has not, in any sense, been made 'easier' by the accommodation, but rather 'different'; the accommodated student has simply been given the same chance to reach her peak raw score as the nonaccommodated student." *Id*. at 166–167.

When considered against the core case of a Braille test, how do Enyart's and Breimhorst's accommodations stack up? Enyart's requests for JAWS and ZoomText seem incredibly close to that core case. Why were those, among all of Enyart's requests, the ones that the NCBE resisted? Do you find their argument in this regard persuasive? Breimhorst's track-ball computer also seems quite analogous to the Braille test: The GMAT does not purport to test for writing or typing *with hands*; if Breimhorst must take the test by handwriting or typing, he will be totally unable to demonstrate the knowledge, understanding, and ability for which the GMAT actually purports to test; and people with hands are unlikely to benefit from a track ball.

What about extra time? An extra-time accommodation seems different than a Braille test on all three key dimensions: Speedy analysis and decision, unlike the ability to see, is a quality for which the bar exam and the GMAT may purport to test; if so, it seems far less problematic to let a disability-induced lack of speed affect Enyart's or Breimhorst's score. Moreover, even if Enyart's and Breimhorst's disabilities slow them down, the lack of extra time does not *totally* prevent them from demonstrating their knowledge, understanding, and abilities; in this sense, the lack of extra time is quite unlike the lack of a Braille test. And many students, with and without disabilities, would benefit from extra time on the GMAT. See, *e.g.*, Colker, *supra*, at 146 ("[T]he empirical literature suggests that *most* test takers improve their performance when offered extra time.").[*] Extra time thus can readily be seen as giving Enyart and Breimhorst "an easier exam, not just a different one." Kelman & Lester, *supra*, at 167.

What, then, is the argument for granting extra time as a testing accommodation? Perhaps processing speed is not really an important value in the program in which the test is administered. That may or may not be a

---

[*]   Whether students with particular disabilities—particularly learning disabilities—benefit more than nondisabled students from extra time is a matter of considerable debate. For reviews of the evidence, see Colker, *supra*, at 147–155; Kelman & Lester, *supra*, at 169–173.

difficult argument to make in the context of the bar exam or the GMAT, but surely there are subjects in which timed tests are given purely for administrative convenience and not because the examiners really care about speed. One might imagine, for example, that processing speed is not particularly important in a history graduate program, where students are being prepared to conduct extensive archival research in which material is synthesized over a long period of time.

Even if processing speed does matter, perhaps timed examinations overemphasize it. Consider law school examinations. It is fairly uncontroversial that processing speed matters for practicing lawyers. Most practicing lawyers encounter circumstances where they must think "on their feet"—in court, in client meetings, in negotiations, et cetera. Many litigators must occasionally write emergency motions; many transactional lawyers must occasionally write memoranda or deal language quickly. And many lawyers work in settings where they must bill a large number of hours *and* be sufficiently productive to justify a high billing rate for those hours. See Kelman & Lester, *supra*, at 180. But the occasions in practice for using the sorts of speedy processing skills that students must use on timed law school exams reflect a small portion of most lawyers' time. See Colker, *supra*, at 203–204. If timed exams test processing speed at the expense of other important virtues, then a person like Breimhorst who is denied extra time "will display mostly his slowness, and not have enough chance to show his other skills." Kelman & Lester, *supra*, at 167; see also *id.* at 177 (finding "the affirmative case for speeded exams in the educational psychology literature" to be "surprisingly weak").

But if the challenged test weights processing speed too heavily, why isn't the proper response to relax or eliminate the time constraints so that the test gives an appropriate weight to processing speed—and then give the same, properly weighted, test to everybody? Professors Kelman and Lester argue that "[t]o give extra time only to students with learning disabilities would both raise fairness concerns for non-LD test takers and put undue pressure on a very imprecise diagnostic system." *Id.* The point can to some extent be generalized to all disabilities (though some, like Breimhorst's lack of hands, do not raise the concern about imprecise diagnosis). Where examiners rank-order students, and a student's success therefore depends significantly on her position vis-a-vis other students, is it fair to give extra time only to those students who have disabilities?

2.   Flagging. Ought it be permissible for standardized testing services to flag the scores of test-takers who received accommodations? If the accommodations were not required by law in the first place, then a testing service has a decent argument that the greater includes the lesser—that it could have denied the accommodations altogether, so a person who receives the accommodations cannot complain that they are conditioned on the flagging of the resulting scores. But where testing accommodations are required by law, flagging seems to undermine the purposes of the requirement by sending the message to admissions officers that the scores of one who received accommodations should be taken less seriously. See Helia Garrido Hull, *Equal Access to Post-Secondary Education: The Sisyphean Impact of Flagging Test Scores of Persons with Disabilities*, 55 Clev. St. L. Rev. 15, 25–26 (2007). Testing services justify flagging on the ground that their tests are standardized based on typical administration protocols; any change to those protocols eliminates the standardized nature of the test and thus introduces problems of validity and reliability. But is that really true? To the extent that testing accommodations are required by the statute, they are required because the standard administration protocols do *not* provide valid results for some individuals with disabilities. The point of the accommodations is to ensure that the test scores for those individuals with disabilities will be just as valid as those of nondisabled test takers. But is it really possible to precisely calibrate the accommodation so that it cancels out the unreliability introduced by administering the test according to standard protocols, without introducing new sources of invalidity? The individualized nature of accommodations makes it impossible to employ the technique that standardized tests rely on for their validity and reliability—and that gives them their name—the technique of standardization. Should standardized testing services be prohibited from informing admissions officers that individuals with disabilities took the tests under other-than-standard conditions?

After the decision denying the motion to dismiss in *Breimhorst*, the Educational Testing Service settled the case by agreeing not to flag scores on the tests it administers. See Hull, *supra*, at 42. The parties to the case "agreed to select a national panel of experts, jointly selected by Disability Rights Advocates and the College Board, to study the issue of flagging on the SAT I," and that panel concluded that "there was 'no evidence to suggest that the magnitude of the overall difference in predictive validity between standard and extended time administration warrants a cautionary flag to be attached to the scores of students who took the test under the condition of extended time.' " *Id.* After the panel reported its conclusions, the College Board agreed to stop flagging on the SAT, and the American College Testing Service agreed to stop flagging on the ACT. See *id.* at 42–43. But "[d]espite the significant change brought about by *Breimhorst*, both the Law School Admission Council (LSAC), which owns and administers the LSAT, and the Association of American Medical Colleges (AAMC), which owns and administers the MCAT, steadfastly refuse to discontinue the use of flags on scores received under nonstandard test conditions." *Id.* at 43. Does the decision to eliminate flagging by ETS, the College Board, and the American College Testing Service suggest that flagging is unnecessary, or are there valid reasons to continue the practice in the admissions tests for law and medical schools?

In 2012, California adopted a statute that prohibits the LSAC from flagging the scores of individuals who receive accommodations on the LSAT. See Cal. Educ. Code § 99161.5(c)(1) ("The test sponsor of the Law School Admission Test shall not notify a test score recipient that the score of any test subject was obtained by a subject who received an accommodation pursuant to this section."). The LSAC has brought state-court litigation to challenge the constitutionality of that statute. In a parallel case pending in federal court, the California Department of Fair Employment and Housing, joined by two sets of intervenors (the United States Department of Justice and three individual plaintiffs) has sued the LSAC for violating the ADA and state law in its provision of testing accommodations; the alleged violations include the flagging of tests. See

Dept. of Fair Employment & Housing v. Law School Admission Council, Inc., 896 F.Supp.2d 849 (N.D.Cal.2012) (denying motion to dismiss). As this book goes to press, both litigations remain pending.

INDEX

References are to Pages